# PETERSON'S
## College Guide for
# Performing *Arts*
## Majors
## 2009

Carole J. Everett
Former Director of Admissions
The Juilliard School

# PETERSON'S
A **nelnet** COMPANY

**About Peterson's, a Nelnet company**

Peterson's (www.petersons.com) is a leading provider of education information and advice, with books and online resources focusing on education search, test preparation, and financial aid. Its Web site offers searchable databases and interactive tools for contacting educational institutions, online practice tests and instruction, and planning tools for securing financial aid. Peterson's serves 110 million education consumers annually.

For more information, contact Peterson's, 2000 Lenox Drive, Lawrenceville, NJ 08648; 800-338-3282; or find us on the World Wide Web at www.petersons.com/about.

Previous editons published as *Peterson's Professional Degree Programs in the Visual & Performing Arts* © 1995, 1996, 1997, 1998, 1999, 2000, 2001, 2002, 2003, 2004, 2005 and as *Peterson's College Guide for Performing Arts Majors* © 2006, 2007

Stephen Clemente, President; Fern A. Oram, Content Director; Bernadette Webster, Operations Director; Roger S. Williams, Sales and Marketing; Therese DeAngelis, Developmental Editor; Jill C. Schwartz, Production Editor; Bret Bollmann, Michael Haines, Sally Ross, Pam Sullivan, Valerie Bolus Vaughan, Copy Editors; Jennifer Fishberg, Research Project Manager; Tim Nelson, Programmer; Ray Golaszewski, Manufacturing Manager; Linda M. Williams, Composition Manager; Janet Garwo, Mimi Kaufman, Danielle Vreeland, Client Relations Representatives

ISSN 1552-7751
ISBN-13: 978-0-7689-2563-0
ISBN-10: 0-7689-2563-0

Printed in the United States of America

10  9  8  7  6  5  4  3  2  1     10  09  08

Fourteenth Edition

## ABOUT THE AUTHOR

An honors graduate of Barnard College of Columbia University, an educator, and a renowned mezzo-soprano who has performed with opera companies and orchestras and on recital tours around the world, Carole Everett also holds an advanced degree from the Universita of Siena, Italy. For seven years she served as the Director of Admissions at The Juilliard School in New York City. She has also worked at the Nightingale-Bamford School, was Head of School at an independent school in St. Croix in the U.S. Virgin Islands, and currently works at St. Luke's School in Greenwich Village. Ms. Everett speaks and consults frequently on college and graduate school admissions and has taught voice, public speaking, reading, current events, and Latin at elementary through post-secondary levels. She is a native of Wellesley, Massachusetts, and lives in New York City and Spoleto, Italy, with her husband, son, and Bernese mountain dog.

Performing *Arts*

# Contents

Performing

*Arts*

# A Note from the Peterson's Editors

As a prospective performing arts major, you probably know where your talent lies and can see yourself becoming a dancer, a musician, or an actor one day. You are one of the lucky college-bound students who already know what they want to study and have one foot solidly on their career path. That part might have been easy. But what's usually not easy is choosing a school or a program. This guide will help you to make the right decisions.

Written by Carole J. Everett, former admissions director at The Juilliard School, *Peterson's College Guide for Performing Arts Majors* takes you step-by-step through the various stages of applying to college, provides insight into the world of performing arts education, and gives you expert advice on everything from auditioning to planning a career.

In the first section of the guide, **The College Admissions Process,** you'll learn how to assess your talent and discover your educational needs and goals—perhaps the most important step in identifying potential schools to place on your "list." The pros and cons of attending a conservatory versus a liberal arts college are explored, as are Early Decision and deferred admission. You'll discover an abundance of practical tips on campus visits, interviews, applications, and financial aid. The College Admissions Timetable sums it all up from sophomore through senior year and keeps you on track.

The guide is then divided into three sections containing in-depth information: **For Dance Majors, For Music Majors,** and **For Theater Majors.** Topics such as health issues for dancers, hiring a photographer to do head shots, and how to make an audition recording are explored. And you'll find some of the best advice available on auditions: what to expect at an audition, how to choose material, how to deal with nerves, taped versus live auditions, things you should never do at an audition, and much more. There are even sample audition evaluation forms that show you just how your dancing, acting, or musical performance will be critiqued and rated. No one who is planning a college audition should be without this invaluable information.

At the end of each of the three sections you'll find essays written by current dance, music, and theater majors, which contain their advice as well as a glimpse into what being a performing arts major is really like. There are checklists to keep you on track throughout the admissions process, and for those thinking ahead there is a chapter on careers in the performing arts that you might never have thought of. There is even a chapter "For Parents," which lists things that parents should do (and not do!) to help their children during the college admission process.

When it's time to get the details on individual schools and programs, turn to the **Profiles of Performing Arts Programs** section. Here you will find all the need-to-know information on accredited professional degree programs located throughout the U.S. and Canada. Some schools have provided even more information about their facilities, faculty, alumni, and special programs in *More About the School* at the end of their profile. There isn't an easier or more efficient way to explore college programs.

For those who already have specifics in mind, the **Quick-Reference Chart** lists schools by state and lets you compare programs at a glance. The **Appendixes** include additional resources, including listings of summer programs and scholarships for performing arts students. The **Indexes** let you locate schools by their majors or concentrations or alphabetically by name.

Peterson's publishes a full line of resources to help guide you through the admission process. Peterson's publications can be found at your local bookstore or library and at your high school guidance office; you can access us online at www.petersons.com.

We welcome any comments or suggestions you may have about this publication and invite you to complete our online survey at www.petersons. com/booksurvey. Or you can fill out the survey at the back of this book, tear it out, and mail it to us at:

Publishing Department
Peterson's, a Nelnet company
2000 Lenox Drive
Lawrenceville, NJ 08648

Your feedback will help us make your education dreams possible.

Remember, there is no "best" school—only the best school for you. Start examining your goals, your interests, your personality, your talents—and by all means, talk with your teachers and guidance counselors. The editors at Peterson's wish you the best of luck in your college search!

# The College Admissions Process

Don't let the college admissions process intimidate you. Colleges and universities all compete for students. Choose eight to ten appropriate schools, pay close attention to your applications, and give the best audition you can. You might find that the hardest part of the process will be choosing which offer of admission to accept.

Performing Arts

# Choosing Your Educational Future

## PERSONAL ASSESSMENT

Choosing a college is a great challenge for every student. When you have special talent in the performing arts, the choice is even more critical and you must make some personal assessments at a rather early stage about priorities, goals, professional commitment, and direction for your future. It is important that you take the time to be brutally honest with yourself as you examine your values, strengths, weaknesses, and dreams. It is also essential that you find a college that is best for you. As a performing artist, you must begin this process early enough to prepare for any auditions required. While most students start the college admissions process in the spring of their junior year, performing arts majors should begin to explore colleges, programs, and audition requirements earlier, and no later than in their sophomore year.

Start your personal assessment by considering the following questions:

- How do I like to spend my time? What makes me happiest? What bores me to tears?

- What am I good at? Where do my academic strengths lie? What do I never want to have to study again?

- Why do I want to go to college? What do I expect to gain? What am I looking forward to?

- Do I want to stay close to home or go away? How often do I imagine myself coming home during the year?

- What kind of surroundings make me happiest? Do I thrive on the pace and opportunities in a city? Am I happiest in the country, a serene, pastoral setting? Do I enjoy suburbia? Am I sensitive to weather—do I hate the cold or heat?

- What kind of people do I like to be around?

- What values are most important to me? What do I care most about?

- What kind of person do I want to become?

3

- What has been the best decision I've made in the past three years? Why?

- What has been the worst decision I've made in the past three years? Why? What did I learn from that experience?

- What decision have I let others (parents, teachers, friends, etc.) make for me? Why? What was the outcome?

- How free do I feel to make my own college decisions? Do my parents generally agree with my plans for college? How important to me are the opinions of family? Friends? Teachers?

- Is there anything preventing me from enrolling in a post-secondary program (college, conservatory, etc.) right out of high school?

- What do I think of general education (liberal arts) versus specialization (conservatory training)? How does this relate to the way I want to spend my time?

- What is my favorite postsecondary program now? What characteristics make this program my favorite?

- How do I feel about the size of an institution? Do I work best in small groups? Do I prefer lots of individual attention? Do I like larger settings?

- How do I respond to competition? Do I thrive on pressure or need a more nurturing environment? Do I want a program in which I must work hard constantly, or would I prefer one in which I can obtain respectable grades without knocking myself out? How would I feel if I were in the middle or the bottom of my class? Is it important to me to be near the top of the class?

- How do I learn best? What teachers and methods of teaching have worked best for me?

- How would I feel about attending a program in which there are few requirements? How much structure is best for me?

- How have I done in high school? Where are my academic strengths? What are my standardized test scores (PSAT, SAT, ACT, SAT Subject Tests)? Is my academic record an accurate measure of any ability? Have I taken any Advanced Placement (AP) courses? What have been my scores on those? What do I consider the best measure of my potential for college work?

Once you have answered these questions and others that you, your parents, your high school counselor, and your teachers will also pose, you can begin your search for the right environment for further study. Guard against choosing the "designer-label" school of the year. Look instead for an institution where you will be able to learn, grow, have fun, make friends, and cultivate your special talents. This is an exciting time. It is also a time when you have much more control over your choices than you probably imagine. Colleges and conservatories all compete for students. If you choose eight to ten appropriate schools and if you do your best in the application, interview, and audition process, you may find yourself with multiple acceptances. You are the consumer and schools need you. You control your future.

## DO YOU HAVE WHAT IT TAKES?

Sometimes it is difficult to know how your talent measures up. Many of you have starred in the high school play, sung solos with a glee club, danced in regular studio recitals, and perhaps even attended district or all-state band, orchestra, or chorus. Everyone in the community raves about your talent, and you think you want to develop it further at college. But how do you really know if you have what it takes? Your answers to the following questions may help you clarify just how dedicated you are to the development of your talent.

### Dancers

- Are you taking classes regularly? In ballet? In modern dance?

- Do you enjoy taking classes?

- What is the background of your teacher(s)? What feedback have you received?

- How many public performances have you done? How did you feel during the rehearsal stage? During the performance? Afterwards?

- Have you auditioned for any competitive summer programs? For regional productions? What was the outcome?

- Do you have the body type suitable for further study in dance? Have you ever had a weight problem?

- What books about dance have you read?

- What performances have you seen?

- Do you feel that you are musical or musically sensitive?

- Do you enjoy the physicality of dance?

- Are you self-motivated regarding dance?

- Do you remember sequences of dance steps well?

- Are you self-disciplined? (Ask yourself this several times.)

- Do you eat, drink, breathe, and dream dance? Are you prepared to make the sacrifices necessary to make your passion to study dance a reality?

- Is there anything else you could pursue that would make you happy? (If you answer "yes" to this, you probably should decide not to follow a full-time dance program of study.)

**Musicians**

- How many years of study have you had on your major instrument?

- Have you studied intensively with a private teacher? What is that teacher's background? What feedback does your teacher give you?

- Do you listen to music regularly? To recordings? To the radio? Do you attend classical concerts as well as alternative performance events?

- Have you prepared the repertoire required for auditions?

- Have you participated in musical events in your school? How did you feel during the rehearsals? During the performances? Afterwards?

- Have you auditioned and been accepted at any competitive programs? All-state programs? District programs? Youth symphonies or community choruses? Bands? Summer programs?

- Have you been a soloist? How often?

- Have you studied any music theory? Sight reading? Music history?

- How many hours a day do you practice?

- Do you have the emotional fortitude to deal with the inevitable rejection that accompanies the audition process?

- Are you realistic about the business nature of the music industry?

- Is there anything else you could pursue that would make you happy? (If you answer "yes" to this, you should probably decide not to follow a full-time music program of study.)

## Actors

- Have you participated in theater productions in your school? How did you feel during the rehearsal stage? During the production? Afterwards?

- Have you taken any acting classes? Singing? Movement? Improvisation?

- Are you aware that real actor training is both physically and emotionally demanding? Are you willing to put in the dedication and concentration for the scope of training that will serve you best?

- What is the background of your principal acting teacher? Your director? What feedback have you received?

- Do you know your "type"?

- Do you memorize well? Quickly?

- What kind of acting are you interested in? Film? TV? Theater?

- Do you have the patience for the hours of memorizing and sometimes tedious rehearsals required of actors?

- Are you resourceful in thinking of ways to support yourself until you get cast as an actor? Will your ego withstand being in "rent" or "day" jobs?

- Do you have the emotional fortitude to deal with the inevitable rejection that accompanies life in the theater?

- Are you aware that show business is really just that: a business? How will you feel about dealing with the business side of the entertainment industry?

- Is there anything else you could pursue that would make you happy? (If you answer "yes" to this, you should probably decide not to follow a full-time theater program of study.)

### Getting Objective Opinions About Your Talent

It is sometimes possible to arrange an "advisory" audition to help you determine your level of expertise. In dance, you might call your regional ballet company and see if they would refer you to a class where you could speak with the teacher afterwards. Does that "objective" teacher think that you are at the level of auditioning for a regional company? A conservatory program? Or, should you consider dance as an avocation?

In theater, it is virtually impossible to do an advisory audition for a selective school program. You might call a casting director or ask a working actor for some advice. It is not wise to send an unsolicited videotape or DVD of your monologues to programs in which you are interested. The admissions committee wants to see you in person or at a regional audition. Your best bet is to participate in your school and community theater group and in summer theater programs. Read lots of plays. Investigate taking private classes, too, if they are offered in your area. For your further education, the best recommendation is a liberal arts environment. Some of the best actors were English, history, or foreign language majors at liberal arts colleges who then did specific training in theater after two or four years of general education.

In classical instrumental music, it is common for well-known teachers to give advisory auditions or consultations. If you live near a conservatory or plan to visit one, write to a teacher in advance and request a consultation or lesson. Be prepared to pay for this, however. See "Researching Teachers for Consultations and Lessons" in **For Music Majors** in this guide. If you do not live in the vicinity of a conservatory, try calling the nearest regional orchestra and asking if the principal player on your instrument is willing to hear you and give an opinion. For popular music, you might ask about sitting in with some "name" players and seeking their opinion and advice. Or you might ask if they would be willing to listen to a live or taped performance and give you an evaluation.

For singers, it is a little bit more difficult to get an objective opinion. At 17 or 18, very few singers have the physical development to reveal the true quality of their voice. While there may seem to be potential, it is usually very raw talent. Unfortunately, some voice teachers are happy to string students along as long as they are paying for regular lessons. Choir directors or directors of musical theater are usually very encouraging of young singers. However, before young singers become deluded with the sense of having a major career in opera or on Broadway, they should seek some objective assessment of their talent. Some colleges and conservatories are now requiring videotapes or DVDs for first-time college applicants as a way of pre-screening. As with theater majors, young singers should plan for at least two years of liberal arts study, including foreign languages (especially French, Italian, and German), literature, history, and economics, as well as music theory, music history, ear-training, and especially sight-singing. Because of everything from basic physical development to hormonal changes in the body, the voice is slower to develop, and so there is time for this general study.

Composers and conductors have an even more difficult time obtaining an early assessment. Composers might write in advance to ask a faculty member to evaluate copies of scores. Conductors might inquire about sending videotapes or DVDs of performances.

## EDUCATION CHOICES

Once you have done some self-evaluation, you will probably find that you fall into one of the following three groups:

- You are sure that you want to focus on your performing art now and will apply only to conservatory or preprofessional programs or audition for companies.

- You are not quite sure that you want to be totally focused on your performing art. You want to keep your options open and plan to apply to conservatories, joint programs, and liberal arts colleges with strong performing arts programs. You will explore Bachelor of Arts (B.A.), Bachelor of Fine Arts (B.F.A.), and/or Bachelor of Music (B.M.) degree programs.

- You are not clear about the level of your talent, or you may think that you have talent in more than one area and want to expand your background before focusing. You think that applying to liberal arts colleges or universities is best for you at this time.

Many students do end up changing their majors. So if you are the least bit uncertain about pursuing an area within the performing arts, you should keep your options open by choosing an institution that has a good department in the area of your main interest but also has general distribution requirements. If you end up changing your major, chances are that it is because another department within the college or university offered courses that inspired you.

While this guide contains profiles of professional performing arts programs, there are many excellent performing arts programs available at colleges that only offer liberal arts undergraduate degrees. Macalester College, Massachusetts Institute of Technology (MIT), Princeton University, Roberts Wesleyan College, Tufts University, Wesleyan University, and Yale University all have impressive undergraduate dance, music, and/or theater programs. Some institutions that award only undergraduate liberal arts degrees offer joint programs with other schools, such as Barnard College and Columbia University that have joint programs with the Manhattan School of Music and/or Juilliard. A separate application and admission to the professional program is usually required, and the professional degree (e.g., B.M.) is actually awarded from the professional school.

In addition, many students choose to study performing arts abroad at some point in their training. The Guildhall School of Music and Drama in London, England, is an internationally renowned conservatory offering programs in music, acting, and technical theater. Music majors are also encouraged to learn about Toho Gakuen in Japan and the Hochschule system in Germany.

Whichever type of program you are applying to, certain procedures in the college admissions process are common to all programs. This guide will discuss various aspects of the entire admissions process and then focus specifically on the unique requirements for dance, music, and theater auditions and applications.

Performing

Arts

# Beginning the College Search

## SURFING THE INTERNET

Almost every college, university, or conservatory has its own Web site. This is a good place to begin your search. Start reviewing Web sites early on. You can read a general description of the school, determine tour information, research teachers and majors, find out about audition dates and application deadlines, and obtain audition repertoire requirements. You will sometimes find a profile of the entering class or a description of the type of student most likely to be admitted. When you analyze that profile, you may be able to get an idea of whether you are the kind of student the institution is looking for.

On the school's Web site, you can also usually request more information about its programs. Most students fill out an online registration form to get on the institution's mailing list for a catalog or viewbook, and sometimes for information about upcoming concerts.

Remember these important points regarding the Internet and college admissions.

- Do NOT use a screen name that is provocative. Such names as Partyboy@hotmail.com, hotdiva@yahoo.com, sexydancer@aol.com, staractor@gmail.com, or anything else that sounds suggestive are not considered in good taste or funny. They reflect poorly on you and should be totally avoided.

- Any contact you make with a college, university, or conservatory over the Internet usually becomes part of your admissions file and is considered formal correspondence with that institution. Therefore, do NOT write in colloquial "Internet language." Whether it is an e-mail to a teacher or admissions representative, contact over the school's message board, or entry on a blog, you must be extremely careful to be proper and discreet and to write in standard English.

Colleges and universities are some of the leaders in using the Internet. Some have put their entire catalog online, including the list of faculty. Others have everything from a virtual tour of the campus to a calendar of upcoming concerts and recitals to their student newspaper available on their Web site. It is worth your time to surf the Internet and visit the Web sites of colleges, conservatories, and universities—but remember that nothing is as memorable as your own visit to a campus to see what it is really like.

There are also interactive Web sites devoted to college search and selection. Petersons.com is a one-stop source of information on college admission. See "Searching for Performing Arts Programs and Scholarships Online" in this guide.

In recent times, some colleges, universities, and conservatories have begun using social networking Web sites such as Facebook.com and MySpace.com. Do not judge a school by the people who are "friends" on these pages. They may or may not be accepted into the school. If you decide to post on one of these sites, be extremely prudent about the content and tone of your post.

## COLLEGE CATALOGS

Much of the information about each school can be gleaned from the college catalog. This publication contains a wealth of material about the size, location, history, philosophy, calendar, costs, admissions policies, financial aid availability, faculty, and degree requirements of a school. Reading them carefully and critically will help illuminate the differences among schools. For instance, if you want to be a theater major at a liberal arts college but you hate to write papers, a college that requires a written senior thesis may not be appropriate. Or, if you are a dancer and never want to take another foreign language course, a program that requires you to demonstrate proficiency in at least one foreign language may not be the one for you. Reading the catalog will help you narrow your list, formulate intelligent questions to ask your interviewer, and give you the most objective information on the policies, procedures, and climate of a campus.

## VIEWBOOKS AND VIDEOS/DVDS

Because of the great competition among schools for qualified students, many colleges have produced glossy viewbooks and professional videos or DVDs to send to prospective students. These are often written and produced by public relations or marketing specialists and include glamorous photos of the campus at its best, with the most photogenic students and perfect views of buildings.

A fairly new company, Collegiate Choice Walking Tours Videos (www. collegiatechoice.com), has nonpromotional videos of more than 350 colleges and universities in the United States, Canada, and nine other countries. While viewbooks, videos, and DVDs can give you some flavor of a campus, they should not replace your own research through a careful reading of the course catalog and a campus visit, if possible.

You can write or send a fax or e-mail to the schools that interest you for catalogs and admissions information. Be prepared to give your name, address, area of concentration, birth date, and social security number. (If you do not have a social security number, now would be a good time to get one; you'll need it for computer identification.) If you write, follow the style of the sample letter:

Sally Smith
1 Main Street
Anywhere, ST
February 15, 2008

Dear Director of Admissions:

I am currently a sophomore at Anywhere High School and am interested in learning more about [name of school]. Please send me your most recent course catalog, an application, and any other admissions information. I am interested in studying dance [or theater or music—specify your instrument] further in college, so any specific information about your program in [your performing art] would be very helpful. I would also like to learn about any financial aid or scholarship information.

Thank you for your attention to this request.

Sincerely,
Sally Smith

Once you have made initial contact with a school, whether by telephone, letter, fax, or e-mail, most schools will establish a computer file on you. They will send you materials and may even deluge you with propaganda. It is your job to assess this information crucially and systematically.

### KEEP A COLLEGE NOTEBOOK

The best way to organize your college information is to set up a "college notebook" or Excel spreadsheet. You can use it to keep track of your mailings, to make checklists for yourself, and to record your impressions of each school.

### BLOGS AND OTHER ONLINE TOOLS TO TRACK YOUR THOUGHTS

Some students have taken to keeping a blog about their journey through the college admission process. I highly urge you NOT to engage in this activity. Remember that a blog is open to everyone on the Internet and anybody can see what you've written. If you are writing about your reflections on College X in a blog, you have no idea who may read your entry. It may be a friend, a teacher, a college admissions representative, or a future employer. And Web sites such as MySpace, Xanga, Facebook, LiveJournal, and Friendster are highly controversial for this purpose. Some students have been suspended or expelled from summer programs or schools for what they have posted online, whether it be photos or indiscreet writings. When it comes to college admission, it is advisable to go back to the old method of pen and paper or even word processing in a private document and to keep your impressions off the Internet.

### NARROWING YOUR SEARCH

After you have reviewed the Web sites and/or read the college catalogs (some students send for twenty-five to fifty catalogs at first), you should be able to narrow your list of preferred schools to about twelve to eighteen that seriously interest you. The list should reflect a range of selectivity, including some "reaches," "possibles," and "safeties." Other means of gathering more information about these schools before deciding to visit include:

- speaking to your high school counselor and reviewing your list;

- speaking with students in your area who attend the college and are home on vacation;

- obtaining names of alumni in your area and speaking with them;

- talking to your current teachers about colleges and conservatories;

- attending college fairs and speaking with admissions representatives;

- meeting admission representatives visiting your high school; and

- attending any group meetings held in selected cities and towns where college and conservatory admissions representatives are available to answer your questions.

The National Association for College Admission Counseling (NACAC) sponsors an annual series of National Performing Arts College Fairs, held in approximately fifteen cities throughout the United States. Most admission directors from colleges, conservatories, and universities listed in this guide attend these important fairs and provide information and answer questions. For exact dates and locations, contact NACAC at www.nacacnet.org, where you can view the list of college fairs, or call 703-836-2222 or 800-822-6285. The NACAC fax is 703-836-8015.

**A Word about Decision Plans**

Colleges and conservatories have many different policies for applying. In narrowing your list, you should also consider whether you want to play a strategy game and juggle application deadlines and decision plans. For instance, if you have decided to apply to liberal arts colleges or universities and have fallen in love with one particular college, you might consider applying via an Early Decision plan, if the college has one. This plan means that you apply early to that one school, and then if you are admitted, you must attend. Other plans include Early Action (you apply early and get an early reply, but you do not have to make the commitment to attend right away), and some institutions have a menu of Early plans—Early Decision Plan I, Early Decision Plan II, and so on. Be sure to read the fine print about these plans very carefully and discuss your options with your college counselor. There are also Rolling Decision plans (often found at state universities, with decisions made on a first-come, first-served basis), Regular Decision plans, and others. There are strategies with deadlines and decision plans. Be a smart applicant and see whether any will work for you.

If you are applying to conservatories, the traditional time to apply is in late November or early December for auditions in January through March, when most conservatories have their main auditions. Read about deadlines carefully. Since some conservatories also have later auditions, you might juggle the audition process, applying to your first choice and auditioning at the earliest audition time, usually in February or March, and attending, if admitted, but doing further auditions later, often in May, if not accepted. However, you do gamble when taking this approach, because some departments may close by that time of year. For more about timing of auditions, see "Music Auditions" in **For Music Majors** in this guide.

# Searching for Performing Arts Programs and Scholarships Online

Choosing a college performing arts program involves a serious commitment of time and resources. Therefore, it is important to have the most up-to-date information about institutions and their programs at your fingertips. The Internet can be a great tool for gathering that information, and one of the best sites to visit during the college selection process is Peterson's Visual & Performing Arts (VPA) channel at www.petersons.com/arts.

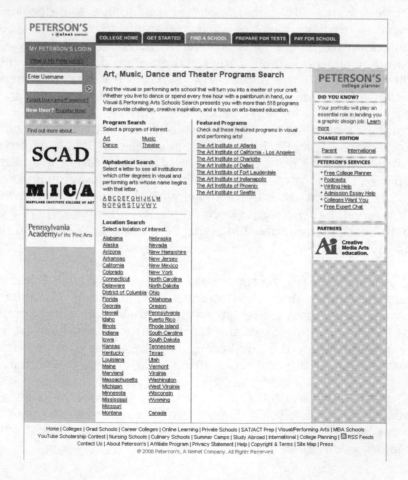

## PETERSON'S VISUAL & PERFORMING ARTS CHANNEL

The VPA channel at www.petersons.com is a one-stop source of information on college programs in the U.S. and Canada. Under "Colleges and Universities," click on "Art, Music, Dance and Theater Programs" in the Quick Links box to access Peterson's comprehensive database of arts programs. If you know what area of dance, theater, or music you're interested in, you can locate a school or program by clicking on the area on the Program Search menu, which provides a list of majors or concentrations. Simply click one of these, and you will see a list of schools that offer a degree program in that field. Or, if you'd like to search by location, you can access lists of schools offering arts programs in any state or in Canada. Finally, if you have a particular school in mind and want to see what programs it offers, you can do an alphabetical search on the school's name and get information about their programs.

You can also request information from some schools by clicking on "Get Free Info." Within minutes, the school will receive your message and mail a catalog, an application, or information on financial aid to you. If you find the perfect school for a friend, you can even send the page to him or her with a message. There also are links to the school's Web site.

## PETERSON'S FREE SCHOLARSHIP SEARCH

Petersons.com is a great site for any college-bound student. There is a wealth of information on undergraduate, graduate, online learning, and study-abroad programs and also some of the best financial aid advice available.

With Peterson's free Scholarship Search on the financial aid channel of Petersons.com (www.petersons.com/finaid), you can explore more than 1.68 million scholarships, grants, and prizes totaling nearly $8 billion and do an individualized search for awards that match your financial and educational needs. In just three easy steps, you can register and complete a customized profile indicating your scholastic and personal background, including intended major, work experience, and a host of other criteria that will allow you to access a list of scholarships that match your needs. Each scholarship is described in detail with eligibility and application requirements, contact information, and links to its e-mail address and Web site. Finding money for college couldn't be easier.

So what are you waiting for? Log on to Petersons.com and let us help you with your college planning!

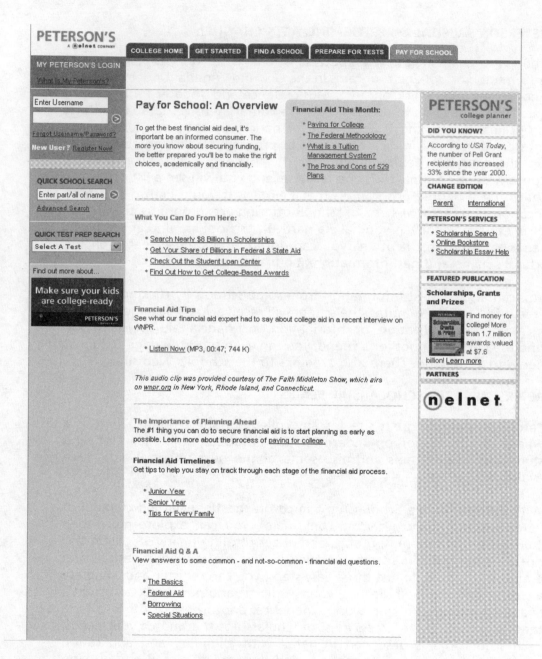

**PETERSON'S**
A nelnet COMPANY

| COLLEGE HOME | GET STARTED | FIND A SCHOOL | PREPARE FOR TESTS | PAY FOR SCHOOL |

MY PETERSON'S LOGIN

What is My Peterson's?

Enter Username

Forgot Username/Password?

**New User?** Register Now!

QUICK SCHOOL SEARCH

Enter part/all of name

Advanced Search

QUICK TEST PREP SEARCH

Select A Test

Find out more about...

Make sure your kids
are college-ready

PETERSON'S

### Pay for School: An Overview

To get the best financial aid deal, it's
important be an informed consumer. The
more you know about securing funding,
the better prepared you'll be to make the right
choices, academically and financially.

**Financial Aid This Month:**
* Paying for College
* The Federal Methodology
* What is a Tuition Management System?
* The Pros and Cons of 529 Plans

**What You Can Do From Here:**

* Search Nearly $8 Billion in Scholarships
* Get Your Share of Billions in Federal & State Aid
* Check Out the Student Loan Center
* Find Out How to Get College-Based Awards

**Financial Aid Tips**
See what our financial aid expert had to say about college aid in a recent interview on
WNPR.

* Listen Now (MP3, 00:47; 744 K)

*This audio clip was provided courtesy of The Faith Middleton Show, which airs
on wnpr.org in New York, Rhode Island, and Connecticut.*

**The Importance of Planning Ahead**
The #1 thing you can do to secure financial aid is to start planning as early as
possible. Learn more about the process of paying for college.

**Financial Aid Timelines**
Get tips to help you stay on track through each stage of the financial aid process.

* Junior Year
* Senior Year
* Tips for Every Family

**Financial Aid Q & A**
View answers to some common - and not-so-common - financial aid questions.

* The Basics
* Federal Aid
* Borrowing
* Special Situations

**PETERSON'S**
college planner

**DID YOU KNOW?**
According to *USA Today*,
the number of Pell Grant
recipients has increased
33% since the year 2000.

**CHANGE EDITION**

Parent    International

**PETERSON'S SERVICES**
* Scholarship Search
* Online Bookstore
* Scholarship Essay Help

**FEATURED PUBLICATION**

**Scholarships, Grants
and Prizes**

Find money for
college! More
than 1.7 million
awards valued
at $7.6
billion! Learn more

**PARTNERS**

nelnet

# College Admissions Timetable

Below is a general outline of how to proceed and pace yourself in the college admissions process. Your actual timetable may differ slightly, depending on the deadlines at the schools you have chosen and audition schedules. Keep an up-to-date spreadsheet with deadlines and use this as a list of guideposts.

## SOPHOMORE YEAR (TENTH GRADE)

### September–October

- Make learning and your education a priority, along with practice in your performing art. Aim for balance.

- Take a practice PSAT/NMSQT in October. This is good practice for junior year, when PSAT scores count toward National Merit® Scholarships. (National Merit Scholarships are based on the scores you achieve on this test when you take it in your junior year.) Note that many schools require that sophomores take a practice PSAT, some make it optional to take, and other schools do not offer it to tenth graders at all. It can be a useful exercise to take it in tenth grade, and you should inquire in September about taking it if your guidance counselor does not have everyone register.

### December

- Obtain your PSAT results. Review the answer sheet. Talk to your guidance counselor about the advisability of taking a test preparation course.

### January–April

- Begin your review of Web sites for colleges and universities.

- Write for college catalogs. Read them, noting audition requirements.

- Obtain a social security number if you do not already have one.

- Investigate the National Foundation for Advancement in the Arts (NFAA or ARTS) annual scholarship competition.

- Meet with your guidance counselor. Discuss course plans—APs, honors, or additional performing arts classes—and about other plans for your future.

- Research taking and registering for any SAT Subject Tests in a subject in which you have done well and which may be required by the school you're interested in attending. Speak to your teacher first.

- Start researching financial aid and scholarship opportunities.

- Keep a file of various documents: reviews, copies of programs, photos, and any papers you have received good comments and grades on, articles you've written for the school newspaper, or stories contributed to the literary magazine.

- Attend college fairs. Find out all you can about schools you are considering.

- Plan your summer to expand your performing experience. Participate in a summer program. Remember to ask for letters of recommendation.

## JUNIOR YEAR (ELEVENTH GRADE)

### September

- Meet with your guidance counselor or college adviser to renew or establish your acquaintance. Review plans; register for the PSAT/NMSQT.

- Strive to do well in your classes this year.

### October

- Take the PSAT (again). Remember that this time it counts for National Merit® Scholarships.

- Obtain information. Surf the Internet and get catalogs and applications from all the schools you are considering.

- Continue to investigate financial aid opportunities.

- Keep your college notebook or spreadsheet up-to-date.

### December

- Review your PSAT/NMSQT results. PSAT scores indicate what areas you need to strengthen for the SAT.

- Register for the SAT or ACT Assessment. Also consider SAT Subject Tests and the TOEFL, if appropriate. Prepare on your own or take a review course.

**March–June**

- Meet with your guidance counselor and parents/guardians to discuss college plans, your testing schedule, course selections for your senior year, college application essay topics, and any other related matters.

- Plan another enriching summer.

- Start your college visits.

- Take the SAT, ACT, TOEFL, and any SAT Subject Tests, if necessary.

- Attend college fairs.

**July–August**

- Continue your college visits and interviews over the summer.

- Continue to surf the Internet, send for applications, visit colleges, and interview.

- Start planning your audition(s).

**SENIOR YEAR (TWELFTH GRADE)**

**September–October**

- Continue your college visits and interviews. Record your reactions in your college notebook.

- Meet with your guidance counselor or college adviser. Discuss your college list and try to narrow it down.

- Consider applying Early Decision to your top-choice school. Check deadlines. November 1 and November 15 are common dates.

- Get letters of recommendation from teachers and former employees.

- Apply for the ARTS recognition scholarship through NFAA. (National Foundation for Advancement in the Arts, 444 Brickell Avenue, Miami, FL 33131; 305-377-1140 or toll-free, 800-970-ARTS; www.artsawards.org.)

- Be sure you have all application forms. Start drafting college application essays.

- Do a run-through of your audition material.

### November

- Meet Early Decision deadline, if appropriate.

- Fill out college application forms. Continue to revise and perfect your essays.

- Take any additional tests: SAT, ACT, TOEFL, or SAT Subject Tests.

- Complete and submit your applications. Proofread them thoroughly and photocopy them before mailing.

- Request that your test results be sent to the colleges that require them.

- Continue practicing for your audition.

### December–January

- Early Decision results are mailed. Celebrate if you were admitted and meet all deadlines for enrollment deposits. If you were deferred or rejected, submit other applications and move on.

- Obtain the FAFSA and CSS/Financial Aid PROFILE® (if applicable) if you are applying for financial aid. Start filling out financial aid forms and be aware of deadlines.

- Have your guidance counselor or college adviser send transcripts and test scores to the schools you've chosen.

- Last chance to take the SAT and ACT!

### February–March

- Attend scheduled auditions.

- Check to make sure that all your financial aid documents are in order.

### April

- Make your decision. Consider with your parents and adviser the pros and cons of each institution.

- Revisit any college if your decision to attend is not crystal clear.

- Notify colleges of your decision by May 1. If a school asks for a decision response before May 1, you have a right to request an extension until the May 1 Candidate's Reply Deadline (CRD).

**May**

- Be sure to notify all colleges by May 1, even if you are on the waiting list.
- Take any AP exams, if applicable.

# Campus Visits

Once you have narrowed your list further, you may want to visit a campus. There is really no substitute for seeing a campus yourself, experiencing the atmosphere, meeting students, sitting in on classes, and picturing yourself in the environment. If a school requires an interview and you are ready, you can combine the campus visit with the interview. "Drop-ins" at an admission office are not necessarily welcome. It's worthwhile to call ahead and schedule an appointment.

## WHEN TO VISIT

You should visit before the application deadline, as the visit is one way for you to determine if you actually want to apply to the school. There are many things to consider when planning the timing of the visit.

### Spring of Junior Year

Many students try to visit three or four colleges during spring break of their junior year. The problem with this is that many college admissions offices are at their busiest at this time, holding auditions or finalizing decisions on students who have applied. Although you may be able to take a campus tour and speak to some students, this may not be a good time for your college interview.

### Summer Between Junior and Senior Years

The advantage of a summer visit is that the admissions office is more relaxed and you may be given more time and personal attention. You can go on a campus tour and see the facilities, but, unless there is a summer session, you cannot get the flavor of the campus in action. You may decide that you like the school and will keep it on your list, but may need to visit again to stay overnight and sit in on classes. Your family may want to include a few summer visits to colleges as part of a vacation trip, or you may plan to visit before your summer program starts or after your summer job ends.

### Fall of Senior Year

This is probably the best time to visit the colleges in which you are most interested. Just be careful not to miss so much time at your own school that you fall behind in your classes. First-semester senior-year grades are

Performing Arts

extremely important. Some high schools set aside college visiting days, and there are also the traditional fall holidays, such as Columbus Day, when many colleges are open and may have classes in session. Be sure to make appointments well in advance of your visit.

## WHEN NOT TO VISIT

It is not a good idea to visit a campus when the admissions office is closed or on major holiday breaks, such as Thanksgiving, Christmas, or New Year's. Other dates to avoid include pre-exam, exam, and jury weeks (when auditions are held). While some colleges have Saturday morning interviews during the busy fall, there are seldom classes you can sit in on over the weekend.

## THE IDEAL VISIT

It is best to arrive on a weekday afternoon. Take an admissions-sponsored guided tour of the campus, stay over in a dormitory with an admissions host or with a friend who attends the school, eat in the cafeteria, and observe and talk to as many students as possible. Try to attend a concert or production that evening. In the morning sit in on some classes, watch a rehearsal or coaching, and speak to faculty members. (Arrange for this in advance.) If an interview is recommended or required, have your interview, preferably after lunch.

### What to Look for When You Visit

You want to gather as much information as possible during your visit. Pick up a copy of the campus newspaper, read bulletin boards to see the variety of activities announced, and look at the ride board. Are students going away every weekend? Get the calendar of events for the week or month during which you are visiting. Does it represent a variety of activities? Look through a yearbook if possible. Observe the people around you. Are they "your kind of people"? Sit in on a rehearsal. What is the level of expertise? Explore the surrounding neighborhood. Do you feel safe? Does it provide the kind of environment that makes you feel comfortable?

### Questions to Ask Your Tour Guide

Here are some general questions you might ask your tour guide or student host. (Specific questions about your area in the performing arts are covered in later sections.)

- How diverse is the student body? Where are students from? Do they represent different racial, ethnic, and economic backgrounds?

- What percentage of the student body are from abroad? Which countries are represented by the most students? Are the foreign students integrated into the community?

- What do students like most about the college? What are the most frequent complaints?

- How would you describe the overall tone (attitude, morale) of the campus?

- What have been the issues or tensions on the campus this year?

- What do students do for fun?

- What do students typically do on a weekend?

- What is the role of fraternities and sororities?

- What sports teams are available?

- What extracurricular activities are strongly supported by the administration?

- Are faculty members generally accessible?

- What is the workload like? How would you describe competition among students?

- What were the cultural highlights of last year? The social highlights?

- What are the housing options for freshmen? For transfers? Are there single-sex floors? Nonsmoking dorms? Quiet study facilities?

- How are roommates chosen?

- What kind of meal plans are offered? Is there vegetarian or kosher food? Must I subscribe to the meal plan if I live in college housing?

- Are student health services provided? Is a doctor, nurse, or psychologist provided at no additional charge?

- How is the library? The media center? The computer facilities? Are there any student complaints about these facilities?

- What is the relationship between the college and the surrounding town or city?

- How are the academics? Are there any outstanding faculty members I should know about?

- When you register for classes, what percentage of courses that you want to take are you able to enroll in?

- Is the campus safe? What are the crime statistics? (Colleges are required to make crime statistics available to the public.)

- Are there any problems with drugs or alcohol?

- How are racial relations on the campus?

- Is there career counseling?

- What career paths do most graduates take?

- If you have questions that your tour guide cannot answer, ask your interviewer or speak to an admissions counselor.

## FOLLOW-UP TO YOUR VISIT

After your visit, it is appropriate to write a thank-you note to your interviewer. It may be just a simple, handwritten note or postcard saying that you enjoyed the conversation and look forward to applying to the school, or you may want to add something about the conversation you had. Often this note becomes part of your file, and admissions officers tend to react favorably to finding a thoughtful note among all the other information there. You should also write a note of thanks to your host, if you stayed over. A note or postcard is better than an e-mail in this case. In recent times, many colleges are using interest demonstrated in a school as one of the key factors in an admissions decision. Thus, if you are truly interested in the school, you really should be certain to write that follow-up correspondence.

Record your impressions in your college notebook as soon as possible after you visit. Be careful not to be overly influenced by personalities on a campus. Although admissions representatives tend to be positive and perky types, anyone can have a bad day. If someone is abrupt or less than friendly, try not to let this color your view of the entire campus. Also, beware of thinking that a school seen on a perfect, sunny, crisp fall day is more appealing than another school seen on a gloomy, rainy day. Be honest with yourself, too. A prestigious school visited under ideal conditions may be seductive, but is it the right match for you?

## IF YOU ARE UNABLE TO VISIT

If financial restrictions, time constraints, or other reasons make it impossible to visit a campus, call the admissions office and find out about alumni and current students who live near you or admissions representatives traveling in your area. Try to schedule an interview with one of these individuals for first-hand information. Also visit the Web site and request the college video or DVD if one exists. Again, if this college truly appeals to you, demonstrating your sincere interest is vitally important and you should make it clear that your inability to travel to the campus at this time is no reflection of the seriousness of your interest.

Performing Arts

# College Interviews

This is your opportunity to be more than just a stack of papers in the admissions office; it's your chance to personalize the admission process. Interviews do not usually make or break admissions decisions, but you should try to have an interview at those schools that are of real interest to you and are realistic choices.

## SCHEDULING YOUR INTERVIEW

When you read the college catalog, note whether an interview is optional or required. (Do not confuse this topic with auditions, which are quite another matter and are discussed later in this book.) Because of staff restrictions, travel difficulties, and financial constraints, very few colleges make the interview mandatory.

If you do decide to have an interview, never just drop in. Try to plan your interviews as part of your campus visit. Don't schedule your first interview to be at your first-choice school; you'll do better after you've had some experience in an interview situation. Try to avoid making your first-choice school your last interview, also, as you want to remain fresh and spontaneous in your responses.

Schedule all Interviews well in advance. And, if you cannot attend an interview appointment, be sure to call and cancel. A cancellation will not be held against, you but a missed appointment probably will be. If you get lost en route to an interview and are running late, be sure to call.

## GETTING READY

Preparing for an interview is important. Practice interviews are helpful to some students. Ask your college counselor to conduct a mock interview with you or have a family friend role-play with you.

Be sure to read the catalog and write down a list of questions that you want to ask. Take time to think about your strengths and weaknesses, and be prepared to speak about them in a positive way. College interviews are not the time for modesty and monosyllabic answers. At the same time, you do not want to sound boastful or arrogant.

Take stock of the extracurricular activities in which you have participated, your hobbies, volunteer work, and other ways that you spend your time.

If there are special circumstances in your life that have affected your academic record, you may want to bring them up at an interview. For instance, if you missed a great deal of school because you had a heavy performance schedule but were able to make up the work, or if your family went through a particularly grueling year, with divorce, unemployment, or sickness, you may want to talk about it with your interviewer. Be careful not to sound as though you are making excuses for yourself, but rather adding to the college's understanding of who you are.

**What to Wear**

Just as there are costumes for performances, there are interview "costumes." For women, a nice skirt (not too short) or pants and a blouse, possibly with a jacket, or a simple dress is recommended, worn with low to medium heels. Men should wear nice pants with a shirt, jacket, and tie, or a turtleneck or shirt with a collar. Be neat and clean.

**WHAT *NOT* TO DO AT YOUR INTERVIEW**

Here are some things you should *not* do at an interview:

- smoke;
- chew gum;
- complain or make excuses;
- swear or use language that is too colloquial;
- exhibit a negative attitude (boredom, arrogance, etc.);
- answer in monosyllables or in single sentences;
- ask questions if you have no interest in the response;
- ask for an evaluation of another school you are considering;
- bring your scrapbook of programs, reviews, articles, or term papers for the interviewer to read;
- dress inappropriately;
- twitch, fidget, or slump in your seat; or
- pretend to be someone you are not. Be yourself!

**TYPICAL INTERVIEW QUESTIONS**

Every interviewer has his or her favorites questions, but there are some common areas that are covered in most interviews. These include:

- your high school experience;

- your personal traits, relationships with others, and family background;

- your interests outside the classroom–hobbies, extracurricular activities, summer vacations, movies you've seen, and so on;

- your values and goals, and how you view the world around you;

- your impressions of the college you are visiting; and

- answering your questions.

You should anticipate questions like these:

- Tell me about your high school. How long have you attended? What are the students like? Do you like your high school? What would you preserve or change about it?

- Which courses have you liked most? Which do you like least? Which have been the most challenging?

- How well do you think your school has prepared you for your future study?

- How would you describe yourself as a student?

- Do you know what you want to major in?

- What has been your most stimulating intellectual experience?

- In what extracurricular activity have you been most involved? How much time do you devote to it?

- Do you have hobbies or special interests?

- After a long, hard day, what do you enjoy doing most? What do you do for fun? For relaxation?

- How have you spent your summer vacations? Why did you decide to spend them that way?

- How would you describe yourself in five adjectives?

- What is your family like? Describe your upbringing. How has your environment influenced your way of thinking?

- How would your friends describe you?

- Which relationships are most important to you? Why?

- Have you ever encountered people who thought and acted differently from you? What viewpoints or actions challenged you the most? How did you respond? What did you learn about yourself?

- What do your friends and family expect of you? What pressures have you felt?

- If you had a year to go anywhere and do whatever you wanted, how would you spend that year?

- What magazines or newspapers do you read regularly?

- What books have you read recently? Are there any authors you particularly like?

- What movie have you seen recently and what did you think of it?

- Who are your favorite dancers or dance companies? Why?

- Who are your favorite actors? Why?

- Who are your favorite musicians? Why?

- Who are your favorite performers? Why?

- How did you choose your particular area in the performing arts? Why do you want to pursue this art form?

- What has been your most memorable performance to date? Why?

- Have you worked with a director, choreographer, or conductor who was particularly challenging or inspirational? Describe the experience.

- Who has been your most memorable teacher? Why?

- Why do you want to go to college?

- Why have you chosen this college to investigate? What first brought us to your attention?

- What do you picture yourself doing ten years from now?

- What do you think of the National Endowment for the Arts (or some current affair in the arts)?

- What distresses you most about the world around you? If you had the opportunity to change the world, where would you start?

- Are there any outside circumstances that have interfered with your performance in school? An after-school job? Long commute back and forth to school? Home responsibilities or

*Performing*

*Arts*

difficulties? Illness? Parental pressure? English not spoken at home? Problems with course scheduling? Extended absences from school due to performance schedules? (Take care not to make excuses for yourself, but to present any difficulties honestly and as positively as possible.)

- What more do you want to know about us?

This last question is your opening to ask your questions. Do not be shy about taking out your list; no one expects you to memorize a list of questions, and you want to be sure that you are learning all that you can during your visit to make the decision as to whether or not this is a campus where you could be happy. Many of the questions regarding campus life were probably answered by your tour guide or student host. Here are some other general questions you may want to ask. (Specific questions about your area in dance, theater, or music are presented later in this guide.)

- Who teaches freshmen? Transfers?

- How does registration work? Is it easy to get the classes I want to take?

- What is the advising system like? What are its strengths and weaknesses?

- Are there any changes anticipated in the curriculum?

- Are there any departments that might be cut or discontinued? Have any departments been discontinued in the past two years?

- Are there any planned cutbacks in faculty? Any new appointments scheduled?

- Are there any new programs under consideration? What are they?

- What percentage of students receive financial aid?

- Are there jobs on campus for students? What is a typical work/study job? Are there jobs in the community?

- Are there any opportunities for internships? Study abroad?

- Are financial aid decisions made separately from admissions decisions? Will applying for financial aid influence admissions decisions?

- Do you offer any merit-based scholarships?

The College Admissions Process

- What is your policy on fee waivers, if I cannot afford the application fee?

- What is the overall financial security of the school? Is tuition increased annually? What additional fees might I anticipate?

- What is the most important factor in admissions decisions?

## AFTER YOUR INTERVIEW

Be sure to write your impressions of the interview in your college notebook. And, most important, write the interviewer a thank-you note. Mention something specific that came up in the conversation. Three lines on nice stationery or even on a postcard should be sufficient.

Performing

*Arts*

# The Application

When you have finally narrowed your list to the eight to ten schools to which you have decided to apply, it is time to approach the applications. Application forms have several components. When you decide to apply to a school, do not go immediately to the school's Web site and fill it out online and submit it quickly. Rather, either download a copy and sit down with the print-out of the application, or if you cannot get the entire document downloaded, start to fill it out as a DRAFT and save as you go along, but do NOT hit "submit" until you have truly reviewed the entire document for completeness. (Note that many colleges now strongly prefer that you use the online application, and in recent times more than one-half of all applicants have applied online.)

If you are applying with hard copy via "snail mail," first, read the application carefully. Then make a photocopy of the application to fill out as your draft. It is important that applications be neat and legible, either typed or printed in black or blue ink. Never submit an application that has been filled out in pencil or an odd color ink or that has been scribbled in haste. Fill out the informational section first and then think about the essay questions, if required.

If you do apply electronically, be sure to run spellcheck and to print out your draft to proofread before sending it. Always print and save a hard copy for yourself. Some schools will ask you also to send a hard copy with the application fee.

## ACADEMIC PROFILE

Colleges will require a copy of your high school transcripts(s). Be sure that you have checked your transcript for accuracy before it is sent by your high school. Many schools will also require college entrance examination scores. Some schools use standardized test scores for placement, and some use them as another indicator in your academic profile. As a performing artist, if you plan to apply to schools that require the SAT, SAT Subject Tests, or ACT and have not received scores that you think are truly representative of your ability, you should consider doing some test preparation and retaking the test to raise your score.

In analyzing your scholastic record, colleges are trying to decide whether you will be able to withstand the academic rigor of their environment.

Taking a full complement of challenging academic courses in high school is important. If you are applying to a conservatory, your academic profile is secondary in consideration to your demonstrated talent, but at liberal arts colleges and for joint programs, the academic profile is more important in establishing the match. If you want to leave all options open for college, the most prudent approach is to take the most challenging assortment of academic courses, including math, science, and foreign language electives. However, if you absolutely know that you are applying to a conservatory, taking an extra year of something in which you are not strong probably won't have any effect on an admissions decision. And by not taking it you may have more time to pursue work in your major or concentration area or have more time to practice. Be sure to speak to your college counselor about this and, if necessary, call a few admissions officers for opinions.

## PERSONAL PROFILE

The personal profile that a college gathers on you consists largely of information that is entirely in your control. This includes your list of extracurricular activities, your recommendations, essays, and any appropriate supplementary materials you send. Let's consider each of these.

### Extracurricular Activities

This term refers to any activity outside of the classroom. Many colleges will ask you to put this information in a table, showing the activity, any position of leadership, hours spent in the activity, etc.

As a performing artist, you may not have joined any clubs in your high school, focusing all your time on one activity. That's great! Do not hesitate to acknowledge such dedication. If you have participated in many activities, draft a list including school activities, any jobs you've held, hobbies, community or volunteer activities, church groups, honors, and awards. The point is to make the list comprehensive, but not exhaustive. Depth in one activity is important, so don't try to pad the list.

### Recommendations

Many colleges request teacher recommendations as well as the college counselor report. Choose teachers who know you well as a student and as a person, who like you, and who write well. You should also choose teachers who will add balance and another dimension to your application. For instance, if you are a musician who also has a passion for mathematics, consider asking your math teacher for a recommendation. When you ask a teacher to write a letter of recommendation, remember to:

- ask politely;

- give the teacher the forms (with the top part with your name, etc., filled out) well before the deadline;

- provide the teacher with stamped envelopes addressed to the colleges; and

- include a cover letter to the teacher that gives the deadlines for each school, a list of your extracurricular activities, or anything else that might be helpful to the teacher in writing your recommendation.

Guidance counselors are often also asked to fill out a counselor recommendation form that may include a checklist and narrative. If you attend a large school where the counselors have many responsibilities other than college guidance, you would do well to establish a relationship with your guidance counselor. Schedule meetings, stop by the office to ask quick questions, and, in general, make yourself known to your counselor.

## Essays

Although most admissions representatives say that an essay will not make or break an application, there have been applicants who essentially "wrote" themselves into acceptance. The essay is another opportunity for the admissions committee to get to know you better. Even if the essay is optional, it's a good idea to provide one. A well-written essay will make your application more memorable and distinctive.

Perhaps the hardest thing about the essay is getting started. One method that has worked well, especially with students in the performing arts, is to set your cassette recorder beside you and start talking. Then play back the cassette and transcribe what you said. Usually this technique will allow you to capture your personal voice and help you over any obstacle that you have about putting your thoughts on paper.

Plan to write several drafts of your college essay. Ask your parents, a trusted friend, your college counselor, and/or a teacher to read it and give their reactions. While some editorial help is not out of line, never allow anyone else to write your essay. Admissions counselors know when you have not submitted your own work. Also, do not allow someone to edit so much that the tone becomes stale or stilted. Do have someone proofread your final draft, however.

The best essays resonate with the personal voice of the applicant, describing ideas in very specific, reflective ways that may reveal fears, fantasies, or insecurities but are always thoughtful, fresh, and spontaneous. The worst essays present a factual, often chronological version of an experience—the orchestra's tour to Europe, for example, or a recent performance—in a way that is totally lacking in creativity or individuality. The orchestra tour to Europe essay that simply describes arriving in Paris, playing at a concert hall, and then taking a bus to the next place is hardly riveting. The same essay telling how you got lost and could not find the stage door, and how you dealt with that situation, becomes specific and says something about you.

There is no "right" essay, but there are several approaches that you should avoid. For example, do not submit a poem as an essay. If you have talent as a poet, consider submitting a few select samples of your poetry as supplementary material instead. Also, do not use the essay to make excuses for something in your background. If you have a special situation, consider writing about it in a separate letter or asking a teacher or your guidance counselor to mention it in his or her letter of recommendation. Do not repeat information from other parts of your application, and avoid writing about trendy topics, your religious beliefs, relationships, sex, drugs or alcohol, or the importance of a college education. Do not try to impress an admissions committee with your vocabulary, revealing that you have thumbed through the thesaurus. Rather, write simply about something you really care about in a personal and specific manner.

Try to limit yourself to the space provided, or type your essay on separate sheets and write, "See essay attached." In general, the quality, not the quantity, is what counts.

### Supplementary Materials

Because you are a performing artist, you will want to document your special talent with carefully chosen additional materials. A letter of recommendation from your dance, theater, or music teacher would be appropriate. Ask colleges about sending cassettes, CDs, DVDs, or videotapes. Some may require them for pre-screening; other schools have neither the staff nor facilities for evaluating these. Do not send:

- additional letters of recommendation from people who do not know you well: congressmen, mayors, the neighbor's uncle who attended your college choice but whom you've never met, and so on. Such letters do not usually add to an understanding of who you are.

- copies of awards or honors. No scrapbooks!

- copies of lengthy reports or term papers. If a college wants a graded paper, they will specify this in the application directions.

- a pile of newspaper clippings about yourself. If you have received many positive reviews, select two or three, but do not send the entire stack and never send original copies.

- copies of programs in which you have participated. Your list of extracurricular activities or resume should reflect this.

- lots of photographs of yourself. One or two good ones, especially if you are a dancer, would be appropriate. An entire portfolio is not.

- every article you've ever written. If you write for the school newspaper, you might send a copy of one or two articles—not every issue of the paper in which one of your articles has appeared.

## DEADLINES

Do yourself and the admissions office a favor by submitting your application before it is actually due. This may also help you in getting the better audition times, if auditions are required, because some schools schedule on a first-come, first-served basis. Drama programs in particular, but also some other programs use the deadline as one way to eliminate applicants. Remember to proofread your application before you mail or transmit it and to keep a copy of it for your files. If sent by standard mail, it is a good idea to include a stamped, self-addressed postcard that says, "College X has received the application from Mary Jones. Signed by admissions: Date: __," which the admissions office can return to you. Also watch for your canceled check to be returned. Things do get lost, and you want to be sure that your application does not go astray. And, if you are using e-mail or otherwise filing electronically, remember to print out a hard copy of whatever you transmit to save for your files, too.

# College Admissions Checklist

Use this convenient checklist to remind yourself of individual college admission requirements and to record the progress of your application procedures.

| | | | | | | | | |
|---|---|---|---|---|---|---|---|---|
| College Name | | | | | | | | |
| College Address | | | | | | | | |
| Application Deadline | | | | | | | | |
| Application Fee | | | | | | | | |
| Required Tests: | Registration Deadline | Testing Date | Registration Deadline | Testing Date | Registration Deadline | Testing Date | Registration Deadline | Testing Date |
| PSAT/NMSQT | | | | | | | | |
| SAT | | | | | | | | |
| ACT | | | | | | | | |
| Others | | | | | | | | |
| Course Requirements Fulfilled | | | | | | | | |
| Personal Interview Required | | | | | | | | |
| Interview Date | | | | | | | | |
| Audition Required | | | | | | | | |
| Audition Date | | | | | | | | |
| Applications Requested | | | | | | | | |
| References Required | | | | | | | | |
| Names/Addresses of References | | | | | | | | |
| References Completed | | | | | | | | |
| Application Filed | | | | | | | | |
| Transcript Forwarded | | | | | | | | |
| College Reply Date | | | | | | | | |
| Financial Interview Required | | | | | | | | |
| Required Financial Forms: | | | | | | | | |
| CSS/PROFILE | | | | | | | | |
| FAFSA | | | | | | | | |
| Other | | | | | | | | |
| Housing Deadline | | | | | | | | |
| Housing Fee | | | | | | | | |
| Housing Application Mailed | | | | | | | | |

Performing Arts

## INTERNATIONAL STUDENTS' CHECKLIST

Any student who is not a citizen or permanent resident of the United States is usually considered an "international" or "foreign" student (the term varies at schools). Many schools recruit abroad and most schools welcome students from abroad. The admissions procedures at most schools are the same for international students as for U.S. applicants. However, there are a few additional aspects international students should take into account.

- Begin your search extra early. International mail takes additional time, and catalogs cannot be faxed at this point.

- Take advantage of the Internet and e-mail in expediting your questions, but always print a hard copy for yourself.

- Determine from each college or university whether you must take the TOEFL (Test of English as a Foreign Language) if English is not your native language. Arrange to take the test, if necessary, so that your scores can be submitted at the required time. Contact www.TOEFL.org or ETS at 609-771-7100 or toll free at 877-863-3546.

- Be sure to study English intensively. There are many good English as a Second Language (ESL) programs both in the United States and abroad and many summer programs in the United States. An Internet search should help you to discover ESL programs available to you.

- Investigate the visa process early. If you must travel to the United States for an audition, many conservatories or colleges will issue you a letter to present to a consulate in order to obtain a B-2 Prospective Student Visa. An I-20 will be issued to admitted students only. Everything regarding visas does take time, so plan ahead.

- Determine a school's policy on financial aid for international students. Government or state loans are not available to students from abroad, and many schools reserve their limited scholarship funds for domestic students. Some schools will not admit a qualified international student who has applied for financial aid. Be sure to ask for the current policy, and do not hesitate to ask for clarification of the policy if you are in doubt.

- Find out whether the school requires a guarantee of financial support in advance.

- Ask about tape or application pre-screening or regional auditions in your country.

- Complete the application on your own, especially the essays. If your English is not good enough to write an acceptable essay, you probably won't be able to understand the lectures or complete the assignments at a U.S. school.

- Be sure that schools know about your academic history in terms of the grading and overall educational system in your country. For instance, if no one from your high school has ever applied to schools in the United States before, you should send a prospectus or profile of your school.

- Some colleges and universities may require that your official transcript be reviewed or translated by the World Education Services (WES). Ask about requirements of the specific schools. The URL for WES is www.wes.org.

- Find out whether it is possible for international students to work while attending the program.

- Ask whether there are quotas on the number of students from a certain country or on international students in general.

- Find out about advisers and other support services for students from abroad.

- Find out if the program is authorized to grant Practical Training status to international students.

**Performing**

*Arts*

# Admissions Outcomes

After the application review and audition, if required, admissions committees will meet to determine whether to admit you, reject you, or place your name on a waiting list. Be aware that the weight of the letter or size of the envelope does not necessarily indicate the admissions decision.

If you are admitted to more than one school, weigh the pros and cons of each institution, perhaps visit again, ask lots of questions, and try to respond to the Office of Admissions in plenty of time before their deadline. Most institutions comply with the guidelines established by the National Association for College Admission Counseling (NACAC) and the College Board, which set the Candidate's Reply Deadline (CRD) as May 1. If a school requires you to make a decision before that deadline or before you have heard from all of your schools, you have every right to question that institution. If, to make an informed decision about your college choice, you need more information, or if your financial aid package has not arrived in time to meet the deadline, call the college and request an extension on the deadline. If you do not contact the college at all by May 1, the admissions staff may assume that you have decided to attend another institution and offer your place to someone on the waiting list. Be certain to contact your college by the deadline stipulated.

If you are rejected, do not despair. See whether you can get feedback about ways in which you might improve before auditioning or applying again. You may want to think about applying another year as a transfer student. Speak to your college counselor about what you might do differently.

A wait list is a positive place to be. It means that a college realized your strengths, but because of a limited number of openings it was not able to offer you admission at this time. Your initial response will probably be disappointment and irritation, but wait a few days before you do anything. Then you will be more able to make a rational decision about whether to remain active on a waiting list or to accept the offer of another college that admitted you right away.

If you want to be considered from the waiting list, now is the time to be even more proactive in demonstrating your desire to attend. Call, send an e-mail, and/or write to the college to say that you want to be considered from the wait list. Include any new information about yourself since your application was reviewed. If it is true, let a college know that if taken off the waiting list, you will enroll. Talk to your college counselor about any further steps you should take, and then be patient. You should probably submit a deposit to your second-choice school to protect yourself, in the event that the first choice does not accept anyone from its wait list. If you are admitted from the wait list, however, and intend to accept the offer of admission and enroll, be sure to immediately contact the school where you gave your deposit so that they may possibly offer your place to someone else. You should never make a deposit at more than one school; multiple deposits are considered unethical in college admissions.

## IF YOU WANT TO DEFER ADMISSION

Often a student who has been admitted will want to take a year to travel or work before enrolling. Many colleges and universities are pleased to grant a deferral of a year. They may give you guidelines about what they will allow you to do with the year. For instance, attending another college usually is not allowed, and they may give a new deadline for committing to enrollment. Some schools may ask for an account of what you have done with your time off.

# Covering Your College Costs

A college education is expensive: more than $150,000 for four years at some of the higher-priced colleges and universities and more than $50,000 at many lower-cost, state-supported colleges. Figuring out how you and your family will come up with the necessary funds to pay for your education requires planning, perseverance, and learning as much as you can about the options available.

For most families, paying the total cost of a student's college education out of savings is not possible. Clearly, the more your family has saved, the better off you will be and the less you will need to earn and borrow. But paying for college should not be looked at merely as a four-year financial commitment. While some of the money you need will likely come from funds that you and your parents have managed to save, some will come from a portion of your or your parents' current income. The rest will come from future earnings, through loans you or your parents will pay off later.

If your family has not saved the total amount or does not have sufficient current income to cover the costs, you can still attend college. That's where financial aid comes in. The amount you and your family will be expected to contribute toward your college expenses will be based upon your and your family's income and assets. But if this is not enough, the rest of the expenses can be met through various financial aid programs.

## FINANCIAL AID BASICS: HOW FINANCIAL AID IS AWARDED

When you apply for aid, your family's financial situation is analyzed using a government-approved formula called the Federal Methodology. The result of this is the amount you and your family are expected to contribute toward your college expenses, called your Expected Family Contribution or EFC. If this is equal to or more than the cost of attendance at a particular college, then you do not demonstrate "financial need." However, even if you don't have financial need, you may still qualify for aid since there are many grants, scholarships, and loans that are not based on financial need.

If the cost of education is greater than your EFC, then you will be eligible for "need-based" assistance. The calculation of "financial need" is very simple:

Total Cost of Attendance
− Expected Family Contribution
Financial Need

The total aid you are awarded by any one college will likely differ from the amount offered by other colleges you may be applying to because, among other things, the costs of attendance are different. Secondly, not all colleges have the same amount of funds available to offer their needy students. But, your EFC should remain about the same regardless of which college you attend. It is the goal of every financial aid office to meet the financial needs of its students and help all families find the information they need to finance the tuition, fees, room and board, and other costs.

## SOURCES OF FINANCIAL AID

The largest single source of aid is the federal government, which awarded more than $97 billion during 2006–07 (College Board, *Trends in Higher Education* series). More than 14 million people apply for financial aid each year. But the federal government is not the only source of financial aid. The colleges and universities themselves are the next-largest source of financial aid. Institutions award an estimated $24 billion to students each year. Some of this aid is awarded to students who have a demonstrated need based on either the Federal Methodology or another formula, the Institutional Methodology, which is used by some colleges to award their own funds in conjunction with other aid. Some aid is not based on need and is called merit aid. Merit-based aid is usually awarded based on a student's academic performance or specific talents or abilities, or to students the institutions most want to attract.

Another source of financial aid is from state governments, awarding more than $6.8 billion per year. All fifty states offer grant and/or scholarship aid, most of which is need-based, but some of which is merit-based. Most state programs award aid only to state residents attending college in their home state, although a few do allow their state aid to be "portable" from state to state.

Other sources of financial aid include private agencies, foundations, corporations, clubs, fraternal and service organizations, civic associations, unions, and religious groups that award grants, scholarships, and low-interest loans. Some employers provide tuition reimbursement benefits for employees and their families.

More information about these different sources of aid is available from high school guidance offices, public libraries, college financial aid offices, and directly from the sponsoring organizations. In addition, Peterson's offers an excellent source of scholarship leads at www.petersons.com/finaid.

## APPLYING FOR FINANCIAL AID

Every student must complete the Free Application for Federal Student Aid (FAFSA) to be considered for federal aid. The FAFSA is available in your high school guidance office and many public libraries, or directly from the U.S. Department of Education. Students are encouraged to apply for aid on the Web by using the electronic FAFSA, which can be accessed at www.fafsa.ed.gov. If you apply online, you and one parent will need to obtain an electronic signature before filing. To get your Personal Identification Number, or PIN, go to www.pin.ed.gov.

To award their own funds, many schools require a second application, the CSS/Financial Aid PROFILE®. The PROFILE asks supplemental questions that some colleges and awarding agencies feel provide a more accurate assessment of the family's ability to pay for college. It is up to the college to decide whether it will use only the FAFSA or both the FAFSA and the PROFILE.

The first thing you will have to do is determine whether you will need to fill out only the FAFSA or whether you will also have to complete the PROFILE. The listings later in this book will tell you what forms are required. You should also read the schools' brochures or speak to someone in the financial aid office to be sure. The PROFILE contains a list of schools and agencies that require the form.

### If the College You're Applying to in 2009 Requires Just the FAFSA

This scenario is pretty simple: Complete the FAFSA sometime after January 1, 2009, being certain to send it in before any college-imposed deadlines. (You are not permitted to send in the 2009–2010 FAFSA before January 1, 2009, which should not pose a problem because most college application deadlines are in February or March.) It is best if you wait until you have all your financial records for the previous year available, but if that is not possible, you can use estimated figures. It is critical to file by the published filing deadline. Filing late can mean the loss of thousands of dollars in assistance.

After you send in your FAFSA, either on paper or electronically, you'll receive a Student Aid Report (SAR) that includes all of the information you reported and shows your EFC. The SAR will be sent to you electronically if you provided an e-mail address. Otherwise, you will receive a paper-copy SAR in the mail. Be sure to review the SAR, checking to see if the information you reported is correct. If you used estimated numbers to complete the FAFSA, you may have to resubmit the SAR with any corrections to the data. The college(s) you have designated on the

FAFSA will receive the information you reported and will use that data to make their decision. In many instances, the colleges you've applied to will ask you to send copies of your and your parents' federal income tax returns for 2008 plus any other documents needed to verify the information you reported.

### If a College Also Requires the CSS/Financial Aid PROFILE®

**Step 1: Register for the PROFILE in the fall of your senior year in high school.**

You can apply for the PROFILE online at http://profileonline.collegeboard.com/index/jsp.

Registration information with a list of the schools requiring the PROFILE is available in most high school guidance offices.

There is a fee for using the PROFILE application ($25 for the first college and $16 for each additional college). You must pay for the service by credit card when you register. If you do not have a credit card, you will be billed.

**Step 2: Fill out your customized PROFILE.**

Once you register, your application will be immediately available online and

- will have questions that must be completed by you and your parents (unless you are considered independent and the colleges or programs selected do not require parent information).

- *may* have supplemental questions needed by one or more of your schools or programs. If required, those will be found in Section Q of the application.

In addition to the PROFILE application, which you complete online, you may be required to complete a Business/Farm Supplement in a traditional paper format. Completion of this form is not part of the "online" process. Instead, instructions about how to download and print the supplemental form are provided if it is required.

If your biological or adoptive parents are separated or divorced and your colleges and programs require it, your noncustodial parent may be asked to complete the Noncustodial PROFILE.

Once you complete and submit your PROFILE Application, your information is processed and sent directly to the colleges and programs that you requested.

## FINANCIAL AID AWARDS

After you've submitted your financial aid application, and usually after you've been accepted for admission, each college will send you a letter containing your financial aid award. Most award letters show the college's budget, how much you and your family are expected to contribute, and the amount and types of aid the college has awarded you. Most students who are eligible for aid are awarded aid from a combination of sources and programs; hence your award is often called a "package." For first-year students, award letters are often sent with the letter of admission, or soon after.

## FINANCIAL AID PROGRAMS

There are three types of financial aid: scholarships (also known as grants or gift aid), loans, and student employment. Scholarships and grants are outright gifts and do not have to be repaid. Loans must be repaid, usually after graduation; the amount you have to pay back is the total you've borrowed plus an interest charge. Student employment is a job arranged for you during the academic year. Loans and student employment programs are generally referred to as self-help aid.

The federal government has two large grant programs, the Federal Pell Grant and the Federal Supplemental Educational Opportunity Grant; a student employment program called the Federal Work-Study Program; and several loan programs, including one for parents of undergraduate students. Students who are Pell Grant eligible and have completed a rigorous high school program may be eligible for the Academic Competitiveness Grant. Additional information on this new federal grant program is available from your college's financial aid office or high school guidance office. For juniors and seniors, there is another new federal scholarship program called National SMART grants. The grants are limited to Pell Grant recipients in selected majors—primarily science, math, and certain foreign languages.

The Subsidized Direct Stafford Student Loan, the Subsidized FFEL Stafford Student Loan, and the Federal Perkins Loan are all need-based, government-subsidized loans. Students who borrow under these programs do not have to pay interest on the loan until after they graduate or leave school. The Unsubsidized Direct Stafford Loan, the Unsubsidized

FFEL Stafford Student Loan, and the Parent Loan (PLUS) program are not based on need, and these loans accrue interest while the student is in school.

A number of federal tax–based programs also help families with incomes up to $110,000. Additional information about the Hope Scholarship, Lifetime Learning tax credits, and other education assistance tax–based programs is available from the IRS. Consult a tax adviser for other educational tax deductions, since income cutoffs can vary from program to program.

**IF YOU DON'T QUALIFY FOR NEED-BASED AID**

If you are not eligible for need-based aid, or the aid you have been awarded is not sufficient, you should look into three other funding sources.

First is the search for merit scholarships, which you can start during your junior year of high school at the initial stages of the aid application process. Merit-based awards are becoming an increasingly important part of college financing plans, and many colleges award these grants to students they especially want to attract. As a result, applying to a school at which your qualifications put you at the top of the entering class may be a good idea since you may receive a merit award. It is also a good idea to look for private scholarships and grants, especially from local service and community groups.

The second source of aid is employment, during both the summer and the academic year. The student employment office at your college should be able to help you locate a job in the area, either on or off campus.

The third source is borrowing through the Unsubsidized FFEL Stafford Student Loan or the Unsubsidized Direct Stafford Student Loan, both of which are open to all students. The terms and conditions are similar to the subsidized loans. The biggest difference is that the borrower is responsible for the interest while still in college, although most lenders permit students to delay paying the interest right away and add the accrued interest to the total amount owed.

After you've secured what you can through scholarships, work, and loans, your parents will have to figure out how they will meet the balance of the college bill. Most colleges offer monthly payment plans that spread the cost out over the academic year. For many parents, the monthly payments still turn out to be more than they can afford, so they can borrow through the Federal Parent Loan for Undergraduate Students (PLUS) program, through one of the many private education loan programs available, or through home equity loans and lines of credit. This spreads the payments out over a longer period and makes the monthly payments smaller. The college financial aid office may offer a list of preferred lenders or banks and institutions they work with on a regular basis. Parents can select any lender they feel offers them the best terms and conditions and are not required to use a financial institution from the school's preferred lender list.

Students and parents who are interested in more information about financing a college education and in learning more about the financial aid application process should read *Peterson's College Money Handbook.*

The College Admissions Process

# For Parents

The college admissions process can be especially stressful to parent-child relations. Here are some pointers for parents of talented young people seeking admission to the best performing arts programs.

Parents SHOULD NOT:

- call or write admissions offices for the child.
- fill out applications.
- write or overly edit essays.
- nag about deadlines.
- dictate college choices.
- ask too many questions during the campus tour. (Let your child take the lead.)
- delay filing financial aid information.
- attend the interview.
- sit in on the audition.
- serve as accompanist at the audition.
- offer too much advice about training.
- try to bribe or otherwise influence an admissions officer or teacher.

Parents SHOULD:

- be supportive.
- help organize the college visits.
- go along on college visits, but use the time to speak with financial aid officers and placement or career counseling officers.
- submit all financial aid documents promptly.
- help set up practice auditions that their child may decide to hold at home or in a local church or auditorium.
- arrange to record on DVD, CD, or videotape practice auditions.

- rent, buy, or borrow the best instrument within one's means for their child to play.

- help their child learn how to care for him or herself best, paying special attention to nutrition, exercise, managing stress, handling rejection, and preventing injuries.

- understand if their child's performing schedule conflicts with family obligations.

- help a child deal with the tensions and frustrations of trying to excel in both academic and artistic endeavors.

The College Admissions Process

# For Dance Majors

Dance programs vary greatly in what is offered and what is required. If you have the passion to become a professional performer and you have positive evaluations from your current teachers and successful auditions for major performing institutions, a B.F.A. program may be the route to pursue.

Performing *Arts*

# Advanced Study in Dance

## AGE

Age is more of a factor in the dance world than in the other performing arts. If you are now a sophomore in high school, one question that you may want to ask yourself is whether it is important for you to finish your high school program. If you do decide to spend all four years in high school, be sure that you are taking regular dance classes and performing as often as possible. If you decide to finish or leave high school at the end of three years, there are other options for you.

## EARLY ADMISSION

Early Admission policies apply to students who want to be admitted to college before completing high school, usually during the junior year. (This is not to be confused with Early Decision policies, which apply to your senior year.) You should think about Early Admission in your freshman year or in your sophomore year, but no later than fall semester of your junior year, so that you will have time to plan ahead. You may approach this in one of two ways: either plan to finish the requirements for high school and graduate early at the end of your junior year, or leave high school at the end of junior year, enroll at a college, and see whether your high school will grant your diploma pending the successful completion of your freshman year.

You may also decide that a high school diploma is not important to you and enroll at the college that admits you as an Early Admission candidate. Some students may also want to take the GED exam.

If you plan to finish high school early, you may have to take a summer course or two and take additional courses during the regular school year. Work closely with your college counselor to see whether this is feasible. Usually you'll need an English or U.S. history requirement to graduate early.

If you decide to leave high school and have your diploma awarded after your freshman year, be sure to get all the terms of such an agreement *in writing*. Does your high school require that you not only successfully complete your freshman year but that you also take certain courses and achieve a certain grade? If your high school does not put the terms in writing, be sure that you or your parents write a letter stating your understanding, and keep a copy of this letter for your files.

## CHOOSING YOUR TEACHERS

It is important that you study with someone who will help you establish the best habits in your early development and teach you a solid technique. As you investigate teachers in your area, here are some questions you might want to ask:

- Where did the teacher go to school?
- Did the teacher dance professionally? With what company?
- Does the teacher talk about placement?
- Does the teacher explain *how* to perform an exercise as well as what to do?
- Does the teacher give corrections?
- Does the teacher save stretching for after you are warmed up?
- Does the teacher stress turnout from the hips rather than from the knees or feet?
- Does the teacher have an awareness of injury prevention?
- Is there any discussion about musicality?
- Are dance classes focused on learning a routine for a dance concert or recital, or is technique taught regularly?

## APPLICATION PHOTOGRAPHS

Often you will be asked to submit a photograph of yourself in dance attire along with your application. Unlike theater applicants trying to find the most appealing head shot, you need not go to the trouble of expensive professional photos. You should have someone take a full-length photograph of you either in color or black-and-white. Some schools specify an exact position they would like to see you in; if so, follow their directions exactly. When specific instructions are not given, the photograph(s) submitted should show you in a flattering pose or dance position, in appropriate dance clothing. If you have a photograph that was taken of you in a performance, this would be fine, also. These photos are used for reference to remember you and should show you at your best. Avoid choosing provocative poses or outrageous attire.

Performing *Arts*

# Dance Auditions

Most major auditions for dance programs are held in January through March, with possible late auditions in May. If you have a choice, try not to do your first audition at your first-choice school. Make sure that you have done plenty of preparation.

**BEFORE YOU AUDITION**

Whether it is for a company, a conservatory, or a dance department at a liberal arts college or university, you should be prepared well in advance of your audition time. Be sure to read carefully and thoroughly the catalog or any audition information that is sent to you.

Things you will need:

- your attire for a ballet class;

- your attire for a modern class;

- any other change of clothing or shoes;

- a cassette tape or CD of the music for your solo or sheet music for a piano accompaniment;

- another copy of your resume and photographs, in case they are requested; and

- any health form that is requested.

If admission is based primarily on your performance in a class or two, be sure that you arrive in plenty of time to do a complete warm-up and to get a good spot in the room. If they arrange you alphabetically for the class, you have no control, but if they arrange you according to the order in which you arrived, you may be in the front if you arrive early enough.

If you are asked to perform a solo that you have choreographed or someone has choreographed for you, be sure to choose material that accentuates your strengths. Many applicants prepare something from the standard repertoire on *pointe*, which shows the outer limits of their technique. It would be better to offer something less demanding that showcases your strengths now. Stay strictly within stipulated time regulations, as well.

Be prepared to speak about your material: the title of the piece, the choreographer, and the composer.

If for some reason you are injured before your audition, it is best to call and consult someone about postponing it. Going to the audition and saying, "I'm not allowed to jump because of an injury" is not going to win you favor with an audition panel.

### Practice

Practice ahead of time. Rehearse everything from how you will enter the room and how you will introduce yourself and your solo piece to what you need to tell the pianist (including the tempo). Go over your solo many times so that you can perform it under almost any circumstance, even a severe case of nerves. Frequently, the students who become nervous in auditions are the ones who have not lived with a piece long enough or rehearsed it enough and have some element of insecurity based on lack of preparation. Since being well prepared can help you relax, Dr. Beth Rom-Rymer, a psychologist in Chicago, says that it sometimes helps if you pretend the audition is two weeks earlier than it is to get the feeling of having gained some extra time. Try to arrange to perform for a group of your peers and for your teacher several months before the audition and record yourself; critique your performance and then do it again, at least a month before the audition. About a week before, try to get a group together and set up a mock audition situation for yourself.

### Music for Your Auditions

You may be asked to perform, with music, a solo that you have choreographed or that someone else has choreographed for you. Be sure you know what player is available for you for playing the music. It would be awful to show up with a CD if there is only a cassette player. If you bring a tape, be sure that it contains only musical accompaniment for your solo and is cued to play.

If you do not bring a CD or tape, most auditions will have a pianist who accompanies the class and is available to play for your solo. If your piece is standard and not too difficult, bring the sheet music for the pianist. Be certain that it is legible, that it is assembled so that it is easy for a pianist to turn pages, and that any cuts or repeats are clearly marked. You may want to talk to the pianist ahead of time or send a copy of the music in advance. Be sure that you and the pianist communicate about the tempo before you begin your solo.

**For Dance Majors**

### What to Wear

Schools and programs usually specify what they would like you to wear at your audition. The norm seems to be:

*For a ballet class:*

Black leotard, pink tights, and ballet shoes for women. White tee shirt, black tights, white socks, and ballet shoes for men. Some programs ask to see you *en pointe.* Be sure you have both ballet and *pointe* shoes with you.

*For a modern class:*

You can be a little more creative here, wearing a different color leotard or unitards, but usually you must be barefoot.

You should be neatly dressed and feel comfortable. Because dance is physical and your body is your instrument, it is important to wear proper attire and not try to hide your body. No big t-shirts or sweats. Your hair should be out of your face and nicely groomed.

### WHAT TO EXPECT

When you arrive at a dance audition, check in and then go to the dressing room. (Never leave valuables in any dressing room.) At the beginning of the audition, you will be put in lines based on the order in which you arrived or in alphabetical order. Often you will be required to wear a number or your name. While you may feel that this is dehumanizing, it helps the audition panel recognize you, and you do not want to be confused with another applicant. You should also be aware that dance auditions are more frequently being recorded nowadays for reference, so try to ignore the camera. Adjudicators may have your file and photos with them and compare to see that you really do look like your photograph.

During the audition, be sure to listen carefully and follow instructions precisely. Perform the material the way it is asked for, even if it is unfamiliar, and be sure to apply any corrections given to the class in general to yourself. Always be courteous to the other dancers.

Many auditions now conduct classes in ballet and modern and then have callbacks. If you do *not* receive a callback, do not assume that you are going to be rejected without confirming that this is the policy. Some schools do not call back the students who are obviously admissible.

## NERVES

While a college interview may make you nervous, an audition may induce a real anxiety attack. The best defense is to be sure that you are so well prepared that you can function almost on automatic pilot. Arrive early and do a careful warm-up, including deep breathing exercises. Also, if you think of an audition as a performance, you may actually be able to develop the positive energy that you bring to the stage. It seems that the word "audition" with the connotation of judgment makes even seasoned performers nervous. Remember that the panel watching the audition really wants you to do well; so do your best and keep your focus on performing with confidence.

## WHAT *NOT* TO DO AT A DANCE AUDITION

- Do not run away after you have finished. Take your appropriate bows and then wait until you are dismissed. Many times there will be an awkward period of silence and then the adjudicators may want to ask you something. If you disappear, an opportunity may be lost.

- Do not wear inappropriate attire. Leave the big t-shirts, sweats, and tights with holes in them at home.

- Do not "play" to the judges. It is best to look a little over their heads.

- Do not choose a solo that you think the audition panel wants to see. Choose something that you love to dance and that is appropriate for your level of development.

- Do not perform a solo that is longer than the time stipulated in the guidelines.

## REGIONAL AUDITIONS

Many conservatories will hold auditions in a number of different cities and sometimes in other countries as well. While doing the audition on the campus gives you an opportunity to see the facilities and probably meet with more faculty, if you have any scheduling conflicts or reasons not to travel to the campus, take the regional audition. They are usually treated as just as valid as an audition on campus, and sometimes, because you may be seen with a smaller group, may give you an advantage. Ask about who will conduct the auditions, which faculty members will teach classes and evaluate the audition, and if a videotape will be made of the audition for other faculty to review.

## DVD OR VIDEOTAPES VS. LIVE AUDITIONS

Some programs will accept a DVD or videotape of your dancing in lieu of a personal audition. The best advice is to use a recording only as a last resort. A live audition is always better than a DVD or videotape. Faculty members like to see applicants in person, whether at a regional audition or on campus, and you may diminish your chances of admission by submitting your audition on DVD or tape. Be sure you call the dance program for exact guidelines on length and content of the DVD or video. International students must be certain that the video is in U.S.-standard VHS format.

If you absolutely must submit a recording as your only possible way of auditioning, do not go for a glitzy professionally produced DVD or video, which will cost you a fortune in production. A well-done (hold the camera steady and have the picture in focus!) home version is fine for this, but remember you are not helping your chances for admission by not attending in person! Do not send an unsolicited recording, as it will probably end up in a pile—unwatched.

## AUDITION EVALUATION CRITERIA

When you audition, the faculty members and administrators in attendance will evaluate your performance in terms of certain criteria established by the school. Forms vary from school to school, but as you will note from the sample forms that follow, many similar criteria are reviewed. Some programs may give you copies of the evaluation or notes on how you might improve; other programs consider this strictly confidential.

## MODERN DANCE AUDITION SHEET
## ABC SCHOOL OF DANCE

Date _____                              Audition No. _____

Auditioning for:                                          Accept _____

_____ regular school only                      Reject _____

_____ summer school only                      Summer school to re-audition

_____ both summer school and regular school

Name: _____     Sex:  M  F _____

Date of Birth: _____   Age: _____   Height: _____   Weight: _____

Past Study:  Years: _____   Classes/week: _____   Studios: _____

### APPEARANCE

|  | good | fair | poor |  | good | fair | poor |
|---|---|---|---|---|---|---|---|
| Body tone |  |  |  | Turnout |  |  |  |
| Carriage of torso |  |  |  | Feet |  |  |  |
| Placement (static) |  |  |  | Hamstring flexibility |  |  |  |
| Abdominal support |  |  |  | Hip flexibility |  |  |  |
| Shape of leg |  |  |  | Lower back strength |  |  |  |

Comments:

### TECHNIQUE

|  | good | fair | poor |  | good | fair | poor |
|---|---|---|---|---|---|---|---|
| Basic dance vocabulary |  |  |  | Coordination |  |  |  |
| Torso flexibility, strength |  |  |  | Placement in space |  |  |  |
| Use of upper back, arms |  |  |  | Learning ability |  |  |  |
| Use of legs and feet |  |  |  |  |  |  |  |

Comments:

### PERFORMANCE

|  | good | fair | poor |  | good | fair | poor |
|---|---|---|---|---|---|---|---|
| Use of space |  |  |  | Musicality |  |  |  |
| Motivation |  |  |  | Projection |  |  |  |
| Phrasing |  |  |  | Technical degree of difficulty |  |  |  |
| Dynamics |  |  |  | Type of music used |  |  |  |

Comments:

Auditioner: _____

**Performing**

**Arts**

**BALLET AUDITIONING SHEET**
**ABC School of Dance**

Date _____   Audition No. _____

Name: _____ Sex: M F _____ Age: _____

Height: _____ Weight: _____ Entering grade level: _____

Past study (years): _____ Classes per week: _____ Studios: _____

| | good | fair | poor | |
|---|---|---|---|---|
| Height | | | | too tall/too short |
| Weight | | | | overweight/underweight |
| Head | | | | small/average/large |
| Neck | | | | long/medium/short |
| Shoulders | | | | sloping/straight/high/narrow/broad |
| Torso | | | | short/medium/long |
| Spine | | | | straight/curved (upper/middle/lower) |
| Hips (pelvis) | | | | small/medium/wide |
| Legs | | | | long/average/short |
| Shape of legs | | | | (stand candidate straight with feet toward en face) straight/bowed top to bottom/bowed between knees and ankles |
| Knees | | | | flat/sway back at knee joints/knees do not straighten/knock-kneed |
| Feet | | | | small/large/flat/no arch/no points/no coupe de pied/stiff in ankle joints |
| Turnout | | | | loose/tight/not from hips |
| Flexibility | | | | |
| Placement (static) | | | | shoulders up/shoulders back/lower back swayed/abdomen dropped/chest dropped/not centered |
| Plié demi | | | | |
| Plié grand | | | | |
| Extension | | | | |
| Adage | | | | good épaulé/poor épaulé/good extension/poor extension/no center |
| Turns en dehors | | | | |
| Turns en dedens | | | | |
| Turns diagonal | | | | |
| Petite allegro | | | | no speed/no turnout/no use of feet |
| Grand allegro | | | | no elevation/no line/no turnout/no use of feet |
| Port de bras | | | | placement of arms/correct position/incorrect positions |
| Quality of movement | | | | coordination/fluidity/carriage/expression |
| Musicality | | | | ahead/behind/cannot count |
| Schooling | | | | correct for age/behind for age/ahead for age |
| Placement (in space) | | | | |
| Presentation | | | | outgoing/withdrawn/unfocused/blank/sullen |
| Energy | | | | |

Outstanding talent _____   COMMENTS:
Scholarship material _____
Accept _____
Further discussion _____
_____
Reject _____   AUDITIONER

For Dance Majors

# THE COLLEGE OF PERFORMING ARTS
## ENTRANCE AUDITION EVALUATION—FORM FOR DANCE DIVISION

| Student Information | For Dance Office Use Only |
|---|---|
| *(Computer Label)* | Admit _____  Waiting List _____<br><br>Reject _____  Re-Audition _____<br><br>Scholarship Decision: _____<br><br>Audition Rating: _____<br><br>Scholarship Rating: _____<br><br>Combined Rating: _____ |

|  | Exceptional | Superior | Very Good | Good | Adequate | Possible | Unacceptable |
|---|---|---|---|---|---|---|---|
| Ballet technique |  |  |  |  |  |  |  |
| Modern technique |  |  |  |  |  |  |  |
| Performance |  |  |  |  |  |  |  |
| Body Proportions |  |  |  |  |  |  |  |
| Musicality |  |  |  |  |  |  |  |

Piece Performed: _____

| Remarks: | Overall Rating (circle one):<br><br>E  S  VG  G  A  P  U<br><br>Accept _____<br>Possible _____<br>Reject _____ |
|---|---|
| The student should be encouraged to re-audition<br>☐ Yes   ☐ No<br><br>Why?<br><br><br>Signed: _____<br><br>Date: _____ | Scholarship Recommendations<br><br>Definitely ☐<br><br>Probably ☐<br><br>Possibly ☐<br><br>No ☐ |

# Health Issues for Dancers

## DEALING WITH INJURIES

If you have had an injury, be honest about it. Many colleges will require that you submit a health form or have an orthopedic evaluation prior to being allowed to take the audition. If you are not honest and a doctor reveals something about a past problem, however small, it does not reflect well on you.

In looking at your future in dance, you must consider how injuries will influence some of your choices. All serious dancers are bound to incur some injuries. You must be brutally honest with yourself about when an injury will have to be taken into account in determining your future training. You should also be sure that you educate yourself about basic health issues, including good nutrition, basic injury prevention, and strengthening exercises, and you should read about how posture and psychology can contribute to injuries. Learn about strapping and padding techniques that support injuries, and become aware of the range of therapies available.

Although some great dancers have survived knee surgery and other injuries, every young dancer must decide whether personal injuries or physical restrictions are severe enough to interfere with career goals. The following books address the topic of dancers and health:

Arnheim, Daniel D. *Dance Injuries: Their Prevention and Care.* 3rd ed. Hightstown, NJ: Princeton Book Company/Dance Horizons Series, 1991.

Hamilton, Linda. *Advice for Dancers: Emotional Counsel and Practical Strategies.* San Francisco: Jossey-Bass, 1998.

Howse, Justin, and Moira McCormack. *Dance Technique and Injury Prevention.* 3rd ed. New York: Routledge, 2000.

Solomon, Ruth, John Solomon, and Sandra Minton. *Preventing Dance Injuries.* 2nd ed. Champaign, IL: Human Kinetics Publishers, 2005.

Spilken, Terry L., M.D. *The Dancer's Foot Book*. Princeton: Princeton Book Company/Dance Horizons Series, 1990.

Vincent, Larry M., M.D., The *Dancer's Book of Health.* Hightstown, NJ: Princeton Book Company/Dance Horizons Series, 1988.

Watkins, Andrea, and Priscilla M. Clarkson. *Dancing Longer, Dancing Stronger: A Dancer's Guide to Improving Technique and Preventing Injuries.* Hightstown, NJ: Princeton Book Company/ Dance Horizons Series, 1990.

The Princeton Book Company/Dance Horizons publishers (www.dance horizons.com) also have a number of DVDs regarding dance and health. Their contact information is: 614 Route 130, Hightstown, NJ 08520; 800-220-7149 or 609-426-0602.

There are a number of Web sites that address issues of dancers' health. Some may be found as links off of ballet company Web sites. Two popular ones, however, are www.foot.com, which addresses foot health and care for dancers, and the International Association for Dance Medicine and Science (IADMS) at www.iadms.org, which is dedicated to improving dancers' health.

## OTHER HEALTH ISSUES

Many conservatory dance programs and also companies have recently been enforcing weight policies for young dancers. While the best dance educators consider this truly risky to both the psychology and natural physical body changes of mid-adolescence, there is an emphasis on thinness in much of the dance world. When you are looking at a college, conservatory, or company, you would be wise to ask about any weight policy.

# A Dance Company vs. College

Dance company Web sites provide a wealth of information. You may learn about their educational outreach programs or summer intensives. If you are a junior or senior in high school and have the opportunity to audition for some companies, by all means take the auditions. You can learn a great deal about yourself and about a company just by auditioning. If you are admitted into the company, you must do some serious thinking about what you want to do. Review your contract very carefully. Some of the concerns you should evaluate include:

- How good is this company? How long do the dancers seem to stay with it? Where do they go from here?

- Are there any reviews of the company that you could read?

- What is the daily routine? How many classes? How many hours of rehearsal? How many performances a week?

- Will you be cast? What are the casting policies? Or are you corps de ballet?

- What do people like most about the company? What are the most common complaints?

- What is the financial profile of the company? Is payroll met regularly? Are there any problems?

- What are the plans for the near future? Any tours? What are the long-range plans?

- Where do most company members live?

Some companies that admit young dancers include the New York City Ballet, Pennsylvania Ballet, and Pittsburgh Ballet, and these companies will usually give you an indication of their interest in you very early on.

Some experienced dancers suggest that the company route is right for only a small number of dancers. These dancers point out that while dancers who join a company and those who follow a college curriculum will probably end up with the same acquired knowledge, the college route telescopes the learning time while the performing route leaves the dancer to learn by trial and error over a span of many years. These dancers also acknowledge that life after your years as a performer are much more difficult if you do not have a college education, and most directors and choreographers have attended college.

Be sure that you distinguish whether you are admitted to the *school* for a company, or to the company itself.

If you are admitted to a company, and your parents object because they want you to go to college, you should point out to them that most colleges do not have an age limit but a dance career does. If you are ready now, you might want to "leap" at the opportunity if the company meets your standards. It should be noted, however, that most modern dancers do have college degrees. In ballet, if you have no company options by age 17, college is a good choice. You might try deferring college admission or taking a year off after high school and doing a lot of auditions, or you could try to graduate from high school early and complete college in three years. By then, you would be 19 or 20 and still young enough to begin a ballet career.

If you are admitted to the school of a company, the decision about whether to enroll at a degree-granting conservatory or at a company school becomes even more difficult. Some of the company schools that you might investigate include the School of American Ballet, Dance Theater of Harlem, Alvin Ailey School, Joffrey, Pennsylvania Ballet School, San Francisco Ballet School, Boston Ballet School, Atlanta School, Graham School, Nikolais School, and Merce Cunningham School. (*Stern's Performing Arts Directory* is a good reference for these programs.) Here are some of the questions you should ask:

- What is a typical schedule for a freshman? Are there any electives?

- Is the dance department embedded within another department of the college?

- What is the reputation of the dance department within the college? Outside?

- How many dance performances are there? Fully produced concerts? Workshops?

- What is the policy on casting?

- What kind of flooring is there in the studios?

- How many studios are there? What are the facilities available to students (if you have not seen them on your campus tour)?

- Who have been the most recent choreographers?

- Who has taught the most recent master classes?
- What kind of technique is taught?
- What kind of repertory is studied?
- How will the audition be run?
- Who evaluates the audition?
- Is it possible to focus on ballet or modern, or do I have to be proficient in both?
- What do most graduates go on to do?
- What companies now employ graduates from your program?
- Do you help with job placement?
- What is the enrollment in the dance department? How many males? How many females? Has this been steady? Is it growing? Diminishing? How many graduate students? How many under-graduates?
- How many technical classes are required per week? In ballet? Modern? Jazz? Ethnic forms (also called international, world, or genre dance on some campuses)? Pas de deux? Pointe? Other?
- What is the difficulty level of technical classes?
- What is the length of dance classes? Size?
- Is there live accompaniment for dance classes?
- Is there an opportunity to choose faculty for specific classes?
- Do you accept DVDs or videotapes in lieu of a personal audition? If so, what special instructions should I know about? Format? Length? Do you accept DVDs or videotapes for pre-screening? Any special directions for these?

**For Dance Majors**

# A Current Dance Major Speaks Out

PAM SOMMER
**Mason Gross School of the Arts**
**Rutgers University**

### WHAT ADVICE CAN YOU GIVE HIGH SCHOOL SENIORS WHO ARE THINKING OF MAJORING IN DANCE IN COLLEGE?

The best advice I can give is that if you love it, GO FOR IT. It is completely normal to have the feelings like "What am I going to do with a dance degree?" But this is the only time in your life you will have the chance to have this experience. Know that it is going to be a challenging experience but that it is worth every minute of it, because rather than spending all day in lecture classes, you spend your time learning and doing what you love. I know that it is the best decision I have made. My time at Mason Gross has taught me more than just dance. I've learned valuable lessons that I will carry with me throughout my life. It's also interesting because you become a family with your class. Since you spend so much time together, you learn to love and grow with one another, which I think is so important. In school you make friends you never thought you would have.

As for choosing your school—really look into it. You have to remember that this is a place you are going to be training seriously and intensively at for four years. It is important to make sure that you love the studio, the style you will be taught, and the teachers you will be working with. Any of these things could determine how you feel about the program and influence your decision.

It is also very important to keep an open mind, since the more styles of dancing you learn, the better. So even if something doesn't appeal to you immediately, don't shut it out right away, because you could be surprised by what you will learn. It is easy to be intimidated by other people but don't be! People will ask you why you want to study dance, isn't that a hobby, what will you do with a degree in dance? All that means is they don't understand the passion in it. There are so many different fields a dancer can go into, and success isn't only measured by how much money you make, but how happy the profession makes you. So, the bottom line is, if you love to dance, don't stop. Learn as much as you possibly can and dance as hard as you can because you only live once.

Performing

**For Dance Majors**

## HOW DID YOU PREPARE FOR BECOMING A DANCE MAJOR WHEN YOU WERE IN HIGH SCHOOL?

I took as many dance classes as I possibly could. Training is so important in the dance world. All good schools are looking for a dancer with drive, determination, and good training, so learn everything you possibly can before you get there. I also taught myself how to budget my time. A dancer's schedule isn't easy. You have to make sure that you learn to prep yourself for very long days and budget your time so that you don't overlap events or wear yourself down.

I also began to talk to people who were attending schools that I was interested in. I asked them what a day was like for them, whether they liked the school, and about the styles taught there, the teachers, and the other students. I felt that the more I knew about a school before enrolling in it, the better prepared I'd be.

I really started focusing on my school work. Honestly, I was never the best of students. I was the one who breezed my way through classes without opening a book. But I knew that wasn't going to fly once I entered college, and in order to stay in the program I would have to pass my academics with good grades. So I began to train myself to do some reading in between classes and aim for better grades. This prepared me for the loads of work and studying I was going to have to accomplish in between dance classes.

## WHAT SHOULD PROSPECTIVE DANCE MAJORS LOOK FOR IN A COLLEGE?

A great faculty. To me, that is what makes or breaks the program. I have fallen in love with Mason Gross because of the teachers. They all care so much about the students and really go out of their way for us in many ways. They make class a positive learning experience instead of a place to feel belittled or insecure. They help us find confidence where we need it and really pay attention to our bodies and individual needs. I feel that I can go up to any of my teachers and talk to them about just about anything, and that is what is important. Like the other students in the class, the faculty also becomes family to you.

Also, check out the facility. Make sure that it looks like a safe and comfortable environment to dance in.

Meet some of the other dancers too. It's important to make sure that you are going to feel comfortable around the people you'll be spending time with because in this major you spend a majority of your day with the same people. Look at the academic program and make sure that it suits your needs—that it is not too easy or too hard—because although you can dance, you also have to survive academically.

I have heard from many dancers at various schools that when you walk into your school, you just know. It feels right. Go with that instinct because it's probably right.

### WHAT IS YOUR TYPICAL DAILY SCHEDULE LIKE?

Busy, busy, busy is all that I can say. Expect early morning classes. I know that in my school, freshmen have an 8:10 ballet class every morning, followed by a 2-hour technique class (modern), followed by two to three more classes every day, not to mention rehearsals for several hours a night and academic school work. During show season, you are usually dancing seven days a week for several hours a day. Make sure you pack a lunch, because a lot of days you won't have a break to eat. Aside from classes and rehearsal, we all know that having a social life is important in college. So the free hour or two you may have in a day is usually spent hanging out with friends. It does get hard sometimes though, when all your friends want to spend a night out and you can't because you have to wake up early and dance. But I can honestly say that you usually don't mind staying in because you enjoy going to class and don't want to be tired for it.

### WHAT WAS THE BIGGEST SURPRISE YOU FOUND ONCE YOU GOT TO COLLEGE?

What I was able to accomplish on my own. I'm not going to lie, I was scared. I didn't know how I was going to survive. But you realize that if you put your mind to something, no matter what is on your plate, you can finish the job and do it well. I was surprised at how independent and self-motivating I can be and that I am capable of more than I could have ever imagined.

### WHAT KINDS OF PERFORMANCES ARE YOU CURRENTLY INVOLVED IN?

I was just involved in the spring dance concert, which included all student choreography. It is such a great experience because not only do you get the chance to perform, but you get to be hands-on throughout the entire production, and that's the part I found the most exciting.

Throughout the year I also performed in faculty concerts and helped to run them. We have to take a class in dance production, and I feel it is one of the most helpful classes I have taken. I now have learned how to hook up and hang lights in a theater, design the lighting for a piece, and work backstage as a show is in progress. In this profession knowing how to do that is so important.

### DO YOU HAVE A CONCENTRATION?

Modern dance is my concentration. Most dance departments now concentrate on modern dance or ballet, since they are the more classical types of training. At some schools you get to choose your concentration, and at others it is chosen for you.

## WHAT CAREER PATH DO YOU HOPE TO FOLLOW?

I leave my doors open to anything. I hope to perform for a while, meet people, and let my path guide me where it may. I believe that it is important to keep an open mind and open heart to everything, and that what you are looking for will find you. But, as contradictory as this may sound, I also believe it is important to have interests in a specific field you wish to go into or something you see yourself doing in the long run. For example, I hope to one day become a dance therapist for special education. I am not limiting myself to only that, but I keep it in mind as a definite place I would like to go. All that I know is that I love what I am doing, and whatever path I may choose, I know that I will never regret a moment of it because I am living my passion.

# Alternative Careers for Dance Majors

If you decide that you do not want to pursue being a performer full-time, or if you find yourself needing to supplement your income, there are many related activities in the performing arts that you might want to consider. One recent study reported that after graduation, only 10 to 15 percent of all performance majors earn their main income from performing. The others are combining performance activities with other occupations or "temping"—working as temporary secretaries, receptionists, or assistants. Following are some examples of alternative career choices for dance majors.

Dance majors might also explore any of these career areas:

- Choreographer
- Teacher
- Director
- Dance or movement therapist
- Director of a dance school or studio
- Labanotation expert
- Model
- Cast member at a theme park or in industrial shows

Performing

Arts

# What to Put in Your College Notebook

You might add a page to your personal college notebook with a chart like this one, listing the areas of dance you are interested in studying.

**AREAS OF DANCE TAUGHT**

☐ Classical Ballet

☐ Modern Dance
  Graham-based technique
  Limon-based technique
  Nikolais-based technique
  Cunningham-based technique

☐ Other:

List: _____

☐ Repertory

☐ Jazz

☐ Tap

☐ Historical Dance

☐ Ethnic forms:
  African
  Indian
  Middle Eastern
  Spanish
  Asian

☐ Other:

List:_____

☐ Movement Techniques
  Alexander
  Feldenkrais®
  Laban movement studies

☐ Other:

List: _____

☐ Dance Composition/
  Choreography

☐ Pedagogy
  (any teacher certification?)

☐ Labanotation

☐ Anatomy

☐ Music

☐ Stagecraft

☐ Acting

☐ Voice

☐ Other:

List: _____

# Questions to Ask Yourself

Here are some questions to ask yourself at various points in the admissions process.

Have I:

- reviewed the program's Web site thoroughly?

- requested catalogs and read them carefully and critically?

- requested applications and made photocopies of the ones in which I am interested?

- started a college notebook to record my impressions of colleges, audition and repertoire requirements, and deadlines?

- obtained a social security number (United States citizens and Permanent Residents)?

- registered for the PSAT/NMSQT?

- obtained information about the ARTS scholarships? (National Foundation for Advancement in the Arts, 444 Brickell Avenue, Miami, FL 33131; 305-377-1140 or 800-970-ARTS (toll-free); www.artsawards.org.)

- made an appointment with my guidance counselor to discuss future plans?

- looked into working with an independent counselor, if appropriate?

- talked with my current dance teacher about plans for my future?

- made arrangements to continue my dance classes?

- discussed high school courses to take?

- discussed which standardized tests to take and when?

- discussed whether tutoring for standardized tests is appropriate for me?

- discussed Early Admission possibilities?

- investigated summer programs and/or jobs and applied as necessary?

78

- investigated sources and policies regarding financial aid and scholarships?

- kept a file of performance programs, DVDs, or videotapes of performances, good term papers, articles, and so on?

- attended college fairs and met with college representatives who visited my school?

- finished my essays and applications and photocopied everything before mailing, or printed a hard copy before submitting online?

- registered for any standardized tests required (SAT, ACT, TOEFL, SAT Subject Tests)?

- met again with my guidance counselor?

- arranged my college visits?

- scheduled interview appointments?

- sent thank-you notes after my college interviews?

- chosen my audition material?

- narrowed my list of colleges?

- settled on decision plans?

- asked for letters of recommendation, if necessary?

- drafted my essays?

- applied for financial aid, if necessary?

- requested that official score reports be sent directly to the colleges that require them?

- done mock (practice) auditions and recorded them for my own critique?

- submitted any performance recording for pre-screening, if required?

- had photographs taken to submit with applications, if necessary?

- prepared a resume?

- requested that a copy of my transcript be sent?

- communicated regularly with my guidance counselor about my progress in the college admissions process and in school?

- kept up with all school work?

- prepared a list of extracurricular activities, if necessary?
- arranged for an accompanist for my audition, if necessary?
- checked that all financial aid documentation is complete?
- read carefully any audition or schedule information sent to me?
- prepared any necessary audition CD or tape of music for my solo piece?
- responded to colleges about any offer of admission?
- requested an extension beyond the May 1 Candidates Reply Deadline, if necessary?
- continued with my regular dance classes?

Performing

*Arts*

# For Music Majors

Whatever program you choose, keep in mind that the vast majority of people with careers in music have extensive formal training. Music is highly structured, and theoretical studies provide the structure that puts music together. Pursuing a degree will not only make you a better, more well-rounded musician, but it will also provide an automatic connection to the arts world that is much more difficult to obtain on your own.

Performing Arts

# Advanced Study in Music

## BACHELOR OF ARTS VS. BACHELOR OF MUSIC

Unlike other performing arts students choosing between a Bachelor of Arts (B.A.) and a Bachelor of Fine Arts (B.F.A.) program, music students will find more differences between Bachelor of Arts and Bachelor of Music (B.M.) programs than just the proportion of courses taken in liberal arts and in applied music. Often, students choosing the route of the B.A. do not want to major in music but do want to take some music courses and continue private lessons. If you want to apply to graduate school on the master's level, it is important that at the bachelor's level you continue your musical study; otherwise you will fall behind in both your major area of study (instrument or voice) and in music history, ear-training, and music theory.

The instrument you play has some bearing on your choice of a program. For instance, singers are encouraged to pursue liberal arts studies for at least two years before turning to more concentrated voice study. If you are a violinist or pianist, however, age seems to be more important, and if you are serious about having a performing career, you may want to focus on a Bachelor of Music degree program. Age seems to matter slightly less for cellists and little for violists and double bass players, in the string family. Most wind, brass, and percussion players can also wait to pursue focused musical studies in a B.M. degree, but flutists are advised to go directly into the B.M. program. Because of the intensely competitive nature of the flute, age does matter more than on other wind instruments.

Popular music, musical theater, and jazz do seem a bit more flexible in admissions and the age factor, so whether to pursue focused musical studies at the undergraduate level or to get a more general education seems to be a matter of personal choice.

There are many well-known musicians whose choices may serve as examples. Some that come to mind immediately are cellist Yo-Yo Ma, who did his undergraduate work at Harvard while continuing his cello studies and doing music programs during the summers; he then went to Juilliard for graduate school. Pianist Emanuel Ax went to Columbia. Flutist Eugenia Zukerman attended Barnard College for two years and then transferred to Juilliard. Guitarists Eliot Fisk and Sharon Isbin did their undergraduate work at Yale. And then there are the legions of musicians who went directly to conservatories. Obviously this is a highly personal decision, and you must do what feels right to you.

# Music Auditions

When you read the college catalog, take careful note of whether an audition is optional or required. All major conservatories and joint programs require auditions, as do many college music departments.

## WHAT TO EXPECT

Music auditions have been portrayed in a variety of movies and plays, sometimes very accurately. *Fame*, *A Chorus Line*, and *Running on Empty* all have that hollow, disembodied voice calling out in a hall, "Thank you," often right before that fiendishly difficult passage that the auditioners have practiced so carefully and are so sure will reveal their most musical moments. To be honest, very few music auditions are pleasant experiences. It is generally conceded that music auditions are an experience unto themselves—neither a performance, nor a lesson, nor a rehearsal, nor a "woodshedding" session. After having prepared for years, you are usually given 10 to 15 minutes to demonstrate your level of achievement, talent, and potential—often in a dry, stuffy room—for a group of faculty members who are known worldwide. Sometimes the faculty members whisper amongst themselves, pass notes, argue about what repertoire to request next from you, or engage in other activities that do not relate to your performance. It can truly be an intimidating experience. If you know what to expect, however, you will be better prepared to handle even the worst situation.

Remember that you have paid for the audition and this is your time, so make every moment count and take some control of the situation yourself. Also remember that even the most jaded, tired person on the audition panel will respond to excellence, so psyche yourself up to do your best, performing music that you love.

## TIMING OF AUDITIONS

If possible, plan to take your audition during the main audition period from a school, usually in January through March, though some auditions are now in November. This is when the school will be filling the greatest number of openings; any further auditions will be held to fill a limited number of vacancies that might exist after the newly admitted applicants from this main audition period have responded to the offer of admission. So, if you wait until May, some departments may be closed already and others may have only a few openings.

Performing

Arts

Schools usually set audition weeks and then contact the faculty to see which day within that week is the best for them to hear auditions. To be safe, block off the entire audition week listed in a school's catalog. You are not able to choose the day that you would like to audition; the school determines this. If you run into a major conflict, call the admissions office and see if there is any way to resolve it.

By submitting your application early, you may secure a better audition time. If you know of a conflict in advance, you might request that your audition be on a certain day, but whether or not your request is honored will be depend on faculty availability. Never try to contact faculty members directly to reschedule an audition; this must go through the admissions office.

Should you need to cancel your audition or postpone it to the later audition period, be sure to call and then follow up with a letter or e-mail. Many admissions offices will take note of your phone call but consider your communication official only when put in writing. If you must cancel on the day of the audition or if you are somehow delayed, be sure to call as soon as possible. Nothing is more frustrating to an audition committee than wasting time waiting for a no-show.

Try to arrive at least one hour ahead of your audition time, but be sure to read any schedule letter sent to you by the school very carefully. Some schools have group activities or speeches you are expected to attend before the auditions start. In any event, you do want to have time to locate the audition room, check in, and find a practice room for a good warm-up. It is a good idea to do a preliminary warm-up before you leave for your audition. Practice rooms or warm-up space may be at a premium, and you may not be altogether comfortable going through your entire warm-up routine surrounded by other applicants.

## WHAT TO WEAR

What you wear to an audition is important. Just as for an interview, you should have an audition outfit. Singers tend to be dressier than instrumentalists. Neatness, cleanliness, and comfort are all important, but so is the fact that you are appearing in a performance. You want to convey to the faculty that you take this audition seriously and have dressed for it appropriately. Recommendations:

Women instrumentalists: a nice skirt (not too short or too long), blouse, and a blazer, if comfortable; or a simple dress (not too frilly, flouncy, or provocative). Low-to-medium heels.

Women singers: a simple dress, neither too short nor too long. Silk, or a silk-like fabric, seems to be the most popular. No glitter, evening gowns,

For Music Majors

fancy recital dresses, plunging necklines, or outrageous stockings. If you want to make a "statement," make it with color, not style. (Brown and beige are not good stage colors.) Be sure that the dress fits well so that you have plenty of room to breathe without bursting any seams, buttons, or zippers. (This happens more often than you would imagine!) Shoes should have low-to-medium heels—no spike heels.

Men (including singers): a nice pair of pants; a shirt, jacket, and tie; and loafers or nice shoes. (The traditional look of gray trousers, white shirt, tie, and navy blue blazer is very popular and appropriate.) If you want to make a "statement," make it with your tie. A nice turtleneck is okay, too. No tuxes, tails, fancy suits, jeans, or sneakers. For singers and wind players, be sure that the shirt is large enough so that you do not have to leave the top button open or loosen your tie.

### WHAT TO BRING WITH YOU

Before you leave for your audition, look at the catalog one more time and reexamine the letter sent to you with your audition schedule. Do you need to bring manuscript paper and pencils? (Conductors and composers often do.) It may also be helpful to take a look at your photocopy or hard copy print-out of the application you submitted, just to refresh your memory about what you wrote. Here are some questions to ask yourself before you leave for the audition.

- Do I have copies of the music that I am prepared to perform?

- Is the music that I am giving to my accompanist in best form? Can they read it easily? Turn pages simply? This music should NOT be stapled, and it should be a clean copy with all notes included and not dropped off the page.

- Do I have a copy of the schedule letter that was sent to me to glance at for reference?

- Do I have all my audition clothing? Shoes?

- Do I have all the equipment I need? This may include a music stand; sticks and brushes (percussionists); your instrument, including mouthpiece, mutes, bows, rosin, etc. (Believe it or not, a guitarist once showed up at Juilliard with his guitar case but no instrument inside!); any extra copies of your audition repertoire list just in case it is requested; tissues or handkerchiefs (for sweaty palms, to wipe your brow, or as a basic prop), and water, if you think you may need it.

Performing

*Arts*

## REPERTOIRE CHOICES

If you do not submit the required repertoire on your application, many schools will not allow you to audition and will reject your application outright, so be sure that you are conforming to the requirements. If you have any doubts, write a letter (do not make a phone call in this case) to the admissions office and ask them if what you are planning meets with the faculty's standards. This is particularly true in piano, where the repertoire is vast and the interpretation of the word "substantial," used in several catalogs, is open to debate.

Be sure to choose music that you really love from within the repertoire requirements; this will make it much more pleasurable to perform under duress. Don't make the mistake of choosing an aria or sonata you think the audition panel wants to hear. You will do well only if you like what you have chosen to perform.

Changing repertoire may be permitted, but be sure that whatever composition you are substituting conforms with the overall requirements. You should write to the admissions office with your change of repertoire, but also announce it at the beginning of your audition. Typing a new "Audition Repertoire List" and having enough copies to distribute to the faculty at the audition is a good thing to do.

## PRACTICE AUDITION

One of the best ways to prepare for the audition is to do it, under mock or concert circumstances, many, many times. Videotape or make a DVD of each mock audition and critique it yourself, as well as seeking the evaluation of others. One pianist from Texas who was admitted to several schools used her mock audition times as an opportunity for fund-raising. She would charge a modest admission, as though this were a mini-concert, and then play and discuss the performance with the audience afterwards.

When you set up these mock auditions for yourself, try out the clothing that you think you will wear. Can you breathe comfortably? Can you walk well in the shoes you have chosen? Also give yourself a number of sample rooms to audition in. While some audition rooms may be concert halls with wonderful acoustics, others are teaching studios with very dead sounds. Get used to performing under a variety of circumstances and don't let anything distract you from doing your best.

**BEFORE YOU AUDITION**

The importance of preparation for your audition cannot be stressed enough. Classical musicians should start with the repertoire. Check your catalog or the school's Web site in your freshman and sophomore years and plan your repertoire accordingly. Usually you must perform from memory. You need to live with your selections long enough to know that you can perform them with total security technically and emotionally. By choosing repertoire early, you also allow yourself time to make a switch if you need or want to.

Popular musicians should also start early with repertoire preparation. If you are required to perform standards, get them in your blood so that you will be able to improvise easily. And, if you plan to perform any original compositions, preparing early will allow you to try out the compositions in a variety of settings and get some feedback from teachers, colleagues, and audiences.

As you read the Web site or catalog, note whether you will be required to take any additional examinations, such as an ear training, sight-reading, or music theory test. If so, be sure to do some review and familiarize yourself with the material as best you can. You may have a melodic dictation. This is usually played by an instructor at the piano. Clef and key will usually be given (e.g., A major), but not time signature or pitch. You will have to determine meter, starting note, and notate the melody correctly. You may also be asked to sight sing; do an analysis of a piece, including identifying chords with Roman numerals and indicating nonharmonic tones by type such as escape tone, appoggiatura, passing tone, upper neighbor, suspension; identify plagal, half, deceptive, or full cadences; or do harmonization with figured bass realizations. Some schools have Web-based practice tests or reviews online. Others have recommended texts. Some common texts for study are:

### Music Theory

Aldwell, Edward, and Carl Schacter. *Harmony and Voice Leading.* New York: Schirmer, 2002.

Clough, John, and Joyce Conley. *Scales, Keys, Intervals, Triads, Rhythm, and Meter.* New York: Norton, 1999.

Fux, John J. *The Study of Counterpoint.* New York: Norton, 1965.

Gauldin, Robert. *Harmonic Practice in Tonal Music.* New York: Norton, 2004.

Kostka, Stefan, and Dorothy Payne. *Tonal Harmony.* New York: McGraw-Hill, 2000.

Marvin, Elizabeth West, and Jane Clendinning. *Musician's Guide to Theory and Analysis.* New York: Norton, 2004.

**Music History**

Burkholder, J. Peter, Donald Grout, and Claude V. Paleisca. *A History of Western Music.* 7th ed. New York: Norton, 2005.

Burkholder, J. Peter, ed. *The Norton Anthology of Western Music and the Norton Recorded Anthology.* 5th ed. New York: Norton, 2005.

Fuller, Sarah. *The European Musical Heritage, 800–1750.* Revised ed. Boston: McGraw-Hill, 2006.

Salzman, Eric. *Twentieth Century Music: An Introduction.* Englewood, NJ: Prentice-Hall, 2001.

**Ear Training**

Fish, Arnold, and Norman Lloyd. *Fundamentals of Ear Training and Sight Singing.* Waveland Press, 1992.

Ottman, Robert. *Music for Sight Singing.* Englewood, NJ: Prentice-Hall, 2003.

**Piano Literature**

Dubal, David. *Art of the Piano: Its Performers, Literature, etc.* Amadeus Press, 2005.

Hinson, Maurice. *Guide to the Pianist's Repertoire.* IN: Indiana University Press, 2001.

Matthews, Denis, ed. *Keyboard Music.* New York: Praeger Publishers, 1972.

**Keyboard Studies**

Morris, R. O. *Preparatory Exercises in Score Reading and Figured Harmony at the Keyboard, Book I.* UK: Oxford University Press.

Once your repertoire is under control, you must begin your mental and emotional preparation for the audition. There are many parallels between music performance and sports. Just as an athlete must have tremendous powers of concentration, so should a musician. You must not allow distractions from the audition panel (often called a "jury" in music) to interfere with your performance. Learn to focus your concentration on the music and your performance of it. Walk into the audition with confidence and a positive attitude. Know the music inside and out and in retrograde inversion, but when you play or sing, perform from the heart.

Some additional tips on preparing for your audition:

- Try to avoid traveling on the day of the audition. Plan to arrive at least a day ahead, more if the location is at a higher altitude and you are a wind or brass player or a singer. Traveling can tire you out, and airplanes can dehydrate you and affect your ears.

- Get a good night's sleep the night before the audition. Do not stay up talking to friends or to other people auditioning.

- Avoid alcohol and caffeine, which can also dehydrate you. Drink lots of water.

## TYPES OF AUDITIONS

Auditions are run in different ways from school to school, but there are some common types of auditions.

### On Campus for a Representative Group of the Faculty

This is the most common type of audition. You arrive at the campus and are told that the auditions for your major field of study (instrument, voice, musical theater, etc.) are being held in a certain room. You locate the room, check in with a monitor, meet your accompanist, have a few minutes to warm up and check tempi, and then are told that the faculty are ready to hear you. You walk into the room and are confronted with 3 to possibly 16 distinguished faculty members. (Piano, violin, and voice seem to have the largest number of audition panel members.) One of these people usually will act as coordinator of the audition. Take your lead from this person. You might say, "Hello, my name is Sally Smith," and proceed to sit down (or stand) and wait for them to get their audition evaluation forms together and acknowledge you. If you are playing with an accompanist, the pianist should already have your music in order. Do not start until the coordinator of the audition tells you to begin. In some auditions, you may be asked some simple questions to help you relax before you play. In other auditions, the atmosphere will be very formal with many moments of silence. Then the coordinator may say something such as, "With what would you like to start today?"

Most schools let you start your audition with a piece of your choosing. You should select that piece very carefully. It need not be the most difficult piece in your repertoire but something that you really love and that shows you off to your best. The audition panel may cut you off while you are in the midst of this piece (tapping a pencil on the table seems to be the most popular technique, but some may clap, and others just speak up), but do not start with an attitude of wondering where they will stop you; this will leave your concentration unfocused. Rather, keep focused and enjoy yourself as best you can, getting "into" the music.

Usually the audition committee will ask you to perform something else from your repertoire list. Before you start that selection, be sure to take a deep breath and focus your mental energy and concentration on this new piece. If you are asked for another selection after this one, follow the same procedure.

Before you start to play or sometimes before you leave an audition, faculty members may ask you a few simple questions, such as, "Where are you from?" "How long have you studied and where?" "How much do you practice each day?" "Do you make your own reeds?" "What kind of horn is that?" "What is the extent of your orchestral experience?", etc. You may or may not be asked about naming your current teacher. Whatever you do, do not be thrown by these questions, and be sure to answer them honestly, thoughtfully, and completely. International students are not allowed to bring translators, so you will want to practice your responses to questions such as these prior to your audition.

Your audition is over when the faculty indicates that you may go. The length of auditions varies, but it tends to be 10 to 15 minutes on average, depending on the instrument. Percussion, accompanying, organ, and jazz auditions are usually a little longer. You may feel that the faculty is being remote, detached, or unfriendly in an audition of this nature. In fact, they are trying to be objective and fair, judging you on the quality of your music-making. You should also realize that sitting for many hours listening intently to auditions is very hard work, and people do get tired and cantankerous. If you take control of your instrument and are as pleasant and confident as possible, the image that you project will help to warm up the room.

### For a Single Faculty Member

Some schools will have you audition only for the faculty member you have indicated you want to study with, or the school will have a one-person department. These auditions may be run like the audition just described or may be more like a lesson or consultation, so that the faculty member sees how you work and whether or not you are responsive to the teaching methods he or she uses. These auditions may be longer, perhaps even 30 minutes. Be prepared to be flexible.

**Regional Auditions**

Regional auditions, sometimes called "external auditions," held in selected cities around the country and, more frequently, internationally, are usually conducted by a member of the administration. Sometimes faculty representatives are present, but usually regional auditions are taped or videotaped, and those tapes are then played for the faculty.

If you cannot go to the campus for a personal audition, which is always preferred, a regional audition is a good alternative. Anticipate walking into the room, introducing yourself, choosing your first selection, and then being asked to play something contrasting from your repertoire list. A third selection may be requested, and you may be asked a few questions before you are dismissed.

**Taped vs. Live Auditions**

Some schools request that audiotapes, CDs, or videotapes be submitted with applications for a pre-screening review to see who should be invited to audition in person. Be sure that you follow the format a school requires: If audio, is it a standard cassette? A CD? If video, must it be American-format VHS? Is a DVD preferred? The audio quality of the tape should be as high as possible, and if it is a video or DVD, be sure that the camera is in focus and that the background is not distracting. (Do not bother with an expensively produced video or DVD. A good home video with high-quality audio is just fine.) You should label your recordings carefully with your name, address, instrument, and the repertoire presented, in the order in which you perform it on the tape. This information should be on the tape, CD, or DVD itself, and also on whatever packaging you send it in. If you make it past this pre-screening, you will be invited to perform in person.

Live auditions are always preferred to recordings, so you should make every effort to arrange to get an on-campus or regional audition. Sending an audiotape, CD, DVD, or videotape for your actual audition may slightly diminish your chances for admission. If you are a prize-winning performer, with many professional credits, then you may present yourself well on recording. Anyone else should really aim to perform in person.

### Making an Audition Recording

Presenting your playing on an audiocassette, CD, DVD, or videotape is difficult. It is essential that you present the highest audio quality possible, while staying within your budget. One musician who has been on the orchestra committee for symphony auditions tells of reviewing tapes that were made on machines with automatic volume control, or even made on telephone answering machines! These people did not win the audition, needless to say. Other reviewers talk of students who spend money on professional videos of almost MTV quality—just not worth it.

While it is probably not worth your time and money to rent a professional recording studio, where rates are often very high and the engineers will often want to put in extra reverb or other effects, you should have good microphones and experiment with their placement. Making a good recording takes time. You will need to go through your pieces several times before you get a "take." Remember that the committee reviewing a cassette or video rarely listens to the entire set of selections, so you should put your very best pieces first. If you are working with an accompanist, set up several times to work on the recording.

Douglas Yeo, bass trombonist with the Boston Symphony, suggests the following method for making an audition tape. Buy, borrow, or rent the best equipment you can, always following the directions the school or program has given you. Set yourself up in a good-sized room, not too big and not too small. Spend one session experimenting with the microphone setup. Use high-quality tape, turn on the machine, and start playing or singing. Play every excerpt or part of a composition more than once, checking the recording set up and carefully noting what you do. Keep the tape rolling throughout this exercise.

After the session, listen to the tape on a good machine and judge the best setup from a sonic perspective. (Never send a recording that you have not reviewed! Many directors of admission tell of assembling faculty members to review tapes, only to find a few with nothing on them!) Then, the next day or even later, repeat the entire process using the setup you liked best. Play through the repertoire as best you can. Later choose your best takes and transfer them, with your very best piece first, to another tape. Listen to the finished product and if you need to, repeat the entire process until you get something you like. You should never splice an audition tape, but choosing your best rendition after several opportunities to perform it is usually permitted. After all this, it may seem even more practical, as well as to your advantage, to attend the personal audition.

## DIFFICULT SITUATIONS TO ANTICIPATE

No matter how well prepared you are, you may still encounter a situation that you could not possibly have anticipated.

**Faculty members who argue among themselves about your repertoire choices.** You have just presented your first selection and now the coordinator asks for something else. Another faculty member does not want to hear that and speaks up. A debate ensues. You should just sit there patiently until this debate is resolved.

**Lack of interest from the faculty.** This may be because you are scheduled right before lunch, when the focus is on food, or right after lunch, when panel members may be sleepy, or late in the day, when they are tired. The best way to handle this situation is to be as energetic and positive as possible, and totally dedicated to the music. If they do not ask you to play a second selection, it does get a little tricky. They may have really liked you and did not need to hear more. On the other hand, if you did not do your very best on that first piece, you might tactfully try suggesting, "Well, I do have my Paganini Caprice and it's really short. Since I've only had 5 minutes of your time, perhaps you'd let me start this." If you do not feel comfortable with this, then stop by the admissions office and let them know what happened.

**Unfortunate remarks by faculty members.** Sometimes you may say the name of your teacher and there may be some history or politics involved, or someone on the audition panel may say something like, "Oh, is that person still teaching?" Do not let this throw you. You are being evaluated on the quality of your music-making, not on who your teacher is.

**Faculty members who stand up and walk around, pass candies among themselves, or engage in some other sort of distracting activity.** Keep your concentration. Some faculty members may move around because they cannot see your embouchure or fingerings from where they are sitting. This does not necessarily mean that they have lost interest or want you to stop. Some may have been sitting for quite a while and need to stand up and stretch.

**Anything out of the blue.** Perhaps the hardest thing at an audition is being asked to do something you had not expected or prepared for. For example, you might be asked to improvise, to sight-read, or to answer questions about a piece you may have studied but are not prepared to play. Since this is your time, take control of the situation and present your strengths. If you have not had much practice at sight-reading and did not anticipate this as any part of your audition, you might say, "I'd be happy to give this a try, but I would love a minute or two to look it over, as I spent my time preparing the specified repertoire for this audition."

What if your accompanist plays poorly? Remember, the faculty is listening to you and is not evaluating the accompanist. Just keep going and do your best. Be sure to rehearse in advance with the accompanist and never be rude to this person.

If an audition really goes poorly, you should contact the admissions office and ask to speak with either the director or assistant director. Be very specific about what transpired. Perhaps another audition can be arranged.

## PARTNERS/ACCOMPANISTS

Most schools require that classical instrumentalists play a sonata or concerto with piano accompaniment. If it is at all feasible, try to bring your own accompanist with whom you have worked regularly. If this is not possible, call in advance (two weeks usually) and get the name of the school's accompanist who is assigned to your instrument. Call that person and ask if he or she would be willing to play for you. If at all possible, arrange to rehearse a day in advance. While this may cost you anywhere between $40 and $750, it is well worth the extra charge, because you will feel more at ease and will have worked out tempi in advance. If the accompanist does not know something on your repertoire list, ask if he or she would like you to send a copy of the composition in advance or if there is someone else he or she might recommend.

Singers should follow essentially the same procedure as classical instrumentalists. It is best to make repertoire selections from the standard repertoire of arias and art songs if you plan to use anyone other than your own accompanist. It is also important to choose the most common editions of arias.

In musical theater, an accompanist is usually provided. Plan what you want to say to the pianist about tempi. You should plan on being cut off after a limited number of measures in your songs.

Popular musicians (jazz) are often invited to sit in with a "house band," or have a rhythm section provided at their audition. Have fun!

Accompanists are usually encouraged to bring their own "partners"— usually a violinist and a singer with whom they have worked in the past. If you are unable to bring your own partners, call the school at least two weeks in advance and get the names of the people the school has assigned for these auditions. See if you can have a rehearsal the day before the audition.

Whenever collaborating with an accompanist, you must present the music in the best form possible. Arrange to have either the original score or very legible photocopies bound in a loose-leaf notebook or pasted onto cardboard. If you are taking any cuts in the music, be sure that they are marked clearly and that you point these out verbally before the audition. If your interpretation has particular nuances with tempi or dynamics, be certain to mention these verbally and have them clearly indicated in the score. An accompanist is a valuable collaborator and can really give you support during your audition. Make sure that you develop a good rapport with this person and prepare as much as possible. It is generally not advantageous to have your parent or teacher accompany you. Better to use the person assigned by the school and rehearse in advance with this person.

## NERVES

Being nervous for an audition in music is de rigueur. In general, the best prescription for nerves is preparation. If you love the compositions you have chosen, focus on the performance aspect of the audition, and cancel out of your mind any sense of judgment, you may have a good time and not be nervous at all. Remember, the people listening want to like you.

Perhaps one of the most typical manifestations of nerves is a memory lapse. You'll be playing along or singing and just go blank. Stop and start up when you left off. If it really is totally gone from your mind and ear, ask the audition panel if you may start again.

Dr. Beth Rom-Rymer, a psychologist in Chicago, did a workshop with members of the Chicago Youth Symphony Orchestra, who shared their feelings about a number of topics, including nerves (_Upbeat,_ Spring 1991, vol. 6, no. 2):

_Many students related to a string player who had such bad stage fright that she had to give up after walking on stage three times, unable to play the piece she had perfected for a competition through many hours of practice. Many other students could empathize with another string player who said he sometimes gets so tense his fingers cramp up and won't move._

*To avoid anxiety before a competition, Dr. Rom-Rymer suggested meditation/relaxation exercises, including cognitive rehearsal for the expected and unforeseen event, using positive and flexible cognitive imagery. You can use your inside as a refuge for relaxing and reverse the anxiety response.*

*When feeling tense muscles during long hours of practice, Dr. Rom-Rymer recommended taking time off to relax the body.*

Diane Nichols, head of Mental Health at the Miller Health Care Institute for Performing Artists in New York City, suggests strategies of quieting the physical and psychological symptoms of performance anxiety:

*Develop a pre-performance ritual. It doesn't matter what the ritual entails as long as you do it regularly to give you a sense of comfort and security. One actor pushes against a wall before every show; a student breakfasts on cereal and bananas before taking an exam. A singer takes a shower. You could lift weights or call Mom; the choice is purely personal.*

*Yawn. Yawning relaxes the jaw, neck, and shoulders and releases tension. It tells the body there's no danger.*

*Talk to yourself. When you're fearful, you lose sight of your strengths. The next time images of hissing audiences cloud your vision, say out loud, "I don't have to be perfect," or some other verbal reminder to put the situation into perspective.*

*Breathe. Before stepping into the spotlight, take two slow, deep breaths. It sounds simple, but once you're in control of your breathing patterns, you'll feel more in control of the situation.*

*Finally, SMILE. Studies show that you can't smile and feel fear at the same time. In addition to relaxing your muscles, smiling engages the listener as your presentation begins.*

## AUDITION EVALUATION CRITERIA

While you are playing or singing, the faculty members will usually be completing forms, evaluating you on a variety of factors. To demystify the process, copies of audition forms from a number of schools are on pages 99 to 101.

### ADDITIONAL EXAMINATIONS

As part of some auditions, you will be asked to take additional examinations. These vary from school to school and are used differently: some for admissions purposes and some for placement. Be sure that you are clear about what is expected of you so that you may prepare appropriately. If you are asked to play a separate orchestral placement examination, which will include sight-reading excerpts, speak with your teacher about common excerpts so that you can look them over in advance. Music theory, music history, piano proficiency (for non-keyboard applicants), and ear training are all fairly common examinations. For applicants for whom English is not the native language, there may be an English examination. There may be a diction evaluation for singers or a foreign language proficiency examination for doctoral students. Help yourself by preparing as best you can in advance.

### WHAT *NOT* TO DO AT A MUSIC AUDITION

- Dress inappropriately.

- Arrive late or forget to cancel the audition.

- Chew gum.

- Forget to introduce yourself.

- Start playing before you are asked to begin.

- Try to talk with a particular faculty member in the audition room.

- Try to listen to other applicants' auditions.

- Make excuses for any slip you may have or curse out loud if this happens to you.

- Tell your life story in answer to a simple question intended to help you relax.

- Leave in the middle of the audition. If you have a tendency towards dryness, particularly as a singer or wind player, bring water into the audition room with you, and be sure you have gone to the bathroom before the audition.

- Cry.

**AUDITION EVALUATION**

Name: _____ ID #: _____ In person: _____ Tape: _____

Address: _____ Phone: _____

Instrument/Voice Part: _____

MAJOR IN:

☐ Piano Pedagogy ☐ Music Education ☐ Music Therapy ☐ Theory/Composition
☐ Performance ☐ Sacred Music ☐ Conducting
☐ Music Minor with possible major in: _____

☐ First Year ☐ Graduate ☐ Transfer from: _____

Repertoire Performed: _____

_____

CIRCLE each characteristic from low (1) to high (10)

| | unacceptable | weak | adequate | very good | outstanding |
|---|---|---|---|---|---|
| A. TONE QUALITY | 1 2 | 3 4 | 5 6 | 7 8 | 9 10 |
| B. TECHNIQUE (articulation, diction) | 1 2 | 3 4 | 5 6 | 7 8 | 9 10 |
| C. INTONATION (except keyboard) | 1 2 | 3 4 | 5 6 | 7 8 | 9 10 |
| D. RHYTHM | 1 2 | 3 4 | 5 6 | 7 8 | 9 10 |
| E. STYLE–INTERPRETATION | 1 2 | 3 4 | 5 6 | 7 8 | 9 10 |
| F. OVERALL MUSICIANSHIP | 1 2 | 3 4 | 5 6 | 7 8 | 9 10 |
| G. MUSIC READING (if checked) | 1 2 | 3 4 | 5 6 | 7 8 | 9 10 |

Performance applicants must score 7 or higher.
Other majors and minors must score 5 or higher.

COMMITTEE RATING

1–10

COMMITTEE EVALUATION: _____

_____

_____

FACULTY RECOMMENDED: ☐ High Award ☐ Moderate ☐ Possible ☐ None

EVALUATORS: _____ _____
_____ _____
_____ _____

**For Music Majors**

# PETERSON COLLEGE
## Conservatory of Music—General

Name: _____     ID: _____

Address: _____     Instrument: _____

_____

Telephone: _____     Audition Location: _____ Tape: _____

Application Date: _____

Wishes to Enter: _____     ASI: _____ PLI: _____

Application Type: _____     HS Grad Date: _____ Program: _____

High School: _____

    Major 1: _____     Major 2: _____

    Major 3: _____     Major 4: _____

HS Rank: _____     SAT: _____     ACT: _____

Teacher 1: _____     _____

Teacher 2: _____     _____

Teacher 3: _____     _____

Teacher 4: _____     _____

Composition 1 _____     _____

Composition 2 _____     _____

Composition 3 _____     _____

Composition 4 _____     _____

Composition 5 _____     _____

Rate the candidate in the following areas
[5 = Superior; 4 = Above Average; 3 = Average; 2 = Below Average; 1 = Poor]

Comments

| | 5 | 4 | 3 | 2 | 1 |
|---|---|---|---|---|---|
| Musical Talent | 5 | 4 | 3 | 2 | 1 |
| Tone | 5 | 4 | 3 | 2 | 1 |
| Intonation | 5 | 4 | 3 | 2 | 1 |
| Technique | 5 | 4 | 3 | 2 | 1 |
| Control | 5 | 4 | 3 | 2 | 1 |
| Rhythmic Accuracy | 5 | 4 | 3 | 2 | 1 |
| Interpretation | 5 | 4 | 3 | 2 | 1 |
| Contrast and Balance | 5 | 4 | 3 | 2 | 1 |
| Articulation | 5 | 4 | 3 | 2 | 1 |
| Sight Reading | 5 | 4 | 3 | 2 | 1 |
| Memory | 5 | 4 | 3 | 2 | 1 |

Rate the audition using the 5–1 scale above
    5   4   3   2   1

On the basis of this audition do you recommend that the applicant be admitted to the conservatory?

☐ Yes    ☐ No    ☐ ?

Do you recommend that the applicant receive special talent scholarship consideration?    ☐ Yes    ☐ No

Faculty examiner: _____     Date: _____

Performing Arts

# PERCUSSION

Name: _____   Address: _____

Performance Medium: _____   Probable Major: _____

Length of Study:  Years: _____  Months: _____   Present Teacher: _____

Personal Audition:  Date: _____  Time: _____   Examiner: _____

Recorded Audition: _____  Transfer: _____   College: _____

| | Superior | Above Average | Average | Below Average | Poor |
|---|---|---|---|---|---|
| **MARIMBA, XYLOPHONE: Composition** | | | | | |
| Tone (touch, evenness of sound) | | | | | |
| Roll | | | | | |
| Technique and Hand Position (dynamics, phrasing) | | | | | |
| Contrast and Balance | | | | | |
| Sight Reading | | | | | |
| Rhythmic Accuracy | | | | | |
| Pitch Accuracy | | | | | |
| Interpretation | | | | | |
| **SNARE DRUM: Composition** | | | | | |
| Tone (touch, evenness of sound) | | | | | |
| Roll | | | | | |
| Technique and Hand Position (dynamics, phrasing) | | | | | |
| Contrast and Balance | | | | | |
| Sight Reading | | | | | |
| Rhythmic Accuracy | | | | | |
| Pitch Accuracy | | | | | |
| Interpretation | | | | | |
| **TIMPANI: Composition** | | | | | |
| Tone (touch, evenness of sound) | | | | | |
| Roll | | | | | |
| Technique and Hand Position (dynamics, phrasing) | | | | | |
| Contrast and Balance | | | | | |
| Sight Reading | | | | | |
| Rhythmic Accuracy | | | | | |
| Pitch Accuracy | | | | | |
| Interpretation | | | | | |
| **MULTIPLE PERCUSSION: Composition** | | | | | |
| Tone (touch, evenness of sound) | | | | | |
| Roll | | | | | |
| Technique and Hand Position (dynamics, phrasing) | | | | | |
| Contrast and Balance | | | | | |
| Sight Reading | | | | | |
| Rhythmic Accuracy | | | | | |
| Pitch Accuracy | | | | | |
| Interpretation | | | | | |
| MUSICAL TALENT | | | | | |
| SENSE OF METER | | | | | |

In the space below please give your comments about the audition. Give special attention to the candidate's strengths and weaknesses. On the basis of this audition, do you recommend that the applicant be admitted to the conservatory?

☐ Yes   ☐ No   ☐ ?   Comments: _____

Faculty examiner: _____

# Advice on Music Specialties

**WOODWIND AND BRASS**

Many woodwind and brass players come from a background that has focused mainly on band music. This is tremendously valuable experience, providing players a fundamental grasp of their instrument and helping them to develop a good musical sense and the ability to phrase, to be part of an ensemble, and to follow a conductor. However, it is recommended that this band training be augmented with an awareness of Western European orchestral tradition. Listen to recordings of the great orchestras, attend orchestra concerts, and learn some standard orchestral excerpts for your audition. (You should also listen to the entire piece and know the excerpt in context.) If there is a youth symphony in your area, audition and try to join this organization or investigate the community orchestra. Read the journals on your instrument.

Some specific tips: Imitate your favorite recordings. Watch DVDs or videos of your favorite soloists and orchestral players. Listen to a passage of a piece and imitate it, like a jazz musician learning a solo. Listen to articulation as well as tone. Take responsibility for teaching yourself. Your own style will come from what you want to hear. Your own point of view is important and you must know what you like. Other recommendations from woodwind and brass players include being sure that you do not warm up too much. Blowing on your chops every few minutes to check them will tire you quickly. Better to spend the time concentrating on breathing deeply and relaxing. Be sure to drink lots of water (neither too hot nor too cold) to avoid "cotton mouth," and avoid soda, tea, coffee, and certainly milk before an audition.

**OBOE AND ENGLISH HORN**

Very few schools will let you major in English horn; most programs require that you major in oboe and play oboe d'amore and English horn as ancillary instruments on which you develop proficiency. Most double reed players complain that very few students develop any dynamic range on the instruments; they leap into playing concerti far too soon, before they have developed a basic technique. Work diligently on your études and learn how to stop and start a note attractively. Work on your breathing. Know also that music preparation involves studying scores, harmony, and theory and having keyboard proficiency and advanced listening skills. You should also know that the politics of the oboe/English horn world often focuses on an American versus European bias and discussions about vibrato. Be sure that whatever department you are joining represents your preference and that you are aware of both camps and have an idea about your future should you choose to play in one style over another. Ask questions about this.

## TROMBONE AND TUBA

Some books worth reading include *The Art of Trombone Playing*, by Edward Kleinhammer (Evanston, IL: Summy-Binchard, 1963), and *Art of Brass Playing*, by Philip Farkas (Bloomington, IN: Brass Publications, 1962). Also recommended is an article on breathing by Arnold Jacobs, which appeared in *The Instrumentalists, Brass Anthology*, and a collection of memoirs of Jacobs' students entitled *Arnold Jacobs: Legacy of a Master*. Trombonists should be acquainted with the Rochut Etude books (3 volumes); *Daily Drills and Technical Studies*, by Max Schlossberg; and the Arban book, *Blazevich Clef Studies*. They should also look at the Bach cello suites, the *David Concerto*, Kopprasch Book I and II, and orchestral excerpts. Tuba players should learn to play both the little and big tuba. Standard orchestral excerpts include *Die Meistersinger, Die Walküre (Ride of the Valkyries)*, Vaughan Williams' *Solo*, and Berlioz' *Hungarian March*.

## STRINGS

In discussing auditions, preparation for auditions, and playing in general, almost every string faculty member and player talked about two things: technical facility and musical intention. It seems tremendously important to string players that you pay special attention to your bow arm, left hand position, basic sound production, vibrato, and intonation. It is also important that you think of the music musically and have definite feelings and thoughts about what you want to convey. Fast fingers without feeling, thought, and emotional involvement is vapid. You must work at all levels in order to prepare properly for an audition.

It is also important that as a string player, you perform on the best instrument available to you at this stage in your development. To present yourself positively, try to play on an instrument that will allow you to have a sound that is uniquely your own and does not stand in your way.

This brings up the whole issue of instrument dealers. You should be aware that some teachers receive large fees, sometimes very large ones, from dealers for convincing students to buy certain instruments. While you may want your teacher to evaluate an instrument for you, and you would want to compensate the teacher for his or her time, buying an instrument just because a teacher suggests it may not be wise. Stop and think about the instrument's suitability for you.

## HARP

It is helpful for harpists to have a background in piano. Because harps are so expensive, some will rent the instrument before they know that they are committed to the harp, and then work to buy their own. (When you go for an audition, be sure to ask if you will be able to use the school's harp or if you need to transport your own—a rare occurrence.)

It is important to get as much playing experience as possible. Often young harpists will offer their services to the local community orchestra in order to learn the basic orchestral excerpts and to get experience playing in an ensemble. Because harpists tend to work so much on their own, it is important to try to reach out and play in ensembles, learning how to relate in chamber groups and develop an ensemble sense of rhythm. The American Harp Society holds an annual conference and has competitions every three years for all levels. There are also regional events. It is a good idea to attend or compete in these American Harp Society gatherings so that you hear other harpists and get a sense of where your level of playing stands among your peers. It should also be noted that harpists have an easier time applying to conservatories at the undergraduate level, and most professional harpists have chosen the route of conservatory training.

## ORGAN

Within the world of organists, there are some who are considered as "antiaquarians" and others who believe that the modern organ as it is now constructed should be the vehicle for the vast repertoire. It is probably worth your while to investigate the philosophical point of view of any department or individual teacher to be sure that you will be in harmony. Be aware that some schools require that organ applicants also audition in piano. Ask questions about the repertoire required.

## PIANO

One practical suggestion offered by many faculty members is that in playing your "mock auditions," you should play on a variety of instruments so that you can play your repertoire no matter what the action or state of repair of the piano.

In speaking to piano faculty members at various institutions, the resounding piece of advice seems to be regarding the audition program. Faculty members stress that you should present what you play best and like to play, which falls within the guidelines required, and not try to play something too difficult just to be impressive. The audition program should fit together and demonstrate lyric qualities, fingers or "chops," and a full range of musical virtues: legato line, sensitivity, and technical solidity. The piano literature is vast and you should be making selections for yourself; however, the following selections are offered as a basic guideline of some repertoire that seems fairly common for auditions:

Babbitt: *Three Compositions for Piano; Partitions*

Bach: *Well-Tempered Clavier,* Books I and II–Preludes and Fugues

Barber: *Sonata*

Bartók: *Suite,* Op. 14; *Sonata*

Beethoven: *Sonatas* (excluding Op. 14, Op. 49, and Op. 79)

Bolcom: *Etudes*

Brahms: *Intermezzi; Variations on a Theme by Handel; E-flat Rhapsody; Sonatas; Variations on a Theme by Paganini*

Chopin: *Ballades; Etudes; Scherzi*

Copland: *Variations*

Corigliano: *Etude Fantasy*

Debussy: *Images; Estampe; L'isle joyeuse; Pour le Piano*

Dello Joio: *Sonata*

Ginastera: *Sonata*

Lees: *Sonatas*

Liszt: *Transcendental Etudes: Vallée d'Obermann; Après une lecture de Dante; 11th Rhapsody; Mephisto Waltz; Funerailles*

Mendelssohn: *Sonata*

Messiaen: *Vingt Regards sur l'Enfant-Jésus* or any of the *Bird Pieces (Catalogue d' oiseaux)*

Persichetti: *Poems*

Prokofiev: *Sonata #3*

Rachmaninoff: *Preludes; Etudes Tableaux; Moments Musicaux*

Ravel: *Jeux d'eau; Sonatine; Gaspard de la nuit*

Rorem: *Barcarolles; Etudes*

Schubert: *Moment Musicale; Impromptus; "little" A major Sonata*

Schumann: *8th Novelette, Abegg Variations, G minor Sonata, Papillon*

Takemitsu: *Les Yeux Clos I and II*

## ACCOMPANISTS (ALSO REFERRED TO AS COLLABORATIVE PIANISTS)

Many of the most famous accompanists stress that it is most important to get your "piano chops" together first, meaning that your level of technical ability should be developed and strong. Thus, very few schools have an undergraduate major in accompanying, and most accompanists major in piano or attend a liberal arts college, keep up their private piano lessons, and then attend a graduate program in accompanying/collaborative piano.

It is important to note that some accompanying programs are only for vocal accompanying, while others are more oriented toward instrumental accompanying. While there are a handful of truly accomplished accompanists who do well in both the vocal and instrumental worlds, most have chosen an area of specialization.

Be aware that if you choose to be a vocal accompanist/coach, you should have your foreign languages and English diction in order. Study French, Italian, German, and Spanish, emphasizing both language and diction. You should have dictionaries in all these languages as part of your library, also. Study the standard vocal literature, including the "hit parade" of arias for each voice category and the song repertoire, including Brahms, Wolf, Schubert, Schumann, Fauré, Debussy, Chausson, Ravel, Italian art songs, works of Dowland and Purcell, and some of the standard American art songs, just to scratch the surface. Those wishing to pursue vocal accompanying should be attending recitals and the opera often. You should listen to recordings of the great singers and try to make arrangements to accompany lessons for a teacher with a reputable voice studio.

If you choose to specialize in instrumental accompanying, you should attend as many master classes as possible, learn as much as imaginable about the various instruments, attend solo and chamber music concerts and recitals, listen to recordings, and study the sonata and concerto repertoire. You should know how to read an orchestral score and reduce it at the piano and be able to render an orchestral accompaniment with the proper inflection to do full justice to the orchestration. You should try to accompany lessons for various teachers, too.

Some wonderful books have been written about being an accompanist. Basic recommended reading includes Bob Spilman, *The Art of Accompanying* (New York: Schirmer Books, 1985), and Gerald Moore's many books, including *Am I Too Loud? Memoirs of an Accompanist* (London: Hamish Hamilton, 1962) and *Singer and Accompanist* (London: Methuen, 1953).

## SINGERS

Do not prepare repertoire that is beyond your ability at this point. For instance, young singers really should not be singing the heavy verismo arias; Mozart is much more appropriate. Be aware that if you do offer Vissi d'arte or other such heavy arias, you are increasing your chances for rejection. Faculty members will note inappropriate repertoire, poor training, and lack of vocal understanding. Sample opera repertoire might include works of Mozart, Bellini, Donizetti, or Handel—no Verdi or Puccini! The point is not to dazzle your audition committee, but to demonstrate your present ability with selections that do not overtax you emotionally but that allow you to show your personality and your language skills. Lieder studies might include songs of Fauré, Schubert, Brahms, the Italian anthology, and Purcell or Dowland. If you are asked to prepare some twentieth-century repertoire, review the songs of Ned Rorem, Richard Hundley, Benjamin Britten, Aaron Copland, Dominic Argento, or Samuel Barber, for example. Your lessons should include good vocalizes, many of which will be special exercises that your teacher devises, such as those in Nicola Vaccai's *Metodo Pratico di Canto* (Practical Singing Method), a classic book first published in 1832 of various musical matters put together in attractive ariettas with Italian texts. Other good books regarding vocal technique that may be illuminating include William Vennard, *Singing—The Mechanism and the Technic* (New York: Carl Fischer, 1967); Johan Sundbert, *The Science of the Singing Voice*

(Northern Illinois University Press, 1987); and Robert Shewen with Judith Coen, *Singing and the Brain* (NY: Roberts Wesleyan College Press, 2005).

Any teacher who says that you have a "big voice" and can handle the "large or heavy repertoire" may be hearing what your voice may become, but if you sing that heavy repertoire before you are physically, technically, or emotionally prepared, you will probably be damaging your vocal apparatus.

Most voice teachers with whom I have spoken say that it is a very rare 18-year-old who should even consider a conservatory. Most would do best studying at a liberal arts college, learning literature and several foreign languages, for at least two years, and taking private voice lessons with a reputable teacher on the side.

It is important that singers be good sight-readers. Although the participation of young would-be soloists in choruses or choirs is controversial among some voice teachers, it is suggested that young singers participate in some choruses or choirs to improve their sight-reading ability and explore a variety of musical styles. Some voice teachers also recommend that singers try to participate in a summer program overseas.

## CHORAL CONDUCTORS

Most choral conductors have a background as an organist or as a singer. Some have majored in music education, augmented with intensive piano studies. The best training for choral conductors seems to be in settings where there is a strong choral tradition, coupled with a good voice department, and opportunities with opera and symphony choruses as well. In the United States right now, many choral programs are in a period of transition, as some of the well-known choral conductor/teachers are retiring. Choral conductors should be as well versed in score-reading, transpositions, languages, and other musical matters, just the same as any other conductor.

## ORCHESTRAL CONDUCTORS

There seems to be much debate about the best training and background for conductors. Many working conductors feel that it is essential for an aspiring conductor to work at the undergraduate level on all of the following: becoming proficient on an instrument, including piano; studying composition and analysis; gaining a background in the humanities, with special attention to literature and art history; taking as much music theory and ear-training as possible; attending as many rehearsals and concerts as possible; and learning foreign languages, including Italian, German, and French.

A common belief is that it is good training to be an assistant to an established conductor, doing an apprenticeship of sorts. The Exxon/ Affiliate Artist program is the most established way of doing this, but it is highly competitive. Concentration in conducting, if desired in a school setting, should come at the graduate level. Be sure to ask how much time is spent in the classroom and how much is spent actually conducting an orchestra. Are your rehearsals recorded for your review? Will you ever have any opportunities to conduct in public? Are various art forms part of your training? Ballet orchestras? Opera? Contemporary ensembles?

In training to be a conductor, there is no substitute for time. Since the development of the conductor's ear is critical, try to sit in on orchestra rehearsals, not just in the audience, but in various sections of the orchestra. It is also important to be aware of the politics of the business and to develop an appropriate presentation of yourself. You must be extremely well organized, able to get along with everyone from the music director and administrative director, to all players in the orchestra, ladies auxiliary committees, and the coat room attendant. You must be prepared to conduct youth concerts, pops concerts, and senior citizen pre-concert lectures, and be part of an organization's sense of civic pride.

## COMPOSERS

There is some consensus about what makes for good piano playing or singing, for instance, but the scope of what is considered good or bad in the composition world is very broad. It is important, therefore, in your investigation that you do careful research about composition departments. Are you comfortable with their philosophy? Do you understand and respect each other's musical idiom? Do you want your life as a composer do be more "academic," i.e., involving teaching and writing on the side, or do you intend to focus on having your music performed? What sort of facilities are available for you to use? Computer publishing programs? How often will you be guaranteed that your music will be played? With what other composers will you have contact and in what forum?

One well-known composer suggested that composition majors look for a department that is strongly oriented toward synthesis and studio technique with a willingness to be on the cutting edge of new techniques in using computers and other technology. He suggested listening to

National Public Radio (NPR), the noncommercial radio broadcast throughout the United States and parts of Canada, especially the "new sounds" of John Schaeffer's program. He also suggested that you hang out at your local music store and become acquainted with the new technology in instruments, get to know who the musicians are in your neighborhood, and go to "alternative" concerts and talk to the performers afterwards.

Other composers stress the importance of having a strong background in music theory and music history, with careful attention to analyzing scores. Learn everything from species counterpoint to the most complex analysis of music and listen to as much music as possible. One composer tells the story of a young person coming to an audition and being asked what composers he likes to listen to. The applicant responded, "Stravinsky." "What of his do you particularly like?" The applicant said, "The Rite of Spring." The professor said, "Oh, have you heard it live or do you have a favorite recording?" "No," said the applicant. "Then have you studied the score in depth?" "No, I've never looked at it," replied the applicant. Learn from this example: Study scores, listen to music of all kinds, attend as many concerts as possible, and talk to as many living composers as you can. Look at scores with an eye toward figuring out orchestration, instrumentation, transpositions, clefs, and the basic layout of the score. Learn as much about computers and their musical applications and software as possible.

At your audition in composition you will probably be asked not only to speak about your compositional choices and technique, but also given detailed questions about the music of the "masters" such as Bach and Beethoven, so prepare accordingly. Also remember that when you send your scores, you should not send the originals.

## JAZZ

Jazz is now sometimes referred to as "classical jazz." Improvising, while the most natural way to make music, requires great skill in the jazz idiom. Jamey Aebersold, a nationally known saxophonist and jazz educator, once wrote in the *International Musician*:

There are several ingredients that go into making a good jazz soloist/improviser:

- Desire to improvise
- Listening to jazz via recordings and live performances
- A method of practice—knowing what and how to practice

- A rhythm section with which to practice and improvise (via live group or play-along "music minus one" recordings)

- Self-esteem, discipline, and determination

Many students of jazz wonder if they will ever be able to play on their instruments the melodies that they hear in their heads. Ms. Aebersold suggests that you begin not only by listening, but by practicing simple melodies such as "Happy Birthday," starting on one note in the middle of the register of your instrument, and then playing it starting on any of the twelve notes of the chromatic scale. This is an excellent way of conditioning your fingers and mind to work together to produce the sounds you are hearing in your head.

It is recommended that jazz musicians do a regular warm-up, which might include playing the first five notes to each chord/scale, playing the seventh and ninth chords, up and down, and variations on this, such as playing the scale up to the ninth and then coming back down the chord. This sort of warm-up conditions your mind and fingers to the scales and chords over which you will improvise.

Transcribing solos or portions of solos from recordings is also highly recommended. Analyze the solo for things like whether the soloist uses scales or bits and pieces of scales; has favorite licks that are used repeatedly; or uses chromatics or passing tones, silence/rests, or rhythmic variety—double time, for instance.

Jazz studies at the college or university level have become very sophisticated, and there are some excellent programs. Many require that you be as proficient on your instrument as any player in the strictly "classical" area. An audition is usually required, either in person or by recording. You are usually asked to perform three pieces. Be sure to offer standards and not present three of your own compositions. Play in the style with which you are most comfortable. If you are not a bebopper, do not feel compelled to present a bebop solo. You may be asked to improvise and even sit in with a house band. Listen well and be positive. Be sure that you have listened to such jazz greats as Charlie Parker, Duke Ellington, Thelonius Monk, Coleman Hawkins, Dizzy Gillespie, Sonny Stitt, and Sonny Rollins; that you have studied privately; and that you have learned by doing—working with a band and getting gigs.

## POPULAR MUSICIANS

Popular musicians vary widely in their training, and they range from having the most sophisticated awareness of music theory and ear-training to having completely unschooled natural talent, enthusiasm, and ability.

Rock musicians traditionally have had about four years of private lessons and have played in bands. Many lack reading skills, but most rock musicians have great ears and, if given a passage, can repeat it with little trouble. To make the leap ahead, rock musicians should study music theory and concentrate on chord/scale relationships along with their playing ability and ensemble experience. Rock musicians would do well to be acquainted with lots of other musical styles, including jazz, R&B, the blues (people like Lightnin' Hopkins, John Lee Hooker, and Muddy Waters, for example), and country music. Also, because rock performances are sometimes almost athletic events, it is important for rock musicians to be in good physical shape.

Those who want to go on in commercial/pop music have also usually had at least three years of private lessons. Singers would do well to listen to Barbra Streisand, Ella Fitzgerald, Aretha Franklin, Frank Sinatra, Bing Crosby, Elvis Presley, and Sarah Vaughan, among others. It is also worthwhile to be exposed to a number of different styles: country music, big band, R&B, church music, folk, the blues, and rock. Diction, rhythm, and good sight-reading are very important skills to develop. Pop singers should also work hard on being as disciplined as the most focused classical musician. Although a few good college programs exist for popular and commercial musicians, this is an area where you learn by doing, so performing as much as possible is vitally important, combined with some good coaching and private instruction.

## MUSICAL THEATER

The best preparation for musical theater is to study voice, dance, and acting. At many auditions you will be required to sing one or two selections from musical theater. In choosing these, offer contrasting styles; one up-tempo number demonstrating your rhythm and performance pizzazz; and then another that has strong emotional content, usually a ballad. At some schools you may be asked to discuss your choices and interpretation. You may also be required to take a dance class, where you may be taught a routine and those evaluating the audition will be reviewing not just how well you move, but how well you take direction and respond to corrections. Be sure to bring appropriate clothing and shoes for this: dance attire or gym shorts or sweats are common for this part of the audition. Ask if you need tap or ballet shoes, or kneepads. Read the school's material to see if anything is specified. For the theater segment of your audition you maybe asked to present a monologue or two or to do a reading. In preparation for this multi-level audition, be sure that you have rehearsed your song with a pianist and not with the Broadway cast recording. Be prepared to be stopped after 16 measures. You should have taken both dance and acting classes and have participated in school and community productions.

In evaluating any college-level musical theater programs, be sure that the training is comprehensive in music, dance, and theater. Like singers, musical theater majors should consider acquiring at least two years of liberal arts studies. Be sure that you spend your summers wisely, however, getting as much experience as possible in summer stock.

For Music Majors

# Researching Teachers for Consultations and Lessons

Choosing the teacher with whom you would like to study is a vitally important decision. Ask your current teacher for recommendations, and then do lots of investigating on your own. Read the biography of the teacher in the catalog. Has the person studied with other people who uphold a tradition that you would like to follow? What is the teacher's performing background? Is the teacher an adjudicator for major competitions? Talk to students who currently work with the person you are considering. Are they pleased with their progress? Do they have regular lessons? During those lessons do they have the teacher's undivided attention?

Because so much of the relationship between teacher and student is personal, you must be sure that the chemistry between you works. This is difficult to determine unless you are able to speak to the teacher directly or, even better, to arrange a sample lesson, often called a consultation. You should be prepared to pay anywhere from $125 to $250 for such a meeting. At that time, you will play or sing for the teacher, see if you can work together, and ask all the questions you want. Do not be intimidated about asking questions about how this person works, where he or she sees your major weaknesses now, and what direction your lessons may take. If a personal meeting is not possible, you might call, write, or send an e-mail to the teacher in care of the school and ask if you could send a recording for his or her evaluation. Then follow up with a telephone conversation.

Famous or big-name teachers are not necessarily the best. You are looking for a teacher who will be best for you at this stage of your development as a performer. While "name" teachers may help somewhat at a certain time in your development, especially with the politics of the business, they may not give you the attention that you need to make progress in your technique. Will you receive a weekly lesson from that teacher, or will you be taught by an assistant?

If you are assigned to a teacher and then discover that the relationship is not working out, do not despair. Still, approach this change with utmost sensitivity and care. A student-teacher relationship is a business agreement of sorts; the teacher is being paid to teach you. If you need to make a change, most conservatories and departments of music have a procedure for this that will involve as little misery on either part as possible. You will need to have a conversation with the teacher or perhaps write the teacher a letter. This may be difficult, but it is better that you make a change than remain trapped in a situation that is not beneficial. Remember that the music world is very small, however, and you never know when you'll encounter this person again. Will they be judging that big competition that is important for your future? Be sure you move on with tremendous good will.

**For Music Majors**

# Questions to Ask at a Campus Visit

- What role does the audition play in my admission? Is it the major criterion, or does my high school or college record count also?

- What role do exams such as ear training play in my admission?

- Is a personal interview required? If so, who conducts the interview?

- What is the music department enrollment?

- What is the enrollment in my instrument? Is there a quota?

- What general education courses are offered? Which are required? Is there any cross-registration with another school?

- How many faculty members work with my instrument? Will I have a wide enough variety of choice in case I want to make a teacher change?

- How often do students have lessons? Am I guaranteed to have lessons with my major teacher? How often do assistants teach major lessons?

- What is the policy on performance evaluations (juries)? How often are they held? Are students ever cut from the program based on a jury?

- What are the facilities like? How many teaching studios? What equipment is in them? How many performance halls are there?

- How many practice rooms are there? What is their availability? (Ask students if they ever have problems securing a practice room.)

- In general, how often do students perform each semester? How many fully produced concerts are there? Informal concerts? Operas? In-school performances (i.e., at a high school)? Recitals? Contemporary music concerts? Other opportunities?

- Is there a program of master classes? Who has taught them most recently?

- Who are some of the well-known alumni of the school?

- What sort of job-placement service does the school provide?

116

- What career paths do most alumni take?

- Is there an alumni network of any sort?

- What is competition like at the school?

- What ensembles will I be required to participate in?

- How are orchestral assignments made? (Ask students whether they think the orchestral assignments are fair.) Is there a policy of rotation within the orchestra?

- Do you have a program for engaging guest conductors? Who have been the recent conductors?

- What is the policy for casting operas? (Ask current students whether they think the policy is fair.)

- What chorus requirements are there for singers?

- Is there an opportunity to get certified in music education?

- What other related courses are taught? Is music engineering, music criticism, or piano tuning taught?

- Is there any affiliation between the school and any other musical organization, such as the local symphony, opera, or jazz clubs?

- Are any tours anticipated?

- Are there exchange programs with any schools?

- During the auditions, are teachers informed about who has applied for them?

- Who evaluates the auditions? How are they run?

- Are chamber music opportunities available? Any requirements for chamber music? Who coaches ensembles?

- Do you hold any sessions on how to audition for orchestras, companies, and so on, for after graduation?

- What is the feeling at this school about regional auditions? Recorded versus live auditions?

- Do you ever defer admissions decisions?

For Music Majors

# A Current Music Major Speaks Out

NATALIA KIENIEWICZ
**Applied Music in Voice (Vocal Performance)**
**University of Delaware**

### WHAT ADVICE CAN YOU GIVE HIGH SCHOOL SENIORS WHO ARE THINKING OF MAJORING IN MUSIC IN COLLEGE?

My best advice is to be prepared to make a commitment to your major: It's not for people who don't know what else to do with themselves. There is nothing wrong with being undeclared. If you love music and think that it is what you want to do with your life, then by all means go for it. But it's not easy, and you shouldn't expect it to be. It's a lot of work and a lot of disappointment sometimes, but when your work pays off, it is incredibly rewarding.

### WHAT SHOULD PROSPECTIVE MUSIC STUDENTS LOOK FOR IN A COLLEGE?

As a music student, it is most important to look for a teacher you can trust to point you in the right direction. A solid program at a school is a great thing, but it doesn't matter how great the program is if you are not developing your technique as a musician. At the same time, I find it important to be in an environment that is at least somewhat positive and inspiring. Backstabbing gets old fast, but at the same time, so does being surrounded by bad musicians.

### HOW DID YOU PREPARE FOR BECOMING A MUSIC MAJOR WHEN YOU WERE IN HIGH SCHOOL?

I worked some on my repertoire, but mostly I tried to develop at least a concept of good singing technique so that when I was looking at colleges I could get a feel for whom I could trust. I asked people I trusted for recommendations of colleges with good teachers and good programs. I looked at the artist histories of current singers I liked to see where they studied— and it wasn't always at a conservatory. In addition, I took language courses in high school that I knew would be beneficial. I managed to get a 4 on the AP German test, and I spent a month of the summer after I graduated in Germany.

Performing

Arts

## WHAT IS YOUR TYPICAL DAILY SCHEDULE LIKE?

I generally wake up around 8 a.m., sometimes earlier if I need to get things done before class. I shower (most of the time), eat breakfast, and drink lots of coffee. It supposedly dehydrates you and is therefore not recommended for singers, but I won't sing very well if I'm falling asleep, so I don't have much of a crisis about it. I'm in class and rehearsal at any time from 9 a.m. until 9:30 p.m., with gaps of an hour or two or three interspersed when I eat lunch, practice, procrastinate, go to work, do homework, and/or (if I'm extremely lucky) nap. Most days I'm done by 5 or 6 p.m. and I can do something fun like yoga or bellydancing or reading. My voice lesson is usually the highlight of my week, work-wise. I take mostly music classes, but since I go to a four-year university, I also have core requirements. I actually really enjoy them, because it gets me out of the music building, and I can exercise a different part of my brain. As a music student, I take a lot of pleasure in having friends outside my department. I was on the school's Ultimate Frisbee team until the end of sophomore year when I found it impossible to make the necessary commitment without compromising my musical studies.

Another sacrifice I had to make because of the enormous commitment that music requires was a rather lucrative job as a waitress. I work 11 hours a week at the University library, which is a flexible work environment. Some semesters I can work more hours, sometimes I can't even hold onto 10 without going crazy. I'm also president of our school's chapter of Amnesty International, which is a fair amount of work but it is incredibly important to me. Additionally, although I don't believe in having a "fall-back plan" (you always end up using it), I do feel like I have garnered a great deal of experience doing this, and I could potentially look for work in the human rights world if I had to.

So when I finally do get home "for good" (sometimes around 6 or 7 p.m., sometimes at 10), I make dinner and mess around on the computer. If I have work to do that I absolutely can't put off, I take care of it. I have study groups, do social things, exercise, or sometimes I lie around and watch a movie. I'm often pretty exhausted when I go to bed. It used to be around 2 or 3 a.m., but these days I try to get to bed around 1. Guess I'm getting old or something.

## WHAT WAS THE BIGGEST SURPRISE YOU FOUND ONCE YOU GOT TO COLLEGE?

I was really surprised to find out what I am capable of and at the same time how far I have to go.

## WHAT KINDS OF PROJECTS ARE YOU CURRENTLY WORKING ON?

I recently gave my Junior Recital, which was a fantastic success after months and months of hard work. I have two competitions this weekend, and a third two weeks from now. This summer, I am participating in a summer opera program in Graz, Austria, at the American Institute of Musical Studies.

## WHAT CAREER PATH DO YOU HOPE TO FOLLOW?

When I graduate, I plan to move overseas to Austria or Germany. This summer, when I am in Graz, I hope to connect with a teacher who will agree to take me on after I graduate. I am lucky enough to have the right to British citizenship, meaning that I can live and work anywhere in the European Union without having to obtain a work visa. I also speak enough German to get around. I plan to take voice lessons and work for awhile, do competitions, and apply for young artist studios at opera companies. After a year or so, I will decide if I want to apply for graduate school.

# Alternative Careers for Music Majors

People trained as musicians may be found in every career from insurance to medicine to college administration. With technological advancements the nature of the music business is constantly changing. Some other related careers include:

- Arranger/orchestrator
- Music critic
- Music copyists (be sure that you know some of the computer programs, such as Finale and Sibelius)
- Recording engineer
- Music therapist
- Instrument builder or repairer
- Music publisher
- Piano tuner
- Music manager
- Music librarian
- Music administrator: schools, orchestras, choruses
- Radio announcer
- Box office manager
- Development director
- Teacher: elementary, secondary, college, or private instruction

If you do decide to teach, be sure that you are proficient on the piano for accompanying choruses or other ensembles. If you plan to teach in a public school, you will need certification, so be certain to take appropriate courses.

# What to Put in Your College Notebook

Use the sample Music Program Rating Sheet below or one of your own design:

<table>
<tr><td colspan="1" align="center">**MUSIC PROGRAM RATING SHEET**</td></tr>
<tr><td>Size of department:<br>Enrollment _____        Teachers _____</td></tr>
<tr><td>Lessons: How often? With major teachers or assistants?</td></tr>
<tr><td>Facilities: Number of teaching studios, practice rooms</td></tr>
<tr><td>Performances: How often? Type (concerts, operas, recitals, etc.)</td></tr>
<tr><td>Master classes: Availability? Recent teachers?</td></tr>
<tr><td>Exchange Programs with other schools?</td></tr>
<tr><td>Affiliation between school and other musical organizations?</td></tr>
<tr><td>Curriculum: General education requirement? Certificate in Music Ed?</td></tr>
<tr><td>Techniques taught:</td></tr>
<tr><td>Audition workshops:</td></tr>
<tr><td>Job placement record:</td></tr>
<tr><td>Famous alumni:</td></tr>
<tr><td>Current students' opinions:</td></tr>
<tr><td>My Personal Reaction:</td></tr>
</table>

Performing

*Arts*

# Questions to Ask Yourself

Here are some questions to ask yourself at various points in the admissions process.

Have I:

- checked out the Web site for any schools or programs of interest?

- requested catalogs and read them carefully and critically?

- requested applications and made photocopies of the ones in which I am interested?

- started a college notebook with my impressions of colleges and notes about audition requirements, dates, etc?

- noted repertoire requirements?

- obtained a social security number (United States and Permanent Residents)?

- registered for the PSAT/NMSQT?

- obtained information about the ARTS scholarships? (National Foundation for Advancement in the Arts, 444 Brickell Avenue, Miami, FL 33131; 305-377-1140 or 800-970-ARTS (toll-free); www.artsawards.org)?

- made an appointment with my guidance counselor?

- looked into working with an independent counselor, if appropriate?

- talked with my current private music teacher about plans for my future?

- made arrangements to continue my music lessons?

- discussed high school courses to take?

- been taking regular private lessons?

- participated regularly in music programs at my school or in the community?

- discussed which standardized tests to take and when?

- discussed whether tutoring for standardized tests is appropriate for me?

- investigated summer programs and/or jobs and applied and taken auditions as necessary?

- investigated sources and policies regarding financial aid and scholarships?

- kept a file of performance programs, DVDs, or videotapes of performances, good term papers, articles, and so on?

- attended college fairs and met with college representatives who visited my school?

- registered for any standardized tests required (SAT, ACT, TOEFL, SAT Subject Tests)?

- met again with my guidance counselor?

- arranged my college visits?

- scheduled any interview appointments?

- sent thank-you notes after my college interviews?

- chosen my audition material?

- narrowed my list of colleges?

- settled on decision plans?

- asked for letters of recommendation, if necessary?

- drafted any essays?

- finished my essays and applications and photocopied everything before mailing?

- applied for financial aid, if necessary?

- requested that official test score reports be sent directly to the colleges that require them?

- done mock auditions and recorded them for my own critique?

- submitted any recordings for pre-screening, if required?

- had photographs taken to submit with applications, if necessary?

- prepared a resume?

- requested that a copy of my transcript be sent to the college?

- communicated regularly with my guidance counselor or guidance adviser about my progress in the college admissions process and in school?

- kept up with all school work?

- prepared a list of extracurricular activities, if necessary?

- arranged for an accompanist for my audition, if necessary?

- checked that all financial aid documentation is complete?

- read carefully any audition or schedule information sent to me?

- prepared photocopies of piano music for my accompanist?

- made copies of any original compositions I intend to perform?

- responded to colleges about any offers of admission?

- requested an extension beyond the May 1 Candidates Reply Deadline, if necessary?

- continued with regular music lessons and ensemble opportunities?

**For Music Majors**

# For Theater Majors

If you're planning on hearing "break a leg" or "lights, camera, action" in your future, be prepared for a lot of competition, starting with your college applications. Keep in mind that theater programs all have their own personality and mission. You'll want to make sure that the one you choose meets your needs, talents, and professional goals.

Performing Arts

# Advanced Study in Theater

"All the world's a stage," and so many young people aspire to be in the spotlight. There is debate among actors about the best training. Some believe that years of training provide a distinct advantage; others suggest relying on natural talent and instincts. There is a school of thought that says that taking too many classes in acting develops a dependency wherein you become a professional student, rather than a professional actor, and another that says that you can never take too many classes in voice, acting, and movement, and you should never stop studying. For a young actor, there are many available options.

## BACHELOR OF ARTS VS. BACHELOR OF FINE ARTS

The essential difference between these two programs involves proportion in course work. In a Bachelor of Arts (B.A.) degree program, you will be expected to study a broad range of courses in the liberal arts and sciences and, at some schools, to fulfill distribution requirements. You might major in theater (called a drama or acting major at some schools) and take a certain number of credit hours in this as your major, but the proportion of liberal arts to theater courses is tilted in the direction of the liberal arts. A Bachelor of Fine Arts (B.F.A.) program is more heavily weighted on the theater side.

For certain people there is a distinct advantage to attending a liberal arts college and majoring in theater. For one thing, the number of students who change their major after freshman year is extremely high. If you were locked into a B.F.A. program, you might have more trouble changing to another major than you would in a B.A. program, where changing majors is common. Another reason to attend a liberal arts college to obtain a B.A. is for the very breadth of learning in a wide range of subjects. When you create a role, you can call more to it if you have a background in literature and history than if you know only the theater. Finally, you are likely to encounter a more diverse student body at a liberal arts college than you would at a specialized school. This very diversity might influence you in creating a role someday.

If you do choose the liberal arts route, look very carefully at the strength of the theater department. In some liberal arts colleges, theater courses are taught through the English department. What is the curriculum? A liberal arts college offering a theater major that teaches only theater history, dramatic literature, and a basic acting course probably does not have the strongest theater department. How many faculty members are there? Do they also work in conjunction with a dance and/or music department? A theater department with fewer than 4 faculty members may not be considered a priority by the administration and may not present to you enough variety in your learning. Investigate carefully.

The B.F.A. program is for students who want to focus immediately on specific theater skills. If you know, without a doubt, that you want to pursue your major in theater and that you want that focus, a good B.F.A. program may be for you.

Most B.F.A. programs, either at conservatories or at universities, require an audition, even if you have been admitted into the main school. Prepare thoroughly for the audition.

*Note for International Students:* If English is not your native language and you speak with a heavy accent, quite bluntly, your chances for admission to a theater program in a competitive U.S. conservatory or B.F.A. program are not strong. A B.A. program will be more flexible.

## RESUMES FOR THEATER STUDENTS

Most theater programs ask for a copy of your resume. If you have had a great deal of experience, putting your resume together will not be a problem. Get in the habit of keeping it up-to-date. If your experience has been limited to high school productions and classes, this is absolutely fine. Present your background and qualifications honestly. Knowing about your previous experience may be useful to the admissions committee, but how you handle the audition will count the most.

There is no one prescribed format for theater resumes. Certain standard background information should appear, however, including your name, address, phone numbers (day, evening, and cell), e-mail address, height, weight, eye and hair color, and voice range, if you sing. Experience may be broken down into categories including theater or stage, musicals, summer stock, film, television, and so on. A high school student might list high school productions, summer work, workshops, and master classes. Include names of your teachers. Mention any specialized skills, such as playing a musical instrument, gymnastics, stage combat, fencing, ice skating, juggling, mime, skateboarding, horseback riding, whistling, or other related skills.

A good resume should be printed in black ink on 8½ × 11 paper (white bond, not colored), word-processed (easy for regular updating), and certainly no longer than two pages; a one-page resume for theater is best. This resume should be attached to your head shot. (See pages 134–136 for three typical resumes: one for a freshman applicant, one for a transfer student, and one for a graduate student.)

## HEAD SHOTS

Many programs will request that you submit a head shot with your resume and application. If you do not have a professional photo, do not allow this to stop you from applying or delay you in sending in your application. Instead, submit the application with a note saying that you are having the head shot done and will submit it as soon as possible.

Your application head shot should look like you and present a pleasant impression. Just as you should go for a somewhat conventional look in your dress for a college interview, you should choose a pose and overall look for your head shot that calls attention to your eyes, your face. Do not wear outrageous jewelry, pose provocatively, or choose a hairstyle that focuses attention on your hair rather than on you. Selective schools claim never to have admitted candidates who submitted head shots that were either in bad taste or particularly weird or inappropriate.

Finding a good photographer to take your head shot can be a challenge. If you do not live in a city, you might ask the photography teacher at your high school for a recommendation, or perhaps he or she might take it for you. Bring along some head shots you like from programs or newspapers as samples. Yearbook photographers who are experienced in photographing in black and white are also a possibility. You do not have to spend an exorbitant amount of money on your head shot. Go for quality with economy, if that is possible. *The Back Stage Handbook for Performing Artists* (Sherry Eaker, editor) has a helpful article about head shots. It suggests that you ask a prospective photographer some of the following questions:

- Have you taken head shots before? Could I see your portfolio? (When reviewing the portfolio, look at the expression in the eyes that the photographer has captured in each photograph. Is the look engaging or vacant? Is the smile genuine or tense? Does the pose capture the "best side" of the person, or just look staged? Does the skin texture look real? Does the photograph have the look of a real person or someone who has been retouched and airbrushed into a homogenized glamorous look? How is the lighting?)

- What format do you use? Digital? Film?

- Do you take Polaroids first? Could I see some before-and-after shots?

- What do you charge for head shots? (Prices generally range from $200 to $1500.) What is included in this fee?

- How many rolls of film do you shoot? What format do you use? Do you give your clients the negatives or charge for them? Do you charge for airbrushing or retouching? Do you do the blowups and reprints yourself, or will you recommend where I can get them done?

- How long will it be before I see the contact sheets?

- How far in advance do I need to book a sitting? How long is a typical sitting?

- Do you require a deposit? Will you refund the deposit or schedule a reshoot if I don't like the results?

- Are hair and make-up included in the price? Will you recommend a stylist?

It is very important that you feel a rapport with the photographer. When you feel comfortable during a photo session, the photographs themselves reflect this. If the chemistry just is not right between you and the photographer, find someone else.

Here are some things you should bring to your photo session:

- changes of clothing, with particular attention to your waist-up look;

- additional make-up;

- hairbrush, comb, and hair styling products;

- extra shaving equipment (for men);

- a favorite photo of yourself;

- anything that will help you to relax, such as tapes (I've known people to bring a favorite stuffed animal or herbal tea);

- any props you want, which you should discuss in advance with your photographer, such as glasses, a book, or a musical instrument; and

- additional jewelry, such as a change of earrings.

Once you have the contact sheets, show them to a variety of people—your parents, teachers, friends, and agent (if you have one)—and seek opinions. Keep track of these opinions on a separate piece of paper. The photographer will probably indicate his or her two favorite choices. Remember that this is a photograph that you will have to live with for probably two or three years before you update it, so choose carefully. Be sure that your head shot has your name on either the front or back, so that if it becomes separated from your resume, the photograph can still be identified.

For Theater Majors

**FRESHMAN RESUME**

## John A. Doe
123 Main Street
Wilmington, Delaware 19807
(302) 123-4567

### EDUCATION

| | |
|---|---|
| A. I. Du Pont High School | Diploma anticipated, June 2009 |

### EXPERIENCE

| | | |
|---|---|---|
| 2009 | This is a Test (Pat) | One-act play<br>A.I. Du Pont High School |
| 2008 | Renaissance Faire<br>St. George and the Dragon (Reginald Brown) | Delaware Theater Company |
| 2008 | Cinderella, Cinderella . . . (Prince Charming) | Wilmington Drama League |
| 2008 | To Kill a Mockingbird (Townsperson) | Delaware Theater Company |
| 2008 | Baby (Father) | One-act play<br>A. I. Du Pont High School |
| 2008 | Zombie Army (Orderly) | Film<br>Cheap Productions, Inc. |

### TRAINING AND EXTRA ACTIVITIES

| | |
|---|---|
| Two years theater/acting class<br>Senior Literary Society | A. I. Du Pont High School |
| One year public speaking | Carson Long Military Institute |
| The Art of Acting | Delaware Technical & Community College |
| Drama Club<br>The International Thespian Society | A. I. Du Pont High School |

### TECHNICAL WORK

| | | |
|---|---|---|
| 2009 | Get Smart | Play. Light and makeup. |

### One-Act Plays

| | | |
|---|---|---|
| 2008 | This Is a Test | A. I. Du Pont High School |
| 2007 | Pink Lemonade | |
| 2007 | Drive-in | |

### AWARDS AND COMPETITION

| | |
|---|---|
| Third Place, Declamation Contest<br>Julius Caesar (Marcus Antonius) | Carson Long Military Institute |

### OTHERS SKILLS

Certified scuba diver.     Juggler.     Expert whistler.

### REFERENCES AND RECOMMENDATIONS

Available upon request.

Performing
*Arts*

## TRANSFER STUDENT RESUME

### MARCIA SMITH

| | |
|---|---|
| 123 4th Avenue | Height: 5'4" |
| New York, New York 10003 | Weight: 120 |
| 212-123-4567—home | Hair: Brown |
| 212-555-1234—cell | Eyes: Brown |

*THEATER*

| | | |
|---|---|---|
| THANK YOU AMY | Amy | Theater in the Square |
| THE DINING ROOM | Ensemble | Tisch School of the Arts, NYU |
| NO COMMENT CAB.A.RET | Sandy | Tisch School of the Arts |
| VESTLESS ATTIRE | Ensemble | The Gas Station |
| CINDERELLA | Cinderella | Boston Children's Theater |
| LUDLOW FAIR | Rachel | Directing Project Williamstown Theater Festival |
| PARLOUR GAMES | Ensemble | Massachusetts College of Art |
| THIRD RAIL | Cathy | Emerson College |

*TELEVISION AND FILM*

| | | |
|---|---|---|
| RAP AROUND (Four Segments) | Jessica | WBZ-TV |
| PUBLIC SERVICE ANNOUNCEMENT | Girl | WBZ-TV |
| CHILDREN AND DIVORCE | | WNEV-TV |
| SIDEWALK | Girl | Tisch School of the Arts |

*SUMMER*

| | | |
|---|---|---|
| Institute Member | 2009 | National Shakespeare Conservatory |
| Apprentice | 2008 | Williamstown Theater Festival |
| Young Critic's Institute | 2007 | Huntington Theater |

*TRAINING*

| | |
|---|---|
| Classes: | Lyric Stage, Wheelock Family Theater, Boston Children's Theater |
| Participant: | Oberlin Theater Institute Circle in the Square Theatre School |
| Currently attending: B.F.A. program | Tisch School of the Arts, New York University |

*AWARDS*

National Foundation for the Advancement in the Arts:
    Arts Recognition and Talent Search Awardee, 2007

National Endowment for the Humanities Scholar:
    Young Critic's Institute–Huntington Theater

Presidential Scholar in the Arts:
    Semifinalist, 2007

*OTHER SKILLS*

Ice skating; Fencing; Mime

**GRADUATE STUDENT RESUME**

# SARA GREEN

Height:        5'6"
Age Range:  18–24

12 EAST 90th STREET, NY, NY 10004
cell: **2 1 2 - 6 6 6 - 1 1 1 1**
home: **2 1 2 - 3 4 5 - 6 7 8 9**

## SAG/AFTRA
AEA (Eligible)

High soprano

## theater

| | | |
|---|---|---|
| BLACK ICE | Lady Die | Kampo Cultural Center/Dean Mitchell |
| CRIMES OF THE HEART | Lenny | Herald Square Players/Boy Byrd |

## films

| | | |
|---|---|---|
| INTERVIEW | Crack Addict | Sony/Steve Buscemi |
| WAIST DEEP | Gang Member | Rogue Prods./Vondie Curtis-Hall |

## television

| | | |
|---|---|---|
| CSI: NY | Angelica | CBS |
| THAT'S SO RAVEN | Church Attendant | DISNEY |
| SCRUBS | Karen (Bar Patron) | NBC |
| LAW & ORDER | Court Stenographer | NBC |
| THE SOPRANOS | Sara B (Homeless Woman) | HBO |
| THE LAKER GIRLS | Laker Cheerleader | CBS (Pilot) |

## commercials/voice-overs        List Available Upon Request

## training

**Commercial:**  Reed-Sweeney-Reed—Pat Sweeney . . . On-Camera Technique
SAG & AFTRA Conservatory—Affiliated Instructors . . . On-Camera Commercial Tech. & Improv.
Hyde Hamlet Casting–Sara Hamlet . . . On-Camera Technique

**Acting:**  Video Perspectives—Boy Byrd . . . Sitcom Workshop
Herbert Berghof Studios—Michael Beckett . . . Scene Study & Technique I, II

**Dance:**  Broadway Dance Center—Sue Samuels . . . Jazz Technique I
Broadway Dance Center—Farnsworth . . . Ballet Technique I
Ruth Williams Dance Studios—Ruth Williams . . . Modern Dance/Ballet

**Voice:**  NY School of Commercial Music—Ruth DeBrow . . . Mezzo-Soprano

**Education:**  B.A. Architecture—Syracuse University
Member of Black Filmmakers Foundation

## special skills

Jamaican, Southern, and New York Dialects; Cheerleader, Syracuse University (3 years); Aerobics/ Weight Training; Roller Skating; Double-Dutch Jumping; Scuba Diving (certified); Licensed Driver; Excellent with Children and Pets. Own Evening Gowns, Nurse Uniform, and selection of 10 Wigs and Hairpieces.

*Performing*

*Arts*

# Theater Auditions

It is very important for theater students to submit applications well in advance of any deadlines. Because there are usually many more applicants to theater programs than can be accepted, one means of elimination that admissions departments use is to observe the deadline strictly. Do not procrastinate in sending your application. And, if possible, schedule your first-choice school as your second or third audition, not your first.

## WHAT TO EXPECT

Most theater auditions consist of presenting monologues of your choice from memory. Some programs may assign required monologues; ask you to improvise; sing *a cappella* (unaccompanied); participate in a movement class; do a group theater activity or "theater game;" possibly do a dance combination; or do a cold reading. Some may also ask you to write an essay while you are there for the audition. A theater audition begins right when you walk in the door of the audition location. The way you greet the receptionist and introduce yourself makes a difference. If you are rude, pushy, withdrawn, or odd, it will make an impression. At an audition, you are *always* being observed.

When you attend an audition, there may be a group warm-up. If so, use this time to make sure that your voice is working and your body is relaxed. Once you enter the audition room, be prepared to answer a few short questions from the audition panel. Questions such as "Where are you from?" or "How did you get here today?" are intended to help you relax. This is not the time to be dramatic or to relate your entire life story, but the chance for you to answer politely and normally. If the audition panel suggests that you "take a few minutes to gather yourself before you present your first monologue," do not use the time to go through your whole warm-up in front of them. Just take a few deep breaths and think about getting into character for the part you will play.

## CHOOSING MONOLOGUES

Some programs will give you a list of suggested monologues. The list is just that: suggestions. You need not choose something from the list, but consider it as a guideline for the type of material the audition panel considers appropriate. Be sure to observe the time limit suggested, usually two monologues, not to exceed 4 minutes. Most often you are asked to present one monologue from the classical repertoire and one contemporary monologue of a contrasting nature. Some may ask for a lighter piece. Remember that a comedic monologue is NOT a stand-up comedy act! While researching monologues on the Internet or glancing through a book of monologues may be somewhat helpful, it is critical to know the whole play and the monologue in context; some audition panels may even ask you questions about the entire play. Many programs specify no dialects or old characters, and some programs are clear in their advice about choosing a character close to your own age. Be sure to read requirements carefully and rehearse well in advance. In some audition rooms, there may be a table and some chairs should you need them. Expect to be interrupted and stopped. Do not read into this; the panel may love you and just be pressed for time. All audition panels anticipate that auditioners may be nervous, and usually the panelists are quite sympathetic. It is a good idea to bring a clearly printed copy of your monologues with you. Some audition panels may follow along and be there to prompt you should you have a memory lapse. In choosing your monologues, give some thought to your "type." Are you an ingénue? A character actor? What age range are you most comfortable playing? Some people will work from a process of elimination: "I'm not a (fill in the blank)." The best advice is to choose a monologue you are comfortable performing and that you can present with conviction. Remember, an audition is a performance.

## SUGGESTED MONOLOGUES FOR AUDITIONS

In surveying various Theater/Drama departments, the following seemed to be some commonly suggested monologues:

| SAMPLE AUDITION SCENES FOR WOMEN | | |
|---|---|---|
| **CLASSICAL** | | |
| Aeschylus | Agamemnon | Clytemnestra (telling how she killed Agamemnon) |
| Beaumont/Fletcher | The Maid's Tragedy | Aspatia, Act II, Scene 1 (line 5) |
| Euripides | Trojan Women | Andromache (gives up son to be killed by Greeks) |
| | Iphigenia at Aulos | Iphigenia |
| Middleton | The Changeling | Beatrice Joanna |

| SAMPLE AUDITION SCENES FOR WOMEN—*continued* | | |
|---|---|---|
| **CLASSICAL—*continued*** | | |
| Shakespeare | The Merchant of Venice | Portia, Act III, Scene 2 (line 149) |
| | All's Well That Ends Well | Helena, Act I, Scene 3 (line 197) |
| | King John | Constance, Act III, Scene 1, (line 43) |
| | Richard III | Anne, Act I, Scene 2 (line 1) |
| | Henry IV, Part 1 | Lady Percy, Act II, Scene 3 (line 40) |
| | Henry IV, Part 2 | Lady Percy, Act II, Scene 3 (line 9) |
| | Hamlet | Ophelia, Act III, Scene 1 (line 158) |
| | Othello | Desdemona, Act I, Scene 3 (line 249) |
| | Comedy of Errors | Adriana, Act II, Scene 2 (line 111) |
| | Midsummer Night's Dream | Helena, Act III, Scene 2 (line 195) |
| | The Winter's Tale | Hermione, Act III, Scene 2 (line 90) |
| | The Winter's Tale | Paulina, Act III, Scene 2 (line 173) |
| | Cymbeline | Imogen, Act III, Scene 6 (line 1) |
| | Henry VI, Part 3 | Queen Margaret, Act I, Scene 1 (line 230) |
| Sophocles | Antigone | Antigone (answering Creon, daring his law) |
| Webster | The White Devil | Vittoria (Trial Scene) |

| SAMPLE AUDITION SCENES FOR WOMEN—*continued* | | |
|---|---|---|
| **CONTEMPORARY** | | |
| Anouilh | The Lark | Joan |
| Chekhov | Three Sisters | Irina |
| | Uncle Vanya | Sonya |
| Elder | Ceremonies in Dark Old Men | Adelaide |
| Giraudoux | Apollo of Bellac | Agnes |
| Hansberry | A Raisin in the Sun | Beneatha |
| McNally | Noon | Allegra |
| Medoff | When You Coming Back, Red Ryder | Angel |
| O'Neill | Beyond the Horizon | Ruth |
| | Mourning Becomes Electra | Lavinia |
| Patrick | Kennedy's Children | Carla |
| Polikov, S. | City Sugar | Nicola, Scene 7 |
| Rabe | In the Boom Boom Room | Chrissie |
| Shange | For Colored Girls . . . | |
| Shaw | Heartbreak House | Ellie |
| | Major Barbara | Barbara |
| Shepard | Tooth of Crime | Becky |
| | Angel City | Miss Scoom |
| | Buried Child | Shelie |
| Strindberg | Easter | Eleanora, Act I |
| Whiting, J. | The Devils | Sister Jeanne, Act I |
| Williams | Summer and Smoke | Alma |
| | Talk to Me Like the Rain | Girl |
| | Cat on a Hot Tin Roof | Maggie |
| | Orpheus Descending | Carol |

| SAMPLE AUDITION SCENES FOR MEN | | |
|---|---|---|
| **CLASSICAL** | | |
| Euripides | Hippolytus | Hippolytus (speech against women, after learning of Phaedra's love) |
| Jonson | The Alchemist | Sir Epicure, Act II, Scene 1 |
| | The Alchemist | Subtle, Act II, Scene 2 |
| Middleton | The Changeling | Deflores |
| Shakespeare | Taming of the Shrew | Petruchio, Act IV, Scene 1 (line 191) |
| | Two Gentlemen of Verona | Proteus, Act II, Scene 6 (line 1) |
| | | Val, Act III, Scene 1 (line 170) |
| | Much Ado About Nothing | Benedick, Act II, Scene 3 (line 7) |
| | Twelfth Night | Sebastian, Act IV, Scene 3 (line 1) |
| | Troilus and Cressida | Ulysses, Act III, Scene 3 (line 145) |
| | Henry VI, Part 3 | Richard of Gloucester, Act III, Scene 2 (line 124) |
| | | Richard, Duke of York, Act I, Scene 4 (line 111) |
| | Henry V | Henry, Act I, Scene 1 (line 259) |
| | | Henry, Act III, Scene 1 (line 1) |
| | Julius Caesar | Brutus, Act III, Scene 2 (line 13) |
| | Othello | Iago, Act I, Scene 3 (line 338) |
| | | Othello, Act III, Scene 3 (line 258) |

| SAMPLE AUDITION SCENES FOR MEN—*continued* | | |
|---|---|---|
| **CLASSICAL—*continued*** | | |
| | Richard II | Mowbray, Act 1, Scene 3 (line 154) |
| | King Lear | Edgar, Act III, Scene 6 (line 102) |
| | Measure for Measure | Claudio, Act III, Scene 1 (line 117) |
| | The Tempest | Ferdinand, Act III, Scene 1 (line 1) |
| | Henry IV, Part 2 | Prince Hal, Act IV, Scene 5 (line 20 or 138) |
| | Pericles | Pericles, Act I, Scene 1 (line 121) |
| | Titus Andronicus | Aaron the Moor, Act IV, Scene 2 (line 88) |
| Sheridan | The Rivals | Jack Absolute |
| Sophocles | Antigone | Messenger's Final Speech |
| Webster | The Duchess of Malfi | Ferdinand, Act III, Scene 2 (line 120) |
| Webster | The Duchess of Malfi | Basola, Act V, Scene 2 (line 328) |
| **CONTEMPORARY** | | |
| Babe | Kid Champion | Kid Bullins |
| | In the Wine Time | Cliff Dawson |
| Chekhov | The Three Sisters | Andrei |
| | The Seagull | Treplev |
| Davis | Mass Appeal | Mark Dolson |
| Elder | Ceremonies in Dark Old Men | Mr. Bluehaven |
| Gordone | No Place to Be Somebody | Johnny Williams |
| Horowitz | The Indian Wants the Bronx | |

| SAMPLE AUDITION SCENES FOR MEN—*continued* | | |
|---|---|---|
| **CONTEMPORARY**—*continued* | | |
| Ibsen | Ghosts | Oswald |
| Inge | Picnic | Hal |
| O'Neill | Beyond the Horizon | Rob |
|  | Ah! Wilderness | Richard |
| Peterson, D. | Does the Tiger Wear a Necktie? | Bickell |
| Peterson, L. | Take a Giant Step | Spencer |
| Rabe | Pavlo Hummel | Pavlo |
|  | Streamers | Billy |
| Shepard | Tooth of Crime | Hoss |
|  | Buried Child | Vince or Tilden |
|  | Curse of the Starving Class | Wesley |
| Wilder | Our Town | George |
|  | The Matchmaker | Cornelius |
| Williams | Sweet Bird of Youth | Chance |
|  | Cat on a Hot Tin Roof | Brick |
|  | The Glass Menagerie | Tom |
| Wilson, L. | Burn This | Pale |

If a program specifies that the classical piece must be in verse or blank verse, some playwrights to consider are the Greeks; Lope de Vega; Christopher Marlowe; William Shakespeare; John Ford; John Webster; Racine in verse translation; William Congreve; Richard Brinsley Sheridan. For comedic monologues, be aware that Victoria Wood and Alan Bennett are frequent choices.

## CHOOSING SONGS

Most theater auditions will include asking you to sing a song unaccompanied. You need not think that you must have had extensive vocal training. The audition panel wants to get a sense of your vocal range and the basic quality of your voice. For musical theater auditions, you may be asked to prepare two songs: usually a ballad, to demonstrate your emotional range, sensitivity to the text, and lyrical phrasing and an up-tempo song to demonstrate your rhythm and showmanship. Choose repertoire that is age appropriate. Be in character when you are singing. And remember that humor helps.

## DANCE

While most theater auditions will include some sort of movement class, others, especially for musical theater, will ask you to do a dance sequence. Ask in advance what kind of shoes you need to bring: tap, ballet, jazz, knee pads, etc. Inquire about what style of dance you might expect at the audition. Pay attention and have fun in this portion of the audition. A smile helps a lot.

## WHAT TO WEAR

Black seems to be the color for theater auditions: women in black dresses, leotards with a skirt, or black pants and a black turtleneck, and men in black pants and turtlenecks. If this is your color, that's fine. The bottom line for your audition is to dress comfortably so that you can move freely, and yet nicely to indicate respect for the situation. Dress for theater auditions seems to be more casual than for classical music auditions. For the basic monologue part of the audition, women should wear a skirt (not too short) and blouse or a dress or pants and a sweater or blouse, and shoes with low to medium heels. Men should choose a turtleneck and pants or a shirt and pants. Suits, or jackets and ties, are not recommended—and neither are sweat suits! Since an actor's body is his or her instrument, it is important to wear something that gives some indication of what shape you are in. Appearance matters for actors. While you do not want to show up in costume for your audition, keeping in mind your characters for your monologues and acknowledging that in a subtle way, may be helpful. You should inquire if there is a required movement class also, and bring appropriate attire for that. For a movement class, you may be asked to remove your jewelry and any piercings. (Remember, it is best to leave valuables at home.) If there are going to be dance auditions, be prepared with tap, jazz, and ballet shoes, as needed. And, if there are callbacks, many audition panelists suggest that you wear the same clothes as you did for the first audition to aid in recognition.

## BEFORE YOU AUDITION

It is important that you know exactly what will be expected of you at the audition. Will you have to write an essay while you are there for the audition, to show that you can write in English? Does the audition schedule involve callbacks? How much time should you realistically set aside for this audition? Be sure to ask enough questions so that you know what to bring with you and what to expect.

## PRACTICE AUDITIONS

The best way to prepare for an audition is to practice often in a mock audition situation. Do this several months in advance and videotape yourself. Ask members of your family, your teachers, and friends to critique your performance as you watch the tape. Remember, though, that audition panels want to see your interpretation of a monologue, not something that has been coached to death and reflects a teacher's version. Be simple and truthful. Do practice auditions often, up to a week before the actual audition, so that you feel totally comfortable about your presentation. Prepare yourself mentally so that you go to every audition with the most positive mental attitude, anticipating success.

## NERVES

What do you do if you walk into the audition room and your knees are shaking, you cannot get a good breath, or your voice is quaking? It helps to remember that everyone else is in the same boat and an attack of nerves is totally normal. Try deep breathing: breathing in on a count of four and out on eight. Do not be ashamed to say, "I'm so nervous," but do not let that be an excuse for yourself. Use the beginning of the audition to relax as best you can, and then to get into the character of the first monologue. If you think of the audition panel as an audience at your performance, you may get past the nerves. It is very important in your overall actor training that you learn to take care of yourself. Educate yourself about nutrition and exercise, how to manage stress, handle rejection, prevent injury, and handle nerves constructively.

## AUDITION EVALUATION CRITERIA

When an audition panel watches and listens to your audition, they are looking for several things. This may include your fluency in English; sense of humor; sense of language; imagination; energy; evidence of having an open mind; intellectual and artistic curiosity; willingness to take risks; work ethic; ability to read, understand, and interpret texts; concentration and focus; your overall physical appearance: body, weight, features; and voice. The audition sheets on pages 148–150 indicate the kinds of things the audition panel are evaluating.

### WHAT *NOT* TO DO AT A THEATER AUDITION

- Do not try to play something other than the core of the part. Play the character and do not get caught up in the language.

- Do not just learn the monologue. Read the entire play and know the context for the monologue.

- Never leave the room during an audition. There are some humorous yet sad stories about applicants who either wanted to make an entrance or exit, in character, for their monologue and walked out of the room, only to discover that the door would not open again. Applicants who think they may get dry should bring water in with them to the audition, so as not to need to leave the room. Also, at the end of the audition, do not leave until the faculty panel invites you to go.

- Do not drag in props or set pieces. A piece of paper for a letter scene may be fine, but anything beyond that is not appropriate. Most places will have a chair or two and a table to use as props if you need them.

- Do not even think of changing costumes between monologues.

- Do not stand too close to the audition panel.

- Do not get up on the audition table.

- Do not use the audition panel as your scene partners. Play slightly above their heads.

- Do not tell the audition panel your life story if you are asked a simple question.

- Do not cry.

- Do not do your warm-up in the audition room. Walk in prepared.

- Do not take forever with your "actor focus moment" before you start your scene.

- Do not change the lyrics of a song.

- Do not offer to sing an original song.

- Do not throw things.

- Do not ask on the spot whether you are getting the callback.

## REGIONAL AUDITIONS

Theater programs will sometimes hold auditions in chosen cities as well as on campus. They will bring along faculty and administration members and treat these auditions as being as valid as any auditions on campus. Because regional auditions are very popular, it is important that you submit your application early, before all audition openings are booked.

## DVDS OR VIDEOTAPES VS. LIVE AUDITIONS

A live audition is always better than a DVD or videotape. If you absolutely must submit a recording as your only possible way of auditioning, do not go for a glitzy professionally produced DVD or video, which will cost you a fortune in production. A well-done (hold the camera steady and have the picture in focus!) home version is fine for this, but remember you are not helping your chances for admission by not attending in person! Do not send an unsolicited recording, as it will probably end up in a pile—unwatched.

For Theater Majors

## ACADEMY OF DRAMATIC ARTS

Audition Notes: _____

Auditioner: _____

Date: _____

Name: _____  Program: _____  M.F.A.: _____  CERTIFICATE: _____

CONTEMPORARY: _____

Is talking immediate:

Are actions used:

Is there a purpose/arc:

Is it spontaneous:

Is there an organic character:

Is it personalized:

Are there clear transitions:

Sense of humor:

Trainable:

CLASSICAL: _____

Vocal quality:

Speech:

Physically alive:

Phrasing:

Sensitivity to language:

Use of actions:

Use of self in the circumstances:

Spontaneity:

| TAKE | POSSIBLE | LOW POSSIBLE | NO |
|---|---|---|---|

COMMENTS:

# Audition Form

**XXX UNIVERSITY**
**Department of Drama**

Audition City: _____ Audition Date: _____

Option: Acting: _____ Musical Theater: _____

_____
Last Name            First Name            Initial

_____
Street         City           State       Zip

_____
Phone        Age         Height         Weight

_____
Language studied                  Years studied

**Musical Theater Option ONLY:**
    Can you read music? _____ Sing? _____
    Play an instrument? _____ If yes, what? _____

_____
High School or College Name         City         State

Is there a reason why you can NOT participate in a strenuous program of development?
_____

_____

| TRAINING . . . outside of high school | Acting | Singing | Dancing |
|---|---|---|---|
| Years studied | _____ | _____ | _____ |
| Teacher's name | _____ | _____ | _____ |

EXPERIENCE . . . list representative roles; if you have a resume, please attach.

| | | | | |
|---|---|---|---|---|
| Play | _____ | _____ | _____ | _____ |
| Role | _____ | _____ | _____ | _____ |
| Date performed | _____ | _____ | _____ | _____ |
| Place perormed | _____ | _____ | _____ | _____ |

| AUDITION | Acting (two pieces REQUIRED) | | Singing (Musical Theater ONLY —two pieces REQUIRED) | |
|---|---|---|---|---|
| Play/Song | | | | |
| Character | _____ | _____ | _____ | _____ |

_____ DO NOT WRITE BELOW THIS LINE _____

012       345       678       9

_____signed _____date

**For Theater Majors**

## PETERSON'S ACTING CONSERVATORY

CITY: _____    DATE: _____

NAME: _____    YES: _____

AGE: _____    NO: _____

POSSIBLE: _____

|  | CLASSICAL | CONTEMPORARY | COLD READING | ADDITIONAL |
|---|---|---|---|---|
| SCENE |  |  |  |  |
| VOICE |  |  |  |  |
| SPEECH |  |  |  |  |
| BODY |  |  |  |  |
| PERFORMANCE |  |  |  |  |

### GENERAL IMPRESSIONS

APPEARANCE:

TRAINING:

ATTITUDE:

POTENTIAL:

OTHER REMARKS:

Signed: _____

**Performing**

*Arts*

# Questions to Ask at a Campus Visit

- What is the enrollment number in the theater department? How many males? Females? Undergraduates? Graduates?

- Is the theater department part of another department?

- How many faculty members are there? How many are full-time? Part-time? What is the student/faculty ratio?

- How many faculty members are working professionally in theater? How many have more of an academic background and approach?

- Do you require an audition? If so, what is required?

- What does the basic curriculum entail? What acting technique is taught?

- What is the philosophy of the program?

- Who are your resident directors?

- Who have been the most recent directors of your productions?

- Do you have a program of master classes or guest speakers? Who has given these in the past two years? Did students have an opportunity to get to know the guests?

- What repertoire is performed?

- How and when do you evaluate a student's progress? Do you have a "cut" after one or two years?

- How often to the students perform each semester? Which of the following types of performing opportunities are available and how frequently: Fully produced productions? Informal workshops? Workshops? In-school performances (i.e., at high schools, etc.)? Off-campus performances?

- Are student-initiated projects encouraged? Is there a budget for these? What are examples of this in the past two years?

- What performing facilities are available for students (if you have not seen them on your campus tour)?

- How many productions are presented by your theater program each year?

- What is the casting policy? (Ask students, "Is the casting policy fair?")

- (At a liberal arts college) Is there a theater club? What is the relationship between the extracurricular theater activities and the theater department?

- Does the college have a relationship with a professional theater company or summer stock theater? If so, which one and what is the relationship?

- Does the college help students obtain an Equity card?

- Are there any restrictions on first-year (freshman) activities in the department? In casting?

- What are the strengths and weaknesses of this program?

- (Ask students) If you had it all to do over again, would you choose this program?

- Who are some renowned alumni?

- What careers do most alumni follow?

- Do you teach auditioning skills?

- Is there any sort of alumni network?

- Is there a technical requirement? If so, what is it?

- Does the school recruit at any Thespian Societies? Which ones? Are there any scholarships available through these?

- Does the school participate in any of the regional events of the American College Theater Festivals?

- Is the program accredited by the National Association of Schools of Theatre?

Performing

Arts

# Current Theater Majors Speak Out

GLYNNIS PURCELL
Theater
American University

## WHAT ADVICE CAN YOU GIVE HIGH SCHOOL SENIORS WHO ARE THINKING OF MAJORING IN THEATER IN COLLEGE?

Get involved in as many shows as possible. Learn to take all kinds of parts, and help out backstage and with lights and sound. The more versatile you are, the better your chances will be of learning what you need to know and getting a role. Always keep a positive outlook: No part or job is too small; it's all what you make it, so have fun!

## WHAT SHOULD PROSPECTIVE PERFORMING ARTS STUDENTS LOOK FOR IN A COLLEGE?

Look for a department and professors who are eager to help you learn. When you go to an audition, it's important to observe the way the judges react; if they take an interest in your piece, then you know they will want to help you every step of the way.

## HOW DID YOU PREPARE FOR BECOMING A THEATER MAJOR WHEN YOU WERE IN HIGH SCHOOL?

I got involved in as many performances as I possibly could. I took every role I was offered, no matter how small, and I if I didn't get a part I offered to work backstage on the production. People respond favorably when they know you're eager to be a part of the show regardless of what you'll be doing—and they'll be more willing to cast you in more substantial roles in future productions.

## WHAT IS YOUR TYPICAL DAILY SCHEDULE LIKE?

When I was a freshman, I had to take general curriculum classes, so that year I wasn't able to take as many theater courses as I wanted to. Now, though, I take two to three theater classes per semester. A typical day begins with a class around 11:30, then a break for lunch, and then two afternoon classes, one of which is usually a theater class.

### WHAT SURPRISED YOU THE MOST ABOUT COLLEGE? WHAT SURPRISED YOU THE MOST ABOUT YOURSELF?

What surprised was the fact that I now had total control over what I was doing and when I did it. You really have to learn to manage your time and money when you're in college; no one else will do it for you. It took a while to get accustomed to that, but I feel as though I grew up a lot in that first year. I was surprised at how much more mature I felt after only one semester. Being in college taught me how to handle my own life and deal with situations as they arise.

### WHAT KINDS OF PROJECTS ARE YOU CURRENTLY WORKING ON?

I'm currently seeking an agent. At the end of last semester, I held the main role in a film produced by friends of mine, and now I have a DVD of the film to show as part of my portfolio. I'm also working on getting into the school's study-abroad program, so that I can attend the British American Drama Academy (BADA) in London next spring.

### WHAT CAREER PATH DO YOU HOPE TO FOLLOW?

I hope to become a film actress. I plan to move to Los Angeles, CA, after I graduate—or perhaps to London if I get into the study-abroad program and all goes well there. No matter where I live, I want to pursue a career in film acting.

### DO YOU HAVE ANY OTHER ADVICE FOR PROSPECTIVE THEATER MAJORS?

Learn to be versatile. If you act like a diva, people will be less likely to work with you or want to be around you. Some of the best and most enjoyable roles are minor parts such as being in the chorus—and you can shine in any role as long as you work hard and do what you love. Good luck!

## ALEXIS BRONKOVIC
**Theater Arts**
**Marymount Manhattan College**

### WHAT ADVICE CAN YOU GIVE HIGH SCHOOL SENIORS WHO ARE THINKING OF MAJORING IN THEATER IN COLLEGE?

I would advise high school students to make sure that they enjoy other parts of the acting profession besides the lights and the applause. Most of your time at school is spent in class and alone in your room memorizing, researching, rehearsing, and auditioning. Even if you are cast in a lot of main stage college plays, they often only run for a few nights. Therefore you have to be able to appreciate the process and not just the end result. If there is one thing that you learn at school, it's that art is a process, not a product. Be prepared to work. The students who truly take their work seriously and aren't afraid to jump in are the students who find success in their classes.

### HOW DID YOU PREPARE FOR BECOMING A THEATER MAJOR WHEN YOU WERE IN HIGH SCHOOL?

I spent much of my time working on high school and community theater productions and working in local playhouses trying to gain as much experience as possible. I wanted to try anything and everything because EVERY experience is a good one. The more auditions you go on, directors you work with, people you meet, and shows you are in, the more it will help.

### WHAT IS YOUR TYPICAL DAILY SCHEDULE LIKE?

This semester I have a lot of theater classes. On Mondays, Wednesdays, and Fridays I head to Times Square for dance class at 9:30 a.m. Typically I walk, because well, I'm broke. But it's great exercise! After that, I walk home to take a quick shower and head to school where I work in the admissions office. I work there from about 12:30 to 4 p.m., and then I head to either acting class or musical theater techniques class. After those classes is when I might head to the library, run errands, rehearse, etc. Then I head home to the residence hall where I can get distracted from work by my friends or else I go on duty (I'm an R.A.). Often these shifts last until 12:30 a.m. On Tuesdays and Thursdays I begin my day with voice and speech class at 10 a.m. After that I have a break to catch up on or start my reading for my 1 p.m. class, which is theater history. We always have textbook pages and a play to read for every class. On Thursdays I take the subway to the West Village for my voice lesson, and then go home, eat dinner, and go to my 7:15–10 p.m. class.

As a theater arts student there are lots of extra hours devoted to rehearsal/lab time. It's not class time and it's not free time—yet it's some of the most important time! It is much needed in order to really get the most out of what you are studying. Be prepared for lots of time commitments to various classes and activities. My acting teacher always says that "you can be as good as want to be." The harder you work, the better you'll get.

### DO YOU HAVE A CONCENTRATION?

I am a Theater Arts major with a concentration in Performance. Basically that means I am an acting major. I have a minor in Musical Theater as well.

## WHAT CAREER PATH DO YOU HOPE TO FOLLOW?

I want to work professionally in the field, but I do not have specific plans. I think that when I am finished here at Marymount I would love to explore some other institutions in Europe to further my education. Many students choose to go to graduate school as well. I do not really know at the moment what I plan to do when I graduate, but I think that that's okay. Studying theater, you have to be prepared for anything. Unexpected opportunities arise all the time, and you have to be flexible and prepared to take advantage of them. I am keeping my options open and plan to follow my instinct. That's the best advice I can give. Follow your heart both in your career choices and in your stage work. It always leads you the right way.

# Alternative Careers for Theater Majors

In addition to the obvious Broadway, film, and television venues, actors should consider expanding their job searches to include off-off Broadway, dinner theater, children's theater, theme parks, cruise lines, summer stock, industrial shows (sometimes called business theater), cabarets, and improvisation groups. Producing your own showcase, creating a one-person show, and becoming involved in museum theater are also ways to launch your career.

However, theater students develop observation, communication, analytical, and critical-thinking skills that can be transferred to a variety of other career fields. Examples of these include:

- Working in the business side of the entertainment industry as personal managers, casting directors, agents, or publicists
- Sales, including telemarketing
- Voice-overs
- Stage management
- Directing
- Technical theater
- Theater design
- Teaching
- Playwriting
- Criticism

Some actors work on the "other side" for a time to observe what other actors do right (and wrong), and then return to the audition circuit hoping to benefit from their business experience. It is a good idea to take some courses in these related areas as part of your actor training.

# What to Put in Your College Notebook

You might want to keep a page of impressions about your theater department visit and include some of the information provided on the Theater Program Rating Sheet below.

---

**THEATER PROGRAM RATING SHEET**

Size of the department: _____
(too large, you will never be cast; too small, not enough variety)

Faculty: _____
(working pros to give realistic approach; academics; combination)

Curriculum: _____

Acting technique: _____
(Is there a specific technique taught? Elaborate.)

Do other courses offered include:

- Alexander Technique
- Dramatic Verse/Literature
- Drama History
- Masks
- Commedia dell'Arte
- Movement
- Music Studies
- Liberal Arts Courses
- Physical Comedy
- Singing
- Speech

- Stage Combat
- Stage Makeup
- Tap Dance
- Voice
- Text Analysis
- Monologue Class
- Audition Workshop
- Period Styles
- Mime
- Improvisation
- Scene Studies

- Acrobatics
- Jazz Dance
- Technical Theater (Scene Shop)
- Design (Scene, Costume, Lighting)
- Directing
- Stage Management
- Arts Management
- Other

Facilities: _____
(full range from state-of-the-art, with computerized lighting boards, trap doors, revolving stage, etc., to bare bones, learning how to cope)

Productions: _____
(number, quality, diversity—If they perform only Shakespeare, how will you find your experience in more modern theater?)

Current students' opinions: _____

Alumni: _____

Job placement record: _____

---

*Performing*

*Arts*

# Questions to Ask Yourself

Here are some questions to ask yourself at various points in the admissions process.

Have I:

- surfed the Internet and seen the Web sites for programs in which I am interested

- requested catalogs and read them carefully and critically?

- requested applications and made photocopies of the ones in which I am interested?

- started a college notebook with my impressions of colleges and notes about audition requirements, dates, etc.?

- noted any requirements about scenes or monologues?

- obtained a social security number (United States and Permanent Residents)?

- registered for the PSAT/NMSQT?

- obtained information about the ARTS scholarships? (National Foundation for Advancement in the Arts, 444 Brickell Avenue, Miami, FL 33131; 305-377-1140 or 800-970-ARTS (toll-free); www.artsawards.org.)

- made an appointment with my guidance counselor?

- looked into working with an independent counselor, if appropriate?

- talked with my current theater or acting teacher about plans for my future?

- participated regularly in school, community, or professional productions?

- made arrangements to continue my involvement in theater activities?

- discussed high school courses to take?

- discussed which standardized tests to take and when?

- discussed whether tutoring for standardized tests is appropriate for me?

# How to Use This Guide

*Peterson's College Guide for Performing Arts Majors* offers detailed information on professional degree programs in Dance, Music, and Theater offered at institutions in the U.S., its territories, and Canada. The guide should be used as a first step toward identifying potential programs; students are encouraged to consult with their school counselors and arts teachers for additional guidance.

## QUICK-REFERENCE CHART

If you want to find out quickly which professional degrees are offered by a specific school, turn to the **Performing Arts Program At-a-Glance** chart. Organized geographically, the chart provides the most basic information about each school in this guide, including:

- *Institution name and location*
- *Professional degrees offered in dance, music, and theater*
- *Total enrollment*
- *Tuition and fees for the 2008–09 or 2007–08 academic year*
- *Profile page reference*

## PROFILES OF PERFORMING ARTS PROGRAMS

This guide profiles professional degree programs only. The **Profiles of Performing Arts Programs** section is organized alphabetically by institution name and divided into three sections:

- Dance Programs
- Music Programs
- Theater Programs

Each profile consists of the following elements:

**Institutional control:** Private institutions are designated as *independent* (nonprofit), *independent/religious* (sponsored by or affiliated with a religious group or having a non-denominational or interdenominational religious orientation), or *proprietary* (profit-making). Public institutions are designated by their primary source of support, such as *federal, state, commonwealth* (Puerto Rico), *territory* (U.S. territories), *county, district* (an administrative unit of public education, often having boundaries different from units of local government), *city, state and local* ("local" refers to county, district, or city), or *state-related* (funded primarily by the state but administered autonomously).

**Student body type:** Categories are *men* (100 percent of student body), *primarily men, women* (100 percent of student body), *primarily women*, and *coed*. A few schools are designated as *undergraduate: women only; graduate: coed* or *undergraduate: men only; graduate: coed.*

**Campus setting:** Setting is designated as *urban, suburban, small town*, or *rural*.

**Degrees:** Many of the degrees listed (both undergraduate and graduate) are purely professional in scope and definition. Institutions may also offer B.A., B.S., M.A., and M.S. degrees that are considered "professional" based upon the prescribed curriculum and course load within the discipline. In a professional degree program, the majority of the curriculum is made up of course work within the particular arts field, while the rest of the program involves traditional liberal arts course work. A professional degree program allows students to focus most of their studies in dance, music, or theater and emphasizes professional training and acquiring professional skills in such areas as performance, exhibition, and education. This section also lists program accreditation by national arts organizations.

**Enrollment:** This data element cites the number of matriculated undergraduate and (if applicable) graduate students in the arts program, both full-time and part-time, as of fall 2007 (or 2006 if 2007 information was not available).

**Student profile:** Whole-figure percentages are given for the total program enrollment broken down into the following categories: *minorities, female, male, international*.

**Faculty:** Numbers are given for undergraduate and graduate (if applicable) faculty members teaching full-time and part-time in the respective area of study. A percentage of full-time faculty members who have appropriate terminal degrees in their field is listed, as is the ratio of undergraduate students to faculty members teaching undergraduate courses. Finally, mention is made if graduate students teach undergraduate courses in the program.

**Student life:** This section lists program-related organizations and campus activities in which performing arts students may participate. The

Performing

*Arts*

availability of housing opportunities designated solely for performing arts students is mentioned here as well.

**Expenses:** Figures are given for the 2008–09 academic year (actual or estimated) or for the 2007–08 academic year if more recent figures were not yet available at the time of data collection. Annual expenses may be expressed as a *comprehensive fee* (this includes full-time tuition, mandatory fees, and college room and board) or as separate figures for full-time *tuition, mandatory fees, college room and board*, or *college room only*. For public institutions where tuition differs according to residence, separate figures are given for area and/or state residents and for out-of-state residents. The tuition structure at some institutions is complex in that freshmen and sophomores may be charged a different rate from that for juniors and seniors, or a professional or vocational division may have a different fee structure than the liberal arts division of the same institution. In such cases, the lowest tuition appears in the profile, followed by the notation minimum. Also, in instances where colleges report room and board costs that vary depending on the type of accommodation and meal plan, the figures given are either for the most common room arrangement and a full meal plan or for the lowest figures, followed by the notation minimum. If the institution charges special program-related fees for students in the visual and performing arts, these are listed as well.

**Financial aid:** This section provides information regarding any college-administered award opportunities dedicated exclusively for undergraduate students in the program. Keep in mind that while these awards are only for students in the program, program students may qualify for other financial aid opportunities at the institution as well.

**Application procedures:** This section indicates if students are admitted directly into the professional program when they enroll for the freshman year or if they must apply for admission into the professional program at some point during their undergraduate career. Admission application deadlines and dates for notification of acceptance or rejection into the program are given either as specific dates or as *continuous* for freshmen and transfers. Continuous means that applications are processed as they are received, and qualified students are accepted as long as there are openings. Continuous notification means that applicants are notified of acceptance or rejection as applications are processed up until the date indicated or until the actual beginning of classes. Application requirements are grouped into either *required* or *recommended*. In addition to these requirements, an institution may indicate if *auditions* are held and where they are held (on or off campus).

Performing

Arts

**Contact:** Information includes the name, title, mailing address, phone number, fax number, and e-mail address of the person to contact for further information. Where applicable, a graduate contact is listed as well.

**More About the School:** A **Special Message** may be included for schools that wish to place additional emphasis on some aspect of their program offerings.

## APPENDIXES

The **Summer Programs in the Performing Arts** appendix lists names and contact information for summer programs that can help high school students develop their talent and skills in dance, music, or theater.

**Scholarships for Performing Artists** contains a partial listing of private scholarships, grants & prizes awarded to college-bound dance, music, or theater students. The awards are based on data collected between January and April 2008 through survey mailings and phone interviews. Every effort has been made to provide up-to-date information. However, changes in particular program information may occur after this book is published. To make sure that you have the most current information, always contact the sponsors directly.

The **Additional Resources** appendix provide readers with lists of various performing arts education organizations that provide support to students in the arts.

## INDEXES

The **Majors and Concentrations** index presents 274 major fields of study. This index is divided into three sections: Dance, Music, and Theater. The majors are listed alphabetically in each section. The terms used for the majors are the most widely used. However, many institutions use different terms for the same or similar areas. In addition, while the term "major" is used in this guide, some schools may use other terms such as concentration, program of study, or field.

The **Alphabetical Listing of Schools** index lists every professional degree-granting institution in the guide alphabetically and gives the page number(s) on which its profile can be found.

## DATA COLLECTION PROCEDURES

The data contained in the college chart, profiles, and indexes were collected through *Peterson's Survey of Professional Degree Programs in the Visual & Performing Arts*. Questionnaires were sent to the more than 1,100 programs that meet the criteria for inclusion outlined below. All data included in this edition have been submitted by officials (usually program directors, department heads, or admissions personnel) at the institutions themselves. In addition, the great majority of institutions that submitted data were contacted directly by Peterson's editorial staff to verify unusual figures, resolve discrepancies, and obtain additional data. All usable information received in time for publication has been included. The omission of any items from an index or profile listing signifies either that the data were not applicable to that institution or that data were not available. Institutions that did not return a survey may be listed with an abbreviated profile in order to ensure a comprehensive reference product. We have every reason to believe that the information presented in this guide is accurate. However, students should check with a specific college or university at the time of application to verify such figures as tuition and fees, which may have changed since the publication of this volume.

## CRITERIA FOR INCLUSION IN THIS BOOK

*Peterson's College Guide for Performing Arts Majors* covers accredited baccalaureate-degree-granting institutions in the United States, U.S. territories, and Canada. Institutions have full accreditation or candidate-for-accreditation (preaccreditation) status granted by an institutional or specialized accrediting body recognized by the U.S. Department of Education or Council for Higher Education Accreditation. Recognized institutional accrediting bodies, which consider each institution as a whole, are the following: the six regional associations of schools and colleges (Middle States, New England, North Central, Northwest, Southern, and Western), each of which is responsible for a specified portion of the United States and its territories; the Association for Biblical Higher Education (ABHE); the Accrediting Council for Independent Colleges and Schools (ACICS); the Accrediting Commission of Career Schools and Colleges of Technology (ACCSCT); the Distance Education and Training Council (DETC); the American Academy for Liberal Education (AALE); the Council on Occupational Education; and the Transnational Association of Christian Colleges and Schools (TRACS). Program registration by the New York State Board of Regents is considered to be the equivalent of institutional accreditation, since the Board requires that all programs offered by an institution meet its standards before recognition is granted. A Canadian institution must be chartered and authorized to grant degrees by the provincial government, affiliated with a chartered institution, or accredited by a recognized U.S. accrediting body. There are recognized specialized accrediting bodies in over forty different fields, each of which is authorized to accredit specific programs in its particular field. This can serve as the equivalent of institutional accreditation for specialized institutions that offer programs in one field only (schools of art, music, optometry, theology, etc.).

In addition, a profiled institution must grant one or more of the following undergraduate professional degrees in dance, music, or theater:

Associate in Occupational Studies
Bachelor of Arts
Bachelor of Arts/Bachelor of Education
Bachelor of Arts/Bachelor of Fine Arts
Bachelor of Arts/Bachelor of Music
Bachelor of Arts/Bachelor of Science
Bachelor of Arts in Music
Bachelor of Church Music
Bachelor of Dance Arts
Bachelor of Education
Bachelor of Fine Arts
Bachelor of Fine Arts/ Master of Arts
Bachelor of Music

Bachelor of Music/Bachelor of Music Education
Bachelor of Music/Bachelor of Science
Bachelor of Musical Arts
Bachelor of Music Education
Bachelor of Music Education/Music Therapy
Bachelor of Music Therapy
Bachelor of Sacred Music
Bachelor of Science
Bachelor of Science/ Bachelor of Fine Arts
Bachelor of Science in Education
Bachelor of Science in Music Education

Many of these institutions also offer advanced degrees at the master's or doctoral level:

Master of Arts
Master of Arts/Doctor of Philosophy
Master of Arts/Master of Fine Arts
Master of Arts/Master of Science
Master of Arts in Education
Master of Arts in Teaching

Master of Church Music
Master of Design
Master of Education
Master of Fine Arts
Master of Humanities
Master of Liturgical Music
Master of Music
Master of Music Education
Master of Music Therapy

Master of Music/Doctor of
 Philosophy
Master of Musical Arts
Master of Professional
 Studies
Master of Public Art
 Studies
Master of Sacred Music
Master of Science
Master of Science in
 Education

Master of Science in
 Physical Education
Master of Science in
 Teaching
Doctor of Arts
Doctor of Education
Doctor of Music
Doctor of Music Education
Doctor of Musical Arts
Doctor of Philosophy

# Quick-Reference Chart

# Performing Arts Programs At-a-Glance

| | Dance | Music | Theater | Enroll- ment | Tuition and Fees | Summer Programs | Page |
|---|---|---|---|---|---|---|---|
| **U.S. AND U.S. TERRITORIES** | | | | | | | |
| **Alabama** | | | | | | | |
| Auburn University | | BMEd, MEd, MS, PhD | BFA | 24,137 | 5834* | Theater | 224, 365 |
| Birmingham-Southern College | | BM, BMEd, MM | | 1,389 | 25,586** | Music | 228 |
| Jacksonville State University | | BA, MA | | 9,077 | 5070* | Music | 265 |
| Samford University | | BM, MM | | 4,485 | 17,920* | | 302 |
| University of Mobile | | BM, BSM | | 1,639 | 13,390* | Music | 333 |
| University of Montevallo | | BM, MM | BFA | 2,948 | 6080* | Music | 334, 398 |
| University of South Alabama | | BFA, BM | BFA | 13,779 | 4822* | | 341, 400 |
| **Alaska** | | | | | | | |
| University of Alaska Anchorage | | BM | | 17,023 | 4400* | | 316 |
| University of Alaska Fairbanks | | BM | | 8,627 | 4756** | Music | 316 |
| **Arizona** | | | | | | | |
| Arizona State University | BFA, MFA | BM, MM, DMA | | 51,481 | 5661** | | 195, 223 |
| Northern Arizona University | | BA, BM, BME, MM | | 21,352 | 4844* | Music | 290 |
| **Arkansas** | | | | | | | |
| Arkansas State University | | | BFA | 10,869 | 6010* | Theater | 364 |
| Harding University | | BMEd | | 6,139 | 12,360* | | 258 |
| Henderson State University | | BM | | 3,603 | 4939** | | 259 |

\* Expenses for 2007–2008.   \*\* Estimated expenses for 2008–2009.   NR = Not reported.
For public institutions where tuition differs according to residence, the in-state tuition and fees are shown.

| | Dance | Music | Theater | Enroll-ment | Tuition and Fees | Summer Programs | Page |
|---|---|---|---|---|---|---|---|
| **Arkansas**—*continued* | | | | | | | |
| Ouachita Baptist University | | BM, BME | | 1,448 | 18,400** | | 295 |
| University of Arkansas | | BM, MM | | 18,648 | 6038* | Music | 317 |
| University of Central Arkansas | | BM, MM | | 12,619 | 6205* | | 319 |
| **California** | | | | | | | |
| California Institute of the Arts | BFA, MFA | BFA, MFA | BFA, MFA | 1,324 | 33,436** | | 197, 234, 369 |
| California State University, Long Beach | BFA, MFA | BM, MM | | 36,868 | 13,564** | | 198, 235 |
| California State University, Los Angeles | | BA, BM, MA, MM | | 21,051 | 3377** | | 236 |
| California State University, Northridge | | BA, BM, MEd, MM | | 34,560 | 3350* | | 236 |
| California State University, Sacramento | | BA, BM, MM | | 28,829 | 4752* | | 236 |
| Chapman University | BFA | BM, BMEd | BFA | 6,022 | 34,700** | | 199, 241, 371 |
| The Colburn School Conservatory of Music | | BM | | | 1400** | | 245 |
| Musicians Institute | | BM | | | NR | Music | 283 |
| San Diego State University | BFA | BM, MA, MM | | 36,559 | 3428* | | 209, 303 |
| San Francisco Conservatory of Music | | BM, MM | | 406 | 29,980* | | 303 |
| San Francisco State University | | BM, MA, MM | | 30,125 | 13,626* | | 304 |
| University of California, Irvine | | BA, BM, MFA | | 26,483 | 8276* | | 318 |
| University of Redlands | | BM, MM | | 2,445 | 30,626* | | 339 |
| University of Southern California | | BM, MA, MM, MMEd, PhD, DMA | BFA, MFA | 33,408 | 35,810* | Theater | 342, 401 |
| University of the Pacific | | BA, BM, MA, MM | | 6,235 | 28,980* | Music | 346 |

* Expenses for 2007–2008.   ** Estimated expenses for 2008–2009.   NR = Not reported.
For public institutions where tuition differs according to residence, the in-state tuition and fees are shown.

| | Dance | Music | Theater | Enroll-ment | Tuition and Fees | Summer Programs | Page |
|---|---|---|---|---|---|---|---|
| **Colorado** | | | | | | | |
| Colorado Christian University | | BM | | 2,221 | 18,350* | | 246 |
| University of Colorado at Boulder | BFA, MFA | BM, BMEd, MM, MMEd, PhD, DMA | BFA, PhD | 31,470 | 7278** | | 212, 321, 394 |
| University of Colorado Denver | | BS | | 20,162 | 5932** | | 322 |
| University of Denver | | BM, MA, MM | | 11,053 | 32,232* | | 323 |
| Western State College of Colorado | | BA | | 2,064 | 3586* | | 356 |
| **Connecticut** | | | | | | | |
| Albertus Magnus College | | | BFA | 2,034 | 21,074* | | 363 |
| Central Connecticut State University | | | BFA | 12,106 | 6734* | | 370 |
| University of Bridgeport | | BM | | 4,752 | 22,860* | | 317 |
| University of Connecticut | | BA, BM, BS, MA, MM, PhD, DMA | BFA, MA, MFA | 23,692 | 9338** | | 322, 395 |
| **Delaware** | | | | | | | |
| University of Delaware | | BM, BMEd, MM | | 19,677 | 8150* | | 323 |
| **District of Columbia** | | | | | | | |
| The Catholic University of America | | BM, MA, MM, MMSM, DMA | | 6,440 | 28,990* | | 239 |
| Howard University | | | BFA | | 13,715* | | 375 |
| **Florida** | | | | | | | |
| The Baptist College of Florida | | BM, BMEd | | 564 | 7850* | | 226 |
| Florida Atlantic University | | BM, MA | BFA, MFA | 26,275 | 3367* | Theater | 255, 374 |

* Expenses for 2007–2008.   ** Estimated expenses for 2008–2009.   NR = Not reported.
For public institutions where tuition differs according to residence, the in-state tuition and fees are shown.

| | Dance | Music | Theater | Enroll-ment | Tuition and Fees | Summer Programs | Page |
|---|---|---|---|---|---|---|---|
| **Florida**—*continued* | | | | | | | |
| Florida State University | BFA, MA, MFA | BM, BMEd, EdD, MA, MM, MMEd, PhD, DM | BFA, MFA | 40,555 | 3355* | | 201, 255, 374 |
| Jacksonville University | BFA | BM, BMEd | BFA | 3,436 | 23,900** | | 202, 265, 378 |
| New World School of the Arts | BFA | BM | BFA | 416 | 3000* | | 204, 287, 382 |
| Palm Beach Atlantic University | | BM | | 3,291 | 20,210* | Music | 296 |
| Stetson University | | BM, BMEd | | 3,721 | 30,216** | | 312 |
| University of Central Florida | | | BFA, MFA | 48,497 | 3620* | | 393 |
| University of Florida | BFA | | BFA, MFA | 51,725 | 3257* | | 212, 395 |
| University of Miami | | BA, BM, BS, MM, MS, DMA | BFA | 15,462 | 33,118* | | 329, 396 |
| The University of Tampa | | BM | | 5,628 | 20,682* | | 343 |
| **Georgia** | | | | | | | |
| Armstrong Atlantic State University | | BA, BMEd | | 6,831 | 3424* | | 223 |
| Augusta State University | | BM | | 6,588 | 3728* | | 225 |
| Brenau University | BFA | BAM, BM | BFA | 916 | 18,800** | Music, Theater | 196, 231, 367 |
| Clayton State University | | BM | | 6,043 | 3354* | | 242 |
| Columbus State University | | BM, MM | | 7,590 | 3514* | | 246 |
| Georgia College & State University | | BA, BMEd, BMT, MMEd, MUST | | 6,249 | 5066* | | 257 |
| Georgia State University | | BM, BS, MM, PhD | | 27,137 | 5485** | | 257 |
| Mercer University | | BM, BMEd, MOM | | 5,253 | 26,960* | Music | 279 |
| Shorter College | | BFA, BM | BFA | 1,394 | 15,160* | | 306, 390 |

\* Expenses for 2007–2008.   \*\* Estimated expenses for 2008–2009.   NR = Not reported.
For public institutions where tuition differs according to residence, the in-state tuition and fees are shown.

| | Dance | Music | Theater | Enroll-ment | Tuition and Fees | Summer Programs | Page |
|---|---|---|---|---|---|---|---|
| **Georgia**—*continued* | | | | | | | |
| University of Georgia | | BM, EdD, MM, MMEd, PhD, DMA | | 33,831 | 5622* | | 324 |
| **Hawaii** | | | | | | | |
| University of Hawaii at Manoa | BFA, MA, MFA | BM, MA, MM, PhD | | 20,357 | 5390* | | 213, 324 |
| **Idaho** | | | | | | | |
| Idaho State University | | BM, BMEd, MEd | | 13,208 | 4400* | Music | 261 |
| University of Idaho | BS | BFA, BM, BMEd, MA, MM | | 11,636 | 4410* | | 213, 325 |
| **Illinois** | | | | | | | |
| Bradley University | | BM | BA, BS | 6,053 | 21,360* | | 231, 367 |
| Columbia College Chicago | BA, BFA | BA, BM, MFA | BA, BFA | 11,499 | 17,634* | Dance, Music, Theater | 200, 246, 371 |
| DePaul University | | BM, BS, MM | BFA, MFA | 23,401 | 24,394** | | 251, 372 |
| Illinois State University | | BA, BM, BMEd, BS, MM, MMEd, MS | BA, BS, MA, MFA, MS | 20,274 | 9019* | Theater | 261, 375 |
| Illinois Wesleyan University | | BM, BMEd | BA, BFA | 2,094 | 30,750* | | 262, 376 |
| Millikin University | | | BA, BFA | 2,376 | 23,845* | | 381 |
| North Park University | | BM, BMEd, MM | | | 16,560* | | 291 |
| Rockford College | | | BFA | 1,566 | 23,500** | | 388 |
| Roosevelt University | | BM, MM | BFA, MA, MFA | 7,163 | 16,980* | | 299, 388 |
| Saint Xavier University | | BM | | 5,675 | 21,236* | | 302 |
| Southern Illinois University Carbondale | | BM, MM | | 20,983 | 8899* | | 308 |
| Southern Illinois University Edwardsville | | BM, MM | | 13,298 | 6408* | | 309 |

* Expenses for 2007–2008.   ** Estimated expenses for 2008–2009.   NR = Not reported.
For public institutions where tuition differs according to residence, the in-state tuition and fees are shown.

Performing

*Arts*

| | Dance | Music | Theater | Enroll-ment | Tuition and Fees | Summer Programs | Page |
|---|---|---|---|---|---|---|---|
| **Illinois**—*continued* | | | | | | | |
| University of Illinois at Urbana–Champaign | BFA, MFA | BM, BME, EdD, MM, MME, PhD, DMA | BFA, MFA, PhD | 42,326 | 11,130* | | 213, 326, 396 |
| VanderCook College of Music | | BMEd, MMEd | | | 18,800* | | 352 |
| Western Illinois University | | BM, MM | | 13,331 | 8272** | | 355 |
| Wheaton College | | BM, BMEd | | 2,895 | 23,730* | | 358 |
| **Indiana** | | | | | | | |
| Butler University | BA, BFA, BS | BA, BM, BS, MM | BA, BS | 4,479 | 26,806* | Dance | 196, 233, 368 |
| Huntington University | | BM | | 1,152 | 19,430* | | 261 |
| Indiana University Bloomington | BS, BSOF | BM, BMEd, BS, MA, MM, MMEd, MS, PhD, DM, DME | | 38,990 | 7837* | Music | 201, 262 |
| Taylor University | | BA, BM, BMEd, BS | | 1,879 | 24,546** | | 313 |
| University of Evansville | | BM, BS | | 2,898 | 24,340* | | 324 |
| Valparaiso University | | BM, BMEd | | 3,872 | 25,200* | | 351 |
| **Iowa** | | | | | | | |
| Coe College | | BM, BMEd | | 1,300 | Can34,610 | | 244 |
| Cornell College | | BM, BMEd | | 1,083 | 26,280* | | 248 |
| Iowa Wesleyan College | | BMEd | | 833 | 18,870* | | 263 |
| Simpson College | | BM | | 2,039 | 24,771** | Music | 306 |
| The University of Iowa | BFA, MFA | | | 29,117 | 6544** | Dance | 213 |
| **Kansas** | | | | | | | |
| Baker University | | BMEd | | 942 | 18,750* | | 225 |
| Emporia State University | | BM, BME, MM | BFA | 6,354 | 3926* | | 253, 373 |
| Fort Hays State University | | BM | | 7,403 | 3355* | | 256 |

\* Expenses for 2007–2008.   \*\* Estimated expenses for 2008–2009.   NR = Not reported.
For public institutions where tuition differs according to residence, the in-state tuition and fees are shown.

| | Dance | Music | Theater | Enroll-ment | Tuition and Fees | Summer Programs | Page |
|---|---|---|---|---|---|---|---|
| **Kansas**—*continued* | | | | | | | |
| Kansas State University | | BM, BMEd, MM | | 22,530 | 6235* | | 268 |
| Washburn University | | BM, BMEd | | 6,901 | 5636* | | 353 |
| Wichita State University | BFA | | BFA | 14,442 | 4770* | | 219, 408 |
| **Kentucky** | | | | | | | |
| Georgetown College | | BM, BMEd | | 1,903 | 22,360* | | 256 |
| Kentucky Wesleyan College | | BM, BME | | 956 | 14,550* | | 269 |
| Morehead State University | | BM, BMEd, MM | | 8,966 | 5280* | | 282 |
| Murray State University | | BM, MMEd | | 10,149 | 5748** | | 283 |
| Northern Kentucky University | | BM | BFA | 14,785 | 6528** | | 291, 384 |
| University of Kentucky | | BM, MA, MM, PhD, DMA | | 25,856 | 7096^ | | 326 |
| University of Louisville | | BM, MAT, MM, MME | | 20,592 | 7564** | | 327 |
| University of the Cumberlands | | BM | | 1,884 | 13,658* | | 345 |
| Western Kentucky University | | BM, MAE | | 19,258 | 6416* | | 355 |
| **Louisiana** | | | | | | | |
| Louisiana State University and Agricultural and Mechanical College | | BM, BMEd, MM, PhD, DMA | | 28,628 | 4543* | | 274 |
| Loyola University New Orleans | | BM, BMEd, BMT, MM, MMEd, MMT | | 4,360 | 28,044** | | 274 |
| Northwestern State University of Louisiana | | BM, BMEd, MM | BS | 9,037 | 3528* | Theater | 292, 384 |
| Southeastern Louisiana University | | BM, BMEd, MM | | 14,757 | 3561* | | 308 |

\* Expenses for 2007–2008.   \*\* Estimated expenses for 2008–2009.   NR = Not reported.
For public institutions where tuition differs according to residence, the in-state tuition and fees are shown.

| | Dance | Music | Theater | Enroll-ment | Tuition and Fees | Summer Programs | Page |
|---|---|---|---|---|---|---|---|
| **Louisiana**—*continued* | | | | | | | |
| Southern University and Agricultural and Mechanical College | | BM, BMEd | | 8,179 | 3706** | | 309 |
| Tulane University | BFA | | BFA, MFA | 10,519 | 36,610* | | 211, 393 |
| University of Louisiana at Lafayette | | BM, BMEd, MM, MMEd | | 16,345 | 3402* | | 326 |
| **Maine** | | | | | | | |
| University of Southern Maine | | BM, MM | | 10,453 | 6866* | Music | 343 |
| **Maryland** | | | | | | | |
| The Johns Hopkins University | | BM, MA, MM, DMA | | 6,257 | 35,900* | | 266 |
| University of Maryland, College Park | | BM, MA, MM, PhD, DMA | | 35,970 | 7969* | Music | 328 |
| **Massachusetts** | | | | | | | |
| Anna Maria College | | BM | | 1,244 | 24,617* | | 222 |
| Berklee College of Music | | BM | | 4,090 | 28,200** | Music | 227 |
| The Boston Conservatory | BFA | BM, MM | BFA, MM | 560 | 30,099* | Dance, Music | 195, 229, 365 |
| Boston University | | BM, MM, DMA | BFA, MFA | 32,053 | 37,050** | Music, Theater | 230, 366 |
| Emerson College | | | BFA, MA | 4,380 | 26,880* | Theater | 373 |
| Gordon College | | BM, MA | | 1,645 | 27,294** | | 258 |
| New England Conservatory of Music | | BM, MM, DMA | | 795 | 33,325** | | 284 |
| Salem State College | | | BFA | 10,085 | 6210* | | 390 |
| University of Massachusetts Amherst | BFA | | | 25,873 | 10,417** | | 214 |
| University of Massachusetts Dartmouth | | BA | | 9,080 | 8592* | | 328 |
| University of Massachusetts Lowell | | BM, MM | | 11,635 | 8731* | Music | 329 |

* Expenses for 2007–2008.   ** Estimated expenses for 2008–2009.   NR = Not reported.
For public institutions where tuition differs according to residence, the in-state tuition and fees are shown.

| | Dance | Music | Theater | Enroll-ment | Tuition and Fees | Summer Programs | Page |
|---|---|---|---|---|---|---|---|
| **Michigan** | | | | | | | |
| Aquinas College | | BM, MAT | | 2,107 | 21,150** | | 223 |
| Central Michigan University | | BM, BME, MM | | 26,611 | 9120* | Music | 240 |
| Cornerstone University | | BMus | | 2,466 | 18,360* | | 249 |
| Marygrove College | | BM | | 2,953 | 14,690* | Music | 277 |
| Northern Michigan University | | BMEd | | 9,111 | 6709* | | 291 |
| Oakland University | | BM, MM, PhD | | 18,081 | 7575* | | 292 |
| University of Michigan | BFA, MFA | BFA, BM, BMA, BS, MA, MM, PhD, DMA | BFA, BTA | 41,042 | 10,447* | Dance, Music | 214, 331, 396 |
| University of Michigan–Flint | | | BFA, BS | 6,883 | 7342* | | 397 |
| Wayne State University | | BA, BM, MA, MM | BFA, MFA, DA | 33,240 | 7844* | | 354, 406 |
| Western Michigan University | BFA | BM, MM | BFA | 24,433 | 7260* | Music | 219, 356, 407 |
| **Minnesota** | | | | | | | |
| Augsburg College | | BA, BM, BMEd, BS | | 3,732 | 24,539* | | 224 |
| Concordia College | | BM | | 2,815 | 24,120** | | 247 |
| Crown College | | BA, BME | | 1,270 | 19,198** | | 249 |
| Minnesota State University Mankato | | BM, BS, MM | | 14,148 | 6050* | Music | 280 |
| St. Cloud State University | | BA, BM, BS, MM | | 15,808 | 5955* | | 301 |
| St. Olaf College | | BM | | 3,040 | 34,300** | | 302 |
| University of Minnesota, Duluth | | BA, BM, MM, MMEd | | 11,184 | 9600* | | 331 |
| University of Minnesota, Twin Cities Campus | BFA | BM, MM, PhD, DMA | BFA, MFA | 50,883 | 7950* | | 214, 332, 397 |

\* Expenses for 2007–2008.   \*\* Estimated expenses for 2008–2009.   NR = Not reported.
For public institutions where tuition differs according to residence, the in-state tuition and fees are shown.

| | Dance | Music | Theater | Enroll-ment | Tuition and Fees | Summer Programs | Page |
|---|---|---|---|---|---|---|---|
| **Mississippi** | | | | | | | |
| Belhaven College | BFA | | | 2,485 | 16,360** | | 195 |
| Delta State University | | BM, BMEd | | 4,091 | 4248* | | 250 |
| Jackson State University | | BM, BMEd, MM, MMEd | | 8,698 | 4432* | Music | 265 |
| Mississippi State University | | BMEd | | 17,039 | 4978* | | 281 |
| University of Mississippi | | BM, MM, DA | | 15,129 | 4932* | | 332 |
| University of Southern Mississippi | | | BFA, MFA | 14,592 | 4914** | | 402 |
| William Carey University | | BA, BM | BFA | 2,493 | 9015* | | 359, 408 |
| **Missouri** | | | | | | | |
| Calvary Bible College and Theological Seminary | | BM, BS | | 329 | 8500* | | 237 |
| Central Methodist University | | BM, BME | | 841 | 17,160* | | 240 |
| Lincoln University | | BMEd | | 3,156 | 6010* | | 273 |
| Lindenwood University | | | BFA, MFA | 9,633 | 13,000** | | 379 |
| Missouri State University | BFA | BFA, BM, BME, BS, MM | | 19,348 | 6606* | Music | 204, 281 |
| Southeast Missouri State University | | BM, BME, MME | | 10,665 | 5925* | | 308 |
| Stephens College | | | BFA | 1,050 | 23,000** | Theater | 392 |
| Truman State University | | BM, MA, MAE | | 5,866 | 6432* | | 315 |
| University of Central Missouri | | BM, BMEd, MA | | 10,918 | 6829* | | 319 |
| University of Missouri–Columbia | | BM, BS, MA, MEd, MM, PhD | | 28,477 | 8099* | | 332 |
| University of Missouri–Kansas City | BFA | BA, BM, BMEd, IPhD, MA, MM, MME, DMA | | 14,442 | 8396** | Music | 215, 333 |

* Expenses for 2007–2008.   ** Estimated expenses for 2008–2009.   NR = Not reported.
For public institutions where tuition differs according to residence, the in-state tuition and fees are shown.

Performing

*Arts*

| | Dance | Music | Theater | Enroll-ment | Tuition and Fees | Summer Programs | Page |
|---|---|---|---|---|---|---|---|
| **Missouri**—*continued* | | | | | | | |
| Webster University | BFA | BM, BMEd, MM | BA, BFA | 8,430 | 19,330* | | 218, 355, 406 |
| **Montana** | | | | | | | |
| Montana State University | | BA, BME | | 12,170 | 5749* | | 281 |
| The University of Montana | BFA | BM, BMEd, MM | BFA, MFA | 13,858 | 5180** | | 215, 333, 397 |
| **Nebraska** | | | | | | | |
| Nebraska Wesleyan University | | BA, BM | BFA | 2,107 | 20,252* | Music, Theater | 284, 381 |
| University of Nebraska at Omaha | | BM, MM | | 14,156 | 5531* | | 334 |
| University of Nebraska–Lincoln | | BM, BME, MM, DMA | BFA, MFA | 22,973 | 6215* | Music | 334, 398 |
| **Nevada** | | | | | | | |
| University of Nevada, Las Vegas | | BM, MM, DMA | | 28,008 | 4583** | Music | 335 |
| University of Nevada, Reno | | | BFA | 16,681 | 4411** | | 398 |
| **New Jersey** | | | | | | | |
| The College of New Jersey | | BM | | 6,964 | 11,307* | | 245 |
| Fairleigh Dickinson University, College at Florham | | | BA | 3,463 | 28,228* | | 373 |
| Montclair State University | BA, BFA | BA, BM, MA | | 16,736 | 8895* | | 204, 282 |
| Rowan University | | BM, MM | | 10,091 | 10,068* | | 300 |
| Rutgers, The State University of New Jersey, Mason Gross School of the Arts | BFA | BM, MM, DMA | BFA, MFA | | NR | Theater | 204, 278, 381 |
| Westminster Choir College of Rider University | | BA, BM, MA, MM, MMEd, MVP | | 452 | NR | Music | 357 |

\* Expenses for 2007–2008.   \*\* Estimated expenses for 2008–2009.   NR = Not reported.
For public institutions where tuition differs according to residence, the in-state tuition and fees are shown.

Performing Arts

| | Dance | Music | Theater | Enroll-ment | Tuition and Fees | Summer Programs | Page |
|---|---|---|---|---|---|---|---|
| **New Mexico** | | | | | | | |
| New Mexico State University | | BM, BMEd, MM | | 16,726 | 4452* | | 285 |
| University of New Mexico | | BM, BMEd, MM | | | 4571* | | 335 |
| **New York** | | | | | | | |
| Adelphi University | | | BFA | 8,354 | 23,255* | | 363 |
| American Academy of Dramatic Arts | | | AOS, Cert | 228 | 20,000** | Theater | 363 |
| Brooklyn College of the City University of New York | | BM, MA, MM | | 15,947 | 4150* | | 232 |
| City College of the City University of New York | | BFA, MA | | 14,536 | 4359* | | 242 |
| The College at Brockport, State University of New York | BFA, MFA | | | 8,303 | 5442** | | 199 |
| Five Towns College | | BM, MM, DMA | BFA | 1,151 | 18,125** | Theater | 254, 374 |
| Fordham University | BFA | | BA | 14,448 | 32,857* | | 201, 375 |
| Houghton College | | BM, MM | | 1,382 | 21,620* | | 260 |
| Ithaca College | | BM, MM | BFA | 6,660 | 28,670* | | 263, 377 |
| The Juilliard School | BFA | AD, BM, MM, DMA | AD, BFA | 832 | 27,150* | Dance, Music | 202, 268, 378 |
| Lehman College of the City University of New York | | BS, MAT | | 10,922 | 4290** | | 272 |
| Long Island University, C.W. Post Campus | BFA | | BFA, MA | 8,361 | 25,950* | | 203, 379 |
| Manhattan School of Music | | BM, MM, DMA | | 854 | NR | | 275 |
| Manhattanville College | | B Mus, BA, BA/MAT, MAT | | 3,023 | 31,620** | | 275 |
| Mannes College The New School for Music | | BM, BS, MM | | 379 | 30,410* | | 276 |
| Marymount Manhattan College | BFA | | BFA | 1,895 | 20,600* | | 203, 380 |
| Nazareth College of Rochester | | BM, MS | | 3,185 | 22,880* | Music | 284 |

\* Expenses for 2007–2008.   \*\* Estimated expenses for 2008–2009.   NR = Not reported.
For public institutions where tuition differs according to residence, the in-state tuition and fees are shown.

| | Dance | Music | Theater | Enroll-ment | Tuition and Fees | Summer Programs | Page |
|---|---|---|---|---|---|---|---|
| **New York**—*continued* | | | | | | | |
| The New School for Jazz and Contemporary Music | | BA/BFA, BFA | | 245 | 30,450* | | 286 |
| New York University | BFA, MFA | BFA, BM, EdD, MA, MM, PhD | BFA, BFA, BS, EdD, MA, MFA, PhD | 41,783 | 35,290* | Music, Theater | 205, 288, 383 |
| Niagara University | | | BFA | 4,116 | 22,300* | | 383 |
| Pace University | | | BFA | 12,912 | 30,158* | | 385 |
| Purchase College, State University of New York | BFA, MFA | BMus, MM | BFA, MFA | 4,265 | 5997** | Theater | 207, 297, 387 |
| Queens College of the City University of New York | | BM, MA, MS | | 18,728 | 4377** | | 298 |
| Russell Sage College | | | BA | 682 | 25,990* | | 389 |
| State University of New York at Binghamton | | BM, MM | | 14,435 | 6012* | | 310 |
| State University of New York at Fredonia | BFA | BFA, BM, BS, MM | BFA | 5,404 | 5542* | | 210, 311, 391 |
| State University of New York College at Potsdam | | BM, MM | | 4,338 | 5406* | Music | 311 |
| Syracuse University | | BA, BM, BS, MM | BFA, BS | 17,677 | 31,686* | Theater | 312, 393 |
| University at Buffalo, the State University of New York | | BA, MA, MM, Mus. B., PhD | | 28,054 | 6217* | | 315 |
| University of Rochester | | BM, MA, MA/PhD, MM, PhD, DMA | | 9,334 | 35,190* | Music | 340 |
| **North Carolina** | | | | | | | |
| Appalachian State University | | BM, BS, MM, MMT | | 15,871 | 4241* | Music | 222 |
| Brevard College | | BA, BM | | 675 | 18,750* | | 232 |
| Catawba College | | | BFA | 1,323 | 22,290* | | 370 |
| Chowan University | | BS | | | 17,030* | | 241 |
| East Carolina University | BFA | BM, MM | BFA | 25,990 | 4368* | Dance | 200, 252, 372 |
| Lenoir-Rhyne College | | BMEd | | 1,626 | 23,070** | | 273 |

* Expenses for 2007–2008.   ** Estimated expenses for 2008–2009.   NR = Not reported.
For public institutions where tuition differs according to residence, the in-state tuition and fees are shown.

| | Dance | Music | Theater | Enroll-ment | Tuition and Fees | Summer Programs | Page |
|---|---|---|---|---|---|---|---|
| **North Carolina—*continued*** | | | | | | | |
| Meredith College | | BM, MM | | 2,202 | 23,550** | | 279 |
| North Carolina Agricultural and Technical State University | | | BFA | 11,098 | 3500* | | 383 |
| North Carolina Central University | | BA, BM | | 8,383 | 3670** | | 289 |
| North Carolina School of the Arts | BFA | BM, MM | BFA, MFA | 864 | 5061* | Dance, Theater | 205, 290, 384 |
| Queens University of Charlotte | | BM | | 2,243 | 22,068** | | 298 |
| The University of North Carolina at Charlotte | | BM | | 22,388 | 4152* | Music | 336 |
| The University of North Carolina at Greensboro | | BM, MM, PhD, DMA | BA, BFA, MEd, MFA | 17,157 | 4029* | | 336, 399 |
| The University of North Carolina Wilmington | | BM | | 11,840 | 4398* | Music | 336 |
| Western Carolina University | | | BFA | 9,056 | 4414** | | 407 |
| **North Dakota** | | | | | | | |
| University of North Dakota | | BM, MM, PhD | BFA | 12,559 | 6130* | Theater | 337, 399 |
| Valley City State University | | BS | | 921 | 5584* | | 351 |
| **Ohio** | | | | | | | |
| Ashland University | | BM | | 2,772 | 24,340** | | 224 |
| Baldwin-Wallace College | | BM, BMEd | | 4,394 | 23,524** | Music | 225 |
| Bowling Green State University | | BM, MM, DMA | | 18,619 | 9060* | Music | 230 |
| Capital University | | BA, BM, MM | | 3,713 | 26,360* | Music | 237 |
| Cedarville University | | B Mus, BMEd | | 3,055 | 21,130* | | 240 |
| Cleveland Institute of Music | | BM, MM, DMA | | 426 | NR | | 243 |
| Cleveland State University | | B Mus, MM | | 15,383 | 7920* | Music | 244 |
| The College of Wooster | | BM, BMEd | | 1,777 | 33,770** | | 245 |

\* Expenses for 2007–2008.  \*\* Estimated expenses for 2008–2009.  NR = Not reported.
For public institutions where tuition differs according to residence, the in-state tuition and fees are shown.

| | Dance | Music | Theater | Enroll-ment | Tuition and Fees | Summer Programs | Page |
|---|---|---|---|---|---|---|---|
| **Ohio**—*continued* | | | | | | | |
| Heidelberg College | | BM | | 1,584 | 19,922** | | 259 |
| Kent State University | BFA | BM, MM | BFA, MFA | 22,819 | 8430** | | 203, 268, 379 |
| Miami University | | BM, MM | | 15,922 | 11,925* | | 280 |
| Oberlin College | | BM, MM, MMT | | 2,774 | 36,282* | Music | 247 |
| Ohio Northern University | | BM | BFA | 3,603 | 30,765** | | 293, 385 |
| The Ohio State University | BFA, MFA, PhD | | | 52,568 | 8676* | Dance | 205 |
| Ohio University | BFA | | BFA, MA, MFA | 20,711 | 8907* | | 206, 385 |
| Ohio Wesleyan University | | BM | | 1,967 | 31,930* | | 293 |
| Otterbein College | | BFA, BM, BMEd | BFA | 3,107 | 25,065* | | 295, 385 |
| The University of Akron | BA, BFA | | | 23,007 | 8382* | | 211 |
| University of Cincinnati | BFA | BM, MM, PhD, DMA | BFA, MFA | 29,319 | 9399* | | 212, 319, 394 |
| University of Dayton | | BM, MEd | | 10,395 | 25,950* | | 322 |
| The University of Toledo | | BM, BMEd, MM, MMEd | | 19,768 | 7927** | Music | 347 |
| Wright State University | BFA | BM, MHUM, MM | BFA | 16,151 | 7278* | | 220, 360, 408 |
| Youngstown State University | | BM, MM | | 13,489 | 6721* | | 361 |
| **Oklahoma** | | | | | | | |
| East Central University | | BS | | 4,463 | 3796* | | 253 |
| Oklahoma Baptist University | | BM, BMEd | | | 15,468** | | 293 |
| Oklahoma City University | | BM, BMEd, MM | | 3,865 | 21,000* | Music | 294 |
| Oklahoma State University | | BM, MM | | 23,005 | 5491* | | 294 |
| Oral Roberts University | | BM, BMEd | | 3,170 | 17,400* | | 294 |

* Expenses for 2007–2008. ** Estimated expenses for 2008–2009. NR = Not reported.
For public institutions where tuition differs according to residence, the in-state tuition and fees are shown.

Performing Arts

| | Dance | Music | Theater | Enroll-ment | Tuition and Fees | Summer Programs | Page |
|---|---|---|---|---|---|---|---|
| **Oklahoma**—*continued* | | | | | | | |
| Southwestern Oklahoma State University | | BM, BMEd, MM | | 5,017 | 3750* | Music | 310 |
| University of Oklahoma | BFA, MFA | | BFA, MA, MFA | 26,205 | 4534* | Dance, Theater | 215, 399 |
| **Oregon** | | | | | | | |
| Marylhurst University | | BM, BMT | | 1,433 | 15,570* | | 278 |
| Southern Oregon University | | | BFA | 4,801 | 5409* | | 391 |
| University of Oregon | | BM, MA, MM, PhD, DMA | | 20,332 | 6036* | | 338 |
| Willamette University | | BM | | 2,720 | 31,968* | | 359 |
| **Pennsylvania** | | | | | | | |
| Bucknell University | | BM | | 3,677 | 39,652** | | 233 |
| Carnegie Mellon University | | BFA, MM | | 10,493 | 39,564** | Music | 238 |
| The Curtis Institute of Music | | BM, MM | | | NR | | 250 |
| Drexel University | | BS, BS/MBA | | 20,682 | 30,440** | Music | 252 |
| Duquesne University | | BM, BS, MM | | 10,296 | 23,950* | Music | 252 |
| Grove City College | | BM | | 2,504 | 11,500* | | 258 |
| Immaculata University | | BM, MA | | 4,038 | 22,650* | | 262 |
| Lebanon Valley College | | BM, BS, MME | | 1,936 | 27,800* | | 272 |
| Mansfield University of Pennsylvania | | BM, MA | | 3,338 | 7004* | | 277 |
| Moravian College | | BM | | 1,917 | 28,388* | | 282 |
| Penn State University Park | | BM, BMA, BME, MA, MM, MME, PhD | BFA, MFA | 43,252 | 12,844* | | 296, 386 |
| Philadelphia Biblical University | | BM | | 1,388 | 17,785** | | 296 |
| Point Park University | BA, BA/BFA | | BA/BFA, MFA | 3,592 | 18,990* | Dance, Theater | 206, 386 |

* Expenses for 2007–2008.   ** Estimated expenses for 2008–2009.   NR = Not reported.
For public institutions where tuition differs according to residence, the in-state tuition and fees are shown.

| | Dance | Music | Theater | Enroll-ment | Tuition and Fees | Summer Programs | Page |
|---|---|---|---|---|---|---|---|
| **Pennsylvania**—*continued* | | | | | | | |
| Seton Hill University | | BM | | 1,967 | 25,006* | | 305 |
| Slippery Rock University of Pennsylvania | BA | | | 8,325 | 6671* | | 210 |
| Susquehanna University | | BM | | 2,039 | 31,080** | | 312 |
| Temple University | | BM, BS, MM, MMT, PhD, DMA | | 34,696 | 10,802* | | 313 |
| The University of the Arts | BFA | BM, MAT, MM | BFA | 2,396 | 30,600** | Dance, Music, Theater | 216, 345, 403 |
| Westminster College | | BM | | 1,593 | 25,530* | | 356 |
| **Puerto Rico** | | | | | | | |
| Conservatory of Music of Puerto Rico | | BM, MM | | | NR | Music | 248 |
| **Rhode Island** | | | | | | | |
| University of Rhode Island | | BA, BA/BS, BM, MM | BFA | 15,650 | 8184* | | 340, 400 |
| **South Carolina** | | | | | | | |
| Anderson University | | BMEd | | 1,902 | 17,400** | | 222 |
| Coker College | | BMEd | | 634 | 18,602* | | 244 |
| Columbia College | BFA | | | 1,510 | 21,650* | | 199 |
| Furman University | | BM | | 2,951 | 31,560* | | 256 |
| Lander University | | BS | | 2,408 | 8278* | | 270 |
| University of South Carolina | | BM, MM, MMEd, PhD, DMA | | 27,272 | 8346** | | 342 |
| Winthrop University | | BM, BME, MM, MME | | 6,382 | 10,210* | Music | 360 |
| **South Dakota** | | | | | | | |
| Northern State University | | BA, BMEd | | 2,578 | 5280* | | 291 |
| South Dakota State University | | BMEd, BS | | 11,645 | 5373* | | 307 |
| The University of South Dakota | | BM, MM | BFA, MFA | 9,243 | 5392* | | 342, 400 |

* Expenses for 2007–2008.   ** Estimated expenses for 2008–2009.   NR = Not reported.
For public institutions where tuition differs according to residence, the in-state tuition and fees are shown.

| | Dance | Music | Theater | Enroll-ment | Tuition and Fees | Summer Programs | Page |
|---|---|---|---|---|---|---|---|
| **Tennessee** | | | | | | | |
| Belmont University | | BM, MM | | 4,756 | 21,110** | | 226 |
| Carson-Newman College | | BM | | 2,012 | 16,980* | | 238 |
| Lambuth University | | BA, BM, BS | | 751 | 17,400* | | 270 |
| Lee University | | BA, BM, BMEd, BS, MCM, MMME | | 4,086 | 10,782* | Music | 272 |
| Tennessee Wesleyan College | | BMEd | | 861 | 17,050** | | 314 |
| The University of Tennessee | | BM, MM | | 29,937 | 6188** | | 344 |
| The University of Tennessee at Chattanooga | | BM, MM | | 9,558 | 5062* | | 344 |
| The University of Tennessee at Martin | BFA | BM | BFA | 7,173 | 5005* | | 216, 344, 402 |
| Vanderbilt University | | BM, BM/MEd | | 11,847 | 35,276* | | 352 |
| **Texas** | | | | | | | |
| Abilene Christian University | | BM | | 4,675 | 17,410* | | 221 |
| Baylor University | | BM, BMEd MM | BFA, MFA | 14,174 | 26,234** | | 226, 365 |
| East Texas Baptist University | | BM | | 1,308 | 14,680* | | 253 |
| Hardin-Simmons University | | BM, MM | | 2,435 | 18,380** | Music | 259 |
| Howard Payne University | | BM | | 1,385 | 17,400** | | 260 |
| Lamar University | | BM, MM, MMEd | | 10,595 | 4607* | | 269 |
| Rice University | | BM, MM, DMA | | 5,243 | 30,479** | | 299 |
| Sam Houston State University | | BM, MM | | 16,454 | 5566* | | 303 |
| Southern Methodist University | BFA, MFA | | BFA, MFA | 10,829 | 33,198** | | 210, 391 |
| Southwestern University | | BM | BFA | 1,294 | 25,740* | Theater | 310, 391 |
| Stephen F. Austin State University | | BM, MA, MM | BFA | 11,607 | 6162* | | 311, 392 |
| Texas A&M University–Kingsville | | BM, MM | | | 4386* | | 314 |

* Expenses for 2007–2008.   ** Estimated expenses for 2008–2009.   NR = Not reported.
For public institutions where tuition differs according to residence, the in-state tuition and fees are shown.

| | Dance | Music | Theater | Enroll-ment | Tuition and Fees | Summer Programs | Page |
|---|---|---|---|---|---|---|---|
| **Texas**—*continued* | | | | | | | |
| Texas Christian University | BFA, MFA | BM, BMEd, MM, MMEd | | 8,668 | 24,868* | Dance | 211, 314 |
| University of Houston | | BM, MM, DMA | BA, MA, MFA | 34,663 | 7450* | | 325, 395 |
| University of North Texas | | BM, MM, MME, DMA | | 34,153 | 6320* | Music | 337 |
| The University of Texas at Austin | | | BFA, MFA, PhD | 50,170 | 7670* | | 402 |
| The University of Texas at San Antonio | | BM, MM | | 28,533 | 6677* | | 345 |
| University of the Incarnate Word | | BA, BMEd, BMT | | 5,752 | 20,260** | | 346 |
| West Texas A&M University | BFA, MA | BM, MA, MM | | 7,502 | NR | Dance | 219, 357 |
| **Utah** | | | | | | | |
| Brigham Young University | | | BA, BFA, MA, MFA | 34,174 | 7680* | Theater | 368 |
| University of Utah | BFA, MA, MFA | BA, BM, BMEd, MA, MM, MMEd, PhD, DMA | BFA | 28,025 | 4986* | | 217, 347, 403 |
| Utah State University | | BM, BS | | 14,893 | 4200* | | 351 |
| Weber State University | | BM, BMEd | | 18,081 | 3663* | | 354 |
| **Virginia** | | | | | | | |
| Christopher Newport University | | BM, MAT | | 4,884 | 10,138* | | 242 |
| James Madison University | | BM, MM, DMA | | 17,918 | 6666* | | 266 |
| Liberty University | | BM, BS | | 27,063 | 15,800* | | 273 |
| Longwood University | | BM | BA, BFA | 4,727 | 8058* | | 274, 380 |
| Norfolk State University | | BM, MM | | | 5322* | Music | 289 |
| Radford University | BFA | BM, MS | | 9,122 | 6176* | Dance, Music | 208, 298 |

* Expenses for 2007–2008.   ** Estimated expenses for 2008–2009.   NR = Not reported.
For public institutions where tuition differs according to residence, the in-state tuition and fees are shown.

| | Dance | Music | Theater | Enroll-ment | Tuition and Fees | Summer Programs | Page |
|---|---|---|---|---|---|---|---|
| **Virginia**—*continued* | | | | | | | |
| Shenandoah University | BFA, MA, MFA, MS | BM, BMT, BS, MM, MME, MMT, MS, DMA | BFA | 3,393 | 23,340** | Music | 209, 305, 390 |
| Virginia Commonwealth University | BFA | BA, BM, MM | BA, BFA, MFA | 31,907 | 6196* | Dance | 218, 352, 405 |
| Virginia Intermont College | | | BFA | 635 | 22,150* | | 406 |
| **Washington** | | | | | | | |
| Central Washington University | | BM, MM | | 10,505 | 5723** | | 241 |
| Cornish College of the Arts | BFA | BM | BFA, BFA | 768 | 24,000* | Dance | 200, 249, 372 |
| Pacific Lutheran University | | BM, BMA, BME | | 3,661 | 25,088* | | 295 |
| University of Puget Sound | | BM | | 2,799 | 31,895* | | 339 |
| University of Washington | | BM, MM, PhD, DMA | | 40,218 | 6385* | | 348 |
| Walla Walla University | | BM | | 1,829 | 21,945* | | 353 |
| Washington State University | | BM, BMEd, MA | | 24,396 | 6866* | | 354 |
| **West Virginia** | | | | | | | |
| Marshall University | | | BFA | 13,808 | 4560* | | 380 |
| West Virginia University | | BM, MM, PhD, DMA | BFA, MFA | 28,113 | 4722* | | 358, 407 |
| **Wisconsin** | | | | | | | |
| Alverno College | | BM | | 2,480 | 17,296* | | 221 |
| Lawrence University | | BA/BM, BM | | 1,451 | 31,080* | | 270 |
| Silver Lake College | | BM, MM | | 832 | 19,194** | | 306 |
| University of Wisconsin–Green Bay | | BM | | 6,083 | 5959* | | 348 |
| University of Wisconsin–Madison | | BM, MMA, MMEd, DMA | | 42,041 | 8047* | Music | 348 |
| University of Wisconsin–Milwaukee | BFA, MFA | BFA, MM | BFA | 29,338 | 7727* | | 218, 349, 404 |

\* Expenses for 2007–2008.  \*\* Estimated expenses for 2008–2009.  NR = Not reported.
For public institutions where tuition differs according to residence, the in-state tuition and fees are shown.

| | Dance | Music | Theater | Enroll-ment | Tuition and Fees | Summer Programs | Page |
|---|---|---|---|---|---|---|---|
| **Wisconsin**—*continued* | | | | | | | |
| University of Wisconsin–Oshkosh | | BM, BMEd | | 12,693 | 5693* | | 349 |
| University of Wisconsin–Stevens Point | | BM, MMEd | | 8,888 | 5834* | Music | 349 |
| University of Wisconsin–Superior | | BM, BMEd | BFA | 2,753 | 5907* | Theater | 350, 404 |
| University of Wisconsin–Whitewater | | | BFA | 10,737 | 6730* | | 404 |
| Viterbo University | | BM | BFA | 3,088 | 19,490** | | 353, 406 |
| **Wyoming** | | | | | | | |
| University of Wyoming | BFA | BM, BMEd, MM, MMEd | BFA | 12,875 | 3554* | Dance | 218, 350, 405 |
| **CANADA** | | | | | | | |
| **Alberta** | | | | | | | |
| University of Alberta | | BM, BM/BEd, MA, MM, PhD, DM | | 36,562 | NR | Music | 316 |
| **British Columbia** | | | | | | | |
| The University of British Columbia | | BM, MA, MM, PhD, DMA | | 43,720 | NR | | 318 |
| **Manitoba** | | | | | | | |
| Brandon University | | BM, BM/BEd, MM | | 3,524 | Can$3464* | | 231 |
| University of Manitoba | | BM, BM/BEd, MM | | 25,516 | NR | Music | 327 |
| **New Brunswick** | | | | | | | |
| Mount Allison University | | BM | | 2,170 | Can$6977* | | 283 |

\* Expenses for 2007–2008.   \*\* Estimated expenses for 2008–2009.   NR = Not reported.
For public institutions where tuition differs according to residence, the in-state tuition and fees are shown.

Performing *Arts*

| | Dance | Music | Theater | Enroll-ment | Tuition and Fees | Summer Programs | Page |
|---|---|---|---|---|---|---|---|
| **Nova Scotia** | | | | | | | |
| Acadia University | | BAIM, BM | | 3,333 | Can$8242* | Music | 221 |
| Dalhousie University | | BA, BM | | 15,440 | Can$7582* | | 250 |
| St. Francis Xavier University | | BA, BM | | 4,969 | Can$7350* | | 301 |
| **Ontario** | | | | | | | |
| Brock University | | BA, Mus.B. | | 17,006 | NR | | 232 |
| Carleton University | | BM | | 23,683 | 5341* | | 238 |
| Lakehead University | | HBA, HBM | | 7,837 | 5128* | | 269 |
| Ryerson University | BFA | | | 30,154 | Can$4921* | | 209 |
| University of Windsor | | | BA, BFA | 15,999 | 5393** | Theater | 403 |
| York University | BFA | BFA | BFA, MFA | 51,420 | Can$5278* | | 220, 361, 409 |
| **Prince Edward Island** | | | | | | | |
| University of Prince Edward Island | | BMus, BMusEd | | 4,075 | Can$5177* | | 338 |
| **Quebec** | | | | | | | |
| McGill University | | BM, BM/BEd, MA, MM, PhD, DM | | 31,081 | Can$3189* | | 279 |
| **Saskatchewan** | | | | | | | |
| University of Regina | | BA, BM, BMEd, MA, MM | | 11,819 | Can$4993* | | 339 |

\* Expenses for 2007–2008.   \*\* Estimated expenses for 2008–2009.   NR = Not reported.
For public institutions where tuition differs according to residence, the in-state tuition and fees are shown.

# Profiles of Performing Arts Programs

# Dance Programs

## Adelphi University
**Garden City, New York**

Independent, coed. Suburban campus. Total enrollment: 8,354. Dance program established 1938.
**Web Site** http://www.adelphi.edu/

## The Ailey School/Fordham College at Lincoln Center
See Fordham University

### *The Katherine K. Herberger College of Fine Arts*
## Arizona State University
**Tempe, Arizona**

State-supported, coed. Suburban campus. Total enrollment: 51,481. Dance program established 1937.
**Degrees** Bachelor of Fine Arts. Majors and concentrations: dance education. Graduate degrees offered: Master of Fine Arts in the area of dance.
**Enrollment** 178 total; 150 undergraduate, 28 graduate.
**Dance Student Profile** 86% females, 14% males, 12% minorities, 2% international.
**Dance Faculty** 14 total (full-time), 17 total (part-time). 81% of full-time faculty have terminal degrees. Graduate students teach a few undergraduate courses. Undergraduate student–faculty ratio: 6:1.
**Student Life** Student groups/activities include Repertory Company. Special housing available for dance students.
**Expenses for 2008–2009** Application fee: $50. State resident tuition: $5409 full-time. Nonresident tuition: $17,697 full-time. Mandatory fees: $252 full-time. College room and board: $8797. College room only: $5247. Special program-related fees: $50 per course for accompanist fee, $50 per course for technology fee.
**Financial Aid** Program-specific awards: 10 in-state tuition scholarships for those demonstrating need/talent ($1206), 1 Sun Angel Scholarship for those demonstrating need/talent ($1100), 8 out-of-state tuition scholarships for those demonstrating need/talent ($3933), 1 Herberger Scholarship for those demonstrating need/talent ($2500), 9 summer study scholarships for those demonstrating need/talent ($500).
**Application Procedures** Students admitted directly into the professional program freshman year. Required: essay, high school transcript, college transcript(s) for transfer students, minimum 3.0 high school GPA, audition, SAT or ACT test scores (minimum composite ACT score of 24). Auditions held 3 times on campus; videotaped performances are permissible as a substitute for live auditions.
**Web Site** http://herbergercollege.asu.edu/dance/
**Undergraduate Contact** Ms. Melissa Phelan, Academic Specialist Advisement, Herberger College of the Arts, Arizona State University, PO Box 872102, Tempe, Arizona 85287-2102; 480-965-9432, fax: 480-965-9073.
**Graduate Contact** Pegge Vissicaro, Graduate Advisor, Dance Department, Arizona State University, PO Box 870304, Tempe, Arizona 85287-0304; 480-965-5029, fax: 480-965-2247, e-mail address: pegge@asu.edu

## Belhaven College
**Jackson, Mississippi**

Independent Presbyterian, coed. Urban campus. Total enrollment: 2,485. Dance program established 1997.

**Degrees** Bachelor of Fine Arts in the area of dance. Majors and concentrations: ballet, modern dance. Program accredited by NASD.
**Enrollment** 65 total; 31 undergraduate, 34 nonprofessional degree.
**Dance Student Profile** 90% females, 10% males, 8% minorities.
**Dance Faculty** 4 undergraduate (full-time), 3 undergraduate (part-time). 50% of full-time faculty have terminal degrees. Graduate students do not teach undergraduate courses. Undergraduate student–faculty ratio: 8:1.
**Student Life** Student groups/activities include Belhaven College Dance Ensemble, DOXA (student organization), Swing Club, Urban Dance Club.
**Expenses for 2008–2009** Application fee: $25. Comprehensive fee: $22,480 includes full-time tuition ($16,360) and college room and board ($6120).
**Financial Aid** Program-specific awards: 500 dance scholarships for program students ($8000).
**Application Procedures** Students apply for admission into the professional program by freshman year. Deadline for freshmen and transfers: July 2. Notification date for freshmen and transfers: August 8. Required: high school transcript, college transcript(s) for transfer students, minimum 2.0 high school GPA, letter of recommendation, audition, SAT or ACT test scores (minimum combined SAT score of 930, minimum composite ACT score of 20), letter of intent, snapshots, completed registration form, dance resumé. Recommended: interview, video. Auditions held twice on campus; videotaped performances are permissible as a substitute for live auditions in special circumstances (scholarships not awarded based on video).
**Web Site** http://arts.belhaven.edu/Dance/default.htm
**Undergraduate Contact** Suzanne Sullivan, Director of Admissions, Belhaven College, 1500 Peachtree Street, Box 153, Jackson, Mississippi 39202; 601-968-5940, e-mail address: ssullivan@belhaven.edu

## The Boston Conservatory
**Boston, Massachusetts**

Independent, coed. Urban campus. Total enrollment: 560. Dance program established 1943.
**Degrees** Bachelor of Fine Arts. Majors and concentrations: dance. Cross-registration with ProArts Consortium. Program accredited by NASM.
**Enrollment** 84 total; all undergraduate.
**Dance Student Profile** 84% females, 16% males, 30% minorities, 5% international.
**Dance Faculty** 7 total (full-time), 15 total (part-time). Graduate students do not teach undergraduate courses. Undergraduate student–faculty ratio: 4:1.
**Student Life** Student groups/activities include The Boston Conservatory Dance Theater, Boston Dance Theater. Special housing available for dance students.
**Expenses for 2007–2008** Application fee: $105. Comprehensive fee: $45,739 includes full-time tuition ($28,300), mandatory fees ($1799), and college room and board ($15,640). Full-time tuition and fees vary according to program. Room and board charges vary according to board plan and housing facility.
**Financial Aid** Program-specific awards: 29 Conservatory Scholarships for those passing audition evaluations ($5000–$33,000), 5 Jan Veen Memorial Scholarships for continuing students ($1000–$5000), 1 Ruth S. Ambrose Award for juniors ($1000–$2000), 1 Anamarie Sarazin Award for junior ballet students ($1000–$2000).
**Application Procedures** Students admitted directly into the professional program freshman year. Deadline for freshmen and transfers: December 1. Notification date for freshmen and

*The Boston Conservatory (continued)*

transfers: April 1. Required: essay, high school transcript, college transcript(s) for transfer students, 2 letters of recommendation, interview, audition, minimum TOEFL score of 550 for international applicants, artistic resumé, minimum 2.7 high school GPA. Auditions held throughout January, February, and March on campus and off campus in Los Angeles, CA; Houston, TX; New York, NY; Washington, DC; St. Petersburg, FL; videotaped performances are permissible as a substitute for live auditions when distance is prohibitive.
**Web Site** http://www.bostonconservatory.edu
**Undergraduate Contact** Admissions Office, The Boston Conservatory, 8 The Fenway, Boston, Massachusetts 02215; 617-912-9153, fax: 617-247-3159, e-mail address: admissions@bostonconservatory.edu

### More About the Conservatory

The Boston Conservatory trains exceptional young performing artists for careers that enrich and transform the human experience. Known for its multidisciplinary environment, the Conservatory offers fully accredited graduate and undergraduate programs in music, dance, and theater, and it presents more than 200 performances each year by students, faculty members, and guest artists. The intimacy of the Conservatory's class settings provides a student-centered atmosphere that is uniquely intensive and supportive.

Since its founding in 1867, the Boston Conservatory has shared its talent and creativity with the city of Boston, the region, and the nation, and it continues to grow today as a vibrant community of artists and educators.

The Boston Conservatory Dance Division is one of the oldest degree-granting dance program in the United States. Founded in 1943 by dance innovator and instructor Jan Veen, the Dance Division was the first to offer ballet and modern training as a core curriculum of study. This tradition continues today with additional study in all styles of dance performance.

Daily technique classes provide professional training in ballet and modern dance. In addition, dancers study choreography, pedagogy, music, jazz, tap, and cultural dance styles.

Versatility for a dancer translates into work and performance opportunities; therefore, the Boston Conservatory curriculum requires students to extend themselves and be knowledgeable about music, literature, dance repertory, dance history, Gyrokinesis, Pilates, Alexander Technique, nutrition, and anatomy. To support the dancer, seminars in health and wellness are scheduled throughout the academic year.

Faculty members are current or former members of some of the most prestigious dance organizations in the United States. Their artistry and professional qualifications offer students a full range of dance technique and teaching methods. Faculty members serve as mentors to dancers, forming a nurturing and supportive relationship. Students are thus able to grow and achieve their dreams within a caring, artistic environment.

Performance experience is provided in both studio and mainstage concerts. The range of work performed runs the gamut of dance repertory, in addition to frequent premieres of new works choreographed by artist faculty members or guest artists commissioned by the school. Mainstage concerts are held in collaboration with the Music Division, offering a unique opportunity to collaborate with musicians as part of the performance preparation.

Boston is a major center of higher education in America, with more than fifty major colleges and universities. The city provides a diverse student population and an endless array of courses, lectures, concerts, and social opportunities. The Conservatory is a member of the Pro-Arts Consortium, in conjunction with five area colleges (Emerson College, Berklee College of Music, School of the Museum of Fine Arts, Massachusetts College of Art, and Boston Architectural Center), offering cross-registration course possibilities to all students.

On-campus housing is provided for freshmen. Housing is available to upperclassmen and graduates on a space-available basis, offering brownstone-style living accommodations just a few steps from the main training and rehearsal buildings. For those students interested in off-campus housing, Boston offers a wide range of architectural styles and rent prices in neighborhoods throughout the city that are all within easy access to the school by public transportation.

The Boston Conservatory strives to meet each student's needs—musically and personally—and provides a nurturing, safe environment in which to study, learn, and grow. The supportive atmosphere of the college extends to student life areas as well. More than a dozen special interest groups and organizations exist on campus, with new ones developing constantly as the student population grows and its needs change. As part of the student services, a number of career seminars are given each year ranging from resume writing and audition anxiety to grant writing and tax laws for the performing artist. In addition, there is an active student government and a student-run newspaper.

# Brenau University
## Gainesville, Georgia

Independent, women only. Small town campus. Total enrollment: 916. Dance program established 1978.
**Degrees** Bachelor of Fine Arts in the areas of arts management, dance, dance education. Majors and concentrations: dance, dance education. Program accredited by NASD.
**Enrollment** 46 total; 41 undergraduate, 5 nonprofessional degree.
**Dance Student Profile** 100% females, 24% minorities.
**Dance Faculty** 3 undergraduate (full-time), 3 undergraduate (part-time). 100% of full-time faculty have terminal degrees. Graduate students do not teach undergraduate courses. Undergraduate student–faculty ratio: 14:1.
**Student Life** Student groups/activities include Faculty Concert, Brenau Opera Company, Brenau Dance Ensemble.
**Expenses for 2008–2009** Application fee: $35. Comprehensive fee: $28,287 includes full-time tuition ($18,550), mandatory fees ($250), and college room and board ($9487).
**Financial Aid** Program-specific awards: dance scholarships for program majors ($1000–$5000).
**Application Procedures** Students admitted directly into the professional program freshman year. Deadline for freshmen and transfers: continuous. Notification date for freshmen and transfers: continuous. Required: high school transcript, college transcript(s) for transfer students, letter of recommendation, interview, audition, SAT or ACT test scores (minimum composite ACT score of 19), minimum 2.5 high school GPA. Recommended: minimum 3.0 high school GPA. Auditions held 4 times on campus; videotaped performances are permissible as a substitute for live auditions when distance is prohibitive.
**Web Site** http://www.brenau.edu/sfah
**Undergraduate Contact** Christina White, Coordinator of Admissions, Admissions, Brenau University, 500 Washington Street, SE, Gainesville, Georgia 30501; 800-252-5119, fax: 770-538-4306, e-mail address: cwhite@brenau.edu

*Jordan College of Fine Arts*
# Butler University
## Indianapolis, Indiana

Independent, coed. Urban campus. Total enrollment: 4,479. Dance program established 1913.
**Degrees** Bachelor of Arts in the area of dance pedagogy; Bachelor of Fine Arts in the area of dance performance; Bachelor of Science in the area of dance arts administration. Majors and concentrations: dance arts administration, dance pedagogy, dance performance. Cross-registration with Indianapolis Consortium for Urban Education. Program accredited by NASD.
**Enrollment** 101 total; all undergraduate.
**Dance Student Profile** 88% females, 12% males, 6% minorities, 3% international.
**Dance Faculty** 6 undergraduate (full-time), 8 undergraduate (part-time). 29% of full-time faculty have terminal degrees.

Graduate students do not teach undergraduate courses. Undergraduate student–faculty ratio: 12:1.

**Student Life** Student groups/activities include Butler Ballet, senior production concerts, summer dance concert and touring.

**Expenses for 2007–2008** Application fee: $35. Comprehensive fee: $35,766 includes full-time tuition ($26,070), mandatory fees ($736), and college room and board ($8960). Full-time tuition and fees vary according to program. Room and board charges vary according to housing facility.

**Financial Aid** Program-specific awards: talent awards.

**Application Procedures** Students admitted directly into the professional program freshman year. Deadline for freshmen and transfers: continuous. Required: essay, high school transcript, college transcript(s) for transfer students, minimum 2.0 high school GPA, letter of recommendation, audition, SAT or ACT test scores, 5x7 photo in dance attire and appropriate pose (for male dancer: attitude derriére, female dancer: arabesque on pointe). Recommended: minimum 3.0 high school GPA, interview, portfolio. Auditions held 18 times on campus; videotaped performances are permissible as a substitute for live auditions when residence is outside contiguous 48 states. Portfolio reviews held on campus.

**Web Site** http://www.butler.edu/dance/

**Undergraduate Contact** Kathy Lang, Admission Representative, Jordan College of Fine Arts, Butler University, Lilly Hall - 138B, 4600 Sunset Avenue, Indianapolis, Indiana 46208; 317-940-9656, fax: 317-940-9658, e-mail address: klang@butler.edu

### More About the University

Butler University is most proud of its tradition of excellence and innovation. Challenging and enabling students to meet their personal and professional goals has guided the University since 1855. Today, Butler is an independent, coeducational, nonsectarian university, with a total undergraduate enrollment of more than 3,900 students. The University is accredited by the North Central Association of Colleges and Schools.

Butler's reputation as one of the finest university dance programs in the nation continues, with a department offering the serious dance student professional-level training with a broad approach to liberal arts education. The Department of Dance was among the first in the nation to offer a dance major centered on ballet technique. Many of its graduates have gone on to prestigious professional careers as dancers, teachers, choreographers, managers, and writers.

Dance majors acquire a strong technical training based on the central focus of ballet; versatility in other techniques; the opportunity to perform extensively in a preprofessional company; broad exposure to academic subjects in dance and other arts; and skills in writing, speaking, and analysis from the humanities, mathematics, and science.

**Campus and Surroundings** Indianapolis, Indiana's state capital and the thirteenth-largest city in the nation, boasts a variety of cultural activities, including the Indianapolis Symphony Orchestra, Dance Kaleidoscope, Indiana Repertory Theatre, the Indianapolis Museum of Art, the Eiteljorg Museum, and the world's largest children's museum. Citywide celebrations are plentiful, including ethnic festivals, art fairs, and outdoor music festivals.

**Program Facilities** Butler's Clowes Memorial Hall is a 2,200-seat performance hall that hosts a variety of events, from community arts groups to national and international touring companies and many University performances. The five dance studios in Lilly Hall are equipped with state-of-the-art resilient L'Air modular flooring, barres and mirrors, pianos, and abundant audiovisual equipment. A new performing arts complex is currently under construction. The first phase of the complex, a 47,000-square-foot addition to Lilly Hall called the Courtyard Building, was completed in spring 2003. This new building houses a choral rehearsal hall, an instrumental rehearsal hall, dance studios, a theater studio, an electronic music lab, and a percussion studio. The second phase, the 140-seat Eidson-Duckwall Recital Hall, was completed in fall 2004. The third phase is a 450-seat performance hall/proscenium theater with adjustable acoustical features.

**Faculty/Alumni** Butler's highly qualified teachers are artist-scholars who combine broad educational backgrounds with professional performing careers, in-depth study, choreography, and teaching in the United States, Europe, and Asia. Their diversity, expertise, and experience contribute to the scope of the program. Faculty members provide a direct link to the important developments of dance not only in America, but worldwide. They are soloists, artistic directors, certified movement analysts, principal dancers, ballet masters, and ballet mistresses. Recent graduates are performing with the American Repertory Ballet, Atlanta Ballet, Ballet Arizona, Ballet Austin, Boston Ballet, Dance Kaleidoscope, Dance Theatre of Harlem, Georgia Ballet, San Diego Ballet, *The Producers'* National Tour, and the Broadway production and national tour of *Movin' Out*.

**Student Performance Opportunities** The Butler Ballet is a preprofessional company offering extensive opportunities for performance. The annual presentation of *The Nutcracker* has been an Indianapolis family tradition for more than twenty years. The company also presents full-length classical ballets, such as *Swan Lake, Giselle, Sleeping Beauty, Cinderella,* or *Coppelia.*

Occasionally, the Butler Ballet produces an original contemporary full-length work such as *The Messiah* or Gustav Holst's *The Planets.* In spring 2003, the company presented the world premiere of a new full-length ballet called *The Willow Maiden.*

Butler Ballet performs three to four productions each year on campus in Clowes Memorial Hall, rated among the top facilities in the region, to a total audience of more than 20,000. Butler Ballet performs with a number of symphonies, notably the Indianapolis Chamber Orchestra. For more than thirty years, the company has toured regionally, providing a unique experience for the students.

**Special Programs** Degrees in dance require 136 credit hours, including study in three areas: technique, performance, and dance academics. Butler is one of very few schools accredited to offer a Bachelor of Fine Arts degree in performance. Butler also offers a Bachelor of Arts in dance-pedagogy and a Bachelor of Science in dance-arts administration. Students may also opt to have dance as a secondary major or minor.

**Cooperative Agreements** Butler University has collaborative relationships with many local arts organizations, including the Indianapolis Opera. The following collaborative groups are located on campus: Dance Kaleidoscope, Indianapolis Symphonic Choir, Indianapolis Chamber Orchestra, American Pianists Association, and the Indianapolis Children's Choir.

**Career Placement Services and Opportunities** Graduates of the dance department excel as dancers, teachers, choreographers, and artistic directors with professional, semi-professional, and regional companies as well as on Broadway or in musical theater and film productions. Some work for universities and private studios while others combine their knowledge with other artistic disciplines to become photographers or designers of costumes, sets, and lighting. Arts management or dance research and criticism are additional career choices. Graduates qualify for a wide variety of careers due to the diverse curricula and personalized advising from Butler's faculty members. The University's Center for Career Planning and Development and the Department of Dance both play an active role in assisting dance majors with job opportunities.

# California Institute of the Arts
## Valencia, California

Independent, coed. Suburban campus. Total enrollment: 1,324. Dance program established 1961.

**Degrees** Bachelor of Fine Arts in the area of dance. Majors and concentrations: dance. Graduate degrees offered: Master of Fine Arts in the areas of dance, integrated media. Program accredited by NASD.

**Enrollment** 90 total; 84 undergraduate, 4 graduate, 2 nonprofessional degree.

*California Institute of the Arts (continued)*

**Dance Student Profile** 78% females, 22% males, 39% minorities, 8% international.

**Dance Faculty** 8 total (full-time), 10 total (part-time). 100% of full-time faculty have terminal degrees. Graduate students do not teach undergraduate courses. Undergraduate student–faculty ratio: 5:1.

**Student Life** Student groups/activities include American College Dance Festival Association. Special housing available for dance students.

**Expenses for 2008–2009** Application fee: $70. Comprehensive fee: $42,084 includes full-time tuition ($32,860), mandatory fees ($576), and college room and board ($8648). College room only: $4985.

**Financial Aid** Program-specific awards: 30–35 Sharon Lund Scholarships for program majors ($2000–$10,000).

**Application Procedures** Students admitted directly into the professional program freshman year. Deadline for freshmen and transfers: January 5. Required: essay, high school transcript, college transcript(s) for transfer students, 2 letters of recommendation, audition. Auditions held 7 times on campus and off campus in New York, NY; Boston, MA; San Francisco, CA; videotaped performances are permissible as a substitute for live auditions with approval from the department and for international students.

**Web Site** http://www.calarts.edu

**Contact** Ms. Zari Wigfall, Admissions Counselor, School of Dance, California Institute of the Arts, 24700 McBean Parkway, Valencia, California 91355; 661-253-7771, fax: 661-253-1562, e-mail address: zwigfall@calarts.edu

### More About the Institute

Located in Valencia in Southern California, the California Institute of the Arts (CalArts) School of Dance offers a Bachelor of Fine Arts (B.F.A.) degree in dance performance/choreography/production and a Master of Fine Arts (M.F.A.) degree in choreography. The B.F.A degree program carries with it a complete component of general studies as presented by the School of Critical Studies. An audition is required of all incoming students. Acceptance into the program is based solely on talent. Information on times, locations, and dates is available from the School of Dance office and the Office of Enrollment Services.

The B.F.A curriculum places a strong emphasis on the individual development of each dancer through modern and ballet techniques, performance opportunities, and dance production and nurtures creative freedom through dance composition and choreography. Because of a low student-faculty ratio, equal importance is placed on studies relating to dance, such as production technology, music, dance history, anatomy, kinesiology, video, digital technologies, production crewing, Pilates, and African and Indonesian dance as electives. Interdisciplinary collaboration is encouraged on all levels, broadening the future of dance in ways that constantly challenge the imagination.

**Program Facilities** The CalArts Sharon Disney Lund Dance Theater is a 50-foot-by-70-foot space used exclusively for dance performances, rehearsals, and classes. This hall features wall-to-wall *L Air* sprung flooring covered with seamless black *Lonstage*. Retractable theater seating allows for many different staging configurations. Seating capacity is usually 125 persons, with a maximum capacity of 250.

In addition to the Sharon Disney Lund Dance Theater, there are three other full-time dance studios available for technique classes, composition classes, and rehearsals. The two larger dance studios measure 36-feet-by-50-feet each. Each studio has one mirrored wall and barres set into the other three walls, and is equipped with a set of eight portable barres, a piano, and power outlets for sound and video equipment. Both spaces have *L Air* sprung floors covered in seamless *Lonstage*. The third studio is 39-feet-by-23-feet and has a sprung wooded floor, a full wall of mirrors, and a chalkboard.

A fully carpeted Pilates body-conditioning studio measures 39-feet-by-23-feet. It has a mirrored wall and includes the following equipment: four Pilates studio reformers, two trapeze tables, one Wunda chair, one whale, four tumbling mats, and one Pacemaster Pro-Plus treadmill.

The School of Dance's array of digital, video, and sound equipment allows M.F.A. and upper-division B.F.A students to experiment with multi-track mixing and video editing techniques while creating movement-themed DVDs as well as Web page design. Digital video is incorporated into documenting all dance works and a variety of other classroom and production purposes.

In downtown Los Angeles, The Roy and Edna Disney/CalArts Theater, otherwise known as REDCAT, is housed as a separate entity in the stunning, Frank Gehry–designed Walt Disney Concert Hall. REDCAT is conceived as a unique platform to showcase CalArts experimental and interdisciplinary work in dance, theater, music, the visual arts, and film/video.

**Faculty and Alumni** The School's faculty consists of well-known, seasoned professional artists who are continuing to pursue and explore dance while teaching. The School of Dance faculty members include Stephan Koplowitz, Dean; Cynthia Young, Associate Dean; Laurence Blake, Assistant Dean; David Kroth; Fontella Boone; Colin Connor; John Gaydos; Kate Fox; Ed Groff; Francesca Penzani; Robin Cox; Rosanna Gamson; Cheryl Montelle; Stephanie Nugent; John Pennington; Mitchell Rose; and Glen Eddy.

The School of Dance has alumni performing in dance and touring companies, choreographing, directing, and teaching. Among these include Dallas McMurray, who dances with the Mark Morrison Company; Brooke Smiley, who tours with Transitions Dance Company in London, England; Jamie Bishton, artistic director of Jamie Bishton/Dance in New York City; Keisha Clarke, who tours with the Garth Fagan Dance Company in Rochester, New York; Qi Zhang, choreographer; Laura Gorenstein, artistic director of Helios Dance Theater in Los Angeles; Dawn Stoppiello, co-artistic director of Troika Ranch in New York City; Yuan-Yuan Wang, choreographer; Jacques Heim, artistic director of the Diavolo Dance Theater in Los Angeles; and others.

**Student Performance/Exhibit Opportunities** The School of Dance's performance schedule features as many as six regularly scheduled dance concerts, Winter and Spring concerts, and three to five graduate thesis dance concerts.

**Special Programs** The School of Dance has an ongoing exchange program with the London Contemporary Dance School. Each fall, two upper-division undergraduates selected by the dean and faculty enjoy the unique opportunity to study abroad for one semester.

# California State University, Long Beach

### Long Beach, California

State-supported, coed. Suburban campus. Total enrollment: 36,868. Dance program established 1970.

**Degrees** Bachelor of Fine Arts in the area of dance. Majors and concentrations: dance. Graduate degrees offered: Master of Fine Arts in the area of dance. Program accredited by NASD.

**Enrollment** 40 undergraduate, 10 graduate, 80 nonprofessional degree.

**Dance Student Profile** 85% females, 15% males, 35% minorities, 10% international.

**Dance Faculty** 10 total (full-time), 17 total (part-time). 90% of full-time faculty have terminal degrees. Graduate students do not teach undergraduate courses. Undergraduate student–faculty ratio: 15:1.

**Student Life** Student groups/activities include Off 7th Dancers.

**Expenses for 2008–2009** Application fee: $55. Nonresident tuition: $10,170 full-time. Mandatory fees: $3394 full-time. College room and board: $7940.

**Financial Aid** Program-specific awards: 1 Fine Arts Affiliates Award for program majors ($1000), 2 Dramatic Allied Arts Guild Awards for program majors ($1000), 4 rotating awards for

program majors ($1000–$1200), 2 Lana Alper Awards for program majors ($2000), 1 Joan Schlaich Award for program majors ($1000), 2–4 Gloria Newman Awards for program majors ($500–$1000), 2–5 new student scholarships for majors ($500–$1500).
**Application Procedures** Students apply for admission into the professional program by sophomore, junior year. Deadline for freshmen: November 30; transfers: March 1. Required: high school transcript, college transcript(s) for transfer students, minimum 2.0 high school GPA, audition, SAT or ACT test scores, self-choreographed solo performance as part of the audition (for transfer students). Recommended: minimum 3.0 high school GPA. Auditions held 3-4 times on campus; videotaped performances are permissible as a substitute for live auditions for out-of-state and international applicants.
**Web Site** http://www.csulb.edu/depts/dance/
**Undergraduate Contact** Susan McLain, Professor, California State University, Long Beach, 1250 Bellflower Boulevard, Long Beach, California 90840-7201; 562-985-7008, fax: 562-985-7896, e-mail address: smsmith@csulb.edu
**Graduate Contact** Judy Allen, Professor, Department of Dance, California State University, Long Beach, 1250 Bellflower Boulevard, Long Beach, California 90840-7201; 562-985-4748, fax: 562-985-7896.

# Chapman University
## Orange, California

Independent, coed. Suburban campus. Total enrollment: 6,022.
**Degrees** Bachelor of Fine Arts in the area of dance performance. Majors and concentrations: performance.
**Enrollment** 78 total; 8 undergraduate, 70 nonprofessional degree.
**Dance Student Profile** 90% females, 10% males, 10% minorities, 1% international.
**Dance Faculty** 4 undergraduate (full-time), 11 undergraduate (part-time). 100% of full-time faculty have terminal degrees. Graduate students do not teach undergraduate courses. Undergraduate student–faculty ratio: 2:1.
**Student Life** Student groups/activities include Chapman Dance Association, American Celebration.
**Expenses for 2008–2009** Application fee: $55. Comprehensive fee: $46,015 includes full-time tuition ($33,760), mandatory fees ($940), and college room and board ($11,315).
**Financial Aid** Program-specific awards: 25 talent awards for incoming students ($5000).
**Application Procedures** Students apply for admission into the professional program by sophomore year. Deadline for freshmen: January 31; transfers: March 15. Required: essay, high school transcript, college transcript(s) for transfer students, minimum 2.0 high school GPA, 2 letters of recommendation, audition, SAT or ACT test scores, recent photograph, resumé. Recommended: interview. Auditions held 9 times on campus; videotaped performances are permissible as a substitute for live auditions with permission of the Department Secretary.
**Web Site** http://www.chapman.edu/sac/dance/
**Undergraduate Contact** Ms. Heather Stoltzfus, Department Secretary, Department of Dance, Chapman University, 1 University Drive, Orange, California 92866; 714-628-1411, fax: 714-628-0405, e-mail address: dance@chapman.edu

# The College at Brockport, State University of New York
## Brockport, New York

State-supported, coed. Small town campus. Total enrollment: 8,303. Dance program established 1970.
**Degrees** Bachelor of Fine Arts. Majors and concentrations: dance. Graduate degrees offered: Master of Fine Arts in the area of dance. Program accredited by NASD.
**Enrollment** 110 total; 40 undergraduate, 10 graduate, 60 nonprofessional degree.
**Dance Student Profile** 95% females, 5% males, 10% minorities, 6% international.

**Dance Faculty** 10 total (full-time), 13 total (part-time). 80% of full-time faculty have terminal degrees. Graduate students do not teach undergraduate courses. Undergraduate student–faculty ratio: 3:1.
**Student Life** Student groups/activities include Dance Club, Scholars Day, Freshman Convocation.
**Expenses for 2008–2009** Application fee: $40. State resident tuition: $4350 full-time. Nonresident tuition: $10,610 full-time. Mandatory fees: $1092 full-time. College room and board: $8597. College room only: $5682.
**Financial Aid** Program-specific awards: 2–3 Friars Foundation Scholarships for talented sophomores, juniors ($2500), 1 Pylyshenko-Strasser Award for freshmen ($1000), 1–3 Lipson Summer Study Awards for returning students ($1000).
**Application Procedures** Students apply for admission into the professional program by freshman year. Deadline for freshmen and transfers: March 22. Required: essay, high school transcript, college transcript(s) for transfer students, minimum 3.0 high school GPA, audition, SAT or ACT test scores. Recommended: letter of recommendation, interview. Auditions held 3 times on campus; videotaped performances are permissible as a substitute for live auditions for international applicants.
**Web Site** http://www.brockport.edu/dance
**Undergraduate Contact** Jacquie Davis, Undergraduate Program Director, Department of Dance, The College at Brockport, State University of New York, Hartwell Hall, Brockport, New York 14420; 585-395-5303, fax: 585-395-5134, e-mail address: jdavis@brockport.edu
**Graduate Contact** Darwin Prioleau, Graduate Program Director, Department of Dance, The College at Brockport, State University of New York, Hartwell Hall, Brockport, New York 14420; 585-395-2153, fax: 585-395-5134, e-mail address: dpriolea@brockport.edu

# College-Conservatory of Music Dance Division
See University of Cincinnati

# Columbia College
## Columbia, South Carolina

Independent United Methodist, Suburban campus. Total enrollment: 1,510. Dance program established 1976.
**Degrees** Bachelor of Fine Arts in the area of dance performance and choreography. Majors and concentrations: choreography, dance performance. Program accredited by NASD.
**Enrollment** 53 total; 9 undergraduate, 44 nonprofessional degree.
**Dance Student Profile** 100% females, 26% minorities.
**Dance Faculty** 4 undergraduate (full-time), 2 undergraduate (part-time). 50% of full-time faculty have terminal degrees. Graduate students do not teach undergraduate courses. Undergraduate student–faculty ratio: 8:1.
**Student Life** Student groups/activities include American College Dance Festival Association, The Power Company-Resident Professional Contemporary Dance Company, South Carolina Dancing Association (SCDA).
**Expenses for 2007–2008** Application fee: $25. Comprehensive fee: $27,882 includes full-time tuition ($21,200), mandatory fees ($450), and college room and board ($6232). Full-time tuition and fees vary according to class time. Room and board charges vary according to board plan and housing facility.
**Financial Aid** Program-specific awards: 10 dance scholarships for program majors ($3000–$5000).
**Application Procedures** Students apply for admission into the professional program by freshman, sophomore year. Deadline for freshmen and transfers: continuous. Required: high school transcript, college transcript(s) for transfer students, minimum 2.0 high school GPA, 4 letters of recommendation, audition, SAT or ACT test scores (minimum composite ACT score of 21). Recommended: essay, interview. Auditions held once and by appointment on campus; recorded music is permissible as a substitute for live auditions for out-of-state applicants and

*Columbia College (continued)*

videotaped performances are permissible as a substitute for live auditions for out-of-state applicants. Portfolio reviews held twice on campus.

**Web Site** http://www.columbiacollegesc.edu

**Undergraduate Contact** Ms. Patty Graham, MA, Associate Professor, Dance Department, Columbia College, 1301 Columbia College Drive, Columbia, South Carolina 29203; 803-786-3668, fax: 803-786-3868, e-mail address: pgraham@colacoll.edu

# Columbia College Chicago

## Chicago, Illinois

Independent, coed. Urban campus. Total enrollment: 11,499. Dance program established 1970.

**Degrees** Bachelor of Arts in the area of dance; Bachelor of Fine Arts in the area of dance. Majors and concentrations: choreography, dance education, performance, teacher certification.

**Enrollment** 295 total; 224 undergraduate, 63 graduate, 8 nonprofessional degree.

**Dance Student Profile** 94% females, 6% males, 31% minorities.

**Dance Faculty** 11 undergraduate (full-time), 31 undergraduate (part-time), 3 graduate (full-time), 4 graduate (part-time). Graduate students do not teach undergraduate courses. Undergraduate student–faculty ratio: 6:1.

**Expenses for 2007–2008** Application fee: $35. Comprehensive fee: $29,652 includes full-time tuition ($17,104), mandatory fees ($530), and college room and board ($12,018). College room only: $9048. Special program-related fees: $5–$415 per course for class fees.

**Financial Aid** Program-specific awards: 2 Forrest Foundation Dance Scholarships ($1500).

**Application Procedures** Students admitted directly into the professional program freshman year. Deadline for freshmen and transfers: continuous. Notification date for freshmen and transfers: continuous. Required: essay, high school transcript, college transcript(s) for transfer students, letter of recommendation, meeting with admissions counselor for a personal interview and possible remediation program attendance for students with less than a 2.0 GPA, audition and portfolio for transfer students. Recommended: minimum 2.0 high school GPA, interview, SAT or ACT test scores. Auditions held on campus. Portfolio reviews held continuously on campus.

**Web Site** http://www.colum.edu

**Undergraduate Contact** Mr. Murphy Monroe, Director, Office of Admissions, Columbia College Chicago, 600 South Michigan Avenue, Chicago, Illinois 60605; 312-344-7133, fax: 312-344-8024, e-mail address: admissions@colum.edu

# Concordia University

## Montreal, Quebec, Canada

Province-supported, coed. Urban campus. Total enrollment: 32,416. Dance program established 1979.

**Web Site** http://www.concordia.ca/

# Cornish College of the Arts

## Seattle, Washington

Independent, coed. Urban campus. Total enrollment: 768 (2006). Dance program established 1914.

**Degrees** Bachelor of Fine Arts in the area of dance. Majors and concentrations: ballet, choreography and performance, modern dance.

**Enrollment** 92 total; all undergraduate.

**Dance Student Profile** 65% females, 35% males, 14% minorities, 3% international.

**Dance Faculty** 6 undergraduate (full-time), 13 undergraduate (part-time). 58% of full-time faculty have terminal degrees. Graduate students do not teach undergraduate courses. Undergraduate student–faculty ratio: 5:1.

**Student Life** Student groups/activities include Cornish Dance Theater.

**Expenses for 2007–2008** Application fee: $35. Tuition: $23,700 full-time. Mandatory fees: $300 full-time.

**Financial Aid** Program-specific awards: Nellie Scholarships for new students, departmental scholarships for new and continuing students, Presidential Scholarships for continuing students.

**Application Procedures** Students admitted directly into the professional program freshman year. Deadline for freshmen and transfers: August 15. Required: essay, high school transcript, college transcript(s) for transfer students, minimum 2.0 high school GPA, audition. Recommended: minimum 3.0 high school GPA, 2 letters of recommendation, interview, SAT or ACT test scores. Auditions held 10 times on campus and off campus in various sites in northern and southern California, Interlochen, MI; Perpich School (Minneapolis, MN); videotaped performances are permissible as a substitute for live auditions when distance is prohibitive.

**Web Site** http://www.cornish.edu

**Undergraduate Contact** Sharron Starling, Director of Admission, Cornish College of the Arts, 1000 Lenora, Seattle, Washington 98121; 800-726-ARTS, fax: 206-720-1011, e-mail address: sstarling@cornish.edu

# East Carolina University

## Greenville, North Carolina

State-supported, coed. Urban campus. Total enrollment: 25,990. Dance program established 1962.

**Degrees** Bachelor of Fine Arts in the areas of dance, dance education. Majors and concentrations: ballet, dance education, jazz dance, modern dance.

**Enrollment** 85 total; 70 undergraduate, 15 nonprofessional degree.

**Dance Student Profile** 75% females, 25% males, 4% minorities, 1% international.

**Dance Faculty** 6 total (full-time), 2 total (part-time). 95% of full-time faculty have terminal degrees. Graduate students do not teach undergraduate courses. Undergraduate student–faculty ratio: 25:1.

**Student Life** Student groups/activities include guest artists/visiting artists, Day of Dance, master classes.

**Expenses for 2007–2008** Application fee: $60. State resident tuition: $2431 full-time. Nonresident tuition: $12,945 full-time. Mandatory fees: $1937 full-time. College room and board: $7150. College room only: $4150. Room and board charges vary according to board plan and housing facility.

**Financial Aid** Program-specific awards: 3 endowed scholarships for program majors ($500–$1000).

**Application Procedures** Students apply for admission into the professional program by sophomore year. Deadline for freshmen: March 15; transfers: April 15. Required: high school transcript, college transcript(s) for transfer students, audition, SAT or ACT test scores. Recommended: minimum 2.0 high school GPA, 3 letters of recommendation. Auditions held twice on campus.

**Web Site** http://www.theatre-dance.ecu.edu

**Undergraduate Contact** Undergraduate Admissions, East Carolina University, Wichard Building, Greenville, North Carolina 27858-4353; 252-328-6640, e-mail address: admis@mail.ecu.edu

# Eastern Michigan University

## Ypsilanti, Michigan

State-supported, coed. Suburban campus. Total enrollment: 22,638. Dance program established 1951.

**Web Site** http://www.emich.edu/

# Feinstein College of Arts and Sciences

See Roger Williams University

# Florida State University
## Tallahassee, Florida

State-supported, coed. Suburban campus. Total enrollment: 40,555. Dance program established 1965.

**Degrees** Bachelor of Fine Arts in the area of dance. Majors and concentrations: dance. Graduate degrees offered: Master of Arts in the areas of American dance studies, dance; Master of Fine Arts in the area of dance. Cross-registration with Florida Agricultural and Mechanical University. Program accredited by NASD.

**Enrollment** 706 total; 73 undergraduate, 33 graduate, 600 nonprofessional degree.

**Dance Student Profile** 92% females, 8% males, 22% minorities.

**Dance Faculty** 18 total (full-time), 1 total (part-time). 55% of full-time faculty have terminal degrees. Graduate students teach about a quarter of undergraduate courses. Undergraduate student–faculty ratio: 4:1.

**Student Life** Student groups/activities include American College Dance Festival Association, Florida Dance Association.

**Expenses for 2007–2008** Application fee: $30. State resident tuition: $3355 full-time. Nonresident tuition: $16,487 full-time. Full-time tuition varies according to location. College room and board: $8000. College room only: $4700. Room and board charges vary according to board plan and housing facility.

**Financial Aid** Program-specific awards: 25 out-of-state tuition waivers for program majors ($2400–$3200), 8 talent and need awards for program majors ($250–$1000).

**Application Procedures** Students admitted directly into the professional program freshman year. Deadline for freshmen: March 3; transfers: July 3. Required: high school transcript, college transcript(s) for transfer students, minimum 3.0 high school GPA, audition, SAT or ACT test scores, video for international applicants. Recommended: 3 letters of recommendation. Auditions held 3 times on campus.

**Web Site** http://dance.fsu.edu/

**Undergraduate Contact** Ms. Janie Brown, Academic Services Coordinator, Department of Dance, Florida State University, Room 148 Montgomery Gym, Tallahassee, Florida 32306-2120; 850-644-1023, fax: 850-644-1277.

**Graduate Contact** Ms. Patricia H. Phillips, Co-Chairperson, Department of Dance, Florida State University, Room 201 Montgomery Gym, Tallahassee, Florida 32306-2120; 850-644-1024, fax: 850-644-1277.

## *The Ailey School/Fordham College at Lincoln Center*
# Fordham University
## New York, New York

Independent Roman Catholic (Jesuit), coed. Urban campus. Total enrollment: 14,448. Dance program established 1998.

**Degrees** Bachelor of Fine Arts in the area of dance. Majors and concentrations: dance.

**Enrollment** 86 undergraduate.

**Dance Student Profile** 60% females, 40% males, 23% minorities, 3% international.

**Dance Faculty** 4 undergraduate (full-time), 56 undergraduate (part-time). Graduate students do not teach undergraduate courses. Undergraduate student–faculty ratio: 12:1.

**Student Life** Student groups/activities include Global Outreach (service), resident advisers, open house dance demonstrations.

**Expenses for 2007–2008** Application fee: $50. Comprehensive fee: $45,157 includes full-time tuition ($31,800), mandatory fees ($1057), and college room and board ($12,300). Room and board charges vary according to board plan and location. Special program-related fees: $60 per semester for physical therapy.

**Application Procedures** Students admitted directly into the professional program freshman year. Deadline for freshmen and transfers: January 15. Notification date for freshmen and transfers: April 1. Required: essay, high school transcript, college transcript(s) for transfer students, letter of recommendation, audition, SAT or ACT test scores, separate BFA application for audition. Auditions held 12 times on campus and off campus in Chicago, IL; Washington DC; Atlanta, GA; Miami, FL; Los Angeles, CA; Houston, TX; Seattle, WA; videotaped performances are permissible as a substitute for live auditions.

**Web Site** http://www.fordham.edu/bfa

**Undergraduate Contact** Dr. Patricia Peek, Director of LC Admission, Undergraduate Admission, Fordham University, 113 West 60th Street, New York, New York 10023; 212-636-6715, e-mail address: peek@fordham.edu

# Friends University
## Wichita, Kansas

Independent, coed. Urban campus. Dance program established 1987.

**Web Site** http://www.friends.edu/

# George Mason University
## Fairfax, Virginia

State-supported, coed. Suburban campus. Total enrollment: 30,332. Dance program established 1980.

**Web Site** http://www.gmu.edu/

# The Hartt School
See University of Hartford

## *Jacobs School of Music*
# Indiana University Bloomington
## Bloomington, Indiana

State-supported, coed. Small town campus. Total enrollment: 38,990. Dance program established 1956.

**Degrees** Bachelor of Science in the area of ballet; Bachelor of Science with an Outside Field in the area of ballet. Majors and concentrations: ballet. Program accredited by NASM.

**Enrollment** 55 total; all undergraduate.

**Dance Student Profile** 82% females, 18% males, 15% minorities.

**Dance Faculty** 4 total (full-time), 2 total (part-time). Graduate students do not teach undergraduate courses. Undergraduate student–faculty ratio: 9:1.

**Student Life** Student groups/activities include dancing with Illinois Opera Theatre, teaching in Pre-College Program (ages 3-18), major ballet performances (3 per year).

**Expenses for 2007–2008** Application fee: $50. State resident tuition: $7000 full-time. Nonresident tuition: $21,479 full-time. Mandatory fees: $837 full-time. Full-time tuition and fees vary according to location and program. College room and board: $6676. College room only: $4172. Room and board charges vary according to board plan and housing facility. Special program-related fees: $150 per course for ballet therapy.

**Financial Aid** Program-specific awards: School of Music Dean's Awards for those demonstrating musical ability and scholastic achievement, minority scholarships for those demonstrating musical ability, scholastic achievement, and financial need, University Grants for those demonstrating musical ability, scholastic achievement, and financial need.

**Application Procedures** Students admitted directly into the professional program freshman year. Deadline for freshmen and transfers: continuous. Required: essay, high school transcript, college transcript(s) for transfer students, minimum 2.0 high school GPA, audition, SAT or ACT test scores. Recommended: minimum 3.0 high school GPA. Auditions held 6 times on campus; videotaped performances are permissible as a substitute for live auditions when the ballet department is contacted ahead of time.

**Web Site** http://www.music.indiana.edu

**Undergraduate Contact** Music Admissions, Jacobs School of Music, Indiana University Bloomington, 1201 East 3rd Street-MU 101, Bloomington, Indiana 47405; 812-855-7998, fax: 812-856-6086, e-mail address: musicadm@indiana.edu

# Jacksonville University

**Jacksonville, Florida**

Independent, coed. Suburban campus. Total enrollment: 3,436. Dance program established 1958.

**Degrees** Bachelor of Fine Arts. Majors and concentrations: dance. Program accredited by NASD.

**Enrollment** 38 total; all undergraduate.

**Dance Student Profile** 58% females, 42% males, 27% minorities, 3% international.

**Dance Faculty** 3 undergraduate (full-time), 1 undergraduate (part-time). 100% of full-time faculty have terminal degrees. Graduate students do not teach undergraduate courses. Undergraduate student–faculty ratio: 12:1.

**Student Life** Student groups/activities include Jacksonville University Dance Theatre, Jacksonville University Dance Ensemble, Alpha Psi Omega.

**Expenses for 2008–2009** Application fee: $30. Comprehensive fee: $32,660 includes full-time tuition ($23,900) and college room and board ($8760). College room only: $5000. Special program-related fees: $15–$80 per course per semester for materials, $50 per course per semester for student choreography production fees.

**Financial Aid** Program-specific awards: 11 dance scholarships for those demonstrating need/talent ($1000–$5300), 1 Phillips Scholarship for those demonstrating exceptional talent ($1000).

**Application Procedures** Students admitted directly into the professional program freshman year. Deadline for freshmen and transfers: continuous. Notification date for freshmen and transfers: continuous. Required: high school transcript, college transcript(s) for transfer students, minimum 2.0 high school GPA, audition, SAT or ACT test scores. Recommended: essay, minimum 3.0 high school GPA, 3 letters of recommendation. Auditions held twice and by appointment on campus; videotaped performances are permissible as a substitute for live auditions if a campus visit is impossible.

**Web Site** http://www.ju.edu

**Undergraduate Contact** Miriam King, Vice President of Enrollment Management, Jacksonville University, 2800 University Boulevard North, Jacksonville, Florida 32211; 904-256-7000, fax: 904-256-7012, e-mail address: admissions@ju.edu

# Jacobs School of Music

See Indiana University Bloomington

# Jordan College of Fine Arts

See Butler University

# The Juilliard School

**New York, New York**

Independent, coed. Urban campus. Total enrollment: 832. Dance program established 1951.

**Degrees** Bachelor of Fine Arts. Majors and concentrations: dance.

**Enrollment** 90 total; all undergraduate.

**Dance Student Profile** 51% females, 49% males, 34% minorities, 11% international.

**Dance Faculty** 12 undergraduate (full-time), 13 undergraduate (part-time). Graduate students do not teach undergraduate courses. Undergraduate student–faculty ratio: 4:1.

**Student Life** Student groups/activities include dance performances, composers/choreographers collaboration, Arts Outreach Program. Special housing available for dance students.

**Expenses for 2007–2008** Application fee: $100. Comprehensive fee: $37,890 includes full-time tuition ($27,150) and college room and board ($10,740).

**Financial Aid** Program-specific awards: 84 merit and/or need-based awards for program majors ($20,873).

**Application Procedures** Students admitted directly into the professional program freshman year. Deadline for freshmen and transfers: December 1. Notification date for freshmen and transfers: April 1. Required: essay, high school transcript, college transcript(s) for transfer students, 2 letters of recommendation, audition, TOEFL for all non-native English speakers. Recommended: photo. Auditions held once on campus and off campus in San Francisco, CA; Houston, TX; Miami, FL; Chicago, IL.

**Web Site** http://www.juilliard.edu

**Undergraduate Contact** Ms. Lee Cioppa, Associate Dean for Admissions, The Juilliard School, 60 Lincoln Center Plaza, New York, New York 10023-6588; 212-799-5000 ext. 223, fax: 212-769-6420, e-mail address: admissions@juilliard.edu

## More About the School

Juilliard aims to create true contemporary dancers—trained equally in classical ballet and modern dance. By teaching dancers the great traditions and disciplines of both past and present, Juilliard opens their eyes and minds to all the choreographic possibilities that lie ahead. Now in its fifty-fifth season, the Juilliard Dance Division is a groundbreaking conservatory dance program whose faculty members and alumni have changed the face of dance around the world.

Established in 1951 by William Schuman during his tenure as president of Juilliard, with the guidance of founding director Martha Hill, Juilliard Dance became the first major teaching institution to combine equal dance instruction in both contemporary and ballet techniques, an idea that was considered heretical in its day. Early faculty members included renowned dance figures, such as Alfredo Corvino, Doris Humphrey, José Limón, Anna Sokolow, Antony Tudor, and Hector Zaraspe. Ms. Hill became Artistic Director Emeritus with the appointment of Muriel Topaz as Director in 1985, and she remained active at Juilliard almost until her death in 1995. In 1992, choreographer and artistic director Benjamin Harkarvy was appointed head of the division, a position he maintained until his death in March 2002.

In July of 2002, master teacher Lawrence Rhodes was appointed the new director of the Dance Division. Since his appointment, Mr. Rhodes' focus remains the students' involvement with a wide variety of dance styles and language, inviting numerous well-known and up-and-coming choreographers to create works and restage classic repertoire for the dancers. Recent choreographers include Aszure Barton, Robert Battle, Ronald K. Brown, Eliot Feld, William Forsythe, Jirí Kylián, Susan Marshall, Mark Morris, Matthew Neenan, Ohad Naharin, David Parker, Twyla Tharp, and Doug Varone. Numerous performances each season also present the year's best work by Juilliard's own young choreographers.

The dance faculty brings to the classroom, the studio, and the stage an extraordinary background of professional accomplishment. All faculty members are active in the world of dance as coaches, adjudicators, choreographers, restagers of works, writers, guest teachers—and as dancers.

The Dance Division's four-year course of study offers students the choice of pursuing a Bachelor of Fine Arts (B.F.A.) degree or a diploma. The core curriculum requires intensive technical study and performance in classical ballet and modern dance and includes courses in repertory, pas de deux, pointe or men's class, dance composition, anatomy, acting, dance history, stagecraft, production, music theory, and elements of performing. The dancers work in an enormous variety of repertory styles and techniques. Traditional courses, such as dance composition, also benefit from guest artists and noted choreographers who work in the studios with Juilliard dancers as part of their weekly schedule. Also offered are electives such as voice and tap and jazz. All dancers are introduced to the techniques of creating new works in beginning choreography classes and are encouraged to present their own choreographed works in informal concerts and workshops showings. Also each year, a Choreographers and Composers program offers collaborations between third-year student choreographers and student composers. A springtime concert, Senior Production, features the work of accomplished choreographers selected from the senior class in a concert produced by the senior class, with lighting design and behind-the-scenes production by the junior class.

In addition, in the fall, each individual class has the opportunity to work with established choreographers in premiere dances as part of the *New Dances* performances. Spring repertory concerts give dancers the opportunity to perform in established works from repertory, including works by distinguished living choreographers as well as classic works by legendary figures such as Martha Graham, José Limón, and Antony Tudor. Facilities include five class and rehearsal studios as well as the Peter J. Sharp Theater and other smaller performance venues. The Juilliard Dance Division also presents programs in Lincoln Center's Clark Theater and in venues throughout the metropolitan region, including New York City public schools.

A seminar class for seniors teaches dancers how to prepare resumes, write grant proposals, and produce their own performances. Juilliard dancers also learn production techniques, how to audition, and how to focus their career ambitions.

Graduates of the division have gone on to dance with virtually every established modern and ballet company in the United States and abroad, and they are also among the directors and administrators of respected companies worldwide. Alumni include noted directors and choreographers, such as Robert Battle, Pina Bausch, Martha Clarke, Mercedes Ellington, Robert Garland, Kazuko Hirabayashi, Saeko Ichinohe, Lar Lubovitch, Bruce Marks, Susan Marshall, Ohad Naharin, and Paul Taylor.

# The Katherine K. Herberger College of Fine Arts

See Arizona State University

# Kent State University

## Kent, Ohio

State-supported, coed. Suburban campus. Total enrollment: 22,819. Dance program established 1980.
**Degrees** Bachelor of Fine Arts in the areas of dance performance, dance education. Majors and concentrations: dance education, dance performance. Program accredited by NASD.
**Enrollment** 85 total; all undergraduate.
**Dance Student Profile** 91% females, 9% males, 20% minorities.
**Dance Faculty** 5 total (full-time), 6 total (part-time). 94% of full-time faculty have terminal degrees. Graduate students do not teach undergraduate courses. Undergraduate student–faculty ratio: 15:1.
**Student Life** Student groups/activities include National Dance Education Organization Student Chapter, Kent Dance Ensemble, Kent Dance Association. Special housing available for dance students.
**Expenses for 2008–2009** Application fee: $30. State resident tuition: $8430 full-time. Nonresident tuition: $15,862 full-time. College room and board: $7200. College room only: $4410.
**Financial Aid** Program-specific awards: 3–6 Creative Arts Awards for program majors ($1800–$3300).
**Application Procedures** Students admitted directly into the professional program freshman year. Deadline for freshmen and transfers: continuous. Required: high school transcript, college transcript(s) for transfer students, minimum 2.0 high school GPA, interview, audition, SAT or ACT test scores (minimum composite ACT score of 21), completion of college preparatory courses. Recommended: minimum 3.0 high school GPA, 3 letters of recommendation. Auditions held 4 times on campus; videotaped performances are permissible as a substitute for live auditions when distance is prohibitive.
**Web Site** http://www.dance.kent.edu
**Undergraduate Contact** Prof. Andrea Shearer, Dance Coordinator, School of Theatre and Dance, Kent State University, PO Box 5190, Kent, Ohio 44242-0001; 330-672-2069, fax: 330-672-4897, e-mail address: ashearer@kent.edu

# Leigh Gerdine College of Fine Arts

See Webster University

# Long Island University, C.W. Post Campus

## Brookville, New York

Independent, coed. Suburban campus. Total enrollment: 8,361. Dance program established 1996.
**Degrees** Bachelor of Fine Arts in the areas of arts management, dance studies. Majors and concentrations: arts management, dance.
**Enrollment** 32 total; all undergraduate.
**Dance Student Profile** 93% females, 7% males, 25% minorities, 5% international.
**Dance Faculty** 2 undergraduate (full-time), 8 undergraduate (part-time). 80% of full-time faculty have terminal degrees. Graduate students do not teach undergraduate courses. Undergraduate student–faculty ratio: 7:1.
**Student Life** Student groups/activities include lecture demonstrations, Post Concert Dance Company, American College Dance Festival Association.
**Expenses for 2007–2008** Application fee: $30. Comprehensive fee: $35,550 includes full-time tuition ($24,700), mandatory fees ($1250), and college room and board ($9600). College room only: $6320. Room and board charges vary according to board plan and housing facility. Special program-related fees: $65 per technique class for accompanist and theater services, $75 per technical theater for class supplies.
**Financial Aid** Program-specific awards: 2 Provost's Awards for dance studies majors ($2000), 12 Post Concert Dance Company Awards for dance studies majors ($2000), 7 freshman incentive awards for dance studies majors ($2000).
**Application Procedures** Students admitted directly into the professional program freshman year. Deadline for freshmen and transfers: continuous. Required: essay, high school transcript, college transcript(s) for transfer students, 2 letters of recommendation, interview, audition, SAT or ACT test scores. Recommended: minimum 3.0 high school GPA. Auditions held 4 times on campus and off campus in Texas Magnet Auditions; videotaped performances are permissible as a substitute for live auditions when distance is prohibitive. Portfolio reviews held 3 times.
**Web Site** http://www.liu.edu
**Undergraduate Contact** Mr. Gary Bergman, Associate Provost for Enrollment Services, Admissions, Long Island University, C.W. Post Campus, 720 Northern Boulevard, Brookville, New York 11548-1300; 516-299-2900, fax: 516-299-2418, e-mail address: enroll@cwpost.liu.edu

# Marymount Manhattan College

## New York, New York

Independent, coed. Urban campus. Total enrollment: 1,895.
**Degrees** Bachelor of Fine Arts in the area of dance. Majors and concentrations: dance.
**Enrollment** 150 total; all undergraduate.
**Dance Student Profile** 85% females, 15% males, 20% minorities, 10% international.
**Dance Faculty** 6 undergraduate (full-time), 30 undergraduate (part-time). 50% of full-time faculty have terminal degrees. Graduate students do not teach undergraduate courses. Undergraduate student–faculty ratio: 26:1.
**Expenses for 2007–2008** Application fee: $60. Comprehensive fee: $32,850 includes full-time tuition ($19,666), mandatory fees ($934), and college room and board ($12,250). College room only: $10,250. Special program-related fees: $15 per credit hour for technique/lab fees.
**Financial Aid** Program-specific awards: competitive talent awards for dance majors ($1000–$4000).
**Application Procedures** Students admitted directly into the professional program freshman year. Deadline for freshmen and transfers: March 25. Required: essay, high school transcript, college transcript(s) for transfer students, minimum 2.0 high school GPA, 2 letters of recommendation, interview, audition, SAT or ACT test scores, 5" x 7" photograph in first arabesque en l'air or tendu a la seconde, dance audition application form.

*Marymount Manhattan College (continued)*

Auditions held 7 times on campus and off campus in San Francisco, CA; Chicago, IL; Miami, FL; videotaped performances are permissible as a substitute for live auditions when distance is prohibitive.
**Web Site** http://marymount.mmm.edu
**Undergraduate Contact** Mr. Anthony Ferro, Recruiter, Department of Dance, Marymount Manhattan College, 221 East 71st Street, New York, New York 10021; 212-517-0610, fax: 212-517-0619, e-mail address: dance@mmm.edu

## Rutgers, The State University of New Jersey
# Mason Gross School of the Arts
### New Brunswick, New Jersey

State-supported, coed. Small town campus. Dance program established 1981.
**Degrees** Bachelor of Fine Arts in the area of dance. Majors and concentrations: modern dance. Program accredited by NASD.
**Enrollment** 101 total; 58 undergraduate, 43 nonprofessional degree.
**Dance Student Profile** 85% females, 15% males, 15% minorities, 1% international.
**Dance Faculty** 7 undergraduate (full-time), 8 undergraduate (part-time). 90% of full-time faculty have terminal degrees. Graduate students do not teach undergraduate courses. Undergraduate student–faculty ratio: 15:1.
**Student Life** Student groups/activities include DancePlus Concert Series, student-produced performances, University Dance Works. Special housing available for dance students.
**Expenses for 2007–2008** Special program-related fees: $50 per 3-credit course for supplies for dance production, $75 per 3-credit course for performance tickets.
**Financial Aid** Program-specific awards: 4 University DanceWorks Awards for BFA dancers ($12,000), 2 Carr Scholarships for BFA dancers ($40,000).
**Application Procedures** Students admitted directly into the professional program freshman year. Deadline for freshmen and transfers: continuous. Notification date for freshmen and transfers: continuous. Required: high school transcript, college transcript(s) for transfer students, minimum 2.0 high school GPA, interview, audition, SAT or ACT test scores. Auditions held 4 times on campus; videotaped performances are permissible as a substitute for live auditions when distance is prohibitive.
**Web Site** http://mgsa.rutgers.edu
**Undergraduate Contact** Office of Undergraduate Admissions, Rutgers, The State University of New Jersey, Mason Gross School of the Arts, PO Box 2101, New Brunswick, New Jersey 08903-2101; 732-445-3777.

# Meadows School of the Arts
See Southern Methodist University

# Missouri State University
### Springfield, Missouri

State-supported, coed. Suburban campus. Total enrollment: 19,348.
**Degrees** Bachelor of Fine Arts in the areas of dance performance, dance studies. Majors and concentrations: dance performance, dance studies.
**Enrollment** 60 total; all undergraduate.
**Dance Student Profile** 90% females, 10% males, 3% minorities, 1% international.
**Dance Faculty** 6 undergraduate (full-time). 100% of full-time faculty have terminal degrees. Graduate students do not teach undergraduate courses. Undergraduate student–faculty ratio: 12:1.
**Student Life** Student groups/activities include Inertia Dance Company, Syncopation Entertainment Troupe.
**Expenses for 2007–2008** Application fee: $35. State resident tuition: $5988 full-time. Nonresident tuition: $11,088 full-time.

Mandatory fees: $618 full-time. Full-time tuition and fees vary according to course load, degree level, location, and program. College room and board: $5312. Room and board charges vary according to board plan and housing facility.
**Financial Aid** Program-specific awards: 4 dance activity awards for upperclass program majors ($2000), 2 out-of-state waivers for upperclass program majors ($2000).
**Application Procedures** Students apply for admission into the professional program by sophomore year. Deadline for freshmen and transfers: August 1. Notification date for freshmen and transfers: continuous. Required: high school transcript, college transcript(s) for transfer students, minimum 2.0 high school GPA, ACT test score only, standing in top 67% of graduating class. Recommended: interview. Auditions held once on campus.
**Web Site** http://www.theatreanddance.missouristate.edu/
**Undergraduate Contact** Mr. Mark Biggs, Head, Acting, Department of Theatre and Dance, Missouri State University, 901 South National, Springfield, Missouri 65804; 417-836-4400, fax: 417-836-4234.

# Montclair State University
### Upper Montclair, New Jersey

State-supported, coed. Suburban campus. Total enrollment: 16,736.
**Degrees** Bachelor of Arts in the area of dance (certification P-12); Bachelor of Fine Arts. Majors and concentrations: dance. Program accredited by NASD.
**Enrollment** 90 total; all undergraduate.
**Dance Student Profile** 97% females, 3% males, 3% minorities, 1% international.
**Dance Faculty** 2 undergraduate (full-time), 6 undergraduate (part-time). 50% of full-time faculty have terminal degrees. Graduate students do not teach undergraduate courses. Undergraduate student–faculty ratio: 7:1.
**Student Life** Student groups/activities include Danceworks, musicals, American College Dance Festival Association.
**Expenses for 2007–2008** Application fee: $55. State resident tuition: $6390 full-time. Nonresident tuition: $13,659 full-time. Mandatory fees: $2505 full-time. College room and board: $9500. College room only: $6350. Room and board charges vary according to board plan and housing facility. Special program-related fees: $50 per class for accompanists and other dance needs.
**Financial Aid** Program-specific awards available.
**Application Procedures** Students admitted directly into the professional program freshman year. Deadline for freshmen: March 1; transfers: May 1. Required: essay, high school transcript, college transcript(s) for transfer students, minimum 2.0 high school GPA, interview, audition, SAT test score only. Recommended: 2 letters of recommendation. Auditions held continuously on campus; videotaped performances are permissible as a substitute for live auditions for international students and U.S. students when distance is prohibitive.
**Web Site** http://www.montclair.edu
**Undergraduate Contact** Ms. Lori Katterhenry, Program Coordinator, Division of Dance, Montclair State University, Normal Avenue, Montclair, New Jersey 07043; 973-655-7080, fax: 973-655-7717, e-mail address: katterhenrl@mail.montclair.edu

# New World School of the Arts
### Miami, Florida

State-supported, coed. Urban campus. Total enrollment: 416. Dance program established 1988.
**Degrees** Bachelor of Fine Arts in the area of dance. Majors and concentrations: performance. Mandatory cross-registration with University of Florida, Miami Dade College. Program accredited by NASD.
**Enrollment** 92 total; all undergraduate.
**Dance Student Profile** 72% females, 28% males, 75% minorities, 1% international.
**Dance Faculty** 5 undergraduate (full-time), 11 undergraduate (part-time). Graduate students do not teach undergraduate courses. Undergraduate student–faculty ratio: 5:1.

**Student Life** Student groups/activities include Florida Dance Association, local dance companies, Student Government.
**Expenses for 2007–2008** Application fee: $0. State resident tuition: $3000 full-time. Nonresident tuition: $10,000 full-time.
**Financial Aid** Program-specific awards: 4 Nations Bank Merit Scholarships for program majors ($2000), 1 Lewis Dorfman Merit Scholarship for program majors ($1000), 1 Patricia Olalde Merit Scholarship for choreography majors ($1000), 10 Dr. Betty Rowen Merit Scholarships for dance education majors ($1500), 25 Miami-Dade College Scholarships for program majors ($1500).
**Application Procedures** Students admitted directly into the professional program freshman year. Deadline for freshmen and transfers: continuous. Notification date for freshmen and transfers: continuous. Required: essay, high school transcript, college transcript(s) for transfer students, 2 letters of recommendation, audition. Recommended: minimum 2.0 high school GPA, interview, SAT or ACT test scores. Auditions held continuously on campus and off campus in Jacksonville, FL; Dallas, TX; videotaped performances are permissible as a substitute for live auditions when distance is prohibitive.
**Web Site** http://www.mdc.edu/nwsa
**Undergraduate Contact** Pamela Neumann, Recruitment and Admissions Coordinator, Student Services, New World School of the Arts, 300 NE 2nd Avenue, Miami, Florida 33132; 305-237-7007, fax: 305-237-3794, e-mail address: nwsaadm@mdc.edu

*Tisch School of the Arts, Department of Dance*
# New York University
## New York, New York

Independent, coed. Urban campus. Total enrollment: 41,783. Dance program established 1965.
**Degrees** Bachelor of Fine Arts. Majors and concentrations: dance. Graduate degrees offered: Master of Fine Arts in the area of dance.
**Enrollment** 103 total; 75 undergraduate, 28 graduate.
**Dance Student Profile** 73% females, 27% males, 11% minorities, 6% international.
**Dance Faculty** 9 total (full-time), 15 total (part-time). Graduate students do not teach undergraduate courses. Undergraduate student–faculty ratio: 5:1.
**Student Life** Student groups/activities include Community Connections, The Collective, Tisch Talent Guild.
**Expenses for 2007–2008** Application fee: $65. Comprehensive fee: $47,490 includes full-time tuition ($33,268), mandatory fees ($2022), and college room and board ($12,200). Full-time tuition and fees vary according to course load and program. Room and board charges vary according to board plan and housing facility.
**Financial Aid** Program-specific awards available.
**Application Procedures** Students admitted directly into the professional program freshman year. Deadline for freshmen: January 15; transfers: April 1. Notification date for freshmen: April 1; transfers: May 15. Required: essay, high school transcript, college transcript(s) for transfer students, 2 letters of recommendation, audition, SAT or ACT test scores. Recommended: minimum 3.0 high school GPA, interview. Auditions held continuously from November through April on campus and off campus in Chicago, IL; San Francisco, CA; Los Angeles, CA; videotaped performances are permissible as a substitute for live auditions for international applicants only.
**Web Site** http://dance.tisch.nyu.edu
**Undergraduate Contact** Ms. Patricia A. Decker, Director of Recruitment, Tisch School of the Arts, New York University, 721 Broadway, 8th Floor, New York, New York 10003-6807; 212-998-1900, fax: 212-995-4060, e-mail address: tisch.recruitment@nyu.edu
**Graduate Contact** Mr. Dan Sandford, Director of Graduate Admissions, Tisch School of the Arts, New York University, 721 Broadway, 8th Floor, New York, New York 10003-6807; 212-998-1900, fax: 212-995-4060, e-mail address: dan.sandford@nyu.edu

# North Carolina School of the Arts
## Winston-Salem, North Carolina

State-supported, coed. Urban campus. Total enrollment: 864. Dance program established 1965.
**Degrees** Bachelor of Fine Arts in the area of dance. Majors and concentrations: ballet, contemporary dance.
**Enrollment** 84 total; 58 undergraduate, 26 nonprofessional degree.
**Dance Student Profile** 74% females, 26% males, 9% minorities, 5% international.
**Dance Faculty** 13 undergraduate (full-time), 1 undergraduate (part-time). 22% of full-time faculty have terminal degrees. Graduate students do not teach undergraduate courses. Undergraduate student–faculty ratio: 5:1.
**Student Life** Special housing available for dance students.
**Expenses for 2007–2008** Application fee: $50. State resident tuition: $3224 full-time. Nonresident tuition: $14,654 full-time. Mandatory fees: $1837 full-time. Full-time tuition and fees vary according to program. College room and board: $6431. College room only: $3289. Room and board charges vary according to board plan and housing facility. Special program-related fees: $60 per year for injury screening fee, $135 per year for educational and technology fee.
**Financial Aid** Program-specific awards: 49 talent/need scholarships for those demonstrating talent and/or need ($2667).
**Application Procedures** Students admitted directly into the professional program freshman year. Deadline for freshmen and transfers: continuous. Required: high school transcript, college transcript(s) for transfer students, 2 letters of recommendation, interview, audition, two photos. Recommended: SAT or ACT test scores. Auditions held by request on campus and off campus in various cities in the U.S.; videotaped performances are permissible as a substitute for live auditions for provisional acceptance.
**Web Site** http://www.ncarts.edu
**Undergraduate Contact** Ms. Sheeler Lawson, Director of Admissions, North Carolina School of the Arts, 1533 South Main Street, Winston-Salem, North Carolina 27117-2189; 336-770-3291, fax: 336-770-3370, e-mail address: admissions@ncarts.edu

# The Ohio State University
## Columbus, Ohio

State-supported, coed. Total enrollment: 52,568. Dance program established 1968.
**Degrees** Bachelor of Fine Arts. Majors and concentrations: dance. Graduate degrees offered: Master of Fine Arts in the areas of choreography, performance, lighting, directing in Labanotation, dance technologies, dance documentation. Doctor of Philosophy in the area of dance studies. Cross-registration with Columbus State. Program accredited by NASD.
**Enrollment** 120 total; 85 undergraduate, 35 graduate.
**Dance Student Profile** 90% females, 10% males, 20% minorities, 4% international.
**Dance Faculty** 20 total (full-time), 10 total (part-time). 85% of full-time faculty have terminal degrees. Graduate students teach a few undergraduate courses. Undergraduate student–faculty ratio: 8:1.
**Student Life** Student groups/activities include Black Dance Alliance, Students Pursuing The Avante-gard. Special housing available for dance students.
**Expenses for 2007–2008** Application fee: $40. State resident tuition: $8406 full-time. Nonresident tuition: $21,015 full-time. Mandatory fees: $270 full-time. Full-time tuition and fees vary according to course load, program, reciprocity agreements, and student level. College room and board: $7365. College room only: $4605. Room and board charges vary according to board plan and housing facility. Special program-related fees: $43 for learning technologies fee.
**Financial Aid** Program-specific awards: 10 dance scholarships for talented dance majors ($1000).
**Application Procedures** Students admitted directly into the professional program freshman year. Deadline for freshmen: February 15; transfers: June 15. Required: essay, high school transcript, college transcript(s) for transfer students, audition, SAT or ACT

*The Ohio State University (continued)*

test scores, minimum 3.0 high school GPA or top 30% of graduating class. Recommended: interview. Auditions held twice on campus; videotaped performances are permissible as a substitute for live auditions for international applicants.
**Web Site** http://www.dance.ohio-state.edu/
**Undergraduate Contact** Misty Kerns, Undergraduate Coordinator, Department of Dance, The Ohio State University, Sullivant Hall, 1813 North High Street, Columbus, Ohio 43210-1307; 614-292-7977, fax: 614-292-0939, e-mail address: ugdance@osu.edu
**Graduate Contact** Misty Kerns, Graduate Coordinator, Department of Dance, The Ohio State University, Sullivant Hall, 1813 North High Street, Columbus, Ohio 43210-1307; 614-292-7977, fax: 614-292-0939, e-mail address: graddance@osu.edu

# Ohio University
## Athens, Ohio

State-supported, coed. Small town campus. Total enrollment: 20,711. Dance program established 1969.
**Degrees** Bachelor of Fine Arts in the area of choreography and performance. Majors and concentrations: dance. Program accredited by NASD.
**Enrollment** 58 total; all undergraduate.
**Dance Student Profile** 92% females, 8% males, 13% minorities, 2% international.
**Dance Faculty** 7 undergraduate (full-time). 70% of full-time faculty have terminal degrees. Graduate students do not teach undergraduate courses. Undergraduate student–faculty ratio: 8:1.
**Student Life** Student groups/activities include The Movement (student performance organization). Special housing available for dance students.
**Expenses for 2007–2008** Application fee: $45. State resident tuition: $8907 full-time. Nonresident tuition: $17,871 full-time. College room and board: $8427. College room only: $4476. Room and board charges vary according to board plan.
**Financial Aid** Program-specific awards: 4–5 Provost Scholarships for talented students ($1000), 1 Ruiz-Lewis Scholarship for minorities and males ($500), 1 Bailin-Stern Scholarship for talented students ($400–$500), 1 Hazeland Carr Liggett Award for talented students ($800), 1–2 Shirley Wimmer Awards for talented students ($1000–$1200), 1 Betty Milhendler Award for talented students ($500), 1 Bill Cratty Award for talented males ($500), 1 Yolanda Molnar Scholarship for talented students ($1000), 1 Margaret Schuette Scholarship for talented students ($1000).
**Application Procedures** Students admitted directly into the professional program freshman year. Deadline for freshmen: February 1; transfers: June 1. Notification date for freshmen: March 15; transfers: June 15. Required: essay, high school transcript, college transcript(s) for transfer students, 2 letters of recommendation, audition, SAT or ACT test scores. Recommended: minimum 3.0 high school GPA, interview. Auditions held twice on campus; videotaped performances are permissible as a substitute for live auditions when distance is prohibitive.
**Web Site** http://www.finearts.ohio.edu/dance
**Undergraduate Contact** Ms. Teresa Holland, Assistant to the Director, School of Dance, Ohio University, Putnam Hall 137, Athens, Ohio 45701; 740-593-1826, fax: 740-593-0749, e-mail address: dance@ohiou.edu

# Point Park University
## Pittsburgh, Pennsylvania

Independent, coed. Urban campus. Total enrollment: 3,592. Dance program established 1968.
**Degrees** Bachelor of Arts in the area of dance pedagogy; Bachelor of Arts/Bachelor of Fine Arts in the area of dance. Majors and concentrations: ballet, dance pedagogy, jazz dance, modern dance. Cross-registration with Carnegie Mellon University, University of Pittsburgh, Chatham College, Robert Morris College, Duquesne University, Carlow College. Program accredited by NASD.

**Enrollment** 254 total; all undergraduate.
**Dance Student Profile** 83% females, 17% males, 18% minorities, 2% international.
**Dance Faculty** 10 undergraduate (full-time), 15 undergraduate (part-time). 90% of full-time faculty have terminal degrees. Graduate students do not teach undergraduate courses. Undergraduate student–faculty ratio: 12:1.
**Student Life** Student groups/activities include Pittsburgh Playhouse Dance Company, American College Dance Festival Association, Point Park College Dance Club.
**Expenses for 2007–2008** Application fee: $40. Comprehensive fee: $27,430 includes full-time tuition ($18,460), mandatory fees ($530), and college room and board ($8440). College room only: $3980. Full-time tuition and fees vary according to program. Room and board charges vary according to board plan and housing facility. Special program-related fees: $395 per term for voice/piano private lessons.
**Financial Aid** Program-specific awards: 22 academic scholarships for those demonstrating talent and academic achievement ($2000–$7500), 24–35 dance scholarships for those demonstrating talent and academic achievement ($1000–$5000), 25 dance apprenticeships for those demonstrating talent ($500–$3500).
**Application Procedures** Students admitted directly into the professional program freshman year. Deadline for freshmen and transfers: May 1. Required: high school transcript, college transcript(s) for transfer students, minimum 2.0 high school GPA, 2 letters of recommendation, audition, SAT or ACT test scores. Auditions held 10 times on campus and off campus in New York, NY; Chicago, IL; Washington, DC; videotaped performances are permissible as a substitute for live auditions if distance is prohibitive or in special circumstances.
**Web Site** http://www.pointpark.edu
**Undergraduate Contact** Mr. Joseph McGoldrick, Director of Artistic Recruitment, Conservatory of Performing Arts, Point Park University, 201 Wood Street, Pittsburgh, Pennsylvania 15222-1984; 412-392-3450, fax: 412-391-2424, e-mail address: jmcgoldrick@pointpark.edu

*More About the Program*

The Conservatory of Performing Arts confers Bachelor of Arts and Bachelor of Fine Arts degrees in dance, dance pedagogy, and theater arts and offers conservatory training within a liberal arts context. Students receive intense training in their concentration as well as a thorough academic education. Because the faculty members believe that performing arts majors develop best in front of a live audience, the program offers varied performing opportunities for students at the Pittsburgh Playhouse of Point Park University.

Nationally renowned, the Pittsburgh Playhouse is the performance facility for the Conservatory of Performing Arts. Here students participate in live-theater/dance experiences before a subscription audience. Consisting of three working theaters, this 70-year-old facility is fully staffed by a production team of designers and artisans who train and supervise student apprentices in building, designing, lighting, and managing shows. The front-of-house staff members as well as the box office and public relations personnel engage all students in the business aspect of running a theater. The season, which features student actors, dancers, designers, and stage managers, consists of five Playhouse Jr. shows for children and five Conservatory Theatre Company dramas/musicals.

Dance students may perform in one of five Playhouse Dance Company productions and a Playhouse Jr. Children's Dance Show as well as a public school outreach program.

The Bachelor of Arts degree in cinema and digital arts is an innovatively designed program, with an emphasis on professional education and liberal arts—both in theory and in practice. Exploring the integration of media and the arts in society as well as the impact of technology on culture, the curriculum provides practical, professional training while developing a sound foundation in the arts and humanities. Theory and aesthetics are taught as an integral part of developing communication and production skills.

In the Conservatory of Performing Arts, it is the mission to educate, train, and artistically equip students with the skills necessary to compete in the commercial media industry. The degree offered is a four-year, 120-credit Bachelor of Arts in film and electronic arts, with concentrations in cinematography, directing, editing and sound, producing, and screenwriting.

This well-rounded educational experience culminates with the annual Point Park Digital Film Festival, presented to showcase graduating senior thesis production projects. Admission to the Film and Electronic Arts program is based on self-discipline, professional attitude, and a commitment to the craft as demonstrated through an interview with the Director of Film.

The B.F.A. degree in film and video production is offered in collaboration with Pittsburgh Filmmakers. Students take their academic courses at Point Park University and their film and video requirements at Pittsburgh Filmmakers' newly built facility in the Oakland section of Pittsburgh. Both institutions work together to ensure students receive a challenging educational experience.

Conservatory faculty members are working professionals in acting, singing, dancing, writing, composing, painting, designing, choreography, and other specialties. Guest artists and master teachers in musical theater, voice and speech, and dance are regularly featured. Past guests include Chita Rivera, Michael Rupert, Jeff Shade, Rob Ashford, Sherry Zunker-Dow, Cicely Berry, Paul Gavert, Patricia Wilde, Albert Poland, Barbara Pontecorvo, Edward Villella, Maxine Sherman, Marshall Swiney, and Claire Bataille. The program also offers many workshops and collaborative efforts of an interdisciplinary nature with other University programs.

During the summer, the Conservatory offers an International Summer Dance program (open by audition) featuring renowned names in the world of dance. The International Summer Dance program offers training in jazz, ballet, Alexander, and modern dance. The program culminates in a recital performance.

The community of Pittsburgh itself is an arts and education center with the Pittsburgh Symphony, Opera, Ballet, and Dance Council and the Pittsburgh Public Theaters supplemented by eight other institutions of higher learning within a 15-minute drive. The whole city is truly the campus of the programs.

Prospective applicants must apply and be accepted by the University. An audition for and an interview with faculty members is required of all prospective majors. Scholarships/apprenticeships from $1000 to $5000 are based on either talent or academics or both. Presidential and special academic full- and part-time awards are highly competitive.

Off-campus auditions are possible at Thespian State Conferences and dance conferences in Chicago; New York; Washington, D.C.; Houston; Detroit; and Louisville, Kentucky. Videotaped auditions are acceptable; prospective students should contact the Conservatory for procedures.

**Program Facilities and Features** At the Conservatory of Performing Arts, facilities include ten dance studios as well as the three-theater complex at the Pittsburgh Playhouse of Point Park University, which offers performance opportunities for students in front of a subscription audience. In addition, students can take advantage of the on-site costume/set construction apprenticeships, 11 private singing and piano instructors; art and design classes; more than 100 dance classes per week, acting classes with a ratio of 1 instructor to 15 students, and the Point Park University Singers. Point Park University is central to many educational, arts, and entertainment activities, and it is within walking distance of boating, swimming, and parks.

Point Park University's widely acclaimed dance program plans to raise the bar yet another notch in fall 2007 when it opens the doors of its new, state-of-the-art, multistudio dance complex. Designed after an extensive benchmarking process that involved some of the world's most prestigious dance companies and schools, the spacious studios and innovative green-building design will create the best of all possible environments for the University's dance students. The new 42,000-square-foot facility will house four studios, one of which can be converted to an informal performance space to allow student choreographers to showcase their talents and hone their skills.

**Alumni** The Conservatory has numerous graduates performing in touring companies, on Broadway, in dance companies, in movies, on TV, and in other theaters. Many more alumni are teaching in schools, on faculties, choreographing, writing, directing, and stage managing across the world. Broadway and national touring productions of *Contact, Cabaret, 42nd St.,* and *Kiss Me Kate* as well as movie and TV credits, including *Pulp Fiction, Inspector Gadget, Wonder Boys, NYPD Blue, Due South, The Guiding Light, Providence, CSI: NYC,* and *Leaving L.A.* are just a few of the vehicles showcasing Conservatory graduates of theater and dance.

# Purchase College, State University of New York
### Purchase, New York

State-supported, coed. Small town campus. Total enrollment: 4,265.
**Degrees** Bachelor of Fine Arts in the area of dance. Majors and concentrations: ballet, composition, modern dance, performance, production. Graduate degrees offered: Master of Fine Arts in the area of dance.
**Enrollment** 176 total; 167 undergraduate, 9 graduate.
**Dance Student Profile** 77% females, 23% males, 26% minorities, 9% international.
**Dance Faculty** 7 undergraduate (full-time), 8 undergraduate (part time), 5 graduate (part-time). 100% of full-time faculty have terminal degrees. Graduate students do not teach undergraduate courses.
**Student Life** Student groups/activities include Downtown Cabaret, lectures/demonstrations at local schools, national and international performance tours, Purchase Dance Corps.
**Expenses for 2008–2009** Application fee: $40. State resident tuition: $4350 full-time. Nonresident tuition: $10,610 full-time. Mandatory fees: $1647 full-time. College room and board: $9484. College room only: $5886.
**Financial Aid** Program-specific awards: 50 dance scholarships/awards ($2626).
**Application Procedures** Students admitted directly into the professional program freshman year. Deadline for freshmen and transfers: April 15. Notification date for freshmen and transfers: May 1. Required: high school transcript, college transcript(s) for transfer students, audition, minimum TOEFL score of 550 for international applicants. Recommended: SAT or ACT test scores. Auditions held 9 times on campus and off campus in Miami, FL; Chicago, IL; San Francisco, CA; Los Angeles, CA; Interlochen, MI; videotaped performances are permissible as a substitute for live auditions for international applicants and applicants from Hawaii and Puerto Rico.
**Web Site** http://www.purchase.edu/dance
**Undergraduate Contact** Shirley Williams, Counselor, Office of Admissions, Purchase College, State University of New York, 735 Anderson Hill Road, Purchase, New York 10577-1400; 914-251-6317, fax: 914-251-6314, e-mail address: shirley.williams@purchase.edu
**Graduate Contact** Ms. Sabrina Johnston, Counselor, Office of Admissions, Purchase College, State University of New York, 735 Anderson Hill Road, Purchase, New York 10577-1400; 914-251-6479, fax: 914-251-6314, e-mail address: sabrina.johnston@purchase.edu

### *More About the College*
Purchase is a preeminent conservatory program from which to launch a career in dance. It offers professional, comprehensive, in-depth, personalized training in modern dance and classical ballet/performance and composition. The Conservatory of Dance curriculum in the School of the Arts has a shared emphasis for all students in performance and composition. Prospective students must audition in person, except for international students residing abroad, who may send videotapes. Scholarships are awarded

*Purchase College, State University of New York (continued)*

based on the talent demonstrated at the entrance audition. Students in the Conservatory are from thirty-six states and nine other countries.

Performance credits are required for graduation. Students may perform in the Purchase Dance Corps concerts, international and national tours, senior project concerts, M.F.A. concerts, lecture demonstrations, galas and fund-raising events, student concerts, studio showings, and workshops. Performance of a major professional repertory piece is required for the B.F.A. senior project. Purchase Dance Corps International Tours have included Amsterdam (1991); Taiwan (1992, 1995, and 2004); Beijing, China (1994); France (1995); Hong Kong (1987, 1990, 1997, and 2006); Germany (2002); and the Kennedy Center in the United States (2004 and 2006).

The four-year composition curriculum involves each student in performance of a sophomore and junior composition showing. The senior choreography project is mentored by a faculty member and monitored by the faculty senior project committee. The senior project concerts, coproduced by 3 to 4 seniors in the Dance Theatre Lab, are culminating artistic and directorial events that serve the student as a bridge to the profession.

The B.F.A. degree conservatory professional training program requires 120 semester credits to graduate: 90 credits in the professional dance curriculum, 30 credits in liberal arts, which fulfill the SUNY-mandated general education requirements. The program emphasizes modern dance technique/classical ballet technique daily, anatomy for dance, music for dance, dance history, dance production, improvisation, ballet and modern partnering, ballet or modern composition, and pointe. The M.F.A. degree is a 60-credit, two-year, residential curriculum in choreography or performance/teaching.

The Conservatory of Dance faculty members are active in the profession as choreographers, teachers, coaches, musicians, and performers. Alumni are performing or have performed in the Martha Graham Dance Company, the Merce Cunningham Dance Company, the Trisha Brown Dance Company, the Frankfurt Ballet, the Houston Ballet, the Parson's Company, the Mark Morris Dance Group, Limón Dance Company, American Ballet Theatre, Feld's Ballet Tech, the Paul Taylor Dance Company, Alvin Ailey American Dance Theatre, and the Bill T. Jones/Arnie Zane Dance Company. Alumni are founders of their own companies or are freelance choreographers. An extensive listing of alumni accomplishments is available on request.

**Campus and Surroundings** On campus, The Performing Arts Center provides professional theaters for performances by the Conservatory students as well as an annual professional concert series of major contemporary and classical companies. Each company provides a master class for students. Companies included are the Miami City Ballet, Alvin Ailey American Dance Theatre, Paul Taylor Dance Company, Hubbard Street, Bill T. Jones, David Parsons, Mark Morris Dance Group, Urban Bush Women, Jant-Bi, and Lyon Opera Ballet.

Purchase College is 35 minutes north of New York City in a suburban setting where students have the best of both worlds. They reside on campus in residence halls or apartment complexes with students from the other arts programs and liberal arts and sciences. The ease of living in a campus setting, combined with the cultural advantages of Manhattan, informs the students' artistic stimulation and knowledge of the real challenges they are likely to face upon graduation. They travel to the city to attend concerts, take classes, go to auditions, visit museums, and absorb the rich culture. New York City is a crucial resource in the education of these future artists. It is the reality check and the constant reminder of what students work for in their programs in the Conservatory.

**Facilities** The award-winning dance building at Purchase College is the first specially built facility in the United States designed exclusively for the training and performance of dance. There are nine fully equipped, light-filled studios; a 270-seat Dance Theatre

Lab, and The Performing Arts Center, with four theaters, where the Purchase Dance Corps performs.

**Faculty** B.F.A. and M.F.A. faculty members have performed with Martha Graham, Merce Cunningham, Alvin Ailey, José Limón, Viola Farber, Mark Morris, New York City Ballet, and the American Ballet Theatre. They choreograph, teach, and/or set masterworks in Asia, Europe, and South America. They produce their own work in Manhattan. The faculty members teach the students daily. Musicians accompany all technique classes.

**Performance Opportunities** Students are required to perform. The Purchase Dance Corps, the performing company of the Conservatory of Dance B.F.A. program, for which all students are eligible to audition, presents two concerts annually of major professional repertory in The Performing Arts Center, including modern works by artists such as Paul Taylor, Merce Cunningham, and Mark Morris; ballets by George Balanchine, Robert Hill, and Gerald Arpino; works by stellar alumni, such as Doug Varone and Nicolo Fonte; and co-commissioned collaborations with the American Ballet Theatre Ballet Studio Company; the Nutcracker Ballet; works by international choreographers Lin Hwai Min, Shen Wei, and Robert Cohan; as well as commissioned pieces by emerging choreographers and works by faculty members, created especially for the Purchase Dance Corps. Additional performance opportunities include B.F.A. senior project concerts and M.F.A. showings and concerts in the Dance Theatre Lab, special fund-raising events and galas, and summer tours to Asia and Europe.

**Special Programs** Student exchange programs in dance are available in London; Amsterdam; Rotterdam; Perth, Australia; or Taipei. The College also offers a B.A. degree in an arts management certificate. A physical therapist is available two days per week.

For additional information, prospective students should visit the Web site at http://www.purchase.edu/dance.

# Radford University
## Radford, Virginia

State-supported, coed. Small town campus. Total enrollment: 9,122. Dance program established 1966.
**Degrees** Bachelor of Fine Arts in the areas of classical dance, contemporary dance. Majors and concentrations: ballet, contemporary dance.
**Enrollment** 74 total; 50 undergraduate, 24 nonprofessional degree.
**Dance Student Profile** 97% females, 3% males, 4% minorities.
**Dance Faculty** 4 undergraduate (full-time), 2 undergraduate (part-time). 100% of full-time faculty have terminal degrees. Graduate students do not teach undergraduate courses. Undergraduate student–faculty ratio: 8:1.
**Student Life** Student groups/activities include Harmony in Motion, Radford University Dance Theatre, Radford University Ballet Theatre. Special housing available for dance students.
**Expenses for 2007–2008** Application fee: $50. State resident tuition: $4026 full-time. Nonresident tuition: $12,360 full-time. Mandatory fees: $2150 full-time. College room and board: $6490. College room only: $3452. Room and board charges vary according to board plan and housing facility.
**Financial Aid** Program-specific awards: 5–10 Arts Society Scholarships for talented dance majors ($500–$2000), 3–5 Horth Scholarships for summer students dance workshop participants ($300–$1200), Academic Common Market Awards for dance majors from Tennessee, West Virginia, Kentucky and Delaware ($5754).
**Application Procedures** Students admitted directly into the professional program freshman year. Deadline for freshmen and transfers: continuous. Required: essay, high school transcript, college transcript(s) for transfer students, minimum 2.0 high school GPA, interview, audition, SAT or ACT test scores. Auditions held continuously by appointment on campus; videotaped performances are permissible as a substitute for live auditions when distance is prohibitive.
**Web Site** http://www.radford.edu/~dance/

Undergraduate Contact Mr. David Kraus, Director, Office of Admissions, Radford University, PO Box 6903, Radford, Virginia 24142; 540-831-5371, fax: 540-831-5138, e-mail address: dwkraus@radford.edu

## Feinstein College of Arts and Sciences
# Roger Williams University
**Bristol, Rhode Island**

Independent, coed. Total enrollment: 5,166. Dance program established 1972.
**Web Site** http://www.rwu.edu/

# Rutgers, The State University of New Jersey

See Mason Gross School of the Arts

# Ryerson University
**Toronto, Ontario, Canada**

Province-supported, coed. Urban campus. Total enrollment: 30,154 (2007). Dance program established 1971.
**Degrees** Bachelor of Fine Arts. Majors and concentrations: dance.
**Enrollment** 120 total; all undergraduate.
**Dance Student Profile** 91% females, 9% males, 5% minorities, 2% international.
**Dance Faculty** 6 undergraduate (full-time), 10 undergraduate (part-time). 20% of full-time faculty have terminal degrees. Graduate students do not teach undergraduate courses. Undergraduate student–faculty ratio: 6:1.
**Expenses for 2007–2008** Application fee: $100 Canadian dollars. Tuition, fee, and room and board charges are reported in Canadian dollars. Province resident tuition: $4373 full-time. Mandatory fees: $548 full-time. Full-time tuition and fees vary according to course load, degree level, and program. College room and board: $7782. Room and board charges vary according to board plan and housing facility. International student tuition: $12,925 full-time. Special program-related fees: $50 per year for theater ticket voucher, $100 per year for subscription series.
**Financial Aid** Program-specific awards: 3 entrance awards ($2500), 1 second-year award for those demonstrating talent and academic achievement ($2000).
**Application Procedures** Students admitted directly into the professional program freshman year. Deadline for freshmen and transfers: March 1. Required: high school transcript, college transcript(s) for transfer students, minimum 3.0 high school GPA, interview, audition, resumé, photo. Recommended: essay, 2 letters of recommendation. Auditions held on campus; videotaped performances are permissible as a substitute for live auditions for those living outside 300-mile radius. Portfolio reviews held once on campus.
**Web Site** http://www.ryerson.ca
**Undergraduate Contact** Pallavi Rathi, Admission Officer, Dance Program, Ryerson University, 350 Victoria Street, Toronto, Ontario M5B 2K3, Canada; 416-979-5000 ext. 6018, fax: 416-979-5221, e-mail address: p2rathi@ryerson.ca

# San Diego State University
**San Diego, California**

State-supported, coed. Urban campus. Total enrollment: 36,559. Dance program established 1970.
**Degrees** Bachelor of Fine Arts in the areas of performance, choreography. Majors and concentrations: contemporary dance.
**Enrollment** 60 total; 30 undergraduate, 30 nonprofessional degree.
**Dance Student Profile** 95% females, 5% males, 30% minorities, 5% international.
**Dance Faculty** 5 total (full-time), 7 total (part-time). 60% of full-time faculty have terminal degrees. Graduate students do not teach undergraduate courses. Undergraduate student–faculty ratio: 12:1.
**Expenses for 2007–2008** Application fee: $55. State resident tuition: $0 full-time. Nonresident tuition: $10,170 full-time. Mandatory fees: $3428 full-time. Full-time tuition and fees vary according to degree level. College room and board: $10,904. Room and board charges vary according to board plan and housing facility. Special program-related fees: $20 per semester for equipment use fee.
**Financial Aid** Program-specific awards: 4–5 scholarships for dance majors ($500–$1000).
**Application Procedures** Students admitted directly into the professional program freshman year. Deadline for freshmen and transfers: November 30. Notification date for freshmen and transfers: April 1. Required: high school transcript, college transcript(s) for transfer students, minimum 3.0 high school GPA, audition, SAT or ACT test scores. Auditions held twice on campus; videotaped performances are permissible as a substitute for live auditions when distance is prohibitive.
**Web Site** http://www.musicdance.sdsu.edu
**Undergraduate Contact** Mrs. Sandra Konar, Music and Dance Student Coordinator, School of Music and Dance, San Diego State University, San Diego, California 92182-7902; 619-594-6032, fax: 619-594-1692, e-mail address: music.dance@sdsu.edu

# Shenandoah Conservatory
See Shenandoah University

## Shenandoah Conservatory
# Shenandoah University
**Winchester, Virginia**

Independent United Methodist, coed. Total enrollment: 3,393.
**Degrees** Bachelor of Fine Arts. Majors and concentrations: dance, dance education. Graduate degrees offered: Master of Arts in the area of dance; Master of Fine Arts in the area of dance; Master of Science.
**Enrollment** 39 total; 25 undergraduate, 2 graduate, 12 nonprofessional degree.
**Dance Student Profile** 92% females, 8% males, 13% international.
**Dance Faculty** 5 total (full-time), 4 total (part-time). 60% of full-time faculty have terminal degrees. Graduate students teach a few undergraduate courses. Undergraduate student–faculty ratio: 3:1.
**Student Life** Student groups/activities include American College Dance Festival Association, Shenandoah Dance Ensembles on tour, Sigma Rho Delta National Dance Fraternity-Epsilon Chapter.
**Expenses for 2008–2009** Application fee: $30. Comprehensive fee: $31,690 includes full-time tuition ($23,040), mandatory fees ($300), and college room and board ($8350).
**Financial Aid** Program-specific awards: 44 talent and academic scholarships for program majors ($3280).
**Application Procedures** Students admitted directly into the professional program freshman year. Deadline for freshmen and transfers: continuous. Required: high school transcript, college transcript(s) for transfer students, minimum 2.0 high school GPA, letter of recommendation, interview, video, audition, portfolio, SAT or ACT test scores. Auditions held 8 times on campus and off campus in New York, NY; Chicago, IL; Boston, MA; videotaped performances are permissible as a substitute for live auditions with permission. Portfolio reviews held 11 times on campus and off campus.
**Web Site** http://www.su.edu/conservatory
**Contact** Mr. David Anthony, Dean, Admissions Office, Shenandoah University, 1460 University Drive, Winchester, Virginia 22601-5195; 540-665-4581, fax: 540-665-4627, e-mail address: admit@su.edu

# Simon Fraser University

Burnaby, British Columbia, Canada

Province-supported, coed. Suburban campus. Total enrollment: 26,128. Dance program established 1993.
**Web Site** http://www.sfu.ca/

# Slippery Rock University of Pennsylvania

Slippery Rock, Pennsylvania

State-supported, coed. Rural campus. Total enrollment: 8,325. Dance program established 1989.
**Degrees** Bachelor of Arts in the area of dance. Majors and concentrations: dance. Program accredited by NASD.
**Enrollment** 90 total; all undergraduate.
**Dance Student Profile** 95% females, 5% males, 3% minorities.
**Dance Faculty** 6 undergraduate (full-time), 1 undergraduate (part-time). 100% of full-time faculty have terminal degrees. Graduate students do not teach undergraduate courses. Undergraduate student–faculty ratio: 15:1.
**Student Life** Student groups/activities include Slippery Rock University Dance Theatre, Slippery Rock University Tour Group, Dance Express. Special housing available for dance students.
**Expenses for 2007–2008** Application fee: $30. State resident tuition: $5178 full-time. Nonresident tuition: $7767 full-time. Mandatory fees: $1493 full-time. Full-time tuition and fees vary according to course load and degree level. College room and board: $7862. College room only: $5618. Room and board charges vary according to board plan, housing facility, and location.
**Financial Aid** Program-specific awards: 1 freshman scholarship for freshmen ($1000), 1 transfer scholarship for transfer students ($1000), 1 Lucy I. Sack Scholarship for dance majors ($1000), 2 summer study scholarships for dance majors ($500).
**Application Procedures** Students admitted directly into the professional program freshman year. Deadline for freshmen and transfers: continuous. Required: essay, high school transcript, college transcript(s) for transfer students, minimum 2.0 high school GPA, interview, audition, SAT or ACT test scores (minimum combined SAT score of 930, minimum composite ACT score of 20). Recommended: minimum 3.0 high school GPA. Auditions held 3 times on campus; videotaped performances are permissible as a substitute for live auditions if campus visit impossible.
**Web Site** http://www.sru.edu
**Undergraduate Contact** Nora Ambrosio, Professor, Dance Department, Slippery Rock University of Pennsylvania, Slippery Rock, Pennsylvania 16057; 724-738-2036, fax: 724-738-4524, e-mail address: nora.ambrosio@sru.edu

## *Meadows School of the Arts*
# Southern Methodist University

Dallas, Texas

Independent, coed. Suburban campus. Total enrollment: 10,829.
**Degrees** Bachelor of Fine Arts in the area of dance performance. Majors and concentrations: ballet, jazz dance, modern dance. Graduate degrees offered: Master of Fine Arts in the area of dance. Program accredited by NASD.
**Enrollment** 82 total; 78 undergraduate, 4 graduate.
**Dance Student Profile** 82% females, 18% males, 19% minorities.
**Dance Faculty** 8 total (full-time), 5 total (part-time). 50% of full-time faculty have terminal degrees. Graduate students do not teach undergraduate courses. Undergraduate student–faculty ratio: 6:1.
**Student Life** Student groups/activities include American Dance Festival, Dallas Morning News Dance Festival, Dance for the Planet. Special housing available for dance students.
**Expenses for 2008–2009** Application fee: $60. Comprehensive fee: $45,073 includes full-time tuition ($29,430), mandatory fees ($3768), and college room and board ($11,875). College room only: $7655.

**Financial Aid** Program-specific awards: Meadows Artistic Scholarships for talented program majors ($1000–$5000).
**Application Procedures** Students apply for admission into the professional program by sophomore year. Deadline for freshmen and transfers: continuous. Required: essay, high school transcript, college transcript(s) for transfer students, letter of recommendation, audition, SAT or ACT test scores. Recommended: minimum 3.0 high school GPA, interview. Auditions held 12 times on campus and off campus in various national venues; videotaped performances are permissible as a substitute for live auditions when distance or schedule is prohibitive.
**Web Site** http://www.smu.edu/meadows/dance
**Undergraduate Contact** Kevin Hofeditz, Associate Dean for Student Affairs, Meadows School of the Arts, Southern Methodist University, PO Box 750356, Dallas, Texas 75275-0356; 214-768-3947, fax: 214-768-3272, e-mail address: hofeditz@mail.smu.edu
**Graduate Contact** Jean Cherry, Coordinator, Graduate Studies, Division of Dance, Southern Methodist University, PO Box 750356, Dallas, Texas 75275-0356; 214-768-3765, fax: 214-768-3272.

# State University of New York at Fredonia

Fredonia, New York

State-supported, coed. Small town campus. Total enrollment: 5,404. Dance program established 2007.
**Degrees** Bachelor of Fine Arts. Majors and concentrations: dance. Program accredited by NAST.
**Enrollment** 12 total; all undergraduate.
**Dance Student Profile** 60% females, 40% males, 5% minorities.
**Dance Faculty** 3 undergraduate (full-time), 1 undergraduate (part-time). 66% of full-time faculty have terminal degrees. Graduate students do not teach undergraduate courses. Undergraduate student–faculty ratio: 4:1.
**Student Life** Student groups/activities include Orchesis Dance (student dance organization).
**Expenses for 2007–2008** Application fee: $40. State resident tuition: $4350 full-time. Nonresident tuition: $10,610 full-time. Mandatory fees: $1192 full-time. College room and board: $8380. College room only: $5050. Room and board charges vary according to board plan and housing facility. Special program-related fees: $35 per semester for dance department fees.
**Financial Aid** Program-specific awards: 6 Jack Cogdill Scholarships for program majors ($1250), 4 Gertrude Prushaw Maytum Scholarships for program majors ($1250), 1 Carol Preuit Award for Dance for program majors ($600), 1 Myers New Major Award for new BFA dance students ($600), 1 Trentillig Scholarship for program major ($1100).
**Application Procedures** Students admitted directly into the professional program freshman year. Deadline for freshmen and transfers: continuous. Required: high school transcript, college transcript(s) for transfer students, 2 letters of recommendation, interview, audition, SAT or ACT test scores. Recommended: minimum 3.0 high school GPA. Auditions held 6 times on campus; videotaped performances are permissible as a substitute for live auditions for international students only.
**Web Site** http://www.fredonia.edu/department/theatre/index.asp
**Undergraduate Contact** Prof. Stephen E. Rees, Chair, Department of Theatre and Dance, State University of New York at Fredonia, 212 Rockefeller Arts Center, Fredonia, New York 14063; 716-673-3596, fax: 716-673-3621, e-mail address: stephen.rees@fredonia.edu

# Sybil B. Harrington College of Fine Arts and Humanities

See West Texas A&M University

# Temple University

Philadelphia, Pennsylvania

State-related, coed. Urban campus. Total enrollment: 34,696. Dance program established 1970.
**Web Site** http://www.temple.edu/

## Texas Christian University
### Fort Worth, Texas

Independent, coed. Suburban campus. Total enrollment: 8,668. Dance program established 1949.
**Degrees** Bachelor of Fine Arts in the area of ballet or modern dance. Majors and concentrations: ballet, modern dance, teacher certification. Graduate degrees offered: Master of Fine Arts in the area of ballet or modern dance. Program accredited by NASD.
**Enrollment** 70 total; all undergraduate.
**Dance Student Profile** 85% females, 15% males, 10% minorities, 2% international.
**Dance Faculty** 6 undergraduate (full-time), 6 undergraduate (part-time). 70% of full-time faculty have terminal degrees. Graduate students do not teach undergraduate courses. Undergraduate student–faculty ratio: 9:1.
**Student Life** Student groups/activities include Chi Tau Epsilon (honor society).
**Expenses for 2007–2008** Application fee: $40. Comprehensive fee: $33,068 includes full-time tuition ($24,820), mandatory fees ($48), and college room and board ($8200). College room only: $5000. Room and board charges vary according to board plan and housing facility.
**Financial Aid** Program-specific awards: 4 Nordan Awards for dance majors ($10,000), 1 Adrienne Perner Scholarship for ballet, female, military family students ($5000).
**Application Procedures** Students admitted directly into the professional program freshman year. Notification date for transfers: continuous. Required: high school transcript, college transcript(s) for transfer students, letter of recommendation, audition, SAT or ACT test scores, photo in first arabesque. Recommended: interview. Auditions held 4 times on campus; videotaped performances are permissible as a substitute for live auditions for international applicants only with specific requirements.
**Web Site** http://www.dance.tcu.edu
**Contact** Ms. Ellen Page Shelton, Director, TCU School for Classical and Contemporary Dance, Texas Christian University, PO Box 297910, Fort Worth, Texas 76129; 817-257-7615, fax: 817-257-7675, e-mail address: e.shelton@tcu.edu

## Tisch School of the Arts, Department of Dance

See New York University

## Towson University
### Towson, Maryland

State-supported, coed. Suburban campus. Total enrollment: 19,758. Dance program established 1982.
**Web Site** http://www.towson.edu/

## Tulane University
### New Orleans, Louisiana

Independent, coed. Urban campus. Total enrollment: 10,519. Dance program established 1940.
**Degrees** Bachelor of Fine Arts. Majors and concentrations: dance. Cross-registration with Loyola University.
**Enrollment** 310 total; 10 undergraduate, 300 nonprofessional degree.
**Dance Student Profile** 90% females, 10% males, 12% minorities, 8% international.
**Dance Faculty** 4 undergraduate (full-time), 8 undergraduate (part-time). 100% of full-time faculty have terminal degrees. Graduate students do not teach undergraduate courses. Undergraduate student–faculty ratio: 3:1.
**Student Life** Student groups/activities include Newcomb Dance Company (student company), Spring Arts, Young Performers (student choreography).

**Expenses for 2007–2008** Application fee: $0. Comprehensive fee: $45,550 includes full-time tuition ($33,500), mandatory fees ($3110), and college room and board ($8940). College room only: $5140. Room and board charges vary according to board plan and housing facility.
**Application Procedures** Students apply for admission into the professional program by freshman year. Deadline for freshmen: January 15; transfers: June 1. Required: essay, high school transcript, college transcript(s) for transfer students, letter of recommendation, audition, SAT or ACT test scores. Recommended: minimum 2.0 high school GPA, minimum 3.0 high school GPA, interview. Auditions held by appointment on campus.
**Web Site** http://www.tulane.edu/~theatre/danceProg.html
**Undergraduate Contact** John Allen, Theatre and Dance, Tulane University, 215 McWilliams Hall, New Orleans, Louisiana 70118; 504-314-7759, fax: 504-865-6737, e-mail address: jallen1@tulane.edu

## The University of Akron
### Akron, Ohio

State-supported, coed. Urban campus. Total enrollment: 23,007. Dance program established 1970.
**Degrees** Bachelor of Arts in the area of dance; Bachelor of Fine Arts in the area of dance. Majors and concentrations: dance. Program accredited by NASD.
**Enrollment** 130 total; 35 undergraduate, 20 graduate, 75 nonprofessional degree.
**Dance Student Profile** 94% females, 6% males, 13% minorities, 2% international.
**Dance Faculty** 10 undergraduate (full-time), 16 undergraduate (part-time). 75% of full-time faculty have terminal degrees. Graduate students do not teach undergraduate courses. Undergraduate student–faculty ratio: 10:1.
**Student Life** Student groups/activities include Ohio Association of Health, Physical Education, Recreation, and Dance, American College Dance Festival Association, OHIODANCE, Association of Arts Administration Educators (AAAE).
**Expenses for 2007–2008** Application fee: $30. State resident tuition: $7218 full-time. Nonresident tuition: $16,467 full-time. Mandatory fees: $1164 full-time. Full-time tuition and fees vary according to course load, degree level, and location. College room and board: $8003. College room only: $4955. Room and board charges vary according to board plan and housing facility. Special program-related fees: $15 per course for trainer, supplies and student support.
**Financial Aid** Program-specific awards available.
**Application Procedures** Students apply for admission into the professional program by sophomore year. Deadline for freshmen and transfers: August 12. Required: high school transcript, college transcript(s) for transfer students, audition, SAT or ACT test scores. Recommended: video. Auditions held twice on campus; videotaped performances are permissible as a substitute for live auditions if a campus visit is impossible.
**Web Site** http://www.uakron.edu/dtaa
**Undergraduate Contact** Neil Sapienza, Acting Director, School of Dance, Theatre, and Arts Administration, The University of Akron, Guzzetta Hall, Akron, Ohio 44325-2502; 330-972-7948, fax: 330-972-7892, e-mail address: nbs@uakron.edu

## The University of Arizona
### Tucson, Arizona

State-supported, coed. Urban campus. Total enrollment: 37,217. Dance program established 1984.
**Web Site** http://www.arizona.edu/

## University of California, Santa Barbara
### Santa Barbara, California

State-supported, coed. Suburban campus. Total enrollment: 21,410. Dance program established 1984.
**Web Site** http://www.ucsb.edu/

## *College-Conservatory of Music Dance Division*
# University of Cincinnati
### Cincinnati, Ohio

State-supported, coed. Urban campus. Total enrollment: 29,319. Dance program established 1964.

**Degrees** Bachelor of Fine Arts in the area of dance. Majors and concentrations: ballet. Program accredited by NASD.

**Enrollment** 47 total; all undergraduate.

**Dance Student Profile** 85% females, 15% males, 2% minorities.

**Dance Faculty** 4 undergraduate (full-time), 4 undergraduate (part-time). 20% of full-time faculty have terminal degrees. Graduate students do not teach undergraduate courses. Undergraduate student–faculty ratio: 7:1.

**Student Life** Student groups/activities include Choreographers Showcase, informal studio showings, Ballet Ensemble.

**Expenses for 2007–2008** Application fee: $40. State resident tuition: $7896 full-time. Nonresident tuition: $22,419 full-time. Mandatory fees: $1503 full-time. Full-time tuition and fees vary according to course load, degree level, location, program, and reciprocity agreements. College room and board: $8799. College room only: $5259. Room and board charges vary according to board plan and housing facility. Special program-related fees: $78 per quarter for technology fee.

**Financial Aid** Program-specific awards: honor awards for program majors ($1000–$8000).

**Application Procedures** Students admitted directly into the professional program freshman year. Deadline for freshmen and transfers: continuous. Notification date for freshmen and transfers: continuous. Required: high school transcript, college transcript(s) for transfer students, minimum 2.0 high school GPA, letter of recommendation, audition, SAT or ACT test scores. Recommended: minimum 3.0 high school GPA. Auditions held 11 times on campus and off campus in Louisville, KY; Toledo, OH; Columbus, OH; Lynchburg, VA; Interlochen, MI; Charlotte, NC; Boston, MA; videotaped performances are permissible as a substitute for live auditions when distance is prohibitive with approval from the division head.

**Web Site** http://www.ccm.uc.edu/dance/

**Undergraduate Contact** Ms. Kelly Hebblethwaite, Admissions Officer, College-Conservatory of Music, University of Cincinnati, PO Box 210003, Cincinnati, Ohio 45221-0003; 513-556-5463, fax: 513-556-1028, e-mail address: kelly.hebblethwaite@uc.edu

# University of Colorado at Boulder
### Boulder, Colorado

State-supported, coed. Suburban campus. Total enrollment: 31,470. Dance program established 1948.

**Degrees** Bachelor of Fine Arts in the area of dance. Majors and concentrations: choreography and performance, contemporary dance. Graduate degrees offered: Master of Fine Arts in the area of dance.

**Enrollment** 102 total; 13 undergraduate, 15 graduate, 74 nonprofessional degree.

**Dance Student Profile** 90% females, 10% males, 14% minorities, 1% international.

**Dance Faculty** 7 total (full-time), 5 total (part-time). 85% of full-time faculty have terminal degrees. Graduate students do not teach undergraduate courses. Undergraduate student–faculty ratio: 2:1.

**Student Life** Student groups/activities include American College Dance Festival Association, Onstage (theater and dance student group), Black College Dance Exchange.

**Expenses for 2008–2009** Application fee: $50. One-time mandatory fee: $112. State resident tuition: $5922 full-time. Nonresident tuition: $25,400 full-time. Mandatory fees: $1356 full-time. College room and board: $9860. Special program-related fees: $10 per course (jazz classes) for tapes and compact discs, $20 per course for guest lecturer fee, $40–$70 per course for accompanist fee (modern, ballet, music theater, African, flamenco).

**Financial Aid** Program-specific awards: 10–12 University Dance Awards for program majors ($250–$1000), 1–3 Redmond Scholarships for upperclass program majors demonstrating talent and academic achievement ($800–$2000), 1 Katherine J.

Lamont Scholarship for program majors ($500–$1000), 1 De Castro Scholarship for program majors ($300–$500), 1 Freshman Scholarship for freshman majors ($300–$600).

**Application Procedures** Students apply for admission into the professional program by sophomore year. Deadline for freshmen: January 15; transfers: April 1. Notification date for freshmen and transfers: continuous. Required: essay, high school transcript, college transcript(s) for transfer students, minimum 2.0 high school GPA, SAT or ACT test scores, letter of application to dance faculty, at least 1 semester as BA student in dance program, enrollment in or completion of beginning composition.

**Web Site** http://www.colorado.edu/TheatreDance

**Undergraduate Contact** Office of Admissions, University of Colorado at Boulder, 030 UCB, Boulder, Colorado 80309; 303-492-6301, fax: 303-492-7115, e-mail address: apply@colorado.edu

**Graduate Contact** Michelle Gipner, Graduate Secretary, Department of Theatre and Dance, University of Colorado at Boulder, 261 UCB, Boulder, Colorado 80309; 303-492-7356, fax: 303-492-7722, e-mail address: michelle.gipner@colorado.edu

# University of Florida
### Gainesville, Florida

State-supported, coed. Suburban campus. Total enrollment: 51,725. Dance program established 1975.

**Degrees** Bachelor of Fine Arts in the area of dance performance. Majors and concentrations: choreography and performance, dance in medicine, dance theater, world dance. Cross-registration with Florida State University System.

**Enrollment** 29 total; all undergraduate.

**Dance Student Profile** 90% females, 10% males, 20% minorities, 1% international.

**Dance Faculty** 6 undergraduate (full-time), 4 undergraduate (part-time). 100% of full-time faculty have terminal degrees. Graduate students do not teach undergraduate courses. Undergraduate student–faculty ratio: 5:1.

**Student Life** Student groups/activities include Edgework Dance Company, Florida Mod Project, Agbedidi Africa. Special housing available for dance students.

**Expenses for 2007–2008** Application fee: $30. State resident tuition: $3257 full-time. Nonresident tuition: $17,841 full-time. College room and board: $7020. College room only: $4530. Room and board charges vary according to board plan. Special program-related fees: $15–$45 for lab fees.

**Financial Aid** Program-specific awards: 5 Constans Theatre and Dance Scholarships for program majors ($500), 5 Ingram Scholarships for program majors ($500), 2 Richardson Scholarships for program majors ($1000), 8 Stoughton Scholarships for program majors ($500), 3 Outstanding Senior Awards for graduating seniors ($500).

**Application Procedures** Students admitted directly into the professional program freshman year. Deadline for freshmen: January 7; transfers: June 7. Required: essay, high school transcript, college transcript(s) for transfer students, minimum 2.0 high school GPA, audition, SAT or ACT test scores. Recommended: minimum 3.0 high school GPA, letter of recommendation. Auditions held twice on campus; videotaped performances are permissible as a substitute for live auditions with approval from the school and in compliance with UF/School of Theatre and Dance video auditions requirements as posted on Web site.

**Web Site** http://www.arts.ufl.edu/theatreanddance

**Undergraduate Contact** Dr. Russella Brandman, Coordinator of Dance, School of Theatre and Dance, University of Florida, PO Box 115900, Gainesville, Florida 32611-5900; 352-273-5054, fax: 352-392-5114, e-mail address: drdance@ufl.edu

## *The Hartt School*
# University of Hartford
### West Hartford, Connecticut

Independent, coed. Suburban campus. Total enrollment: 7,290. Dance program established 1994.

**Web Site** http://www.hartford.edu/

# University of Hawaii at Manoa
## Honolulu, Hawaii

State-supported, coed. Urban campus. Total enrollment: 20,357. Dance program established 1965.

**Degrees** Bachelor of Fine Arts in the area of dance. Majors and concentrations: dance theater. Graduate degrees offered: Master of Arts in the areas of dance ethnology, dance education; Master of Fine Arts in the area of dance.

**Enrollment** 57 total; 40 undergraduate, 17 graduate.

**Dance Student Profile** 90% females, 10% males, 70% minorities, 10% international.

**Dance Faculty** 5 total (full-time), 9 total (part-time). 80% of full-time faculty have terminal degrees. Graduate students teach a few undergraduate courses. Undergraduate student–faculty ratio: 10:1.

**Student Life** Student groups/activities include American College Dance Festival Association, Council of Dance Administrators, London Contemporary Dance School Exchange Program.

**Expenses for 2007–2008** Application fee: $50. State resident tuition: $5136 full-time. Nonresident tuition: $14,400 full-time. Mandatory fees: $254 full-time. College room and board: $7185. College room only: $4527.

**Financial Aid** Program-specific awards: 2 Department of Theatre and Dance tuition waivers for BA and BFA dance students, John Young Scholarship Fund Awards for dance majors ($2500).

**Application Procedures** Students apply for admission into the professional program by freshman year. Deadline for freshmen and transfers: May 7. Required: college transcript(s) for transfer students, minimum 3.0 high school GPA, audition, SAT or ACT test scores, minimum TOEFL score of 600 for international applicants. Auditions held once on campus.

**Web Site** http://www2.hawaii.edu/~uhmdance

**Undergraduate Contact** Ms. Peggy Gaither Adams, Undergraduate Advisor, Department of Theatre and Dance, University of Hawaii at Manoa, 1770 East West Road, Honolulu, Hawaii 96822; 808-956-3264, fax: 808-956-4234, e-mail address: adamsp@hawaii.edu

**Graduate Contact** Mr. Gregg Lizenbery, Director and Graduate Chair of Dance, Department of Theatre and Dance, University of Hawaii at Manoa, 1770 East West Road, Honolulu, Hawaii 96822; 808-956-2464, fax: 808-956-4234, e-mail address: lgreg@hawaii.edu

# University of Idaho
## Moscow, Idaho

State-supported, coed. Small town campus. Total enrollment: 11,636.

**Degrees** Bachelor of Science in the area of dance. Majors and concentrations: dance.

**Enrollment** 30 total; all undergraduate.

**Dance Student Profile** 90% females, 10% males, 20% minorities.

**Dance Faculty** 2 total (full-time), 4 total (part-time). 100% of full-time faculty have terminal degrees. Graduate students do not teach undergraduate courses. Undergraduate student–faculty ratio: 15:1.

**Student Life** Student groups/activities include Dance Major Club. Special housing available for dance students.

**Expenses for 2007–2008** Application fee: $40. Area resident tuition: $0 full-time. State resident tuition: $0 full-time. Nonresident tuition: $10,080 full-time. Mandatory fees: $4410 full-time. Full-time tuition and fees vary according to degree level and program. College room and board: $6424. Room and board charges vary according to board plan and housing facility.

**Financial Aid** Program-specific awards: 1 Freshman Scholarship for dance majors ($1000), 5 Bookstore Dance Scholarships for dance majors ($1000).

**Application Procedures** Students admitted directly into the professional program freshman year. Required: essay, high school transcript, college transcript(s) for transfer students, minimum 2.0 high school GPA, audition, SAT or ACT test scores. Auditions held twice on campus; videotaped performances are permissible as a substitute for live auditions.

**Web Site** http://www.dance.uidaho.edu

**Undergraduate Contact** Greg Halloran, Director, Division of Health, Physical Education, Recreation, and Dance, University of Idaho, Physical Education Building, Room 101, Moscow, Idaho 83844-2401; 208-885-2184, fax: 208-885-5929, e-mail address: halloran@uidaho.edu

# University of Illinois at Urbana–Champaign
## Champaign, Illinois

State-supported, coed. Urban campus. Total enrollment: 42,326. Dance program established 1949.

**Degrees** Bachelor of Fine Arts in the area of dance. Majors and concentrations: choreography and performance, dance. Graduate degrees offered: Master of Fine Arts in the area of dance. Program accredited by NASD.

**Enrollment** 74 total; 60 undergraduate, 14 graduate.

**Dance Student Profile** 92% females, 8% males, 9% minorities, 5% international.

**Dance Faculty** 11 total (full-time), 7 total (part-time). 88% of full-time faculty have terminal degrees. Graduate students teach a few undergraduate courses. Undergraduate student–faculty ratio: 8:1.

**Student Life** Student groups/activities include Illini Union Board Musicals, Student Dance Movement.

**Expenses for 2007–2008** Application fee: $40. State resident tuition: $8440 full-time. Nonresident tuition: $22,526 full-time. Mandatory fees: $2690 full-time. Full-time tuition and fees vary according to course load, program, and student level. College room and board: $8196. Room and board charges vary according to board plan and housing facility. Entering degree-seeking students are guaranteed the same tuition rates for 4 years.

**Financial Aid** Program-specific awards: talented student awards.

**Application Procedures** Students admitted directly into the professional program freshman year. Deadline for freshmen and transfers: continuous. Notification date for freshmen and transfers: continuous. Required: essay, high school transcript, college transcript(s) for transfer students, minimum 3.0 high school GPA, interview, audition, SAT or ACT test scores. Auditions held 3 times on campus; videotaped performances are permissible as a substitute for live auditions when distance is prohibitive.

**Web Site** http://www.dance.uiuc.edu/

**Undergraduate Contact** Linda Lehovec, Associate Professor, Department of Dance, University of Illinois at Urbana–Champaign, 907 1/2 West Nevada, Urbana, Illinois 61801-3810; 217-333-1010, fax: 217-333-3000.

**Graduate Contact** Mrs. Cindi Howard, Program Coordinator, Department of Dance, University of Illinois at Urbana–Champaign, 907 1/2 West Nevada, Urbana, Illinois 61801-3810; 217-333-1011, fax: 217-333-3000, e-mail address: choward1@uiuc.edu

# The University of Iowa
## Iowa City, Iowa

State-supported, coed. Small town campus. Total enrollment: 29,117. Dance program established 1987.

**Degrees** Bachelor of Fine Arts. Majors and concentrations: dance. Graduate degrees offered: Master of Fine Arts in the area of dance. Program accredited by NASD.

**Enrollment** 191 total; 6 undergraduate, 11 graduate, 174 nonprofessional degree.

**Dance Student Profile** 94% females, 6% males, 6% minorities, 1% international.

**Dance Faculty** 9 total (full-time). 55% of full-time faculty have terminal degrees. Graduate students do not teach undergraduate courses. Undergraduate student–faculty ratio: 2:1.

**Student Life** Student groups/activities include American College Dance Festival Association. Special housing available for dance students.

**Expenses for 2008–2009** Application fee: $40. State resident tuition: $5548 full-time. Nonresident tuition: $19,662 full-time. Mandatory fees: $996 full-time. College room and board: $7673.

*The University of Iowa (continued)*

**Financial Aid** Program-specific awards: 5 Upper Classmen Iowa Center for the Arts Scholarships for upper classman program majors ($1000), 1 Iowa Center for the Arts Scholarship for incoming freshmen ($5000), 1 T. J. Myers Memorial Scholarship for male incoming freshmen ($1000), 1 dance scholarship for program majors ($1000), 2 Francoise Martinet Scholarships for program majors ($1000), 6 Dance Foundation Scholarships for program majors ($1000).
**Application Procedures** Students apply for admission into the professional program by sophomore year. Deadline for freshmen and transfers: April 1. Required: high school transcript, college transcript(s) for transfer students, audition, SAT or ACT test scores, audition or video for placement and scholarship consideration, minimum 2.5 high school GPA. Recommended: essay, minimum 3.0 high school GPA, 3 letters of recommendation, interview, resumé. Auditions held 4 times on campus; videotaped performances are permissible as a substitute for live auditions when distance is prohibitive or for financial reasons.
**Web Site** http://www.uiowa.edu/~dance
**Undergraduate Contact** Charlotte Adams, Associate Professor, Dance Department, The University of Iowa, E114 Halsey Hall, Iowa City, Iowa 52242; 319-335-2185, fax: 319-335-3246, e-mail address: charlotte-adams@uiowa.edu
**Graduate Contact** Armando Duarte, Professor, Dance Department, The University of Iowa, E114 Halsey Hall, Iowa City, Iowa 52242; 319-335-2186, fax: 319-335-3246, e-mail address: armando-duarte@uiowa.edu

# University of Massachusetts Amherst

## Amherst, Massachusetts

State-supported, coed. Total enrollment: 25,873. Dance program established 1974.
**Degrees** Bachelor of Fine Arts. Majors and concentrations: dance. Cross-registration with Amherst College, Hampshire College, Mount Holyoke College, Smith College.
**Enrollment** 45 total; 30 undergraduate, 15 nonprofessional degree.
**Dance Student Profile** 92% females, 8% males, 10% minorities.
**Dance Faculty** 3 undergraduate (full-time), 1 undergraduate (part-time). Graduate students teach a few undergraduate courses. Undergraduate student–faculty ratio: 14:1.
**Student Life** Student groups/activities include Alive With Dance, Dance Team, Music Theater Guild.
**Expenses for 2008–2009** Application fee: $40. State resident tuition: $1714 full-time. Nonresident tuition: $9937 full-time. Mandatory fees: $8703 full-time. College room and board: $8114. College room only: $4524.
**Financial Aid** Program-specific awards: 12 Chancellor's Talent Awards for program students.
**Application Procedures** Students admitted directly into the professional program freshman year. Deadline for freshmen: January 15; transfers: May 2. Notification date for freshmen: April 15; transfers: June 1. Required: essay, high school transcript, college transcript(s) for transfer students, audition, SAT or ACT test scores. Auditions held 4 times on campus; videotaped performances are permissible as a substitute for live auditions when distance is prohibitive, if auditions are full, or in special circumstances.
**Web Site** http://www.umass.edu/hfa
**Undergraduate Contact** Ms. Mary Lou Laurenza, Director of Dance Admissions, Dance Program, University of Massachusetts Amherst, 11 Totman, Amherst, Massachusetts 01003; 413-545-6064, fax: 413-545-0220, e-mail address: mllauren@dance.umass.edu

# University of Michigan

## Ann Arbor, Michigan

State-supported, coed. Suburban campus. Total enrollment: 41,042. Dance program established 1929.
**Degrees** Bachelor of Fine Arts in the area of dance. Majors and concentrations: choreography and performance, modern dance. Graduate degrees offered: Master of Fine Arts in the area of dance.

**Enrollment** 399 total; 64 undergraduate, 10 graduate, 325 nonprofessional degree.
**Dance Student Profile** 90% females, 10% males, 7% minorities, 2% international.
**Dance Faculty** 11 total (full-time), 3 total (part-time). 90% of full-time faculty have terminal degrees. Graduate students do not teach undergraduate courses. Undergraduate student–faculty ratio: 7:1.
**Expenses for 2007–2008** Application fee: $40. State resident tuition: $10,258 full-time. Nonresident tuition: $31,112 full-time. Mandatory fees: $189 full-time. Full-time tuition and fees vary according to course load, degree level, location, program, and student level. College room and board: $8190. Room and board charges vary according to board plan and housing facility.
**Financial Aid** Program-specific awards: dance merit scholarships for incoming students.
**Application Procedures** Students admitted directly into the professional program freshman year. Deadline for freshmen and transfers: December 1. Required: essay, high school transcript, college transcript(s) for transfer students, minimum 3.0 high school GPA, 2 letters of recommendation, audition, SAT or ACT test scores (minimum combined SAT score of 1650, minimum composite ACT score of 24), written personal statement. Auditions held 5 times on campus; videotaped performances are permissible as a substitute for live auditions with permission of the chair.
**Web Site** http://www.music.umich.edu
**Undergraduate Contact** Ms. Laura Strozeski, Assistant Dean for Enrollment Management and Student Services, School of Music Office of Admissions and Student Services, University of Michigan, 2240 Moore Building, 1100 Baits Drive, Ann Arbor, Michigan 48109-2085; 734-764-0593, fax: 734-763-5097, e-mail address: music.admissions@umich.edu
**Graduate Contact** Bill De Young, Chair, Department of Dance, University of Michigan, 1310 North University Court, Ann Arbor, Michigan 48109-2217; 734-763-5460, fax: 734-763-5962, e-mail address: bdyj@umich.edu

# University of Minnesota, Twin Cities Campus

## Minneapolis, Minnesota

State-supported, coed. Urban campus. Total enrollment: 50,883. Dance program established 1987.
**Degrees** Bachelor of Fine Arts. Majors and concentrations: dance. Program accredited by NASD.
**Enrollment** 1,100 total; 100 undergraduate, 1,000 nonprofessional degree.
**Dance Student Profile** 83% females, 17% males, 16% minorities, 2% international.
**Dance Faculty** 5 undergraduate (full-time), 38 undergraduate (part-time). 100% of full-time faculty have terminal degrees. Graduate students do not teach undergraduate courses. Undergraduate student–faculty ratio: 4:1.
**Student Life** Student groups/activities include West Bank Arts Quarter Collective, Student Dance Coalition. Special housing available for dance students.
**Expenses for 2007–2008** Application fee: $45. One-time mandatory fee: $1000. State resident tuition: $7950 full-time. Nonresident tuition: $19,580 full-time. Full-time tuition varies according to program and reciprocity agreements. College room and board: $7062. College room only: $4184. Room and board charges vary according to board plan, housing facility, and location. Special program-related fees: $55 for musician accompanist fee.
**Financial Aid** Program-specific awards: 1 Jenwilla Scholarship for dance majors ($1000), 1 Sealy Scholarship for incoming freshman ($2500), 1 Nadine Jette-Sween Scholarship for dance majors ($2000), 1 Marion Haynes Andrus Scholarship for dance majors ($1000), 1 Tom and Ellie Crosby Scholarship for incoming freshmen or newly declared dance majors ($1000), 1 Robert Moulton Memorial Scholarship for dance majors ($2000), 1 Barbara Barker Scholarship for dance majors ($2000), 1–3 Gertrude Lippincott Scholarships for incoming freshman ($6000), 1 Stefannie Valencia Kierlen Memorial Scholarship for dance

majors ($1000), 1 Marge Maddux Scholarship for incoming freshman ($2500), 1 Hope-Supan Scholarship for incoming freshman ($3000).
**Application Procedures** Students admitted directly into the professional program freshman year. Deadline for freshmen and transfers: continuous. Required: essay, high school transcript, college transcript(s) for transfer students, interview, audition, SAT or ACT test scores, core subjects. Recommended: minimum 3.0 high school GPA, letter of recommendation. Auditions held 3 times on campus; videotaped performances are permissible as a substitute for live auditions when distance or financial circumstances are prohibitive.
**Web Site** http://dance.umn.edu
**Undergraduate Contact** Office of Admissions, University of Minnesota, Twin Cities Campus, 240 Williamson Hall, 231 Pillsbury Drive, SE, Minneapolis, Minnesota 55455; 612-625-2008.

## University of Missouri–Kansas City
### Kansas City, Missouri

State-supported, coed. Urban campus. Total enrollment: 14,442. Dance program established 1907.
**Degrees** Bachelor of Fine Arts. Majors and concentrations: dance.
**Enrollment** 72 total; all undergraduate.
**Dance Student Profile** 75% females, 25% males, 10% minorities, 2% international.
**Dance Faculty** 5 undergraduate (full-time), 3 undergraduate (part-time). 100% of full-time faculty have terminal degrees. Graduate students do not teach undergraduate courses. Undergraduate student–faculty ratio: 10:1.
**Student Life** Student groups/activities include Dance Students Association.
**Expenses for 2008–2009** Application fee: $35. State resident tuition: $7368 full-time. Nonresident tuition: $18,459 full-time. Mandatory fees: $1028 full-time. College room and board: $7841. College room only: $5460.
**Financial Aid** Program-specific awards: endowed scholarships for program majors ($700–$2500).
**Application Procedures** Students admitted directly into the professional program freshman year. Deadline for freshmen and transfers: March 7. Notification date for freshmen and transfers: continuous. Required: high school transcript, college transcript(s) for transfer students, minimum 2.0 high school GPA, 3 letters of recommendation, audition, ACT score for state residents, SAT or ACT score for out-of-state residents. Recommended: minimum 3.0 high school GPA. Auditions held by appointment on campus; videotaped performances are permissible as a substitute for live auditions for provisional acceptance.
**Web Site** http://www.umkc.edu/conservatory
**Undergraduate Contact** Dr. James T. Elswick, Associate Director of Admissions, Conservatory of Music and Dance, University of Missouri–Kansas City, 5227 Holmes Road, Kansas City, Missouri 64110; 816-235-2900, fax: 816-235-5264, e-mail address: cadmissions@umkc.edu

## The University of Montana
### Missoula, Montana

State-supported, coed. Total enrollment: 13,858. Dance program established 1972.
**Degrees** Bachelor of Fine Arts in the area of dance. Majors and concentrations: choreography and performance, dance education.
**Enrollment** 37 total; 15 undergraduate, 22 nonprofessional degree.
**Dance Student Profile** 95% females, 5% males, 1% minorities.
**Dance Faculty** 4 undergraduate (full-time), 2 undergraduate (part-time). 100% of full-time faculty have terminal degrees. Graduate students do not teach undergraduate courses. Undergraduate student–faculty ratio: 17:1.
**Student Life** Student groups/activities include Headwaters Dance Company, UM Student Dance Ensemble.
**Expenses for 2008–2009** Application fee: $30. State resident tuition: $3739 full-time. Nonresident tuition: $15,014 full-time. Mandatory fees: $1441 full-time. College room and board:

$6258. College room only: $2808. Special program-related fees: $20–$60 for class materials/accompanist fee (selected classes).
**Financial Aid** Program-specific awards: 2 departmental scholarships for program majors ($500–$1000), 2 Alexander Dean Awards for program majors ($500), 1 Kliber Memorial Award for program majors ($1000), 7 Odyssey Scholarships for program majors ($200–$400).
**Application Procedures** Students apply for admission into the professional program by freshman year. Deadline for freshmen and transfers: March 1. Notification date for freshmen and transfers: continuous. Required: essay, high school transcript, college transcript(s) for transfer students, minimum 2.0 high school GPA, audition, SAT or ACT test scores (minimum combined SAT score of 1540, minimum composite ACT score of 22). Recommended: see www.sfa.umt.edu/drama. Auditions held once at the end of freshman year on campus.
**Web Site** http://www.sfa.umt.edu/drama
**Undergraduate Contact** Erin McDaniel, Administrative Assistant, Department of Drama/Dance, The University of Montana, PARTV 196, Missoula, Montana 59812; 406-243-4481, fax: 406-243-5726, e-mail address: umtheatredance@umontana.edu

## The University of North Carolina at Greensboro
### Greensboro, North Carolina

State-supported, coed. Urban campus. Total enrollment: 17,157. Dance program established 1948.
**Web Site** http://www.uncg.edu/

## University of Oklahoma
### Norman, Oklahoma

State-supported, coed. Suburban campus. Total enrollment: 26,205. Dance program established 1963.
**Degrees** Bachelor of Fine Arts in the area of dance. Majors and concentrations: ballet, modern dance. Graduate degrees offered: Master of Fine Arts in the area of dance.
**Enrollment** 83 total; 78 undergraduate, 5 graduate.
**Dance Student Profile** 87% females, 13% males, 25% minorities, 4% international.
**Dance Faculty** 11 total (full-time), 4 total (part-time). 67% of full-time faculty have terminal degrees. Graduate students do not teach undergraduate courses. Undergraduate student–faculty ratio: 5:1.
**Student Life** Student groups/activities include Student Advisory Council.
**Expenses for 2007–2008** Application fee: $40. State resident tuition: $2609 full-time. Nonresident tuition: $9900 full-time. Mandatory fees: $1925 full-time. Full-time tuition and fees vary according to course load, location, program, and reciprocity agreements. College room and board: $7058. College room only: $3854. Room and board charges vary according to board plan and housing facility. Special program-related fees: $110 per course for accompanist.
**Financial Aid** Program-specific awards: 15–20 tuition waivers for out-of-state program students ($1500–$4000), 10–20 Barnett Foundation Scholarships for exceptional dancers ($300–$800), 2–6 Everett Foundation Scholarships for male ballet majors ($1000), 4–6 fee waivers for state residents ($500–$1000), 2 Busken Scholarships for junior/senior ballet majors ($2000).
**Application Procedures** Students admitted directly into the professional program freshman year. Deadline for freshmen and transfers: continuous. Notification date for freshmen and transfers: continuous. Required: high school transcript, minimum 3.0 high school GPA, 2 letters of recommendation, audition, SAT or ACT test scores (minimum composite ACT score of 24), minimum SAT score of 1090 for state residents; 1170 for nonresidents, minimum ACT score of 24 for state residents; 26 for nonresidents. Recommended: college transcript(s) for transfer students, interview. Auditions held twice on campus; videotaped performances are permissible as a substitute for live auditions when distance is prohibitive.
**Web Site** http://www.ou.edu/finearts

*University of Oklahoma (continued)*

**Undergraduate Contact** Ms. Kate O'Brien-Hamoush, Staff Assistant, School of Dance, University of Oklahoma, 560 Parrington Oval, Room 1000, Norman, Oklahoma 73019; 405-325-4051, fax: 405-325-7024, e-mail address: dance@ou.edu

**Graduate Contact** Prof. Jeremy Lindberg, Graduate Liaison, School of Dance, University of Oklahoma, 560 Parrington Oval, Room 1000, Norman, Oklahoma 73019; 405-325-5312, fax: 405-325-7024, e-mail address: jlindberg@ou.edu

# University of Southern Mississippi
## Hattiesburg, Mississippi

State-supported, coed. Suburban campus. Total enrollment: 14,592. Dance program established 1982.
**Web Site** http://www.usm.edu/

# University of South Florida
## Tampa, Florida

State-supported, coed. Urban campus. Total enrollment: 44,870.
**Web Site** http://www.usf.edu

# The University of Tennessee at Martin
## Martin, Tennessee

State-supported, coed. Small town campus. Total enrollment: 7,173. Dance program established 1999.
**Degrees** Bachelor of Fine Arts in the area of fine and performing arts. Majors and concentrations: dance education.
**Enrollment** 2 total; all undergraduate.
**Dance Faculty** 1 undergraduate (full-time). 100% of full-time faculty have terminal degrees. Graduate students do not teach undergraduate courses.
**Student Life** Student groups/activities include UTM Dance Ensemble.
**Expenses for 2007–2008** Application fee: $30. State resident tuition: $4150 full-time. Nonresident tuition: $14,190 full-time. Mandatory fees: $855 full-time. College room and board: $4446. College room only: $2160. Room and board charges vary according to board plan and housing facility.
**Financial Aid** Program-specific awards available.
**Application Procedures** Students admitted directly into the professional program freshman year. Deadline for freshmen and transfers: continuous. Required: high school transcript, college transcript(s) for transfer students, audition, SAT or ACT test scores, ACT score of 21 and high school GPA of 2.50, or ACT score of 18 and high school GPA of 2.85. Auditions held once on campus; videotaped performances are permissible as a substitute for live auditions whenever needed.
**Web Site** http://www.utm.edu/departments/chfa/finearts/
**Undergraduate Contact** Mr. Douglas J. Cook, Chair, Department of Art, Dance and Theatre, The University of Tennessee at Martin, 102 Fine Arts Building, Martin, Tennessee 38238; 731-881-7400, fax: 731-881-7415, e-mail address: dcook@utm.edu

# The University of Texas at Austin
## Austin, Texas

State-supported, coed. Urban campus. Total enrollment: 50,170. Dance program established 1938.
**Web Site** http://www.utexas.edu/

# The University of the Arts
## Philadelphia, Pennsylvania

Independent, coed. Total enrollment: 2,396. Dance program established 1947.
**Degrees** Bachelor of Fine Arts in the areas of dance, dance education, modern dance, ballet, jazz dance. Majors and concentrations: ballet, dance, dance education, jazz dance, modern dance. Program accredited by NASD.

**Enrollment** 278 total; all undergraduate.
**Dance Student Profile** 77% females, 23% males, 38% minorities, 1% international.
**Dance Faculty** 10 undergraduate (full-time), 34 undergraduate (part-time). 30% of full-time faculty have terminal degrees. Graduate students do not teach undergraduate courses. Undergraduate student–faculty ratio: 6:1.
**Student Life** Student groups/activities include Student Government. Special housing available for dance students.
**Expenses for 2008–2009** Application fee: $60. Tuition: $29,500 full-time. Mandatory fees: $1100 full-time. College room only: $7047.
**Financial Aid** Program-specific awards: 35 merit scholarships for incoming students ($1000–$12,000).
**Application Procedures** Students admitted directly into the professional program freshman year. Deadline for freshmen and transfers: continuous. Notification date for freshmen and transfers: September 1. Required: essay, high school transcript, college transcript(s) for transfer students, minimum 2.0 high school GPA, letter of recommendation, audition, SAT or ACT test scores, resume. Recommended: minimum 3.0 high school GPA, interview, photo. Auditions held 9 times on campus and off campus in various locations in California; videotaped performances are permissible as a substitute for live auditions if student lives more than 200 miles from Philadelphia.
**Web Site** http://www.uarts.edu
**Undergraduate Contact** Susan Gandy, Director of Admission, The University of the Arts, 320 South Broad Street, Philadelphia, Pennsylvania 19102; 800-616-ARTS ext. 6049, fax: 215-717-6045, e-mail address: admissions@uarts.edu

## More About the University

The University of the Arts embraces all the arts. Here, students discover a community of creative individuals whose passion and commitment spur them to create works that make a lasting impact on society. Located on the Avenue of the Arts in the heart of Center City Philadelphia, UArts is next to the Kimmel Center for the Performing Arts. The University offers undergraduate and graduate degree programs to 2,300 full-time students from forty states and thirty other countries.

The UArts School of Dance offers an environment in which students develop an individual artistic vision while learning to be thoughtful, well-rounded artists and people. Students are prepared to dance professionally at the highest level through a rigorous studio experience and excellent instruction. As dance majors at UArts, students go beyond technique and explore the full expressive potential of dance—its beauty and power, elegance, and athleticism.

Over 200 students are enrolled, making it one of the largest dance departments in the United States. Students complete a two-year core curriculum before specializing in classical ballet, modern, jazz, or dance education. Students take classes in ballet, modern, jazz, tap, African, Brazilian, and Spanish as well as choreography, music, and repertory. Liberal arts courses and electives complete the core. Aspiring young artists are prepared to pursue careers as professional performers, dance educators, or choreographers.

The School of Dance includes nine state-of-the-art, spacious, fully-equipped, well-lit dance studios with lockers, dressing rooms, showers, and lounges. Students perform in the UArts Dance Theater, a 200-seat theater used exclusively for dance. The magnificent, historic 1,800-seat Merriam Theater is home to the School's winter and spring concerts. The University of the Arts maintains a strong relationship with local and national arts organizations, including the Philadelphia Dance Alliance, Dance Affiliates, PHILADANCO, the American Dance Festival, and Jacob's Pillow.

The UArts faculty of acclaimed professionals guides students as they strengthen their bodies and refine their technique. Students train with professionals who are familiar with the world of dance and its demands. Faculty come from many prominent areas of dance, including the National Ballet of Hungary, the Alvin Ailey American Dance Theater, the Pennsylvania Ballet, Dance Theater of Harlem, Momix, the Martha Graham Dance Company, PHILADANCO, New York City Ballet, the Broadway stage, and many more.

UArts alumni have gone on to perform with such prominent companies as Pilobolus, Alvin Ailey, the Joffrey Ballet, Jose Limon, Bejart, Cirque du Soleil, Rumble, Momix, and PHILADANCO. They have appeared in the Broadway productions of Evita, Cats, and The Lion King, and many alumni dance in film, video productions, and musical revues on cruise ships and cabarets. Alumni have also become dance teachers in high schools, colleges, and private dance studios, full- or part-time. Those who choose to pursue advanced degrees in dance have received prestigious teaching assistantships and fellowships. Graduates have found numerous choreographic opportunities in companies throughout the world, and several have established their own companies.

UArts' Summer World of Dance, the Pre-College Summer Institute at UArts, is a unique environment where high school juniors and seniors ages 16–18 can find their way in the world as artists, thinkers, creators, and performers. This two-week intensive course is designed to provide the serious dancer with an opportunity to hone his or her skills and explore new techniques and styles within a university environment. Students within the dance program take a full day of classes, workshops, and rehearsals within the University's studios. All courses in the dance program are taught by professionals in the fields who teach in the undergraduate program in the School of Dance.

In the spring of 2008, the University of the Arts hosted the ninth National High School Dance Festival, welcoming more the 1,500 students in grades 9–12 representing ninety high schools with 300 teachers and principals and 100 college recruiters and vendors. The Festival also offers a full day of scholarship auditions and more than 300 master classes in subject areas including ballet, modern, jazz, tap, hip hop, musical theater, salsa, African, Pilates, massage, stretch, injury prevention, nutrition, and more.

The University of the Arts has made a strong commitment to providing a supportive living and learning environment. The University offers four undergraduate residence halls. All are furnished and have bathroom and kitchen facilities in each apartment. Each building has 24-hour security and maintenance.

Financial aid and scholarships are available. Admission is based on both an audition and a review of academic credentials.

## Ballet Department
# University of Utah
### Salt Lake City, Utah

State-supported, coed. Urban campus. Total enrollment: 28,025. Dance program established 1951.
**Degrees** Bachelor of Fine Arts in the area of ballet. Majors and concentrations: ballet. Graduate degrees offered: Master of Arts in the area of ballet; Master of Fine Arts in the area of ballet.
**Enrollment** 312 total; 110 undergraduate, 8 graduate, 194 nonprofessional degree.
**Dance Student Profile** 90% females, 10% males, 10% minorities, 5% international.
**Dance Faculty** 7 total (full-time), 10 total (part-time). 43% of full-time faculty have terminal degrees. Graduate students teach a few undergraduate courses. Undergraduate student–faculty ratio: 15:1.
**Student Life** Student groups/activities include collaborative concerts, student guest artist opportunities, senior concert. Special housing available for dance students.
**Expenses for 2007–2008** Application fee: $35. State resident tuition: $4269 full-time. Nonresident tuition: $14,945 full-time. Mandatory fees: $717 full-time. Full-time tuition and fees vary according to course level, course load, degree level, program, reciprocity agreements, and student level. College room and board: $5778. College room only: $2890. Room and board charges vary according to board plan and housing facility.

Contact university directly for part-time tuition costs. Special program-related fees: $5–$15 for live accompanists, $10 for hydrostatic weighing of students.
**Financial Aid** Program-specific awards: 6 Willam F. Christensen Scholarships for resident incoming program students ($2000), 25–40 departmental scholarships for program students ($600–$6000), 1–2 Honors at Entrance/Presidential Scholarships for ballet majors demonstrating high academic achievement ($2280–$7000), 1 Fine Arts Advisory Board Award for juniors or seniors ($2000), 1 Kennecott Award for juniors/seniors ($2000).
**Application Procedures** Students admitted directly into the professional program freshman year. Deadline for freshmen and transfers: March 1. Notification date for freshmen and transfers: May 31. Required: high school transcript, college transcript(s) for transfer students, minimum 2.0 high school GPA, 2 letters of recommendation, audition, SAT or ACT test scores, 2 photographs in ballet poses (women on pointe), application form (ballet majors). Recommended: essay, minimum 3.0 high school GPA. Auditions held twice on campus; videotaped performances are permissible as a substitute for live auditions when distance is prohibitive or time constraints exist (request instructions).
**Web Site** http://www.ballet.utah.edu
**Undergraduate Contact** Ms. Pamela Rasmussen, Administrative Assistant, Ballet Department, University of Utah, 330 S 1500 E, Room 112, Salt Lake City, Utah 84112-0280; 801-581-8231, fax: 801-581-5442, e-mail address: pamela.rasmussen@utah.edu
**Graduate Contact** Prof. Richard Wacko, Graduate Advisor, Ballet Department, University of Utah, 330 S 1500 E, Room 112, Salt Lake City, Utah 84112-0280; 801-587-3742, fax: 801-581-5442, e-mail address: richard.wacko@utah.edu

## Department of Modern Dance
# University of Utah
### Salt Lake City, Utah

State-supported, coed. Urban campus. Total enrollment: 28,025. Dance program established 1940.
**Degrees** Bachelor of Fine Arts. Majors and concentrations: modern dance. Graduate degrees offered: Master of Fine Arts in the area of modern dance.
**Enrollment** 100 total; 80 undergraduate, 20 graduate.
**Dance Student Profile** 90% females, 10% males, 10% minorities, 5% international.
**Dance Faculty** 10 total (full-time), 2 total (part-time). 90% of full-time faculty have terminal degrees. Graduate students do not teach undergraduate courses. Undergraduate student–faculty ratio: 6:1.
**Student Life** Student groups/activities include American College Dance Festival Association, Associated Student Organization, Student Dance Company. Special housing available for dance students.
**Expenses for 2007–2008** Application fee: $35. State resident tuition: $4269 full-time. Nonresident tuition: $14,945 full-time. Mandatory fees: $717 full-time. Full-time tuition and fees vary according to course level, course load, degree level, program, reciprocity agreements, and student level. College room and board: $5778. College room only: $2890. Room and board charges vary according to board plan and housing facility. Contact university directly for part-time tuition costs. Special program-related fees: $8–$15 per class for equipment use fee, musicians.
**Financial Aid** Program-specific awards: 3 Hayes Scholarships for state residents, 15 departmental scholarships for program students.
**Application Procedures** Students admitted directly into the professional program freshman year. Deadline for freshmen: August 25; transfers: April 1. Required: high school transcript, college transcript(s) for transfer students, minimum 3.0 high school GPA, audition. Auditions held 3 times on campus and off campus in various cities; videotaped performances are permissible as a substitute for live auditions.
**Web Site** http://www.dance.utah.edu
**Undergraduate Contact** Department of Modern Dance, University of Utah, 330 S 1500 E, Room 106, Salt Lake City, Utah 84112-0280; 801-581-7327, fax: 801-581-5442.

*University of Utah (continued)*

**Graduate Contact** Mr. Steve Koester, Director of Graduate Studies, Department of Modern Dance, University of Utah, 330 South 1500 East, Room 106, Salt Lake City, Utah 84112-0280; 801-581-7327, fax: 801-581-5442, e-mail address: stephen.koester@utah.edu

## University of Wisconsin–Milwaukee
### Milwaukee, Wisconsin

State-supported, coed. Urban campus. Total enrollment: 29,338. Dance program established 1965.
**Degrees** Bachelor of Fine Arts in the areas of dance (K-12 certification option), musical theatre. Majors and concentrations: contemporary dance, dance education, music theater. Graduate degrees offered: Master of Fine Arts in the area of dance.
**Enrollment** 125 total; 100 undergraduate, 25 graduate.
**Dance Student Profile** 90% females, 10% males, 15% minorities.
**Dance Faculty** 9 undergraduate (full-time), 6 graduate (full-time), 23 total (part-time). 66% of full-time faculty have terminal degrees. Graduate students do not teach undergraduate courses. Undergraduate student–faculty ratio: 11:1.
**Student Life** Student groups/activities include Terpsichorean People.
**Expenses for 2007–2008** Application fee: $35. State resident tuition: $6960 full-time. Nonresident tuition: $16,686 full-time. Mandatory fees: $767 full-time. Full-time tuition and fees vary according to location, program, and reciprocity agreements. College room only: $3620. Room charges vary according to housing facility. Special program-related fees: $20 per credit for guest artists, workshops, performance expenses.
**Financial Aid** Program-specific awards available.
**Application Procedures** Students admitted directly into the professional program freshman year. Required: essay, high school transcript, college transcript(s) for transfer students, interview, audition, ACT test score only (minimum composite ACT score of 17). Auditions held on campus.
**Web Site** http://arts.uwm.edu/dance
**Undergraduate Contact** Office Manager, Department of Dance, University of Wisconsin–Milwaukee, PO Box 413, Milwaukee, Wisconsin 53201-0413; 414-229-2571, e-mail address: danceinfo@uwm.edu
**Graduate Contact** Simone Ferro, Director of Graduate Studies in Dance, Department of Dance, University of Wisconsin–Milwaukee, PO Box 413, Milwaukee, Wisconsin 53201; 414-229-4178, e-mail address: sferro@uwm.edu

## University of Wyoming
### Laramie, Wyoming

State-supported, coed. Total enrollment: 12,875. Dance program established 1972.
**Degrees** Bachelor of Fine Arts in the area of dance. Majors and concentrations: ballet, jazz dance, modern dance.
**Enrollment** 65 total; 40 undergraduate, 25 nonprofessional degree.
**Dance Student Profile** 90% females, 10% males, 15% minorities, 1% international.
**Dance Faculty** 12 undergraduate (full-time), 1 undergraduate (part-time). 90% of full-time faculty have terminal degrees. Graduate students do not teach undergraduate courses. Undergraduate student–faculty ratio: 10:1.
**Student Life** Student groups/activities include Associated Students of the Performing Arts.
**Expenses for 2007–2008** Application fee: $40. One-time mandatory fee: $40. State resident tuition: $2820 full-time. Nonresident tuition: $9660 full-time. Mandatory fees: $734 full-time. Full-time tuition and fees vary according to course load, location, program, and reciprocity agreements. College room and board: $7274. College room only: $3158. Room and board charges vary according to board plan and housing facility.
**Financial Aid** Program-specific awards: 21 departmental awards for program majors ($2575).

**Application Procedures** Students admitted directly into the professional program freshman year. Deadline for freshmen and transfers: August 31. Required: high school transcript, college transcript(s) for transfer students, SAT or ACT test scores, audition for scholarship consideration, minimum 2.5 high school GPA. Recommended: letter of recommendation, interview, audition. Auditions held twice on campus and off campus in Rocky Mountain Theatre Association Festival locations; videotaped performances are permissible as a substitute for live auditions if a campus visit is impossible.
**Web Site** http://www.uwyo.edu/th&d/
**Undergraduate Contact** Leigh Selting, Head, Department of Theatre and Dance, University of Wyoming, Department 3951, 1000 East University Avenue, Laramie, Wyoming 82071-3951; 307-766-2198, fax: 307-766-2197, e-mail address: selting@uwyo.edu

## Virginia Commonwealth University
### Richmond, Virginia

State-supported, coed. Urban campus. Total enrollment: 31,907. Dance program established 1981.
**Degrees** Bachelor of Fine Arts in the area of dance and choreography. Majors and concentrations: modern dance. Program accredited by NASD.
**Enrollment** 80 total; all undergraduate.
**Dance Student Profile** 85% females, 15% males, 30% minorities.
**Dance Faculty** 8 undergraduate (full-time), 14 undergraduate (part-time). 63% of full-time faculty have terminal degrees. Graduate students do not teach undergraduate courses. Undergraduate student–faculty ratio: 10:1.
**Student Life** Student groups/activities include public performances, dance festivals.
**Expenses for 2007–2008** Application fee: $40. State resident tuition: $4482 full-time. Nonresident tuition: $16,858 full-time. Mandatory fees: $1714 full-time. College room and board: $7567. College room only: $4497. Room and board charges vary according to board plan. Special program-related fees: $30 per course for dance course fees, $75–$265 per semester for School of the Arts major fees.
**Financial Aid** Program-specific awards: Oates Dance Education Scholarship for full-time students who wish to teach dance (K-12), Carpenter Foundation Scholarship for full-time students, School of the Arts Scholarship in Dance for incoming freshman.
**Application Procedures** Students admitted directly into the professional program freshman year. Deadline for freshmen and transfers: continuous. Notification date for freshmen and transfers: continuous. Required: high school transcript, college transcript(s) for transfer students, minimum 2.0 high school GPA, 2 letters of recommendation, audition, SAT or ACT test scores. Recommended: essay. Auditions held 4 times on campus; videotaped performances are permissible as a substitute for live auditions when distance is prohibitive.
**Web Site** http://www.vcu.edu/artweb/dance/
**Undergraduate Contact** Dr. James Frazier, Chair, Department of Dance and Choreography, Virginia Commonwealth University, 1315 Floyd Avenue, Box 843007, Richmond, Virginia 23284-3007; 804-828-1711, fax: 804-828-7356, e-mail address: jfrazier@vcu.edu

## Virginia Intermont College
### Bristol, Virginia

Independent, coed. Small town campus. Total enrollment: 635.
**Web Site** http://www.vic.edu/

### *Leigh Gerdine College of Fine Arts*
## Webster University
### St. Louis, Missouri

Independent, coed. Suburban campus. Total enrollment: 8,430. Dance program established 1970.
**Degrees** Bachelor of Fine Arts. Majors and concentrations: dance. Cross-registration with various colleges in St. Louis.

**Enrollment** 40 total; all undergraduate.

**Dance Student Profile** 93% females, 7% males, 5% minorities.

**Dance Faculty** 2 undergraduate (full-time), 5 undergraduate (part-time). Graduate students do not teach undergraduate courses.

**Student Life** Student groups/activities include Dance Club, Fine Arts Club.

**Expenses for 2007–2008** Application fee: $35. Comprehensive fee: $27,550 includes full-time tuition ($19,330) and college room and board ($8220). College room only: $4100. Full-time tuition varies according to program. Room and board charges vary according to board plan and housing facility.

**Application Procedures** Students admitted directly into the professional program freshman year. Deadline for freshmen and transfers: May 1. Required: essay, high school transcript, college transcript(s) for transfer students, letter of recommendation, audition, SAT or ACT test scores (minimum combined SAT score of 1500, minimum composite ACT score of 21). Recommended: minimum 2.0 high school GPA. Auditions held 12 times on campus; videotaped performances are permissible as a substitute for live auditions when distance is prohibitive.

**Web Site** http://www.webster.edu

**Undergraduate Contact** Carrie Indelicato, Auditions Coordinator, Office of Admissions, Webster University, 470 East Lockwood Avenue, St. Louis, Missouri 63119-3194; 314-968-7001, fax: 314-968-7115, e-mail address: cgeorge@webster.edu

# Western Michigan University
## Kalamazoo, Michigan

State-supported, coed. Urban campus. Total enrollment: 24,433. Dance program established 1972.

**Degrees** Bachelor of Fine Arts in the area of dance. Majors and concentrations: dance. Program accredited by NASD.

**Enrollment** 79 total; 8 undergraduate, 71 nonprofessional degree.

**Dance Student Profile** 90% females, 10% males, 10% minorities.

**Dance Faculty** 8 undergraduate (full-time), 6 undergraduate (part-time). 75% of full-time faculty have terminal degrees. Graduate students do not teach undergraduate courses. Undergraduate student–faculty ratio: 2:1.

**Student Life** Student groups/activities include Orchesis Dance Society, Western Dance Project (student touring ensemble), university musicals and operas.

**Expenses for 2007–2008** Application fee: $35. One-time mandatory fee: $300. State resident tuition: $6570 full-time. Nonresident tuition: $16,116 full-time. Mandatory fees: $690 full-time. Full-time tuition and fees vary according to course load, location, and student level. College room and board: $7042. College room only: $3725. Room and board charges vary according to board plan. Special program-related fees: $10 for guest speakers, $25–$70 per technique course for accompanying fee, guest artists fee, equipment.

**Financial Aid** Program-specific awards: 8–10 Jean Warner Labelle Dance Scholarships for outstanding majors ($500), 1–4 Dalton New Dance Major Scholarships for incoming students ($500), 1–6 Exceptional Dance Major Scholarships for talented program majors ($750), 4–6 Outstanding Dance Major Scholarships for outstanding program majors ($1000–$2000), 1–4 Partners in Dance Scholarships for outstanding majors ($500–$1000), 1 Wendy L. Cornish Scholarship for outstanding major ($600), 1 Ethel Perry Eaton Dance Scholarship for outstanding majors ($500), 1 Arthur and Martha Hearron Dance Scholarship for outstanding major ($750).

**Application Procedures** Students apply for admission into the professional program by sophomore year. Deadline for freshmen and transfers: May 1. Notification date for freshmen and transfers: continuous. Required: high school transcript, college transcript(s) for transfer students, minimum 2.0 high school GPA, audition, SAT or ACT test scores, high school transcripts for transfer students with fewer than 26 transferable credit hours. Auditions held 3 times (October, November, and February) on campus and off campus in Detroit, MI; videotaped performances are permissible as a substitute for live auditions for international applicants.

**Web Site** http://www.wmich.edu/dance

**Undergraduate Contact** Jane Baas, Associate Professor of Dance and Academic Advisor, Department of Dance, Western Michigan University, 1903 West Michigan Avenue, Kalamazoo, Michigan 49008-5417; 269-387-5845, fax: 269-387-5820, e-mail address: jane.baas@wmich.edu

## Sybil B. Harrington College of Fine Arts and Humanities
# West Texas A&M University
## Canyon, Texas

State-supported, coed. Small town campus. Total enrollment: 7,502. Dance program established 1984.

**Degrees** Bachelor of Fine Arts. Majors and concentrations: dance. Graduate degrees offered: Master of Arts in the area of interdisciplinary studies.

**Enrollment** 14 total; 13 undergraduate, 1 graduate.

**Dance Student Profile** 60% females, 40% males, 16% minorities, 1% international.

**Dance Faculty** 2 total (full-time), 1 total (part-time). Graduate students do not teach undergraduate courses. Undergraduate student–faculty ratio: 7:1.

**Student Life** Student groups/activities include American College Dance Festival Association, Dance for the Planet, community outreach performances.

**Expenses for 2008–2009** Application fee: $25.

**Financial Aid** Program-specific awards: 10 Endowed Scholarships for dancers ($1000).

**Application Procedures** Students admitted directly into the professional program freshman year. Deadline for freshmen and transfers: August 1. Notification date for freshmen and transfers: August 1. Required: high school transcript, college transcript(s) for transfer students, minimum 2.0 high school GPA, audition, SAT or ACT test scores, minimum 2.5 high school GPA for out-of-state students. Recommended: essay, 2 letters of recommendation, interview. Auditions held at various times on campus; videotaped performances are permissible as a substitute for live auditions when distance is prohibitive.

**Web Site** http://www.wtamu.edu/academic/fah/mus

**Contact** Mr. Edward Truitt, Director of Dance, Department of Art, Theatre, and Dance, West Texas A&M University, Box 60747, Canyon, Texas 79016-0001; 806-651-2820, fax: 806-651-2818.

# Wichita State University
## Wichita, Kansas

State-supported, coed. Urban campus. Total enrollment: 14,442. Dance program established 1978.

**Degrees** Bachelor of Fine Arts in the area of performing arts/dance. Majors and concentrations: dance. Program accredited by NASD.

**Enrollment** 39 total; all undergraduate.

**Dance Student Profile** 90% females, 10% males, 10% minorities.

**Dance Faculty** 3 undergraduate (full-time), 5 undergraduate (part-time). 100% of full-time faculty have terminal degrees. Graduate students do not teach undergraduate courses. Undergraduate student–faculty ratio: 7:1.

**Student Life** Student groups/activities include Kansas Dance Festival, Mid-America Dance Network, American College Dance Festival Association, Wichita Contemporary Dance Theatre Touring Company. Special housing available for dance students.

**Expenses for 2007–2008** Application fee: $30. State resident tuition: $3912 full-time. Nonresident tuition: $11,259 full-time. Mandatory fees: $858 full-time. Full-time tuition and fees vary according to course load. College room and board: $5580. Room and board charges vary according to board plan and housing facility. Special program-related fees: $12 per course for live accompanying fees for specific courses.

**Financial Aid** Program-specific awards: 16–18 Miller Dance Scholarships for incoming students ($600–$1200), 4 City Dance Scholarships for incoming and continuing students ($300–$1200), 1 Kim Stephens Scholarship for continuing students ($600), 1 Mildred McCoy Armstrong Award for continuing

*Wichita State University (continued)*

students ($275), 1 Martha Fleming Award for continuing students ($300), 2 Lulu Donavia Scholarships for out of state students ($2500).

**Application Procedures** Students admitted directly into the professional program freshman year. Deadline for freshmen and transfers: continuous. Required: high school transcript, college transcript(s) for transfer students, minimum 2.0 high school GPA, SAT or ACT test scores. Recommended: audition. Auditions held once and by arrangement on campus.

**Web Site** http://www.wichita.edu

**Undergraduate Contact** Ms. Gina Crabtree, Director of Admissions, Undergraduate Admissions, Wichita State University, 1845 Fairmount, Wichita, Kansas 67260-0124; 316-978-3085.

# Wright State University

## Dayton, Ohio

State-supported, coed. Suburban campus. Total enrollment: 16,151.

**Degrees** Bachelor of Fine Arts. Majors and concentrations: dance.

**Dance Faculty** Graduate students do not teach undergraduate courses.

**Student Life** Student groups/activities include Dayton Ballet II Company, Dayton Contemporary Dance Company II.

**Expenses for 2007–2008** Application fee: $30. State resident tuition: $7278 full-time. Nonresident tuition: $14,004 full-time. College room and board: $7180. Special program-related fees: $190 per quarter for private voice lessons.

**Financial Aid** Program-specific awards: Theatre Arts Talent Scholarship for acting, dance, motion picture production, and design/technology students, merit scholarships for all majors.

**Application Procedures** Students admitted directly into the professional program freshman year. Deadline for freshmen and transfers: March 1. Required: high school transcript, college transcript(s) for transfer students, interview, audition, SAT or ACT test scores, dance photograph. Auditions held twice on campus; videotaped performances are permissible as a substitute for live auditions when distance is prohibitive.

**Web Site** http://www.wright.edu/tdmp

**Undergraduate Contact** Ms. Victoria Oleen, Managing Director, Department of Theatre, Dance & Motion Pictures, Wright State University, 3640 Colonel Glenn Highway, T148 CAC, Dayton, Ohio 45435; 937-775-3072, fax: 937-775-3787, e-mail address: victoria.oleen@wright.edu

# York University

## Toronto, Ontario, Canada

Province-supported, coed. Urban campus. Total enrollment: 51,420. Dance program established 1970.

**Degrees** Bachelor of Fine Arts in the areas of dance performance, composition. Majors and concentrations: ballet, composition, modern dance. Cross-registration with University of Chichester (United Kingdom).

**Enrollment** 262 total; 194 undergraduate, 68 nonprofessional degree.

**Dance Student Profile** 98% females, 2% males, 2% international.

**Dance Faculty** 15 total (full-time), 17 total (part-time). 92% of full-time faculty have terminal degrees. Graduate students teach a few undergraduate courses. Undergraduate student–faculty ratio: 7:1.

**Student Life** Student groups/activities include Dance Students Association, Creative Arts Students Association.

**Expenses for 2007–2008** Application fee: $175 Canadian dollars. Tuition, fee, and room and board charges are reported in Canadian dollars. Comprehensive fee: $11,664 includes full-time tuition ($5278) and college room and board ($6386). College room only: $3986. Full-time tuition varies according to course load, degree level, and program. Room and board charges vary according to board plan and housing facility. International student tuition: $15,278 full-time. Special program-related fees: $20 per year for studio/conditioning equipment/lockers.

**Financial Aid** Program-specific awards: 2 talent awards for applicants with outstanding auditions ($1000), 5 Harry Rowe Bursaries for those demonstrating achievement or potential in artistic or scholarly work ($1000–$2000), Fine Arts Bursaries for academically qualified students demonstrating financial need, 1 Spedding Memorial Award for applicants showing excellence in choreography and demonstrating need ($550), 1 Manorama Thakkar Award in Indian Dance for those demonstrating academic/artistic excellence and achievement in Indian dance studies ($500), Dance Department Awards for those demonstrating exceptional talent and need, 1 Menaka Thakkar Award in World Dance for 3rd- or 4th- year students demonstrating excellence in world dance ($500), 10 IMASCO Performing Arts Awards for 2nd- or 3rd-year students demonstrating outstanding ability and sound academic standing ($3000).

**Application Procedures** Students admitted directly into the professional program freshman year. Deadline for freshmen and transfers: February 1. Notification date for freshmen: June 16; transfers: continuous. Required: essay, high school transcript, minimum 3.0 high school GPA, interview, audition, 2 letters of recommendation and video if applicant cannot audition in person. Recommended: 2 letters of recommendation. Auditions held 10 times on campus; videotaped performances are permissible as a substitute for live auditions when distance is prohibitive.

**Web Site** http://www.yorku.ca/finearts/dance/

**Undergraduate Contact** Susan Wessels, Coordinator, Recruitment and Liaison, Student and Academic Services, York University, 201R Goldfarb Centre of Fine Arts, 4700 Keele Street, Toronto, Ontario M3J 1P3, Canada; 416-736-2100 ext. 77141, fax: 416-736-5447, e-mail address: swessels@yorku.ca

# Music Programs

## Aaron Copland School of Music
See Queens College of the City University of New York

## Abilene Christian University
### Abilene, Texas

Independent, coed. Urban campus. Total enrollment: 4,675. Music program established 1906.

**Degrees** Bachelor of Music in the areas of voice performance, piano performance, vocal music education, instrumental music education, piano teaching (with band tract, vocal tract, or orchestra tract). Majors and concentrations: instrumental music, piano, vocal music. Cross-registration with Hardin-Simmons University. Program accredited by NASM.

**Enrollment** 75 total; all undergraduate.

**Music Student Profile** 57% females, 43% males, 5% minorities, 7% international.

**Music Faculty** 12 undergraduate (full-time), 12 undergraduate (part-time). 60% of full-time faculty have terminal degrees. Graduate students do not teach undergraduate courses. Undergraduate student–faculty ratio: 17:1.

**Student Life** Student groups/activities include Children's Theater, Sing Song, Homecoming Musical.

**Expenses for 2007–2008** Application fee: $25. Comprehensive fee: $23,760 includes full-time tuition ($16,710), mandatory fees ($700), and college room and board ($6350). College room only: $2950. Full-time tuition and fees vary according to course load. Room and board charges vary according to board plan and housing facility. Special program-related fees: $215–$325 per credit hour for private lessons.

**Financial Aid** Program-specific awards: 40 budgeted awards for musically qualified program majors ($1500), 10 endowed awards for program majors ($1000).

**Application Procedures** Students admitted directly into the professional program freshman year. Deadline for freshmen and transfers: August 31. Required: high school transcript, college transcript(s) for transfer students, 2 letters of recommendation, audition, SAT or ACT test scores. Recommended: interview. Auditions held once in February, once in March, and by appointment on campus; recorded music is permissible as a substitute for live auditions when distance is prohibitive and videotaped performances are permissible as a substitute for live auditions when scheduling is difficult.

**Web Site** http://www.acu.edu/music

**Undergraduate Contact** Kara Taylor, Recruiting Supervisor, Music Department, Abilene Christian University, ACU Station, Box 28274, Abilene, Texas 79699; 325-674-2197, fax: 325-674-2608.

## Acadia University
### Wolfville, Nova Scotia, Canada

Province-supported, coed. Small town campus. Total enrollment: 3,333. Music program established 1926.

**Degrees** Bachelor of Arts in Music in the areas of music business, music (in combination with an outside field), arts administration, music technology; Bachelor of Music in the areas of performance, composition, music theory/history, music education, music therapy, music theater, arts administration, music pedagogy, jazz studies. Majors and concentrations: arts administration, composition, harpsichord, jazz studies, music, music business, music education, music history, music pedagogy, music technology, music theater, music theory, music therapy, piano/organ, stringed instruments, voice, wind and percussion instruments. Program accredited by CUMS.

**Enrollment** 150 total; 120 undergraduate, 30 nonprofessional degree.

**Music Student Profile** 75% females, 25% males, 5% minorities, 4% international.

**Music Faculty** 8 total (full-time), 19 total (part-time). 100% of full-time faculty have terminal degrees. Graduate students do not teach undergraduate courses. Undergraduate student–faculty ratio: 11:1.

**Student Life** Student groups/activities include music ensembles, public performances.

**Expenses for 2007–2008** Application fee: $25 Canadian dollars. Tuition, fee, and room and board charges are reported in Canadian dollars. Province resident tuition: $8062 full-time. Mandatory fees: $180 full-time. Full-time tuition and fees vary according to course level, course load, degree level, and program. College room and board: $8284. College room only: $5107. Room and board charges vary according to board plan and housing facility.

**Financial Aid** Program-specific awards: 40 endowed awards for program majors ($400–$7500), 12 alumni awards for program majors ($400–$5000).

**Application Procedures** Students admitted directly into the professional program freshman year. Deadline for freshmen and transfers: continuous. Notification date for freshmen and transfers: continuous. Required: high school transcript, college transcript(s) for transfer students, 3 letters of recommendation, interview, audition, music theory test, minimum 2.5 high school GPA. Recommended: minimum 3.0 high school GPA. Auditions held 6 times on campus; recorded music is permissible as a substitute for live auditions when distance is prohibitive and videotaped performances are permissible as a substitute for live auditions when distance is prohibitive.

**Web Site** http://ace.acadiau.ca/arts/music/index.html

**Undergraduate Contact** Barbara Jordan, Administrative Secretary, School of Music, Acadia University, Wolfville, Nova Scotia B0P 1X0, Canada; 902-542-2201 ext. 1512, e-mail address: bjordan@acadiau.ca

## Alverno College
### Milwaukee, Wisconsin

Independent Roman Catholic, Suburban campus. Total enrollment: 2,480 (2007).

**Degrees** Bachelor of Music in the area of music therapy. Majors and concentrations: music therapy. Program accredited by NASM, AMTA.

**Enrollment** 13 total; all undergraduate.

**Music Student Profile** 99% females, 1% males, 35% minorities, 1% international.

**Music Faculty** 1 undergraduate (full-time), 2 undergraduate (part-time). 100% of full-time faculty have terminal degrees. Graduate students do not teach undergraduate courses. Undergraduate student–faculty ratio: 7:1.

**Student Life** Student groups/activities include Music Therapy Club.

**Expenses for 2007–2008** Application fee: $20. Comprehensive fee: $23,402 includes full-time tuition ($16,896), mandatory fees ($400), and college room and board ($6106). Full-time tuition and fees vary according to class time and program. Room and board charges vary according to board plan and housing facility. Special program-related fees: $100–$250 per credit for private lessons.

**Application Procedures** Students admitted directly into the professional program freshman year. Deadline for freshmen and transfers: continuous. Required: essay, high school transcript, college transcript(s) for transfer students, interview, audition, ACT test score only, placement assessment. Auditions held 3 times on campus; recorded music is permissible as a substitute

*Alverno College (continued)*

for live auditions for out-of-state applicants and videotaped performances are permissible as a substitute for live auditions for out-of-state applicants.

**Web Site** http://www.alverno.edu

**Undergraduate Contact** Kim Wankowski, Director, Admissions Department, Alverno College, 3400 South 43rd Street, PO Box 343922, Milwaukee, Wisconsin 53234-3922; 414-382-6100, fax: 414-382-6354, e-mail address: kim.wankowski@alverno.edu

# Anderson University
## Anderson, South Carolina

Independent Baptist, coed. Suburban campus. Total enrollment: 1,902. Music program established 1911.

**Degrees** Bachelor of Music Education in the areas of vocal music, instrumental. Majors and concentrations: choral music education, instrumental music education. Program accredited by NASM.

**Music Student Profile** 60% females, 40% males, 15% minorities, 4% international.

**Music Faculty** 6 undergraduate (full-time), 5 undergraduate (part-time). 83% of full-time faculty have terminal degrees. Graduate students do not teach undergraduate courses. Undergraduate student–faculty ratio: 7:1.

**Student Life** Student groups/activities include Music Educators National Conference Student Chapter, The Playhouse of Anderson University, National Association of Teachers of Singing student auditions.

**Expenses for 2008–2009** Application fee: $25. Comprehensive fee: $24,450 includes full-time tuition ($17,400) and college room and board ($7050). College room only: $3600. Special program-related fees: $225 per credit hour for private music lessons.

**Financial Aid** Program-specific awards: 10–15 merit scholarships for program majors ($1500–$6000).

**Application Procedures** Students apply for admission into the professional program by freshman year. Deadline for freshmen and transfers: continuous. Notification date for freshmen and transfers: continuous. Required: high school transcript, college transcript(s) for transfer students, minimum 2.0 high school GPA, interview, audition, SAT or ACT test scores. Recommended: minimum 3.0 high school GPA. Auditions held continuously on campus; recorded music is permissible as a substitute for live auditions when distance is prohibitive and videotaped performances are permissible as a substitute for live auditions in special circumstances.

**Web Site** http://andersonuniversity.edu

**Undergraduate Contact** James Clark, Chair, Music Department, College of Visual & Performing Arts, Anderson University, 316 Boulevard, Anderson, South Carolina 29621; 864-231-2124, fax: 864-231-2083, e-mail address: jclark@andersonuniversity.edu

# Angelo State University
## San Angelo, Texas

State-supported, coed. Urban campus. Total enrollment: 6,239. Music program established 1966.

**Web Site** http://www.angelo.edu/

# Anna Maria College
## Paxton, Massachusetts

Independent Roman Catholic, coed. Rural campus. Total enrollment: 1,244. Music program established 1947.

**Degrees** Bachelor of Music in the areas of music education, music therapy, music education and music therapy, piano performance, vocal performance. Majors and concentrations: music education, music therapy, piano performance, voice performance. Cross-registration with Worcester Consortium. Program accredited by AMTA.

**Enrollment** 35 total; all undergraduate.

**Music Student Profile** 70% females, 30% males.

**Music Faculty** 5 undergraduate (full-time), 16 undergraduate (part-time). 50% of full-time faculty have terminal degrees.

Graduate students do not teach undergraduate courses. Undergraduate student–faculty ratio: 6:1.

**Student Life** Student groups/activities include Music Education Club, Music Educators National Conference, Music Therapy Club.

**Expenses for 2007–2008** Application fee: $40. Comprehensive fee: $33,532 includes full-time tuition ($22,360), mandatory fees ($2257), and college room and board ($8915). Full-time tuition and fees vary according to program. Room and board charges vary according to board plan. Special program-related fees: $1650 per semester for private lessons, instrument rental.

**Financial Aid** Program-specific awards: 8 music scholarships for program majors ($1281).

**Application Procedures** Students admitted directly into the professional program freshman year. Deadline for freshmen and transfers: continuous. Required: essay, high school transcript, college transcript(s) for transfer students, minimum 2.0 high school GPA, 3 letters of recommendation, audition, SAT or ACT test scores. Recommended: interview. Auditions held by appointment on campus; recorded music is permissible as a substitute for live auditions when distance is prohibitive and videotaped performances are permissible as a substitute for live auditions when distance is prohibitive. Portfolio reviews held by appointment on campus; the submission of slides may be substituted for portfolios when distance is prohibitive.

**Web Site** http://www.annamaria.edu

**Undergraduate Contact** Mr. Tim Donahue, Director of Admissions, Anna Maria College, Box U, Paxton, Massachusetts 01612-1198; 508-849-3365, fax: 508-849-3362, e-mail address: tdonahue@annamaria.edu

*Mariam Cannon Hayes School of Music*

# Appalachian State University
## Boone, North Carolina

State-supported, coed. Small town campus. Total enrollment: 15,871.

**Degrees** Bachelor of Music in the areas of music education, performance, composition, sacred music, music therapy; Bachelor of Science in the area of music industry studies. Majors and concentrations: composition, music, music business, music education, music therapy, piano/organ, sacred music, stringed instruments, voice, wind and percussion instruments. Graduate degrees offered: Master of Music in the areas of music education, performance, composition; Master of Music Therapy in the area of music therapy. Program accredited by NASM.

**Enrollment** 490 total; 465 undergraduate, 25 graduate.

**Music Student Profile** 56% females, 44% males, 5% minorities, 2% international.

**Music Faculty** 16 undergraduate (full-time), 20 undergraduate (part-time), 24 graduate (full-time). 80% of full-time faculty have terminal degrees. Graduate students teach a few undergraduate courses. Undergraduate student–faculty ratio: 12:1.

**Student Life** Student groups/activities include Music Educators National Conference, Music and Entertainment Industry Student Association, music fraternities and sororities.

**Expenses for 2007–2008** Application fee: $50. State resident tuition: $2221 full-time. Nonresident tuition: $11,963 full-time. Mandatory fees: $2020 full-time. College room and board: $5990. College room only: $3250. Room and board charges vary according to board plan and housing facility.

**Financial Aid** Program-specific awards: 30 School of Music Awards for program majors ($750–$1500), 4 Hayes Scholarships for program majors ($1000–$5000), 1 Presser Award for program majors ($4000), 20 Appal PIE Awards for program majors ($2500), 4 White Scholarships for program majors ($3000).

**Application Procedures** Students admitted directly into the professional program freshman year. Deadline for freshmen and transfers: April 1. Notification date for freshmen and transfers: July 1. Required: high school transcript, college transcript(s) for transfer students, interview, audition, SAT or ACT test scores. Recommended: minimum 3.0 high school GPA. Auditions held 5 times on campus; recorded music is permissible as a substitute for live auditions when distance is prohibitive and videotaped performances are permissible as a substitute for live auditions when distance is prohibitive.

**Web Site** http://www.music.appstate.edu

**Undergraduate Contact** Ms. Cara Osborne, Receptionist, Mariam Cannon Hayes School of Music, Appalachian State University, PO Box 32096, Boone, North Carolina 28608; 828-262-3020, fax: 828-262-6446, e-mail address: harbinsonwg@appstate.edu

**Graduate Contact** Dr. Nancy Schneeloch Bingham, Coordinator of Graduate Studies in Music, Mariam Cannon Hayes School of Music, Appalachian State University, PO Box 32096, Boone, North Carolina 28608; fax: 828-262-6446, e-mail address: schneelochna@appstate.edu

# Aquinas College
## Grand Rapids, Michigan

Independent Roman Catholic, coed. Suburban campus. Total enrollment: 2,107. Music program established 1944.

**Degrees** Bachelor of Music in the areas of choral supervision, instrumental supervision, liturgical music. Majors and concentrations: liturgical music, music education. Graduate degrees offered: Master of Arts in Teaching.

**Enrollment** 35 total; 23 undergraduate, 12 nonprofessional degree.

**Music Student Profile** 65% females, 35% males, 11% minorities, 1% international.

**Music Faculty** 3 total (full-time), 22 total (part-time). 33% of full-time faculty have terminal degrees. Graduate students do not teach undergraduate courses. Undergraduate student–faculty ratio: 12:1.

**Student Life** Student groups/activities include Music Educators National Conference, National Association of Teachers of Singing, Association of National Pastoral Musicians.

**Expenses for 2008–2009** Application fee: $0. Comprehensive fee: $27,828 includes full-time tuition ($21,150) and college room and board ($6678). College room only: $3084. Special program-related fees: $5 per semester for locker rental, $30 per semester for instrument rental, $280 per semester for private lesson fee.

**Financial Aid** Program-specific awards: 2 departmental awards for students taking private lessons ($240–$560), 24 Audrey E. Mohler Awards for music education majors ($500–$3000), 1 Dr. R. Bruce Early Award for undergraduate Jazz students ($600), 1 Sisters Emmanuel and Evangelista Award for private piano students ($400), 3 Ernest "Bud" Kretschner Awards for private lessons students ($560), 2 Benny Carew Awards for jazz ensemble and/or vocal jazz members ($500), 1 Sr. Henry Suso Lerczak Award for freshmen music majors ($250), 1 Margaret Bailey Osborn Award for junior or senior music majors ($500), 2 Mary Jane Kirchgessner Awards for band or chorus members ($500), 4 Darlene Gray Scholarships for continuing education music students ($250–$600), 2 Chuck and Stella Royce Awards for choral and band music major ($1000), 1 Maxine Hattem Memorial Award for liturgical music majors ($1000), 1 Marin Family Scholarship for theology and music majors ($1000), 2 Eugene Hopkins Awards for pianist music majors ($350).

**Application Procedures** Students admitted directly into the professional program freshman year. Deadline for freshmen and transfers: continuous. Notification date for freshmen and transfers: continuous. Required: high school transcript, college transcript(s) for transfer students, letter of recommendation, SAT or ACT test scores, video or audition for scholarship consideration. Recommended: essay, minimum 3.0 high school GPA, video, audition. Auditions held 6 times on campus; recorded music is permissible as a substitute for live auditions if unable to visit campus and videotaped performances are permissible as a substitute for live auditions if unable to visit campus.

**Web Site** http://www.aquinas.edu

**Undergraduate Contact** Ms. Paula Meehan, Dean of Admissions, Aquinas College, 1607 Robinson Road, SE, Grand Rapids, Michigan 49506; 616-459-8281 ext. 5205, fax: 616-732-4435.

**Graduate Contact** Ms. Nanette Clatterbuck, Dean of School of Education, Aquinas College, 1607 Robinson Road, SE, Grand Rapids, Michigan 49506; 616-459-8281 ext. 5422, fax: 616-732-4487, e-mail address: clattnan@aquinas.edu

# Arizona State University
## Tempe, Arizona

State-supported, coed. Suburban campus. Total enrollment: 51,481. Music program established 1946.

**Degrees** Bachelor of Music in the areas of choral music, general music, instrumental music, music theater, performance, music theory and composition, music therapy, jazz performance, piano accompanying. Majors and concentrations: collaborative piano, jazz, music education, music theater, music theory and composition, music therapy, piano/organ, stringed instruments, voice, wind and percussion instruments. Graduate degrees offered: Master of Music in the areas of choral music, general music, instrumental music, music theater, performance, music theater direction, performance pedagogy, music theory, composition, piano accompanying. Doctor of Musical Arts in the areas of choral music, instrumental music, performance. Program accredited by NASM, AMTA.

**Enrollment** 775 total; 450 undergraduate, 300 graduate, 25 nonprofessional degree.

**Music Student Profile** 53% females, 47% males, 11% minorities, 7% international.

**Music Faculty** 75 total (full-time), 30 total (part-time). 75% of full-time faculty have terminal degrees. Graduate students teach a few undergraduate courses. Undergraduate student–faculty ratio: 7:1.

**Student Life** Student groups/activities include Music Therapy Student Organization, Music Educators National Conference Student Chapter. Special housing available for music students.

**Expenses for 2008–2009** Application fee: $50. State resident tuition: $5409 full-time. Nonresident tuition: $17,697 full-time. Mandatory fees: $252 full-time. College room and board: $8797. College room only: $5247. Special program-related fees: $100 per semester for studio lesson fee.

**Financial Aid** Program-specific awards: 165 tuition waivers for out-of-state program students ($8000), 167 tuition waivers for state residents ($2000), 100 cash awards for program students ($500).

**Application Procedures** Students admitted directly into the professional program freshman year. Deadline for freshmen and transfers: March 1. Required: essay, high school transcript, college transcript(s) for transfer students, minimum 3.0 high school GPA, 3 letters of recommendation, audition, SAT or ACT test scores, portfolio for composition applicants, School of Music application. Auditions held 5 times on campus; recorded music is permissible as a substitute for live auditions when distance is prohibitive or in special circumstances and videotaped performances are permissible as a substitute for live auditions when distance is prohibitive or in special circumstances.

**Web Site** http://music.asu.edu/bravo

**Undergraduate Contact** Dr. Karen Bryan, Associate Director, School of Music, Arizona State University, Box 870405, Tempe, Arizona 85287-0405; 480-965-5069, fax: 480-727-6544.

**Graduate Contact** Dr. Robert Spring, Associate Director, School of Music, Arizona State University, Box 870405, Tempe, Arizona 85287-0405; 480-965-3371.

# Arkansas Tech University
## Russellville, Arkansas

State-supported, coed. Small town campus. Total enrollment: 7,476. Music program established 1950.

**Web Site** http://www.atu.edu/

# Armstrong Atlantic State University
## Savannah, Georgia

State-supported, coed. Total enrollment: 6,831. Music program established 1935.

**Degrees** Bachelor of Arts in the area of music (performance and composition); Bachelor of Music Education. Majors and concentrations: choral music education, composition, instrumental music education, music education, performance and composition. Program accredited by NASM.

*Armstrong Atlantic State University (continued)*

**Enrollment** 60 total; 40 undergraduate, 20 nonprofessional degree.

**Music Student Profile** 50% females, 50% males, 20% minorities, 4% international.

**Music Faculty** 7 undergraduate (full-time), 14 undergraduate (part-time). 86% of full-time faculty have terminal degrees. Graduate students do not teach undergraduate courses. Undergraduate student–faculty ratio: 5:1.

**Student Life** Student groups/activities include Collegiate Music Educators National Conference.

**Expenses for 2007–2008** Application fee: $25. State resident tuition: $2868 full-time. Nonresident tuition: $11,472 full-time. Mandatory fees: $556 full-time. Full-time tuition and fees vary according to program and student level. College room only: $5000. Room charges vary according to housing facility. Special program-related fees: $90 per semester for applied music fee.

**Financial Aid** Program-specific awards: 30 departmental awards for program majors ($600).

**Application Procedures** Students admitted directly into the professional program freshman year. Deadline for freshmen and transfers: continuous. Notification date for freshmen and transfers: continuous. Required: high school transcript, college transcript(s) for transfer students, minimum 2.0 high school GPA, interview, audition, SAT or ACT test scores, music theory placement test. Recommended: minimum 3.0 high school GPA. Auditions held by appointment on campus; recorded music is permissible as a substitute for live auditions for out-of-state applicants and videotaped performances are permissible as a substitute for live auditions for out-of-state applicants.

**Web Site** http://www.finearts.armstrong.edu

**Undergraduate Contact** Dr. Tom Cato, Head, Department of Art, Music and Theatre, Armstrong Atlantic State University, 11935 Abercorn Street, Savannah, Georgia 31419; 912-927-5325, fax: 912-921-5492, e-mail address: finearts@mail.armstrong.edu

# Ashland University
## Ashland, Ohio

Independent, coed. Small town campus. Total enrollment: 2,772.

**Degrees** Bachelor of Music. Majors and concentrations: music education. Program accredited by NASM.

**Enrollment** 47 total; 40 undergraduate, 7 nonprofessional degree.

**Music Student Profile** 70% females, 30% males, 5% minorities.

**Music Faculty** 9 undergraduate (full-time), 12 undergraduate (part-time). 78% of full-time faculty have terminal degrees. Graduate students do not teach undergraduate courses. Undergraduate student–faculty ratio: 4:1.

**Student Life** Student groups/activities include Music Educators National Conference, Kappa Kappa Psi.

**Expenses for 2008–2009** Application fee: $0. Comprehensive fee: $33,216 includes full-time tuition ($23,550), mandatory fees ($790), and college room and board ($8876). College room only: $4768. Special program-related fees: $297 per semester for private music lessons.

**Financial Aid** Program-specific awards: 40 scholarships for program majors ($2800).

**Application Procedures** Students admitted directly into the professional program freshman year. Deadline for freshmen and transfers: continuous. Required: essay, high school transcript, college transcript(s) for transfer students, 2 letters of recommendation, audition, SAT or ACT test scores. Recommended: minimum 3.0 high school GPA, interview. Auditions held 5 times and by appointment on campus; videotaped performances are permissible as a substitute for live auditions when distance is prohibitive.

**Web Site** http://www.ashland.edu

**Undergraduate Contact** Cathy Rowland, Administrative Assistant, Department of Music, Ashland University, 401 College Avenue, Ashland, Ohio 44805; 419-289-5100, fax: 419-289-5638, e-mail address: crowlan1@ashland.edu

# Auburn University
## Auburn University, Alabama

State-supported, coed. Small town campus. Total enrollment: 24,137. Music program established 1935.

**Degrees** Bachelor of Music Education. Majors and concentrations: choral music education, instrumental music education. Graduate degrees offered: Master of Education in the areas of choral, instrumental music; Master of Science in the areas of choral, instrumental music education. Doctor of Philosophy in the area of music education. Program accredited by NASM.

**Enrollment** 95 total; 79 undergraduate, 16 graduate.

**Music Student Profile** 51% females, 49% males, 2% minorities.

**Music Faculty** 11 total (full-time), 8 total (part-time). 90% of full-time faculty have terminal degrees. Graduate students teach a few undergraduate courses.

**Student Life** Student groups/activities include Phi Mu Alpha, Kappa Kappa Psi, Collegiate Music Educators National Conference.

**Expenses for 2007–2008** Application fee: $25. State resident tuition: $5490 full-time. Nonresident tuition: $15,990 full-time. Mandatory fees: $344 full-time. Full-time tuition and fees vary according to course load, program, and reciprocity agreements. College room only: $3200. Room charges vary according to housing facility. Special program-related fees: $156 per hour for private lessons.

**Financial Aid** Program-specific awards: Hargis Scholarships for band participants, music scholarships for music education students.

**Application Procedures** Students apply for admission into the professional program by sophomore year. Deadline for freshmen and transfers: July 7. Required: high school transcript, college transcript(s) for transfer students, ACT test score only. Recommended: audition. Auditions held 3 times on campus; recorded music is permissible as a substitute for live auditions and videotaped performances are permissible as a substitute for live auditions.

**Web Site** http://www.auburn.edu/

**Contact** Dr. Kimberly C. Walls, Coordinator of Music Education, Department of Curriculum and Teaching, Auburn University, 5040 Haley Center, Auburn University, Alabama 36849-5420; 334-844-6892, fax: 334-844-6789, e-mail address: kim.walls@auburn.edu

# Augsburg College
## Minneapolis, Minnesota

Independent Lutheran, coed. Urban campus. Total enrollment: 3,732. Music program established 1922.

**Degrees** Bachelor of Arts in the area of music; Bachelor of Music in the areas of performance, education; Bachelor of Music Education; Bachelor of Science in the area of music therapy. Majors and concentrations: music, music education, music performance, music therapy. Cross-registration with Associated Colleges of the Twin Cities (Hamline University, Macalester College, College of St. Catherine, University of St. Thomas). Program accredited by NASM.

**Enrollment** 110 total; all undergraduate.

**Music Student Profile** 65% females, 35% males, 1% minorities, 1% international.

**Music Faculty** 8 undergraduate (full-time), 28 undergraduate (part-time). 50% of full-time faculty have terminal degrees. Graduate students do not teach undergraduate courses. Undergraduate student–faculty ratio: 10:1.

**Student Life** Student groups/activities include receptions/dinners, concerts/recitals.

**Expenses for 2007–2008** Application fee: $25. Comprehensive fee: $31,441 includes full-time tuition ($24,046), mandatory fees ($493), and college room and board ($6902). College room only: $3534. Room and board charges vary according to board plan and housing facility. Special program-related fees: $15 per semester for instrument rental, $380–$790 per semester for lessons (MUP courses).

**Financial Aid** Program-specific awards: 40 scholarships for program majors ($200–$10,000).

**Application Procedures** Students apply for admission into the professional program by sophomore year. Deadline for freshmen and transfers: April 1. Required: essay, high school transcript, college transcript(s) for transfer students, minimum 2.0 high school GPA, SAT or ACT test scores, audition for scholarship consideration. Recommended: 2 letters of recommendation. Auditions held once on campus; recorded music is permissible as a substitute for live auditions when distance is prohibitive and videotaped performances are permissible as a substitute for live auditions when distance is prohibitive.

**Web Site** http://www.augsburg.edu/music

**Undergraduate Contact** Admissions, Augsburg College, 2211 Riverside Avenue, Minneapolis, Minnesota 55454; 612-330-1001, fax: 612-330-1590.

# Augusta State University
## Augusta, Georgia

State-supported, coed. Urban campus. Total enrollment: 6,588. Music program established 1971.

**Degrees** Bachelor of Music in the areas of performance, music education. Majors and concentrations: music education, piano/organ, stringed instruments, voice, wind and percussion instruments. Program accredited by NASM.

**Enrollment** 91 total; 44 undergraduate, 47 nonprofessional degree.

**Music Student Profile** 48% females, 52% males, 23% minorities, 3% international.

**Music Faculty** 11 undergraduate (full-time), 16 undergraduate (part-time). 85% of full-time faculty have terminal degrees. Graduate students do not teach undergraduate courses. Undergraduate student–faculty ratio: 8:1.

**Student Life** Student groups/activities include American String Teachers Association, Collegiate Music Educators National Conference, Phi Mu Epsilon.

**Expenses for 2007–2008** Application fee: $30. State resident tuition: $3192 full-time. Nonresident tuition: $12,792 full-time. Mandatory fees: $536 full-time. College room and board: $9600. College room only: $4920. Special program-related fees: $38–$68 per semester for applied music fee.

**Financial Aid** Program-specific awards: 12–15 Maxwell Fund Awards for program majors ($300–$600), 4–6 Church Scholarships for choir singers ($1200–$1500), 1 Mary Byrd Scholarship for students from Columbia County, Georgia ($1500), 3–4 Pamplin Scholarships for program majors ($300–$600), 1 Sweet Adelines Award for vocal majors ($800), 1 Garden City Chorus Award1 for vocal majors ($800), 8 Cleon Mauldin Scholarships for program majors ($1000).

**Application Procedures** Students apply for admission into the professional program by sophomore year. Deadline for freshmen and transfers: July 18. Required: high school transcript, college transcript(s) for transfer students, minimum 2.0 high school GPA, 2 letters of recommendation, SAT or ACT test scores. Recommended: audition. Auditions held 4 times on campus and off campus in Aiken, SC; Thomson, GA; Harlem, GA; recorded music is permissible as a substitute for live auditions when distance is prohibitive and videotaped performances are permissible as a substitute for live auditions when distance is prohibitive.

**Web Site** http://www.aug.edu

**Undergraduate Contact** Dr. Angela Morgan, Chair, Fine Arts Department, Augusta State University, 2500 Walton Way, Augusta, Georgia 30904-2200; 706-737-1453, fax: 706-667-4937, e-mail address: amorgan@aug.edu

# Baker University
## Baldwin City, Kansas

Independent United Methodist, coed. Small town campus. Total enrollment: 942. Music program established 1858.

**Degrees** Bachelor of Music Education. Majors and concentrations: music education. Program accredited by NASM, NCATE.

**Enrollment** 35 total; all undergraduate.

**Music Student Profile** 55% females, 45% males, 2% minorities.

**Music Faculty** 6 undergraduate (full-time), 9 undergraduate (part-time). 83% of full-time faculty have terminal degrees.

Graduate students do not teach undergraduate courses. Undergraduate student–faculty ratio: 8:1.

**Student Life** Student groups/activities include Collegiate Music Educators National Conference.

**Expenses for 2007–2008** Application fee: $0. One-time mandatory fee: $80. Comprehensive fee: $24,900 includes full-time tuition ($18,750) and college room and board ($6150). College room only: $2850. Full-time tuition varies according to location and program. Room and board charges vary according to board plan and housing facility. Special program-related fees: $170 per credit for applied music fee.

**Financial Aid** Program-specific awards: 130 participation awards for band, chorus, and orchestra members ($1000–$3000), academic scholarships for musicians ($3000–$6000).

**Application Procedures** Students admitted directly into the professional program freshman year. Deadline for freshmen and transfers: continuous. Required: high school transcript, letter of recommendation, interview, audition, SAT or ACT test scores, minimum 2.7 high school GPA. Recommended: minimum 3.0 high school GPA. Auditions held 5 times and by appointment on campus; recorded music is permissible as a substitute for live auditions when distance is prohibitive and videotaped performances are permissible as a substitute for live auditions when distance is prohibitive.

**Web Site** http://www.bakeru.edu

**Undergraduate Contact** Dr. John Buehler, Chairman, Department of Music, Baker University, PO Box 65, Baldwin City, Kansas 66006-0065; 785-594-8400, fax: 785-594-4546.

# Baldwin-Wallace College
## Berea, Ohio

Independent Methodist, Suburban campus. Total enrollment: 4,394. Music program established 1898.

**Degrees** Bachelor of Music in the areas of performance, music theater, music therapy, composition, music history and literature, music theory; Bachelor of Music Education in the area of integrated instrumental/vocal music education. Majors and concentrations: arts management, brass, classical guitar, composition, music education, music history and literature, music theater, music theory, music therapy, performance, piano/organ, stringed instruments, voice, wind and percussion instruments. Cross-registration with Case Western Reserve University, Cleveland Institute of Music, Cleveland State University, John Carroll University, Hiram College, Lake Erie College, Ursuline College, Notre Dame College of Ohio, David N. Meyers College, and several community colleges. Program accredited by NASM, NCATE.

**Enrollment** 268 total; 250 undergraduate, 18 nonprofessional degree.

**Music Student Profile** 60% females, 40% males, 12% minorities, 1% international.

**Music Faculty** 28 undergraduate (full-time), 44 undergraduate (part-time). 75% of full-time faculty have terminal degrees. Graduate students do not teach undergraduate courses. Undergraduate student–faculty ratio: 4:1.

**Student Life** Student groups/activities include Northcoast Student Music Therapists, Ohio Collegiate Music Educators Association Student Chapter, American String Teachers Association, Arts Management Association, Arts Nova (Music Theatre), Mu Phi Epsilon, Con Council, American Choral Directors Association.

**Expenses for 2008–2009** Application fee: $25. Comprehensive fee: $31,252 includes full-time tuition ($23,524) and college room and board ($7728). College room only: $3776.

**Financial Aid** Program-specific awards: 42 Griffiths Scholarships for musicians ($3500), Conservatory Merit Awards for musicians, 34 Conservatory Talent Awards for musicians ($3000).

**Application Procedures** Students admitted directly into the professional program freshman year. Deadline for freshmen and transfers: March 1. Notification date for freshmen: June 1; transfers: August 1. Required: essay, high school transcript, college transcript(s) for transfer students, 2 letters of recommendation, audition, SAT or ACT test scores. Recommended: interview, minimum 2.8 high school GPA. Auditions held 6 times on campus; 6 times off-campus on campus and off campus in Tampa, FL; Chicago, IL; Interlochen, MI; Dallas, TX; Houston, TX;

*Baldwin-Wallace College (continued)*

recorded music is permissible as a substitute for live auditions except music theater applicants and videotaped performances are permissible as a substitute for live auditions except music theater.

**Web Site** http://www.bw.edu/conservatory
**Undergraduate Contact** Ms. Anita S. Evans, Associate Director of Admission, Conservatory of Music, Baldwin-Wallace College, 275 Eastland Road, Berea, Ohio 44017; 440-826-2367, fax: 440-826-3239, e-mail address: aevans@bw.edu

# Ball State University

## Muncie, Indiana

State-supported, coed. Suburban campus. Total enrollment: 19,849. Music program established 1945.
**Web Site** http://www.bsu.edu/

# The Baptist College of Florida

## Graceville, Florida

Independent Southern Baptist, coed. Small town campus. Total enrollment: 564. Music program established 1960.
**Degrees** Bachelor of Music in the area of church music; Bachelor of Music Education. Majors and concentrations: church music, music education. Program accredited by NASM.
**Enrollment** 49 total; 24 undergraduate, 25 nonprofessional degree.
**Music Student Profile** 55% females, 45% males, 6% minorities, 2% international.
**Music Faculty** 5 undergraduate (full-time), 4 undergraduate (part-time). 80% of full-time faculty have terminal degrees. Graduate students do not teach undergraduate courses. Undergraduate student–faculty ratio: 5:1.
**Student Life** Student groups/activities include Spring Concert, Christmas concert, Senior Adult Day.
**Expenses for 2007–2008** Application fee: $20. Comprehensive fee: $11,586 includes full-time tuition ($7500), mandatory fees ($350), and college room and board ($3736). Full-time tuition and fees vary according to course load and location. Room and board charges vary according to board plan and housing facility. Special program-related fees: $25 per semester for class instruction (applied), $30 per semester for recital fee, $175–$275 per semester for private lessons.
**Financial Aid** Program-specific awards: 7 music scholarships for music majors ($500).
**Application Procedures** Students admitted directly into the professional program freshman year. Deadline for freshmen and transfers: August 1. Notification date for freshmen and transfers: August 15. Required: high school transcript, college transcript(s) for transfer students, minimum 2.0 high school GPA, 3 letters of recommendation, interview, audition, ACT test score only. Auditions held 5-6 times on campus.
**Web Site** http://www.baptistcollege.edu
**Undergraduate Contact** Mrs. Sandra K. Richards, Director of Marketing, The Baptist College of Florida, 5400 College Drive, Graceville, Florida 32440-1898; 850-263-3261 ext. 460, fax: 850-263-7506, e-mail address: admissions@baptistcollege.edu

# Baylor University

## Waco, Texas

Independent Baptist, coed. Urban campus. Total enrollment: 14,174. Music program established 1903.
**Degrees** Bachelor of Music in the area of classical music; Bachelor of Music Education in the area of classical music. Majors and concentrations: classical music, music, music education, opera, piano/organ, sacred music, stringed instruments, voice, wind and percussion instruments. Graduate degrees offered: Master of Music in the area of classical music. Program accredited by NASM.
**Enrollment** 365 total; 293 undergraduate, 64 graduate, 8 nonprofessional degree.

**Music Student Profile** 52% females, 48% males, 16% minorities, 2% international.
**Music Faculty** 61 total (full-time), 20 total (part-time). 74% of full-time faculty have terminal degrees. Graduate students teach a few undergraduate courses. Undergraduate student–faculty ratio: 5:1.
**Student Life** Student groups/activities include professional fraternities and sororities, Music Educators National Conference Student Chapter, Baylor Association of Church Musicians.
**Expenses for 2008–2009** Application fee: $50. Comprehensive fee: $34,464 includes full-time tuition ($23,664), mandatory fees ($2570), and college room and board ($8230). College room only: $4000. Special program-related fees: $50 per course for lab fees, $163 per credit hour for applied music fee.
**Financial Aid** Program-specific awards: 1 competitive scholarship for organ majors, 37 general scholarships for program majors, 65 incentive scholarships for program majors.
**Application Procedures** Students admitted directly into the professional program freshman year. Deadline for freshmen and transfers: continuous. Required: high school transcript, college transcript(s) for transfer students, minimum 2.0 high school GPA, audition, SAT or ACT test scores. Recommended: minimum 3.0 high school GPA. Auditions held 4 times on campus; recorded music is permissible as a substitute for live auditions if a campus visit is impossible.
**Web Site** http://www.baylor.edu/music/
**Undergraduate Contact** Ms. Deloris Acevedo, Secretary, School of Music, Baylor University, 1 Bear Place, #97408, Waco, Texas 76798-7408; 254-710-7681, fax: 254-710-1191, e-mail address: deloris_acevedo@baylor.edu
**Graduate Contact** Dr. David Music, Director of Graduate Studies, School of Music, Baylor University, 1 Bear Place, #97408, Waco, Texas 76798-7408; 254-710-2360, fax: 254-710-1191, e-mail address: david_music@baylor.edu

# Belmont University

## Nashville, Tennessee

Independent Baptist, coed. Urban campus. Total enrollment: 4,756. Music program established 1951.
**Degrees** Bachelor of Music. Majors and concentrations: church music, classical performance, commercial music, composition, music education, music theater, music theory, piano pedagogy. Graduate degrees offered: Master of Music in the areas of performance, pedagogy, church music, music education, composition. Program accredited by NASM.
**Enrollment** 557 total; 505 undergraduate, 52 graduate.
**Music Student Profile** 55% females, 45% males, 10% minorities, 1% international.
**Music Faculty** 35 total (full-time), 80 total (part-time). 59% of full-time faculty have terminal degrees. Graduate students teach a few undergraduate courses. Undergraduate student–faculty ratio: 11:1.
**Student Life** Student groups/activities include International Association for Jazz Education, Phi Mu Alpha, Sigma Alpha Iota.
**Expenses for 2008–2009** Application fee: $35. Comprehensive fee: $31,110 includes full-time tuition ($20,070), mandatory fees ($1040), and college room and board ($10,000). College room only: $6300. Special program-related fees: $30–$100 per semester for material fees, $150–$300 per semester for applied lessons.
**Financial Aid** Program-specific awards: 6–16 endowed scholarships for talented applicants ($1000–$2000), 20–25 music scholarships for talented applicants ($1000–$2000).
**Application Procedures** Students admitted directly into the professional program freshman year. Deadline for freshmen and transfers: June 1. Required: essay, high school transcript, college transcript(s) for transfer students, minimum 3.0 high school GPA, letter of recommendation, audition, SAT or ACT test scores, Basic Musicianship Test. Auditions held 5 times on campus; videotaped performances are permissible as a substitute for live auditions if a campus visit is impossible.
**Web Site** http://www.belmont.edu/music/
**Undergraduate Contact** Dr. Sharon F. Gregg, Director of Admissions, School of Music, Belmont University, 1900 Belmont Boulevard,

Nashville, Tennessee 37212-3757; 615-460-6408, fax: 615-386-0239, e-mail address: greggs@mail.belmont.edu

**Graduate Contact** Dr. Robert B. Gregg, Director of Graduate Studies, School of Music, Belmont University, 1900 Belmont Boulevard, Nashville, Tennessee 37212-3757; 615-460-6408, fax: 615-386-0239, e-mail address: greggr@mail.belmont.edu

### More About the University

The Wilson Music Building and Massey Performing Arts Center provide ample rehearsal and practice rooms, spacious teaching studios, fully equipped classrooms, and computer, piano, and music technology labs. Multiple performance areas include a recital hall, a large concert hall, and a historic antebellum mansion. Guest artists frequently perform and hold master classes.

**Faculty** Undergraduate and graduate music students from thirty states and various countries prepare at Belmont for careers as performers, church musicians, composers, music teachers, and studio musicians. Faculty members are graduates of some of the most prestigious institutions and hold such honors as Composer of the Year awards, listings in *Who's Who in Music*, Outstanding Educator of America, Grammy Award nominations, professionally released recordings, and Metropolitan Opera Regional Finalist.

**Student Performance** Ensemble opportunities include Oratorio Chorus, Chorale, Chamber Singers, Women's Choir, Company (show choir), Jazzmin, Southbound (country ensemble), Phoenix (top 40 ensemble), Session (a capella women's ensemble), Opera and Musical Theatre workshops, Wind Ensemble, Symphony Orchestra, Jazz Ensemble and small jazz groups, Brass and Woodwind Quintets, String Quartets, Rock Combo, Belmont Pops, Bluegrass, and Percussion Ensemble. Belmont's proximity to downtown Nashville and Music Row allows for involvement in professional recording projects and productions of leading arts organizations.

**Special Programs** International music opportunities are growing with the Russian Academy of Music in Moscow and with Germany's Hochschule für Musik Dresden, Karl Maria von Weber. The Commercial Music Program, a unique approach to the study of popular styles, continues to develop course work in music technology to stay current with developing technological advances as they impact music composition, copying, and performance. There is also a vocal arts lab utilizing state-of-the-art technology to assist students in the development of proper technique.

# Benjamin T. Rome School of Music

See The Catholic University of America

# Berklee College of Music

## Boston, Massachusetts

Independent, coed. Urban campus. Total enrollment: 4,090. Music program established 1945.

**Degrees** Bachelor of Music in the areas of performance, music synthesis, music education, composition, contemporary writing and production, film scoring, jazz composition, music business/management, music production and engineering, music therapy, professional music, songwriting. Majors and concentrations: composition, contemporary writing and production, film scoring, jazz composition, music business/management, music education, music engineering and production, music synthesis, music therapy, performance, professional music, songwriting. Cross-registration with ProArts Consortium: Boston Architectural Center, School of the Museum of Fine Arts, Massachusetts College of Art, Boston Conservatory, Emerson College.

**Enrollment** 4,090 total; all undergraduate.

**Music Student Profile** 28% females, 72% males, 25% minorities, 22% international.

**Music Faculty** 514 total undergraduate. Graduate students do not teach undergraduate courses. Undergraduate student–faculty ratio: 8:1.

**Student Life** Student groups/activities include Berklee Cares (community action response education service), Women Musician's Network (WMN), Boston Jazz Society-Student Chapter. Special housing available for music students.

**Expenses for 2008–2009** Application fee: $150. One-time mandatory fee: $650. Comprehensive fee: $43,160 includes full-time tuition ($27,500), mandatory fees ($700), and college room and board ($14,960).

**Financial Aid** Program-specific awards: 637 Live Auditions (North American, European, Asian and Latin American Tour Awards) for entering students ($9314), 52 Berklee Entering Student Talent (BEST) Scholarships for entering students ($4625), 127 Berklee Achievement Scholarships (BAS) for continuing students ($4662), 727 Live Auditions (North American, European, Asian and Latin American Tour Awards) for continuing students ($8553).

**Application Procedures** Students admitted directly into the professional program freshman year. Deadline for freshmen and transfers: February 1. Notification date for freshmen and transfers: March 31. Required: essay, high school transcript, college transcript(s) for transfer students, minimum 2.0 high school GPA, 2 letters of recommendation, interview, audition, English reference letter for international applicants, audition for scholarship consideration. Recommended: minimum 3.0 high school GPA, SAT or ACT test scores, TOEFL score for international applicants. Auditions held 45 times on campus and off campus in domestic and international sites; recorded music is permissible as a substitute for live auditions at discretion of Board of Admissions and videotaped performances are permissible as a substitute for live auditions at discretion of Board of Admissions.

**Web Site** http://www.berklee.edu

**Undergraduate Contact** Damien Bracken, Director of Admissions, Berklee College of Music, 1140 Boylston Street, Boston, Massachusetts 02215-3693; 617-747-2222, fax: 617-747-2047, e-mail address: admissions@berklee.edu

### More About the College

Berklee attracts the most creative music students in the world, those who know that no other music college or institution offers such a rich diversity of people, music, and programs. They come to Berklee to discover their true music calling, pushing themselves past their own expectations and into the forefront of every aspect of the global music community.

Founded in 1945, Berklee is the world's largest accredited music college and the premier institution for the study of contemporary music. The College's nearly 4,000 students, from seventy-eight countries, and more than 400 faculty members interact in an environment designed to provide the most complete learning experience possible, including all of the opportunities and challenges presented by a career in the contemporary music industry. Using Berklee's extensive facilities, students develop musical competencies in such areas as composition, performance, and recording/production and also learn to make the informed business decisions necessary to career success.

Berklee was founded on two revolutionary ideas: that musicianship could be taught through the music of the time and

*Berklee College of Music (continued)*

that students need practical, professional skills for successful, sustainable music careers. While Berklee's bedrock philosophy has not changed, the music around has and requires that the College evolve with it. For more than half a century, Berklee has demonstrated its commitment to this approach by wholeheartedly embracing change.

Berklee continually updates its curriculum and technology to make them more relevant, and it attracts diverse students who reflect the multiplicity of influences in today's music. The College prepares students for a lifetime of professional and personal growth through the study of the arts, sciences, and humanities. Berklee is also developing new initiatives to reach and influence an ever-widening audience.

More than a college, Berklee has become the world's singular learning lab for the music of today—and tomorrow. Berklee is a microcosm of the music world, reflecting the interplay between music and culture, and an environment where aspiring music professionals learn how to integrate new ideas, adapt to changing musical genres, and showcase their distinctive skills in an evolving community. The College is at the center of a widening network of industry professionals who use their openness, virtuosity, and versatility to take music in surprising new directions.

Berklee students focus on their musicianship, on the technologies that help shape this art form, on the intricacies and realities of the business and promotion of music, or on the leading thinking in music education and music therapy.

Students at Berklee start bands of their own, participate in regularly scheduled ensembles, go on tour, and take advantage of internships throughout the industry. They record student projects, score films, write, practice, and perform.

What separates Berklee College of Music from everywhere else is the people who make it up. It is the faculty and staff members, the students, and the alumni who compose the extraordinary community. Every year, a common passion and a common spirit of innovation draw remarkable people from all over the world to Boston and Berklee.

Berklee offers a Bachelor of Music (B.M.) degree program and a four-year program leading to the professional diploma. Students may choose to major in composition, contemporary writing and production, film scoring, jazz composition, music business/management, music education, music production and engineering, music synthesis, music therapy, performance, professional music, and songwriting. The College also offers a five-year, dual-major option in which students graduate with an even more marketable education that expands their career options in the music industry.

Berklee students have the chance to work in the College's state-of-the-art music technology facilities, using some of the most sophisticated recording and synthesis equipment currently available, in addition to facilities specifically designed for the areas of composition, arranging, and film scoring. The facilities at Berklee are furnished with the instruments and equipment that are being used in the world beyond the classroom. Berklee's performance facilities include the Berklee Performance Center, a 1,200-seat concert hall hosting more than 300 concerts by students, faculty members, and others each year; four recital halls equipped with a variety of sound reinforcement systems; more than forty ensemble rooms; seventy-five private instruction studios; 300 private practice rooms; and an outdoor concert pavilion.

The personal attention students receive from teachers at Berklee guides them beyond the theoretical so that they can apply what they have learned in their next ensemble rehearsal, evening jam session, or gig. Berklee faculty members teach all instruction. The teachers are talented artists who demonstrate their commitment to music education in the classroom—and beyond. Most faculty members also write and arrange music, perform in concert halls and clubs, make recordings, or perform on television and radio—some do it all. All faculty members bring to the classroom their knowledge of music and the wisdom that comes from professional music experience.

Berklee awards $12.5 million in scholarships each year to students from all over the world who demonstrate the potential to succeed in today's music industry.

Prospective students who are ready to live, breathe, and play music on a different scale should go to http://www.berklee.edu for admissions information.

## Bernice Young Jones School of Fine Arts

See Ouachita Baptist University

## Berry College
### Mount Berry, Georgia

Independent interdenominational, coed. Suburban campus. Total enrollment: 1,858. Music program established 1969. **Web Site** http://www.berry.edu/

## Birmingham-Southern College
### Birmingham, Alabama

Independent Methodist, coed. Urban campus. Total enrollment: 1,389. Music program established 1922.

**Degrees** Bachelor of Music in the areas of classical performance, composition, music history, church music; Bachelor of Music Education. Majors and concentrations: church music, classical music, composition, guitar, music education, music history, opera, piano/organ, stringed instruments, voice, wind and percussion instruments. Graduate degrees offered: Master of Music in the areas of composition, organ, piano, voice. Cross-registration with University of Alabama at Birmingham, Samford University, University of Montevallo. Program accredited by NASM.

**Enrollment** 44 total; 20 undergraduate, 4 graduate, 20 nonprofessional degree.

**Music Student Profile** 60% females, 40% males, 20% minorities, 20% international.

**Music Faculty** 10 undergraduate (full-time), 15 undergraduate (part-time). 100% of full-time faculty have terminal degrees. Graduate students do not teach undergraduate courses. Undergraduate student–faculty ratio: 2:1.

**Student Life** Student groups/activities include ensemble performances, opera productions, music theater productions.

**Expenses for 2008–2009** Application fee: $25. Comprehensive fee: $34,691 includes full-time tuition ($24,780), mandatory fees ($806), and college room and board ($9105). College room only: $5245. Special program-related fees: $160–$300 per course for private lessons.

**Financial Aid** Program-specific awards: 2–3 music theater scholarships for program majors and minors ($3000–$16,000), 7–8 music performance scholarships for program majors and minors ($4000–$18,000), 1–2 music composition awards for program majors ($4000–$18,000).

**Application Procedures** Students admitted directly into the professional program freshman year. Deadline for freshmen and transfers: May 1. Required: essay, high school transcript, college transcript(s) for transfer students, minimum 2.0 high school GPA, SAT or ACT test scores, portfolio for composition majors. Recommended: letter of recommendation, interview, audition. Auditions held twice on campus; recorded music is permissible as a substitute for live auditions when distance is prohibitive and videotaped performances are permissible as a substitute for live auditions when distance is prohibitive. Portfolio reviews held once on campus.

**Web Site** http://www.bsc.edu

**Undergraduate Contact** Ms. Sheri Salmon, Associate Vice President of Admissions, Birmingham-Southern College, 900 Arkadelphia Road, Box 549033, Birmingham, Alabama 35254; 205-226-4686, fax: 205-226-4696, e-mail address: ssalmon@bsc.edu

**Graduate Contact** Dr. Lester Seigel, Music, Birmingham-Southern College, 900 Arkadelphia Road, Box 549033, Birmingham, Alabama 35254; 205-226-4957, fax: 205-226-3058, e-mail address: lseigel@bsc.edu

# Blair School of Music

See Vanderbilt University

# The Boston Conservatory

## Boston, Massachusetts

Independent, coed. Urban campus. Total enrollment: 560. Music program established 1867.

**Degrees** Bachelor of Music in the areas of composition, performance. Majors and concentrations: brass, composition, guitar, harp, marimba, opera, piano, saxophone, stringed instruments, voice, wind and percussion instruments. Graduate degrees offered: Master of Music in the areas of composition, choral conducting, performance, opera, music education, orchestral conducting. Cross-registration with ProArts Consortium. Program accredited by NASM.

**Enrollment** 354 total; 180 undergraduate, 174 graduate.

**Music Student Profile** 60% females, 40% males, 20% minorities, 18% international.

**Music Faculty** 29 total (full-time), 94 total (part-time). Graduate students do not teach undergraduate courses.

**Student Life** Student groups/activities include Music Educators National Conference, Phi Mu Alpha Sinfonia, Sigma Alpha Iota. Special housing available for music students.

**Expenses for 2007–2008** Application fee: $105. Comprehensive fee: $45,739 includes full-time tuition ($28,300), mandatory fees ($1799), and college room and board ($15,640). Full-time tuition and fees vary according to program. Room and board charges vary according to board plan and housing facility. Special program-related fees: $65 per year for music education lab fees.

**Financial Aid** Program-specific awards: 195 merit scholarships for artistically talented students ($5000–$32,000).

**Application Procedures** Students admitted directly into the professional program freshman year. Deadline for freshmen and transfers: December 1. Notification date for freshmen and transfers: April 1. Required: essay, high school transcript, college transcript(s) for transfer students, 2 letters of recommendation, audition, SAT or ACT test scores, video for some programs, and portfolio for composition majors, interview for some majors, minimum TOEFL score of 550 for international applicants, artistic resumé, minimum 2.7 high school GPA. Auditions held during the months of February and March on campus and off campus in Atlanta, GA; Houston, TX; Seattle, WA; Los Angeles, CA; Toronto; Interlochen, MI; and Washington, DC; recorded music is permissible as a substitute for live auditions when distance is prohibitive and videotaped performances are permissible as a substitute for live auditions when distance is prohibitive. Portfolio reviews held on campus.

**Web Site** http://www.bostonconservatory.edu

**Contact** Admissions Office, The Boston Conservatory, 8 The Fenway, Boston, Massachusetts 02215; 617-536-9153, fax: 617-247-3159, e-mail address: admissions@bostonconservatory.edu

## More About the Conservatory

The Boston Conservatory trains exceptional young performing artists for careers that enrich and transform the human experience. Known for its multidisciplinary environment, the Conservatory offers fully accredited graduate and undergraduate programs in music, dance, theater, and music education, and it presents more than 200 performances each year by students, faculty members, and guest artists. The intimacy of the Conservatory's class settings provides a student-centered atmosphere that is uniquely intensive and supportive.

Since its founding in 1867, the Boston Conservatory has shared its talent and creativity with the city of Boston, the region, and the nation, and it continues to grow today as a vibrant community of artists and educators.

Music students work with artist faculty members and teachers who are passionately dedicated to working to develop students' musical abilities to their utmost potential. With more than 300 concerts being offered each year, performance experience is a core part of the curriculum. Students participate in orchestra, choral ensembles, chamber groups, and pit work for the dance, opera, and musical theater main-stage productions that are produced throughout the academic year.

Stylistic versatility is a distinct advantage for the aspiring musician. The Boston Conservatory's programs in music provide students with the technical skills and performance experiences—in an array of musical styles and settings—necessary to prepare them for a variety of future paths as professional musicians.

The scale of the program is purposefully small and designed to give students individual attention. With personalized one-on-one training, small class sizes, master classes, guest artists, special events, and countless cultural activities available throughout Boston, the Boston Conservatory fully immerses students in their craft while exposing them to some of the world's top musicians.

Faculty at The Boston Conservatory includes members of the Boston Symphony Orchestra and Boston Pops as well as numerous professional soloists, ensemble players, conductors, and composers with international careers.

Music students have abundant and varied opportunities to perform—as soloists, as orchestra and ensemble players, and as members of chamber groups and chorales as well as in recitals and opera productions. In addition, because of the presence of programs in dance and theater on the same campus, the Boston Conservatory is one of only a handful of schools in the world that can offer classical musicians comprehensive training in standard classical and new music repertoire as well as significant exposure to the music of Broadway and beyond. In fact, many instrumentalists choose the Boston Conservatory specifically for the opportunity to perform in a symphonic orchestra one month, a ballet orchestra the next, and a Broadway-style pit band after that.

Music alumni of the Boston Conservatory are teaching, performing, and conducting with many of the world's great companies, including the Berlin Philharmonic, Boston Symphony Orchestra, Metropolitan Opera, and Santa Fe Opera.

Boston is a major center of higher education in America, with more than fifty major colleges and universities. The city provides a diverse student population and an endless array of courses, lectures, concerts, and social opportunities. The Conservatory is a member of the Pro-Arts Consortium, in conjunction with five area colleges (Emerson College, Berklee College of Music, School of the Museum of Fine Arts, Massachusetts College of Art, and Boston Architectural Center), offering extensive cross-registration course possibilities to all students.

On-campus housing is provided for freshmen and to upperclassmen and graduates on a space-available basis, offering brownstone-style living accommodations just a few steps from the main training and rehearsal buildings. For those students interested in off-campus housing, Boston offers a wide range of architectural styles and rent prices in neighborhoods throughout the city that are all within easy access to the school by public transportation.

The Boston Conservatory strives to meet each student's needs—musically and personally—and provides a nurturing, safe environment in which to study, learn, and grow. The supportive atmosphere of the college extends to student life areas as well. More than a dozen special interest groups and organizations exist on campus, with new ones developing constantly as the student population grows and needs change. As part of the student services, a number of career seminars are given each year ranging from resume writing and audition anxiety to grant writing and tax laws for the performing artist. In addition, there is an active student government and a student-run newspaper.

# Boston University

## Boston, Massachusetts

Independent, coed. Urban campus. Total enrollment: 32,053. Music program established 1872.

**Degrees** Bachelor of Music in the areas of performance, music education, music theory and composition, musicology. Majors and concentrations: brass, composition, music education, musicology, percussion, piano, stringed instruments, voice, wind instruments. Graduate degrees offered: Master of Music in the areas of performance, music education, music theory, composition, orchestral and choral conducting, historical performance, musicology. Doctor of Musical Arts in the areas of performance, music education, composition, orchestral and choral conducting, historical performance, musicology. Cross-registration with Boston College, Brandeis University, Tufts University, Hebrew College. Program accredited by NASM.

**Enrollment** 512 total; 188 undergraduate, 324 graduate.

**Music Student Profile** 60% females, 40% males, 27% international.

**Music Faculty** 50 total (full-time), 80 total (part-time). 75% of full-time faculty have terminal degrees. Graduate students teach a few undergraduate courses.

**Student Life** Student groups/activities include symphonic orchestra, symphonic chorus, marching band, concert band, pep band, jazz ensemble. Special housing available for music students.

**Expenses for 2008–2009** Application fee: $75. Comprehensive fee: $48,468 includes full-time tuition ($36,540), mandatory fees ($510), and college room and board ($11,418). College room only: $7420.

**Financial Aid** Program-specific awards: 60 grants-performance awards for freshmen and transfers ($6000–$30,000).

**Application Procedures** Students admitted directly into the professional program freshman year. Deadline for freshmen: January 1; transfers: April 1. Notification date for freshmen and transfers: June 1. Required: essay, high school transcript, college transcript(s) for transfer students, 2 letters of recommendation, audition, SAT or ACT test scores, portfolio for composition majors. Recommended: minimum 3.0 high school GPA, interview, resumé. Auditions held 40 times on campus and off campus in various cities; recorded music is permissible as a substitute for live auditions when distance is prohibitive (beyond a 300-mile radius). Portfolio reviews held as needed on campus.

**Web Site** http://www.bu.edu/cfa

**Contact** Tracy Rider, Director of Admissions and Student Affairs, School of Music, Boston University, 855 Commonwealth Avenue, Boston, Massachusetts 02215; 617-353-3341, fax: 617-353-7455, e-mail address: cfamusic@bu.edu

### More About the University

Boston University College of Fine Arts (CFA) is a small, conservatory-style school within a major university, offering outstanding professional training in music, the theater, and visual arts. The college was begun as the College of Music in 1873 and is the oldest degree-granting school of music in the nation.

The school offers the Bachelor of Music, the Master of Music, the Doctor of Musical Arts, the Artist Diploma, the Performance Diploma, and a certificate from the Opera Institute. The school prepares its students for careers as performers, composers, educators, and scholars. The faculty members are committed to providing outstanding opportunities for students to study, create, and perform.

**Campus Surroundings** Boston University—independent, coeducational, nonsectarian—is an internationally recognized center of higher education and research. The University is located in the heart of Boston, along the banks of the Charles River and adjacent to the historic Back Bay district of Boston. Boston University is perfectly situated to enjoy both the charm and beauty of the city and its cultural and recreational attractions. Boston is a city rich in music, and students have the opportunity to listen to some of the world's greatest musicians. Students benefit from the many major musical organizations, museums and galleries, and theaters that make Boston a rich and varied cultural environment.

**Program Facilities** The College of Fine Arts houses a 485-seat concert hall, music studios and practice rooms, a curriculum lab, recording studio and three electronic music studios. Students also perform at the 650-seat Tsai Performance Center on the campus. The Boston University Symphony performs annually at Boston's Symphony Hall. The Opera Institute performs at the Boston University Theatre, an 850-seat proscenium house that is also the home of the Huntingdon Theatre Company.

**Faculty, Resident Artists, and Alumni** The School of Music thrives under the instruction of some of the world's top musicians. The faculty includes accomplished solo performers as well as members of the Boston Symphony Orchestra, the Boston Lyric Opera, the Boston Pops, and the Handel and Hayden Society. The Muir String quartet and Allea III, a contemporary music ensemble, are in residence. Boston Baroque, America's leading Baroque orchestra and chorus, is the resident ensemble in support of the school's historic performance program. Notable alumni include Fred A. Bronstein, President of the Dallas Symphony Orchestra; Ikuno Mizuno-Spire, the first woman to play first violin with the Boston Symphony Orchestra; Peter Chapman, trumpet, the Boston Symphony Orchestra; Edward Atkatz, percussion, Chicago Symphony Orchestra; opera singers Dominique LaBelle and Stephen Salters; and Anthony Tommasini, music critic of the *New York Times*.

**Student Performance Opportunities** More than 400 student and faculty performances are held throughout the year. Ensembles include the Symphony Orchestra, Chamber Orchestra, Wind Ensemble Opera Workshop, and Women's Chorale. All-University organizations include the Jazz Ensemble, Concert Band, Pep Band, and Marching Band.

**Special Programs** Students at the Boston University College of Fine Arts may take advantage of a wide range of academic and extracurricular activities. Through the Collaborative Degree Program (BUCOP), students may obtain a dual degree in two of the University's schools and colleges and can minor in liberal arts, communications, or business. Students are encouraged to spend the fall semester of their junior year at the Royal College of Music in London.

# Bowling Green State University

## Bowling Green, Ohio

State-supported, coed. Small town campus. Total enrollment: 18,619. Music program established 1917.

**Degrees** Bachelor of Music in the areas of music education, performance, music history and literature, composition, jazz studies, world music. Majors and concentrations: brass, composition, guitar, harp, jazz, music, music education, music history, music history and literature, piano accompanying, piano pedagogy, piano/organ, stringed instruments, voice, wind and percussion instruments, world music. Graduate degrees offered: Master of Music in the areas of music education, performance, composition, music theory, music history, ethnomusicology. Doctor of Musical Arts in the area of composition/performance. Cross-registration with University of Toledo. Program accredited by NASM.

**Enrollment** 551 total; 430 undergraduate, 121 graduate.

**Music Student Profile** 52% females, 48% males, 7% minorities, 3% international.

**Music Faculty** 53 total (full-time), 29 total (part-time). 100% of full-time faculty have terminal degrees. Graduate students teach a few undergraduate courses. Undergraduate student–faculty ratio: 7:1.

**Student Life** Student groups/activities include Ohio Collegiate Music Educators Association, professional music fraternities and sororities, American Choral Directors Association. Special housing available for music students.

**Expenses for 2007–2008** Application fee: $40. State resident tuition: $7778 full-time. Nonresident tuition: $15,086 full-time. Mandatory fees: $1282 full-time. College room and board: $6878. College room only: $4200. Room and board charges vary according to board plan and housing facility. Special program-related fees: $100 per year for music equipment fee, $180 per year for applied music lesson fee.

**Financial Aid** Program-specific awards: 115 Music Talent Awards for top musicians ($2200).
**Application Procedures** Students admitted directly into the professional program freshman year. Deadline for freshmen and transfers: continuous. Notification date for freshmen and transfers: continuous. Required: high school transcript, college transcript(s) for transfer students, audition, SAT or ACT test scores, minimum 2.5 high school GPA. Recommended: essay, minimum 3.0 high school GPA, 2 letters of recommendation, interview. Auditions held 6 times on campus; recorded music is permissible as a substitute for live auditions when distance is prohibitive and videotaped performances are permissible as a substitute for live auditions when distance is prohibitive.
**Web Site** http://www.bgsu.edu/colleges/music/index.html
**Undergraduate Contact** Dr. Kathleen Moss, Coordinator of Music Admissions, College of Musical Arts, Bowling Green State University, 1031 Moore Musical Arts Center, Bowling Green, Ohio 43403-0290; 419-372-8577, fax: 419-372-2938, e-mail address: kmoss@bgnet.bgsu.edu
**Graduate Contact** Dr. Robert Satterlee, Coordinator of Graduate Admissions, College of Musical Arts, Bowling Green State University, 1031 Moore Musical Arts Center, Bowling Green, Ohio 43403-0290; 419-372-2182, fax: 419-372-2938.

## Boyer College of Music and Dance

See Temple University

## Bradley University

### Peoria, Illinois

Independent, coed. Suburban campus. Total enrollment: 6,053. Music program established 1921.
**Degrees** Bachelor of Music in the areas of composition, music education, performance. Majors and concentrations: composition, music education, performance. Program accredited by NASM.
**Enrollment** 107 total; 63 undergraduate, 44 nonprofessional degree.
**Music Student Profile** 54% females, 46% males, 11% minorities, 4% international.
**Music Faculty** 9 undergraduate (full-time), 18 undergraduate (part-time). 80% of full-time faculty have terminal degrees. Graduate students do not teach undergraduate courses. Undergraduate student–faculty ratio: 8:1.
**Student Life** Student groups/activities include Music Educators National Conference, Phi Mu Alpha Sinfonia, Sigma Alpha Iota.
**Expenses for 2007–2008** Application fee: $35. Comprehensive fee: $28,410 includes full-time tuition ($21,200), mandatory fees ($160), and college room and board ($7050). College room only: $4100. Full-time tuition and fees vary according to student level. Room and board charges vary according to board plan. Special program-related fees: $165 per hour for applied music fee.
**Financial Aid** Program-specific awards: 66 music scholarships for program majors ($1560).
**Application Procedures** Students admitted directly into the professional program freshman year. Deadline for freshmen and transfers: continuous. Required: high school transcript, college transcript(s) for transfer students, minimum 2.0 high school GPA, audition, SAT or ACT test scores. Recommended: letter of recommendation. Auditions held continuously on campus; recorded music is permissible as a substitute for live auditions when distance is prohibitive and videotaped performances are permissible as a substitute for live auditions when distance is prohibitive.
**Web Site** http://music.bradley.edu
**Undergraduate Contact** Ms. Nickie Roberson, Director of Admissions, Office of Undergraduate Admissions, Bradley University, Swords Hall, Peoria, Illinois 61625; 800-447-6460, fax: 309-677-2797, e-mail address: admissions@bradley.edu

## Brandon University

### Brandon, Manitoba, Canada

Province-supported, coed. Small town campus. Total enrollment: 3,524 (2006). Music program established 1963.

**Degrees** Bachelor of Music in the areas of music education, performance, honours music; Bachelor of Music/Bachelor of Education. Majors and concentrations: music, music education, performance. Graduate degrees offered: Master of Music in the areas of performance and literature: piano and strings, music education. Program accredited by CUMS.
**Enrollment** 160 total; 140 undergraduate, 20 graduate.
**Music Faculty** 19 total (full-time), 10 total (part-time). Graduate students do not teach undergraduate courses. Undergraduate student–faculty ratio: 7:1.
**Expenses for 2007–2008** Application fee: $60 Canadian dollars. Tuition, fee, and room and board charges are reported in Canadian dollars. Province resident tuition: $3019 full-time. Canadian resident tuition: $3019 full-time. Mandatory fees: $445 full-time. Full-time tuition and fees vary according to class time, course load, degree level, location, and program. College room and board: $7033. College room only: $4172. Room and board charges vary according to location.
**Financial Aid** Program-specific awards: Vasey Memorial Scholarship ($3900), Cowan Bursary ($750), 2 Don Wright Scholarships in Music Education for instrumental/choral/vocal students ($2837), 2 Jane Vasey Memorial Scholarships ($1900), The Kay & G. R. Rowe Scholarship ($1350), Shirley Craig Scholarship ($1000), R. D. Bell String Scholarships, Helen C. Riesberry Scholarship ($1000).
**Application Procedures** Students admitted directly into the professional program freshman year. Deadline for freshmen and transfers: May 2. Required: high school transcript, college transcript(s) for transfer students, 2 letters of recommendation, audition. Auditions held 8 times on campus; recorded music is permissible as a substitute for live auditions when distance is prohibitive and videotaped performances are permissible as a substitute for live auditions when distance is prohibitive.
**Web Site** http://www.brandonu.ca
**Undergraduate Contact** Heather Beesley, Administrative Assistant, School of Music, Brandon University, 270 18th Street, Brandon, Manitoba R7A 6A9, Canada; 204-727-7388, fax: 204-728-6839, e-mail address: music@brandonu.ca
**Graduate Contact** Dr. Art Bower, Chair, Graduate Music Department, Brandon University, School of Music, Brandon, Manitoba R7A 6A9, Canada; 204-727-7436, fax: 204-728-6839, e-mail address: bower@brandonu.ca

## Brenau University

### Gainesville, Georgia

Independent, women only. Small town campus. Total enrollment: 916. Music program established 1878.
**Degrees** Bachelor of Music in the areas of performance, music education; Bachelor of Arts in Music in the area of music. Majors and concentrations: choral music education, piano, voice. Program accredited by NCATE.
**Enrollment** 25 total; 20 undergraduate, 5 nonprofessional degree.
**Music Student Profile** 100% females, 20% minorities, 3% international.
**Music Faculty** 3 undergraduate (full-time), 2 undergraduate (part-time). 100% of full-time faculty have terminal degrees. Graduate students do not teach undergraduate courses. Undergraduate student–faculty ratio: 10:1.
**Student Life** Student groups/activities include opera company, Lahier Chamber Singers, Mu Phi Epsilon. Special housing available for music students.
**Expenses for 2008–2009** Application fee: $35. Comprehensive fee: $28,287 includes full-time tuition ($18,550), mandatory fees ($250), and college room and board ($9487). Special program-related fees: $150 per semester for accompanist.
**Financial Aid** Program-specific awards: music scholarships for program majors ($3000–$5000).
**Application Procedures** Students admitted directly into the professional program freshman year. Deadline for freshmen and transfers: continuous. Required: high school transcript, college transcript(s) for transfer students, minimum 2.0 high school GPA, letter of recommendation, interview, audition, SAT or ACT test scores (minimum combined SAT score of 900, minimum composite ACT score of 19). Recommended: minimum 3.0 high school GPA. Auditions held twice and by appointment on

*Brenau University (continued)*

campus; recorded music is permissible as a substitute for live auditions when distance is prohibitive and videotaped performances are permissible as a substitute for live auditions when distance is prohibitive.
**Web Site** http://www.brenau.edu/sfah/music
**Undergraduate Contact** Dean of Admissions, Brenau University, 500 Washington Street, SE, Gainesville, Georgia 30501; 800-252-5119, fax: 770-538-4306, e-mail address: wcadmissions@brenau.edu

# Brevard College

## Brevard, North Carolina

Independent United Methodist, coed. Small town campus. Total enrollment: 675. Music program established 1995.
**Degrees** Bachelor of Arts in the area of music teaching; Bachelor of Music in the area of performance. Majors and concentrations: composition, jazz studies, music teaching. Program accredited by NASM.
**Enrollment** 45 total; 12 undergraduate, 33 nonprofessional degree.
**Music Student Profile** 60% females, 40% males, 10% minorities, 5% international.
**Music Faculty** 8 undergraduate (full-time), 11 undergraduate (part-time). 75% of full-time faculty have terminal degrees. Graduate students do not teach undergraduate courses. Undergraduate student–faculty ratio: 6:1.
**Student Life** Student groups/activities include workshops and master classes with visiting artists/performers, Music Educators National Conference (MENC) Student Chapter, Percussive Arts Society Student Chapter.
**Expenses for 2007–2008** Application fee: $30. Comprehensive fee: $25,800 includes full-time tuition ($18,700), mandatory fees ($50), and college room and board ($7050). Full-time tuition and fees vary according to course load. Room and board charges vary according to board plan and housing facility. Special program-related fees: $100 for recital fee, $125 per credit hour for applied music fee.
**Financial Aid** Program-specific awards: 12–20 music audition awards for freshmen and transfers ($3000).
**Application Procedures** Students apply for admission into the professional program by sophomore year. Deadline for freshmen and transfers: continuous. Required: high school transcript, college transcript(s) for transfer students, minimum 2.0 high school GPA, interview, audition, SAT or ACT test scores, placement test in theory and instrument, keyboard placement. Recommended: 1-2 letters of recommendation. Auditions held 4 times and by appointment on campus; recorded music is permissible as a substitute for live auditions when distance is prohibitive and videotaped performances are permissible as a substitute for live auditions when distance is prohibitive.
**Web Site** http://www.brevard.edu
**Undergraduate Contact** Prof. S. Kay Hoke, Chair, Division of Fine Arts, Department of Music, Brevard College, One Brevard College Drive, Brevard, North Carolina 28712; 828-884-8211, fax: 828-884-3790, e-mail address: music@brevard.edu

# Brewton-Parker College

## Mt. Vernon, Georgia

Independent Southern Baptist, coed. Rural campus. Total enrollment: 1,034. Music program established 1964.
**Web Site** http://www.bpc.edu/

# Brigham Young University

## Provo, Utah

Independent, coed. Suburban campus. Total enrollment: 34,174. Music program established 1878.
**Web Site** http://www.byu.edu/

# Brock University

## St. Catharines, Ontario, Canada

Province-supported, coed. Urban campus. Total enrollment: 17,006.
**Degrees** Bachelor of Arts. Majors and concentrations: music. Program accredited by CUMS.
**Enrollment** 60 total; all undergraduate.
**Music Student Profile** 85% females, 15% males, 5% minorities, 3% international.
**Music Faculty** 6 undergraduate (full-time), 15 undergraduate (part-time). 100% of full-time faculty have terminal degrees. Graduate students do not teach undergraduate courses. Undergraduate student–faculty ratio: 11:1.
**Student Life** Student groups/activities include performances at on-campus and off-campus functions, Music Society.
**Expenses for 2007–2008** Application fee: $115 Canadian dollars. Tuition, fee, and room and board charges are reported in Canadian dollars. Special program-related fees: $50 per year for practice room rental, $1200 per year for music lesson fee for non-MusB students.
**Financial Aid** Program-specific awards: 1 Sir Isaac Brock Scholarship for junior and senior program majors ($475), 1 Senior Scholarship in Music I for junior program majors ($425), 1 Senior Scholarship in Music II for senior program majors ($425), 1 A. Whitmore Griffin Award in Music for junior and senior program majors ($2400).
**Application Procedures** Students admitted directly into the professional program freshman year. Deadline for freshmen and transfers: June 1. Notification date for freshmen and transfers: June 30. Required: essay, high school transcript, college transcript(s) for transfer students, minimum 3.0 high school GPA, 2 letters of recommendation, interview, audition, 2 years of theory study, photograph, questionnaire. Recommended: 4 years of keyboard study. Auditions held 5 times and by appointment on campus; recorded music is permissible as a substitute for live auditions for international applicants and videotaped performances are permissible as a substitute for live auditions for international applicants.
**Web Site** http://www.brocku.ca
**Undergraduate Contact** Natalie Fedj, Administrative Assistant, Department of Music, Brock University, 500 Glenridge Avenue, St. Catharines, Ontario L2S 3A1, Canada; 905-688-5550 ext. 3817, fax: 905-688-2789, e-mail address: music@brocku.ca

# Brooklyn College of the City University of New York

## Brooklyn, New York

State and locally supported, coed. Urban campus. Total enrollment: 15,947 (2007). Music program established 1963.
**Degrees** Bachelor of Music in the areas of performance, composition, music education. Majors and concentrations: classical music, composition, music, music education, opera, performance, stringed instruments, voice, wind and percussion instruments. Graduate degrees offered: Master of Arts in the area of music education; Master of Music in the areas of performance, composition. Cross-registration with City University of New York System.
**Enrollment** 230 total; 100 undergraduate, 110 graduate, 20 nonprofessional degree.
**Music Student Profile** 60% females, 40% males, 30% minorities, 25% international.
**Music Faculty** 20 total (full-time), 40 total (part-time). 85% of full-time faculty have terminal degrees. Graduate students teach a few undergraduate courses. Undergraduate student–faculty ratio: 10:1.
**Student Life** Student groups/activities include music for convocations, commencements, and community concerts, Conservatory Concert Series, Arts Council events and performances.
**Expenses for 2007–2008** Application fee: $65. State resident tuition: $4000 full-time. Nonresident tuition: $8762 full-time. Mandatory fees: $150 full-time. Special program-related fees: $75 per semester for technology fee, $115 per semester for student and university fees.

**Financial Aid** Program-specific awards: 20 music scholarships for qualified students ($300–$2000).

**Application Procedures** Students admitted directly into the professional program freshman year. Deadline for freshmen and transfers: continuous. Notification date for freshmen and transfers: August 15. Required: high school transcript, college transcript(s) for transfer students, minimum 3.0 high school GPA, audition, SAT test score only, minimum TOEFL score of 550 for international students, portfolio for composition students. Recommended: letter of recommendation, interview. Auditions held 4 times on campus; recorded music is permissible as a substitute for live auditions when distance is prohibitive and videotaped performances are permissible as a substitute for live auditions when distance is prohibitive. Portfolio reviews held continuously, September through May on campus.

**Web Site** http://bcmusic.org

**Undergraduate Contact** Dr. Jonathan Babcock, Deputy Chairman, Conservatory of Music, Brooklyn College of the City University of New York, 2900 Bedford Avenue, Brooklyn, New York 11210; 718-951-5000 ext. 2888, fax: 718-951-4502, e-mail address: jbabcock@brooklyn.cuny.edu

**Graduate Contact** Stephanie Jensen-Moulton, Deputy Chairman, Conservatory of Music, Brooklyn College of the City University of New York, 2900 Bedford Avenue, Brooklyn, New York 11210; 718-951-5954, fax: 718-951-4502, e-mail address: sjensenmoulton@brooklyn.cuny.edu

# Bucknell University

## Lewisburg, Pennsylvania

Independent, coed. Small town campus. Total enrollment: 3,677. Music program established 1892.

**Degrees** Bachelor of Music in the areas of performance, music education, music history, music composition. Majors and concentrations: composition, music education, music history, piano/organ, stringed instruments, voice, wind instruments. Program accredited by NASM.

**Enrollment** 53 total; 28 undergraduate, 25 nonprofessional degree.

**Music Student Profile** 60% females, 40% males, 5% minorities.

**Music Faculty** 10 undergraduate (full-time), 16 undergraduate (part-time). 88% of full-time faculty have terminal degrees. Graduate students do not teach undergraduate courses. Undergraduate student–faculty ratio: 2:1.

**Expenses for 2008–2009** Application fee: $60. Comprehensive fee: $48,380 includes full-time tuition ($39,434), mandatory fees ($218), and college room and board ($8728). College room only: $4912. Special program-related fees: $350 per semester for lessons for non-majors.

**Financial Aid** Program-specific awards: preferential awards for program majors demonstrating need ($2000).

**Application Procedures** Students admitted directly into the professional program freshman year. Deadline for freshmen: January 1; transfers: April 1. Notification date for freshmen: April 1; transfers: July 1. Required: essay, high school transcript, college transcript(s) for transfer students, minimum 3.0 high school GPA, audition, SAT or ACT test scores. Recommended: 3 letters of recommendation, interview. Auditions held 4 times on campus; recorded music is permissible as a substitute for live auditions if a campus visit is impossible and videotaped performances are permissible as a substitute for live auditions if a campus visit is impossible.

**Web Site** http://www.bucknell.edu/music

**Undergraduate Contact** Ms. Brenda Ross, Secretary, Department of Music, Bucknell University, Lewisburg, Pennsylvania 17837; 570-577-1216, fax: 570-577-1215, e-mail address: bross@bucknell.edu

## Jordan College of Fine Arts
# Butler University

## Indianapolis, Indiana

Independent, coed. Urban campus. Total enrollment: 4,479. Music program established 1896.

**Degrees** Bachelor of Arts in the areas of music theory, music history, music composition, piano pedagogy, applied music; Bachelor of Music in the areas of performance, composition, piano pedagogy. music education; Bachelor of Science in the area of arts administration/music. Majors and concentrations: applied music, brass, composition, jazz studies, music education, music history and literature, music theory, performance, piano, piano pedagogy, stringed instruments, voice, wind and percussion instruments. Graduate degrees offered: Master of Music in the areas of performance, composition, conducting, music theory, music history, piano pedagogy, music education. Cross-registration with Indianapolis Consortium for Urban Education. Program accredited by NASM.

**Enrollment** 233 total; 197 undergraduate, 36 graduate.

**Music Student Profile** 54% females, 46% males, 6% minorities, 3% international.

**Music Faculty** 28 total (full-time), 28 total (part-time). 41% of full-time faculty have terminal degrees. Graduate students do not teach undergraduate courses. Undergraduate student–faculty ratio: 6:1.

**Student Life** Student groups/activities include Music Educators National Conference Student Chapter, Butler Community Arts School, music fraternities and sororities.

**Expenses for 2007–2008** Application fee: $35. Comprehensive fee: $35,766 includes full-time tuition ($26,070), mandatory fees ($736), and college room and board ($8960). Full-time tuition and fees vary according to program. Room and board charges vary according to housing facility. Special program-related fees: $170 per credit hour for one-on-one instruction.

**Financial Aid** Program-specific awards: audition awards for program majors.

**Application Procedures** Students admitted directly into the professional program freshman year. Deadline for freshmen and transfers: continuous. Required: essay, high school transcript, college transcript(s) for transfer students, minimum 2.0 high school GPA, letter of recommendation, audition, SAT or ACT test scores, music application. Recommended: minimum 3.0 high school GPA, interview. Auditions held 5 times on campus; recorded music is permissible as a substitute for live auditions when distance is prohibitive and videotaped performances are permissible as a substitute for live auditions when distance is prohibitive.

**Web Site** http://www.butler.edu/music/

**Contact** Ms. Kathy Lang, Admission Representative, Jordan College of Fine Arts, Butler University, Lilly Hall - 138B, 4600 Sunset Avenue, Indianapolis, Indiana 46208; 317-940-9656, fax: 317-940-9658, e-mail address: klang@butler.edu

### More About the University

**B**utler University is most proud of its tradition of excellence and innovation. Challenging and enabling students to meet their personal and professional goals has guided the University since 1855. Today, Butler is an independent, coeducational, nonsectarian university, with a total undergraduate enrollment of more than 3,900 students. The University is accredited by the North Central Association of Colleges and Schools.

As one of America's oldest music institutions, Butler's programs prepare young musicians to become outstanding teachers, solo artists, and leaders in the cultural community. Programs in performance combine quality private study, engaging classroom work, and a variety of performance ensembles. Aspiring musicians/teachers pursue diverse field experiences in their first year of study. The arts administration program prepares talented artistic students for careers in arts-related, not-for-profit organizations and in the business world. Arts administration students regularly intern at the Kennedy Center, the San Francisco Opera, Kentucky Center for the Arts, and many of Indianapolis's finest cultural institutions.

**Campus and Surroundings** Indianapolis, Indiana's state capital and the thirteenth-largest city in the nation, boasts a variety of cultural activities, including the Indianapolis Symphony Orchestra, Indiana Repertory Theatre, Indianapolis Chamber Orchestra, the Indianapolis Museum of Art, and the world's largest children's museum. Citywide celebrations are plentiful, including ethnic festivals, art fairs, and outdoor music festivals.

*Butler University (continued)*

**Program Facilities** Clowes Memorial Hall is a 2,200-seat performance hall that hosts a variety of events, from community arts groups to national and international touring companies and many University performances. A new performing arts complex is currently under construction. The first phase of the complex, a 47,000-square-foot addition to Lilly Hall called the Courtyard Building, was completed in spring 2003. This new building houses a choral rehearsal hall, an instrumental rehearsal hall, dance studios, a theater studio, an electronic music lab, and a percussion studio. The second phase, the 140-seat Eidson-Duckwall Recital Hall, was completed in fall 2004. The third phase is a 450-seat performance hall/proscenium theater with adjustable acoustical features.

**Faculty/Alumni** Studio instruction at Butler is always with professional members of the faculty, and classrooms are led by outstanding scholar educators. The award-winning group includes editors of definitive editions of the songs by Debussy and Schubert; nationally known composers in demand as composers-in-residence; an outstanding performing faculty; individual artists with opera companies and orchestras throughout the world; winners in the Metropolitan Opera Auditions, MacAllister Awards, Bodky Competition, and the Van Cliburn Competition; and conductors who have given the downbeat on the podium in the world's great concert halls.

Butler's program prepares students for the future with its graduates pursuing master's programs at the Eastman School of Music, Peabody Conservatory, Boston University, Florida State University, the University of Michigan, and Indiana University.

**Student Performance Opportunities** In addition to numerous solo recital opportunities, students participate in a variety of large and small ensembles. Instrumental students may play in groups that range from chamber-style winds, string quartets, and piano trios to the larger Symphonic Wind Ensemble and the University's full-scale Butler Symphony Orchestra. Singers might find themselves in intimate ensembles like the Jordan Jazz or Madrigal Singers or in larger staged productions of the Butler Opera and the University Choir or Butler Chorale. Students regularly combine forces to present titan works, such as Orff's *Carmin Burana*, Beethoven's *Choral Symphony*, or Bernstein's *Candide*.

**Special Programs** Butler has a strong commitment to new programs, technology, and facilities, including a new recording industry studies major, in collaboration with the media arts department that places students in studios for hands-on learning experiences. Each year, more than 30 visiting artists perform on campus and interact with students. Butler music students have worked with the likes of Yo-Yo Ma, Andre Watts, Richard Stolzman, Denyce Graves, Jeffrey Kahane, Cleo Laine, Dale Warland, Marvin Hamlisch, John Holloway, H. Robert Reynolds, Karel Haus, and Suzanne Vega.

**Cooperative Agreements** Butler University has collaborative relationships with many local arts organizations, including the Indianapolis Opera. The following are located on campus: Dance Kaleidoscope, Indianapolis Symphonic Choir, Indianapolis Chamber Orchestra, American Pianists Association, and the Indianapolis Children's Choir.

**Career Placement Services and Opportunities** Butler students sing, play, conduct, teach, and inspire. Students with undergraduate Butler music degrees continue their studies at some of the country's finest advanced-study programs, including Indiana University, the Manhattan School of Music, the Juilliard Opera Program, Florida State University, and the Eastman School of Music.

Former Butler students are on the stage and in the pit for major Broadway shows like *Les Misérables, Blast!*, and *Phantom of the Opera*. The music education program has a 99 percent placement for teachers. Butler's music education students are regularly cited as outstanding young educators by the Music Educators National Conference and hold teaching positions at public and private

schools all over the country. Butler has maestros on the podium at the Warner Brothers Orchestra, Evansville Philharmonic, Ft. Smith Symphony, and on Broadway.

# California Institute of the Arts
## Valencia, California

Independent, coed. Suburban campus. Total enrollment: 1,324. Music program established 1961.

**Degrees** Bachelor of Fine Arts in the areas of music composition, musical arts, performance, world music, jazz, music technology, performer/composer. Majors and concentrations: classical music, composition, harp, jazz, music technology, musical arts, new media, performer/composer, piano, stringed instruments, voice, wind and percussion instruments, world music. Graduate degrees offered: Master of Fine Arts in the areas of music composition, performance, world music, composition/new media, jazz, performer/composer, integrated media-music, performer/composer-African American improvisational music. Program accredited by NASM.

**Enrollment** 255 total; 152 undergraduate, 103 graduate.

**Music Student Profile** 28% females, 72% males, 24% minorities, 8% international.

**Music Faculty** 32 total (full-time), 26 total (part-time). 80% of full-time faculty have terminal degrees. Graduate students do not teach undergraduate courses. Undergraduate student–faculty ratio: 5:1.

**Student Life** Student groups/activities include Community Arts Partnership (CAP), off-campus performance groups, Intercultural Arts Project (ICAP). Special housing available for music students.

**Expenses for 2008–2009** Application fee: $70. Comprehensive fee: $42,084 includes full-time tuition ($32,860), mandatory fees ($576), and college room and board ($8648). College room only: $4985.

**Financial Aid** Program-specific awards: CalArts Scholarships for students demonstrating talent ($2000–$22,000), Minority Scholarships ($2000–$22,000).

**Application Procedures** Students admitted directly into the professional program freshman year. Deadline for freshmen and transfers: January 5. Required: essay, high school transcript, college transcript(s) for transfer students, 2 letters of recommendation, audition, portfolio for composition, music technology, experimental sound practices applicants, recorded audition for jazz applicants, video recording for world music applicants (excluding transfer students). Recommended: interview. Auditions held by appointment on campus and off campus in New York, NY; Chicago, IL; Interlochen, MI; Valencia, CA; San Francisco, CA; recorded music is permissible as a substitute for live auditions whenever needed and videotaped performances are permissible as a substitute for live auditions whenever sound reading is not available. Portfolio reviews held on campus.

**Web Site** http://www.calarts.edu

**Contact** Ms. Harmony Jiroudek, Admissions Counselor, California Institute of the Arts, 24700 McBean Parkway, Valencia, California 91355; 661-255-1050, fax: 661-253-7710, e-mail address: hjiroudek@calarts.edu

### More About the Institute

The School of Music at California Institute of the Arts (CalArts) strives to create a learning environment to support the informed, creative music maker. High standards, a focus on new and experimental forms, and a respect for great musical traditions are the School's hallmark and its formula for success. In addition to cross-stylistic collaborations within the School of Music, students work with visual artists, filmmakers, animators, dancers, actors, and writers from the five other schools at CalArts.

The School of Music offers rigorous training in a unique variety of musical styles and cultures, from chamber and orchestral music to computer music, from opera to interdisciplinary performance, from jazz improvisation to the musical traditions of Africa, India, and Indonesia. With approximately 250 students and a 5:1 student-faculty ratio, the School of Music offers one of the most intimate learning environments available. Every student works closely with a mentor, a faculty member who serves as that student's artistic and academic advisor.

**Programs of Study** The School of Music offers undergraduate programs that lead to a Bachelor of Fine Arts (B.F.A.) degree or a Certificate of Fine Arts. Graduate programs lead to a Master of Fine Arts (M.F.A.) degree or an Advanced Certificate of Fine Arts. Prospective students are invited to apply to the following degree programs: Composition Program (B.F.A., M.F.A.), with a specialization available in experimental sound practices for M.F.A. only; Jazz Studies Program (B.F.A., M.F.A.); Multifocus Programs in Performance (B.F.A., M.F.A.), including the Wind/Brass/String Instruments Program, the Harp Program, the Piano/Keyboard/Collaborative Keyboard Program, the Guitar Program, the Percussion/World Percussion Program, and the Voice Program; Multi Focus Music Technologies Program (B.F.A. only); Performer/Composer Program (Upper-division B.F.A., M.F.A. only), with a specialization available in African American improvisational music; World Music Performance Program (B.F.A., M.F.A.), with specializations available in African music and dance (M.F.A. only), Balinese and Javanese music and dance (M.F.A. only), North Indian music (M.F.A. only), and World Percussion (M.F.A. only).

Every B.F.A. student pursues course work in three areas: the School of Music core curriculum, the critical studies undergraduate requirements, and his or her specialized program curriculum.

M.F.A. students concentrate primarily on advanced work in their respective programs. They are generally not required to take core curriculum and critical studies courses. M.F.A. students may be required, however, to take core curriculum courses to strengthen their musical skills and/or theoretical knowledge. Qualified graduate applicants may also apply to be considered for a supplemental concentration in integrated media (IM), a course of study focused on interdisciplinary work with digital media.

All B.F.A. and M.F.A. programs offered by the School of Music have their own integral curriculum. The School, however, encourages courses of study that draw on the resources of several programs. Faculty mentors guide students in designing such courses of study.

The School of Music offers more than 200 courses each semester. Music students may also take advantage of numerous elective courses offered throughout CalArts. In order to graduate, students must complete all program and course requirements and pass regular faculty member reviews of their artistic and academic progress.

**Program Facilities** Most large-ensemble performances take place in the Roy O. Disney Music Hall, a multipurpose space with adaptable acoustics, lighting, and sound features. This hall is used for both traditional and experimental events. Additional concerts are presented in the Walt Disney Modular Theater and the Main Gallery.

An important new addition to the School of Music's resources is the Roy and Edna Disney/CalArts Theater (REDCAT), a performance and exhibition space that opened in November 2003 in downtown Los Angeles. Housed as a separate entity in the Frank Gehry-designed Walt Disney Concert Hall complex (the new home of the Los Angeles Philharmonic Orchestra), REDCAT features CalArts student, alumni, and faculty member work as well as that of visiting artists.

The School of Music has more than twenty-five practice rooms, many with pianos, including special rooms for piano and percussion majors. All rooms are available around-the-clock when school is in session.

CalArts' sizable instrument collection features fifty pianos, three harpsichords, an organ, and a celesta; three harps; various strings, woodwinds, brass, and early European instruments; numerous orchestral and nontraditional percussion instruments; Balinese and Javanese gamelans; African drum ensembles; and sarods, sitars, tabla, and other Indian instruments.

The School of Music has extensive state-of-the-art facilities for using computers and interactive media to create, perform, record,

and print music. Studios support classes in composition, synthesis, and scoring; digital recording, editing, and processing; multimedia design; telecommunications; and software and hardware development. All studios are open around the clock during academic sessions.

**Faculty, Resident Artists, Alumni** CalArts' faculty features innovators and leaders in each specialty—composers, performers, and producers who have distinguished themselves at the highest levels. All faculty members are practicing professionals and can prepare students for the demands of a global music community.

The School of Music regularly invites celebrated artists in a variety of specialties to share their experience and insights with students and to supplement the expertise of regular faculty members. They may perform, conduct their compositions, give master classes and workshops, and teach courses or lessons.

CalArts alumni have made their mark on every aspect of musicmaking, including professors at distinguished music schools, performing and recording artists, composers, computer musicians, and the like.

**Student Performance/Exhibit Opportunities** The School of Music's performance schedule features more than 250 concerts every year, running the gamut from informal noon concerts and student-organized jam sessions to formal on-campus evening events and performances at high-profile venues throughout the Los Angeles area. Faculty members play alongside students at many of these concerts.

# California State University, Fullerton
## Fullerton, California

State-supported, coed. Suburban campus. Total enrollment: 37,130. Music program established 1960.
**Web Site** http://www.fullerton.edu/

# California State University, Long Beach
## Long Beach, California

State-supported, coed. Suburban campus. Total enrollment: 36,868. Music program established 1949.
**Degrees** Bachelor of Music in the areas of performance, music history and literature, composition, jazz studies, music education. Majors and concentrations: classical music, composition, jazz, music, music education, music history, opera, piano, stringed instruments, voice, wind and percussion instruments. Graduate degrees offered: Master of Music in the areas of composition, conducting, performance, music history, music theory, opera, jazz studies. Cross-registration with California State University System. Program accredited by NASM.
**Enrollment** 640 total; 519 undergraduate, 91 graduate, 30 nonprofessional degree.
**Music Student Profile** 52% females, 48% males, 40% minorities, 5% international.
**Music Faculty** 21 total (full-time), 75 total (part-time). 85% of full-time faculty have terminal degrees. Graduate students teach a few undergraduate courses. Undergraduate student–faculty ratio: 20:1.
**Student Life** Student groups/activities include American Choral Directors Association, Music Educators National Conference, professional music fraternities.
**Expenses for 2008–2009** Application fee: $55. Nonresident tuition: $10,170 full-time. Mandatory fees: $3394 full-time. College room and board: $7940. Special program-related fees: $25 per semester for practice room, instrument fee, locker room fee.
**Financial Aid** Program-specific awards: 80 music scholarships for program majors ($700).
**Application Procedures** Students admitted directly into the professional program freshman year. Deadline for freshmen: November 30; transfers: February 1. Required: high school transcript, college transcript(s) for transfer students, minimum 3.0 high school GPA, audition, SAT or ACT test scores. Auditions held 4

*California State University, Long Beach (continued)*

times on campus; recorded music is permissible as a substitute for live auditions when distance is prohibitive and videotaped performances are permissible as a substitute for live auditions when distance is prohibitive.

**Web Site** http://www.csulb.edu/~music

**Undergraduate Contact** Dr. Lee Vail, Undergraduate Advisor, Department of Music, California State University, Long Beach, 1250 Bellflower Boulevard, Long Beach, California 90840-7101; 562-985-4399, fax: 562-985-2490, e-mail address: lvail@csulb.edu

**Graduate Contact** Dr. Kristine Forney, Director of Graduate Studies, Department of Music, California State University, Long Beach, 1250 Bellflower Boulevard, Long Beach, California 90840-7101; 562-984-4788, fax: 562-985-2490, e-mail address: kforney@csulb.edu

# California State University, Los Angeles

## Los Angeles, California

State-supported, coed. Urban campus. Total enrollment: 21,051. Music program established 1952.

**Degrees** Bachelor of Arts in the area of general music; Bachelor of Music in the areas of performance, composition, jazz studies, music education. Majors and concentrations: composition, jazz, music, music education, piano, stringed instruments, voice, wind and percussion instruments. Graduate degrees offered: Master of Arts in the areas of music education, musicology, general music; Master of Music in the areas of commercial music, composition, performance, conducting, Afro Latin music. Cross-registration with California State University System. Program accredited by NASM.

**Enrollment** 273 total; 163 undergraduate, 110 graduate.

**Music Student Profile** 60% females, 40% males, 80% minorities, 10% international.

**Music Faculty** 15 total (full-time), 46 total (part-time). 80% of full-time faculty have terminal degrees. Graduate students do not teach undergraduate courses. Undergraduate student–faculty ratio: 13:1.

**Student Life** Student groups/activities include Music Educators National Conference, American Choral Directors Association, International Association for Jazz Education.

**Expenses for 2008–2009** Application fee: $55. State resident tuition: $0 full-time. Nonresident tuition: $11,513 full-time. Mandatory fees: $3377 full-time. College room and board: $8406. College room only: $5094. Special program-related fees: $25 per quarter for practice room fee.

**Financial Aid** Program-specific awards: 15 Friends of Music Scholarships for music majors ($600–$1200), 12 general music scholarships for music majors ($600–$1200).

**Application Procedures** Students apply for admission into the professional program by freshman year. Deadline for freshmen and transfers: June 30. Required: essay, high school transcript, college transcript(s) for transfer students, minimum 2.0 high school GPA, audition, portfolio, two letters of recommendation (for music education majors only). Recommended: SAT or ACT test scores. Auditions held 4 times and by appointment on campus; recorded music is permissible as a substitute for live auditions when distance is prohibitive and videotaped performances are permissible as a substitute for live auditions when distance is prohibitive. Portfolio reviews held continuously on campus.

**Web Site** http://www.calstatela.edu/academic/music/

**Contact** David Connors, Chair, Department of Music, California State University, Los Angeles, 5151 State University Drive, Los Angeles, California 90032; 323-343-4060, fax: 323-343-4063, e-mail address: dconnor@calstatela.edu

# California State University, Northridge

## Northridge, California

State-supported, coed. Urban campus. Total enrollment: 34,560 (2007). Music program established 1958.

**Degrees** Bachelor of Arts in the areas of music therapy, music industry; Bachelor of Music in the areas of performance, jazz, composition. Majors and concentrations: classical guitar, commercial and media writing, composition, jazz studies, keyboard, music education, music industry, music therapy, orchestral strings, percussion instruments performance, vocal music, wind instruments. Graduate degrees offered: Master of Education in the area of music education; Master of Music in the areas of performance, conducting, composition. Cross-registration with California State University System. Program accredited by NASM.

**Enrollment** 643 total; 559 undergraduate, 68 graduate, 16 nonprofessional degree.

**Music Student Profile** 43% females, 57% males, 32% minorities, 9% international.

**Music Faculty** 23 total (full-time), 45 total (part-time). 42% of full-time faculty have terminal degrees. Graduate students do not teach undergraduate courses. Undergraduate student–faculty ratio: 15:1.

**Student Life** Student groups/activities include California Music Educators Association Student Chapter, American Association of Music Therapy Student Chapter, Sigma Alpha Iota. Special housing available for music students.

**Expenses for 2007–2008** Application fee: $55. State resident tuition: $0 full-time. Nonresident tuition: $8136 full-time. Mandatory fees: $3350 full-time. College room and board: $9350. College room only: $5413. Room and board charges vary according to board plan and housing facility. Special program-related fees: $10 per semester for piano classes, piano lessons, use of instruments.

**Financial Aid** Program-specific awards: 25 University Scholarships for program students ($1000), 250 departmental scholarships for program students ($1100).

**Application Procedures** Students admitted directly into the professional program freshman year. Deadline for freshmen and transfers: continuous. Required: essay, high school transcript, college transcript(s) for transfer students, minimum 2.0 high school GPA, 2 letters of recommendation, interview, audition, portfolio. Recommended: minimum 3.0 high school GPA. Auditions held 3-4 times on campus; recorded music is permissible as a substitute for live auditions when distance is prohibitive and videotaped performances are permissible as a substitute for live auditions when distance is prohibitive. Portfolio reviews held 3-4 times.

**Web Site** http://www.csun.edu/~amc1700/

**Undergraduate Contact** Lea Clará, Undergraduate Advisor/Coordinator, Department of Music, California State University, Northridge, 18111 Nordhoff Street, Northridge, California 91330-8314; 818-677-3181, fax: 818-677-3255, e-mail address: music@csun.edu

**Graduate Contact** Dr. John Roscigno, Graduate Advisor, Department of Music, California State University, Northridge, 18111 Nordhoff Street, Northridge, California 91330-8314; 818-677-3064, fax: 818-677-2646.

# California State University, Sacramento

## Sacramento, California

State-supported, coed. Urban campus. Total enrollment: 28,829. Music program established 1947.

**Degrees** Bachelor of Arts in the areas of music, music management; Bachelor of Music in the areas of voice, piano, organ, orchestral instruments, guitar, music theory/composition, music education, jazz studies. Majors and concentrations: guitar, jazz studies, music, music education, music management, music theory and composition, piano/organ/harpsichord, stringed instruments, voice, wind and percussion instruments. Graduate degrees offered: Master of Music in the areas of conducting, composition, music education, music history and literature, performance. Cross-registration with University of California-Davis, Los Rios Community College District. Program accredited by NASM.

**Enrollment** 285 total; 200 undergraduate, 35 graduate, 50 nonprofessional degree.

**Music Student Profile** 59% females, 41% males, 5% international.

**Music Faculty** 22 total (full-time), 30 total (part-time). 100% of full-time faculty have terminal degrees. Graduate students do not teach undergraduate courses. Undergraduate student–faculty ratio: 12:1.

**Student Life** Student groups/activities include Music Educators National Conference, Mu Phi Epsilon, Pi Kappa Lambda.

**Expenses for 2007–2008** Application fee: $55. State resident tuition: $0 full-time. Nonresident tuition: $12,942 full-time. Mandatory fees: $4752 full-time. College room and board: $8598. College room only: $5778. Room and board charges vary according to board plan. Special program-related fees: $40 per semester for music service fee.

**Financial Aid** Program-specific awards: 30–50 music awards for program majors ($150–$2000).

**Application Procedures** Students admitted directly into the professional program freshman year. Deadline for freshmen and transfers: continuous. Required: high school transcript, college transcript(s) for transfer students, minimum 2.0 high school GPA, audition, SAT or ACT test scores, portfolio for theory/composition applicants. Recommended: essay, minimum 3.0 high school GPA, video. Auditions held 4 times on campus; recorded music is permissible as a substitute for live auditions if a campus visit is impossible and videotaped performances are permissible as a substitute for live auditions if a campus visit is impossible. Portfolio reviews held 4 times on campus.

**Web Site** http://www.csus.edu/music

**Undergraduate Contact** Mr. Mark Allen, Admissions Counselor, Department of Music, California State University, Sacramento, 6000 J Street, Sacramento, California 95819-6015; 916-278-6543, e-mail address: music@csus.edu

**Graduate Contact** Dr. Ernie Hills, Graduate Coordinator, Department of Music, California State University, Sacramento, 6000 J Street, Sacramento, California 95819-6015; 916-278-5191, e-mail address: hills@csus.edu

# Calvary Bible College and Theological Seminary

### Kansas City, Missouri

Independent nondenominational, coed. Suburban campus. Total enrollment: 329 (2007). Music program established 1955.

**Degrees** Bachelor of Music in the areas of music education, music performance and pedagogy; Bachelor of Science in the area of church music. Majors and concentrations: church music, music education, piano pedagogy, piano performance, vocal pedagogy, voice performance.

**Enrollment** 25 total.

**Music Student Profile** 66% females, 34% males, 10% minorities.

**Music Faculty** 3 undergraduate (full-time), 2 undergraduate (part-time). 67% of full-time faculty have terminal degrees. Graduate students do not teach undergraduate courses. Undergraduate student–faculty ratio: 5:1.

**Student Life** Student groups/activities include musicals, dramas, oratorios.

**Expenses for 2007–2008** Application fee: $25. Comprehensive fee: $12,500 includes full-time tuition ($7800), mandatory fees ($700), and college room and board ($4000). College room only: $1800. Special program-related fees: $50 per semester for accompanist fee, $125 per semester for private lessons.

**Financial Aid** Program-specific awards: 3–6 Music Department Scholarships for music majors ($700).

**Application Procedures** Students admitted directly into the professional program freshman year. Deadline for freshmen and transfers: July 15. Required: high school transcript, college transcript(s) for transfer students, 2 letters of recommendation, audition, SAT or ACT test scores. Auditions held whenever needed on campus; recorded music is permissible as a substitute for live auditions if a campus visit is impossible and videotaped performances are permissible as a substitute for live auditions if a campus visit is impossible.

**Web Site** http://www.calvary.edu

**Undergraduate Contact** Paul Vander Mey, Chairman, Music Department, Calvary Bible College and Theological Seminary, 15800 Calvary Road, Kansas City, Missouri 64147; 816-322-0110 ext. 1354, fax: 816-331-4474, e-mail address: musicdir@calvary.edu

# Cameron University

### Lawton, Oklahoma

State-supported, coed. Small town campus. Total enrollment: 5,475.

**Web Site** http://www.cameron.edu/

# Campbellsville University

### Campbellsville, Kentucky

Independent, coed. Small town campus. Total enrollment: 2,376 (2007). Music program established 1957.

**Web Site** http://www.campbellsville.edu/

# Capital University

### Columbus, Ohio

Independent, coed. Suburban campus. Total enrollment: 3,713. Music program established 1918.

**Degrees** Bachelor of Arts in the area of music; Bachelor of Music in the areas of music education, composition, jazz studies, music industry, performance, keyboard pedagogy, music theater, music merchandising, music media, music technology. Majors and concentrations: composition, jazz studies, keyboard pedagogy, music education, music industry, music media, music merchandising, music performance, music technology. Graduate degrees offered: Master of Music in the area of music education with an emphasis in Kodaly. Cross-registration with Higher Education Council of Columbus. Program accredited by NASM.

**Enrollment** 247 total; 205 undergraduate, 42 graduate.

**Music Student Profile** 54% females, 46% males, 3% minorities, 2% international.

**Music Faculty** 27 total (full-time), 22 total (part-time). 41% of full-time faculty have terminal degrees. Graduate students do not teach undergraduate courses. Undergraduate student–faculty ratio: 4:1.

**Student Life** Student groups/activities include Ohio Collegiate Music Educators Association, Phi Mu Alpha/Phi Beta/Sigma Alpha Iota/Tau Beta Sigma, Music and Entertainment Industry Student Association.

**Expenses for 2007–2008** Application fee: $25. Comprehensive fee: $33,180 includes full-time tuition ($26,360) and college room and board ($6820). Full-time tuition varies according to course load, degree level, program, and student level. Room and board charges vary according to board plan and housing facility. Special program-related fees: $150 per semester for group lesson, $315–$395 per semester for private lessons.

**Financial Aid** Program-specific awards: music scholarships for program majors ($500–$10,000), participation awards for non-music majors ($500–$1000), music grants for program majors with exceptional talent or needed instruments ($500–$1000), composition awards for composition majors ($500–$1000).

**Application Procedures** Students admitted directly into the professional program freshman year. Deadline for freshmen: April 15; transfers: continuous. Notification date for freshmen and transfers: continuous. Required: high school transcript, college transcript(s) for transfer students, letter of recommendation, audition, SAT or ACT test scores (minimum composite ACT score of 18), minimum 2.6 high school GPA, minimum 2.25 college GPA for transfers, college report form for transfer students. Recommended: minimum 3.0 high school GPA, interview. Auditions held 5 times on campus; videotaped performances are permissible as a substitute for live auditions for out-of-state students only.

**Web Site** http://www.capital.edu

**Undergraduate Contact** Ms. Meagan M. Webb, Assistant Director of Admission, Admissions, Capital University, 1 College and Main, Columbus, Ohio 43209; 614-236-6101 ext. 6574, fax: 614-236-6926, e-mail address: admissions@capital.edu

**Graduate Contact** Dr. Sandra Mathias, Professor of Music and Education, Conservatory of Music, Capital University, 1 College and Main, Columbus, Ohio 43209; 614-236-6267, fax: 614-236-6935, e-mail address: smathias@capital.edu

# Carleton University

## Ottawa, Ontario, Canada

Province-supported, coed. Urban campus. Total enrollment: 23,683 (2006). Music program established 1967.

**Degrees** Bachelor of Music in the areas of performance, composition, musical research. Majors and concentrations: classical music, computer music, ethnomusicology, jazz, music, music media, music technology, piano/organ, popular music, sociology of music, stringed instruments, voice, wind and percussion instruments. Cross-registration with University of Ottawa. Program accredited by CUMS.

**Enrollment** 145 total; 82 undergraduate, 63 nonprofessional degree.

**Music Student Profile** 57% females, 43% males, 4% international.

**Music Faculty** 8 undergraduate (full-time). 100% of full-time faculty have terminal degrees. Graduate students do not teach undergraduate courses. Undergraduate student–faculty ratio: 18:1.

**Student Life** Student groups/activities include fund-raising events, term-end concerts of performance groups, off-campus venue appearances.

**Expenses for 2007–2008** Application fee: $85 Canadian dollars. Province resident tuition: $4794 full-time. Mandatory fees: $547 full-time. Full-time tuition and fees vary according to course level, course load, degree level, and program. College room and board: $7247. Room and board charges vary according to board plan and housing facility. International student tuition: $14,936 full-time.

**Financial Aid** Program-specific awards: 3 Jack Barwick Awards for program majors ($500), 2 MacDonald Club Awards for program majors ($500), 2 Bettina Oppenheimer Awards for seniors ($1000), 1 music award for sophomores ($300), 1 Helen Nininger Scholarship for program majors ($1000), 1 Robert Fleming Memorial Award for composition/Canadian music students ($1500), 2 CHIN/CJLL Radio Awards for program majors ($1250).

**Application Procedures** Students admitted directly into the professional program freshman year. Deadline for freshmen and transfers: April 1. Notification date for freshmen: June 15; transfers: June 30. Required: high school transcript, college transcript(s) for transfer students, audition, Canadian OAC of 6. Recommended: interview. Auditions held several times on campus; recorded music is permissible as a substitute for live auditions when distance is prohibitive and videotaped performances are permissible as a substitute for live auditions when distance is prohibitive.

**Web Site** http://www.carleton.ca

**Undergraduate Contact** Suzanne Blanchard, Director of Admissions, Carleton University, 1125 Colonel By Drive, Ottawa, Ontario K1S 5B6, Canada; 613-520-3663 ext. 3609, fax: 613-520-3517, e-mail address: suzanne_blanchard@carlton.ca

# Carnegie Mellon University

## Pittsburgh, Pennsylvania

Independent, coed. Urban campus. Total enrollment: 10,493. Music program established 1913.

**Degrees** Bachelor of Fine Arts in the areas of music performance, composition. Majors and concentrations: composition, instrumental music, piano/organ, voice. Graduate degrees offered: Master of Music in the areas of composition, conducting, performance, music education. Cross-registration with Pittsburgh Council on Higher Education. Program accredited by NASM.

**Enrollment** 260 total; 140 undergraduate, 70 graduate, 50 nonprofessional degree.

**Music Student Profile** 55% females, 45% males, 4% minorities, 20% international.

**Music Faculty** 70 total (full-time), 20 total (part-time). 33% of full-time faculty have terminal degrees. Graduate students do not teach undergraduate courses. Undergraduate student–faculty ratio: 4:1.

**Student Life** Student groups/activities include Greek Sing, carnival, Scotch 'n Soda (student-run theater group).

**Expenses for 2008–2009** Application fee: $70. Comprehensive fee: $49,614 includes full-time tuition ($39,150), mandatory fees ($414), and college room and board ($10,050). College room only: $5890.

**Financial Aid** Program-specific awards: 20–40 music scholarships for program majors.

**Application Procedures** Students admitted directly into the professional program freshman year. Deadline for freshmen and transfers: December 1. Notification date for freshmen and transfers: March 15. Required: essay, high school transcript, college transcript(s) for transfer students, 3 letters of recommendation, audition, SAT or ACT test scores. Recommended: minimum 3.0 high school GPA, interview, video. Auditions held 15 times on campus and off campus in New York, NY; recorded music is permissible as a substitute for live auditions if a campus visit is impossible and videotaped performances are permissible as a substitute for live auditions if a campus visit is impossible.

**Web Site** http://music.web.cmu.edu/

**Contact** Ms. Michele McGregor, Director of Recruitment and Enrollment, School of Music, Carnegie Mellon University, 5000 Forbes Avenue, Pittsburgh, Pennsylvania 15213-3890; 412-268-4118, fax: 412-268-3222, e-mail address: mtmcgreg@andrew.cmu.edu

# The Carroll McDaniel Petrie School of Music

See Converse College

# Carson-Newman College

## Jefferson City, Tennessee

Independent Southern Baptist, coed. Small town campus. Total enrollment: 2,012. Music program established 1888.

**Degrees** Bachelor of Music in the areas of applied music, church music, music education, music theory, composition. Majors and concentrations: church music, composition, keyboard, music education, music theory, voice. Program accredited by NASM.

**Enrollment** 116 total; 98 undergraduate, 18 nonprofessional degree.

**Music Student Profile** 67% females, 33% males, 3% minorities.

**Music Faculty** 12 undergraduate (full-time), 11 undergraduate (part-time). 71% of full-time faculty have terminal degrees. Graduate students do not teach undergraduate courses.

**Student Life** Student groups/activities include Delta Omicron benefit recitals, American Guild of Organists projects, Institute for Church Music.

**Expenses for 2007–2008** Application fee: $25. Comprehensive fee: $22,340 includes full-time tuition ($16,200), mandatory fees ($780), and college room and board ($5360). College room only: $2320. Full-time tuition and fees vary according to class time and course load. Room and board charges vary according to board plan, gender, and housing facility. Special program-related fees: $100–$200 per semester hour for applied music lesson fees.

**Financial Aid** Program-specific awards: 80 performance scholarships for program majors ($4000).

**Application Procedures** Students admitted directly into the professional program freshman year. Deadline for freshmen and transfers: continuous. Required: high school transcript, college transcript(s) for transfer students, minimum 2.0 high school GPA, 2 letters of recommendation, audition, SAT or ACT test scores, 24 hours of credit and minimum 2.0 college GPA for transfer students, theory placement exam. Auditions held 3 times and by appointment on campus; recorded music is permissible as a substitute for live auditions when distance is prohibitive and videotaped performances are permissible as a substitute for live auditions when distance is prohibitive.

**Web Site** http://www.cn.edu/music

**Undergraduate Contact** Dr. Tom Huebner, Vice President for Enrollment Management, Undergraduate Admissions, Carson-Newman College, Box 72025, Jefferson City, Tennessee 37760; 800-678-9061, fax: 865-471-3502, e-mail address: thuebner@cn.edu

*Benjamin T. Rome School of Music*
# The Catholic University of America
## Washington, District of Columbia

Independent, coed. Urban campus. Total enrollment: 6,440. Music program established 1965.

**Degrees** Bachelor of Music in the areas of vocal performance, instrumental performance, composition, musical theatre, general-choral music education, instrumental music education, combined general choral and instrumental music education, music history and literature. Majors and concentrations: choral music education, composition, instrumental music education, instrumental performance, music history and literature, music theater, voice performance. Graduate degrees offered: Master of Arts in the areas of music history, music theory; Master of Music in the areas of vocal performance, instrumental performance, accompanying, chamber music, pedagogy, composition, instrumental conducting; Master of Music in Sacred Music in the areas of choral music, composition, organ and voice. Doctor of Musical Arts in the areas of vocal performance, instrumental performance, accompanying, chamber music, composition, instrumental conducting, pedagogy. sacred music. Cross-registration with Consortium of Universities of the Washington Metropolitan Area. Program accredited by NASM.

**Enrollment** 313 total; 187 undergraduate, 125 graduate, 1 nonprofessional degree.

**Music Student Profile** 65% females, 35% males, 9% minorities, 6% international.

**Music Faculty** 17 total (full-time), 110 total (part-time). 71% of full-time faculty have terminal degrees. Graduate students teach a few undergraduate courses.

**Student Life** Student groups/activities include drama department productions and student-run productions, Music Educators National Conference Student Chapter, Sigma Alpha Iota.

**Expenses for 2007–2008** Application fee: $55. One-time mandatory fee: $400. Comprehensive fee: $39,798 includes full-time tuition ($27,700), mandatory fees ($1290), and college room and board ($10,808). College room only: $6224. Full-time tuition and fees vary according to program. Room and board charges vary according to board plan and housing facility. Special program-related fees for applied music, $35–$50 per semester for practice room fee, $50 for recital fee.

**Financial Aid** Program-specific awards: 110 music performance scholarships for musically qualified applicants ($1000–$13,000).

**Application Procedures** Students admitted directly into the professional program freshman year. Deadline for freshmen: February 1; transfers: June 1. Required: essay, high school transcript, college transcript(s) for transfer students, minimum 3.0 high school GPA, letter of recommendation, audition, SAT or ACT test scores. Recommended: interview, SAT. Auditions held approximately once per month on campus; recorded music is permissible as a substitute for live auditions if a campus visit is impossible and videotaped performances are permissible as a substitute for live auditions if a campus visit is impossible.

**Web Site** http://music.cua.edu

**Undergraduate Contact** Dr. Amy Antonelli, Assistant Dean, Benjamin T. Rome School of Music, The Catholic University of America, Washington, District of Columbia 20064; 202-319-5414, fax: 202-319-6280.

**Graduate Contact** Dr. Joseph Santo, Assistant Dean of Graduate Studies, Benjamin T. Rome School of Music, The Catholic University of America, Washington, District of Columbia 20064; 202-319-5414, fax: 202-319-6280.

### More About the School

As Washington, D.C.'s only university school of music, the Benjamin T. Rome School of Music is both professionally competitive and personally supportive. The School has an excellent location and offers numerous performance opportunities both on and off campus in the city of Washington. Through its comprehensive graduate and undergraduate programs, the Benjamin T. Rome School of Music is committed to excellence and personal attention. The School of Music is a professional school within a liberal arts university.

Undergraduate students study with an outstanding full-time faculty of artists-scholars and an extensive part-time faculty, including members of the National Symphony Orchestra, Washington National Opera Orchestra, Philadelphia Orchestra, Baltimore Symphony Orchestra, and the Metropolitan Opera Orchestra. Piano faculty members perform internationally in solo, chamber, and orchestra programs. Voice faculty members have performance experience or are currently performing with nationally and internationally renowned opera houses, such as the Metropolitan Opera and La Scala. Undergraduates benefit from teaching by scholars whose research includes Gregorian chant, medieval music, opera, musical theater, and twentieth-century music. In addition, many of the world's greatest performers hold master classes at the Catholic University of America, including Andre Watts, Brian Stokes Mitchell, Faith Prince, John Corigliano, Renata Scotto, and Joseph Kalichstein.

The School of Music offers the Bachelor of Music (B.M.) degree, with majors in performance (orchestral instruments, organ, piano, and voice), music education (choral, orchestral, and combined) composition, music history, musical theater, and literature (honors program). Students may pursue dual degrees in music and another discipline. Students who wish to major in music without the rigorous musical training demanded in the B.M. curriculum may pursue a B.A. with a concentration in music and/or minor in music.

With a present enrollment of 350 music majors, the School schedules numerous concerts, recitals, and special events throughout each academic year. As performance is the focus of all the degree programs, more than 200 performances are presented each year. In addition to solo recitals and chamber music, the CUA Symphony Orchestra, Chorus, and Chamber Choir perform throughout the academic year. These concerts are highlighted by a nationally televised Christmas concert, concerto and vocal competitions, fully staged opera and musical theater productions, and a yearly week-long festival of the arts that includes symposia, films, concerts, and musical theater productions. In 2006, the School of Music was invited to participate in the prestigious Prague Spring Festival. Members of the orchestra and chorus performed Defiant Requiem, a concert drama about the Verdi Requiem at Terezin, 1943–1944, with recollections, historic film, and a full performance of Verdi's score. The production was conceived, written, and conducted by Murry Sidlin, dean of the School of Music.

Music alumni and faculty members have won many awards and maintain high professional visibility as performers, music educators, composers, liturgical musicians, and scholars. Among those who have received national and international recognition are Grammy Award winners John Aler (opera) and Robert Shafer (choral conductor). Graduates of the School of Music have performed on Broadway, off-Broadway, in touring companies and regional theaters; at the Metropolitan Opera, Vienna Opera, and York City Opera; and with virtually every major symphony orchestra in the United States.

Catholic University is housed on a spacious 144-acre campus in the heart of Washington, D.C. The campus provides an impressive combination of collegiate and city life. Student life is culturally dynamic in a city that is famous for museums, monuments, and landmarks, such as Capitol Hill, the Smithsonian Institution, the Library of Congress, the National Zoo, and the John F. Kennedy Center for the Performing Arts. Most attractions are just minutes from campus via Metrorail, a modern subway system that stops adjacent to the campus.

The School of Music performance spaces include the acoustically excellent Ward Recital Hall (120 seats), Hartke Theatre (590 seats), and St. Vincent's Chapel (400 seats). School of Music performances are also held at the Basilica of the National Shrine of the Immaculate Conception on the campus of CUA, at St. Matthew's Cathedral, and at the Concert Hall and the Millennium Stage of the John F. Kennedy Center for the Performing Arts. Music students have also performed in many of the regional theaters in and around Washington.

*The Catholic University of America (continued)*

There are numerous internships available in Washington, D.C. Music students have interned at local television stations, local theaters, the Washington Performing Arts Society, Washington National Opera, and the John F. Kennedy Center for the Performing Arts.

# Cedarville University

## Cedarville, Ohio

Independent Baptist, coed. Rural campus. Total enrollment: 3,055. Music program established 1887.

**Degrees** Bachelor of Music Education in the areas of choral music education, instrumental music education. Majors and concentrations: brass instruments performance, church music, composition, keyboard pedagogy, music education, piano/organ performance, stringed instrument performance, voice performance, wind and percussion instruments performance. Program accredited by NASM.

**Enrollment** 111 total; 92 undergraduate, 19 nonprofessional degree.

**Music Student Profile** 69% females, 31% males, 3% minorities.

**Music Faculty** 14 undergraduate (full-time), 17 undergraduate (part-time). 64% of full-time faculty have terminal degrees. Graduate students do not teach undergraduate courses. Undergraduate student–faculty ratio: 8:1.

**Student Life** Student groups/activities include Music Educators National Conference.

**Expenses for 2007–2008** Application fee: $30. Comprehensive fee: $26,140 includes full-time tuition ($19,680), mandatory fees ($1450), and college room and board ($5010). College room only: $2684. Room and board charges vary according to board plan. Special program-related fees: $30 per semester for lab fee, $40 per semester for methods fee, $75 per semester for recital fee, $200 per semester for practice room fee.

**Financial Aid** Program-specific awards: 36 music scholarships for those demonstrating musical achievement ($1000–$4000).

**Application Procedures** Students apply for admission into the professional program by freshman year. Deadline for freshmen and transfers: continuous. Required: essay, high school transcript, college transcript(s) for transfer students, minimum 2.0 high school GPA, 2 letters of recommendation, audition, SAT or ACT test scores (minimum composite ACT score of 22). Recommended: minimum 3.0 high school GPA, portfolio. Auditions held 4 times and by appointment on campus; recorded music is permissible as a substitute for live auditions (video tape or signed affidavit preferred) and videotaped performances are permissible as a substitute for live auditions if a campus visit is impossible.

**Web Site** http://www.cedarville.edu

**Undergraduate Contact** Ms. Pam Miller, Administrative Assistant, Music and Art Department, Cedarville University, 251 North Main Street, Cedarville, Ohio 45314; 937-766-7728, fax: 937-766-7661, e-mail address: millerp@cedarville.edu

## *Hurley School of Music*
# Centenary College of Louisiana

## Shreveport, Louisiana

Independent United Methodist, coed. Suburban campus. Total enrollment: 938. Music program established 1936.

**Web Site** http://www.centenary.edu/

## *The Swinney Conservatory of Music*
# Central Methodist University

## Fayette, Missouri

Independent Methodist, coed. Small town campus. Total enrollment: 841 (2007). Music program established 1927.

**Degrees** Bachelor of Music in the areas of piano, organ, voice; Bachelor of Music Education. Majors and concentrations: classical music, instrumental music, music education, piano/organ, voice. Program accredited by NASM.

**Enrollment** 50 total; 45 undergraduate, 5 nonprofessional degree.

**Music Student Profile** 60% females, 40% males, 6% minorities.

**Music Faculty** 6 undergraduate (full-time), 5 undergraduate (part-time). 100% of full-time faculty have terminal degrees. Graduate students do not teach undergraduate courses.

**Student Life** Student groups/activities include Phi Mu Alpha, Music Educators National Conference, Sigma Alpha Iota.

**Expenses for 2007–2008** Application fee: $20. Comprehensive fee: $22,880 includes full-time tuition ($16,430), mandatory fees ($730), and college room and board ($5720). College room only: $2820. Room and board charges vary according to board plan and housing facility. Special program-related fees: $75 for applied lesson fee.

**Financial Aid** Program-specific awards: 30–50 music scholarships for program majors, music ensemble members ($5000–$16,000).

**Application Procedures** Students admitted directly into the professional program freshman year. Deadline for freshmen and transfers: continuous. Required: high school transcript, college transcript(s) for transfer students, minimum 2.0 high school GPA, interview, audition, SAT or ACT test scores (minimum composite ACT score of 18). Recommended: letter of recommendation. Auditions held continuously on campus; recorded music is permissible as a substitute for live auditions when distance is prohibitive or if a campus visit is impossible and videotaped performances are permissible as a substitute for live auditions when distance is prohibitive or if a campus visit is impossible.

**Web Site** http://www.centralmethodist.edu

**Undergraduate Contact** Office of Admissions, Central Methodist University, 411 Central Methodist Square, Fayette, Missouri 65248; 660-248-6249, fax: 660-248-1872, e-mail address: admissions@cmc.edu

# Central Michigan University

## Mount Pleasant, Michigan

State-supported, coed. Small town campus. Total enrollment: 26,611. Music program established 1900.

**Degrees** Bachelor of Music in the areas of performance, music theory/composition; Bachelor of Music Education. Majors and concentrations: music education, music theory and composition, orchestral instruments, piano/organ, voice. Graduate degrees offered: Master of Music in the areas of music education, performance, composition, conducting, piano pedagogy. Program accredited by NASM.

**Enrollment** 625 total; 504 undergraduate, 121 graduate.

**Music Student Profile** 55% females, 45% males, 4% minorities, 1% international.

**Music Faculty** 34 total (full-time), 8 total (part-time). 76% of full-time faculty have terminal degrees. Graduate students teach a few undergraduate courses. Undergraduate student–faculty ratio: 14:1.

**Student Life** Student groups/activities include student ensembles, preprofessional student associations, music service fraternity and sororities. Special housing available for music students.

**Expenses for 2007–2008** Application fee: $35. State resident tuition: $9120 full-time. Nonresident tuition: $21,210 full-time. Full-time tuition varies according to student level. College room and board: $7236. College room only: $3618. Room and board charges vary according to board plan, housing facility, location, and student level. Costs at Central Michigan University are based upon a guaranteed undergraduate tuition plan called the CMU Promise. The CMU Promise to new and transfer undergraduate students is one unchanging tuition rate for up to five years. In addition to fixing the. Special program-related fees: $5 per semester for locker rental, $40–$75 per semester for private lessons.

**Financial Aid** Program-specific awards: 71 music scholarships for program majors ($1000–$2000).

**Application Procedures** Students admitted directly into the professional program freshman year. Deadline for freshmen and transfers: March 16. Notification date for freshmen and transfers: April 15. Required: high school transcript, college transcript(s) for transfer students, minimum 2.0 high school GPA, audition, SAT or ACT test scores. Recommended: minimum 3.0

high school GPA. Auditions held 4 times on campus; recorded music is permissible as a substitute for live auditions for out-of-state applicants and videotaped performances are permissible as a substitute for live auditions for out-of-state applicants.
**Web Site** http://www.mus.cmich.edu
**Graduate Contact** Dr. Daniel Steele, Graduate Coordinator, School of Music, Central Michigan University, Room 162, Mount Pleasant, Michigan 48859; 989-774-3281, fax: 989-774-3766, e-mail address: daniel.steele@cmich.edu

## Central Washington University
### Ellensburg, Washington

State-supported, coed. Small town campus. Total enrollment: 10,505. Music program established 1958.
**Degrees** Bachelor of Music in the areas of music education, performance, composition, music theory, pedagogy, jazz. Majors and concentrations: guitar, jazz, music, music education, music theory and composition, piano/organ, stringed instruments, voice, wind and percussion instruments. Graduate degrees offered: Master of Music in the areas of music education, performance, composition, conducting, pedagogy. Program accredited by NASM.
**Enrollment** 270 total; 202 undergraduate, 16 graduate, 52 nonprofessional degree.
**Music Student Profile** 50% females, 50% males, 5% minorities, 1% international.
**Music Faculty** 20 undergraduate (full-time), 12 undergraduate (part-time). 50% of full-time faculty have terminal degrees. Graduate students teach a few undergraduate courses. Undergraduate student–faculty ratio: 7:1.
**Student Life** Student groups/activities include Music Educators National Conference Student Chapter, American Choral Directors Association, American String Teachers Association. Special housing available for music students.
**Expenses for 2008–2009** Application fee: $50. State resident tuition: $4841 full-time. Nonresident tuition: $14,713 full-time. Mandatory fees: $882 full-time. College room and board: $8052. Special program-related fees: $15 for instrument repair, $40 per quarter for recital fee, $60 per applied music course for lab fee.
**Financial Aid** Program-specific awards: 40 Music Department Scholarships for program majors ($800).
**Application Procedures** Students admitted directly into the professional program freshman year. Deadline for freshmen and transfers: May 1. Required: high school transcript, college transcript(s) for transfer students, minimum 2.0 high school GPA, 2 letters of recommendation, audition, SAT or ACT test scores. Auditions held throughout the school year on campus; recorded music is permissible as a substitute for live auditions when distance is prohibitive and videotaped performances are permissible as a substitute for live auditions when distance is prohibitive.
**Web Site** http://www.cwu.edu/~music
**Contact** Dr. Peter Gries, Chair, Department of Music, Central Washington University, 400 East Eighth Avenue, Ellensburg, Washington 98926-7458; 509-963-1216, fax: 509-963-1239, e-mail address: griesp@cwu.edu

## Chapman University
### Orange, California

Independent, coed. Suburban campus. Total enrollment: 6,022. Music program established 1932.
**Degrees** Bachelor of Music in the areas of performance, conducting, composition, music therapy; Bachelor of Music Education. Majors and concentrations: composition, conducting, music education, music therapy, piano/organ, stringed instruments, voice, wind and percussion instruments. Program accredited by NASM.
**Enrollment** 197 total; 185 undergraduate, 12 nonprofessional degree.
**Music Student Profile** 60% females, 40% males, 15% minorities, 10% international.
**Music Faculty** 14 undergraduate (full-time), 36 undergraduate (part-time). 70% of full-time faculty have terminal degrees.

Graduate students do not teach undergraduate courses. Undergraduate student–faculty ratio: 4:1.
**Student Life** Student groups/activities include American Choral Directors Association Student Chapter, American Association of Music Therapy Student Chapter, American String Teachers Association.
**Expenses for 2008–2009** Application fee: $55. Comprehensive fee: $46,015 includes full-time tuition ($33,760), mandatory fees ($940), and college room and board ($11,315). Special program-related fees: $125 per unit for private lessons.
**Financial Aid** Program-specific awards: 75 talent awards for talented students ($10,000).
**Application Procedures** Students admitted directly into the professional program freshman year. Deadline for freshmen: January 31; transfers: March 15. Required: essay, high school transcript, college transcript(s) for transfer students, letter of recommendation, audition, SAT or ACT test scores. Recommended: minimum 2.0 high school GPA. Auditions held by appointment on campus; recorded music is permissible as a substitute for live auditions when distance is prohibitive and videotaped performances are permissible as a substitute for live auditions when distance is prohibitive.
**Web Site** http://www.chapman.edu/music/index.html
**Undergraduate Contact** Mr. Michael Pelly, Director of Admissions, Chapman University, 1 University Drive, Orange, California 92866; 714-997-6711, fax: 714-997-6713, e-mail address: pelly@chapman.edu

## Chicago College of Performing Arts - The Music Conservatory

See Roosevelt University

## Chowan University
### Murfreesboro, North Carolina

Independent Baptist, coed. Rural campus. Music program established 2000.
**Degrees** Bachelor of Science in the area of music education. Majors and concentrations: choral music, instrumental music. Program accredited by NASM, NCATE.
**Enrollment** 16 total; 5 undergraduate, 11 nonprofessional degree.
**Music Student Profile** 44% females, 56% males, 38% minorities.
**Music Faculty** 4 undergraduate (full-time), 7 undergraduate (part-time). 75% of full-time faculty have terminal degrees. Graduate students do not teach undergraduate courses. Undergraduate student–faculty ratio: 1:1.
**Student Life** Student groups/activities include Chowan Singers, Chowan Winds, Meherrin Chamber Orchestra.
**Expenses for 2007–2008** Application fee: $20. Comprehensive fee: $24,030 includes full-time tuition ($16,750), mandatory fees ($280), and college room and board ($7000). College room only: $3300. Room and board charges vary according to board plan. Special program-related fees: $315 per semester for applied music fee.
**Financial Aid** Program-specific awards: 12–15 Music Scholarships for new students ($1500–$4000).
**Application Procedures** Students apply for admission into the professional program by junior year. Deadline for freshmen and transfers: continuous. Required: high school transcript, college transcript(s) for transfer students, interview, audition, SAT or ACT test scores. Auditions held 5 times on campus; recorded music is permissible as a substitute for live auditions if student unable to come to campus and videotaped performances are permissible as a substitute for live auditions if student unable to come to campus.
**Web Site** http://www.chowan.edu/academics/school-arts-sciences.htm#music
**Undergraduate Contact** Dr. Gregory B. Parker, Chair, Department of Music, Chowan University, 1 University Place, Murfreesboro, North Carolina 27855; 252-398-6201, fax: 252-398-6213, e-mail address: parkeg@chowan.edu

# Christopher Newport University

## Newport News, Virginia

State-supported, coed. Suburban campus. Total enrollment: 4,884. Music program established 1984.

**Degrees** Bachelor of Music. Majors and concentrations: choral music education, composition, instrumental music education, jazz studies, music history and literature, music theory, performance. Graduate degrees offered: Master of Arts in Teaching. Cross-registration with any state university in Virginia. Program accredited by NASM.

**Enrollment** 135 total; 125 undergraduate, 10 graduate.

**Music Student Profile** 50% females, 50% males, 10% minorities.

**Music Faculty** 12 total (full-time), 25 total (part-time). 100% of full-time faculty have terminal degrees. Graduate students do not teach undergraduate courses. Undergraduate student–faculty ratio: 17:1.

**Student Life** Student groups/activities include Phi Mu Alpha Sinfonia, Sigma Alpha Iota, Music Educators National Conference, Pi Kappa Lambda.

**Expenses for 2007–2008** Application fee: $45. State resident tuition: $7050 full-time. Nonresident tuition: $14,150 full-time. Mandatory fees: $3088 full-time. Full-time tuition and fees vary according to course load and degree level. College room and board: $8500. Room and board charges vary according to board plan and housing facility. Special program-related fees: $150 per course (1 credit) for applied music fees.

**Financial Aid** Program-specific awards: 1 Friend of Music Endowed Scholarship for program majors ($2500), 1 Gloucester-Matthews County Endowed Scholarship for program majors ($500), 3 Mark U. Reimer Endowed Scholarships for program majors ($1100), 1 John W. and Cathleen B. Gaines Endowed Music Scholarship for program majors ($1500), 1 William S. Brown Endowed Scholarship for jazz students ($1100), 1 Marguerite K. Carter Endowed Scholarship for violin majors ($1800), 1 Alumni Endowed Scholarship for program majors ($1000), 2 Ella Fitzgerald Endowed Scholarships for jazz students ($2000), 1 Mark Lee McCoy Endowed Scholarship for program majors ($1000), 1 Jeffrey Brown Endowed Scholarship for piano majors ($1000), 1 Charles Cooper Endowed Scholarship for program majors ($800), 1 Ed D'Alfonso Endowed Scholarship for instrumental music education majors ($2000), 2 Presidential Music Scholarships for program majors ($2000), 1 Virginia Purtle Scholarship for voice majors ($1500), 4 David Reynolds Endowed Scholarships for voice majors ($1000), 1 Robert Carrol Smith Scholarship for piano majors ($2100).

**Application Procedures** Students apply for admission into the professional program by sophomore year. Deadline for freshmen and transfers: August 1. Required: essay, high school transcript, college transcript(s) for transfer students, minimum 3.0 high school GPA, 2 letters of recommendation, interview, audition, SAT or ACT test scores (minimum combined SAT score of 1190, minimum composite ACT score of 20). Auditions held 4 times on campus; recorded music is permissible as a substitute for live auditions when distance is prohibitive and videotaped performances are permissible as a substitute for live auditions when distance is prohibitive (beyond a 250-mile radius).

**Web Site** http://www.music.cnu.edu

**Undergraduate Contact** Ms. Patricia Cavender, Director of Admissions, Christopher Newport University, 1 University Place, Newport News, Virginia 23606; 757-594-7206, fax: 757-594-7333, e-mail address: cavender@cnu.edu

# City College of the City University of New York

## New York, New York

State and locally supported, coed. Urban campus. Total enrollment: 14,536. Music program established 1973.

**Degrees** Bachelor of Fine Arts in the areas of jazz performance, classical performance, music and technology. Majors and concentrations: acoustic recording, classical music, jazz, music, performance, sonic arts. Graduate degrees offered: Master of Arts in the areas of musicology, theory, composition, performance (classical and jazz). Cross-registration with other senior colleges within City University of New York.

**Enrollment** 230 total; 100 undergraduate, 30 graduate, 100 nonprofessional degree.

**Music Student Profile** 40% females, 60% males, 70% minorities, 50% international.

**Music Faculty** 15 total (full-time), 20 total (part-time). 90% of full-time faculty have terminal degrees. Graduate students teach a few undergraduate courses. Undergraduate student–faculty ratio: 8:1.

**Student Life** Student groups/activities include Friends of Music, gospel choir.

**Expenses for 2007–2008** Application fee: $65. State resident tuition: $4080 full-time. Nonresident tuition: $8640 full-time. Mandatory fees: $279 full-time. Full-time tuition and fees vary according to class time, course load, and program. College room only: $8250. Special program-related fees: $25 per course for technology fee.

**Financial Aid** Program-specific awards: 2 Friar Foundation Awards for BFA applicants passing audition evaluation ($750), 2 Rosalind Joel Scholarships for talented performers ($3000), 1 Ben Jablonsky Scholarship for jazz composers/arrangers ($750).

**Application Procedures** Students apply for admission into the professional program by sophomore, junior year. Deadline for freshmen and transfers: continuous. Required: high school transcript, college transcript(s) for transfer students, minimum 3.0 high school GPA, audition for performance majors. Recommended: interview, audition. Auditions held twice on campus; recorded music is permissible as a substitute for live auditions when distance is prohibitive and videotaped performances are permissible as a substitute for live auditions when distance is prohibitive.

**Web Site** http://www.ccny.cuny.edu/music/

**Undergraduate Contact** Mr. Alan Sabal, Associate Director of Admissions, City College of the City University of New York, Admissions A100B, 138th Street and Convent Avenue, New York, New York 10031; 212-650-6444, fax: 212-650-6417.

**Graduate Contact** Prof. Shaugn O'Donnell, MA Supervisor, Music Department, City College of the City University of New York, Shepard Hall 72, 160 Convent Avenue, New York, New York 10031; 212-650-7683, fax: 212-650-5428, e-mail address: sodonnell@ccny.cuny.edu

# Claire Trevor School of the Arts

See University of California, Irvine

# Clayton State University

## Morrow, Georgia

State-supported, coed. Suburban campus. Total enrollment: 6,043. Music program established 1992.

**Degrees** Bachelor of Music in the areas of performance, composition, music education. Majors and concentrations: composition, keyboard, stringed instruments, voice, wind and percussion instruments. Cross-registration with all eighteen schools affiliated with The Atlanta Regional Consortium for Higher Education. Program accredited by NASM.

**Enrollment** 58 total; 30 undergraduate, 28 nonprofessional degree.

**Music Faculty** 7 undergraduate (full-time), 14 undergraduate (part-time). 100% of full-time faculty have terminal degrees. Graduate students do not teach undergraduate courses.

**Student Life** Student groups/activities include MENC-The National Association for Music Education, Mu Phi Epsilon, Society of Composers.

**Expenses for 2007–2008** Application fee: $40. State resident tuition: $2640 full-time. Nonresident tuition: $10,516 full-time. Mandatory fees: $714 full-time. Full-time tuition and fees vary according to course load.

**Financial Aid** Program-specific awards: Spivey Scholarships for program majors.

**Application Procedures** Students admitted directly into the professional program freshman year. Deadline for freshmen and transfers: July 17. Notification date for freshmen and transfers:

continuous. Required: high school transcript, college transcript(s) for transfer students, minimum 2.0 high school GPA, SAT or ACT test scores (minimum composite ACT score of 17). Recommended: audition. Auditions held 6 times and by arrangement on campus; recorded music is permissible as a substitute for live auditions for out-of-state applicants and videotaped performances are permissible as a substitute for live auditions for out-of-state applicants.

**Web Site** http://www.clayton.edu

**Undergraduate Contact** Dr. Douglas Wheeler, Head, Department of Music, Clayton State University, 2000 Clayton State Boulevard, Morrow, Georgia 30260; 678-466-4758, fax: 678-466-4769, e-mail address: douglaswheeler@clayton.edu

# Cleveland Institute of Music
## Cleveland, Ohio

Independent, coed. Urban campus. Music program established 1920.

**Degrees** Bachelor of Music in the areas of piano, harpsichord, organ, voice, violin, viola, cello, double bass, harp, classical guitar, flute, oboe, clarinet, bassoon, trumpet, horn, trombone, bass trombone, tuba, percussion, audio recording, composition, eurhythmics. Majors and concentrations: audio recording technology, classical guitar, composition, eurhythmics, harp, harpsichord, piano/organ, stringed instruments, voice, wind and percussion instruments. Graduate degrees offered: Master of Music in the areas of piano, harpsichord, organ, voice, violin, viola, cello, double bass, harp, classical guitar, flute, oboe, clarinet, bassoon, trumpet, horn, trombone, bass trombone, tuba, Suzuki violin or cello pedagogy, percussion, composition, orchestral conducting. Doctor of Musical Arts in the areas of piano, organ, collaborative piano, voice, violin, viola, cello, double bass, harp, classical guitar, flute, oboe, clarinet, bassoon, trombone, bass trombone, tuba, percussion, composition, horn, trumpet, harpsichord. Mandatory cross-registration with Case Western Reserve University. Program accredited by NASM.

**Enrollment** 453 total; 223 undergraduate, 230 graduate.

**Music Student Profile** 55% females, 45% males, 10% minorities, 25% international.

**Music Faculty** 42 total (full-time), 69 total (part-time). 15% of full-time faculty have terminal degrees. Graduate students do not teach undergraduate courses. Undergraduate student–faculty ratio: 7:1.

**Student Life** Student groups/activities include orchestra, opera, chamber music. Special housing available for music students.

**Expenses for 2007–2008** Special program-related fees: $150 per year for accompanist fee.

**Financial Aid** Program-specific awards: 417 Cleveland Institute of Music Scholarships for program students ($13,278), 40 Cleveland Institute of Music Loans for program students ($1669).

**Application Procedures** Students admitted directly into the professional program freshman year. Deadline for freshmen and transfers: December 1. Notification date for freshmen and transfers: April 1. Required: essay, high school transcript, college transcript(s) for transfer students, 2 letters of recommendation, audition, SAT or ACT test scores. Recommended: minimum 3.0 high school GPA, interview. Auditions held several times on campus; recorded music is permissible as a substitute for live auditions with approval from the department (DVDs only) and videotaped performances are permissible as a substitute for live auditions with approval from the department (DVDs only).

**Web Site** http://www.cim.edu

**Undergraduate Contact** Mr. William Fay, Director of Admission, Cleveland Institute of Music, 11021 East Boulevard, Cleveland, Ohio 44106; 216-795-3107, fax: 216-795-3161, e-mail address: william.fay@case.edu

### More About the Institute

The mission of the Cleveland Institute of Music (CIM) is to provide exceptionally talented students from around the world an outstanding and thoroughly professional education in the art of music performance and related musical disciplines. The Institute embraces the legacy of the past and promotes the continuing evolution of music within a supportive and nurturing environment. The Institute also provides rigorous training in programs for gifted precollege musicians and serves as a resource for the community with training for individuals of all ages and abilities.

A guiding principle at the Institute maintains that a liberal arts education contributes to a broad, humanistic perspective and is a vital component of the undergraduate curriculum. Equally important is the faculty's commitment to incorporating new technologies to complement and enhance the educational program.

The distinguished faculty of the Institute aims to develop the full artistic potential of all its students. Through performance and teaching, the faculty and administration are dedicated to passing along their knowledge and love for this great art and to providing the bridge to an exciting and fulfilling career.

Founded in 1920, the Cleveland Institute of Music maintains its current size of approximately 400 undergraduate and graduate students and 90 full- and part-time faculty members by controlling enrollment through carefully balanced admission policies. In admitting the optimum rather than an unlimited number of students to each performance area, CIM provides personal, individual attention for each student and maximizes the number of performance opportunities.

The unusually intense performance environment encourages students to develop multifaceted skills that include solo, chamber, orchestral, and operatic literature. This approach leads students to focus on solo expertise as well as to develop the collaborative abilities necessary for small and large ensemble work. The key is access to faculty members and visiting artists in a challenging but supportive atmosphere of private lessons, master classes, repertoire classes, concerts, and recitals.

Orchestral studies are designed to develop and maintain the discipline and skill necessary to make the smoothest possible transition from school to professional life. Regularly scheduled sectional rehearsals and orchestral repertoire classes are conducted by principals of The Cleveland Orchestra. The Institute's two symphony orchestras present approximately twenty concerts during the academic year, including multiple performances of fully staged operas. These ensembles also provide a vehicle through which student composers may hear and record readings of their works.

The sequence of opera courses is devoted to the principles of theory and practice of the various arts that combine to create an operatic performance. Emphasis is placed on vocal, musical, stylistic, linguistic, and dramatic techniques. Study stresses the application of these elements to role preparation for operas of different historical periods.

CIM is located in University Circle, a cultural, educational, and scientific research center situated approximately 3 miles east of downtown Cleveland. University Circle comprises more than thirty institutions that together constitute one of the largest diversified cultural complexes in the world. Located within easy walking distance of CIM are Case Western Reserve University, where CIM students have access to all facilities and liberal arts course offerings, and Severance Hall, home of The Cleveland Orchestra, the rehearsals of which are open to CIM students by special arrangement. Also easily accessible are numerous other University Circle institutions, such as the Cleveland Museum of Art, Cleveland Institute of Art, Cleveland Play House, Cleveland Museum of Natural History, Western Reserve Historical Society, Crawford Auto-Aviation Museum, and Cleveland Botanical Garden.

**Program Facilities** CIM recently completed a $40-million expansion project that added practice, teaching, and performance space to its facility. The project provided two major additions, including a new state-of-the-art recital hall and new façade in the addition at its main entrance. The recital hall seats 250 people in an acoustically outstanding space for recitals and chamber music. Another addition at the rear of the main building includes practice rooms, teaching studios, audio recording and distance learning studios, administrative space, and a new student lounge and outdoor patio.

*Cleveland Institute of Music (continued)*

Cleveland Institute of Music's main building includes a concert hall, classrooms, teaching studios, practice rooms, a library, a eurhythmics studio, an orchestra library, an opera theater workshop and studio, and a music store. Through connection of the entire facility to Case Western Reserve University's computer network, CIM also provides wireless Internet access as well as a Technology Learning Center that enables students to become aware of and accustomed to the ways in which music and technology go hand in hand.

CIM's Robinson Music Library contains 52,309 books and scores, 110 periodical subscriptions, and an audiovisual collection of 26,813 items in the Library Media Center. Through the Institute's relationship with CWRU, CIM students have access to additional library resources, especially those at the CWRU Music Department. CWRU holdings include more than 2,471,504 volumes, 2,548,156 microforms, and 20,265 current serial subscriptions. A shared online system with CWRU permits the viewing of CWRU library holdings from online public catalogs at CIM. There is also wireless computer access in the library.

The residence hall, Cutter House, is adjacent to CIM. In addition to the usual amenities, each room has fiber-optic computer access. Also adjacent is the Hazel Road Annex, an additional facility for individual practice, chamber music, rehearsal and coaching, master classes, and class recitals.

**Faculty** The distinguished faculty includes the principals and many section players of The Cleveland Orchestra, with which CIM has a close relationship. All collegiate-level music instruction is conducted by CIM faculty members and not by teaching assistants. Liberal arts, music education, and music history courses are taught by the faculty of Case Western Reserve University.

# Cleveland State University
## Cleveland, Ohio

State-supported, coed. Urban campus. Total enrollment: 15,383. Music program established 1964.
**Degrees** Majors and concentrations: composition, guitar, harp, music education, music therapy, piano/organ, stringed instruments, voice, wind and percussion instruments. Graduate degrees offered: Master of Music in the areas of performance, education, composition, history. Program accredited by NASM.
**Enrollment** 189 total; 111 undergraduate, 64 graduate, 14 nonprofessional degree.
**Music Student Profile** 51% females, 49% males, 11% minorities, 4% international.
**Music Faculty** 13 total (full-time), 52 total (part-time). 100% of full-time faculty have terminal degrees. Graduate students do not teach undergraduate courses. Undergraduate student–faculty ratio: 17:1.
**Student Life** Student groups/activities include Ohio Collegiate Music Educators Association, Mu Phi Epsilon, American Choral Directors Association.
**Expenses for 2007–2008** Application fee: $30. State resident tuition: $7920 full-time. Nonresident tuition: $10,664 full-time. Full-time tuition varies according to program. College room and board: $8100. College room only: $5200. Room and board charges vary according to board plan and housing facility. Special program-related fees: $114–$342 per 1-3 credit hours for music therapy, $200–$325 per 1-2 credit hours for music lessons.
**Financial Aid** Program-specific awards: 99 music scholarships for program majors ($3135).
**Application Procedures** Students admitted directly into the professional program freshman year. Deadline for freshmen and transfers: continuous. Notification date for freshmen and transfers: continuous. Required: high school transcript, college transcript(s) for transfer students, minimum 2.0 high school GPA, interview, audition, SAT or ACT test scores (minimum combined SAT score of 750, minimum composite ACT score of 16), portfolio for composition applicants. Auditions held by appointment on campus; recorded music is permissible as a substitute for live

auditions when distance is prohibitive and videotaped performances are permissible as a substitute for live auditions when distance is prohibitive. Portfolio reviews held as needed on campus.
**Web Site** http://www.csuohio.edu/music
**Undergraduate Contact** Alexandra Vago, School Recruiter, Music Department, Cleveland State University, 2121 Euclid Avenue, Cleveland, Ohio 44115; 216-687-5039, fax: 216-687-9279, e-mail address: a.vago@csuohio.edu
**Graduate Contact** Dr. Birch P. Browning, Assistant Professor, Music Department, Cleveland State University, 2121 Euclid Avenue, Cleveland, Ohio 44115; 216-687-3768, fax: 216-687-9279, e-mail address: b.browning@csuohio.edu

# Coe College
## Cedar Rapids, Iowa

Independent, coed. Urban campus. Total enrollment: 1,300 (2007). Music program established 1920.
**Degrees** Bachelor of Music in the areas of performance, music education, music theory/composition; Bachelor of Music Education in the area of vocal and instrumental. Majors and concentrations: classical music, guitar, harpsichord, music, music education, music theory and composition, piano/organ, stringed instruments, voice, wind and percussion instruments. Cross-registration with Mount Mercy College. Program accredited by NASM.
**Enrollment** 54 total; 39 undergraduate, 15 nonprofessional degree.
**Music Student Profile** 54% females, 46% males, 7% minorities.
**Music Faculty** 5 undergraduate (full-time), 25 undergraduate (part-time). 100% of full-time faculty have terminal degrees. Graduate students do not teach undergraduate courses. Undergraduate student–faculty ratio: 8:1.
**Student Life** Student groups/activities include Pi Kappa Lambda, Mu Phi Epsilon, Phi Mu Alpha.
**Expenses for 2008–2009** Application fee: $30. Comprehensive fee: $34,610. Special program-related fees: $175–$450 per term for private lessons.
**Financial Aid** Program-specific awards: Marshall Full-Tuition Scholarships for program majors ($26,100), music scholarships for program majors ($2000).
**Application Procedures** Students apply for admission into the professional program by sophomore year. Deadline for freshmen and transfers: March 1. Notification date for freshmen and transfers: March 15. Required: essay, high school transcript, college transcript(s) for transfer students, 2 letters of recommendation, SAT or ACT test scores. Recommended: minimum 3.0 high school GPA, interview, audition. Auditions held twice on campus; recorded music is permissible as a substitute for live auditions when distance is prohibitive and videotaped performances are permissible as a substitute for live auditions when distance is prohibitive.
**Web Site** http://www.coe.edu
**Undergraduate Contact** Ms. Sharon Kay Stang, Recruiting Coordinator, Music Department, Coe College, 1220 1st Avenue, NE, Cedar Rapids, Iowa 52402; 319-399-8640, fax: 319-399-8209, e-mail address: sstang@coe.edu

# Coker College
## Hartsville, South Carolina

Independent, coed. Small town campus. Total enrollment: 634. Music program established 1908.
**Degrees** Bachelor of Music Education. Majors and concentrations: music education. Program accredited by NASM.
**Enrollment** 8 total; all undergraduate.
**Music Student Profile** 60% females, 40% males, 26% minorities, 3% international.
**Music Faculty** 3 undergraduate (full-time), 1 undergraduate (part-time). 100% of full-time faculty have terminal degrees. Graduate students do not teach undergraduate courses. Undergraduate student–faculty ratio: 2:1.

**Student Life** Student groups/activities include Music Educators National Conference, National Association of Teachers of Singing, Music Teachers National Association. Special housing available for music students.

**Expenses for 2007–2008** Application fee: $15. Comprehensive fee: $24,522 includes full-time tuition ($18,072), mandatory fees ($530), and college room and board ($5920). College room only: $3070. Special program-related fees: $20 per hour for accompanist fee (vocal only).

**Financial Aid** Program-specific awards: 5–10 Wilds Music Scholarships for music majors ($1000–$3000), 2 Goodson Music Scholarships for musically talented performers ($2000), 1–2 Anna White Hill Scholarships for non-music major/chorale singers ($250), 1–2 Bethea Scholarships for those demonstrating need and living in Dillon/Marion area ($500–$2000), 1 Brittain Music Scholarship for program students (piano preferred) ($3000), 1 Cottingham Music Scholarship for program students (piano preferred) ($1000), 1 Edwards Music Scholarship for program students with B average ($500), 1 McLeod Music Scholarship for program students with B average ($500).

**Application Procedures** Students admitted directly into the professional program freshman year. Deadline for freshmen and transfers: continuous. Required: high school transcript, college transcript(s) for transfer students, letter of recommendation, audition, SAT or ACT test scores (minimum composite ACT score of 17). Recommended: minimum 3.0 high school GPA, interview, minimum 2.5 high school GPA. Auditions held by arrangement on campus; recorded music is permissible as a substitute for live auditions when distance is prohibitive and videotaped performances are permissible as a substitute for live auditions when distance is prohibitive. Portfolio reviews held by appointment on campus.

**Web Site** http://www.coker.edu

**Undergraduate Contact** Shelli Wilson, Admissions Counselor, Coker College, 300 East College Avenue, Hartsville, South Carolina 29550; 843-383-8050, fax: 843-383-8056, e-mail address: swilson@coker.edu

# The Colburn School Conservatory of Music

## Los Angeles, California

Independent, coed. Urban campus. Total enrollment: 96. Music program established 2003.

**Degrees** Bachelor of Music. Majors and concentrations: performance. Program accredited by NASM.

**Enrollment** 67 total; 30 undergraduate, 37 graduate.

**Music Student Profile** 55% females, 45% males, 3% minorities, 39% international.

**Music Faculty** 8 total (full-time), 14 total (part-time). Graduate students do not teach undergraduate courses.

**Student Life** Special housing available for music students.

**Expenses for 2008–2009** Application fee: $100. Comprehensive fee: $1400 includes full-time tuition ($0), mandatory fees ($1400), and college room and board ($0). All students receive monetary support which covers tuition, room and board.

**Financial Aid** Program-specific awards: full tuition, room, board for all enrolled students.

**Application Procedures** Students admitted directly into the professional program freshman year. Deadline for freshmen and transfers: January 15. Notification date for freshmen and transfers: May 1. Required: essay, high school transcript, college transcript(s) for transfer students, 2 letters of recommendation, interview, audition, minimum TOEFL score of 500 for international students. Recommended: SAT or ACT test scores. Auditions held once on campus.

**Web Site** http://www.colburnschool.edu

**Undergraduate Contact** Mr. Hank Mou, Admissions Specialist, The Colburn School Conservatory of Music, 200 South Grand Avenue, Los Angeles, California 90012; 213-621-2200 ext. 218, fax: 213-621-2110, e-mail address: admissions@colburnschool.edu

# The College of New Jersey

## Ewing, New Jersey

State-supported, coed. Suburban campus. Total enrollment: 6,964. Music program established 1916.

**Degrees** Bachelor of Music in the areas of performance, music education. Majors and concentrations: accordion, music education, performance, piano, stringed instruments, voice, wind and percussion instruments. Program accredited by NASM, NCATE.

**Enrollment** 152 total; all undergraduate.

**Music Student Profile** 57% females, 43% males, 14% minorities.

**Music Faculty** 13 undergraduate (full-time), 33 undergraduate (part-time). 100% of full-time faculty have terminal degrees. Graduate students do not teach undergraduate courses. Undergraduate student–faculty ratio: 4:1.

**Student Life** Student groups/activities include Music Educators National Conference, American String Teachers Association, Pi Kappa Lambda.

**Expenses for 2007–2008** Application fee: $60. State resident tuition: $8072 full-time. Nonresident tuition: $15,295 full-time. Mandatory fees: $3235 full-time. College room and board: $9242. College room only: $6680. Room and board charges vary according to board plan.

**Financial Aid** Program-specific awards: 1 Eric L. Maybury Award for music education majors ($400), 1 Helena Hoffman Classical Music Scholarship for those demonstrating high academic and performance achievement ($100), 5–10 talent scholarships for those demonstrating talent ($750–$1000), 1 Hy Frank Music Scholarship for music education students (non voice/keyboard) ($1500), 1 Thomas H. Kean Scholarship for junior and senior New Jersey residents ($2500), 1 Laurenti Family Art Fund for Mercer County resident music majors ($1000), 1 George and Christine Krauss Scholarship for music education majors ($500), 1 Barbara Meyers Pelson Fund for music education majors ($2700), 1 Nicholas Crocker Fund for sophomore, or junior music majors ($1000).

**Application Procedures** Students admitted directly into the professional program freshman year. Deadline for freshmen and transfers: February 1. Notification date for freshmen: April 1; transfers: April 15. Required: essay, high school transcript, college transcript(s) for transfer students, minimum 3.0 high school GPA, 2 letters of recommendation, interview, audition, SAT or ACT test scores. Auditions held 9 times on campus.

**Web Site** http://www.tcnj.edu/~music

**Undergraduate Contact** Dr. Suzanne L. Hickman, Chair, Department of Music, The College of New Jersey, PO Box 7718, Ewing, New Jersey 08628-0718; 609-771-2551, fax: 609 637 5102, e-mail address: hickman@tcnj.edu

# College of Santa Fe

## Santa Fe, New Mexico

Independent, coed. Suburban campus. Total enrollment: 672. Music program established 1992.

**Web Site** http://www.csf.edu

# The College of Wooster

## Wooster, Ohio

Independent, coed. Small town campus. Total enrollment: 1,777. Music program established 1872.

**Degrees** Bachelor of Music in the areas of performance, music theory/composition, music history/literature, composition; Bachelor of Music Education in the areas of public school teaching, music therapy. Majors and concentrations: composition, music education, music history and literature, music therapy, piano/organ, stringed instruments, voice, wind and percussion instruments. Mandatory cross-registration with Baldwin-Wallace College (music therapy courses only). Program accredited by NASM, AMTA.

**Enrollment** 39 total; 29 undergraduate, 10 nonprofessional degree.

**Music Student Profile** 43% females, 57% males, 5% minorities.

*The College of Wooster (continued)*

**Music Faculty** 9 undergraduate (full-time), 17 undergraduate (part-time). 67% of full-time faculty have terminal degrees. Graduate students do not teach undergraduate courses. Undergraduate student–faculty ratio: 5:1.

**Student Life** Student groups/activities include Student Music Association.

**Expenses for 2008–2009** Application fee: $40. Comprehensive fee: $42,420 includes full-time tuition ($33,770) and college room and board ($8650). College room only: $3860. Special program-related fees: $376 per semester for music lessons in secondary instrument only.

**Financial Aid** Program-specific awards: 8–15 music performance scholarships for talented musicians ($2000–$8000).

**Application Procedures** Students admitted directly into the professional program freshman year. Deadline for freshmen: February 15; transfers: June 1. Notification date for freshmen: March 25. Required: essay, high school transcript, college transcript(s) for transfer students, 2 letters of recommendation, SAT or ACT test scores. Recommended: minimum 2.0 high school GPA, interview.

**Web Site** http://www.wooster.edu/music

**Undergraduate Contact** Dean of Admissions, The College of Wooster, 1101 North Bever Street, Wooster, Ohio 44691; 800-877-9905.

# Colorado Christian University
## Lakewood, Colorado

Independent interdenominational, coed. Suburban campus. Total enrollment: 2,221 (2007). Music program established 1914.

**Degrees** Bachelor of Music in the areas of music ministry, choral music education, instrumental music education, general music education. Majors and concentrations: classical music, contemporary Christian music, jazz, music, music education, piano/organ, sound recording technology, stringed instruments, voice, wind and percussion instruments. Program accredited by NASM.

**Enrollment** 40 total; 16 undergraduate, 24 nonprofessional degree.

**Music Student Profile** 47% females, 53% males, 10% minorities.

**Music Faculty** 6 undergraduate (full-time), 19 undergraduate (part-time). 50% of full-time faculty have terminal degrees. Graduate students do not teach undergraduate courses. Undergraduate student–faculty ratio: 7:1.

**Student Life** Student groups/activities include music ministry in local churches, music theater productions, contemporary Christian music ensembles/chapel teams.

**Expenses for 2007–2008** Application fee: $50. Comprehensive fee: $25,975 includes full-time tuition ($18,200), mandatory fees ($150), and college room and board ($7625). College room only: $4415. Special program-related fees: $25 per semester for instrument rentals, $60 per semester for ensemble fee, $100 per semester for instrumental accompanying fee, $100 per semester for vocal accompanying fee.

**Financial Aid** Program-specific awards: 51 music scholarships for program students ($1500), 5 ensemble scholarships for program students ($200).

**Application Procedures** Students apply for admission into the professional program by sophomore year. Deadline for freshmen and transfers: continuous. Notification date for freshmen and transfers: continuous. Required: essay, high school transcript, college transcript(s) for transfer students, minimum 2.0 high school GPA, 3 letters of recommendation, interview, audition, SAT or ACT test scores. Recommended: minimum 3.0 high school GPA, video. Auditions held 3 times on campus; videotaped performances are permissible as a substitute for live auditions if a campus visit is impossible.

**Web Site** http://www.ccu.edu

**Undergraduate Contact** Mr. Ron Rex, Vice President, University Advancement, Colorado Christian University, 8787 West Alameda Avenue, Lakewood, Colorado 80226; 800-44-FAITH, fax: 303-963-3001.

# Colorado State University
## Fort Collins, Colorado

State-supported, coed. Urban campus. Total enrollment: 27,569. Music program established 1937.

**Web Site** http://www.colostate.edu/

# Columbia College Chicago
## Chicago, Illinois

Independent, coed. Urban campus. Total enrollment: 11,499. Music program established 1970.

**Degrees** Bachelor of Arts in the area of music; Bachelor of Music in the area of music. Majors and concentrations: composition, directing, instrumental jazz, instrumental performance, jazz performance, jazz studies, jazz voice, voice performance. Graduate degrees offered: Master of Fine Arts in the area of music composition for the screen.

**Enrollment** 408 total; 399 undergraduate, 9 graduate.

**Music Student Profile** 29% females, 71% males, 31% minorities, 1% international.

**Music Faculty** 15 total (full-time), 28 total (part-time). Graduate students do not teach undergraduate courses. Undergraduate student–faculty ratio: 9:1.

**Student Life** Student groups/activities include Columbia Urban Music Association.

**Expenses for 2007–2008** Application fee: $35. Comprehensive fee: $29,652 includes full-time tuition ($17,104), mandatory fees ($530), and college room and board ($12,018). College room only: $9048. Special program-related fees: $5–$415 per course for class fees.

**Financial Aid** Program-specific awards: The Music Department Scholarship for full-time students.

**Application Procedures** Students admitted directly into the professional program freshman year. Deadline for freshmen and transfers: continuous. Notification date for freshmen and transfers: continuous. Required: essay, high school transcript, college transcript(s) for transfer students, letter of recommendation, meeting with admissions counselor for a personal interview and possible remediation program attendance for students with less than a 2.0 GPA, audition for transfer students. Recommended: minimum 2.0 high school GPA, interview, SAT or ACT test scores. Auditions held only by appointment on campus.

**Web Site** http://www.colum.edu

**Undergraduate Contact** Mr. Murphy Monroe, Director, Office of Admissions, Columbia College Chicago, 600 South Michigan Avenue, Chicago, Illinois 60605; 312-344-7133, fax: 312-344-8024, e-mail address: admissions@colum.edu

**Graduate Contact** Mr. Robert Garcia, Director of Graduate Admission, Graduate School Admission, Columbia College Chicago, 600 South Michigan Avenue, Chicago, Illinois 60605; 312-344-7262, fax: 312-344-8047, e-mail address: rgarcia@colum.edu

*Schwob School of Music*
# Columbus State University
## Columbus, Georgia

State-supported, coed. Suburban campus. Total enrollment: 7,590. Music program established 1969.

**Degrees** Bachelor of Music in the areas of performance, piano pedagogy, music education. Majors and concentrations: guitar, music education, piano pedagogy, piano/organ, stringed instruments, voice, wind and percussion instruments. Graduate degrees offered: Master of Music in the area of music education. Program accredited by NASM, NCATE.

**Enrollment** 213 total; 179 undergraduate, 8 graduate, 26 nonprofessional degree.

**Music Student Profile** 46% females, 54% males, 25% minorities, 6% international.

**Music Faculty** 21 total (full-time), 16 total (part-time). 48% of full-time faculty have terminal degrees. Graduate students do not teach undergraduate courses. Undergraduate student–faculty ratio: 8:1.

**Student Life** Student groups/activities include Music Educators National Conference Student Chapter, Mu Phi Epsilon, Phi Mu Alpha Sinfonia.

**Expenses for 2007–2008** Application fee: $25. State resident tuition: $2868 full-time. Nonresident tuition: $11,472 full-time. Mandatory fees: $646 full-time. College room and board: $6220. College room only: $2420. Room and board charges vary according to board plan and location. Special program-related fees: $82 per semester for private lessons.

**Financial Aid** Program-specific awards: 140 Patrons of Music Awards ($2700).

**Application Procedures** Students admitted directly into the professional program freshman year. Deadline for freshmen and transfers: July 30. Notification date for freshmen and transfers: July 30. Required: high school transcript, college transcript(s) for transfer students, interview, audition, SAT or ACT test scores, college preparatory curriculum. Recommended: minimum 3.0 high school GPA, 2 letters of recommendation. Auditions held 3 times and by appointment on campus; recorded music is permissible as a substitute for live auditions for out-of-state applicants and videotaped performances are permissible as a substitute for live auditions for out-of-state applicants.

**Web Site** http://music.colstate.edu

**Undergraduate Contact** Ms. Diane E. Andrae, Admissions Secretary, Schwob School of Music, Columbus State University, 4225 University Avenue, Columbus, Georgia 31907-5645; 706-649-7224, fax: 706-649-7369, e-mail address: andrae_diane@colstate.edu

**Graduate Contact** Dr. Deborah Jacobs, Graduate Studies Coordinator, Schwob School of Music, Columbus State University, 4225 University Avenue, Columbus, Georgia 31907-5645; 706-649-7243, fax: 706-649-7369, e-mail address: jacobs_deborah@colstate.edu

# Concordia College
## Moorhead, Minnesota

Independent, coed. Suburban campus. Total enrollment: 2,815. Music program established 1932.

**Degrees** Bachelor of Music in the areas of music education, performance, music theory. Majors and concentrations: composition, music education, music theory, piano/organ, stringed instruments, voice, wind and percussion instruments. Cross-registration with Minnesota State University Moorhead, North Dakota State University. Program accredited by NASM.

**Enrollment** 185 total; all undergraduate.

**Music Student Profile** 62% females, 38% males, 2% minorities, 2% international.

**Music Faculty** 26 undergraduate (full-time), 17 undergraduate (part-time). 50% of full-time faculty have terminal degrees. Graduate students do not teach undergraduate courses. Undergraduate student–faculty ratio: 5:1.

**Student Life** Student groups/activities include Music Educators National Conference Student Chapter, American Choral Directors Association Student Chapter.

**Expenses for 2008–2009** Application fee: $20. Comprehensive fee: $30,280 includes full-time tuition ($23,925), mandatory fees ($195), and college room and board ($6160). College room only: $2760. Special program-related fees: $50 for applied music fees use of instruments, practice rooms.

**Financial Aid** Program-specific awards: 75 music performance scholarships for freshmen ($10,000).

**Application Procedures** Students apply for admission into the professional program by freshman year. Deadline for freshmen and transfers: continuous. Notification date for freshmen and transfers: September 5. Required: high school transcript, minimum 2.0 high school GPA, audition, SAT or ACT test scores, proficiency exams for transfer students. Auditions held 4-6 times on campus and off campus in Minneapolis, MN; recorded music is permissible as a substitute for live auditions when distance is prohibitive and videotaped performances are permissible as a substitute for live auditions when distance is prohibitive.

**Web Site** http://www.cord.edu/dept/music/

**Undergraduate Contact** Mr. Omar Correa, Vice President of Admissions, Concordia College, 901 8th Street South, Moorhead, Minnesota 56562; 218-299-3004.

# Concordia University
## Montreal, Quebec, Canada

Province-supported, coed. Urban campus. Total enrollment: 32,416. Music program established 1975.

**Web Site** http://www.concordia.ca/

## Oberlin College
# The Conservatory of Music at Oberlin College
## Oberlin, Ohio

Independent, coed. Small town campus. Total enrollment: 2,774. Music program established 1865.

**Degrees** Bachelor of Music in the areas of performance, music education, composition, music history, electronic and computer music, jazz studies, music theory, accompanying. Majors and concentrations: accompanying, brass, composition, electronic music, historical performance, jazz, music education, music theory, musicology, piano/organ, stringed instruments, voice, wind and percussion instruments. Graduate degrees offered: Master of Music in the areas of historical performance, opera theater, conducting; Master of Music in Teaching in the area of music education. Program accredited by NASM.

**Enrollment** 584 total; 572 undergraduate, 12 graduate.

**Music Student Profile** 52% females, 48% males, 16% minorities, 13% international.

**Music Faculty** 70 total (full-time), 21 total (part-time). 90% of full-time faculty have terminal degrees. Graduate students do not teach undergraduate courses. Undergraduate student–faculty ratio: 7:1.

**Expenses for 2007–2008** Application fee: $35. Comprehensive fee: $46,362 includes full-time tuition ($36,064), mandatory fees ($218), and college room and board ($10,080). College room only: $4850. Full-time tuition and fees vary according to course load. Room and board charges vary according to board plan and housing facility.

**Financial Aid** Program-specific awards: 220 Oberlin College Scholarships for those demonstrating need ($2000–$34,000), 200 Oberlin Conservatory Dean's Scholarships for those demonstrating talent and academic achievement ($2000–$36,000), 10 Oberlin College Prize Funds for those with academic merit ($50–$4000), 15 Oberlin Conservatory/Aspen-John H. Stern Scholarships for enrolled students ($1500), 220 work-study awards for program majors ($500–$1600).

**Application Procedures** Students admitted directly into the professional program freshman year. Deadline for freshmen and transfers: December 1. Notification date for freshmen and transfers: April 1. Required: essay, high school transcript, college transcript(s) for transfer students, 2 letters of recommendation, audition, SAT or ACT test scores, transfer release form (for transfer applicants), DVD (for recorded audition). Recommended: minimum 3.0 high school GPA, interview, video. Auditions held 28 times on campus and off campus in Atlanta, GA; Boston, MA; Chicago, IL; Denver, CO; Houston, TX; Interlochen, MI; Idyllwild, CA; Los Angeles, CA; Minneapolis, MN; New York, NY; Portland, OR; San Francisco, CA; Seattle, WA; Washington, DC; videotaped performances are permissible as a substitute for live auditions if of good quality.

**Web Site** http://www.oberlin.edu/con

**Contact** Mr. Michael Manderen, Director of Conservatory Admissions, Conservatory of Music, Oberlin College, 39 West College Street, Oberlin, Ohio 44074; 440-775-8413, fax: 440-775-6972, e-mail address: conservatory.admissions@oberlin.edu

### More About the Conservatory

**W**ithin the Conservatory, which is housed in a modern complex designed by Minoru Yamasaki, are ensemble rehearsal rooms, two excellent concert halls, and 153 individual practice rooms. The Conservatory houses one of the largest collection of Steinway pianos in the world, and the campus is also home to twenty-five organs. Other features include numerous

*The Conservatory of Music at Oberlin College (continued)*

instrument collections, seven acoustically isolated and optimized electronic music studios, and a library that rivals those in the nation's largest university music schools.

The Conservatory of Music and the College of Arts and Sciences share the same campus. As a result, Conservatory students can take courses in both the College and the Conservatory in the same semester and can simultaneously pursue majors in both divisions, completing majors leading to both the B.Mus. and the B.A. degrees after five years. Twenty-five to 30 percent of the Conservatory's students are in the Double Degree Program. In addition, the Conservatory offers dual-degree programs, open only to Oberlin's own undergraduates, which combine bachelor's degree study in performance with graduate study leading to the master's degree in conducting, opera theater, or music teaching.

The Oberlin Conservatory is one of the few major music schools in the country devoted primarily to the education of undergraduate musicians. As a division of Oberlin College, the Conservatory is also recognized for being paired with a preeminent college of the liberal arts and sciences. These factors allow the conservatory to offer its students the essential components of excellent musical training: an accomplished faculty, outstanding facilities, an extensive curriculum drawing on both divisions of Oberlin College, and an active cultural life centered on campus and drawing on Cleveland as well.

"You're at Oberlin? What do you play?" Every Oberlinian has heard this question even though the Conservatory of Music is but one fourth the size of its partner, the College of Arts and Sciences. Yet it is natural that the name Oberlin should evoke thoughts of music. Built up by an amateur cellist (Charles Grandison Finney) and funded mainly by a former piano student (Charles Martin Hall), Oberlin College created America's first professorship in music in 1835. Oberlin's Conservatory of Music, established in 1865, is the country's first continuously operating conservatory. Even before the Civil War, a visitor, Thomas Hastings, pronounced the Oberlin choir "the finest in the land." A century later, Igor Stravinsky was similarly effusive over the Conservatory's young instrumentalists.

Oberlin has been the source of much innovation in American musical education. It established the country's first full-time chair in music history (1892), offered the country's first four-year degree program in public school music (1921), introduced to the United States the renowned Suzuki method of string pedagogy (1958), pioneered a program in electronic music (1969), and created the American-Soviet Youth Orchestra, composed of 100 young musicians from the United States and the former U.S.S.R., the first arts exchange produced jointly by the two countries (1988).

Conservatory alumni include well-known composers, conductors, performers, and teachers. Some, like David Zinman, conductor, have gained public renown. Others, like jazz pioneer Will Marion Cook—whom Duke Ellington called "my conservatory"—are revered mainly by specialists. Today's Oberlin graduates are to be found in virtually every major American orchestra as well as in international orchestras from Berlin to Hong Kong. Its singers and pianists are no less ubiquitous, as are Oberlinians in the many new allied fields of music.

The Oberlin Conservatory of Music has taken great pains to both educate and train its students. More than ever, technical proficiency is essential to success in music; however, the day when a pianist could simply perfect a limited repertoire of classics in order to launch a career is past. Increasingly, musicians need to master worlds of sound that were scarcely imaginable when they were students. Only the most well-educated minds can attain such flexibility. Oberlin is committed to providing its students a balanced combination of professional training and comprehensive education.

# Conservatory of Music of Puerto Rico
## San Juan, Puerto Rico

Commonwealth-supported, coed. Urban campus. Music program established 1959.

**Degrees** Bachelor of Music in the area of performance and music education. Majors and concentrations: composition, jazz, music education, performance. Graduate degrees offered: Master of Music in the area of music education. Cross-registration with Sacred Heart University. Program accredited by NASM.

**Enrollment** 392 total; 331 undergraduate, 45 graduate, 16 nonprofessional degree.

**Music Student Profile** 28% females, 72% males, 100% minorities, 5% international.

**Music Faculty** 43 undergraduate (full-time), 32 undergraduate (part-time), 3 graduate (part-time). 3% of full-time faculty have terminal degrees. Graduate students do not teach undergraduate courses. Undergraduate student–faculty ratio: 5:1.

**Student Life** Student groups/activities include community outreach activities/concerts, recruitment visits, institutional committees.

**Expenses for 2007–2008** Special program-related fees: $35 per course for accompanist fee.

**Financial Aid** Program-specific awards: 17 Angel Ramos Foundation Grants for undergraduate students ($472), 20 Programa de becas for undergraduate students ($283), 129 Programa Ayoda Suplementaria for undergraduate students ($192), 4 Banco Popular Foundation Grants for undergraduate students ($728).

**Application Procedures** Students admitted directly into the professional program freshman year. Deadline for freshmen and transfers: February 28. Required: high school transcript, college transcript(s) for transfer students, minimum 2.0 high school GPA, letter of recommendation, audition, SAT or ACT test scores, birth certificate, vaccination certificate, essay and interview for music education applicants. Recommended: interview. Auditions held once on campus; videotaped performances are permissible as a substitute for live auditions for out-of-state students.

**Web Site** http://www.cmpr.edu

**Undergraduate Contact** Eutimia Santiago, Director of Admission, Student Affairs Office, Conservatory of Music of Puerto Rico, 350 Rafael Lamar Street, San Juan, Puerto Rico 00918-2199; 787-751-0160 ext. 275, fax: 787-758-8268.

**Graduate Contact** Eutimia Santiago, Director of Admission, Student Affairs Office, Conservatory of Music of Puerto Rico, 350 Rafael Lamor Street, San Juan, Puerto Rico 00918-2199; 787-751-0160 ext. 275, fax: 787-758-8268.

*The Carroll McDaniel Petrie School of Music*
# Converse College
## Spartanburg, South Carolina

Independent, Total enrollment: 1,881. Music program established 1889.

**Web Site** http://www.converse.edu/

# Cornell College
## Mount Vernon, Iowa

Independent Methodist, coed. Small town campus. Total enrollment: 1,083. Music program established 1853.

**Degrees** Bachelor of Music; Bachelor of Music Education. Majors and concentrations: music education, performance.

**Enrollment** 40 total; 30 undergraduate, 10 nonprofessional degree.

**Music Student Profile** 60% females, 40% males, 10% minorities, 5% international.

**Music Faculty** 5 undergraduate (full-time), 18 undergraduate (part-time). 100% of full-time faculty have terminal degrees. Graduate students do not teach undergraduate courses. Undergraduate student–faculty ratio: 5:1.

**Expenses for 2007–2008** Application fee: $30. Comprehensive fee: $33,250 includes full-time tuition ($26,100), mandatory fees

($180), and college room and board ($6970). College room only: $3250. Room and board charges vary according to board plan and housing facility.

**Financial Aid** Program-specific awards: 10 Trustees Music Scholar Awards for music majors and minors ($15,000), 4 WFK Music Scholarships for music majors and minors, Horace Alden Miller (HAMM) Award for music majors and minors ($5000).

**Application Procedures** Students apply for admission into the professional program by sophomore year. Deadline for freshmen and transfers: continuous. Required: essay, high school transcript, college transcript(s) for transfer students, minimum 2.0 high school GPA, letter of recommendation, audition, SAT or ACT test scores. Recommended: interview. Auditions held once and by appointment on campus; recorded music is permissible as a substitute for live auditions if a campus visit is impossible and videotaped performances are permissible as a substitute for live auditions if a campus visit is impossible.

**Web Site** http://www.cornellcollege.edu

**Undergraduate Contact** Jonathan Stroud, Director of Admissions, Cornell College, 600 First Street West, Mount Vernon, Iowa 52314-1098; 319-895-4477, fax: 319-895-4451.

## Cornerstone University
### Grand Rapids, Michigan

Independent nondenominational, coed. Suburban campus. Total enrollment: 2,466. Music program established 1945.

**Degrees** Bachelor of Music in the areas of performance, composition, contemporary Christian music, music education. Majors and concentrations: composition, contemporary Christian music, music education, piano/organ, voice, wind and percussion instruments. Program accredited by NASM.

**Enrollment** 99 total; 92 undergraduate, 7 nonprofessional degree.

**Music Student Profile** 51% females, 49% males, 10% minorities, 1% international.

**Music Faculty** 7 undergraduate (full-time), 26 undergraduate (part-time). 14% of full-time faculty have terminal degrees. Graduate students do not teach undergraduate courses. Undergraduate student–faculty ratio: 10:1.

**Student Life** Student groups/activities include pep band, Spring Musical, worship band.

**Expenses for 2007–2008** Application fee: $25. Comprehensive fee: $24,660 includes full-time tuition ($18,040), mandatory fees ($320), and college room and board ($6300). Room and board charges vary according to board plan. Special program-related fees: $40 per course for music recital fee, $240–$480 per credit hour for private instruction fee.

**Financial Aid** Program-specific awards: 65 music scholarships for talented instrumentalists and vocalists ($500–$6500).

**Application Procedures** Students admitted directly into the professional program freshman year. Deadline for freshmen and transfers: continuous. Required: essay, high school transcript, college transcript(s) for transfer students, 2 letters of recommendation, audition, SAT or ACT test scores (minimum combined SAT score of 1350, minimum composite ACT score of 19), minimum 2.5 high school GPA (4.0 scale). Recommended: minimum 3.0 high school GPA, interview. Auditions held continuously on campus; recorded music is permissible as a substitute for live auditions when distance is prohibitive and videotaped performances are permissible as a substitute for live auditions when distance is prohibitive. Portfolio reviews held continuously on campus.

**Web Site** http://www.cornerstone.edu/academics/fine_arts

**Undergraduate Contact** Dr. Donna M. Bohn, Chair, Division of Fine Arts, Cornerstone University, 1001 East Beltline Avenue, NE, Grand Rapids, Michigan 49525; 616-222-1543, fax: 616-222-1540, e-mail address: donna.bohn@cornerstone.edu

## Cornish College of the Arts
### Seattle, Washington

Independent, coed. Urban campus. Total enrollment: 768 (2006). Music program established 1914.

**Degrees** Bachelor of Music in the areas of jazz performance, classical and new music performance, composition. Majors and concentrations: classical music, composition, electronic music, instrumental music, jazz, voice, world music.

**Enrollment** 129 total; all undergraduate.

**Music Student Profile** 65% females, 35% males, 14% minorities, 3% international.

**Music Faculty** 13 undergraduate (full-time), 21 undergraduate (part-time). 58% of full-time faculty have terminal degrees. Graduate students do not teach undergraduate courses. Undergraduate student–faculty ratio: 5:1.

**Expenses for 2007–2008** Application fee: $35. Tuition: $23,700 full-time. Mandatory fees: $300 full-time. Special program-related fees: $700 per year for private lessons (amount may vary by major).

**Financial Aid** Program-specific awards: Nellie Scholarships for new students, departmental scholarships for new and continuing students, Presidential Scholarships for continuing students.

**Application Procedures** Students admitted directly into the professional program freshman year. Deadline for freshmen and transfers: August 15. Notification date for freshmen and transfers: August 30. Required: essay, high school transcript, college transcript(s) for transfer students, minimum 2.0 high school GPA, audition. Recommended: 2 letters of recommendation, interview, SAT or ACT test scores. Auditions held 20 times on campus and off campus in San Francisco, CA; recorded music is permissible as a substitute for live auditions when distance is prohibitive.

**Web Site** http://www.cornish.edu

**Undergraduate Contact** Sharron Starling, Director of Admission, Cornish College of the Arts, 1000 Lenora, Seattle, Washington 98121; 800-726-ARTS, fax: 206-720-1011, e-mail address: sstarling@cornish.edu

## Covenant College
### Lookout Mountain, Georgia

Independent, coed. Suburban campus. Total enrollment: 1,063. Music program established 1964.

**Web Site** http://www.covenant.edu/

## The Crane School of Music
See State University of New York College at Potsdam

## Crown College
### St. Bonifacius, Minnesota

Independent, coed. Suburban campus. Total enrollment: 1,270. Music program established 1980.

**Degrees** Bachelor of Arts in the areas of vocal, piano, instrumental, church music, worship arts; Bachelor of Music Education in the area of vocal music education. Majors and concentrations: church music, music, music education, piano, voice.

**Enrollment** 30 total; all undergraduate.

**Music Student Profile** 52% females, 48% males.

**Music Faculty** 2 total (full-time), 10 total (part-time). 70% of full-time faculty have terminal degrees. Graduate students do not teach undergraduate courses. Undergraduate student–faculty ratio: 4:1.

**Student Life** Student groups/activities include American Choral Directors Association Student Chapter, Music Educators National Conference Student Chapter, Minnesota Music Educators Association Student Chapter.

**Expenses for 2008–2009** Application fee: $35. Comprehensive fee: $26,564 includes full-time tuition ($19,198) and college room and board ($7366). College room only: $3834. Special program-related fees: $175 per semester for credit lesson fee, $250 per semester for non-credit lesson fee.

**Financial Aid** Program-specific awards: 130 music participation grants for music performers ($100–$315), 12 scholarships for program majors ($200–$2000).

**Application Procedures** Students apply for admission into the professional program by sophomore year. Deadline for freshmen and transfers: continuous. Notification date for freshmen and

*Crown College (continued)*

transfers: continuous. Required: high school transcript, college transcript(s) for transfer students, 4 letters of recommendation, interview, ACT test score only (minimum composite ACT score of 18), audition for scholarship consideration, minimum 2.5 high school GPA, portfolio for music education applicants. Recommended: minimum 3.0 high school GPA, audition. Auditions held as needed on campus; recorded music is permissible as a substitute for live auditions when distance is prohibitive and videotaped performances are permissible as a substitute for live auditions when distance is prohibitive. Portfolio reviews held as needed on campus.

**Web Site** http://www.crown.edu

**Undergraduate Contact** Mr. Mitch Fisk, Director of Admissions, Crown College, 8700 College View Drive, St. Bonifacius, Minnesota 55375; 952-446-4142, fax: 952-446-4149, e-mail address: info@crown.edu

## Culver-Stockton College

### Canton, Missouri

Independent, coed. Rural campus. Total enrollment: 849. Music program established 1925.

**Web Site** http://www.culver.edu/

## The Curtis Institute of Music

### Philadelphia, Pennsylvania

Independent, coed. Urban campus. Music program established 1924.

**Degrees** Bachelor of Music in the area of performance. Majors and concentrations: brass, composition, conducting, harpsichord, piano/organ, stringed instruments, voice, wind and percussion instruments. Graduate degrees offered: Master of Music in the area of opera. Cross-registration with University of Pennsylvania. Program accredited by NASM.

**Enrollment** 158 total.

**Music Student Profile** 55% females, 45% males, 46% international.

**Music Faculty** 2 total (full-time), 86 total (part-time). Graduate students do not teach undergraduate courses.

**Student Life** Student groups/activities include symphony concerts, operas, chamber concerts.

**Expenses for 2007–2008** Special program-related fees: $2100 per year for comprehensive fee (includes textbooks).

**Financial Aid** Program-specific awards: tuition scholarships for program students, supplemental financial assistance awards for those demonstrating need.

**Application Procedures** Students admitted directly into the professional program freshman year. Deadline for freshmen and transfers: December 15. Notification date for freshmen and transfers: April 15. Required: high school transcript, college transcript(s) for transfer students, 4 letters of recommendation, audition, SAT test score only. Auditions held once on campus.

**Web Site** http://www.curtis.edu

**Contact** Mr. Chris Hodges, Director of Admissions, The Curtis Institute of Music, 1726 Locust Street, Philadelphia, Pennsylvania 19103; 215-893-5262 ext. 3117, fax: 215-893-0194.

## Dalhousie University

### Halifax, Nova Scotia, Canada

Province-supported, coed. Total enrollment: 15,440 (2007). Music program established 1967.

**Degrees** Bachelor of Arts in the area of music and theater; Bachelor of Music in the areas of composition, history, church music, performance, music instruction, self-directed study, contemporary music. Majors and concentrations: brass, classical guitar, composition, music history, music instruction, musicology, piano/organ, stringed instruments, voice, wind and percussion instruments. Cross-registration with Atlantic School of Theology (for church music majors only), University of Kings College.

**Enrollment** 113 total; 89 undergraduate, 24 nonprofessional degree.

**Music Student Profile** 50% females, 50% males, 99% minorities, 4% international.

**Music Faculty** 12 undergraduate (full-time), 23 undergraduate (part-time). 100% of full-time faculty have terminal degrees. Graduate students do not teach undergraduate courses. Undergraduate student–faculty ratio: 5:1.

**Student Life** Student groups/activities include Symphony Nova Scotia, Nova Scotia Choral Federation.

**Expenses for 2007–2008** Application fee: $45 Canadian dollars. Tuition, fee, and room and board charges are reported in Canadian dollars. Province resident tuition: $6800 full-time. Mandatory fees: $782 full-time. College room and board: $7575. International student tuition: $13,250 full-time. Special program-related fees: $850 per year for applied skills and electroacoustic classes.

**Financial Aid** Program-specific awards: 1–2 Don Wright Excellence Scholarships for first year students ($3000–$6000), 6 Don Wright Scholarships for music instruction students ($500–$2000), 1 Halifax Ladies Musical Club Scholarship for first-year students ($500), 24 Effie Mae Ross and Campbell Scholarships for in-course students ($500–$3000), 1 L. D. Currie Memorial Scholarship for in-course students ($750), 1 Elizabeth Meyerhof Scholarship for fourth-year students ($3000), 1 David Peters Keyboard Scholarship for piano or organ majors ($900), 1 Bornoff/Gramie Memorial String Scholarship for 4th-year string students ($300), 3 James and Abbie Campbell Incentive Scholarships for incoming students ($500–$1250), 10 Effie May Ross Entrance Scholarships ($500–$3000), 1 Elvira Gonnella Scholarship for 3rd-and 4th-year voice students ($1600), 1 Tietje Zonneveld Scholarship in Piano Studies for senior piano students ($1000), 1 Charles and Mary MacLennan Bursary in Music for in-course students ($2500), 1 Margaret Newcomb Layton Harrigan Brink Bursary for in-course students from Nova Scotia ($500).

**Application Procedures** Students admitted directly into the professional program freshman year. Deadline for freshmen: April 1; transfers: June 1. Notification date for freshmen: June 1; transfers: September 1. Required: high school transcript, college transcript(s) for transfer students, minimum 3.0 high school GPA, interview, audition, portfolio for composition applicants, SAT for U.S. applicants only. Recommended: letter of recommendation. Auditions held 4-5 times from March through May on campus; videotaped performances are permissible as a substitute for live auditions when distance is prohibitive. Portfolio reviews held as needed on campus.

**Web Site** http://music.dal.ca

**Undergraduate Contact** Dr. Steven Baur, Student Advisor, Department of Music, Dalhousie University, Room 514 Arts Center, Halifax, Nova Scotia B3H 4R2, Canada; 902-494-6502, fax: 902-494-2801, e-mail address: steven.baur@dal.ca

## Dana School of Music

See Youngstown State University

## Delta State University

### Cleveland, Mississippi

State-supported, coed. Small town campus. Total enrollment: 4,091.

**Degrees** Bachelor of Music in the areas of voice, piano, instrumental performance; Bachelor of Music Education in the areas of vocal music education, instrumental music education. Majors and concentrations: piano/organ, voice, wind and percussion instruments. Program accredited by NASM.

**Enrollment** 84 total; all undergraduate.

**Music Student Profile** 49% females, 51% males, 15% minorities, 2% international.

**Music Faculty** 13 total (full-time), 4 total (part-time). 87% of full-time faculty have terminal degrees. Graduate students do not teach undergraduate courses. Undergraduate student–faculty ratio: 6:1.

**Student Life** Student groups/activities include Phi Mu Alpha, Mu Phi Epsilon, Pi Kappa Lambda.

**Expenses for 2007–2008** Application fee: $15. State resident tuition: $4248 full-time. Nonresident tuition: $10,258 full-time. College room and board: $4876. College room only: $2626. Room and board charges vary according to board plan and housing facility. Special program-related fees: $10 for music computer lab fee, $15 for string methods and materials lab fee, $20 for keyboard lab fee, $50 per credit hour for applied fee.
**Financial Aid** Program-specific awards: 232 music scholarships for members of ensembles ($1600).
**Application Procedures** Students admitted directly into the professional program freshman year. Deadline for freshmen and transfers: continuous. Required: high school transcript, audition, SAT or ACT test scores. Auditions held by appointment on campus; recorded music is permissible as a substitute for live auditions when distance is prohibitive and videotaped performances are permissible as a substitute for live auditions when distance is prohibitive.
**Web Site** http://www.deltastate.edu
**Undergraduate Contact** Dr. David Schubert, Chair, Department of Music, Delta State University, PO Box 3256, Cleveland, Mississippi 38733; 662-846-4606, fax: 662-846-4605, e-mail address: schubert@deltastate.edu

# DePaul University
## Chicago, Illinois

Independent Roman Catholic, coed. Urban campus. Total enrollment: 23,401. Music program established 1912.
**Degrees** Bachelor of Music in the areas of composition, jazz studies, performing arts management, music education, performance; Bachelor of Science in the area of sound recording technology. Majors and concentrations: brass, composition, jazz studies, music business, music education, piano, sound recording technology, stringed instruments, voice, wind and percussion instruments. Graduate degrees offered: Master of Music in the areas of composition, music education, performance, jazz studies. Program accredited by NASM.
**Enrollment** 399 total; 300 undergraduate, 90 graduate, 9 nonprofessional degree.
**Music Student Profile** 44% females, 56% males, 15% minorities, 10% international.
**Music Faculty** 22 total (full-time), 95 total (part-time). 88% of full-time faculty have terminal degrees. Graduate students do not teach undergraduate courses. Undergraduate student–faculty ratio: 8:1.
**Student Life** Student groups/activities include Music Educators National Conference.
**Expenses for 2008–2009** Application fee: $40. Comprehensive fee: $34,349 includes full-time tuition ($23,820), mandatory fees ($574), and college room and board ($9955). College room only: $7390. Special program-related fees: $20 for music education instrument rental, $200 per quarter for vocal accompanist fee.
**Financial Aid** Program-specific awards: 250 music performance awards for program majors ($3000–$15,000).
**Application Procedures** Students admitted directly into the professional program freshman year. Deadline for freshmen and transfers: January 15. Notification date for freshmen and transfers: April 1. Required: essay, high school transcript, college transcript(s) for transfer students, letter of recommendation, audition, SAT or ACT test scores (minimum composite ACT score of 22), minimum 2.75 high school GPA. Recommended: minimum 3.0 high school GPA, interview. Auditions held January and February on campus; recorded music is permissible as a substitute for live auditions for students outside the continental U.S. and videotaped performances are permissible as a substitute for live auditions for students outside the continental U.S..
**Web Site** http://music.depaul.edu
**Contact** Mr. Ross Beacraft, Director of Admission, School of Music, DePaul University, 804 West Belden Avenue, Chicago, Illinois 60614-3296; 800-433-7285 ext. 57444, fax: 773-325-7429, e-mail address: rbeacraf@depaul.edu

### More About the School

DePaul University School of Music graduates are currently performing with the Chicago and Boston Symphony Orchestra; the Berlin Philharmonic; the Los Angeles Philharmonic; the Philadelphia, Buffalo, Charleston, Jacksonville, Memphis, Winnipeg, and Kitchener-Waterloo Symphony Orchestras; the Metropolitan, Houston, Chicago Lyric, Berlin, Zurich, Montreal, Boston, Glimmerglass, Santa Fe, and Minnesota Opera Companies; and touring in musical theater productions across the country. Jazz studies majors have gone on to work in Chicago's commercial recording studios; recorded and toured with Maynard Ferguson, Chick Corea, Frank Mantooth, Woody Herman, Chicago Jazz Ensemble, Alanis Morissette, and Mighty Blue Kings; and released CDs for Reference, Corridor, River North, and Mesa/Bluemoon recordings.

Formed in 1923, the School of Music provides approximately 400 music majors from the United States, Canada, South and Central America, Europe, Asia, and Australia the opportunity to study with a world-class faculty. Students work with 100 full- and part-time faculty members who are members of the Chicago Symphony, the Lyric Opera, and Chicago's major chamber music ensembles and recording and jazz artists. In addition, students receive master classes with such major artists as Renee Flemming, Susan Mentzer, Phillip Glass, Elliot Carter, George Pearle, Phil Smith, Joseph Alessi, John Faddis, Bobbi Shew, and Phil Woods.

The School of Music is located on DePaul's beautiful Lincoln Park Campus in one of Chicago's most desirable neighborhoods. Students are less than 15 minutes from Symphony Center, the Civic Opera House, the Art Institute, Auditorium Theater, and literally dozens of other concert, theater, and jazz venues. Practice rooms are open from 7 a.m. until midnight, seven days a week. There are separate facilities for piano and percussion majors.

DePaul has great pride in the quality of its performing ensembles. Students have the opportunity to perform and read major repertoire with DePaul Symphony Orchestra, DePaul Chamber Orchestra, DePaul Wind Ensemble, Wind Symphony, DePaul Jazz Ensemble, Jazz Orchestra & Jazz Workshop, DePaul Opera Theater, Concert Choir, and Chamber Choir. All performance majors are also required to participate in chamber music, a very important part of music at DePaul. Student performances are given in the Lincoln Park Campus Recital and Concert Halls, Orchestra Hall at Symphony Center, and the Merle Reskin Theatre. In addition, many students perform with the Civic Orchestra of Chicago, the many regional and metropolitan orchestras, theater orchestras, jazz ensembles, and churches in the area.

The School of Music offers undergraduate degrees in Performance, Music Education, Jazz Studies, Composition, Performing Arts Administration, and Sound Recording Technology. Graduate degrees are offered in Performance, Music Education, Jazz Studies, and Composition. All applicants are required to audition. The School requires a live on-campus audition but accepts an audiotape or videotape from applicants outside the continental United States. The application deadline for freshman and transfer students is January 15. All auditions must be completed by February 28.

To view a video about the School of Music, students should use the following link: http://vision2012.depaul.edu/video/video.aspx?id=som&src=wmv.

For more information, prospective students should contact: Mr. Ross Beacraft, Director of Admissions, DePaul University School of Music, 804 West Belden, Chicago, Illinois 60614. Phone: 773-325-7444 or 800-4-DePaul Ext. 7444 (toll-free). Fax: 773-325-7429. E-mail: musicadmissions@depaul.edu. Web site: http://music.depaul.edu.

# DePauw University
## Greencastle, Indiana

Independent, coed. Small town campus. Total enrollment: 2,398. Music program established 1884.
**Web Site** http://www.depauw.edu/

# Dorothy F. Schmidt College of Arts and Letters

See Florida Atlantic University

# Drexel University

## Philadelphia, Pennsylvania

Independent, coed. Urban campus. Total enrollment: 20,682. Music program established 2001.

**Degrees** Bachelor of Science in the area of music; Bachelor of Science/Master of Business Administration. Majors and concentrations: music industry. Graduate degrees offered: Bachelor of Science/Master of Business Administration.

**Enrollment** 193 total; all undergraduate.

**Music Student Profile** 30% females, 70% males, 1% international.

**Music Faculty** 10 total (full-time), 40 total (part-time). 100% of full-time faculty have terminal degrees. Graduate students do not teach undergraduate courses. Undergraduate student–faculty ratio: 15:1.

**Student Life** Student groups/activities include Drexel Players (theater group), musical ensembles.

**Expenses for 2008–2009** Application fee: $75. Comprehensive fee: $42,575 includes full-time tuition ($28,500), mandatory fees ($1940), and college room and board ($12,135). College room only: $7275. Special program-related fees: $500 per term for private music lessons.

**Financial Aid** Program-specific awards: 108 Performing Arts Scholarships ($1000).

**Application Procedures** Students admitted directly into the professional program freshman year. Deadline for freshmen: December 1. Notification date for freshmen: March 1. Required: high school transcript, minimum 2.0 high school GPA, 2 letters of recommendation, portfolio, SAT or ACT test scores (minimum composite ACT score of 27), minimum 1200 combined critical reading/math SAT. Recommended: essay, minimum 3.0 high school GPA, interview, video, audition. Auditions held by appointment on campus; recorded music is permissible as a substitute for live auditions and videotaped performances are permissible as a substitute for live auditions. Portfolio reviews held on campus; the submission of slides may be substituted for portfolios.

**Web Site** http://www.drexel.edu/comad

**Undergraduate Contact** David Miller, Director of Recruitment, Dean's Office, College of Media Arts and Design, Drexel University, 33rd and Market Streets, Philadelphia, Pennsylvania 19104; 215-895-1675, fax: 215-895-4917, e-mail address: ddm22@drexel.edu

## *The Mary Pappert School of Music*

# Duquesne University

## Pittsburgh, Pennsylvania

Independent Roman Catholic, coed. Urban campus. Total enrollment: 10,296. Music program established 1926.

**Degrees** Bachelor of Music in the areas of performance, music technology; Bachelor of Science in the areas of music education, music therapy. Majors and concentrations: music education, music performance, music technology, music therapy. Graduate degrees offered: Master of Music in the areas of performance, sacred music, music theory/composition, music technology, music education. Cross-registration with Pittsburgh Council on Higher Education. Program accredited by NASM.

**Enrollment** 369 total; 285 undergraduate, 75 graduate, 9 nonprofessional degree.

**Music Student Profile** 43% females, 57% males, 21% minorities, 10% international.

**Music Faculty** 26 total (full-time), 73 total (part-time). 100% of full-time faculty have terminal degrees. Graduate students do not teach undergraduate courses. Undergraduate student–faculty ratio: 8:1.

**Student Life** Student groups/activities include Mu Phi Epsilon, Music Educators National Conference, Music Therapy Club.

**Expenses for 2007–2008** Application fee: $50. Comprehensive fee: $32,496 includes full-time tuition ($22,054), mandatory fees ($1896), and college room and board ($8546). College room only: $4662. Full-time tuition and fees vary according to program. Room and board charges vary according to board plan and housing facility.

**Financial Aid** Program-specific awards: 70 School of Music Talent Awards for program students ($2000–$20,000).

**Application Procedures** Students admitted directly into the professional program freshman year. Deadline for freshmen and transfers: May 1. Notification date for freshmen and transfers: August 15. Required: essay, high school transcript, college transcript(s) for transfer students, minimum 2.0 high school GPA, 2 letters of recommendation, audition, SAT or ACT test scores, theory examination, musicianship examination, compositions (for composition majors) (portfolio), piano placement exam. Recommended: minimum 3.0 high school GPA, interview. Auditions held 12 times on campus and off campus in Washington, DC area; recorded music is permissible as a substitute for live auditions if a campus visit is impossible and videotaped performances are permissible as a substitute for live auditions if a campus visit is impossible.

**Web Site** http://www.music.duq.edu/

**Undergraduate Contact** Mr. Paul Cukanna, Dean of Admissions, Duquesne University, 600 Forbes Avenue, Pittsburgh, Pennsylvania 15282; 412-396-6222, fax: 412-396-5644.

**Graduate Contact** Mr. Nicholas Jordanoff, Director of Music Admissions, School of Music, Duquesne University, 600 Forbes Avenue, Pittsburgh, Pennsylvania 15282; 412-396-5983, fax: 412-396-5479, e-mail address: jordanof@duq.edu

# East Carolina University

## Greenville, North Carolina

State-supported, coed. Urban campus. Total enrollment: 25,990. Music program established 1909.

**Degrees** Bachelor of Music in the areas of performance, music education, piano pedagogy, sacred music, theory/composition, music therapy, music theater, jazz studies. Majors and concentrations: jazz performance, music education, music theater, music theory and composition, music therapy, piano pedagogy, piano/organ, sacred music, stringed instruments, voice, wind and percussion instruments. Graduate degrees offered: Master of Music in the areas of accompanying, sacred music, music education, composition, performance, piano pedagogy, Suzuki pedagogy, music therapy, choral conducting, jazz performance, theory, voice pedagogy, instrumental conducting. Program accredited by NASM, AMTA.

**Enrollment** 295 total; 235 undergraduate, 60 graduate.

**Music Student Profile** 50% females, 50% males, 11% minorities, 1% international.

**Music Faculty** 50 total (full-time), 11 total (part-time). 94% of full-time faculty have terminal degrees. Graduate students teach a few undergraduate courses. Undergraduate student–faculty ratio: 6:1.

**Student Life** Student groups/activities include music sororities and fraternities, Music Educators National Conference, American Choral Directors Association. Special housing available for music students.

**Expenses for 2007–2008** Application fee: $60. State resident tuition: $2431 full-time. Nonresident tuition: $12,945 full-time. Mandatory fees: $1937 full-time. College room and board: $7150. College room only: $4150. Room and board charges vary according to board plan and housing facility. Special program-related fees: $35 per credit hour for applied music fee.

**Financial Aid** Program-specific awards: 75 music scholarships for music majors ($500–$7000).

**Application Procedures** Students admitted directly into the professional program freshman year. Deadline for freshmen: March 15; transfers: April 15. Required: high school transcript, college transcript(s) for transfer students, minimum 2.0 high school GPA, interview, audition, SAT or ACT test scores, minimum combined SAT score of 1000 for out-of-state applicants, musicianship test (written and aural). Recommended: essay, minimum 3.0 high school GPA, 2 letters of recommendation. Auditions held 8 times on campus; recorded music is permissible as a substitute for live

auditions if a campus visit is impossible and videotaped performances are permissible as a substitute for live auditions if a campus visit is impossible.
**Web Site** http://www.ecu.edu/music
**Undergraduate Contact** Mr. Christopher Ulffers, Assistant Director, School of Music, East Carolina University, A.J. Fletcher Music Center, Greenville, North Carolina 27858-4353; 252-328-4281, fax: 252-328-6258, e-mail address: ulffersj@ecu.edu
**Graduate Contact** Dr. Thomas Huener, Director of Graduate Studies, School of Music, East Carolina University, A.J. Fletcher Music Center, Greenville, North Carolina 27858-4353; 252-328-6851, fax: 252-328-6258, e-mail address: huenert@ecu.edu

## East Central University
### Ada, Oklahoma

State-supported, coed. Small town campus. Total enrollment: 4,463. Music program established 1909.
**Degrees** Bachelor of Science in the areas of music, music education. Majors and concentrations: music education, piano/organ, voice, wind and percussion instruments. Program accredited by NASM.
**Enrollment** 65 total; all undergraduate.
**Music Student Profile** 50% females, 50% males, 1% minorities.
**Music Faculty** 8 undergraduate (full-time), 6 undergraduate (part-time). 90% of full-time faculty have terminal degrees. Graduate students do not teach undergraduate courses. Undergraduate student–faculty ratio: 15:1.
**Student Life** Student groups/activities include Music Educators National Conference Student Chapter, Kappa Kappa Psi.
**Expenses for 2007–2008** Application fee: $20. State resident tuition: $2662 full-time. Nonresident tuition: $8135 full-time. Mandatory fees: $1134 full-time. Full-time tuition and fees vary according to course load. College room and board: $3860. College room only: $1500. Room and board charges vary according to board plan and housing facility. Special program-related fees: $3 per semester for class instrument rental fee, $10 per semester for organ rental, $36 per credit hour for private lessons.
**Application Procedures** Students admitted directly into the professional program freshman year. Deadline for freshmen and transfers: continuous. Required: high school transcript, college transcript(s) for transfer students, minimum 2.0 high school GPA, audition, ACT test score only (minimum composite ACT score of 20). Auditions held continuously on campus; recorded music is permissible as a substitute for live auditions if a campus visit is impossible and videotaped performances are permissible as a substitute for live auditions If a campus visit is impossible. Portfolio reviews held on campus; the submission of slides may be substituted for portfolios when distance is prohibitive.
**Web Site** http://www.ecok.edu
**Undergraduate Contact** Dr. Mark S. Hollingsworth, Chair, Department of Music, Box P-6, East Central University, 1100 East 14th Street, Ada, Oklahoma 74820; 580-310-5474, fax: 580-310-5752, e-mail address: mholling@ecok.edu

## Eastern Illinois University
### Charleston, Illinois

State-supported, coed. Small town campus. Total enrollment: 12,179. Music program established 1928.
**Web Site** http://www.eiu.edu/

## Eastern Michigan University
### Ypsilanti, Michigan

State-supported, coed. Suburban campus. Total enrollment: 22,638.
**Web Site** http://www.emich.edu/

## Eastman School of Music of the University of Rochester

See University of Rochester

## East Tennessee State University
### Johnson City, Tennessee

State-supported, coed. Small town campus. Total enrollment: 13,119. Music program established 1949.
**Web Site** http://www.etsu.edu/

## East Texas Baptist University
### Marshall, Texas

Independent Baptist, coed. Small town campus. Total enrollment: 1,308. Music program established 1912.
**Degrees** Bachelor of Music. Majors and concentrations: music education, piano performance, sacred music, voice performance. Program accredited by NASM.
**Enrollment** 201 total; 83 undergraduate, 118 nonprofessional degree.
**Music Student Profile** 60% females, 40% males, 5% minorities, 5% international.
**Music Faculty** 9 undergraduate (full-time), 9 undergraduate (part-time). 56% of full-time faculty have terminal degrees. Graduate students do not teach undergraduate courses. Undergraduate student–faculty ratio: 9:1.
**Student Life** Student groups/activities include Sigma Alpha Iota, Tau Beta Sigma, Kappa Kappa Psi.
**Expenses for 2007–2008** Application fee: $25. Comprehensive fee: $19,343 includes full-time tuition ($14,680) and college room and board ($4663). College room only: $2000. Room and board charges vary according to board plan and housing facility. Special program-related fees: $40 for recital accompanist, $100 per credit hour for applied music fee, $125 per credit hour for applied music accompanist.
**Financial Aid** Program-specific awards: 61 music scholarships for program majors ($1500–$2400), 33 ensemble scholarships for ensemble players ($300–$1000).
**Application Procedures** Students admitted directly into the professional program freshman year. Deadline for freshmen and transfers: August 1. Required: essay, high school transcript, college transcript(s) for transfer students, minimum 2.0 high school GPA, interview, audition, SAT or ACT test scores (minimum composite ACT score of 18), portfolio for scholarship consideration, 860 minimal combined SAT reading and math, only. Recommended: letter of recommendation. Auditions held 10 times on campus; recorded music is permissible as a substitute for live auditions when distance is prohibitive or scheduling is difficult and videotaped performances are permissible as a substitute for live auditions when distance is prohibitive or if scheduling is difficult. Portfolio reviews held 4 times on campus.
**Web Site** http://www.etbu.edu
**Undergraduate Contact** Melissa Fitts, Director of Admissions, East Texas Baptist University, 1209 North Grove, Marshall, Texas 75670; 800-804-3828 ext. 002, fax: 903-923-2000, e-mail address: mfitts@etbu.edu

## Elmhurst College
### Elmhurst, Illinois

Independent, coed. Suburban campus. Total enrollment: 3,107 (2007). Music program established 1938.
**Web Site** http://www.elmhurst.edu/

## Emporia State University
### Emporia, Kansas

State-supported, coed. Small town campus. Total enrollment: 6,354. Music program established 1925.
**Degrees** Bachelor of Music in the area of performance; Bachelor of Music Education in the areas of instrumental music education, vocal music education. Majors and concentrations: music education, piano, stringed instruments, voice, wind and percussion instruments. Graduate degrees offered: Master of Music in the areas of performance, music education. Program accredited by NASM.

*Emporia State University (continued)*

**Enrollment** 104 total; 88 undergraduate, 16 graduate.
**Music Student Profile** 55% females, 45% males, 5% minorities, 3% international.
**Music Faculty** 13 total (full-time), 7 total (part-time). 13% of full-time faculty have terminal degrees. Graduate students do not teach undergraduate courses. Undergraduate student–faculty ratio: 6:1.
**Student Life** Student groups/activities include Collegiate Music Educators National Conference, Kappa Kappa Psi, Tau Beta Sigma.
**Expenses for 2007–2008** Application fee: $30. State resident tuition: $3140 full-time. Nonresident tuition: $11,190 full-time. Mandatory fees: $786 full-time. Full-time tuition and fees vary according to degree level. College room and board: $5581. College room only: $2832. Room and board charges vary according to board plan and housing facility.
**Financial Aid** Program-specific awards: 60 endowed scholarships for talented students ($800–$1500), 5 academic scholarships for those with a minimum 3.75 GPA ($500–$1000).
**Application Procedures** Students apply for admission into the professional program by sophomore year. Deadline for freshmen and transfers: continuous. Required: high school transcript, college transcript(s) for transfer students, SAT or ACT test scores, theory skills evaluation for transfer students. Recommended: audition. Auditions held 4 times on campus; recorded music is permissible as a substitute for live auditions for out-of-state applicants and videotaped performances are permissible as a substitute for live auditions for out-of-state applicants.
**Web Site** http://www.emporia.edu/music
**Undergraduate Contact** Dr. Marie Miller, Chair, Department of Music, Emporia State University, Box 4029, Emporia, Kansas 66801; 620-341-5431, fax: 620-341-5601, e-mail address: mmiller@emporia.edu
**Graduate Contact** Dr. Andrew Houchins, Director, Graduate Studies in Music, Department of Music, Emporia State University, Box 4029, Emporia, Kansas 66801; 620-341-6089, fax: 620-341-5601, e-mail address: ahouchin@emporia.edu

# Fisk University

## Nashville, Tennessee

Independent, coed. Urban campus. Total enrollment: 890 (2006). Music program established 1866.
**Web Site** http://www.fisk.edu/

# Five Towns College

## Dix Hills, New York

Independent, coed. Suburban campus. Total enrollment: 1,151. Music program established 1972.
**Degrees** Bachelor of Music in the areas of jazz/commercial music, music education. Majors and concentrations: audio recording technology, composition/songwriting, music business, music education, performance. Graduate degrees offered: Master of Music in the areas of composition arranging, music history, music performance, audio recording technology. Doctor of Musical Arts in the areas of composition and arranging, music history and literature, music performance, music education. Program accredited by NCATE.
**Enrollment** 266 total; 225 undergraduate, 41 graduate.
**Music Student Profile** 45% females, 55% males, 16% minorities, 1% international.
**Music Faculty** 13 undergraduate (full-time), 29 undergraduate (part-time), 3 graduate (full-time), 4 graduate (part-time). 45% of full-time faculty have terminal degrees. Graduate students do not teach undergraduate courses. Undergraduate student–faculty ratio: 13:1.
**Student Life** Student groups/activities include Music Theatre Production Society, Audio Recording Society, Music Educators National Conference Student Chapter.
**Expenses for 2008–2009** Application fee: $35. Comprehensive fee: $29,875 includes full-time tuition ($17,400), mandatory fees ($725), and college room and board ($11,750). Special program-

related fees: $10 per semester for piano lab fee, $150–$350 per semester for film/video lab, $750 per semester for private music instruction.
**Financial Aid** Program-specific awards: 110 Music Program Awards for musical performers ($1000–$7000).
**Application Procedures** Students admitted directly into the professional program freshman year. Deadline for freshmen and transfers: continuous. Required: essay, high school transcript, college transcript(s) for transfer students, minimum 2.0 high school GPA, 2 letters of recommendation, audition, SAT or ACT test scores (minimum composite ACT score of 19), personal statement. Recommended: minimum 3.0 high school GPA, interview. Auditions held on an individual basis on campus; recorded music is permissible as a substitute for live auditions for international applicants or when distance is prohibitive and videotaped performances are permissible as a substitute for live auditions when distance is prohibitive.
**Web Site** http://www.ftc.edu
**Undergraduate Contact** Jerry Cohen, Dean of Enrollment, Five Towns College, 305 North Service Road, Dix Hills, New York 11746; 631-424-7000 ext. 2110, fax: 631-424-7008.
**Graduate Contact** Dr. Jill Miller-Thorn, Chair of Graduate Program, Music Division, Five Towns College, 305 North Service Road, Dix Hills, New York 11746; 631-424-7000 ext. 2142, fax: 631-656-2172.

### More About the College

Nestled on nearly 40 rolling acres at Dix Hills, Long Island, New York, Five Towns College is a comprehensive institution of higher education with a well-rounded music, media, and performing arts environment. Through its five major divisions—Music, Business, Liberal Arts, Fine Arts, and Childhood Education—the College offers more than thirty different programs of study leading to associate, bachelor's, master's and doctoral degrees.

The College awards a Bachelor of Music degree in jazz/commercial music, with major areas of concentration in performance, composition/songwriting, musical theater, and audio recording technology and music business. These programs are designed for students pursuing careers as professional performers, composers, recording engineers, music business executives, or producers.

The College also offers a Bachelor of Music degree program in music education. The Music Education Program is designed for students interested in a career as a teacher of music in a public or private school and leads to New York State Certification. In addition, the College offers a master's degree program (grades K–12) leading to a Master of Music (M.M.) in jazz/commercial music or music education as well as a Doctor of Musical Arts (D.M.A.).

Five Towns College offers the Bachelor of Fine Arts (B.F.A.) degree program in theater, with major areas of concentration in acting and musical theater. The theater program is designed for students who are interested in a career in the performing arts field as an actor, entertainer, director, stage manager, lighting or sound engineer, or any other related aspect of the entertainment industry.

For students interested in nonperforming careers in the music industry, Five Towns College offers the Bachelor of Professional Studies (B.P.S.) degree program in business management, with major areas of concentration in audio recording technology and music business. A Bachelor of Fine Art degree (B.F.A.) in film/video is also available to those interested in pursuing filmmaking, commercial video production, and television production. These programs are designed for students planning to pursue careers in management, record labels, retail, and marketing with firms in the areas of record and music production, broadcasting, concert promotion, radio, television, theater, and communications. The program is intended for students who are interested in developing their business and technical expertise.

Five Towns College offers the Bachelor of Science (B.S.) degree in elementary teacher education (grades 1–6), with areas of concentration in music and theater or elective offerings in a variety of fields. Students teach in neighboring school districts to gain experience. Upon completion of the program, students are licensed by the State of New York.

A Bachelor of Science (B.S.) in mass communication is offered, with concentrations in broadcasting and journalism, and students are able to broadcast on the college radio station WFTU (AM/FM).

Students who attend Five Towns College benefit from the institution's excellent reputation for preparing students for entry into the entertainment industry. In addition to its highly qualified faculty, the College has facilities that are state-of-the-art. The College is also equipped with a film/video production facility and sound stages of various sizes. The Dix Hills Center for the Performing Arts has been described as "acoustically perfect." The Five Towns College library consists of more than 35,000 print and nonprint materials and has a significant collection of recorded music. The Five Towns College Living/Learning Center is a complex of four residence halls. Students reside in single- and double-occupancy rooms, each equipped with a private bathroom, high-speed Internet access, and satellite TV.

Five Towns College is fully accredited by the Middle States Association and the New York State Board of Regents.

**Program Facilities** Performance spaces include the Dix Hills Center for the Performing Arts (500 seats), the Student Center, and The Upbeat Café. In addition, the College is equipped with 16-, 24-, 48-, and 72-channel state-of-the-art recording studios as well as a MIDI technology laboratory. The College's film/video studios are equipped with both linear and nonlinear digital-editing suites as well as AVID nonlinear editing suites. The College operates WFTU, a 1,000-watt commercial radio station, and Radio Five Towns, a low-power on-campus radio station.

**Faculty, Resident Artists, and Alumni** The many gifted and talented musicians and educators who compose the Five Towns College faculty bring a vast array of backgrounds and experiences to campus. The faculty is exemplary in both their academic and performance credentials. Artists-in-residence include the Township Theatre Group, Wes Belcamp, and Peter Rogine. Representative visiting artists include Don Grusin, the Sea Cliff Chamber Players, the Sound Symphony Orchestra, and the Gilbert & Sullivan Light Opera Theatre Company of Long Island. John Sebastian, Ian McDonald, Steve Howe, Arvell Shaw, J.Geils, Jimmy Vivino, Sal Salvador, Arlen Roth, Tuck and Patti, and Special EFX are just a few of the artists/clinicians who appeared at the College the past few seasons. Alumni work throughout the music industry in numerous capacities, such as musicians, business managers, audio recording engineers, and music educators.

**Student Performance** Students have the opportunity to perform in ensembles of every size and instrumentation. The most popular ensembles include the Concert Choir, Stage Band, Guitar Ensemble, and Percussion Ensemble. Students are invited to participate in any of the major theatrical productions produced on campus each year by the Play Production Workshop and the Light Opera Company. These include musicals, operettas, comedies, dramas, and children's theater productions. The Upbeat Café and the Student Center provide informal venues for students to gather, perform, and collaborate each afternoon.

**Special Programs** The College is a member of the Phi Sigma National Honor Society and hosts a student chapter of the Music Educators National Conference (MENC). Numerous festivals and performances are held each year, including a Stage Band Festival and Music Industry Conference. Past events have included the Classic American Guitar Show, the Long Island Media Arts Show, and the Great American Songbook.

*Dorothy F. Schmidt College of Arts and Letters*
# Florida Atlantic University
**Boca Raton, Florida**

State-supported, coed. Suburban campus. Total enrollment: 26,275. Music program established 1963.

**Degrees** Bachelor of Music in the areas of music performance, music education, jazz studies, music business, commercial music. Majors and concentrations: commercial music, composition, jazz, music business, music technology, piano, stringed instruments, voice, wind and percussion instruments. Graduate degrees offered: Master of Arts in the area of music. Program accredited by NASM.
**Enrollment** 305 total; 250 undergraduate, 35 graduate, 20 nonprofessional degree.
**Music Student Profile** 50% females, 50% males, 10% minorities, 2% international.
**Music Faculty** 19 undergraduate (full-time), 20 undergraduate (part-time), 19 graduate (full-time), 20 graduate (part-time). 75% of full-time faculty have terminal degrees. Graduate students teach a few undergraduate courses. Undergraduate student–faculty ratio: 5:1.
**Student Life** Student groups/activities include Music Teachers National Association, Collegiate Music Educators National Conference, International Association for Jazz Education, American Choral Directors Association, Kappa Kappa Psi.
**Expenses for 2007–2008** Application fee: $30. State resident tuition: $3367 full-time. Nonresident tuition: $16,431 full-time. Full-time tuition varies according to course load. College room and board: $8610. Room and board charges vary according to board plan and housing facility.
**Financial Aid** Program-specific awards: 60 music scholarships for program majors and ensemble participants ($400–$2000).
**Application Procedures** Students admitted directly into the professional program freshman year. Deadline for freshmen: June 1; transfers: July 1. Required: high school transcript, college transcript(s) for transfer students, minimum 2.0 high school GPA, audition, SAT or ACT test scores. Auditions held 4 times on campus; recorded music is permissible as a substitute for live auditions when distance is prohibitive and videotaped performances are permissible as a substitute for live auditions when distance is prohibitive.
**Web Site** http://www.fau.edu
**Undergraduate Contact** Dr. Heather Coltman, Chair, Department of Music, Florida Atlantic University, 777 Glades Road, Boca Raton, Florida 33431; 561-297-3820, fax: 561-297-2944, e-mail address: coltman@fau.edu
**Graduate Contact** Heather Coltman, Graduate Coordinator Associate Professor, Department of Music, Florida Atlantic University, 777 Glades Road, Boca Raton, Florida 33431; 561-297-3820, fax: 561-297-2944, e-mail address: coltman@fau.edu

# Florida State University
**Tallahassee, Florida**

State-supported, coed. Suburban campus. Total enrollment: 40,555. Music program established 1900.
**Degrees** Bachelor of Music in the areas of performance, piano pedagogy, composition, music history/literature, music theory, music theater, music therapy; Bachelor of Music Education in the areas of instrumental music education, choral music education, general music education. Majors and concentrations: classical music, composition, jazz, music, music education, music history and literature, music theater, music theory, music therapy, piano/organ, stringed instruments, voice, wind and percussion instruments. Graduate degrees offered: Master of Arts in the area of arts administration; Master of Music in the areas of performance, accompanying, piano pedagogy, choral conducting, opera, instrumental conducting, jazz, theory, composition, ethnomusicology, historical musicology, music therapy; Master of Music Education in the areas of instrumental music education, choral music education, general music education. Doctor of Music in the areas of composition, performance; Doctor of Education in the area of music education; Doctor of Philosophy in the areas of music education, music theory, ethnomusicology, historical musicology. Program accredited by NASM, NCATE.
**Enrollment** 1,136 total; 516 undergraduate, 406 graduate, 214 nonprofessional degree.
**Music Student Profile** 51% females, 49% males, 22% minorities, 7% international.

*Florida State University (continued)*

**Music Faculty** 90 total (full-time), 7 total (part-time). 80% of full-time faculty have terminal degrees. Graduate students teach about a quarter of undergraduate courses. Undergraduate student–faculty ratio: 8:1.

**Student Life** Student groups/activities include Collegiate Music Educators National Conference, American Choral Directors Association, American String Teachers Association. Special housing available for music students.

**Expenses for 2007–2008** Application fee: $30. State resident tuition: $3355 full-time. Nonresident tuition: $16,487 full-time. Full-time tuition varies according to location. College room and board: $8000. College room only: $4700. Room and board charges vary according to board plan and housing facility. Special program-related fees: $30 per recital for student degree recital (staff and recording), $60 per recital for non-degree recital, $90 per semester for music, instrument, equipment fees.

**Financial Aid** Program-specific awards: 70 out-of-state tuition waivers for program majors ($10,000), 200 general scholarships for program majors ($250–$3000).

**Application Procedures** Students admitted directly into the professional program freshman year. Deadline for freshmen and transfers: December 1. Required: essay, high school transcript, college transcript(s) for transfer students, minimum 3.0 high school GPA, letter of recommendation, audition, SAT or ACT test scores. Auditions held 4 times on campus; recorded music is permissible as a substitute for live auditions when distance is prohibitive.

**Web Site** http://www.music.fsu.edu

**Undergraduate Contact** Dr. Ted Stanley, Program Director for Undergraduate Studies, College of Music, Florida State University, Tallahassee, Florida 32306-1180; 850-644-4833, fax: 850-644-2033, e-mail address: tstanley@fsu.edu

**Graduate Contact** Dr. Seth Beckman, Assistant Dean/Director of Graduate Studies, College of Music, Florida State University, Tallahassee, Florida 32306-1180; 850-644-5848, fax: 850-644-2033, e-mail address: sbeckman@admin.fsu.edu

# Fort Hays State University
### Hays, Kansas

State-supported, coed. Small town campus. Total enrollment: 7,403 (2007). Music program established 1902.

**Degrees** Bachelor of Music in the areas of performance, music education, theory/composition. Majors and concentrations: music education, music theory and composition, piano, stringed instruments, voice, wind and percussion instruments. Program accredited by NASM.

**Enrollment** 82 total; 60 undergraduate, 22 nonprofessional degree.

**Music Student Profile** 50% females, 50% males, 7% minorities, 7% international.

**Music Faculty** 13 undergraduate (full-time), 2 undergraduate (part-time). 70% of full-time faculty have terminal degrees. Graduate students do not teach undergraduate courses. Undergraduate student–faculty ratio: 6:1.

**Student Life** Student groups/activities include Collegiate Music Educators National Conference, Phi Mu Alpha Sinfonia, Sigma Alpha Iota.

**Expenses for 2007–2008** Application fee: $30. State resident tuition: $3355 full-time. Nonresident tuition: $10,543 full-time. Full-time tuition varies according to course load and location. College room and board: $6011. Room and board charges vary according to board plan, housing facility, and student level. Special program-related fees: $20 per semester for instrument usage.

**Financial Aid** Program-specific awards: 20–30 Awards of Excellence in Music for freshmen ($500), 40–60 music scholarships for program students ($800).

**Application Procedures** Students admitted directly into the professional program freshman year. Deadline for freshmen and transfers: February 15. Required: high school transcript, college transcript(s) for transfer students, 2 letters of recommendation, audition, ACT test score only (minimum composite ACT score of 21). Auditions held 3 times on campus; recorded music is permissible as a substitute for live auditions when distance is prohibitive and videotaped performances are permissible as a substitute for live auditions when distance is prohibitive.

**Web Site** http://www.fhsu.edu/music/

**Undergraduate Contact** Tricia Cline, Director, Admissions Department, Fort Hays State University, 600 Park Street, Hays, Kansas 67601; 785-628-5660, e-mail address: tigers@fhsu.edu

# Friends University
### Wichita, Kansas

Independent, coed. Urban campus.
**Web Site** http://www.friends.edu/

# Frost School of Music
See University of Miami

# Furman University
### Greenville, South Carolina

Independent, coed. Suburban campus. Total enrollment: 2,951.

**Degrees** Bachelor of Music in the areas of performance, church music, music education, music theory. Majors and concentrations: church music, music education, music theory, performance, piano/organ, stringed instruments, voice, wind and percussion instruments. Program accredited by NASM.

**Enrollment** 161 total; 119 undergraduate, 42 nonprofessional degree.

**Music Student Profile** 61% females, 39% males, 7% minorities.

**Music Faculty** 19 undergraduate (full-time), 18 undergraduate (part-time). 94% of full-time faculty have terminal degrees. Graduate students do not teach undergraduate courses. Undergraduate student–faculty ratio: 12:1.

**Student Life** Student groups/activities include Phi Mu Alpha, Sigma Alpha Iota.

**Expenses for 2007–2008** Comprehensive fee: $39,624 includes full-time tuition ($31,040), mandatory fees ($520), and college room and board ($8064). College room only: $4256. Room and board charges vary according to board plan and housing facility. Special program-related fees: $50 per term for lab fee for private lessons, $210–$420 per term for private noncredit lessons.

**Financial Aid** Program-specific awards: 16 Daniel Scholarships for program majors ($5000–$10,000), 12 Timmons Scholarships for program majors ($5000–$12,000), 132 general music scholarships for program students ($2000–$12,000), 6 Gunter Scholarships for program majors ($5000–$10,000), 5 Lusby Scholarships for strings students ($5000–$10,000).

**Application Procedures** Students apply for admission into the professional program by sophomore year. Deadline for freshmen and transfers: January 15. Notification date for freshmen: March 15. Required: essay, high school transcript, college transcript(s) for transfer students, SAT or ACT test scores, audition for scholarship consideration, audition for ensembles and/or private lessons. Recommended: 2 letters of recommendation. Auditions held 4 times on campus; recorded music is permissible as a substitute for live auditions when distance is prohibitive and videotaped performances are permissible as a substitute for live auditions when distance is prohibitive.

**Web Site** http://www.furman.edu

**Undergraduate Contact** Mr. Woody O'Cain, Admissions Director, Furman University, Greenville, South Carolina 29613; 864-294-2034, fax: 864-294-3127, e-mail address: woody.o'cain@furman.edu

# Georgetown College
### Georgetown, Kentucky

Independent, coed. Suburban campus. Total enrollment: 1,903. Music program established 1840.

**Degrees** Bachelor of Music in the area of church music; Bachelor of Music Education in the areas of vocal music education,

instrumental music education. Majors and concentrations: church music, music education. Cross-registration with University of Oxford (England).
**Enrollment** 13 total; 7 undergraduate, 6 nonprofessional degree.
**Music Student Profile** 60% females, 40% males, 3% minorities.
**Music Faculty** 6 undergraduate (full-time), 8 undergraduate (part-time). 100% of full-time faculty have terminal degrees. Graduate students do not teach undergraduate courses. Undergraduate student–faculty ratio: 13:1.
**Student Life** Student groups/activities include Music Educators National Conference Student Chapter, Delta Omicron, National Association of Teachers of Singing.
**Expenses for 2007–2008** Application fee: $30. Comprehensive fee: $28,740 includes full-time tuition ($22,360) and college room and board ($6380). College room only: $3080. Room and board charges vary according to board plan and housing facility. Special program-related fees: $130 per semester for piano class, $175–$300 per semester for applied fees.
**Financial Aid** Program-specific awards: 12–15 Music Department Scholarships ($200–$3000), 25–50 college grants in music ($200–$3000).
**Application Procedures** Students admitted directly into the professional program freshman year. Deadline for freshmen and transfers: April 15. Required: essay, high school transcript, college transcript(s) for transfer students, interview, audition, SAT or ACT test scores. Auditions held 5 times and by appointment on campus; recorded music is permissible as a substitute for live auditions when distance is prohibitive and videotaped performances are permissible as a substitute for live auditions when distance is prohibitive.
**Web Site** http://spider.georgetowncollege.edu/music/
**Undergraduate Contact** Dr. Sonny Burnette, Chair, Department of Music, Georgetown College, 400 East College Street, Georgetown, Kentucky 40324-1696; 502-863-8112, e-mail address: sonny_burnette@georgetowncollege.edu

# Georgia College & State University
## Milledgeville, Georgia

State-supported, coed. Small town campus. Total enrollment: 6,249. Music program established 1935.
**Degrees** Bachelor of Arts in the area of music performance; Bachelor of Music Education in the areas of choral music, instrumental music, elementary music; Bachelor of Music Therapy. Majors and concentrations: choral music education, composition, instrumental music education, music, music education, music performance, music therapy. Graduate degrees offered: Master of Music Education in the areas of choral music, instrumental music, elementary music; Master of Music Therapy. Program accredited by NASM, NCATE, AMTA.
**Enrollment** 107 total; 92 undergraduate, 15 graduate.
**Music Student Profile** 64% females, 36% males, 9% minorities, 2% international.
**Music Faculty** 13 undergraduate (full-time), 21 undergraduate (part-time). 100% of full-time faculty have terminal degrees. Graduate students do not teach undergraduate courses. Undergraduate student–faculty ratio: 7:1.
**Student Life** Student groups/activities include Music Educators National Conference Student Chapter, American Choral Directors Association Student Chapter, Phi Mu Alpha/Sigma Alpha Iota.
**Expenses for 2007–2008** Application fee: $40. State resident tuition: $4208 full-time. Nonresident tuition: $16,830 full-time. Mandatory fees: $858 full-time. Full-time tuition and fees vary according to student level. College room and board: $7380. College room only: $3990. Room and board charges vary according to board plan and housing facility. Special program-related fees: $75 per course for student teaching fee, $150 per course for applied music fees.
**Financial Aid** Program-specific awards: 6 Outstanding Student Scholarships for those demonstrating talent and academic achievement ($1000), 4–5 Max Noah Scholarships for music majors ($600), 4–5 Foundation Scholarships for music majors ($400).
**Application Procedures** Students admitted directly into the professional program freshman year. Deadline for freshmen and

transfers: continuous. Required: high school transcript, college transcript(s) for transfer students, letter of recommendation, interview, audition, SAT or ACT test scores, completion of College Preparatory Curriculum (CPC) with no deficiencies, essay. Recommended: minimum 3.0 high school GPA. Auditions held 3 times and by appointment on campus; recorded music is permissible as a substitute for live auditions on a case-by-case basis and videotaped performances are permissible as a substitute for live auditions on a case-by-case basis.
**Web Site** http://www.gcsu.edu/music
**Undergraduate Contact** Dr. Todd Shiver, Director of Bands, Department of Music and Theatre, Georgia College & State University, Box 066, Milledgeville, Georgia 31061; 478-445-4226, fax: 478-445-1633, e-mail address: todd.shiver@gcsu.edu
**Graduate Contact** Dr. Patti Tolbert, Director of Masters in Music Education, Department of Music and Theatre, Georgia College & State University, Box 066, Milledgeville, Georgia 31061; 478-445-4966, e-mail address: patti.tolbert@gcsu.edu

# Georgia Southern University
## Statesboro, Georgia

State-supported, coed. Total enrollment: 16,841. Music program established 1967.
**Web Site** http://www.georgiasouthern.edu/

# Georgia State University
## Atlanta, Georgia

State-supported, coed. Urban campus. Total enrollment: 27,137. Music program established 1958.
**Degrees** Bachelor of Music in the areas of music education, performance, jazz studies, composition, sound recording; Bachelor of Science in the area of music management. Majors and concentrations: composition, jazz studies, music education, music management, performance, sound recording technology. Graduate degrees offered: Master of Music in the areas of music education, performance, composition, jazz studies, music theory, conducting, piano pedagogy, sacred music. Doctor of Philosophy in the area of music education. Cross-registration with Georgia State University System, Emory University. Program accredited by NASM.
**Enrollment** 430 total; 345 undergraduate, 70 graduate, 15 nonprofessional degree.
**Music Student Profile** 50% females, 50% males, 15% minorities, 10% international.
**Music Faculty** 29 undergraduate (full-time), 34 undergraduate (part-time). 64% of full-time faculty have terminal degrees. Graduate students teach a few undergraduate courses. Undergraduate student–faculty ratio: 10:1.
**Student Life** Student groups/activities include Pi Kappa Lambda.
**Expenses for 2008–2009** Application fee: $50. State resident tuition: $4497 full-time. Nonresident tuition: $17,985 full-time. Mandatory fees: $988 full-time. College room and board: $9230. College room only: $6746. Special program-related fees: $10 for locker, $50 per semester for use of recording studios/equipment, $50 per recital for use of hall.
**Financial Aid** Program-specific awards: 2 The Charles Thomas Wurm Music Scholarships for program majors ($1000), 1 The Friends of Rick Bell Jazz Scholarship for jazz majors ($1000), 1 The Haskell Boyter Choral Scholarship for voice majors ($1000), 1 The Thomas M. Brumby Keyboard Scholarship for keyboard majors ($1000), 1 The Friends of Music Scholarship for program majors ($1000), 1 The Montgomery Music Scholarship for program majors ($1000), 1 The National Association for Recording Arts and Sciences Award for music technology majors ($1000), 1 The Presser Foundation Music Scholarship for program majors ($4000), 2 Bill Lowery Awards for music management majors ($1000), 4 Alfredo Barili Awards for strings majors ($1000), 2 Charles and Rosemary Hall Scholarships for music management students ($1000).
**Application Procedures** Students admitted directly into the professional program freshman year. Deadline for freshmen: March 1; transfers: June 1. Required: high school transcript, college transcript(s) for transfer students, minimum 2.0 high school GPA,

*Georgia State University (continued)*

audition, SAT test score only, portfolio review for composition applicants. Recommended: essay, minimum 3.0 high school GPA, 2 letters of recommendation, portfolio. Auditions held 3 times on campus; recorded music is permissible as a substitute for live auditions when distance is prohibitive and videotaped performances are permissible as a substitute for live auditions when distance is prohibitive. Portfolio reviews held 3 times on campus.
**Web Site** http://www.music.gsu.edu
**Contact** Mr. David Smart, Admissions & Enrollment Coordinator, School of Music, Georgia State University, PO Box 4097, Atlanta, Georgia 30302-4097; 404-651-3676, fax: 404-651-3213, e-mail address: smart@gsu.edu

## Gordon College
### Wenham, Massachusetts

Independent nondenominational, coed. Suburban campus. Total enrollment: 1,645.
**Degrees** Bachelor of Music in the areas of music performance, music education. Majors and concentrations: classical music, music, music education, piano/organ, stringed instruments, voice, wind and percussion instruments. Graduate degrees offered: Master of Arts in the area of music education. Cross-registration with Christian College Coalition, Northeast Consortium of Colleges and Universities in Massachusetts. Program accredited by NASM.
**Enrollment** 105 total; 91 undergraduate, 7 graduate, 7 nonprofessional degree.
**Music Faculty** 15 total (full-time), 40 total (part-time). 75% of full-time faculty have terminal degrees. Graduate students do not teach undergraduate courses. Undergraduate student–faculty ratio: 9:1.
**Student Life** Student groups/activities include Music Educators National Conference Student Chapter, American Choral Directors Association Student Chapter.
**Expenses for 2008–2009** Application fee: $50. Comprehensive fee: $34,718 includes full-time tuition ($26,132), mandatory fees ($1162), and college room and board ($7424).
**Financial Aid** Program-specific awards: music grants for program majors ($2000).
**Application Procedures** Students admitted directly into the professional program freshman year. Deadline for freshmen and transfers: continuous. Required: essay, high school transcript, college transcript(s) for transfer students, 2 letters of recommendation, interview, audition, SAT or ACT test scores. Recommended: minimum 2.0 high school GPA. Auditions held 7 times on campus; recorded music is permissible as a substitute for live auditions when distance is prohibitive and videotaped performances are permissible as a substitute for live auditions when distance is prohibitive.
**Web Site** http://www.gordon.edu/music
**Undergraduate Contact** Mr. Keith Groen, Undergraduate Program Coordinator, Department of Music, Gordon College, 255 Grapevine Road, Wenham, Massachusetts 01984; 978-867-4273, fax: 978-867-4655.
**Graduate Contact** Graduate Program Coordinator, Gordon College, Wenham, Massachusetts 01964.

## Grace College
### Winona Lake, Indiana

Independent, coed. Small town campus. Total enrollment: 1,403. Music program established 1948.
**Web Site** http://www.grace.edu/

## Grand Valley State University
### Allendale, Michigan

State-supported, coed. Small town campus. Total enrollment: 23,464. Music program established 1968.
**Web Site** http://www.gvsu.edu/

## The Greatbatch School of Music
See Houghton College

## Grove City College
### Grove City, Pennsylvania

Independent Presbyterian, coed. Small town campus. Total enrollment: 2,504. Music program established 1876.
**Degrees** Bachelor of Music in the areas of music education, music and religion, music and business, music and performing arts. Majors and concentrations: music, music and business, music and performing arts, music and religion, music education.
**Enrollment** 102 total; all undergraduate.
**Music Student Profile** 60% females, 40% males.
**Music Faculty** 7 undergraduate (full-time), 29 undergraduate (part-time). 100% of full-time faculty have terminal degrees. Graduate students do not teach undergraduate courses. Undergraduate student–faculty ratio: 20:1.
**Student Life** Student groups/activities include Music Educators National Conference Student Chapter, Kappa Kappa Psi.
**Expenses for 2007–2008** Application fee: $50. Comprehensive fee: $17,634 includes full-time tuition ($11,500) and college room and board ($6134). Full-time tuition varies according to course load. Room and board charges vary according to housing facility. Special program-related fees: $275 per semester for private lessons; 1/2 hour lesson, $335 per semester for organ; private 1/2 hour lesson, $365 per semester for harp; private 1/2 hour lesson.
**Financial Aid** Program-specific awards: 6 music awards for upperclassmen.
**Application Procedures** Students apply for admission into the professional program by sophomore year. Deadline for freshmen: February 1; transfers: August 1. Notification date for freshmen: March 15. Required: essay, high school transcript, college transcript(s) for transfer students, minimum 3.0 high school GPA, 2 letters of recommendation, interview, audition, SAT or ACT test scores. Recommended: video. Auditions held 5 times and by appointment on campus; recorded music is permissible as a substitute for live auditions when distance is prohibitive and videotaped performances are permissible as a substitute for live auditions when distance is prohibitive.
**Web Site** http://www.gcc.edu
**Undergraduate Contact** Dr. Edwin Arnold, Chair, Department of Music and Fine Arts, Grove City College, 100 Campus Drive, Grove City, Pennsylvania 16127; 724-458-2084, fax: 724-458-2164, e-mail address: eparnold@gcc.edu

## Harding University
### Searcy, Arkansas

Independent, coed. Small town campus. Total enrollment: 6,139. Music program established 1934.
**Degrees** Bachelor of Music Education. Majors and concentrations: instrumental music, vocal music. Program accredited by NASM.
**Enrollment** 55 total; 30 undergraduate, 25 nonprofessional degree.
**Music Student Profile** 60% females, 40% males, 5% minorities, 5% international.
**Music Faculty** 10 undergraduate (full-time), 6 undergraduate (part-time). 60% of full-time faculty have terminal degrees. Graduate students do not teach undergraduate courses. Undergraduate student–faculty ratio: 3:1.
**Student Life** Student groups/activities include Collegiate Music Educators National Conference, American Choral Directors Association, National Association of Teachers of Singing.
**Expenses for 2007–2008** Application fee: $35. Comprehensive fee: $17,938 includes full-time tuition ($11,940), mandatory fees ($420), and college room and board ($5578). College room only: $2810. Full-time tuition and fees vary according to course load. Room and board charges vary according to board plan and housing facility. Special program-related fees: $425 per semester hour for private lessons.
**Financial Aid** Program-specific awards: 55 departmental scholarships for music majors ($1500).

**Application Procedures** Students apply for admission into the professional program by junior year. Deadline for freshmen and transfers: continuous. Required: high school transcript, college transcript(s) for transfer students, interview, audition, SAT or ACT test scores, music fundamentals competency. Recommended: minimum 2.0 high school GPA. Auditions held 3 times on campus; recorded music is permissible as a substitute for live auditions when distance is prohibitive and videotaped performances are permissible as a substitute for live auditions when distance is prohibitive.
**Web Site** http://www.harding.edu/music/
**Undergraduate Contact** Mr. Glenn Dillard, Director of Admissions, Harding University, Box 12255, Searcy, Arkansas 72149-0001; 800-477-4407, fax: 501-279-4865.

# Hardin-Simmons University
## Abilene, Texas

Independent Baptist, coed. Urban campus. Total enrollment: 2,435. Music program established 1926.
**Degrees** Bachelor of Music in the areas of performance, music education, church music, music theory/composition. Majors and concentrations: church music, music business, music education, music performance, music theory and composition. Graduate degrees offered: Master of Music in the areas of performance, music education, music theory/composition, church music. Cross-registration with Abilene Christian University, McMurry University. Program accredited by NASM.
**Enrollment** 98 total; 71 undergraduate, 7 graduate, 20 nonprofessional degree.
**Music Student Profile** 56% females, 44% males, 7% minorities.
**Music Faculty** 18 total (full-time), 7 total (part-time). 71% of full-time faculty have terminal degrees. Graduate students do not teach undergraduate courses. Undergraduate student–faculty ratio: 10:1.
**Student Life** Student groups/activities include Music Educators National Conference Student Chapter, Phi Mu Alpha, Sigma Alpha Iota.
**Expenses for 2008–2009** Application fee: $50. Comprehensive fee: $23,560 includes full-time tuition ($17,400), mandatory fees ($980), and college room and board ($5180). College room only: $2492. Special program-related fees: $15 per semester for music performance facilities fee, $130 per credit hour for private instruction.
**Financial Aid** Program-specific awards: 1 Irl Allison Award for pianists/returning students ($400), 6 Foreman Awards for cowboy band /returning students ($1890), 1 Hamilton Award for vocalists/returning students ($1600), 1 Lacewell Award for church music majors ($2500), 4 Reeves Awards for program majors ($2475), 1 Shaw Award for church music majors ($1400), 1 Presser Award for outstanding music majors ($4200).
**Application Procedures** Students admitted directly into the professional program freshman year. Deadline for freshmen and transfers: continuous. Required: high school transcript, college transcript(s) for transfer students, minimum 2.0 high school GPA, audition, SAT or ACT test scores (minimum composite ACT score of 18), two letters of recommendation for scholarship consideration. Auditions held 4 times on campus; recorded music is permissible as a substitute for live auditions if a campus visit is impossible and videotaped performances are permissible as a substitute for live auditions if a campus visit is impossible.
**Web Site** http://www.hsutx.edu/academics/music/index.html
**Undergraduate Contact** Shane Davidson, Associate Vice President of Enrollment Services, Hardin-Simmons University, Box 16050, Abilene, Texas 79698-6050; 915-670-1207, fax: 915-670-1527.
**Graduate Contact** Dr. Leigh Anne Hunsaker, Program Director, School of Music, Hardin-Simmons University, Box 16230, Abilene, Texas 79698-6230; 915-670-1391, fax: 915-670-5873.

# The Hartt School

See University of Hartford

# Hastings College
## Hastings, Nebraska

Independent Presbyterian, coed. Small town campus. Total enrollment: 1,138. Music program established 1882.
**Web Site** http://www.hastings.edu/

# Heidelberg College
## Tiffin, Ohio

Independent, coed. Small town campus. Total enrollment: 1,584. Music program established 1886.
**Degrees** Bachelor of Music in the areas of composition, performance, music industry, music education. Majors and concentrations: composition, music, music education, music industry, piano/organ, stringed instruments, voice, wind and percussion instruments. Program accredited by NASM.
**Enrollment** 80 total; 65 undergraduate, 15 nonprofessional degree.
**Music Student Profile** 50% females, 50% males, 3% minorities, 1% international.
**Music Faculty** 9 undergraduate (full-time), 15 undergraduate (part-time). 88% of full-time faculty have terminal degrees. Graduate students do not teach undergraduate courses. Undergraduate student–faculty ratio: 6:1.
**Student Life** Student groups/activities include Ohio Collegiate Music Educators National Conference, American Choral Directors Association, Tau Mu Sigma. Special housing available for music students.
**Expenses for 2008–2009** Application fee: $25. Comprehensive fee: $28,060 includes full-time tuition ($19,464), mandatory fees ($458), and college room and board ($8138). College room only: $3852.
**Financial Aid** Program-specific awards: 20–25 music scholarships for program majors ($2000–$3000), 10 endowed music awards for program majors ($500–$1000).
**Application Procedures** Students admitted directly into the professional program freshman year. Deadline for freshmen and transfers: continuous. Required: high school transcript, college transcript(s) for transfer students, minimum 2.0 high school GPA, 2 letters of recommendation, interview, audition, SAT or ACT test scores. Recommended: essay. Auditions held 3 times as needed on campus; recorded music is permissible as a substitute for live auditions when distance is prohibitive and videotaped performances are permissible as a substitute for live auditions when distance is prohibitive.
**Web Site** http://www.heidelberg.edu/
**Undergraduate Contact** Dr. Douglas McConnell, Chair, Department of Music, Heidelberg College, 310 East Market Street, Tiffin, Ohio 44883; 419-448-2073, fax: 419-448-2124, e-mail address: dmcconne@heidelberg.edu

# Henderson State University
## Arkadelphia, Arkansas

State-supported, coed. Small town campus. Total enrollment: 3,603.
**Degrees** Bachelor of Music in the areas of performance (with vocal or instrumental area of study), music education (with vocal or instrumental area of study), composition. Majors and concentrations: composition, music education, performance, strings, voice, wind and percussion instruments. Cross-registration with Ouachita Baptist University. Program accredited by NASM.
**Enrollment** 125 total; 80 undergraduate, 45 nonprofessional degree.
**Music Student Profile** 47% females, 53% males, 1% minorities, 1% international.
**Music Faculty** 13 undergraduate (full-time), 4 undergraduate (part-time). 98% of full-time faculty have terminal degrees. Graduate students do not teach undergraduate courses. Undergraduate student–faculty ratio: 9:1.
**Student Life** Student groups/activities include elementary music workshops, Phi Mu Alpha, Kappa Kappa Psi.

*Henderson State University (continued)*

**Expenses for 2008–2009** Application fee: $0. State resident tuition: $3936 full-time. Nonresident tuition: $7872 full-time. Mandatory fees: $1003 full-time. College room and board: $4860. Special program-related fees: $40–$60 per credit hour for applied music fees.

**Financial Aid** Program-specific awards: 55–100 band scholarships for band members ($800–$2000), 30–50 music scholarships for program majors/non-majors ($1000–$1600).

**Application Procedures** Students admitted directly into the professional program freshman year. Deadline for freshmen and transfers: continuous. Required: high school transcript, college transcript(s) for transfer students, minimum 2.0 high school GPA, SAT or ACT test scores (minimum composite ACT score of 19). Recommended: interview, audition. Auditions held continuously on campus and off campus in various schools in Arkansas; recorded music is permissible as a substitute for live auditions when distance is prohibitive and videotaped performances are permissible as a substitute for live auditions when distance is prohibitive; must have references.

**Web Site** http://www.hsu.edu/music/

**Undergraduate Contact** Mr. Tom Gattin, Registrar, Admissions Office, Henderson State University, Box 7534, Arkadelphia, Arkansas 71999-0001; 870-230-5135, fax: 870-230-5144.

# Holy Names University

## Oakland, California

Independent Roman Catholic, coed, primarily women. Urban campus. Total enrollment: 1,114. Music program established 1880.

**Web Site** http://www.hnu.edu/

## *The Greatbatch School of Music*

# Houghton College

## Houghton, New York

Independent Wesleyan, coed. Rural campus. Total enrollment: 1,382. Music program established 1946.

**Degrees** Bachelor of Music in the areas of applied music, music education, composition. Majors and concentrations: brass, composition, guitar, music education, organ, piano, stringed instruments, voice, wind and percussion instruments. Graduate degrees offered: Master of Music in the areas of collaborative performance, composition, conducting, performance. Program accredited by NASM.

**Enrollment** 120 total; 100 undergraduate, 5 graduate, 15 nonprofessional degree.

**Music Student Profile** 60% females, 40% males, 5% minorities, 5% international.

**Music Faculty** 13 total (full-time), 22 total (part-time). 80% of full-time faculty have terminal degrees. Graduate students do not teach undergraduate courses. Undergraduate student–faculty ratio: 7:1.

**Student Life** Student groups/activities include Pi Kappa Lambda, New York State Music Educators Association, Music Educators National Conference. Special housing available for music students.

**Expenses for 2007–2008** Application fee: $40. Comprehensive fee: $28,480 includes full-time tuition ($21,620) and college room and board ($6860). College room only: $3640. Full-time tuition varies according to class time, program, and reciprocity agreements. Room and board charges vary according to board plan and housing facility. Special program-related fees: $630 per hour for private lessons.

**Financial Aid** Program-specific awards: 20–30 performance grants for program majors ($1000–$8000), 1 Presidential Scholarship for program majors ($15,000).

**Application Procedures** Students admitted directly into the professional program freshman year. Deadline for freshmen and transfers: continuous. Required: essay, high school transcript, college transcript(s) for transfer students, minimum 2.0 high school GPA, 2 letters of recommendation, audition, SAT or ACT

test scores. Recommended: minimum 3.0 high school GPA, interview. Auditions held 7 times on campus; recorded music is permissible as a substitute for live auditions when distance is prohibitive and videotaped performances are permissible as a substitute for live auditions when distance is prohibitive.

**Web Site** http://campus.houghton.edu/orgs/music/

**Undergraduate Contact** Connie Van Slyke, Administrative Assistant, The Greatbatch School of Music, Houghton College, 1 Willard Avenue, Houghton, New York 14744; 585-567-9400, fax: 585-567-9517, e-mail address: music@houghton.edu

**Graduate Contact** Mindy Airhart, Graduate Communications Assistant, The Greatbatch School of Music, Houghton College, 1 Willard Avenue, Houghton, New York 14744; 585-567-9400, fax: 585-567-9517, e-mail address: music@houghton.edu

# Howard Payne University

## Brownwood, Texas

Independent, coed. Small town campus. Total enrollment: 1,385. Music program established 1900.

**Degrees** Bachelor of Music in the areas of piano, organ, voice, instrumental music, piano pedagogy and accompanying, church music, choral music education, instrumental music education. Majors and concentrations: accompanying, choral music education, church music, instrumental music education, piano pedagogy, piano/organ, voice, wind and percussion instruments. Program accredited by NASM.

**Enrollment** 61 total; all undergraduate.

**Music Student Profile** 50% females, 50% males, 3% minorities, 4% international.

**Music Faculty** 9 undergraduate (full-time), 3 undergraduate (part-time). 60% of full-time faculty have terminal degrees. Graduate students do not teach undergraduate courses. Undergraduate student–faculty ratio: 5:1.

**Student Life** Student groups/activities include Music Educators National Conference, American Choral Directors Association, Southern Baptist Church Music Conference, Texas Music Educators Association.

**Expenses for 2008–2009** Application fee: $25. Comprehensive fee: $21,860 includes full-time tuition ($16,350), mandatory fees ($1050), and college room and board ($4460). College room only: $1980. Special program-related fees: $100 per course for applied music fees, $100 per course for piano accompanying fees, $330 per semester for computer lab use.

**Financial Aid** Program-specific awards: 1 Turner Music Award for program majors ($1000), 1 Presser Award for program majors ($4000), 1 Schubert Music Award for program majors ($150), 100 music scholarships for program majors/minors ($400–$2000).

**Application Procedures** Students admitted directly into the professional program freshman year. Deadline for freshmen and transfers: continuous. Required: high school transcript, college transcript(s) for transfer students, interview, audition, SAT or ACT test scores (minimum composite ACT score of 19). Recommended: minimum 3.0 high school GPA, letter of recommendation. Auditions held 4 times at student's convenience on campus; recorded music is permissible as a substitute for live auditions if a campus visit is impossible and videotaped performances are permissible as a substitute for live auditions if a campus visit is impossible.

**Web Site** http://www.hputx.edu/music

**Undergraduate Contact** Ms. Cheryl Mangrum, Director, Enrollment Services, Howard Payne University, 1000 Fisk Street, HPU Station 828, Brownwood, Texas 76801-2794; 915-649-8020, fax: 915-649-8901, e-mail address: cmangrum@hputx.edu

# Howard University

## Washington, District of Columbia

Independent, coed. Urban campus. Music program established 1902.

**Web Site** http://www.howard.edu/

# Hugh A. Glauser School of Music

See Kent State University

## Hugh Hodgson School of Music
See University of Georgia

## Hunter College of the City University of New York
**New York, New York**

State and locally supported, coed. Urban campus. Total enrollment: 20,845. Music program established 1975.
**Web Site** http://www.hunter.cuny.edu/

## Huntington University
**Huntington, Indiana**

Independent, coed. Small town campus. Total enrollment: 1,152. Music program established 1897.
**Degrees** Bachelor of Music in the areas of music performance, music education. Majors and concentrations: church music, music, music business, music education. Program accredited by NASM.
**Enrollment** 23 total; 16 undergraduate, 7 nonprofessional degree.
**Music Student Profile** 70% females, 30% males.
**Music Faculty** 4 undergraduate (full-time), 19 undergraduate (part-time). 75% of full-time faculty have terminal degrees. Graduate students do not teach undergraduate courses. Undergraduate student–faculty ratio: 4:1.
**Expenses for 2007–2008** Application fee: $20. Comprehensive fee: $26,160 includes full-time tuition ($18,980), mandatory fees ($450), and college room and board ($6730). College room only: $3130. Room and board charges vary according to board plan. Special program-related fees: $265 per half-hour lesson for private instruction and practice room fee.
**Financial Aid** Program-specific awards: 19 performance grants for program majors/minors ($1426).
**Application Procedures** Students admitted directly into the professional program freshman year. Deadline for freshmen and transfers: continuous. Required: high school transcript, college transcript(s) for transfer students, minimum 2.0 high school GPA, audition, SAT or ACT test scores. Auditions held as needed on campus.
**Web Site** http://www.huntington.edu
**Undergraduate Contact** Mr. Jeffrey Berggren, Executive Director of Enrollment Management, Admissions Department, Huntington University, 2303 College Avenue, Huntington, Indiana 46750; 260-356-6000, fax: 260-356-9448.

## Hurley School of Music
See Centenary College of Louisiana

## Idaho State University
**Pocatello, Idaho**

State-supported, coed. Small town campus. Total enrollment: 13,208. Music program established 1940.
**Degrees** Bachelor of Music in the area of performance; Bachelor of Music Education. Majors and concentrations: guitar, music, music education, organ, piano, stringed instruments, voice, wind and percussion instruments. Graduate degrees offered: Master of Education in the area of music education. Program accredited by NASM.
**Enrollment** 85 total; 67 undergraduate, 5 graduate, 13 nonprofessional degree.
**Music Student Profile** 60% females, 40% males, 2% minorities.
**Music Faculty** 12 total (full-time), 11 total (part-time). 67% of full-time faculty have terminal degrees. Graduate students do not teach undergraduate courses. Undergraduate student–faculty ratio: 6:1.
**Student Life** Student groups/activities include Music Educators National Conference Student Chapter, American Choral Directors Association Student Chapter.

**Expenses for 2007–2008** Application fee: $40. State resident tuition: $2882 full-time. Nonresident tuition: $11,566 full-time. Mandatory fees: $1518 full-time. Full-time tuition and fees vary according to program and reciprocity agreements. College room and board: $4950. College room only: $2250. Room and board charges vary according to board plan and housing facility. Special program-related fees: $160–$320 per lesson for applied music fee.
**Financial Aid** Program-specific awards: 80 ensemble scholarships for program majors/minors ($350–$1000), 2 Missal Band Scholarships for band majors ($1000), 7 Berryman Endowment Awards for program majors ($500–$600), 6 Phoenix Endowment Awards for program majors ($500–$600), 11 Department of Music Endowment Awards for program majors ($350–$500), 1 Anderson Vocal Scholarship for vocal majors ($1000–$1200), 75 marching band scholarships for instrumentalists ($500–$800), 20 Grayson Endowment Awards for vocal majors ($500–$1000), 1 Kwiat Endowment Award for piano majors ($350).
**Application Procedures** Students apply for admission into the professional program by sophomore year. Deadline for freshmen: August 1; transfers: continuous. Notification date for freshmen and transfers: continuous. Required: high school transcript, college transcript(s) for transfer students, minimum 2.0 high school GPA, letter of recommendation, interview, audition, placement examinations in piano and theory, SAT or ACT (ACT preferred). Recommended: essay, minimum 3.0 high school GPA. Auditions held 3-4 times on campus and off campus in various Idaho locations; recorded music is permissible as a substitute for live auditions when distance is prohibitive and videotaped performances are permissible as a substitute for live auditions when distance is prohibitive.
**Web Site** http://www.isu.edu/music
**Contact** Dr. Randy A. Earles, Chairman, Department of Music, Idaho State University, Box 8099, Pocatello, Idaho 83209-8099; 208-282-3636, fax: 208-282-4884, e-mail address: earlrand@isu.edu

## Illinois State University
**Normal, Illinois**

State-supported, coed. Urban campus. Total enrollment: 20,274. Music program established 1913.
**Degrees** Bachelor of Arts in the area of musical theatre; Bachelor of Music in the areas of performance, music therapy, music composition; Bachelor of Music Education; Bachelor of Science in the area of music business. Majors and concentrations: classical guitar, classical music, composition, music, music business, music education, music theater, music therapy, piano/organ, stringed instruments, voice, wind and percussion instruments. Graduate degrees offered: Master of Music in the areas of performance, music composition, music therapy; Master of Music Education; Master of Science. Program accredited by NASM.
**Enrollment** 331 total; 266 undergraduate, 65 graduate.
**Music Student Profile** 57% females, 43% males, 12% minorities, 6% international.
**Music Faculty** 43 total (full-time). 65% of full-time faculty have terminal degrees. Graduate students teach a few undergraduate courses. Undergraduate student–faculty ratio: 6:1.
**Student Life** Student groups/activities include National Association of Music Therapy, Music Educators National Conference, Tau Beta Sigma. Special housing available for music students.
**Expenses for 2007–2008** Application fee: $40. State resident tuition: $6990 full-time. Nonresident tuition: $14,310 full-time. Mandatory fees: $2029 full-time. Full-time tuition and fees vary according to course load. College room and board: $6848. College room only: $3560. Room and board charges vary according to board plan, housing facility, and location. Special program-related fees: $10 per semester for locker rental, $15 per degree for practice room usage.
**Financial Aid** Program-specific awards: 16 tuition waivers for program majors and minors ($300–$3700), 20 talent grants-in-aid for program majors and minors ($200–$2600), 20 endowed scholarships for enrolled music majors.
**Application Procedures** Students admitted directly into the professional program freshman year. Deadline for freshmen and transfers: March 1. Notification date for freshmen and transfers:

*Illinois State University (continued)*

April 15. Required: essay, high school transcript, college transcript(s) for transfer students, minimum 2.0 high school GPA, audition, SAT or ACT test scores. Recommended: 3 letters of recommendation. Auditions held 6 times on campus; recorded music is permissible as a substitute for live auditions for out-of-state applicants and videotaped performances are permissible as a substitute for live auditions for out-of-state applicants.
**Web Site** http://www.music.ilstu.edu
**Undergraduate Contact** Mrs. Janet Tulley, Assistant to the Director, School of Music, Illinois State University, Campus Box 5660, Normal, Illinois 61790-5660; 309-438-3566, fax: 309-438-5833, e-mail address: jatulle@ilstu.edu
**Graduate Contact** Dr. Angelo Favis, Graduate Music Admissions Director, School of Music, Illinois State University, Campus Box 5660, Normal, Illinois 61790-5660; 309-438-8960, fax: 309-438-5833, e-mail address: alfavis@ilstu.edu

# Illinois Wesleyan University
## Bloomington, Illinois

Independent, coed. Suburban campus. Total enrollment: 2,094. Music program established 1897.
**Degrees** Bachelor of Music in the areas of performance, composition; Bachelor of Music Education in the areas of vocal music education, instrumental music education. Majors and concentrations: brass instruments performance, classical music, composition, music, music education, piano, stringed instruments, voice, wind and percussion instruments. Program accredited by NASM.
**Enrollment** 200 total; 160 undergraduate, 40 nonprofessional degree.
**Music Student Profile** 56% females, 44% males, 7% minorities, 3% international.
**Music Faculty** 18 undergraduate (full-time), 31 undergraduate (part-time). 100% of full-time faculty have terminal degrees. Graduate students do not teach undergraduate courses. Undergraduate student–faculty ratio: 11:1.
**Student Life** Student groups/activities include Music Educators National Conference Student Chapter, Phi Mu Alpha/Delta Omicron, Sigma Alpha Iota. Special housing available for music students.
**Expenses for 2007–2008** Application fee: $0. Comprehensive fee: $37,780 includes full-time tuition ($30,580), mandatory fees ($170), and college room and board ($7030). College room only: $4330. Room and board charges vary according to board plan and housing facility. Special program-related fees: $315 per semester for private music lessons beyond curricular requirements.
**Financial Aid** Program-specific awards: 16–40 Music Talent Awards for program students ($6500–$28,986).
**Application Procedures** Students admitted directly into the professional program freshman year. Deadline for freshmen: March 1; transfers: April 1. Notification date for freshmen: April 1; transfers: May 1. Required: essay, high school transcript, college transcript(s) for transfer students, minimum 3.0 high school GPA, interview, audition, SAT or ACT test scores (minimum composite ACT score of 23), portfolio for composition majors. Recommended: 2 letters of recommendation. Auditions held 6 times and by appointment on campus; recorded music is permissible as a substitute for live auditions when distance is prohibitive and videotaped performances are permissible as a substitute for live auditions when distance is prohibitive. Portfolio reviews held 6 times and by appointment on campus.
**Web Site** http://www.iwu.edu
**Undergraduate Contact** Ms. Laura Dolan, Music Admissions Coordinator, School of Music, Illinois Wesleyan University, PO Box 2900, Bloomington, Illinois 61702; 309-556-3063, fax: 309-556-3411, e-mail address: ldolan@iwu.edu

# Immaculata University
## Immaculata, Pennsylvania

Independent Roman Catholic, coed, primarily women. Suburban campus. Total enrollment: 4,038. Music program established 1921.

**Degrees** Bachelor of Music in the areas of music education, music therapy. Majors and concentrations: music education, music therapy. Graduate degrees offered: Master of Arts in the area of music therapy. Program accredited by NASM, AMTA.
**Enrollment** 100 total; 60 undergraduate, 21 graduate, 19 nonprofessional degree.
**Music Student Profile** 81% females, 19% males, 9% minorities, 2% international.
**Music Faculty** 6 undergraduate (full-time), 25 undergraduate (part-time), 2 graduate (full-time). 80% of full-time faculty have terminal degrees. Graduate students do not teach undergraduate courses. Undergraduate student–faculty ratio: 8:1.
**Student Life** Student groups/activities include Men's Glee Club, various musical ensembles, Music Educators National Conference Student Chapter, American Music Therapy Association Student Chapter, Annual Institute for Music and Healing, chorale, symphony, madrigals.
**Expenses for 2007–2008** Application fee: $35. Comprehensive fee: $32,450 includes full-time tuition ($22,650) and college room and board ($9800). College room only: $5260. Full-time tuition varies according to student level. Room and board charges vary according to housing facility. Special program-related fees: $320–$610 per course for private applied music lessons.
**Financial Aid** Program-specific awards: 1 Cheryl Thatcher Award for music therapy students ($1000), 36 music scholarships for music majors ($36,000), 1 Borelli Award for program juniors or seniors ($1000), 1 Almira Doutt Award for program juniors or seniors ($1000).
**Application Procedures** Students admitted directly into the professional program freshman year. Deadline for freshmen and transfers: continuous. Required: high school transcript, college transcript(s) for transfer students, minimum 2.0 high school GPA, letter of recommendation, audition, SAT or ACT test scores (minimum combined SAT score of 1000). Recommended: essay, interview, video. Auditions held 8 times on campus; recorded music is permissible as a substitute for live auditions if a campus visit is impossible and videotaped performances are permissible as a substitute for live auditions if a campus visit is impossible.
**Web Site** http://www.immaculata.edu
**Undergraduate Contact** Ms. Becky Bowlby, Director of Admission, Immaculata University, 1145 King Road, Immaculata, Pennsylvania 19345; 610-647-4400 ext. 3046, fax: 610-251-1668, e-mail address: rbowlby@immaculata.edu
**Graduate Contact** Dr. Brian Abrams, Chair, Graduate Music Therapy Program, Music Therapy Department, Immaculata University, PO Box 697, Immaculata, Pennsylvania 19345-0697; 610-647-4400 ext. 3490, fax: 610-251-1668, e-mail address: babrams@immaculata.edu

# Indiana State University
## Terre Haute, Indiana

State-supported, coed. Small town campus. Total enrollment: 10,543.
**Web Site** http://web.indstate.edu/

*Jacobs School of Music*
# Indiana University Bloomington
## Bloomington, Indiana

State-supported, coed. Small town campus. Total enrollment: 38,990. Music program established 1910.
**Degrees** Bachelor of Music in the areas of performance, composition, early music, jazz studies; Bachelor of Music Education in the areas of choral-general teaching, instrumental teaching, choral and instrumental teaching area; Bachelor of Science in the areas of audio recording, music and an outside field. Majors and concentrations: audio recording technology, bassoon, cello, choral music education, clarinet, classical guitar, composition, double bass, early music, euphonium, flute, harp, horn, instrumental music education, jazz studies, oboe, organ, percussion, performance, piano, saxophone, trombone, trumpet, tuba, viola, violin, voice. Graduate degrees offered: Master of Arts in the area of musicology; Master of Music in the areas of

choral conducting, composition, early music, instrumental conducting, jazz studies, music theory, organ and church music, wind conducting, performance, computer music composition; Master of Music Education; Master of Science in the areas of music theater scenic techniques, stage direction for opera, music education. Doctor of Music in the areas of choral conducting, composition, early music, instrumental conducting, organ and church music, wind conducting, performance, brass pedagogy; Doctor of Music Education; Doctor of Philosophy in the areas of music theory, musicology, music education. Program accredited by NASM.

**Enrollment** 1,633 total; 801 undergraduate, 818 graduate, 14 nonprofessional degree.

**Music Student Profile** 51% females, 49% males, 10% minorities, 20% international.

**Music Faculty** 170 total (full-time), 23 total (part-time). Graduate students teach about a quarter of undergraduate courses. Undergraduate student–faculty ratio: 18:1.

**Student Life** Student groups/activities include opera theater, choral ensembles, singing Hoosiers, instrumental ensembles (orchestra, band, jazz, chamber groups).

**Expenses for 2007–2008** Application fee: $50. State resident tuition: $7000 full-time. Nonresident tuition: $21,479 full-time. Mandatory fees: $837 full-time. Full-time tuition and fees vary according to location and program. College room and board: $6676. College room only: $4172. Room and board charges vary according to board plan and housing facility. Special program-related fees: $10 per semester for locker rental, $35 per recital for recital recording, $35 per program for recital program printing, $50 per course for electronic course, $150 per course for ballet therapy, $800 per semester for applied music fee.

**Financial Aid** Program-specific awards: School of Music Dean's Award for those demonstrating musical ability and scholastic achievement, minority scholarships for minority students demonstrating musical ability, scholastic achievement, and financial need, University Grants for those demonstrating musical ability, scholastic achievement, and financial need.

**Application Procedures** Students admitted directly into the professional program freshman year. Deadline for freshmen and transfers: December 1. Notification date for freshmen and transfers: May 1. Required: essay, high school transcript, college transcript(s) for transfer students, minimum 2.0 high school GPA, interview, video, audition, portfolio, SAT or ACT test scores. Recommended: minimum 3.0 high school GPA. Auditions held 3 times on campus; recorded music is permissible as a substitute for live auditions and videotaped performances are permissible as a substitute for live auditions. Portfolio reviews held 3 times on campus.

**Web Site** http://www.music.indiana.edu

**Contact** Music Admissions, Jacobs School of Music, Indiana University Bloomington, 1201 East 3rd Street- MU 101, Bloomington, Indiana 47405; 812-855-7998, fax: 812-856-6086, e-mail address: musicadm@indiana.edu

# Indiana University–Purdue University Fort Wayne

**Fort Wayne, Indiana**

State-supported, coed. Urban campus. Total enrollment: 11,943. Music program established 1967.

**Web Site** http://www.ipfw.edu/

# Indiana University South Bend

**South Bend, Indiana**

State-supported, coed. Suburban campus. Total enrollment: 7,517. Music program established 1965.

**Web Site** http://www.iusb.edu/

# Iowa State University of Science and Technology

**Ames, Iowa**

State-supported, coed. Suburban campus. Total enrollment: 26,160. Music program established 1967.

**Web Site** http://www.iastate.edu/

# Iowa Wesleyan College

**Mount Pleasant, Iowa**

Independent United Methodist, coed. Small town campus. Total enrollment: 833.

**Degrees** Bachelor of Music Education. Majors and concentrations: music education. Cross-registration with Southeastern Community College.

**Enrollment** 12 total; 11 undergraduate, 1 nonprofessional degree.

**Music Student Profile** 55% females, 45% males, 18% minorities, 18% international.

**Music Faculty** 4 undergraduate (full-time), 6 undergraduate (part-time). 100% of full-time faculty have terminal degrees. Graduate students do not teach undergraduate courses. Undergraduate student–faculty ratio: 3:1.

**Student Life** Student groups/activities include Music Educators National Conference Student Chapter, American Choral Directors Association Student Chapter.

**Expenses for 2007–2008** Application fee: $0. Comprehensive fee: $24,750 includes full-time tuition ($18,870) and college room and board ($5880). College room only: $2430.

**Financial Aid** Program-specific awards: 5–8 Goodell Music Scholarships for incoming students ($3000–$6000).

**Application Procedures** Students apply for admission into the professional program by sophomore year. Deadline for freshmen and transfers: continuous. Required: essay, high school transcript, college transcript(s) for transfer students, minimum 2.0 high school GPA, letter of recommendation, audition, SAT or ACT test scores (minimum combined SAT score of 900, minimum composite ACT score of 19), audition for scholarship consideration. Recommended: interview. Auditions held by appointment on campus; recorded music is permissible as a substitute for live auditions when distance is prohibitive (beyond 200-mile radius) and videotaped performances are permissible as a substitute for live auditions when distance is prohibitive.

**Web Site** http://www.iwc.edu

**Undergraduate Contact** Mr. Mark Petty, Director, Admissions Department, Iowa Wesleyan College, 601 North Main Street, Mount Pleasant, Iowa 52641; 319-385-6231, fax: 319-385-6296, e-mail address: admit@iwc.edu

# Ithaca College

**Ithaca, New York**

Independent, coed. Small town campus. Total enrollment: 6,660. Music program established 1892.

**Degrees** Bachelor of Music in the areas of composition, jazz studies, music education, performance, performance/music education, music theory, music in combination with an outside field, recording. Majors and concentrations: brass, guitar, jazz, jazz studies, music education, music theory, performance, piano/organ, recording arts and sciences, stringed instruments, voice, wind and percussion instruments. Graduate degrees offered: Master of Music in the areas of brasses, composition, conducting, music education, performance, strings, Suzuki pedagogy, woodwinds. Cross-registration with Cornell University, Wells College. Program accredited by NASM.

**Enrollment** 532 total; 466 undergraduate, 47 graduate, 19 nonprofessional degree.

**Music Student Profile** 53% females, 47% males, 9% minorities, 1% international.

**Music Faculty** 63 undergraduate (full-time), 31 undergraduate (part-time). 98% of full-time faculty have terminal degrees. Graduate students teach a few undergraduate courses. Undergraduate student–faculty ratio: 7:1.

*Ithaca College (continued)*

**Student Life** Student groups/activities include American Choral Directors Association, Music Educators National Conference, American String Teachers Association.

**Expenses for 2007–2008** Application fee: $60. Comprehensive fee: $39,398 includes full-time tuition ($28,670) and college room and board ($10,728). College room only: $5604.

**Financial Aid** Program-specific awards: 1 Reginald Allen Scholarship for voice major with a GPA of 3.0 or greater (preference for ALANA students) ($2000), 1 Ronald Baston Scholarship for voice major ($1080), 2 Les Brown Scholarships for outstanding junior instramentalists ($1837), 1 Margery Dubois Scholarship for program major ($1255), 1 Charles Hockett Music Scholarship for composition major ($1045), 1 Herbert C. Mueller Memorial Scholarship for trumpet major ($572), 9 Clinton B. Ford Music Scholars for talented stringed instrumentalists ($1000–$2840), 16 Ithaca Premier Talent Scholarships for program majors ($10,000–$16,000), 13 Leo A. & Frances MacArthur Keilocker Scholars for talented stringed instrumentalists ($1500–$4000), 17 Col. George S. Howard '25 Scholarships for talented wind instrumentalists ($1686), 10 Iola Angood Taylor Scholarships for students from public school music programs ($1684), 8 Robert S. Boothroyd Scholarships for outstanding music students ($1925), 4 Allan H. Treman Music Scholarships for outstanding music students ($1325), 1 Gretchen Haller/Haenchen Music Scholarship for those demonstrating financial need (vocal performance preference) ($536), 4 James J. Whalen Young Artists for freshmen music majors ($12,170–$15,670).

**Application Procedures** Students admitted directly into the professional program freshman year. Deadline for freshmen: February 1; transfers: March 1. Notification date for freshmen: April 15. Required: essay, high school transcript, college transcript(s) for transfer students, letter of recommendation, audition, SAT or ACT test scores, two original music scores for composition applicants. Recommended: minimum 3.0 high school GPA, interview. Auditions held 12 times on campus and off campus in New York, NY; Washington, DC; Philadelphia, PA; Boston, MA; recorded music is permissible as a substitute for live auditions when distance is prohibitive or scheduling is difficult and videotaped performances are permissible as a substitute for live auditions when distance is prohibitive or scheduling is difficult (video preferred).

**Web Site** http://www.ithaca.edu/music

**Undergraduate Contact** Mr. Gerard Turbide, Director, Admission, Ithaca College, 100 Job Hall, Ithaca, New York 14850-7020; 607-274-3124, fax: 607-274-1900, e-mail address: admission@ithaca.edu

**Graduate Contact** Dean of Graduate and Professional Studies, Ithaca College, 111 Towers Concourse, Ithaca, New York 14850-7142; 607-274-3527, fax: 607-274-1263, e-mail address: gps@ithaca.edu

### More About the College

Since its founding in 1892 as a conservatory of music, Ithaca College has been nurturing and developing its musical character. The College remains dedicated to the goals of its founder, W. Grant Egbert, who said, "It is my plan to build a school of music second to none in the excellence of its faculty, the soundness of its educational ideals, and the superior quality of instruction."

As the conservatory evolved into a college with expanded academic offerings, the programs in music retained their position of prominence. Today, Ithaca's School of Music is counted among the nation's leading schools devoted primarily to undergraduate study. Students benefit from a blend of first-class faculty members, innovative programs, and outstanding facilities.

Students in the School of Music take about one quarter of their academic work in the liberal arts, primarily through the School of Humanities and Sciences. Additional electives from the Schools of Business, Communications, and Health Sciences and Human Performance and the Division of Interdisciplinary and International Studies are also available. The interaction between these schools and the division is another advantage to an Ithaca education: physics majors can be found working in the electroacoustic music studios, television-radio majors may take

courses such as Music and the Media, and music students play in the pit orchestra for theater productions and perform on sound tracks for student filmmakers. The planned studies option allows students to create their own degree programs that take advantage of the broad array of courses and majors—some 2,000 courses and more than 100 degree programs are offered.

Students who come to the Ithaca College School of Music are already dedicated to the idea of mastering voice, piano, guitar, organ, or any of the standard orchestral and band instruments. At Ithaca they continue their training under a faculty of performing professionals who are dedicated to teaching undergraduates. Students prepare for their musical performances through weekly private lessons and hour-long repertory classes with their major teachers and fellow students. Repertory classes provide opportunities for students to perform for each other, review performance techniques, and meet guest artists such as Vladimir Felstman, Midori, Emanuel Ax, Richard Stoltzman, Christian Tetzlaff, and the Guarneri String Quartet. As soloists and with ensembles, students become part of the rich musical life of the school, where more than 300 recitals, concerts, musicals, and operas are given each year.

All degree programs emphasize performance. Each year, some 500 undergraduate and 40 graduate students are involved in live performances—on campus, in the Ithaca community, throughout the northeastern United States, and at national and international concert venues. In addition, several ensembles tour annually and have won critical acclaim for their work in New York City at Lincoln Center, St. Patrick's Cathedral, and Carnegie Hall; throughout New England; in Washington, D.C., and other cities; and in international venues such as London's Royal Academy of Music and the University of Limerick in Ireland.

The city of Ithaca is one of the country's premier college towns, with about 26,000 students at Ithaca College and Cornell University. Surrounded by magnificent gorges, lakes, and countryside in the Finger Lakes region of New York State, Ithaca is a thriving cultural center. The community supports an impressive array of concerts, art galleries, movies, and theater productions. Among the artists who have performed in town recently are Ladysmith Black Mambazo, Itzhak Perlman, Arlo Guthrie, Branford Marsalis, Yo-Yo Ma, and Janos Starker.

Ithaca College's combination of a resident faculty, an emphasis on undergraduate performance, and access to a wide spectrum of liberal arts courses makes it an excellent choice among the major music schools in the nation.

**Program Facilities** Performance spaces include Ford Hall Auditorium (735 seats), the Hockett Family Recital Hall (250 seats), and Nabenhauer Recital Hall (150 seats). Electroacoustic music studios, computer-assisted instruction facilities, a professionally equipped recording studio, and a full complement of practice instruments are available. Some ninety practice rooms are open to students, and there are forty Steinway grand pianos included in the 167 pianos at the school. The library has extensive holdings of music and recordings. A 69,000-square-foot music building addition has nearly doubled the existing space and includes increased rehearsal space, a computer classroom and lab, and a music education resource center.

**Faculty, Resident Artists, and Alumni** Faculty members perform nationally and regionally; many are scholars in the fields of music education, theory, composition, and history. Resident faculty ensembles include the Ithaca Brass, Ithaca Wind Quintet, and Ariadne String Quartet. Alumni hold positions in major orchestras and opera companies, perform in many prestigious chamber ensembles, sing on Broadway, and are recognized jazz recording artists. They also hold teaching positions in secondary schools and universities and are successful in arts administration, music publishing, audio technology, and music business.

**Student Performance Opportunities** Every student is required to perform in a major ensemble each semester; many participate in more than one. There are more than twenty student ensembles, including symphony orchestra, chamber orchestra, wind ensemble, concert band, symphonic band, brass choir, percussion ensemble, guitar ensemble, choir, chorus, women's chorale, madrigal singers, vocal jazz ensemble, opera workshop, and jazz workshop, as well as other numerous chamber ensembles.

**Special Programs** Students may study abroad at the Ithaca College London Center or in one of about fifty affiliated programs worldwide. The Office of Career Services offers special assistance geared to music students, and alumni also actively serve as career opportunity resources.

# Jackson State University

## Jackson, Mississippi

State-supported, coed. Urban campus. Total enrollment: 8,698.
**Degrees** Bachelor of Music in the areas of piano performance, vocal and instrumental performance, church music, music technology; Bachelor of Music Education in the areas of instrumental music education, vocal music education, piano music education, jazz music education. Majors and concentrations: church music, jazz, music education, music technology, piano, stringed instruments, voice, wind and percussion instruments. Graduate degrees offered: Master of Music in the areas of performance, church music; Master of Music Education. Program accredited by NASM.
**Enrollment** 137 total; 125 undergraduate, 12 graduate.
**Music Student Profile** 45% females, 55% males, 3% international.
**Music Faculty** 7 graduate (full-time), 3 total (part-time). 55% of full-time faculty have terminal degrees. Graduate students do not teach undergraduate courses. Undergraduate student–faculty ratio: 5:1.
**Student Life** Student groups/activities include Music Educators National Conference, Music Teachers National Association, Tau Beta Sigma, Phi Mu Alpha Sinfonia.
**Expenses for 2007–2008** Application fee: $0. State resident tuition: $4432 full-time. Nonresident tuition: $9974 full-time. College room and board: $5600. College room only: $3400. Room and board charges vary according to board plan.
**Financial Aid** Program-specific awards: 250 music scholarships for talented program majors ($1000).
**Application Procedures** Students admitted directly into the professional program freshman year. Deadline for freshmen and transfers: July 1. Required: high school transcript, audition, SAT or ACT test scores (minimum composite ACT score of 16), minimum 2.5 high school GPA. Recommended: 3 letters of recommendation, video, portfolio. Auditions held 3 times on campus and off campus in St. Louis, MO; Chicago, IL; Detroit, MI; Atlanta, GA; Hattiesburg, MS; Clarksdale, MS; Memphis, TN; recorded music is permissible as a substitute for live auditions when distance is prohibitive and videotaped performances are permissible as a substitute for live auditions when distance is prohibitive.
**Web Site** http://www.jsums.edu
**Undergraduate Contact** Dr. Jimmie James Jr., Chair, Department of Music, Jackson State University, PO Box 17055, Jackson, Mississippi 39217; 601-979-2141, fax: 601-979-2568, e-mail address: jimmie.james@jsums.edu
**Graduate Contact** Dr. Johnny Anthony, Associate Professor, Department of Music, Jackson State University, PO Box 17055, Jackson, Mississippi 39217; 601-979-2141, fax: 601-979-2568, e-mail address: johnny.anthony@jsums.edu

# Jacksonville State University

## Jacksonville, Alabama

State-supported, coed. Small town campus. Total enrollment: 9,077. Music program established 1960.
**Degrees** Bachelor of Arts in the area of music education. Majors and concentrations: music, music education. Graduate degrees offered: Master of Arts in the area of music education. Program accredited by NASM.
**Enrollment** 250 total; 210 undergraduate, 25 graduate, 15 nonprofessional degree.

**Music Student Profile** 45% females, 55% males, 12% minorities, 5% international.
**Music Faculty** 16 undergraduate (full-time), 7 undergraduate (part-time), 5 graduate (full-time). 75% of full-time faculty have terminal degrees. Graduate students do not teach undergraduate courses. Undergraduate student–faculty ratio: 12:1.
**Student Life** Student groups/activities include Music Educators National Conference Student Chapter, Phi Mu Alpha Sinfonia, Sigma Alpha Iota, Pi Kappa Lambda. Special housing available for music students.
**Expenses for 2007–2008** Application fee: $20. State resident tuition: $5070 full-time. Nonresident tuition: $10,140 full-time. College room and board: $3763. Room and board charges vary according to board plan and housing facility.
**Financial Aid** Program-specific awards: 75–100 band scholarships for wind and percussion majors ($200–$2000), 25–50 choral scholarships for vocal/choral majors ($200–$2000), 10–15 vocal scholarships for voice majors ($200–$2000), 10–15 piano scholarships for piano majors ($200–$2000), 10–15 jazz scholarships for jazz ensemble participants ($200–$2000).
**Application Procedures** Students admitted directly into the professional program freshman year. Deadline for freshmen and transfers: continuous. Required: high school transcript, college transcript(s) for transfer students, minimum 2.0 high school GPA, SAT or ACT test scores. Recommended: interview, audition. Auditions held 4 times on campus; recorded music is permissible as a substitute for live auditions if a campus visit is impossible and videotaped performances are permissible as a substitute for live auditions if a campus visit is impossible.
**Web Site** http://music.jsu.edu/
**Undergraduate Contact** Ms. Kelly Osterbind, Registrar, Office of Admissions and Records, Jacksonville State University, 700 Pelham Road North, Jacksonville, Alabama 36265; 256-782-5400.
**Graduate Contact** Dr. William Carr, Dean, College of Graduate Studies and Continuing Education, Jacksonville State University, 700 Pelham Road North, Jacksonville, Alabama 36265; 256-782-5329.

# Jacksonville University

## Jacksonville, Florida

Independent, coed. Suburban campus. Total enrollment: 3,436. Music program established 1958.
**Degrees** Bachelor of Music in the areas of performance, composition and theory; Bachelor of Music Education. Majors and concentrations: music, music education, music theory and composition, voice performance. Program accredited by NASM.
**Enrollment** 69 total; all undergraduate.
**Music Student Profile** 58% females, 42% males, 27% minorities, 3% international.
**Music Faculty** 12 undergraduate (full-time), 11 undergraduate (part-time). 33% of full-time faculty have terminal degrees. Graduate students do not teach undergraduate courses. Undergraduate student–faculty ratio: 4:1.
**Student Life** Student groups/activities include Mu Phi Epsilon, Florida National Music Educators Conference Student Chapter, Pi Kappa Lambda.
**Expenses for 2008–2009** Application fee: $30. Comprehensive fee: $32,660 includes full-time tuition ($23,900) and college room and board ($8760). College room only: $5000.
**Financial Aid** Program-specific awards: 52 music awards for those demonstrating need and talent ($750–$7000), 4 Phillips Scholarships for those demonstrating exceptional talent ($1000–$4000), 1 orchestra award for those demonstrating need and talent ($3000), 1 band award for those demonstrating need and talent ($3000), 1 Larson Scholarship for those demonstrating exceptional talent ($4000), 1 Warren Scholarship for those demonstrating exceptional talent ($1000), 2 Sheldon Bryan Scholarships for those demonstrating exceptional talent ($2000–$6000).
**Application Procedures** Students admitted directly into the professional program freshman year. Deadline for freshmen and transfers: continuous. Notification date for freshmen and transfers: continuous. Required: high school transcript, college transcript(s) for transfer students, minimum 2.0 high school GPA, audition, SAT or ACT test scores. Recommended: essay, minimum 3.0 high school GPA, 2 letters of recommendation. Auditions

*Jacksonville University (continued)*

held 5 times and by appointment on campus; recorded music is permissible as a substitute for live auditions if a campus visit is impossible and videotaped performances are permissible as a substitute for live auditions if a campus visit is impossible.
**Web Site** http://www.ju.edu
**Undergraduate Contact** Ms. Miriam King, Vice President of Enrollment Management, Jacksonville University, 2800 University Boulevard North, Jacksonville, Florida 32211; 904-256-7000, fax: 904-256-7012, e-mail address: admissions@ju.edu

## Jacobs School of Music
See Indiana University Bloomington

## James Madison University
### Harrisonburg, Virginia

State-supported, coed. Small town campus. Total enrollment: 17,918. Music program established 1934.
**Degrees** Bachelor of Music in the areas of music industry, music education, performance, composition, music theatre. Majors and concentrations: accompanying, composition, music business, music education, music theater, piano, stringed instruments, voice, wind and percussion instruments. Graduate degrees offered: Master of Music in the areas of performance, music education, conducting, music theory/composition. Doctor of Musical Arts in the areas of performance, conducting. Program accredited by NASM.
**Enrollment** 400 total; 375 undergraduate, 25 graduate.
**Music Student Profile** 50% females, 50% males, 8% minorities, 1% international.
**Music Faculty** 45 total (full-time), 15 total (part-time). 78% of full-time faculty have terminal degrees. Graduate students do not teach undergraduate courses. Undergraduate student–faculty ratio: 13:1.
**Student Life** Student groups/activities include Music Educators National Conference, Kappa Kappa Psi, Sigma Alpha Iota, Pi Kappa Lambda.
**Expenses for 2007–2008** Application fee: $40. State resident tuition: $3420 full-time. Nonresident tuition: $14,140 full-time. Mandatory fees: $3246 full-time. College room and board: $7108. College room only: $3712. Room and board charges vary according to board plan and housing facility.
**Financial Aid** Program-specific awards: 50 music performance awards for program majors ($100–$2000).
**Application Procedures** Students apply for admission into the professional program by freshman year. Deadline for freshmen: January 15; transfers: February 1. Notification date for freshmen: March 25; transfers: April 1. Required: essay, high school transcript, college transcript(s) for transfer students, minimum 3.0 high school GPA, 3 letters of recommendation, audition, SAT or ACT test scores, music aptitude test, piano placement test. Recommended: interview. Auditions held 3 times on campus; recorded music is permissible as a substitute for live auditions when distance is prohibitive and videotaped performances are permissible as a substitute for live auditions when distance is prohibitive.
**Web Site** http://www.jmu.edu/music/
**Undergraduate Contact** Dr. Michele M. Kirkdorffer, Music Admissions, School of Music, James Madison University, MSC 7301, Harrisonburg, Virginia 22807; 540-568-6197, fax: 540-568-7819, e-mail address: music_admit@jmu.edu
**Graduate Contact** Dr. Mary Jean Speare, Director of Graduate Studies, School of Music, James Madison University, MSC 7301, Harrisonburg, Virginia 22807; 540-568-6197, fax: 540-568-7819, e-mail address: spearemj@jmu.edu

## John J. Cali School of Music
See Montclair State University

## John M. Long School of Music
See Troy University

*Peabody Conservatory of Music*
## The Johns Hopkins University
### Baltimore, Maryland

Independent, coed. Urban campus. Total enrollment: 6,257.
**Degrees** Bachelor of Music in the areas of composition, performance, recording arts and sciences, music education, jazz performance, computer music. Majors and concentrations: composition, computer music, jazz performance, music education, performance, recording arts and sciences. Graduate degrees offered: Master of Arts in the area of acoustical studies; Master of Music in the areas of composition, performance, conducting, music education, musicology, computer music, theory pedagogy, performance pedagogy, early music. Doctor of Musical Arts in the areas of composition, performance, conducting. Cross-registration with Maryland Institute College of Art, Loyola College. Program accredited by NASM.
**Enrollment** 654 total; 312 undergraduate, 342 graduate.
**Music Student Profile** 51% females, 49% males, 13% minorities, 25% international.
**Music Faculty** 77 total (full-time), 80 total (part-time). 37% of full-time faculty have terminal degrees. Graduate students do not teach undergraduate courses. Undergraduate student–faculty ratio: 15:1.
**Student Life** Special housing available for music students.
**Expenses for 2007–2008** Application fee: $70. One-time mandatory fee: $500. Comprehensive fee: $46,992 includes full-time tuition ($35,900) and college room and board ($11,092). College room only: $6340. Room and board charges vary according to board plan and housing facility. Special program-related fees: $150 per year for technology fee.
**Financial Aid** Program-specific awards: performance scholarships for talented applicants with financial need and those who fulfill school needs for a balanced ensemble ($1000–$15,000).
**Application Procedures** Students admitted directly into the professional program freshman year. Deadline for freshmen and transfers: April 15. Notification date for freshmen and transfers: June 10. Required: essay, high school transcript, college transcript(s) for transfer students, minimum 3.0 high school GPA, 3 letters of recommendation, audition, SAT test score only, TOEFL score for international students. Recommended: interview. Auditions held 12 times on campus and off campus in New York, NY; Boston, MA; Atlanta, GA; Chicago, IL; San Francisco, CA; Los Angeles, CA; recorded music is permissible as a substitute for live auditions when distance is prohibitive (beyond 300-mile radius).
**Web Site** http://www.peabody.jhu.edu/
**Contact** Mr. David Lane, Director of Admissions, Peabody Conservatory of Music, The Johns Hopkins University, 1 East Mount Vernon Place, Baltimore, Maryland 21202; 410-659-8110, e-mail address: admissions@peabody.jhu.edu

### More About the Conservatory

The Admissions office at the Peabody Institute understands how daunting the college-search process can be to an aspiring artist. Students are likely to be clicking on Web sites and collecting literature from many colleges, conservatories, and universities. The college viewbooks they receive generally paint a wholly appealing picture of life at the school—no scheduling problems, an exquisite campus, incredibly talented students, and understanding faculty members—one could imagine that a Carnegie Hall debut is only a step away. How does a student make a wise choice and separate the fantasies from realities?

As the Director of Admissions at Peabody has said, "If a student and I do our jobs well, it is likely he or she will be happy with the final school selected. We need to see if what Peabody has to offer fits a student's needs."

Of course, Peabody has much to offer. Recently celebrating its 150th anniversary, the school was founded in 1857. The advantage of this age is that Peabody has been turning out top quality musicians for more than a century, and the music world has come to assume that anyone who graduates from Peabody is a good performer. When students are asked how they heard about the school, they often reply, "I don't know. I think I've always known about Peabody."

Peabody is one of the schools of The Johns Hopkins University. Therefore, Peabody students have access to the resources of the University. A shuttle bus runs hourly between the campuses. Double degrees, music minors, etc., can be shared with the schools of Arts and Sciences and Engineering. Thus, Peabody graduates are simultaneously graduates of JHU. If the Carnegie Hall fantasy doesn't work out, a Peabody/Hopkins diploma is a powerful credential to have on a resume.

The focus of Peabody's student body, which is made up of about 675 students, is classical music and jazz. All Peabody undergraduates—even those majoring in music education or recording arts and sciences—must complete the same performance curriculum as those majoring in performance.

Students can write or call Peabody for application materials, or to learn details about the school's philosophy, audition requirements, faculty members, and the financial side of things. In any case, the Peabody Institute wishes every student planning to pursue a music career the best of luck in finding the right school.

# Jordan College of Fine Arts
See Butler University

# Juilliard Jazz
See The Juilliard School

*Juilliard Jazz*
# The Juilliard School
**New York, New York**

Independent, coed. Urban campus. Total enrollment: 832. Music program established 2003.
**Degrees** Artist's Diploma; Bachelor of Music. Majors and concentrations: jazz studies. Graduate degrees offered: Master of Music. Cross-registration with Barnard College and Columbia College (Columbia University).
**Enrollment** 32 total; 13 undergraduate, 19 graduate.
**Music Student Profile** 100% males, 56% minorities, 10% international.
**Music Faculty** 7 total (full-time), 12 total (part-time). Graduate students do not teach undergraduate courses.
**Student Life** Student groups/activities include Juilliard Jazz Orchestra and Ensemble, composer-performer collaboration, tour opportunities and bookings in metro area clubs, International Association for Jazz Education. Special housing available for music students.
**Expenses for 2007–2008** Application fee: $100. Comprehensive fee: $37,890 includes full-time tuition ($27,150) and college room and board ($10,740).
**Financial Aid** Program-specific awards: 12 merit and/or need-based awards for program majors ($30,086).
**Application Procedures** Students admitted directly into the professional program freshman year. Deadline for freshmen: December 1. Notification date for freshmen: April 1. Required: essay, high school transcript, college transcript(s) for transfer students, letter of recommendation, audition, pre-audition audio performance tape, TOEFL for all students for whom English is not a native language. Auditions held once on campus.
**Web Site** http://www.juilliard.edu
**Contact** Ms. Lee Cioppa, Associate Dean for Admissions, The Juilliard School, 60 Lincoln Center Plaza, New York, New York 10023-6588; 212-799-5000 ext. 223, fax: 212-769-6420, e-mail address: admissions@juilliard.edu

## *More About the School*

The Juilliard School, located at Manhattan's Lincoln Center, represents more than 100 years of the finest performing arts education in North America. Each year, Juilliard presents more than 700 performances in dance, drama, and music. Juilliard's central mission is to educate talented performing musicians, dancers, and actors so that they may achieve the highest artistic standards as well as become leaders in their professions.

The Dance Division, founded in 1951, aims to create true contemporary dancers—trained equally in classical ballet and modern dance. The Dance Division's four-year course of study offers students the choice of pursuing a Bachelor of Fine Arts degree or a diploma. In addition to daily technique classes, dancers refine their skills in focused study of repertory, pas de deux, pointe or men's class, dance composition, anatomy, acting, dance history, stagecraft, production, music theory, and elements of performing. The dancers work in an enormous variety of repertory styles and techniques. Also offered are electives such as voice, tap, and jazz. All dancers have the opportunity to work with living choreographers on newly commissioned works, established repertory, and their own compositions.

Since 1968, the Drama Division has become one of the most respected training programs for actors in the English-speaking world. The classical theater training program offers students the choice of pursuing a Bachelor of Fine Arts degree or a diploma. Each of the drama classes, numbering around 18 students, moves as a group through the four years of the program, whose major emphasis is on dramatic interpretation the students' ability to bring their bodies and voices into harmony with the characters being portrayed. The training integrates the whole artist—voice, body, mind, and emotion—to become characters from any tradition, classical to contemporary. Actors refine the tools of their craft in acting, Alexander technique, comedy, mask, music, singing, and speech classes. Acting classes and rehearsal projects focus on the styles, conventions, and inner worlds of plays. Students learn and explore how they may transform their total selves into living characters in those worlds. All the hard work and excitement culminate in the fourth year, as students again act in four full-scale productions in different styles.

The Drama Division also offers a one-year, tuition-free, graduate-level playwriting program. The Lila Acheson Wallace American Playwrights Program, under the direction of Christopher Durang and Marsha Norman, encourages and aids the development of new and diverse voices in the American theater.

The Music Division offers a four-year undergraduate program leading to a Bachelor of Music degree, or a three year diploma program. Graduate-level degree programs lead to the Master of Music or Doctor of Musical Arts degrees. Graduate-level programs concentrating exclusively on performance include the graduate diploma and the artist diploma. With individualized instruction from members of a superb faculty and with continual performance opportunities at the school, around the city, the country, and the world, Juilliard helps its music students transform their passions and skills into artistic maturity. Students of orchestral instruments have ample opportunities to play in large ensembles, including the Juilliard Orchestra. Juilliard ensembles perform at the finest venues in New York: Alice Tully Hall, Avery Fisher Hall, and Carnegie Hall. Those interested in twentieth and twenty-first century music can play in the New Juilliard Ensemble. The AXIOM ensemble is dedicated to performing the masterworks of the twentieth century. At any given time, some 120 separate chamber ensembles are also at work at Juilliard. Student musicians form their own groups, audition for faculty coaches, and attend weekly coaching sessions that culminate each semester in performances around the building and beyond.

The Vocal Arts Department offers a comprehensive training program for singers at all stages of development. In addition to private lessons, voice majors receive professional vocal coaching, a process that combines musical instruction with guidance in diction, language and text, movement, and character development.

*The Juilliard School (continued)*

In performances for the Juilliard community and the public, vocalists explore the entire spectrum of opera and art song repertoire. The advanced Juilliard Opera Center accepts artists who have already completed their formal education and who demonstrate significant potential for careers as operatic performers. This program offers singers performance experience and an intensive course of practical study that helps provide a successful transition from an academic to a professional environment.

In 2001, Juilliard married America's greatest indigenous art form with the same standards of training and performance set by the classical division. Juilliard now offers a four-year Jazz Studies Bachelor of Music program, as well as graduate-level Master of Music, graduate diploma, and artist diploma programs. Courses include jazz improvisation, jazz history, composition and arranging, harmony and counterpoint, and the business of jazz. The Jazz Studies program integrates a balanced classroom education with a well-developed performance and touring program. The Juilliard Jazz Orchestra, Ensembles, students, and alumni perform regularly at local clubs such as Birdland, Triad, Swing 46, Blue Note, and Jazz at Lincoln Center's Dizzy's Club *Coca-Cola*. The Juilliard Jazz Orchestra and Ensembles have traveled internationally to locations including Costa Rica, Japan, Spain, France, Italy, and Qatar. National touring locations have included New Orleans, St. Louis, Wisconsin, South Carolina, and Utah.

Aspiring artists in all divisions obtain an education that is truly unique, with a long-standing tradition of excellence that is reflected in the achievements of alumni; a world-class faculty; an institution based in New York City at Lincoln Center, with contacts in the performing arts all around the city, the nation, and the world; and an institutional philosophy that nurtures the complete artist and the complete human being.

## *Music Division*
# The Juilliard School
### New York, New York

Independent, coed. Urban campus. Total enrollment: 832. Music program established 1905.
**Degrees** Artist's Diploma; Bachelor of Music in the area of music performance. Majors and concentrations: bassoon, clarinet, composition, double bass, flute, French horn, guitar, harp, harpsichord, horn, oboe, organ, percussion, piano, trombone, trumpet, tuba, viola, violin, violoncello, voice. Graduate degrees offered: Master of Music. Doctor of Musical Arts. Cross-registration with Columbia University, Barnard College.
**Enrollment** 601 total; 325 undergraduate, 276 graduate.
**Music Student Profile** 47% females, 53% males, 38% minorities, 31% international.
**Music Faculty** 84 total (full-time), 108 total (part-time). Graduate students teach a few undergraduate courses. Undergraduate student–faculty ratio: 2:1.
**Student Life** Student groups/activities include orchestra and symphony concerts around Manhattan, mainstage opera productions, chamber music concerts. Special housing available for music students.
**Expenses for 2007–2008** Application fee: $100. Comprehensive fee: $37,890 includes full-time tuition ($27,150) and college room and board ($10,740).
**Financial Aid** Program-specific awards: 224 merit and/or need-based awards for program majors ($27,278).
**Application Procedures** Students admitted directly into the professional program freshman year. Deadline for freshmen and transfers: December 1. Notification date for freshmen and transfers: April 1. Required: essay, high school transcript, college transcript(s) for transfer students, letter of recommendation, interview, audition, TOEFL score for non-native English speakers, pre-screening audio tape for composition, flute, percussion, piano, violin, cello, voice, viola, double bass. Auditions held once on campus.
**Web Site** http://www.juilliard.edu

**Contact** Ms. Lee Cioppa, Associate Dean for Admissions, The Juilliard School, 60 Lincoln Center Plaza, New York, New York 10023-6588; 212-799-5000 ext. 223, fax: 212-769-6420, e-mail address: admissions@juilliard.edu

# J. William Fulbright College of Arts and Sciences
See University of Arkansas

# Kansas State University
### Manhattan, Kansas

State-supported, coed. Suburban campus. Total enrollment: 22,530.
**Degrees** Bachelor of Music in the areas of performance, composition, music theater; Bachelor of Music Education. Majors and concentrations: composition, music, music education, music theater, piano/organ, stringed instruments, voice, wind and percussion instruments. Graduate degrees offered: Master of Music in the areas of music education, performance, music history and literature, composition. Program accredited by NASM.
**Enrollment** 165 total; 130 undergraduate, 15 graduate, 20 nonprofessional degree.
**Music Student Profile** 55% females, 45% males, 5% minorities, 5% international.
**Music Faculty** 26 total (full-time), 2 total (part-time). 92% of full-time faculty have terminal degrees. Graduate students teach a few undergraduate courses.
**Student Life** Student groups/activities include Music Educators National Conference Student Chapter, American Choral Directors Association, music fraternities and sororities.
**Expenses for 2007–2008** Application fee: $30. State resident tuition: $5625 full-time. Nonresident tuition: $15,360 full-time. Mandatory fees: $610 full-time. College room and board: $6084. Room and board charges vary according to board plan.
**Financial Aid** Program-specific awards: 50 Music Service Guild Awards for freshmen program majors ($500).
**Application Procedures** Students admitted directly into the professional program freshman year. Deadline for freshmen and transfers: continuous. Required: high school transcript, college transcript(s) for transfer students, ACT test score only (minimum composite ACT score of 21). Recommended: audition. Auditions held 3 times on campus; recorded music is permissible as a substitute for live auditions if a campus visit is impossible and videotaped performances are permissible as a substitute for live auditions if a campus visit is impossible.
**Web Site** http://www.ksu.edu/
**Undergraduate Contact** Dr. Paul Hunt, Head, Music Department, Kansas State University, McCain 109, Manhattan, Kansas 66506; 785-532-5740, fax: 785-532-3813, e-mail address: music@ksu.edu
**Graduate Contact** Dr. Frederick Burrack, Director of Graduate Studies, Music Department, Kansas State University, McCain 109, Manhattan, Kansas 66506; 785-532-3807, fax: 785-532-5764, e-mail address: fburrack@ksu.edu

# Kennesaw State University
### Kennesaw, Georgia

State-supported, coed. Suburban campus. Total enrollment: 20,603. Music program established 1984.
**Web Site** http://www.kennesaw.edu/

## *Hugh A. Glauser School of Music*
# Kent State University
### Kent, Ohio

State-supported, coed. Suburban campus. Total enrollment: 22,819. Music program established 1913.

**Degrees** Bachelor of Music in the areas of performance, theory, composition, music education. Majors and concentrations: composition, music education, music theory, performance. Graduate degrees offered: Master of Music in the areas of performance, conducting, music education. Program accredited by NASM.

**Enrollment** 229 total; 92 undergraduate, 79 graduate, 58 nonprofessional degree.

**Music Student Profile** 45% females, 55% males, 7% minorities, 6% international.

**Music Faculty** 32 total (full-time), 14 total (part-time). 90% of full-time faculty have terminal degrees. Graduate students teach a few undergraduate courses. Undergraduate student–faculty ratio: 7:1.

**Student Life** Student groups/activities include Music Educators National Conference Student Chapter, Delta Omicron, Ohio College Music Educators Association. Special housing available for music students.

**Expenses for 2008–2009** Application fee: $30. State resident tuition: $8430 full-time. Nonresident tuition: $15,862 full-time. College room and board: $7200. College room only: $4410. Special program-related fees: $40 per credit hour for applied lesson fee for accompanists for instruction, juries, recitals.

**Financial Aid** Program-specific awards: 20 School of Music Scholarships for all music students ($100–$5000).

**Application Procedures** Students admitted directly into the professional program freshman year. Deadline for freshmen and transfers: continuous. Required: high school transcript, college transcript(s) for transfer students, minimum 2.0 high school GPA, audition, SAT or ACT test scores (minimum composite ACT score of 21), completion of college preparatory courses. Recommended: minimum 3.0 high school GPA. Auditions held 6 times on campus; recorded music is permissible as a substitute for live auditions and videotaped performances are permissible as a substitute for live auditions.

**Web Site** http://dept.kent.edu/music

**Undergraduate Contact** Mr. Dana Brown, Coordinator of Undergraduate Studies, Hugh A. Glauser School of Music, Kent State University, PO Box 5190, Kent, Ohio 44242-0001; 330-672-2172, fax: 330-672-7837, e-mail address: dabrown@kent.edu

**Graduate Contact** Dr. Ralph Lorenz, Graduate Coordinator, Hugh A. Glauser School of Music, Kent State University, PO Box 5190, Kent, Ohio 44242-0001; 330-672-2172, fax: 330-672-7837, e-mail address: rlorenz@kent.edu

# Kentucky Wesleyan College

## Owensboro, Kentucky

Independent Methodist, coed. Suburban campus. Total enrollment: 956. Music program established 1958.

**Degrees** Bachelor of Music in the area of music performance; Bachelor of Music Education in the area of music education. Majors and concentrations: brass instruments performance, guitar, organ, percussion, piano, strings, voice, wind instruments. Cross-registration with Brescia University.

**Enrollment** 46 total; 21 undergraduate, 25 nonprofessional degree.

**Music Student Profile** 58% females, 42% males, 4% minorities, 2% international.

**Music Faculty** 3 undergraduate (full-time), 7 undergraduate (part-time). 100% of full-time faculty have terminal degrees. Graduate students do not teach undergraduate courses. Undergraduate student–faculty ratio: 8:1.

**Student Life** Student groups/activities include Kentucky Wesleyan Band, Kentucky Wesleyan Singers, Kentucky Wesleyan Players.

**Expenses for 2007–2008** Application fee: $0. Comprehensive fee: $20,500 includes full-time tuition ($14,100), mandatory fees ($450), and college room and board ($5950). College room only: $2700. Full-time tuition and fees vary according to course load. Special program-related fees: $50 per credit hour for applied music fee.

**Financial Aid** Program-specific awards: 30–35 music scholarships for program majors ($2000).

**Application Procedures** Students admitted directly into the professional program freshman year. Deadline for freshmen and transfers: continuous. Required: high school transcript, college transcript(s) for transfer students, minimum 2.0 high school GPA, audition, SAT or ACT test scores. Recommended: essay, minimum 3.0 high school GPA, 3 letters of recommendation, interview. Auditions held 4 times and by appointment on campus and off campus in various cities by special arrangement; recorded music is permissible as a substitute for live auditions and videotaped performances are permissible as a substitute for live auditions.

**Web Site** http://www.kwc.edu

**Undergraduate Contact** Dr. Diane K. Earle, Director of Music Program, Music Department, Kentucky Wesleyan College, 3000 Frederica Street, Owensboro, Kentucky 42302-1039; 270-852-3617, fax: 270-926-3196, e-mail address: dearle@kwc.edu

# Lakehead University

## Thunder Bay, Ontario, Canada

Province-supported, coed. Suburban campus. Total enrollment: 7,837. Music program established 1988.

**Degrees** Honors Bachelor of Arts in the area of music; Honors Bachelor of Music in the area of music. Majors and concentrations: classical music. Program accredited by CUMS.

**Enrollment** 55 total; all undergraduate.

**Music Student Profile** 50% females, 50% males, 5% minorities.

**Music Faculty** 3 undergraduate (full-time), 20 undergraduate (part-time). 100% of full-time faculty have terminal degrees. Graduate students do not teach undergraduate courses. Undergraduate student–faculty ratio: 4:1.

**Student Life** Student groups/activities include ensembles concerts (chamber, vocal, new music), student recitals, Lakehead University Music Association (student group).

**Expenses for 2007–2008** Application fee: $105 Canadian dollars. Canadian resident tuition: $4500 full-time. Mandatory fees: $628 full-time. Full-time tuition and fees vary according to location and program. College room and board: $7030. College room only: $5380. Room and board charges vary according to board plan, housing facility, and location. International student tuition: $12,000 full-time.

**Financial Aid** Program-specific awards: 1 Munro Family Memorial Prize for program majors ($725), 5 A. L. Musselman Awards for program majors ($297–$800), 1 Westlake Music Scholarship for continuing students ($450), 1 Ranta Entrance Award for incoming students ($300), 1 Lakehead University Music Festival Scholarship for incoming students ($1226), 1 Westlake Music Scholarship for incoming students ($450), 1 Canadian Scholars Press Music Bursary for program majors ($500), 1 Westlake Music Bursary for continuing students ($750), 2 Wilma C. Ayre Memorial Bursaries for continuing students ($300), 10 William H. Buset Memorial Bursaries for program majors ($1000).

**Application Procedures** Students admitted directly into the professional program freshman year. Deadline for freshmen and transfers: continuous. Required: high school transcript, college transcript(s) for transfer students, minimum 2.0 high school GPA, interview, audition, music theory entrance test. Auditions held by appointment on campus; recorded music is permissible as a substitute for live auditions for out-of-town applicants and videotaped performances are permissible as a substitute for live auditions for out-of-town applicants.

**Web Site** http://www.lakeheadu.ca

**Undergraduate Contact** Office of Admissions, Lakehead University, 955 Oliver Road, Thunder Bay, Ontario P7B 5E1, Canada; 807-343-8500, fax: 807-343-8156, e-mail address: admissions@lakeheadu.ca

# Lamar University

## Beaumont, Texas

State-supported, coed. Suburban campus. Total enrollment: 10,595 (2006). Music program established 1953.

**Degrees** Bachelor of Music in the areas of performance, composition, music education. Majors and concentrations: composition, music education, piano, stringed instruments, voice, wind and percussion instruments. Graduate degrees offered: Master of Music in the area of performance; Master of Music Education. Program accredited by NASM.

**Enrollment** 140 total; 130 undergraduate, 10 graduate.

*Lamar University (continued)*

**Music Student Profile** 50% females, 50% males, 20% minorities, 1% international.

**Music Faculty** 14 total (full-time), 12 total (part-time). 91% of full-time faculty have terminal degrees. Graduate students do not teach undergraduate courses. Undergraduate student–faculty ratio: 8:1.

**Student Life** Student groups/activities include Delta Omicron, Phi Mu Alpha Sinfonia, Pi Kappa Lambda.

**Expenses for 2007–2008** Application fee: $0. State resident tuition: $3240 full-time. Nonresident tuition: $9912 full-time. Mandatory fees: $1367 full-time. Full-time tuition and fees vary according to course load. College room and board: $5888. College room only: $3990. Room and board charges vary according to board plan and housing facility. Special program-related fees: $50 per hour for applied music fee ($150 maximum).

**Financial Aid** Program-specific awards: 45–50 band scholarships for band students ($300–$4000), 20–25 choir scholarships for choir students ($300–$4000), 5–10 orchestra scholarships for orchestra students ($700–$2000), 20–30 endowed scholarships for program majors ($300–$3000).

**Application Procedures** Students admitted directly into the professional program freshman year. Deadline for freshmen and transfers: continuous. Required: high school transcript, college transcript(s) for transfer students, audition, SAT or ACT test scores, THEA scores. Recommended: interview. Auditions held continuously with 4 set dates on campus; recorded music is permissible as a substitute for live auditions when distance is prohibitive and videotaped performances are permissible as a substitute for live auditions when distance is prohibitive.

**Web Site** http://www.lamar.edu

**Undergraduate Contact** Dr. Kim Ellis, Professor, Department of Music, Theatre & Dance, Lamar University, PO Box 10044, Beaumont, Texas 77710; 409-880-8149, fax: 409-880-8143, e-mail address: kim.ellis@lamar.edu

**Graduate Contact** Dr. Robert M. Culbertson Jr., Director of Graduate Studies in Music, Department of Music, Theatre & Dance, Lamar University, PO Box 10044, Beaumont, Texas 77710; 409-880-8073, fax: 409-880-8143, e-mail address: robert. culbertson@lamar.edu

# Lambuth University
## Jackson, Tennessee

Independent United Methodist, coed. Urban campus. Total enrollment: 751. Music program established 1924.

**Degrees** Bachelor of Arts in the area of entertainment & music industry; Bachelor of Music in the areas of music, performance (vocal and instrumental), music education, church music, general music; Bachelor of Science in the area of entertainment & music industry. Majors and concentrations: church music, music education, music industry, performance. Cross-registration with Union University, Freed-Hardeman University.

**Enrollment** 25 total; all undergraduate.

**Music Student Profile** 54% females, 46% males, 21% minorities, 3% international.

**Music Faculty** 4 undergraduate (full-time), 3 undergraduate (part-time). 80% of full-time faculty have terminal degrees. Graduate students do not teach undergraduate courses. Undergraduate student–faculty ratio: 4:1.

**Student Life** Student groups/activities include musicians for theater performances, jazz band.

**Expenses for 2007–2008** Application fee: $25. Comprehensive fee: $24,560 includes full-time tuition ($17,000), mandatory fees ($400), and college room and board ($7160). College room only: $3410. Room and board charges vary according to housing facility. Special program-related fees: $100–$200 per semester for applied music lesson fee.

**Financial Aid** Program-specific awards: 5–10 Faculty Select Awards for Music for program majors ($2500), 50–75 Music Scholarships for band/choir majors and group members ($500–$5000).

**Application Procedures** Students admitted directly into the professional program freshman year. Deadline for freshmen and transfers: continuous. Required: essay, high school transcript, college transcript(s) for transfer students, minimum 2.0 high

school GPA, 2 letters of recommendation, SAT or ACT test scores, letter of good standing for transfer students. Recommended: interview, audition. Auditions held 3 times and by appointment on campus; recorded music is permissible as a substitute for live auditions when distance is prohibitive and videotaped performances are permissible as a substitute for live auditions when distance is prohibitive.

**Web Site** http://www.lambuth.edu

**Undergraduate Contact** Ms. Cherine Heckman, Vice President for Enrollment Management, Lambuth University, 705 Lambuth Boulevard, Jackson, Tennessee 38301; 731-425-3223, fax: 731-425-3496, e-mail address: heckman@lambuth.edu

# Lamont School of Music

See University of Denver

# Lander University
## Greenwood, South Carolina

State-supported, coed, primarily women. Small town campus. Total enrollment: 2,408. Music program established 1872.

**Degrees** Bachelor of Science in the areas of instrumental music education, vocal music education. Majors and concentrations: instrumental music, keyboard, music education, voice. Cross-registration with University of Plymouth (England). Program accredited by NASM.

**Enrollment** 39 total; all undergraduate.

**Music Student Profile** 66% females, 34% males, 26% minorities, 2% international.

**Music Faculty** 6 undergraduate (full-time), 8 undergraduate (part-time). 80% of full-time faculty have terminal degrees. Graduate students do not teach undergraduate courses. Undergraduate student–faculty ratio: 11:1.

**Student Life** Student groups/activities include Music Educators National Conference, Phi Mu Alpha Sinfonia Fraternity.

**Expenses for 2007–2008** Application fee: $35. State resident tuition: $7728 full-time. Nonresident tuition: $14,616 full-time. Mandatory fees: $550 full-time. Full-time tuition and fees vary according to course load and degree level. College room and board: $5940. College room only: $3650. Room and board charges vary according to board plan and housing facility. Special program-related fees: $40 per semester for applied music fee.

**Financial Aid** Program-specific awards: 1 Kerhoulas Award for incoming students ($500), 1 White Award for instrumentalists ($1500), 1 Hutto Award for voice majors ($150), 2 Lenti Awards for piano majors ($900), 1 Scofield Scholarship for voice majors ($300), 1 Wilkins Scholarship for concert band/jazz ensemble members ($150), 1 Lenna Clifford Scholarship for violin or piano majors ($1000–$2000).

**Application Procedures** Students admitted directly into the professional program freshman year. Deadline for freshmen and transfers: continuous. Required: high school transcript, college transcript(s) for transfer students, letter of recommendation, audition, SAT or ACT test scores, music theory test, minimum 2.5 high school GPA. Recommended: minimum 3.0 high school GPA, interview, standing in top 50% of graduating class. Auditions held 2-3 times on campus; recorded music is permissible as a substitute for live auditions when distance is prohibitive and videotaped performances are permissible as a substitute for live auditions when distance is prohibitive.

**Web Site** http://www.lander.edu

**Undergraduate Contact** Mr. Jonathan Reece, Director of Admissions, Lander University, 320 Stanley Avenue, Greenwood, South Carolina 29649; 864-388-8307, fax: 864-388-8890, e-mail address: jreece@lander.edu

# Lawrence University
## Appleton, Wisconsin

Independent, coed. Small town campus. Total enrollment: 1,451. Music program established 1874.

**Degrees** Bachelor of Arts/Bachelor of Music in the areas of liberal arts in combination with music performance, music education, theory-composition; Bachelor of Music in the areas of music education, music theory-composition, performance. Majors and concentrations: choral music, classical guitar, classical music, instrumental music, jazz, music, music education, music theory and composition, performance, piano/organ, stringed instruments, voice, wind and percussion instruments. Program accredited by NASM.

**Enrollment** 1,405 total; 295 undergraduate, 1,110 nonprofessional degree.

**Music Student Profile** 54% females, 46% males, 8% minorities, 10% international.

**Music Faculty** 38 undergraduate (full-time), 26 undergraduate (part-time). 96% of full-time faculty have terminal degrees. Graduate students do not teach undergraduate courses. Undergraduate student–faculty ratio: 6:1.

**Student Life** Student groups/activities include Phi Mu Alpha Sinfonia, Sigma Alpha Iota, WLFM-FM (campus radio station).

**Expenses for 2007–2008** Application fee: $40. Comprehensive fee: $37,770 includes full-time tuition ($30,846), mandatory fees ($234), and college room and board ($6690). College room only: $3081. Room and board charges vary according to board plan.

**Financial Aid** Program-specific awards: 20–30 performance awards for top auditions ($2000–$12,000), 10–12 Trustee Awards for top auditions ($10,000), Institutional Grants for those demonstrating need ($21,000), 5–10 music education scholarships for those demonstrating potential during participation in on-campus workshop ($7000), 1–5 theory/composition scholarships for those selected by faculty based on portfolios ($7000).

**Application Procedures** Students admitted directly into the professional program freshman year. Deadline for freshmen: January 15; transfers: May 15. Notification date for freshmen: April 1; transfers: June 1. Required: essay, high school transcript, college transcript(s) for transfer students, 3 letters of recommendation, audition. Recommended: minimum 3.0 high school GPA, interview. Auditions held 14 times on campus and off campus in New York, NY; Washington, D.C.; Boston, MA; Denver, CO; Interlochen, MI; Los Angeles, CA; San Francisco, CA; Portland, OR; Seattle, WA; Houston, TX; Atlanta, GA; recorded music is permissible as a substitute for live auditions when distance is prohibitive to campus or a regional site (over 350 miles) and videotaped performances are permissible as a substitute for live auditions when distance is prohibitive to campus or a regional site (over 350 miles).

**Web Site** http://www.lawrence.edu

**Undergraduate Contact** Nathan Ament, Director of Conservatory Admissions, Lawrence University, PO Box 599, Appleton, Wisconsin 54912-0599; 920-832-6508, fax: 920-832-6782, e-mail address: nathan.ament@lawrence.edu

## More About the University

The Lawrence Conservatory of Music is a nationally recognized conservatory devoted exclusively to the education of undergraduate musicians within a college of the liberal arts and sciences.

The faculty of performers, composers, scholars, and pedagogues provide individual attention and guidance to the more than 350 music majors and the many college students who participate in the Conservatory's activities.

Music facilities are housed within three adjoining buildings: the Music-Drama Center, the Memorial Chapel, and the Ruth Harwood Shattuck Hall of Music. The music library, located in the Media Center of the University library, holds more than 30,000 recordings and scores as well as music reference works.

Music students choose from five degree programs: the Bachelor of Music degree in performance, the Bachelor of Music degree in music education (instrumental; general; choral/general; instrumental/general; choral/general/instrumental), the Bachelor of Music degree in theory-composition, the Bachelor of Arts degree in music, and the double degree. The Lawrence five-year double-degree program permits students to earn a Bachelor of Music degree and a Bachelor of Arts degree in a discipline other than music. The combined degree program provides both professional-level study of music and a rigorous academic program of study. In addition, students may design their own majors or pursue a double major within the Bachelor of Music degree. The curriculum in the Conservatory of Music seeks to ensure that all music students, regardless of their major, graduate with a thorough and firm grounding in music theory and analysis, music history and literature, and both solo and ensemble performance.

At Lawrence, music is not isolated from the other disciplines. All music majors complete a core curriculum in the college in addition to their Conservatory course work. Conservatory students live in the same residence halls and dine with college students, taking full advantage of the residential nature of the liberal arts institution. While the degree curriculum within the Conservatory is intense and focused in music, it allows students to explore the liberal arts and sciences through an array of courses taught by an accomplished faculty. The study of music at Lawrence occurs within the context of the liberal arts, thereby providing a well-rounded, broad-based understanding of music.

This preparation and training have allowed Lawrence's students and ensembles to receive national and international awards; major ensembles have performed at regional and national music conferences and have recorded CDs for national distribution; students have placed as finalists and winners in the Metropolitan Opera auditions, the Concert Artists Guild Competition, the MTNA Solo and Chamber Music Competitions, the Grace Vamos Competition, and *Down Beat* magazine's Outstanding Jazz Big Band Award and Outstanding Jazz Composition Award competitions, among others. Each summer, a number of conservatory students continue their studies at festivals such as Tanglewood and Aspen.

Lawrence University is committed to the development of intellect and talent, the acquisition of knowledge and understanding, and the cultivation of judgment and values. The University prepares students for lives of service, achievement, leadership, and personal fulfillment. Lawrence Conservatory graduates are counted not only among the ranks of professional orchestras and opera companies, Grammy Award winners, university faculties, elementary and high school teachers, college administrators, and composers, but also among authors, medical and law professionals, and public servants.

**Program Facilities** The Conservatory's facilities include the Memorial Chapel (concert hall of 1,250 seats); Harper Recital Hall (250 seats); Miller Hall (150-seat rehearsal hall); a large ensemble rehearsal hall (315 seats); a jazz rehearsal/recording studio; percussion studios; a recording studio with recording, editing, and production capabilities; a Macintosh-based computer lab, offering MIDI technology in conjunction with Finale, Symphony, and Vivace programs; Cloak Theatre (experimental black box); Stansbury Theatre (proscenium theater of 500 seats); WLFM campus radio station; historical instruments, such as an 1815 Broadwood piano and a Guarneri violin; and the forty-one-stop mechanical action organ by John Brombaugh.

**Faculty and Resident Artists** There are 38 full-time faculty members and 23 part-time faculty members. Artists-in-residence include faculty chamber ensembles and baritone Dale Duesing. Recent visiting artists include Emanuel Ax, Midori, The Saint Paul Chamber Orchestra, Wayne Shorter, Wynton Marsalis, Diane Reeves, the American Brass Quintet, and the Vermeer String Quartet.

**Student Performance Opportunities** Ensembles include Symphony Orchestra, Chamber Orchestra, Collegium Musicum, Wind Ensemble, Symphonic Band, Jazz Ensemble, Percussion Ensemble, African and Brazilian Drumming Ensembles, Cello Ensemble, Low Brass Choir, Horn Choir, Concert Choir, Viking Chorale, Cantala, Opera Theatre, Music Theatre, Jazz Singers, and numerous chamber ensembles and small jazz groups.

**Special Programs** The Conservatory offers a five-year double-degree (B.A./B.Mus.) program; music education certification (K–12); fifty-five off-campus programs, both domestic and international; academic advising; residence hall life; a counseling

*Lawrence University (continued)*

center; a career center; a writing skills lab; more than 100 campus clubs and organizations; twenty-three varsity sports; and numerous club and intramural sports.

# Lebanon Valley College
## Annville, Pennsylvania

Independent United Methodist, coed. Small town campus. Total enrollment: 1,936. Music program established 1932.

**Degrees** Bachelor of Music in the area of music recording technology; Bachelor of Science in the area of music education. Majors and concentrations: music education, music technology. Graduate degrees offered: Master of Music Education in the area of music education. Program accredited by NASM.

**Enrollment** 374 total; 226 undergraduate, 100 graduate, 48 nonprofessional degree.

**Music Student Profile** 45% females, 55% males, 3% minorities.

**Music Faculty** 14 undergraduate (full-time), 25 undergraduate (part-time), 4 graduate (full-time), 2 graduate (part-time). 70% of full-time faculty have terminal degrees. Graduate students do not teach undergraduate courses. Undergraduate student–faculty ratio: 16:1.

**Student Life** Student groups/activities include Audio Engineering Society, Music Educators National Conference Student Chapter.

**Expenses for 2007–2008** Application fee: $30. Comprehensive fee: $35,230 includes full-time tuition ($27,125), mandatory fees ($675), and college room and board ($7430). College room only: $3630. Room and board charges vary according to board plan and housing facility. Special program-related fees: $120 per unit for private instruction.

**Financial Aid** Program-specific awards: 4 Carmean String Scholarships for string players ($1000), 6 Carmean Talent Awards for musically talented students ($1000).

**Application Procedures** Students apply for admission into the professional program by sophomore year. Deadline for freshmen and transfers: continuous. Notification date for freshmen and transfers: April 1. Required: high school transcript, college transcript(s) for transfer students, audition. Recommended: essay, 2 letters of recommendation, interview. Auditions held by appointment on campus; recorded music is permissible as a substitute for live auditions for international applicants or when distance is prohibitive and videotaped performances are permissible as a substitute for live auditions for international applicants or when distance is prohibitive.

**Web Site** http://www.lvc.edu

**Undergraduate Contact** Dr. Barry Hill, Director, Music Recording Technology, Department of Music, Lebanon Valley College, Blair Music Center, Annville, Pennsylvania 17003; 717-867-6285, fax: 717-867-6390, e-mail address: hill@lvc.edu

**Graduate Contact** Dr. Mark Mecham, Chair and Director of MME Program, Music, Lebanon Valley College, Blair Music Center, Annville, Pennsylvania 17003; 717-867-6275, fax: 717-867-6390, e-mail address: mecham@lvc.edu

# Lee University
## Cleveland, Tennessee

Independent, coed. Small town campus. Total enrollment: 4,086.

**Degrees** Bachelor of Arts in the area of church music; Bachelor of Music in the area of performance; Bachelor of Music Education in the areas of vocal/general music education, instrumental music education, keyboard; Bachelor of Science in the area of music business emphasis. Majors and concentrations: applied music, church music, music business, piano, stringed instruments, voice, wind and percussion instruments. Graduate degrees offered: Master of Church Music; Master of Music in Music Education in the areas of music performance, music education with teacher certification. Program accredited by NASM.

**Enrollment** 253 total; 167 undergraduate, 39 graduate, 47 nonprofessional degree.

**Music Student Profile** 57% females, 43% males, 15% minorities, 9% international.

**Music Faculty** 20 total (full-time), 31 total (part-time). 65% of full-time faculty have terminal degrees. Graduate students do not teach undergraduate courses. Undergraduate student–faculty ratio: 15:1.

**Student Life** Student groups/activities include opera theatre, Music Drama Workshop, Choral Union.

**Expenses for 2007–2008** Application fee: $25. Comprehensive fee: $16,058 includes full-time tuition ($10,392), mandatory fees ($390), and college room and board ($5276). College room only: $2556. Room and board charges vary according to board plan and housing facility. Special program-related fees: $130 per semester for accompanist fee, $200 per semester for practice room rental, lesson fee.

**Financial Aid** Program-specific awards: 27 endowed scholarships for program majors ($1250), 245 performance scholarships for ensemble members ($705).

**Application Procedures** Students apply for admission into the professional program by sophomore year. Deadline for freshmen and transfers: continuous. Required: high school transcript, college transcript(s) for transfer students, audition, SAT or ACT test scores. Recommended: 3 letters of recommendation, interview. Auditions held 4 times on campus; recorded music is permissible as a substitute for live auditions when distance is prohibitive and videotaped performances are permissible as a substitute for live auditions when distance is prohibitive.

**Web Site** http://music.leeuniversity.edu/

**Undergraduate Contact** Ms. Celia Narus, Assistant to the Dean, School of Music, Lee University, PO Box 3450, Cleveland, Tennessee 37320-3450; 423-614-8240, fax: 423-614-8242, e-mail address: cnarus@leeuniversity.edu

**Graduate Contact** Dr. Stephen W. Plate, Dean, School of Music, Lee University, PO Box 3450, Cleveland, Tennessee 37320-3450; 423-614-8240, fax: 423-614-8242, e-mail address: splate@leeuniversity.edu

# Lehman College of the City University of New York
## Bronx, New York

State and locally supported, coed. Urban campus. Total enrollment: 10,922. Music program established 1942.

**Degrees** Bachelor of Science in the area of music. Majors and concentrations: composition, instrumental performance, music education, percussion, voice. Graduate degrees offered: Master of Arts in Teaching in the area of music education. Cross-registration with City University of New York colleges.

**Enrollment** 85 total; 36 undergraduate, 49 graduate.

**Music Student Profile** 56% females, 44% males, 60% minorities, 4% international.

**Music Faculty** 7 total (full-time), 9 total (part-time). 100% of full-time faculty have terminal degrees. Graduate students do not teach undergraduate courses.

**Student Life** Student groups/activities include stage bands, chorus, ensembles, orchestra.

**Expenses for 2008–2009** Application fee: $65. State resident tuition: $4000 full-time. Nonresident tuition: $10,800 full-time. Mandatory fees: $290 full-time.

**Financial Aid** Program-specific awards: Bellezeller Scholarship for music students.

**Application Procedures** Students admitted directly into the professional program freshman year. Deadline for freshmen and transfers: continuous. Required: high school transcript, college transcript(s) for transfer students, minimum 2.0 high school GPA, interview, audition. Recommended: essay, portfolio, SAT or ACT test scores. Auditions held by appointment on campus; recorded music is permissible as a substitute for live auditions at the discretion of the chair and videotaped performances are permissible as a substitute for live auditions at the discretion of the chair. Portfolio reviews held by appointment on campus.

**Web Site** http://www.lehman.cuny.edu

**Undergraduate Contact** Clarence Wilkes, Director of Admissions, Lehman College of the City University of New York, 250 Bedford Park Boulevard West, Shuster Hall 155, Bronx, New York 10468; 718-960-8706, fax: 718-960-8712.

**Graduate Contact** Office of Graduate Admissions, Lehman College of the City University of New York, Shuster Hall, Room 150, Bronx, New York 10468; 718-960-8702, fax: 718-960-8713.

# Leigh Gerdine College of Fine Arts
See Webster University

# Lenoir-Rhyne College
## Hickory, North Carolina

Independent Lutheran, coed. Small town campus. Total enrollment: 1,626. Music program established 1900.
**Degrees** Bachelor of Music Education in the areas of vocal /choral music education, keyboard music education, instrumental music education. Majors and concentrations: piano/organ, stringed instruments, voice, wind and percussion instruments. Program accredited by NCATE.
**Enrollment** 45 total; all undergraduate.
**Music Student Profile** 70% females, 30% males, 1% minorities.
**Music Faculty** 7 total (full-time), 8 total (part-time). 60% of full-time faculty have terminal degrees. Graduate students do not teach undergraduate courses. Undergraduate student–faculty ratio: 8:1.
**Student Life** Student groups/activities include Suzuki Program, Youth Percussion Program, youth chorus.
**Expenses for 2008–2009** Application fee: $35. Comprehensive fee: $31,220 includes full-time tuition ($23,070) and college room and board ($8150). Special program-related fees: $85 per half-hour lesson for applied music fee.
**Financial Aid** Program-specific awards: 10 talent scholarships for program majors ($5000), 5 music minor scholarships for music minors ($2000), 10 music participation scholarships (ensemble) for vocalists and instrumentalists ($2500).
**Application Procedures** Students admitted directly into the professional program freshman year. Deadline for freshmen and transfers: continuous. Required: high school transcript, college transcript(s) for transfer students, 2 letters of recommendation, audition, SAT or ACT test scores (minimum composite ACT score of 20), minimum 2.5 high school GPA. Recommended: interview. Auditions held 3 times and by appointment on campus; recorded music is permissible as a substitute for live auditions when distance is prohibitive or scheduling is difficult and videotaped performances are permissible as a substitute for live auditions when distance is prohibitive or scheduling is difficult.
**Web Site** http://www.lrc.edu
**Undergraduate Contact** Dr. Daniel Kiser, Chair, School of Fine Arts, Lenoir-Rhyne College, Box 7355, Hickory, North Carolina 28603; 828-328-1741, fax: 828-328-7037, e-mail address: kiser@lrc.edu

# Liberty University
## Lynchburg, Virginia

Independent nondenominational, coed. Suburban campus. Total enrollment: 27,063. Music program established 1971.
**Degrees** Bachelor of Music in the areas of choral music, instrumental music, instrumental music education, choral music education; Bachelor of Science in the area of worship and music ministry. Majors and concentrations: music, music education. Program accredited by NCATE.
**Enrollment** 100 total; all undergraduate.
**Music Student Profile** 51% females, 49% males, 10% minorities, 2% international.
**Music Faculty** 15 undergraduate (full-time), 5 undergraduate (part-time). 80% of full-time faculty have terminal degrees. Graduate students do not teach undergraduate courses. Undergraduate student–faculty ratio: 15:1.
**Student Life** Student groups/activities include Music Educators National Conference.
**Expenses for 2007–2008** Application fee: $50. Comprehensive fee: $21,200 includes full-time tuition ($14,850), mandatory fees ($950), and college room and board ($5400). Special program-related fees: $30 per semester for practice room rental, $150 per year for wind ensemble.

**Financial Aid** Program-specific awards: 11 Fine Arts Scholarships for program majors ($500–$1000), 80–100 marching band service awards for marching band members ($200–$500), 40–50 Concert Band Service Awards for concert band members ($300–$500).
**Application Procedures** Students apply for admission into the professional program by sophomore year. Deadline for freshmen and transfers: August 1. Required: high school transcript, college transcript(s) for transfer students, 3 letters of recommendation, SAT test score only. Recommended: interview, audition. Auditions held 4 times on campus; recorded music is permissible as a substitute for live auditions when distance is prohibitive and videotaped performances are permissible as a substitute for live auditions when distance is prohibitive.
**Web Site** http://www.liberty.edu/academics/musicandhumanities
**Undergraduate Contact** Dr. John W. Hugo, Chairman, Department of Music and Humanities, Liberty University, 1971 University Boulevard, Lynchburg, Virginia 24502-2269; 804-582-2318, fax: 804-582-2891, e-mail address: musicandhumanities@liberty.edu

# Lincoln University
## Jefferson City, Missouri

State-supported, coed. Small town campus. Total enrollment: 3,156. Music program established 1951.
**Degrees** Bachelor of Music Education. Majors and concentrations: instrumental music education, piano, vocal music education. Program accredited by NASM.
**Enrollment** 49 total; 42 undergraduate, 7 nonprofessional degree.
**Music Student Profile** 26% females, 74% males, 66% minorities, 4% international.
**Music Faculty** 6 undergraduate (full-time), 3 undergraduate (part-time). 83% of full-time faculty have terminal degrees. Graduate students do not teach undergraduate courses. Undergraduate student–faculty ratio: 12:1.
**Student Life** Student groups/activities include Music Educators National Conference, Kappa Kappa Psi, Phi Mu Alpha.
**Expenses for 2007–2008** Application fee: $20. State resident tuition: $5520 full-time. Nonresident tuition: $10,050 full-time. Mandatory fees: $490 full-time. Full-time tuition and fees vary according to location. College room and board: $4590. College room only: $2358. Room and board charges vary according to board plan and housing facility. Special program-related fees: $69 per semester for applied lab fees.
**Financial Aid** Program-specific awards: 20 music scholarships for program majors ($1200), 55 service awards for ensemble players ($500).
**Application Procedures** Students apply for admission into the professional program by sophomore year. Deadline for freshmen and transfers: July 15. Required: high school transcript, college transcript(s) for transfer students, audition, SAT or ACT test scores, theory test, performance on piano, minimum 2.0 high school GPA for out-of-state students. Auditions held 4 times on campus and off campus in St. Louis, MO; Kansas City, MO; Chicago, IL; recorded music is permissible as a substitute for live auditions for provisional acceptance and videotaped performances are permissible as a substitute for live auditions for provisional acceptance.
**Web Site** http://www.lincolnu.edu
**Undergraduate Contact** Mohammed Khaleel, Director of Admissions, Lincoln University, 820 Chestnut Street, Jefferson City, Missouri 65102-0029; 573-681-5599, fax: 573-681-5566.

# Lionel Hampton School of Music
See University of Idaho

# Long Island University, C.W. Post Campus
## Brookville, New York

Independent, coed. Suburban campus. Total enrollment: 8,361. Music program established 1956.
**Web Site** http://www.liu.edu/

# Longwood University

**Farmville, Virginia**

State-supported, coed. Total enrollment: 4,727.

**Degrees** Bachelor of Music in the areas of performance, education, piano pedagogy. Majors and concentrations: brass, music education, piano, piano pedagogy, voice, wind and percussion instruments. Cross-registration with Hampden-Sydney College. Program accredited by NASM.

**Enrollment** 61 undergraduate, 4 nonprofessional degree.

**Music Student Profile** 60% females, 40% males, 10% minorities.

**Music Faculty** 7 undergraduate (full-time), 9 undergraduate (part-time). 86% of full-time faculty have terminal degrees. Graduate students do not teach undergraduate courses. Undergraduate student–faculty ratio: 9:1.

**Student Life** Student groups/activities include Music Educators National Conference, Sigma Alpha Iota, Phi Mu Alpha.

**Expenses for 2007–2008** Application fee: $40. State resident tuition: $4249 full-time. Nonresident tuition: $12,450 full-time. Mandatory fees: $3809 full-time. Full-time tuition and fees vary according to course load. College room and board: $6740. College room only: $3840. Room and board charges vary according to board plan, housing facility, and location. Special program-related fees: $178 per semester for applied music fee.

**Financial Aid** Program-specific awards: 4 Hull Scholarships for music majors ($1455), 1 Haga Scholarship for junior and senior music majors ($1000), 2 Holiday Dinner Scholarships for music majors ($500–$1000), 7 Foundation Scholarships for music majors ($500), 7 Cole Scholarships for music majors ($750–$1500), 1 Pauline Boehm Haga Scholarship for music education majors with highest GPA ($861), 3 Roy Clark Scholarships for music majors ($985), 1 Mary Pucket Asher King Scholarship for music majors ($543).

**Application Procedures** Students admitted directly into the professional program freshman year. Deadline for freshmen and transfers: March 1. Required: essay, high school transcript, college transcript(s) for transfer students, minimum 2.0 high school GPA, interview, audition, SAT or ACT test scores. Recommended: 2 letters of recommendation. Auditions held 6 times and by appointment on campus; recorded music is permissible as a substitute for live auditions for out-of-state applicants and videotaped performances are permissible as a substitute for live auditions for out-of-state applicants.

**Web Site** http://web.longwood.edu/music

**Undergraduate Contact** Dr. Charles Kinzer, Chair, Department of Music, Longwood University, 201 High Street, Wygal Building, Farmville, Virginia 23909; 434-395-2495, fax: 434-395-2149, e-mail address: kinzerce@longwood.edu

# Louisiana State University and Agricultural and Mechanical College

**Baton Rouge, Louisiana**

State-supported, coed. Urban campus. Total enrollment: 28,628.

**Degrees** Bachelor of Music in the areas of performance, composition; Bachelor of Music Education in the areas of instrumental music education, vocal music education. Majors and concentrations: composition, harp, music education, organ, piano, piano pedagogy, stringed instruments, voice, wind and percussion instruments. Graduate degrees offered: Master of Music in the areas of performance, theory, musicology, music education, piano pedagogy, conducting. Doctor of Musical Arts in the areas of performance, conducting; Doctor of Philosophy in the areas of music education, musicology, music theory, composition. Cross-registration with Southern University and Agricultural and Mechanical College, Baton Rouge Community College. Program accredited by NASM.

**Enrollment** 442 total; 282 undergraduate, 160 graduate.

**Music Student Profile** 49% females, 51% males, 15% minorities, 9% international.

**Music Faculty** 50 total (full-time), 8 total (part-time). 100% of full-time faculty have terminal degrees. Graduate students teach a few undergraduate courses. Undergraduate student–faculty ratio: 10:1.

**Student Life** Student groups/activities include music fraternities and sororities, student chapters of American Choral Directors Association, Music Educators National Conference, Music Teachers National Association.

**Expenses for 2007–2008** Application fee: $40. State resident tuition: $2981 full-time. Nonresident tuition: $11,281 full-time. Mandatory fees: $1562 full-time. College room and board: $6852. College room only: $4130. Room and board charges vary according to board plan and housing facility. Special program-related fees: $10 per year for locker rental fee, $75 for senior recital fee.

**Financial Aid** Program-specific awards: 100 School of Music Scholarships for talented students ($1000–$11,300).

**Application Procedures** Students admitted directly into the professional program freshman year. Deadline for freshmen and transfers: April 15. Required: high school transcript, college transcript(s) for transfer students, minimum 3.0 high school GPA, audition, SAT or ACT test scores (minimum composite ACT score of 22). Recommended: essay, 2 letters of recommendation, essay (for full scholarship consideration). Auditions held 3 times and by appointment on campus; recorded music is permissible as a substitute for live auditions if a live audition is impossible and videotaped performances are permissible as a substitute for live auditions if a live audition is impossible.

**Web Site** http://www.music.lsu.edu

**Undergraduate Contact** Ms. Carol Larsen, Assistant to the Dean for Undergraduate Programs, School of Music, Louisiana State University and Agricultural and Mechanical College, 102 School of Music, Baton Rouge, Louisiana 70803; 225-578-3261, fax: 225-578-2562, e-mail address: clarse1@lsu.edu

**Graduate Contact** Dr. Sara Lynn Baird, Associate Dean, Director of Graduate Studies, School of Music, Louisiana State University and Agricultural and Mechanical College, 102 School of Music, Baton Rouge, Louisiana 70803; 225-578-3261, fax: 225-578-2562, e-mail address: sbaird@lsu.edu

# Louisiana Tech University

**Ruston, Louisiana**

State-supported, coed. Small town campus. Total enrollment: 10,564. Music program established 1959.

**Web Site** http://www.latech.edu/

# Loyola University New Orleans

**New Orleans, Louisiana**

Independent Roman Catholic (Jesuit), coed. Urban campus. Total enrollment: 4,360. Music program established 1932.

**Degrees** Bachelor of Music in the areas of performance, piano pedagogy, jazz studies, theory, composition, music industry; Bachelor of Music Education in the area of vocal and instrumental music; Bachelor of Music Therapy. Majors and concentrations: guitar performance, instrumental performance, jazz studies, keyboard performance, music industry, music with elective studies, voice performance. Graduate degrees offered: Master of Music in the area of performance; Master of Music Education; Master of Music Therapy. Cross-registration with Xavier University of Louisiana, Tulane University, Notre Dame Seminary, Southern University at New Orleans. Program accredited by NASM.

**Enrollment** 353 total; 327 undergraduate, 26 graduate.

**Music Student Profile** 49% females, 51% males, 15% minorities, 3% international.

**Music Faculty** 24 total (full-time), 37 total (part-time). 62% of full-time faculty have terminal degrees. Graduate students do not teach undergraduate courses. Undergraduate student–faculty ratio: 6:1.

**Student Life** Student groups/activities include Loyola Association of Music Therapy Students, Music Educators National Conference Student Chapter, Loyola University Community Action Program.

**Expenses for 2008–2009** Application fee: $20. Comprehensive fee: $37,438 includes full-time tuition ($27,168), mandatory fees

($876), and college room and board ($9394). College room only: $5488. Special program-related fees: $100 for student teaching fee.

**Financial Aid** Program-specific awards: 52 music scholarships for music majors ($4500).

**Application Procedures** Students admitted directly into the professional program freshman year. Deadline for freshmen and transfers: May 1. Notification date for freshmen and transfers: May 1. Required: essay, high school transcript, college transcript(s) for transfer students, minimum 2.0 high school GPA, 2 letters of recommendation, audition, SAT or ACT test scores (minimum composite ACT score of 21), portfolio for composition and music business majors, interview for music industry majors. Auditions held 3 times on campus; recorded music is permissible as a substitute for live auditions when distance is prohibitive and videotaped performances are permissible as a substitute for live auditions when distance is prohibitive. Portfolio reviews held 3 times on campus.

**Web Site** http://www.music.loyno.edu

**Contact** Dr. Anthony Decuir, Associate Dean, College of Music, Loyola University New Orleans, 6363 Saint Charles Avenue, New Orleans, Louisiana 70118; 504-865-3037, fax: 504-865-2852, e-mail address: decuir@loyno.edu

# Manhattan School of Music
## New York, New York

Independent, coed. Urban campus. Total enrollment: 854. Music program established 1917.

**Degrees** Bachelor of Music in the areas of classical performance, classical composition, jazz/jazz composition. Graduate degrees offered: Master of Music in the areas of classical performance, classical composition, jazz/jazz composition, orchestral performance, contemporary music performance. Doctor of Musical Arts in the areas of classical performance, classical composition, jazz arts advancement. Cross-registration with Barnard College.

**Enrollment** 823 total; 399 undergraduate, 424 graduate.

**Music Student Profile** 52% females, 48% males, 19% minorities, 31% international.

**Music Faculty** 68 total (full-time), 185 total (part-time). 20% of full-time faculty have terminal degrees. Graduate students teach a few undergraduate courses. Undergraduate student–faculty ratio: 10:1.

**Student Life** Student groups/activities include orchestra, opera studio, chamber ensembles. Special housing available for music students.

**Expenses for 2008–2009** Application fee: $100.

**Financial Aid** Program-specific awards: MSM Scholarship for high merit students with need ($15,000), President's Award for high merit students, non-need ($5000).

**Application Procedures** Students admitted directly into the professional program freshman year. Deadline for freshmen and transfers: December 1. Notification date for freshmen and transfers: April 1. Required: essay, high school transcript, college transcript(s) for transfer students, minimum 2.0 high school GPA, 2 letters of recommendation, audition, list of performance experience. Recommended: minimum 3.0 high school GPA, SAT or ACT test scores, pre-screen (CD for voice, flute, jazz, cello, violin, composition, clarinet, piano, and viola applicants). Auditions held once on campus; videotaped performances are permissible as a substitute for live auditions for applicants living outside North America and for cello, double bass, and tuba applicants.

**Web Site** http://www.msmnyc.edu

**Contact** Ms. Amy A. Anderson, Associate Dean of Enrollment Management, Manhattan School of Music, 120 Claremont Avenue, New York, New York 10027-4698; 212-749-2802 ext. 4501, fax: 212-749-3025, e-mail address: admission@msmnyc.edu

### More About the School

Since 1917, Manhattan School of Music (MSM) has prepared gifted young musicians to assume their place on the world's stages.

In selecting MSM, students choose to work with faculty members who are themselves performers with international reputations. They choose to be with students from around the world who come together to create an environment remarkable not just for its intensity, but for genuine friendliness and cooperation. And, of course, they choose New York itself, a major center of music and art in America.

While many fine music conservatories are acknowledged for their ability to develop talents and skills, MSM has a particular combination of strengths that make it an excellent place from which to launch a career.

With extensive performance opportunities on campus as well as the chance to freelance and begin to develop a network of professional contacts, students undergo remarkable changes here: they start to function as professional musicians while they are still in school. It is this powerful convergence of opportunity and training that gives students the chance to go as far as their talent, intelligence, and courage can take them.

Alumni are the School's best examples of this training. Here are just a few of MSM alumni from 1970 to the present: Laura Albeck, Metropolitan Opera Orchestra; Robert Anderson, Minnesota Orchestra; Gerald Appleman, New York Philharmonic; Karen Beardsley, soprano, New York City Opera; Elizabeth Burkhardt, Atlanta Symphony; John Carabella, New York Philharmonic; Ron Carter, jazz bassist; Harry Connick Jr., singer; Todd Coolman, jazz bassist; Alison Dalton, Chicago Symphony; Jacqui Danilow, Metropolitan Opera Orchestra; Garry Dial, jazz pianist; James Dooley, San José Symphony; Don Ehrlich, San Francisco Symphony; Desiree Elsevier, Metropolitan Opera Orchestra; Mary Ewing, New York Philharmonic; Lauren Flannigan, soprano, Metropolitan Opera; Anna Garzuly, Gewandhaus Orchestra (Leipzig); Susan Graham, mezzo-soprano, Metropolitan Opera; Andrea Gruber, soprano, Metropolitan Opera; Laura Hamilton, Metropolitan Opera Orchestra; Herbie Hancock, jazz pianist; Stefon Harris, jazz vibraphonist; Louella Hasbun, San José Symphony; Douglas Hedwig, Metropolitan Opera Orchestra; Frank Hosticka, Metropolitan Opera Orchestra; Simon James, Seattle Symphony; Richard Jensen, Cincinnati Symphony; Henry Kao, New Jersey Symphony; Gilad Karni, Bamburger Sinfoniker; Kemal Khan, conductor; Christopher Komer, New Jersey Symphony; Dawn Kotoski, soprano, Metropolitan Opera; Morris Lang, New York Philharmonic; Michael Leonhart, Grammy Award winner; Igor Leschishin, Kennedy Center Opera Orchestra; Roy Lewis, Manhattan String Quartet; Douglas Lindsay, Cincinnati Symphony; George Manahan, Music Director, New York City Opera; Marvis Martin, soprano, Metropolitan Opera; Kerri McDermott, New York Philharmonic; Peter McGinnis, jazz trombonist; Sharon Meekins, Metropolitan Opera Orchestra; Warren Mok, tenor, Berlin Opera; Jane Monheit, jazz vocalist; Jason Moran, jazz pianist; Frank Morelli, Orpheus Chamber Orchestra; June Morganstern, Chicago Lyric Opera Orchestra; Elmar Oliveira, concert violinist; Susan Quittmeyer, mezzo-soprano, Metropolitan Opera; Max Roach, jazz artist; Tatiana Ruhland, Dresden Philharmonic; Bruce Smith, Detroit Symphony; Dawn Stahler, Dallas Symphony; James Stubbs, Metropolitan Opera Orchestra; Stewart Taylor, Israel Philharmonic; Dawn Upshaw, soprano, Metropolitan Opera; Roland Vasquez, jazz drummer; Rosa Vento, soprano, Vienna State Opera; Geraldine Walther, San Francisco Symphony; Bing Wang, Los Angeles Philharmonic; Mark Wells, Canadian Opera Orchestra; Virginia Chen Wells, Toronto Symphony; Thomas Wetzel, Milwaukee Symphony; Timothy Wilson, San Francisco Opera Orchestra; Carol Wincenc, concert flutist; Naomi Youngstein, New Jersey Symphony; and Dolora Zajick, mezzo-soprano, Metropolitan Opera.

# Manhattanville College
## Purchase, New York

Independent, coed. Suburban campus. Total enrollment: 3,023. Music program established 1937.

**Degrees** Bachelor of Arts in the area of music; Bachelor of Arts/Master of Arts in Teaching in the area of music education.

*Manhattanville College (continued)*

Majors and concentrations: music, music education, music management, music theater. Graduate degrees offered: Master of Arts in Teaching in the area of music education; Bachelor of Arts/Master of Arts in Teaching in the area of music education. Cross-registration with Purchase College-State University of New York.

**Enrollment** 94 total; 82 undergraduate, 12 graduate.

**Music Student Profile** 68% females, 32% males, 22% minorities, 8% international.

**Music Faculty** 4 undergraduate (full-time), 20 undergraduate (part-time), 2 graduate (part-time). 100% of full-time faculty have terminal degrees. Graduate students do not teach undergraduate courses. Undergraduate student–faculty ratio: 8:1.

**Student Life** Student groups/activities include Music Educators National Conference, Music Teachers National Association.

**Expenses for 2008–2009** Application fee: $65. Comprehensive fee: $44,660 includes full-time tuition ($30,400), mandatory fees ($1220), and college room and board ($13,040). College room only: $7740. Special program-related fees: $60 per semester for instrument rental, $720 per semester for instrumental and vocal instruction (includes practice room).

**Financial Aid** Program-specific awards: departmental awards ($2000–$5000).

**Application Procedures** Students admitted directly into the professional program freshman year. Deadline for freshmen and transfers: continuous. Required: essay, high school transcript, college transcript(s) for transfer students, minimum 2.0 high school GPA, 2 letters of recommendation, audition, SAT or ACT test scores, high school transcript for transfer applicants with fewer than 45 credits. Recommended: minimum 3.0 high school GPA, interview. Auditions held 6 times on campus; recorded music is permissible as a substitute for live auditions for international applicants and in special circumstances and videotaped performances are permissible as a substitute for live auditions for international applicants and in special circumstances.

**Web Site** http://www.mville.edu

**Undergraduate Contact** Mr. Jose Flores, Director of Admissions, Manhattanville College, 2900 Purchase Street, Purchase, New York 10577; 800-328-4553, fax: 914-694-1732, e-mail address: admissions@mville.edu

**Graduate Contact** Alyce Poli, Director, Graduate Education Admissions, School of Education, Manhattanville College, 2900 Purchase Street, Purchase, New York 10577; 914-323-3208, e-mail address: polia@mville.edu

## The New School
# Mannes College The New School for Music

### New York, New York

Independent, coed. Urban campus. Total enrollment: 379. Music program established 1916.

**Degrees** Bachelor of Music in the areas of orchestral instruments, piano, voice, composition, music theory, orchestral and choral conducting, harpsichord, classic guitar; Bachelor of Science in the areas of orchestral instruments, piano, harpsichord, voice, classical guitar, orchestral conducting, choral conducting, composition, theory. Majors and concentrations: classical guitar, composition, conducting, guitar, harpsichord, music theory, performance, piano, stringed instruments, voice, wind and percussion instruments. Graduate degrees offered: Master of Music in the areas of orchestral instruments, piano, voice, composition, music theory, orchestral and choral conducting, harpsichord, classic guitar. Cross-registration with The New School.

**Enrollment** 379 total; 189 undergraduate, 182 graduate, 8 nonprofessional degree.

**Music Student Profile** 60% females, 40% males, 28% minorities, 48% international.

**Music Faculty** 5 total (full-time), 151 total (part-time). Graduate students do not teach undergraduate courses. Undergraduate student–faculty ratio: 6:1.

**Expenses for 2007–2008** Application fee: $100. Comprehensive fee: $42,160 includes full-time tuition ($29,800), mandatory fees ($610), and college room and board ($11,750). College room only: $8750. Room and board charges vary according to board plan.

**Financial Aid** Program-specific awards: merit scholarships for above-average students.

**Application Procedures** Students admitted directly into the professional program freshman year. Deadline for freshmen and transfers: December 1. Notification date for freshmen and transfers: June 1. Required: essay, high school transcript, college transcript(s) for transfer students, letter of recommendation, interview, audition, TOEFL for international students for whom English is a second language. Recommended: minimum 2.0 high school GPA. Auditions held twice on campus.

**Web Site** http://www.mannes.edu

**Contact** Ms. Georgia Schmitt, Director of Admissions, Mannes College The New School for Music, 150 West 85th Street, New York, New York 10024; 212-580-0210 ext. 4805, fax: 212-580-1738, e-mail address: schmittg@newschool.edu

### More About the College

For students at Mannes College in New York City, music is a part of life both in and out of the classroom. Students at this world-renowned classical music conservatory benefit from and contribute to the city's rich musical and cultural life.

Mannes is alone among New York City's major conservatories in being part of a liberal arts university—The New School—allowing students to focus on performance while being able to access insightful courses in all the liberal arts.

At Mannes, small classes and a small student body (fewer than 300 students and a 2:1 student-faculty ratio) ensure that each student receives personalized instruction and has close interaction with faculty and staff members, administrators, and peers. Undergraduates can earn a Bachelor of Music, Bachelor of Science, or an undergraduate diploma in orchestral instruments, piano, harpsichord, voice, classical guitar, orchestral conducting, choral conducting, composition, or theory. Mannes also offers Master of Music degrees and Professional Studies Diplomas. At Mannes, older students frequently act as mentors for their younger colleagues, for example in the Mannes Orchestra, which includes about half of Mannes' college students.

For aspiring musicians, there is no substitute for the experience gained by performing. Mannes presents hundreds of performances by students, faculty members, and artists-in-residence each year in its two concert halls. In addition, Mannes offers unsurpassed opportunities for students to perform at major venues throughout New York City, including Carnegie Hall and Lincoln Center. In 2008, the *New York Times* praised the Mannes Orchestra for a "lustrous, driven performance" at Carnegie Hall and the Mannes Opera for a performance of Francis Poulenc's "Dialogues of the Carmelites" at the Kaye Playhouse, which lived up to the program's "stellar reputation for the quality of its productions and the excellence of its student singers."

As part of the curriculum, performance courses are balanced with techniques of music courses to give students solid training in the language of music. Through ear training, dictation, keyboard skills, theory, and analysis courses, students deepen their understanding of the structures of music. In addition, students receive private lessons with one of the school's 150 distinguished faculty members and study a curriculum that is tailored to meet their particular needs. The Mannes Opera program, led by Metropolitan Opera conductor Joseph Colaneri and featuring the vocal guidance of legendary opera singer Regina Resnik, is considered among the top in the country, producing full-staged professional operas every year. As Anne Midgette has written in the *New York Times,* "People in the opera would often ask: Where are all the good, healthy young voices? Here's an answer: At Mannes College...."

When they are not practicing or attending classes, students have plenty of opportunities for relaxation and recreation in Mannes' residential Upper West Side neighborhood. Students can dine on any sort of food imaginable, explore Central Park, walk to major museums and nearby theaters, and attend live performances at concert halls throughout the city, most of which are within minutes of Mannes.

Students at Mannes have access to everything aspiring musicians need. The Federal-style building Mannes calls home offers classrooms, practice rooms, a state-of-the-art computer lab, and the Scherman Music Library, which features a collection that includes 8,000 books, 30,000 scores, 9,000 recordings, 300 video recordings, many music-related periodicals, specialized databases, and electronic resources, as well as study carrels, computers, and a complete music and listening library. The New School also offers the facilities of the Fogelman Social Science and Humanities Library, located on the downtown campus, and, through a consortium known as the Research Library Association of South Manhattan, the Bobst Library at New York University and the consortium's online catalog, Bobcat, are accessible on the Internet.

The pursuit of instrumental and vocal mastery is complemented by classes in literature, history, and liberal arts. Degree candidates have access to The New School's broad liberal arts curriculum, and Mannes students share resources with The New School's other divisions: The New School for General Studies, The New School for Social Research, Milano The New School for Management and Urban Policy, Parsons The New School for Design, Eugene Lang College The New School for Liberal Arts, The New School for Drama, and The New School for Jazz and Contemporary Music.

The performance faculty at Mannes includes active professionals from all areas of the music world—concert artists, chamber musicians, successful freelancers, established composers, and members of such leading organizations as the New York Philharmonic, Metropolitan Opera, Orpheus Chamber Orchestra, New York City Opera, and Philadelphia Orchestra.

Students also have access to a network of thousands of successful alumni who are putting their training to work on stages around the world. Mannes's distinguished alumni include Frederica von Stade, Richard Goode, Murray Perahia, JoAnn Falletta, and Kaori Sato. For more information about Mannes, students should visit http://www.newschool.edu/mannes.

# Mansfield University of Pennsylvania
## Mansfield, Pennsylvania

State-supported, coed. Small town campus. Total enrollment: 3,338. Music program established 1880.

**Degrees** Bachelor of Music in the areas of music education, performance, elective studies in business. Majors and concentrations: music, music business, music education, music performance, piano, stringed instruments, voice, wind and percussion instruments. Graduate degrees offered: Master of Arts in the areas of music education, instrumental conducting, choral conducting. Program accredited by NASM.

**Enrollment** 241 total; 200 undergraduate, 16 graduate, 25 nonprofessional degree.

**Music Student Profile** 60% females, 40% males, 4% minorities, 1% international.

**Music Faculty** 19 undergraduate (full-time), 4 undergraduate (part-time), 19 graduate (full-time), 4 graduate (part-time). 94% of full-time faculty have terminal degrees. Graduate students do not teach undergraduate courses. Undergraduate student–faculty ratio: 12:1.

**Student Life** Student groups/activities include Music Educators National Conference Student Chapter, Mid-Atlantic Regional Association of Music Therapy Students, American Choral Directors Association.

**Expenses for 2007–2008** Application fee: $25. State resident tuition: $5177 full-time. Nonresident tuition: $12,944 full-time. Mandatory fees: $1827 full-time. College room and board: $6236. College room only: $2326. Room and board charges vary according to board plan. Special program-related fees: $25 per department for recording and program fee, $30 per course for instrument rental fee for all techniques courses.

**Financial Aid** Program-specific awards: 5 Kreuscher Awards for program majors ($1000), 1 Darrin-Dye Award for freshmen program majors ($1000), 1 Doud Award for freshmen program majors ($3400), 2 Music Department Scholarships for freshmen program majors ($1000–$2000), 5 Jones Awards for voice program majors ($2000), 1 Frances Award for freshman program majors ($1000), 1 Ruc Scholarship for upperclass students from Pennsylvania ($1000).

**Application Procedures** Students admitted directly into the professional program freshman year. Deadline for freshmen and transfers: February 28. Required: high school transcript, college transcript(s) for transfer students, minimum 2.0 high school GPA, 2 letters of recommendation, interview, audition, SAT or ACT test scores, theory placement test, piano proficiency test, aural skills test. Recommended: essay, minimum 3.0 high school GPA. Auditions held 8 times on campus; recorded music is permissible as a substitute for live auditions when distance is prohibitive and without editing and videotaped performances are permissible as a substitute for live auditions when distance is prohibitive and without editing.

**Web Site** http://www.music.mansfield.edu

**Contact** Dr. Adam F. Brennan, Chairperson, Department of Music, Mansfield University of Pennsylvania, Butler Center 110, Mansfield, Pennsylvania 16933; 570-662-4710, fax: 570-662-4114, e-mail address: abrennan@mansfield.edu

# Wands L. Bass School of Music
See Oklahoma City University

# Mariam Cannon Hayes School of Music
See Appalachian State University

# Marygrove College
## Detroit, Michigan

Independent Roman Catholic, coed, primarily women. Urban campus. Total enrollment: 2,953 (2007). Music program established 1927.

*Marygrove College (continued)*

**Degrees** Bachelor of Music in the areas of performance (voice, organ or piano), piano pedagogy, music education, sacred music (choral, organ, or piano emphasis), theory and composition. Majors and concentrations: electronic music, music education, music theory and composition, performance, piano pedagogy, sacred music. Cross-registration with University of Detroit Mercy.
**Enrollment** 33 total; 28 undergraduate, 5 nonprofessional degree.
**Music Student Profile** 75% females, 25% males, 75% minorities, 1% international.
**Music Faculty** 4 undergraduate (full-time), 7 undergraduate (part-time). 100% of full-time faculty have terminal degrees. Graduate students do not teach undergraduate courses. Undergraduate student–faculty ratio: 9:1.
**Student Life** Student groups/activities include Music Teachers National Association Student Chapter, Marygrove College Chorale, Lyric Theatre Program.
**Expenses for 2007–2008** Application fee: $25. One-time mandatory fee: $25. Comprehensive fee: $21,290 includes full-time tuition ($14,380), mandatory fees ($310), and college room and board ($6600). Room and board charges vary according to board plan. Special program-related fees: $25 per semester for choir fee, $65 per credit hour for private lessons.
**Financial Aid** Program-specific awards: 2–4 music scholarships for talented students ($500–$1000), Distinguished Student Awards for talented students ($2000–$9000), Admissions Talent Awards for talented students ($3000–$9000).
**Application Procedures** Students admitted directly into the professional program freshman year. Deadline for freshmen and transfers: continuous. Required: high school transcript, college transcript(s) for transfer students, SAT or ACT test scores, minimum 2.7 high school GPA, minimum 2.0 college GPA for transfer applicants, audition for scholarship consideration. Recommended: interview, audition. Auditions held twice on campus; recorded music is permissible as a substitute for live auditions for international applicants and videotaped performances are permissible as a substitute for live auditions for international applicants.
**Web Site** http://www.marygrove.edu
**Undergraduate Contact** John Ambrose, Director of Admissions, Marygrove College, 8425 West McNichols Road, Detroit, Michigan 48221; 313-927-1236, fax: 313-864-6670, e-mail address: adm@marygrove.edu

# Marylhurst University

## Marylhurst, Oregon

Independent Roman Catholic, coed. Suburban campus. Total enrollment: 1,433. Music program established 1961.
**Degrees** Bachelor of Music in the areas of composition, performance; Bachelor of Music Therapy. Majors and concentrations: composition, jazz, music performance, music therapy, piano pedagogy, piano performance, voice pedagogy, voice performance. Program accredited by NASM.
**Enrollment** 57 total; 43 undergraduate, 14 nonprofessional degree.
**Music Student Profile** 65% females, 35% males, 20% minorities, 5% international.
**Music Faculty** 2 undergraduate (full-time), 30 undergraduate (part-time). 100% of full-time faculty have terminal degrees. Graduate students do not teach undergraduate courses. Undergraduate student–faculty ratio: 6:1.
**Expenses for 2007–2008** Application fee: $20. Tuition: $15,120 full-time. Mandatory fees: $450 full-time. Full-time tuition and fees vary according to course load, degree level, and program. Special program-related fees: $30 per course for music therapy practicum, $100 per course for private music lessons.
**Financial Aid** Program-specific awards: 8 departmental scholarships for all music majors ($300–$3000).
**Application Procedures** Students admitted directly into the professional program freshman year. Deadline for freshmen and transfers: continuous. Required: essay, high school transcript, college transcript(s) for transfer students, minimum 3.0 high school GPA, letter of recommendation, interview, audition, portfolio. Auditions held 3 times on campus; recorded music is permissible as a substitute for live auditions when distance is prohibitive or in special circumstances and videotaped performances are permissible as a substitute for live auditions when distance is prohibitive or in special circumstances.
**Web Site** http://www.marylhurst.edu/music
**Undergraduate Contact** Office of Admissions, Marylhurst University, PO Box 261, Marylhurst, Oregon 97036-0261; 503-699-6268, fax: 503-635-6585, e-mail address: studentinfo@marylhurst.edu

# The Mary Pappert School of Music

See Duquesne University

*Rutgers, The State University of New Jersey*
# Mason Gross School of the Arts

## New Brunswick, New Jersey

State-supported, coed. Small town campus. Music program established 1976.
**Degrees** Bachelor of Music in the areas of music education, jazz, performance. Majors and concentrations: classical music, jazz, music education. Graduate degrees offered: Master of Music in the areas of performance, jazz, music education, collaborative piano, instrumental, choral, and orchestral conducting. Doctor of Musical Arts in the areas of performance, music education, collaborative piano, instrumental, choral, and orchestral conducting. Program accredited by NASM.
**Enrollment** 454 total; 212 undergraduate, 196 graduate, 46 nonprofessional degree.
**Music Student Profile** 40% females, 60% males, 10% minorities, 15% international.
**Music Faculty** 25 undergraduate (full-time), 45 undergraduate (part-time), 8 graduate (full-time), 2 graduate (part-time). 100% of full-time faculty have terminal degrees. Graduate students teach about a quarter of undergraduate courses. Undergraduate student–faculty ratio: 3:1.
**Student Life** Student groups/activities include National Association of Teachers.
**Financial Aid** Program-specific awards: 13 Benefit Series Awards for those with artistic merit ($500–$3500), 15 Marryott Scholarships for those with artistic merit ($500–$4000), 5 Douglass Noe Awards for those with artistic merit ($500–$2500), 3 Douglass Shaw Awards for those with artistic merit ($500–$1500), 5 Douglass Waksman Awards for those with artistic merit ($500–$2000), Lockfeld Awards in Jazz for those with artistic merit ($1000), Jean Hooper Awards for those with artistic merit ($2500), 4 W. Robert and Leone Schare Scholarships for those with artistic merit ($500–$1700).
**Application Procedures** Students admitted directly into the professional program freshman year. Deadline for freshmen: continuous; transfers: March 15. Notification date for freshmen and transfers: May 1. Required: high school transcript, college transcript(s) for transfer students, minimum 2.0 high school GPA, interview, audition, SAT or ACT test scores. Auditions held 4 times on campus; recorded music is permissible as a substitute for live auditions when distance is prohibitive or scheduling is difficult and videotaped performances are permissible as a substitute for live auditions when distance is prohibitive or scheduling is difficult.
**Web Site** http://www.rutgers.edu
**Undergraduate Contact** Dr. Antonius Bittmann, Chairman, Music Department, Rutgers, The State University of New Jersey, Mason Gross School of the Arts, Marryott Music Building, New Brunswick, New Jersey 08901; 732-932-8860, fax: 732-932-1517.
**Graduate Contact** Dr. Richard Chrisman, Graduate Director, Music Department, Rutgers, The State University of New Jersey, Mason Gross School of the Arts, Marryott Music Building, New Brunswick, New Jersey 08901; 732-932-9272, fax: 732-932-1517, e-mail address: chrisman@rci.rutgers.edu

## Schulich School of Music
# McGill University
### Montreal, Quebec, Canada

Province-supported, coed. Urban campus. Total enrollment: 31,081. Music program established 1904.

**Degrees** Bachelor of Music in the areas of composition, music history, music theory, performance (piano, voice, orchestral instruments, church music, early music, jazz); Bachelor of Music/Bachelor of Education in the area of music education (concurrent program). Majors and concentrations: composition, early music, jazz performance, music education, music history, music theory, performance. Graduate degrees offered: Master of Arts in the areas of music education, music technology, musicology, theory; Master of Music in the areas of composition, performance, sound recording. Doctor of Music in the areas of composition, performance; Doctor of Philosophy in the areas of composition, music education, music technology, musicology, sound recording theory. Cross-registration with any Quebec university; also bi-lateral exchange agreement with Sibelius Academy in Finland. Program accredited by CUMS.

**Enrollment** 863 total; 557 undergraduate, 253 graduate, 53 nonprofessional degree.

**Music Student Profile** 51% females, 49% males, 12% international.

**Music Faculty** 62 total (full-time), 193 total (part-time). 44% of full-time faculty have terminal degrees. Graduate students teach about a quarter of undergraduate courses. Undergraduate student–faculty ratio: 10:1.

**Student Life** Student groups/activities include performances at various campus functions, paying engagements in Montreal area.

**Expenses for 2007–2008** Application fee: $80 Canadian dollars. Tuition, fee, and room and board charges are reported in Canadian dollars. Province resident tuition: $1768 full-time. Canadian resident tuition: $5140 full-time. Mandatory fees: $1421 full-time. Full-time tuition and fees vary according to class time, course load, degree level, location, program, and student level. College room and board: $10,400. Room and board charges vary according to board plan, gender, housing facility, and location. Special program-related fees: $666 for private lesson fee (variable), $700 per 30 credits for instruments, practice rooms, ensemble music, society fee.

**Financial Aid** Program-specific awards: 10–12 Schulich Scholarships for candidates with exceptional musical skills ($5000), 2–5 McGill Major Awards for freshmen with high academic standing ($5000–$8000), 12 music entrance scholarships for candidates with exceptional musical skills ($2000), 2 Lloyd Carr Harris String Scholarships for string players with exceptional musical skills ($10,000).

**Application Procedures** Students admitted directly into the professional program freshman year. Deadline for freshmen and transfers: January 15. Notification date for freshmen and transfers: March 30. Required: high school transcript, college transcript(s) for transfer students, minimum 3.0 high school GPA, letter of recommendation, audition, statement of intent, portfolio for composition majors, screening tape for jazz piano and female voice, music education letter in support of suitability. Recommended: SAT or ACT test scores. Auditions held once on campus; recorded music is permissible as a substitute for live auditions when distance is prohibitive or a scheduling conflict exists (students not eligible for scholarships if audition is taped or video) and videotaped performances are permissible as a substitute for live auditions when distance is prohibitive or a scheduling conflict exists (students not eligible for scholarships if audition is taped or video). Portfolio reviews held once on campus.

**Web Site** http://www.mcgill.ca/music

**Contact** Mr. Patrick O'Neill, Admissions Officer, Schulich School of Music, McGill University, 555 Sherbrooke Street West, Montreal, Quebec H3A 1E3, Canada; 514-398-4546, fax: 514-398-8873, e-mail address: undergradadmissions.music@mcgill.ca

# McLean School of Music
### See Middle Tennessee State University

# Meadows School of the Arts/Division of Music
### See Southern Methodist University

# Mercer University
### Macon, Georgia

Independent Baptist, coed. Suburban campus. Total enrollment: 5,253. Music program established 1978.

**Degrees** Bachelor of Music in the area of performance; Bachelor of Music Education. Majors and concentrations: composition, guitar, harpsichord, music education, music theory, piano/organ, stringed instruments, voice, wind and percussion instruments. Graduate degrees offered: Master of Music in the areas of church music, performance with an emphasis in church music, conducting. Program accredited by NASM.

**Enrollment** 70 total; 35 undergraduate, 35 nonprofessional degree.

**Music Student Profile** 50% females, 50% males, 12% minorities, 1% international.

**Music Faculty** 13 undergraduate (full-time), 15 undergraduate (part-time). 100% of full-time faculty have terminal degrees. Graduate students do not teach undergraduate courses. Undergraduate student–faculty ratio: 5:1.

**Student Life** Student groups/activities include Music Educators National Conference Student Chapter, American Choral Directors Association Student Chapter, Mu Phi Epsilon.

**Expenses for 2007–2008** Application fee: $50. Comprehensive fee: $34,975 includes full-time tuition ($26,760), mandatory fees ($200), and college room and board ($8015). College room only: $3980. Full-time tuition and fees vary according to class time, course load, and location. Room and board charges vary according to board plan, housing facility, and location. Special program-related fees: $218 per semester for lesson fee.

**Financial Aid** Program-specific awards: 40 music scholarships for music majors ($1000–$6000).

**Application Procedures** Students apply for admission into the professional program by sophomore year. Deadline for freshmen and transfers: continuous. Notification date for freshmen and transfers: continuous. Required: high school transcript, college transcript(s) for transfer students, minimum 2.0 high school GPA, letter of recommendation, audition, SAT or ACT test scores, list of extracurricular activities. Auditions held 4 times and by appointment on campus; recorded music is permissible as a substitute for live auditions when distance is prohibitive and videotaped performances are permissible as a substitute for live auditions when distance is prohibitive.

**Web Site** http://www.mercer.edu/music/

**Undergraduate Contact** Director of Admissions, Mercer University, 1400 Coleman Avenue, Macon, Georgia 31207; 478-301-2650, fax: 478-301-4120.

**Graduate Contact** Dr. John E. Simons, Director, Townsend School of Music, Mercer University, 1400 Coleman Avenue, Macon, Georgia 31207; 478-301-2748, fax: 478-301-5633.

# Meredith College
### Raleigh, North Carolina

Independent, Urban campus. Total enrollment: 2,202. Music program established 1899.

**Degrees** Bachelor of Music in the areas of performance, music education. Majors and concentrations: classical music, composition, music, music education, piano pedagogy, piano/organ, stringed instruments, voice, wind and percussion instruments. Graduate degrees offered: Master of Music in the area of performance/pedagogy. Cross-registration with North Carolina State University and Cooperating Raleigh Colleges Consortium. Program accredited by NASM.

**Enrollment** 70 total; 40 undergraduate, 10 graduate, 20 nonprofessional degree.

**Music Student Profile** 100% females, 5% international.

*Meredith College (continued)*

**Music Faculty** 9 total (full-time), 25 total (part-time). 100% of full-time faculty have terminal degrees. Graduate students do not teach undergraduate courses. Undergraduate student–faculty ratio: 5:1.

**Student Life** Student groups/activities include Sigma Alpha Iota, Pi Kappa Lambda, Collegiate Music Educators National Conference.

**Expenses for 2008–2009** Application fee: $40. Comprehensive fee: $30,290 includes full-time tuition ($23,500), mandatory fees ($50), and college room and board ($6740). College room only: $3370. Special program-related fees: $150–$300 per semester for applied music fee, $380 per semester for professional accompanist fee (if applicable).

**Financial Aid** Program-specific awards: 1 Excellence in Music Scholarship for incoming freshmen ($7500), 1 Robert H. Lewis Award for incoming freshmen ($6000), 3 music talent scholarships for incoming freshmen ($500–$1500), 1 Mary Perry Beddingfield Award for incoming freshmen ($1000).

**Application Procedures** Students admitted directly into the professional program freshman year. Deadline for freshmen and transfers: continuous. Required: high school transcript, college transcript(s) for transfer students, minimum 2.0 high school GPA, 2 letters of recommendation, interview, audition, SAT test score only. Recommended: essay. Auditions held at various times on campus; recorded music is permissible as a substitute for live auditions when distance is prohibitive or scheduling is difficult and videotaped performances are permissible as a substitute for live auditions when distance is prohibitive or scheduling is difficult.

**Web Site** http://www.meredith.edu

**Undergraduate Contact** Ms. Heidi Fletcher, Director, Office of Admissions, Meredith College, 3800 Hillsborough Street, Raleigh, North Carolina 27607-5298; 800-637-3348, fax: 919-760-2348, e-mail address: admissions@meredith.edu

**Graduate Contact** Director, John E. Weems Graduate School, Meredith College, 3800 Hillsborough Street, Raleigh, North Carolina 27607-5298; 919-760-8423, fax: 919-760-2898, e-mail address: gradmusic@meredith.edu

# Metropolitan State College of Denver
**Denver, Colorado**

State-supported, coed. Urban campus. Music program established 1965.
**Web Site** http://www.mscd.edu/

# Miami University
**Oxford, Ohio**

State-related, coed. Small town campus. Total enrollment: 15,922. Music program established 1929.

**Degrees** Bachelor of Music in the areas of performance, music education. Majors and concentrations: harp, music, music education, piano/organ, stringed instruments, voice, wind and percussion instruments. Graduate degrees offered: Master of Music in the areas of performance, music education. Program accredited by NASM, NCATE.

**Enrollment** 250 total; 225 undergraduate, 25 graduate.

**Music Student Profile** 50% females, 50% males, 5% minorities, 1% international.

**Music Faculty** 31 total (full-time), 12 total (part-time). 50% of full-time faculty have terminal degrees. Graduate students teach a few undergraduate courses. Undergraduate student–faculty ratio: 6:1.

**Student Life** Student groups/activities include Music Educators National Conference, American Choral Directors Association, professional music fraternities and sororities.

**Expenses for 2007–2008** Application fee: $45. State resident tuition: $9910 full-time. Nonresident tuition: $22,362 full-time. Mandatory fees: $2015 full-time. College room and board: $8600. College room only: $4410. Room and board charges vary according to board plan and housing facility. Special program-related fees: $150 per semester for fee for hour lesson.

**Financial Aid** Program-specific awards: 40 music talent awards for music majors ($4000).

**Application Procedures** Students admitted directly into the professional program freshman year. Deadline for freshmen: January 31; transfers: May 1. Notification date for freshmen: March 15; transfers: June 1. Required: essay, high school transcript, college transcript(s) for transfer students, minimum 2.0 high school GPA, audition, SAT or ACT test scores. Recommended: minimum 3.0 high school GPA, 3 letters of recommendation, interview. Auditions held 15 times on campus; recorded music is permissible as a substitute for live auditions when distance is prohibitive and videotaped performances are permissible as a substitute for live auditions when distance is prohibitive.

**Web Site** http://www.muohio.edu/music/

**Undergraduate Contact** Barbara Wright, Administrative Assistant, Department of Music, Miami University, 119 Center for the Performing Arts, Oxford, Ohio 45056; 513-529-3014, fax: 513-529-3027, e-mail address: wrightbk@muohio.edu

**Graduate Contact** Dr. Claire Boge, Director of Graduate Studies, Department of Music, Miami University, 119 Center for the Performing Arts, Oxford, Ohio 45056; 513-529-3014, fax: 513-529-3027, e-mail address: bogecl@muohio.edu

*McLean School of Music*
# Middle Tennessee State University
**Murfreesboro, Tennessee**

State-supported, coed. Total enrollment: 23,246. Music program established 1911.
**Web Site** http://www.mtsu.edu/

# Midwestern State University
**Wichita Falls, Texas**

State-supported, coed. Urban campus. Total enrollment: 6,027. Music program established 1954.
**Web Site** http://www.mwsu.edu/

# Millikin University
**Decatur, Illinois**

Independent, coed. Suburban campus. Total enrollment: 2,376. Music program established 1901.
**Web Site** http://www.millikin.edu/

# Minnesota State University Mankato
**Mankato, Minnesota**

State-supported, coed. Small town campus. Total enrollment: 14,148.

**Degrees** Bachelor of Music in the areas of voice, piano, winds, strings, percussion, organ; Bachelor of Science in the areas of music education (instrumental, choral/vocal), music industry. Majors and concentrations: music, music education, music industry, piano/organ, stringed instruments, voice, wind and percussion instruments. Graduate degrees offered: Master of Music in the areas of performance, music education, choral conducting, wind band conducting. Program accredited by NASM.

**Enrollment** 110 total; 90 undergraduate, 10 graduate, 10 nonprofessional degree.

**Music Student Profile** 60% females, 40% males, 8% minorities, 4% international.

**Music Faculty** 14 total (full-time), 8 total (part-time). 91% of full-time faculty have terminal degrees. Graduate students do not teach undergraduate courses. Undergraduate student–faculty ratio: 10:1.

**Student Life** Student groups/activities include Music Educators National Conference, American Choral Directors Association, International Association for Jazz Education.

**Expenses for 2007–2008** Application fee: $20. State resident tuition: $5308 full-time. Nonresident tuition: $11,370 full-time.

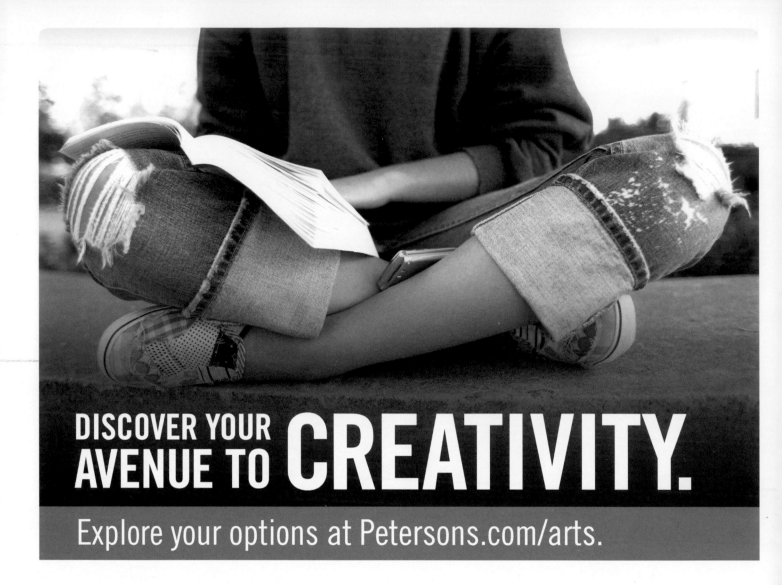

# DISCOVER YOUR AVENUE TO CREATIVITY.

## Explore your options at Petersons.com/arts.

When you're looking for a professional program in the visual arts, such as painting, drawing, and sculpture, or performing arts, including music, dance, and theater, check out these helpful resources at Petersons.com:

- A comprehensive search for Bachelor of Fine Arts programs
- A customized scholarship search
- Free information from schools you contact
- Advice articles
- Financial aid information

**VISIT PETERSONS.COM/ARTS TODAY.**

**PETERSON'S**
A nelnet COMPANY

Mandatory fees: $742 full-time. Full-time tuition and fees vary according to course load and reciprocity agreements. College room and board: $5354. Room and board charges vary according to board plan. Special program-related fees: $10–$35 per term for instrument rental.

**Financial Aid** Program-specific awards: 1 Stewart Ross Band Scholarship for band instrumentalists ($600), 1 Nancy Cora Williams Scholarship for music education majors ($500), 1 Van Sickle Endowment Award for string or voice majors ($600), 1 Een Endowment Award for program majors ($470), 16 talent grants for incoming freshmen ($600), 7 Stein Scholarships for music majors ($350), 7 Music Foundation Awards for music majors ($450), 4 Mankato Symphony Awards for orchestra students ($1250), 2 Kiyo Suyematsu Scholarships for music majors ($1500), 1 Lindberg Woodwind Scholarship for woodwind players (especially double reeds) ($1000).

**Application Procedures** Students apply for admission into the professional program by freshman year. Deadline for freshmen and transfers: continuous. Required: high school transcript, college transcript(s) for transfer students, minimum 2.0 high school GPA, 3 letters of recommendation, interview, audition, SAT or ACT test scores. Recommended: minimum 3.0 high school GPA. Auditions held as needed on campus; recorded music is permissible as a substitute for live auditions when distance is prohibitive and videotaped performances are permissible as a substitute for live auditions when distance is prohibitive. Portfolio reviews held twice on campus.

**Web Site** http://www.intech.mnsu.edu/music

**Undergraduate Contact** Dr. John Lindberg, Chair, Music Department, Minnesota State University Mankato, PAC 202, Mankato, Minnesota 56002-8400; 507-389-2118, fax: 507-389-2922, e-mail address: john.lindberg@mankato.msus.edu

**Graduate Contact** Dr. David Dickau, Graduate Coordinator, Music Department, Minnesota State University Mankato, PAC 202, Mankato, Minnesota 56002-8400; 507-389-5546, fax: 507-389-2922.

# Mississippi State University

## Mississippi State, Mississippi

State-supported, coed. Total enrollment: 17,039. Music program established 1957.

**Degrees** Bachelor of Music Education in the areas of instrumental music education, vocal music education, keyboard music education, guitar music education. Majors and concentrations: guitar music education, instrumental music education, keyboard music education, vocal music education. Program accredited by NASM.

**Enrollment** 106 total; 72 undergraduate, 34 nonprofessional degree.

**Music Student Profile** 60% females, 40% males, 18% minorities, 3% international.

**Music Faculty** 20 undergraduate (full-time), 2 undergraduate (part-time). 90% of full-time faculty have terminal degrees. Graduate students do not teach undergraduate courses. Undergraduate student–faculty ratio: 5:1.

**Student Life** Student groups/activities include Music Educators National Conference, Phi Mu Alpha Sinfonia, Sigma Alpha Iota, American Choral Directors Association (ACDA), Kappa Kappa Psi.

**Expenses for 2007–2008** Application fee: $25. State resident tuition: $4978 full-time. Nonresident tuition: $11,469 full-time. College room and board: $6951. College room only: $3716. Room and board charges vary according to board plan, housing facility, and student level.

**Financial Aid** Program-specific awards: 2–3 Thomas Piano Scholarships for keyboard majors, 1–2 Cheryl Prewitt Scholarships for voice majors, 70 music scholarships for incoming freshmen and transfers, 400 service scholarships for choir and band members, 1–2 Kaufman Endowment Awards for those demonstrating musical and academic achievement, 1–2 Hal Polk Scholarships for instrumental majors, 1–2 music education faculty scholarships.

**Application Procedures** Students admitted directly into the professional program freshman year. Deadline for freshmen and transfers: continuous. Required: high school transcript, college transcript(s) for transfer students, audition, SAT or ACT test scores (minimum composite ACT score of 20). Auditions held 4 times and by appointment on campus; recorded music is

permissible as a substitute for live auditions when distance is prohibitive and in special circumstances with permission and videotaped performances are permissible as a substitute for live auditions with permission of professor or committee.

**Web Site** http://music.msstate.edu

**Undergraduate Contact** Dr. Michael Brown, Professor and Head, Department of Music, Mississippi State University, Box 9734, Mississippi State, Mississippi 39762; 662-325-3070, fax: 662-325-0250.

# Mississippi University for Women

## Columbus, Mississippi

State-supported, coed, primarily women. Small town campus. Total enrollment: 2,379. Music program established 1935.

**Web Site** http://www.muw.edu/

# Missouri State University

## Springfield, Missouri

State-supported, coed. Suburban campus. Total enrollment: 19,348. Music program established 1908.

**Degrees** Bachelor of Fine Arts in the area of musical theater; Bachelor of Music in the areas of music/performance, music/composition; Bachelor of Music Education in the area of instrumental/vocal music education; Bachelor of Science in the areas of music education, electronic arts. Majors and concentrations: electronic arts, music, music education, music theater. Graduate degrees offered: Master of Music in the areas of performance, pedagogy, composition, conducting, music education. Program accredited by NASM.

**Enrollment** 295 total; 260 undergraduate, 35 graduate.

**Music Student Profile** 55% females, 45% males, 5% minorities, 3% international.

**Music Faculty** 30 total (full-time), 22 total (part-time). 100% of full-time faculty have terminal degrees. Graduate students teach a few undergraduate courses. Undergraduate student–faculty ratio: 13:1.

**Expenses for 2007–2008** Application fee: $35. State resident tuition: $5988 full-time. Nonresident tuition: $11,088 full-time. Mandatory fees: $618 full-time. Full-time tuition and fees vary according to course load, degree level, location, and program. College room and board: $5312. Room and board charges vary according to board plan and housing facility.

**Financial Aid** Program-specific awards available.

**Application Procedures** Students admitted directly into the professional program freshman year. Deadline for freshmen and transfers: continuous. Notification date for freshmen and transfers: continuous. Required: audition. Auditions held three times on campus; recorded music is permissible as a substitute for live auditions and videotaped performances are permissible as a substitute for live auditions.

**Web Site** http://www.missouristate.edu/music/

**Undergraduate Contact** Dr. Roger Stoner, Head, Music Department, Missouri State University, 901 South National, Springfield, Missouri 65897; 417-836-5648, fax: 417-836-7665, e-mail address: rogerstoner@missouristate.edu

**Graduate Contact** Dr. Robert Quebbeman, Graduate Advisor, Music Department, Missouri State University, 901 South National, Springfield, Missouri 65897; 417-836-5729, fax: 417-836-7665, e-mail address: robertquebbeman@missourstate.edu

# Montana State University

## Bozeman, Montana

State-supported, coed. Small town campus. Total enrollment: 12,170. Music program established 1967.

**Degrees** Bachelor of Arts in the area of music; Bachelor of Music Education. Majors and concentrations: music education, piano/organ, stringed instruments, studio teaching, voice, wind and percussion instruments. Program accredited by NASM.

**Enrollment** 96 total; all undergraduate.

**Music Student Profile** 52% females, 48% males.

*Montana State University (continued)*

**Music Faculty** 11 undergraduate (full-time), 9 undergraduate (part-time). 100% of full-time faculty have terminal degrees. Graduate students do not teach undergraduate courses. Undergraduate student–faculty ratio: 6:1.

**Student Life** Student groups/activities include Kappa Kappa Psi (Beta), Collegiate Music Educators National Conference, American Choral Directors Association.

**Expenses for 2007–2008** Application fee: $30. State resident tuition: $5749 full-time. Nonresident tuition: $16,274 full-time. Full-time tuition varies according to course load. College room and board: $6780. Room and board charges vary according to board plan and housing facility. Special program-related fees: $3 per course for music, $15 per course for lab fee/instrument maintenance, $75 per semester for applied music fee.

**Financial Aid** Program-specific awards: 30 fee waivers for program majors ($2067), 6 Intermountain Opera Awards for state resident program majors ($1200), 49 music performance awards for program majors ($100–$1500).

**Application Procedures** Students admitted directly into the professional program freshman year. Deadline for freshmen and transfers: continuous. Required: high school transcript, audition for scholarship consideration. Auditions held continuously on campus; recorded music is permissible as a substitute for live auditions when distance is prohibitive and videotaped performances are permissible as a substitute for live auditions when distance is prohibitive.

**Web Site** http://www.montana.edu/wwwmusic

**Undergraduate Contact** Ms. Carole Oeschger, Administrative Officer, Department of Music, Montana State University, PO Box 173420, Bozeman, Montana 59717-0342; 406-994-1911, fax: 406-994-6656, e-mail address: oeschger@montana.edu

## *John J. Cali School of Music*
# Montclair State University
### Upper Montclair, New Jersey

State-supported, coed. Suburban campus. Total enrollment: 16,736. Music program established 1963.

**Degrees** Bachelor of Arts in the area of music therapy; Bachelor of Music in the areas of performance, music theory/composition, musical theater, music education. Majors and concentrations: classical music, music, music education, music theater, music theory and composition, music therapy, performance, piano/organ, stringed instruments, voice, wind and percussion instruments. Graduate degrees offered: Master of Arts in the areas of performance, theory/composition, music education, music therapy. Program accredited by NASM.

**Enrollment** 320 total; 240 undergraduate, 50 graduate, 30 nonprofessional degree.

**Music Student Profile** 60% females, 40% males, 30% minorities, 15% international.

**Music Faculty** 16 total (full-time), 52 total (part-time). 100% of full-time faculty have terminal degrees. Graduate students do not teach undergraduate courses. Undergraduate student–faculty ratio: 3:1.

**Student Life** Student groups/activities include Sigma Alpha Iota, Phi Mu Alpha Sinfonia, Music Educators National Conference.

**Expenses for 2007–2008** Application fee: $55. State resident tuition: $6390 full-time. Nonresident tuition: $13,659 full-time. Mandatory fees: $2505 full-time. College room and board: $9500. College room only: $6350. Room and board charges vary according to board plan and housing facility. Special program-related fees: $50 per semester for instrument rental, $100 per recital for recital recording fee, $400 per semester for applied music fees.

**Financial Aid** Program-specific awards: 1–10 Griffiths Piano Scholarships for piano majors ($100–$500), 1–10 Ravina Strings Awards for strings majors ($100–$500), 1–10 Howe Scholarships for music majors ($100–$500), 1 Hooper Scholarship for instrumental majors ($5000).

**Application Procedures** Students apply for admission into the professional program by sophomore year. Deadline for freshmen: March 1; transfers: May 1. Notification date for freshmen

and transfers: continuous. Required: high school transcript, college transcript(s) for transfer students, interview, audition, SAT test score only, portfolio for theory/composition applicants. Recommended: essay, 2 letters of recommendation. Auditions held 5 times on campus; recorded music is permissible as a substitute for live auditions when distance is prohibitive and videotaped performances are permissible as a substitute for live auditions when distance is prohibitive. Portfolio reviews held 5 times and by appointment on campus.

**Web Site** http://www.montclair.edu/music

**Contact** Admissions Chairperson, Department of Music, Montclair State University, 1 Normal Avenue, Montclair, New Jersey 07043; 973-655-7610, fax: 973-655-5279, e-mail address: music@mail.montclair.edu

# Moores School of Music
See University of Houston

# Moravian College
### Bethlehem, Pennsylvania

Independent, coed. Suburban campus. Total enrollment: 1,917. Music program established 1982.

**Degrees** Bachelor of Music in the areas of performance, composition, music education, sacred music. Majors and concentrations: composition, instrumental music, jazz, music education, performance, sacred music, voice. Cross-registration with Lehigh University, Lafayette College, Muhlenberg College, DeSales University, Cedar Crest College. Program accredited by NASM.

**Enrollment** 92 total; 85 undergraduate, 7 nonprofessional degree.

**Music Student Profile** 66% females, 34% males, 9% minorities.

**Music Faculty** 6 undergraduate (full-time), 40 undergraduate (part-time). 83% of full-time faculty have terminal degrees. Graduate students do not teach undergraduate courses. Undergraduate student–faculty ratio: 5:1.

**Student Life** Student groups/activities include Music Educators National Conference, Delta Omicron, American Choral Directors Association.

**Expenses for 2007–2008** Application fee: $40. Comprehensive fee: $36,381 includes full-time tuition ($27,873), mandatory fees ($515), and college room and board ($7993). College room only: $4491. Room and board charges vary according to board plan and housing facility. Special program-related fees: $160 per semester for set of lessons (electives) beyond degree requirement (maximum of 3 lessons).

**Financial Aid** Program-specific awards: 15 Ina Love Thursby Scholarships for those demonstrating need ($1000), 9 Arthur Hugo Awards for incoming freshmen demonstrating need and talent ($3000), 1 Richard and Monica Shantz Award for seniors demonstrating need ($1000), 1 John H. Reimers Music Scholarship for junior and senior music majors demonstrating excellence in performance and academics ($500).

**Application Procedures** Students admitted directly into the professional program freshman year. Deadline for freshmen: September 1; transfers: continuous. Required: essay, high school transcript, college transcript(s) for transfer students, minimum 2.0 high school GPA, 3 letters of recommendation, audition, SAT or ACT test scores. Recommended: interview. Auditions held 3-4 times on campus; recorded music is permissible as a substitute for live auditions if distance is prohibitive and videotaped performances are permissible as a substitute for live auditions if distance is prohibitive.

**Web Site** http://www.moravian.edu/academics/departments/music/index.htm

**Undergraduate Contact** Mr. James Earl Barnes, Chair, Music Department, Moravian College, 1200 Main Street, Bethlehem, Pennsylvania 18018; 610-861-1672, fax: 610-861-1657, e-mail address: mejeb01@moravian.edu

# Morehead State University
### Morehead, Kentucky

State-supported, coed. Small town campus. Total enrollment: 8,966. Music program established 1937.

**Degrees** Bachelor of Music in the areas of performance, jazz studies; Bachelor of Music Education. Majors and concentrations: jazz, music education, piano/organ, stringed instruments, voice, wind and percussion instruments. Graduate degrees offered: Master of Music in the areas of performance, music education. Program accredited by NASM, NCATE.
**Enrollment** 248 total; 221 undergraduate, 22 graduate, 5 nonprofessional degree.
**Music Student Profile** 60% females, 40% males, 6% minorities, 8% international.
**Music Faculty** 27 undergraduate (full-time), 8 undergraduate (part-time), 16 graduate (full-time). 78% of full-time faculty have terminal degrees. Graduate students do not teach undergraduate courses. Undergraduate student–faculty ratio: 14:1.
**Student Life** Student groups/activities include concerts, recitals, master classes (guest artists). Special housing available for music students.
**Expenses for 2007–2008** Application fee: $0. State resident tuition: $5280 full-time. Nonresident tuition: $13,340 full-time. Full-time tuition varies according to course load and reciprocity agreements. College room and board: $5620. Room and board charges vary according to board plan and housing facility. Special program-related fees: $10–$20 per semester for instrument rental, $30–$90 per semester for private lessons.
**Financial Aid** Program-specific awards: 40 music scholarships for program majors and minors ($2500).
**Application Procedures** Students admitted directly into the professional program freshman year. Deadline for freshmen and transfers: June 15. Notification date for freshmen: August 1. Required: high school transcript, college transcript(s) for transfer students, minimum 2.0 high school GPA, SAT or ACT test scores. Recommended: minimum 3.0 high school GPA, 2 letters of recommendation, interview, video, audition. Auditions held 3 times on campus; recorded music is permissible as a substitute for live auditions when distance is prohibitive and videotaped performances are permissible as a substitute for live auditions when distance is prohibitive.
**Web Site** http://www.moreheadstate.edu/music
**Undergraduate Contact** Dr. M. Scott McBride, Chair, Department of Music, Morehead State University, Baird Music Hall #106, Morehead, Kentucky 40351-1689; 606-783-2473, fax: 606-783-5447, e-mail address: s.mcbride@moreheadstate.edu
**Graduate Contact** Dr. David Oyen, Graduate Studies Coordinator, Department of Music, Morehead State University, Baird Music Hall #250, Morehead, Kentucky 40351-1689; 606-783-2404, fax: 606-783-5447, e-mail address: d.oyen@moreheadstate.edu

## Mount Allison University
### Sackville, New Brunswick, Canada

Province-supported, coed. Small town campus. Total enrollment: 2,170. Music program established 1874.
**Degrees** Bachelor of Music. Majors and concentrations: music. Program accredited by CUMS.
**Enrollment** 87 total; 73 undergraduate, 14 nonprofessional degree.
**Music Student Profile** 70% females, 30% males.
**Music Faculty** 11 undergraduate (full-time), 5 undergraduate (part-time). 81% of full-time faculty have terminal degrees. Graduate students do not teach undergraduate courses. Undergraduate student–faculty ratio: 7:1.
**Student Life** Student groups/activities include symphonic band, choral society, chamber orchestra, chamber choir, instrumental jazz ensemble, opera workshop, Garnet and Gold, Ethel Peak Music Society.
**Expenses for 2007–2008** Application fee: $50 Canadian dollars. Tuition, fee, and room and board charges are reported in Canadian dollars. Province resident tuition: $6720 full-time. Mandatory fees: $257 full-time. Full-time tuition and fees vary according to course load. College room and board: $6795. College room only: $3530. Room and board charges vary according to board plan. International student tuition: $13,440 full-time.
**Financial Aid** Program-specific awards: 5 Blakie Scholarships for freshmen program majors ($1000), 1 Robert Marsh Scholarship

for freshmen program majors ($1000), 2 Gladys Muttart Scholarships for freshmen program majors ($1250), 4 Pickard Scholarships for freshmen program majors ($6000), 1 Carleton Elliott Scholarship for freshmen program majors ($2000), 3 Department of Music Scholarships for freshmen program majors ($1500), 1 Howard Brown Scholarship for freshmen program majors ($6700).
**Application Procedures** Students admitted directly into the professional program freshman year. Deadline for freshmen and transfers: February 15. Required: high school transcript, college transcript(s) for transfer students, minimum 3.0 high school GPA, interview, audition, music theory examination, completion of college preparatory courses. Recommended: 2 letters of recommendation. Auditions held 3 times and by appointment on campus; recorded music is permissible as a substitute for live auditions if a campus visit is impossible and videotaped performances are permissible as a substitute for live auditions if a campus visit is impossible.
**Web Site** http://www.mta.ca/music/
**Undergraduate Contact** Head, Department of Music, Mount Allison University, 134 Main Street, Sackville, New Brunswick E4L 1A6, Canada; 506-364-2374, fax: 506-364-2376, e-mail address: music@mta.ca

## Murray State University
### Murray, Kentucky

State-supported, coed. Small town campus. Total enrollment: 10,149. Music program established 1930.
**Degrees** Bachelor of Music in the areas of performance, music education. Majors and concentrations: music, music business, music education, piano/organ, stringed instruments, voice, wind and percussion instruments. Graduate degrees offered: Master of Music Education. Program accredited by NASM.
**Enrollment** 197 total; 145 undergraduate, 16 graduate, 36 nonprofessional degree.
**Music Student Profile** 45% females, 55% males, 2% minorities, 4% international.
**Music Faculty** 22 total (full-time), 7 total (part-time). 81% of full-time faculty have terminal degrees. Graduate students do not teach undergraduate courses. Undergraduate student–faculty ratio: 8:1.
**Student Life** Student groups/activities include Music Educators National Conference, Phi Mu Alpha Sinfonia, Sigma Alpha Iota.
**Expenses for 2008–2009** Application fee: $30. State resident tuition: $4932 full-time. Nonresident tuition: $7426 full-time. Mandatory fees: $816 full-time. College room and board: $6004. College room only: $3278. Special program-related fees: $50–$100 per semester for lesson fees.
**Financial Aid** Program-specific awards: 30–88 Music/University Scholarships for program majors ($500–$3000).
**Application Procedures** Students apply for admission into the professional program by sophomore year. Deadline for freshmen and transfers: continuous. Required: high school transcript, college transcript(s) for transfer students, audition, ACT test score only (minimum composite ACT score of 18), interview for scholarship consideration. Recommended: letter of recommendation. Auditions held 4 times on campus; recorded music is permissible as a substitute for live auditions when distance is prohibitive and videotaped performances are permissible as a substitute for live auditions when distance is prohibitive.
**Web Site** http://www.murraystate.edu/music
**Contact** Dr. Pamela Wurgler, Chair, Department of Music, Murray State University, 504 Fine Arts Building, Murray, Kentucky 42071-3342; 270-809-6339, fax: 270-809-3965, e-mail address: pamela.wurgler@murraystate.edu

## Musicians Institute
### Hollywood, California

Proprietary, coed. Music program established 1994.
**Degrees** Bachelor of Music in the area of commercial music. Majors and concentrations: bass, guitar, keyboard, percussion, voice. Mandatory cross-registration with Los Angeles City College. Program accredited by NASM.

*Musicians Institute (continued)*

**Enrollment** 67 total; all undergraduate.

**Music Faculty** 20 total (full-time), 20 total (part-time). 75% of full-time faculty have terminal degrees. Graduate students do not teach undergraduate courses.

**Student Life** Student groups/activities include recording sessions, clinics, live concerts.

**Expenses for 2007–2008** Special program-related fees: $50–$200 per quarter for lab fees.

**Financial Aid** Program-specific awards: 5 partial scholarships ($500–$2000), 3 Stanley Clark Awards ($2500–$5000).

**Application Procedures** Students admitted directly into the professional program freshman year. Deadline for freshmen and transfers: July 15. Required: essay, high school transcript, college transcript(s) for transfer students, minimum 2.0 high school GPA, 2 letters of recommendation, video, audition, SAT or ACT test scores (minimum composite ACT score of 21), minimum TOEFL score of 500 for international applicants, recorded music performance. Recommended: interview. Portfolio reviews held continuously on campus.

**Web Site** http://www.mi.edu

**Undergraduate Contact** Steve Lunn, Director of Admissions, Admissions, Musicians Institute, 1655 North McCadden Place, Hollywood, California 90028; 323-462-1384, fax: 323-462-1575.

# Nazareth College of Rochester

### Rochester, New York

Independent, coed. Suburban campus. Total enrollment: 3,185. Music program established 1924.

**Degrees** Bachelor of Music in the area of music. Majors and concentrations: music education, music history, music theory, music therapy, performance. Graduate degrees offered: Master of Science in the area of education (music). Cross-registration with Rochester Area Colleges Inter-Institutional Undergraduate Student Enrollment Program. Program accredited by NASM, AMTA.

**Enrollment** 225 total; 185 undergraduate, 40 graduate.

**Music Student Profile** 78% females, 22% males, 3% minorities, 2% international.

**Music Faculty** 13 undergraduate (full-time), 40 undergraduate (part-time). 92% of full-time faculty have terminal degrees. Graduate students do not teach undergraduate courses. Undergraduate student–faculty ratio: 17:1.

**Student Life** Student groups/activities include Music Educators National Conference Student Chapter, Music Therapy Club, Pi Kappa Lambda Honor Society: Theta Lambda Chapter.

**Expenses for 2007–2008** Application fee: $40. Comprehensive fee: $32,380 includes full-time tuition ($21,900), mandatory fees ($980), and college room and board ($9500). College room only: $5230. Room and board charges vary according to board plan and housing facility. Special program-related fees: $35 per course for music therapy clinic fee, $178 per course for group lessons, $178 per course for voice or instrument lessons for minors, $335 per course for voice or instrument lessons for majors.

**Financial Aid** Program-specific awards: 8 Honors Music Scholarships for incoming freshmen passing audition evaluations ($2000–$6000), 5 Gerald Wilmot Music Scholarships for honors juniors or seniors ($1000–$2500), 2 Lewis Dollinger Scholarships for honors juniors or seniors ($1000), 1 Presser Scholarship for seniors ($4000).

**Application Procedures** Students admitted directly into the professional program freshman year. Deadline for freshmen and transfers: continuous. Required: essay, high school transcript, college transcript(s) for transfer students, minimum 2.0 high school GPA, 2 letters of recommendation, interview, audition. Recommended: SAT or ACT test scores. Auditions held 9 times on campus; recorded music is permissible as a substitute for live auditions with subsequent live audition upon enrollment and videotaped performances are permissible as a substitute for live auditions with subsequent live audition upon enrollment.

**Web Site** http://www.naz.edu/dept/music/

**Undergraduate Contact** Mr. Tom DaRin, Vice President for Enrollment Management, Nazareth College of Rochester, 4245 East Avenue, Rochester, New York 14618; 585-389-2860, fax: 585-389-2939.

**Graduate Contact** Dr. Mary Carlson, Program Director for Graduate and Undergraduate Music Education, Music Department, Nazareth College of Rochester, 4245 East Avenue, Rochester, New York 14618; 585-389-2697, fax: 585-389-2939, e-mail address: mccarlso@naz.edu

# Nebraska Wesleyan University

### Lincoln, Nebraska

Independent United Methodist, coed. Suburban campus. Total enrollment: 2,107. Music program established 1903.

**Degrees** Bachelor of Arts in the area of music; Bachelor of Music in the areas of performance, music education. Majors and concentrations: music education, music performance. Program accredited by NASM.

**Enrollment** 67 total; all undergraduate.

**Music Student Profile** 76% females, 24% males, 4% minorities.

**Music Faculty** 8 undergraduate (full-time), 14 undergraduate (part-time). 75% of full-time faculty have terminal degrees. Graduate students do not teach undergraduate courses. Undergraduate student–faculty ratio: 8:1.

**Student Life** Student groups/activities include Mu Phi Epsilon, Music Educators National Conference, American Choral Directors Association.

**Expenses for 2007–2008** Application fee: $20. One-time mandatory fee: $120. Comprehensive fee: $25,592 includes full-time tuition ($19,930), mandatory fees ($322), and college room and board ($5340). Full-time tuition and fees vary according to class time, course load, degree level, location, and program. Room and board charges vary according to board plan.

**Financial Aid** Program-specific awards: 39 music scholarships for program majors ($500–$3500), 24 ensemble participation grants for non-music majors ($300–$1500).

**Application Procedures** Students admitted directly into the professional program freshman year. Deadline for freshmen and transfers: continuous. Required: high school transcript, college transcript(s) for transfer students, audition, ACT test score only, must be in top half of high school graduating class or have ACT of 21 or better. Recommended: interview. Auditions held 6 times on campus; recorded music is permissible as a substitute for live auditions if a campus visit is impossible and videotaped performances are permissible as a substitute for live auditions if a campus visit is impossible.

**Web Site** http://music.nebrwesleyan.edu/

**Undergraduate Contact** Ms. Patricia Karthauser, Vice President for Enrollment and Marketing, Nebraska Wesleyan University, 5000 St. Paul Avenue, Lincoln, Nebraska 68504-2794; 402-465-2551, fax: 402-465-2179, e-mail address: pkart@nebrwesleyan.edu

# New England Conservatory of Music

### Boston, Massachusetts

Independent, coed. Urban campus. Total enrollment: 795. Music program established 1867.

**Degrees** Bachelor of Music in the areas of composition, historical performance, music history, music theory, performance. Majors and concentrations: classical music, composition, contemporary improvisation, historical performance, jazz, music history, music theory, performance, piano, stringed instruments, voice, wind and percussion instruments. Graduate degrees offered: Master of Music in the areas of composition, historical performance, music theory, collaborative piano, conducting, musicology, vocal pedagogy, performance. Doctor of Musical Arts in the areas of performance, composition. Cross-registration with Northeastern University, Tufts University, Simmons College. Program accredited by NASM.

**Enrollment** 389 undergraduate, 394 graduate.

**Music Student Profile** 50% females, 50% males, 15% minorities, 29% international.

**Music Faculty** 89 total (full-time), 123 total (part-time). Graduate students teach a few undergraduate courses. Undergraduate student–faculty ratio: 4:1.

**Student Life** Special housing available for music students.

**Expenses for 2008–2009** Application fee: $100. Comprehensive fee: $44,925 includes full-time tuition ($32,900), mandatory fees ($425), and college room and board ($11,600). Special program-related fees: $60 per year for practice room fee for percussion majors, $100 per semester for registration fee for any electronic music course, $130 per year for practice room fee for collaborative piano, piano, harpsichord, jazz piano, percussion and jazz percussion majors only.

**Application Procedures** Students admitted directly into the professional program freshman year. Deadline for freshmen and transfers: December 1. Notification date for freshmen and transfers: April 1. Required: essay, high school transcript, college transcript(s) for transfer students, 2 letters of recommendation, audition, portfolio for composition majors, artistic resumé, repertoire list, minimum 2.75 high school GPA. Recommended: SAT or ACT test scores. Auditions held multiple dates in February on campus; recorded music is permissible as a substitute for live auditions when distance is prohibitive and videotaped performances are permissible as a substitute for live auditions when distance is prohibitive (for some majors). Portfolio reviews held as needed on campus.

**Web Site** http://www.newenglandconservatory.edu

**Contact** Ms. Chris Daly, Director of Admissions, New England Conservatory of Music, 290 Huntington Avenue, Boston, Massachusetts 02115; 617-585-1101, fax: 617-585-1115, e-mail address: christina.daly@newenglandconservatory.edu

### More About the Conservatory

Recognized nationally and internationally as a leader among music schools, New England Conservatory (NEC) offers rigorous training in an intimate, nurturing community to 750 undergraduate, graduate, and doctoral music students from around the world. Its faculty of 225 boasts internationally esteemed artist-teachers and scholars. Its alumni go on to fill orchestra chairs, concert hall stages, jazz clubs, recording studios, and arts management positions worldwide. NEC faculty members and alumni make up almost half of the Boston Symphony Orchestra and have been honored with Grammy Awards, MacArthur Fellowships, and Naumburg Awards.

NEC is the most enduring independent school of music in the United States, founded in 1867 by educational maverick Eben Tourjée, and making history ever since with jazz instruction and professional chamber music programs, to name a few milestones. Opening its doors in 1903, Jordan Hall is literally at the heart of NEC's main building and is renowned for its wonderful acoustics. It serves as the stage for both NEC student concerts and the world's leading concert artists.

NEC's performance-focused curriculum provides a wealth of solo and ensemble experiences for students, including required recitals and participation in four orchestras, three choruses, two wind ensembles, large and small jazz ensembles, new music groups, and a wide variety of chamber music groups. Additionally, the opera department presents two full-length staged operas with orchestra each year as well as several programs of opera scenes.

As seasoned concert soloists, orchestra and chamber musicians, veterans of the world's premier opera stages, and jazz legends, NEC's diverse faculty members form a musical network that spans the globe and enhances the careers of graduates. In the past few years, some of the foremost performer/teachers in the world have joined the faculty, including Donald Weilerstein and Miriam Fried, violin; Kim Kashkashian and Martha Strongin Katz, viola; Paul Katz, cello; Paula Robison, flute; John Ferrillo, oboe; Bruce Brubaker and Alexander Korsantia, piano; Vinson Cole, Delores Ziegler, Lorraine Nubar, Luretta Bybee, and Patricia Misslin, voice; and jazz musicians Anthony Coleman, Billy Hart, Dave Holland, Robin Eubanks, and Brad Shepik. The addition of these teachers to the existing strong faculty has created an incomparable music-training program.

Boston itself is one of the world's great music centers and is a capital of higher education. NEC students have the opportunity to benefit from cross-registration for classes at Tufts University, Northeastern University, and Simmons College. New England Conservatory also partners with Tufts University to offer a five-year dual-bachelor's-degree program and with Harvard University to offer a five-year program leading to a Bachelor of Arts degree from Harvard and a Master of Music degree from NEC. NEC's thriving Performance Outreach program provides performance opportunities for students in the Boston area and beyond and helps young musicians develop the skills to communicate with audiences of all ages and backgrounds. Performance sites include social, civic, cultural, and educational organizations that have forged partnerships with NEC. The Music Referral Service brokers professional engagements for students in the city and surrounding area. The Career Services Center also provides comprehensive information on employment opportunities, summer festivals, competitions, private teaching referrals, and resume and career counseling—all the essential materials needed to expand a musician's horizons.

NEC alumni are renowned as soloists—with singer Denyce Graves, today's Carmen of choice, and jazz clarinetist Don Byron currently at the top of their respective fields. Many are also extending their art form: in the classical world, violinist Lara St. John; and in the jazz world, all three members of Medeski, Martin & Wood. Alumni are principals or section players in professional orchestras in the United States and around the world, teach at major music schools, and influence the future of music in other ways. Three such notable alums are Los Angeles Philharmonic Executive Director Deborah Borda, St. Paul Chamber Orchestra President and Managing Director Bruce Coppock, and Curtis Institute's new director, Roberto Diaz. Alumni composers Richard Danielpour, Michael Gandolfi, and Lee Hyla write music that is being avidly performed—and Gandolfi also teaches at NEC. Students and alumni have also enjoyed impressive successes at international competitions in recent years, including the Metropolitan Opera National Auditions, Naumburg Award, William Kapell International Piano Competition, Young Concert Artists International Auditions, Concert Artists Guild Auditions, Banff International Chamber Music Competition, Fischoff National Chamber Music Competition, Irving M. Klein International String Competition, and Italy's Paolo Borciani Chamber Music Competition.

# New Mexico State University
### Las Cruces, New Mexico

State-supported, coed. Suburban campus. Total enrollment: 16,726. Music program established 1905.

**Degrees** Bachelor of Music in the areas of performance, piano pedagogy, music business; Bachelor of Music Education in the areas of vocal music education, instrumental music education. Majors and concentrations: music, music business, music education, piano, piano pedagogy, stringed instruments, voice performance, wind and percussion instruments. Graduate degrees offered: Master of Music in the areas of accompanying, performance, music education, conducting. Program accredited by NASM.

**Enrollment** 32 total; 23 undergraduate, 9 graduate.

**Music Student Profile** 46% females, 54% males, 61% minorities, 1% international.

**Music Faculty** 17 total (full-time), 8 total (part-time). 94% of full-time faculty have terminal degrees. Graduate students teach a few undergraduate courses. Undergraduate student–faculty ratio: 14:1.

**Student Life** Student groups/activities include Sigma Alpha Iota, Music Educators National Conference Student Chapter.

**Expenses for 2007–2008** Application fee: $20. State resident tuition: $3274 full-time. Nonresident tuition: $13,002 full-time. Mandatory fees: $1178 full-time. College room and board: $5766. College room only: $3322. Room and board charges vary according to board plan and gender.

*New Mexico State University (continued)*

**Financial Aid** Program-specific awards: 1 Theodore Presser Scholarship for junior program majors ($1500), 1 Vivien B. Head Scholarship for program majors, 1 Ray Tross Scholarship for woodwind majors, band, choir, and orchestra service grants for musically talented performers, 1 Ruthena C. King Memorial Award for music majors residing in Otero County, 1 Elenore Ward Memorial Scholarship for instrumentalists, music majors, 1 Frederick and Norma Sell Scholarship for instrumentalists, 1 Wooten Scholarship for music majors, 1 8va Scholarship for music majors, trumpet.

**Application Procedures** Students admitted directly into the professional program freshman year. Deadline for freshmen and transfers: April 15. Notification date for freshmen and transfers: July 1. Required: high school transcript, college transcript(s) for transfer students, audition, SAT or ACT test scores. Recommended: minimum 3.0 high school GPA, 3 letters of recommendation, interview. Auditions held continuously on campus and off campus in various New Mexico cities; recorded music is permissible as a substitute for live auditions.

**Web Site** http://www.nmsu.edu/~music

**Contact** Dr. Greg Fant, Head, Music Department, New Mexico State University, MSC 3F, Las Cruces, New Mexico 88003; 505-646-2421, fax: 505-646-8199, e-mail address: music@nmsu.edu

## The New School

See Mannes College The New School for Music

## The New School

See The New School for Jazz and Contemporary Music

*The New School*
# The New School for Jazz and Contemporary Music
**New York, New York**

Independent, coed. Urban campus. Total enrollment: 245. Music program established 1986.

**Degrees** Bachelor of Arts/Bachelor of Fine Arts in the area of liberal arts/jazz; Bachelor of Fine Arts in the area of jazz. Majors and concentrations: commercial jazz, composition, instrumental jazz, jazz, jazz and African-American music, jazz bass, jazz composing and arranging, jazz composition, jazz drums, jazz guitar, jazz performance, jazz piano, jazz saxophone, jazz studies, jazz trombone, jazz trumpet, jazz voice, jazz/music technology, studio music and jazz, studio/jazz guitar. Cross-registration with Eugene Lang College The New School for Liberal Arts.

**Enrollment** 245 total; all undergraduate.

**Music Student Profile** 20% females, 80% males, 23% minorities, 22% international.

**Music Faculty** 2 total (full-time), 64 total (part-time). 100% of full-time faculty have terminal degrees. Graduate students do not teach undergraduate courses. Undergraduate student–faculty ratio: 10:1.

**Student Life** Student groups/activities include Jazz Student Council, university committees.

**Expenses for 2007–2008** Application fee: $40. Comprehensive fee: $42,200 includes full-time tuition ($29,800), mandatory fees ($650), and college room and board ($11,750). College room only: $8750. Room and board charges vary according to board plan.

**Financial Aid** Program-specific awards: jazz scholarships for those demonstrating talent/ability, University Scholar Awards for minority students.

**Application Procedures** Students admitted directly into the professional program freshman year. Deadline for freshmen and transfers: January 1. Notification date for freshmen and transfers: April 1. Required: high school transcript, college

transcript(s) for transfer students, minimum 2.0 high school GPA, letter of recommendation, audition, TOEFL score for international applicants, personal statement. Auditions held 15 times on campus and off campus in selected high schools; recorded music is permissible as a substitute for live auditions when distance is prohibitive.

**Web Site** http://www.newschool.edu/jazz

**Undergraduate Contact** Ms. Teri Lucas, Director of Admissions, The New School for Jazz and Contemporary Music, 55 West 13th Street, New York, New York 10011; 212-229-5896 ext. 4589, fax: 212-229-8936, e-mail address: jazzadm@newschool.edu

### More About the School

Located in the heart of Greenwich Village, The New School for Jazz and Contemporary Music offers talented musicians an exceptional opportunity to train with professional artists from New York City's celebrated jazz community. The teaching model at the School is based on the tradition of artist as mentor and is implemented by accomplished career musicians with significant links to the history and evolution of jazz, blues, pop, and new genres. Students benefit from the expert training associated with a conservatory as well as the generative spirit and vigor of jazz that flows through the school. This environment extends past the walls of the school and into the streets and studios, clubs, and concert halls of New York City—one of the music capitals of the world.

Alumni of The New School for Jazz and Contemporary Music have become some of today's top jazz stars and recording artists, including Roy Hargrove, Brad Mehldau, Marcus Strickland, Robert Glasper, and Greg Kurstin (of the bird and the bee). In the contemporary music realm, a number of current students and alumni perform with Grammy Award-winning bands and artists such as Diddy, Al Green, Beyoncé, Jay-Z, and James Taylor.

With a large percentage of the student body from outside the United States, The New School for Jazz and Contemporary Music is a truly multicultural universe. Bachelor of Fine Arts students do the core of their work in classrooms and in private studios with exceptional musician-educators, gaining direct exposure to modern music's traditions and practices in an intellectual context that encourages both exploration and innovation.

No aspiring musician can expect to make it in this highly competitive industry without real-world performance experience. Students at The New School for Jazz and Contemporary Music have ample opportunities to perform at school and in professional venues with their peers, as well as with current stars of the jazz

world. Indeed, many well-known alumni started their careers while they were undergraduates. Students perform each semester in a variety of ensembles and venues. Ensembles include the Thelonious Monk Ensemble, the Electric Miles Ensemble, Rhythm Section and Vocal accompaniment, the Charlie Parker Ensemble, the Afro–Cuban Jazz Orchestra, and the Art Blakey Ensemble.

The New School for Jazz and Contemporary Music is one of eight schools that make up The New School, a major urban university, and students can take advantage of everything the university has to offer. There are numerous opportunities for cross-registration, and students can enroll in everything from humanities courses at Eugene Lang College The New School for Liberal Arts to art and design courses at Parsons The New School for Design and classical music instruction at Mannes College The New School for Music. Students are encouraged to participate in artistic collaborations and performances with students from other schools.

Taking full advantage of the university setting, The New School for Jazz and Contemporary Music and Eugene Lang College The New School for Liberal Arts have structured a five-year dual-degree program in which students simultaneously complete a music B.F.A. and a liberal arts B.A. For more information, students should visit http://www.newschool.edu/babfa.

**Location** New York City is one of the great capitals of the jazz world, and the school is located in one of the city's most exciting neighborhoods—Greenwich Village—where the arts, politics, and commerce come together. Musical inspiration is everywhere in this fast-paced urban environment, from historic performance venues like the Village Vanguard or the Blue Note, to the city's parks and even its subway stations. As one student put it, "There's no place like New York City to study people and no place like Greenwich Village to study jazz."

**Program Facilities** The School's 20,000-square-foot state-of-the-art facility on West 13th Street was designed specifically to help young artists realize their goal of becoming effective music professionals. The facility offers administrative, classroom, practice, and rehearsal space—all constructed with the highest quality and attention to acoustics, soundproofing, and aesthetics. All classrooms are fully dedicated with Yamaha grand pianos, drum kits, amplifiers, vocal PA systems, and full-component stereo systems. Specialized instrumental practice and teaching rooms are offered, as well as an MP3 listening library and keyboard/MIDI labs. Concert and recording needs are served in an intimate and beautiful performance space seating 120, with full capacity for professional sound, lighting, and recording. A second studio is used for additional recording and engineering, with both studios connected to the university's server and Internet sites. Additional university performance facilities within a two-block radius include a 170-seat auditorium and an excellent and acoustically balanced concert hall with a capacity of 500.

**Alumni** The New School for Jazz and Contemporary Music's alumni include Lucien Ban, Miri Ben-Ari, Peter Bernstein, Walter Blanding Jr., Avashi Cohen, Jesse Davis, John Ellis, Rebecca Coupe Franks, Robert Glasper, Aaron Goldberg, Larry Goldings, Roy Hargrove, Susie Ibarra, Ali Jackson, Ori Kaplan, Greg Kurstin, Gregoire Maret, Virginia Mayhew, Carlos McKinney, Brad Mehldau, Shedrick Mitchell, Vickie Natale, Bilal Oliver, John Popper, Jaz Sawyer, Woody Shaw III, Alex Skolnick, E. J. Strickland, Marcus Strickland, Manuel Valera, and Sam Yahel.

**Faculty** Faculty members at The New School for Jazz and Contemporary Music include Ahmed Abdullah, trumpet; Junko Arita, voice; Jane Ira Bloom, saxophone; Richard Boukas, guitar; Joanne Brackeen, piano; Cecil Bridgewater, trumpet; Brian Camelio, guitar; Jeff Carney, bass; Joe Chambers, drums; Haim Cotton, piano; Andrew Cyrille, drums; Gerard D'Angelo, piano; Armen Donelian, piano; Mario Escalera, woodwinds; Ray Gallon, piano; Hal Galper, piano; George Garzone, saxophone; Dave Glasser, saxophone; Dan Greenblatt, saxophone; Chico Hamilton, drums; Billy Harper, saxophone; Richard Harper, voice, trom-

bone; Gerry Hemingway, percussion; Adam Holzman, keyboard; Satoshi Inoue, guitar; Vic Juris, guitar; Michael Karn, saxophone; Bill Kirchner, woodwinds; Janet Lawson, voice; Lee Ann Ledgerwood, piano; Elisabeth Lohninger, voice; Amy London, voice; David Lopato, piano; Arun Luthra, saxophone; Ed MacEachen, guitar; Junior Mance, piano; Andy McKee, bass; Andy Milne, piano; Kirk Nurock, piano; Jimmy Owens, trumpet; Charli Persip, drums; Ron Petrides, guitar; Benny Powell, trombone; Robert Sadin, composition; Bobby Sanabria, percussion; David Schnitter, saxophone; Kenneth Scott, voice; Harel Shachal, saxophones; Rich Shemaria, piano; Jim Snidero, saxophone; Joan Stiles, piano; Rory Stuart, guitar; Francesca Tanksley, piano; Charles Tolliver, trumpet; Johannes Wallmann, piano; Reggie Workman, bass; Peter Zak, piano; and Amir Ziv, drums

**Special Programs** Throughout the school year, The New School for Jazz and Contemporary Music offers master classes, lectures, performances, and workshops featuring top artists and industry leaders. Recent guests include Barry Harris, Pat Metheny, Roy Hargrove, Christian McBride, Steffon Harris, Bob Hurwitz, and Arturo O'Farril. Faculty members, students, and affiliated artists appear weekly on stages and in clubs throughout the city and the greater metropolitan area. Performances presented by the School include more than 150 student recitals and concerts each year, weekly professional sessions at the legendary Sweet Rhythm jazz club, and a series of concerts showcasing faculty members with alumni or current students. Students have also appeared at a number of high-visibility venues, including Jazz at Lincoln Center's Dizzy's Club Coca-Cola, and performed live at radio stations WBGO and WBAI. Students have access to an outreach office providing professional industry internships and a gig office that links students to professional performance opportunities.

# New World School of the Arts
## Miami, Florida

State-supported, coed. Urban campus. Total enrollment: 416. Music program established 1988.

**Degrees** Bachelor of Music in the areas of instrumental studies, vocal studies, composition/electronic music. Majors and concentrations: bass, bassoon, cello, clarinet, composition, flute, French horn, guitar, oboe, percussion, piano, saxophone, trombone, trumpet, tuba, viola, violin, voice. Mandatory cross-registration with University of Florida, Miami-Dade College. Program accredited by NASM.

**Enrollment** 62 total; all undergraduate.

**Music Student Profile** 58% females, 42% males, 73% minorities, 16% international.

**Music Faculty** 5 undergraduate (full-time), 12 undergraduate (part-time). 85% of full-time faculty have terminal degrees. Graduate students do not teach undergraduate courses. Undergraduate student–faculty ratio: 3:1.

**Student Life** Student groups/activities include Student Government, opera ensemble, chamber orchestra.

**Expenses for 2007–2008** Application fee: $0. State resident tuition: $3000 full-time. Nonresident tuition: $10,000 full-time.

**Financial Aid** Program-specific awards: 25–30 NWSA Music Scholarships for talented music students ($2000).

**Application Procedures** Students admitted directly into the professional program freshman year. Deadline for freshmen and transfers: continuous. Notification date for freshmen and transfers: continuous. Required: essay, high school transcript, college transcript(s) for transfer students, 2 letters of recommendation, audition. Recommended: minimum 2.0 high school GPA, interview, SAT or ACT test scores. Auditions held by appointment on campus; recorded music is permissible as a substitute for live auditions when distance is prohibitive or if a campus visit is impossible and videotaped performances are permissible as a substitute for live auditions when distance is prohibitive or if a campus visit is impossible.

**Web Site** http://www.mdc.edu/nwsa

**Undergraduate Contact** Pamela Neumann, Recruitment and Admissions Coordinator, Student Services, New World School of the

*New World School of the Arts (continued)*

Arts, 300 North East 2nd Avenue, Miami, Florida 33132; 305-237-7007, fax: 305-237-3794, e-mail address: nwsaadm@mdc.edu

## Tisch School of the Arts, Clive Davis Department of Recorded Music

# New York University

**New York, New York**

Independent, coed. Urban campus. Total enrollment: 41,783. Music program established 2003.
**Degrees** Bachelor of Fine Arts. Majors and concentrations: recorded music.
**Enrollment** 102 total; all undergraduate.
**Music Student Profile** 38% females, 62% males, 15% minorities, 3% international.
**Music Faculty** 5 undergraduate (full-time), 30 undergraduate (part-time). 60% of full-time faculty have terminal degrees. Graduate students do not teach undergraduate courses. Undergraduate student–faculty ratio: 3:1.
**Student Life** Student groups/activities include Audio Engineering Society (AES).
**Expenses for 2007–2008** Application fee: $65. Comprehensive fee: $47,490 includes full-time tuition ($33,268), mandatory fees ($2022), and college room and board ($12,200). Full-time tuition and fees vary according to course load and program. Room and board charges vary according to board plan and housing facility. Special program-related fees: $230 per semester for lab fee.
**Application Procedures** Students admitted directly into the professional program freshman year. Deadline for freshmen: January 15; transfers: April 1. Notification date for freshmen: April 1; transfers: May 15. Required: essay, high school transcript, college transcript(s) for transfer students, 2 letters of recommendation, portfolio, SAT or ACT test scores. Recommended: minimum 3.0 high school GPA.
**Web Site** http://clivedavisdept.tisch.nyu.edu
**Undergraduate Contact** Ms. Patricia A. Decker, Director of Recruitment, Tisch School of the Arts, New York University, 721 Broadway, 8th Floor, New York, New York 10003; 212-998-1900, fax: 212-995-4060, e-mail address: tisch.recruitment@nyu.edu

## Steinhardt School of Culture, Education, and Human Development, Department of Music and Performing Arts Professions

# New York University

**New York, New York**

Independent, coed. Urban campus. Total enrollment: 41,783.
**Degrees** Bachelor of Music in the areas of performance (instrumental, piano, and vocal), theory and composition, music business, music technology, music education. Majors and concentrations: instrumental performance, music business, music education, music technology, music theory and composition, piano performance, vocal performance. Graduate degrees offered: Master of Arts in the areas of music education, music therapy, music business, music education (for college and university faculty), performing arts administration; Master of Music in the areas of instrumental performance (classical and jazz), vocal performance (classical or music theatre), music theory and composition, music technology. Doctor of Education in the areas of music education (all grades), music education (for college and university faculty); Doctor of Philosophy in the areas of music performance and composition, music education (all grades), music education (for college and university faculty), music technology. Program accredited by AMTA.
**Enrollment** 1,220 total; 652 undergraduate, 568 graduate.
**Music Student Profile** 49% females, 51% males, 18% minorities, 19% international.

**Music Faculty** 26 total (full-time), 300 total (part-time). 70% of full-time faculty have terminal degrees. Graduate students teach a few undergraduate courses. Undergraduate student–faculty ratio: 2:1.
**Student Life** Student groups/activities include various performance opportunities on campus and throughout New York City (symphony orchestras, string and wind chamber ensembles, choirs, operas, music theatre productions, jazz ensembles), internships, student teaching, and other fieldwork, Village Records.
**Expenses for 2007–2008** Application fee: $65. Comprehensive fee: $47,490 includes full-time tuition ($33,268), mandatory fees ($2022), and college room and board ($12,200). Full-time tuition and fees vary according to course load and program. Room and board charges vary according to board plan and housing facility. Special program-related fees: $75 for recital fee, $90 for music and music education private instruction fee.
**Financial Aid** Program-specific awards: 5–10 talent awards for performance students.
**Application Procedures** Students admitted directly into the professional program freshman year. Deadline for freshmen: January 15; transfers: April 1. Notification date for freshmen: April 1; transfers: continuous. Required: essay, high school transcript, college transcript(s) for transfer students, 3 letters of recommendation, audition, SAT or ACT test scores, strong high school GPA. Auditions held 12 times on campus; recorded music is permissible as a substitute for live auditions when distance is prohibitive and videotaped performances are permissible as a substitute for live auditions when distance is prohibitive.
**Web Site** http://www.steinhardt.nyu.edu/perf-arts2008
**Undergraduate Contact** Ms. Candice MacLusky, Assistant Director of Undergraduate Admissions, New York University, 22 Washington Square North, New York, New York 10011-9191; 212-998-4500, fax: 212-995-4902.
**Graduate Contact** Mr. John Myers, Director of Enrollment Services, Office of Graduate Admissions, New York University, 82 Washington Square East, 3rd Floor, New York, New York 10003-6680; 212-998-5030, fax: 212-995-4328, e-mail address: steinhardt.gradadmissions@nyu.edu

### More About the University

**N**YU's Steinhardt School of Culture, Education, and Human Development offers a diverse range of undergraduate and graduate programs in applied psychology, art, communication, education, health, and music. Our School has a long history of connecting theory to applied learning experiences through dozens of affiliations and partnerships with urban institutions, building communities within and beyond our classrooms, and nurturing the human spirit. Our faculty members are intellectually adventurous and socially conscious. Our students study in the expansive environment of a great research university and use the urban neighborhoods of New York City and countries around the world as their laboratories. Now in our 118th year of educating artists, professionals, scholars, and researchers, we are applying our creativity and knowledge where it is needed most.

Baccalaureate programs in the Department of Music and Performing Arts Professions combine intense professional training in music performance, composition, technology, music business, dance, or theater with a solid liberal arts core in the humanities and the social and natural sciences. In seminars, master classes, and selected classes, undergraduate students join advanced graduate students and faculty members in a collaborative environment that fosters creativity of the highest order.

Facilities and resources include practice rooms, ensemble rehearsal rooms, teaching studios, the Frederick Loewe Theatre, two recital rooms, the Black Box recital theater, and the restored Provincetown Playhouse; 12 computer music and recording studios; multimedia laboratories; digital recording and editing rooms featuring Digidesign Pro Tools and Sonic Solutions multitrack systems; 5.1 surround sound; a multitrack facility featuring analog and digital recording, automated inline console, outboard effects, and MIDI processing for live and studio performance; Village Records (a full-service record company providing experience in all aspects of record production and promotion); the Nordoff-Robbins Center for Music Therapy (an international outreach and training center for music therapists); the NYU Arts and Media Studio (advanced hardware platforms for computer music, graphics, and animation); and the Elmer Holmes Bobst Library (open stack; more than 3.4 million volumes), which includes the Avery Fisher Center for Music and Media. The Kimmel Center for University Life includes a 900-seat state-of-the-art theater, a second 540-seat theater, a 150-seat recital room, and additional ensemble rehearsal rooms and private practice rooms.

**Faculty, Resident Artists, and Alumni** Faculty members are internationally acclaimed artists, composers, scholars, industry executives, and members of such renowned music organizations as the New York Philharmonic and the Metropolitan Opera. They include Joe Lovano, Robin Eubanks, Brian Lynch, Chris Potter, John Scofield, and Kenny Werner (jazz); Martin Canin, Eduardus Halim, Miyoko Lotto, and Seymour Bernstein (piano); Stanley Drucker and Esther Lamneck (clarinet); Pamela Frank, Anton Miller, and Martin Beaver (violin); and David Elliott (music education). Currently in residence: Combo Nuvo, the New Hudson Saxophone Quartet, the NYU Music Theatre Repertory Ensemble, the NYU New Music Ensemble, and the Quintet of the Americas. Composers in residence have included George Perle, Milton Babbitt, Ned Rorem, Roger Reynolds, Lukas Foss, Emil Sein, Morton Subotnik, and George Crumb.

**Student Performance Opportunities** Student composers and performers are regularly featured in concerts and recitals at NYU, Carnegie Recital Hall, Merkin Hall, Lincoln Center, and landmark jazz clubs and new music venues in Greenwich Village and SoHo and are involved in national and international tours. Performance ensembles include string, brass, and woodwind chamber music ensembles; chamber symphony; two symphony orchestras; concert wind ensemble; Washington Square Woodwind Ensemble; trio-to-septet jazz ensembles; two big-band concert ensembles; new music and dance ensemble; percussion ensembles; Choral Arts Society; Women's Choir; opera workshop; music theater ensemble; All-University Gospel Choir; University Singers; Jazz Choir; and Composers Ensemble. An active NYU composers' forum features visiting composers and provides ongoing opportunities for students' work to be performed. Several mainstage and workshop musical theater and opera productions are presented each year.

Added to this are the excitement and opportunities of New York City that enable students to build important career alliances and professional opportunities. World-class artists regularly provide seminars and master classes and often join students in performances on and off campus. Music business and technology students as well as performance and composition majors gain hands-on experience through internships at leading recording companies, publishing houses, and concert management and

public relations firms. Students in music education gain the finest student experiences in the country's largest public school system.

**Special Programs** A selection of special programs are also offered: Interactive Arts Performance Series; Stephen F. Temmer Tonmeister Studies (advanced recording technology); annual summer composer's seminar; summer musical theater at Washington Square; summer Kodály Workshop for music educators; summer string quartet, woodwind quintet, jazz guitar, piano, harp, and Broadway percussion performance institutes; summer musical theater; and a summer study-abroad new music and dance program in Florence, Italy.

# Nicholls State University
## Thibodaux, Louisiana

State-supported, coed. Small town campus. Total enrollment: 6,865. Music program established 1967.
**Web Site** http://www.nicholls.edu

# Norfolk State University
## Norfolk, Virginia

State-supported, coed. Urban campus. Music program established 1952.
**Degrees** Bachelor of Music in the areas of media, music education. Majors and concentrations: music education, music media, piano/organ, stringed instruments, voice, wind and percussion instruments. Graduate degrees offered: Master of Music in the areas of performance, theory and composition, music education. Cross-registration with Old Dominion University. Program accredited by NASM.
**Enrollment** 190 total; 180 undergraduate, 10 graduate.
**Music Student Profile** 40% females, 60% males, 90% minorities, 1% international.
**Music Faculty** 22 total (full-time), 6 total (part-time). 47% of full-time faculty have terminal degrees. Graduate students do not teach undergraduate courses. Undergraduate student–faculty ratio: 3:1.
**Student Life** Student groups/activities include Music Educators National Conference, American Choral Directors Association, Intercollegiate Music Association.
**Expenses for 2007–2008** State resident tuition: $2700 full-time. Nonresident tuition: $13,620 full-time. Mandatory fees: $2622 full-time. Full-time tuition and fees vary according to course load. College room and board: $6909. College room only: $4402. Room and board charges vary according to board plan and housing facility. Special program-related fees: $35 per applied lesson for miscellaneous music fees.
**Financial Aid** Program-specific awards: 200 band scholarships for band students ($1000–$2000), 30 choir scholarships for choir students ($2000), 20 jazz ensemble scholarships for jazz players ($500).
**Application Procedures** Students admitted directly into the professional program freshman year. Deadline for freshmen and transfers: August 1. Required: high school transcript, college transcript(s) for transfer students, minimum 2.0 high school GPA, audition, SAT or ACT test scores. Auditions held 4 times on campus.
**Web Site** http://www.nsu.edu/
**Undergraduate Contact** Dr. Ernest Brown, Head, Department of Music, Norfolk State University, 700 Park Avenue, Norfolk, Virginia 23504; 757-823-8544, fax: 757-823-2605, e-mail address: ejbrown@nsu.edu
**Graduate Contact** Mrs. Geraldine Boone, Coordinator, Department of Music, Norfolk State University, 700 Park Avenue, Norfolk, Virginia 23504; 757-823-8025, fax: 757-823-2605.

# North Carolina Central University
## Durham, North Carolina

State-supported, coed. Urban campus. Total enrollment: 8,383.
**Degrees** Bachelor of Arts in the areas of music education, music (concentration in music industry, sacred music, ethnomusicology);

*North Carolina Central University (continued)*

Bachelor of Music in the area of jazz studies. Majors and concentrations: brass instruments performance, ethnomusicology, guitar, jazz studies, music education, music industry, piano/organ, sacred music, stringed instruments, voice, wind and percussion instruments. Cross-registration with all universities in the UNC system. Program accredited by NCATE.
**Enrollment** 140 total; all undergraduate.
**Music Student Profile** 11% minorities, 1% international.
**Music Faculty** 17 undergraduate (full-time), 9 undergraduate (part-time). 35% of full-time faculty have terminal degrees. Graduate students do not teach undergraduate courses. Undergraduate student–faculty ratio: 7:1.
**Student Life** Student groups/activities include Tau Beta Sigma, Kappa Kappa Psi, Intercollegiate Music Association, Collegiate Music Educators National Conference (CMENC), National Association for Teachers of Singing (NATS), Phi Mu Alpha.
**Expenses for 2008–2009** Application fee: $30. State resident tuition: $2218 full-time. Nonresident tuition: $11,962 full-time. Mandatory fees: $1452 full-time. College room and board: $6015. College room only: $3433.
**Financial Aid** Program-specific awards: 1–2 Otelia Stewart Scholarships for juniors and seniors ($1000), 25–30 music scholarships for band, jazz band, choir participants ($1000–$5000).
**Application Procedures** Students admitted directly into the professional program freshman year. Deadline for freshmen and transfers: continuous. Required: high school transcript, college transcript(s) for transfer students, audition, SAT or ACT test scores, confidential statement for transfer students, campus safety questions on application, fee. Recommended: minimum 2.0 high school GPA, 2 letters of recommendation. Auditions held 6-8 times on campus and off campus in various sites (varies by faculty); recorded music is permissible as a substitute for live auditions if a campus visit is impossible.
**Web Site** http://www.nccu.edu/
**Undergraduate Contact** Department of Music, North Carolina Central University, 1801 Fayetteville Street, Durham, North Carolina 27707; 919-530-6319, fax: 919-530-7540.

# North Carolina School of the Arts
## Winston-Salem, North Carolina

State-supported, coed. Urban campus. Total enrollment: 864. Music program established 1965.
**Degrees** Bachelor of Music in the area of music performance. Majors and concentrations: classical music, composition, guitar, harp, performance, piano/organ, saxophone, stringed instruments, voice, wind and percussion instruments. Graduate degrees offered: Master of Music in the areas of music performance, opera, voice performance.
**Enrollment** 175 total; 99 undergraduate, 45 graduate, 31 nonprofessional degree.
**Music Student Profile** 40% females, 60% males, 10% minorities, 8% international.
**Music Faculty** 28 total (full-time), 6 total (part-time). 90% of full-time faculty have terminal degrees. Graduate students do not teach undergraduate courses. Undergraduate student–faculty ratio: 4:1.
**Student Life** Special housing available for music students.
**Expenses for 2007–2008** Application fee: $50. State resident tuition: $3224 full-time. Nonresident tuition: $14,654 full-time. Mandatory fees: $1837 full-time. Full-time tuition and fees vary according to program. College room and board: $6431. College room only: $3289. Room and board charges vary according to board plan and housing facility. Special program-related fees: $135 per year for educational and technology fee, $160 for music course fee.
**Financial Aid** Program-specific awards: 91 talent/need scholarships for those demonstrating talent and/or need ($3178).
**Application Procedures** Students admitted directly into the professional program freshman year. Deadline for freshmen and transfers: continuous. Required: high school transcript, 2 letters of recommendation, interview, audition, portfolio for composition applicants. Recommended: SAT or ACT test scores. Auditions held several times on campus and off campus in various cities in the U.S.; recorded music is permissible as a substitute for live auditions for provisional acceptance and videotaped performances are permissible as a substitute for live auditions for provisional acceptance. Portfolio reviews held several times on campus.
**Web Site** http://www.ncarts.edu
**Contact** Ms. Sheeler Lawson, Director of Admissions, North Carolina School of the Arts, 1533 South Main Street, Winston-Salem, North Carolina 27117-2189; 336-770-3291, fax: 336-770-3370, e-mail address: admissions@ncarts.edu

# Northern Arizona University
## Flagstaff, Arizona

State-supported, coed. Small town campus. Total enrollment: 21,352.
**Degrees** Bachelor of Arts in the area of music; Bachelor of Music in the area of performance; Bachelor of Music Education in the areas of choral/general, instrumental/general. Majors and concentrations: choral music education, instrumental music education, instrumental performance, piano accompanying, piano performance, voice performance. Graduate degrees offered: Master of Music in the areas of performance, music education, music history/musicology, music theory/composition, conducting, Suzuki violin/viola. Program accredited by NASM.
**Enrollment** 400 total; 320 undergraduate, 80 graduate.
**Music Student Profile** 60% females, 40% males, 3% minorities, 3% international.
**Music Faculty** 28 total (full-time), 16 total (part-time). 90% of full-time faculty have terminal degrees. Graduate students teach a few undergraduate courses. Undergraduate student–faculty ratio: 13:1.
**Student Life** Student groups/activities include music fraternities and sororities, Music Educators National Conference Student Chapter, American Choral Directors Association Student Chapter.
**Expenses for 2007–2008** Application fee: $25. State resident tuition: $4594 full-time. Nonresident tuition: $14,428 full-time. Mandatory fees: $250 full-time. Full-time tuition and fees vary according to location and program. College room and board: $6572. College room only: $3624. Room and board charges vary according to board plan and housing facility. Special program-related fees: $25–$50 per semester for class fees (various courses), $74 per semester for private lessons.
**Financial Aid** Program-specific awards: 60–90 tuition waiver scholarships for program majors and minors ($1300–$5516), 25 endowed scholarships for program majors and minors ($500–$4000).
**Application Procedures** Students admitted directly into the professional program freshman year. Deadline for freshmen and transfers: continuous. Required: high school transcript, college transcript(s) for transfer students, minimum 2.0 high school GPA, audition, SAT or ACT test scores. Recommended: 3 letters of recommendation. Auditions held 5 times and by request on campus; recorded music is permissible as a substitute for live auditions when distance is prohibitive and videotaped performances are permissible as a substitute for live auditions when distance is prohibitive.
**Web Site** http://www.nau.edu/music
**Undergraduate Contact** Dr. Rick Stamer, Associate Director, School of Music, Northern Arizona University, PO Box 6040, Flagstaff, Arizona 86011-6040; 928-523-3731, fax: 928-523-5111, e-mail address: rick.stamer@nau.edu
**Graduate Contact** Dr. Judith Cloud, Coordinator of Graduate Studies, School of Music, Northern Arizona University, PO Box 6040, Flagstaff, Arizona 86011-6040; 928-523-2770, fax: 928-523-5111.

# Northern Illinois University
## De Kalb, Illinois

State-supported, coed. Small town campus. Total enrollment: 25,254.
**Web Site** http://www.niu.edu/

# Northern Kentucky University

## Highland Heights, Kentucky

State-supported, coed. Suburban campus. Total enrollment: 14,785. Music program established 1969.
**Degrees** Bachelor of Music in the areas of performance, music education. Majors and concentrations: guitar, music education, piano, piano pedagogy, stringed instruments, voice, wind and percussion instruments. Cross-registration with Greater Cincinnati Consortium of Colleges and Universities. Program accredited by NASM.
**Enrollment** 137 total; 96 undergraduate, 41 nonprofessional degree.
**Music Student Profile** 50% females, 50% males, 1% minorities, 5% international.
**Music Faculty** 22 undergraduate (full-time), 18 undergraduate (part-time). 100% of full-time faculty have terminal degrees. Graduate students do not teach undergraduate courses. Undergraduate student–faculty ratio: 12:1.
**Student Life** Student groups/activities include Sigma Alpha Iota, Phi Mu Alpha, Music Educators National Conference Student Chapter.
**Expenses for 2008–2009** Application fee: $40. State resident tuition: $6528 full-time. Nonresident tuition: $11,952 full-time. College room and board: $6560. Special program-related fees: $350 per semester for private music lessons.
**Financial Aid** Program-specific awards: 18 University Scholarships for musically talented students ($1500), 10 private scholarships for musically talented students ($3000).
**Application Procedures** Students apply for admission into the professional program by sophomore year. Deadline for freshmen and transfers: August 1. Required: high school transcript, college transcript(s) for transfer students, SAT or ACT test scores, audition, music theory test, and music history test for transfers. Recommended: 2 letters of recommendation, audition. Auditions held 4 times on campus; recorded music is permissible as a substitute for live auditions and videotaped performances are permissible as a substitute for live audition is impossible.
**Web Site** http://www.nku.edu/~music
**Undergraduate Contact** Office of Admissions, Northern Kentucky University, Lucas Administrative Center, Highland Heights, Kentucky 41099-1005; 859-572-5220, fax: 859-572-6665, e-mail address: admitnku@nku.edu

# Northern Michigan University

## Marquette, Michigan

State-supported, coed. Small town campus. Total enrollment: 9,111. Music program established 1969.
**Degrees** Bachelor of Music Education. Majors and concentrations: choral music education, instrumental music education. Program accredited by NASM.
**Enrollment** 60 total; all undergraduate.
**Music Student Profile** 55% females, 45% males, 3% international.
**Music Faculty** 11 undergraduate (full-time). 90% of full-time faculty have terminal degrees. Graduate students do not teach undergraduate courses. Undergraduate student–faculty ratio: 5:1.
**Student Life** Student groups/activities include Music Educators National Conference, Marquette Symphony Orchestra, Marquette Chorale Society.
**Expenses for 2007–2008** Application fee: $30. State resident tuition: $6144 full-time. Nonresident tuition: $10,080 full-time. Mandatory fees: $565 full-time. Full-time tuition and fees vary according to location. College room and board: $7220. College room only: $3606. Room and board charges vary according to board plan and housing facility.
**Financial Aid** Program-specific awards: 20 scholarships for talented program majors ($1000).
**Application Procedures** Students apply for admission into the professional program by freshman year. Deadline for freshmen and transfers: continuous. Required: high school transcript, college transcript(s) for transfer students, SAT or ACT test scores (minimum composite ACT score of 20), minimum 2.7 high school

GPA. Recommended: letter of recommendation, audition. Auditions held as needed for voice and instrumental applicants on campus; recorded music is permissible as a substitute for live auditions if a campus visit is impossible and videotaped performances are permissible as a substitute for live auditions if a campus visit is impossible.
**Web Site** http://www.nmu.edu/departments/music/
**Undergraduate Contact** Dr. Donald Grant, Head, Music Department, Northern Michigan University, 1401 Presque Isle Avenue, Marquette, Michigan 49855; 906-227-2563, fax: 906-227-2165.

# Northern State University

## Aberdeen, South Dakota

State-supported, coed. Small town campus. Total enrollment: 2,578. Music program established 1940.
**Degrees** Bachelor of Arts in the area of music; Bachelor of Music Education in the areas of instrumental music, vocal music, composite (instrumental and vocal). Majors and concentrations: instrumental music, piano/organ, stringed instruments, voice. Program accredited by NASM.
**Enrollment** 105 total; all undergraduate.
**Music Student Profile** 60% females, 40% males.
**Music Faculty** 13 undergraduate (full-time), 1 undergraduate (part-time). 80% of full-time faculty have terminal degrees. Graduate students do not teach undergraduate courses. Undergraduate student–faculty ratio: 8:1.
**Student Life** Student groups/activities include Music Educators National Conference, Sigma Alpha Iota, Phi Mu Alpha Sinfonia. Special housing available for music students.
**Expenses for 2007–2008** Application fee: $20. State resident tuition: $2478 full-time. Nonresident tuition: $7872 full-time. Mandatory fees: $2802 full-time. Full-time tuition and fees vary according to course level, course load, and reciprocity agreements. College room and board: $4499. College room only: $2378. Room and board charges vary according to board plan.
**Financial Aid** Program-specific awards: 45 music scholarships for incoming freshmen/transfers ($800).
**Application Procedures** Students admitted directly into the professional program freshman year. Deadline for freshmen and transfers: August 15. Notification date for freshmen and transfers: continuous. Required: high school transcript, college transcript(s) for transfer students, minimum 2.0 high school GPA, audition, SAT or ACT test scores. Recommended: 3 letters of recommendation. Auditions held once and by appointment on campus; recorded music is permissible as a substitute for live auditions when distance is prohibitive and videotaped performances are permissible as a substitute for live auditions when distance is prohibitive.
**Web Site** http://www.northern.edu
**Undergraduate Contact** Admissions Office, Northern State University, Dacotah Hall Room 101, 1200 South Jay Street, Aberdeen, South Dakota 57401-7198; 605-626-2544, fax: 605-626-2587, e-mail address: admissions@northern.edu

# North Park University

## Chicago, Illinois

Independent, coed. Urban campus. Music program established 1960.
**Degrees** Bachelor of Music in the areas of performance, music in worship; Bachelor of Music Education. Majors and concentrations: brass, music education, music in worship, piano, stringed instruments, voice, wind instruments. Graduate degrees offered: Master of Music in the area of vocal performance. Program accredited by NASM.
**Enrollment** 45 total; 24 undergraduate, 5 graduate, 16 nonprofessional degree.
**Music Student Profile** 71% females, 29% males, 15% minorities, 2% international.
**Music Faculty** 6 undergraduate (full-time), 27 undergraduate (part-time), 4 graduate (part-time). 83% of full-time faculty have terminal degrees. Graduate students do not teach undergraduate courses. Undergraduate student–faculty ratio: 8:1.

*North Park University (continued)*

**Student Life** Student groups/activities include Student Performance Awards Competition, Chicago-area competitions.

**Expenses for 2007–2008** Application fee: $20. Comprehensive fee: $23,890 includes full-time tuition ($16,500), mandatory fees ($60), and college room and board ($7330). College room only: $4100. Full-time tuition and fees vary according to program. Room and board charges vary according to board plan, housing facility, and student level.

**Financial Aid** Program-specific awards: 20 music scholarships for freshmen and transfer students ($1000–$4000), 14 named music scholarships for continuing students ($300–$1500), 3 Presidential Honors Music Scholarships for freshmen and transfers ($6000).

**Application Procedures** Students apply for admission into the professional program by sophomore year. Deadline for freshmen and transfers: continuous. Required: essay, high school transcript, college transcript(s) for transfer students, letter of recommendation, interview, SAT or ACT test scores (minimum composite ACT score of 17), audition for scholarship consideration. Recommended: minimum 2.0 high school GPA, audition. Auditions held 3 times and by appointment on campus; recorded music is permissible as a substitute for live auditions if a campus visit is impossible and videotaped performances are permissible as a substitute for live auditions if a campus visit is impossible.

**Web Site** http://www.northpark.edu

**Undergraduate Contact** Mr. Joseph Lill, Music Admission Coordinator, School of Music, North Park University, 3225 West Foster Avenue, Chicago, Illinois 60625; 773-244-5634, fax: 773-244-5230, e-mail address: jlill@northpark.edu

**Graduate Contact** Mr. Joseph Lill, Graduate Admissions Coordinator, School of Music, North Park University, 3225 West Foster Avenue, Chicago, Illinois 60625; 773-244-5634, fax: 773-244-5230, e-mail address: jlill@northpark.edu

# Northwestern State University of Louisiana

**Natchitoches, Louisiana**

State-supported, coed. Small town campus. Total enrollment: 9,037. Music program established 1883.

**Degrees** Bachelor of Music in the areas of performance, sacred music; Bachelor of Music Education in the areas of instrumental music education, vocal music education, piano music education. Majors and concentrations: music, music education, piano/organ, sacred music, voice, wind and percussion instruments. Graduate degrees offered: Master of Music in the areas of instrumental music, vocal music, piano, music education. Cross-registration with Louisiana State University in Shreveport, Louisiana State University and Agricultural and Mechanical College. Program accredited by NASM.

**Enrollment** 191 total; 176 undergraduate, 15 graduate.

**Music Student Profile** 40% females, 60% males, 10% minorities, 1% international.

**Music Faculty** 21 total (full-time), 11 total (part-time). 80% of full-time faculty have terminal degrees. Graduate students teach a few undergraduate courses. Undergraduate student–faculty ratio: 8:1.

**Student Life** Student groups/activities include professional fraternities and sororities, Music Educators National Conference. Special housing available for music students.

**Expenses for 2007–2008** Application fee: $20. State resident tuition: $2240 full-time. Nonresident tuition: $8318 full-time. Mandatory fees: $1288 full-time. Full-time tuition and fees vary according to course load. College room and board: $5850. College room only: $3700. Room and board charges vary according to board plan, housing facility, and location.

**Financial Aid** Program-specific awards: 300 band awards for incoming freshmen ($800–$2000), 100 choir awards for incoming freshmen ($800–$1500), 20 Deer Scholarships for music majors ($2000), 20 Magale Scholarships for music majors ($200–$1200), 30 orchestra awards for music majors ($1000–$3000), 10 keyboard awards for music majors ($1000–$3000).

**Application Procedures** Students admitted directly into the professional program freshman year. Deadline for freshmen and

transfers: August 15. Notification date for freshmen: August 15. Required: high school transcript, college transcript(s) for transfer students, minimum 2.0 high school GPA, 3 letters of recommendation, audition, SAT or ACT test scores. Recommended: interview, video, portfolio. Auditions held by appointment on campus; recorded music is permissible as a substitute for live auditions with approval from the department and videotaped performances are permissible as a substitute for live auditions with approval from the department. Portfolio reviews held by appointment on campus.

**Web Site** http://www.nsula.edu/capa/

**Undergraduate Contact** Ms. Jana Lucky, Director, Office of Admissions, Northwestern State University of Louisiana, College Avenue, Natchitoches, Louisiana 71497; 318-357-4503, fax: 318-357-5906.

**Graduate Contact** Dr. Steve Horton, Dean, Graduate Studies, Northwestern State University of Louisiana, College Avenue, Natchitoches, Louisiana 71497; 318-357-5851, fax: 318-357-5019.

# Northwestern University

**Evanston, Illinois**

Independent, coed. Suburban campus. Total enrollment: 18,028. Music program established 1895.

**Web Site** http://www.northwestern.edu/

# Notre Dame de Namur University

**Belmont, California**

Independent Roman Catholic, coed. Suburban campus. Total enrollment: 1,491. Music program established 1851.

**Web Site** http://www.ndnu.edu

# Nyack College

**Nyack, New York**

Independent, coed. Suburban campus. Total enrollment: 3,250. Music program established 1947.

**Web Site** http://www.nyack.edu

# Oakland City University

**Oakland City, Indiana**

Independent General Baptist, coed. Rural campus. Total enrollment: 2,007.

**Web Site** http://www.oak.edu/

# Oakland University

**Rochester, Michigan**

State-supported, coed. Suburban campus. Total enrollment: 18,081. Music program established 1972.

**Degrees** Bachelor of Music in the areas of performance, composition, music education. Majors and concentrations: composition, instrumental performance, keyboard, music education, voice. Graduate degrees offered: Master of Music in the areas of music education, conducting, performance, composition, pedagogy. Doctor of Philosophy in the area of music education. Program accredited by NASM.

**Enrollment** 400 total; 200 undergraduate, 60 graduate, 140 nonprofessional degree.

**Music Student Profile** 77% females, 23% males, 7% minorities.

**Music Faculty** 14 total (full-time), 60 total (part-time). 82% of full-time faculty have terminal degrees. Graduate students do not teach undergraduate courses. Undergraduate student–faculty ratio: 19:1.

**Student Life** Student groups/activities include MENC–The National Association for Music Education, ensembles.

**Expenses for 2007–2008** Application fee: $40. State resident tuition: $7575 full-time. Nonresident tuition: $17,625 full-time. Full-time tuition varies according to program and student level. College room and board: $6670. Room and board charges vary

according to housing facility. Special program-related fees: $13–$85 per credit for applied music lessons or classes.
**Financial Aid** Program-specific awards: music scholarships for talented students ($750–$2000).
**Application Procedures** Students admitted directly into the professional program freshman year. Deadline for freshmen and transfers: July 15. Required: high school transcript, audition, SAT or ACT test scores, minimum 2.5 high school GPA. Auditions held 3 times on campus; recorded music is permissible as a substitute for live auditions if a campus visit is impossible and videotaped performances are permissible as a substitute for live auditions if a campus visit is impossible.
**Web Site** http://www.otus.oakland.edu/mtd
**Undergraduate Contact** John-Paul White, Director of Undergraduate Music Education, Department of Music, Theatre, and Dance, Oakland University, 315 Varner Hall, Rochester, Michigan 48309; 248-370-2030, fax: 248-370-2041.
**Graduate Contact** Jackie Wiggins, Department of Music, Theatre, and Dance, Oakland University, 211 Varner Hall, Rochester, Michigan 48309; 248-370-2030, fax: 248-370-2041, e-mail address: jwiggins@oakland.edu

## Oberlin College

See The Conservatory of Music at Oberlin College

## Ohio Northern University

### Ada, Ohio

Independent, coed. Small town campus. Total enrollment: 3,603. Music program established 1871.
**Degrees** Bachelor of Music. Majors and concentrations: composition, music and business, music education, music performance. Cross-registration with multiple colleges and universities. Program accredited by NASM, NCATE.
**Enrollment** 84 total; 70 undergraduate, 14 nonprofessional degree.
**Music Student Profile** 65% females, 35% males, 4% minorities.
**Music Faculty** 8 undergraduate (full-time), 18 undergraduate (part-time). 63% of full-time faculty have terminal degrees. Graduate students do not teach undergraduate courses. Undergraduate student–faculty ratio: 3:1.
**Student Life** Student groups/activities include Ohio Music Education Association, National Association of Teachers of Singing, National Federation of Music Clubs.
**Expenses for 2008–2009** Application fee: $30. Comprehensive fee: $38,655 includes full-time tuition ($30,555), mandatory fees ($210), and college room and board ($7890). College room only: $3945. Special program-related fees: $25 per quarter for private lessons, $250 per year for recital fee.
**Financial Aid** Program-specific awards: 30 Snyder Scholarships for top musicians ($8000–$10,000), 30 Dean's Talent Awards for top musicians ($5000–$8000).
**Application Procedures** Students admitted directly into the professional program freshman year. Deadline for freshmen and transfers: continuous. Required: high school transcript, college transcript(s) for transfer students, minimum 2.0 high school GPA, audition, SAT or ACT test scores. Auditions held 5 times on campus; recorded music is permissible as a substitute for live auditions for out-of-state applicants and videotaped performances are permissible as a substitute for live auditions for out-of-state applicants.
**Web Site** http://www.onu.edu
**Undergraduate Contact** Dennis Kratzer, Recruitment Coordinator, Music Department, Ohio Northern University, 525 South Main Street, Ada, Ohio 45810; 419-772-2153, fax: 419-772-2488, e-mail address: d-kratzer@onu.edu

## Ohio University

### Athens, Ohio

State-supported, coed. Small town campus. Total enrollment: 20,711. Music program established 1946.
**Web Site** http://www.ohio.edu/

## Ohio Wesleyan University

### Delaware, Ohio

Independent United Methodist, coed. Small town campus. Total enrollment: 1,967. Music program established 1877.
**Degrees** Bachelor of Music in the areas of performance, music education. Majors and concentrations: music education, music performance, piano/organ, stringed instruments, voice, wind and percussion instruments. Program accredited by NASM.
**Enrollment** 43 total; 35 undergraduate, 8 nonprofessional degree.
**Music Student Profile** 65% females, 35% males, 10% minorities, 4% international.
**Music Faculty** 8 undergraduate (full-time), 10 undergraduate (part-time). 100% of full-time faculty have terminal degrees. Graduate students do not teach undergraduate courses. Undergraduate student–faculty ratio: 4:1.
**Student Life** Student groups/activities include Mu Phi Epsilon Student Chapter, Music Educators National Conference Student Chapter.
**Expenses for 2007–2008** Application fee: $35. Comprehensive fee: $39,960 includes full-time tuition ($31,510), mandatory fees ($420), and college room and board ($8030). College room only: $4000. Room and board charges vary according to board plan.
**Financial Aid** Program-specific awards: Ruth Wilson Music Scholarships for program majors, Edward D. and Laura Rich Cleary Music Education Memorial Scholarship for music education majors, Edith Mahon Davis Music Education Scholarship for music education majors, Ohio Wesleyan University Merit Scholarships for program majors, Edith M. Keller Scholarship in Music Education for music education majors, Col. George Howard Instrumental Music Scholarship for instrumental majors.
**Application Procedures** Students admitted directly into the professional program freshman year. Deadline for freshmen and transfers: March 1. Required: essay, high school transcript, college transcript(s) for transfer students, letter of recommendation, audition, SAT or ACT test scores. Recommended: interview, video. Auditions held 6 scheduled times and by appointment on campus; recorded music is permissible as a substitute for live auditions when distance is prohibitive and videotaped performances are permissible as a substitute for live auditions when distance is prohibitive.
**Web Site** http://www.owu.edu/~musicd
**Undergraduate Contact** Admissions, Ohio Wesleyan University, Slocum Hall, 61 South Sandusky Street, Delaware, Ohio 43015; 740-368-2000, fax: 740-368-3314.

## Oklahoma Baptist University

### Shawnee, Oklahoma

Independent Southern Baptist, coed. Music program established 1917.
**Degrees** Bachelor of Music in the areas of voice/keyboard, music performance, church music, composition; Bachelor of Music Education in the areas of vocal music education, instrumental music education. Majors and concentrations: music education, music theory and composition, piano, sacred music, stringed instruments, voice, wind and percussion instruments. Program accredited by NASM.
**Enrollment** 77 total; 75 undergraduate, 2 nonprofessional degree.
**Music Student Profile** 66% females, 34% males, 8% minorities, 1% international.
**Music Faculty** 16 undergraduate (full-time), 7 undergraduate (part-time). 65% of full-time faculty have terminal degrees. Graduate students do not teach undergraduate courses. Undergraduate student–faculty ratio: 9:1.
**Student Life** Student groups/activities include Music Educators National Conference, Sigma Alpha Iota, Phi Mu Alpha Sinfonia.
**Expenses for 2008–2009** Application fee: $25. One-time mandatory fee: $25. Comprehensive fee: $20,668 includes full-time tuition ($15,468) and college room and board ($5200). Special program-related fees: $900 per course for applied music fees.
**Financial Aid** Program-specific awards: 74 music scholarships for program majors ($1450).
**Application Procedures** Students admitted directly into the professional program freshman year. Deadline for freshmen and

*Oklahoma Baptist University (continued)*

transfers: continuous. Required: high school transcript, college transcript(s) for transfer students, minimum 2.0 high school GPA, audition, SAT or ACT test scores. Auditions held 4 times on campus; recorded music is permissible as a substitute for live auditions when distance is prohibitive and videotaped performances are permissible as a substitute for live auditions when distance is prohibitive.
**Web Site** http://www.okbu.edu
**Undergraduate Contact** Mr. Bruce Perkins, Dean of Admissions, Oklahoma Baptist University, Box 61174, 500 West University, Shawnee, Oklahoma 74804; 800-654-3285, fax: 405-878-2046, e-mail address: bruce.perkins@okbu.edu

## *Wands L. Bass School of Music*
# Oklahoma City University
### Oklahoma City, Oklahoma

Independent United Methodist, coed. Urban campus. Total enrollment: 3,865. Music program established 1904.
**Degrees** Bachelor of Music in the areas of performance, music theater, composition, piano pedagogy, music business, church music; Bachelor of Music Education in the areas of vocal music education, instrumental music education. Majors and concentrations: church music, composition, music, music business, music education, music theater, piano/organ, stringed instruments, voice, wind and percussion instruments. Graduate degrees offered: Master of Music in the areas of performance, composition, music theater, opera performance, conducting. Program accredited by NASM.
**Enrollment** 351 total; 294 undergraduate, 57 graduate.
**Music Student Profile** 55% females, 45% males, 13% minorities, 10% international.
**Music Faculty** 24 total (full-time), 27 total (part-time). 54% of full-time faculty have terminal degrees. Graduate students do not teach undergraduate courses. Undergraduate student–faculty ratio: 14:1.
**Student Life** Student groups/activities include American String Teachers Association, Sigma Alpha Iota, Music Educators National Conference.
**Expenses for 2007–2008** Application fee: $30. Comprehensive fee: $29,400 includes full-time tuition ($19,600), mandatory fees ($1400), and college room and board ($8400). College room only: $4650. Full-time tuition and fees vary according to program. Room and board charges vary according to board plan and housing facility. Special program-related fees: $190 per credit hour for applied music fee, $250 per semester for facilities fee, $300 per semester for accompanist fee (vocal only).
**Financial Aid** Program-specific awards: 200 Music Talent Awards for program majors and performers ($4500).
**Application Procedures** Students admitted directly into the professional program freshman year. Deadline for freshmen and transfers: continuous. Notification date for freshmen and transfers: August 20. Required: essay, high school transcript, college transcript(s) for transfer students, minimum 2.0 high school GPA, audition, SAT or ACT test scores (minimum composite ACT score of 22), minimum 2.5 high school GPA, standing in top 50% of graduating class, portfolio for composition majors. Recommended: minimum 3.0 high school GPA. Auditions held 6 times on campus; recorded music is permissible as a substitute for live auditions if a campus visit is impossible and videotaped performances are permissible as a substitute for live auditions if a campus visit is impossible.
**Web Site** http://www.okcu.edu/music
**Undergraduate Contact** Ms. Mary Mowry, Coordinator of Student Services, Wands L. Bass School of Music, Oklahoma City University, 2501 North Blackwelder, Oklahoma City, Oklahoma 73106; 405-208-5980, fax: 405-208-5971, e-mail address: mamowry@okcu.edu
**Graduate Contact** Dr. David Steffens, Graduate Studies Advisor, Wands L. Bass School of Music, Oklahoma City University, 2501 North Blackwelder, Oklahoma City, Oklahoma 73106; 405-208-5981, fax: 405-208-5791, e-mail address: dsteffens@okcu.edu

# Oklahoma State University
### Stillwater, Oklahoma

State-supported, coed. Small town campus. Total enrollment: 23,005. Music program established 1902.
**Degrees** Bachelor of Music in the areas of performance, music education, music business. Majors and concentrations: music business, music education, piano/organ, stringed instruments, voice, wind and percussion instruments. Graduate degrees offered: Master of Music in the area of pedagogy and performance. Program accredited by NASM.
**Enrollment** 179 total; 148 undergraduate, 15 graduate, 16 nonprofessional degree.
**Music Student Profile** 49% females, 51% males, 18% minorities, 1% international.
**Music Faculty** 25 total (full-time), 8 total (part-time). 52% of full-time faculty have terminal degrees. Graduate students teach a few undergraduate courses. Undergraduate student–faculty ratio: 4:1.
**Student Life** Student groups/activities include professional music fraternities and sororities.
**Expenses for 2007–2008** Application fee: $40. One-time mandatory fee: $70. State resident tuition: $3585 full-time. Nonresident tuition: $13,010 full-time. Mandatory fees: $1906 full-time. Full-time tuition and fees vary according to program and student level. College room and board: $6267. College room only: $3267. Room and board charges vary according to board plan and housing facility. Special program-related fees: $10 per credit for organ rental, $15 per credit for class piano fee, $25 per credit for ensemble enrollment fee, $25 per credit for applied lessons.
**Financial Aid** Program-specific awards: 190–230 music scholarships for program majors and musicians ($100–$3500).
**Application Procedures** Students admitted directly into the professional program freshman year. Deadline for freshmen and transfers: continuous. Required: high school transcript, college transcript(s) for transfer students, minimum 3.0 high school GPA, audition, ACT test score only (minimum composite ACT score of 24). Auditions held continuously on campus and off campus in various locations in Oklahoma; recorded music is permissible as a substitute for live auditions if a campus visit is impossible and videotaped performances are permissible as a substitute for live auditions if a campus visit is impossible.
**Web Site** http://music.okstate.edu
**Undergraduate Contact** Prof. Julia C. Combs, Head, Department of Music, Oklahoma State University, 132 Seretean Center, Stillwater, Oklahoma 74078-4077; 405-744-6133, fax: 405-744-9324, e-mail address: julie.combs@okstate.edu
**Graduate Contact** Dr. D. Allen Scott, Graduate Program Coordinator, Department of Music, Oklahoma State University, 132 Seretean Center, Stillwater, Oklahoma 74078-4077; 405-744-6149, fax: 405-744-9324, e-mail address: allen.scott@okstate.edu

# Oral Roberts University
### Tulsa, Oklahoma

Independent interdenominational, coed. Urban campus. Total enrollment: 3,170. Music program established 1963.
**Degrees** Bachelor of Music in the areas of sacred music, composition, performance, composition/technology; Bachelor of Music Education in the areas of vocal music education, instrumental music education. Majors and concentrations: composition, music education, piano, sacred music, stringed instruments, voice, wind and percussion instruments. Program accredited by NASM.
**Enrollment** 51 total; all undergraduate.
**Music Student Profile** 52% females, 48% males, 13% minorities, 5% international.
**Music Faculty** 14 undergraduate (full-time), 21 undergraduate (part-time). 59% of full-time faculty have terminal degrees. Graduate students do not teach undergraduate courses. Undergraduate student–faculty ratio: 3:1.
**Student Life** Student groups/activities include opera and musical productions, Family Christmas Concert, oratorio presentations.
**Expenses for 2007–2008** Application fee: $35. Comprehensive fee: $24,750 includes full-time tuition ($17,000), mandatory fees

($400), and college room and board ($7350). Special program-related fees: $40 per course for music ensemble fee, $55 per course for music equipment, $250 per semester for applied music lesson fee.

**Financial Aid** Program-specific awards: 150 talent awards for music majors, minors, or participants ($500–$5000), 25 special awards ($500–$2000).

**Application Procedures** Students admitted directly into the professional program freshman year. Deadline for freshmen and transfers: continuous. Required: essay, high school transcript, college transcript(s) for transfer students, minimum 2.0 high school GPA, 2 letters of recommendation, audition, SAT or ACT test scores (minimum composite ACT score of 20). Auditions held by appointment on campus; recorded music is permissible as a substitute for live auditions when distance is prohibitive and videotaped performances are permissible as a substitute for live auditions when distance is prohibitive. Portfolio reviews held as needed on campus.

**Web Site** http://www.oru.edu

**Undergraduate Contact** Mrs. LaDonna Thornton, Secretary, Music Department, Oral Roberts University, 7777 South Lewis Avenue, Tulsa, Oklahoma 74171; 918-495-7500, fax: 918-495-7502, e-mail address: lthornton@oru.edu

# Otterbein College
## Westerville, Ohio

Independent United Methodist, coed. Suburban campus. Total enrollment: 3,107. Music program established 1847.

**Degrees** Bachelor of Fine Arts in the area of musical theater; Bachelor of Music in the area of performance; Bachelor of Music Education in the areas of vocal, general, and instrumental music education. Majors and concentrations: classical music, music, music education, music theater, piano/organ, stringed instruments, voice, wind and percussion instruments. Cross-registration with Ohio State University, Capital University, Columbus State Community College. Program accredited by NASM.

**Enrollment** 200 total; 130 undergraduate, 70 nonprofessional degree.

**Music Student Profile** 60% females, 40% males, 2% minorities, 5% international.

**Music Faculty** 10 undergraduate (full-time), 45 undergraduate (part-time). 90% of full-time faculty have terminal degrees. Graduate students do not teach undergraduate courses. Undergraduate student–faculty ratio: 3:1.

**Student Life** Student groups/activities include Ohio Student Music Educators Association, Delta Omicron, Music and Entertainment Industry Students Association. Special housing available for music students.

**Expenses for 2007–2008** Application fee: $25. Comprehensive fee: $32,214 includes full-time tuition ($25,065) and college room and board ($7149). College room only: $3399. Full-time tuition varies according to course load and program. Room and board charges vary according to housing facility. Special program-related fees: $750–$1500 per year for private applied music lessons.

**Financial Aid** Program-specific awards: 30–40 Music Talent Awards for program majors ($2000–$7000).

**Application Procedures** Students admitted directly into the professional program freshman year. Deadline for freshmen and transfers: continuous. Required: high school transcript, college transcript(s) for transfer students, minimum 2.0 high school GPA, audition, SAT or ACT test scores. Recommended: interview. Auditions held continuously on campus and off campus; recorded music is permissible as a substitute for live auditions when distance is prohibitive and videotaped performances are permissible as a substitute for live auditions when distance is prohibitive.

**Web Site** http://www.otterbein.edu/admission/music.html

**Undergraduate Contact** Debbie Byrne, Admission Counselor/Arts Recruiter, Admissions Office, Otterbein College, Westerville, Ohio 43081; 614-823-1219, fax: 614-823-1200, e-mail address: dbyrne@otterbein.edu

*Bernice Young Jones School of Fine Arts*
# Ouachita Baptist University
## Arkadelphia, Arkansas

Independent Baptist, coed. Small town campus. Total enrollment: 1,448. Music program established 1886.

**Degrees** Bachelor of Music in the areas of performance, musical theater, church music, music theory/composition; Bachelor of Music Education in the areas of choral music education, instrumental music education. Majors and concentrations: church music, music, music education, music theater, piano/organ, voice, wind and percussion instruments. Cross-registration with Henderson State University. Program accredited by NASM.

**Enrollment** 160 total; 121 undergraduate, 39 nonprofessional degree.

**Music Student Profile** 55% females, 45% males, 4% minorities, 4% international.

**Music Faculty** 16 undergraduate (full-time), 11 undergraduate (part-time). 76% of full-time faculty have terminal degrees. Graduate students do not teach undergraduate courses. Undergraduate student–faculty ratio: 6:1.

**Student Life** Student groups/activities include Phi Mu Alpha Sinfonia, Sigma Alpha Iota, Tau Beta Sigma.

**Expenses for 2008–2009** Application fee: $50. Comprehensive fee: $23,930 includes full-time tuition ($18,000), mandatory fees ($400), and college room and board ($5530). Special program-related fees: $125 per semester for 30-minute weekly private instruction in all instruments.

**Financial Aid** Program-specific awards: 70–80 music scholarships for program majors ($1000–$5000), 50 band scholarships for non-music majors ($2000).

**Application Procedures** Students admitted directly into the professional program freshman year. Deadline for freshmen and transfers: February 15. Notification date for freshmen and transfers: continuous. Required: high school transcript, college transcript(s) for transfer students, audition, SAT or ACT test scores (minimum composite ACT score of 20), minimum 2.75 high school GPA for regular admission, ACT score of 17 for conditional admission. Auditions held twice and by appointment on campus; recorded music is permissible as a substitute for live auditions if a campus visit is impossible and videotaped performances are permissible as a substitute for live auditions if a campus visit is impossible.

**Web Site** http://www.obu.edu/finearts/

**Undergraduate Contact** Dr. Scott Holsclaw, Dean, Bernice Young Jones School of Fine Arts, Ouachita Baptist University, Box 3771, Arkadelphia, Arkansas 71998-0001; 870-245-5129, fax: 870-245-5500, e-mail address: holsclaws@obu.edu

# Pacific Lutheran University
## Tacoma, Washington

Independent, coed. Suburban campus. Total enrollment: 3,661. Music program established 1891.

**Degrees** Bachelor of Music in the area of performance; Bachelor of Musical Arts in the area of music combined with an outside field; Bachelor of Music Education in the areas of choral music, band, orchestra. Majors and concentrations: composition, music education, performance. Program accredited by NASM.

**Enrollment** 176 total; all undergraduate.

**Music Student Profile** 60% females, 40% males, 8% minorities, 5% international.

**Music Faculty** 15 undergraduate (full-time), 35 undergraduate (part-time). 60% of full-time faculty have terminal degrees. Graduate students do not teach undergraduate courses. Undergraduate student–faculty ratio: 15:1.

**Student Life** Student groups/activities include Music Educators National Conference, American Choral Directors Association, Mu Phi Epsilon.

**Expenses for 2007–2008** Application fee: $40. Comprehensive fee: $32,800 includes full-time tuition ($25,088) and college room and board ($7712). College room only: $3720. Full-time tuition varies according to course load. Room and board charges vary according to board plan and housing facility. Special program-

*Pacific Lutheran University (continued)*

related fees: $100–$650 per year for ensemble tours (domestic), $200–$400 per semester for private lessons.

**Financial Aid** Program-specific awards: 100–120 music scholarships for incoming freshmen demonstrating need and talent ($1000–$5000), 150 music scholarships for continuing program students ($1000–$5000).

**Application Procedures** Students admitted directly into the professional program freshman year. Deadline for freshmen and transfers: continuous. Required: essay, high school transcript, college transcript(s) for transfer students, 2 letters of recommendation, SAT or ACT test scores, minimum 2.5 high school GPA, audition for scholarship consideration. Auditions held once on campus; recorded music is permissible as a substitute for live auditions and videotaped performances are permissible as a substitute for live auditions.

**Web Site** http://www.plu.edu/music

**Undergraduate Contact** Nita Muir, Administrative Assistant, Department of Music, Pacific Lutheran University, Tacoma, Washington 98447; 253-535-7603, fax: 253-535-8669, e-mail address: muirnl@plu.edu

## Pacific Union College

**Angwin, California**

Independent Seventh-day Adventist, coed. Rural campus. Total enrollment: 1,375. Music program established 1967.

**Web Site** http://www.puc.edu/

## Palm Beach Atlantic University

**West Palm Beach, Florida**

Independent nondenominational, coed. Urban campus. Total enrollment: 3,291. Music program established 1994.

**Degrees** Bachelor of Music in the areas of performance, church music, music education, music composition. Majors and concentrations: church music, composition, instrumental performance, keyboard performance, music education, voice performance. Program accredited by NASM.

**Enrollment** 75 total; 43 undergraduate, 32 nonprofessional degree.

**Music Student Profile** 67% females, 33% males, 14% minorities, 1% international.

**Music Faculty** 10 undergraduate (full-time), 22 undergraduate (part-time). 50% of full-time faculty have terminal degrees. Graduate students do not teach undergraduate courses. Undergraduate student–faculty ratio: 5:1.

**Student Life** Student groups/activities include Collegiate Music Educators National Conference, National Association of Teachers of Singing (local chapter).

**Expenses for 2007–2008** Application fee: $30. Comprehensive fee: $28,296 includes full-time tuition ($19,950), mandatory fees ($260), and college room and board ($8086). College room only: $4270. Full-time tuition and fees vary according to course load, degree level, location, program, and reciprocity agreements. Room and board charges vary according to board plan and housing facility. Special program-related fees: $75–$265 per course for applied fees.

**Financial Aid** Program-specific awards: 1 Eleanor Doverspike Scholarship for program majors ($1500), 50–80 music scholarships for program majors ($5000), 2 Brown Vargas Scholarships for BFA students ($750), 8 John and Sheila Rinker Scholarships for performance majors ($2000), 1 Colonel Struble Scholarship for program majors ($1500).

**Application Procedures** Students admitted directly into the professional program freshman year. Deadline for freshmen and transfers: continuous. Required: essay, high school transcript, college transcript(s) for transfer students, minimum 2.0 high school GPA, 2 letters of recommendation, audition, SAT or ACT test scores. Recommended: minimum 3.0 high school GPA, interview, video. Auditions held continuously on campus; videotaped performances are permissible as a substitute for live auditions when distance is prohibitive.

**Web Site** http://www.pba.edu

**Undergraduate Contact** Mr. Buckley A. James, Vice President for Enrollment Services, Admissions Department, Palm Beach Atlantic University, PO Box 24708, West Palm Beach, Florida 33416; 800 238-3998, fax: 561-803-2115, e-mail address: admit@pba.edu

## Peabody Conservatory of Music

See The Johns Hopkins University

## Penn State University Park

**University Park, Pennsylvania**

State-related, coed. Small town campus. Total enrollment: 43,252. Music program established 1929.

**Degrees** Bachelor of Music in the areas of performance, composition; Bachelor of Musical Arts in the area of performance; Bachelor of Music Education. Majors and concentrations: composition, music education, piano, stringed instruments, voice, wind and percussion instruments. Graduate degrees offered: Master of Arts in the areas of theory and history (integrative), theory, musicology; Master of Music in the areas of performance, conducting, piano pedagogy and performance, voice pedagogy and performance, composition/theory; Master of Music Education in the area of music education. Doctor of Philosophy in the area of music education. Program accredited by NASM.

**Enrollment** 335 total; 262 undergraduate, 73 graduate.

**Music Student Profile** 55% females, 45% males, 7% minorities.

**Music Faculty** 50 total (full-time), 10 total (part-time). 52% of full-time faculty have terminal degrees. Graduate students teach a few undergraduate courses. Undergraduate student–faculty ratio: 6:1.

**Student Life** Special housing available for music students.

**Expenses for 2007–2008** Application fee: $50. State resident tuition: $12,284 full-time. Nonresident tuition: $23,152 full-time. Mandatory fees: $560 full-time. Full-time tuition and fees vary according to course level, location, program, and student level. College room and board: $7180. College room only: $3820. Room and board charges vary according to board plan, housing facility, and location. Special program-related fees: $175–$250 per semester for applied music lesson fee.

**Financial Aid** Program-specific awards: 73 music scholarships for program majors ($2000).

**Application Procedures** Students apply for admission into the professional program by sophomore year. Deadline for freshmen and transfers: continuous. Required: high school transcript, college transcript(s) for transfer students, audition, SAT or ACT test scores. Recommended: interview. Auditions held 4 times on campus; recorded music is permissible as a substitute for live auditions when distance is prohibitive and videotaped performances are permissible as a substitute for live auditions when distance is prohibitive.

**Web Site** http://www.music.psu.edu/

**Undergraduate Contact** Ms. Irene Kohute, Undergraduate Music Admissions Coordinator, School of Music, Penn State University Park, 233 Music Building, University Park, Pennsylvania 16802-1503; 814-863-0418, fax: 814-865-6785, e-mail address: music-ug-adm@psu.edu

**Graduate Contact** Ms. Lisa Stamm, Graduate Admissions Secretary, School of Music, Penn State University Park, 233 Music Building, University Park, Pennsylvania 16802; 814-865-1052, fax: 814-865-6785, e-mail address: music-gr-adm@psu.edu

## Philadelphia Biblical University

**Langhorne, Pennsylvania**

Independent nondenominational, coed. Suburban campus. Total enrollment: 1,388. Music program established 1969.

**Degrees** Bachelor of Music in the areas of performance, music education, church music, composition. Majors and concentrations: church music, composition, guitar, music education, piano/organ, stringed instruments, voice, wind and percussion instruments. Program accredited by NASM.

**Enrollment** 49 total; all undergraduate.

**Music Student Profile** 63% females, 37% males, 14% minorities, 8% international.

**Music Faculty** 7 undergraduate (full-time), 24 undergraduate (part-time). 71% of full-time faculty have terminal degrees. Graduate students do not teach undergraduate courses. Undergraduate student–faculty ratio: 9:1.

**Student Life** Student groups/activities include Music Educators National Conference, American Choral Directors Association, Pennsylvania Music Teachers Association.

**Expenses for 2008–2009** Application fee: $25. Comprehensive fee: $24,935 includes full-time tuition ($17,450), mandatory fees ($335), and college room and board ($7150). College room only: $3750. Special program-related fees: $20–$30 for junior/senior recital fees, $25 per credit for instrumental rental fee for class brass, strings, woodwinds, percussion, $135 per credit for applied lessons in fall and spring semester, $270 per credit for summer private lessons.

**Financial Aid** Program-specific awards: 49 music scholarships for freshmen ($600–$3000).

**Application Procedures** Students admitted directly into the professional program freshman year. Deadline for freshmen and transfers: continuous. Required: high school transcript, college transcript(s) for transfer students, minimum 2.0 high school GPA, 3 letters of recommendation, interview, audition, SAT or ACT test scores (minimum combined SAT score of 920, minimum composite ACT score of 19). Auditions held 7 times on campus; recorded music is permissible as a substitute for live auditions when distance is prohibitive (beyond 300-mile radius) and videotaped performances are permissible as a substitute for live auditions when distance is prohibitive (beyond 300-mile radius).

**Web Site** http://www.pbu.edu

**Undergraduate Contact** Mrs. Rebecca Olson, Recruitment-Coordinator, School of Music and Performing Arts, Philadelphia Biblical University, 200 Manor Avenue, Langhorne, Pennsylvania 19047; 215-702-4324, fax: 215-702-4342.

# Pittsburg State University

**Pittsburg, Kansas**

State-supported, coed. Small town campus. Total enrollment: 7,087. Music program established 1914.

**Web Site** http://www.pittstate.edu/

# Potter College of Arts and Letters

See Western Kentucky University

# Prairie View A&M University

**Prairie View, Texas**

State-supported, coed. Small town campus. Total enrollment: 8,382. Music program established 1920.

**Web Site** http://www.pvamu.edu/

# Purchase College, State University of New York

**Purchase, New York**

State-supported, coed. Small town campus. Total enrollment: 4,265.

**Degrees** Bachelor of Music in the areas of performance, composition, production. Majors and concentrations: bass, cello, classical guitar, classical music, composition, historical performance, horn, jazz, jazz studies, opera, percussion, piano/organ, production, stringed instruments, studio composition, trombone, trumpet, tuba, viola, violin, voice, wind instruments. Graduate degrees offered: Master of Music in the areas of performance, composition.

**Enrollment** 450 total; 339 undergraduate, 111 graduate.

**Music Student Profile** 29% females, 71% males, 13% minorities, 8% international.

**Music Faculty** 21 undergraduate (full-time), 48 undergraduate (part-time). 90% of full-time faculty have terminal degrees.

Graduate students do not teach undergraduate courses. Undergraduate student–faculty ratio: 10:1.

**Student Life** Student groups/activities include Downtown Cabaret, Ballet and Arts in Education performances, performances in the community.

**Expenses for 2008–2009** Application fee: $40. State resident tuition: $4350 full-time. Nonresident tuition: $10,610 full-time. Mandatory fees: $1647 full-time. College room and board: $9484. College room only: $5886. Special program-related fees: $50 for audition, $1900 per year for applied music fees.

**Financial Aid** Program-specific awards: 130 music scholarships/awards ($2500).

**Application Procedures** Students admitted directly into the professional program freshman year. Deadline for freshmen and transfers: June 1. Notification date for freshmen and transfers: July 1. Required: high school transcript, college transcript(s) for transfer students, audition, SAT or ACT test scores, minimum TOEFL score of 550 for international applicants, portfolio for composition majors. Recommended: essay, minimum 3.0 high school GPA, 2 letters of recommendation, interview. Auditions held 4 times on campus; recorded music is permissible as a substitute for live auditions when distance is prohibitive or in special circumstances and videotaped performances are permissible as a substitute for live auditions when distance is prohibitive or in special circumstances. Portfolio reviews held 4 times on campus.

**Web Site** http://www.purchase.edu/music

**Undergraduate Contact** James Gibson, Admissions Counselor, Purchase College, State University of New York, 735 Anderson Hill Road, Purchase, New York 10577-1400; 914-251-6305, fax: 914-251-6314, e-mail address: james.gibson@purchase.edu

**Graduate Contact** Ms. Sabrina Johnston, Counselor, Admissions, Purchase College, State University of New York, 735 Anderson Hill Road, Purchase, New York 10577-1400; 914-251-6479, fax: 914-251-6739, e-mail address: sabrina.johnston@purchase.edu

## More About the College

The Conservatory of Music at Purchase College offers a comprehensive musical education at both the undergraduate and graduate levels for gifted students seeking professional training in music. All students who enter the Conservatory of Music have been admitted as the result of an audition process. Purchase is an intimate community of approximately 450 students studying with distinguished and dedicated faculty members who are as committed to their teaching as they are to their own careers as performers, composers, and scholars.

The Conservatory of Music offers the following degrees: Bachelor of Music, Performer's Certificate, Master of Music, and Artist's Diploma. Areas of study include instrumental performance: woodwinds (flute, oboe, clarinet, bassoon), brass (trumpet, horn, trombone, tuba), strings (violin, viola, cello, bass), classical guitar, harp, percussion, and piano (also organ/harpsichord); voice/opera studies; jazz studies; composition; studio composition; and studio production.

The core undergraduate curriculum for the Bachelor of Music degree is similar throughout the four years for all areas of study: students take private or small-group study; ensemble; a series of skills courses in music theory, history, and musicianship; and courses specific to their primary area of study. All students perform here—early, classical, contemporary, jazz, electro-acoustic, and commercial—and the opportunities to perform are numerous.

The 30-credit general education program in the liberal arts and sciences supports the Conservatory curriculum and provides a broad education that enhances the musical education and better prepares the students to function successfully as thoughtful, responsible, and contributive members to society.

The Master of Music degree is an intensive program designed to provide advanced training for students seeking professional careers in music. Other training opportunities include the one- or two-year Performer's Certificate, a postbaccalaureate program, and the Artist's Diploma postgraduate program.

The Conservatory of Music provides the serious, developing musician an educational experience that encourages excellence

*Purchase College, State University of New York (continued)*

within the context of a nurturing and supportive learning environment. Instruction in the classroom and studio is significantly enhanced by a regular series of concerts, including faculty and guest artist recitals, master classes, workshops and special events. Among those who have offered their musical gifts and special insights to the Conservatory of Music community are Emanuel Ax, Colorado Quartet, Misha Dichter, Emerson Quartet, Vladimir Feltsman, Guarneri Quartet, Matt Haimovitz, Jimmy Heath, Freddie Hubbard, Marilyn Horne, Juilliard Quartet, Lang Lang, Jennifer Larmore, Branford Marsalis, Midori, New Millennium Ensemble, Charles Niedich, Garrick Ohlssohn, Orpheus, Frederic Rzewski, Clark Terry, Tokyo Quartet, and Yo-Yo Ma.

The Conservatory of Music at Purchase College is one of the few conservatories in the nation producing fully mounted opera productions predominantly for undergraduates. The opera program has won the National Opera Association's "Best Production of the Year" awards for *Hansel and Gretel* (2004), *Dialogues of the Carmelites* (2005), and *The Coronation of Poppea* (2007). The jazz curriculum is performance-driven and includes both large and small ensemble work. The majority of the studio production and composition students work professionally while still at Purchase because of the contacts and opportunities offered to them by the faculty. The other major areas of study also provide similar intensive training and resources in support of professional development.

## Aaron Copland School of Music
# Queens College of the City University of New York
### Flushing, New York

State and locally supported, coed. Urban campus. Total enrollment: 18,728. Music program established 1937.
**Degrees** Bachelor of Music in the area of performance. Majors and concentrations: brass, composition, piano/organ, stringed instruments, voice, wind and percussion instruments. Graduate degrees offered: Master of Arts in the areas of performance, composition, musicology, music theory, jazz performance, jazz composition, conducting; Master of Science in the area of music education.
**Enrollment** 350 total; 250 undergraduate, 100 graduate.
**Music Student Profile** 50% females, 50% males, 50% minorities, 35% international.
**Music Faculty** 26 total (full-time), 44 total (part-time). 90% of full-time faculty have terminal degrees. Graduate students teach a few undergraduate courses. Undergraduate student–faculty ratio: 15:1.
**Student Life** Student groups/activities include Music Educators National Conference, Music Students Association.
**Expenses for 2008–2009** Application fee: $65. State resident tuition: $4000 full-time. Nonresident tuition: $8640 full-time. Mandatory fees: $377 full-time.
**Financial Aid** Program-specific awards: 1–3 Boris Schwarz Scholarships for string majors ($250–$500), 2 Zatkin Scholarships-Opera Awards for voice majors ($250–$500), 1 Edward Downes Scholarship for voice majors ($250–$500), 25 departmental scholarships for those demonstrating talent/financial need ($200–$1000), 2 Castellini Awards for string majors ($1000), 2 Rosenfeld Awards for string majors ($1000), 1–2 Novack Scholarships for theory students ($500–$1000), 5–10 LeFrak Scholarships for performance majors ($200–$1000).
**Application Procedures** Students admitted directly into the professional program freshman year. Deadline for freshmen and transfers: March 15. Notification date for freshmen and transfers: continuous. Required: essay, high school transcript, college transcript(s) for transfer students, minimum 3.0 high school GPA, 3 letters of recommendation, audition. Recommended: portfolio, SAT or ACT test scores. Auditions held twice on campus; recorded music is permissible as a substitute for live

auditions when distance is prohibitive and videotaped performances are permissible as a substitute for live auditions when distance is prohibitive. Portfolio reviews held twice on campus.
**Web Site** http://www.qc.edu
**Undergraduate Contact** Dr. Jonathan Irving, Special Assistant to the Director, Aaron Copland School of Music, Queens College of the City University of New York, 65-30 Kissena Boulevard, Flushing, New York 11367; 718-997-3802, fax: 718-997-3849, e-mail address: jonathan_irving@qc.edu
**Graduate Contact** Prof. William Rothstein, Graduate Advisor, Aaron Copland School of Music, Queens College of the City University of New York, 65-30 Kissena Boulevard, Flushing, New York 11367; 718-997-3863, fax: 817-997-3849, e-mail address: wrothstein@qc.cuny.edu

# Queens University of Charlotte
### Charlotte, North Carolina

Independent Presbyterian, coed. Suburban campus. Total enrollment: 2,243. Music program established 1857.
**Degrees** Bachelor of Music in the areas of music therapy, applied music performance. Majors and concentrations: guitar, harp, music therapy, piano/organ, stringed instruments, voice, wind and percussion instruments. Cross-registration with 13 member colleges of the Charlotte Area Educational Consortium. Program accredited by NASM, AMTA.
**Enrollment** 41 total; 28 undergraduate, 13 nonprofessional degree.
**Music Student Profile** 97% females, 3% males, 3% minorities, 1% international.
**Music Faculty** 6 undergraduate (full-time), 16 undergraduate (part-time). 66% of full-time faculty have terminal degrees. Graduate students do not teach undergraduate courses. Undergraduate student–faculty ratio: 4:1.
**Student Life** Student groups/activities include Music Therapy Club, Drama Club.
**Expenses for 2008–2009** Application fee: $40. Comprehensive fee: $29,950 includes full-time tuition ($22,068) and college room and board ($7882). Special program-related fees: $25 per credit hour for accompanist fee, $100 per semester credit hour for private music instruction.
**Financial Aid** Program-specific awards: music major awards for program majors ($500–$3000), music minor awards for program minors ($500–$1000), 1–3 Stegner Music Scholarships for music majors ($500–$3000), 1 Lammers Music Scholarship for music majors ($5000), 1 Kennedy Scholarship for music majors ($500), 1–2 O'Quinn Scholarships for music majors ($2500), 2 Hamrich Scholarships for music majors ($1450).
**Application Procedures** Students admitted directly into the professional program freshman year. Deadline for freshmen and transfers: continuous. Required: essay, high school transcript, college transcript(s) for transfer students, minimum 2.0 high school GPA, 2 letters of recommendation, interview, audition, SAT or ACT test scores. Recommended: portfolio. Auditions held 3 times and by appointment on campus; videotaped performances are permissible as a substitute for live auditions if student has already visited the campus or when distance is prohibitive. Portfolio reviews held twice a year (minimum) on campus.
**Web Site** http://www.queens.edu
**Undergraduate Contact** Mr. Brian Ralph, Vice President of Enrollment Management, CAS Admissions, Queens University of Charlotte, 1900 Selwyn Avenue, Charlotte, North Carolina 28274; 800-849-0202, fax: 704-337-2503, e-mail address: ralphb@queens.edu

# Radford University
### Radford, Virginia

State-supported, coed. Small town campus. Total enrollment: 9,122.
**Degrees** Bachelor of Music. Majors and concentrations: composition, music and technology, music business, music education, music therapy. Graduate degrees offered: Master of Science in the area of music therapy. Program accredited by NASM.

**Enrollment** 97 total; 60 undergraduate, 19 graduate, 18 nonprofessional degree.
**Music Student Profile** 54% females, 46% males, 14% minorities, 4% international.
**Music Faculty** 16 total (full-time), 9 total (part-time). 56% of full-time faculty have terminal degrees. Graduate students teach a few undergraduate courses. Undergraduate student–faculty ratio: 2:1.
**Student Life** Student groups/activities include Music Therapy Student Organization, Music Educators National Conference Student Chapter, Arts and Entertainment Business Association. Special housing available for music students.
**Expenses for 2007–2008** Application fee: $50. State resident tuition: $4026 full-time. Nonresident tuition: $12,360 full-time. Mandatory fees: $2150 full-time. College room and board: $6490. College room only: $3452. Room and board charges vary according to board plan and housing facility.
**Financial Aid** Program-specific awards: 2–4 Arts Society Awards for freshmen ($4000), 3 Ingram-Lee Awards for program majors ($1200), 1 Presser Award for seniors ($4000), 1 May Award for program majors ($850), 1 Vickers Award for program majors ($1000), 1 Grabeal Award for program majors ($750), 1 Jason Rooker Memorial Award for music therapy majors ($500), 1 Bondurant Award for music business majors ($500).
**Application Procedures** Students apply for admission into the professional program by freshman year. Deadline for freshmen: April 1; transfers: June 1. Notification date for freshmen and transfers: continuous. Required: high school transcript, college transcript(s) for transfer students, minimum 2.0 high school GPA, audition, SAT or ACT test scores. Recommended: essay, minimum 3.0 high school GPA. Auditions held continuously by appointment on campus; recorded music is permissible as a substitute for live auditions if unedited and videotaped performances are permissible as a substitute for live auditions if unedited.
**Web Site** http://www.radford.edu/~musc-web/
**Undergraduate Contact** Mr. David Kraus, Director, Office of Admissions, Radford University, PO Box 6903, Radford, Virginia 24142; 540-831-5371, fax: 540-831-5138, e-mail address: dwkraus@radford.edu
**Graduate Contact** Ms. Sharon Gunter, Admissions Coordinator, College of Graduate and Extended Education, Radford University, PO Box 6928, Radford, Virginia 24142; 540-831-5724, e-mail address: gradcoll@radford.edu

## *Shepherd School of Music*
## Rice University
### Houston, Texas

Independent, coed. Urban campus. Total enrollment: 5,243. Music program established 1974.
**Degrees** Bachelor of Music in the areas of performance, music theory, composition, musicology. Majors and concentrations: composition, music, music history, music theory, piano/organ, stringed instruments, voice, wind and percussion instruments. Graduate degrees offered: Master of Music in the areas of performance, music theory, composition, musicology, conducting. Doctor of Musical Arts in the areas of performance, composition.
**Enrollment** 300 total; 120 undergraduate, 180 graduate.
**Music Student Profile** 54% females, 46% males, 5% minorities, 20% international.
**Music Faculty** 38 total (full-time), 27 total (part-time). 99% of full-time faculty have terminal degrees. Graduate students teach a few undergraduate courses. Undergraduate student–faculty ratio: 5:1.
**Student Life** Student groups/activities include symphony orchestra, chamber ensembles, opera.
**Expenses for 2008–2009** Application fee: $60. Comprehensive fee: $41,229 includes full-time tuition ($29,960), mandatory fees ($519), and college room and board ($10,750). College room only: $7150.
**Financial Aid** Program-specific awards: merit awards for program majors ($1000).
**Application Procedures** Students admitted directly into the professional program freshman year. Deadline for freshmen: January

2; transfers: March 15. Notification date for freshmen: April 1; transfers: May 15. Required: essay, high school transcript, college transcript(s) for transfer students, 2 letters of recommendation, interview, audition, portfolio, SAT or ACT test scores, two SAT subject exam scores, portfolio for composition students, ACT (writing component). Recommended: minimum 3.0 high school GPA. Auditions held on campus; recorded music is permissible as a substitute for live auditions if a live audition is impossible and videotaped performances are permissible as a substitute for live auditions if a live audition is impossible. Portfolio reviews held on campus.
**Web Site** http://www.rice.edu/music
**Undergraduate Contact** Mr. Bradley Blunt, Director of Music Admissions, Shepherd School of Music, Rice University, PO Box 1892, Houston, Texas 77251; 713-348-3032, fax: 713-348-5317, e-mail address: bblunt@rice.edu
**Graduate Contact** Mr. Grimaldo Robles, Admissions Assistant, Shepherd School of Music, Rice University, PO Box 1892, Houston, Texas 77251; 713-348-3578, fax: 713-348-5317, e-mail address: grobles@rice.edu

## Rider University
See Westminster College of the Arts of Rider University

## *Chicago College of Performing Arts - The Music Conservatory*
## Roosevelt University
### Chicago, Illinois

Independent, coed. Urban campus. Total enrollment: 7,163. Music program established 1867.
**Degrees** Bachelor of Music in the areas of jazz studies, classical performance, music education, composition. Majors and concentrations: composition, jazz studies, music education, stringed instruments, voice, wind and percussion instruments. Graduate degrees offered: Master of Music in the areas of classical performance, composition, orchestral studies (winds/brass/percussion only). Program accredited by NASM.
**Enrollment** 347 total; 211 undergraduate, 126 graduate, 10 nonprofessional degree.
**Music Student Profile** 50% females, 50% males, 47% minorities, 30% international.
**Music Faculty** 25 total (full-time), 90 total (part-time). 55% of full-time faculty have terminal degrees. Graduate students do not teach undergraduate courses. Undergraduate student–faculty ratio: 11:1.
**Student Life** Student groups/activities include Music Educators National Conference.
**Expenses for 2007–2008** Application fee: $25. Comprehensive fee: $26,828 includes full-time tuition ($16,680), mandatory fees ($300), and college room and board ($9848). College room only: $6824. Full-time tuition and fees vary according to course load and program. Room and board charges vary according to board plan and housing facility.
**Financial Aid** Program-specific awards: 200 music scholarships for music majors ($9000).
**Application Procedures** Students admitted directly into the professional program freshman year. Deadline for freshmen and transfers: January 15. Notification date for freshmen and transfers: April 1. Required: essay, high school transcript, college transcript(s) for transfer students, minimum 2.0 high school GPA, audition, SAT or ACT test scores (minimum composite ACT score of 20), interview (for music education and composition), composition portfolio (music composition only). Recommended: minimum 3.0 high school GPA, letter of recommendation. Auditions held 15 times on campus; recorded music is permissible as a substitute for live auditions when distance is prohibitive (over 500 miles from Chicago) and videotaped performances are permissible as a substitute for live auditions when distance is prohibitive (over 500 miles from Chicago).
**Web Site** http://ccpa.roosevelt.edu
**Contact** Heather McCowen, Assistant Dean for Enrollment and Student Services, Chicago College of Performing Arts, Room 918,

*Roosevelt University (continued)*

Roosevelt University, 430 South Michigan Avenue, Chicago, Illinois 60605; 312-341-3789, fax: 312-341-6358, e-mail address: music@roosevelt.edu

### More About the Conservatory

The Music Conservatory at Roosevelt University's Chicago College of Performing Arts provides professional training and education within the context of a vibrant university in a world-class city. It is a place where musical genres from classical to jazz are valued, where the energies of one discipline spill over to enliven other artistic endeavors, where preparing to be a teacher is as important as preparing to be a performer or scholar, and where students come to enhance their unique talents and polish them to perfection.

The Music Conservatory is well situated on the top floors of the historic landmark Auditorium Building, designed by world-famous architects Dankmar Adler and Louis Sullivan. The building includes the 3,800-seat Auditorium Theatre, renowned for its beauty and exquisite acoustics. Located on the corner of Michigan Avenue and Congress Parkway, this edifice is now an integral part of the "educational corridor" of more than 50,000 students enrolled in various institutions in the famous downtown Loop. Across the street are the Pritzker Music Pavilion of Millennium Park, the magnificent Buckingham Fountain, and the sparkling beauty of Lake Michigan. The new state-of-the-art residence hall, the University Center of Chicago, is located just one block away on the corner of State Street and Congress Parkway.

Within walking distance are many of the city's major cultural institutions, including Symphony Center, home of the Chicago Symphony Orchestra; the Lyric Opera; the Jazz Showcase; the Goodman, Chicago, Oriental, and Cadillac theaters; the Art Institute; the Field Museum of Natural History; and the "Magnificent Mile" of shops and galleries. This ideal location provides opportunities for learning from some of the most accomplished musicians in the world, from principals in the Chicago Symphony to Grammy-nominated jazz artists.

**Faculty** *Violin:* Shmuel Ashkenasi (First Violin, Vermeer Quartet); Robert Chen (Co-Concertmaster, Chicago Symphony); Nathan Cole (Chicago Symphony); Cyrus Forough; Vadim Gluzman (Concert Artist); Stefan Hersh (Former Principal Second Violin, Minnesota Orchestra/Former violinist, Chicago String Quartet); Yang Liu (Concert Artist); Laura Park Chen (Lyric Opera of Chicago, Head of Strings); *Viola:* Li-Kuo Chang (Assistant Principal, Chicago Symphony); Roger Chase (Former Guest Principal, Berlin Philharmonic); Lawrence Neuman (Chicago Symphony); *Cello:* Tanya Carey (Former Assistant Principal, Milwaukee Symphony); Barbara Haffner (Assistant Principal, Lyric Opera of Chicago); Richard Hirschl (Chicago Symphony); Kenneth Olsen (Assistant Principal, Chicago Symphony); John Sharp (Principal, Chicago Symphony); Wendy Warner (Concert Artist); *Bass:* Andrew Anderson (Lyric Opera of Chicago); Stephen Lester (Chicago Symphony); *Harp:* Sarah Bullen (Principal, Chicago Symphony); *Flute:* Dionne Hansen-Jackson (Assistant Principal, Lyric Opera of Chicago); Donald Peck (Principal Flute Emeritus, Chicago Symphony); *Oboe:* Eugene Izotov (Principal, Chicago Symphony); Peggy Michel (Music of the Baroque); Grover Schiltz (English Horn, Chicago Symphony); *Clarinet:* Gregory Smith (Chicago Symphony); Carolee Smith; John Bruce Yeh (Assistant Principal, Chicago Symphony); *Bassoon:* Dennis Michel (Chicago Symphony, Head of Winds); Theodore Soluri (Principal, Milwaukee Symphony); *Saxophone:* Jan Berry; *Horn:* Dale Clevenger (Principal, Chicago Symphony); Alice Render; *Trumpet:* Tage Larsen (Chicago Symphony); Channing Philbrick (Co-Assistant Principal, Lyric Opera of Chicago); Chris Martin (Principal, Chicago Symphony); Mark Ridenour (Assistant Principal, Chicago Symphony); *Trombone:* Jay Friedman (Principal, Chicago Symphony, Head of Brass); Peter Ellefson; *Tuba:* Gene Pokorny, masterclasses (Principal,

Chicago Symphony); Charles Schuchat (Former Principal, Israel Philharmonic); *Percussion:* Edward Harrison (Principal Timpanist, Lyric Opera of Chicago); Vadim Karpinos (Chicago Symphony); *Orchestral Seminar:* Henry Fogel (President, American Symphony Orchestra League); *Piano:* Emilio del Rosario; Ani Gogova; Kuang-Hao Huang; Ludmila Lazar; Meng-Chieh Liu; Solomon Mikowsky; Jorge Federico Osorio; *Guitar:* Denis Azabagic; Paul Henry; Pamela Kimmel, Head of Guitar; *Voice:* Michael Best, Head of Voice; Matthew Chellis; Mark Crayton; Judith Haddon; David Holloway, Chair of Performance; Jonita Lattimore; Elizabeth Norman; Samuel Ramey, masterclasses; Richard Stilwell; Tracy Watson; Dana Brown, vocal coach; Giulio Favario, vocal coach; Scott Gilmore, vocal coach; James Gandre, performance class; *Music Education:* Charles Groeling; Mary Jo Ferneding; Cheryl Frazes Hill, Head of Music Education; July Moe; John Thomson; *Composition:* Stacy Garrop; Kyong-Mee Choi; *Jazz Studies:* Neal Alger, guitar; Jackie Allen, voice; Ruben Alvarez, Latin percussion; Rob Amster, bass; Steve Berry, trombone; John Blane, trombone; Linda Clifford, voice; Jo Ann Daugherty, piano; Carey Deadman, trumpet; Jerry DiMuzio, saxophone; Jim Gailloreto, saxophone; Tom Garling, trombone; Phil Gratteau, drum set; Roger Harris, piano; Art Hoyle, trumpet; Roger Ingram, trumpet; Henry Johnson, guitar; Scott Mason, bass; John McLean, guitar; Paul Mertens, saxophone; Jeff Morrow, voice; Dave Onderdonk, guitar; Rob Parton, trumpet; Judy Roberts, voice; Marlene Rosenberg, bass; Ron Ruvio, trumpet; Fred Simon, piano; Mike Smith, saxophone; Colleen Timler, voice; Jim Trompeter, piano; Paul Wertico, Interim Head of Jazz, drum set; Brad Wheeler, saxophone; *Theory and Music History:* Charles Brauner, music history; Linda Berna, music history and theory; Donald Chen, theory and conducting orchestral studies; Stuart Folse, music theory; Ani Gogova, keyboard studies; Phyllis Hill, keyboard studies; William Hussey, music theory; Lucia Marchi, music history; Rudy Marcozzi, music theory and history, Chair of Academic Music Studies; Gregory Reish, music history; David Schrader, music history and performance practice; *Conductors:* Cheryl Frazes Hill, Director of Choral Activities; Jay Friedman, Principal Guest Conductor; Anne Heider, Resident Choral Conductor; Jane Glover, Guest Conductor, 2007–08; Stephen Squires, Principal Conductor.

**Student Performance Opportunities** There are more than 200 concerts, recitals, operas, and theater performances presented each year. Ensembles include Symphony Orchestra, Chamber Orchestra, Conservatory Chorus, Wind Ensemble, Women's Chorus, Opera, Jazz Ensembles, Chamber Music, New Music Ensemble, Guitar Ensemble, and Collegium Musicum.

**Programs and Additional Information** The Bachelor of Music degree is offered in performance studies, composition, jazz studies, and music education. The Master of Music degree is offered in performance, orchestral studies, and composition. A Performance Diploma is available in instrumental performance (classical), opera (a joint program with Chicago Opera Theater), and orchestral studies.

There is a diverse student body from forty states and twenty-three other countries. Roosevelt University offers exclusive ESL preparation. The Music Scholarship program is open to both U.S. and international applicants.

# Rowan University
### Glassboro, New Jersey

State-supported, coed. Suburban campus. Total enrollment: 10,091. Music program established 1958.

**Degrees** Bachelor of Music in the areas of applied music, jazz, music education, composition. Majors and concentrations: composition, jazz, music education, performance. Graduate degrees offered: Master of Music in the areas of applied music, jazz, composition. Program accredited by NASM.

**Enrollment** 174 undergraduate, 31 graduate.

**Music Student Profile** 60% females, 40% males, 18% minorities, 5% international.

**Music Faculty** 19 total (full-time), 40 total (part-time). 80% of full-time faculty have terminal degrees. Graduate students do not teach undergraduate courses. Undergraduate student–faculty ratio: 7:1.

**Student Life** Student groups/activities include Music Educators National Conference Student Chapter, Pi Kappa Lambda, Phi Mu Alpha.

**Expenses for 2007–2008** Application fee: $50. State resident tuition: $7308 full-time. Nonresident tuition: $14,616 full-time. Mandatory fees: $2760 full-time. Full-time tuition and fees vary according to degree level. College room and board: $9242. College room only: $5862. Room and board charges vary according to board plan and housing facility. Special program-related fees: $6 per credit for lab fees, $15 per quarter for instrument rental.

**Financial Aid** Program-specific awards: 20 Department of Music Scholarships for music students ($4000).

**Application Procedures** Students admitted directly into the professional program freshman year. Deadline for freshmen: March 15; transfers: April 15. Notification date for freshmen: May 1. Required: high school transcript, college transcript(s) for transfer students, letter of recommendation, audition, SAT or ACT test scores, portfolio for composition applicants. Auditions held 5 times on campus; recorded music is permissible as a substitute for live auditions when distance is prohibitive and videotaped performances are permissible as a substitute for live auditions when distance is prohibitive. Portfolio reviews held throughout the year on campus.

**Web Site** http://www.rowan.edu

**Undergraduate Contact** Dr. Robert Rawlins, Chair, Department of Music, Rowan University, 201 Mullica Hill Road, Glassboro, New Jersey 08028-1702; 856-256-4557, fax: 856-256-4644, e-mail address: rawlinsr@rowan.edu

**Graduate Contact** Bryan Appleby-Wineberg, Assistant Professor, Department of Music, Rowan University, 201 Mullica Hill Road, Glassboro, New Jersey 08028-1702; 856-256-4500 ext. 3526, fax: 856-256-4644, e-mail address: applebywineberg@rowan.edu

# The Rudi E. Scheidt School of Music

See University of Memphis

# Rutgers, The State University of New Jersey

See Mason Gross School of the Arts

# St. Cloud State University

### St. Cloud, Minnesota

State-supported, coed. Suburban campus. Total enrollment: 15,808. Music program established 1869.

**Degrees** Bachelor of Arts in the area of music; Bachelor of Music in the areas of performance, piano pedagogy; Bachelor of Science in the area of music education. Majors and concentrations: jazz, music education, music theory and composition, performance, piano pedagogy. Graduate degrees offered: Master of Music in the areas of education, conducting, piano pedagogy. Program accredited by NASM.

**Enrollment** 155 total; 110 undergraduate, 45 graduate.

**Music Student Profile** 50% females, 50% males, 3% minorities, 4% international.

**Music Faculty** 18 total (full-time), 7 total (part-time). 90% of full-time faculty have terminal degrees. Graduate students do not teach undergraduate courses. Undergraduate student–faculty ratio: 18:1.

**Student Life** Student groups/activities include Sigma Alpha Iota, Music Educators National Conference Student Chapter, American Choral Directors Association Student Chapter.

**Expenses for 2007–2008** Application fee: $20. State resident tuition: $5247 full-time. Nonresident tuition: $11,389 full-time. Mandatory fees: $708 full-time. Full-time tuition and fees vary according to course load and reciprocity agreements. College room and board: $5592. College room only: $3596. Room and board charges vary according to board plan and housing facility. Special program-related fees: $55 per credit for private lessons, $60 per year for instrument rental.

**Financial Aid** Program-specific awards: 20 Endowed/Foundation Scholarships for talented students ($1500), 7 David Swenson Memorial Awards for percussion students ($3500).

**Application Procedures** Students apply for admission into the professional program by freshman year. Deadline for freshmen and transfers: continuous. Required: high school transcript, college transcript(s) for transfer students, minimum 2.0 high school GPA, ACT test score only (minimum composite ACT score of 25), audition for scholarship consideration. Auditions held twice on campus; recorded music is permissible as a substitute for live auditions by arrangement with department and videotaped performances are permissible as a substitute for live auditions by arrangement with department.

**Web Site** http://www.stcloudstate.edu/music

**Undergraduate Contact** Mr. Jeff Rhodes, Director of Admissions, Admissions, St. Cloud State University, 720 4th Avenue South, St. Cloud, Minnesota 56301-4498; 320-308-3981, fax: 320-308-2243, e-mail address: scsu4u@stcloudstate.edu

**Graduate Contact** Mr. Dennis Nunes, Dean, School of Graduate Studies, St. Cloud State University, 720 4th Avenue South, St. Cloud, Minnesota 56301-4498; 320-308-2113, fax: 320-308-5371, e-mail address: graduatestudies@stcloudstate.edu

# St. Francis Xavier University

### Antigonish, Nova Scotia, Canada

Independent Roman Catholic, coed. Small town campus. Total enrollment: 4,969.

**Degrees** Bachelor of Arts in the area of music; Bachelor of Music in the areas of jazz performance, jazz composition/arranging. Majors and concentrations: bass, brass, jazz guitar, jazz performance, piano, voice, wind and percussion instruments.

**Enrollment** 80 total.

**Music Student Profile** 20% females, 80% males, 3% minorities, 1% international.

**Music Faculty** 9 undergraduate (full-time), 4 undergraduate (part-time). 100% of full-time faculty have terminal degrees. Graduate students do not teach undergraduate courses. Undergraduate student–faculty ratio: 9:1.

**Student Life** Student groups/activities include Nova Scotia Music Educators Association, Music Society, Big Band.

**Expenses for 2007–2008** Application fee: $40 Canadian dollars. Tuition, fee, and room and board charges are reported in Canadian dollars. Comprehensive fee: $13,845 includes full-time tuition ($6205), mandatory fees ($1145), and college room and board ($6495). Full-time tuition and fees vary according to course load. Room and board charges vary according to board plan and housing facility. International student tuition: $12,410 full-time.

**Financial Aid** Program-specific awards: 3 music scholarships for program majors ($1000), 8 music bursaries for program majors ($250–$500).

**Application Procedures** Students apply for admission into the professional program by sophomore year. Deadline for freshmen and transfers: August 1. Notification date for freshmen and transfers: August 15. Required: high school transcript, college transcript(s) for transfer students, audition. Recommended: 2 letters of recommendation. Auditions held continuously on campus; recorded music is permissible as a substitute for live auditions if certified by a teacher and videotaped performances are permissible as a substitute for live auditions if certified by a teacher.

**Web Site** http://www.stfx.ca/academic/music

**Undergraduate Contact** Director of Admissions, St. Francis Xavier University, PO Box 5000, Antigonish, Nova Scotia B2G 2W5, Canada; 902-867-2219, fax: 902-867-2329.

# Saint Mary's College

### Notre Dame, Indiana

Independent Roman Catholic, women only. Suburban campus. Total enrollment: 1,604. Music program established 1894.

**Web Site** http://www.saintmarys.edu/

# St. Olaf College

**Northfield, Minnesota**

Independent Lutheran, coed. Small town campus. Total enrollment: 3,040. Music program established 1895.

**Degrees** Bachelor of Music in the areas of performance, music education, church music, theory/composition. Majors and concentrations: church music, music education, music theory and composition, piano performance, piano/organ performance, stringed instruments, voice performance, wind and percussion instruments. Cross-registration with Carleton College. Program accredited by NASM.

**Enrollment** 273 total; 109 undergraduate, 164 nonprofessional degree.

**Music Student Profile** 55% females, 45% males, 6% minorities, 2% international.

**Music Faculty** 28 undergraduate (full-time), 33 undergraduate (part-time). 85% of full-time faculty have terminal degrees. Graduate students do not teach undergraduate courses. Undergraduate student–faculty ratio: 11:1.

**Student Life** Student groups/activities include Music Educators National Conference, Phi Kappa Lampda, American Choral Directors Association.

**Expenses for 2008–2009** Application fee: $0. Comprehensive fee: $42,200 includes full-time tuition ($34,300) and college room and board ($7900). College room only: $3650.

**Financial Aid** Program-specific awards: 50 Christiansen Music Scholarships for music and non-music majors ($7000), 50 Cassler Scholarships for music and non-music majors ($1000–$4000), 125 performance study scholarships for music majors ($720–$1440).

**Application Procedures** Deadline for freshmen: December 1; transfers: February 15. Notification date for freshmen: February 1; transfers: May 1. Required: essay, high school transcript, college transcript(s) for transfer students, 2 letters of recommendation, audition, SAT or ACT test scores, piano and aural screenings (held on campus), music resumé. Recommended: minimum 3.0 high school GPA, portfolio for theory/composition applicants. Auditions held once on campus; recorded music is permissible as a substitute for live auditions for provisional acceptance and videotaped performances are permissible as a substitute for live auditions if a live audition is impossible. Portfolio reviews held by request on campus.

**Web Site** http://www.stolaf.edu/depts/music/

**Undergraduate Contact** Ms. Mary Hakes, Music Admissions Coordinator, Department of Music, St. Olaf College, 1520 St. Olaf Avenue, Northfield, Minnesota 55057-1098; 507-786-3297, fax: 507-786-3527, e-mail address: music@stolaf.edu

# Saint Xavier University

**Chicago, Illinois**

Independent Roman Catholic, coed. Urban campus. Total enrollment: 5,675. Music program established 1847.

**Degrees** Bachelor of Music in the areas of performance, music education. Majors and concentrations: music education, piano, stringed instruments, voice, wind and percussion instruments. Program accredited by NASM.

**Enrollment** 33 total; 28 undergraduate, 5 nonprofessional degree.

**Music Student Profile** 70% females, 30% males, 15% minorities.

**Music Faculty** 5 undergraduate (full-time), 10 undergraduate (part-time). 60% of full-time faculty have terminal degrees. Graduate students do not teach undergraduate courses. Undergraduate student–faculty ratio: 6:1.

**Student Life** Student groups/activities include Collegiate Music Educators National Conference.

**Expenses for 2007–2008** Application fee: $25. Comprehensive fee: $28,862 includes full-time tuition ($21,016), mandatory fees ($220), and college room and board ($7626). College room only: $4442. Full-time tuition and fees vary according to course load. Room and board charges vary according to board plan and housing facility. Special program-related fees: $100 per credit per semester for accompanist fee.

**Financial Aid** Program-specific awards: 3 Sinon Catherine O'Donohue Keyboard Scholarships for keyboard students ($2000), 2 Sister Gabrielle McShane Awards for vocalists/instrumentalists

($2000), 20 ensemble awards for ensemble performers ($750–$5000), 8 talent awards for voice/band/orchestra participants ($1000–$7000).

**Application Procedures** Students apply for admission into the professional program by sophomore year. Deadline for freshmen and transfers: continuous. Required: essay, high school transcript, college transcript(s) for transfer students, minimum 2.0 high school GPA, letter of recommendation, interview, audition, SAT or ACT test scores. Auditions held 4-5 times and by appointment on campus; recorded music is permissible as a substitute for live auditions and videotaped performances are permissible as a substitute for live auditions for out-of-state and international applicants.

**Web Site** http://www.sxu.edu

**Undergraduate Contact** Dr. Greg Coutts, Chair, Music Department, Saint Xavier University, 3700 West 103rd Street, Chicago, Illinois 60655; 773-298-3424, fax: 773-779-9061, e-mail address: coutts@sxu.edu

# Salem College

**Winston-Salem, North Carolina**

Independent religious, Urban campus. Total enrollment: 992. Music program established 1879.

**Web Site** http://www.salem.edu/

# Samford University

**Birmingham, Alabama**

Independent Baptist, coed. Suburban campus. Total enrollment: 4,485. Music program established 1949.

**Degrees** Bachelor of Music in the areas of performance, church music, music theory/composition, music education, musical theatre. Majors and concentrations: church music, music education, music theater, music theory and composition, piano/organ, stringed instruments, voice, wind and percussion instruments. Graduate degrees offered: Master of Music in the areas of church music, music education, piano performance/pedagogy. Program accredited by NASM.

**Enrollment** 101 undergraduate, 13 graduate, 2 nonprofessional degree.

**Music Student Profile** 55% females, 45% males, 3% minorities, 1% international.

**Music Faculty** 18 total (full-time), 14 total (part-time). 80% of full-time faculty have terminal degrees. Graduate students do not teach undergraduate courses. Undergraduate student–faculty ratio: 8:1.

**Student Life** Student groups/activities include Phi Mu Alpha Sinfonia, Delta Omicron, Music Educators National Conference Student Chapter.

**Expenses for 2007–2008** Application fee: $35. Comprehensive fee: $24,240 includes full-time tuition ($17,920) and college room and board ($6320). College room only: $3220. Full-time tuition varies according to course load. Room and board charges vary according to board plan and housing facility. Special program-related fees: $50 per credit hour for applied music fee.

**Financial Aid** Program-specific awards: 55 music scholarships for program majors ($1000), 35 band scholarships for band members ($500–$3000).

**Application Procedures** Students admitted directly into the professional program freshman year. Deadline for freshmen and transfers: March 1. Notification date for freshmen and transfers: May 1. Required: essay, high school transcript, college transcript(s) for transfer students, 2 letters of recommendation, audition, SAT or ACT test scores, music theory placement exam, piano proficiency exam. Recommended: minimum 3.0 high school GPA. Auditions held 4 times in February on campus; videotaped performances are permissible as a substitute for live auditions in special circumstances and when scheduling is difficult.

**Web Site** http://www.samford.edu/schools/performingarts/degrees.html

**Undergraduate Contact** Dr. Billy Strickland, Associate Dean for Music, Division of Music, Samford University, PO Box 292242, 800

Lakeshore Drive, Birmingham, Alabama 35229; 205-726-2826, fax: 205-726-2165, e-mail address: bjstrick@samford.edu
**Graduate Contact** Dr. Moya Nordlund, Assistant Dean for Graduate Studies, Division of Music, Samford University, PO Box 292242, 800 Lakeshore Drive, Birmingham, Alabama 35229; 205-726-2496, fax: 205-726-2165, e-mail address: mlnordlu@samford.edu

## Sam Houston State University

### Huntsville, Texas

State-supported, coed. Small town campus. Total enrollment: 16,454. Music program established 1938.
**Degrees** Bachelor of Music in the areas of performance, music theory/composition, music therapy, teacher certification. Majors and concentrations: music, music education, music theory and composition, music therapy, piano/organ, stringed instruments, voice, wind and percussion instruments. Graduate degrees offered: Master of Music in the areas of performance, music theory/composition, conducting. Program accredited by NASM.
**Enrollment** 350 total; 276 undergraduate, 19 graduate, 55 nonprofessional degree.
**Music Student Profile** 56% females, 44% males, 35% minorities, 2% international.
**Music Faculty** 25 total (full-time), 27 total (part-time). 72% of full-time faculty have terminal degrees. Graduate students do not teach undergraduate courses. Undergraduate student–faculty ratio: 7:1.
**Student Life** Student groups/activities include American Association of Music Therapy Student Chapter, Sigma Alpha Iota, Kappa Kappa Psi.
**Expenses for 2007–2008** Application fee: $35. State resident tuition: $4170 full-time. Nonresident tuition: $12,510 full-time. Mandatory fees: $1396 full-time. Full-time tuition and fees vary according to course load. College room and board: $6046. College room only: $3460. Room and board charges vary according to board plan and housing facility. Special program-related fees: $20 for recital recording fee, $30 for recital hall rental fee.
**Financial Aid** Program-specific awards: 82 scholarships for program students ($200–$2000).
**Application Procedures** Students admitted directly into the professional program freshman year. Deadline for freshmen and transfers: continuous. Required: high school transcript, college transcript(s) for transfer students, 3 letters of recommendation, interview, audition, SAT or ACT test scores. Recommended: minimum 3.0 high school GPA. Auditions held 4 times on campus; recorded music is permissible as a substitute for live auditions with permission of the chair and videotaped performances are permissible as a substitute for live auditions when distance is prohibitive.
**Web Site** http://www.shsu.edu/~music
**Undergraduate Contact** Dr. James M. Bankhead, Director, School of Music, Sam Houston State University, PO Box 2208, Huntsville, Texas 77341-2208; 936-294-1360, fax: 936-294-3765, e-mail address: bankhead@shsu.edu
**Graduate Contact** Dr. Scott Plugge, Graduate Student Advisor, School of Music, Sam Houston State University, PO Box 2208, Huntsville, Texas 77341-2208; 936-294-1360, fax: 936-294-3765, e-mail address: plugge@shsu.edu

## San Diego State University

### San Diego, California

State-supported, coed. Urban campus. Total enrollment: 36,559. Music program established 1898.
**Degrees** Bachelor of Music in the areas of performance, jazz studies, composition, music education, electro-acoustic music, professional studies. Majors and concentrations: classical music, composition, electroacoustic studies, guitar, jazz, music, music education, piano/organ, professional studies, stringed instruments, voice, wind and percussion instruments, world music instruments. Graduate degrees offered: Master of Arts in the areas of music, piano pedagogy, ethnomusicology, theory,

musicology; Master of Music in the areas of performance, jazz studies, composition, conducting. Cross-registration with University of California, San Diego.
**Enrollment** 340 total; 250 undergraduate, 50 graduate, 40 nonprofessional degree.
**Music Student Profile** 55% females, 45% males, 40% minorities, 5% international.
**Music Faculty** 20 total (full-time), 34 total (part-time). 60% of full-time faculty have terminal degrees. Graduate students teach a few undergraduate courses. Undergraduate student–faculty ratio: 17:1.
**Student Life** Student groups/activities include Phi Mu Alpha, Tau Beta Sigma, Sigma Alpha Iota.
**Expenses for 2007–2008** Application fee: $55. State resident tuition: $0 full-time. Nonresident tuition: $10,170 full-time. Mandatory fees: $3428 full-time. Full-time tuition and fees vary according to degree level. College room and board: $10,904. Room and board charges vary according to board plan and housing facility. Special program-related fees: $20 per semester for equipment use fee, $20 per semester for instrument use fee, $20 per semester for piano practice room.
**Financial Aid** Program-specific awards: 40–50 scholarships for music majors ($500–$4000).
**Application Procedures** Students admitted directly into the professional program freshman year. Deadline for freshmen and transfers: November 30. Notification date for freshmen and transfers: April 1. Required: high school transcript, college transcript(s) for transfer students, minimum 3.0 high school GPA, audition, SAT or ACT test scores. Auditions held twice on campus; videotaped performances are permissible as a substitute for live auditions when distance is prohibitive.
**Web Site** http://www.musicdance.sdsu.edu
**Undergraduate Contact** Mrs. Sandra Konar, Music and Dance Student Coordinator, School of Music and Dance, San Diego State University, San Diego, California 92182-7902; 619-594-6032, fax: 619-594-1692, e-mail address: music.dance@sdsu.edu
**Graduate Contact** Prof. Martin Chambers, Graduate Advisor - Music, School of Music and Dance, San Diego State University, San Diego, California 92182-7902; 619-594-6031, fax: 619-594-1692, e-mail address: music.dance@sdsu.edu

## San Francisco Conservatory of Music

### San Francisco, California

Independent, coed. Urban campus. Total enrollment: 406. Music program established 1917.
**Degrees** Bachelor of Music in the areas of classical guitar, composition, keyboard instruments, orchestral instruments, voice. Majors and concentrations: classical guitar, composition, piano/organ, stringed instruments, voice, wind and percussion instruments. Graduate degrees offered: Master of Music in the areas of chamber music, classical guitar, composition, conducting, keyboard instruments, orchestral instruments, piano accompanying, voice. Program accredited by NASM.
**Enrollment** 397 total; 212 undergraduate, 185 graduate.
**Music Student Profile** 60% females, 40% males, 22% minorities, 28% international.
**Music Faculty** 30 total (full-time), 73 total (part-time). 50% of full-time faculty have terminal degrees. Graduate students do not teach undergraduate courses. Undergraduate student–faculty ratio: 5:1.
**Student Life** Student groups/activities include Student Government Organization.
**Expenses for 2007–2008** Application fee: $100. One-time mandatory fee: $174. Tuition: $29,700 full-time. Mandatory fees: $280 full-time.
**Financial Aid** Program-specific awards: 120 Conservatory Scholarships for undergraduates ($13,500).
**Application Procedures** Students admitted directly into the professional program freshman year. Deadline for freshmen and transfers: December 1. Notification date for freshmen and transfers: April 1. Required: high school transcript, college transcript(s) for transfer students, minimum 2.0 high school GPA, 2 letters of recommendation, audition, minimum TOEFL score of 500/173 or minimum of 61 on TOEFL iBT for students for whom English is not the first language. Recommended: essay, SAT or

*San Francisco Conservatory of Music (continued)*

ACT test scores. Auditions held 5 times: January, February, March, May, and November on campus and off campus in Boston, MA; New York, NY; Chicago, IL; Interlochen, MI; Houston, TX; Oberlin, OH; Idyllwild, CA; videotaped performances are permissible as a substitute for live auditions for non-voice applicants residing outside of northern California and international applicants.

**Web Site** http://www.sfcm.edu

**Contact** Ms. Melissa Cocco-Mitten, Assistant Director of Admission, San Francisco Conservatory of Music, 50 Oak Street, San Francisco, California 94102; 800-899-7326, fax: 415-503-6299, e-mail address: admit@sfcm.edu

### More About the Conservatory

The San Francisco Conservatory of Music (SFCM), founded in 1917, is a nationally prominent conservatory with an international reputation and student body. Enrollment is kept small (400 total students) to ensure close student-faculty interaction and frequent and regular performance opportunities for every student throughout the program. Significant personal attention for each student and a collaborative and intimate atmosphere guarantee that students receive intense and rigorous preparation for careers in music.

The Bay Area's public transportation provides quick access to downtown San Francisco and the Civic Center, the city's cultural center and the site of the Conservatory's new, state-of-the-art facility, which opened in the fall of 2006. From its new location at Civic Center, the Conservatory will strengthen ties with the San Francisco Symphony, the Opera, and other arts and educational organizations, further developing its intellectual and musical collaborations. Students already enjoy free tickets to the symphony, the ballet, the opera, and various theatrical offerings. Museums, galleries, and the remarkable physical beauty of San Francisco—its parks, beaches, views, and neighborhoods—provide much to explore and enjoy.

Performing is a major aspect of student life at SFCM. Students not only present their required solo and chamber recitals but also participate actively in the major ensembles, collaborate with classmates and faculty members in performances, and have positions with Bay Area choirs, orchestras, and other ensembles.

Every year, the Conservatory's Community Service Program sends students into the community, both as soloists and ensembles, to perform at hospitals, senior centers, schools, and other institutions. The popular Music To Go! program offers some 1,000 paid-performance opportunities each year to students who audition to be on call for private and corporate events throughout the Bay Area. Outside the Conservatory, students augment their study as members of regional opera companies, orchestras, chamber music ensembles, and choruses; this also allows students to make important professional connections while they are still students. Alumni are counted among the members of national and

international arts organizations, including the Chicago Symphony, Glyndebourne Festival Opera, Israel Philharmonic, Los Angeles Philharmonic, Metropolitan Opera, Minnesota Orchestra, National Symphony Orchestra, San Francisco Opera and Opera Orchestra and Ballet Orchestra, Peabody Trio, Tokyo Philharmonic Orchestra, and Stuttgart Staatsoper.

San Francisco's Conservatory of Music students receive instruction from a world-class faculty in an atmosphere that is at once intense and informal. From the studio to the classroom, SFCM faculty members are passionately committed to the development of the individual, both artistically and intellectually. Personal attention is a hallmark of an SFCM education.

**Program Facilities** New facilities include a concert hall (435 seats), sure to be one of the finest concert halls of its size in California; the Sol Joseph Recital Hall (130 seats); the Osher Salon (100 seats), a multiuse performance/teaching space; a new, roof-top library, offering more than 40,000 volumes, scores, and periodicals and more than 10,000 recordings; a computer center and the electronic composition studio; two professional recording studios; a roof garden; forty-two practice rooms; forty-four teaching studios; fourteen classrooms; a student lounge; and a café.

**Faculty, Visiting Artists, and Alumni** SFCM faculty members are past and present members of the San Francisco Symphony, San Francisco Ballet Orchestra, San Francisco Opera and Opera Orchestra, Philharmonia Baroque Orchestra, Smithson Quartet, Francesca Trio, and others and perform internationally as soloists and chamber musicians. Recent master classes have been presented by John Adams, Gil Shaham, Ned Rorem, Paula Robison, Lynn Harrell, Jerry Hadley, Thomas Hampson, Richard Goode, Leon Fleisher, Manuel Barrueco, Yo-Yo Ma, Hakan Hardenberger, Menachem Pressler, Gil Kalish, and Frederica von Stade. Nationally known alumni include pianist-conductor Jeffrey Kahane, pianist Robin Sutherland, Pulitzer Prize–winning composer Aaron Jay Kernis, guitarist David Tanenbaum, and Naumburg Award–winning cellist Hai-Ye Ni. Yehudi Menuhin and Isaac Stern studied at the Conservatory as children.

**Student Performance Opportunities** Approximately 400 events are presented at the Conservatory each year, featuring solo and chamber recitals by students and faculty members, small ensembles, fully staged operas, and symphonic programs. Conservatory ensembles include the Orchestra, Opera Theatre, Opera Workshop, Musical Theatre Workshop, Baroque Ensemble, Guitar Ensemble, Percussion Ensemble, New Music Ensemble, and a host of other smaller, specialized groups. Chamber music, especially for strings and piano, is a signature program at SFCM.

# San Francisco State University
## San Francisco, California

State-supported, coed. Urban campus. Total enrollment: 30,125. Music program established 1930.

**Degrees** Bachelor of Music in the areas of music education, performance, composition, music history and literature. Majors and concentrations: composition, instrumental performance, jazz performance, music education, music history and literature, voice, voice performance. Graduate degrees offered: Master of Arts in the areas of music education, music history, music composition; Master of Music in the areas of classical performance, chamber music, conducting. Cross-registration with University of California, Berkeley; California State University, Hayward. Program accredited by NASM.

**Enrollment** 350 total; 100 undergraduate, 30 graduate, 220 nonprofessional degree.

**Music Student Profile** 54% females, 46% males, 10% minorities, 5% international.

**Music Faculty** 15 total (full-time), 40 total (part-time). 57% of full-time faculty have terminal degrees. Graduate students do not teach undergraduate courses. Undergraduate student–faculty ratio: 12:1.

**Student Life** Student groups/activities include California Music Educators Association.

**Expenses for 2007–2008** Application fee: $55. Nonresident tuition: $10,170 full-time. Mandatory fees: $3456 full-time. Full-time tuition and fees vary according to degree level. College room and board: $9896. College room only: $6388. Room and board charges vary according to board plan and housing facility. Special program-related fees: $25 for instrument rental, $25 per year for ear lab fee.

**Financial Aid** Program-specific awards: Paul Pone Forgivable Loan Scholarships for academically and artistically talented program majors, Edward Nagel Scholarships for students interested in music and business, 1 Wayne Peterson Prize in Music Composition ($4000).

**Application Procedures** Students admitted directly into the professional program freshman year. Deadline for freshmen and transfers: continuous. Required: high school transcript, college transcript(s) for transfer students, minimum 2.0 high school GPA, audition, SAT or ACT test scores, minimum TOEFL score of 550 for international applicants, theory and ear training placement exam, piano class placement exam. Auditions held 6 times on campus; recorded music is permissible as a substitute for live auditions when distance is prohibitive and videotaped performances are permissible as a substitute for live auditions when distance is prohibitive.

**Web Site** http://www.sfsu.edu/~smd

**Undergraduate Contact** Enrollment Services, San Francisco State University, 1600 Holloway Avenue, San Francisco, California 94132; 415-338-1431, fax: 415-338-3294.

**Graduate Contact** Graduate Studies, San Francisco State University, 1600 Holloway Avenue, San Francisco, California 94132; 415-338-2234.

# San Jose State University
## San Jose, California

State-supported, coed. Urban campus. Total enrollment: 29,604 (2007). Music program established 1847.
**Web Site** http://www.sjsu.edu/

# Schulich School of Music
See McGill University

# Schwob School of Music
See Columbus State University

# Setnor School of Music
See Syracuse University

# Seton Hall University
## South Orange, New Jersey

Independent Roman Catholic, coed. Suburban campus. Total enrollment: 9,637 (2006). Music program established 1968.
**Web Site** http://www.shu.edu/

# Seton Hill University
## Greensburg, Pennsylvania

Independent Roman Catholic, coed. Small town campus. Total enrollment: 1,967. Music program established 1918.
**Degrees** Bachelor of Music in the areas of performance, music education, sacred music, music therapy. Majors and concentrations: music education, music performance, music therapy, sacred music. Cross-registration with Saint Vincent College, University of Pittsburgh at Greensburg. Program accredited by NASM, AMTA.
**Enrollment** 89 total; 74 undergraduate, 15 nonprofessional degree.

**Music Student Profile** 60% females, 40% males, 3% minorities, 3% international.

**Music Faculty** 5 undergraduate (full-time), 19 undergraduate (part-time). 80% of full-time faculty have terminal degrees. Graduate students do not teach undergraduate courses. Undergraduate student–faculty ratio: 10:1.

**Student Life** Student groups/activities include Music Educators National Conference, Pennsylvania Music Educators Association Student Chapter, American Guild of Organists.

**Expenses for 2007–2008** Application fee: $35. Comprehensive fee: $32,746 includes full-time tuition ($24,806), mandatory fees ($200), and college room and board ($7740). Room and board charges vary according to board plan and housing facility. Special program-related fees: $15 for large ensembles, $15–$50 for music education methods course fee, $130 for private instruction on a secondary instrument, $260 for private instruction on a major instrument.

**Financial Aid** Program-specific awards: 7 division scholarships for incoming students ($3500), 2 Gabriel Burda Scholarships for incoming students ($4000), 4 string quartet scholarships for string players ($1500), 1 Highberger Scholarship for incoming students ($1000), 1 Choral Society Scholarship for incoming students ($500), 1 symphonic winds scholarship for incoming students ($1000), 1–4 Mildred Gardner Music Scholarships for incoming students from Westmoreland County, PA ($1000–$4000).

**Application Procedures** Students admitted directly into the professional program freshman year. Deadline for freshmen and transfers: continuous. Notification date for freshmen and transfers: continuous. Required: high school transcript, college transcript(s) for transfer students, minimum 2.0 high school GPA, audition, SAT or ACT test scores. Recommended: essay, minimum 3.0 high school GPA, letter of recommendation, interview. Auditions held 3 times and by appointment on campus; recorded music is permissible as a substitute for live auditions if a campus visit is impossible and videotaped performances are permissible as a substitute for live auditions if a campus visit is impossible.

**Web Site** http://www.setonhill.edu

**Undergraduate Contact** Ms. Sherrie Bett, Director, Admissions Office, Seton Hill University, Seton Hill Drive, Greensburg, Pennsylvania 15601; 724-838-4255, fax: 724-830-4611, e-mail address: admit@setonhill.edu

# Shenandoah Conservatory
See Shenandoah University

*Shenandoah Conservatory*
# Shenandoah University
## Winchester, Virginia

Independent United Methodist, coed. Total enrollment: 3,393.
**Degrees** Bachelor of Music in the areas of church music, commercial music, composition, jazz studies, music education, performance, piano accompanying, music with elective studies, music theater accompanying; Bachelor of Music Therapy; Bachelor of Science in the area of arts management. Majors and concentrations: arts management, church music, composition, jazz, music education, music production and recording technology, music theater accompanying, music therapy, music with elective studies, performance, piano accompanying, piano/organ, stringed instruments, voice, wind and percussion instruments. Graduate degrees offered: Master of Music in the areas of composition, conducting, performance, church music, dance accompanying, piano accompanying, pedagogy; Master of Music Education; Master of Music Therapy; Master of Science in the areas of arts administration, music. Doctor of Musical Arts in the areas of music education, performance. Program accredited by NASM.
**Enrollment** 397 total; 240 undergraduate, 135 graduate, 22 nonprofessional degree.
**Music Student Profile** 34% females, 66% males, 7% international.

*Shenandoah University (continued)*

**Music Faculty** 41 total (full-time), 39 total (part-time). 70% of full-time faculty have terminal degrees. Graduate students teach a few undergraduate courses. Undergraduate student–faculty ratio: 3:1.

**Student Life** Student groups/activities include music fraternities and sororities, Music Educators National Conference Student Chapter, Student Association of Music Therapy.

**Expenses for 2008–2009** Application fee: $30. Comprehensive fee: $31,690 includes full-time tuition ($23,040), mandatory fees ($300), and college room and board ($8350). Special program-related fees: $125 per half-hour lesson for private voice and piano lessons, $250 per one-hour lesson for private music lessons for majors.

**Financial Aid** Program-specific awards: 189 talent and academic scholarships for program students ($4066).

**Application Procedures** Students admitted directly into the professional program freshman year. Deadline for freshmen and transfers: continuous. Required: high school transcript, college transcript(s) for transfer students, minimum 2.0 high school GPA, letter of recommendation, interview, video, audition, SAT or ACT test scores, portfolio for composition majors. Auditions held 11 times on campus and off campus in New York, NY; Chicago, IL; Boston, MA; recorded music is permissible as a substitute for live auditions with permission and videotaped performances are permissible as a substitute for live auditions with permission. Portfolio reviews held 11 times on campus and off campus in NYC, Chicago, Boston.

**Web Site** http://www.su.edu/conservatory

**Contact** Mr. David Anthony, Dean, Admissions Office, Shenandoah University, 1460 University Drive, Winchester, Virginia 22601-5195; 540-665-4581, fax: 540-665-4627, e-mail address: admit@su.edu

# Shepherd School of Music

See Rice University

# Shorter College

## Rome, Georgia

Independent Baptist, coed. Small town campus. Total enrollment: 1,394. Music program established 1938.

**Degrees** Bachelor of Fine Arts in the areas of musical theater, musical direction; Bachelor of Music in the areas of voice, piano, organ, piano pedagogy, music education, church music. Majors and concentrations: church music, music education, music theater, organ, piano, piano pedagogy, voice. Program accredited by NASM.

**Enrollment** 111 total; 108 undergraduate, 3 nonprofessional degree.

**Music Student Profile** 66% females, 34% males, 7% minorities.

**Music Faculty** 13 undergraduate (full-time), 6 undergraduate (part-time). 66% of full-time faculty have terminal degrees. Graduate students do not teach undergraduate courses. Undergraduate student–faculty ratio: 12:1.

**Student Life** Student groups/activities include Mu Phi Epsilon, Phi Mu Alpha Sinfonia.

**Expenses for 2007–2008** Application fee: $25. Comprehensive fee: $22,160 includes full-time tuition ($14,850), mandatory fees ($310), and college room and board ($7000). College room only: $3800. Full-time tuition and fees vary according to course load. Room and board charges vary according to board plan and housing facility. Special program-related fees: $250 per semester for private applied lessons.

**Financial Aid** Program-specific awards: 40 music scholarships for music majors ($500–$4000).

**Application Procedures** Students admitted directly into the professional program freshman year. Deadline for freshmen and transfers: continuous. Required: essay, high school transcript, college transcript(s) for transfer students, minimum 2.0 high school GPA, interview, audition, SAT or ACT test scores, music theory examination, minimum 2.0 college GPA for transfer students. Recommended: letter of recommendation. Auditions held 4 times and by appointment on campus; recorded music is

permissible as a substitute for live auditions for international students and U.S. students from a great distance and videotaped performances are permissible as a substitute for live auditions for international students and U.S. students from a great distance.

**Web Site** http://www.shorter.edu/

**Undergraduate Contact** Dr. Alan B. Wingard, Dean, School of the Arts, Shorter College, 315 Shorter Avenue, Rome, Georgia 30165; 706-233-7247, fax: 706-236-1517, e-mail address: awingard@shorter.edu

# Silver Lake College

## Manitowoc, Wisconsin

Independent Roman Catholic, coed. Rural campus. Total enrollment: 832. Music program established 1960.

**Degrees** Bachelor of Music in the areas of music education, music. Majors and concentrations: choral music education, instrumental music education, music, music education, music education-Kodaly. Graduate degrees offered: Master of Music in the area of music education. Program accredited by NASM.

**Enrollment** 47 total; 15 undergraduate, 30 graduate, 2 nonprofessional degree.

**Music Student Profile** 80% females, 20% males, 4% minorities, 10% international.

**Music Faculty** 5 total (full-time), 7 total (part-time). 80% of full-time faculty have terminal degrees. Graduate students do not teach undergraduate courses. Undergraduate student–faculty ratio: 4:1.

**Student Life** Student groups/activities include sophomore, senior, and honors recitals, major seasonal concerts, Music Educators National Conference Collegiate Chapter.

**Expenses for 2008–2009** Application fee: $35. Comprehensive fee: $24,644 includes full-time tuition ($19,194) and college room and board ($5450). College room only: $4900.

**Financial Aid** Program-specific awards: music ensemble grants for music majors ($500–$1000), Ginzl Endowed Music Scholarships for music majors ($500–$1000), Dunne Memorial Endowed Awards for music majors ($2000–$2500), Music Department Scholarships for music majors ($500–$1000), Jagemann Memorial Scholarships for music majors ($500–$1000), talent incentive grants ($250–$500).

**Application Procedures** Students admitted directly into the professional program freshman year. Deadline for freshmen and transfers: continuous. Required: high school transcript, college transcript(s) for transfer students, minimum 2.0 high school GPA, audition, ACT test score only (minimum composite ACT score of 19), high school transcript for transfer applicants with fewer than 30 credits. Auditions held 5 times on campus.

**Web Site** http://www.sl.edu/music/

**Undergraduate Contact** Jamie Grant, Associate Director of Admissions, Silver Lake College, 2406 South Alverno Road, Manitowoc, Wisconsin 54220-9319; 920-686-6186, fax: 920-684-7082, e-mail address: jgrant@silver.sl.edu

**Graduate Contact** Cindy St. John, Associate Director of Admissions, Silver Lake College, 2406 South Alverno Road, Manitowoc, Wisconsin 54220-9319; 920-686-6350, fax: 920-684-7082, e-mail address: cstjohn@silver.sl.edu

# Simon Fraser University

## Burnaby, British Columbia, Canada

Province-supported, coed. Suburban campus. Total enrollment: 26,128. Music program established 1992.

**Web Site** http://www.sfu.ca/

# Simpson College

## Indianola, Iowa

Independent United Methodist, coed. Small town campus. Total enrollment: 2,039. Music program established 1900.

**Degrees** Bachelor of Music in the areas of classical music, piano/organ, voice, winds and percussion music, vocal music education, instrumental music education, guitar. Majors and concentrations: brass, classical guitar, classical music, music education, performance, piano/organ, voice, wind and percussion instruments. Program accredited by NASM.

**Enrollment** 105 total; 95 undergraduate, 10 nonprofessional degree.

**Music Student Profile** 60% females, 40% males, 4% minorities, 1% international.

**Music Faculty** 14 undergraduate (full-time), 15 undergraduate (part-time). 75% of full-time faculty have terminal degrees. Graduate students do not teach undergraduate courses. Undergraduate student–faculty ratio: 7:1.

**Student Life** Student groups/activities include Phi Mu Alpha Sinfonia, Mu Phi Epsilon, Music Educators National Conference.

**Expenses for 2008–2009** Application fee: $0. One-time mandatory fee: $100. Comprehensive fee: $31,759 includes full-time tuition ($24,414), mandatory fees ($357), and college room and board ($6988). College room only: $3354. Special program-related fees: $50 per semester for recital fee, $50 per semester for accompanist fee, $235 per credit hour for lesson fee.

**Financial Aid** Program-specific awards: 70–80 music scholarships for program majors ($2000–$5000).

**Application Procedures** Students apply for admission into the professional program by sophomore year. Deadline for freshmen and transfers: August 1. Notification date for freshmen and transfers: June 30. Required: essay, high school transcript, college transcript(s) for transfer students, minimum 2.0 high school GPA, letter of recommendation, audition, SAT or ACT test scores (minimum composite ACT score of 21). Recommended: minimum 3.0 high school GPA, interview, video. Auditions held twice plus special auditions on campus; recorded music is permissible as a substitute for live auditions if a campus visit is impossible and videotaped performances are permissible as a substitute for live auditions if a campus visit is impossible.

**Web Site** http://www.simpson.edu

**Undergraduate Contact** Dr. Maria DiPalma, Chairperson, Department of Music, Simpson College, 701 North Street, Indianola, Iowa 50125-1297; 515-961-1570, fax: 515-961-1498, e-mail address: admiss@simpson.edu

### More About the College

The Simpson College Conservatory of Music was founded in 1891. In 1940, it became the Music Department at Simpson and has developed and maintained a position of preeminence among schools offering serious musical training in the Midwest.

Simpson combines the atmosphere of a fine small liberal arts college with a distinguished program in music education and music performance. Students at Simpson are given the opportunity to work with superior teachers in private study and in small classes and are given extraordinary opportunities for both ensemble and solo performances. Here, every student is an individual and treated as such, often having the opportunity for upper-division directed studies in such areas as conducting, vocal repertory, ethnomusicology, Kodaly and Orff techniques, and opera coaching.

The Middle Ages, the Renaissance, the great operatic repertory of the nineteenth century, and the vitality of twentieth-century musical thought and American jazz are living, breathing, exciting, and viable entities in the music department. Visiting artists such as Chanticleer, soprano Evelyn Lear, and jazz great Maynard Ferguson give recitals and master classes. Alumni artists like John Osborn, a tenor who is performing internationally at the Metropolitan Opera, Vienna Stadsoper, National Opera, and Glimmerglass; Kimm Julian, well-known baritone with regional opera companies and in Europe; and Beverly O'Reagan Thiele, soprano who sings with the New York City Opera and the Metropolitan Opera, also return for recitals and master classes. Distinguished music educators on the national scene appear regularly to participate in the music education workshop series for students and area teachers.

Indianola and the Blank Performing Arts Center are the home of the Des Moines Metro Opera, one of America's leading regional opera companies, and a number of students become a part of its staff each summer.

Simpson is a remarkable place for a young musician to watch, listen, and grow. It is a place where each student is challenged to develop his or her musical and artistic gifts to the fullest and counseled carefully on realistic career goals and the steps to be taken beyond the Simpson years.

# Slippery Rock University of Pennsylvania

### Slippery Rock, Pennsylvania

State-supported, coed. Rural campus. Total enrollment: 8,325. Music program established 1960.

**Web Site** http://www.sru.edu/

# South Dakota State University

### Brookings, South Dakota

State-supported, coed. Total enrollment: 11,645. Music program established 1906.

**Degrees** Bachelor of Music Education in the areas of vocal music education, instrumental music education, general music education; Bachelor of Science in the area of music merchandising. Majors and concentrations: music education, music merchandising. Program accredited by NASM.

**Enrollment** 97 total; 78 undergraduate, 19 nonprofessional degree.

**Music Student Profile** 56% females, 44% males, 2% minorities, 2% international.

**Music Faculty** 14 undergraduate (full-time), 1 undergraduate (part-time). 79% of full-time faculty have terminal degrees. Graduate students do not teach undergraduate courses. Undergraduate student–faculty ratio: 15:1.

**Student Life** Student groups/activities include Music Educators National Conference, Music Industry Club.

**Expenses for 2007–2008** Application fee: $20. State resident tuition: $2478 full-time. Nonresident tuition: $3716 full-time. Mandatory fees: $2895 full-time. Full-time tuition and fees vary according to course load, location, program, and reciprocity agreements. College room and board: $5240. College room only: $2348. Room and board charges vary according to board plan and housing facility.

**Financial Aid** Program-specific awards: 30–45 music scholarships for music majors and minors ($600–$1500).

**Application Procedures** Students admitted directly into the professional program freshman year. Deadline for freshmen and transfers: June 23. Notification date for freshmen and transfers: continuous. Required: high school transcript, college transcript(s) for transfer students, audition, ACT test score only (minimum composite ACT score of 18), minimum 2.6 high school GPA or standing in top 60% of graduating class or ACT of 18. Recommended: 2 letters of recommendation. Auditions held twice on campus and off campus in Rapid City, SD; Minneapolis, MN; Sioux City, IA; recorded music is permissible as a substitute

*South Dakota State University (continued)*

for live auditions when distance is prohibitive and videotaped performances are permissible as a substitute for live auditions when distance is prohibitive.
**Web Site** http://www3.sdstate.edu/Academics/ CollegeOfArtsAndSciences/Music/
**Undergraduate Contact** Dr. David Reynolds, Head, Music Department, South Dakota State University, LMH Box 2212, Brookings, South Dakota 57007; 605-688-5188, fax: 605-688-4307, e-mail address: paul.reynolds@sdstate.edu

# Southeastern Louisiana University

## Hammond, Louisiana

State-supported, coed. Small town campus. Total enrollment: 14,757. Music program established 1946.
**Degrees** Bachelor of Music in the areas of instrumental music, vocal music, keyboard; Bachelor of Music Education in the areas of instrumental music education, vocal music education. Majors and concentrations: band, guitar, music education, piano, strings, voice. Graduate degrees offered: Master of Music in the areas of theory, performance. Cross-registration with Southern University and Agricultural and Mechanical College. Program accredited by NASM, NCATE.
**Enrollment** 209 total; 191 undergraduate, 18 graduate.
**Music Student Profile** 42% females, 58% males, 14% minorities, 10% international.
**Music Faculty** 19 total (full-time), 15 total (part-time). 75% of full-time faculty have terminal degrees. Graduate students teach a few undergraduate courses.
**Student Life** Student groups/activities include Phi Mu Alpha Sinfonia, Music Educators National Conference, Delta Omicron, Kappa Kappa Psi. Special housing available for music students.
**Expenses for 2007–2008** Application fee: $20. State resident tuition: $2216 full-time. Nonresident tuition: $8216 full-time. Mandatory fees: $1345 full-time. Full-time tuition and fees vary according to course load. College room and board: $5990. College room only: $3780. Room and board charges vary according to board plan and housing facility.
**Financial Aid** Program-specific awards: 200 performance grants for music majors ($1000).
**Application Procedures** Students admitted directly into the professional program freshman year. Deadline for freshmen and transfers: continuous. Required: high school transcript, college transcript(s) for transfer students, audition, minimum ACT score of 20, standing in top 50% of high school class, or 2.0 GPA. Auditions held 10 times on campus and off campus in various locations; recorded music is permissible as a substitute for live auditions when distance is prohibitive and videotaped performances are permissible as a substitute for live auditions when distance is prohibitive.
**Web Site** http://www.selu.edu/music
**Undergraduate Contact** Dr. David Evenson, Head, Department of Music and Dramatic Arts, Southeastern Louisiana University, SLU Box 10815, Hammond, Louisiana 70402; 985-549-2184, fax: 985-549-2892, e-mail address: devenson@selu.edu
**Graduate Contact** Dr. Andrew Seigel, Graduate Coordinator, Department of Music and Dramatic Arts, Southeastern Louisiana University, SLU Box 10815, Hammond, Louisiana 70402; 985-549-2184, fax: 985-549-2892, e-mail address: aseigel@selu.edu

# Southeast Missouri State University

## Cape Girardeau, Missouri

State-supported, coed. Small town campus. Total enrollment: 10,665.
**Degrees** Bachelor of Music in the area of performance; Bachelor of Music Education in the areas of instrumental music education, vocal music education. Majors and concentrations: composition, harpsichord, music, music education, piano/organ, stringed instruments, voice, wind and percussion instruments. Graduate degrees offered: Master of Music Education. Cross-registration with selected institutions in southeast Missouri. Program accredited by NASM.

**Enrollment** 115 total; 95 undergraduate, 15 graduate, 5 nonprofessional degree.
**Music Student Profile** 55% females, 45% males, 5% minorities, 3% international.
**Music Faculty** 18 total (full-time), 4 total (part-time). 89% of full-time faculty have terminal degrees. Graduate students do not teach undergraduate courses. Undergraduate student–faculty ratio: 9:1.
**Student Life** Student groups/activities include Collegiate Music Educators National Conference, Phi Mu Alpha Sinfonia, Sigma Alpha Iota.
**Expenses for 2007–2008** Application fee: $25. State resident tuition: $5304 full-time. Nonresident tuition: $9699 full-time. Mandatory fees: $621 full-time. Full-time tuition and fees vary according to course load and location. College room and board: $5923. College room only: $3661. Room and board charges vary according to board plan and housing facility. Special program-related fees: $10–$30 per semester for locker rental, $25 per key for key fee, $25 per instrument for instrument rental, $75 per credit hour for applied music lesson fee.
**Financial Aid** Program-specific awards: 4 Bea Limbaugh Scholarships for music students ($1200), 4 Margaret Woods Allen Piano Scholarships for piano students ($3200), 1 Charles Cox Scholarship for music students ($770), 1 Leroy Mason Scholarship for music students ($850), 1 Harold Lichtenegger Scholarship for music students ($1300), 1 O.L. Wilcox Scholarship for music students.
**Application Procedures** Students apply for admission into the professional program by sophomore, junior year. Deadline for freshmen and transfers: March 15. Required: high school transcript, college transcript(s) for transfer students, minimum 2.0 high school GPA, 2 letters of recommendation, interview, audition, ACT test score only (minimum composite ACT score of 18), minimum 2.0 college GPA for transfer students. Auditions held continuously on campus; recorded music is permissible as a substitute for live auditions when distance is prohibitive and videotaped performances are permissible as a substitute for live auditions when distance is prohibitive. Portfolio reviews held on campus.
**Web Site** http://www5.semo.edu/music/
**Undergraduate Contact** Mr. Barry W. Bernhardt, Undergraduate Admissions, Department of Music, Southeast Missouri State University, 1 University Plaza, Cape Girardeau, Missouri 63701; 573-651-2335, fax: 573-651-2431.
**Graduate Contact** Dr. Robert Conger, Graduate Admissions, Department of Music, Southeast Missouri State University, 1 University Plaza, Cape Girardeau, Missouri 63701; 573-651-2141, fax: 573-651-2431.

# Southern Adventist University

## Collegedale, Tennessee

Independent Seventh-day Adventist, coed. Small town campus. Total enrollment: 2,640.
**Web Site** http://www.southern.edu/

# Southern Arkansas University–Magnolia

## Magnolia, Arkansas

State-supported, coed. Small town campus. Total enrollment: 3,147.
**Web Site** http://www.saumag.edu/

# Southern Illinois University Carbondale

## Carbondale, Illinois

State-supported, coed. Rural campus. Total enrollment: 20,983.
**Degrees** Bachelor of Music in the areas of performance, piano pedagogy, music theory/composition, music education. Majors and concentrations: classical music, guitar, music education,

music theory and composition, opera, piano pedagogy, piano/organ, stringed instruments, voice, wind and percussion instruments. Graduate degrees offered: Master of Music in the areas of performance, piano pedagogy, music theory/composition, music history/literature, opera/music theater, music education. Program accredited by NASM.

**Enrollment** 270 total; 170 undergraduate, 40 graduate, 60 nonprofessional degree.

**Music Student Profile** 45% females, 55% males, 5% minorities, 18% international.

**Music Faculty** 30 total (full-time), 3 total (part-time). 85% of full-time faculty have terminal degrees. Graduate students do not teach undergraduate courses. Undergraduate student–faculty ratio: 7:1.

**Student Life** Student groups/activities include Collegiate Music Educators National Conference, Phi Mu Alpha Sinfonia, Mu Phi Epsilon.

**Expenses for 2007–2008** Application fee: $30. State resident tuition: $6348 full-time. Nonresident tuition: $15,870 full-time. Mandatory fees: $2551 full-time. Full-time tuition and fees vary according to course load. College room and board: $6666. College room only: $3650. Room and board charges vary according to board plan and housing facility. Special program-related fees: $20 per semester for instrument rental.

**Financial Aid** Program-specific awards: 20–30 music scholarships for musically talented students ($300–$2000).

**Application Procedures** Students admitted directly into the professional program freshman year. Deadline for freshmen and transfers: continuous. Notification date for freshmen: August 15. Required: high school transcript, college transcript(s) for transfer students, audition, ACT test score only (minimum composite ACT score of 21). Auditions held 3 times and by appointment on campus; recorded music is permissible as a substitute for live auditions for out-of-state applicants and videotaped performances are permissible as a substitute for live auditions for international applicants and out-of-state applicants.

**Web Site** http://www.siu.edu/~music

**Undergraduate Contact** Dr. Jeanine Wagner, Undergraduate Advisor, School of Music, Southern Illinois University Carbondale, Mailcode 4302, Carbondale, Illinois 62901; 618-453-5815, fax: 618-453-5808, e-mail address: jwagner@siu.edu

**Graduate Contact** Dr. Frank Stemper, Graduate Advisor, School of Music, Southern Illinois University Carbondale, Mailcode 4302, Carbondale, Illinois 62901; 618-536-8742, fax: 618-453-5808, e-mail address: fstemp@siu.edu

# Southern Illinois University Edwardsville

## Edwardsville, Illinois

State-supported, coed. Suburban campus. Total enrollment: 13,298. Music program established 1958.

**Degrees** Bachelor of Music in the areas of performance, music education, jazz performance, musical theater, theory/composition, music merchandising. Majors and concentrations: jazz, music education, music history and literature, music merchandising, music theater, music theory and composition, performance. Graduate degrees offered: Master of Music in the areas of music education, performance. Program accredited by NASM.

**Enrollment** 239 total; 184 undergraduate, 35 graduate, 20 nonprofessional degree.

**Music Student Profile** 55% females, 45% males, 10% minorities, 5% international.

**Music Faculty** 22 total (full-time), 21 total (part-time). 68% of full-time faculty have terminal degrees. Graduate students teach a few undergraduate courses. Undergraduate student–faculty ratio: 5:1.

**Student Life** Student groups/activities include Sigma Alpha Iota, Phi Mu Alpha Sinfonia, Music Educators National Conference. Special housing available for music students.

**Expenses for 2007–2008** Application fee: $30. Area resident tuition: $5228 full-time. State resident tuition: $5938 full-time. Nonresident tuition: $13,069 full-time. Mandatory fees: $1180 full-time. College room and board: $6750. College room only: $3970.

Special program-related fees: $10 for music methods fee, $20 per course for private applied lessons, $30 for ensemble fee.

**Financial Aid** Program-specific awards: 20–40 Music Talent Awards for those demonstrating talent and academic achievement ($100–$1000), 20 Provost Scholarships for those demonstrating talent and academic achievement ($2000).

**Application Procedures** Students admitted directly into the professional program freshman year. Deadline for freshmen and transfers: April 1. Notification date for freshmen and transfers: August 19. Required: high school transcript, college transcript(s) for transfer students, audition, SAT or ACT test scores, minimum 2.5 high school GPA. Recommended: letter of recommendation. Auditions held 3 times and by appointment on campus; recorded music is permissible as a substitute for live auditions when distance is prohibitive and videotaped performances are permissible as a substitute for live auditions when distance is prohibitive.

**Web Site** http://www.siue.edu/MUSIC/

**Undergraduate Contact** John Bell, Music Department, Southern Illinois University Edwardsville, Box 1771, Edwardsville, Illinois 62026-1771; 618-650-3900, fax: 618-692-5988, e-mail address: admis@siue.edu

**Graduate Contact** Darryl Coan, Director of Graduate Studies, Department of Music, Southern Illinois University Edwardsville, Box 1771, Edwardsville, Illinois 62026-1771; 618-650-3900, fax: 618-692-5988.

*Meadows School of the Arts/Division of Music*
# Southern Methodist University
## Dallas, Texas

Independent, coed. Suburban campus. Total enrollment: 10,829.
**Web Site** http://www.smu.edu/

# Southern University and Agricultural and Mechanical College
## Baton Rouge, Louisiana

State-supported, coed. Suburban campus. Total enrollment: 8,179. Music program established 1937.

**Degrees** Bachelor of Music in the area of performance; Bachelor of Music Education. Majors and concentrations: instrumental music, music education, piano, voice, wind and percussion instruments. Cross-registration with Louisiana State University, Southeastern Louisiana University. Program accredited by NASM.

**Enrollment** 135 total.

**Music Student Profile** 26% females, 74% males, 99% minorities, 1% international.

**Music Faculty** 9 undergraduate (full-time), 8 undergraduate (part-time). 22% of full-time faculty have terminal degrees. Graduate students do not teach undergraduate courses. Undergraduate student–faculty ratio: 10:1.

**Student Life** Student groups/activities include Phi Mu Alpha Sinfonia, Mu Phi Epsilon/Sigma Iota.

**Expenses for 2008–2009** Application fee: $20. State resident tuition: $3706 full-time. Nonresident tuition: $9498 full-time. College room and board: $6504.

**Financial Aid** Program-specific awards: 12 choir/vocal awards for choir singers ($100–$500), 10–15 music awards for program majors ($100–$500), 6 transfer scholarships for transfer students ($1000).

**Application Procedures** Students admitted directly into the professional program freshman year. Deadline for freshmen and transfers: continuous. Notification date for freshmen and transfers: continuous. Required: high school transcript, college transcript(s) for transfer students, audition, SAT or ACT test scores, medical history, good conduct letter. Auditions held twice and by appointment on campus; recorded music is permissible as a substitute for live auditions for out-of-state applicants and videotaped performances are permissible as a substitute for live auditions for out-of-state applicants.

**Web Site** http://www.subr.edu

*Southern University and Agricultural and Mechanical College (continued)*

**Undergraduate Contact** Mrs. Tracie Abraham, Director of Admissions, Southern University and Agricultural and Mechanical College, PO Box 9901, Southern University Station, Baton Rouge, Louisiana 70813; 225-771-2430.

# Southwestern Oklahoma State University

## Weatherford, Oklahoma

State-supported, coed. Small town campus. Total enrollment: 5,017.

**Degrees** Bachelor of Music in the areas of music therapy, music theory/composition, performance/instrumental, vocal, keyboard, music with elective studies in business; Bachelor of Music Education in the areas of instrumental music education, vocal/keyboard music education. Majors and concentrations: composition, music, music and business, music education, music theory, music therapy, performance, piano/organ, stringed instruments, voice, wind and percussion instruments. Graduate degrees offered: Master of Music in the area of performance and music education. Program accredited by NASM, AMTA.

**Enrollment** 150 total; 130 undergraduate, 10 graduate.

**Music Student Profile** 60% females, 40% males, 5% minorities, 5% international.

**Music Faculty** 13 total (full-time), 6 total (part-time). 70% of full-time faculty have terminal degrees. Graduate students teach a few undergraduate courses. Undergraduate student–faculty ratio: 10:1.

**Student Life** Student groups/activities include music fraternities and sororities, American Music Therapy Association, Music Educators National Conference.

**Expenses for 2007–2008** Application fee: $15. State resident tuition: $3000 full-time. Nonresident tuition: $7800 full-time. Mandatory fees: $750 full-time. Full-time tuition and fees vary according to program. College room and board: $3800. College room only: $1500. Room and board charges vary according to board plan. Special program-related fees: $50 per credit hour for applied lessons fee.

**Financial Aid** Program-specific awards: ensemble music scholarships for ensemble performers, music scholarships for those passing audition evaluations.

**Application Procedures** Students admitted directly into the professional program freshman year. Deadline for freshmen and transfers: continuous. Required: high school transcript, college transcript(s) for transfer students, SAT or ACT test scores (minimum composite ACT score of 19), audition for transfer students. Recommended: audition. Auditions held continuously by appointment on campus; recorded music is permissible as a substitute for live auditions when distance is prohibitive and videotaped performances are permissible as a substitute for live auditions when distance is prohibitive.

**Web Site** http://www.swosu.edu

**Undergraduate Contact** Ms. Marla Russ, Administrative Assistant, Department of Music, Southwestern Oklahoma State University, 100 Campus Drive, Weatherford, Oklahoma 73096; 580-774-3708, fax: 580-774-3714, e-mail address: marla.russ@swosu.edu

**Graduate Contact** Dr. Dennis Widen, Assistant Professor, Department of Music, Southwestern Oklahoma State University, 100 Campus Drive, Weatherford, Oklahoma 73096; 580-774-3216, fax: 580-774-3714, e-mail address: dennis.widen@swosu.edu

# Southwestern University

## Georgetown, Texas

Independent Methodist, coed. Suburban campus. Total enrollment: 1,294.

**Degrees** Bachelor of Music in the areas of performance, music education, music theory, music literature, sacred music. Majors and concentrations: guitar, organ, piano, stringed instruments, voice, wind and percussion instruments. Program accredited by NASM.

**Enrollment** 42 total; 17 undergraduate, 25 nonprofessional degree.

**Music Student Profile** 60% females, 40% males, 20% minorities.

**Music Faculty** 9 undergraduate (full-time), 19 undergraduate (part-time). 100% of full-time faculty have terminal degrees. Graduate students do not teach undergraduate courses.

**Student Life** Student groups/activities include Pi Kappa Lambda, Delta Omicron, Texas Music Educators Association.

**Expenses for 2007–2008** Application fee: $40. Comprehensive fee: $33,870 includes full-time tuition ($25,740) and college room and board ($8130). College room only: $4410. Room and board charges vary according to board plan and housing facility. Special program-related fees: $170 per semester for half-hour weekly private lessons, $340 per semester for one-hour weekly private lessons.

**Financial Aid** Program-specific awards: 25 music scholarships for talented program majors ($3500–$10,000).

**Application Procedures** Students admitted directly into the professional program freshman year. Deadline for freshmen: February 15; transfers: continuous. Notification date for freshmen: May 1; transfers: continuous. Required: essay, high school transcript, college transcript(s) for transfer students, minimum 2.0 high school GPA, audition, SAT or ACT test scores, minimum 3.0 college GPA for transfer students. Recommended: minimum 3.0 high school GPA, letter of recommendation, interview. Auditions held 2-3 times on campus; recorded music is permissible as a substitute for live auditions when distance is prohibitive and videotaped performances are permissible as a substitute for live auditions when distance is prohibitive.

**Web Site** http://www.southwestern.edu

**Undergraduate Contact** Dr. Kiyoshi Tamagawa, Chair, Department of Music, Southwestern University, Box 770, Georgetown, Texas 78627; 512-863-1356, fax: 512-863-1422.

# State University of New York at Binghamton

## Binghamton, New York

State-supported, coed. Suburban campus. Total enrollment: 14,435.

**Degrees** Bachelor of Music in the area of performance. Majors and concentrations: organ, piano, stringed instruments, voice, wind and percussion instruments. Graduate degrees offered: Master of Music in the areas of performance, composition, conducting, music history. Program accredited by NASM.

**Enrollment** 86 total; 6 undergraduate, 30 graduate, 50 nonprofessional degree.

**Music Faculty** 9 total (full-time), 25 total (part-time). 75% of full-time faculty have terminal degrees. Graduate students do not teach undergraduate courses.

**Expenses for 2007–2008** Application fee: $40. State resident tuition: $4350 full-time. Nonresident tuition: $10,610 full-time. Mandatory fees: $1662 full-time. College room and board: $9188. College room only: $5662. Room and board charges vary according to board plan and housing facility. Special program-related fees: $15 per year for practice room fee.

**Financial Aid** Program-specific awards: 9 endowed scholarships for music majors ($500–$2500).

**Application Procedures** Students apply for admission into the professional program by freshman year. Deadline for freshmen and transfers: January 15. Required: essay, high school transcript, college transcript(s) for transfer students, audition, SAT or ACT test scores. Auditions held as needed on campus.

**Web Site** http://music.binghamton.edu/

**Undergraduate Contact** Timothy LeFebvre, Director of Undergraduate Studies, Department of Music, State University of New York at Binghamton, PO Box 6000, Binghamton, New York 13902-6000; 607-777-2530, fax: 607-777-4425, e-mail address: lefebvre@binghamton.edu

**Graduate Contact** Dr. Bruce Borton, Director of Graduate Studies, Department of Music, State University of New York at Binghamton, PO Box 6000, Binghamton, New York 13902-6000; 607-777-6109, fax: 607-777-4425, e-mail address: bborton@binghamton.edu

# State University of New York at Fredonia

**Fredonia, New York**

State-supported, coed. Small town campus. Total enrollment: 5,404. Music program established 1931.

**Degrees** Bachelor of Fine Arts in the area of music theater; Bachelor of Music in the areas of music education, performance, composition; Bachelor of Science in the areas of sound recording technology, music therapy. Majors and concentrations: brass, composition, guitar, music education, music therapy, piano, sound recording technology, stringed instruments, voice, wind and percussion instruments. Graduate degrees offered: Master of Music in the areas of music education, performance, theory/composition. Program accredited by NASM, AMTA.

**Enrollment** 583 total; 515 undergraduate, 41 graduate, 27 nonprofessional degree.

**Music Student Profile** 53% females, 47% males, 8% minorities, 2% international.

**Music Faculty** 42 total (full-time), 45 total (part-time). 90% of full-time faculty have terminal degrees. Graduate students teach a few undergraduate courses. Undergraduate student–faculty ratio: 13:1.

**Student Life** Student groups/activities include Music Educators National Conference Student Chapter, National Association of Music Therapy Student Chapter, professional music fraternities.

**Expenses for 2007–2008** Application fee: $40. State resident tuition: $4350 full-time. Nonresident tuition: $10,610 full-time. Mandatory fees: $1192 full-time. College room and board: $8380. College room only: $5050. Room and board charges vary according to board plan and housing facility. Special program-related fees: $225 per semester for comprehensive music fee (all majors).

**Financial Aid** Program-specific awards: 40–50 Hillman Foundation Awards for program majors ($500–$1500), 10–15 piano scholarships for program majors ($500–$2000).

**Application Procedures** Students admitted directly into the professional program freshman year. Deadline for freshmen and transfers: continuous. Required: high school transcript, college transcript(s) for transfer students, 2 letters of recommendation, audition, SAT or ACT test scores. Auditions held 6 times on campus and off campus in Suffolk County, Long Island, NY; Albany, NY; recorded music is permissible as a substitute for live auditions when distance is prohibitive and videotaped performances are permissible as a substitute for live auditions when distance is prohibitive.

**Web Site** http://www.fredonia.edu/som/

**Undergraduate Contact** Mr. Barry Kilpatrick, Assistant Director (Admissions), School of Music, State University of New York at Fredonia, Mason Hall, Fredonia, New York 14063; 716-673-3153, fax: 716-673-3154, e-mail address: barry.kilpatrick@fredonia.edu

**Graduate Contact** Ms. Patricia Corron, Graduate Advisor, School of Music, State University of New York at Fredonia, Mason Hall, Fredonia, New York 14063; 716-673-4636, fax: 716-673-3154, e-mail address: patricia.corron@fredonia.edu

## *The Crane School of Music*
# State University of New York College at Potsdam

**Potsdam, New York**

State-supported, coed. Total enrollment: 4,338. Music program established 1886.

**Degrees** Bachelor of Music in the areas of music education, musical studies, performance, business of music. Majors and concentrations: classical music, guitar, harp, jazz studies, music, music and business, music education, musical studies, piano, piano pedagogy, special music education, stringed instruments, voice, wind and percussion instruments. Graduate degrees offered: Master of Music in the areas of music education, performance, composition. Cross-registration with State Univer-

sity of New York College of Technology at Canton, St. Lawrence University, Clarkson College. Program accredited by NASM.

**Enrollment** 605 total; 567 undergraduate, 34 graduate, 4 nonprofessional degree.

**Music Student Profile** 50% females, 50% males, 4% minorities, 1% international.

**Music Faculty** 61 undergraduate (full-time), 19 undergraduate (part-time). 15% of full-time faculty have terminal degrees. Graduate students do not teach undergraduate courses. Undergraduate student–faculty ratio: 7:1.

**Student Life** Student groups/activities include Music Educators National Conference, Phi Mu Alpha Sinfonia, Sigma Alpha Iota.

**Expenses for 2007–2008** Application fee: $40. State resident tuition: $4350 full-time. Nonresident tuition: $10,610 full-time. Mandatory fees: $1056 full-time. College room and board: $8420. College room only: $4920. Room and board charges vary according to board plan and housing facility. Special program-related fees: $30–$60 per year for community performance series fee, $150 per semester for instrument maintenance.

**Financial Aid** Program-specific awards: 100 endowed scholarships for program students ($851).

**Application Procedures** Students admitted directly into the professional program freshman year. Deadline for freshmen and transfers: March 1. Notification date for freshmen and transfers: April 1. Required: high school transcript, college transcript(s) for transfer students, letter of recommendation, audition, SAT or ACT test scores, 80% average out of 100% in high school, portfolio for composition majors only. Recommended: essay, interview. Auditions held 9 times on campus and off campus in Albany, NY; Rochester, NY; locations on Long Island; recorded music is permissible as a substitute for live auditions for out-of-state and international applicants and videotaped performances are permissible as a substitute for live auditions for out-of-state and international applicants.

**Web Site** http://www.potsdam.edu/crane/

**Undergraduate Contact** Thomas W. Nesbitt, Director, Admissions Office, State University of New York College at Potsdam, Potsdam, New York 13676; 315-267-2180.

**Graduate Contact** Dr. Glenn Guiles, Associate Dean, The Crane School of Music, State University of New York College at Potsdam, 44 Pierrepont Avenue, Potsdam, New York 13676; 315-267-2775, fax: 315-267-2413.

# Steinhardt School of Culture, Education, and Human Development, Department of Music and Performing Arts Professions

See New York University

# Stephen F. Austin State University

**Nacogdoches, Texas**

State-supported, coed. Small town campus. Total enrollment: 11,607. Music program established 1923.

**Degrees** Bachelor of Music in the areas of performance, composition, music education. Majors and concentrations: music education, music theory and composition, orchestral instruments, piano pedagogy, piano/organ, voice, wind and percussion instruments. Graduate degrees offered: Master of Arts in the areas of music education, music; Master of Music in the areas of performance, conducting, accompanying, opera. Program accredited by NASM.

**Enrollment** 336 total; 302 undergraduate, 34 graduate.

**Music Student Profile** 59% females, 41% males, 28% minorities, 2% international.

**Music Faculty** 29 total (full-time), 7 total (part-time). 75% of full-time faculty have terminal degrees. Graduate students teach a few undergraduate courses. Undergraduate student–faculty ratio: 11:1.

**Student Life** Student groups/activities include Texas Music Educators Association, National Association of Teachers of Singing, Music Teachers National Association.

*Stephen F. Austin State University (continued)*

**Expenses for 2007–2008** Application fee: $35. State resident tuition: $4410 full-time. Nonresident tuition: $12,750 full-time. Mandatory fees: $1752 full-time. Full-time tuition and fees vary according to course load. College room and board: $6885. Room and board charges vary according to board plan and housing facility. Special program-related fees: $15 per class for elementary music education fee, $15 per class for computer lab fee, $15 per class for ensemble materials fees, $15 for recital fee, $20 per credit hour for applied music lesson fee, $61 per credit hour for accompanist, keyboard maintenance.

**Financial Aid** Program-specific awards: 12 Young Artists Scholarship Awards for incoming freshmen ($5000–$12,000), 75 music activity scholarships for program students ($600–$8000).

**Application Procedures** Students admitted directly into the professional program freshman year. Deadline for freshmen and transfers: continuous. Notification date for freshmen and transfers: continuous. Required: high school transcript, college transcript(s) for transfer students, audition, SAT or ACT test scores (minimum combined SAT score of 850, minimum composite ACT score of 18), SAT or ACT (minimums vary according to high school rank). Auditions held as needed on campus; recorded music is permissible as a substitute for live auditions when distance is prohibitive and videotaped performances are permissible as a substitute for live auditions when distance is prohibitive.

**Web Site** http://www.music.sfasu.edu

**Contact** Dr. Ronald E. Anderson, Director, School of Music, Stephen F. Austin State University, Box 13043, SFA Station, Nacogdoches, Texas 75962; 936-468-4602, fax: 936-468-5810, e-mail address: randerson@sfasu.edu

## Stetson University
### DeLand, Florida

Independent, coed. Small town campus. Total enrollment: 3,721. Music program established 1883.

**Degrees** Bachelor of Music in the areas of performance, music theory and composition, elective studies in an outside field (business, other), music technology; Bachelor of Music Education in the areas of vocal music education, instrumental music education. Majors and concentrations: guitar, interdisciplinary studies, music, music education, music technology, music theory and composition, piano/organ, stringed instruments, voice, wind and percussion instruments. Program accredited by NASM.

**Enrollment** 200 total; all undergraduate.

**Music Student Profile** 55% females, 45% males, 12% minorities, 3% international.

**Music Faculty** 26 undergraduate (full-time), 20 undergraduate (part-time). 95% of full-time faculty have terminal degrees. Graduate students do not teach undergraduate courses. Undergraduate student–faculty ratio: 5:1.

**Student Life** Student groups/activities include Collegiate Music Educators National Conference, Phi Mu Alpha, Sigma Alpha Iota, American Choral Directors Association.

**Expenses for 2008–2009** Application fee: $40. Comprehensive fee: $38,652 includes full-time tuition ($28,456), mandatory fees ($1760), and college room and board ($8436). College room only: $4776. Special program-related fees: $25 per course for practice room fee.

**Financial Aid** Program-specific awards: 255 endowed music scholarships for program students ($5500), 250 merit awards for program students ($5000).

**Application Procedures** Students admitted directly into the professional program freshman year. Deadline for freshmen: March 15; transfers: March 1. Notification date for freshmen: April 1; transfers: continuous. Required: essay, high school transcript, college transcript(s) for transfer students, interview, audition, portfolio, SAT or ACT test scores, portfolio and interview for composition and music technology applicants. Recommended: minimum 3.0 high school GPA. Auditions held 4 times and scheduled as needed on campus and off campus in various locations; recorded music is permissible as a substitute for live auditions if a campus visit is impossible; video performance audition may be permitted and videotaped performances are permissible as a substitute for live auditions if a campus visit is impossible. Portfolio reviews held as needed on campus; the submission of slides may be substituted for portfolios if campus visit is impossible then electronic transmission by arrangement with professor.

**Web Site** http://www.stetson.edu

**Undergraduate Contact** Tammy Shistle, Music Admissions Counselor, School of Music, Stetson University, 421 North Woodland Boulevard, Unit 8399, DeLand, Florida 32720; 386-822-8975, fax: 386-822-8948.

## Susquehanna University
### Selinsgrove, Pennsylvania

Independent, coed. Suburban campus. Total enrollment: 2,039. Music program established 1899.

**Degrees** Bachelor of Music in the areas of performance, music education. Majors and concentrations: brass, music education, performance, piano/organ, stringed instruments, voice, wind and percussion instruments. Program accredited by NASM.

**Enrollment** 98 total; 74 undergraduate, 24 nonprofessional degree.

**Music Student Profile** 61% females, 39% males, 1% minorities.

**Music Faculty** 11 undergraduate (full-time), 18 undergraduate (part-time). 90% of full-time faculty have terminal degrees. Graduate students do not teach undergraduate courses. Undergraduate student–faculty ratio: 10:1.

**Student Life** Student groups/activities include Music Educators National Conference Student Chapter, Phi Mu Alpha Sinfonia, Sigma Alpha Iota.

**Expenses for 2008–2009** Application fee: $35. Comprehensive fee: $39,480 includes full-time tuition ($30,700), mandatory fees ($380), and college room and board ($8400). College room only: $4400.

**Financial Aid** Program-specific awards: 1 Isaacs Scholarship for program majors ($10,000), music scholarships for program majors ($2000–$5000), performance grants for program majors and non-majors ($1000–$1500).

**Application Procedures** Students admitted directly into the professional program freshman year. Deadline for freshmen: March 1; transfers: continuous. Notification date for freshmen: continuous. Required: essay, high school transcript, college transcript(s) for transfer students, 2 letters of recommendation, audition. Recommended: interview, SAT or ACT test scores. Auditions held 5 times on campus; recorded music is permissible as a substitute for live auditions in special circumstances and videotaped performances are permissible as a substitute for live auditions in special circumstances.

**Web Site** http://www.susqu.edu/music/

**Undergraduate Contact** Ms. Lois Purcell, Music Admissions Coordinator, Department of Music, Susquehanna University, 514 University Avenue, Selinsgrove, Pennsylvania 17870; 570-372-4309, fax: 570-372-2789, e-mail address: musicdept@susqu.edu

## The Swinney Conservatory of Music
See Central Methodist University

## Sybil B. Harrington College of Fine Arts and Humanities
See West Texas A&M University

*Setnor School of Music*
## Syracuse University
### Syracuse, New York

Independent, coed. Urban campus. Total enrollment: 17,677. Music program established 1877.

**Degrees** Bachelor of Arts in the area of music; Bachelor of Music in the areas of music composition, music education, music industry, performance; Bachelor of Science in the area of recording and allied entertainment industries. Majors and concentrations: composition, music, music business, music education, performance. Graduate degrees offered: Master of Music in the areas of music composition, music education, organ, percussion, piano, strings, voice, wind instruments. Program accredited by NASM.

**Enrollment** 222 total; 198 undergraduate, 24 graduate.

**Music Student Profile** 68% females, 32% males, 6% minorities.

**Music Faculty** 19 total (full-time), 51 total (part-time). 92% of full-time faculty have terminal degrees. Graduate students teach a few undergraduate courses. Undergraduate student–faculty ratio: 9:1.

**Student Life** Student groups/activities include Sigma Alpha Iota, Music Educators National Conference, Pi Kappa Lambda.

**Expenses for 2007–2008** Application fee: $70. Comprehensive fee: $42,626 includes full-time tuition ($30,470), mandatory fees ($1216), and college room and board ($10,940). College room only: $5660. Room and board charges vary according to board plan and housing facility. Special program-related fees: $800 per semester for private lessons in program requirement, practice room fees, lab fees.

**Financial Aid** Program-specific awards: 36 Special Music Awards for talented program majors ($18,000).

**Application Procedures** Students admitted directly into the professional program freshman year. Deadline for freshmen and transfers: January 1. Notification date for freshmen: March 1; transfers: August 15. Required: essay, high school transcript, college transcript(s) for transfer students, minimum 3.0 high school GPA, 2 letters of recommendation, SAT or ACT test scores, high school counselor evaluation, audition for BA and BM degree programs. Recommended: interview. Auditions held 10 times on campus and off campus in New York, NY; videotaped performances are permissible as a substitute for live auditions if a live audition is impossible.

**Web Site** http://vpa.syr.edu/

**Undergraduate Contact** Director, CVPA Recruitment and Admissions, College of Visual and Performing Arts, Syracuse University, 202P Crouse College, Syracuse, New York 13244-1010; 315-443-2769, fax: 315-443-1935, e-mail address: admissu@syr.edu

**Graduate Contact** Graduate School, Syracuse University, Suite 303 Bowne Hall, Syracuse, New York 13244; 315-443-3028, fax: 315-443-3423, e-mail address: gradschl@syr.edu

# Taylor University
## Upland, Indiana

Independent interdenominational, coed. Rural campus. Total enrollment: 1,879. Music program established 1970.

**Degrees** Bachelor of Arts in the area of music; Bachelor of Music in the areas of performance, composition; Bachelor of Music Education in the area of music education; Bachelor of Science in the areas of music/management, music/marketing, music/theatre arts. Majors and concentrations: composition, guitar, music education, piano/organ, stringed instruments, theater arts studies, voice, wind and percussion instruments. Cross-registration with Taylor University-Fort Wayne Campus. Program accredited by NASM.

**Enrollment** 65 total; 45 undergraduate, 20 nonprofessional degree.

**Music Student Profile** 52% females, 48% males, 5% minorities, 5% international.

**Music Faculty** 8 undergraduate (full-time), 20 undergraduate (part-time). 100% of full-time faculty have terminal degrees. Graduate students do not teach undergraduate courses. Undergraduate student–faculty ratio: 15:1.

**Student Life** Student groups/activities include Music Educators National Conference, National Association of Schools of Singing, Marion Philharmonic Orchestra.

**Expenses for 2008–2009** Application fee: $25. Comprehensive fee: $30,898 includes full-time tuition ($24,314), mandatory fees ($232), and college room and board ($6352). College room only: $3144. Special program-related fees: $196 per semester for applied lesson fee.

**Financial Aid** Program-specific awards: 20 music scholarships for music majors ($3000–$7000), 20 music merit awards for music majors ($1500–$3000), 20 applied music awards for music majors ($1000–$1500).

**Application Procedures** Students admitted directly into the professional program freshman year. Deadline for freshmen and transfers: February 1. Notification date for freshmen and transfers: continuous. Required: essay, high school transcript, college transcript(s) for transfer students, minimum 3.0 high school GPA, 3 letters of recommendation, interview, audition, SAT or ACT test scores. Auditions held 4 times on campus; recorded music is permissible as a substitute for live auditions when distance is prohibitive and videotaped performances are permissible as a substitute for live auditions when distance is prohibitive.

**Web Site** http://www.tayloru.edu

**Undergraduate Contact** Mr. Steve Mortland, Admissions Department, Taylor University, 236 West Reade Avenue, Upland, Indiana 46989; 317-998-5206, e-mail address: stmortlan@tayloru.edu

## *Boyer College of Music and Dance*
# Temple University
## Philadelphia, Pennsylvania

State-related, coed. Urban campus. Total enrollment: 34,696. Music program established 1962.

**Degrees** Bachelor of Music in the areas of composition, jazz arranging and composition, jazz performance (instrumental and vocal), music education, music history, music theory, music therapy, piano pedagogy, performance (instrumental, piano, harpsichord, voice); Bachelor of Science in the area of music. Majors and concentrations: composition, harpsichord, instrumental performance, jazz composition, jazz performance, music education, music history, music theory, music therapy, piano, piano pedagogy, voice performance. Graduate degrees offered: Master of Music in the areas of choral conducting, composition, music education, music history, opera, orchestral performance, piano accompanying and chamber music, piano accompanying and opera coaching, piano pedagogy, piano performance, string pedagogy, harpsichord performance; Master of Music Therapy. Doctor of Musical Arts in the areas of composition, performance (instrumental, piano, voice); Doctor of Philosophy in the areas of music education, music therapy. Program accredited by NASM.

**Enrollment** 578 total; 353 undergraduate, 201 graduate, 24 nonprofessional degree.

**Music Student Profile** 55% females, 45% males, 29% minorities, 11% international.

**Music Faculty** 47 total (full-time), 150 total (part-time). 95% of full-time faculty have terminal degrees. Graduate students teach a few undergraduate courses. Undergraduate student–faculty ratio: 10:1.

**Student Life** Student groups/activities include music, band, and honor societies, Music Educators National Conference Student Chapter. Special housing available for music students.

**Expenses for 2007–2008** Application fee: $50. State resident tuition: $10,252 full-time. Nonresident tuition: $18,770 full-time. Mandatory fees: $550 full-time. Full-time tuition and fees vary according to course load, program, and reciprocity agreements. College room and board: $8518. College room only: $5604. Room and board charges vary according to board plan and housing facility. Special program-related fees: $8–$30 per course for lab fees, $150 per course for private lesson fee.

**Financial Aid** Program-specific awards: music awards for those demonstrating musical merit ($500–$12,000), academic grants for those demonstrating high academic merit ($1000–$8000).

**Application Procedures** Students admitted directly into the professional program freshman year. Deadline for freshmen and transfers: March 1. Notification date for freshmen and transfers: September 1. Required: essay, high school transcript, college transcript(s) for transfer students, audition, SAT or ACT test scores, portfolio for composition and jazz arranging/composition applicants, interview for music theory applicants, minimum 2.75 high school GPA, minimum 3.0 high school GPA for music therapy and music education applicants. Recommended: minimum 3.0 high school GPA, 2 letters of recommendation, interview. Auditions held 6 times on campus and off campus in Atlanta, GA; Interlochen, MI; recorded music is permissible as a substitute for live auditions when distance is

*Temple University (continued)*

prohibitive and videotaped performances are permissible as a substitute for live auditions when distance is prohibitive. Portfolio reviews held continuously on campus.
**Web Site** http://www.temple.edu/boyer
**Contact** Kristi Johnston, Associate Director of Recruitment and Financial Aid, Boyer College of Music and Dance, Temple University, 2001 North 13th Street, Philadelphia, Pennsylvania 19122; 215-204-6810, fax: 215-204-4957, e-mail address: kristi. johnston@temple.edu

# Tennessee Technological University
## Cookeville, Tennessee

State-supported, coed. Small town campus. Total enrollment: 10,321. Music program established 1948.
**Web Site** http://www.tntech.edu/

# Tennessee Wesleyan College
## Athens, Tennessee

Independent United Methodist, coed. Small town campus. Total enrollment: 861. Music program established 1955.
**Degrees** Bachelor of Music Education in the areas of teaching, church music. Majors and concentrations: church music, music education.
**Enrollment** 10 total; 6 undergraduate, 4 nonprofessional degree.
**Music Student Profile** 70% females, 30% males, 10% international.
**Music Faculty** 2 undergraduate (full-time), 2 undergraduate (part-time). 50% of full-time faculty have terminal degrees. Graduate students do not teach undergraduate courses. Undergraduate student–faculty ratio: 3:1.
**Student Life** Student groups/activities include Music Educators National Conference, Alpha Psi Omega.
**Expenses for 2008–2009** Application fee: $25. Comprehensive fee: $22,880 includes full-time tuition ($16,500), mandatory fees ($550), and college room and board ($5830).
**Financial Aid** Program-specific awards: 20 scholarships for choir participants ($1000–$6000).
**Application Procedures** Students admitted directly into the professional program freshman year. Deadline for freshmen and transfers: continuous. Required: high school transcript, college transcript(s) for transfer students, minimum 2.0 high school GPA, letter of recommendation, SAT or ACT test scores (minimum composite ACT score of 19), audition for scholarship consideration. Recommended: audition. Auditions held by appointment on campus; recorded music is permissible as a substitute for live auditions when distance is prohibitive and videotaped performances are permissible as a substitute for live auditions when distance is prohibitive.
**Web Site** http://www.twcnet.edu
**Undergraduate Contact** Dr. Janice Ryberg, Chair, Fine Arts Department, Tennessee Wesleyan College, PO Box 40, Athens, Tennessee 37371; 423-746-5229, fax: 423-744-9968, e-mail address: jlryberg@twcnet.edu

# Texas A&M University–Commerce
## Commerce, Texas

State-supported, coed. Small town campus. Total enrollment: 8,882. Music program established 1917.
**Web Site** http://www.tamu-commerce.edu/

# Texas A&M University–Corpus Christi
## Corpus Christi, Texas

State-supported, coed. Suburban campus. Total enrollment: 8,585 (2007). Music program established 1972.
**Web Site** http://www.tamucc.edu/

# Texas A&M University–Kingsville
## Kingsville, Texas

State-supported, coed. Small town campus. Music program established 1930.
**Degrees** Bachelor of Music in the areas of music education, performance. Majors and concentrations: music education, performance. Graduate degrees offered: Master of Music in the area of music education. Program accredited by NASM.
**Enrollment** 222 total; 202 undergraduate, 20 graduate.
**Music Student Profile** 30% females, 70% males, 90% minorities.
**Music Faculty** 16 total (full-time), 7 total (part-time). 70% of full-time faculty have terminal degrees. Graduate students do not teach undergraduate courses. Undergraduate student–faculty ratio: 12:1.
**Student Life** Student groups/activities include Sigma Alpha Iota, Tau Beta Sigma, Kappa Kappa Psi, Phi Mu Alpha.
**Expenses for 2007–2008** Application fee: $15. State resident tuition: $4386 full-time. Nonresident tuition: $11,058 full-time. Full-time tuition varies according to course load. Special program-related fees: $5 per course for lab fees, $50 per credit hour for applied music.
**Financial Aid** Program-specific awards: 75 departmental awards for music majors ($200–$600), 30 All-State Honor Dormitory Scholarships for music majors ($2800).
**Application Procedures** Students admitted directly into the professional program freshman year. Deadline for freshmen and transfers: continuous. Required: high school transcript, college transcript(s) for transfer students, 3 letters of recommendation, audition, SAT or ACT test scores (minimum composite ACT score of 21), completion of college preparatory courses, Texas Academic Skills Program test. Recommended: minimum 3.0 high school GPA. Auditions held 3 times on campus; recorded music is permissible as a substitute for live auditions when distance is prohibitive and videotaped performances are permissible as a substitute for live auditions when distance is prohibitive.
**Web Site** http://www.tamuk.edu/music
**Undergraduate Contact** Dr. Paul Hageman, Chair, Department of Music, Texas A&M University–Kingsville, Box 174, Kingsville, Texas 78363; 361-593-2806, fax: 361-593-2816, e-mail address: paul.hageman@tamuk.edu
**Graduate Contact** Dr. Nancy King Sanders, Graduate Coordinator, Department of Music, Texas A&M University–Kingsville, Box 174, Kingsville, Texas 78363; 361-593-2157, fax: 361-593-2816.

# Texas Christian University
## Fort Worth, Texas

Independent, coed. Suburban campus. Total enrollment: 8,668. Music program established 1873.
**Degrees** Bachelor of Music in the areas of performance, piano pedagogy, music theory-composition, church music; Bachelor of Music Education in the areas of vocal music education, instrumental music education. Majors and concentrations: church music, guitar, music, music education, music theory and composition, piano pedagogy, piano/organ, stringed instruments, voice, wind and percussion instruments. Graduate degrees offered: Master of Music in the areas of performance, pedagogy, musicology, music theory/composition/computer music; Master of Music Education. Program accredited by NASM.
**Enrollment** 243 total; 190 undergraduate, 44 graduate, 9 nonprofessional degree.
**Music Student Profile** 59% females, 41% males, 12% minorities, 20% international.
**Music Faculty** 35 total (full-time), 28 total (part-time). 85% of full-time faculty have terminal degrees. Graduate students do not teach undergraduate courses. Undergraduate student–faculty ratio: 8:1.
**Student Life** Student groups/activities include professional music societies, American String Teachers Association, Music Educators Organization.
**Expenses for 2007–2008** Application fee: $40. Comprehensive fee: $33,068 includes full-time tuition ($24,820), mandatory fees ($48), and college room and board ($8200). College room only: $5000. Room and board charges vary according to board plan

and housing facility. Special program-related fees: $50 per semester for applied lessons, $50–$100 per semester for organ practice fees/piano practice fees.
**Financial Aid** Program-specific awards: choral scholarships for vocalists ($800–$23,000), orchestra scholarships for string players ($800–$23,000), band scholarships for band instrumentalists ($800–$23,000), Music Department Scholarships for program majors ($800–$23,000).
**Application Procedures** Students apply for admission into the professional program by freshman year. Deadline for freshmen: February 15; transfers: August 1. Notification date for freshmen: March 15; transfers: August 15. Required: essay, high school transcript, college transcript(s) for transfer students, 2 letters of recommendation, audition, SAT or ACT test scores, portfolio for theory/composition majors. Recommended: minimum 3.0 high school GPA, interview. Auditions held continuously by appointment on campus and off campus in various locations; recorded music is permissible as a substitute for live auditions when distance is prohibitive and videotaped performances are permissible as a substitute for live auditions when distance is prohibitive. Portfolio reviews held by appointment on campus.
**Web Site** http://www.music.tcu.edu
**Undergraduate Contact** Paul Cortese, Assistant Director, School of Music, Texas Christian University, TCU Box 297500, Fort Worth, Texas 76129; 817-257-6606, fax: 817-257-5818, e-mail address: p.cortese@tcu.edu
**Graduate Contact** Dr. Joseph Butler, Director of Graduate Studies, College of Fine Arts, Texas Christian University, TCU Box 298000, Fort Worth, Texas 76129; 817-257-7098, fax: 817-257-7703, e-mail address: h.j.butler@tcu.edu

## Texas State University–San Marcos
**San Marcos, Texas**

State-supported, coed. Suburban campus. Total enrollment: 28,121. Music program established 1903.
**Web Site** http://www.txstate.edu/

## Texas Tech University
**Lubbock, Texas**

State-supported, coed. Urban campus. Total enrollment: 28,257. Music program established 1923.
**Web Site** http://www.ttu.edu/

## Tisch School of the Arts, Clive Davis Department of Recorded Music
See New York University

## Towson University
**Towson, Maryland**

State-supported, coed. Suburban campus. Total enrollment: 19,758. Music program established 1966.
**Web Site** http://www.towson.edu/

## Trinity University
**San Antonio, Texas**

Independent, coed. Urban campus. Total enrollment: 2,679. Music program established 1975.
**Web Site** http://www.trinity.edu/

### John M. Long School of Music
## Troy University
**Troy, Alabama**

State-supported, coed. Small town campus. Total enrollment: 28,953. Music program established 1965.
**Web Site** http://www.troy.edu/

## Truman State University
**Kirksville, Missouri**

State-supported, coed. Small town campus. Total enrollment: 5,866. Music program established 1940.
**Degrees** Bachelor of Music in the area of performance. Majors and concentrations: brass, composition, piano, stringed instruments, voice, wind and percussion instruments. Graduate degrees offered: Master of Arts in the areas of performance, conducting, composition, research; Master of Art Education. Program accredited by NASM.
**Enrollment** 190 total; 65 undergraduate, 16 graduate, 109 nonprofessional degree.
**Music Student Profile** 51% females, 49% males, 1% minorities, 1% international.
**Music Faculty** 21 total (full-time), 4 total (part-time). 95% of full-time faculty have terminal degrees. Graduate students do not teach undergraduate courses. Undergraduate student–faculty ratio: 10:1.
**Student Life** Student groups/activities include Phi Mu Alpha, Sigma Alpha Iota, Collegiate Music Educators National Conference.
**Expenses for 2007–2008** Application fee: $0. One-time mandatory fee: $250. State resident tuition: $6210 full-time. Nonresident tuition: $10,820 full-time. Mandatory fees: $222 full-time. College room and board: $5815. Room and board charges vary according to housing facility. Special program-related fees: $60–$110 per semester for private lessons.
**Financial Aid** Program-specific awards: 21 endowed scholarships for program majors ($300–$1500), 100 service scholarships for program majors and non-majors ($300–$1500).
**Application Procedures** Students admitted directly into the professional program freshman year. Deadline for freshmen and transfers: May 1. Notification date for freshmen: December 5. Required: essay, high school transcript, college transcript(s) for transfer students, audition, SAT or ACT test scores. Recommended: portfolio. Auditions held continuously on campus and off campus in Kansas City, MO; St. Louis, MO; Chicago, IL; Des Moines, IA; recorded music is permissible as a substitute for live auditions with approval from the department and videotaped performances are permissible as a substitute for live auditions with approval from the department.
**Web Site** http://www.truman.edu
**Undergraduate Contact** Mr. Dan Peterson, Director of Bands, Music, Truman State University, 100 East Normal, Ophelia Parrish 1101, Kirksville, Missouri 63501; 660-785-4417, fax: 660-785-7463, e-mail address: pete@truman.edu
**Graduate Contact** Dr. Warren Gooch, Professor of Music, Music, Truman State University, 100 East Normal, Ophelia Parrish 1101, Kirksville, Missouri 63501; 660-785-4417, fax: 660-785-7463, e-mail address: wgooch@truman.edu

## Union University
**Jackson, Tennessee**

Independent Southern Baptist, coed. Small town campus. Total enrollment: 3,229. Music program established 1920.
**Web Site** http://www.uu.edu/

## University at Buffalo, the State University of New York
**Buffalo, New York**

State-supported, coed. Total enrollment: 28,054. Music program established 1958.
**Degrees** Bachelor of Arts in the area of music. Majors and concentrations: brass, classical guitar, double bass, electric bass, harpsichord, piano/organ, stringed instruments, voice, wind and percussion instruments. Graduate degrees offered: Master of Arts in the areas of music history, music theory, composition; Master of Music in the area of music performance. Doctor of Philosophy in the areas of historical musicology and music theory, composition.

*University at Buffalo, the State University of New York (continued)*

**Enrollment** 122 total; 50 undergraduate, 72 graduate.
**Music Student Profile** 45% females, 55% males, 1% minorities, 40% international.
**Music Faculty** 7 undergraduate (full-time), 17 undergraduate (part-time), 10 graduate (full-time). 65% of full-time faculty have terminal degrees. Graduate students teach a few undergraduate courses. Undergraduate student–faculty ratio: 3:1.
**Student Life** Student groups/activities include concert band, UB Symphony Orchestra, university chorus and choir.
**Expenses for 2007–2008** Application fee: $40. State resident tuition: $4350 full-time. Nonresident tuition: $10,610 full-time. Mandatory fees: $1867 full-time. College room and board: $8620. College room only: $5360. Room and board charges vary according to board plan and housing facility. Special program-related fees: $75 per semester for computer music lab.
**Financial Aid** Program-specific awards: 9 departmental scholarships for program majors ($200–$2500), 4 Garahee Awards for program majors ($400), 3 D. Bernard and Jill L. Simon Awards for program majors ($750), 2–3 Performing Arts Honors Awards for program majors ($2500), 2 Talentships (Honors) for program majors ($2500).
**Application Procedures** Students apply for admission into the professional program by sophomore year. Deadline for freshmen and transfers: continuous. Required: essay, high school transcript, college transcript(s) for transfer students, minimum 2.0 high school GPA, 2 letters of recommendation, audition, SAT or ACT test scores, minimum TOEFL score of 550 (paper-based) or 213 (computer-based) for international students. Recommended: minimum 3.0 high school GPA. Auditions held 3 times on campus and off campus in New York, NY; recorded music is permissible as a substitute for live auditions if scheduling is difficult and videotaped performances are permissible as a substitute for live auditions if scheduling is impossible.
**Web Site** http://www.music.buffalo.edu/
**Contact** Student Programs ATC, Department of Music, University at Buffalo, the State University of New York, 226 Baird Hall, Buffalo, New York 14260; 716-645-2758 ext. 1248, fax: 716-645-3824, e-mail address: mus-info@buffalo.edu

# The University of Alabama
## Tuscaloosa, Alabama

State-supported, coed. Suburban campus. Total enrollment: 25,544. Music program established 1905.
**Web Site** http://www.ua.edu/

# University of Alaska Anchorage
## Anchorage, Alaska

State-supported, coed. Urban campus. Total enrollment: 17,023 (2007).
**Degrees** Bachelor of Music in the areas of performance, music education. Majors and concentrations: classical music, music, music education, piano/organ, stringed instruments, voice, wind and percussion instruments. Program accredited by NASM.
**Enrollment** 78 total; 58 undergraduate, 20 nonprofessional degree.
**Music Student Profile** 60% females, 40% males, 10% minorities, 25% international.
**Music Faculty** 8 undergraduate (full-time), 20 undergraduate (part-time). 65% of full-time faculty have terminal degrees. Graduate students do not teach undergraduate courses. Undergraduate student–faculty ratio: 3:1.
**Student Life** Student groups/activities include Music Educators National Conference Student Chapter.
**Expenses for 2007–2008** Application fee: $40. State resident tuition: $3840 full-time. Nonresident tuition: $12,810 full-time. Mandatory fees: $560 full-time. Full-time tuition and fees vary according to course level. College room and board: $8230. College room only: $4630. Room and board charges vary according to board plan and housing facility.

**Financial Aid** Program-specific awards: 1 music scholarship for incoming students ($2400).
**Application Procedures** Students admitted directly into the professional program freshman year. Deadline for freshmen and transfers: July 1. Required: high school transcript, college transcript(s) for transfer students. Recommended: minimum 2.0 high school GPA.
**Web Site** http://www.uaa.alaska.edu/music
**Undergraduate Contact** Deborah Ginsburg, Student Success Coordinator, College of Arts and Sciences, University of Alaska Anchorage, 3211 Providence Drive, Anchorage, Alaska 99508; 907-786-1357, fax: 907-786-4630, e-mail address: andmg@uaa.alaska.edu

# University of Alaska Fairbanks
## Fairbanks, Alaska

State-supported, coed. Small town campus. Total enrollment: 8,627.
**Degrees** Bachelor of Music in the areas of performance, secondary music education, elementary music education. Majors and concentrations: classical music, jazz, music education, piano/organ, stringed instruments, voice, wind and percussion instruments. Program accredited by NASM.
**Enrollment** 84 total; 35 undergraduate, 49 nonprofessional degree.
**Music Student Profile** 50% females, 50% males, 1% minorities, 1% international.
**Music Faculty** 9 total (full-time), 14 total (part-time). 67% of full-time faculty have terminal degrees. Graduate students teach a few undergraduate courses.
**Expenses for 2008–2009** Application fee: $40. State resident tuition: $4020 full-time. Nonresident tuition: $13,440 full-time. Mandatory fees: $736 full-time. College room and board: $6030. College room only: $3440. Special program-related fees: $5 per semester for locker rental, $40 per semester for instrument rental fee, $150 per semester for private lessons.
**Financial Aid** Program-specific awards: 1–4 Friends of Music Awards for program majors ($500), 1–2 Glenmede Awards for string players ($500), 1–2 Fejes Music Scholarships for program majors ($500), 3–6 Fairbanks Symphony Scholarships for program majors ($500–$1000), 1 Anderson/DeRamus Scholarship for African-American program majors ($700), 1 Pearl Berry-Boyd Scholarship for program majors ($500).
**Application Procedures** Students apply for admission into the professional program by freshman year. Deadline for freshmen and transfers: August 2. Required: high school transcript, college transcript(s) for transfer students, 3 letters of recommendation, SAT or ACT test scores, audition for entry into BM program. Recommended: audition. Auditions held in December and May on campus; recorded music is permissible as a substitute for live auditions with later audition on campus and videotaped performances are permissible as a substitute for live auditions with later audition on campus.
**Web Site** http://www.uaf.edu
**Undergraduate Contact** Admissions and Records, University of Alaska Fairbanks, Signers' Hall, Suite 102, Fairbanks, Alaska 99775-0060; 907-474-7521, fax: 907-474-5379, e-mail address: admissions@uaf.edu

# University of Alberta
## Edmonton, Alberta, Canada

Province-supported, coed. Urban campus. Total enrollment: 36,562 (2007). Music program established 1947.
**Degrees** Bachelor of Music in the areas of school music, performance, music theory and composition, music history and literature, world music; Bachelor of Music/Bachelor of Education in the areas of secondary music education, elementary music education. Majors and concentrations: classical music, composition, guitar, harp, music education, music history and literature, music theory and composition, piano/organ, stringed instruments, voice, wind and percussion instruments, world music. Graduate degrees offered: Master of Arts in the areas of music (ethnomusicology, musicology, theory); Master of Music in the

areas of applied music, composition, choral conducting. Doctor of Music in the areas of keyboard performance, choral conducting, composition; Doctor of Philosophy in the areas of music, ethnomusicology, musicology, theory. Cross-registration with Grant MacEwan Community College. Program accredited by CUMS.
**Enrollment** 392 total; 135 undergraduate, 57 graduate, 200 nonprofessional degree.
**Music Student Profile** 60% females, 40% males, 10% minorities, 6% international.
**Music Faculty** 21 total (full-time), 54 total (part-time). 90% of full-time faculty have terminal degrees. Graduate students teach a few undergraduate courses. Undergraduate student–faculty ratio: 10:1.
**Expenses for 2007–2008** Special program-related fees: $30 per year for lockers and keys.
**Financial Aid** Program-specific awards: 2 Hrapko Family Scholarships in Music for academically and artistically talented students ($1000), 1 Alberta Baroque Music Society Scholarship for academically and artistically talented students ($1250), 10–35 Beryl Barns Memorial Awards for academically and artistically talented students ($500–$2000), 2 Richard Eaton Scholarships in Music and Voice for academically and artistically talented students ($2000–$4000), 1 Abigal Edith Condell Memorial Scholarship in Music for academically and artistically talented students ($1500), 1 Edmonton Musical Club Scholarship in Music for academically and artistically talented students ($1500), 2 FM105 Easy Rock Prizes for academically and artistically talented students ($1250), 1 John Newman Memorial Scholarship for Performance of Contemporary Music for academically and artistically talented students ($1250), 12 Peace River Pioneer Memorial Scholarships in Music for academically and artistically talented students ($750–$1500), 1 Mary Stinson Prize in Piano Accompaniment for academically and artistically talented students ($1250), 4–5 Universiade '83 Scholarships for academically and artistically talented students ($2000), 1 Margo Fraser Memorial Scholarship for academically and artistically talented students ($2500), 1 Edmonton Composer's Concert Society Scholarship for academically and artistically talented students ($500), 1 Edmonton Opera Guild Award for academically and artistically talented students ($2000), 1 Edna and John Bullock Memorial Scholarship for academically and artistically talented students ($1000), 1 Ernesto B. Lejano Scholarship in Piano Performance for academically and artistically talented students ($1250), 1 Lois Field Scholarship in Music Education for academically and artistically talented students ($500), 1 Luc Barton Memorial Scholarship in Music for academically and artistically talented students ($1000), 1 Frantisek Cikaneck Memorial Award for academically and artistically talented students ($600), 1 Ernest Dalwood Clarinet Prize for academically and artistically talented students ($1000), Harry Farmer Scholarship in Organ Performance for academically and artistically talented students, 1 Charles Gale Memorial Scholarship in Music ($750), 1 Margarita Heron Pine Lake String Prize for academically and artistically talented students ($250), 1 Marek Jablonski Prize for academically and artistically talented students ($500), 1 Marion Wray Lauder Memorial Scholarship for academically and artistically talented students ($500), 1 Leeder Memorial Scholarship in Voice for academically and artistically talented students ($1000), Carol Mallett Scholarship for academically and artistically talented students ($3500), 1 St. David's Welsh Society Award in Choral Music ($1000), 1 Lloyd Thomas Award ($2000), 1 Varagur Vaikunta and Sarada Srinivasan Memorial Scholarship in Ethromusicology ($500), 2 Vienna Opera Ball Society Scholarship ($1250), 1 Wiebe Johnson Scholarship in Voice ($1000).
**Application Procedures** Students admitted directly into the professional program freshman year. Deadline for freshmen and transfers: May 1. Notification date for freshmen and transfers: June 15. Required: high school transcript, college transcript(s) for transfer students, minimum 2.0 high school GPA, audition, music rudiments exam, aural skills exam, portfolio for composition applicants. Recommended: minimum 3.0 high school GPA, interview. Auditions held twice on campus; recorded music is permissible as a substitute for live auditions when distance is prohibitive and videotaped performances are permissible as a

substitute for live auditions when distance is prohibitive. Portfolio reviews held continuously on campus.
**Web Site** http://www.ualberta.ca/music
**Undergraduate Contact** Ms. Jill Younghusband, Executive Assistant, Department of Music, University of Alberta, FAB 3-82, Edmonton, Alberta T6G 2C9, Canada; 780-492-0602, fax: 780-492-9246, e-mail address: jilly@ualberta.ca
**Graduate Contact** Donna Maskell, Graduate Programs Administrator, Department of Music, University of Alberta, FAB 3-82, Edmonton, Alberta T6G 2C9, Canada; 780-492-0603, fax: 780-492-9246, e-mail address: dmaskell@ualberta.ca

## *J. William Fulbright College of Arts and Sciences*
# University of Arkansas
### Fayetteville, Arkansas

State-supported, coed. Suburban campus. Total enrollment: 18,648. Music program established 1952.
**Degrees** Bachelor of Music in the areas of performance, music education, composition, music theory. Majors and concentrations: composition, guitar, music business, music education, music theory, piano/organ, stringed instruments, voice, wind and percussion instruments. Graduate degrees offered: Master of Music in the areas of performance, music education, composition, music history, music theory, conducting. Program accredited by NASM.
**Enrollment** 380 total; 300 undergraduate, 30 graduate, 50 nonprofessional degree.
**Music Student Profile** 48% females, 52% males, 16% minorities, 5% international.
**Music Faculty** 29 undergraduate (full-time), 29 graduate (full-time), 10 total (part-time). 95% of full-time faculty have terminal degrees. Graduate students teach a few undergraduate courses. Undergraduate student–faculty ratio: 9:1.
**Student Life** Student groups/activities include drama department productions, North Arkansas Symphony Orchestra, North Arkansas Symphony Chorus.
**Expenses for 2007–2008** Application fee: $40. State resident tuition: $4772 full-time. Nonresident tuition: $13,226 full-time. Mandatory fees: $1266 full-time. Full-time tuition and fees vary according to program. College room and board: $7017. College room only: $4387. Room and board charges vary according to board plan and housing facility.
**Financial Aid** Program-specific awards: 102 music scholarships for music major and non-major ensemble members ($1200–$4200), 215 band scholarships for music major and non-major ensemble members ($1200–$3500), 25 Inspirational Singers Awards for gospel choir members ($1200–$2500).
**Application Procedures** Students apply for admission into the professional program by sophomore year. Deadline for freshmen and transfers: May 1. Required: essay, high school transcript, minimum 3.0 high school GPA, audition, SAT or ACT test scores. Auditions held by appointment on campus; recorded music is permissible as a substitute for live auditions when distance is prohibitive and videotaped performances are permissible as a substitute for live auditions when distance is prohibitive.
**Web Site** http://www.uark.edu/depts/uamusic
**Contact** Dr. Ronda Mains, Associate Chair, Department of Music, University of Arkansas, 201 Music Building, Fayetteville, Arkansas 72701; 479-575-4701, fax: 479-575-5409, e-mail address: rmains@uark.edu

# University of Arkansas at Monticello
### Monticello, Arkansas

State-supported, coed. Small town campus. Total enrollment: 3,187. Music program established 1935.
**Web Site** http://www.uamont.edu/

# University of Bridgeport
### Bridgeport, Connecticut

Independent, coed. Urban campus. Total enrollment: 4,752.

*University of Bridgeport (continued)*

**Degrees** Bachelor of Music. Majors and concentrations: jazz studies, music education, performance.
**Enrollment** 32 total; all undergraduate.
**Music Student Profile** 34% females, 66% males, 50% minorities, 13% international.
**Music Faculty** 2 undergraduate (full-time), 9 undergraduate (part-time). 100% of full-time faculty have terminal degrees. Graduate students do not teach undergraduate courses. Undergraduate student–faculty ratio: 8:1.
**Expenses for 2007–2008** Application fee: $25. Comprehensive fee: $32,860 includes full-time tuition ($21,150), mandatory fees ($1710), and college room and board ($10,000). College room only: $5200. Full-time tuition and fees vary according to program. Room and board charges vary according to board plan and student level. Special program-related fees: $425 per credit hour for private lessons.
**Financial Aid** Program-specific awards: 5–20 Music Department Scholarships for music majors ($3500–$19,310).
**Application Procedures** Students admitted directly into the professional program freshman year. Deadline for freshmen and transfers: continuous. Required: essay, high school transcript, college transcript(s) for transfer students, audition, SAT or ACT test scores. Recommended: minimum 2.0 high school GPA, 2 letters of recommendation, interview. Auditions held as needed on campus; recorded music is permissible as a substitute for live auditions when distance is prohibitive and videotaped performances are permissible as a substitute for live auditions when distance is prohibitive.
**Web Site** http://www.bridgeport.edu
**Undergraduate Contact** Ms. Audrey A. Ashton Savage, Vice President Enrollment Management, University of Bridgeport, 126 Park Avenue, Wahlstrom Library, Bridgeport, Connecticut 06604; 800-EXCEL-UB, fax: 203-576-4941, e-mail address: admit@bridgeport.edu

# The University of British Columbia
### Vancouver, British Columbia, Canada

Province-supported, coed. Urban campus. Total enrollment: 43,720. Music program established 1959.
**Degrees** Bachelor of Music in the areas of composition, general studies, elementary education stream, secondary education stream, guitar, music scholarship, opera, orchestral instruments, organ, piano, voice. Majors and concentrations: composition, guitar, harpsichord, music, music education, music scholarship, opera, orchestral instruments, piano/organ, voice. Graduate degrees offered: Master of Arts in the areas of ethnomusicology, musicology, music theory; Master of Music in the areas of composition, piano, organ, voice, orchestral instruments, opera, guitar, harpsichord, choral conducting. Doctor of Musical Arts in the areas of composition, piano, voice, orchestral instruments; Doctor of Philosophy in the areas of ethnomusicology, musicology, music theory. Program accredited by CUMS.
**Enrollment** 393 total; 266 undergraduate, 127 graduate.
**Music Student Profile** 61% females, 39% males, 5% international.
**Music Faculty** 29 total (full-time), 54 total (part-time). 70% of full-time faculty have terminal degrees. Graduate students teach a few undergraduate courses. Undergraduate student–faculty ratio: 3:1.
**Student Life** Student groups/activities include student ensembles, opera productions, musical theatre.
**Expenses for 2008–2009** Application fee: $100 Canadian dollars.
**Financial Aid** Program-specific awards: scholarships for program students ($1000–$3000).
**Application Procedures** Students admitted directly into the professional program freshman year. Deadline for freshmen and transfers: February 28. Notification date for freshmen and transfers: April 30. Required: high school transcript, college transcript(s) for transfer students, 2 letters of recommendation, audition, music theory examination, original music scores for composition applicants, minimum 2.5 high school GPA, video audition for out-of-town applicants, original essay for music scholarship applicants. Auditions held once on campus; recorded music is permissible as a substitute for live auditions when

distance is prohibitive and videotaped performances are permissible as a substitute for live auditions when distance is prohibitive. Portfolio reviews held once on campus.
**Web Site** http://www.music.ubc.ca
**Undergraduate Contact** Ms. Rayne Graham, Academic Advisor, Recruitment and Admissions, School of Music, The University of British Columbia, 6361 Memorial Road, Vancouver, British Columbia V6T 1Z2, Canada; 604-822-5502, fax: 604-822-4884, e-mail address: music.advisor@ubc.ca
**Graduate Contact** Ms. Miriam Nechemia, Admissions Officer, School of Music, The University of British Columbia, 6361 Memorial Road, Vancouver, British Columbia V6T 1Z2, Canada; 604-822-5750, fax: 604-822-4884, e-mail address: music.admissions@ubc.ca

# University of Calgary
### Calgary, Alberta, Canada

Province-supported, coed. Urban campus. Music program established 1967.
**Web Site** http://www.ucalgary.ca/

*Claire Trevor School of the Arts*
# University of California, Irvine
### Irvine, California

State-supported, coed. Total enrollment: 26,483. Music program established 1965.
**Degrees** Bachelor of Arts in the area of music; Bachelor of Music in the areas of voice, piano, wind and percussion instruments, stringed instruments, jazz instrumental. Majors and concentrations: bassoon, clarinet, composition, double bass, flute, French horn, guitar, harp, jazz, lute, oboe, percussion, piano, trombone, trumpet, tuba, viola, violin, violoncello, voice. Graduate degrees offered: Master of Fine Arts in the area of music. Cross-registration with University of California System.
**Enrollment** 145 total; 125 undergraduate, 20 graduate.
**Music Student Profile** 70% females, 30% males, 65% minorities, 10% international.
**Music Faculty** 12 total (full-time), 25 total (part-time). 100% of full-time faculty have terminal degrees. Graduate students teach a few undergraduate courses. Undergraduate student–faculty ratio: 12:1.
**Student Life** Student groups/activities include Kappa Kappa Psi Lambda Alpha Chapter. Special housing available for music students.
**Expenses for 2007–2008** Application fee: $60. State resident tuition: $0 full-time. Nonresident tuition: $19,620 full-time. Mandatory fees: $8276 full-time. College room and board: $10,547. Room and board charges vary according to board plan and housing facility.
**Financial Aid** Program-specific awards: 4 Rawlins Scholarships for strings or piano majors ($5000), 1 Harry and Marjorie Slim Scholarship for instrumental or voice majors ($1000), 1 Tierney Scholarship for instrumental or voice majors ($4200), Artsbridge Scholarships for instrumental or voice majors ($2500), 10–12 music scholarships for instrumental or voice majors ($1000), 1 Winifred Smith Scholarship for cello (preferred), violin/piano students ($5000), 1 Phyllis Kovach Vacca Scholarship for cello (preferred), piano students ($1500).
**Application Procedures** Students admitted directly into the professional program freshman year. Deadline for freshmen and transfers: November 30. Notification date for freshmen and transfers: continuous. Required: essay, high school transcript, college transcript(s) for transfer students, audition, SAT or ACT test scores, minimum 3.0 college GPA for transfer students, SAT. Recommended: minimum 3.0 high school GPA. Auditions held once on campus; recorded music is permissible as a substitute for live auditions when distance is prohibitive and videotaped performances are permissible as a substitute for live auditions when distance is prohibitive.
**Web Site** http://www.arts.uci.edu

**Undergraduate Contact** Admissions Counselor, Office of Admissions and Relations with Schools, University of California, Irvine, 206 Administration Building, Irvine, California 92697-1075; 949-824-6703.

**Graduate Contact** Mr. Robin Buck, Associate Professor, Department of Music, University of California, Irvine, 303 Music and Media Building, 726, Irvine, California 92697-2775; 949-824-3803, fax: 949-824-4914, e-mail address: rbuck@uci.edu

# University of California, Santa Barbara

**Santa Barbara, California**

State-supported, coed. Suburban campus. Total enrollment: 21,410. Music program established 1976.
**Web Site** http://www.ucsb.edu/

# University of Central Arkansas

**Conway, Arkansas**

State-supported, coed. Small town campus. Total enrollment: 12,619. Music program established 1908.
**Degrees** Bachelor of Music in the areas of performance, music education, composition. Majors and concentrations: brass, composition, music, music education, piano/organ, stringed instruments, voice, wind and percussion instruments. Graduate degrees offered: Master of Music in the areas of performance, music theory, music education, choral conducting, instrumental conducting. Program accredited by NASM.
**Enrollment** 177 total; 159 undergraduate, 18 graduate.
**Music Student Profile** 50% females, 50% males, 15% minorities, 10% international.
**Music Faculty** 30 total (full-time), 8 total (part-time). 88% of full-time faculty have terminal degrees. Graduate students do not teach undergraduate courses. Undergraduate student–faculty ratio: 5:1.
**Student Life** Student groups/activities include Music Teachers National Association competitions, Arkansas Symphony Orchestra.
**Expenses for 2007–2008** Application fee: $0. State resident tuition: $4830 full-time. Nonresident tuition: $9660 full-time. Mandatory fees: $1375 full-time. College room and board: $4600. College room only: $2680. Room and board charges vary according to board plan and housing facility. Special program-related fees: $25–$40 per credit hour for practice room fees.
**Financial Aid** Program-specific awards: 143 music scholarships for wind, brass, percussion, orchestral, vocal, and keyboard students ($200–$2500).
**Application Procedures** Students apply for admission into the professional program by freshman year. Deadline for freshmen and transfers: continuous. Required: college transcript(s) for transfer students, 3 letters of recommendation, audition, SAT or ACT test scores. Recommended: high school transcript, minimum 3.0 high school GPA, interview. Auditions held 3 times and by appointment on campus; recorded music is permissible as a substitute for live auditions when distance is prohibitive, in special circumstances, or for international applicants and videotaped performances are permissible as a substitute for live auditions when distance is prohibitive, in special circumstances, or for international applicants.
**Web Site** http://www.uca.edu/divisions/academic/music
**Undergraduate Contact** Ms. Jann Bryant, Instructor, Department of Music, University of Central Arkansas, UCA 201 Donaghey Avenue, Conway, Arkansas 72035-0001; 501-450-5755, fax: 501-450-5773, e-mail address: jannb@uca.edu
**Graduate Contact** Dr. Jane Dahlenburg, Graduate Advisor, Department of Music, University of Central Arkansas, UCA 201 Donaghey Avenue, Conway, Arkansas 72035-0001; 501-450-3301, fax: 501-450-5773, e-mail address: dahlen@uca.edu

# University of Central Missouri

**Warrensburg, Missouri**

State-supported, coed. Small town campus. Total enrollment: 10,918. Music program established 1920.

**Degrees** Bachelor of Music in the areas of instrumental music, jazz/commercial music, piano pedagogy, music technology; Bachelor of Music Education in the areas of instrumental music education, vocal music education. Majors and concentrations: jazz, music education, music technology, piano pedagogy, piano/organ, stringed instruments, voice, wind and percussion instruments. Graduate degrees offered: Master of Arts in the areas of theory and composition, history and literature, music education, performance, piano pedagogy, conducting. Program accredited by NASM.
**Enrollment** 228 total; 202 undergraduate, 20 graduate, 6 nonprofessional degree.
**Music Student Profile** 36% females, 64% males, 7% minorities, 1% international.
**Music Faculty** 2 graduate (part-time), 22 total (full-time). 95% of full-time faculty have terminal degrees. Graduate students do not teach undergraduate courses. Undergraduate student–faculty ratio: 8:1.
**Student Life** Student groups/activities include Phi Mu Alpha Sinfonia, Sigma Alpha Iota, Music Educators National Conference. Special housing available for music students.
**Expenses for 2007–2008** Application fee: $30. State resident tuition: $6225 full-time. Nonresident tuition: $11,845 full-time. Mandatory fees: $604 full-time. Full-time tuition and fees vary according to course load and location. College room and board: $5846. College room only: $3746. Room and board charges vary according to board plan and housing facility. Special program-related fees: $15 per course for instrument acquisition and maintenance, $35 per course for music technology courses.
**Financial Aid** Program-specific awards: 10–12 achievement awards for program majors ($300), 30–35 Foundation Awards for program majors and minors ($500–$2000), 150–175 service awards for ensemble performers ($200–$1000).
**Application Procedures** Students admitted directly into the professional program freshman year. Deadline for freshmen and transfers: continuous. Required: high school transcript, college transcript(s) for transfer students, minimum 2.0 high school GPA, audition, ACT test score only (minimum composite ACT score of 21). Recommended: letter of recommendation. Auditions held at student's convenience on campus; recorded music is permissible as a substitute for live auditions if a campus visit is impossible and videotaped performances are permissible as a substitute for live auditions if a campus visit is impossible.
**Web Site** http://www.cmsu.edu/
**Undergraduate Contact** Mr. Paul Orscheln, Director of Admissions, University of Central Missouri, Ward Edwards 1422, Warrensburg, Missouri 64093; 660-543-4290, fax: 660-543-8517.
**Graduate Contact** Dr. Franklin Fenley, Graduate Coordinator, Department of Music, University of Central Missouri, Warrensburg, Missouri 64093; 660-543-4974, fax: 660-543-8271, e-mail address: fenley@ucmo.edu

# University of Cincinnati

See University of Cincinnati College Conservatory of Music

*University of Cincinnati*
# University of Cincinnati College Conservatory of Music

**Cincinnati, Ohio**

State-supported, coed. Urban campus. Total enrollment: 29,319. Music program established 1867.
**Degrees** Bachelor of Music in the areas of performance, music education, jazz, theory/history/composition. Majors and concentrations: classical guitar, composition, harpsichord, jazz, music, music education, music history, music theory, piano/organ, stringed instruments, voice, wind and percussion instruments. Graduate degrees offered: Master of Music in the areas of performance, music education, theory/history/composition, conducting, collaborative piano. Doctor of Musical Arts in the areas of performance, composition, conducting; Doctor of Philosophy

*University of Cincinnati College Conservatory of Music (continued)*

in the areas of music theory, musicology. Cross-registration with Greater Cincinnati Consortium of Colleges and Universities. Program accredited by NASM.

**Enrollment** 996 total; 356 undergraduate, 613 graduate.

**Music Student Profile** 49% females, 51% males, 9% minorities, 24% international.

**Music Faculty** 70 total (full-time), 50 total (part-time). 73% of full-time faculty have terminal degrees. Graduate students teach a few undergraduate courses. Undergraduate student–faculty ratio: 5:1.

**Student Life** Student groups/activities include Student Artist Program, music fraternities and sororities. Special housing available for music students.

**Expenses for 2007–2008** Application fee: $40. State resident tuition: $7896 full-time. Nonresident tuition: $22,419 full-time. Mandatory fees: $1503 full-time. Full-time tuition and fees vary according to course load, degree level, location, program, and reciprocity agreements. College room and board: $8799. College room only: $5259. Room and board charges vary according to board plan and housing facility.

**Financial Aid** Program-specific awards: 300 endowed scholarships for program majors ($1600–$4500), 185 Cincinnatus Awards for top academic scholars based on test scores and high school GPA ($2000–$20,000).

**Application Procedures** Students admitted directly into the professional program freshman year. Deadline for freshmen and transfers: December 1. Notification date for freshmen and transfers: continuous. Required: high school transcript, college transcript(s) for transfer students, letter of recommendation, interview, audition, SAT or ACT test scores. Recommended: minimum 3.0 high school GPA. Auditions held 15 times on campus and off campus in Atlanta, GA; Chicago, IL; Interlochen, MI; Los Angeles, CA; New York, NY; San Francisco, CA; recorded music is permissible as a substitute for live auditions with approval from the department and videotaped performances are permissible as a substitute for live auditions with approval from the department.

**Web Site** http://www.ccm.uc.edu

**Undergraduate Contact** Mr. P.J. Woolston, Senior Admissions Officer, College-Conservatory of Music, University of Cincinnati, PO Box 210003, Cincinnati, Ohio 45221-0003; 513-556-9479, fax: 513-556-1028, e-mail address: pj.woolston@uc.edu

**Graduate Contact** Mr. Paul R. Hillner, Assistant Dean, College-Conservatory of Music, University of Cincinnati, PO Box 210003, Cincinnati, Ohio 45221-0003; 513-556-9478, fax: 513-556-1028, e-mail address: paul.hillner@uc.edu

## More About the University

The University of Cincinnati College-Conservatory of Music (CCM) is the result of the merger of two distinguished schools of music—the Cincinnati Conservatory of Music, established in 1867, and the College of Music at Cincinnati, established in 1878. This merger in 1955, and subsequent union with the University of Cincinnati (UC) in 1962, brought together the professional training in the performing arts and media of a city long noted for its support in these areas.

Cited in the *New York Times* as one of the nation's leading conservatories, CCM is among the nation's most comprehensive performing arts schools, housing not only the standard disciplines of instrumental performance, voice, musicology, theory, and composition but also music education, conducting, musical theater, drama, opera, theater design and production (makeup, lighting, scene design, stage management, costuming, sound design, and theater production), electronic media, jazz and studio music, dance, arts administration, accompanying, opera coaching, and directing. (The last four programs listed are at the graduate level only.)

Performing groups are continually recognized for their outstanding achievements. The jazz ensemble has regularly won the *Down Beat* magazine award for the best student ensemble; the National Opera Association has honored the CCM opera program with thirty-three first-place awards in the past nineteen years; and the wind department has been featured at major conventions and

conferences in this country and in Japan and currently has more than twelve CDs on the market. Six additional outstanding CDs have been produced by the CCM Philharmonia Orchestra, the Faculty Jazz Ensemble, and the Ensemble for Eighteenth Century Music. All have been recorded commercially.

As the first music school in the United States to offer courses in classical ballet, CCM's dance division is the founding institution and affiliate of the Cincinnati Ballet. Both Cincinnati Ballet and Cincinnati Opera offer numerous performance opportunities to dance majors. The dance division also offers continual ballet performance experience, featuring works by division faculty members and guest choreographers, as well as the opportunity to work with notable guest artists, including Bart Cook, Vivi Flindt, Sean Curren, Adam Skulte, and Laura Alonzo, among others. Other opportunities exist in productions by CCM's opera and musical theater programs.

Theater training offers a unique opportunity for CCM students because of the combination of instruction in vocal coaching, dance, opera, musical theater, drama, theater design and production, and arts administration within one division. Students have the opportunity to share in a wide-ranging scope of classes, major productions, workshop productions, master classes, and internships. This remarkable sharing of experiences among experts in all areas of theater and arts administration allows students exposure to a wealth of learning opportunities. In addition, the division manages CCM's major theater and concert venues. Technical facilities currently include a state-of-the-art computerized lighting control mechanism for the theaters. The technical support area, which opened in 1997, includes an 8,500-square-foot scene shop; a 3,000-square-foot costume shop plus wig, make-up, and prosthetics studios; a 1,500-square-foot design/drafting studio; an 800-square-foot light lab; and CAD drafting stations. The United States Institute of Technical Theater (USITT) has honored these programs with more than thirty awards in the past ten years.

In addition to the strengths of the College-Conservatory of Music, students have the resources of a major university at their disposal. The libraries of the University constitute a nationally recognized research center, with holdings that include 3.2 million bound volumes and more than 42,000 serial subscriptions. They also offer access to an expanding number of libraries throughout the state via the OhioLINK online catalog. University Libraries is also a founding member of the Association of Research Libraries.

Student-support offices serve the entire University population and offer academic counseling and tutoring, resume and interview skills training, psychological and personal counseling, student health clinics, day-care centers, special programming for ethnic groups and women, and a host of center activities, such as special-interest clubs, student government, and intramural sports.

The extensive physical facilities of the University provide residence halls for students; banking services; swimming, tennis, track, volleyball, basketball, racquetball/handball, and bowling; plus a movie theater and more than six restaurants ranging from fast food to table service. A state-of-the-art recreational facility opened in February 2006.

Cincinnati, "North America's most livable city" (*Places Rated Almanac*, 1993), is bordered on the south by the Ohio River and truly offers something for everyone. Nearby are Mt. Adams and the adjoining Eden Park, a stylish urban area perched on top of a hill with spectacular views of the city and the Ohio River and the home of the Playhouse in the Park, Cincinnati Art Museum, and Krohn Conservatory. Within walking distance of UC is University Village, offering inexpensive restaurants and shops, and just beyond is Ludlow Avenue in Clifton's Gaslight District, with its boutiques, restaurants, and tree-lined streets. At the heart of downtown, just a 5-minute bus ride away, is Fountain Square—the place Cincinnatians go to celebrate, demonstrate, welcome hometown heroes, or bring in the new year. Also downtown are numerous and diverse cultural opportunities, including the Cincinnati Symphony Orchestra and Cincinnati Pops, Cincinnati Opera, Cincinnati Ballet, Ensemble Theatre of Cincinnati, Broadway Series, Cincinnati Museum Center at Union Terminal, Contemporary Arts Center, Taft Museum of Art, National Underground Railroad Freedom Center, and more.

Both of CCM's founding schools, the Cincinnati Conservatory of Music and the College of Music of Cincinnati, were charter members of the National Association of Schools of Music (NASM), in which CCM continues to play a vital leadership role. Theater programs have received accreditation from the National Association of Schools of Theater (NAST) and the University/Resident Theater Association (URTA), and the dance program holds accreditation from the National Association of Schools of Dance (NASD).

**Program Facilities** In 1999, CCM celebrated the grand opening of its campus village, a collection of renovated and new buildings that significantly enhance the college's teaching and performance capabilities. The complex stresses the synergy between the performing arts and electronic media and effectively accommodates nearly 900 public performances each year. With the help of its design architect, Henry N. Cobb, the college has produced a physical environment that truly reflects and advances its reputation as one of the finest and most comprehensive training centers for the performing arts and electronic media. The Corbett Center for the Performing Arts houses the elegant 738-seat Corbett Auditorium, the 380-seat Patricia Corbett Theater, the 140-seat Watson Recital Hall, the flexible Cohen Family Studio Theater, three dance studios, and four large rehearsal rooms. CCM's theater production wing includes the scene and costume shops, various design-oriented classrooms, labs, jazz studios, and ensemble rehearsal rooms. The Dieterle Vocal Arts Center is the home to the voice, opera, choral, and accompanying departments. It has nineteen faculty studios, three private coaching rooms, the Italo Tajo Archive Room, two warm-up rooms, the 100-seat choral rehearsal room, and the choral library. The Center is also the location of the Nippert Rehearsal Studio, a large, grand opera–scale rehearsal space with dressing rooms and technical support so that the space can double as a performance venue for workshops and concerts. Memorial Hall houses teaching studios for piano, harpsichord, strings, and winds, plus practice rooms, chamber music rehearsal rooms, and the electronic music studios. The computer music studio, used by composers, researchers, and performers, contains a Genelec multichannel audio system, workstations, and peripherals for sampling, editing, synthesis, signal processing, algorithmic composition, programming, and controller development. Mary Emery Hall, the home of the academic offices and the electronic media division, is the newest addition to the CCM Village. Highlights include the Bartlett Television Studio and the J. Ralph Corbett Audio Production Center, a master classroom, smart classrooms with audio/video link-up to the University library, and the stunning Robert J. Werner Recital Hall, a 300-seat intimate performing space for chamber music and solo recitals. The Gorno Memorial Music Library houses more than 170,000 volumes, including books, music scores, periodicals, and numerous special collections of rare books, music, and recordings.

**Faculty, Resident Artists, and Alumni** CCM has more than 150 faculty members including Kurt Sassmannshaus (violin), Masao Kawasaki (viola), Yehuda Hanani (violoncello), Al Laszlo (double bass), William Winstead (bassoon), Randy Gardner (horn), Mark Ostoich (oboe), Brad Garner (flute), Awadagin Pratt (piano), and James Tocco (piano and chamber music). Ensembles-in-Residence include Percussion Group Cincinnati, the Pridonoff Piano Duo, and the Cincinnati Children's Choir. Alumni continue to hold key positions in the performing and media arts. Numbered among them are American and European opera stars Kathleen Battle, Barbara Daniels, David Daniels, Catherine Keen, David Malis, Deborah Polaski, Stanford Olsen, and Mark Oswald; producers Earl Hamner (*The Waltons* and *Falcon Crest*) and Dan Guntzelman (*Growing Pains*); musical theater stars Faith Prince, Lee Roy Reams, Michele Pawk, Jason Graae, Jim Walton, Vicki Lewis, and Ashley Brown; prima ballerina Suzanne Farrell; jazz great Al Hirt; composers Albert Hague (*Plain and Fancy*, *Redhead*, *How the Grinch Stole Christmas*), Randy Edelman (*Last of the Mohicans*, *While You Were Sleeping*), Stephen Flaherty (*Once on This Island*, *Ragtime*, *Seussical*), theatrical producer Kevin McCollum (*Rent*, *Avenue Q.*, *The Drowsy Chaperone*), and a host of international competition winners and instrumentalists who hold positions in the major orchestras, both in the United States and in Europe.

**Student Performance Opportunities** Nearly 900 performances a year take place at CCM by two large orchestras, three chamber orchestras, two wind ensembles, five choruses, more than forty chamber groups, dance productions and choreographers' workshops, jazz ensembles, early music ensembles, brass choir, and twenty-four mainstage and workshop productions in opera, musical theater, and drama.

# University of Colorado at Boulder
## Boulder, Colorado

State-supported, coed. Suburban campus. Total enrollment: 31,470. Music program established 1920.

**Degrees** Bachelor of Music in the areas of composition, musicology, all major instruments, voice, voice theater; Bachelor of Music Education in the areas of instrumental music education, choral music education, general music. Majors and concentrations: brass, composition, music education, musicology, opera, performance, piano/organ, stringed instruments, voice, wind and percussion instruments. Graduate degrees offered: Master of Music in the areas of performance, composition, conducting, musicology, performance and pedagogy; Master of Music Education in the areas of general, instrumental (band), string, and vocal music. Doctor of Musical Arts in the areas of performance, composition, conducting, performance and pedagogy; Doctor of Philosophy in the areas of music education, musicology. Cross-registration with University of Colorado System. Program accredited by NASM.

**Enrollment** 510 total; 280 undergraduate, 230 graduate.

*University of Colorado at Boulder (continued)*

**Music Student Profile** 46% females, 54% males, 14% minorities, 8% international.
**Music Faculty** 58 total (full-time), 15 total (part-time). 75% of full-time faculty have terminal degrees. Graduate students teach a few undergraduate courses. Undergraduate student–faculty ratio: 6:1.
**Student Life** Student groups/activities include Sigma Alpha Iota, Phi Mu Alpha, Music Educators National Conference.
**Expenses for 2008–2009** Application fee: $50. One-time mandatory fee: $112. State resident tuition: $5922 full-time. Nonresident tuition: $25,400 full-time. Mandatory fees: $1356 full-time. College room and board: $9860. Special program-related fees: $15 per class for music course fees.
**Financial Aid** Program-specific awards: 200 music scholarships for program majors ($3500).
**Application Procedures** Students admitted directly into the professional program freshman year. Deadline for freshmen and transfers: February 1. Notification date for freshmen and transfers: July 1. Required: essay, high school transcript, college transcript(s) for transfer students, minimum 2.0 high school GPA, letter of recommendation, audition, SAT or ACT test scores. Recommended: minimum 3.0 high school GPA. Auditions held weekly in February and by appointment on campus; recorded music is permissible as a substitute for live auditions when distance is prohibitive and videotaped performances are permissible as a substitute for live auditions when distance is prohibitive.
**Web Site** http://www.colorado.edu/music
**Undergraduate Contact** Dr. James Austin, Associate Dean for Undergraduate Studies, College of Music, University of Colorado at Boulder, Campus Box 301, Boulder, Colorado 80309-0301; 303-492-6354, fax: 303-492-5619, e-mail address: ugradmus@colorado.edu
**Graduate Contact** Dr. Steven Bruns, Associate Dean for Graduate Studies, College of Music, University of Colorado at Boulder, Campus Box 301, Boulder, Colorado 80309-0301; 303-492-2207, fax: 303-492-5619, e-mail address: gradmusc@colorado.edu

# University of Colorado Denver

## Denver, Colorado

State-supported, coed. Urban campus. Total enrollment: 20,162. Music program established 1973.
**Degrees** Bachelor of Science in the area of music. Majors and concentrations: music management, music performance, music technology. Cross-registration with Metropolitan State College of Denver, Community College System of Colorado. Program accredited by NASM.
**Enrollment** 560 total; 68 undergraduate, 492 nonprofessional degree.
**Music Student Profile** 22% females, 78% males, 15% minorities, 2% international.
**Music Faculty** 14 undergraduate (full-time), 24 undergraduate (part-time). 93% of full-time faculty have terminal degrees. Graduate students do not teach undergraduate courses. Undergraduate student–faculty ratio: 9:1.
**Student Life** Student groups/activities include Audio Engineering Society, Music and Entertainment Industry Student Organization.
**Expenses for 2008–2009** Application fee: $50. State resident tuition: $5054 full-time. Nonresident tuition: $17,010 full-time. Mandatory fees: $878 full-time. College room and board: $9990. College room only: $5940.
**Financial Aid** Program-specific awards: 3 Mike Barney Memorial Scholarship Fund Awards for music students ($500), Deborah and Larry Melnick Endowed Scholarship for fine arts majors, 1 Donna Bogard Scholarship in Voice for voice students demonstrating merit and with minimum 3.0 GPA ($1000).
**Application Procedures** Students admitted directly into the professional program freshman year. Deadline for freshmen and transfers: April 1. Notification date for freshmen and transfers: May 1. Required: high school transcript, college transcript(s) for transfer students, minimum 2.0 high school GPA, SAT or ACT test scores, audition for music technology, management, and

performance majors, music audiation exam. Recommended: minimum 3.0 high school GPA. Auditions held on campus; recorded music is permissible as a substitute for live auditions for out-of-state applicants and videotaped performances are permissible as a substitute for live auditions for out-of-state applicants.
**Web Site** http://www.cudenver.edu/cam
**Undergraduate Contact** Leah Haloin, Administrative Assistant, Department of Music & Entertainment Industry Studies, University of Colorado Denver, Campus Box 162, PO Box 173364, Denver, Colorado 80217-3364; 303-556-2279, fax: 303-556-2335.

# University of Connecticut

## Storrs, Connecticut

State-supported, coed. Rural campus. Total enrollment: 23,692.
**Degrees** Bachelor of Arts in the areas of music, jazz; Bachelor of Music in the areas of vocal performance, instrumental performance, music theory; Bachelor of Science in the area of music education. Majors and concentrations: jazz, music education, music history/theory, piano/organ, stringed instruments, voice, wind and percussion instruments. Graduate degrees offered: Master of Arts in the areas of music theory, musicology; Master of Music in the areas of performance, performance with conducting (instrumental, choral), music education. Doctor of Musical Arts in the areas of performance, conducting; Doctor of Philosophy in the areas of music theory and history, music education. Program accredited by NASM.
**Enrollment** 256 total; 188 undergraduate, 68 graduate.
**Music Student Profile** 56% females, 44% males, 9% minorities, 3% international.
**Music Faculty** 24 total (full-time), 24 total (part-time). 100% of full-time faculty have terminal degrees. Graduate students teach a few undergraduate courses. Undergraduate student–faculty ratio: 9:1.
**Student Life** Student groups/activities include Music Educators National Conference Student Chapter, American Choral Directors Association Student Chapter. Special housing available for music students.
**Expenses for 2008–2009** Application fee: $70. State resident tuition: $7200 full-time. Nonresident tuition: $21,912 full-time. Mandatory fees: $2138 full-time. College room and board: $9300. College room only: $4210. Special program-related fees: $230 per course for applied music fee.
**Financial Aid** Program-specific awards: 1–2 Victor Borge Awards for those demonstrating talent and academic achievement ($1000–$3000), 1 Dean's Scholarship for those demonstrating talent and academic achievement ($2000), 20–25 departmental scholarships for program students ($1000–$4600).
**Application Procedures** Students admitted directly into the professional program freshman year. Deadline for freshmen and transfers: February 1. Notification date for freshmen and transfers: July 1. Required: high school transcript, college transcript(s) for transfer students, audition, SAT test score only. Recommended: minimum 3.0 high school GPA. Auditions held 4 times on campus; recorded music is permissible as a substitute for live auditions when distance is prohibitive (beyond a 150-mile radius) and videotaped performances are permissible as a substitute for live auditions when distance is prohibitive (beyond a 150-mile radius).
**Web Site** http://www.sfa.uconn.edu
**Undergraduate Contact** Deborah Trahan, Administrative Assistant, Music Department, University of Connecticut, 1295 Storrs Road, Unit 1012, Storrs, Connecticut 06269-1012; 860-486-3728, fax: 860-486-3796, e-mail address: music@uconn.edu
**Graduate Contact** Dr. Richard Bass, Director of Graduate Studies, Music Department, University of Connecticut, 1295 Storrs Road, Unit 1012, Storrs, Connecticut 06269-1012; 860-486-4197, fax: 860-486-3796, e-mail address: richard.bass@uconn.edu

# University of Dayton

## Dayton, Ohio

Independent Roman Catholic, coed. Suburban campus. Total enrollment: 10,395.

**Degrees** Bachelor of Music in the areas of music therapy, music education, music composition, music performance. Majors and concentrations: composition, music, music education, music therapy, performance. Graduate degrees offered: Master of Education in the area of music. Cross-registration with Southwestern Ohio Council for Higher Education. Program accredited by NASM, AMTA.

**Enrollment** 155 total; 110 undergraduate, 35 graduate, 10 nonprofessional degree.

**Music Student Profile** 65% females, 35% males, 1% minorities.

**Music Faculty** 15 undergraduate (full-time), 36 undergraduate (part-time). 75% of full-time faculty have terminal degrees. Graduate students do not teach undergraduate courses. Undergraduate student–faculty ratio: 15:1.

**Student Life** Student groups/activities include music fraternity and sorority, Ohio Collegiate Music Education Association, Music Therapy Club.

**Expenses for 2007–2008** Application fee: $50. Comprehensive fee: $33,670 includes full-time tuition ($24,880), mandatory fees ($1070), and college room and board ($7720). College room only: $4550. Full-time tuition and fees vary according to program. Room and board charges vary according to board plan, housing facility, and student level. Special program-related fees: $75 per course for pedagogy classes, $150–$250 per semester for lesson fees.

**Financial Aid** Program-specific awards: 10–13 Music Talent Awards for program students ($5000), 12–18 Reichard Awards for program students ($500), 12–18 band grants for band members.

**Application Procedures** Students admitted directly into the professional program freshman year. Deadline for freshmen and transfers: continuous. Notification date for freshmen and transfers: continuous. Required: essay, high school transcript, college transcript(s) for transfer students, minimum 2.0 high school GPA, 2 letters of recommendation, interview, audition, SAT or ACT test scores, portfolio for composition applicants. Recommended: minimum 3.0 high school GPA. Auditions held 4 times and by appointment on campus; recorded music is permissible as a substitute for live auditions if a campus visit is impossible and videotaped performances are permissible as a substitute for live auditions if a campus visit is impossible. Portfolio reviews held once on campus.

**Web Site** http://www.udayton.edu/~music

**Undergraduate Contact** Mrs. Jeanie Smith, Coordinator, Music Admissions, Department of Music, University of Dayton, 300 College Park, Dayton, Ohio 45469-0290; 937-229-3936, fax: 937-229-3916, e-mail address: jean.smith@notes.udayton.edu

**Graduate Contact** Dr. Linda Hartley, Coordinator, Graduate Studies in Music Education, Department of Music, University of Dayton, 300 College Park, Dayton, Ohio 45469-0290; 937-229-3232, fax: 937-229-3916, e-mail address: lhartley@udayton.edu

# University of Delaware

## Newark, Delaware

State-related, coed. Small town campus. Total enrollment: 19,677. Music program established 1938.

**Degrees** Bachelor of Music in the areas of applied vocal and instrumental music, music theory and composition; Bachelor of Music Education in the areas of instrumental music education, choral music education. Majors and concentrations: classical music, music, music education, music theory and composition, piano, stringed instruments, voice, wind and percussion instruments. Graduate degrees offered: Master of Music in the areas of instrumental performance, teaching, voice, strings, instrumental conducting, composition. Program accredited by NASM.

**Enrollment** 255 total; 172 undergraduate, 21 graduate, 62 nonprofessional degree.

**Music Student Profile** 52% females, 48% males, 3% minorities, 1% international.

**Music Faculty** 30 undergraduate (full-time), 25 undergraduate (part-time), 30 graduate (full-time), 20 graduate (part-time). 67% of full-time faculty have terminal degrees. Graduate students teach a few undergraduate courses. Undergraduate student–faculty ratio: 4:1.

**Student Life** Student groups/activities include Sigma Alpha Iota, Phi Mu Alpha, Music Educators National Conference. Special housing available for music students.

**Expenses for 2007–2008** Application fee: $70. State resident tuition: $7340 full-time. Nonresident tuition: $18,590 full-time. Mandatory fees: $810 full-time. College room and board: $7948. College room only: $4748. Room and board charges vary according to housing facility.

**Application Procedures** Students admitted directly into the professional program freshman year. Deadline for freshmen and transfers: March 1. Notification date for freshmen and transfers: April 15. Required: essay, high school transcript, college transcript(s) for transfer students, minimum 3.0 high school GPA, audition, SAT or ACT test scores, musicality test. Recommended: 2 letters of recommendation, interview. Auditions held 4 times on campus; recorded music is permissible as a substitute for live auditions when distance is prohibitive and videotaped performances are permissible as a substitute for live auditions when distance is prohibitive.

**Web Site** http://www.music.udel.edu

**Undergraduate Contact** Mr. Lou Hirsh, Associate Provost for Enrollment Services, University of Delaware, 116 Hullihen Hall, Newark, Delaware 19716; 302-831-8125, fax: 302-831-6905.

**Graduate Contact** Dr. Lawrence Stomberg, Chair, Department of Music, University of Delaware, Amy DuPont Music Building, Newark, Delaware 19716; 302-831-8732, fax: 302-831-3589, e-mail address: lstom@udel.edu

## *Lamont School of Music*

# University of Denver

## Denver, Colorado

Independent, coed. Total enrollment: 11,053. Music program established 1931.

**Degrees** Bachelor of Music in the areas of performance, jazz, composition, commercial music, audio production. Majors and concentrations: accordion, arranging, audio production, classical music, commercial music, composition, guitar, harp, jazz, music, piano/organ, stringed instruments, voice, wind and percussion instruments. Graduate degrees offered: Master of Arts in the areas of music theory, music history and literature; Master of Music in the areas of performance, composition, conducting, piano pedagogy, Suzuki pedagogy. Program accredited by NASM.

**Enrollment** 315 total; 235 undergraduate, 61 graduate, 19 nonprofessional degree.

**Music Student Profile** 50% females, 50% males, 14% minorities, 16% international.

**Music Faculty** 24 total (full-time), 28 total (part-time). 18% of full-time faculty have terminal degrees. Graduate students teach a few undergraduate courses. Undergraduate student–faculty ratio: 7:1.

**Student Life** Student groups/activities include professional music fraternities and sororities, ensemble groups. Special housing available for music students.

**Expenses for 2007–2008** Application fee: $50. Comprehensive fee: $41,910 includes full-time tuition ($31,428), mandatory fees ($804), and college room and board ($9678). College room only: $6015. Full-time tuition and fees vary according to class time, course load, and program. Room and board charges vary according to board plan and housing facility. Special program-related fees: $85 per year for chamber music .

**Financial Aid** Program-specific awards: 206 music activity grants for program majors ($17,992), 10 endowed awards for specific program majors ($32,428), 7 endowed full-tuition awards for program majors ($32,428).

**Application Procedures** Students admitted directly into the professional program freshman year. Deadline for freshmen: February 1; transfers: March 15. Required: essay, high school transcript, college transcript(s) for transfer students, minimum 3.0 high school GPA, 2 letters of recommendation, interview, audition, SAT or ACT test scores, pre-screening auditions for jazz studies and commercial music major application. Recommended: video. Auditions held 4 times on campus; recorded music is permissible as a substitute for live auditions if a campus visit is impossible and videotaped performances are permissible as a substitute for live auditions if a campus visit is impossible.

**Web Site** http://www.du.edu/lamont

*University of Denver (continued)*

**Contact** Director of Admissions, Lamont School of Music, University of Denver, 2344 East Iliff Avenue, Denver, Colorado 80208; 303-871-6973, fax: 303-871-6382.

# University of Evansville
## Evansville, Indiana

Independent, coed. Urban campus. Total enrollment: 2,898. Music program established 1933.

**Degrees** Bachelor of Music in the areas of performance, music therapy, music education; Bachelor of Science in the area of music management. Majors and concentrations: classical guitar, music education, music management, music performance, music therapy, piano/organ, stringed instruments, voice, wind and percussion instruments. Program accredited by NASM.

**Enrollment** 124 total; all undergraduate.

**Music Student Profile** 69% females, 31% males, 6% minorities, 2% international.

**Music Faculty** 17 undergraduate (full-time), 9 undergraduate (part-time). 100% of full-time faculty have terminal degrees. Graduate students do not teach undergraduate courses. Undergraduate student–faculty ratio: 5:1.

**Student Life** Student groups/activities include American Music Therapy Association Student Chapter, Music Educators National Conference Student Chapter, Phi Mu Alpha/Sigma Alpha Iota.

**Expenses for 2007–2008** Application fee: $35. Comprehensive fee: $31,990 includes full-time tuition ($23,710), mandatory fees ($630), and college room and board ($7650). College room only: $3890. Room and board charges vary according to board plan and housing facility. Special program-related fees: $285 per credit hour for applied music fee.

**Financial Aid** Program-specific awards: 100 academic scholarships for those demonstrating talent and academic achievement ($11,000).

**Application Procedures** Students admitted directly into the professional program freshman year. Deadline for freshmen: May 1; transfers: June 1. Required: essay, high school transcript, college transcript(s) for transfer students, minimum 2.0 high school GPA, audition, SAT or ACT test scores. Recommended: minimum 3.0 high school GPA, 2 letters of recommendation. Auditions held 4 times on campus; recorded music is permissible as a substitute for live auditions when distance is prohibitive and videotaped performances are permissible as a substitute for live auditions when distance is prohibitive.

**Web Site** http://music.evansville.edu

**Undergraduate Contact** Eva Key, Music Admission Coordinator, Department of Music, University of Evansville, 1800 Lincoln Avenue, Evansville, Indiana 47722; 812-488-2742, fax: 812-488-2101, e-mail address: music@evansville.edu

*Hugh Hodgson School of Music*
# University of Georgia
## Athens, Georgia

State-supported, coed. Suburban campus. Total enrollment: 33,831. Music program established 1928.

**Degrees** Bachelor of Music in the areas of performance, composition, music therapy, music theory, music education. Majors and concentrations: composition, music education, music theory, music therapy, piano/organ, stringed instruments, voice, wind and percussion instruments. Graduate degrees offered: Master of Music in the areas of musicology, composition, music literature, performance; Master of Music Education in the areas of music education, music therapy. Doctor of Musical Arts in the areas of performance, composition, music education, conducting; Doctor of Education in the area of music education; Doctor of Philosophy in the areas of musicology/ethnomusicology, music theory, music education. Cross-registration with University System of Georgia. Program accredited by NASM, NCATE, AMTA.

**Enrollment** 401 total; 236 undergraduate, 139 graduate, 26 nonprofessional degree.

**Music Student Profile** 50% females, 50% males, 14% minorities, 8% international.

**Music Faculty** 56 undergraduate (full-time), 6 undergraduate (part-time), 40 graduate (full-time), 1 graduate (part-time). 80% of full-time faculty have terminal degrees. Graduate students do not teach undergraduate courses. Undergraduate student–faculty ratio: 10:1.

**Student Life** Student groups/activities include Music Educators National Conference, Music Teachers National Association, American Music Therapy Association.

**Expenses for 2007–2008** Application fee: $50. State resident tuition: $4496 full-time. Nonresident tuition: $19,600 full-time. Mandatory fees: $1126 full-time. Full-time tuition and fees vary according to course load, location, program, and student level. College room and board: $7292. College room only: $4010. Room and board charges vary according to board plan and housing facility. Special program-related fees: $50 for stage managing and recording engineer for recital.

**Financial Aid** Program-specific awards: 113 music scholarships for music majors ($1250).

**Application Procedures** Students apply for admission into the professional program by sophomore year. Deadline for freshmen: January 15; transfers: April 1. Notification date for freshmen: May 1; transfers: July 1. Required: essay, high school transcript, college transcript(s) for transfer students, minimum 3.0 high school GPA, letter of recommendation, interview, audition, SAT or ACT test scores. Recommended: portfolio for composition applicants. Auditions held 4 times and by appointment on campus; recorded music is permissible as a substitute for live auditions when distance is prohibitive or scheduling is difficult and videotaped performances are permissible as a substitute for live auditions when distance is prohibitive or scheduling is difficult. Portfolio reviews held by appointment on campus.

**Web Site** http://www.music.uga.edu

**Undergraduate Contact** Ms. Suzanne Caruso, Administrative Coordinator, School of Music, University of Georgia, Music Building, Athens, Georgia 30602-3153; 706-542-2764, fax: 706-542-2773, e-mail address: scaruso@uga.edu

**Graduate Contact** Ms. Susan LeCroy, Administrative Coordinator, School of Music, University of Georgia, Music Building, Athens, Georgia 30602-3153; 706-542-2743, fax: 706-542-2773, e-mail address: shlecroy@uga.edu

*The Hartt School*
# University of Hartford
## West Hartford, Connecticut

Independent, coed. Suburban campus. Total enrollment: 7,290. Music program established 1920.

**Web Site** http://www.hartford.edu/

# University of Hawaii at Manoa
## Honolulu, Hawaii

State-supported, coed. Urban campus. Total enrollment: 20,357. Music program established 1947.

**Degrees** Bachelor of Music in the areas of composition, performance. Majors and concentrations: composition, guitar, music education, piano, stringed instruments, voice, wind and percussion instruments. Graduate degrees offered: Master of Arts in the areas of ethnomusicology, musicology, music education, theory; Master of Music in the areas of composition, performance. Doctor of Philosophy in the area of music. Program accredited by NASM.

**Enrollment** 182 total; 129 undergraduate, 53 graduate.

**Music Student Profile** 47% females, 53% males, 80% minorities, 20% international.

**Music Faculty** 22 total (full-time), 34 total (part-time). 100% of full-time faculty have terminal degrees. Graduate students teach a few undergraduate courses. Undergraduate student–faculty ratio: 6:1.

**Student Life** Student groups/activities include American Choral Directors Association Student Chapter, Circle of Fifths (departmental student organization), Music Educators National Conference Student Chapter.

**Expenses for 2007–2008** Application fee: $50. State resident tuition: $5136 full-time. Nonresident tuition: $14,400 full-time. Mandatory fees: $254 full-time. College room and board: $7185. College room only: $4527.

**Financial Aid** Program-specific awards: 160 tuition waivers for band and orchestra members ($1400–$4260), 30 scholarships for program majors ($200–$4000).

**Application Procedures** Students admitted directly into the professional program freshman year. Deadline for freshmen and transfers: April 15. Notification date for freshmen and transfers: June 1. Required: high school transcript, college transcript(s) for transfer students, minimum 2.0 high school GPA, letter of recommendation, audition, SAT or ACT test scores, standing in top 40% of class for transfer students. Recommended: minimum 3.0 high school GPA, interview, portfolio. Auditions held twice and by appointment on campus; recorded music is permissible as a substitute for live auditions for out-of-state applicants and videotaped performances are permissible as a substitute for live auditions for out-of-state applicants. Portfolio reviews held once and by appointment for composition applicants on campus.

**Web Site** http://www.hawaii.edu/uhmmusic

**Undergraduate Contact** Dr. Jane Moulin, Undergraduate Chair, Music Department, University of Hawaii at Manoa, 2411 Dole Street, Honolulu, Hawaii 96822; 808-956-7707, fax: 808-956-9657, e-mail address: moulin@hawaii.edu

**Graduate Contact** Dr. Lesley Wright, Graduate Chair, Music Department, University of Hawaii at Manoa, 2411 Dole Street, Honolulu, Hawaii 96822; 808-956-7795, fax: 808-956-9657, e-mail address: wright@hawaii.edu

## *Moores School of Music*
# University of Houston
### Houston, Texas

State-supported, coed. Urban campus. Total enrollment: 34,663. Music program established 1927.

**Degrees** Bachelor of Music in the areas of applied music, music with teaching certificate, music theory, composition, music with elective studies. Majors and concentrations: composition, music business, music education, music theory, piano/organ, stringed instruments, voice, wind and percussion instruments. Graduate degrees offered: Master of Music in the areas of applied music, music theory, composition, music literature, music education, accompanying and chamber music, performance and pedagogy. Doctor of Musical Arts in the areas of performance, conducting, composition, music education. Program accredited by NASM.

**Enrollment** 385 undergraduate, 119 graduate, 37 nonprofessional degree.

**Music Student Profile** 43% females, 57% males, 36% minorities, 11% international.

**Music Faculty** 16 undergraduate (full-time), 30 undergraduate (part-time), 17 graduate (full-time), 12 graduate (part-time). 57% of full-time faculty have terminal degrees. Graduate students teach a few undergraduate courses. Undergraduate student–faculty ratio: 7:1.

**Student Life** Student groups/activities include Phi Mu Alpha Sinfonia, Sigma Alpha Iota, Kappa Kappa Psi.

**Expenses for 2007–2008** Application fee: $50. State resident tuition: $4826 full-time. Nonresident tuition: $13,166 full-time. Mandatory fees: $2624 full-time. Full-time tuition and fees vary according to course level, course load, degree level, location, program, reciprocity agreements, and student level. College room and board: $6651. College room only: $3778. Room and board charges vary according to board plan and housing facility. Special program-related fees: $10–$55 per semester for some music courses, $200 per semester for applied music courses, $225 per semester for music major fee.

**Financial Aid** Program-specific awards: 384 music scholarships for program students ($2000), 220 band grants for program students ($500).

**Application Procedures** Students apply for admission into the professional program by sophomore, junior year. Deadline for freshmen: April 2; transfers: May 1. Required: essay, high school transcript, college transcript(s) for transfer students, minimum 2.0 high school GPA, audition, SAT or ACT test scores. Recommended: minimum 3.0 high school GPA, 3 letters of recommendation, interview. Auditions held 3 times on campus; recorded music is permissible as a substitute for live auditions when distance is prohibitive or scheduling is difficult and videotaped performances are permissible as a substitute for live auditions when distance is prohibitive or scheduling is difficult.

**Web Site** http://www.music.uh.edu

**Undergraduate Contact** Ms. Kris Lytle, Academic Advisor (undergraduate), Moores School of Music, University of Houston, Houston, Texas 77204-4017; 713-743-3172, fax: 713-743-3166, e-mail address: kmlytle@uh.edu

**Graduate Contact** Mr. Douglas Goldberg, Graduate Advisor, Moores School of Music, University of Houston, Houston, Texas 77204-4017; 713-743-3314, fax: 713-743-3166, e-mail address: gradmusic@uh.edu

## *Lionel Hampton School of Music*
# University of Idaho
### Moscow, Idaho

State-supported, coed. Small town campus. Total enrollment: 11,636. Music program established 1893.

**Degrees** Bachelor of Fine Arts in the area of musical theater; Bachelor of Music in the areas of performance, composition, business; Bachelor of Music Education in the areas of instrumental music education, choral music education. Majors and concentrations: composition, music and business, music education, music theater, piano/organ, stringed instruments, voice, wind and percussion instruments. Graduate degrees offered: Master of Arts in the area of music history; Master of Music in the areas of performance, music education, pedagogy, accompanying, composition. Cross-registration with Washington State University. Program accredited by NASM.

**Enrollment** 269 total; 216 undergraduate, 20 graduate, 33 nonprofessional degree.

**Music Student Profile** 49% females, 51% males, 9% minorities, 1% international.

**Music Faculty** 23 total (full-time), 7 total (part-time). 61% of full-time faculty have terminal degrees. Graduate students teach a few undergraduate courses. Undergraduate student–faculty ratio: 7:1.

**Student Life** Student groups/activities include Sigma Alpha Iota/Phi Mu Alpha Sinfonia (music societies), Pi Kappa Lambda (music honorary fraternity), Music Educators National Conference Student Chapter. Special housing available for music students.

**Expenses for 2007–2008** Application fee: $40. Area resident tuition: $0 full-time. State resident tuition: $0 full-time. Nonresident tuition: $10,080 full-time. Mandatory fees: $4410 full-time. Full-time tuition and fees vary according to degree level and program. College room and board: $6424. Room and board charges vary according to board plan and housing facility. Special program-related fees: $25–$50 per semester for lab fee for equipment maintenance in specific courses, $200 per semester for non-major fee (1 credit), $270 per semester for lesson fee (2-3 credits).

**Financial Aid** Program-specific awards: 106 music merit scholarships for those passing audition evaluations ($500–$2500), 16 out-of-state tuition waivers for out-of-state program majors ($10,000).

**Application Procedures** Students admitted directly into the professional program freshman year. Deadline for freshmen and transfers: August 1. Notification date for freshmen and transfers: continuous. Required: high school transcript, college transcript(s) for transfer students, minimum 2.0 high school GPA, audition, SAT or ACT test scores. Auditions held once and as needed on campus; recorded music is permissible as a substitute for live auditions by request and videotaped performances are permissible as a substitute for live auditions by request.

**Web Site** http://www.uidaho.edu/LS/Music

*University of Idaho (continued)*

**Undergraduate Contact** Dr. Susan Hess, Assistant Director, Lionel Hampton School of Music, University of Idaho, PO Box 444015, Moscow, Idaho 83844-4253; 208-885-6231, fax: 208-885-7254, e-mail address: music@uidaho.edu

**Graduate Contact** Dr. Mary DuPree, Graduate Studies Committee Chair, Lionel Hampton School of Music, University of Idaho, Moscow, Idaho 83844-4015; 208-885-6231, fax: 208-885-7254, e-mail address: mdupree@uidaho.edu

# University of Illinois at Urbana–Champaign
## Champaign, Illinois

State-supported, coed. Urban campus. Total enrollment: 42,326. Music program established 1895.

**Degrees** Bachelor of Music in the areas of performance, composition/theory, music history, open studies, jazz; Bachelor of Music Education in the areas of instrumental, choral, general. Majors and concentrations: classical music, composition, individualized major, jazz, music education, music history, music theory, piano/organ/harpsichord, stringed instruments, voice, wind and percussion instruments. Graduate degrees offered: Master of Music in the areas of musicology, composition, theory, performance and literature, choral conducting, instrumental conducting, vocal accompanying and coaching, piano pedagogy, jazz; Master of Music Education. Doctor of Musical Arts in the areas of composition, piano, organ, harpsichord, choral music, voice, string instruments, wind instruments, percussion instruments, vocal accompanying and coaching, jazz; Doctor of Education in the area of music education; Doctor of Philosophy in the areas of musicology, music education. Cross-registration with Parkland College. Program accredited by NASM.

**Enrollment** 772 total; 434 undergraduate, 338 graduate.

**Music Student Profile** 55% females, 45% males, 5% minorities, 16% international.

**Music Faculty** 74 total (full-time), 16 total (part-time). 93% of full-time faculty have terminal degrees. Graduate students teach about a quarter of undergraduate courses. Undergraduate student–faculty ratio: 7:1.

**Student Life** Student groups/activities include Music Educators National Conference, Sigma Alpha Iota, Phi Mu Alpha Sinfonia.

**Expenses for 2007–2008** Application fee: $40. State resident tuition: $8440 full-time. Nonresident tuition: $22,526 full-time. Mandatory fees: $2690 full-time. Full-time tuition and fees vary according to course load, program, and student level. College room and board: $8196. Room and board charges vary according to board plan and housing facility. Entering degree-seeking students are guaranteed the same tuition rates for 4 years. Special program-related fees: $834 per year for additional music equipment and instructional support.

**Financial Aid** Program-specific awards: 5 Thomas J. Smith Scholarships for female students from Illinois ($8500), 35 performance awards for program majors ($1500–$10,000).

**Application Procedures** Students admitted directly into the professional program freshman year. Deadline for freshmen: January 1; transfers: March 1. Required: essay, high school transcript, college transcript(s) for transfer students, letter of recommendation, interview, audition, SAT or ACT test scores (minimum composite ACT score of 20), standing in top 40% of graduating class, portfolio for composition/theory and music history applicants, basic musicianship exam. Recommended: minimum 3.0 high school GPA. Auditions held 8 times on campus and off campus in New York, NY; Los Angeles, CA; recorded music is permissible as a substitute for live auditions on a case-by-case basis. Portfolio reviews held 8 times on campus.

**Web Site** http://www.music.uiuc.edu

**Contact** Joyce Griggs, Assistant Director for Enrollment Management and Student Services, School of Music, University of Illinois at Urbana–Champaign, 1114 West Nevada Street, Urbana, Illinois 61801; 217-244-0551, fax: 217-244-4585, e-mail address: griggs@uiuc.edu

# The University of Iowa
## Iowa City, Iowa

State-supported, coed. Small town campus. Total enrollment: 29,117. Music program established 1856.

**Web Site** http://www.uiowa.edu/

# University of Kansas
## Lawrence, Kansas

State-supported, coed. Suburban campus. Total enrollment: 28,569. Music program established 1877.

**Web Site** http://www.ku.edu

# University of Kentucky
## Lexington, Kentucky

State-supported, coed. Urban campus. Total enrollment: 25,856. Music program established 1918.

**Degrees** Bachelor of Music in the areas of performance, music education. Majors and concentrations: music education, music history, piano/organ, stringed instruments, voice, wind and percussion instruments. Graduate degrees offered: Master of Arts in the areas of musicology, music theory; Master of Music in the areas of performance, music composition, music education, conducting, sacred music. Doctor of Musical Arts in the areas of performance, composition, conducting; Doctor of Philosophy in the areas of musicology, music theory, music education. Program accredited by NASM.

**Enrollment** 386 total; 276 undergraduate, 90 graduate, 20 nonprofessional degree.

**Music Student Profile** 53% females, 47% males, 7% minorities, 2% international.

**Music Faculty** 40 total (full-time), 5 total (part-time). 53% of full-time faculty have terminal degrees. Graduate students teach about a quarter of undergraduate courses. Undergraduate student–faculty ratio: 8:1.

**Student Life** Student groups/activities include Music Educators National Conference Student Chapter, Percussive Arts Society Student Chapter, music fraternities and sororities. Special housing available for music students.

**Expenses for 2007–2008** Application fee: $40. State resident tuition: $6302 full-time. Nonresident tuition: $14,102 full-time. Mandatory fees: $794 full-time. Full-time tuition and fees vary according to degree level, program, reciprocity agreements, and student level. College room and board: $7973. College room only: $3785. Room and board charges vary according to board plan and housing facility. Special program-related fees: $50 per semester for applied music fee.

**Financial Aid** Program-specific awards: 100 grants-in-aid for program majors/minors ($1500–$7500).

**Application Procedures** Students admitted directly into the professional program freshman year. Deadline for freshmen and transfers: August 1. Notification date for freshmen and transfers: August 23. Required: high school transcript, college transcript(s) for transfer students, minimum 2.0 high school GPA, audition, SAT or ACT test scores. Recommended: letter of recommendation, interview. Auditions held 3 times on campus; recorded music is permissible as a substitute for live auditions if a campus visit is impossible and videotaped performances are permissible as a substitute for live auditions if a campus visit is impossible.

**Web Site** http://www.uky.edu/FineArts/Music

**Undergraduate Contact** Gordon Cole, Director of Undergraduate Studies, School of Music, University of Kentucky, 105 Fine Arts Building, Lexington, Kentucky 40506; 859-257-8181.

**Graduate Contact** Dr. Cecilia Wang, Director of Graduate Studies, School of Music, University of Kentucky, 105 Fine Arts Building, Lexington, Kentucky 40506-0022; 859-257-8176, fax: 859-257-9576.

# University of Louisiana at Lafayette
## Lafayette, Louisiana

State-supported, coed. Urban campus. Total enrollment: 16,345.

**Degrees** Bachelor of Music in the areas of performance, composition, media, jazz, theory, conducting; Bachelor of Music Education in the area of instrumental and vocal. Majors and concentrations: jazz studies, music education, music media, music theory and composition, performance, piano pedagogy. Graduate degrees offered: Master of Music in the areas of performance, conducting, music theory/composition; Master of Music Education. Program accredited by NASM.

**Enrollment** 246 total; 219 undergraduate, 27 graduate.

**Music Faculty** 22 total (full-time), 8 total (part-time). 75% of full-time faculty have terminal degrees. Graduate students teach a few undergraduate courses. Undergraduate student–faculty ratio: 10:1.

**Student Life** Student groups/activities include Music Educators National Conference, Sigma Alpha Iota, Phi Mu Alpha.

**Expenses for 2007–2008** Application fee: $25. State resident tuition: $3402 full-time. Nonresident tuition: $9582 full-time. Full-time tuition varies according to course load. College room and board: $3820. Room and board charges vary according to housing facility. Special program-related fees: $30 per credit hour for standard fees.

**Financial Aid** Program-specific awards: marching band stipend for all students in marching band ($500), 100 marching band housing awards for all students in marching band, 25 fellowships for all music students ($200).

**Application Procedures** Students admitted directly into the professional program freshman year. Deadline for freshmen and transfers: continuous. Required: high school transcript, college transcript(s) for transfer students, minimum 2.0 high school GPA, audition, SAT or ACT test scores. Auditions held in February and March on campus; recorded music is permissible as a substitute for live auditions when distance is prohibitive or scheduling is difficult and videotaped performances are permissible as a substitute for live auditions when distance is prohibitive or scheduling is difficult.

**Web Site** http://music.louisiana.edu/

**Undergraduate Contact** Dr. Garth Alper, Director, School of Music, University of Louisiana at Lafayette, Box 41207, Lafayette, Louisiana 70504-1207; 337-482-6016, fax: 337-482-5017, e-mail address: garth@louisiana.edu

**Graduate Contact** Dr. Andrea Loewy, Director of Graduate Studies, School of Music, University of Louisiana at Lafayette, Box 41207, Lafayette, Louisiana 70504-1207; 337-482-5214, fax: 337-482-5017, e-mail address: akloewy@aol.com

# University of Louisiana at Monroe
## Monroe, Louisiana

State-supported, coed. Urban campus. Total enrollment: 8,549. Music program established 1957.
**Web Site** http://www.ulm.edu/

# University of Louisville
## Louisville, Kentucky

State-supported, coed. Urban campus. Total enrollment: 20,592. Music program established 1932.

**Degrees** Bachelor of Music in the areas of performance, music history, music theory, composition, music education, music therapy. Majors and concentrations: music education, music history, music performance, music theory and composition, music therapy, piano pedagogy, piano/organ, stringed instruments, voice, wind and percussion instruments. Graduate degrees offered: Master of Arts in Teaching in the areas of instrumental music education, vocal music education; Master of Music in the areas of performance, music history, music theory/composition, jazz performance; Master of Music Education in the areas of instrumental music education, vocal music education. Cross-registration with Metroversity. Program accredited by NASM.

**Enrollment** 325 total; 174 undergraduate, 62 graduate, 89 nonprofessional degree.

**Music Student Profile** 47% females, 53% males, 12% minorities, 7% international.

**Music Faculty** 33 total (full-time), 38 total (part-time). 70% of full-time faculty have terminal degrees. Graduate students do not teach undergraduate courses. Undergraduate student–faculty ratio: 9:1.

**Student Life** Student groups/activities include Phi Mu Alpha Symphonic, Delta Omicron, Music Educators National Conference Student Chapter, International Association of Jazz Educators, American Musicological Society. Special housing available for music students.

**Expenses for 2008–2009** Application fee: $40. State resident tuition: $7564 full-time. Nonresident tuition: $18,354 full-time. College room and board: $6058. College room only: $4068. Special program-related fees: $5 per semester for practice room key/lock, $100 per semester for accompanist fee.

**Financial Aid** Program-specific awards: 1 Sister Cities Award for program majors ($12,000), 1 Presser Award for academically qualified applicants ($4000), 1 Babb Award for composition majors ($2000), 150 performance awards for music majors ($3200).

**Application Procedures** Students admitted directly into the professional program freshman year. Deadline for freshmen: June 2; transfers: July 2. Required: high school transcript, college transcript(s) for transfer students, minimum 2.0 high school GPA, 2 letters of recommendation, interview, audition, SAT or ACT test scores (minimum composite ACT score of 21), minimum 2.75 high school GPA, essay for music history applicants, portfolio for composition and music theory applicants, video for piano pedagogy and conducting applicants. Auditions held 4-6 times on campus; recorded music is permissible as a substitute for live auditions when distance is prohibitive and videotaped performances are permissible as a substitute for live auditions when distance is prohibitive.

**Web Site** http://www.louisville.edu/music

**Undergraduate Contact** Amanda Boyd, Admissions Coordinator, School of Music, University of Louisville, Louisville, Kentucky 40292; 502-852-1623, fax: 502-852-0520, e-mail address: amanda.boyd@louisville.edu

**Graduate Contact** Dr. Jean Christensen, Director of Graduate Studies, School of Music, University of Louisville, Louisville, Kentucky 40292; 502-852-0540, fax: 502-852-0520, e-mail address: jean.christensen@louisville.edu

# University of Manitoba
## Winnipeg, Manitoba, Canada

Province-supported, coed. Suburban campus. Total enrollment: 25,516. Music program established 1964.

**Degrees** Bachelor of Music in the areas of performance, history, general music, composition; Bachelor of Music/Bachelor of Education. Majors and concentrations: composition, music, music education, music history, performance. Graduate degrees offered: Master of Music in the areas of performance, composition, choral and wind conducting.

**Enrollment** 260 total; 240 undergraduate, 20 graduate.

**Music Student Profile** 10% minorities, 5% international.

**Music Faculty** 22 total (full-time), 42 total (part-time). 55% of full-time faculty have terminal degrees. Graduate students do not teach undergraduate courses. Undergraduate student–faculty ratio: 4:1.

**Student Life** Student groups/activities include University Orchestra, wind and jazz ensembles, university choirs.

**Expenses for 2007–2008** Application fee: $75 Canadian dollars. Tuition varies by major. Contact institution directly for tuition information.

**Financial Aid** Program-specific awards: University of Manitoba Entrance Scholarships for entering students with 85.1 or higher in best five academic subjects combined with excellence in performance audition ($800–$2000), 28 Faculty of Music Scholarships for excellent auditions ($200–$2000), 7 Faculty of Music Bursaries for those demonstrating financial need ($150–$1500), 6 prizes for best performance in musical competitions ($100–$1000).

**Application Procedures** Students admitted directly into the professional program freshman year. Deadline for freshmen and transfers: January 15. Notification date for freshmen and transfers: June 1. Required: essay, high school transcript, college

*University of Manitoba (continued)*

transcript(s) for transfer students, minimum 2.0 high school GPA, 2 letters of recommendation, interview, audition, theory assessment, portfolios for composition applicants only. Recommended: minimum 3.0 high school GPA. Auditions held once on campus and off campus in Calgary, AB; Camrose, AB; recorded music is permissible as a substitute for live auditions out-of-province applicants and videotaped performances are permissible as a substitute for live auditions out-of-province applicants. Portfolio reviews held on campus.
**Web Site** http://umanitoba.ca/music
**Undergraduate Contact** Susan Leeson, Registrar, Faculty of Music, University of Manitoba, 65 Dafoe Road, Winnipeg, Manitoba R3T 2N2, Canada; 204-474-9133, fax: 204-474-7546, e-mail address: sleeson@cc.umanitoba.ca
**Graduate Contact** Susan Leeson, Registrar, Faculty of Music, University of Manitoba, 65 DaFoe Road, Winnipeg, Manitoba R3T 2N2, Canada; 204-474-9133, fax: 204-474-7546, e-mail address: sleeson@cc.umanitoba.ac

## University of Maryland, College Park

### College Park, Maryland

State-supported, coed. Suburban campus. Total enrollment: 35,970. Music program established 1964.
**Degrees** Bachelor of Music in the areas of theory, composition, music performance, music education. Majors and concentrations: choral music education, composition, instrumental music education, music theory, piano, stringed instruments, voice, wind and percussion instruments. Graduate degrees offered: Master of Arts in the areas of ethnomusicology, music history and literature, music theory; Master of Music in the areas of performance, theory/composition, music education. Doctor of Musical Arts in the areas of performance, composition; Doctor of Philosophy in the areas of musicology, ethnomusicology, theory, music education. Cross-registration with University of Maryland System. Program accredited by NASM.
**Enrollment** 582 total; 243 undergraduate, 339 graduate.
**Music Student Profile** 55% females, 45% males, 30% minorities, 20% international.
**Music Faculty** 45 total (full-time), 49 total (part-time). 53% of full-time faculty have terminal degrees. Graduate students teach a few undergraduate courses. Undergraduate student–faculty ratio: 3:1.
**Student Life** Student groups/activities include Phi Mu Alpha, Sigma Alpha Iota, Pi Kappa Lambda.
**Expenses for 2007–2008** Application fee: $55. State resident tuition: $6566 full-time. Nonresident tuition: $20,005 full-time. Mandatory fees: $1403 full-time. College room and board: $8854. College room only: $5287. Room and board charges vary according to board plan. Special program-related fees: $300 per semester for applied music fee for private lessons.
**Financial Aid** Program-specific awards: 10 Creative and Performing Arts Scholarships for program majors ($7500), 35 Director's Scholarships for program majors ($1000–$10,000), 15 Endowed Funds Awards for program majors ($1000–$15,000).
**Application Procedures** Students admitted directly into the professional program freshman year. Deadline for freshmen and transfers: December 1. Notification date for freshmen and transfers: March 1. Required: essay, high school transcript, college transcript(s) for transfer students, minimum 3.0 high school GPA, 2 letters of recommendation, audition, SAT or ACT test scores, portfolio for composition applicants. Recommended: interview, record of co-curricular activities. Auditions held once on campus; recorded music is permissible as a substitute for live auditions when distance is prohibitive (beyond a 250-mile radius) and videotaped performances are permissible as a substitute for live auditions when distance is prohibitive (beyond a 250-mile radius). Portfolio reviews held as needed on campus.
**Web Site** http://www.music.umd.edu
**Contact** Mrs. Ashley Fleming, Director of Admissions, School of Music, University of Maryland, College Park, Clarice Smith Performing Arts Center, College Park, Maryland 20742-9504; 301-405-8435, fax: 301-314-7966, e-mail address: musicadmissions@umd.edu

## University of Massachusetts Amherst

### Amherst, Massachusetts

State-supported, coed. Total enrollment: 25,873. Music program established 1968.
**Web Site** http://www.umass.edu/

## University of Massachusetts Dartmouth

### North Dartmouth, Massachusetts

State-supported, coed. Suburban campus. Total enrollment: 9,080. Music program established 1964.
**Degrees** Bachelor of Arts in the area of music. Majors and concentrations: music, music education, world/African-American music. Cross-registration with University of Massachusetts System, Southeastern Association for Cooperation in Higher Education in Massachusetts.
**Enrollment** 81 total; all undergraduate.
**Music Student Profile** 35% females, 65% males, 11% minorities.
**Music Faculty** 4 total (full-time), 22 total (part-time). 75% of full-time faculty have terminal degrees. Graduate students do not teach undergraduate courses. Undergraduate student–faculty ratio: 7:1.
**Student Life** Student groups/activities include Kekeli African Drum and Dance, jazz, pep, and concert bands, chorus.
**Expenses for 2007–2008** Application fee: $40. State resident tuition: $1417 full-time. Nonresident tuition: $11,999 full-time. Mandatory fees: $7175 full-time. Full-time tuition and fees vary according to program and reciprocity agreements. College room and board: $8432. College room only: $5670. Room and board charges vary according to board plan and housing facility. Special program-related fees: $343 per semester for CVPA fee, $420 per course for applied music fee.
**Financial Aid** Program-specific awards: 1 Alda Alves and Bruce Yenawine Scholarship for CVPA students ($1000), 1 Lillian Telles Jenkins Scholarship for CVPA students ($400), 4 Ayuko Ito Scholarships for CVPA students ($1000), 1 Clement Yeager Scholarship for CVPA students ($700–$2500).
**Application Procedures** Students admitted directly into the professional program freshman year. Deadline for freshmen and transfers: continuous. Notification date for freshmen and transfers: continuous. Required: high school transcript, college transcript(s) for transfer students, minimum 2.0 high school GPA, audition, SAT or ACT test scores. Recommended: essay, minimum 3.0 high school GPA, 3 letters of recommendation. Auditions held monthly from January to May on campus; videotaped performances are permissible as a substitute for live auditions (non-New England students should contact department for requirements).
**Web Site** http://www.umassd.edu/cvpa
**Undergraduate Contact** Mr. Steven T. Briggs, Director of Admissions, University of Massachusetts Dartmouth, 285 Old Westport Road, North Dartmouth, Massachusetts 02747-2300; 508-999-8606, fax: 508-999-8755, e-mail address: admissions@umassd.edu

### More About the University

"A world of sound . . . a community of musicians."

All candidates for a Bachelor of Arts (B.A.) in music follow a standard core curriculum. Each student may also choose an option in music education or world music/jazz studies.

Students are given a thorough grounding in the performance and historical background of the Western music tradition. Graduates may further their studies or pursue careers in a variety of related fields. The education program develops skillful teachers who are in demand throughout New England. Students are exposed to Western, African American/jazz, and World music—allowing them to bring diverse experiences into the classroom. State-of-the-art facilities and course content in music technology enable students to function at the cutting edge of today's music scene, from sound recording and manipulation to electronic composition and video scoring. Jazz and world music studios open students to the music and dance of the world's peoples, including the dynamic traditions of Africa, Asia, the Americas, and the African American heritage. At UMass Dartmouth, the global approach to education in a university setting prepares culturally aware graduates for careers in the performing arts and teaching.

**Facilities and Equipment** The music facilities of the College of Visual and Performing Arts (CVPA) include an 800-seat auditorium, an intimate 200-seat recital hall, computer-aided music stations, an electronic clavinova piano lab, two electronic music studios for electronic composition, recording technology and sound production capabilities, Steinway concert grand pianos, traditional and non-Western percussion instruments (Gamelan, steel drums), individual practice rooms, and a campuswide computer network.

**Faculty** The performance faculty members are accomplished musicians who perform in recital halls and on concert stages, both internationally and in the United States. The composition and academic faculty members are noted for their publications, academic papers, and creative work—recognized during the past academic year with a Rome Prize in Music and a Fulbright Scholar Award.

**Performance Opportunities** Students have opportunities to perform in the following groups: University Chorus, Wind Ensemble, Concert Band, Large and Small Jazz Ensembles, Brass Ensemble, West African Drum and Dance Ensemble, Laptop Ensemble, Contemporary Jazz and Jazz Vocal Ensembles, Guitar Ensemble, Javanese Gamelan, and Percussion Ensemble. The Department of Music presents a Guest Artist Recital Series, a Faculty Recital Series, and community concerts as well as student ensemble and solo recitals.

**Special Programs** Music Minor: Students majoring in another field may pursue a minor in music, emphasizing performance, music theory, or jazz.

**Study Abroad** Students are encouraged to pursue fieldwork study and research abroad in a culture relevant to their area of concentration. This work may fulfill specific course requirements with prior approval. All study abroad should be planned in consultation with the student's faculty adviser and the Department of Music Chairperson.

**Requirements for Admission** All candidates must pass an entrance audition and take an advisory exam to assess background and determine potential. Candidates are expected to have some facility on their instrument and to have some preparation in fundamental concepts of music theory. All applicants must also follow the University of Massachusetts Dartmouth's admissions procedures that are detailed in the University Catalogue.

# University of Massachusetts Lowell
## Lowell, Massachusetts

State-supported, coed. Urban campus. Total enrollment: 11,635. Music program established 1894.
**Degrees** Bachelor of Music in the areas of performance, music business, sound recording technology, music studies. Majors and concentrations: music business, music studies, performance, sound recording technology. Graduate degrees offered: Master of Music in the areas of music education, sound recording technology. Program accredited by NASM, NCATE.
**Enrollment** 332 total; 310 undergraduate, 22 graduate.
**Music Student Profile** 36% females, 64% males, 12% minorities, 10% international.
**Music Faculty** 12 total (full-time), 42 total (part-time). 100% of full-time faculty have terminal degrees. Graduate students do not teach undergraduate courses. Undergraduate student–faculty ratio: 13:1.
**Student Life** Student groups/activities include Society of Professional Audio Recording Services, Music Educators National Conference, Audio Engineering Society, Entertainment and Music Industry Association.

**Expenses for 2007–2008** Application fee: $60. State resident tuition: $1454 full-time. Nonresident tuition: $8567 full-time. Mandatory fees: $7277 full-time. College room and board: $6978. College room only: $4331. Room and board charges vary according to board plan and housing facility.
**Financial Aid** Program-specific awards available.
**Application Procedures** Students apply for admission into the professional program by sophomore year. Deadline for freshmen and transfers: continuous. Required: high school transcript, college transcript(s) for transfer students, 2 letters of recommendation, audition, SAT test score only, minimum 3.0 for sound recording technology. Recommended: minimum 2.5 high school GPA. Auditions held 4 times on campus; recorded music is permissible as a substitute for live auditions when distance is prohibitive and videotaped performances are permissible as a substitute for live auditions when distance is prohibitive.
**Web Site** http://www.uml.edu
**Undergraduate Contact** Dr. Paula Telesco, Chair, Department of Music, University of Massachusetts Lowell, 35 Wilder Street, Suite 3, Lowell, Massachusetts 01854-3083; 978-934-3850, fax: 978-934-3034, e-mail address: paula_telesco@uml.edu
**Graduate Contact** Dr. Nicholas Tobin, Graduate Coordinator, Department of Music, University of Massachusetts Lowell, 35 Wilder Street, Suite 3, Lowell, Massachusetts 01854-3083; 978-934-3879, fax: 978-934-3034, e-mail address: rnicholas_tobin@uml.edu

## The Rudi E. Scheidt School of Music
# University of Memphis
## Memphis, Tennessee

State-supported, coed. Urban campus. Total enrollment: 20,379. Music program established 1953.
**Web Site** http://www.memphis.edu/

## Frost School of Music
# University of Miami
## Coral Gables, Florida

Independent, coed. Suburban campus. Total enrollment: 15,462. Music program established 1926.
**Degrees** Bachelor of Arts; Bachelor of Music in the areas of performance composition, studio music and jazz, music engineering technology, music business, music education, music therapy, musical theatre; Bachelor of Science in the area of music engineering technology. Majors and concentrations: composition, composition/commercial music and production, instrumental performance, keyboard performance, music, music business and entertainment, music education, music engineering technology, music theater, music therapy, performance, studio music and jazz, vocal performance. Graduate degrees offered: Master of Music in the areas of accompanying and chamber music, conducting, electronic music, jazz performance, jazz pedagogy, keyboard performance and pedagogy, media writing/production, music education, theory, composition, music therapy, music business and entertainment industries, musicology, studio jazz writing, performance; Master of Science in the area of music engineering. Doctor of Musical Arts in the areas of accompanying and chamber music, composition, jazz composition, conducting, keyboard performance and pedagogy, performance, jazz performance. Program accredited by NASM.
**Enrollment** 724 total; 500 undergraduate, 210 graduate, 14 nonprofessional degree.
**Music Student Profile** 40% females, 60% males, 29% minorities, 11% international.
**Music Faculty** 58 total (full-time), 56 total (part-time). 80% of full-time faculty have terminal degrees. Graduate students teach a few undergraduate courses. Undergraduate student–faculty ratio: 7:1.
**Student Life** Student groups/activities include Phi Mu Alpha Sinfonia, Sigma Alpha Iota, Pi Kappa Lambda.

*University of Miami (continued)*

**Expenses for 2007–2008** Application fee: $65. Comprehensive fee: $42,724 includes full-time tuition ($32,422), mandatory fees ($696), and college room and board ($9606). College room only: $5762.

**Financial Aid** Program-specific awards: need-based grants, loans for those demonstrating need ($2000–$15,000), 222 Frost School of Music Scholarships for those demonstrating musical and/or academic talent ($2000–$31,288).

**Application Procedures** Students admitted directly into the professional program freshman year. Deadline for freshmen and transfers: January 15. Notification date for freshmen and transfers: April 1. Required: essay, high school transcript, college transcript(s) for transfer students, 3 letters of recommendation, audition, SAT or ACT test scores, portfolio for music theory/composition. Recommended: minimum 3.0 high school GPA. Auditions held 14 times on campus and off campus in Atlanta, GA; Boston, MA; Chicago, IL; Dallas, TX; Houston, TX; New York, NY; Philadelphia, PA; Los Angeles, CA; Washington, DC; recorded music is permissible as a substitute for live auditions when distance is prohibitive and videotaped performances are permissible as a substitute for live auditions when distance is prohibitive.

**Web Site** http://www.music.miami.edu

**Undergraduate Contact** Ms. Karen Kerr, Director of Admission and Recruitment, Frost School of Music, University of Miami, PO Box 248165, Coral Gables, Florida 33124; 305-284-2241, fax: 305-284-6475, e-mail address: kmkerr@miami.edu

**Graduate Contact** Dr. Edward P. Asmus, Associate Dean, Frost School of Music, University of Miami, PO Box 248165, Coral Gables, Florida 33124; 305-284-2241, fax: 305-284-6475, e-mail address: ed.asmus@miami.edu

## More About the University

Each year, students from across the United States and approximately forty countries pursue undergraduate and graduate study at the Frost School of Music at the University of Miami. The Frost School enjoys a reputation as a comprehensive and innovative music school, with more than three dozen degree, certificate, diploma, and international exchange program options available.

Since its founding in 1926 and accreditation in 1939 by the National Association of Schools of Music, the Frost School of Music has become one of the largest schools of its kind in a private institution of higher learning in the United States. The Frost School pioneered innovative programs in music business and entertainment industries, music engineering, and studio music and jazz. Since its inception, strong programs in composition/theory, performance, and music education have been a part of the curriculum. Flexible, well-rounded music instruction, designed to give graduates a professional edge, remains a hallmark of the Frost School.

More than 58 full-time faculty members and 56 adjunct faculty members are active in the classroom and as dedicated music professionals. The diverse nature of the programs in the Frost School of Music has attracted a faculty with a broad outlook in its approach to music education, and its members impart and encourage diversity in the music classroom.

Students choosing the Frost School of Music are focused and serious about their studies and are eager for the academic and performance opportunities available to them at the University of Miami. The low ratio of students to faculty members fosters close academic bonding. Every music student enjoys one-on-one studio instruction.

Many of the more than 4,500 students who have graduated from the Frost School of Music have distinguished themselves professionally. Alumni provide a veritable "Who's Who" of both performance and related musical careers. Frost School of Music graduates perform with major orchestras, operas, and jazz ensembles. Their compositions range from orchestral and operatic music to film and video scores. Some graduates are among the top

solo performing artists in the country; others excel as arrangers, recording engineers, editors, therapists, teachers, publishers, distributors, and retailers.

The Frost School of Music is situated on the University's Coral Gables campus, minutes from the city of Miami, where students enjoy a delightful climate that lends itself to a wide range of activities. All the cultural advantages of a metropolitan center are available to Frost School of Music students. In addition to being the home of the New World Symphony and the Florida Grand Opera, the Miami area is regularly included in concert tours of major symphonies, concert artists, jazz performers, and opera companies. Music students are able to participate in master classes given frequently by visiting artists performing in the greater Miami area.

**Facilities** The music complex includes a 600-seat concert hall and 150-seat recital hall, five newly renovated rehearsal halls, two state-of-the-art recording studios, two computer/MIDI keyboard labs, two multimedia classrooms, instructional studios, practice rooms, and classrooms.

The Marta and Austin Weeks Music Library and Technology Center, the newest and largest branch of the University of Miami Libraries, showcases a wide range of resources. Among the nationally known collections housed in the 22,500-square-foot facility are sound recordings, musical theater archives, musical scores, musical manuscripts, research collections, and a wealth of e-resources. This state-of-the-art research facility was built at a cost of $9.9 million.

The 5,200-square-foot Music Technology Center houses a Music Engineering Lab, two Keyboard/Computer Labs, a Multimedia Instruction and Learning Lab (MILL), an Electronic Music Lab, and a Media-Writing and Production Lab. All of the labs contain computers with flat-panel displays, sophisticated software packages for program-specific work, 5.1 Surround Sound™ monitoring, audio/video playback systems, and video projection capabilities.

**Faculty and Alumni** There are more than 114 faculty members. Faculty members perform with the Florida Grand Opera, Miami City Ballet Orchestra, the Naples Philharmonic, and various jazz ensembles. Academic faculty members are widely published and recognized in their various fields. Alumni include Grammy winners Bruce Hornsby and Jon Secada; opera stars Marvis Martin and Sandra Lopez; television star Dawnn Lewis; Keith Buterbaugh, Raoul in *Phantom of the Opera;* Gary Fry, arranger and producer of more than 1,800 commercials; Sam Pilafian, founder of the Empire Brass Quintet and Travelin' Light; and Matt Pierson, Senior Vice President/General Manager Jazz for Warner Brothers Records.

**Performance** The Frost School of Music serves as a major cultural resource for the Greater Miami area, presenting more than 300 musical events annually. Complementing on-campus recitals and concerts by students and faculty members are programs by guest artists, composers, conductors, and lecturers from virtually every corner of the world. Festival Miami, a monthlong international music festival held each fall, typically features performances by an array of faculty and guest artists, student ensembles, composers, and conductors, including many premiere performances of new compositions. Several of the Frost School's more than fifty ensembles have performed in tours around the United States and the world.

# University of Michigan
## Ann Arbor, Michigan

State-supported, coed. Suburban campus. Total enrollment: 41,042. Music program established 1984.

**Degrees** Bachelor of Fine Arts in the area of musical theatre. Majors and concentrations: music theater.

**Enrollment** 80 total; all undergraduate.

**Music Student Profile** 50% females, 50% males, 20% minorities.

Music Faculty 9 total undergraduate. Graduate students do not teach undergraduate courses. Undergraduate student–faculty ratio: 9:1.

Expenses for 2007–2008 Application fee: $40. State resident tuition: $10,258 full-time. Nonresident tuition: $31,112 full-time. Mandatory fees: $189 full-time. Full-time tuition and fees vary according to course load, degree level, location, program, and student level. College room and board: $8190. Room and board charges vary according to board plan and housing facility.

Financial Aid Program-specific awards available.

Application Procedures Students admitted directly into the professional program freshman year. Deadline for freshmen and transfers: December 1. Required: essay, high school transcript, college transcript(s) for transfer students, minimum 3.0 high school GPA, 2 letters of recommendation, audition, SAT or ACT test scores (minimum combined SAT score of 1650, minimum composite ACT score of 24), typed resumé (bring to audition), recent photograph (bring to audition), brief personal statement (bring to audition). Auditions held 10 times on campus and off campus in Chicago, IL; New York, NY.

Web Site http://www.music.umich.edu

Undergraduate Contact Ms. Laura Strozeski, Assistant Dean for Enrollment Management and Student Services, Office of Admissions and Student Services, University of Michigan, 2290 Moore Building, 1100 Baits Drive, Ann Arbor, Michigan 48109-2085; 734-764-0593, fax: 734-763-5097, e-mail address: music.admissions@umich.edu

# University of Michigan

## Ann Arbor, Michigan

State-supported, coed. Suburban campus. Total enrollment: 41,042. Music program established 1880.

Degrees Bachelor of Fine Arts in the areas of performing arts technology, jazz and improvisation, jazz studies, jazz and contemplative studies, design, production; Bachelor of Music in the areas of composition, music and technology, music education, music history, music theory, performance; Bachelor of Musical Arts in the areas of composition, jazz studies, music history, music theory, performance; Bachelor of Science in the area of sound engineering. Majors and concentrations: composition, jazz, music education, music history, music technology, music theory, performing arts technology, piano/organ, stringed instruments, voice, wind and percussion instruments. Graduate degrees offered: Master of Arts in the areas of composition, media arts, musicology, music theory; Master of Music in the areas of arts administration, church music, composition, conducting, improvisation, piano pedagogy and performance, collaborative piano, chamber music, early keyboard instruments, music education, performance: strings, voice, winds and percussion. Doctor of Musical Arts in the areas of collaborative piano, composition, conducting, organ performance, harpsichord performance, piano pedagogy and performance, piano performance, string instruments, voice, wind instruments; Doctor of Philosophy in the areas of music education, music theory, composition, musicology and music theory. Program accredited by NASM.

Enrollment 1,049 total; 777 undergraduate, 272 graduate.

Music Student Profile 52% females, 48% males, 17% minorities, 7% international.

Music Faculty 140 total (full-time), 35 total (part-time). 45% of full-time faculty have terminal degrees. Graduate students teach a few undergraduate courses. Undergraduate student–faculty ratio: 8:1.

Student Life Student groups/activities include Music Educators National Conference, Pi Kappa Lambda, Sigma Alpha Iota/Phi Mu Alpha.

Expenses for 2007–2008 Application fee: $40. State resident tuition: $10,258 full-time. Nonresident tuition: $31,112 full-time. Mandatory fees: $189 full-time. Full-time tuition and fees vary according to course load, degree level, location, program, and student level. College room and board: $8190. Room and board charges vary according to board plan and housing facility.

Financial Aid Program-specific awards: 163 merit awards for program students ($7067).

Application Procedures Students admitted directly into the professional program freshman year. Deadline for freshmen and transfers: December 1. Required: essay, high school transcript, college transcript(s) for transfer students, minimum 3.0 high school GPA, 2 letters of recommendation, audition, SAT or ACT test scores (minimum combined SAT score of 1650, minimum composite ACT score of 24), portfolio for composition and performing arts technology students, interview for music education and technology applicants. Auditions held 15 times on campus and off campus in New York, NY; Los Angeles, CA; Houston, TX; recorded music is permissible as a substitute for live auditions in some programs when distance is prohibitive and videotaped performances are permissible as a substitute for live auditions when distance is prohibitive. Portfolio reviews held continuously on campus.

Web Site http://www.music.umich.edu

Contact Ms. Laura Strozeski, Assistant Dean for Enrollment Management and Student Services, School of Music, University of Michigan, 1100 Baits Drive, Ann Arbor, Michigan 48109-2085; 734-764-0593, fax: 734-763-5097, e-mail address: music.admissions@umich.edu

# University of Minnesota, Duluth

## Duluth, Minnesota

State-supported, coed. Suburban campus. Total enrollment: 11,184. Music program established 1942.

Degrees Bachelor of Arts in the area of music; Bachelor of Music in the areas of jazz studies, performance, music education, theory-composition. Majors and concentrations: jazz studies, music education, music theory and composition, performance. Graduate degrees offered: Master of Music in the area of performance; Master of Music Education. Cross-registration with University of Wisconsin-Superior, College of St. Scholastica. Program accredited by NASM.

Enrollment 508 total; 147 undergraduate, 9 graduate, 352 nonprofessional degree.

Music Student Profile 50% females, 50% males, 7% minorities.

Music Faculty 19 total (full-time), 18 total (part-time). 100% of full-time faculty have terminal degrees. Graduate students teach a few undergraduate courses. Undergraduate student–faculty ratio: 7:1.

Student Life Student groups/activities include Music Educators National Conference, American Choral Directors Association, International Association for Jazz Education.

Expenses for 2007–2008 Application fee: $35. State resident tuition: $7700 full-time. Nonresident tuition: $17,327 full-time. Mandatory fees: $1900 full-time. Full-time tuition and fees vary according to course load, degree level, program, and reciprocity agreements. College room and board: $5904. College room only: $3868. Special program-related fees: $115–$235 per semester for lesson fees (music majors).

Financial Aid Program-specific awards: 1 Eric Tobias Johnson Scholarship for program majors ($250), 4 String Quartet Scholarships for string players ($1250), 4 Rand Scholarships for music education majors ($800), 1 Edson Scholarship for program majors ($1200), 2 Murphy Scholarships for program majors ($1250), 2 Bernstein Jazz Scholarships for jazz players ($1100), 1 Comella Scholarship for music education majors ($1000), 1 Faricy Scholarship for trumpet players ($1500), 1–3 Gauger Scholarships for keyboardists ($300), 1 Gendein Scholarship for state residents ($750), 2 Gershgol Scholarships for program majors ($800), 1 Oreck Scholarship for program majors ($500), 8 Gregg Johnson Scholarships for program majors ($1200), opera scholarship for voice performance majors.

Application Procedures Students admitted directly into the professional program freshman year. Deadline for freshmen and transfers: continuous. Required: college transcript(s) for transfer students, letter of recommendation, interview, audition, SAT or ACT test scores. Recommended: high school transcript. Auditions held 4 times and by request on campus; recorded music is permissible as a substitute for live auditions when distance is prohibitive and videotaped performances are permissible as a substitute for live auditions when distance is prohibitive.

Web Site http://www.d.umn.edu/music/

*University of Minnesota, Duluth (continued)*

**Undergraduate Contact** Kathy Neff, Chair, Scholarship Committee, Department of Music, University of Minnesota, Duluth, 231 H, 1201 Ordean Court, Duluth, Minnesota 55812; 218-726-7090, fax: 218-726-8210, e-mail address: kneff@d.umn.edu

**Graduate Contact** Dr. Judith Kritzmire, Head, Department of Music, University of Minnesota, Duluth, 231 H, 1201 Ordean Court, Duluth, Minnesota 55812; 218-726-8260, fax: 218-726-8210, e-mail address: jkritzmi@d.umn.edu

# University of Minnesota, Twin Cities Campus

## Minneapolis, Minnesota

State-supported, coed. Urban campus. Total enrollment: 50,883. Music program established 1902.

**Degrees** Bachelor of Music in the areas of performance, music education, music therapy. Majors and concentrations: guitar, harp, music education, music therapy, piano/organ, stringed instruments, voice, wind and percussion instruments. Graduate degrees offered: Master of Music in the areas of performance, choral conducting, orchestral conducting, wind/band conducting, accompanying/coaching. Doctor of Musical Arts in the areas of performance, conducting, accompanying/coaching; Doctor of Philosophy in the areas of composition, music education/music therapy, musicology/ethnomusicology, theory. Program accredited by NASM.

**Enrollment** 571 total; 280 undergraduate, 254 graduate, 37 nonprofessional degree.

**Music Student Profile** 60% females, 40% males, 8% minorities, 14% international.

**Music Faculty** 47 total (full-time), 33 total (part-time). 64% of full-time faculty have terminal degrees. Graduate students teach a few undergraduate courses. Undergraduate student–faculty ratio: 4:1.

**Student Life** Student groups/activities include Music Educators National Conference, Music Therapy Club, music fraternities and sororities. Special housing available for music students.

**Expenses for 2007–2008** Application fee: $45. One-time mandatory fee: $1000. State resident tuition: $7950 full-time. Nonresident tuition: $19,580 full-time. Full-time tuition varies according to program and reciprocity agreements. College room and board: $7062. College room only: $4184. Room and board charges vary according to board plan, housing facility, and location. Special program-related fees: $5–$90 per semester for practice rooms, $50–$220 per semester for applied music lessons.

**Financial Aid** Program-specific awards: 75–100 School of Music Scholarships for exceptionally talented students ($1000–$7500).

**Application Procedures** Students admitted directly into the professional program freshman year. Deadline for freshmen: December 15; transfers: continuous. Notification date for freshmen and transfers: continuous. Required: high school transcript, college transcript(s) for transfer students, interview, audition, SAT or ACT test scores, minimum 2.5 college GPA for transfer students. Recommended: 2 letters of recommendation. Auditions held 6 times on campus; recorded music is permissible as a substitute for live auditions when distance is prohibitive and videotaped performances are permissible as a substitute for live auditions when distance is prohibitive.

**Web Site** http://www.music.umn.edu

**Undergraduate Contact** Mr. Aaron J. Rosenberger, Recruitment Coordinator, School of Music, University of Minnesota, Twin Cities Campus, 2106 4th Street South, Minneapolis, Minnesota 55455; 612-624-2847, fax: 612-624-8001, e-mail address: rosen510@umn.edu

**Graduate Contact** Mr. Stanley H. Rothrock, Graduate Student Services, School of Music, University of Minnesota, Twin Cities Campus, 2106 4th Street South, Minneapolis, Minnesota 55455; 612-624-0071, fax: 612-624-8001, e-mail address: roth0228@umn.edu

# University of Mississippi

## University, Mississippi

State-supported, coed. Small town campus. Total enrollment: 15,129. Music program established 1926.

**Degrees** Bachelor of Music in the areas of performance, instrumental music education, vocal music education, keyboard music education. Majors and concentrations: music education, music theory, piano/organ, stringed instruments, voice, wind and percussion instruments. Graduate degrees offered: Master of Music in the areas of performance, instrumental music education, vocal music education, choral conducting, music theory, keyboard music education. Doctor of Arts in the areas of music theory, music literature, music education. Program accredited by NASM.

**Enrollment** 233 total; 141 undergraduate, 62 graduate, 30 nonprofessional degree.

**Music Student Profile** 43% females, 57% males, 7% minorities, 3% international.

**Music Faculty** 24 total (full-time), 9 total (part-time). 75% of full-time faculty have terminal degrees. Graduate students do not teach undergraduate courses. Undergraduate student–faculty ratio: 8:1.

**Student Life** Student groups/activities include Music Educators National Conference, American Choral Directors Association.

**Expenses for 2007–2008** Application fee: $50. State resident tuition: $4932 full-time. Nonresident tuition: $11,436 full-time. College room and board: $6578. College room only: $3300. Room and board charges vary according to board plan and housing facility. Special program-related fees: $35 per semester hour for applied lesson fee.

**Financial Aid** Program-specific awards: 150 band scholarships for wind and percussion players ($1500), 25 orchestra scholarships for stringed instrument players ($500–$1500), 75 chorus scholarships for vocalists ($500–$1500), 15 piano scholarships for pianists ($1000–$2000), 4 special scholarships for music majors ($1000–$2000).

**Application Procedures** Students apply for admission into the professional program by sophomore year. Deadline for freshmen and transfers: April 1. Required: high school transcript, college transcript(s) for transfer students, minimum 2.0 high school GPA, interview, audition, SAT or ACT test scores (minimum composite ACT score of 20). Recommended: 2 letters of recommendation. Auditions held by appointment on campus; recorded music is permissible as a substitute for live auditions with special permission and videotaped performances are permissible as a substitute for live auditions with special permission.

**Web Site** http://www.olemiss.edu/depts/music/

**Undergraduate Contact** Dr. Charles Gates, Chair and Professor, Music Department, University of Mississippi, 164 Scruggs Hall, University, Mississippi 38677; 662-915-7268, fax: 662-915-1230.

**Graduate Contact** Dr. Alan Spurgeon, Professor, Music Department, University of Mississippi, 162 Scruggs Hall, University, Mississippi 38677; 662-915-7268, fax: 662-915-1230.

# University of Missouri–Columbia

## Columbia, Missouri

State-supported, coed. Suburban campus. Total enrollment: 28,477. Music program established 1912.

**Degrees** Bachelor of Music in the areas of performance, theory, history, composition; Bachelor of Science in the area of music education. Majors and concentrations: composition, music education, music history, music theory, piano, stringed instruments, voice, wind and percussion instruments. Graduate degrees offered: Master of Arts in the area of music history; Master of Education in the area of music education; Master of Music in the areas of band conducting, choral conducting, orchestra conducting, piano, strings, winds, percussion, voice, music theory, composition, accompanying, piano pedagogy. Doctor of Philosophy in the area of music education. Program accredited by NASM.

**Enrollment** 215 total; 155 undergraduate, 45 graduate, 15 nonprofessional degree.

**Music Student Profile** 53% females, 47% males, 10% minorities, 8% international.

**Music Faculty** 34 total (full-time), 5 total (part-time). 66% of full-time faculty have terminal degrees. Graduate students teach a few undergraduate courses. Undergraduate student–faculty ratio: 5:1.

**Expenses for 2007–2008** Application fee: $45. State resident tuition: $7077 full-time. Nonresident tuition: $17,733 full-time. Mandatory fees: $1022 full-time. Full-time tuition and fees vary according to course load, program, and reciprocity agreements. College room and board: $7002. College room only: $3752. Room and board charges vary according to board plan and housing facility. Special program-related fees: $194 per semester for applied music fee.

**Financial Aid** Program-specific awards: 80 music scholarships for band, orchestra, chorus participants ($800).

**Application Procedures** Students admitted directly into the professional program freshman year. Deadline for freshmen and transfers: April 1. Notification date for freshmen and transfers: continuous. Required: high school transcript, college transcript(s) for transfer students, minimum 2.0 high school GPA, audition, ACT test score only. Recommended: 2 letters of recommendation. Auditions held 4 times on campus; recorded music is permissible as a substitute for live auditions when distance is prohibitive and videotaped performances are permissible as a substitute for live auditions when distance is prohibitive.

**Web Site** http://www.music.missouri.edu

**Contact** Mr. Dan L. Willett, Director of Graduate and Undergraduate Studies in Music, School of Music, University of Missouri–Columbia, 138 Fine Arts, Columbia, Missouri 65211; 573-882-0933, fax: 573-884-7444, e-mail address: willettd@missouri.edu

# University of Missouri–Kansas City
## Kansas City, Missouri

State-supported, coed. Urban campus. Total enrollment: 14,442. Music program established 1907.

**Degrees** Bachelor of Arts in the area of music therapy; Bachelor of Music in the areas of composition, instrumental music, voice, piano pedagogy, music, applied music, jazz and studio music; Bachelor of Music Education in the areas of music education, music therapy. Majors and concentrations: composition, guitar, music education, music theory, music therapy, piano/organ, stringed instruments, studio music and jazz, voice, wind and percussion instruments. Graduate degrees offered: Master of Arts in the area of music therapy; Master of Music in the areas of composition, applied music, voice, conducting; Master of Music Education in the area of music education. Doctor of Musical Arts in the areas of performance, composition, conducting. Program accredited by NASM, AMTA.

**Enrollment** 650 total; 380 undergraduate, 270 graduate.

**Music Student Profile** 57% females, 43% males, 10% minorities, 10% international.

**Music Faculty** 48 total (full-time), 30 total (part-time). 80% of full-time faculty have terminal degrees. Graduate students teach a few undergraduate courses. Undergraduate student–faculty ratio: 12:1.

**Student Life** Student groups/activities include Collegiate Music Educators National Conference, Music Therapy Association, American Choral Directors Association.

**Expenses for 2008–2009** Application fee: $35. State resident tuition: $7368 full-time. Nonresident tuition: $18,459 full-time. Mandatory fees: $1028 full-time. College room and board: $7841. College room only: $5460. Special program-related fees: $194 per semester for applied lesson fee.

**Financial Aid** Program-specific awards: music awards for program majors ($500–$12,000).

**Application Procedures** Students admitted directly into the professional program freshman year. Deadline for freshmen and transfers: March 7. Notification date for freshmen and transfers: continuous. Required: high school transcript, college transcript(s) for transfer students, minimum 2.0 high school GPA, 3 letters of recommendation, audition, ACT score for state residents, SAT or ACT score for out-of-state residents, portfolio for composition applicants. Recommended: minimum 3.0 high school GPA. Auditions held 5 times on campus; recorded music is permissible as a substitute for live auditions for provisional

acceptance and videotaped performances are permissible as a substitute for live auditions for provisional acceptance. Portfolio reviews held continuously on campus.

**Web Site** http://www.umkc.edu/conservatory

**Contact** Dr. James Elswick, Associate Director of Admissions, Conservatory of Music and Dance, University of Missouri–Kansas City, 5227 Holmes Road, Kansas City, Missouri 64110; 816-235-2900, fax: 816-235-5264, e-mail address: cadmissions@umkc.edu

# University of Mobile
## Mobile, Alabama

Independent Southern Baptist, coed. Suburban campus. Total enrollment: 1,639. Music program established 1996.

**Degrees** Bachelor of Music in the areas of church music, musical theatre; Bachelor of Sacred Music. Majors and concentrations: church music, music education, music theater. Program accredited by NASM.

**Enrollment** 126 total; 65 undergraduate, 61 nonprofessional degree.

**Music Student Profile** 43% females, 57% males, 8% minorities, 1% international.

**Music Faculty** 11 undergraduate (full-time), 25 undergraduate (part-time). 45% of full-time faculty have terminal degrees. Graduate students do not teach undergraduate courses. Undergraduate student–faculty ratio: 6:1.

**Student Life** Student groups/activities include Music Educators National Conference, Voices of Mobile, Christmas Spectacular, chamber singers, wind ensemble, Ram Corps, Exit 13, Sounds of Mobile, Ramtonz, piano ensemble, opera workshop, university singers, guitar ensemble, Rambunctious, Shofar, string ensemble, jazz band, Impact.

**Expenses for 2007–2008** Application fee: $30. Comprehensive fee: $20,530 includes full-time tuition ($12,780), mandatory fees ($610), and college room and board ($7140). College room only: $4260. Full-time tuition and fees vary according to course load. Room and board charges vary according to housing facility.

**Financial Aid** Program-specific awards: 1 Cummings Performance Fund Award, 1 Tim Hudmon Music Scholarship, 1 Melvin Memorial Fund Award, 1 Murphry Memorial Fund Award, 1 Megginson Sinclair Scholarship for organ majors ($1000), 68 departmental scholarships for music students ($1000), 1 Bergdolt Scholarship for full-time music majors.

**Application Procedures** Students admitted directly into the professional program freshman year. Deadline for freshmen and transfers: continuous. Required: high school transcript, college transcript(s) for transfer students, interview, audition, SAT or ACT test scores (minimum combined SAT score of 980, minimum composite ACT score of 21), minimum 2.75 high school GPA (4.0 scale). Auditions held weekly on campus. Portfolio reviews held weekly on campus.

**Web Site** http://www.umobile.edu

**Undergraduate Contact** Mrs. Tracey Ciongoli, Assistant to the Director/Dean, Center for Performing Arts, University of Mobile, 5735 College Parkway, Mobile, Alabama 36613-2842; 251-442-2320, fax: 251-442-2526, e-mail address: tciongol@mail.umobile.edu

# The University of Montana
## Missoula, Montana

State-supported, coed. Total enrollment: 13,858. Music program established 1893.

**Degrees** Bachelor of Music in the areas of performance, composition, music technology; Bachelor of Music Education. Majors and concentrations: composition, instrumental music, music education, music technology, piano/organ, voice. Graduate degrees offered: Master of Music in the areas of performance, theory, technology/composition, music education, musical theater. Program accredited by NASM.

**Enrollment** 235 total; 220 undergraduate, 15 graduate.

**Music Student Profile** 50% females, 50% males, 4% minorities, 2% international.

*The University of Montana (continued)*

**Music Faculty** 21 total (full-time), 6 total (part-time). 100% of full-time faculty have terminal degrees. Graduate students teach a few undergraduate courses. Undergraduate student–faculty ratio: 11:1.

**Student Life** Student groups/activities include Collegiate Music Educators National Conference.

**Expenses for 2008–2009** Application fee: $30. State resident tuition: $3739 full-time. Nonresident tuition: $15,014 full-time. Mandatory fees: $1441 full-time. College room and board: $6258. College room only: $2808. Special program-related fees: $85 per semester for music fees.

**Financial Aid** Program-specific awards: 90 awards for music majors ($1000).

**Application Procedures** Students admitted directly into the professional program freshman year. Deadline for freshmen and transfers: August 15. Required: high school transcript, college transcript(s) for transfer students, audition, SAT or ACT test scores, minimum 2.5 high school GPA. Recommended: interview. Auditions held by appointment on campus; recorded music is permissible as a substitute for live auditions when distance is prohibitive and videotaped performances are permissible as a substitute for live auditions if audio quality is excellent.

**Web Site** http://www.sfa.umt.edu/music

**Contact** Dr. Stephen Kalm, Chair, Department of Music, The University of Montana, Missoula, Montana 59812-7992; 406-243-6880, fax: 406-243-2441.

# University of Montevallo

## Montevallo, Alabama

State-supported, coed. Small town campus. Total enrollment: 2,948. Music program established 1924.

**Degrees** Bachelor of Music in the areas of performance, composition, instrumental music education, choral music education, piano pedagogy. Majors and concentrations: composition, guitar, music, music education, piano pedagogy, piano/organ, voice, wind and percussion instruments. Graduate degrees offered: Master of Music in the areas of performance, music education. Cross-registration with Samford University, Birmingham-Southern University, University of Alabama at Birmingham, Miles College. Program accredited by NASM.

**Enrollment** 86 total; 78 undergraduate, 2 graduate, 6 nonprofessional degree.

**Music Student Profile** 60% females, 40% males, 21% minorities.

**Music Faculty** 11 total (full-time), 14 total (part-time). 91% of full-time faculty have terminal degrees. Graduate students do not teach undergraduate courses. Undergraduate student–faculty ratio: 6:1.

**Student Life** Student groups/activities include Collegiate Music Educators National Conference (CMENC).

**Expenses for 2007–2008** Application fee: $25. State resident tuition: $5850 full-time. Nonresident tuition: $11,700 full-time. Mandatory fees: $230 full-time. Full-time tuition and fees vary according to course load. College room and board: $4360. Special program-related fees: $65 per credit hour for applied music fees.

**Financial Aid** Program-specific awards: 40 College of Fine Arts Awards for talented students ($1000), 26 music awards for talented students ($850).

**Application Procedures** Students admitted directly into the professional program freshman year. Deadline for freshmen and transfers: continuous. Required: high school transcript, college transcript(s) for transfer students, minimum 2.0 high school GPA, interview, audition, SAT or ACT test scores (minimum composite ACT score of 18), music theory entrance test. Recommended: 2 letters of recommendation. Auditions held 3 times in February and March and by appointment on campus; videotaped performances are permissible as a substitute for live auditions with prior approval.

**Web Site** http://www.montevallo.edu/music

**Undergraduate Contact** Dr. Robert Wright, Chair, Department of Music, University of Montevallo, Station 6670, Montevallo, Alabama 35115; 205-665-6670, fax: 205-665-6676, e-mail address: wrightr@montevallo.edu

**Graduate Contact** Dr. Lori Ardovino, Coordinator of Graduate Studies, Department of Music, University of Montevallo, Station 6670, Montevallo, Alabama 35115; 205-665-6672, fax: 205-665-6676, e-mail address: ardovinl@montevallo.edu

# University of Nebraska at Omaha

## Omaha, Nebraska

State-supported, coed. Urban campus. Total enrollment: 14,156. Music program established 1918.

**Degrees** Bachelor of Music in the areas of music education, music performance, music composition, music technology. Majors and concentrations: classical music, composition, music, music education, music performance, music technology, piano/organ, stringed instruments, voice, wind and percussion instruments. Graduate degrees offered: Master of Music in the areas of music education, music performance, conducting. Cross-registration with University of Nebraska System, Metro Community College Omaha. Program accredited by NASM.

**Enrollment** 235 total; 200 undergraduate, 35 graduate.

**Music Student Profile** 51% females, 49% males, 10% minorities, 6% international.

**Music Faculty** 15 undergraduate (full-time), 30 undergraduate (part-time), 14 graduate (full-time), 24 graduate (part-time). 95% of full-time faculty have terminal degrees. Graduate students do not teach undergraduate courses. Undergraduate student–faculty ratio: 9:1.

**Student Life** Student groups/activities include Music Educators National Conference Student Chapter, Kappa Kappa Psi (band professional sorority and fraternity), Music Teachers National Association Student Chapter.

**Expenses for 2007–2008** Application fee: $45. State resident tuition: $4643 full-time. Nonresident tuition: $13,680 full-time. Mandatory fees: $888 full-time. Full-time tuition and fees vary according to course load and reciprocity agreements. College room and board: $6810. College room only: $4610. Room and board charges vary according to board plan. Special program-related fees: $45 per semester for facilities fee (instrument use, piano tuning), $100 per credit hour for applied fee.

**Financial Aid** Program-specific awards: 150 Athletic Bands Scholarships for band participants ($250–$600), 30–40 music scholarships for program majors ($500–$9000), 20–25 ensemble scholarships for ensemble participants ($200–$800), 6–10 Jazz Program Scholarships for majors ($500–$1000).

**Application Procedures** Students admitted directly into the professional program freshman year. Deadline for freshmen and transfers: August 1. Required: high school transcript, college transcript(s) for transfer students, audition, ACT test score only (minimum composite ACT score of 19). Recommended: 2 letters of recommendation. Auditions held 5 times on campus; recorded music is permissible as a substitute for live auditions when distance is prohibitive and videotaped performances are permissible as a substitute for live auditions when distance is prohibitive.

**Web Site** http://music.unomaha.edu

**Undergraduate Contact** Dr. James R. Saker, Chair, Scholarship Recruitment Committee, Department of Music, University of Nebraska at Omaha, Strauss Performing Arts Center, Omaha, Nebraska 68182-0245; 402-554-2251, fax: 402-554-2252, e-mail address: jsaker@mail.unomaha.edu

**Graduate Contact** Dr. Roger Foltz, Chair, Graduate Program Committee, Department of Music, University of Nebraska at Omaha, Strauss Performing Arts Center, Omaha, Nebraska 68182-0245; 402-554-2474, fax: 402-554-2252, e-mail address: rfoltz@unomaha.edu

# University of Nebraska–Lincoln

## Lincoln, Nebraska

State-supported, coed. Urban campus. Total enrollment: 22,973. Music program established 1898.

**Degrees** Bachelor of Music; Bachelor of Music Education. Majors and concentrations: composition, music education, music history, music theory, performance. Graduate degrees offered: Master of Music in the areas of music theory, composition, performance, conducting, music education. Doctor of Musical Arts in the areas of performance, composition, conducting. Program accredited by NASM.

**Enrollment** 370 total; 200 undergraduate, 140 graduate, 30 nonprofessional degree.

**Music Student Profile** 49% females, 51% males, 8% minorities, 2% international.

**Music Faculty** 42 total (full-time), 8 total (part-time). 100% of full-time faculty have terminal degrees. Graduate students teach a few undergraduate courses. Undergraduate student–faculty ratio: 5:1.

**Student Life** Student groups/activities include Sigma Alpha Iota, Music Educators National Conference, Mu Phi Epsilon. Special housing available for music students.

**Expenses for 2007–2008** Application fee: $45. State resident tuition: $5085 full-time. Nonresident tuition: $15,105 full-time. Mandatory fees: $1130 full-time. Full-time tuition and fees vary according to course load. College room and board: $6523. College room only: $3441. Room and board charges vary according to board plan and housing facility. Special program-related fees: $15 per instrument for instrument rental, $20 per semester for ensemble fees, $25 per semester for applied fees.

**Financial Aid** Program-specific awards: 150 endowed awards for music majors ($100–$6000).

**Application Procedures** Students admitted directly into the professional program freshman year. Deadline for freshmen and transfers: July 1. Required: high school transcript, college transcript(s) for transfer students, audition, ACT test score only (minimum composite ACT score of 22). Auditions held 2 times on campus; recorded music is permissible as a substitute for live auditions for out-of-state applicants and videotaped performances are permissible as a substitute for live auditions for out-of-state applicants.

**Web Site** http://www.unl.edu/music/

**Contact** Ms. Susan Tribby, Admissions Coordinator, School of Music, University of Nebraska–Lincoln, 108 Westbrook Music Building, Lincoln, Nebraska 68588-0100; 402-472-6845, fax: 402-472-8962, e-mail address: stribby@unl.edu

# University of Nevada, Las Vegas
## Las Vegas, Nevada

State-supported, coed. Urban campus. Total enrollment: 28,008. Music program established 1968.

**Degrees** Bachelor of Music in the areas of jazz, applied music, composition, music education. Majors and concentrations: classical music, composition, jazz, music education, piano, stringed instruments, voice, wind and percussion instruments. Graduate degrees offered: Master of Music in the areas of performance, theory and composition, music education, jazz, conducting. Doctor of Musical Arts in the areas of applied music, conducting. Program accredited by NASM.

**Enrollment** 417 total; 280 undergraduate, 117 graduate, 20 nonprofessional degree.

**Music Student Profile** 61% females, 39% males, 8% minorities, 6% international.

**Music Faculty** 15 undergraduate (full-time), 31 undergraduate (part-time), 13 graduate (full-time), 4 graduate (part-time). 50% of full-time faculty have terminal degrees. Graduate students teach about a quarter of undergraduate courses. Undergraduate student–faculty ratio: 14:1.

**Student Life** Student groups/activities include American Choral Directors Association, Music Educators National Conference, American String Teachers Association.

**Expenses for 2008–2009** Application fee: $60. State resident tuition: $4005 full-time. Nonresident tuition: $15,100 full-time. Mandatory fees: $578 full-time. College room and board: $9808. College room only: $6232. Special program-related fees: $50 per semester for practice room fee, $250–$500 per semester for private lessons.

**Financial Aid** Program-specific awards: 30 departmental scholarships for program majors ($500–$8500), 60 band scholarships for band members ($500–$8500), 30 orchestra scholarships for orchestra members ($500–$8500), 30 chorus scholarships for vocal students ($500–$8500), 40 marching band scholarships for marching band members ($750).

**Application Procedures** Students admitted directly into the professional program freshman year. Deadline for freshmen and transfers: February 1. Notification date for freshmen and transfers: September 1. Required: high school transcript, college transcript(s) for transfer students, audition, SAT or ACT test scores, minimum 2.5 high school GPA. Recommended: interview. Auditions held 4 times and by appointment on campus; recorded music is permissible as a substitute for live auditions for out-of-state applicants and videotaped performances are permissible as a substitute for live auditions for out-of-state applicants.

**Web Site** http://music.unlv.edu

**Undergraduate Contact** Bill Bernatis, Associate Chair, Department of Music, University of Nevada, Las Vegas, 4505 South Maryland Parkway, Las Vegas, Nevada 89154-5025; 702-895-3713, fax: 702-895-4239, e-mail address: bill.bernatis@unlv.edu

**Graduate Contact** Dr. Janis McKay, Graduate Coordinator, Department of Music, University of Nevada, Las Vegas, 4505 South Maryland Parkway, Las Vegas, Nevada 89154-5025; 702-895-3929, fax: 702-895-4239, e-mail address: janis.mckay@unlv.edu

# University of New Hampshire
## Durham, New Hampshire

State-supported, coed. Small town campus. Total enrollment: 15,053. Music program established 1923.

**Web Site** http://www.unh.edu/

# University of New Mexico
## Albuquerque, New Mexico

State-supported, coed. Urban campus.

**Degrees** Bachelor of Music in the areas of performance, music theory/composition; Bachelor of Music Education. Majors and concentrations: jazz studies, music, music education, music theory and composition, opera, piano/organ, string pedagogy, stringed instruments, voice, wind and percussion instruments. Graduate degrees offered: Master of Music in the areas of performance, conducting, music education, piano accompaniment, music theory/composition, music history and literature. Program accredited by NASM.

**Enrollment** 290 total; 200 undergraduate, 70 graduate, 20 nonprofessional degree.

**Music Student Profile** 60% females, 40% males, 10% minorities, 5% international.

**Music Faculty** 28 total (full-time), 25 total (part-time). 40% of full-time faculty have terminal degrees. Graduate students teach a few undergraduate courses. Undergraduate student–faculty ratio: 10:1.

**Student Life** Student groups/activities include Music Educators National Conference, Collegiate Chorale, Jazz Festival.

**Expenses for 2007–2008** Application fee: $20. State resident tuition: $4571 full-time. Nonresident tuition: $14,942 full-time. College room and board: $7020. College room only: $4100. Room and board charges vary according to board plan and housing facility. Special program-related fees: $10–$50 per course for lab and visiting artists and clinicians fees, $25–$150 per 1-4 credit hours for applied fees.

**Financial Aid** Program-specific awards: 15 Friends of Music Awards for juniors and seniors ($1800), 7 music achievement awards for program students ($2000), 7 wind symphony awards for program students ($2000), 6 Jones Scholarships for program students ($1500), 1 orchestra scholarship for program students ($1400), 2 Anderson Awards for program students ($1250), 13 University Bands Awards for program students ($1200), 30 individual scholarships for program students ($500–$2000), 1 Presser Award for undergraduate senior ($4200).

**Application Procedures** Students admitted directly into the professional program freshman year. Deadline for freshmen and transfers: July 24. Notification date for freshmen and transfers: August 24. Required: essay, high school transcript, college transcript(s) for transfer students, minimum 2.0 high school GPA, 3 letters of recommendation, audition, SAT or ACT test scores. Recommended: interview, video, portfolio for composition majors. Auditions held 3 times and by request on campus; recorded music is permissible as a substitute for live auditions

*University of New Mexico (continued)*

when distance is prohibitive and videotaped performances are permissible as a substitute for live auditions when distance is prohibitive. Portfolio reviews held by request on campus.
**Web Site** http://www.unm.edu
**Undergraduate Contact** Mr. Keith Lemmons, Undergraduate Advisor, Department of Music, University of New Mexico, Fine Arts Center, Room 1105, Albuquerque, New Mexico 87131-1411; 505-277-4905, fax: 505-277-0708, e-mail address: klemmons@unm.edu
**Graduate Contact** Mr. Karl Hinterbichler, Graduate Coordinator, Department of Music, University of New Mexico, Fine Arts Center, Albuquerque, New Mexico 87131-1411; 505-277-4331, fax: 505-277-0708, e-mail address: khtbn@unm.edu

# The University of North Carolina at Charlotte

## Charlotte, North Carolina

State-supported, coed. Suburban campus. Total enrollment: 22,388. Music program established 1990.
**Degrees** Bachelor of Music in the areas of performance, music education. Majors and concentrations: music education, piano/organ performance, stringed instrument performance, voice, wind and percussion instruments performance. Cross-registration with Charlotte Area Educational Consortium.
**Enrollment** 99 total; 98 undergraduate, 1 graduate.
**Music Student Profile** 50% females, 50% males, 10% minorities, 5% international.
**Music Faculty** 14 total (full-time), 15 total (part-time). 80% of full-time faculty have terminal degrees. Graduate students do not teach undergraduate courses. Undergraduate student–faculty ratio: 7:1.
**Student Life** Student groups/activities include Music Educators National Conference, Phi Mu Alpha Sinfonia, Sigma Alpha Iota.
**Expenses for 2007–2008** Application fee: $50. State resident tuition: $2460 full-time. Nonresident tuition: $12,873 full-time. Mandatory fees: $1692 full-time. Full-time tuition and fees vary according to course load. College room and board: $6034. College room only: $3064. Room and board charges vary according to board plan and housing facility. Special program-related fees: $45 per credit hour for applied music courses.
**Financial Aid** Program-specific awards: 12 Music Department Scholarships for music majors ($1500), 12 Stone Scholarships for incoming freshmen ($2000), 1 Fleet-Green Jazz Scholarship for freshmen ($500), 1 Conboy Piano Scholarship for freshman music majors ($1000), 5 Robinson Scholarships for music majors ($2000), 5 Beck Scholarships for music majors ($2000), 4 String Scholarships for music majors ($5000).
**Application Procedures** Students admitted directly into the professional program freshman year. Deadline for freshmen and transfers: continuous. Required: high school transcript, college transcript(s) for transfer students, minimum 2.0 high school GPA, 3 letters of recommendation, audition, SAT or ACT test scores, medical history, completed audition application form. Recommended: minimum 3.0 high school GPA. Auditions held 6 times on campus; recorded music is permissible as a substitute for live auditions when distance is prohibitive and videotaped performances are permissible as a substitute for live auditions when distance is prohibitive.
**Web Site** http://www.uncc.edu/music
**Undergraduate Contact** Denise Shropshire, Administrative Secretary, Department of Music, The University of North Carolina at Charlotte, 9201 University City Boulevard, Rowe Arts 124, Charlotte, North Carolina 28223-0001; 704-687-2472, fax: 704-687-6806, e-mail address: dlshrops@uncc.edu

# The University of North Carolina at Greensboro

## Greensboro, North Carolina

State-supported, coed. Urban campus. Total enrollment: 17,157. Music program established 1892.

**Degrees** Bachelor of Music in the areas of performance, music education, composition, jazz performance. Majors and concentrations: classical music, composition, jazz, music education, piano/organ, stringed instruments, voice, wind and percussion instruments. Graduate degrees offered: Master of Music in the areas of performance, music education, composition, music theory, vocal pedagogy. Doctor of Musical Arts in the area of performance; Doctor of Philosophy in the area of music education. Cross-registration with Bennett College, Elon College, Greensboro College, Guilford College, High Point University, Guilford Technical Community College, North Carolina Agricultural and Technical State University. Program accredited by NASM.
**Enrollment** 579 total; 321 undergraduate, 189 graduate, 69 nonprofessional degree.
**Music Student Profile** 55% females, 45% males, 21% minorities, 1% international.
**Music Faculty** 60 total (full-time), 10 total (part-time). 82% of full-time faculty have terminal degrees. Graduate students teach a few undergraduate courses. Undergraduate student–faculty ratio: 8:1.
**Student Life** Student groups/activities include Collegiate Music Educators National Conference, Phi Mu Alpha Sinfonia, Mu Phi Epsilon.
**Expenses for 2007–2008** Application fee: $45. State resident tuition: $2458 full-time. Nonresident tuition: $13,726 full-time. Mandatory fees: $1571 full-time. College room and board: $6051. College room only: $3427.
**Financial Aid** Program-specific awards: 150–175 music scholarships for program students ($1000–$6000).
**Application Procedures** Students admitted directly into the professional program freshman year. Deadline for freshmen and transfers: August 1. Notification date for freshmen and transfers: continuous. Required: high school transcript, college transcript(s) for transfer students, audition, SAT or ACT test scores, minimum of 16 high school units. Auditions held 4 times and by appointment; recorded music is permissible as a substitute for live auditions and videotaped performances are permissible as a substitute for live auditions.
**Web Site** http://www.uncg.edu/mus/
**Undergraduate Contact** Ms. Dianna Carter, Director of Undergraduate Advising, School of Music, The University of North Carolina at Greensboro, PO Box 26170, Greensboro, North Carolina 27402-6170; 336-334-3638, fax: 336-334-5497, e-mail address: dtcarter@uncg.edu
**Graduate Contact** Dr. David Nelson, Associate Dean and Director of Academic Programs, School of Music, The University of North Carolina at Greensboro, PO Box 26170, Greensboro, North Carolina 27402-6170; 336-334-5789, fax: 336-334-5497.

# The University of North Carolina at Pembroke

## Pembroke, North Carolina

State-supported, coed. Rural campus. Total enrollment: 5,937. Music program established 1928.
**Web Site** http://www.uncp.edu/

# The University of North Carolina Wilmington

## Wilmington, North Carolina

State-supported, coed. Urban campus. Total enrollment: 11,840. Music program established 1986.
**Degrees** Bachelor of Music in the areas of performance, music education. Majors and concentrations: instrumental music, jazz studies, keyboard, music education, vocal music. Cross-registration with Cape Fear Community College. Program accredited by NASM.
**Enrollment** 75 total; all undergraduate.
**Music Student Profile** 47% females, 53% males, 6% minorities.
**Music Faculty** 13 undergraduate (full-time), 13 undergraduate (part-time). 100% of full-time faculty have terminal degrees.

Graduate students do not teach undergraduate courses. Undergraduate student–faculty ratio: 5:1.

**Student Life** Student groups/activities include jazz band, wind symphony orchestra, pep band.

**Expenses for 2007–2008** Application fee: $45. State resident tuition: $2413 full-time. Nonresident tuition: $12,376 full-time. Mandatory fees: $1985 full-time. Full-time tuition and fees vary according to course load. College room and board: $6998. Room and board charges vary according to board plan and housing facility.

**Financial Aid** Program-specific awards: 3 departmental awards for music majors ($750), Levent Chen Scholarship for viola majors ($500), 1 Johanna Rehder Scholarship for voice majors ($500), jazz awards for jazz ensemble participants ($250–$500), 1 William F. Adcock Jr. Scholarship for rising senior music majors ($1500), 1 Cape Fear Jazz Appreciation Society Scholarship for jazz majors ($1000), Outstanding Music Education Major Award.

**Application Procedures** Students admitted directly into the professional program freshman year. Deadline for freshmen: April 15; transfers: continuous. Required: essay, high school transcript, college transcript(s) for transfer students, minimum 3.0 high school GPA, 2 letters of recommendation, audition, SAT or ACT test scores. Recommended: interview, video. Auditions held 10 times on campus; recorded music is permissible as a substitute for live auditions when distance is prohibitive and videotaped performances are permissible as a substitute for live auditions when distance is prohibitive.

**Web Site** http://www.uncw.edu/music

**Undergraduate Contact** Dr. Frank Bongiorno, Chair, Department of Music, The University of North Carolina Wilmington, 601 South College Road, Wilmington, North Carolina 20403-5975; 910-962-3390, fax: 910-962-7106, e-mail address: uncwmus@uncwil.edu

# University of North Dakota
## Grand Forks, North Dakota

State-supported, coed. Urban campus. Total enrollment: 12,559. Music program established 1883.

**Degrees** Bachelor of Music in the areas of performance, music education, music therapy. Majors and concentrations: music education, music therapy, piano/organ, strings, voice, wind and percussion instruments. Graduate degrees offered: Master of Music in the areas of music education, composition, vocal performance, vocal pedagogy, keyboard performance, keyboard pedagogy, instrumental conducting, choral conducting. Doctor of Philosophy in the areas of teaching and learning, music education. Program accredited by NASM.

**Enrollment** 88 total; 58 undergraduate, 11 graduate, 19 nonprofessional degree.

**Music Student Profile** 55% females, 45% males, 6% minorities, 6% international.

**Music Faculty** 17 total (full-time), 9 total (part-time). 50% of full-time faculty have terminal degrees. Graduate students teach a few undergraduate courses. Undergraduate student–faculty ratio: 4:1.

**Student Life** Student groups/activities include Music Educators National Conference, American Choral Directors Association, Sigma Alpha Delta/Pi Kappa Lambda.

**Expenses for 2007–2008** Application fee: $35. State resident tuition: $5025 full-time. Nonresident tuition: $13,418 full-time. Mandatory fees: $1105 full-time. Full-time tuition and fees vary according to degree level, program, and reciprocity agreements. College room and board: $5203. College room only: $2137. Room and board charges vary according to board plan and housing facility. Special program-related fees: $75 per semester for applied music fees.

**Financial Aid** Program-specific awards: 77 music scholarships for program majors/minors/participants ($300–$1500).

**Application Procedures** Students admitted directly into the professional program freshman year. Deadline for freshmen and transfers: continuous. Required: high school transcript, college transcript(s) for transfer students, audition, ACT test score only. Auditions held 3 times on campus and off campus in various cities in North Dakota and Minnesota; recorded music is permissible as a substitute for live auditions when distance is prohibitive and videotaped performances are permissible as a substitute for live auditions when distance is prohibitive.

**Web Site** http://www2.und.edu/undmusic/

**Undergraduate Contact** Dr. Royce Blackburn, Music Department, University of North Dakota, Box 7125, Grand Forks, North Dakota 58202; 701-777-2644, fax: 701-777-3320, e-mail address: royce_blackburn@und.nodak.edu

**Graduate Contact** Dr. Gary Towne, Director of Graduate Studies, Music Department, University of North Dakota, Box 7125, Grand Forks, North Dakota 58202; 701-777-2836, fax: 701-777-3320, e-mail address: gary_towne@und.nodak.edu

# University of Northern Colorado
## Greeley, Colorado

State-supported, coed. Total enrollment: 12,219. Music program established 1895.

**Web Site** http://www.unco.edu/

# University of North Texas
## Denton, Texas

State-supported, coed. Suburban campus. Total enrollment: 34,153.

**Degrees** Bachelor of Music in the areas of composition, theory, music history and literature, performance, jazz studies, music education. Majors and concentrations: composition, jazz, music education, music history and literature, music theory, piano/organ/harpsichord, stringed instruments, voice, wind and percussion instruments. Graduate degrees offered: Master of Music in the areas of theory, composition, musicology, jazz studies, conducting, organ, piano, voice, performance, music education; Master of Music Education. Doctor of Musical Arts in the areas of performance, composition, conducting. Program accredited by NASM.

**Enrollment** 1,600 total; 1,050 undergraduate, 550 graduate.

**Music Faculty** 100 total (full-time), 100 total (part-time). 100% of full-time faculty have terminal degrees. Graduate students teach a few undergraduate courses. Undergraduate student–faculty ratio: 13:1.

**Student Life** Student groups/activities include Sigma Alpha Iota, Phi Mu Alpha Sinfonia, NT 40. Special housing available for music students.

**Expenses for 2007–2008** Application fee: $40. State resident tuition: $4390 full-time. Nonresident tuition: $12,730 full-time. Mandatory fees: $1930 full-time. Full-time tuition and fees vary according to course load. College room and board: $5490. Room and board charges vary according to board plan and housing facility. Special program-related fees: $10 per semester for instrument rental, $10–$40 per semester for practice room fee, $30–$60 per semester for applied lesson fee.

**Financial Aid** Program-specific awards: music scholarships for out-of-state students ($200–$2000).

**Application Procedures** Students admitted directly into the professional program freshman year. Deadline for freshmen and transfers: April 15. Required: high school transcript, college transcript(s) for transfer students, 3 letters of recommendation, audition, SAT or ACT test scores, taped audition for jazz applicants. Auditions held 3 times on campus and off campus in Chicago, IL; Interlochen, MI; New York, NY; Santa Barbara, CA; recorded music is permissible as a substitute for live auditions if a live audition is impossible (for provisional acceptance) and videotaped performances are permissible as a substitute for live auditions (for provisional acceptance).

**Web Site** http://www.music.unt.edu

**Undergraduate Contact** Carol Pollard, Undergraduate Advisor, College of Music, University of North Texas, PO Box 311367, Denton, Texas 76203-1367; 940-565-3781, fax: 940-565-2002, e-mail address: cpollard@music.unt.edu

**Graduate Contact** Cari Geer, Administrative Assistant, Graduate Music Office, University of North Texas, PO Box 311367, Denton, Texas 76203-1367; 940-565-3721, fax: 940-565-2002, e-mail address: cgeer@music.unt.edu

# University of Oregon

## Eugene, Oregon

State-supported, coed. Urban campus. Total enrollment: 20,332. Music program established 1886.

**Degrees** Bachelor of Music in the areas of music composition, music education, music performance, jazz studies. Majors and concentrations: composition, jazz, music, music education, piano/organ, stringed instruments, voice, wind and percussion instruments. Graduate degrees offered: Master of Arts in the areas of music theory, musicology; Master of Music in the areas of conducting, piano pedagogy, music composition, music performance, music education, jazz studies, intermedia music technology, string pedagogy. Doctor of Musical Arts in the areas of music performance, music composition; Doctor of Philosophy in the areas of music composition, music education, musicology, music theory. Program accredited by NASM.

**Enrollment** 433 total; 284 undergraduate, 149 graduate.

**Music Student Profile** 44% females, 56% males, 14% minorities, 7% international.

**Music Faculty** 46 total (full-time), 19 total (part-time). 95% of full-time faculty have terminal degrees. Graduate students teach a few undergraduate courses. Undergraduate student–faculty ratio: 8:1.

**Student Life** Student groups/activities include Oregon Bach Festival, Oregon Festival of American Music, Suzuki Strings Program. Special housing available for music students.

**Expenses for 2007–2008** Application fee: $50. One-time mandatory fee: $250. State resident tuition: $4494 full-time. Nonresident tuition: $17,250 full-time. Mandatory fees: $1542 full-time. Full-time tuition and fees vary according to class time, course load, program, and reciprocity agreements. College room and board: $7849. Room and board charges vary according to board plan and housing facility. Special program-related fees: $10–$50 per term for instrument rental, $10 per term for piano lab fee, $20 per term for organ, harpsichord, or percussion fee, $20 per term for ensemble fee, $20 per term for music education class instrument fee, $50–$200 per term for accompanying fee, $50 per credit for private lessons, $75 per term for synthesizer lab fee, $100 per recital for recital and recording fee, $100 per term for music major fee, $135 per term for group lessons.

**Financial Aid** Program-specific awards: 1 Presser Scholarship for outstanding juniors and seniors ($4200), 2 Corbett Scholarships for Oregon students ($1750), 8 Stauffer Scholarships for male graduates of Oregon high schools ($1000), 2 Mu Phi Epsilon Patron Scholarships for program students ($1000), 4 Polastri Scholarships for voice majors ($2000), 50 Ruth Lorraine Close Scholarships for music majors ($2000), 1 Dorthy Pederson Fahlman Piano Scholarship for piano majors ($1500), 6 Virginia Whitfield Scholarships for music education majors ($1500), 1 Bailey Vocal Scholarship for voice majors ($2000), 8 School of Music general scholarships for music ($850), 1 Atwood Music Scholarship for music majors ($3000), 1 Robert and Leona Anderson DeArmond Scholarship for voice majors ($2500), 1 Robert and Margaret Guitteau Scholarship for music majors ($1500), 2 Maude and H.B. Densmore Memorial Scholarships for voice majors ($1500), 2 Mu Phi Epsilon Patrons Scholarships for music majors ($1500), 20 School of Music Dean's Scholarships ($3000), 1 Bella Voce Scholarship for voice majors ($3000), 1 Moore Scholarship for voice majors ($750), 1 Musgrove Scholarship for voice majors ($1000), 2 Gilkey Scholarships for violin majors ($4000), 5 Parsell Scholarships for violin majors ($1300), 1 Newman Scholarship for program students ($1500), 1 Lotta Carll Scholarship for music advance majors ($3000), 1 Mitchell Scholarship for music majors ($2000), 1 McClure Scholarship for music majors ($1000), 1 Kammerer Scholarship for jazz majors ($900), 2 Culp Scholarships for music majors ($2000), 1 Doran Scholarship for voice or piano majors ($1500), 1 Easley Scholarship for piano or organ ($1000).

**Application Procedures** Students admitted directly into the professional program freshman year. Deadline for freshmen: January 15; transfers: May 15. Notification date for freshmen and transfers: continuous. Required: high school transcript, college transcript(s) for transfer students, minimum 3.0 high school GPA, audition, SAT or ACT test scores. Recommended: essay, 3 letters of recommendation. Auditions held once on campus; recorded music is permissible as a substitute for live auditions when distance is prohibitive and videotaped performances are permissible as a substitute for live auditions when distance is prohibitive.

**Web Site** http://music.uoregon.edu/

**Undergraduate Contact** Ms. Kathy McNulty, Undergraduate Admissions Assistant, School of Music and Dance, University of Oregon, 1225 University of Oregon, Eugene, Oregon 97403-1225; 541-346-5268, fax: 541-346-0723, e-mail address: audition@uoregon.edu

**Graduate Contact** Ms. Kathy McNulty, Admissions Assistant, School of Music and Dance, University of Oregon, 1225 University of Oregon, Eugene, Oregon 97403-1225; 541-346-5268, fax: 541-346-0723, e-mail address: gmusadm@uoregon.edu

# University of Portland

## Portland, Oregon

Independent Roman Catholic, coed. Urban campus. Total enrollment: 3,667. Music program established 1901.

**Web Site** http://www.up.edu/

# University of Prince Edward Island

## Charlottetown, Prince Edward Island, Canada

Province-supported, coed. Small town campus. Total enrollment: 4,075. Music program established 1969.

**Degrees** Bachelor of Music in the areas of general music, theory, musicology, performance; Bachelor of Music Education. Majors and concentrations: guitar, music education, music history, music theory and composition, performance, piano/organ, voice, wind and percussion instruments. Program accredited by CUMS.

**Enrollment** 63 total; 60 undergraduate, 3 nonprofessional degree.

**Music Student Profile** 65% females, 35% males, 1% international.

**Music Faculty** 6 undergraduate (full-time), 13 undergraduate (part-time). 80% of full-time faculty have terminal degrees. Graduate students do not teach undergraduate courses. Undergraduate student–faculty ratio: 6:1.

**Student Life** Student groups/activities include University of Prince Edward Island Music Society.

**Expenses for 2007–2008** Application fee: $50 Canadian dollars. Tuition, fee, and room and board charges are reported in Canadian dollars. Province resident tuition: $4440 full-time. Mandatory fees: $737 full-time. Full-time tuition and fees vary according to course load and degree level. College room and board: $8720. Room and board charges vary according to board plan and housing facility. International student tuition: $8760 full-time. Special program-related fees: $60 per year for instrument rental, locker, telephone, practice room rental, $150 for cost of sessional defraging applied music faculty.

**Financial Aid** Program-specific awards: 5–10 Mary O. Kinch Returning Scholarships for 2nd, 3rd, 4th, 5th year students ($500–$1500), 1 Tersteeg Music Scholarship for 3rd-5th year students ($350), 1 Bevan-MacRae Music Award for 3rd-5th year students ($250), 8 Music Alumni Scholarships for freshmen ($200–$750), 3 Music Society Scholarships for sophomores, juniors, and seniors ($125), 1 Claude and Dr. Bernice Bell Award for program students (renewable for 4 years) ($1000), 1 Elsie Cuthbertson Memorial Music Scholarship for program students ($250), 1 Frances Dindial Memorial Music Scholarship for freshmen ($800), 1 Eleanor Wheler Scholarship for entering students (renewable for 4 years) ($1000), 1 Mathis Music Award for voice or horn majors ($250), 1 Reesor Music Award for organ majors ($300), 6–12 Mary O. Kinch Entrance Awards for entering students ($1600–$20,000), 2 Mary O. Kinch Music Education Scholarships for 5th year students ($800), 1 Florence Simmons Award for organ majors ($500), 1 Christine Burdett Award for 2nd, 3rd, 4th, 5th year students ($750), 1 James A. Ready Scholarship for program students ($1000).

**Application Procedures** Students admitted directly into the professional program freshman year. Deadline for freshmen and transfers: August 15. Notification date for freshmen and transfers: August 25. Required: high school transcript, college transcript(s) for transfer students, letter of recommendation, interview, audition, music theory test, ear test. Recommended:

essay, minimum 3.0 high school GPA, resumé. Auditions held 4 times on campus; recorded music is permissible as a substitute for live auditions when distance is prohibitive (with later audition on campus) and videotaped performances are permissible as a substitute for live auditions when distance is prohibitive (with later audition on campus).
**Web Site** http://www.upei.ca/music
**Undergraduate Contact** Ms. Gloria J. Jay, Audition Coordinator, Department of Music, University of Prince Edward Island, 550 University Avenue, Charlottetown, Prince Edward Island C1A 4P3, Canada; 902-566-0507, fax: 902-566-0777, e-mail address: gjay@upei.ca

# University of Puget Sound
## Tacoma, Washington

Independent, coed. Suburban campus. Total enrollment: 2,799. Music program established 1892.
**Degrees** Bachelor of Music in the areas of performance, music education, with elective studies in business. Majors and concentrations: classical music, harp, harpsichord, music, music business, music education, piano/organ, stringed instruments, voice, wind and percussion instruments. Program accredited by NASM.
**Enrollment** 625 total; 125 undergraduate, 500 nonprofessional degree.
**Music Student Profile** 54% females, 46% males, 12% minorities, 3% international.
**Music Faculty** 12 undergraduate (full-time), 24 undergraduate (part-time). 90% of full-time faculty have terminal degrees. Graduate students do not teach undergraduate courses. Undergraduate student–faculty ratio: 11:1.
**Student Life** Student groups/activities include Music Educators National Conference, Phi Mu Alpha Sinfonia, Sigma Alpha Iota. Special housing available for music students.
**Expenses for 2007–2008** Application fee: $40. Comprehensive fee: $40,160 includes full-time tuition ($31,700), mandatory fees ($195), and college room and board ($8265). College room only: $4610. Full-time tuition and fees vary according to course load. Room and board charges vary according to board plan and housing facility. Special program-related fees: $95 per semester for applied music lessons.
**Financial Aid** Program-specific awards: 100 music scholarships for continuing students ($5000), 35 music scholarships for incoming students ($5000).
**Application Procedures** Students admitted directly into the professional program freshman year. Deadline for freshmen and transfers: February 1. Notification date for freshmen: June 1. Required: essay, high school transcript, college transcript(s) for transfer students, 3 letters of recommendation, audition, SAT or ACT test scores. Recommended: minimum 3.0 high school GPA, interview. Auditions held once and by appointment on campus and off campus in Denver, CO; Minneapolis, MN; San Francisco, CA; recorded music is permissible as a substitute for live auditions when distance is prohibitive and videotaped performances are permissible as a substitute for live auditions when distance is prohibitive.
**Web Site** http://www.ups.edu/music
**Undergraduate Contact** Music Admission Coordinator, School of Music, University of Puget Sound, 1500 North Warner Street, #1076, Tacoma, Washington 98416-1076; 253-879-3730, fax: 253-879-2906, e-mail address: music.admission@ups.edu

# University of Redlands
## Redlands, California

Independent, coed. Small town campus. Total enrollment: 2,445. Music program established 1907.
**Degrees** Bachelor of Music in the areas of performance, music education, composition. Majors and concentrations: composition, music education, piano/organ, stringed instruments, voice, wind and percussion instruments. Graduate degrees offered: Master of Music in the areas of performance, music education, composition. Program accredited by NASM.

**Enrollment** 154 total; 75 undergraduate, 18 graduate, 61 nonprofessional degree.
**Music Student Profile** 60% females, 40% males, 12% minorities, 3% international.
**Music Faculty** 14 total (full-time), 27 total (part-time). 86% of full-time faculty have terminal degrees. Graduate students do not teach undergraduate courses.
**Student Life** Student groups/activities include Sigma Alpha Iota, Phi Mu Alpha Sinfonia, Music Educators National Conference Student Chapter.
**Expenses for 2007–2008** Application fee: $45. Comprehensive fee: $40,408 includes full-time tuition ($30,326), mandatory fees ($300), and college room and board ($9782). College room only: $5456. Room and board charges vary according to board plan and housing facility.
**Financial Aid** Program-specific awards: music merit awards for incoming freshmen, area specific awards for program students.
**Application Procedures** Students admitted directly into the professional program freshman year. Deadline for freshmen and transfers: May 1. Notification date for freshmen: September 1; transfers: August 1. Required: essay, high school transcript, college transcript(s) for transfer students, minimum 3.0 high school GPA, 2 letters of recommendation, audition, SAT or ACT test scores (minimum composite ACT score of 25), portfolio for composition majors. Recommended: interview. Auditions held 3 times on campus; recorded music is permissible as a substitute for live auditions when distance is prohibitive (beyond a 200-mile radius) and videotaped performances are permissible as a substitute for live auditions when distance is prohibitive (beyond a 200-mile radius). Portfolio reviews held continuously on campus.
**Web Site** http://www.redlands.edu/music
**Undergraduate Contact** Mr. Brad Andrews, Assistant Director of Music Admissions, School of Music, University of Redlands, 1200 East Colton Avenue, Box 3080, Redlands, California 92373; 909-748-8014, fax: 909-335-5183, e-mail address: music@redlands.edu
**Graduate Contact** Mr. Brad Andrews, Admissions Coordinator, School of Music, University of Redlands, 1200 East Colton Avenue, Box 3080, Redlands, California 92373; 909-748-8014, fax: 909-335-5183, e-mail address: music@redlands.edu

# University of Regina
## Regina, Saskatchewan, Canada

Province-supported, coed. Urban campus. Total enrollment: 11,819. Music program established 1968.
**Degrees** Bachelor of Arts in the areas of music theory (honors), music history (honors); Bachelor of Music in the areas of performance, composition, music history, theory, comprehensive; Bachelor of Music Education in the area of secondary music education. Majors and concentrations: brass, composition, music education, music history, music theory, piano/organ, stringed instruments, voice, wind and percussion instruments. Graduate degrees offered: Master of Arts in the areas of musicology, music theory; Master of Music in the areas of performance, composition, conducting. Program accredited by CUMS.
**Enrollment** 68 undergraduate, 11 graduate.
**Music Student Profile** 60% females, 40% males, 4% minorities, 3% international.
**Music Faculty** 10 total (full-time), 13 total (part-time). 50% of full-time faculty have terminal degrees. Graduate students teach a few undergraduate courses. Undergraduate student–faculty ratio: 7:1.
**Student Life** Student groups/activities include Saskatchewan Music Educators Association, Music Students Association, Saskatchewan Band Association.
**Expenses for 2007–2008** Application fee: $85 Canadian dollars. Tuition, fee, and room and board charges are reported in Canadian dollars. Province resident tuition: $4551 full-time. Mandatory fees: $442 full-time. Full-time tuition and fees vary according to course load and program. College room and board: $6772. College room only: $4272. Room and board charges vary according to board plan and housing facility. International student tuition: $8627 full-time.

*University of Regina (continued)*

**Financial Aid** Program-specific awards: 1 Bachelor of Music Entrance Scholarship for Saskatchewan residents ($1300), 1 Violet Ewing Entrance Scholarships for freshmen program majors ($1000), 1 Laubach Scholarships for strings majors ($2250), 6 music scholarships for piano or voice majors ($175–$2000), 1 Dr. James McConica Entrance Scholarships for instrumental majors ($2500), 1 Frank Connell Memorial Scholarships for music education majors ($500), 1 Oswell Robinson Scholarships for Bachelor of Music students ($500).

**Application Procedures** Students admitted directly into the professional program freshman year. Deadline for freshmen and transfers: July 31. Required: high school transcript, college transcript(s) for transfer students, minimum 2.0 high school GPA, interview, audition. Auditions held 5 times on campus; recorded music is permissible as a substitute for live auditions when distance is prohibitive and videotaped performances are permissible as a substitute for live auditions when distance is prohibitive.

**Web Site** http://www.uregina.ca/finearts/

**Undergraduate Contact** Office of the Registrar, University of Regina, Regina, Saskatchewan S4S 0A2, Canada; 306-585-4591, fax: 306-337-2525.

**Graduate Contact** Faculty of Graduate Studies and Research, University of Regina, Regina, Saskatchewan S4S 0A2, Canada; 306-585-4161, fax: 306-337-2444.

# University of Rhode Island
## Kingston, Rhode Island

State-supported, coed. Small town campus. Total enrollment: 15,650. Music program established 1933.

**Degrees** Bachelor of Arts in the areas of music, music history and literature, jazz studies, music and communication studies, music and psychology, music and elementary education; Bachelor of Arts/Bachelor of Science in the areas of music and business administration, music and computer science; Bachelor of Music in the areas of music education, music composition, music performance. Majors and concentrations: composition, jazz studies, music, music and business administration, music and communication studies, music and computer science, music and elementary education, music and psychology, music education, music history and literature, music performance. Graduate degrees offered: Master of Music in the areas of music education, performance. Program accredited by NASM, NCATE.

**Enrollment** 171 total; 126 undergraduate, 20 graduate, 25 nonprofessional degree.

**Music Student Profile** 50% females, 50% males, 8% minorities, 5% international.

**Music Faculty** 16 total (full-time), 22 total (part-time). 90% of full-time faculty have terminal degrees. Graduate students do not teach undergraduate courses. Undergraduate student–faculty ratio: 8:1.

**Student Life** Student groups/activities include Music Educators National Conference Student Chapter, Kappa Kappa Psi/Tau Beta Sigma, American Choral Directors Association Student Chapter.

**Expenses for 2007–2008** Application fee: $50. State resident tuition: $6440 full-time. Nonresident tuition: $21,294 full-time. Mandatory fees: $1744 full-time. Full-time tuition and fees vary according to reciprocity agreements. College room and board: $8732. College room only: $5016. Room and board charges vary according to board plan and housing facility. Special program-related fees: $200 per semester for applied music lesson fee.

**Financial Aid** Program-specific awards: 45 music scholarships for program majors ($250–$8000), 4 Honors String Quartet Scholarships for top string players ($4577–$11,603), 25 University Centennial Scholarships for academically and musically talented students ($1000–$21,000).

**Application Procedures** Students admitted directly into the professional program freshman year. Deadline for freshmen and transfers: continuous. Notification date for freshmen and transfers: continuous. Required: high school transcript, college transcript(s) for transfer students, audition, SAT or ACT test scores, minimum 2.5 college GPA for transfer students. Recommended: minimum 3.0 high school GPA, 2 letters of recommen-

dation, interview, video. Auditions held 6 times on campus; recorded music is permissible as a substitute for live auditions with approval from the department and videotaped performances are permissible as a substitute for live auditions with approval from the department.

**Web Site** http://www.uri.edu/artsci/mus

**Undergraduate Contact** Mr. John Dempsey, Professor, Department of Music, University of Rhode Island, Fine Arts Center, Kingston, Rhode Island 02881; 401-874-2782, fax: 401-874-2772, e-mail address: music@etal.uri.edu

**Graduate Contact** Dr. Manabu T. Takasawa, Coordinator, Graduate Studies in Music, Department of Music, University of Rhode Island, Fine Arts Center, Kingston, Rhode Island 02881; 401-874-2790, fax: 401-874-2772, e-mail address: takasawa@uri.edu

## *Eastman School of Music of the University of Rochester*
# University of Rochester
## Rochester, New York

Independent, coed. Suburban campus. Total enrollment: 9,334. Music program established 1921.

**Degrees** Bachelor of Music in the areas of composition, music education, music theory, performance, jazz studies (performance and/or writing), musical arts. Majors and concentrations: applied music, brass, composition, jazz, jazz composition, jazz performance, jazz studies, music education, music theory, musical arts, piano/organ, stringed instruments, voice, wind and percussion instruments. Graduate degrees offered: Master of Arts in the areas of composition, music education, music theory pedagogy, ethnomusicology; Master of Arts/Doctor of Philosophy in the areas of musicology, music theory; Master of Music in the areas of jazz studies (performance ør writing), composition, choral or orchestral conducting, music education, performance & literature (instrumental, vocal, woodwind doubling), piano accompanying & chamber music, early music, opera performance or stage directing. Doctor of Musical Arts in the areas of composition, conducting (choral, orchestral, wind ensemble), music education, performance and literature, piano accompanying and chamber music, jazz studies, early music; Doctor of Philosophy in the areas of composition, music education, musicology, music theory. Cross-registration with all local Rochester colleges, if the course is not offered on the home campus. Program accredited by NASM.

**Enrollment** 941 total; 509 undergraduate, 432 graduate.

**Music Student Profile** 50% females, 50% males, 12% minorities, 20% international.

**Music Faculty** 94 total (full-time), 53 total (part-time). 51% of full-time faculty have terminal degrees. Graduate students teach about a quarter of undergraduate courses. Undergraduate student–faculty ratio: 5:1.

**Student Life** Student groups/activities include community outreach and performance, Music Educators National Conference, professional music fraternities and sororities. Special housing available for music students.

**Expenses for 2007–2008** Application fee: $50. Comprehensive fee: $45,830 includes full-time tuition ($34,380), mandatory fees ($810), and college room and board ($10,640). College room only: $6200. Room and board charges vary according to board plan. Special program-related fees: $135 for organ fee, $240 for comprehensive fee.

**Financial Aid** Program-specific awards: 510 merit-based scholarships for those demonstrating talent and academic achievement ($5000–$15,000), 408 financial aid awards for those demonstrating need ($1000–$15,000).

**Application Procedures** Students admitted directly into the professional program freshman year. Deadline for freshmen and transfers: December 1. Notification date for freshmen and transfers: April 15. Required: high school transcript, college transcript(s) for transfer students, minimum 2.0 high school GPA, 3 letters of recommendation, audition, portfolio for composition majors, interview for theory majors, essay, interview, and skills test for music education applicants, minimum TOEFL 79-80 iBT for non-native English speakers, pre-screening recording for some instruments (see application). Recommended: minimum 3.0 high school GPA, interview, SAT or ACT test scores. Auditions held 23 times on campus and off campus in Atlanta, GA; Chicago, IL; Houston, TX; Los Angeles, CA; Portland, OR; Boston, MA; Dallas, TX; Greenville, SC; Idyllwild and San Francisco, CA; Washington, DC; New York, NY; Seoul, Korea; Taipei; Hong Kong; Singapore; Bangkok; recorded music is permissible as a substitute for live auditions if a campus visit is impossible (some exceptions) and videotaped performances are permissible as a substitute for live auditions if a campus visit is impossible (some exceptions). Portfolio reviews held on campus.

**Web Site** http://www.esm.rochester.edu

**Contact** Dr. Adrian Daly, Director of Admissions, Eastman School of Music, University of Rochester, 26 Gibbs Street, Rochester, New York 14604; 585-274-1060, fax: 585-232-8601, e-mail address: admissions@esm.rochester.edu

### More About the School

One of the world's preeminent music schools, the Eastman School of Music was founded in 1921 by Rochester industrialist and philanthropist George Eastman (founder of Eastman Kodak) as the first professional school within the University of Rochester. Maintaining the highest standards for artistry, intelligent musicianship, and scholarship, the School's comprehensive programs provide outstanding performance and teaching faculty, broad and continuous playing experience, and innovative approaches to career development. Eastman is recognized nationally and internationally for the quality and intensity of its disciplinary training and for its unique opportunities for musical leadership and community enrichment.

There are 900 students enrolled in the collegiate division: 500 undergraduate and 400 graduate students. Current students hail from forty-three states and twenty other countries; 24 percent of the students are international. Each year, about 280 new students enroll, selected from more than 2,100 applicants. Eastman students regularly win Down Beat awards, BMI grants, ASCAP Foundation grants, Fulbright Scholarships, and other national and international awards and competitions.

Eastman students enjoy a collaborative musical environment not found at other "conservatory" programs. In addition, they belong to the larger University of Rochester community. Some students earn minors or even second degrees at the college.

The Sibley Music Library offers more than 350,000 books and scores, 600 music periodicals, and 90,000 audio and video recordings, including the Ruth T. Watanabe Special Collections Department of manuscripts, rare editions, and an audio repository capturing the performance history of the Eastman School since 1933. The Rare Books section contains 150,000 items, including autographs of works by Beethoven, Brahms, Haydn, Schubert, Debussy, Weill, and Copland.

Bachelor's, master's, and doctoral degrees are offered. The B.M. degree is awarded in applied music (performance), composition, jazz studies and contemporary media, music

education, theory, and musical arts, and there is an innovative honors curriculum that allows students to craft an individualized, cross-disciplinary program of study that culminates in a major senior project.

Undergraduates have the option of completing double degrees, a B.M. and a B.A. or B.S., or taking a fifth year under the University's Take Five program or the Eastman School's Forte program for music education majors.

Graduate degrees (M.M., M.A., D.M.A., or Ph.D.) are offered in composition, conducting, performance, music education, music theory, theory pedagogy, musicology, ethnomusicology, early music, jazz studies and contemporary media, and piano accompanying and chamber music.

**Faculty and Alumni** Eastman's faculty consists of more than 130 performers, composers, conductors, scholars, and educators, including Guggenheim Fellows, ASCAP Award recipients, recording artists, and acclaimed musicians. Eastman's full-time, resident faculty members know their students personally, becoming mentors and lifelong friends.

Eastman alumni are members of all leading American orchestras, including conducting and principal chair positions, and also perform all around the world as members of the New York Philharmonic, Philadelphia Orchestra, Boston Symphony, London Symphony, Hong Kong Symphony Orchestra, New Zealand Philharmonic, Cleveland Orchestra, and Chicago Symphony. Voice alumni perform with major opera companies, including the Metropolitan Opera and the Vienna State Opera, and Eastman's Sacred Music graduates hold top positions in churches and synagogues.

Eastman graduates hold key administrative positions with national cultural and performing arts organizations, including the St. Louis Symphony, National Endowment for the Arts, Detroit Symphony, Boston Symphony, St. Louis Symphony, Manhattan School of Music, Opera America, Columbia Artists Management, and BMG. Prominent Eastman graduates include soprano Renée Fleming and tenor Anthony Dean Griffey; jazz musicians Ron Carter, Maria Schneider, Steve Gadd, and Chuck Mangione; and composers Dominick Argento, Michael Torke, George Walker, Alexander Courage (Star Trek), Jeff Beal (Monk), and Charles Strouse (Annie).

**Special Programs** Eastman's Institute for Music Leadership (IML) is bridging the gap between the academic and professional music world. Created in 2001, the IML is a vital hub for creating, sharing, and implementing ideas and programs that will ensure the vitality and relevance of music in the twenty-first century. IML teaches tomorrow's music leaders to become entrepreneurs who understand how to develop and implement a sound business plan without sacrificing their ideals and ideas for their art.

All chamber music groups take part in the innovative Music For All Program, performing at various locations in the community such as schools, hospitals, and businesses. Preparing these programs challenges the students to synthesize their theoretical, historical, and instrumental or vocal training—and to develop the performance and communication skills necessary to relate to the wide range of audiences.

# University of South Alabama
## Mobile, Alabama

State-supported, coed. Suburban campus. Total enrollment: 13,779. Music program established 1965.

**Degrees** Bachelor of Fine Arts in the area of music theater; Bachelor of Music in the areas of performance, music education, business. Majors and concentrations: interdisciplinary studies, music education, music industry, music theater, performance. Program accredited by NASM, NCATE.

**Enrollment** 90 total.

**Music Student Profile** 75% females, 25% males, 5% minorities, 5% international.

*University of South Alabama (continued)*

**Music Faculty** 12 total (full-time), 12 total (part-time). 100% of full-time faculty have terminal degrees. Graduate students do not teach undergraduate courses. Undergraduate student–faculty ratio: 7:1.

**Student Life** Student groups/activities include Music Educators National Conference, Sigma Alpha Iota, Phi Mu Alpha.

**Expenses for 2007–2008** Application fee: $35. State resident tuition: $4020 full-time. Nonresident tuition: $8040 full-time. Mandatory fees: $802 full-time. College room and board: $4820. College room only: $2590. Room and board charges vary according to board plan, housing facility, and location. Special program-related fees: $60–$180 per semester for private lessons.

**Financial Aid** Program-specific awards: 85 music scholarships for ensemble performers ($200–$1500), 1 Theodore Presser Award for senior music majors ($4200), 2 Chester Piano Scholarships for enrolled piano students ($300–$500), 3 Laidlaw Scholarships for enrolled music majors ($1500–$2000), 1 Mike Bartels Award for percussion majors ($250–$350).

**Application Procedures** Students admitted directly into the professional program freshman year. Deadline for freshmen and transfers: August 10. Required: high school transcript, college transcript(s) for transfer students, minimum 2.0 high school GPA, audition, SAT or ACT test scores. Auditions held 4 times on campus; recorded music is permissible as a substitute for live auditions when distance is prohibitive.

**Web Site** http://www.southalabama.edu/music/

**Undergraduate Contact** Dr. Greg Gruner, Chairman, Department of Music, University of South Alabama, Laidlaw Performing Arts Center, Room 1072, Mobile, Alabama 36688; 251-460-6136 ext. 6804, fax: 251-460-7328, e-mail address: ggruner@jaguar1.usouthal.edu

# University of South Carolina
## Columbia, South Carolina

State-supported, coed. Total enrollment: 27,272. Music program established 1937.

**Degrees** Bachelor of Music in the areas of performance, music education, music theory/composition, jazz studies. Majors and concentrations: guitar, jazz, music education, music theory and composition, piano/organ, stringed instruments, voice, wind and percussion instruments. Graduate degrees offered: Master of Music in the areas of composition, performance, piano pedagogy, music history, music theory, conducting, jazz studies, opera theater; Master of Music Education. Doctor of Musical Arts in the areas of composition, performance, piano pedagogy, conducting; Doctor of Philosophy in the area of music education. Program accredited by NASM, NCATE.

**Enrollment** 460 total; 336 undergraduate, 119 graduate, 5 nonprofessional degree.

**Music Student Profile** 42% females, 58% males, 16% minorities, 10% international.

**Music Faculty** 44 total (full-time), 12 total (part-time). 90% of full-time faculty have terminal degrees. Graduate students teach a few undergraduate courses. Undergraduate student–faculty ratio: 10:1.

**Student Life** Student groups/activities include Preparatory Program (applied instruction for community), String Project, Children's Music Development Center. Special housing available for music students.

**Expenses for 2008–2009** Application fee: $50. State resident tuition: $7946 full-time. Nonresident tuition: $21,232 full-time. Mandatory fees: $400 full-time. College room and board: $6946. College room only: $4376. Special program-related fees: $45–$290 for applied music fee, $174–$347 for recital fee.

**Financial Aid** Program-specific awards: 200 music scholarships for program majors and minors ($500–$4100).

**Application Procedures** Students admitted directly into the professional program freshman year. Deadline for freshmen: March 1; transfers: June 1. Notification date for freshmen and transfers: continuous. Required: high school transcript, college transcript(s) for transfer students, minimum 2.0 high school GPA, audition, SAT or ACT test scores (minimum composite ACT score of 24). Recommended: minimum 3.0 high school GPA. Auditions

held 5 times on campus; recorded music is permissible as a substitute for live auditions when distance is prohibitive for provisional acceptance and videotaped performances are permissible as a substitute for live auditions when distance is prohibitive for provisional acceptance.

**Web Site** http://www.music.sc.edu/index.html

**Undergraduate Contact** Ms. Jean Smith, Administrative Assistant, School of Music, University of South Carolina, Columbia, South Carolina 29208; 803-777-4335, fax: 803-777-6508, e-mail address: ugmusic@mozart.sc.edu

**Graduate Contact** Ms. Jammie Turner, Administrative Assistant, School of Music, University of South Carolina, Columbia, South Carolina 29208; 803-777-4106, fax: 803-777-6508, e-mail address: gradmusic@mozart.sc.edu

# The University of South Dakota
## Vermillion, South Dakota

State-supported, coed. Small town campus. Total enrollment: 9,243. Music program established 1882.

**Degrees** Bachelor of Music in the areas of performance, music education, musical arts. Majors and concentrations: brass, music education, piano/organ, stringed instruments, voice, wind and percussion instruments. Graduate degrees offered: Master of Music in the areas of music education, performance, music history, history of musical instruments. Cross-registration with South Dakota State University System. Program accredited by NASM.

**Enrollment** 141 total; 111 undergraduate, 30 graduate.

**Music Student Profile** 65% females, 35% males, 8% minorities, 6% international.

**Music Faculty** 17 total (full-time), 4 total (part-time). 90% of full-time faculty have terminal degrees. Graduate students teach a few undergraduate courses. Undergraduate student–faculty ratio: 7:1.

**Student Life** Student groups/activities include Music Educators National Conference.

**Expenses for 2007–2008** Application fee: $20. State resident tuition: $2478 full-time. Nonresident tuition: $7872 full-time. Mandatory fees: $2914 full-time. Full-time tuition and fees vary according to course load and reciprocity agreements. College room and board: $5174. College room only: $2503. Room and board charges vary according to board plan and housing facility.

**Financial Aid** Program-specific awards: 100 music scholarships for program majors ($200–$4000).

**Application Procedures** Students apply for admission into the professional program by freshman year. Deadline for freshmen and transfers: continuous. Required: high school transcript, college transcript(s) for transfer students, audition, SAT or ACT test scores (minimum composite ACT score of 19), 4 years of high school English (grade of C or above), 3 years of high school advanced math, social sciences and lab science, 1 year of fine arts, minimum 2.6 high school GPA. Auditions held twice on campus; recorded music is permissible as a substitute for live auditions when distance is prohibitive and videotaped performances are permissible as a substitute for live auditions when distance is prohibitive.

**Web Site** http://www.usd.edu/cfa/Music

**Undergraduate Contact** Dr. Larry Schou, Chair, Music Department, The University of South Dakota, CFA 114a, 414 East Clark Street, Vermillion, South Dakota 57069; 605-677-5274, fax: 605-677-5988, e-mail address: lschou@usd.edu

**Graduate Contact** Dr. David Moskowitz, Coordinator of Graduate Music Studies, Music Department, The University of South Dakota, CFA 114a, 414 East Clark Street, Vermillion, South Dakota 57069; 605-677-5716, fax: 605-677-5988, e-mail address: dmoskowi@usd.edu

*USC Thornton School of Music*
# University of Southern California
## Los Angeles, California

Independent, coed. Urban campus. Total enrollment: 33,408. Music program established 1884.

**Degrees** Bachelor of Music in the areas of performance, composition, jazz studies, music industry, vocal arts. Majors and concentrations: classical guitar, composition, jazz studies, music, music industry, piano/organ, stringed instruments, studio/jazz guitar, voice, wind and percussion instruments. Graduate degrees offered: Master of Arts in the areas of music history and literature, early music, teaching music; Master of Music in the areas of choral music, sacred music, composition, jazz studies, music education, conducting, performance, keyboard collaborative arts, vocal arts; Master of Music Education. Doctor of Musical Arts in the areas of choral music, sacred music, music education, early music performance, performance, keyboard collaborative arts, vocal arts, jazz studies; Doctor of Philosophy in the area of historical musicology. Program accredited by NASM.
**Enrollment** 1,071 total; 589 undergraduate, 444 graduate, 38 nonprofessional degree.
**Music Student Profile** 49% females, 51% males, 37% minorities, 14% international.
**Music Faculty** 225 total. 80% of full-time faculty have terminal degrees. Graduate students teach a few undergraduate courses. Undergraduate student–faculty ratio: 6:1.
**Student Life** Student groups/activities include Music Industry Connection, Thornton Outreach Programs, Music Educators National Conference and Music Teachers National Association. Special housing available for music students.
**Expenses for 2007–2008** Application fee: $65. Comprehensive fee: $46,668 includes full-time tuition ($35,212), mandatory fees ($598), and college room and board ($10,858). College room only: $5992. Full-time tuition and fees vary according to program. Room and board charges vary according to board plan and housing facility. Special program-related fees: $325 per course unit for individual instruction fees.
**Financial Aid** Program-specific awards: music scholarships for music performance majors.
**Application Procedures** Students admitted directly into the professional program freshman year. Deadline for freshmen and transfers: December 1. Notification date for freshmen: April 1. Required: essay, high school transcript, college transcript(s) for transfer students, minimum 3.0 high school GPA, 3 letters of recommendation, SAT or ACT test scores, resumé/repertoire list, three original scores for composition applicants, audition for most majors. Recommended: interview. Auditions held 3 times and by appointment on campus and off campus in New York, NY; recorded music is permissible as a substitute for live auditions if a campus visit is impossible (except vocalists), see Web site for details and videotaped performances are permissible as a substitute for live auditions if a campus visit is impossible (except pianists), see Web site for details.
**Web Site** http://www.usc.edu/music
**Contact** Mr. Phillip Placenti, Assistant Dean for Admission and Financial Aid, USC Thornton School of Music, University of Southern California, University Park Campus-UUC 218, Los Angeles, California 90089-2991; 213-740-8986, fax: 213-740-8995, e-mail address: uscmusic@thornton.usc.edu

## University of Southern Maine
### Portland, Maine

State-supported, coed. Suburban campus. Total enrollment: 10,453. Music program established 1957.
**Degrees** Bachelor of Music in the areas of music education, performance. Majors and concentrations: classical music, jazz, music education, music theater, piano pedagogy. Graduate degrees offered: Master of Music in the areas of performance, conducting, composition, jazz studies, music education. Cross-registration with Greater Portland Alliance of Colleges and Universities. Program accredited by NASM.
**Enrollment** 213 total; 158 undergraduate, 22 graduate, 33 nonprofessional degree.
**Music Student Profile** 50% females, 50% males, 2% minorities, 1% international.
**Music Faculty** 15 total (full-time), 36 total (part-time). 66% of full-time faculty have terminal degrees. Graduate students do not teach undergraduate courses. Undergraduate student–faculty ratio: 10:1.

**Student Life** Student groups/activities include Music Educators National Conference, American String Teachers Association, International Association for Jazz Education. Special housing available for music students.
**Expenses for 2007–2008** Application fee: $40. State resident tuition: $5940 full-time. Nonresident tuition: $16,410 full-time. Mandatory fees: $926 full-time. Full-time tuition and fees vary according to course load, degree level, and reciprocity agreements. College room and board: $8038. College room only: $4140. Room and board charges vary according to board plan, housing facility, and location. Special program-related fees: $100 per credit hour for applied music fees.
**Financial Aid** Program-specific awards: 10–15 music talent scholarships for program majors ($750–$5000).
**Application Procedures** Students admitted directly into the professional program freshman year. Deadline for freshmen and transfers: September 1. Required: essay, high school transcript, college transcript(s) for transfer students, minimum 2.0 high school GPA, letter of recommendation, audition, SAT or ACT test scores. Recommended: minimum 3.0 high school GPA, interview. Auditions held 9 times on campus and off campus in Western Massachusetts; Aroostook County, ME; Vermont; recorded music is permissible as a substitute for live auditions on a case-by-case basis and videotaped performances are permissible as a substitute for live auditions on a case-by-case basis.
**Web Site** http://www.usm.maine.edu/~mus
**Undergraduate Contact** Dr. E. Scott Harris, Director, School of Music, University of Southern Maine, 37 College Avenue, Gorham, Maine 04038-1032; 207-780-5265, fax: 207-780-5527, e-mail address: music@usm.maine.edu
**Graduate Contact** Dr. Michele Kaschub, Director, Graduate Studies, School of Music, University of Southern Maine, 37 College Avenue, Gorham, Maine 04038-1032; 207-780-5587, fax: 207-780-5527, e-mail address: kaschub@usm.maine.edu

## University of South Florida
### Tampa, Florida

State-supported, coed. Urban campus. Total enrollment: 44,870. Music program established 1960.
**Web Site** http://www.usf.edu

## The University of Tampa
### Tampa, Florida

Independent, coed. Urban campus. Total enrollment: 5,628. Music program established 1933.
**Degrees** Bachelor of Music. Majors and concentrations: music education, music performance. Program accredited by NASM.
**Enrollment** 53 total; 30 undergraduate, 23 nonprofessional degree.
**Music Faculty** 6 undergraduate (full-time), 19 undergraduate (part-time). 85% of full-time faculty have terminal degrees. Graduate students do not teach undergraduate courses. Undergraduate student–faculty ratio: 12:1.
**Student Life** Student groups/activities include Phi Mu Alpha, Sigma Alpha Iota.
**Expenses for 2007–2008** Application fee: $40. Comprehensive fee: $28,298 includes full-time tuition ($19,700), mandatory fees ($982), and college room and board ($7616). College room only: $4076. Full-time tuition and fees vary according to class time. Room and board charges vary according to board plan and housing facility. Special program-related fees: $100 per credit hour for applied music.
**Financial Aid** Program-specific awards: 25 University Talent Scholarships for music majors ($2500).
**Application Procedures** Students admitted directly into the professional program freshman year. Deadline for freshmen and transfers: May 1. Notification date for freshmen and transfers: continuous. Required: essay, high school transcript, college transcript(s) for transfer students, 2 letters of recommendation, audition, SAT or ACT test scores, music theory placement test. Recommended: evidence of constructive extracurricular activities. Auditions held 3 times and by appointment on campus; recorded music is permissible as a substitute for live auditions

*The University of Tampa (continued)*

when distance is prohibitive and videotaped performances are permissible as a substitute for live auditions when distance is prohibitive.

**Web Site** http://www.ut.edu

**Undergraduate Contact** Ms. Barbara Strickler, Vice President for Enrollment Management, The University of Tampa, 401 West Kennedy Boulevard, Tampa, Florida 33606-1490; 813-253-6228, fax: 813-258-7398.

# The University of Tennessee

## Knoxville, Tennessee

State-supported, coed. Urban campus. Total enrollment: 29,937. Music program established 1947.

**Degrees** Bachelor of Music in the areas of music theory/composition, studio music and jazz, piano, organ, piano pedagogy and literature, sacred music, strings, voice, woodwind, brass, percussion instruments, instrumental and vocal music education. Majors and concentrations: jazz, music, music education, music theory and composition, piano pedagogy, piano/organ, sacred music, stringed instruments, voice, wind and percussion instruments. Graduate degrees offered: Master of Music in the areas of accompanying, choral conducting, composition, instrumental conducting, jazz, music education, music theory, musicology, organ, piano, piano literature and pedagogy, strings, voice, winds and percussion instruments. Program accredited by NASM.

**Enrollment** 392 total; 326 undergraduate, 66 graduate.

**Music Student Profile** 40% females, 60% males, 8% minorities, 4% international.

**Music Faculty** 40 total (full-time), 11 total (part-time). 90% of full-time faculty have terminal degrees. Graduate students teach a few undergraduate courses. Undergraduate student–faculty ratio: 6:1.

**Student Life** Student groups/activities include Sigma Alpha Iota, Phi Mu Alpha, MENC-The National Association for Music Education.

**Expenses for 2008–2009** Application fee: $30. State resident tuition: $5376 full-time. Nonresident tuition: $18,216 full-time. Mandatory fees: $812 full-time. College room and board: $6676. College room only: $3516. Special program-related fees: $60–$120 per semester for private lessons.

**Financial Aid** Program-specific awards: 200 music scholarships for high school seniors ($2000).

**Application Procedures** Students apply for admission into the professional program by freshman year. Deadline for freshmen and transfers: continuous. Required: high school transcript, college transcript(s) for transfer students, minimum 2.0 high school GPA, audition, SAT or ACT test scores. Auditions held 3 times on campus; recorded music is permissible as a substitute for live auditions when distance is prohibitive and videotaped performances are permissible as a substitute for live auditions when distance is prohibitive.

**Web Site** http://www.music.utk.edu

**Undergraduate Contact** Ms. Barbara Murphy, Associate Director for Undergraduate Studies, School of Music, The University of Tennessee, Music Building, 1741 Volunteer Boulevard, Knoxville, Tennessee 37996-2600; 865-974-3241, fax: 865-974-1941, e-mail address: music@utk.edu

**Graduate Contact** Ms. Angela Batey, Associate Director for Graduate Studies, School of Music, The University of Tennessee, 211 Music Building, 1741 Volunteer Boulevard, Knoxville, Tennessee 37996-2600; 865-974-3241, fax: 865-974-1941, e-mail address: music@utk.edu

# The University of Tennessee at Chattanooga

## Chattanooga, Tennessee

State-supported, coed. Urban campus. Total enrollment: 9,558. Music program established 1933.

**Degrees** Bachelor of Music in the areas of performance, music theory/composition, music education. Majors and concentrations: music education, music theory and composition, piano/organ, stringed instruments, voice, wind and percussion instruments. Graduate degrees offered: Master of Music in the areas of music education, performance. Program accredited by NASM.

**Enrollment** 100 total; 76 undergraduate, 11 graduate, 13 nonprofessional degree.

**Music Student Profile** 65% females, 35% males, 10% minorities, 4% international.

**Music Faculty** 15 total (full-time), 18 total (part-time). 100% of full-time faculty have terminal degrees. Graduate students do not teach undergraduate courses. Undergraduate student–faculty ratio: 5:1.

**Student Life** Student groups/activities include Music Educators National Conference Student Chapter, Sigma Alpha Iota, Phi Mu Alpha Sinfonia.

**Expenses for 2007–2008** Application fee: $30. State resident tuition: $3972 full-time. Nonresident tuition: $9962 full-time. Mandatory fees: $1090 full-time. College room and board: $7555. College room only: $5055. Room and board charges vary according to board plan and housing facility. Special program-related fees: $60–$120 per semester for applied music fee.

**Financial Aid** Program-specific awards: 70 performance grants for ensemble participants ($400–$2000).

**Application Procedures** Students admitted directly into the professional program freshman year. Deadline for freshmen and transfers: continuous. Required: high school transcript, college transcript(s) for transfer students, minimum 2.0 high school GPA, letter of recommendation, SAT or ACT test scores, audition for scholarship consideration. Recommended: essay, audition. Auditions held 3 times on campus; recorded music is permissible as a substitute for live auditions when distance is prohibitive and videotaped performances are permissible as a substitute for live auditions.

**Web Site** http://www.utc.edu/Academic/Music/

**Undergraduate Contact** Dr. Lee Harris, Head, Music Department, The University of Tennessee at Chattanooga, 615 McCallie Avenue, Chattanooga, Tennessee 37403; 423-425-4601, fax: 423-425-4603, e-mail address: lee-harris@utc.edu

**Graduate Contact** Dr. Monte Coulter, Coordinator, Graduate Programs in Music, Music Department, The University of Tennessee at Chattanooga, 615 McCallie Avenue, Chattanooga, Tennessee 37403; 423-425-4601, fax: 423-425-4603, e-mail address: monte-coulter@utc.edu

# The University of Tennessee at Martin

## Martin, Tennessee

State-supported, coed. Small town campus. Total enrollment: 7,173. Music program established 1970.

**Degrees** Bachelor of Music in the areas of music education, performance, performance pedagogy. Majors and concentrations: music education, performance. Program accredited by NASM.

**Enrollment** 93 total; 85 undergraduate, 8 nonprofessional degree.

**Music Student Profile** 41% females, 59% males, 13% minorities, 1% international.

**Music Faculty** 13 undergraduate (full-time), 4 undergraduate (part-time). 92% of full-time faculty have terminal degrees. Graduate students do not teach undergraduate courses. Undergraduate student–faculty ratio: 6:1.

**Student Life** Student groups/activities include Phi Mu Alpha Sinfonia, Sigma Alpha Iota, Music Educators National Conference.

**Expenses for 2007–2008** Application fee: $30. State resident tuition: $4150 full-time. Nonresident tuition: $14,190 full-time. Mandatory fees: $855 full-time. College room and board: $4446. College room only: $2160. Room and board charges vary according to board plan and housing facility. Special program-related fees: $150 per semester for applied music fee.

**Financial Aid** Program-specific awards: 77 music scholarships ($800–$4800).

**Application Procedures** Students apply for admission into the professional program by sophomore year. Deadline for freshmen and transfers: continuous. Required: high school transcript, college transcript(s) for transfer students, audition, ACT score of 21 and high school GPA of 2.50, or ACT score of 18 and high school GPA of 2.85. Auditions held 3 times on campus.

**Web Site** http://www.utm.edu/music

**Undergraduate Contact** Dr. Jeremy W. Kolwinska, Chair, Department of Music, The University of Tennessee at Martin, 102 Fine Arts Building, Martin, Tennessee 38238; 731-881-7402, fax: 731-881-7515, e-mail address: jeremyk@utm.edu

# The University of Texas at San Antonio

## San Antonio, Texas

State-supported, coed. Suburban campus. Total enrollment: 28,533. Music program established 1975.

**Degrees** Bachelor of Music in the areas of performance, composition, music marketing, music education. Majors and concentrations: classical guitar, classical music, composition, music education, music marketing, piano/organ, stringed instruments, voice, wind and percussion instruments. Graduate degrees offered: Master of Music in the areas of performance, music education, conducting, piano pedagogy. Program accredited by NASM.

**Enrollment** 300 total; 270 undergraduate, 30 graduate.

**Music Student Profile** 50% females, 50% males, 50% minorities, 5% international.

**Music Faculty** 25 total (full-time), 32 total (part-time). 95% of full-time faculty have terminal degrees. Graduate students do not teach undergraduate courses. Undergraduate student–faculty ratio: 11:1.

**Student Life** Student groups/activities include Music Educators National Conference Student Chapter, Sigma Alpha Iota, Phi Mu Alpha Sinfonia.

**Expenses for 2007–2008** Application fee: $40. State resident tuition: $4530 full-time. Nonresident tuition: $12,780 full-time. Mandatory fees: $2147 full-time. Full-time tuition and fees vary according to course load. College room and board: $8169. College room only: $5616. Room and board charges vary according to board plan and housing facility. Special program-related fees: $20 per course for instrument users fee, $100 per course for private lesson fee.

**Financial Aid** Program-specific awards: 90 Department of Music Scholarships for program majors ($2000).

**Application Procedures** Students admitted directly into the professional program freshman year. Deadline for freshmen and transfers: July 1. Notification date for freshmen and transfers: August 1. Required: high school transcript, college transcript(s) for transfer students, audition, SAT or ACT test scores. Auditions held 4 times on campus; recorded music is permissible as a substitute for live auditions when distance is prohibitive and videotaped performances are permissible as a substitute for live auditions when distance is prohibitive.

**Web Site** http://music.utsa.edu

**Undergraduate Contact** Dr. Diana Allan, Associate Professor, Department of Music, The University of Texas at San Antonio, One UTSA Circle, San Antonio, Texas 78249-1130; 210-458-4354, fax: 210-458-4381.

**Graduate Contact** Dr. Kasandra Keeling, Associate Professor, Department of Music, The University of Texas at San Antonio, One UTSA Circle, San Antonio, Texas 78249-1130; 210-458-4354, fax: 210-458-4381.

# The University of the Arts

## Philadelphia, Pennsylvania

Independent, coed. Total enrollment: 2,396. Music program established 1870.

**Degrees** Bachelor of Music in the areas of instrumental performance, vocal performance, composition in jazz studies. Majors and concentrations: composition, instrumental performance, vocal performance. Graduate degrees offered: Master of Arts in Teaching in the area of music education; Master of Music in the area of jazz studies. Program accredited by NASM.

**Enrollment** 237 total; 220 undergraduate, 17 graduate.

**Music Student Profile** 80% females, 20% males, 20% minorities, 1% international.

**Music Faculty** 12 total (full-time), 82 total (part-time). 33% of full-time faculty have terminal degrees. Graduate students do not teach undergraduate courses. Undergraduate student–faculty ratio: 4:1.

**Student Life** Student groups/activities include Music Educators National Conference, National Academy of Recording Arts and Sciences, International Association for Jazz Education. Special housing available for music students.

**Expenses for 2008–2009** Application fee: $60. Tuition: $29,500 full-time. Mandatory fees: $1100 full-time. College room only: $7047.

**Financial Aid** Program-specific awards: 55 merit scholarships for incoming students ($1000–$12,000).

**Application Procedures** Students admitted directly into the professional program freshman year. Deadline for freshmen and transfers: continuous. Notification date for freshmen and transfers: September 1. Required: essay, high school transcript, college transcript(s) for transfer students, minimum 2.0 high school GPA, letter of recommendation, audition, SAT or ACT test scores, resume, audition repertoire. Recommended: minimum 3.0 high school GPA. Auditions held 9 times on campus and off campus in various locations in California; recorded music is permissible as a substitute for live auditions with approval from the department and videotaped performances are permissible as a substitute for live auditions with approval from the department.

**Web Site** http://www.uarts.edu

**Contact** Susan Gandy, Director of Admission, The University of the Arts, 320 South Broad Street, Philadelphia, Pennsylvania 19102; 800-616-ARTS ext. 6049, fax: 215-717-6045, e-mail address: admissions@uarts.edu

# University of the Cumberlands

## Williamsburg, Kentucky

Independent Kentucky Baptist, coed. Rural campus. Total enrollment: 1,884. Music program established 1968.

**Degrees** Bachelor of Music in the areas of music education, church music. Majors and concentrations: church music, instrumental music, piano, vocal music.

**Enrollment** 54 total; 49 undergraduate, 5 nonprofessional degree.

**Music Student Profile** 55% females, 45% males, 2% minorities, 2% international.

**Music Faculty** 8 undergraduate (full-time), 1 undergraduate (part-time). 50% of full-time faculty have terminal degrees. Graduate students do not teach undergraduate courses. Undergraduate student–faculty ratio: 9:1.

**Student Life** Student groups/activities include Collegiate Music Educators National Conference, American Choral Directors Association, National Association of Teachers of Singing competitions.

**Expenses for 2007–2008** Application fee: $30. Comprehensive fee: $20,284 includes full-time tuition ($13,298), mandatory fees ($360), and college room and board ($6626). Special program-related fees: $5 per semester for locker rental, $50 for instrument maintenance, $75 per semester for applied lesson fee.

**Financial Aid** Program-specific awards: 10–15 music scholarships for program majors ($400–$5000).

**Application Procedures** Students admitted directly into the professional program freshman year. Deadline for freshmen and transfers: continuous. Required: essay, high school transcript, college transcript(s) for transfer students, minimum 2.0 high school GPA, 3 letters of recommendation, SAT or ACT test scores. Recommended: interview, audition. Auditions held continuously on campus and off campus in Louisville, KY; recorded music is permissible as a substitute for live auditions when distance is prohibitive and videotaped performances are permissible as a substitute for live auditions when distance is prohibitive.

**Web Site** http://www.ucumberlands.edu/

**Undergraduate Contact** Dr. Jeff C. Smoak Jr., Chair, Music Department, University of the Cumberlands, 7525 College Station Drive, Williamsburg, Kentucky 40769; 606-539-4332, fax: 606-539-4332, e-mail address: jsmoak@ucumberlands.edu

# University of the Incarnate Word

## San Antonio, Texas

Independent Roman Catholic, coed. Urban campus. Total enrollment: 5,752. Music program established 1932.

**Degrees** Bachelor of Arts in the areas of composition, performance; Bachelor of Music Education; Bachelor of Music Therapy. Majors and concentrations: brass, composition, music, music education, music industry, music therapy, piano/organ, stringed instruments, voice, wind and percussion instruments. Cross-registration with Our Lady of the Lake University of San Antonio, St. Mary's University of San Antonio, Alamo Community Colleges. Program accredited by NASM.

**Enrollment** 66 total; all undergraduate.

**Music Student Profile** 65% females, 35% males, 60% minorities, 10% international.

**Music Faculty** 6 undergraduate (full-time), 18 undergraduate (part-time). 83% of full-time faculty have terminal degrees. Graduate students do not teach undergraduate courses. Undergraduate student–faculty ratio: 6:1.

**Student Life** Student groups/activities include American Music Therapy Association, Music Industries Club.

**Expenses for 2008–2009** Application fee: $20. Comprehensive fee: $27,640 includes full-time tuition ($19,400), mandatory fees ($860), and college room and board ($7380). College room only: $4250. Special program-related fees: $170 per semester for private lessons.

**Financial Aid** Program-specific awards: 1 Sarah Eliz Bell Endowed Scholarship for program majors ($1200), 1 Hortense Buchanan Award for program majors ($100), 1 Lamar Moreau Award for program majors ($100), 1 Sister Margaret Alacoque Colothan Endowed Scholarship for program majors ($700), 8 music scholarships for program majors ($500–$4000), 3 music minor scholarships for program minors ($500–$800).

**Application Procedures** Students apply for admission into the professional program by sophomore year. Deadline for freshmen and transfers: continuous. Required: high school transcript, college transcript(s) for transfer students, minimum 2.0 high school GPA, 2 letters of recommendation, interview, video, audition, SAT or ACT test scores. Auditions held twice on campus; recorded music is permissible as a substitute for live auditions with 2 letters of recommendation and videotaped performances are permissible as a substitute for live auditions with 2 letters of recommendation.

**Web Site** http://www.uiw.edu

**Undergraduate Contact** William Gokelman, Chair of Music, Music Department, University of the Incarnate Word, 4301 Broadway, San Antonio, Texas 78209; 210-829-3848, fax: 210-829-3880, e-mail address: gokelman@uiwtx.edu

# University of the Pacific

## Stockton, California

Independent, coed. Suburban campus. Total enrollment: 6,235. Music program established 1878.

**Degrees** Bachelor of Arts in the areas of music, music management, jazz studies; Bachelor of Music in the areas of performance, music education, music therapy, music composition, music management. Majors and concentrations: brass, composition, jazz studies, music, music education, music management, music therapy, piano, stringed instruments, voice, wind and percussion instruments. Graduate degrees offered: Master of Arts in the area of music therapy; Master of Music in the area of music education. Program accredited by NASM, AMTA.

**Enrollment** 183 total; 171 undergraduate, 3 graduate, 9 nonprofessional degree.

**Music Student Profile** 55% females, 45% males, 20% minorities, 10% international.

**Music Faculty** 23 total (full-time), 21 total (part-time). 65% of full-time faculty have terminal degrees. Graduate students do not teach undergraduate courses. Undergraduate student–faculty ratio: 7:1.

**Student Life** Student groups/activities include Music Educators National Conference Student Chapter, Music Therapy Association, professional music fraternities.

**Expenses for 2007–2008** Application fee: $60. Comprehensive fee: $38,190 includes full-time tuition ($28,480), mandatory fees ($500), and college room and board ($9210). College room only: $4610. Room and board charges vary according to board plan and housing facility. Special program-related fees: $10–$15 per semester for practice room fee, $70–$125 per credit for applied music fee.

**Financial Aid** Program-specific awards: 118 music scholarships for those demonstrating talent and need ($3000–$15,000), 29 Conservatory Performance Scholarships for those demonstrating musical achievement ($1000–$9600).

**Application Procedures** Students admitted directly into the professional program freshman year. Deadline for freshmen and transfers: February 15. Required: essay, high school transcript, college transcript(s) for transfer students, letter of recommendation, interview, audition, SAT or ACT test scores. Recommended: minimum 3.0 high school GPA. Auditions held 4 times on campus; recorded music is permissible as a substitute for live auditions if a campus visit is impossible and videotaped performances are permissible as a substitute for live auditions if a campus visit is impossible.

**Web Site** http://www.pacific.edu/conservatory

**Undergraduate Contact** Mrs. Katherine Harper, Coordinator of Student Services, Conservatory of Music, University of the Pacific, 3601 Pacific Avenue, Stockton, California 95211; 209-946-2418, fax: 209-946-2770, e-mail address: conservatory@pacific.edu

**Graduate Contact** Robin Lattin, Recruitment Administrator, Office of Research and Graduate Studies, University of the Pacific, 3601 Pacific Avenue, Stockton, California 95211; 209-946-2261, fax: 209-946-2858, e-mail address: gradschool@pacific.edu

## *More About the Conservatory*

With its talented students, dedicated faculty members, distinguished guest artists, and diverse range of performances, the Conservatory of Music at the University of the Pacific has been recognized as one of the top music schools for more than 128 years. The Conservatory is a charter member of the National Association of Schools of Music (1928) and was the first accredited professional school of music in the western United States. The mission of the Conservatory is to provide superior educational opportunities, to be a significant musical resource for the University and the community, and to have a significant impact on the future of music.

Bachelor's degrees in jazz studies, music, music composition, music education, music history, music management, music performance, and music therapy and master's degrees in music education and music therapy are offered.

Conservatory students are musically talented, intellectually gifted, and inquisitive. In addition to studies within their majors, students take courses throughout the University as part of their general education program. The close relationship among all the academic units of the University ensures a broad range of educational opportunities.

**Campus and Surroundings** Stockton (population 290,000), situated between San Francisco and the Sierra Nevada, is California's largest inland port. The area provides unlimited cultural and recreational opportunities within a short drive, including entertainment in San Francisco; skiing, camping, and backpacking in the Sierra Nevada; and waterskiing and boating in the California Delta area.

**Program Facilities** The activities of the Conservatory of Music are centered around four buildings. The beautiful 950-seat Faye Spanos Concert Hall opened in 1927 and underwent extensive renovation in 1988. The building houses several faculty studios, practice rooms, and the Conservatory administration offices. The intimate 120-seat Recital Hall has a wonderful acoustical environment, perfect for recitals, master classes, workshops, and other presentations. The Rehearsal Center houses the Instrumental Rehearsal Hall, Choral Rehearsal Hall, two faculty offices, and the band and orchestra music libraries. Buck Hall is the center of most of the classroom teaching in the Conservatory. It houses four large classrooms, a conference and seminar room, a ProTools-based composition studio, and many faculty offices and teaching studios. In the summer of 2006, the Conservatory designed and installed a state-of-the-art music technology laboratory in Buck Hall for both classroom instruction and Conservatory student use. The lab is based on nineteen Apple computers running current versions of Logic Pro 7, a digital audio workstation; Sibelius for music notation; Final Cut Studio 2 (Final Cut Pro, Motion, Soundtrack Pro, Color, Compressor, and DVD Studio Pro) for audio and video editing; Photoshop for image editing; Dreamweaver for Web design; and other supporting software. There is also a 5.1 surround-sound system for the composition and analysis of music for film.

A fifth building, Owen Hall, is located west of the Conservatory, near the center of the campus. Owen Hall houses the keyboard laboratory, several faculty studios, and approximately twenty individual practice rooms. It also contains rehearsal facilities for the Brubeck Institute Jazz Quintet. A ProTools recording studio for recording technique classes, planned to be added in 2008, will also allow faculty members and students to make professional-quality recordings.

**Faculty, Resident Artists, and Alumni** Conservatory faculty members are well qualified to teach, perform, and mentor students throughout their collegiate experiences and into their professional careers. They are dedicated and committed to providing high-quality educational and performance experiences for students and the community.

**Student Performance Opportunities** Musical performance is the core element of being a music major at the University of the Pacific. The Conservatory of Music has a proud tradition of excellence in its student music presentations and in the success of its graduates who enter the world of performance. The musical life of the campus is rich and varied, with more than 120 performances each year by Conservatory students, faculty members, and visiting artists from throughout the country and beyond. Solo performance opportunities abound in the Conservatory. There are also many opportunities for students to perform in a wide variety of ensembles.

**Special Programs** Dave Brubeck, the legendary icon of jazz and American music, graduated from the Conservatory of Music at the College of the Pacific in 1942. Brubeck gave his entire archival collection of his life's work to the University of the Pacific in 2000. In turn, the University created the Brubeck Institute to honor its distinguished alumnus. Students in the jazz studies program participate in and benefit from all clinics, workshops, and other on-campus experiences provided to the Brubeck Institute's Fellowship Program. They also have access to the Brubeck Archive and participate in the annual Brubeck Festival. Exceptional jazz studies majors are encouraged to audition for the Fellowship Program.

# The University of Toledo
**Toledo, Ohio**

State-supported, coed. Total enrollment: 19,768. Music program established 1948.
**Degrees** Bachelor of Music in the area of performance studies; Bachelor of Music Education. Majors and concentrations: jazz, music business, music education, music production and recording technology, piano/organ, stringed instruments, voice, wind and percussion instruments. Graduate degrees offered: Master of Music in the area of performance studies; Master of Music Education. Cross-registration with Bowling Green State University. Program accredited by NASM.
**Enrollment** 150 total; 115 undergraduate, 35 graduate.
**Music Student Profile** 52% females, 48% males, 10% minorities, 5% international.
**Music Faculty** 22 total (full-time), 12 total (part-time). 95% of full-time faculty have terminal degrees. Graduate students teach a few undergraduate courses. Undergraduate student–faculty ratio: 6:1.
**Student Life** Student groups/activities include Mu Phi Epsilon, Music Educators National Conference, Ohio Music Teachers Association. Special housing available for music students.

**Expenses for 2008–2009** Application fee: $40. State resident tuition: $6816 full-time. Nonresident tuition: $15,627 full-time. Mandatory fees: $1111 full-time. College room and board: $8446. College room only: $5496. Special program-related fees: $23–$40 per semester for ensemble and lab fees, $53–$83 per course for applied music fees.
**Financial Aid** Program-specific awards: endowed awards ($300–$5000).
**Application Procedures** Students admitted directly into the professional program freshman year. Deadline for freshmen and transfers: continuous. Required: high school transcript, college transcript(s) for transfer students, minimum 2.0 high school GPA, audition, ACT test score only. Recommended: letter of recommendation. Auditions held 4 times and by appointment on campus; recorded music is permissible as a substitute for live auditions for international applicants and on a case-by-case basis and videotaped performances are permissible as a substitute for live auditions for international applicants and on a case-by-case basis.
**Web Site** http://www.music.utoledo.edu
**Undergraduate Contact** Carolyn Boyle, Secretary, Department of Music, The University of Toledo, 2801 West Bancroft, Toledo, Ohio 43606-3390; 419-530-2448, fax: 419-530-8483, e-mail address: carolyn.boyle@utoledo.edu
**Graduate Contact** Dr. David Jex, Professor, Department of Music, The University of Toledo, 2801 West Bancroft, Toledo, Ohio 43606-3390; 419-530-4560, fax: 419-530-8483, e-mail address: djex@pop3.utoledo.edu

# University of Tulsa
**Tulsa, Oklahoma**

Independent, coed. Urban campus. Total enrollment: 4,165.
**Web Site** http://www.utulsa.edu/

# University of Utah
**Salt Lake City, Utah**

State-supported, coed. Urban campus. Total enrollment: 28,025. Music program established 1908.
**Degrees** Bachelor of Arts in the area of music; Bachelor of Music in the areas of performance, music education, theory, composition, history and literature; Bachelor of Music Education in the areas of instrumental music, choral music. Majors and concentrations: brass, composition, harp, jazz, music education, music history and literature, music theory, organ, piano, stringed instruments, voice, wind and percussion instruments, woodwind instruments. Graduate degrees offered: Master of Arts in the area of musicology; Master of Music in the areas of composition, history/literature, performance, music education, conducting, theory, musicology, collaborative piano, jazz studies; Master of Music Education. Doctor of Musical Arts in the areas of conducting, brass, piano, strings, voice, woodwinds; Doctor of Philosophy in the areas of composition, music education. Program accredited by NASM.
**Enrollment** 427 total; 309 undergraduate, 79 graduate, 39 nonprofessional degree.
**Music Student Profile** 52% females, 48% males, 14% minorities, 5% international.
**Music Faculty** 32 total (full-time), 55 total (part-time). 80% of full-time faculty have terminal degrees. Graduate students teach a few undergraduate courses. Undergraduate student–faculty ratio: 10:1.
**Student Life** Student groups/activities include Music Educators National Conference, world-wide competitions.
**Expenses for 2007–2008** Application fee: $35. State resident tuition: $4269 full-time. Nonresident tuition: $14,945 full-time. Mandatory fees: $717 full-time. Full-time tuition and fees vary according to course level, course load, degree level, program, reciprocity agreements, and student level. College room and board: $5778. College room only: $2890. Room and board charges vary according to board plan and housing facility. Contact university directly for part-time tuition costs. Special program-related fees: $60 per year for practice rooms, $190–$380 per semester for private lessons.

*University of Utah (continued)*

**Financial Aid** Program-specific awards: 180–190 music scholarships for music majors ($500–$3300).

**Application Procedures** Students admitted directly into the professional program freshman year. Deadline for freshmen and transfers: July 1. Required: high school transcript, college transcript(s) for transfer students, minimum 2.0 high school GPA, audition. Recommended: essay, minimum 3.0 high school GPA, 3 letters of recommendation, interview, video, portfolio, ACT test score only. Auditions held 2-3 times on campus; recorded music is permissible as a substitute for live auditions when distance is prohibitive and videotaped performances are permissible as a substitute for live auditions when distance is prohibitive. Portfolio reviews held as needed on campus.

**Web Site** http://www.music.utah.edu/

**Contact** Dr. David Power, Associate Director for Academic Affairs, School of Music, University of Utah, 204 DGH-1375 East Presidents Circle, Salt Lake City, Utah 84112-0030; 801-581-6762, fax: 801-581-5683.

# University of Washington
## Seattle, Washington

State-supported, coed. Urban campus. Total enrollment: 40,218. Music program established 1911.

**Degrees** Bachelor of Music in the areas of performance, jazz studies, composition, music education. Majors and concentrations: composition, guitar, harp, jazz, music education, music history, music theory, orchestral instruments, piano/organ, stringed instruments, voice. Graduate degrees offered: Master of Music in the areas of performance, composition, conducting, opera production. Doctor of Musical Arts in the areas of performance, composition, conducting, opera production; Doctor of Philosophy in the areas of music education, music history, music theory, ethnomusicology. Program accredited by NASM.

**Enrollment** 312 total; 120 undergraduate, 152 graduate, 40 nonprofessional degree.

**Music Student Profile** 49% females, 51% males, 16% minorities, 4% international.

**Music Faculty** 36 total (full-time), 25 total (part-time). 51% of full-time faculty have terminal degrees. Graduate students teach a few undergraduate courses. Undergraduate student–faculty ratio: 2:1.

**Student Life** Student groups/activities include Music Educators National Conference (MENC), Music Student Association (MSA), Kappa Kappa Psi.

**Expenses for 2007–2008** Application fee: $50. State resident tuition: $6385 full-time. Nonresident tuition: $22,131 full-time. Full-time tuition varies according to course load. College room and board: $8337. Room and board charges vary according to board plan and housing facility. Special program-related fees: $15 per year for concert pass, $88 per summer quarter for applied music lesson fee, $111 per quarter for applied music lesson fee.

**Financial Aid** Program-specific awards: 83 music scholarships for music majors ($300–$6500).

**Application Procedures** Students admitted directly into the professional program freshman year. Deadline for freshmen: January 15; transfers: February 15. Required: essay, college transcript(s) for transfer students, minimum 2.0 high school GPA, audition, SAT or ACT test scores, transcripts for non-traditional students, athletes, and students who attended high school outside of the U.S., interview for music education applicants, portfolio, SAT/ACT scores, and transcripts after 2 years of study for composition applicants. Recommended: minimum 3.0 high school GPA. Auditions held 4 times on campus; videotaped performances are permissible as a substitute for live auditions if distance is prohibitive (beyond 1000-mile radius). Portfolio reviews held 3 times on campus.

**Web Site** http://www.music.washington.edu

**Contact** Jenni Cole, Admissions and Outreach Coordinator, School of Music, University of Washington, Box 353450, Seattle, Washington 98195-3450; 206-685-9872, fax: 206-616-6879, e-mail address: somadmit@u.washington.edu

# University of West Georgia
## Carrollton, Georgia

State-supported, coed. Small town campus. Total enrollment: 10,677. Music program established 1966.

**Web Site** http://www.westga.edu/

# University of Wisconsin–Green Bay
## Green Bay, Wisconsin

State-supported, coed. Suburban campus. Total enrollment: 6,083. Music program established 1971.

**Degrees** Bachelor of Music in the areas of music education, performance. Majors and concentrations: bass, guitar, music education, piano/organ, voice, wind and percussion instruments. Program accredited by NASM.

**Enrollment** 118 total; 32 undergraduate, 86 nonprofessional degree.

**Music Student Profile** 60% females, 40% males, 7% minorities, 1% international.

**Music Faculty** 11 undergraduate (full-time), 10 undergraduate (part-time). 73% of full-time faculty have terminal degrees. Graduate students do not teach undergraduate courses. Undergraduate student–faculty ratio: 9:1.

**Student Life** Student groups/activities include American Choral Directors Association College Chapter, Music Educators National Conference Student Chapter, Jazz Society.

**Expenses for 2007–2008** Application fee: $44. State resident tuition: $4819 full-time. Nonresident tuition: $12,392 full-time. Mandatory fees: $1140 full-time. Full-time tuition and fees vary according to reciprocity agreements. College room and board: $5200. College room only: $3200. Room and board charges vary according to housing facility. Special program-related fees: $25 per semester for instrument rental fee.

**Financial Aid** Program-specific awards: 3 jazz scholarships for program majors ($500), 2 piano accompanying awards for program majors ($500), 15 music merit scholarships ($750).

**Application Procedures** Students apply for admission into the professional program by sophomore year. Deadline for freshmen and transfers: continuous. Required: high school transcript, college transcript(s) for transfer students, 2 letters of recommendation, interview, audition, ACT test score only. Recommended: essay, minimum 3.0 high school GPA. Auditions held 3 times and by appointment on campus.

**Web Site** http://www.uwgb.edu/music/

**Undergraduate Contact** Dr. Sarah Meredith, Associate Professor of Music, Music Program, University of Wisconsin–Green Bay, 2420 Nicolet Drive, Green Bay, Wisconsin 54311-7001; 920-465-2637, fax: 920-465-2890, e-mail address: meredits@uwgb.edu

# University of Wisconsin–Madison
## Madison, Wisconsin

State-supported, coed. Urban campus. Total enrollment: 42,041. Music program established 1895.

**Degrees** Bachelor of Music in the areas of performance, music education. Majors and concentrations: brass, composition, music education, music history/theory, piano/organ, stringed instruments, voice, wind and percussion instruments. Graduate degrees offered: Master of Musical Arts in the areas of brass instruments, choral conducting, composition, music education, ethnomusicology, musicology, instrumental conducting-orchestra, instrumental conducting-wind ensemble, opera, organ, percussion, piano, piano-accompanying, piano pedagogy/performance; Master of Music Education. Doctor of Musical Arts in the areas of brass instruments, choral conducting, composition, instrumental conducting-orchestra, instrumental conducting-wind ensemble, organ, piano, stringed instruments, voice, woodwind instruments. Program accredited by NASM.

**Enrollment** 450 total; 200 undergraduate, 175 graduate, 75 nonprofessional degree.

**Music Student Profile** 50% females, 50% males, 10% minorities, 7% international.

**Music Faculty** 51 total (full-time), 3 total (part-time). 50% of full-time faculty have terminal degrees. Graduate students teach a few undergraduate courses. Undergraduate student–faculty ratio: 9:1.

**Student Life** Student groups/activities include Sigma Alpha Iota/Phi Mu Alpha, Music Educators National Conference Student Chapter, Music Teachers National Association Student Chapter.

**Expenses for 2007–2008** Application fee: $44. State resident tuition: $7188 full-time. Nonresident tuition: $21,440 full-time. Mandatory fees: $859 full-time. Full-time tuition and fees vary according to degree level, program, and reciprocity agreements. Special program-related fees: $30 per semester for recital recording, $40 per recital for non-required recital fee, $50 per fall/spring for locker rental, $60–$65 per semester for practice room.

**Financial Aid** Program-specific awards: 40–50 endowed scholarships for program majors ($500–$5000), 40 Music Clinic Scholarships for in-state program majors ($5000–$5500).

**Application Procedures** Students apply for admission into the professional program by freshman, sophomore year. Deadline for freshmen: February 1; transfers: March 1. Notification date for freshmen: March 10; transfers: April 30. Required: high school transcript, college transcript(s) for transfer students, 2 letters of recommendation, interview, audition, minimum 2.5 high school GPA. Recommended: minimum 3.0 high school GPA. Auditions held 3 times and by appointment on campus; recorded music is permissible as a substitute for live auditions when distance is prohibitive and videotaped performances are permissible as a substitute for live auditions in some cases when distance is prohibitive.

**Web Site** http://www.wisc.edu/music

**Undergraduate Contact** Prof. Marc Fink, Associate Director, School of Music, University of Wisconsin–Madison, 1621 Humanities, Madison, Wisconsin 53706; 608-263-3623, fax: 608-262-8876, e-mail address: mdfink@facstaff.wisc.edu

**Graduate Contact** Dr. Pamela Potter, Director of Graduate Studies, School of Music, University of Wisconsin–Madison, 4531 Humanities, Madison, Wisconsin 53706; 608-262-9295, fax: 608-262-8876.

# University of Wisconsin–Milwaukee
## Milwaukee, Wisconsin

State-supported, coed. Urban campus. Total enrollment: 29,338.

**Degrees** Bachelor of Fine Arts in the areas of music, performance, music history and literature, music composition technology, music education/general, music education/instrumental, music education/choral. Majors and concentrations: brass, composition, guitar, music education, piano/organ, stringed instruments, voice, wind and percussion instruments. Graduate degrees offered: Master of Music in the areas of performance, music theory/composition, conducting, music education, music history and literature, collaborative piano, string pedagogy, chamber music performance, music history and literature/library and information science. Program accredited by NASM.

**Enrollment** 506 total; 380 undergraduate, 101 graduate, 25 nonprofessional degree.

**Music Student Profile** 25% females, 75% males, 70% minorities, 25% international.

**Music Faculty** 25 total (full-time), 45 total (part-time). 95% of full-time faculty have terminal degrees. Graduate students do not teach undergraduate courses.

**Student Life** Student groups/activities include Delta Omicron, Collegiate Music Educators National Conference.

**Expenses for 2007–2008** Application fee: $35. State resident tuition: $6960 full-time. Nonresident tuition: $16,686 full-time. Mandatory fees: $767 full-time. Full-time tuition and fees vary according to location, program, and reciprocity agreements. College room only: $3620. Room charges vary according to housing facility.

**Financial Aid** Program-specific awards: 90 music scholarships for program students ($200–$1000).

**Application Procedures** Students admitted directly into the professional program freshman year. Deadline for freshmen and transfers: continuous. Notification date for freshmen and transfers: continuous. Required: essay, high school transcript, college transcript(s) for transfer students, audition, portfolio. Auditions held 4 times on campus; recorded music is permissible as a substitute for live auditions when distance is prohibitive and videotaped performances are permissible as a substitute for live auditions when distance is prohibitive. Portfolio reviews held on campus.

**Web Site** http://www.uwm.edu/

**Undergraduate Contact** Music Department, University of Wisconsin–Milwaukee, PO Box 413, Milwaukee, Wisconsin 53201; 414-229-4393, fax: 414-229-2776.

**Graduate Contact** Director Graduate Studies, Music Department, University of Wisconsin–Milwaukee, PO Box 413, Milwaukee, Wisconsin 53201; 414-229-2286, fax: 414-229-2776.

# University of Wisconsin–Oshkosh
## Oshkosh, Wisconsin

State-supported, coed. Suburban campus. Total enrollment: 12,693. Music program established 1952.

**Degrees** Bachelor of Music in the areas of performance, music industry; Bachelor of Music Education in the areas of general music, choral music, instrumental music. Majors and concentrations: brass, music business/music industry, music education, piano, sound recording technology, stringed instruments, voice, wind and percussion instruments. Program accredited by NASM.

**Enrollment** 214 total; 198 undergraduate, 16 nonprofessional degree.

**Music Student Profile** 48% females, 52% males, 6% minorities, 3% international.

**Music Faculty** 17 undergraduate (full-time), 9 undergraduate (part-time). 82% of full-time faculty have terminal degrees. Graduate students do not teach undergraduate courses. Undergraduate student–faculty ratio: 13:1.

**Student Life** Student groups/activities include Music Educators National Conference Student Chapter, Oshkosh Recording Association. Special housing available for music students.

**Expenses for 2007–2008** Application fee: $35. State resident tuition: $5693 full-time. Nonresident tuition: $13,266 full-time. College room and board: $5746. College room only: $3162.

**Financial Aid** Program-specific awards: 4 Willcockson Prizes in the Arts for incoming freshmen ($1000), 1 Henry Pensis Award for double reed players ($300), 1 Stanley Linton Music Education Award for music education students ($300), 1 Roger Dennis Music Education Award for music education students ($300), 1 Richard K. Porter Vocal Performance Award for voice students ($150), 1 Patricia Radford Fell Award for piano students ($300), 15 music scholarships for music majors ($1000–$3000), 3 Thoma Awards for pianists ($1000).

**Application Procedures** Students admitted directly into the professional program freshman year. Deadline for freshmen and transfers: April 1. Required: high school transcript, audition, ACT test score only. Auditions held 4 times on campus; recorded music is permissible as a substitute for live auditions when distance is prohibitive and videotaped performances are permissible as a substitute for live auditions when distance is prohibitive.

**Web Site** http://www.uwosh.edu/departments/music

**Undergraduate Contact** Admissions Office, University of Wisconsin–Oshkosh, 800 Algoma Boulevard, Oshkosh, Wisconsin 54901; 920-424-0202, fax: 920-424-1207.

# University of Wisconsin–Stevens Point
## Stevens Point, Wisconsin

State-supported, coed. Small town campus. Total enrollment: 8,888. Music program established 1928.

**Degrees** Bachelor of Music. Majors and concentrations: jazz studies, music education, music literature, performance. Graduate degrees offered: Master of Music Education in the areas of instrumental music education, choral music education, jazz pedagogy, studio pedagogy, Suzuki talent education. Program accredited by NASM.

*University of Wisconsin–Stevens Point (continued)*

**Enrollment** 234 total; 186 undergraduate, 8 graduate, 40 nonprofessional degree.

**Music Student Profile** 60% females, 40% males, 3% minorities, 1% international.

**Music Faculty** 21 undergraduate (full-time), 4 undergraduate (part-time). 90% of full-time faculty have terminal degrees. Graduate students do not teach undergraduate courses. Undergraduate student–faculty ratio: 15:1.

**Student Life** Student groups/activities include Music Educators National Conference, American String Teachers Association.

**Expenses for 2007–2008** Application fee: $35. State resident tuition: $4819 full-time. Nonresident tuition: $12,392 full-time. Mandatory fees: $1015 full-time. Full-time tuition and fees vary according to course load and reciprocity agreements. College room and board: $4832. College room only: $2944.

**Financial Aid** Program-specific awards: music scholarships for those demonstrating talent, academic achievement, and need.

**Application Procedures** Students apply for admission into the professional program by sophomore year. Deadline for freshmen: January 15; transfers: February 15. Required: high school transcript, college transcript(s) for transfer students, audition, SAT or ACT test scores (minimum composite ACT score of 18). Recommended: 2 letters of recommendation. Auditions held 3 times and by appointment on campus; recorded music is permissible as a substitute for live auditions when distance is prohibitive and videotaped performances are permissible as a substitute for live auditions when distance is prohibitive.

**Web Site** http://www.uwsp.edu/music/

**Undergraduate Contact** Dr. Robert Kase, Chair, Music Department, University of Wisconsin–Stevens Point, Fine Arts Center, Stevens Point, Wisconsin 54481; 715-346-3107, fax: 715-346-2718, e-mail address: rkase@uwsp.edu

**Graduate Contact** Dr. Patricia Holland, Coordinator of Graduate Studies, Music Department, University of Wisconsin–Stevens Point, Fine Arts Center, Stevens Point, Wisconsin 54481; 715-346-3119, fax: 715-346-2718, e-mail address: pholland@uwsp. edu

# University of Wisconsin–Superior

## Superior, Wisconsin

State-supported, coed. Suburban campus. Total enrollment: 2,753. Music program established 1939.

**Degrees** Bachelor of Music in the areas of performance, jazz studies; Bachelor of Music Education in the areas of instrumental music, choral/general music. Majors and concentrations: guitar, harpsichord, jazz performance, music education, piano/organ, stringed instruments, voice, wind and percussion instruments. Cross-registration with University of Minnesota, Duluth; College of St. Scholastica. Program accredited by NASM.

**Enrollment** 50 total; 35 undergraduate, 15 nonprofessional degree.

**Music Student Profile** 60% females, 40% males, 1% minorities, 2% international.

**Music Faculty** 8 undergraduate (full-time), 14 undergraduate (part-time). 100% of full-time faculty have terminal degrees. Graduate students do not teach undergraduate courses. Undergraduate student–faculty ratio: 4:1.

**Student Life** Student groups/activities include Music Educators National Conference Student Chapter, American Choral Directors Association Student Chapter, Music Teachers National Association Student Chapter.

**Expenses for 2007–2008** Application fee: $35. State resident tuition: $4969 full-time. Nonresident tuition: $12,572 full-time. Mandatory fees: $938 full-time. Full-time tuition and fees vary according to reciprocity agreements. College room and board: $4720. College room only: $2770. Room and board charges vary according to board plan and housing facility.

**Financial Aid** Program-specific awards: 1 NBC Keyboard Award for pianists and organists ($1000), 10 Foundation Awards for incoming freshmen ($500), 1 Rock Scholarship for junior and senior pianists ($1000), 1 McLean Award for pianists and violinists ($500), 3 string scholarships for string players ($600).

**Application Procedures** Students apply for admission into the professional program by freshman year. Deadline for freshmen

and transfers: continuous. Required: high school transcript, college transcript(s) for transfer students, interview, audition, ACT test score only, standing in top half of graduating class, minimum composite ACT score of 21 or standing in top third of class. Recommended: 2 letters of recommendation. Auditions held 3 times or by arrangement on campus; recorded music is permissible as a substitute for live auditions when distance is prohibitive and videotaped performances are permissible as a substitute for live auditions when distance is prohibitive.

**Web Site** http://www.uwsuper.edu/music

**Undergraduate Contact** Dr. Beth Gilbert, Chair, Department of Music, University of Wisconsin–Superior, Box 2000, Superior, Wisconsin 54880-2898; 715-394-8117, fax: 715-394-8578, e-mail address: bgilbert@uwsuper.edu

# University of Wisconsin–Whitewater

## Whitewater, Wisconsin

State-supported, coed. Small town campus. Total enrollment: 10,737. Music program established 1947.

**Web Site** http://www.uww.edu/

# University of Wyoming

## Laramie, Wyoming

State-supported, coed. Total enrollment: 12,875.

**Degrees** Bachelor of Music in the area of music performance; Bachelor of Music Education. Majors and concentrations: music education, music performance. Graduate degrees offered: Master of Music in the area of performance; Master of Music Education. Cross-registration with Wyoming community colleges. Program accredited by NASM.

**Enrollment** 161 total; 148 undergraduate, 9 graduate, 4 nonprofessional degree.

**Music Student Profile** 65% females, 35% males, 7% minorities, 5% international.

**Music Faculty** 15 undergraduate (full-time), 15 undergraduate (part-time), 9 graduate (full-time). 90% of full-time faculty have terminal degrees. Graduate students do not teach undergraduate courses. Undergraduate student–faculty ratio: 18:1.

**Student Life** Student groups/activities include Wyoming Music Educators Association, band fraternities, Kappa Kappa Psi, Tau Beta Sigma, marching band.

**Expenses for 2007–2008** Application fee: $40. One-time mandatory fee: $40. State resident tuition: $2820 full-time. Nonresident tuition: $9660 full-time. Mandatory fees: $734 full-time. Full-time tuition and fees vary according to course load, location, program, and reciprocity agreements. College room and board: $7274. College room only: $3158. Room and board charges vary according to board plan and housing facility. Special program-related fees: $35 per semester for practice room fees, $125–$250 per semester for lesson fees.

**Financial Aid** Program-specific awards: 20 private awards for music majors ($300–$500), 205 general scholarships for all students who participate in music ($200–$7000).

**Application Procedures** Students admitted directly into the professional program freshman year. Deadline for freshmen and transfers: August 28. Notification date for freshmen and transfers: continuous. Required: high school transcript, college transcript(s) for transfer students, minimum 2.0 high school GPA, 3 letters of recommendation, audition, SAT or ACT test scores. Recommended: interview, portfolio. Auditions held twice and by appointment on campus; recorded music is permissible as a substitute for live auditions when distance is prohibitive and videotaped performances are permissible as a substitute for live auditions when distance is prohibitive. Portfolio reviews held once per semester and by appointment on campus.

**Web Site** http://www.uwyo.edu/music

**Undergraduate Contact** Office of Admissions, University of Wyoming, Department 3435, 1000 East University Avenue, Laramie, Wyoming 82071; 307-766-5160, fax: 307-766-4042.

**Graduate Contact** Dean, Graduate School, University of Wyoming, Department 3108, 1000 East University Avenue, Laramie, Wyoming 82071; 307-766-2287, fax: 307-766-4042.

Music Programs 351

# USC Thornton School of Music

See University of Southern California

# Utah State University

**Logan, Utah**

State-supported, coed. Urban campus. Total enrollment: 14,893. Music program established 1969.
**Degrees** Bachelor of Music in the areas of music education, performance, piano pedagogy; Bachelor of Science in the area of music therapy. Majors and concentrations: guitar performance, individualized major, music education, music therapy, piano pedagogy, piano performance, stringed instrument performance, voice performance, wind and percussion instruments performance. Program accredited by NASM, AMTA.
**Enrollment** 353 total; all undergraduate.
**Music Student Profile** 70% females, 30% males, 3% minorities, 2% international.
**Music Faculty** 21 undergraduate (full-time), 35 undergraduate (part-time). 70% of full-time faculty have terminal degrees. Graduate students do not teach undergraduate courses. Undergraduate student–faculty ratio: 20:1.
**Student Life** Student groups/activities include Music Therapy Student Association, Kappa Kappa Psi (band fraternity), Tau Beta Sigma (band sorority), Music Educators National Conference Student Chapter, American String Teachers Association, American Choral Directors Association.
**Expenses for 2007–2008** Application fee: $40. State resident tuition: $3615 full-time. Nonresident tuition: $11,640 full-time. Mandatory fees: $585 full-time. Full-time tuition and fees vary according to course load and student level. College room and board: $4580. College room only: $1600. Room and board charges vary according to board plan and housing facility. Special program-related fees: $8 per semester for instrument locker rentals, $9–$25 per semester for keyboards, instrument rental, $45 per semester for piano/organ practice rooms, $208 per semester for private instruction (non-majors), $358 per semester for private instruction (majors).
**Financial Aid** Program-specific awards: scholarships for performance and education students, marching band members ($150–$2000).
**Application Procedures** Students apply for admission into the professional program by freshman year. Deadline for freshmen and transfers: continuous. Required: high school transcript, college transcript(s) for transfer students, interview, audition, ACT test score only, minimum 2.5 high school GPA. Recommended: minimum 3.0 high school GPA, video. Auditions held at various times on campus; recorded music is permissible as a substitute for live auditions when distance is prohibitive and videotaped performances are permissible as a substitute for live auditions when distance is prohibitive.
**Web Site** http://www.usu.edu/music/
**Undergraduate Contact** Dorothy Kent, Staff Assistant, Department of Music, Utah State University, 4015 Old Main Hill, Logan, Utah 84322-4015; 435-797-3036, fax: 435-797-1862, e-mail address: musicdep@cc.usu.edu

# Valley City State University

**Valley City, North Dakota**

State-supported, coed. Small town campus. Total enrollment: 921. Music program established 1892.
**Degrees** Bachelor of Science in the area of music education. Majors and concentrations: music education. Program accredited by NASM.
**Enrollment** 40 total; 20 undergraduate, 10 nonprofessional degree.
**Music Student Profile** 65% females, 35% males, 5% minorities.
**Music Faculty** 5 undergraduate (full-time), 7 undergraduate (part-time). 60% of full-time faculty have terminal degrees. Graduate students do not teach undergraduate courses. Undergraduate student–faculty ratio: 6:1.

**Student Life** Student groups/activities include Music Educators National Conference, Music Teachers National Association, National Association of Teachers of Singing, Nationally Federated Music Clubs.
**Expenses for 2007–2008** Application fee: $35. State resident tuition: $3941 full-time. Nonresident tuition: $10,522 full-time. Mandatory fees: $1643 full-time. Full-time tuition and fees vary according to course load, location, program, and reciprocity agreements. College room and board: $3880. College room only: $1510. Room and board charges vary according to board plan and housing facility. Special program-related fees: $15 per semester for band instrument rental, $25–$100 per semester for accompanists, $50–$100 per credit for applied lessons.
**Financial Aid** Program-specific awards: 35 Friends of Music Scholarships for program majors, minors, participants ($150–$1800).
**Application Procedures** Students admitted directly into the professional program freshman year. Required: high school transcript, college transcript(s) for transfer students, interview, audition, SAT or ACT test scores, theory placement exam, piano placement exam. Auditions held 3 times on campus; recorded music is permissible as a substitute for live auditions when distance is prohibitive and videotaped performances are permissible as a substitute for live auditions when distance is prohibitive.
**Web Site** http://www.vcsu.nodak.edu
**Undergraduate Contact** Dr. Diana Skroch, Chair, Department of Music, Valley City State University, 101 College Street SW, Valley City, North Dakota 58072; 800-532-8641 ext. 37273, fax: 701-845-7288, e-mail address: diana.skroch@vcsu.edu

# Valparaiso University

**Valparaiso, Indiana**

Independent, coed. Small town campus. Total enrollment: 3,872. Music program established 1925.
**Degrees** Bachelor of Music in the areas of church music, performance, composition; Bachelor of Music Education in the area of combined vocal and instrumental music. Majors and concentrations: church music, composition, music, music education, piano/organ, stringed instruments, voice, wind and percussion instruments. Program accredited by NASM.
**Enrollment** 133 total; 68 undergraduate, 65 nonprofessional degree.
**Music Student Profile** 55% females, 45% males, 5% minorities.
**Music Faculty** 10 undergraduate (full-time), 26 undergraduate (part-time). 100% of full-time faculty have terminal degrees. Graduate students do not teach undergraduate courses. Undergraduate student–faculty ratio: 12:1.
**Student Life** Student groups/activities include American Guild of Organists, Music Educators National Conference, Music Enterprises Student Association.
**Expenses for 2007–2008** Application fee: $30. Comprehensive fee: $32,350 includes full-time tuition ($24,360), mandatory fees ($840), and college room and board ($7150). College room only: $4430. Room and board charges vary according to housing facility and student level. Special program-related fees: $325 per course for studio instruction fee.
**Financial Aid** Program-specific awards: 35–40 music scholarships for performers ($1000–$4000).
**Application Procedures** Students admitted directly into the professional program freshman year. Deadline for freshmen and transfers: continuous. Notification date for freshmen and transfers: August 15. Required: high school transcript, college transcript(s) for transfer students, SAT or ACT test scores, video or audition, theory diagnostic test. Recommended: essay, letter of recommendation, interview. Auditions held twice on campus; recorded music is permissible as a substitute for live auditions by arrangement with department and videotaped performances are permissible as a substitute for live auditions when distance is prohibitive or if a campus visit is impossible.
**Web Site** http://www.valpo.edu/music/
**Undergraduate Contact** Dr. Linda C. Ferguson, Chair, Department of Music, Valparaiso University, Center for the Arts, Valparaiso, Indiana 46383-6493; 219-464-5454, fax: 219-464-5244, e-mail address: linda.ferguson@valpo.edu

*Blair School of Music*

# Vanderbilt University

## Nashville, Tennessee

Independent, coed. Urban campus. Total enrollment: 11,847. Music program established 1986.

**Degrees** Bachelor of Music in the areas of performance, musical arts, composition/music theory; Bachelor of Music/Master of Education in the area of musical arts/education. Majors and concentrations: music education, music theory and composition, musical arts, performance. Graduate degrees offered: Bachelor of Music/Master of Education in the area of musical arts/education. Program accredited by NASM.

**Enrollment** 180 total; all undergraduate.

**Music Student Profile** 55% females, 45% males, 10% minorities.

**Music Faculty** 30 undergraduate (full-time), 40 undergraduate (part-time). 32% of full-time faculty have terminal degrees. Graduate students do not teach undergraduate courses.

**Student Life** Student groups/activities include Pi Kappa Lambda/Sigma Alpha Iota, Voice Majors Association, Phi Mu Alpha Sinfonia, Sigma Alpha Iota Sorority, Music Educators National Conference.

**Expenses for 2007–2008** Application fee: $50. Comprehensive fee: $46,722 includes full-time tuition ($34,414), mandatory fees ($862), and college room and board ($11,446). College room only: $7456. Room and board charges vary according to board plan.

**Financial Aid** Program-specific awards: 1 Harold Sterling Vanderbilt Scholarship for program majors ($21,930), 1–50 Blair Dean's Honor Scholarships for program majors ($1000–$10,000), Blair Help Loans for program majors ($500–$2400), 1 Frances Hampton Currey Music Scholarship for program majors ($32,000), 1 Laura Kemp Goad Honor Scholarship for program majors ($32,000), 1 Joel and Stella Hargrove Scholarship for program majors ($5000), 1 Rae S. Miller Piano Scholarship for piano majors ($5000), 1 Wilda and William Moennig Scholarship for program majors ($12,000), 1 Del Sawyer Trumpet Scholarship for trumpet majors ($32,000), 1 William and Saidee Jarrell Award for program majors ($4000).

**Application Procedures** Students admitted directly into the professional program freshman year. Deadline for freshmen and transfers: continuous. Notification date for freshmen and transfers: April 1. Required: essay, high school transcript, college transcript(s) for transfer students, 2 letters of recommendation, audition, SAT or ACT test scores, portfolio for composition applicants. Recommended: minimum 3.0 high school GPA, video for voice majors. Auditions held 12 times on campus and off campus in Washington, DC; Interlochen, MI; Los Angeles, CA; Houston, TX; Dallas, TX, Boston, Portland, Seattle; recorded music is permissible as a substitute for live auditions for musical arts or performance majors (except in percussion); when distance is prohibitive and videotaped performances are permissible as a substitute for live auditions for percussion majors when distance is prohibitive. Portfolio reviews held by appointment on campus.

**Web Site** http://www.vanderbilt.edu

**Undergraduate Contact** Dr. Dwayne Sagen, Assistant Dean, Blair School of Music, Vanderbilt University, 2400 Blakemore Avenue, Nashville, Tennessee 37212-3499; 615-322-7679, fax: 615-343-0324, e-mail address: dwayne.p.sagen@vanderbilt.edu

# VanderCook College of Music

## Chicago, Illinois

Independent, coed. Urban campus. Music program established 1928.

**Degrees** Bachelor of Music Education. Majors and concentrations: choral music education, instrumental music education. Graduate degrees offered: Master of Music Education in the areas of instrumental music education, choral music education, music education with certification. Cross-registration with Illinois Institute of Technology. Program accredited by NASM.

**Enrollment** 321 total; 114 undergraduate, 207 graduate.

**Music Student Profile** 47% females, 53% males, 20% minorities, 2% international.

**Music Faculty** 13 total (full-time), 30 total (part-time). 46% of full-time faculty have terminal degrees. Graduate students do not teach undergraduate courses. Undergraduate student–faculty ratio: 3:1.

**Student Life** Student groups/activities include Music Educators National Conference Student Chapter, Phi Mu Alpha Sinfonia, Midwest Clinic.

**Expenses for 2007–2008** Application fee: $35. Comprehensive fee: $27,630 includes full-time tuition ($17,980), mandatory fees ($820), and college room and board ($8830). College room only: $4550. Special program-related fees: $70 per class for techniques classes, $125 per semester for computer lab use.

**Financial Aid** Program-specific awards: 75 talent awards for voice and instrument majors ($2500), 30 tuition assistance grants for program majors ($500), 30 VCM Apprentice Grants for program majors ($1000), 15 academic awards for program majors ($1000).

**Application Procedures** Students admitted directly into the professional program freshman year. Deadline for freshmen and transfers: continuous. Notification date for freshmen and transfers: continuous. Required: essay, high school transcript, college transcript(s) for transfer students, minimum 3.0 high school GPA, 3 letters of recommendation, interview, audition, SAT or ACT test scores (minimum combined SAT score of 1000, minimum composite ACT score of 20), minimum TOEFL score of 500 for international applicants. Auditions held 7 times yearly and by appointment on campus; recorded music is permissible as a substitute for live auditions for out-of-state applicants or if a campus visit is impossible and videotaped performances are permissible as a substitute for live auditions for out-of-state applicants or if a campus visit is impossible.

**Web Site** http://www.vandercook.edu

**Undergraduate Contact** Ms. Patty O'Kelley, Director of Student Recruitment, VanderCook College of Music, 3140 South Federal Street, Chicago, Illinois 60616; 800-448-2655 ext. 241, fax: 312-225-5211, e-mail address: pokelley@vandercook.edu

**Graduate Contact** Ms. Amy Lenting, Director of Admissions and Retention, VanderCook College of Music, 3140 South Federal Street, Chicago, Illinois 60616; 800-448-2655 ext. 230, fax: 312-225-5211, e-mail address: alenting@vandercook.edu

# Virginia Commonwealth University

## Richmond, Virginia

State-supported, coed. Urban campus. Total enrollment: 31,907.

**Degrees** Bachelor of Arts in the areas of music, music with emphasis in music business; Bachelor of Music in the areas of music education, performance, jazz studies. Majors and concentrations: guitar, jazz, music business, music education, piano/organ, stringed instruments, voice, wind and percussion instruments. Graduate degrees offered: Master of Music in the area of music education. Program accredited by NASM.

**Enrollment** 302 total; 258 undergraduate, 26 graduate, 18 nonprofessional degree.

**Music Student Profile** 60% females, 40% males, 30% minorities, 2% international.

**Music Faculty** 20 total (full-time), 41 total (part-time). 56% of full-time faculty have terminal degrees. Graduate students teach a few undergraduate courses. Undergraduate student–faculty ratio: 10:1.

**Student Life** Student groups/activities include ensembles.

**Expenses for 2007–2008** Application fee: $40. State resident tuition: $4482 full-time. Nonresident tuition: $16,858 full-time. Mandatory fees: $1714 full-time. College room and board: $7567. College room only: $4497. Room and board charges vary according to board plan. Special program-related fees: $30 per course for music course, $75–$265 per semester for arts major fee, $175–$335 for private music lessons.

**Financial Aid** Program-specific awards: Jessica McCain Memorial Scholarship for strings/music education students, Jesus Silva Merit Scholarship for guitar students, Sue Durden Scholarship in Music for full-time students, Waverly M. Cole Music Fund for organ students.

**Application Procedures** Students admitted directly into the professional program freshman year. Deadline for freshmen and transfers: continuous. Required: essay, high school transcript, college transcript(s) for transfer students, minimum 2.0 high school GPA, letter of recommendation, interview, audition, SAT or ACT test scores. Auditions held 5 times and by appointment on campus; recorded music is permissible as a substitute for live auditions when distance is prohibitive and videotaped performances are permissible as a substitute for live auditions when distance is prohibitive.

**Web Site** http://www.vcumusic.org

**Undergraduate Contact** Undergraduate Admissions Coordinator, Department of Music, Virginia Commonwealth University, 922 Park Avenue, PO Box 842004, Richmond, Virginia 23284-2004; 804-828-1166, fax: 804-827-0230, e-mail address: music@vcu.edu

**Graduate Contact** Ms. Linda Johnston, Administrative Coordinator, Department of Music, Virginia Commonwealth University, 922 Park Avenue, PO Box 842004, Richmond, Virginia 23284-2004; 804-828-8008, fax: 804-827-0230, e-mail address: gradmus@vcu.edu

# Viterbo University

## La Crosse, Wisconsin

Independent Roman Catholic, coed. Suburban campus. Total enrollment: 3,088. Music program established 1944.

**Degrees** Bachelor of Music in the areas of music performance, music education. Majors and concentrations: music education, music pedagogy, opera, performance. Program accredited by NASM, NCATE.

**Enrollment** 51 total; all undergraduate.

**Music Student Profile** 74% females, 26% males.

**Music Faculty** 7 undergraduate (full-time), 3 undergraduate (part-time). 57% of full-time faculty have terminal degrees. Graduate students do not teach undergraduate courses. Undergraduate student–faculty ratio: 7:1.

**Student Life** Student groups/activities include Music Educators National Conference, American Choral Directors Association (ACDA), Viterbo Preparatory School of Arts.

**Expenses for 2008–2009** Application fee: $25. Comprehensive fee: $25,870 includes full-time tuition ($19,000), mandatory fees ($490), and college room and board ($6380). College room only: $2910. Special program-related fees: $265 per credit for applied music fee.

**Financial Aid** Program-specific awards: 7 Fine Arts Scholarships for incoming program majors ($1000), 1 Richard Record Music Scholarship for incoming male voice major ($500), 1 Sister Antoinette DeLorbe Music Scholarship for current music majors ($500), 1 Sister Annarose Glum Music Education Scholarship for current music education majors ($1200), 1 Sister Marlene Weisenbeck Piano Scholarship for current piano majors ($500), 2 Sister Lucilda Meyer Music Scholarships for current music majors ($500).

**Application Procedures** Students admitted directly into the professional program freshman year. Deadline for freshmen and transfers: August 1. Required: high school transcript, college transcript(s) for transfer students, minimum 2.0 high school GPA, interview, audition, SAT or ACT test scores. Recommended: minimum 3.0 high school GPA. Auditions held 4 times on campus; recorded music is permissible as a substitute for live auditions when distance is prohibitive and videotaped performances are permissible as a substitute for live auditions when distance is prohibitive.

**Web Site** http://www.viterbo.edu/SchoolofFineArts.aspx

**Undergraduate Contact** Dr. Roland Nelson, Director of Admissions, Viterbo University, 900 Viterbo Drive, La Crosse, Wisconsin 54601; 608-796-3012, fax: 608-796-3020.

# Walla Walla University

## College Place, Washington

Independent Seventh-day Adventist, coed. Small town campus. Total enrollment: 1,829. Music program established 1892.

**Degrees** Bachelor of Music in the areas of performance, music education. Majors and concentrations: bass, brass, cello, guitar, harp, harpsichord, music education, organ, percussion, piano, viola, violin, voice, wind instruments. Cross-registration with Whitman College. Program accredited by NASM.

**Enrollment** 8 undergraduate, 18 nonprofessional degree.

**Music Student Profile** 58% females, 42% males, 8% minorities, 5% international.

**Music Faculty** 6 undergraduate (full-time), 10 undergraduate (part-time). 84% of full-time faculty have terminal degrees. Graduate students do not teach undergraduate courses. Undergraduate student–faculty ratio: 3:1.

**Student Life** Student groups/activities include Music Club.

**Expenses for 2007–2008** Application fee: $40. Comprehensive fee: $27,000 includes full-time tuition ($21,735), mandatory fees ($210), and college room and board ($5055). College room only: $2655. Full-time tuition and fees vary according to course load and degree level. Room and board charges vary according to housing facility and location. Special program-related fees: $240 per credit hour per quarter for applied lessons.

**Financial Aid** Program-specific awards: 35 music lesson scholarships for program students ($3000), 1 Soper Award for program students ($2000), 1 Ogden Award for program students.

**Application Procedures** Students apply for admission into the professional program by freshman year. Deadline for freshmen and transfers: September 30. Notification date for freshmen and transfers: continuous. Required: high school transcript, college transcript(s) for transfer students, minimum 2.0 high school GPA, 3 letters of recommendation, audition, SAT or ACT test scores. Auditions held once and by arrangement on campus; recorded music is permissible as a substitute for live auditions when distance is prohibitive and videotaped performances are permissible as a substitute for live auditions when distance is prohibitive.

**Web Site** http://music.wwc.edu

**Undergraduate Contact** Matthew James, Chair, Department of Music, Walla Walla University, 204 South College Avenue, College Place, Washington 99324-1198; 509-527-2561, fax: 509-527-2177, e-mail address: music_department@wallawalla.edu

# Wartburg College

## Waverly, Iowa

Independent Lutheran, coed. Small town campus. Total enrollment: 1,810. Music program established 1952.

**Web Site** http://www.wartburg.edu/

# Washburn University

## Topeka, Kansas

City-supported, coed. Urban campus. Total enrollment: 6,901.

**Degrees** Bachelor of Music in the area of music performance; Bachelor of Music Education. Majors and concentrations: instrumental performance, keyboard, music, music education, piano/organ, stringed instruments, vocal music, voice, wind and percussion instruments. Program accredited by NASM.

**Enrollment** 100 total; 84 undergraduate, 16 nonprofessional degree.

**Music Student Profile** 52% females, 48% males, 10% minorities, 4% international.

**Music Faculty** 13 undergraduate (full-time), 20 undergraduate (part-time). 80% of full-time faculty have terminal degrees. Graduate students do not teach undergraduate courses. Undergraduate student–faculty ratio: 7:1.

**Student Life** Student groups/activities include pep band, marching band.

**Expenses for 2007–2008** Application fee: $20. State resident tuition: $5550 full-time. Nonresident tuition: $12,600 full-time. Mandatory fees: $86 full-time. College room and board: $5281. College room only: $2941. Room and board charges vary according to board plan and housing facility.

**Financial Aid** Program-specific awards: 60 music endowments for program majors ($200–$5000).

**Application Procedures** Students admitted directly into the professional program freshman year. Deadline for freshmen and transfers: continuous. Required: high school transcript, college transcript(s) for transfer students, audition, ACT test score only.

*Washburn University (continued)*

Recommended: 2 letters of recommendation, interview. Auditions held 2 times on campus; recorded music is permissible as a substitute for live auditions when distance is prohibitive and videotaped performances are permissible as a substitute for live auditions when distance is prohibitive.
**Web Site** http://www.washburn.edu/cas
**Undergraduate Contact** Ann Marie Snook, Scholarship Coordinator, Music Department, Washburn University, 1700 Southwest College, Topeka, Kansas 66621; 785-670-1522, fax: 785-670-1042, e-mail address: annmarie.snook@washburn.edu

# Washington State University
## Pullman, Washington

State-supported, coed. Rural campus. Total enrollment: 24,396. Music program established 1904.
**Degrees** Bachelor of Music in the areas of voice, keyboard, instruments, composition, music with elective studies in music business, theater, performance; Bachelor of Music Education in the areas of choral music education, instrumental music education, general music education. Majors and concentrations: composition, flute, jazz, music education, percussion, piano/organ, saxophone, stringed instruments, trumpet, voice, wind and percussion instruments. Graduate degrees offered: Master of Arts in the areas of performance, music education, composition, jazz. Program accredited by NASM.
**Enrollment** 187 total; 137 undergraduate, 25 graduate, 25 nonprofessional degree.
**Music Student Profile** 50% females, 50% males, 10% minorities, 6% international.
**Music Faculty** 23 total (full-time), 6 total (part-time). 90% of full-time faculty have terminal degrees. Graduate students teach a few undergraduate courses. Undergraduate student–faculty ratio: 10:1.
**Student Life** Student groups/activities include Music Educators National Conference Student Chapter, American Choral Directors Association Student Chapter, Music Teachers National Association Student Chapter. Special housing available for music students.
**Expenses for 2007–2008** Application fee: $50. State resident tuition: $5812 full-time. Nonresident tuition: $16,126 full-time. Mandatory fees: $1054 full-time. Full-time tuition and fees vary according to location and reciprocity agreements. College room and board: $7316. College room only: $3556. Room and board charges vary according to board plan, housing facility, and location. Special program-related fees: $10–$50 per semester for computer lab use, $10 per semester for instrument rental, $32 per semester for applied lessons.
**Financial Aid** Program-specific awards: 35 Visual and Performing Arts Awards for program students ($500–$1200).
**Application Procedures** Students apply for admission into the professional program by freshman, sophomore year. Deadline for freshmen and transfers: August 16. Notification date for freshmen and transfers: August 22. Required: high school transcript, college transcript(s) for transfer students, minimum 2.0 high school GPA, audition, SAT or ACT test scores. Auditions held by appointment or on campus audition days on campus and off campus in various locations in the Washington area; recorded music is permissible as a substitute for live auditions if a campus visit is impossible.
**Web Site** http://libarts.wsu.edu/musicandtheatre
**Undergraduate Contact** Richard Kaiehn, Music Program Coordinator, School of Music and Theatre Arts, Washington State University, PO Box 645300, Pullman, Washington 99164-5300; 509-335-3898, fax: 509-335-4245.
**Graduate Contact** Dr. Julie Wieck, Coordinator of Graduate Programs in Music, School of Music and Theatre Arts, Washington State University, PO Box 645300, Pullman, Washington 99164-5300; 509-335-3898, fax: 509-335-4245.

# Wayne State University
## Detroit, Michigan

State-supported, coed. Urban campus. Total enrollment: 33,240. Music program established 1918.

**Degrees** Bachelor of Arts in the area of music; Bachelor of Music in the areas of jazz studies, music education, music technology, music business, performance, theory/composition. Majors and concentrations: jazz, music business, music education, music technology, music theory and composition, piano/organ, stringed instruments, voice, wind and percussion instruments. Graduate degrees offered: Master of Arts in the area of music; Master of Music in the areas of composition/theory, conducting, jazz performance, music education, performance. Program accredited by NASM.
**Enrollment** 375 total; 350 undergraduate, 25 graduate.
**Music Student Profile** 33% females, 67% males, 31% minorities, 5% international.
**Music Faculty** 16 total (full-time), 65 total (part-time). 70% of full-time faculty have terminal degrees. Graduate students do not teach undergraduate courses. Undergraduate student–faculty ratio: 21:1.
**Student Life** Student groups/activities include Delta Omicron, Phi Mu Alpha, Mu Phi Epsilon. Special housing available for music students.
**Expenses for 2007–2008** Application fee: $30. State resident tuition: $6783 full-time. Nonresident tuition: $15,534 full-time. Mandatory fees: $1061 full-time. Full-time tuition and fees vary according to course load and student level. College room and board: $6702. Room and board charges vary according to board plan and housing facility. Special program-related fees: $15–$75 per course for course materials fees, $160–$320 per course for private instruction fee.
**Financial Aid** Program-specific awards: 65 talent-based scholarships for program majors ($2700), activity awards for ensemble participants ($100–$2000), 35 honor awards for students demonstrating high academic and musical achievement ($500–$4500).
**Application Procedures** Students admitted directly into the professional program freshman year. Deadline for freshmen and transfers: June 1. Notification date for freshmen and transfers: August 30. Required: high school transcript, college transcript(s) for transfer students, interview, audition, SAT or ACT test scores (minimum composite ACT score of 21), minimum 2.75 high school GPA. Recommended: minimum 3.0 high school GPA. Auditions held 4 times on campus; recorded music is permissible as a substitute for live auditions when distance is prohibitive and videotaped performances are permissible as a substitute for live auditions when distance is prohibitive.
**Web Site** http://www.music.wayne.edu
**Undergraduate Contact** Dr. Norah Duncan, Associate Chair, Department of Music, Wayne State University, 1321 Old Main, Detroit, Michigan 48202; 313-577-1795, fax: 313-577-5420.
**Graduate Contact** Dr. Mary Wischusen, Graduate Director, Department of Music, Wayne State University, 1321 Old Main, Detroit, Michigan 48202; 313-577-1795, fax: 313-577-5420.

# Weber State University
## Ogden, Utah

State-supported, coed. Urban campus. Total enrollment: 18,081. Music program established 1998.
**Degrees** Bachelor of Music in the areas of performance, pedagogy; Bachelor of Music Education. Majors and concentrations: music education, pedagogy, performance. Program accredited by NASM.
**Enrollment** 125 total; 106 undergraduate, 19 nonprofessional degree.
**Music Student Profile** 70% females, 30% males, 2% minorities, 3% international.
**Music Faculty** 12 total (full-time), 24 total (part-time). 100% of full-time faculty have terminal degrees. Graduate students do not teach undergraduate courses. Undergraduate student–faculty ratio: 9:1.
**Student Life** Student groups/activities include National Association of Teachers of Singing, Music Educators National Conference, Music Teachers National Association, American String Teachers Association.
**Expenses for 2007–2008** Application fee: $30. State resident tuition: $2988 full-time. Nonresident tuition: $10,459 full-time. Mandatory fees: $675 full-time. College room and board: $5328.

College room only: $2142. Room and board charges vary according to board plan and housing facility. Special program-related fees: $258 per semester for private music lessons (non-majors/minors), $350 per semester for private music lessons (majors/minors).

**Financial Aid** Program-specific awards: 122 activity waivers for participants in music groups ($1400–$2900), 1 Presser Scholarship for outstanding music students ($4200), 26 Donor Scholarships for music majors ($300–$1500).

**Application Procedures** Students admitted directly into the professional program freshman year. Deadline for freshmen and transfers: continuous. Required: high school transcript, college transcript(s) for transfer students, audition, ACT test score only. Recommended: minimum 3.0 high school GPA, letter of recommendation. Auditions held twice on campus; recorded music is permissible as a substitute for live auditions when distance is prohibitive and videotaped performances are permissible as a substitute for live auditions when distance is prohibitive.

**Web Site** http://www.weber.edu

**Undergraduate Contact** Dr. Michael Palumbo, Chair, Department of Performing Arts, Weber State University, 1905 University Circle, Ogden, Utah 84408-1905; 801-626-6991, fax: 801-626-6811, e-mail address: mpalumbo@weber.edu

*Leigh Gerdine College of Fine Arts*
# Webster University
## St. Louis, Missouri

Independent, coed. Suburban campus. Total enrollment: 8,430. Music program established 1925.

**Degrees** Bachelor of Music in the areas of jazz studies, vocal performance, composition, piano performance, instrumental performance; Bachelor of Music Education in the areas of choral music education, instrumental music education, jazz studies. Majors and concentrations: classical music, composition, guitar, jazz performance, jazz/music technology, music, music education, piano/organ, stringed Instruments, voice, wind and percussion instruments. Graduate degrees offered: Master of Music in the areas of piano, vocal performance, composition, music education, church music, orchestral performance. Cross-registration with various colleges in St. Louis.

**Enrollment** 162 total; 97 undergraduate, 50 graduate, 15 nonprofessional degree.

**Music Student Profile** 60% females, 40% males, 10% minorities, 5% international.

**Music Faculty** 11 total (full-time), 52 total (part-time). 75% of full-time faculty have terminal degrees. Graduate students teach a few undergraduate courses. Undergraduate student–faculty ratio: 10:1.

**Student Life** Student groups/activities include Music Educators National Conference, International Association for Jazz Education.

**Expenses for 2007–2008** Application fee: $35. Comprehensive fee: $27,550 includes full-time tuition ($19,330) and college room and board ($8220). College room only: $4100. Full-time tuition varies according to program. Room and board charges vary according to board plan and housing facility. Special program-related fees: $200–$400 per course for applied music fee.

**Financial Aid** Program-specific awards: 14 Buder Scholarships for continuing students and transfers ($1000–$6000), 6 jazz awards for upperclassmen ($1000–$2500), 1 Opera Award for undergraduates ($1000), 12 Merit/Audition Awards for entering students ($1500).

**Application Procedures** Students admitted directly into the professional program freshman year. Deadline for freshmen and transfers: continuous. Required: essay, high school transcript, college transcript(s) for transfer students, 2 letters of recommendation, interview, audition, SAT or ACT test scores (minimum combined SAT score of 1500, minimum composite ACT score of 21), minimum 2.5 high school GPA, completion of candidacy examination at end of sophomore year. Auditions held 12 times on campus; videotaped performances are permissible as a substitute for live auditions when distance is prohibitive.

**Web Site** http://www.webster.edu/depts/finearts/music/music.html

**Undergraduate Contact** Carrie Indelicato, Auditions Coordinator, Office of Admissions, Webster University, 470 East Lockwood Avenue, St. Louis, Missouri 63119-3194; 314-968-7001, fax: 314-968-7115, e-mail address: cgeorge@webster.edu

**Graduate Contact** Dr. Glen Bauer, Director of Graduate Studies in Music, Department of Music, Webster University, 470 East Lockwood Avenue, St. Louis, Missouri 63119-3194; 314-968-7037, fax: 314-963-6048, e-mail address: bauerga@webster.edu

# Western Carolina University
## Cullowhee, North Carolina

State-supported, coed. Rural campus. Total enrollment: 9,056. Music program established 1952.

**Web Site** http://www.wcu.edu/

# Western Illinois University
## Macomb, Illinois

State-supported, coed. Small town campus. Total enrollment: 13,331. Music program established 1901.

**Degrees** Bachelor of Music in the areas of performance, music education, theory/composition, jazz studies. Graduate degrees offered: Master of Music in the areas of performance, piano pedagogy, music education, theory/composition, conducting, music history/literature, jazz studies. Program accredited by NASM, NCATE.

**Enrollment** 250 total; 230 undergraduate, 20 graduate.

**Music Student Profile** 55% females, 45% males, 10% minorities, 5% international.

**Music Faculty** 36 total (full-time), 6 total (part-time). 95% of full-time faculty have terminal degrees. Graduate students do not teach undergraduate courses. Undergraduate student–faculty ratio: 6:1.

**Student Life** Student groups/activities include Music Teachers National Association, National Association of Music Business Institutes, Music Educators National Conference. Special housing available for music students.

**Expenses for 2008–2009** Application fee: $30. State resident tuition: $6456 full-time. Nonresident tuition: $9684 full-time. Mandatory fees: $1816 full-time. College room and board: $7210. College room only: $4350.

**Financial Aid** Program-specific awards: 100 talent grants for ensemble participants ($2500), 120 endowed scholarships for music majors ($1000).

**Application Procedures** Students admitted directly into the professional program freshman year. Deadline for freshmen and transfers: continuous. Required: high school transcript, college transcript(s) for transfer students, minimum 2.0 high school GPA, 4 letters of recommendation, audition, SAT or ACT test scores, sight-reading, sight-singing, piano placement screening, theory placement screening, pitch matching. Auditions held 3 times on campus and off campus in Naperville, Illinois; recorded music is permissible as a substitute for live auditions when distance is prohibitive and videotaped performances are permissible as a substitute for live auditions when distance is prohibitive. Portfolio reviews held twice on campus.

**Web Site** http://www.wiu.edu/music

**Undergraduate Contact** Mrs. Yvonne Oliver, Auditions Coordinator, School of Music, Western Illinois University, 1 University Circle, Macomb, Illinois 61455; 309-298-1087, fax: 309-298-1968, e-mail address: yl-oliver@wiu.edu

**Graduate Contact** Dr. Brian Locke, Director of Graduate Studies, School of Music, Western Illinois University, 1 University Circle, Macomb, Illinois 61455; 309-298-1544, fax: 309-298-1968, e-mail address: b-locke@wiu.edu

*Potter College of Arts and Letters*
# Western Kentucky University
## Bowling Green, Kentucky

State-supported, coed. Suburban campus. Total enrollment: 19,258. Music program established 1948.

*Western Kentucky University (continued)*

**Degrees** Bachelor of Music in the areas of performance, music education (K-12). Majors and concentrations: guitar, music education, piano, stringed instruments, voice, wind and percussion instruments. Graduate degrees offered: Master of Art Education in the area of music education. Program accredited by NASM.
**Enrollment** 165 total; 100 undergraduate, 25 graduate, 40 nonprofessional degree.
**Music Student Profile** 55% females, 45% males, 9% minorities, 1% international.
**Music Faculty** 21 undergraduate (full-time), 15 undergraduate (part-time), 5 graduate (full-time). 66% of full-time faculty have terminal degrees. Graduate students do not teach undergraduate courses. Undergraduate student–faculty ratio: 10:1.
**Student Life** Student groups/activities include music fraternities and sororities, musical production sponsored by Theater Department.
**Expenses for 2007–2008** Application fee: $35. State resident tuition: $6416 full-time. Nonresident tuition: $15,470 full-time. Full-time tuition varies according to course load, location, program, and reciprocity agreements. College room and board: $5704. College room only: $3360. Room and board charges vary according to board plan and housing facility. Special program-related fees: $20 per year for practice room/locker rental, $50 per semester for applied lessons.
**Financial Aid** Program-specific awards: 70 talent grants for program majors ($1500–$3000), 18 scholarships for majors and minors ($300–$1500).
**Application Procedures** Students admitted directly into the professional program freshman year. Deadline for freshmen and transfers: continuous. Required: high school transcript, college transcript(s) for transfer students, minimum 2.0 high school GPA, audition, SAT or ACT test scores (minimum combined SAT score of 930, minimum composite ACT score of 20). Recommended: minimum 3.0 high school GPA. Auditions held 3 times and by appointment on campus; recorded music is permissible as a substitute for live auditions for out-of-state applicants and videotaped performances are permissible as a substitute for live auditions for out-of-state applicants.
**Web Site** http://www.wku.edu/Music/
**Undergraduate Contact** Office of Admissions, Western Kentucky University, 1906 College Heights Blvd., Potter Hall 127, Bowling Green, Kentucky 42101; 270-745-5422.
**Graduate Contact** Office of Graduate Studies and Research, Western Kentucky University, 1906 College Heights Blvd., Wetherby 207, Bowling Green, Kentucky 42101; 800-896-6960, e-mail address: graduate.studies@wku.edu

# Western Michigan University
## Kalamazoo, Michigan

State-supported, coed. Urban campus. Total enrollment: 24,433. Music program established 1913.
**Degrees** Bachelor of Music in the areas of performance, music education, jazz studies, music therapy, music composition. Majors and concentrations: classical music, composition, jazz, music, music education, music therapy, piano/organ, stringed instruments, voice, wind and percussion instruments. Graduate degrees offered: Master of Music in the areas of performance, music education, composition, conducting, music therapy. Program accredited by NASM.
**Enrollment** 441 total; 375 undergraduate, 66 graduate.
**Music Student Profile** 50% females, 50% males, 9% minorities, 5% international.
**Music Faculty** 38 total (full-time), 15 total (part-time). 88% of full-time faculty have terminal degrees. Graduate students teach a few undergraduate courses. Undergraduate student–faculty ratio: 12:1.
**Student Life** Student groups/activities include Collegiate Music Educators National Conference, music fraternities, Student Music Therapists Association.
**Expenses for 2007–2008** Application fee: $35. One-time mandatory fee: $300. State resident tuition: $6570 full-time. Nonresident tuition: $16,116 full-time. Mandatory fees: $690 full-time.

Full-time tuition and fees vary according to course load, location, and student level. College room and board: $7042. College room only: $3725. Room and board charges vary according to board plan. Special program-related fees: $7 per semester for applied music fee, $150 per semester for music major fee.
**Financial Aid** Program-specific awards: 80 School of Music Scholarships for program majors ($500–$7000).
**Application Procedures** Students admitted directly into the professional program freshman year. Deadline for freshmen and transfers: continuous. Required: high school transcript, college transcript(s) for transfer students, audition, SAT or ACT test scores. Recommended: minimum 3.0 high school GPA, letter of recommendation. Auditions held 4 times on campus; recorded music is permissible as a substitute for live auditions when distance is prohibitive and videotaped performances are permissible as a substitute for live auditions when distance is prohibitive.
**Web Site** http://www.wmich.edu/music
**Undergraduate Contact** Ms. Margaret J. Hamilton, Assistant Director, School of Music, Western Michigan University, 1903 West Michigan Avenue, Kalamazoo, Michigan 49008-5434; 269-387-4672, fax: 269-387-1113, e-mail address: margaret.hamilton@wmich.edu
**Graduate Contact** Dr. David S. Smith, Coordinator of Graduate Studies, School of Music, Western Michigan University, 1903 West Michigan Avenue, Kalamazoo, Michigan 49008-5434; 269-387-4672, fax: 269-387-1113, e-mail address: music-grad@wmich.edu

# Western State College of Colorado
## Gunnison, Colorado

State-supported, coed. Small town campus. Total enrollment: 2,064. Music program established 1911.
**Degrees** Bachelor of Arts in the area of music (music education emphasis). Majors and concentrations: music education. Program accredited by NASM.
**Enrollment** 30 total; 12 undergraduate, 18 nonprofessional degree.
**Music Student Profile** 53% females, 47% males, 13% minorities.
**Music Faculty** 5 undergraduate (full-time), 3 undergraduate (part-time). 40% of full-time faculty have terminal degrees. Graduate students do not teach undergraduate courses. Undergraduate student–faculty ratio: 2:1.
**Student Life** Student groups/activities include choir, symphony band, orchestra.
**Expenses for 2007–2008** Application fee: $30. State resident tuition: $2688 full-time. Nonresident tuition: $11,520 full-time. Mandatory fees: $898 full-time. Full-time tuition and fees vary according to course load. College room and board: $7226. College room only: $3930. Room and board charges vary according to board plan and housing facility.
**Application Procedures** Students admitted directly into the professional program freshman year. Deadline for freshmen and transfers: continuous. Required: high school transcript, college transcript(s) for transfer students, minimum 2.0 high school GPA, letter of recommendation, SAT or ACT test scores. Recommended: essay, minimum 3.0 high school GPA, interview, video, audition. Auditions held 5 times and by arrangement on campus; recorded music is permissible as a substitute for live auditions and videotaped performances are permissible as a substitute for live auditions.
**Web Site** http://www.western.edu/music
**Undergraduate Contact** Dr. Martha Violett, Chair, Music Department, Department of Music, Western State College of Colorado, 101 Quigley Hall, Gunnison, Colorado 81231; 970-943-3054, fax: 970-943-2329, e-mail address: mviolett@western.edu

# Westminster College
## New Wilmington, Pennsylvania

Independent, coed. Small town campus. Total enrollment: 1,593 (2006). Music program established 1947.

**Degrees** Bachelor of Music. Majors and concentrations: music education, performance, sacred music. Program accredited by NASM.
**Enrollment** 87 total; 65 undergraduate, 22 nonprofessional degree.
**Music Student Profile** 74% females, 26% males, 2% minorities.
**Music Faculty** 7 undergraduate (full-time), 25 undergraduate (part-time). 86% of full-time faculty have terminal degrees. Graduate students do not teach undergraduate courses. Undergraduate student–faculty ratio: 2:1.
**Student Life** Student groups/activities include Music Educators National Conference, Mu Phi Epsilon, American Choral Directors Association.
**Expenses for 2007–2008** Application fee: $35. Comprehensive fee: $33,200 includes full-time tuition ($24,430), mandatory fees ($1100), and college room and board ($7670). Room and board charges vary according to board plan.
**Financial Aid** Program-specific awards: music scholarships for program majors ($800–$2500).
**Application Procedures** Students admitted directly into the professional program freshman year. Deadline for freshmen and transfers: continuous. Required: essay, high school transcript, college transcript(s) for transfer students, minimum 2.0 high school GPA, 2 letters of recommendation, SAT or ACT test scores (minimum combined SAT score of 900, minimum composite ACT score of 19), audition on primary instrument or voice, sight singing, rhythmic reading, theory placement exam, minimum SAT score of 900 (reading/math only). Recommended: minimum 3.0 high school GPA, interview. Auditions held 8 times on campus; recorded music is permissible as a substitute for live auditions when distance is prohibitive and videotaped performances are permissible as a substitute for live auditions when distance is prohibitive.
**Web Site** http://www.westminster.edu/acad/music/overview.cfm
**Undergraduate Contact** Brad P. Tokar, Dean of Admissions, Admissions, Westminster College, 319 South Market Street, New Wilmington, Pennsylvania 16172-0001; 724-946-7100, fax: 724-946-6171.

## Rider University
# Westminster College of the Arts of Rider University
### Princeton, New Jersey

Independent, coed. Small town campus. Music program established 1926.
**Degrees** Bachelor of Arts in the areas of music, fine arts (music concentration); Bachelor of Music in the areas of sacred music, music education, theory and composition, organ performance, voice performance, music theater, piano. Majors and concentrations: music, music education, music theater, music theory and composition, organ performance, piano, sacred music, voice performance. Graduate degrees offered: Master of Arts in the area of teaching (music); Master of Music in the areas of sacred music, music education, choral conducting, piano pedagogy and performance, piano accompanying and coaching, composition, organ performance, voice pedagogy and performance, piano performance; Master of Music Education in the area of music education; Master of Voice Pedagogy in the area of voice pedagogy. Cross-registration with Princeton University, Princeton Ballet School. Program accredited by NASM, NCATE.
**Enrollment** 546 total; 416 undergraduate, 130 graduate.
**Music Student Profile** 63% females, 37% males, 20% minorities, 7% international.
**Music Faculty** 38 undergraduate (full-time), 65 undergraduate (part-time), 27 graduate (full-time), 29 graduate (part-time). 92% of full-time faculty have terminal degrees. Graduate students do not teach undergraduate courses. Undergraduate student–faculty ratio: 7:1.
**Student Life** Student groups/activities include Music Teachers National Association, Music Educators National Conference, American Choral Directors Association, National Association of Teachers of Singing. Special housing available for music students.

**Expenses for 2007–2008** Special program-related fees: $125 per semester for senior student teaching.
**Financial Aid** Program-specific awards: 117 Rider Grants for undergraduates ($4462), 221 merit scholarships for undergraduates ($8961), 34 Leadership Scholarships for proven leaders ($1734), 3 Music Theatre Awards for music theatre majors ($10,667), 154 endowed scholarships for qualifying students ($2887), 35 Recognition Awards for undergraduates ($4000), 60 Rider Advantage Awards for enrolled freshmen ($1342).
**Application Procedures** Students admitted directly into the professional program freshman year. Deadline for freshmen: continuous. Required: essay, high school transcript, college transcript(s) for transfer students, 2 letters of recommendation, audition, SAT or ACT test scores, repertoire list, TOEFL score and certification of finances (international students only), institutional music exam, interview for BA, music education, and sacred music applicants. Recommended: minimum 3.0 high school GPA. Auditions held approximately 8-10 times on campus and off campus in various locations; recorded music is permissible as a substitute for live auditions when student resides more than 500 miles from campus and videotaped performances are permissible as a substitute for live auditions when student resides more than 500 miles from campus.
**Web Site** http://www.rider.edu/westminster
**Contact** Ms. Katherine Shields, Senior Associate Director of Admission, Westminster College of the Arts of Rider University, 101 Walnut Lane, Princeton, New Jersey 08540-3899; 609-921-7100 ext. 8103, fax: 609-921-2538, e-mail address: kshields@rider.edu

## Sybil B. Harrington College of Fine Arts and Humanities
# West Texas A&M University
### Canyon, Texas

State supported, coed. Small town campus. Total enrollment: 7,502. Music program established 1916.
**Degrees** Bachelor of Music in the areas of performance, music therapy, composition, music with elective studies in business, music (all-level certification). Majors and concentrations: composition, music, piano/organ, stringed instruments, voice, wind and percussion instruments. Graduate degrees offered: Master of Arts in the area of music; Master of Music in the area of performance. Program accredited by NASM.
**Enrollment** 213 total; 203 undergraduate, 10 graduate.
**Music Student Profile** 50% females, 50% males, 10% minorities, 2% international.
**Music Faculty** 24 total (full-time), 3 total (part-time). 66% of full-time faculty have terminal degrees. Graduate students do not teach undergraduate courses. Undergraduate student–faculty ratio: 20:1.
**Expenses for 2008–2009** Application fee: $25. Special program-related fees: $60 per semester for applied music fee.
**Financial Aid** Program-specific awards available.
**Application Procedures** Students admitted directly into the professional program freshman year. Deadline for freshmen and transfers: continuous. Required: high school transcript, college transcript(s) for transfer students, 2 letters of recommendation, audition, SAT or ACT test scores. Auditions held 3 times on campus; recorded music is permissible as a substitute for live auditions if a campus visit is impossible and videotaped performances are permissible as a substitute for live auditions if a campus visit is impossible.
**Web Site** http://www.wtamu.edu/academic/fah/mus
**Undergraduate Contact** Donna Flatt, Secretary, Department of Music and Dance, West Texas A&M University, WTAMU Box 60879, Canyon, Texas 79016; 806-651-2840, fax: 806-651-2958, e-mail address: dflatt@mail.wtamu.edu
**Graduate Contact** Dr. Robert Hansen, Professor, Department of Music and Dance, West Texas A&M University, WTAMU Box 60879, Canyon, Texas 79016; 806-651-2850, fax: 806-651-2958.

# West Virginia University

## Morgantown, West Virginia

State-supported, coed. Small town campus. Total enrollment: 28,113. Music program established 1897.

**Degrees** Bachelor of Music in the areas of music history, composition, performance, music education. Majors and concentrations: brass, composition, jazz, music education, music performance, piano/organ, stringed instruments, voice, wind and percussion instruments. Graduate degrees offered: Master of Music in the areas of performance, composition, music history, music education. Doctor of Musical Arts in the areas of piano, voice, organ, percussion/world music, orchestral instruments; Doctor of Philosophy in the area of music education. Program accredited by NASM.

**Enrollment** 340 total; 260 undergraduate, 80 graduate.

**Music Student Profile** 49% females, 51% males, 4% minorities, 8% international.

**Music Faculty** 34 total (full-time), 14 total (part-time). 95% of full-time faculty have terminal degrees. Graduate students teach a few undergraduate courses. Undergraduate student–faculty ratio: 8:1.

**Student Life** Student groups/activities include Music Educators National Conference, Music Teachers National Association. Special housing available for music students.

**Expenses for 2007–2008** Application fee: $25. State resident tuition: $4722 full-time. Nonresident tuition: $14,600 full-time. Full-time tuition varies according to location, program, and reciprocity agreements. College room and board: $7046. Room and board charges vary according to board plan, housing facility, and location. Special program-related fees: $15 per semester for practice room fee, $150 per semester for music lessons.

**Financial Aid** Program-specific awards: 1–2 Carolyn and Clifford Brown Music Alumni Scholarships for music majors ($1000), 1 Frank E. and Margaret S. Lorince Scholarship for music majors ($2000), 6 Music Faculty Recognition Scholarships for music majors ($1000), 2–3 Eleanor Tucker Donley Memorial Scholarships for music majors ($1000), 12 Ida Cope Tait Music Scholarships for music majors ($500–$1000), 2 Edith Roberts Williams Music Scholarships for music majors ($1000), 5 Morgantown Music Club Scholarships for music majors ($500), 14 Loyalty Permanent Endowments Awards for music majors ($500–$1000), 56 fine arts scholarships for music majors, 20 performing arts scholarships for music majors ($1000).

**Application Procedures** Students admitted directly into the professional program freshman year. Deadline for freshmen and transfers: continuous. Notification date for freshmen and transfers: August 7. Required: high school transcript, college transcript(s) for transfer students, minimum 2.0 high school GPA, 2 letters of recommendation, audition, SAT or ACT test scores. Recommended: interview. Auditions held 3 times and by appointment on campus; recorded music is permissible as a substitute for live auditions when distance is prohibitive and videotaped performances are permissible as a substitute for live auditions when distance is prohibitive.

**Web Site** http://www.wvu.edu/~music

**Undergraduate Contact** Director, Undergraduate Admissions, Music Department, West Virginia University, College of Creative Arts, PO Box 6111, Morgantown, West Virginia 26506-6111; 304-293-5511, fax: 304-293-7491.

**Graduate Contact** Ms. Cynthia Anderson, Director of Graduate Studies, Music Department, West Virginia University, College of Creative Arts, PO Box 6111, Morgantown, West Virginia 26506-6111; 304-293-5511 ext. 3171, fax: 304-293-7491, e-mail address: cynthia.anderson@mail.wvu.edu

# West Virginia Wesleyan College

## Buckhannon, West Virginia

Independent, coed. Small town campus. Total enrollment: 1,276. Music program established 1937.

**Web Site** http://www.wvwc.edu/

## *Wheaton Conservatory of Music*

# Wheaton College

## Wheaton, Illinois

Independent nondenominational, coed. Suburban campus. Total enrollment: 2,895. Music program established 1882.

**Degrees** Bachelor of Music in the areas of performance, composition, music history/literature, elective studies; Bachelor of Music Education. Majors and concentrations: collaborative piano, composition, conducting, media music studies, music education, music history and literature, pedagogy, piano/organ, stringed instruments, voice. Program accredited by NASM.

**Enrollment** 210 total; 200 undergraduate, 10 nonprofessional degree.

**Music Student Profile** 64% females, 36% males, 17% minorities, 5% international.

**Music Faculty** 20 undergraduate (full-time), 41 undergraduate (part-time). 95% of full-time faculty have terminal degrees. Graduate students do not teach undergraduate courses. Undergraduate student–faculty ratio: 7:1.

**Student Life** Student groups/activities include Music Educators National Conference, American Guild of Organists, National Association of Teachers of Singing.

**Expenses for 2007–2008** Application fee: $50. Comprehensive fee: $30,982 includes full-time tuition ($23,730) and college room and board ($7252). College room only: $4288. Room and board charges vary according to board plan and housing facility. Special program-related fees: $30 per credit hour for music course fee, $145 per semester for ensemble fee, $290–$565 per semester for performance course.

**Financial Aid** Program-specific awards: 2 Cording Awards for those demonstrating talent ($2000), 8 Presidential Honor Awards for those demonstrating talent ($5000), 8 Special Achievement Awards for those demonstrating talent ($1000–$5000), 2 Schulteiss Awards for those demonstrating talent ($3000).

**Application Procedures** Students admitted directly into the professional program freshman year. Deadline for freshmen: January 10; transfers: March 1. Notification date for transfers: April 1. Required: essay, high school transcript, college transcript(s) for transfer students, 4 letters of recommendation, audition, SAT or ACT test scores, portfolio for composition applicants. Recommended: minimum 3.0 high school GPA, interview. Auditions held 5 times on campus; recorded music is permissible as a substitute for live auditions when distance is prohibitive and videotaped performances are permissible as a substitute for live auditions when distance is prohibitive.

**Web Site** http://www.wheaton.edu/Conservatory/index.html

**Undergraduate Contact** Ms. Debbie Rodgers, Admissions Counselor, Wheaton Conservatory of Music, Wheaton College, 501 East College Avenue, Wheaton, Illinois 60187; 800-222-2419 ext. 3, fax: 630-752-5341, e-mail address: music@wheaton.edu

### *More About the Conservatory*

Wheaton College, founded in 1860, is an independent, nondenominational, Christian liberal arts college. The Conservatory of Music, established in 1882, exists to produce professional musicians equipped to pursue varied careers in music and the arts.

Wheaton's historic campus is located 25 miles west of Chicago. The city is only 45 minutes by train or car. Among Chicago's many cultural attractions are the Lyric Opera of Chicago, Chicago Symphony Orchestra, many theaters, art museums, and jazz and chamber music performances. Wheaton is a residential college with shopping, trains, and churches all within walking distance. Representing more than forty countries and all fifty states, 200 Conservatory students, 2,400 undergraduate liberal arts students, and 500 graduate students form the Wheaton College community.

**Program Facilities** Wheaton's primary music facility is McAlister Hall, which houses teaching studios and practice rooms. Performances take place in Edman Memorial Chapel, with seating for 2,350; Pierce Chapel, with seating for 600; and the 500-seat Barrows Auditorium. The state-of-the-art music technol-

ogy lab features sixteen Macintosh workstations for sound synthesis and digital recording. There are more than ninety pianos on campus, including six concert grands, and four pipe organs, including a 50-stop, 70-rank, four-manual, dual-console mechanical action pipe organ built in 2001 by the Casavant Organ Company of Canada. The music library holds more than 28,000 items that include recordings, complete scores, and reference books.

**Faculty, Alumni, and Visiting Artists** Ninety percent of the full-time Conservatory faculty members have doctoral degrees. Faculty artists are in demand as performers and lecturers across the nation and abroad. Choral conductors Mary Hopper and Paul Wiens have led Wheaton College choral ensembles in appearances at the American Choral Directors Association national conventions in New York and Florida. Baritone Gerard Sundberg performed recently in New Zealand, as well as regularly with the Atlanta Symphony Orchestra. Pianists Daniel Horn and Karen Redekopp Edwards are active soloists and collaborators both here and abroad.

Alumni pursue varied careers in opera and concert music (Stephen Morscheck, Sylvia McNair, and Wendy White), jazz (Deanna Witkowski), orchestral conducting (John Nelson, Ensemble Orchestral de Paris), composition (Marty O'Donnell, composer of soundtracks for the video game series Halo I, II and III), and orchestral performance (Douglas Yeo, bass trombonist, Boston Symphony Orchestra and Eric Carlson, trombonist, Philadelphia Orchestra). In addition, alumni actively and successfully pursue careers in schools, churches, and contemporary music venues all over the world.

The Artist Series at Wheaton College offers students an opportunity to attend performances by world-class musicians on campus (http://www.ArtistSeries.org). Recent performances and master classes include Pinchas Zuckerman, the Chicago Symphony Orchestra, and Ladysmith Black Mambazo.

**Student Performance Opportunities** Wheaton Conservatory has eight music ensembles, which are open by audition to the entire campus. For singers: Concert Choir, Men's Glee Club, Opera Music Theater, and Women's Chorale. For instrumentalists: Jazz Ensemble, Percussion Ensemble, Symphony Orchestra, and Symphonic Band. In addition, chamber ensembles and soloists rehearse and perform regularly on and off campus. Large-scale productions, touring, and recording projects are a regular part of the Conservatory schedule. Five annual competitions—the

Concerto Competition (winning soloist performs with the Symphony Orchestra), the Composition Competition, the Chamber Music Competition, the Nordin Vocal Competition, and the Foster String Competition—afford students additional opportunities to perform.

**Special Programs** Off-campus study opportunities include Arts in London, a four-week program offered on alternate years in May. Course selection may include but is not limited to art survey, English cathedral music, musical theater, pop Shakespeare, songwriting, and world music. Wheaton's music ensembles tour regularly both nationally and regionally. International touring opportunities exist as well, including Music and Ministry in the Great Cities of Europe, a three-week trip offered on alternate years.

# Wheaton Conservatory of Music
See Wheaton College

# Willamette University
## Salem, Oregon

Independent United Methodist, coed. Urban campus. Total enrollment: 2,720. Music program established 1842.
**Degrees** Bachelor of Music in the areas of music performance, music (emphasis in music education) composition. Majors and concentrations: composition, instrumental performance, music, music education, voice. Program accredited by NASM.
**Enrollment** 52 total; all undergraduate.
**Music Student Profile** 60% females, 40% males, 3% minorities, 12% international.
**Music Faculty** 10 undergraduate (full-time), 22 undergraduate (part-time). 97% of full-time faculty have terminal degrees. Graduate students do not teach undergraduate courses. Undergraduate student–faculty ratio: 4:1.
**Student Life** Student groups/activities include Music Educators National Conference Student Chapter, Mu Phi Epsilon.
**Expenses for 2007–2008** Application fee: $50. Comprehensive fee: $39,538 includes full-time tuition ($31,760), mandatory fees ($208), and college room and board ($7570). Full time tuition and fees vary according to course load. Room and board charges vary according to board plan and housing facility. Special program-related fees: $5 for locker rental fee, $300–$600 for applied music fee.
**Financial Aid** Program-specific awards: 30 music scholarship awards for talented performers ($1000–$6000), 20 named music scholarships for talented performers ($500–$1500).
**Application Procedures** Students apply for admission into the professional program by freshman year. Deadline for freshmen: March 1; transfers: continuous. Notification date for freshmen and transfers: April 1. Required: essay, high school transcript, college transcript(s) for transfer students, 2 letters of recommendation, SAT or ACT test scores. Recommended: minimum 3.0 high school GPA, interview, audition, portfolio. Auditions held 3 times and through miscellaneous ad hoc auditions on campus; recorded music is permissible as a substitute for live auditions if a live audition is impossible and videotaped performances are permissible as a substitute for live auditions if a live audition is impossible.
**Web Site** http://www.willamette.edu/cla/music
**Undergraduate Contact** Ms. Teresa Hudkins, Director of Admissions, Willamette University, 900 State Street, Salem, Oregon 97301; 503-370-6303, fax: 503-375-5363, e-mail address: thudkins@willamette.edu

## Winters School of Music
# William Carey University
## Hattiesburg, Mississippi

Independent Southern Baptist, coed. Small town campus. Total enrollment: 2,493 (2007). Music program established 1966.

*William Carey University (continued)*

**Degrees** Bachelor of Arts in the area of music; Bachelor of Music in the areas of music education, church music, performance, music therapy. Majors and concentrations: choral music education, church music, guitar, music, music education, music therapy, organ, performance, piano, voice. Program accredited by NASM.
**Enrollment** 75 total; 70 undergraduate, 5 nonprofessional degree.
**Music Student Profile** 66% females, 34% males, 10% minorities, 6% international.
**Music Faculty** 9 undergraduate (full-time), 1 undergraduate (part-time). 78% of full-time faculty have terminal degrees. Graduate students do not teach undergraduate courses. Undergraduate student–faculty ratio: 5:1.
**Student Life** Student groups/activities include Delta Omicron, Music Educators National Conference.
**Expenses for 2007–2008** Application fee: $20. Comprehensive fee: $12,825 includes full-time tuition ($8700), mandatory fees ($315), and college room and board ($3810). College room only: $1500. Full-time tuition and fees vary according to degree level and location. Room and board charges vary according to board plan, housing facility, and location. Special program-related fees: $50 per course for applied music fee.
**Financial Aid** Program-specific awards: 75 departmental awards for program majors ($500–$5000).
**Application Procedures** Students admitted directly into the professional program freshman year. Deadline for freshmen and transfers: continuous. Required: high school transcript, college transcript(s) for transfer students, audition, SAT or ACT test scores (minimum composite ACT score of 17). Recommended: minimum 2.0 high school GPA. Auditions held continuously on campus and off campus in various regional cities; recorded music is permissible as a substitute for live auditions when distance is prohibitive and videotaped performances are permissible as a substitute for live auditions when distance is prohibitive.
**Web Site** http://www.wmcarey.edu/academics/music/
**Undergraduate Contact** Dr. Mark Hugh Malone, Dean, Winters School of Music, William Carey University, 498 Tuscan Avenue, Hattiesburg, Mississippi 39401; 601-318-6177, fax: 601-318-6176, e-mail address: music@wmcarey.edu

# Winters School of Music

See William Carey University

# Winthrop University

**Rock Hill, South Carolina**

State-supported, coed. Suburban campus. Total enrollment: 6,382. Music program established 1886.
**Degrees** Bachelor of Music in the area of performance; Bachelor of Music Education in the areas of choral music education, instrumental music education. Majors and concentrations: guitar, music education, piano/organ, stringed instruments, voice, wind and percussion instruments. Graduate degrees offered: Master of Music in the areas of performance, choral conducting, wind instrumental conducting; Master of Music Education. Program accredited by NASM.
**Enrollment** 205 total; 133 undergraduate, 21 graduate, 51 nonprofessional degree.
**Music Student Profile** 49% females, 51% males, 25% minorities, 4% international.
**Music Faculty** 18 total (full-time), 20 total (part-time). 83% of full-time faculty have terminal degrees. Graduate students do not teach undergraduate courses. Undergraduate student–faculty ratio: 12:1.
**Student Life** Student groups/activities include Delta Omicron, Phi Mu Alpha Sinfonia, Music Educators National Conference.
**Expenses for 2007–2008** Application fee: $40. State resident tuition: $10,210 full-time. Nonresident tuition: $19,034 full-time. Full-time tuition varies according to degree level. College room and board: $5800. College room only: $3670. Room and board charges vary according to board plan and housing facility. Special program-related fees: $100–$275 per semester for applied music fees for private instruction.

**Financial Aid** Program-specific awards: 30–70 music scholarships for above-average freshmen and continuing students with exceptional artistic ability ($500–$3500).
**Application Procedures** Students admitted directly into the professional program freshman year. Deadline for freshmen: May 1; transfers: June 1. Required: high school transcript, college transcript(s) for transfer students, minimum 2.0 high school GPA, audition, SAT or ACT test scores. Recommended: essay, minimum 3.0 high school GPA, 2 letters of recommendation, interview, video. Auditions held 5 times on campus; recorded music is permissible as a substitute for live auditions with written statement from teacher and videotaped performances are permissible as a substitute for live auditions with personal/taped statement from teacher.
**Web Site** http://www.winthrop.edu
**Contact** Dr. Donald M. Rogers, Chair, Department of Music, Winthrop University, 129 Music Conservatory, Rock Hill, South Carolina 29733; 803-323-2255, fax: 803-323-2343, e-mail address: rogersd@winthrop.edu

# Wittenberg University

**Springfield, Ohio**

Independent, coed. Suburban campus. Total enrollment: 2,078. Music program established 1931.
**Web Site** http://www.wittenberg.edu/

# Wright State University

**Dayton, Ohio**

State-supported, coed. Suburban campus. Total enrollment: 16,151. Music program established 1966.
**Degrees** Bachelor of Music in the areas of performance, music history and literature, music education. Majors and concentrations: music education, music history and literature, piano/organ, stringed instruments, voice, wind and percussion instruments. Graduate degrees offered: Master of Humanities in the area of music; Master of Music in the areas of music education, performance. Cross-registration with Southern Ohio Consortium of Higher Education. Program accredited by NASM.
**Enrollment** 200 total; 130 undergraduate, 20 graduate, 50 nonprofessional degree.
**Music Student Profile** 60% females, 40% males, 15% minorities, 5% international.
**Music Faculty** 16 total (full-time), 24 total (part-time). 71% of full-time faculty have terminal degrees. Graduate students teach a few undergraduate courses. Undergraduate student–faculty ratio: 3:1.
**Student Life** Student groups/activities include Collegiate Music Educators National Conference, American Choral Directors Association.
**Expenses for 2007–2008** Application fee: $30. State resident tuition: $7278 full-time. Nonresident tuition: $14,004 full-time. College room and board: $7180. Special program-related fees: $15 for instrument rental fee, $50 for junior, senior recital fee, $150–$300 per quarter for applied music lesson fee.
**Financial Aid** Program-specific awards: 5 string scholarships for string players ($1500), 45 music scholarships for program majors ($1500), 25 Arts Gala Scholarships for music majors from the Miami Valley ($1500).
**Application Procedures** Students admitted directly into the professional program freshman year. Deadline for freshmen and transfers: continuous. Required: essay, high school transcript, college transcript(s) for transfer students, minimum 2.0 high school GPA, 3 letters of recommendation, audition, SAT or ACT test scores. Auditions held 4 times on campus; recorded music is permissible as a substitute for live auditions when distance is prohibitive and videotaped performances are permissible as a substitute for live auditions when distance is prohibitive.
**Web Site** http://www.wright.edu/music
**Undergraduate Contact** Victoria Chadbourne, Promotions and Outreach Coordinator, Department of Music, Wright State University, 3640 Colonel Glenn Highway, Dayton, Ohio 45435; 937-775-2787, fax: 937-775-3786, e-mail address: music@wright.edu

**Graduate Contact** Dr. Hank Dahlman, Graduate Studies in Music, Department of Music, Wright State University, 3640 Colonel Glenn Highway, Dayton, Ohio 45435; 937-775-3721, fax: 937-775-3786, e-mail address: hank.dahlman@wright.edu

# York University
## Toronto, Ontario, Canada

Province-supported, coed. Urban campus. Total enrollment: 51,420. Music program established 1969.
**Degrees** Bachelor of Fine Arts in the areas of music performance, composition. Majors and concentrations: classical performance, composition, electronic music, improvisation, jazz, world music.
**Enrollment** 526 total; 399 undergraduate, 127 nonprofessional degree.
**Music Student Profile** 52% females, 48% males, 1% international.
**Music Faculty** 23 total (full-time), 57 total (part-time). 94% of full-time faculty have terminal degrees. Graduate students teach a few undergraduate courses. Undergraduate student–faculty ratio: 9:1.
**Student Life** Student groups/activities include York Music Students Association, Creative Arts Students Association.
**Expenses for 2007–2008** Application fee: $175 Canadian dollars. Tuition, fee, and room and board charges are reported in Canadian dollars. Comprehensive fee: $11,664 includes full-time tuition ($5278) and college room and board ($6386). College room only: $3986. Full-time tuition varies according to course load, degree level, and program. Room and board charges vary according to board plan and housing facility. International student tuition: $15,278 full-time. Special program-related fees: $10–$40 per course for material fees.
**Financial Aid** Program-specific awards: 3 talent awards for applicants with outstanding auditions ($1000), Harry Rowe Bursaries for students with demonstrated achievement or potential in artistic or scholarly work, Oscar Peterson Scholarship for outstanding jazz performers, 1 Ella Fitzgerald Award for Jazz Performance for those demonstrating artistic excellence ($1500), 1 Sorbara Award for outstanding achievement in composition ($2500), 10 IMASCO Performing Arts Awards for 2nd- or 3rd-year students demonstrating outstanding ability and sound academic standing ($3000), 1 Douglas Menzie Phillips Jazz Scholarship for outstanding achievement in jazz performance ($2500), 1 Nancy Scoular Underhill Piano Award for 2nd-year pianists who demonstrate exceptional promise/ability ($1000).
**Application Procedures** Students admitted directly into the professional program freshman year. Deadline for freshmen and transfers: February 1. Notification date for freshmen: June 16; transfers: continuous. Required: essay, high school transcript, college transcript(s) for transfer students, minimum 3.0 high school GPA, audition, SAT, ACT or Canadian equivalent, theory exercise, questionnaire/statement. Recommended: 2 letters of recommendation. Auditions held 5 times on campus; recorded music is permissible as a substitute for live auditions if distance is prohibitive.
**Web Site** http://www.finearts.yorku.ca/music/index.htm
**Undergraduate Contact** Susan Wessels, Coordinator, Recruitment and Liaison, Student and Academic Services, York University, 4700 Keele Street, 201R Goldfarb Centre of Fine Arts, Toronto, Ontario M3J 1P3, Canada; 416-736-2100 ext. 77141, fax: 416-736-5447, e-mail address: swessels@yorku.ca

*Dana School of Music*
# Youngstown State University
## Youngstown, Ohio

State-supported, coed. Urban campus. Total enrollment: 13,489. Music program established 1941.
**Degrees** Bachelor of Music in the areas of performance, music education, applied music, composition, jazz studies, music recording. Majors and concentrations: classical music, jazz, music education, music recording, music theory and composition, piano/organ, stringed instruments, voice, wind and percussion instruments. Graduate degrees offered: Master of Music in the areas of performance, music education, music theory and composition, music history and literature, jazz studies. Program accredited by NASM.
**Enrollment** 310 total; 275 undergraduate, 35 graduate.
**Music Student Profile** 60% females, 40% males, 4% minorities, 1% international.
**Music Faculty** 14 undergraduate (full-time), 31 undergraduate (part-time), 13 graduate (full-time). 90% of full-time faculty have terminal degrees. Graduate students teach a few undergraduate courses. Undergraduate student–faculty ratio: 8:1.
**Student Life** Student groups/activities include New Music Society, Jazz Society, Ohio Collegiate Music Education Association. Special housing available for music students.
**Expenses for 2007–2008** Application fee: $30. State resident tuition: $6492 full-time. Nonresident tuition: $12,165 full-time. Mandatory fees: $229 full-time. Full-time tuition and fees vary according to course load. College room and board: $6740. Room and board charges vary according to board plan and housing facility. Special program-related fees: $55 per credit hour for applied music fee.
**Financial Aid** Program-specific awards: 50 Youngstown State University Foundation Music Awards for program students ($800), 2 University Grants-in-Aid for program students ($1800), 2 Monday Musical Awards for program students ($1000), 10 Showcase Awards for program students ($600), 12 named music scholarships for program students ($1000).
**Application Procedures** Students admitted directly into the professional program freshman year. Deadline for freshmen and transfers: continuous. Required: high school transcript, college transcript(s) for transfer students, letter of recommendation, audition, SAT or ACT test scores. Recommended: minimum 3.0 high school GPA, interview. Auditions held 4 times on campus; recorded music is permissible as a substitute for live auditions when distance is prohibitive and videotaped performances are permissible as a substitute for live auditions when distance is prohibitive.
**Web Site** http://www.fpa.ysu.edu/music/index.html
**Undergraduate Contact** Meredith Young, Executive Director, Enrollment Management, Youngstown State University, 1 University Plaza, Youngstown, Ohio 44555; 330-941-2000, fax: 330-941-3674, e-mail address: emyoung@ysu.edu
**Graduate Contact** Dr. Darla Funk, Coordinator of Graduate Studies/Music, Dana School of Music, Youngstown State University, 1 University Plaza, Youngstown, Ohio 44555; 330-941-3636, fax: 330-941-1490, e-mail address: djfunk@ysu.edu

# Theater Programs

## Adelphi University

### Garden City, New York

Independent, coed. Suburban campus. Total enrollment: 8,354. Theater program established 1974.

**Degrees** Bachelor of Fine Arts in the area of theater. Majors and concentrations: acting, technical theater. Program accredited by NAST.

**Enrollment** 140 total; all undergraduate.

**Theater Student Profile** 60% females, 40% males, 18% minorities, 2% international.

**Theater Faculty** 6 undergraduate (full-time), 11 undergraduate (part-time). 100% of full-time faculty have terminal degrees. Graduate students do not teach undergraduate courses. Undergraduate student–faculty ratio: 15:1.

**Student Life** Student groups/activities include INTERACT, Alpha Psi Omega. Special housing available for theater students.

**Expenses for 2007–2008** Application fee: $35. Comprehensive fee: $33,155 includes full-time tuition ($21,800), mandatory fees ($1455), and college room and board ($9900). Full-time tuition and fees vary according to course level, location, and program. Room and board charges vary according to board plan and housing facility.

**Financial Aid** Program-specific awards: 8–10 Barnes Scholarships for freshmen actors ($4000–$9000), 8–10 talent awards for actors, tech/design students ($2000–$9000).

**Application Procedures** Students admitted directly into the professional program freshman year. Deadline for freshmen and transfers: continuous. Required: essay, high school transcript, college transcript(s) for transfer students, 2 letters of recommendation, SAT or ACT test scores, portfolio for technical theater majors, audition for acting applicants, minimum 2.5 high school GPA (4.0 scale). Auditions held 10 times on campus; videotaped performances are permissible as a substitute for live auditions when distance is prohibitive. Portfolio reviews held continuously on campus; the submission of slides may be substituted for portfolios when distance is prohibitive.

**Web Site** http://www.adelphi.edu

**Undergraduate Contact** Mr. Nicholas Petron, Chair, Department of Performing Arts, Adelphi University, Post Hall, Room 4, Garden City, New York 11530; 516-877-4930, fax: 516-877-4926, e-mail address: petron@adelphi.edu

### More About the University

Adelphi University is a nationally acclaimed university located near New York City. Founded in 1896, it is also the oldest private coeducational institution of higher education on Long Island. With a new performing arts facility featuring state-of-the art performance, teaching, and rehearsal spaces, an excellent reputation, and proximity to New York City, Adelphi provides numerous opportunities for those majoring in dance, music, or theater arts.

Adelphi is one of the most selective private institutions on Long Island, currently enrolling more than 8,300 students from thirty-six states and forty-seven other countries in more than fifty areas of study.

Adelphi is one of Princeton Review's "The Best Northeastern Colleges" and one of only twenty-six private schools in the country selected as a "Best Buy" by the *Fiske Guide to Colleges* for two years in a row.

Adelphi is committed to combining the best of conservatory and liberal arts education, offering access to rigorous training, exceptional resources, and a campus and community noted for its vitality, convenience, and safety.

Adelphi offers the following performing arts programs: dance, music, performing arts with specialization in acting, and performing arts with specialization in design technology. Students interested in a broader and more intense curricular and extracurricular program can apply for dual entry to the Honors College and to the performing arts program of their choice.

**Campus and Surroundings** Located near Long Island's parks and beaches, Adelphi's 75-acre main campus in Garden City, New York, is only 45 minutes from New York City, offering the combined advantages of a major metropolitan area and a safe, suburban campus environment. In 2006, the new Fine Arts and Facilities Building opened on the south end of the campus, providing state-of-the-art studio and exhibition space for the visual arts.

**Program Facilities** In fall 2008, a new 53,500-square-foot center is scheduled to open. The center features a three-story, 500-seat auditorium with state-of-the-art acoustics, dance studios, a black-box theater, lesson and practice rooms for instruments and voice, and a digital studio.

**Faculty, Resident Artists, and Alumni** Famous Adelphi alumni in the arts include Jonathan Larson, author of the Pulitzer Prize–winning Broadway musical *Rent;* Alice Hoffman, *New York Times* best-selling author; and hip-hop artist Chuck D of Public Enemy. Well-known faculty members include Frank Augustyn, host and cowriter of the Bravo ballet series Footnotes, and Paul Moravec, winner of the 2004 Pulitzer Prize for Music.

## Albertus Magnus College

### New Haven, Connecticut

Independent Roman Catholic, coed. Suburban campus. Total enrollment: 2,034. Theater program established 1971.

**Degrees** Bachelor of Fine Arts. Majors and concentrations: performance.

**Theater Student Profile** 66% females, 34% males, 28% minorities.

**Theater Faculty** 1 total (full-time). 100% of full-time faculty have terminal degrees. Graduate students do not teach undergraduate courses.

**Student Life** Student groups/activities include Non Equity Professional Theatre/ACT 2 Theatre.

**Expenses for 2007–2008** Application fee: $35. Comprehensive fee: $29,981 includes full-time tuition ($20,166), mandatory fees ($908), and college room and board ($8907). Full-time tuition and fees vary according to class time and program. Special program-related fees: $20–$100 per course for material fees for some studio classes.

**Financial Aid** Program-specific awards available.

**Application Procedures** Students apply for admission into the professional program by sophomore year. Deadline for freshmen and transfers: continuous. Required: high school transcript, college transcript(s) for transfer students, minimum 2.0 high school GPA, 2 letters of recommendation, SAT or ACT test scores. Recommended: essay, interview.

**Web Site** http://www.albertus.edu

**Undergraduate Contact** Mr. Richard Lolatte, Dean of Admissions, Albertus Magnus College, 700 Prospect Street, New Haven, Connecticut 06511; 203-773-8501, fax: 203-773-5248, e-mail address: admissions@albertus.edu

## American Academy of Dramatic Arts

### New York, New York

Independent, coed. Urban campus. Theater program established 1884.

*American Academy of Dramatic Arts (continued)*

**Degrees** Associate in Occupational Studies in the areas of acting, dramatic arts; Certificate in the area of advanced studies in actor training. Majors and concentrations: acting. Program accredited by NAST.
**Enrollment** 251 total; all undergraduate.
**Theater Student Profile** 64% females, 36% males, 13% minorities, 29% international.
**Theater Faculty** 7 undergraduate (full-time), 19 undergraduate (part-time). 28% of full-time faculty have terminal degrees. Graduate students do not teach undergraduate courses. Undergraduate student–faculty ratio: 16:1.
**Expenses for 2008–2009** Application fee: $50. Tuition: $19,500 full-time. Mandatory fees: $500 full-time. Special program-related fees: $400 per year for library and classroom materials.
**Financial Aid** Program-specific awards: 2–3 Spencer Tracy Scholarships for sophomores ($1000–$3000), 2–6 Greta Nissen Scholarships for female sophomores demonstrating need ($1500–$4000), 1–2 Julie Harris Scholarships for sophomores ($500–$1500), 2–4 Henrietta Alice Metcalf Memorial Scholarships for sophomores ($500–$3000), 1–2 Kirk Douglas Scholarships for sophomores ($1500–$2500), 1–3 Harryetta Peterka Scholarships for sophomores ($1000–$3000), 1–3 Samuel Freeman Scholarships for sophomores ($1000–$2000), 1–2 Princess Grace Scholarships for sophomores ($1000–$2000), 1–3 W.K. Hearst Scholarships for sophomores ($1000–$3000), 1–3 Neil Simon Scholarships for sophomores ($1000–$2000), 2–4 Dina Merrill Scholarships for sophomores ($1500–$3000).
**Application Procedures** Students admitted directly into the professional program freshman year. Deadline for freshmen and transfers: continuous. Required: essay, high school transcript, college transcript(s) for transfer students, 2 letters of recommendation, interview, audition. Recommended: minimum 2.0 high school GPA, SAT or ACT test scores. Auditions held bi-weekly on campus and off campus in various cities in the U.S..
**Web Site** http://www.aada.org
**Undergraduate Contact** Ms. Karen Higginbotham, Director of Admissions, American Academy of Dramatic Arts, 120 Madison Avenue, New York, New York 10016-7004; 212-686-0620 ext. 315, fax: 212-696-1284, e-mail address: admissions-ny@aada.org

### More About the Academy

Whether students aspire to the stages of Broadway or the soundstages of Burbank, the American Academy of Dramatic Arts (AADA) has both the location and the program to move them closer to their dream. Founded in 1884 as the first acting school in America, the Academy stresses practical, professional training for stage, film, and television. With campuses in both New York City and Los Angeles, the Academy offers the aspiring actor a stimulating, inspiring environment and a fertile ground for professional and personal growth.

The Academy has a full-time, two-year, college-accredited conservatory program; a third-year of advanced performance and professional showcase (Academy Company); and a six-week Summer Program. It also offers evening and Saturday programs for those unable to commit to full-time training. For students who desire a bachelor's degree, the Academy has articulation agreements with St. John's University and Hunter College in New York and Antioch University in Los Angeles. For more information, students should call the Admissions Office on the New York campus at 800-463-8990 or 800-222-2867 (toll-free) in Los Angeles.

The Academy alumni list is an impressive one, with prominent names from all aspects of the entertainment industry, past and present, including 5 Kennedy Center honorees. AADA alumni have been nominated for a total of 72 Oscars, 211 Emmys, and 82 Tonys, with Spencer Tracy, Cecil B. DeMille, Grace Kelly, Robert Redford, Kim Cattrall, Paul Rudd, and Adrien Brody among their ranks.

Academy students come from all parts of the United States, from Canada, and from other countries as well, extending to Europe and Asia and South America and involving such countries as Singapore and Azerbaijan. The Academy goes to great lengths to invite talent from around the world to enlarge its tradition and to integrate its work in the world community of artists. The Academy community is enriched by the cultures and contributions of talented actors from this country and the fellowship of actors that exists worldwide.

Approximately 60 percent of the entering students are recent high school graduates. Others transfer to the Academy from traditional colleges to study acting in a more concentrated, professional environment. The program is highly structured, focusing on acting, voice and speech, and movement, with an emphasis on self-discipline, self-discovery, and, above all, individuality. At each stage of development, students' classroom knowledge is evaluated through performance projects, scene work, or onstage performances. Students who do extremely well in the program may be invited to join the Academy Company, which offers actors further performance opportunities, often in the presence of casting directors, agents, and other industry professionals.

Students invited to the second year may apply to transfer from one campus to the other.

In place of on-campus student housing, the AADA offers a variety of attractive off-campus options through special arrangements with a local housing resource for student housing or other types of housing services, depending upon the student's choice of location.

Scholarships are awarded on the basis of merit and need and may supplement other forms of financial aid. First Year scholarships are determined by the student's admission application and audition. Second Year and Academy Company students may apply for scholarships by writing to the Academy's Scholarship Committee.

**Facilities** AADA New York is housed in the six-story landmark Stanford White Building in the heart of midtown Manhattan. AADA Los Angeles is located in the heart of Hollywood, adjacent to the former Charlie Chaplin studios. Each site includes classrooms, rehearsal halls, movement studios, production and costume departments, a library/learning center, a video studio, and theaters.

**Faculty** The Academy's faculty is composed of seasoned instructors, trained by master teachers, and working professional guest directors, all well-trained within their own disciplines and examples of the excellence that the Academy hopes to instill in its students.

**Student Performances** Students perform roles in four first-year performance projects and at least three second-year projects and full productions. Academy Company performs, on average, twelve fully-mounted productions each year and a final showcase.

**Career Advisement** Seminars offered by career counselors provide the practical information actors need to initiate professional careers. The Academy also offers Q&A events with professional actors who generously share their experiences and advice. In addition, the Academy is host to SAG Foundation events that provide SAG members and Academy students the opportunity to participate in conversations with celebrities as well as career advice seminars.

# Arkansas State University
## State University, Arkansas

State-supported, coed. Small town campus. Total enrollment: 10,869. Theater program established 1958.
**Degrees** Bachelor of Fine Arts in the area of theatre. Majors and concentrations: acting, design technology, directing, music theater.
**Enrollment** 40 total; all undergraduate.
**Theater Student Profile** 60% females, 40% males, 5% minorities, 5% international.
**Theater Faculty** 6 undergraduate (full-time). 100% of full-time faculty have terminal degrees. Graduate students do not teach undergraduate courses. Undergraduate student–faculty ratio: 8:1.

**Student Life** Student groups/activities include The ASU Theatre.
**Expenses for 2007–2008** Application fee: $15. State resident tuition: $4620 full-time. Nonresident tuition: $12,000 full-time. Mandatory fees: $1390 full-time. Full-time tuition and fees vary according to course load, location, and program. College room and board: $4710. Room and board charges vary according to board plan and housing facility.
**Financial Aid** Program-specific awards: 17 theater arts scholarships for program majors ($1000).
**Application Procedures** Students apply for admission into the professional program by sophomore year. Deadline for freshmen and transfers: continuous. Required: high school transcript, SAT or ACT test scores, minimum 2.3 high school GPA. Recommended: 2 letters of recommendation, interview and portfolio for production applicants, video and audition for performance applicants. Auditions held twice on campus and off campus in various sites in Arkansas; recorded music is permissible as a substitute for live auditions when distance is prohibitive and videotaped performances are permissible as a substitute for live auditions when distance is prohibitive. Portfolio reviews held once on campus; the submission of slides may be substituted for portfolios when distance is prohibitive.
**Web Site** http://www.astate.edu
**Undergraduate Contact** Mr. Bob W. Simpson, Chair, Department of Theatre, Arkansas State University, PO Box 2309, State University, Arkansas 72467; 870-972-2037, fax: 870-972-2830, e-mail address: bsimpson@astate.edu

# Auburn University
## Auburn University, Alabama

State-supported, coed. Small town campus. Total enrollment: 24,137. Theater program established 1945.
**Degrees** Bachelor of Fine Arts In the areas of performance (acting and music theatre tracks), production (design/tech & management tracks). Majors and concentrations: design technology, music theater performance, performance, production management. Program accredited by NAST.
**Enrollment** 70 total; 11 undergraduate, 59 nonprofessional degree.
**Theater Student Profile** 60% females, 40% males, 5% minorities.
**Theater Faculty** 9 undergraduate (full-time), 2 undergraduate (part-time). 100% of full-time faculty have terminal degrees. Graduate students do not teach undergraduate courses. Undergraduate student–faculty ratio: 8:1.
**Student Life** Student groups/activities include Auburn University Players, Alpha Psi Omega.
**Expenses for 2007–2008** Application fee: $25. State resident tuition: $5490 full-time. Nonresident tuition: $15,990 full-time. Mandatory fees: $344 full-time. Full-time tuition and fees vary according to course load, program, and reciprocity agreements. College room only: $3200. Room charges vary according to housing facility.
**Financial Aid** Program-specific awards: 10 Malone Fund Scholarships for entering students ($1000), 10 AIV Theatre Patron Scholarship Fund for performance and production majors ($1000).
**Application Procedures** Students apply for admission into the professional program by sophomore year. Deadline for freshmen and transfers: April 1. Required: high school transcript, college transcript(s) for transfer students, minimum 2.0 high school GPA, letter of recommendation, audition, portfolio, SAT or ACT test scores, audition for performance applicants, portfolio for design technology and production management majors, audition/portfolio for scholarship applicants. Auditions held once on campus. Portfolio reviews held once on campus.
**Web Site** http://www.auburnuniversitytheatre.org
**Undergraduate Contact** Prof. Dan LaRocque, Chair, Department of Theatre, Auburn University, 211 Telfair Peet Theatre, Auburn, Alabama 36849-5422; 334-844-4748, fax: 334-844-4743, e-mail address: larocdj@auburn.edu

# Baylor University
## Waco, Texas

Independent Baptist, coed. Urban campus. Total enrollment: 14,174. Theater program established 1947.
**Degrees** Bachelor of Fine Arts in the areas of performance, design. Majors and concentrations: design, performance. Graduate degrees offered: Master of Fine Arts in the area of directing. Program accredited by NAST.
**Enrollment** 104 total; 60 undergraduate, 4 graduate, 40 nonprofessional degree.
**Theater Student Profile** 60% females, 40% males, 12% minorities.
**Theater Faculty** 15 total (full-time). 93% of full-time faculty have terminal degrees. Graduate students do not teach undergraduate courses. Undergraduate student–faculty ratio: 20:1.
**Student Life** Student groups/activities include Student Theater Society.
**Expenses for 2008–2009** Application fee: $50. Comprehensive fee: $34,464 includes full-time tuition ($23,664), mandatory fees ($2570), and college room and board ($8230). College room only: $4000. Special program-related fees: $50 per course for lab fee.
**Financial Aid** Program-specific awards: 8–10 theater scholarships for upperclass program students ($500–$1800).
**Application Procedures** Students admitted directly into the professional program freshman year. Deadline for freshmen: March 1; transfers: continuous. Required: high school transcript, college transcript(s) for transfer students, audition, portfolio, SAT or ACT test scores. Recommended: interview. Auditions held 8 times on campus and off campus in Texas Theatre Association locations; recorded music is permissible as a substitute for live auditions and videotaped performances are permissible as a substitute for live auditions. Portfolio reviews held 9 times on campus and off campus in Texas Theatre Association locations; the submission of slides may be substituted for portfolios.
**Web Site** http://www.baylor.edu/
**Undergraduate Contact** Ms. Lisa Denman, Lecturer, Department of Theater Arts, Baylor University, BU Box 97262, Waco, Texas 76798; 254-710-1861, fax: 254-710-1765, e-mail address: lisa_denman@baylor.edu
**Graduate Contact** Dr. Marion Castleberry, Head of Graduate Program, Department of Theater Arts, Baylor University, BU Box 97262, Waco, Texas 76798; 254-710-6481, fax: 254-710-1765.

# The Boston Conservatory
## Boston, Massachusetts

Independent, coed. Urban campus. Total enrollment: 560. Theater program established 1940.
**Degrees** Bachelor of Fine Arts in the area of musical theater. Majors and concentrations: music theater. Graduate degrees offered: Master of Music in the area of musical theater. Cross-registration with ProArts Consortium. Program accredited by NASM.
**Enrollment** 216 total; 199 undergraduate, 17 graduate.
**Theater Student Profile** 59% females, 41% males, 10% minorities, 2% international.
**Theater Faculty** 16 total (full-time), 20 total (part-time). Graduate students do not teach undergraduate courses. Undergraduate student–faculty ratio: 6:1.
**Student Life** Student groups/activities include Cabaret, Hoofers Dance Troupe. Special housing available for theater students.
**Expenses for 2007–2008** Application fee: $105. Comprehensive fee: $45,739 includes full-time tuition ($28,300), mandatory fees ($1799), and college room and board ($15,640). Full-time tuition and fees vary according to program. Room and board charges vary according to board plan and housing facility.
**Financial Aid** Program-specific awards: 65 Conservatory Theater Scholarships for program majors ($5000–$20,000).
**Application Procedures** Students admitted directly into the professional program freshman year. Deadline for freshmen and transfers: December 1. Notification date for freshmen and transfers: April 1. Required: essay, high school transcript, college transcript(s) for transfer students, 2 letters of recommendation, interview, audition, minimum TOEFL score of 550 for interna-

*The Boston Conservatory (continued)*

tional applicants, artistic resumé, minimum 2.7 high school GPA. Auditions held during the months of January, February, and March on campus and off campus in Chicago, IL; Houston, TX; Los Angeles, CA; San Francisco, CA; New York, NY; Atlanta, GA; videotaped performances are permissible as a substitute for live auditions if a campus visit or regional audition is impossible.
**Web Site** http://www.bostonconservatory.edu
**Contact** Admissions Office, The Boston Conservatory, 8 The Fenway, Boston, Massachusetts 02215; 617-912-9153, fax: 617-247-3159, e-mail address: admissions@bostonconservatory.edu

## More About the Conservatory

The Boston Conservatory trains exceptional young performing artists for careers that enrich and transform the human experience. Known for its multidisciplinary environment, the Conservatory offers fully accredited graduate and undergraduate programs in music, dance, and theater, and it presents more than 200 performances each year by students, faculty members, and guest artists. The intimacy of the Conservatory's class settings provides a student-centered atmosphere that is uniquely intensive and supportive.

Since its founding in 1867, the Boston Conservatory has shared its talent and creativity with the city of Boston, the region, and the nation, and it continues to grow today as a vibrant community of artists and educators.

The Boston Conservatory was one of the first colleges to offer integrated training in theater, encompassing acting, voice, and dance. Beginning as a full acting/drama program in the 1930s, the Theater Division now trains the "triple threat" actor/singer, offering a complete musical theater and acting curriculum coupled with music and voice study and a full range of dance (ballet, modern, tap, jazz, and styles). The B.F.A. theater program offers in-depth courses in theater academics and cultural liberal arts.

The Theater Division faculty is composed of experienced performers and teachers committed to bringing out the best each student has to offer. Potential is acknowledged and developed within a strong interactive musical theater curriculum. Frequent in-class performances with appropriate coaching and critique give guidance and constant evaluation of the student's work.

Performance opportunities are available throughout the year, from in-class and studio work to mainstage productions. All major productions are directed by faculty members or guest directors and have an open, professional casting policy in order for the most qualified person to get the role regardless of class standing. Technical and stagecraft experience is provided, and production assistance is required for freshmen during major runs.

In addition to these opportunities, the studio theater offers small-scale productions throughout the year, directed by faculty members, graduate students, and senior directors.

The Boston Conservatory's alumni can be seen performing on Broadway in *Mamma Mia, The Drowsy Chaperone,* and *The Little Mermaid;* in national tours of *Wicked, Beauty and the Beast,* and *Miss Saigon;* at the Globe Theater in London; on television in *Law and Order, Judging Amy,* and *The Young and the Restless;* and as producers, directors, and creators of Broadway, touring, and television productions, such as *Forbidden Broadway* and *MADTV.*

The Boston area provides varied outside work in theater and dance as well as industrials. Regional theater productions often cast students in both lead and ensemble parts.

Boston is a major center of higher education in America, with more than fifty major colleges and universities. The city provides a diverse student population and an endless array of courses, lectures, concerts, and social opportunities. The Conservatory is a member of the Pro-Arts Consortium, in conjunction with five area colleges (Emerson College, Berklee College of Music, School of the Museum of Fine Arts, Massachusetts College of Art, and Boston Architectural Center), offering cross-registration course possibilities to all students.

On-campus housing is provided for freshmen. Housing is available to upperclassmen and graduates on a space-available basis, offering brownstone-style living accommodations just a few steps from the main training and rehearsal buildings. For those students interested in off-campus housing, Boston offers a wide range of architectural styles and rent prices in neighborhoods throughout the city, which are all within easy access to the school by public transportation.

The Boston Conservatory strives to meet each student's needs—musically and personally—and provides a nurturing, safe environment in which to study, learn, and grow. The supportive atmosphere of the college extends to student life areas as well. More than a dozen special interest groups and organizations exist on campus, with new ones developing constantly as the student population grows and its needs change. As part of the student services, a number of career seminars are given each year ranging from resume writing and audition anxiety to grant writing and tax laws for the performing artist. In addition, there is an active student government and a student-run newspaper.

# Boston University
## Boston, Massachusetts

Independent, coed. Urban campus. Total enrollment: 32,053. Theater program established 1950.
**Degrees** Bachelor of Fine Arts in the areas of acting, design, stage management, theatre arts. Majors and concentrations: acting, costume design, costume production, lighting design, set design, sound design, stage management, technical production, theater arts studies. Graduate degrees offered: Master of Fine Arts in the areas of directing, theater education, scene design, technical production, costume design, costume production, lighting design.
**Enrollment** 230 total; 190 undergraduate, 40 graduate.
**Theater Student Profile** 67% females, 33% males, 7% minorities.
**Theater Faculty** 20 total (full-time), 7 total (part-time). Graduate students do not teach undergraduate courses.
**Student Life** Special housing available for theater students.
**Expenses for 2008–2009** Application fee: $75. Comprehensive fee: $48,468 includes full-time tuition ($36,540), mandatory fees ($510), and college room and board ($11,418). College room only: $7420.
**Financial Aid** Program-specific awards: 12 grants/performance awards for program students ($2000–$8000).
**Application Procedures** Students admitted directly into the professional program freshman year. Deadline for freshmen: January 1; transfers: April 1. Notification date for freshmen: April 15. Required: essay, high school transcript, 2 letters of recommendation, audition, portfolio, SAT or ACT test scores, audition for acting and independent theater study applicants, portfolio for design, technical production, and stage management applicants. Auditions held 20 times on campus and off campus in New York, NY; Chicago, IL; San Francisco, CA; Los Angeles, CA; Washington, DC. Portfolio reviews held 10 times on campus and off campus in New York, NY; Chicago, IL; San Francisco, CA; the submission of slides may be substituted for portfolios when distance is prohibitive.
**Web Site** http://www.bu.edu/cfa/theatre
**Contact** Mr. Paolo DiFabio, Associate Director for Theatre Performance, Theatre Arts Department, Boston University, 855 Commonwealth Avenue, Room 470, Boston, Massachusetts 02215; 617-353-3390, fax: 617-353-4363.

## More About the University

Boston University College of Fine Arts (CFA) is a small, conservatory-style school within a major university, offering outstanding professional training in music, the theater, and visual arts. The college was begun as the College of Music in 1873, and the School of Theater was organized in 1950. The School of Theatre enrolls approximately 250 students and offers the Bachelor of Fine Arts (B.F.A.) and the Master of Fine Arts (M.F.A.). A theater conservatory within the embrace of a metropolitan university, the School offers programs in acting, directing, design, production, management, theater education, and theater arts. The programs foster the synthesis of imagination, intellectual inquiry, and technical skill by combining rigorous training with study in a traditional liberal arts curriculum. The School of Theatre offers unique educational experiences for students possessed of theatrical imagination and professional promise.

**Campus Surroundings** Boston University—independent, coeducational, nonsectarian—is an internationally recognized center of higher education and research. The University is located in the heart of Boston, along the banks of the Charles River and adjacent to the historic Back Bay district of Boston. Boston University is perfectly situated to enjoy both the charm and beauty of the city and its cultural and recreational attractions. Students benefit from the many major theaters, musical organizations, and museums and galleries that make Boston a rich and varied cultural environment.

**Program Facilities** Performance spaces include the Boston University Theatre, an 850-seat proscenium house; the Lane Comley Studio 210, a 100-seat black-box space; and the TheatreLab, a 100-seat proscenium studio. The theater is equipped with a computerized lighting system, shops for scenery and costume construction, and an electronic sound studio. There are three movement studios and six additional rehearsal studios.

**Faculty, Resident Artists, and Alumni** Faculty members are not only master teachers but are also accomplished professionals who maintain vital careers in the theater. Distinguished faculty members include Nicholas Martin, Artistic Director of the Huntington Theatre Company, and Jim Petosa, Director of the School of Theatre and Artistic Director of the Olney Theatre Center outside Washington, D.C. Guest artists have included actors Jason Alexander, Claire Bloom, and Campbell Scott and designers Ralph Funicello and Desmond Heeley. Alumni include actors Geena Davis, Julianne Moore, Michael Chiklis, Ginnifer Goodwin, and Olympia Dukakis; Stewart Lane, Tony Award-winning Broadway producer; Nina Tassler, President of CBS Television, Drama Division; Craig Lucas, Tony-nominated playwright and screen writer; and theater designer, Wynn P. Thomas, whose credits include *A Beautiful Mind* and *Analyze This.*

**Student Performance Opportunities** The School of Theatre produces six fully mounted productions each year as well as ten to twenty workshop productions directed by faculty members and graduate and undergraduate students. An annual festival of new plays provides a showcase for work by undergraduate playwrights.

**Special Programs** The Huntington Theatre Company, one of Boston's leading professional companies, is in residence at the Boston University Theatre. A variety of assistantships and internships are available for students in the areas of design, production, directing, stage management, and theater management. Advanced acting majors have the opportunity to audition for understudy assignments and supporting roles in Huntington Theatre productions. Through the Professional Theatre Initiative, School of Theatre students gain professional opportunities with the Huntingdon Theatre Company, the Boston Playwrights Theatre, the Williamstown Theatre Festival, and the Olney Theatre Center. In addition, students are encouraged to study abroad at the London Academy of Music and Dramatic Arts (LAMDA) in their junior year. A postgraduate program, the Los Angeles Internship Program, offers a semester of study and work in the heart of the film and television. The program provides an unparalleled introduction to the theater, film, and television industries and is appropriate for any student interested in an entertainment career. Students can also earn minors in dance, liberal arts, business, or communications.

# Bradley University
## Peoria, Illinois

Independent, coed. Suburban campus. Total enrollment: 6,053. Theater program established 1978.
**Degrees** Bachelor of Arts in the areas of theater arts, performance, production; Bachelor of Science in the areas of theater performance, production, theater arts. Majors and concentrations: performance, theater production. Program accredited by NAST.
**Enrollment** 59 total; 25 undergraduate, 34 nonprofessional degree.
**Theater Student Profile** 54% females, 46% males, 11% minorities, 4% international.
**Theater Faculty** 5 undergraduate (full-time), 2 undergraduate (part-time). 100% of full-time faculty have terminal degrees. Graduate students do not teach undergraduate courses. Undergraduate student–faculty ratio: 10:1.
**Student Life** Student groups/activities include Alpha Psi Omega, United States Institute for Theater Technology (USITT), Met (lab theatre), Bar-be-que Kittens (improv).
**Expenses for 2007–2008** Application fee: $35. Comprehensive fee: $28,410 includes full-time tuition ($21,200), mandatory fees ($160), and college room and board ($7050). College room only: $4100. Full-time tuition and fees vary according to student level. Room and board charges vary according to board plan.
**Financial Aid** Program-specific awards: 17 theater scholarships for theater majors ($2352).
**Application Procedures** Students admitted directly into the professional program freshman year. Deadline for freshmen and transfers: continuous. Required: high school transcript, college transcript(s) for transfer students, minimum 2.0 high school GPA, interview, audition, portfolio, SAT or ACT test scores, portfolio and audition for scholarship consideration. Recommended: 3 letters of recommendation. Auditions held 4 times on campus; recorded music is permissible as a substitute for live auditions when distance is prohibitive and videotaped performances are permissible as a substitute for live auditions when distance is prohibitive. Portfolio reviews held 4 times on campus; the submission of slides may be substituted for portfolios when distance is prohibitive.
**Web Site** http://theatre.bradley.edu
**Undergraduate Contact** Ms. Nickie Roberson, Director of Admissions, Office of Undergraduate Admissions, Bradley University, Swords Hall, Peoria, Illinois 61625; 800-447-6460, fax: 309-677-2797, e-mail address: admissions@bradley.edu

# Brenau University
## Gainesville, Georgia

Independent, women only. Small town campus. Total enrollment: 916. Theater program established 1979.
**Degrees** Bachelor of Fine Arts in the area of theatre arts (musical theatre emphasis and arts management theatre emphasis). Majors and concentrations: arts management, music theater. Mandatory cross-registration with Gainesville State College.
**Enrollment** 46 total; 13 undergraduate, 33 nonprofessional degree.
**Theater Student Profile** 90% females, 10% males, 1% minorities.
**Theater Faculty** 5 undergraduate (full-time), 1 undergraduate (part-time). 100% of full-time faculty have terminal degrees. Graduate students do not teach undergraduate courses. Undergraduate student–faculty ratio: 10:1.
**Student Life** Student groups/activities include Gainesville Theatre Alliance, Alpha Psi Omega, Wonder Quest Children's Theatre. Special housing available for theater students.
**Expenses for 2008–2009** Application fee: $35. Comprehensive fee: $28,287 includes full-time tuition ($18,550), mandatory fees ($250), and college room and board ($9487).
**Financial Aid** Program-specific awards: 20 talent scholarships for program majors ($1500–$5000).
**Application Procedures** Students admitted directly into the professional program freshman year. Deadline for freshmen and transfers: continuous. Required: essay, high school transcript, college transcript(s) for transfer students, minimum 2.0 high

*Brenau University (continued)*

school GPA, audition, SAT or ACT test scores (minimum composite ACT score of 19), health certificate, 950 combined SAT (critical reading and math only). Recommended: minimum 3.0 high school GPA, interview, portfolio, 1-2 letters of recommendation. Auditions held 8 times and by appointment on campus; videotaped performances are permissible as a substitute for live auditions when distance is prohibitive. Portfolio reviews held upon request on campus; the submission of slides may be substituted for portfolios when distance is prohibitive.

**Web Site** http://www.brenau.edu

**Undergraduate Contact** Christina Jackson, Admissions Coordinator, Brenau University, 500 Washington Street, SE, Gainesville, Georgia 30501; 770-534-6100, fax: 770-538-4306, e-mail address: cjackson@brenau.edu

# Brigham Young University
## Provo, Utah

Independent, coed. Suburban campus. Total enrollment: 34,174. Theater program established 1920.

**Degrees** Bachelor of Arts in the area of theater education; Bachelor of Fine Arts in the area of acting. Majors and concentrations: acting, theater education. Graduate degrees offered: Master of Arts in the area of theater and media arts; Master of Fine Arts in the area of production design. Program accredited by NAST.

**Enrollment** 275 total; 47 undergraduate, 15 graduate, 213 nonprofessional degree.

**Theater Student Profile** 59% females, 41% males.

**Theater Faculty** 5 undergraduate (full-time), 12 undergraduate (part-time), 12 graduate (full-time). 100% of full-time faculty have terminal degrees. Graduate students teach a few undergraduate courses. Undergraduate student–faculty ratio: 7:1.

**Student Life** Student groups/activities include main stage productions, senior project.

**Expenses for 2007–2008** Application fee: $30. Comprehensive fee: $14,140 includes full-time tuition ($7680) and college room and board ($6460). Room and board charges vary according to board plan and housing facility. Latter Day Saints full-time student $3840 per year.

**Application Procedures** Students apply for admission into the professional program by freshman year. Required: essay, college transcript(s) for transfer students, 3 letters of recommendation, interview, audition, SAT or ACT test scores, approved graduation plan, application packet. Auditions held twice on campus; recorded music is permissible as a substitute for live auditions if a campus visit is impossible and videotaped performances are permissible as a substitute for live auditions if a campus visit is impossible.

**Web Site** http://tma.byu.edu

**Undergraduate Contact** Roxanna Boyer, Department Assistant, Department of Theatre and Media Arts, Brigham Young University, D-581 HFAC, Provo, Utah 84602; 801-422-6242, fax: 801-422-0654, e-mail address: roxanna_boyer@byu.edu

**Graduate Contact** Kim Poole, Graduate Secretary, Department of Theatre and Media Arts, Brigham Young University, D-581-HFAC, Provo, Utah 84602; 801-422-3750, fax: 801-422-0654, e-mail address: kim_poole@byu.edu

## *Jordan College of Fine Arts - Department of Theatre*
# Butler University
## Indianapolis, Indiana

Independent, coed. Urban campus. Total enrollment: 4,479.

**Degrees** Bachelor of Arts in the area of theatre; Bachelor of Science in the area of arts administration/theatre. Majors and concentrations: theater, theater arts administration. Cross-registration with Indianapolis Consortium for Urban Education. Program accredited by NAST.

**Enrollment** 81 total; all undergraduate.

**Theater Student Profile** 67% females, 33% males, 7% minorities.

**Theater Faculty** 5 undergraduate (full-time), 5 undergraduate (part-time). 60% of full-time faculty have terminal degrees. Graduate students do not teach undergraduate courses. Undergraduate student–faculty ratio: 12:1.

**Student Life** Student groups/activities include Study Abroad partnership with Hong Kong Academy for Performing Arts and Flinders University, Australia, Alpha Psi Omega, Phoenix Theatre, Indiana Repertory Theatre.

**Expenses for 2007–2008** Application fee: $35. Comprehensive fee: $35,766 includes full-time tuition ($26,070), mandatory fees ($736), and college room and board ($8960). Full-time tuition and fees vary according to program. Room and board charges vary according to housing facility.

**Financial Aid** Program-specific awards: talent audition awards.

**Application Procedures** Students admitted directly into the professional program freshman year. Deadline for freshmen and transfers: continuous. Required: high school transcript, college transcript(s) for transfer students, minimum 2.0 high school GPA, interview, audition, SAT or ACT test scores, head shot photo, theatre application. Recommended: minimum 3.0 high school GPA, letter of recommendation, portfolio. Auditions held 6 times on campus.

**Web Site** http://www.butler.edu/theatre

**Undergraduate Contact** Ms. Kathy Lang, Admission Representative, Jordan College of Fine Arts, Butler University, Lilly Hall - 138B, 4600 Sunset Avenue, Indianapolis, Indiana 46208; 800-368-6852 ext. 9656, fax: 317-940-9658, e-mail address: klang@butler.edu

### More About the University

**B**utler University is most proud of its tradition of excellence and innovation. Challenging and enabling students to meet their personal and professional goals has guided the University since 1855. Today, Butler is an independent, coeducational, nonsectarian university, with a total undergraduate enrollment of more than 3,900 students. The University is accredited by the North Central Association of Colleges and Schools.

Butler Theatre is an award-winning undergraduate program accredited by the National Association of Schools of Theatre (NAST). The Butler program offers a choice of two degrees: Bachelor of Arts (B.A.) in theater and Bachelor of Science (B.S.) in arts administration. The program fosters a creative environment where students develop practical and critical skills, create exciting work, and commit fully to the collaborative process of making theater. Through its professional ties in the Indiana Repertory Theatre, the program provides students regular interaction with professional theater artists, technicians, and administrators, and it facilitates professional experience through internships and contract employment.

**Campus and Surroundings** Indianapolis, Indiana's state capital and the thirteenth-largest city in the nation, has a variety of cultural activities, including the Indiana Repertory Theatre, Phoenix Theatre, Indianapolis Symphony Orchestra, Dance Kaleidoscope, the Indianapolis Museum of Art, and the world's largest children's museum. Citywide celebrations are plentiful, including ethnic festivals, art fairs, and outdoor music festivals.

**Program Facilities** The Lilly Hall Studio Theatre is the venue for most main stage productions. Robertson Studio 33 is the space used for classes in voice, acting, and directing and for student-directed productions and rehearsals. Butler's Clowes Memorial Hall is a 2,200-seat performance hall that hosts a variety of events, from community arts groups to national and international touring companies and many University performances. A new performing arts complex is currently under construction. The first phase of the complex, a 47,000-square-foot addition to Lilly Hall called the Courtyard Building, was completed in spring 2003. This new building houses a choral rehearsal hall, an instrumental rehearsal hall, dance studios, a theater studio, an electronic music lab, and a percussion studio. The second phase, the 140-seat Eidson-Duckwall Recital Hall, was completed in fall 2004. The third phase is a 450-seat performance hall/proscenium theater with adjustable acoustical features.

**Special Programs** Butler is committed to experiencing theater as a global art form, in theory and in practice. The University runs a comprehensive study-abroad program, which encourages students in their junior year to study at a university overseas for one semester. The following countries have emerged as the most popular destinations for theater majors: Australia, United Kingdom, Ireland, Spain, Germany, China (Hong Kong), and South America.

Created in 2002, Butler International Theatre Exchange (BITE) is an annual workshop for students, educators, and theater professionals in Indiana who are devoted to exploring transnational processes of creating live performances with master artists and theater companies from around the world. Each exchange is structured around a twelve-day intensive program of training, held during Butler's first summer session in May.

**Cooperative Agreements** Butler Theatre enjoys a creative partnership with the Indiana Repertory Theatre (IRT), Indiana's largest, fully professional regional theater located in the heart of the city of Indianapolis. The benefits of this partnership include a freshman orientation program that provides first-semester theater majors access to the artistic, administrative, and technical staff of the IRT as an introduction to professional theater practice; a stage management training program taught by the IRT's senior stage management team; and professional internships for juniors and seniors in all areas of the theater's operation. An increasing number of theater majors have made their professional acting debuts at the IRT during their four years of study.

**Faculty/Alumni** Butler's faculty members have expertise in stage directing, acting, performance theory, costume design, play analysis, stage lighting, arts administration, children's theater, technical direction, and auditioning and voice. *BeckettWorks* received ACF National Artistic Achievement Awards for Directing (Department Chair John Green) and Scenic Lighting and Design (Assistant Professor Madeleine Sobota.) Associate Professor Diane Timmerman had her 90-minute adaptations of five Shakespeare plays published by Smith and Krauss.

Butler alumni work in a range of theater careers, including an education assistant at the Chicago Shakespeare Theatre, a marketing manager at the Yale Repertory Theatre, an owner of a casting agency, and actors in Los Angeles and Chicago. Other alumni are technical directors, costumer designers, stage managers, and soundboard operators.

**Student Performance Opportunities** Butler Theater stages between fifteen and twenty shows each year, including four major productions directed by faculty members and guest artists, student-directed honors theses productions and independent projects, faculty and student-directed works in progress, and plays written by students.

In 2000 and 2003, the department was invited to tour Ireland with productions of plays by Samuel Beckett and W.B. Yeats. In 2004, the department went to Italy, and in 2005, it went to Australia. The department also went to St. Petersburg, Russia, in 2006.

**Career Placement Services and Opportunities** With a liberal arts education and practical experience, Butler graduates are prepared for success in many careers. Collaborative partnerships with professional theaters provide networking and internship opportunities for theater students. A sampling of internships include the following positions: production at the Phoenix Theatre; sound at the Indiana Repertory Theatre; stage manager for the Phoenix Theatre, Civic Theatre, and Edyvean Repertory Theatre; marketing for *Fosse* at the Shubert Theatre in Chicago; public relations for the Indiana Arts Commission; internships at Denver Center Theatre Academy and Steppenwolf Theatre in Chicago; and acting at venues around the country. Graduates often find employment at the venues where they served as interns.

# California Institute of the Arts
## Valencia, California

Independent, coed. Suburban campus. Total enrollment: 1,324. Theater program established 1961.
**Degrees** Bachelor of Fine Arts in the areas of acting, design and production. Majors and concentrations: acting, costume design, lighting design, puppetry, set design, sound design, stage management, technical direction. Graduate degrees offered: Master of Fine Arts in the area of acting design and production. Program accredited by NAST.
**Enrollment** 284 total; 157 undergraduate, 127 graduate.
**Theater Student Profile** 57% females, 43% males, 33% minorities, 6% international.
**Theater Faculty** 31 total (full-time), 13 total (part-time). 80% of full-time faculty have terminal degrees. Graduate students do not teach undergraduate courses. Undergraduate student–faculty ratio: 7:1.
**Student Life** Student groups/activities include Community Arts Partnership (CAP). Special housing available for theater students.
**Expenses for 2008–2009** Application fee: $70. Comprehensive fee: $42,084 includes full-time tuition ($32,860), mandatory fees ($576), and college room and board ($8648). College room only: $4985.
**Financial Aid** Program-specific awards: CalArts Scholarships for students demonstrating talent ($6000–$15,000).
**Application Procedures** Students admitted directly into the professional program freshman year. Deadline for freshmen and transfers: January 5. Required: essay, high school transcript, college transcript(s) for transfer students, audition for acting applicants, portfolio for design applicants. Recommended: 2 letters of recommendation, interview. Auditions held 15 times on campus and off campus in New York, NY; Chicago, IL. Portfolio reviews held continuously for design majors (on campus) on campus and off campus in New York, NY; Chicago, IL.
**Web Site** http://www.calarts.edu
**Contact** Mr. Seth Stewart, Admissions Counselor, California Institute of the Arts, 24700 McBean Parkway, Valencia, California 91355; 661-222-2716, fax: 661-253-7710, e-mail address: sstewart@calarts.edu

### More About the Institute

The California Institute of the Arts (CalArts) School of Theater trains students from a global perspective and historical precedent while preparing them for current performance practice. The School's mission is to promote a cultural and aesthetic diversity of viewpoint, experience, and expression.

**Programs of Study** The School of Theater offers undergraduate degrees in acting, costume, lighting, scene, sound design, management, and technical direction. Undergraduate programs lead to a Bachelor in Fine Arts (B.F.A.) degree.

The CalArts School of Theater supports and broadens the work of burgeoning artists from multiple disciplines. The School of Theater's relatively small size (a 7:1 student-faculty ratio) allows for small classes, and one-on-one instruction. Every student works closely with his or her mentor, a faculty member who serves as that student's artistic and academic adviser. Students gain essential practical experience through full School of Theater productions and various other performances, including an annual New Works Festival.

**Facilities** On-campus performance spaces include four black box theaters, a thrust stage, and a cabaret-style stage. Chief among them is the Walt Disney Modular Theater, or the MOD, a vast black box that can be arranged to support an unlimited range of stage and seating configurations. The School of Theater operates shops and labs for scenery, costumes, props, sound, lighting, and computers.

Off-campus, CalArts' dramatic performance space in downtown Los Angeles, REDCAT (Roy and Edna Disney/CalArts Theater), opened in 2003 as part of the Frank Gehry-designed Walt Disney Concert Hall complex. REDCAT provides numerous opportunities for School of Theater students, both as a

*California Institute of the Arts (continued)*

performance venue for select productions and as a forum for acquiring professional experience in design, production, and management.

**Faculty and Alumni** Leading professional theater artists in every area of practice comprise the School of Theater faculty. Each member of the faculty is committed to fostering the ambitions of the next generation of theater artists. Faculty members include Jon Gottlieb, Marissa Chibas, Travis Preston, Erik Ehn, Carl Hancock Rux, Carol Bixler, Fran Bennett, Martha Ferrara, Ellen McCartney, Christopher Barreca, Mary Heilman, Mary Lou Rosato, and Stephanie Young.

Faculty members are in constant contact with noted theater companies and current stage, film, and television productions, they are uniquely able to recommend students for valuable apprenticeships and internships.

Alumni from the School of Theater pursue careers across a variety of media and performance arenas. Distinguished members of this group include Don Cheadle ('86), Ed Harris ('76), Jennifer Elise Cox ('91), Bill Irwin ('72), Daniel K. Boland ('95), and Barbara Inglehart ('86).

**Special Programs** The Center for New Performance at CalArts (CNP) is the professional producing arm of CalArts. Dedicated to the creation of adventurous projects that challenge and redefine the boundaries of contemporary performance, the Center for New Performance enables current students, faculty members, alumni, and guest artists to collaborate in producing new, vital, boundary-crossing performances.

Housed in the CalArts School of Theater, the Cotsen Center for the Puppetry of the Arts is an interdisciplinary laboratory for the study and exploration of puppets and performing objects in theater, film, dance, and art. It allows School of Theater students to incorporate the use of performing objects into their theatrical vocabularies, or concentrate on work centered on puppets and other performing objects.

CalArts champions cross-pollination in the arts. In addition to various collaborations within the School of Theater, students work with writers, musicians, composers, choreographers, filmmakers, animators, and visual artists throughout CalArts.

School of Theater students have access to valuable teaching and community engagement experience through Community Arts Partnership (CAP) workshops and classes at community art centers throughout Los Angeles.

**Cooperative Agreements** Most Center for New Theater projects are performed under the Actors Equity Association Contact with the University/Resident Theater Association (U/RTA); an employment agreement devised to develop and expand both professional theater and advance training laboratories. This agreement allows students to garner equity points toward participation in the Actors Equity Association.

The School of Theater features exchange programs with the Royal Scottish Academy of Music and Drama and the Toi Whakaari New Zealand Drama School. Graduate directors and stage managers may have internships with the Sundance Theater Laboratory.

# Carnegie Mellon University
**Pittsburgh, Pennsylvania**

Independent, coed. Urban campus. Total enrollment: 10,493. Theater program established 1914.
**Web Site** http://www.cmu.edu/

# Catawba College
**Salisbury, North Carolina**

Independent, coed. Small town campus. Total enrollment: 1,323. Theater program established 1956.

**Degrees** Bachelor of Fine Arts. Majors and concentrations: acting and directing, costume design, lighting/sound design, music theater, scenic design, theater arts/drama, theater management.
**Enrollment** 132 total; 12 undergraduate, 120 nonprofessional degree.
**Theater Student Profile** 58% females, 42% males, 9% minorities.
**Theater Faculty** 7 undergraduate (full-time), 6 undergraduate (part-time). 100% of full-time faculty have terminal degrees. Graduate students do not teach undergraduate courses. Undergraduate student–faculty ratio: 8:1.
**Student Life** Student groups/activities include Alpha Psi Omega, Blue Masque Drama Club.
**Expenses for 2007–2008** Application fee: $30. Comprehensive fee: $29,990 includes full-time tuition ($22,290) and college room and board ($7700). Full-time tuition varies according to class time.
**Financial Aid** Program-specific awards: 25 theater arts scholarships and academic awards for incoming freshmen and transfers ($1100).
**Application Procedures** Students apply for admission into the professional program by freshman year. Deadline for freshmen and transfers: continuous. Required: high school transcript, college transcript(s) for transfer students, minimum 3.0 high school GPA, 2 letters of recommendation, interview, audition, portfolio, SAT or ACT test scores. Recommended: essay. Auditions held 5 times on campus and off campus in North Carolina Theatre Conference Meeting sites; recorded music is permissible as a substitute for live auditions and videotaped performances are permissible as a substitute for live auditions when distance is prohibitive. Portfolio reviews held 5 times on campus and off campus in North Carolina Theatre Conference Meeting sites; the submission of slides may be substituted for portfolios.
**Web Site** http://www.catawba.edu/academic/theatrearts/
**Undergraduate Contact** Dr. Woodrow Hood, Chair, Theatre Arts Department, Catawba College, 2300 West Innes Street, Salisbury, North Carolina 28144; 704-637-4771, fax: 704-637-4207, e-mail address: wbhood@catawba.edu

# Central Connecticut State University
**New Britain, Connecticut**

State-supported, coed. Suburban campus. Total enrollment: 12,106. Theater program established 1973.
**Degrees** Bachelor of Fine Arts. Majors and concentrations: acting, costume design, dance, directing, educational theater, technical theater.
**Enrollment** 86 total; all undergraduate.
**Theater Student Profile** 55% females, 45% males, 5% minorities.
**Theater Faculty** 7 undergraduate (full-time), 2 undergraduate (part-time). 100% of full-time faculty have terminal degrees. Graduate students do not teach undergraduate courses. Undergraduate student–faculty ratio: 16:1.
**Student Life** Student groups/activities include Theatre Unlimited (student producing organization), community outreach programs in children's theater and workshops.
**Expenses for 2007–2008** Application fee: $50. State resident tuition: $3346 full-time. Nonresident tuition: $10,831 full-time. Mandatory fees: $3388 full-time. Full-time tuition and fees vary according to course level, course load, and reciprocity agreements. College room and board: $8146. College room only: $4748. Room and board charges vary according to board plan.
**Financial Aid** Program-specific awards: 2 Thad Torp Memorial Scholarships for juniors ($4000), 1 acting scholarship for sophomores ($1000).
**Application Procedures** Students admitted directly into the professional program freshman year. Deadline for freshmen: May 1; transfers: continuous. Required: high school transcript, college transcript(s) for transfer students, letter of recommendation, SAT test score only, audition for acting majors. Recommended: minimum 2.0 high school GPA, interview, portfolio. Auditions held once on campus. Portfolio reviews held as needed on campus; the submission of slides may be substituted for portfolios for executed design projects.
**Web Site** http://www.ccsu.edu

**Undergraduate Contact** Associate Director, Undergraduate Admissions, Office of Admissions, Central Connecticut State University, PO Box 4010, 1615 Stanley Street, New Britain, Connecticut 06050; 860-832-CCSU, fax: 860-832-2295, e-mail address: admissions@ccsu.edu

# Chapman University

## Orange, California

Independent, coed. Suburban campus. Total enrollment: 6,022.
**Degrees** Bachelor of Fine Arts in the area of theatre performance. Majors and concentrations: performance.
**Enrollment** 141 total; 22 undergraduate, 119 nonprofessional degree.
**Theater Student Profile** 74% females, 26% males, 20% minorities, 5% international.
**Theater Faculty** 6 undergraduate (full-time), 9 undergraduate (part-time). 80% of full-time faculty have terminal degrees. Graduate students do not teach undergraduate courses. Undergraduate student–faculty ratio: 5:1.
**Student Life** Student groups/activities include Shakespeare Orange County-Summer Professional Theaters, American Celebration, Performing Arts Society of Chapman.
**Expenses for 2008–2009** Application fee: $55. Comprehensive fee: $46,015 includes full-time tuition ($33,760), mandatory fees ($940), and college room and board ($11,315). Special program-related fees: $75 per course for introduction technology courses; materials fees, $75 per course for introduction theater courses, theater tickets, $85 per course for theatrical makeup kits, $100 per course for stagecraft, theatrical design, one-act production fees.
**Financial Aid** Program-specific awards: 40 talent awards for new incoming students only ($2000).
**Application Procedures** Students apply for admission into the professional program by sophomore year. Deadline for freshmen: January 31; transfers: March 15. Required: essay, high school transcript, college transcript(s) for transfer students, minimum 2.0 high school GPA, 2 letters of recommendation, audition, SAT or ACT test scores, recent photograph, resumé, supplemental theatre application. Recommended: interview, video. Auditions held 2 times per month (October through February) on campus; videotaped performances are permissible as a substitute for live auditions with permission of the Senior Department Secretary. Portfolio reviews held 2 times per month (October through February) on campus; the submission of slides may be substituted for portfolios if submission of portfolio is otherwise not possible.
**Web Site** http://www.chapman.edu/comm/td/
**Undergraduate Contact** Ms. Bonnie Walker, Senior Department Secretary, Department of Theatre, Chapman University, 1 University Drive, Orange, California 92866; 714-744-7087, fax: 714-744-7015, e-mail address: tdoffice@chapman.edu

# Chicago College of Performing Arts - The Theatre Conservatory

See Roosevelt University

# College of Santa Fe

## Santa Fe, New Mexico

Independent, coed. Suburban campus. Total enrollment: 672. Theater program established 1965.
**Web Site** http://www.csf.edu

# Columbia College Chicago

## Chicago, Illinois

Independent, coed. Urban campus. Total enrollment: 11,499. Theater program established 1969.
**Degrees** Bachelor of Arts in the areas of acting, directing, theater design, music theater performance; Bachelor of Fine Arts in the areas of acting, directing, theatrical design. Majors and concentrations: acting, costume design, directing, lighting design, playwriting, set design, technical theatre/design, theater design.
**Enrollment** 700 total; all undergraduate.
**Theater Student Profile** 60% females, 40% males, 26% minorities.
**Theater Faculty** 24 total (full-time), 50 total (part-time). Graduate students do not teach undergraduate courses. Undergraduate student–faculty ratio: 9:1.
**Student Life** Student groups/activities include Black Actor's Guild.
**Expenses for 2007–2008** Application fee: $35. Comprehensive fee: $29,652 includes full-time tuition ($17,104), mandatory fees ($530), and college room and board ($12,018). College room only: $9048. Special program-related fees: $5–$415 per course for class fees (depends on class-related activities).
**Financial Aid** Program-specific awards: 1 Freshman Achievement in Theater Award for theater students ($1500), 1 David Talbot Cox Scholarship for students with concentration in directing ($3000), 1 Betty Garrett Music Theater Scholarship for music theater majors ($1000).
**Application Procedures** Students admitted directly into the professional program freshman year. Deadline for freshmen and transfers: continuous. Notification date for freshmen and transfers: continuous. Required: essay, high school transcript, college transcript(s) for transfer students, letter of recommendation, meeting with admissions counselor for a personal interview and possible remediation program attendance for students with less than a 2.0 GPA, audition and portfolio for transfer students. Recommended: minimum 2.0 high school GPA, interview, SAT or ACT test scores. Portfolio reviews held continuously on campus.
**Web Site** http://www.colum.edu
**Undergraduate Contact** Mr. Murphy Monroe, Director, Office of Admissions, Columbia College Chicago, 600 South Michigan Avenue, Chicago, Illinois 60605; 312-344-7133, fax: 312-344-8024, e-mail address: admissions@colum.edu

# Concordia University

## Montreal, Quebec, Canada

Province-supported, coed. Urban campus. Total enrollment: 32,416. Theater program established 1975.
**Web Site** http://www.concordia.ca/

# Cornish College of the Arts

## Seattle, Washington

Independent, coed. Urban campus. Total enrollment: 768 (2006). Theater program established 1914.
**Degrees** Bachelor of Fine Arts in the area of theater. Majors and concentrations: acting, original works, performing arts.
**Enrollment** 191 total; all undergraduate.
**Theater Student Profile** 65% females, 35% males, 14% minorities, 3% international.
**Theater Faculty** 16 undergraduate (full-time), 11 undergraduate (part-time). 58% of full-time faculty have terminal degrees. Graduate students do not teach undergraduate courses. Undergraduate student–faculty ratio: 10:1.
**Expenses for 2007–2008** Application fee: $35. Tuition: $23,700 full-time. Mandatory fees: $300 full-time. Special program-related fees: $175 per year for supplies.
**Financial Aid** Program-specific awards: Presidential Scholarships for continuing students, Nellie Scholarships for new students, departmental scholarships for new and continuing students.
**Application Procedures** Students admitted directly into the professional program freshman year. Deadline for freshmen and transfers: August 15. Notification date for freshmen and transfers: August 30. Required: essay, high school transcript, college transcript(s) for transfer students, minimum 2.0 high school GPA, audition. Recommended: minimum 3.0 high school GPA, 2 letters of recommendation, interview, SAT or ACT test scores, current resumé/head shot. Auditions held 12 times on campus and off campus in all unified audition sites; videotaped performances are permissible as a substitute for live auditions when distance is prohibitive.
**Web Site** http://www.cornish.edu

*Cornish College of the Arts (continued)*

**Undergraduate Contact** Sharron Starling, Director of Admission, Cornish College of the Arts, 1000 Lenora, Seattle, Washington 98121; 800-726-ARTS, fax: 206-720-1011, e-mail address: sstarling@cornish.edu

# Cornish College of the Arts

## Seattle, Washington

Independent, coed. Urban campus. Total enrollment: 768 (2006). Theater program established 1914.

**Degrees** Bachelor of Fine Arts in the area of performance production. Majors and concentrations: costume design, lighting design, set design, sound design, stage management, technical direction.

**Enrollment** 47 total; all undergraduate.

**Theater Student Profile** 53% females, 47% males, 14% minorities, 3% international.

**Theater Faculty** 5 undergraduate (full-time), 4 undergraduate (part-time). 58% of full-time faculty have terminal degrees. Graduate students do not teach undergraduate courses. Undergraduate student–faculty ratio: 5:1.

**Expenses for 2007–2008** Application fee: $35. Tuition: $23,700 full-time. Mandatory fees: $300 full-time. Special program-related fees: $150 per year for supplies.

**Financial Aid** Program-specific awards: Nellie Scholarships for new students, departmental scholarships for new and continuing students, Presidential Scholarships for continuing students.

**Application Procedures** Students admitted directly into the professional program freshman year. Deadline for freshmen and transfers: August 15. Notification date for freshmen and transfers: August 30. Required: essay, high school transcript, college transcript(s) for transfer students, minimum 2.0 high school GPA, portfolio. Recommended: minimum 3.0 high school GPA, 2 letters of recommendation, interview, audition, SAT or ACT test scores. Auditions held 20 times on campus and off campus in Las Vegas, NV; Los Angeles, CA; San Francisco, CA; videotaped performances are permissible as a substitute for live auditions when distance is prohibitive. Portfolio reviews held continuously on campus and off campus in various cities; the submission of slides may be substituted for portfolios when distance is prohibitive.

**Web Site** http://www.cornish.edu

**Undergraduate Contact** Sharron Starling, Director of Admission, Cornish College of the Arts, 1000 Lenora, Seattle, Washington 98121; 800-726-ARTS, fax: 206-720-1011, e-mail address: sstarling@cornish.edu

# DePaul University

## Chicago, Illinois

Independent Roman Catholic, coed. Urban campus. Total enrollment: 23,401. Theater program established 1925.

**Degrees** Bachelor of Fine Arts. Majors and concentrations: acting, costume design, costume technology, dramaturgy/criticism, lighting design, playwriting, scenic design, stage management, theater arts studies, theater management, theater technology. Graduate degrees offered: Master of Fine Arts in the areas of acting, directing, arts leadership.

**Enrollment** 330 total; 290 undergraduate, 40 graduate.

**Theater Student Profile** 55% females, 45% males, 18% minorities, 1% international.

**Theater Faculty** 28 total (full-time), 54 total (part-time). 95% of full-time faculty have terminal degrees. Graduate students do not teach undergraduate courses. Undergraduate student–faculty ratio: 12:1.

**Student Life** Student groups/activities include new student mentors, The Theatre School Student Government, STARS (Support Tomorrow's Rising Stars).

**Expenses for 2008–2009** Application fee: $40. Comprehensive fee: $34,349 includes full-time tuition ($23,820), mandatory fees ($574), and college room and board ($9955). College room only: $7390.

**Financial Aid** Program-specific awards: 6 performance scholarships for incoming actors ($8000), 40–50 design/tech and theater studies scholarships for incoming program majors (except acting) ($3000–$9000), 50–60 merit scholarships for upperclass program majors ($1500–$12,000).

**Application Procedures** Students admitted directly into the professional program freshman year. Deadline for freshmen and transfers: January 15. Notification date for freshmen and transfers: March 15. Required: high school transcript, college transcript(s) for transfer students, 3 letters of recommendation, interview, audition, portfolio, SAT or ACT test scores (minimum composite ACT score of 20), minimum 2.5 high school GPA, photo/resumé, minimum SAT 1000 (critical reading/math). Recommended: essay. Auditions held 25-30 times on campus and off campus in Los Angeles, CA; San Francisco, CA; New York, NY; Houston, TX; Atlanta, GA; Miami, FL. Portfolio reviews held 8 times (off campus only in February) on campus and off campus in Los Angeles, CA; San Francisco, CA; New York, NY; (off-campus only in February); the submission of slides may be substituted for portfolios if a campus visit is impossible or in special circumstances.

**Web Site** http://theatreschool.depaul.edu

**Contact** Jason Beck, Director of Admissions, The Theatre School, DePaul University, 2135 North Kenmore Avenue, Chicago, Illinois 60614-4111; 773-325-7999 ext. 57999, fax: 773-325-7920, e-mail address: theatreadmissions@depaul.edu

# Dorothy F. Schmidt College of Arts and Letters

See Florida Atlantic University

# East Carolina University

## Greenville, North Carolina

State-supported, coed. Urban campus. Total enrollment: 25,990. Theater program established 1962.

**Degrees** Bachelor of Fine Arts in the area of theatre arts. Majors and concentrations: acting, design production, music theater, stage management, theater education.

**Enrollment** 210 total; 200 undergraduate, 10 nonprofessional degree.

**Theater Student Profile** 55% females, 45% males, 1% minorities, 1% international.

**Theater Faculty** 19 undergraduate (full-time), 4 undergraduate (part-time). 95% of full-time faculty have terminal degrees. Graduate students do not teach undergraduate courses. Undergraduate student–faculty ratio: 10:1.

**Student Life** Student groups/activities include East Carolina Playhouse, East Carolina Summer Theatre, studio theater workshops.

**Expenses for 2007–2008** Application fee: $60. State resident tuition: $2431 full-time. Nonresident tuition: $12,945 full-time. Mandatory fees: $1937 full-time. College room and board: $7150. College room only: $4150. Room and board charges vary according to board plan and housing facility.

**Financial Aid** Program-specific awards: 16 scholarships for program majors demonstrating merit ($800).

**Application Procedures** Students apply for admission into the professional program by sophomore year. Deadline for freshmen: March 15; transfers: April 15. Required: high school transcript, college transcript(s) for transfer students, audition, SAT test score only. Recommended: minimum 2.0 high school GPA, 3 letters of recommendation. Auditions held once on campus.

**Web Site** http://www.theatre-dance.ecu.edu

**Undergraduate Contact** Undergraduate Admissions, East Carolina University, Wichard Building, Greenville, North Carolina 27858; 252-328-6640, e-mail address: admis@mail.ecu.edu

# Elon University

## Elon, North Carolina

Independent, coed. Suburban campus. Total enrollment: 5,456. Theater program established 1991.

**Web Site** http://www.elon.edu/

# Emerson College

## Boston, Massachusetts

Independent, coed. Urban campus. Total enrollment: 4,380. Theater program established 1919.

**Degrees** Bachelor of Fine Arts in the area of performing arts. Majors and concentrations: acting, music theater, production management, stage management, theater design/technology. Graduate degrees offered: Master of Arts in the area of theater education. Cross-registration with Boston Conservatory of Music, Massachusetts College of Art, Berklee College of Music, School of the Museum of Fine Arts, Boston Architectural Center.

**Enrollment** 575 total; 375 undergraduate, 200 nonprofessional degree.

**Theater Student Profile** 60% females, 40% males, 10% minorities, 5% international.

**Theater Faculty** 22 undergraduate (full-time), 40 undergraduate (part-time). 95% of full-time faculty have terminal degrees. Graduate students do not teach undergraduate courses. Undergraduate student–faculty ratio: 16:1.

**Student Life** Student groups/activities include Emerson Comedy Troupes, Musical Theatre Society, Mercutio Drama Ensemble. Special housing available for theater students.

**Expenses for 2007–2008** Application fee: $65. Comprehensive fee: $38,256 includes full-time tuition ($26,880) and college room and board ($11,376).

**Financial Aid** Program-specific awards: 10 Emerson Stage Scholarships for performing arts freshmen ($3000), 50 Dean's Scholarships for performing arts freshmen ($8000), 50 Trustee Scholarships for honors program admission students ($17,624), 1272 Emerson Grants for those demonstrating financial need ($12,062).

**Application Procedures** Students admitted directly into the professional program freshman year. Deadline for freshmen: January 5; transfers: March 1. Notification date for freshmen: April 1; transfers: May 1. Required: essay, high school transcript, college transcript(s) for transfer students, 2 letters of recommendation, audition, portfolio, SAT or ACT test scores, portfolio for design/technology and stage/production management, interview for design/technology and stage/production management. Recommended: minimum 3.0 high school GPA, interview. Auditions held 25 times on campus and off campus in Los Angeles, CA; San Francisco, CA; Chicago, IL; Miami, FL; Atlanta, GA; New York City, NY; Houston, TX; videotaped performances are permissible as a substitute for live auditions for international students living overseas. Portfolio reviews held 10-14 times on campus.

**Web Site** http://www.emerson.edu

**Undergraduate Contact** Ms. Sara S. Ramirez, Director of Admission, Emerson College, 120 Boylston Street, Boston, Massachusetts 02116-4624; 617-824-8600, fax: 617-824-8609.

**Graduate Contact** Dr. Robert W. Colby, Graduate Program Director, Department of Performing Arts, Emerson College, 120 Boylston Street, Boston, Massachusetts 02116-4624; 617-824-8780, fax: 617-824-8799, e-mail address: robert_colby@emerson.edu

# Emporia State University

## Emporia, Kansas

State-supported, coed. Small town campus. Total enrollment: 6,354. Theater program established 1913.

**Degrees** Bachelor of Fine Arts. Majors and concentrations: theater.

**Enrollment** 85 total; all undergraduate.

**Theater Student Profile** 50% females, 50% males, 5% minorities, 2% international.

**Theater Faculty** 7 undergraduate (full-time), 3 undergraduate (part-time). 100% of full-time faculty have terminal degrees. Graduate students do not teach undergraduate courses. Undergraduate student–faculty ratio: 15:1.

**Student Life** Student groups/activities include Educational Theatre Company, Zoiks! - Improvisational Comedy Troupe.

**Expenses for 2007–2008** Application fee: $30. State resident tuition: $3140 full-time. Nonresident tuition: $11,190 full-time. Mandatory fees: $786 full-time. Full-time tuition and fees vary according to degree level. College room and board: $5581.

College room only: $2832. Room and board charges vary according to board plan and housing facility.

**Financial Aid** Program-specific awards: 1 Anderson Scholarship for outstanding theater students ($1100), 1 Bruder Scholarship for outstanding theater students ($2500), 1 Wise Scholarship for outstanding theater students ($1600), 1 Pflaum Scholarship for outstanding theater students ($1300), 1 Karl Malden Scholarship for outstanding theater students ($2500), 1 Gilson Scholarship for future secondary teachers in theater ($600), 1 Halgedahl Scholarship for outstanding students in musical theater ($1200), 1 Frederickson Scholarship for outstanding theater students ($1100), 1 Matheny Scholarship for outstanding theater students ($1500), 1 Lehman Scholarship for outstanding new theater students ($1300), 1 Hill Scholarship for outstanding theater students ($1000).

**Application Procedures** Students admitted directly into the professional program freshman year. Deadline for freshmen and transfers: continuous. Required: high school transcript, college transcript(s) for transfer students, ACT test score only (minimum composite ACT score of 21). Recommended: 2 letters of recommendation, interview, audition, portfolio. Auditions held twice on campus; recorded music is permissible as a substitute for live auditions if a campus visit is impossible and videotaped performances are permissible as a substitute for live auditions if a campus visit is impossible. Portfolio reviews held twice on campus; the submission of slides may be substituted for portfolios if a campus visit is impossible.

**Web Site** http://www.emporia.edu/theatre

**Undergraduate Contact** Jim Bartrutt, Director of Theatre, Department of Communication and Theatre, Emporia State University, 1200 Commercial, Campus Box 4033, Emporia, Kansas 66801-5087; 620-341-5256, fax: 620-341-6031, e-mail address: bartrufj@emporia.edu

# Fairleigh Dickinson University, College at Florham

## Madison, New Jersey

Independent, coed. Suburban campus. Total enrollment: 3,463. Theater program established 2001.

**Degrees** Bachelor of Arts in the areas of theater arts, fine arts (theater concentration). Majors and concentrations: theater arts/drama.

**Enrollment** 75 total; all undergraduate.

**Theater Student Profile** 60% females, 40% males, 15% minorities, 10% international.

**Theater Faculty** 4 undergraduate (full-time), 8 undergraduate (part-time). 80% of full-time faculty have terminal degrees. Graduate students do not teach undergraduate courses. Undergraduate student–faculty ratio: 15:1.

**Student Life** Student groups/activities include Playwrights Theatre of New Jersey, main stage productions, Starshine (student-run drama club).

**Expenses for 2007–2008** Application fee: $40. Comprehensive fee: $38,210 includes full-time tuition ($27,620), mandatory fees ($608), and college room and board ($9982). College room only: $6074. Room and board charges vary according to board plan and housing facility.

**Financial Aid** Program-specific awards: Col. Fairleigh Dickinson Awards for theater majors ($9000).

**Application Procedures** Students admitted directly into the professional program freshman year. Deadline for freshmen and transfers: continuous. Required: high school transcript, college transcript(s) for transfer students, 2 letters of recommendation, audition, SAT test score only, minimum 2.8 high school GPA. Recommended: interview. Auditions held regularly on campus; videotaped performances are permissible as a substitute for live auditions. the submission of slides may be substituted for portfolios.

**Web Site** http://arts.fdu.edu

**Undergraduate Contact** Admissions Office, Fairleigh Dickinson University, College at Florham, 285 Madison Avenue, Madison, New Jersey 07940; 973-443-8900.

# Feinstein College of Arts and Sciences

See Roger Williams University

# Five Towns College

**Dix Hills, New York**

Independent, coed. Suburban campus. Total enrollment: 1,151. Theater program established 1999.

**Degrees** Bachelor of Fine Arts in the areas of theater arts, film/video production. Majors and concentrations: audio recording technology, film and video production, music theater. Program accredited by NCATE.

**Enrollment** 70 total; all undergraduate.

**Theater Student Profile** 65% females, 35% males, 12% minorities, 2% international.

**Theater Faculty** 5 undergraduate (full-time), 2 undergraduate (part-time). Graduate students do not teach undergraduate courses. Undergraduate student–faculty ratio: 13:1.

**Student Life** Student groups/activities include drama workshop, opera workshop.

**Expenses for 2008–2009** Application fee: $35. Comprehensive fee: $29,875 includes full-time tuition ($17,400), mandatory fees ($725), and college room and board ($11,750). Special program-related fees: $750 per semester for private music instruction (when applicable).

**Financial Aid** Program-specific awards: 40 scholarships for theatre students ($4000–$7000).

**Application Procedures** Students admitted directly into the professional program freshman year. Deadline for freshmen and transfers: continuous. Required: essay, high school transcript, college transcript(s) for transfer students, minimum 2.0 high school GPA, 2 letters of recommendation, audition, SAT or ACT test scores, personal statement. Recommended: minimum 3.0 high school GPA, interview, video, portfolio. Auditions held by appointment on campus; recorded music is permissible as a substitute for live auditions when distance is prohibitive and videotaped performances are permissible as a substitute for live auditions when distance is prohibitive. Portfolio reviews held annually on campus.

**Web Site** http://www.ftc.edu

**Undergraduate Contact** Jerry Cohen, Dean of Enrollment, Admissions Office, Five Towns College, 305 North Service Road, Dix Hills, New York 11746; 631-656-2110, fax: 631-656-2172.

## *Dorothy F. Schmidt College of Arts and Letters*
# Florida Atlantic University

**Boca Raton, Florida**

State-supported, coed. Suburban campus. Total enrollment: 26,275. Theater program established 1972.

**Degrees** Bachelor of Fine Arts in the area of acting. Majors and concentrations: acting. Graduate degrees offered: Master of Fine Arts in the areas of acting, design technical.

**Enrollment** 98 total; 16 undergraduate, 19 graduate, 63 nonprofessional degree.

**Theater Student Profile** 68% females, 32% males, 40% minorities, 1% international.

**Theater Faculty** 9 total (full-time), 3 total (part-time). 100% of full-time faculty have terminal degrees. Graduate students teach a few undergraduate courses. Undergraduate student–faculty ratio: 11:1.

**Student Life** Student groups/activities include Alpha Psi Omega, Coalition for the Advancement of Students in Theater.

**Expenses for 2007–2008** Application fee: $30. State resident tuition: $3367 full-time. Nonresident tuition: $16,431 full-time. Full-time tuition varies according to course load. College room and board: $8610. Room and board charges vary according to board plan and housing facility. Special program-related fees: $50 per course for lab fee for technical theater.

**Financial Aid** Program-specific awards: 20 Esther Griswold Awards for program majors ($1000–$2000), 3 Harold Burris-Meyer Scholarships for technical students ($500).

**Application Procedures** Students apply for admission into the professional program by sophomore year. Deadline for freshmen and transfers: June 1. Notification date for freshmen and transfers: July 1. Required: high school transcript, college transcript(s) for transfer students, minimum 3.0 high school GPA, 3 letters of recommendation, audition, SAT or ACT test scores (minimum combined SAT score of 1050, minimum composite ACT score of 23). Recommended: interview. Auditions held 5 times on campus and off campus in Florida Theatre Conference sites and state thespian conference sites.

**Web Site** http://www.fau.edu/divdept/schmidt/theatre/index.htm

**Contact** Dr. Richard J. Gamble, Chair, Theatre Department, Florida Atlantic University, 777 Glades Road, Box 3091, Boca Raton, Florida 33431-6498; 561-297-3810, fax: 561-297-2180, e-mail address: gamble@fau.edu

# Florida International University

**Miami, Florida**

State-supported, coed. Urban campus. Total enrollment: 38,290. Theater program established 1982.

**Web Site** http://www.fiu.edu/

# Florida State University

**Tallahassee, Florida**

State-supported, coed. Suburban campus. Total enrollment: 40,555. Theater program established 1973.

**Degrees** Bachelor of Fine Arts in the areas of acting, music theatre. Majors and concentrations: acting, music theater. Graduate degrees offered: Master of Fine Arts in the areas of acting, costume design, directing, lighting design, scenic design, theater management, technical production, professional writing. Program accredited by NAST.

**Enrollment** 507 total; 80 undergraduate, 95 graduate, 332 nonprofessional degree.

**Theater Student Profile** 61% females, 39% males, 14% minorities, 1% international.

**Theater Faculty** 24 total (full-time). 92% of full-time faculty have terminal degrees. Graduate students teach a few undergraduate courses. Undergraduate student–faculty ratio: 14:1.

**Student Life** Student groups/activities include Florida Theatre Conference, Southeastern Theatre Conference, United States Institute for Theatre Technology.

**Expenses for 2007–2008** Application fee: $30. State resident tuition: $3355 full-time. Nonresident tuition: $16,487 full-time. Full-time tuition varies according to location. College room and board: $8000. College room only: $4700. Room and board charges vary according to board plan and housing facility.

**Financial Aid** Program-specific awards: 2 Presidential Scholarships for program students ($1500), 5 Patron's Scholarships for program students ($1000), 1 Hoffman Chair Scholarship for program students ($1000), 3 Fallon Scholarships for program students ($500), 12–18 School of Theatre Scholarships for program students ($500–$1000), 25 scholarships for program students ($750–$1000).

**Application Procedures** Students admitted directly into the professional program freshman year. Deadline for freshmen and transfers: continuous. Required: high school transcript, college transcript(s) for transfer students, 2 letters of recommendation, SAT or ACT test scores, interview for design technology applicants, audition for acting and music theater applicants, portfolio for design technology applicants. Auditions held 11 times on campus and off campus in Florida Theatre Conference sites, United Auditions, Teens Educational Theatre Association, Miami, FL. Portfolio reviews held 4-5 times on campus and off campus in Florida Theatre Conference sites.

**Web Site** http://theatre.fsu.edu

**Contact** Barbara Thomas, Program Assistant, School of Theatre, Florida State University, 329 Fine Arts Building, Tallahassee, Florida 32306-1160; 850-644-7234, fax: 850-644-7246, e-mail address: bgthomas@admin.fsu.edu

# Fordham University
**New York, New York**

Independent Roman Catholic (Jesuit), coed. Urban campus. Total enrollment: 14,448. Theater program established 1968.
**Degrees** Bachelor of Arts in the area of theatre. Majors and concentrations: acting, directing, playwriting, theater design and production. Cross-registration with various study abroad programs.
**Enrollment** 119 total; all undergraduate.
**Theater Student Profile** 52% females, 48% males, 25% minorities, 3% international.
**Theater Faculty** 9 undergraduate (full-time), 21 undergraduate (part-time). 100% of full-time faculty have terminal degrees. Graduate students do not teach undergraduate courses. Undergraduate student–faculty ratio: 4:1.
**Student Life** Student groups/activities include Mainstage Theatre productions (www.fordham.edu/theatre/shows), studio theatre productions.
**Expenses for 2007–2008** Application fee: $50. Comprehensive fee: $45,157 includes full-time tuition ($31,800), mandatory fees ($1057), and college room and board ($12,300). Room and board charges vary according to board plan and location.
**Financial Aid** Program-specific awards available.
**Application Procedures** Students admitted directly into the professional program freshman year. Deadline for freshmen: January 15; transfers: July 1. Notification date for freshmen: April 1; transfers: continuous. Required: essay, high school transcript, college transcript(s) for transfer students, minimum 3.0 high school GPA, letter of recommendation, video, audition, SAT or ACT test scores (minimum combined SAT score of 1100), live or video audition (for theatre/acting); call 212-636-7778 or e-mail theatredept@fordham.edu, live interview (for theatre/directing), live interview and writing sample (for theatre/playwriting), live interview and portfolio (for theatre/design and production). Auditions held 7 times on campus and off campus in Chicago, IL; San Francisco, CA; Los Angeles, CA; videotaped performances are permissible as a substitute for live auditions video audition must adhere to monologue requirements posted on webside: www.fordham.edu.theatr. Portfolio reviews held 7 times on campus and off campus in Chicago, IL; San Francisco, CA; Los Angeles, CA; the submission of slides may be substituted for portfolios with permission from Head of Design Program.
**Web Site** http://www.fordham.edu/theatre
**Undergraduate Contact** Eva Patton, Theatre Program Administrator, Theatre and Visual Arts, Fordham University, 113 West 60th Street, Room 423, New York, New York 10023; 212-636-6338, fax: 212-636-7003, e-mail address: patton@fordham.edu

# The Hartt School
See University of Hartford

# Hofstra University
**Hempstead, New York**

Independent, coed. Suburban campus. Total enrollment: 12,490. Theater program established 1956.
**Web Site** http://www.hofstra.edu/

# Howard University
**Washington, District of Columbia**

Independent, coed. Urban campus. Theater program established 1960.
**Degrees** Bachelor of Fine Arts. Majors and concentrations: acting, dance arts, music theater, theater arts administration, theater education, theater technology. Cross-registration with Consortium of Universities of the Washington Metropolitan Area. Program accredited by NAST.
**Enrollment** 143 total; all undergraduate.
**Theater Student Profile** 95% females, 5% males, 100% minorities.
**Theater Faculty** 14 undergraduate (full-time), 12 undergraduate (part-time). 92% of full-time faculty have terminal degrees.

Graduate students do not teach undergraduate courses. Undergraduate student–faculty ratio: 6:1.
**Student Life** Student groups/activities include Student Play Festival, Fine Arts Festival.
**Expenses for 2007–2008** Application fee: $45. Comprehensive fee: $20,691 includes full-time tuition ($12,910), mandatory fees ($805), and college room and board ($6976). College room only: $4278. Room and board charges vary according to board plan and housing facility.
**Financial Aid** Program-specific awards: Special Talent Awards for continuing students, Trustee Awards for continuing students.
**Application Procedures** Students admitted directly into the professional program freshman year. Deadline for freshmen and transfers: February 15. Notification date for freshmen and transfers: April 1. Required: essay, high school transcript, college transcript(s) for transfer students, minimum 2.0 high school GPA, 2 letters of recommendation, interview, audition, SAT or ACT test scores, resumé. Auditions held once on campus.
**Web Site** http://www.howard.edu/collegefinearts/theatre
**Undergraduate Contact** Director, Office of Admissions, Howard University, 2400 6th Street, NW, Washington, District of Columbia 20059; 202-806-2763, fax: 202-806-6226, e-mail address: askem@howard.edu

# Idaho State University
**Pocatello, Idaho**

State-supported, coed. Small town campus. Total enrollment: 13,208. Theater program established 1924.
**Web Site** http://www.isu.edu/

# Illinois State University
**Normal, Illinois**

State-supported, coed. Urban campus. Total enrollment: 20,274. Theater program established 1970.
**Degrees** Bachelor of Arts; Bachelor of Science. Majors and concentrations: acting, dance, production/design, theater arts/drama, theater education. Graduate degrees offered: Master of Arts in the area of theater; Master of Fine Arts in the area of theater; Master of Science in the area of theater. Program accredited by NAST.
**Enrollment** 353 total; 323 undergraduate, 30 graduate.
**Theater Student Profile** 60% females, 40% males, 12% minorities, 2% international.
**Theater Faculty** 29 total (full-time), 3 total (part-time). 97% of full-time faculty have terminal degrees. Graduate students teach a few undergraduate courses. Undergraduate student–faculty ratio: 14:1.
**Student Life** Student groups/activities include Illinois State University Theatre, Cross Roads Theatre (minority-based theater), Illinois Shakespeare Festival (professional summer theater).
**Expenses for 2007–2008** Application fee: $40. State resident tuition: $6990 full-time. Nonresident tuition: $14,310 full-time. Mandatory fees: $2029 full-time. Full-time tuition and fees vary according to course load. College room and board: $6848. College room only: $3560. Room and board charges vary according to board plan, housing facility, and location.
**Financial Aid** Program-specific awards: 7 Friends of the Arts Scholarships for those demonstrating need ($500), 20 ISU tuition scholarships for those demonstrating talent ($1200), 7 Talent Grants ($500).
**Application Procedures** Students admitted directly into the professional program freshman year. Deadline for freshmen and transfers: continuous. Required: high school transcript, college transcript(s) for transfer students, minimum 2.0 high school GPA, audition, portfolio, SAT or ACT test scores (minimum composite ACT score of 23), audition/portfolio (design students) for those seeking admission in acting, dance or design/production. Auditions held 4-5 times on campus and off campus in Chicago, IL; videotaped performances are permissible as a substitute for live auditions approval of school of theatre. Portfolio reviews held 4-5 times; the submission of slides may be substituted for portfolios.
**Web Site** http://www.cfa.ilstu.edu/theatre

*Illinois State University (continued)*

**Undergraduate Contact** Admissions Office, Illinois State University, Normal, Illinois 61790; 309-438-8284, fax: 309-438-3932, e-mail address: admissions@illinoisstate.edu

**Graduate Contact** Graduate School, Illinois State University, Normal, Illinois 61790; 309-438-2583, fax: 309-438-7912, e-mail address: admissions@illinoisstate.edu

# Illinois Wesleyan University
## Bloomington, Illinois

Independent, coed. Suburban campus. Total enrollment: 2,094. Theater program established 1948.

**Degrees** Bachelor of Arts in the area of theatre arts; Bachelor of Fine Arts in the areas of acting, music theatre, theatre design and technology. Majors and concentrations: acting, music theater, theater arts studies, theater design/technology.

**Enrollment** 112 total; 67 undergraduate, 45 nonprofessional degree.

**Theater Student Profile** 63% females, 37% males, 1% minorities.

**Theater Faculty** 8 undergraduate (full-time), 12 undergraduate (part-time). 100% of full-time faculty have terminal degrees. Graduate students do not teach undergraduate courses. Undergraduate student–faculty ratio: 12:1.

**Student Life** Student groups/activities include Comedy Improv Group, Sketch Comedy Group.

**Expenses for 2007–2008** Application fee: $0. Comprehensive fee: $37,780 includes full-time tuition ($30,580), mandatory fees ($170), and college room and board ($7030). College room only: $4330. Room and board charges vary according to board plan and housing facility. Special program-related fees: $40–$250 for course fees.

**Financial Aid** Program-specific awards: talent awards for entering freshmen ($5000–$12,000).

**Application Procedures** Students admitted directly into the professional program freshman year. Deadline for freshmen and transfers: continuous. Required: essay, high school transcript, college transcript(s) for transfer students, minimum 3.0 high school GPA, SAT or ACT test scores (minimum composite ACT score of 23), portfolio for design applicants, audition for acting and music theater applicants, on-campus interview for BA applicants. Recommended: interview. Auditions held 4 times on campus; videotaped performances are permissible as a substitute for live auditions with special permission from School of Theatre Arts. Portfolio reviews held 4 times on campus; the submission of slides may be substituted for portfolios with special permission from School of Theatre Arts.

**Web Site** http://titan.iwu.edu/~theatre

**Undergraduate Contact** Ms. Bernadette Brennan, Recruitment Coordinator, Theatre Admission Office, Illinois Wesleyan University, PO Box 2900, Bloomington, Illinois 61702-2900; 309-556-3944, fax: 309-556-3558, e-mail address: theatre@titan.iwu.edu

## More About the Programs

The School of Theatre Arts at Illinois Wesleyan University (IWU) offers Bachelor of Arts in Theatre Arts, Bachelor of Fine Arts in Acting, Bachelor of Fine Arts in Music Theatre, and Bachelor of Fine Arts in Theatre Design and Technology programs as well as minors in theater arts, theater dance, and arts management (offered with the Department of Business Administration).

Students in the School of Theatre Arts programs work closely with an exceptional faculty that gives personal attention to the development of each student. A selective and limited enrollment ensures close mentoring relationships with faculty members. Furthermore, because IWU is strictly an undergraduate university, students play all the roles in productions as well as have opportunities to direct and design major productions.

In addition to obtaining an excellent training in theater arts, the students are strengthened by the University's liberal arts curriculum, which ensures that they receive a broad education in a variety of disciplines across campus. Students graduate from these programs ready to succeed, having developed their own network of contacts through alumni, internships, summer-stock job opportunities, and visitors who come to campus to deliver master classes or to serve as guest designers, directors, or choreographers. Students begin their careers with excellent resumes, a game plan in place, and a superior educational foundation.

The Bachelor of Arts in Theatre Arts allows students a broad range of exploration and study of the theatre, giving them the opportunity to become theatre artists and scholars whose expertise spans more than one facet of the discipline. Although students earning this degree may go on to pursue professional careers in acting, design, or some other theatrical specialization, this course of study uniquely prepares them for the intellectual and aesthetic challenges of the contemporary theatre. This program is intended for the following types of students: the student who aspires to a professional career in directing, playwriting, dramaturgy, theatre management, or other subdiscipline that requires a broad understanding of theatre arts (student actors and designers in the B.A. have the full range of opportunities to participate in the production season open to them); the student who intends to pursue graduate training as a theatre scholar or who aspires to teach at the university level; the student who wishes to double major in theatre arts and a second area; and the student who intends to teach on the high school level (these students are required to double major in another area in which they will be certified to teach, with theatre listed as a secondary area of expertise on the certificate.

The Bachelor of Fine Arts in Theatre Arts is for the student who aspires to an acting career. This well-rounded preprofessional curriculum includes applied training in acting, movement, voice, and dance as well as academically oriented courses like dramatic theory, history, and literature. All students are also exposed to the technical and design areas through course work and production experiences. In addition to intensive course work, B.F.A. actors often have the opportunity to apply their craft on stage in the University's active production season.

The Bachelor of Fine Arts in Music Theatre is for the student who aspires to a performance career in music theatre. This well-rounded preprofessional curriculum requires each student to enroll in a balanced mix of theatre, music, and dance courses, including both applied skills courses like acting, voice lessons, and modern dance and academically oriented courses like dramatic theory, history, and literature. All students are also

exposed to the technical and design areas through course work and production experiences. In addition to intensive course work, B.F.A. Music Theatre students often have the opportunity to apply their craft on stage in the University's active production season.

The Bachelor of Fine Arts in Theatre Design and Technology is for the student who aspires to a career as a designer or technician for the theatre. This well-rounded preprofessional curriculum includes applied training in drawing, rendering, stage craft, construction, drafting, and painting as well as academically oriented courses like dramatic theory, history, and literature. All design/tech students also receive some performance training and have the opportunity to audition for roles. In addition to intensive course work, B.F.A. designers and technicians often have the opportunity to apply their crafts behind the scenes in the University's active production season.

The minor in theatre arts is for students majoring in another field but who wish to pursue their theatrical interest at the college level. Theatre minors take a sampling of performance, technical, and academic courses in theatre and participate actively in the production season.

The minor in theatre dance provides students with training in performance, dance technique (modern, jazz, tap, and ballet), and choreography. It encompasses the physical workings of the body in dance technique as well as the creative and theatrical aspects of the discipline.

The minor in arts management (offered with the Department of Business Administration) is for the student who aspires to manage his or her own theatre, work in arts development, or fulfill any management function within a professional theatre. It is an excellent complement to the B.A. in Theatre Arts.

**Campus and Surroundings** Illinois Wesleyan University is located on a parklike campus in Bloomington's historic northside residential district. The twin cities of Bloomington/Normal, with a combined population of over 125,000, offer all the amenities and cultural activities found in a major metropolitan area. The cities are located midway between Chicago and St. Louis, which are easily accessed by car, bus, or train within 2–3 hours.

**Program Facilities** The School of Theatre Arts has a variety of performance facilities, including the McPherson Theatre, a fully equipped 280-seat proscenium/thrust theatre; the Kirkpatrick Laboratory Theatre, a black-box theatre with flexible seating; the Phoenix Theatre, for experimental theatre productions; and the Dance Studios, used primarily for dance rehearsals.

**Faculty, Resident Artists, and Alumni** Recent graduates have pursued graduate studies at Yale School of Drama, New York University, Opera Institute at Boston University, Indiana University, and University of California, Davis, among others. IWU alumni include Richard Jenkins, *The Visitor, Six Feet Under;* Frankie Faison, *The Wire, Mississippi Burning, The Thomas Crown Affair;* Amanda Denhert, Professor of Theatre at Northwestern University; Mariann Mayberry, Steppenwolf Theatre; Anne Girard, Writer, *Blue Collar TV;* Kevin Dunn, *Transformers, Dave, Godzilla,* and *The Black Dahlia.*

**Special Programs** Illinois Wesleyan students also pursue a number of off-campus opportunities, including internships (in Chicago, New York and San Francisco), study abroad (in places such as Dublin, Moscow, and London), and summer work. Recently, students have worked in the summer at Steppenwolf Theatre Company (Chicago), Rocky Mountain Repertory (Colorado), St. Louis Shakespeare (Missouri), Bigfork Summer Playhouse (Montana) Great River Shakespeare (Minnesota), and Maine State Music Theatre (Maine), among many locations.

# Ithaca College

**Ithaca, New York**

Independent, coed. Small town campus. Total enrollment: 6,660. Theater program established 1927.

**Degrees** Bachelor of Fine Arts in the areas of acting, musical theater, theatrical production arts. Majors and concentrations: acting, music theater, theater design, theater production, theater technology. Cross-registration with Cornell University, Wells College. Program accredited by NAST.

**Enrollment** 264 total; 146 undergraduate, 118 nonprofessional degree.

**Theater Student Profile** 61% females, 39% males, 14% minorities, 1% international.

**Theater Faculty** 19 undergraduate (full-time), 9 undergraduate (part-time). 95% of full-time faculty have terminal degrees. Graduate students do not teach undergraduate courses. Undergraduate student–faculty ratio: 12:1.

**Student Life** Student groups/activities include American College Theatre Festival, No Bucks Theater, IC Triple Threat Theater.

**Expenses for 2007–2008** Application fee: $60. Comprehensive fee: $39,398 includes full-time tuition ($28,670) and college room and board ($10,728). College room only: $5604.

**Financial Aid** Program-specific awards: 2 Peter Bergstrom Scholarships for acting or musical theater majors ($3300), 5 Richard M. Clark Memorial Scholarships for talented program majors ($1700–$3045), 1 George Hoerner Memorial Scholarship for technical theater and scenic design major ($2228), 1 Theater Arts Alumni Memorial Scholarship for junior or senior theater arts major ($2430), 25 Jane Woods Werly Memorial Scholarships for sophomore, junior, or senior musical theater majors ($770–$5300), 12 Ithaca Premier Talent Scholarships for theater arts majors ($10,000–$16,000), 1 Cissy Cheskis Scholarship for theater arts major ($700), 1 Laura Hinkley Hauer '21 Scholarship for theater arts major ($770), Friars Scholarships for theater arts majors, 1 Katherine B. "Toby" Clarey Memorial Scholarship for talented acting or musical theater major ($1355).

**Application Procedures** Students admitted directly into the professional program freshman year. Deadline for freshmen: February 1; transfers: March 1. Notification date for freshmen: April 15. Required: essay, high school transcript, college transcript(s) for transfer students, letter of recommendation, SAT or ACT test scores, audition for acting and musical theater applicants, portfolio and interview for production arts applicants. Recommended: minimum 3.0 high school GPA. Auditions held 15-20 times for acting and musical theater applicants on campus and off campus in New York, NY; Houston, TX; Dallas, TX; Washington, DC; Chicago, IL; Los Angeles, CA; videotaped performances are permissible as a substitute for live auditions when distance is prohibitive. Portfolio reviews held 15-20 times and by appointment on campus and off campus in New York, NY; Houston, TX; Dallas, TX; Washington, DC; Chicago, IL; Los Angeles, CA; the submission of slides may be substituted for portfolios when distance is prohibitive.

**Web Site** http://www.ithaca.edu/lis.php

**Undergraduate Contact** Mr. Gerard Turbide, Director, Admission, Ithaca College, 100 Job Hall, Ithaca, New York 14850-7020; 607 274-3124, fax: 607-274-1900, e-mail address: admission@ithaca.edu

## More About the College

The Department of Theatre Arts offers a powerful combination of intensive classroom and performance experience that has made it one of the most effective and highly respected training programs in the nation. The goal is to prepare students for careers in the theater and entertainment businesses. It is a highly selective program, taught by faculty members whose academic training and professional theater experience have prepared them for the focused, personalized instruction that is the key to successful theatrical training.

The Bachelor of Fine Arts programs in acting and musical theater are performance oriented, providing professional training and experience. The Bachelor of Fine Arts in theatrical production arts and the Bachelor of Science in theater arts management prepare students to enter the design, technical, and managerial areas of the theater and entertainment industry. As with other programs at Ithaca College, the emphasis is on learning by doing. Students pursuing the technology concentration in production, for example, are involved in scenic carpentry, costume construction, drafting, electronics, sound, properties, stage management, and technical direction. The theatrical design concentration provides instruction in scenic design, costume design, lighting design,

*Ithaca College (continued)*

figure drawing, rendering, and art history, in addition to the technical areas. Students pursuing the Bachelor of Science in theater arts management have the opportunity to develop knowledge in marketing, advertising, publicity, fundraising, grant writing, accounting, personnel management, and other areas. For students who elect the liberal arts–based drama degree, courses include directing, acting, theater history, stagecraft, dramatic literature, dance, stage management, dramaturgy, and playwriting.

In addition to the annual senior showcase for New York City agents and casting directors, students and faculty members travel to see plays and participate in special theater events. Faculty members advise students about summer stock opportunities, graduate program admission, and work after graduation, taking extra time with individual students to prepare them for auditions or interviews. Design, technical, and theater arts management students have an outstanding record of acceptance at some of the nation's finest graduate programs.

Students direct all No Bucks Theatre productions; seniors may also direct studio theater productions. Student playwrights are encouraged to submit their plays for production.

Theater students may take advantage of courses outside their major within the School of Humanities and Sciences or in the College's Schools of Business, Communications, Health Sciences and Human Performance, and Music and the Division of Interdisciplinary and International Studies. A comprehensive college, Ithaca offers some 2,000 courses and more than 100 different degree programs. Theater students may be particularly interested in exploring communications courses in areas such as audio production or film directing.

The city of Ithaca is one of the country's premier college towns, with about 26,000 students at Ithaca College and Cornell University. Surrounded by magnificent gorges, lakes, and countryside in the Finger Lakes region of New York State, Ithaca is a thriving cultural center. The community supports an impressive array of concerts, gallery shows, and movies as well as theater productions mounted by two local theater companies.

The combination of excellent undergraduate theater programs, a vibrant community, and a beautiful location make Ithaca College an exceptional choice for talented and motivated young artists who wish to make the theater and entertainment business their profession.

**Program Facilities** Performance facilities at Ithaca include a 520-seat proscenium theater, a 280-seat flexible theater, and a small studio theater, all featuring state-of-the-art equipment. Modern studios for acting, dance, and design combine with shops and workrooms for scenery, costumes, sound, electrics, and props to create a stimulating environment for artistic work. The school is a fully accredited member of the National Association of Schools of Theatre.

**Faculty, Resident Artists, and Alumni** With 18 full-time theater faculty members and an extensive professional staff, the Department of Theatre Arts offers small classes and individualized instruction. Since there are no graduate students, many production opportunities in acting, directing, managing, technical direction, and design exist for the undergraduate student. Guest artists regularly visit campus, sharing their experience and insights and becoming valuable professional contacts. Ithaca alumni in the theater and entertainment world also actively provide career assistance.

**Student Performance Opportunities** The main-stage season includes six productions; the studio season, six to eight productions. The department, the College, and the local community offer many additional opportunities.

**Special Programs** One of the most popular options for theater students is a semester at Ithaca College's London Center. Students spend their time studying and seeing plays—as many as twenty-five productions in a semester. Senior theater majors have an opportunity to participate in a field study for a week in New York City. Ithaca alumni discuss the theater and entertainment business, and qualified acting and musical theater majors present their annual showcase for agents and casting directors at an off Broadway theater.

# Jacksonville University
## Jacksonville, Florida

Independent, coed. Suburban campus. Total enrollment: 3,436.
**Degrees** Bachelor of Fine Arts in the area of theater arts. Majors and concentrations: theater arts studies.
**Enrollment** 40 total; all undergraduate.
**Theater Student Profile** 58% females, 42% males, 27% minorities, 3% international.
**Theater Faculty** 4 undergraduate (full-time). 100% of full-time faculty have terminal degrees. Graduate students do not teach undergraduate courses. Undergraduate student–faculty ratio: 10:1.
**Student Life** Student groups/activities include Alpha Psi Omega, theater productions, performance outreach to local schools.
**Expenses for 2008–2009** Application fee: $30. Comprehensive fee: $32,660 includes full-time tuition ($23,900) and college room and board ($8760). College room only: $5000.
**Financial Aid** Program-specific awards: 7 Theater Scholarships for those demonstrating need/talent ($1000–$2000).
**Application Procedures** Students admitted directly into the professional program freshman year. Deadline for freshmen and transfers: continuous. Notification date for freshmen and transfers: continuous. Required: high school transcript, college transcript(s) for transfer students, minimum 2.0 high school GPA, audition, SAT or ACT test scores. Recommended: essay, minimum 3.0 high school GPA, letter of recommendation. Auditions held by appointment on campus; videotaped performances are permissible as a substitute for live auditions if visit to campus is not possible.
**Web Site** http://www.ju.edu
**Undergraduate Contact** Miriam King, Vice President of Enrollment Management, Jacksonville University, 2800 University Boulevard North, Jacksonville, Florida 32211; 904-745-7000, fax: 904-745-7012.

# Johnny Carson School of Theatre and Film

See University of Nebraska–Lincoln

# Johnson State College
## Johnson, Vermont

State-supported, coed. Rural campus. Total enrollment: 1,867.
Theater program established 1982.
**Web Site** http://www.johnsonstatecollege.edu/

# Jordan College of Fine Arts - Department of Theatre

See Butler University

# The Juilliard School
## New York, New York

Independent, coed. Urban campus. Total enrollment: 832.
Theater program established 1968.
**Degrees** Artist's Diploma in the area of playwriting; Bachelor of Fine Arts in the area of drama. Majors and concentrations: theater arts/drama. Cross-registration with Barnard and Columbia Colleges (Columbia University).
**Enrollment** 81 total; 73 undergraduate, 8 graduate.
**Theater Student Profile** 47% females, 53% males, 40% minorities, 5% international.

**Theater Faculty** 21 total (full-time), 5 total (part-time). Graduate students do not teach undergraduate courses. Undergraduate student–faculty ratio: 3:1.

**Student Life** Student groups/activities include public drama performances, Cabaret performance, collaboration between undergraduate actors and graduate playwrights. Special housing available for theater students.

**Expenses for 2007–2008** Application fee: $100. Comprehensive fee: $37,890 includes full-time tuition ($27,150) and college room and board ($10,740).

**Financial Aid** Program-specific awards: 70 merit and need-based awards for program majors ($30,188).

**Application Procedures** Students admitted directly into the professional program freshman year. Deadline for freshmen: December 1. Notification date for freshmen: April 1. Required: essay, high school transcript, college transcript(s) for transfer students, letter of recommendation, audition, resumé, TOEFL for all non-native English speakers. Recommended: photo. Auditions held once on campus and off campus in Chicago, IL; San Francisco, CA.

**Web Site** http://www.juilliard.edu

**Undergraduate Contact** Ms. Lee Cioppa, Associate Dean for Admissions, The Juilliard School, 60 Lincoln Center Plaza, New York, New York 10023-6588; 212-799-5000 ext. 223, fax: 212-769-6420, e-mail address: admissions@juilliard.edu

## Kent State University

### Kent, Ohio

State-supported, coed. Suburban campus. Total enrollment: 22,819. Theater program established 1983.

**Degrees** Bachelor of Fine Arts in the areas of design/technology, musical theater. Majors and concentrations: design technology, entertainment arts, music theater, theater arts/drama. Graduate degrees offered: Master of Fine Arts in the areas of acting, design/technology. Program accredited by NAST, NASD.

**Enrollment** 200 total; 35 undergraduate, 15 graduate, 150 nonprofessional degree.

**Theater Student Profile** 57% females, 43% males, 12% minorities, 1% international.

**Theater Faculty** 13 total (full-time), 5 total (part-time). 94% of full-time faculty have terminal degrees. Graduate students teach a few undergraduate courses. Undergraduate student–faculty ratio: 15:1.

**Student Life** Student groups/activities include Alpha Psi Omega, United States Institute for Theatre Technology, Musical Theatre Students Organization. Special housing available for theater students.

**Expenses for 2008–2009** Application fee: $30. State resident tuition: $8430 full-time. Nonresident tuition: $15,862 full-time. College room and board: $7200. College room only: $4410. Special program-related fees: $25–$50 per semester for design technology courses (materials).

**Financial Aid** Program-specific awards: 12 Creative Arts Awards for program majors ($1800–$3300).

**Application Procedures** Students admitted directly into the professional program freshman year. Deadline for freshmen and transfers: continuous. Required: high school transcript, college transcript(s) for transfer students, minimum 2.0 high school GPA, audition, portfolio, SAT or ACT test scores (minimum composite ACT score of 21), completion of college preparatory courses. Recommended: minimum 3.0 high school GPA, 3 letters of recommendation, interview. Auditions held twice on campus and off campus in Southeastern Theatre Conference sites, Ohio Theatre Alliance sites, United States Institute for Theatre Technology Conference sites. Portfolio reviews held twice on campus and off campus in Southeastern Theatre Conference sites, United States Institute for Theatre Technology Conference sites; the submission of slides may be substituted for portfolios when distance is prohibitive.

**Web Site** http://www.theatre.kent.edu

**Undergraduate Contact** Prof. Steve Zapytowski, Undergraduate Coordinator, School of Theatre and Dance, Kent State University, PO Box 5190, Kent, Ohio 44242-0001; 330-672-2082, fax: 330-672-2889, e-mail address: szapytow@kent.edu

**Graduate Contact** Dr. Rosemarie K. Bank, Graduate Coordinator, School of Theatre and Dance, Kent State University, PO Box 5190, Kent, Ohio 44242; 330-672-2082, fax: 330-672-2889, e-mail address: rbank@kent.edu

## Lamar D. Fain College of Fine Arts

See Midwestern State University

## Leigh Gerdine College of Fine Arts

See Webster University

## Lindenwood University

### St. Charles, Missouri

Independent Presbyterian, coed. Suburban campus. Total enrollment: 9,633.

**Degrees** Bachelor of Fine Arts in the area of theater. Majors and concentrations: acting, arts management, design, directing, music theater, technical theater, theater education. Graduate degrees offered: Master of Fine Arts in the area of theater. Cross-registration with Maryville University of St. Louis, Missouri Baptist College, Fontbonne University, Webster University, Missouri Valley College.

**Theater Faculty** 5 undergraduate (full-time), 3 undergraduate (part-time), 5 graduate (full-time), 3 graduate (part-time). 90% of full-time faculty have terminal degrees. Graduate students do not teach undergraduate courses.

**Student Life** Student groups/activities include mainstage and black box productions, dinner theater productions, musical theater productions.

**Expenses for 2008–2009** Application fee: $30. Comprehensive fee: $19,500 includes full-time tuition ($12,700), mandatory fees ($300), and college room and board ($6500). College room only: $3400. Special program-related fees: $25–$65 per class for computer studio fees, make-up kit fees.

**Financial Aid** Program-specific awards: talent awards and scholarships for high school students, talent awards and scholarships for transfer students.

**Application Procedures** Students admitted directly into the professional program freshman year. Deadline for freshmen and transfers: continuous. Required: high school transcript, college transcript(s) for transfer students, minimum 2.0 high school GPA, interview, audition, ACT test score only. Recommended: essay, minimum 3.0 high school GPA, letter of recommendation. Auditions held continuously on campus and off campus in various locations; recorded music is permissible as a substitute for live auditions when distance is prohibitive and videotaped performances are permissible as a substitute for live auditions when distance is prohibitive. Portfolio reviews held continuously on campus and off campus in various locations; the submission of slides may be substituted for portfolios when distance is prohibitive.

**Web Site** http://www.lindenwood.edu/

**Undergraduate Contact** Mr. Ted Gregory, Director, Theatre Department, Lindenwood University, 209 South Kings Highway, St. Charles, Missouri 63301; 636-949-4966, fax: 636-949-4910, e-mail address: tgregory@lindenwood.edu

## Long Island University, C.W. Post Campus

### Brookville, New York

Independent, coed. Suburban campus. Total enrollment: 8,361.

**Degrees** Bachelor of Fine Arts in the area of theater. Majors and concentrations: acting, arts management, dance, film, production/design, theater arts/drama. Graduate degrees offered: Master of Arts in the area of theater.

**Enrollment** 127 total; 120 undergraduate, 7 graduate.

**Theater Student Profile** 59% females, 41% males, 30% minorities, 5% international.

*Long Island University, C.W. Post Campus (continued)*

**Theater Faculty** 9 total (full-time), 9 total (part-time). 90% of full-time faculty have terminal degrees. Graduate students do not teach undergraduate courses. Undergraduate student–faculty ratio: 7:1.

**Student Life** Student groups/activities include Post Theatre Students Association, American College Theatre Festival.

**Expenses for 2007–2008** Application fee: $30. Comprehensive fee: $35,550 includes full-time tuition ($24,700), mandatory fees ($1250), and college room and board ($9600). College room only: $6320. Room and board charges vary according to board plan and housing facility. Special program-related fees: $60–$75 per semester for production materials, $65 per class for dance accompanists.

**Financial Aid** Program-specific awards: 15 Theatre Department Awards for program majors ($1000–$2000).

**Application Procedures** Students admitted directly into the professional program freshman year. Deadline for freshmen and transfers: continuous. Notification date for freshmen and transfers: continuous. Required: essay, high school transcript, college transcript(s) for transfer students, minimum 2.0 high school GPA, 2 letters of recommendation, interview, video, audition, SAT or ACT test scores, audition and interview for acting applicants, portfolio for design production majors. Recommended: minimum 3.0 high school GPA. Auditions held 6 times on campus and off campus in Southeastern Theatre Conference sites, Texas Magnet School auditions, International Thespian Society sites; recorded music is permissible as a substitute for live auditions if a campus visit is impossible and videotaped performances are permissible as a substitute for live auditions if a campus visit is impossible. Portfolio reviews held by appointment on campus and off campus in International Thespian Society sites, Texas Magnate auditions, Southeastern Theatre Conference auditions; the submission of slides may be substituted for portfolios if a campus visit is impossible.

**Web Site** http://www.liu.edu

**Undergraduate Contact** Gary Bergman, Associate Provost for Enrollment Services, Admissions, Long Island University, C.W. Post Campus, 720 Northern Boulevard, Brookville, New York 11548; 516-299-2900, fax: 516-299-2418, e-mail address: enroll@cwpost.liu.edu

**Graduate Contact** Dr. Cara Gargano, Chair, Department of Theatre, Film, and Dance, Long Island University, C.W. Post Campus, 720 Northern Boulevard, Brookville, New York 11548; 516-299-2353, fax: 516-299-3824.

# Longwood University
## Farmville, Virginia

State-supported, coed. Total enrollment: 4,727. Theater program established 1966.

**Degrees** Bachelor of Arts in the area of theatre; Bachelor of Fine Arts in the area of theatre. Majors and concentrations: performance, technical theater/stage management, theater education. Cross-registration with Hampden-Sydney College. Program accredited by NAST.

**Enrollment** 50 total; 20 undergraduate, 30 nonprofessional degree.

**Theater Student Profile** 56% females, 44% males, 2% minorities.

**Theater Faculty** 4 undergraduate (full-time), 2 undergraduate (part-time). 100% of full-time faculty have terminal degrees. Graduate students do not teach undergraduate courses. Undergraduate student–faculty ratio: 12:1.

**Student Life** Student groups/activities include Alpha Psi Omega. Special housing available for theater students.

**Expenses for 2007–2008** Application fee: $40. State resident tuition: $4249 full-time. Nonresident tuition: $12,450 full-time. Mandatory fees: $3809 full-time. Full-time tuition and fees vary according to course load. College room and board: $6740. College room only: $3840. Room and board charges vary according to board plan, housing facility, and course load.

**Application Procedures** Students apply for admission into the professional program by sophomore year. Deadline for freshmen and transfers: continuous. Notification date for freshmen and transfers: June 1. Required: essay, high school transcript, college transcript(s) for transfer students, SAT or ACT test scores, minimum 2.3 college GPA for transfers, minimum 2.5 high school GPA. Recommended: minimum 3.0 high school GPA.

**Web Site** http://www.longwood.edu/theatre

**Undergraduate Contact** Dr. Gene Muto, Theatre Program Coordinator, Department of Communication Studies and Theatre, Longwood University, 201 High Street, Farmville, Virginia 23909-1899; 434-395-2643, fax: 434-395-2680, e-mail address: theatre@longwood.edu

# Marshall University
## Huntington, West Virginia

State-supported, coed. Urban campus. Total enrollment: 13,808. Theater program established 1933.

**Degrees** Bachelor of Fine Arts in the area of theater. Majors and concentrations: performance, theater production.

**Enrollment** 55 total; all undergraduate.

**Theater Student Profile** 60% females, 40% males, 4% minorities.

**Theater Faculty** 5 undergraduate (full-time), 5 undergraduate (part-time). 80% of full-time faculty have terminal degrees. Graduate students do not teach undergraduate courses. Undergraduate student–faculty ratio: 11:1.

**Student Life** Student groups/activities include United States Institute for Theater Technology (USITT), West Virginia Theater Conference/Southeastern Theatre Conference, American College Theater Festival (ACTF).

**Expenses for 2007–2008** Application fee: $30. State resident tuition: $4360 full-time. Nonresident tuition: $11,264 full-time. Mandatory fees: $200 full-time. Full-time tuition and fees vary according to degree level, location, program, and reciprocity agreements. College room and board: $6818. College room only: $3944. Room and board charges vary according to board plan and housing facility. Special program-related fees: $25 per credit for specialized supplies.

**Financial Aid** Program-specific awards: 10 tuition waivers for program majors ($500–$6000), 6 theater stipends for program majors ($500–$2000), 8 theater scholarships for program majors ($1500).

**Application Procedures** Students apply for admission into the professional program by sophomore year. Deadline for freshmen and transfers: continuous. Notification date for freshmen and transfers: continuous. Required: high school transcript, college transcript(s) for transfer students, minimum 2.0 high school GPA, SAT or ACT test scores (minimum composite ACT score of 21). Recommended: letter of recommendation, interview, audition, portfolio. Auditions held upon request on campus and off campus; videotaped performances are permissible as a substitute for live auditions if a campus visit is impossible. Portfolio reviews held upon request on campus; the submission of slides may be substituted for portfolios if a campus visit is impossible.

**Web Site** http://www.marshall.edu/cofa/

**Undergraduate Contact** Howard L. Reynolds, Chair, Theatre Department, Marshall University, One John Marshall Drive, Huntington, West Virginia 25755-2240; 304-696-2546, fax: 304-696-6582, e-mail address: reynoldsh@marshall.edu

# Mars Hill College
## Mars Hill, North Carolina

Independent Baptist, coed. Small town campus. Total enrollment: 1,250. Theater program established 1980.

**Web Site** http://www.mhc.edu/

# Marymount Manhattan College
## New York, New York

Independent, coed. Urban campus. Total enrollment: 1,895. Theater program established 1977.

**Degrees** Bachelor of Fine Arts. Majors and concentrations: acting. Cross-registration with Hunter College of the City University of New York.

**Enrollment** 435 total; 156 undergraduate, 279 nonprofessional degree.

**Theater Student Profile** 61% females, 39% males, 18% minorities, 5% international.
**Theater Faculty** 15 undergraduate (full-time), 60 undergraduate (part-time). 80% of full-time faculty have terminal degrees. Graduate students do not teach undergraduate courses. Undergraduate student–faculty ratio: 12:1.
**Student Life** Student groups/activities include STAM (Student Theatre at Marymount), MMC Shakespeare Company.
**Expenses for 2007–2008** Application fee: $60. Comprehensive fee: $32,850 includes full-time tuition ($19,666), mandatory fees ($934), and college room and board ($12,250). College room only: $10,250. Special program-related fees: $15 per credit for studio/performance courses.
**Financial Aid** Program-specific awards: competitive merit scholarships for freshmen program majors ($1000–$4000), transfer competitive merit scholarships for transfer program majors ($1000–$4000).
**Application Procedures** Students admitted directly into the professional program freshman year. Deadline for freshmen and transfers: March 4. Notification date for freshmen and transfers: continuous. Required: essay, high school transcript, college transcript(s) for transfer students, letter of recommendation, interview, audition, SAT or ACT test scores, minimum 2.8 high school GPA. Recommended: minimum 3.0 high school GPA. Auditions held 6 times on campus and off campus in Dallas, TX; Chicago, IL; San Francisco, CA; videotaped performances are permissible as a substitute for live auditions when distance is prohibitive.
**Web Site** http://marymount.mmm.edu
**Undergraduate Contact** Prof. David Mold, Director of Theater Admissions, Theatre Arts Department, Marymount Manhattan College, 221 East 71st Street, New York, New York 10021; 212-774-0767, fax: 212-774-0770, e-mail address: theatre@mmm.edu

## Rutgers, The State University of New Jersey
# Mason Gross School of the Arts
### New Brunswick, New Jersey

State-supported, coed. Small town campus. Theater program established 1976.
**Degrees** Bachelor of Fine Arts in the area of theater arts. Majors and concentrations: acting, design technology, production and management specialties, stage management. Graduate degrees offered: Master of Fine Arts in the area of theater arts.
**Enrollment** 272 total; 122 undergraduate, 74 graduate, 76 nonprofessional degree.
**Theater Student Profile** 49% females, 51% males, 22% minorities.
**Theater Faculty** 16 total (full-time), 35 total (part-time). Graduate students do not teach undergraduate courses. Undergraduate student–faculty ratio: 15:1.
**Student Life** Special housing available for theater students.
**Expenses for 2007–2008** Special program-related fees: $30–$100 per year for class supplies, models, transportation to museums, salon costumes, tickets, $3300 per year for professional acting program fee.
**Application Procedures** Students admitted directly into the professional program freshman year. Deadline for freshmen: continuous; transfers: March 15. Required: high school transcript, college transcript(s) for transfer students, minimum 2.0 high school GPA, SAT or ACT test scores, audition for acting majors, portfolio for design majors, interview for production and design majors. Recommended: essay, 2 letters of recommendation. Auditions held one weekend in late February on campus and off campus in New York, NY; Chicago, IL; San Francisco, CA; Los Angeles, CA; Miami, FL; videotaped performances are permissible as a substitute for live auditions when distance is prohibitive. Portfolio reviews held by appointment on campus; the submission of slides may be substituted for portfolios when distance is prohibitive.
**Web Site** http://mgsa.rutgers.edu/theater/thea.html
**Undergraduate Contact** Assistant Vice President for University Undergraduate Admissions, Rutgers, The State University of New Jersey, Mason Gross School of the Arts, PO Box 2101, New Brunswick, New Jersey 08901-8527; 732-445-3770, fax: 732-445-0237.

**Graduate Contact** Mr. Donald J. Taylor, Director of Graduate and Professional Admissions, Rutgers, The State University of New Jersey, Mason Gross School of the Arts, Van Nest Hall, Room 204, New Brunswick, New Jersey 08901-8527; 732-932-7711, fax: 732-932-8231.

# Meadows School of the Arts
See Southern Methodist University

## Lamar D. Fain College of Fine Arts
# Midwestern State University
### Wichita Falls, Texas

State-supported, coed. Urban campus. Total enrollment: 6,027.
**Web Site** http://www.mwsu.edu/

# Millikin University
### Decatur, Illinois

Independent, coed. Suburban campus. Total enrollment: 2,376. Theater program established 1985.
**Degrees** Bachelor of Arts in the area of theatre; Bachelor of Fine Arts in the areas of musical theatre, acting, technical theatre, directing, theatre administration, stage management. Majors and concentrations: acting, music theater, stage management, theater arts administration, theater arts/drama, theater design/technology.
**Enrollment** 200 total; 120 undergraduate, 80 nonprofessional degree.
**Theater Student Profile** 66% females, 34% males, 5% minorities, 1% international.
**Theater Faculty** 12 undergraduate (full-time), 5 undergraduate (part-time). 100% of full-time faculty have terminal degrees. Graduate students do not teach undergraduate courses. Undergraduate student–faculty ratio: 16:1.
**Student Life** Student groups/activities include Alpha Psi Omega, Children's Theater, Opera Theatre.
**Expenses for 2007–2008** Application fee: $0. Comprehensive fee: $31,055 includes full-time tuition ($23,250), mandatory fees ($595), and college room and board ($7210). College room only: $4010. Full-time tuition and fees vary according to course load. Room and board charges vary according to board plan and housing facility.
**Financial Aid** Program-specific awards: 135 talent awards for musical theatre, acting, directing majors ($1200–$2000), 10 talent awards for technology majors ($2000).
**Application Procedures** Students admitted directly into the professional program freshman year. Deadline for freshmen and transfers: continuous. Required: high school transcript, letter of recommendation, interview, audition, portfolio, SAT or ACT test scores. Auditions held continuously until deadline on campus and off campus in Louisville, KY; Normal, IL; Urbana, IL; Plano, TX; Birmingham, AL. Portfolio reviews held continuously for technology applicants on campus and off campus in Louisville, KY; Normal, IL; Urbana, IL.
**Web Site** http://www.millikin.edu
**Undergraduate Contact** Laura Ledford, Chair, Department of Theatre and Dance, Millikin University, 1184 West Main Street, Decatur, Illinois 62522; 217-424-6282, fax: 217-424-3993, e-mail address: lledford@millikin.edu

# Nebraska Wesleyan University
### Lincoln, Nebraska

Independent United Methodist, coed. Suburban campus. Total enrollment: 2,107. Theater program established 1958.
**Degrees** Bachelor of Fine Arts in the area of theater. Majors and concentrations: acting, creative writing, directing, music theater, production management, theater design/technology, theater management. Cross-registration with University of Nebraska-Lincoln.

*Nebraska Wesleyan University (continued)*

**Enrollment** 75 total; 40 undergraduate, 35 nonprofessional degree.

**Theater Student Profile** 54% females, 46% males, 5% minorities, 2% international.

**Theater Faculty** 5 undergraduate (full-time), 4 undergraduate (part-time). 100% of full-time faculty have terminal degrees. Graduate students do not teach undergraduate courses. Undergraduate student–faculty ratio: 8:1.

**Student Life** Student groups/activities include Wesleyan Theatre Company (service organization), American College Theatre Festival.

**Expenses for 2007–2008** Application fee: $20. One-time mandatory fee: $120. Comprehensive fee: $25,592 includes full-time tuition ($19,930), mandatory fees ($322), and college room and board ($5340). Full-time tuition and fees vary according to class time, course load, degree level, location, and program. Room and board charges vary according to board plan.

**Financial Aid** Program-specific awards: 10–15 theater scholarships for program majors ($1250).

**Application Procedures** Students admitted directly into the professional program freshman year. Deadline for freshmen and transfers: May 1. Notification date for freshmen and transfers: continuous. Required: essay, high school transcript, college transcript(s) for transfer students, minimum 3.0 high school GPA, 2 letters of recommendation, interview, SAT or ACT test scores (minimum composite ACT score of 20). Recommended: audition, portfolio. Auditions held by appointment on campus; videotaped performances are permissible as a substitute for live auditions when distance is prohibitive. Portfolio reviews held by appointment on campus; the submission of slides may be substituted for portfolios.

**Web Site** http://www.nebrwesleyan.edu/depts/commta/

**Undergraduate Contact** Dr. Jay Scott Chipman, Director of Theatre, Communication and Theatre Arts Department, Nebraska Wesleyan University, 5000 St. Paul Avenue, Lincoln, Nebraska 68504; 402-465-2386, fax: 402-456-2179, e-mail address: jsc@nebrwesleyan.edu

# New World School of the Arts
## Miami, Florida

State-supported, coed. Urban campus. Total enrollment: 416. Theater program established 1988.

**Degrees** Bachelor of Fine Arts in the area of theater. Majors and concentrations: acting, music theater. Mandatory cross-registration with University of Florida, Miami Dade College. Program accredited by NAST.

**Enrollment** 72 total; all undergraduate.

**Theater Student Profile** 54% females, 46% males, 38% minorities, 4% international.

**Theater Faculty** 5 undergraduate (full-time), 20 undergraduate (part-time). 90% of full-time faculty have terminal degrees. Graduate students do not teach undergraduate courses. Undergraduate student–faculty ratio: 3:1.

**Student Life** Student groups/activities include Florida Theatre Association, State Thespians, Florida Association of Theater Education.

**Expenses for 2007–2008** Application fee: $0. State resident tuition: $3000 full-time. Nonresident tuition: $10,000 full-time.

**Financial Aid** Program-specific awards: 1 Robert Brenner Merit Scholarship for music theater majors ($1000), 1 Annett Foosaner Merit Scholarship for program majors ($1000), 2 Donald Khan Merit Scholarships for program majors ($1000), 1 Betty Ann Merit Scholarship for program majors ($1000), 1 Douglas Fairbanks/Southern Bell Merit Scholarship for program majors ($1000), 1 Tommy Tune Merit Scholarship for music theater majors ($500), 1 George Abbott Merit Scholarship for music theater majors ($500), 4 Nations Bank Merit Scholarships for program majors ($2000), 25 Miami-Dade Community College Merit Scholarships for program majors ($1500).

**Application Procedures** Students admitted directly into the professional program freshman year. Deadline for freshmen and transfers: continuous. Notification date for freshmen and transfers: continuous. Required: essay, high school transcript, college transcript(s) for transfer students, 2 letters of recommendation, audition. Recommended: minimum 2.0 high school GPA, interview, SAT or ACT test scores. Auditions held continuously on campus and off campus in Southeastern Theatre Conference sites and Florida Theatre Conference sites; videotaped performances are permissible as a substitute for live auditions for out-of-state applicants.

**Web Site** http://www.mdc.edu/nwsa

**Undergraduate Contact** Pamela Neumann, Recruitment and Admissions Coordinator, Student Services, New World School of the Arts, 300 NE 2nd Avenue, Miami, Florida 33132; 305-237-7007, fax: 305-237-3794, e-mail address: nwsaadm@mdc.edu

*Tisch School of the Arts, Department of Drama, Undergraduate*
# New York University
## New York, New York

Independent, coed. Urban campus. Total enrollment: 41,783. Theater program established 1974.

**Degrees** Bachelor of Fine Arts. Majors and concentrations: theater.

**Enrollment** 1,358 total; all undergraduate.

**Theater Faculty** 37 undergraduate (full-time), 89 undergraduate (part-time). 63% of full-time faculty have terminal degrees. Graduate students teach a few undergraduate courses. Undergraduate student–faculty ratio: 10:1.

**Student Life** Student groups/activities include Community Connections, Tisch Talent Guild, The Collective.

**Expenses for 2007–2008** Application fee: $65. Comprehensive fee: $47,490 includes full-time tuition ($33,268), mandatory fees ($2022), and college room and board ($12,200). Full-time tuition and fees vary according to course load and program. Room and board charges vary according to board plan and housing facility.

**Application Procedures** Students admitted directly into the professional program freshman year. Deadline for freshmen: January 15; transfers: April 1. Notification date for freshmen: April 1; transfers: May 15. Required: essay, high school transcript, college transcript(s) for transfer students, 2 letters of recommendation, interview, audition, SAT or ACT test scores, artistic review as described on Web site. Recommended: minimum 3.0 high school GPA. Auditions held continuously from 2 1/2 months on campus and off campus in Chicago, IL; San Francisco, CA; Atlanta, GA; Los Angeles, CA; Houston, TX; videotaped performances are permissible as a substitute for live auditions when live audition is not possible.

**Web Site** http://drama.tisch.nyu.edu

**Undergraduate Contact** Ms. Patricia A. Decker, Director of Recruitment, Tisch School of the Arts, New York University, 721 Broadway, 8th Floor, New York, New York 10003-6807; 212-998-1900, fax: 212-995-4060, e-mail address: tisch.recruitment@nyu.edu

*Tisch School of the Arts, Rita and Burton Goldberg Department of Dramatic Writing*
# New York University
## New York, New York

Independent, coed. Urban campus. Total enrollment: 41,783. Theater program established 1980.

**Degrees** Bachelor of Fine Arts. Majors and concentrations: dramatic writing. Graduate degrees offered: Master of Fine Arts in the area of dramatic writing.

**Enrollment** 250 total; 206 undergraduate, 44 graduate.

**Theater Student Profile** 49% females, 51% males, 16% minorities, 4% international.

**Theater Faculty** 14 undergraduate (full-time), 20 undergraduate (part-time), 15 graduate (full-time), 26 graduate (part-time). 100% of full-time faculty have terminal degrees. Graduate students teach a few undergraduate courses. Undergraduate student–faculty ratio: 5:1.

**Student Life** Student groups/activities include Community Connections, The Collective, Tisch Talent Guild.

**Expenses for 2007–2008** Application fee: $65. Comprehensive fee: $47,490 includes full-time tuition ($33,268), mandatory fees ($2022), and college room and board ($12,200). Full-time tuition and fees vary according to course load and program. Room and board charges vary according to board plan and housing facility.

**Application Procedures** Students admitted directly into the professional program freshman year. Deadline for freshmen: January 15; transfers: April 1. Notification date for freshmen: April 1; transfers: May 15. Required: essay, high school transcript, college transcript(s) for transfer students, 2 letters of recommendation, portfolio, SAT or ACT test scores. Recommended: minimum 3.0 high school GPA.

**Web Site** http://ddw.tisch.nyu.edu

**Undergraduate Contact** Ms. Patricia A. Decker, Director of Recruitment, Tisch School of the Arts, New York University, 721 Broadway, 8th Floor, New York, New York 10003-6807; 212-998-1900, fax: 212-995-4060.

**Graduate Contact** Mr. Dan Sandford, Director of Graduate Admissions, Tisch School of the Arts, New York University, 721 Broadway, 8th Floor, New York, New York 10003-6807; 212-998-1900, fax: 212-995-4060, e-mail address: dan.sandford@nyu.edu

*Steinhardt School of Culture, Education, and Human Development, Department of Music and Performing Arts Professions*

# New York University

### New York, New York

Independent, coed. Urban campus. Total enrollment: 41,783.

**Degrees** Bachelor of Science in the area of educational theatre. Majors and concentrations: educational theater. Graduate degrees offered: Master of Arts in the areas of educational theatre (all grades), educational theatre (with English 7-12 or social studies 7-12), educational theatre in colleges and communities, drama therapy. Doctor of Education in the areas of teachers of educational theatre in high schools, educational theatre in colleges and communities; Doctor of Philosophy in the areas of teachers of educational theatre in high schools, educational theatre in colleges and communities.

**Enrollment** 212 total; 40 undergraduate, 172 graduate.

**Theater Student Profile** 81% females, 19% males, 13% minorities, 6% international.

**Theater Faculty** 6 total (full-time), 26 total (part-time). 83% of full-time faculty have terminal degrees. Graduate students teach a few undergraduate courses. Undergraduate student–faculty ratio: 2:1.

**Student Life** Student groups/activities include Black Box Studio, the Provincetown Playhouse, and community venues, New Plays for Young Audiences and Looking for Shakespeare, study abroad program with drama pioneers in England, Ireland, Brazil, and Puerto Rico.

**Expenses for 2007–2008** Application fee: $65. Comprehensive fee: $47,490 includes full-time tuition ($33,268), mandatory fees ($2022), and college room and board ($12,200). Full-time tuition and fees vary according to course load and program. Room and board charges vary according to board plan and housing facility.

**Application Procedures** Students admitted directly into the professional program freshman year. Deadline for freshmen: January 15; transfers: April 1. Notification date for freshmen: April 1; transfers: continuous. Required: essay, high school transcript, college transcript(s) for transfer students, 3 letters of recommendation, audition, SAT or ACT test scores, strong high school GPA. Auditions held continuously on campus; videotaped performances are permissible as a substitute for live auditions when distance is prohibitive.

**Web Site** http://www.steinhardt.nyu.edu/perf-arts2008

**Undergraduate Contact** Ms. Candice MacLusky, Assistant Director of Undergraduate Admissions, New York University, 22 Washington Square North, New York, New York 10011-9191; 212-998-4500, fax: 212-995-4902.

**Graduate Contact** Mr. John Myers, Director of Enrollment Services, Office of Graduate Admissions, New York University, 82

Washington Square East, 3rd Floor, New York, New York 10003-6680; 212-998-5030, fax: 212-995-4328, e-mail address: steinhardt.gradadmissions@nyu.edu

# Niagara University

### Niagara University, New York

Independent, coed. Suburban campus. Total enrollment: 4,116. Theater program established 1981.

**Degrees** Bachelor of Fine Arts in the area of theater arts. Majors and concentrations: acting, music theater, technical theater, theater arts/drama.

**Enrollment** 91 total; all undergraduate.

**Theater Student Profile** 63% females, 37% males, 10% minorities, 12% international.

**Theater Faculty** 6 undergraduate (full-time), 12 undergraduate (part-time). 100% of full-time faculty have terminal degrees. Graduate students do not teach undergraduate courses. Undergraduate student–faculty ratio: 6:1.

**Student Life** Student groups/activities include NU Players, P.E.A.N. U.T.S. (outreach program in elementary schools).

**Expenses for 2007–2008** Application fee: $30. Comprehensive fee: $31,600 includes full-time tuition ($21,400), mandatory fees ($900), and college room and board ($9300). Special program-related fees: $770 per year for lab fees.

**Financial Aid** Program-specific awards: 40 departmental scholarships for program majors.

**Application Procedures** Students admitted directly into the professional program freshman year. Deadline for freshmen and transfers: continuous. Required: high school transcript, college transcript(s) for transfer students, interview, SAT or ACT test scores, audition for scholarship consideration. Recommended: minimum 3.0 high school GPA, audition. Auditions held once (usually in April) on campus.

**Web Site** http://www.niagara.edu

**Undergraduate Contact** Dr. Sharon O. Watkinson, Chair, Theater and Fine Arts Department, Niagara University, Niagara University, New York 14109; 800-462-2111, fax: 716-286-8710, e-mail address: admissions@niagara.edu

# North Carolina Agricultural and Technical State University

### Greensboro, North Carolina

State supported, coed. Urban campus. Total enrollment: 11,098. Theater program established 1898.

**Degrees** Bachelor of Fine Arts in the area of acting and theater technology. Majors and concentrations: acting, theater technology. Cross-registration with University of North Carolina System. Program accredited by NAST.

**Enrollment** 75 total; all undergraduate.

**Theater Student Profile** 60% females, 40% males, 98% minorities.

**Theater Faculty** 5 undergraduate (full-time), 4 undergraduate (part-time). 100% of full-time faculty have terminal degrees. Graduate students do not teach undergraduate courses. Undergraduate student–faculty ratio: 12:1.

**Student Life** Student groups/activities include American College Theatre Festival, University/Resident Theatre Association, Southeastern Theatre Conference.

**Expenses for 2007–2008** Application fee: $45. State resident tuition: $1994 full-time. Nonresident tuition: $11,436 full-time. Mandatory fees: $1506 full-time. Full-time tuition and fees vary according to student level. College room only: $2956. Room charges vary according to housing facility.

**Financial Aid** Program-specific awards: 5 Chancellor's Awards for freshmen ($1000), 3 tuition remissions for out-of-state students ($950), 1 D.E. Coffey Scholarship for theater majors interested in costuming ($1000), 1–4 departmental scholarships ($200–$500).

**Application Procedures** Students apply for admission into the professional program by freshman year. Deadline for freshmen and transfers: July 15. Required: high school transcript, college transcript(s) for transfer students, minimum 2.0 high school GPA, interview, audition, portfolio, SAT or ACT test scores, minimum combined SAT score of 820 for in-state applicants; 920 for

*North Carolina Agricultural and Technical State University (continued)*

out-of-state applicants, minimum composite ACT score of 17 for in-state applicants; 21 for out-of-state applicants. Recommended: 2 letters of recommendation. Auditions held twice on campus and off campus in Southeastern Theatre Conference venues; recorded music is permissible as a substitute for live auditions if pianist is not available and videotaped performances are permissible as a substitute for live auditions for out-of-state applicants and those unable to make live auditions. Portfolio reviews held twice on campus.

**Web Site** http://www.ncat.edu

**Undergraduate Contact** Frankie Day, Program Chair/Executive Director of Theatre, Division of Theatre Arts, North Carolina Agricultural and Technical State University, 1601 East Market Street, NCB 302-E Building A, Greensboro, North Carolina 27411; 336-334-7852, fax: 336-334-4741, e-mail address: frankie@ncat.edu

# North Carolina School of the Arts
## Winston-Salem, North Carolina

State-supported, coed. Urban campus. Total enrollment: 864. Theater program established 1965.

**Degrees** Bachelor of Fine Arts in the area of design and production. Majors and concentrations: acting, costume design, costume technology, lighting design, makeup and wig design, scene painting, scenic design, sound design, stage automation, stage management, technical direction. Graduate degrees offered: Master of Fine Arts in the area of design and production.

**Enrollment** 308 total; 223 undergraduate, 32 graduate, 53 nonprofessional degree.

**Theater Student Profile** 47% females, 53% males, 8% minorities, 2% international.

**Theater Faculty** 34 total (full-time). 50% of full-time faculty have terminal degrees. Graduate students do not teach undergraduate courses. Undergraduate student–faculty ratio: 8:1.

**Student Life** Special housing available for theater students.

**Expenses for 2007–2008** Application fee: $50. State resident tuition: $3224 full-time. Nonresident tuition: $14,654 full-time. Mandatory fees: $1837 full-time. Full-time tuition and fees vary according to program. College room and board: $6431. College room only: $3289. Room and board charges vary according to board plan and housing facility. Special program-related fees: $135 per year for educational and technology fee, $150 per year for School of Drama fee.

**Financial Aid** Program-specific awards: 124 talent/need scholarships ($2493).

**Application Procedures** Students admitted directly into the professional program freshman year. Deadline for freshmen and transfers: March 1. Required: high school transcript, college transcript(s) for transfer students, 2 letters of recommendation, interview, audition, portfolio. Recommended: SAT or ACT test scores. Auditions held by request on campus and off campus in New York, NY; Seattle, WA; Houston, TX; Chicago, IL; Miami, FL; San Francisco, CA; Los Angeles, CA. Portfolio reviews held 10 times on campus.

**Web Site** http://www.ncarts.edu

**Contact** Ms. Sheeler Lawson, Director of Admissions, North Carolina School of the Arts, 1533 South Main Street, Winston-Salem, North Carolina 27117-2189; 336-770-3291, fax: 336-770-3370, e-mail address: admissions@ncarts.edu

# Northern Kentucky University
## Highland Heights, Kentucky

State-supported, coed. Suburban campus. Total enrollment: 14,785. Theater program established 1970.

**Degrees** Bachelor of Fine Arts. Majors and concentrations: acting, acting and directing, dance, design technology, music theater, playwriting, stage management, theater. Cross-registration with University of Cincinnati, Thomas More College, Xavier University.

**Enrollment** 160 total; 40 undergraduate, 120 nonprofessional degree.

**Theater Student Profile** 50% females, 50% males, 3% minorities, 2% international.

**Theater Faculty** 15 undergraduate (full-time), 12 undergraduate (part-time). 100% of full-time faculty have terminal degrees. Graduate students do not teach undergraduate courses. Undergraduate student–faculty ratio: 12:1.

**Student Life** Student groups/activities include Student Theater, Stage One-Student Service Organization, tour troupes.

**Expenses for 2008–2009** Application fee: $40. State resident tuition: $6528 full-time. Nonresident tuition: $11,952 full-time. College room and board: $6560. Special program-related fees: $90 per semester for private lessons (optional).

**Financial Aid** Program-specific awards: 4 Corbett Scholarships for program majors ($2500), 13 Theater Department Scholarships for program majors ($2500).

**Application Procedures** Students apply for admission into the professional program by freshman, sophomore, junior year. Deadline for freshmen and transfers: continuous. Required: high school transcript, college transcript(s) for transfer students, audition, portfolio, SAT or ACT test scores. Recommended: minimum 2.0 high school GPA, 3 letters of recommendation, interview. Auditions held twice on campus; videotaped performances are permissible as a substitute for live auditions if a campus visit is impossible and only for scholarship consideration, not BFA acceptance. Portfolio reviews held twice on campus.

**Web Site** http://www.nku.edu/start/

**Undergraduate Contact** Office of Admissions, Northern Kentucky University, Lucas Administrative Centre, 4th Floor, Highland Heights, Kentucky 41099; 859-572-5220, fax: 859-572-6665, e-mail address: admitnku@nku.edu

# Northwestern State University of Louisiana
## Natchitoches, Louisiana

State-supported, coed. Small town campus. Total enrollment: 9,037. Theater program established 1953.

**Degrees** Bachelor of Science in the area of theater. Majors and concentrations: dance, music theater, performance/directing, theater design/technology. Program accredited by NAST.

**Enrollment** 106 total; all undergraduate.

**Theater Student Profile** 63% females, 37% males, 15% minorities, 1% international.

**Theater Faculty** 8 undergraduate (full-time), 4 undergraduate (part-time). 100% of full-time faculty have terminal degrees. Graduate students do not teach undergraduate courses. Undergraduate student–faculty ratio: 19:1.

**Student Life** Student groups/activities include Northwestern Theatre, Northwestern Summer Theatre, Tap Rep. Class-Act (Musical Theatre), Out-on-a-Limb (Improv). Special housing available for theater students.

**Expenses for 2007–2008** Application fee: $20. State resident tuition: $2240 full-time. Nonresident tuition: $8318 full-time. Mandatory fees: $1288 full-time. Full-time tuition and fees vary according to course load. College room and board: $5850. College room only: $3700. Room and board charges vary according to board plan, housing facility, and location.

**Financial Aid** Program-specific awards: 92 performance scholarships for theatre majors ($500–$1000).

**Application Procedures** Students apply for admission into the professional program by freshman year. Deadline for freshmen and transfers: July 1. Required: high school transcript, college transcript(s) for transfer students, minimum 2.0 high school GPA, 3 letters of recommendation, interview, audition, portfolio, SAT or ACT test scores (minimum combined SAT score of 940, minimum composite ACT score of 20). Recommended: minimum 3.0 high school GPA. Auditions held as needed on campus and off campus in Plano, TX; Little Rock, AR; videotaped performances are permissible as a substitute for live auditions accepted before established audition dates. Portfolio reviews held on campus and off campus in Plano, TX; Little Rock, AR; the submission of slides may be substituted for portfolios accepted before established audition dates.

**Web Site** http://www.nsula.edu/theatre/

**Undergraduate Contact** University Registrar and Admissions Office, Northwestern State University of Louisiana, Natchitoches, Louisiana 71497; 800-807-8849.

# Ohio Northern University
## Ada, Ohio

Independent, coed. Small town campus. Total enrollment: 3,603. Theater program established 1964.

**Degrees** Bachelor of Fine Arts. Majors and concentrations: international theatre production, music theater, theater arts/drama. Cross-registration with multiple college and universities.
**Enrollment** 120 total; all undergraduate.
**Theater Student Profile** 65% females, 35% males, 5% minorities.
**Theater Faculty** 8 total (full-time), 2 total (part-time). 100% of full-time faculty have terminal degrees. Graduate students do not teach undergraduate courses. Undergraduate student–faculty ratio: 8:1.
**Student Life** Student groups/activities include Theta Alpha Phi, Touring Children's Company, Touring Broadway Revue.
**Expenses for 2008–2009** Application fee: $30. Comprehensive fee: $38,655 includes full-time tuition ($30,555), mandatory fees ($210), and college room and board ($7890). College room only: $3945.
**Financial Aid** Program-specific awards: 10–12 talent awards for program majors ($2000–$10,000).
**Application Procedures** Students admitted directly into the professional program freshman year. Deadline for freshmen and transfers: continuous. Notification date for freshmen and transfers: continuous. Required: high school transcript, college transcript(s) for transfer students, interview, audition, portfolio, SAT or ACT test scores, minimum 2.5 high school GPA, minimum 2.0 college GPA for transfer students, portfolio for technology students. Recommended: essay, minimum 3.0 high school GPA, 2 letters of recommendation, video. Auditions held by appointment on campus; videotaped performances are permissible as a substitute for live auditions if a campus visit is impossible. Portfolio reviews held by appointment on campus.
**Web Site** http://www.onu.edu
**Undergraduate Contact** Ms. Jennifer Walton, Recruitment Coordinator, Ohio Northern University, 525 South Main Street, Ada, Ohio 45810; 419-772-2056, fax: 419-772-1856, e-mail address: j-walton.2@onu.edu

# Ohio University
## Athens, Ohio

State-supported, coed. Small town campus. Total enrollment: 20,711. Theater program established 1890.

**Degrees** Bachelor of Fine Arts in the areas of performance, production, design and technology, theater arts/drama. Majors and concentrations: performance, playwriting, theater design and production, theater management, theater technology. Graduate degrees offered: Master of Arts in the areas of history and criticism, theater (general); Master of Fine Arts in the areas of professional actor training, professional director training, professional playwriting, production, design and technology. Program accredited by NAST.
**Enrollment** 212 total; 145 undergraduate, 67 graduate.
**Theater Student Profile** 57% females, 43% males, 5% minorities, 3% international.
**Theater Faculty** 21 total (full-time). 91% of full-time faculty have terminal degrees. Graduate students teach a few undergraduate courses. Undergraduate student–faculty ratio: 12:1.
**Student Life** Student groups/activities include Ohio Valley Summer Theater, Monomoy Theatre, Cincinnati Playhouse in the Park. Special housing available for theater students.
**Expenses for 2007–2008** Application fee: $45. State resident tuition: $8907 full-time. Nonresident tuition: $17,871 full-time. College room and board: $8427. College room only: $4476. Room and board charges vary according to board plan.
**Financial Aid** Program-specific awards: 15–25 Provost Talent Scholarships for incoming freshmen ($1500), 29 Dean's Scholarships for continuing students ($1000–$1500), 1 Third Century Scholarship for incoming freshmen ($3500), 1 President's

Scholarship for incoming freshmen ($2500), 17 departmental scholarships for continuing students ($500–$1500).
**Application Procedures** Students apply for admission into the professional program by freshman year. Deadline for freshmen: February 2; transfers: continuous. Required: high school transcript, college transcript(s) for transfer students, minimum 3.0 high school GPA, SAT or ACT test scores (minimum composite ACT score of 21), audition for scholarship consideration, portfolio for production design/technology applicants for scholarship consideration, writing sample for playwriting applicants for scholarship consideration. Auditions held twice in the winter on campus. Portfolio reviews held twice in the winter on campus.
**Web Site** http://www.ohiou.edu/theater
**Contact** Ms. Barbara Fiocchi, Secretary, School of Theater, Ohio University, 307 Kantner Hall, Athens, Ohio 45701; 740-593-4818, fax: 740-593-4817, e-mail address: theater@ohio.edu

# Otterbein College
## Westerville, Ohio

Independent United Methodist, coed. Suburban campus. Total enrollment: 3,107.

**Degrees** Bachelor of Fine Arts. Majors and concentrations: acting, design technology, music theater, music theatre/dance. Cross-registration with members of the Higher Education Council of Columbus. Program accredited by NAST, NASM.
**Enrollment** 105 total; 82 undergraduate, 23 nonprofessional degree.
**Theater Student Profile** 58% females, 42% males, 13% minorities, 3% international.
**Theater Faculty** 12 undergraduate (full-time), 20 undergraduate (part-time). 90% of full-time faculty have terminal degrees. Graduate students do not teach undergraduate courses. Undergraduate student–faculty ratio: 8:1.
**Student Life** Student groups/activities include Cap and Dagger (local theater honorary).
**Expenses for 2007–2008** Application fee: $25. Comprehensive fee: $32,214 includes full-time tuition ($25,065) and college room and board ($7149). College room only: $3399. Full-time tuition varies according to course load and program. Room and board charges vary according to housing facility. Special program-related fees: $555 per quarter for private voice lessons (one hour weekly).
**Financial Aid** Program-specific awards: 20–35 theater talent awards for program majors ($3000–$6000), 5 dance talent awards for minors ($750–$1000).
**Application Procedures** Students admitted directly into the professional program freshman year. Deadline for freshmen and transfers: February 1. Notification date for freshmen and transfers: April 1. Required: high school transcript, college transcript(s) for transfer students, interview, audition, portfolio, SAT or ACT test scores, 2 letters of recommendation for design/technology applicants. Recommended: minimum 2.5 high school GPA. Auditions held 12 times on campus and off campus in New York, NY; Chicago, IL; Los Angeles, CA; videotaped performances are permissible as a substitute for live auditions for out-of-state applicants with approval from the department. Portfolio reviews held at student's convenience on campus and off campus in New York, NY; Chicago, IL; Los Angeles; the submission of slides may be substituted for portfolios for out-of-state applicants with approval from the department.
**Web Site** http://www.otterbein.edu/theatre
**Undergraduate Contact** Debbie Byrne, Assistant Director of Admission, Office of Admission, Otterbein College, One Otterbein College, Westerville, Ohio 43081-2006; 800-488-8144, fax: 614-823-1200, e-mail address: dbyrne@otterbein.edu

# Pace University
## New York, New York

Independent, coed. Urban campus. Total enrollment: 12,912. Theater program established 1988.

*Pace University (continued)*

**Degrees** Bachelor of Fine Arts in the areas of acting, musical theatre. Majors and concentrations: acting, directing, music theater, set design, theater management.
**Enrollment** 152 total; 85 undergraduate, 19 graduate, 48 nonprofessional degree.
**Theater Student Profile** 70% females, 30% males, 12% minorities, 2% international.
**Theater Faculty** 8 total (full-time), 10 total (part-time). 100% of full-time faculty have terminal degrees. Graduate students do not teach undergraduate courses. Undergraduate student–faculty ratio: 15:1.
**Student Life** Student groups/activities include Honors Program.
**Expenses for 2007–2008** Application fee: $45. Comprehensive fee: $40,478 includes full-time tuition ($29,454), mandatory fees ($704), and college room and board ($10,320). Room and board charges vary according to board plan and housing facility.
**Application Procedures** Students admitted directly into the professional program freshman year. Deadline for freshmen and transfers: continuous. Required: essay, high school transcript, college transcript(s) for transfer students, minimum 2.0 high school GPA, 2 letters of recommendation, interview, audition, portfolio, SAT or ACT test scores, audition for performance majors, portfolio for design/technical theater majors. Recommended: video. Auditions held continuously on campus; videotaped performances are permissible as a substitute for live auditions when distance is prohibitive. Portfolio reviews held continuously on campus; the submission of slides may be substituted for portfolios if campus visit is impossible.
**Web Site** http://www.pace.edu/page.cfm?doc_id=9255
**Undergraduate Contact** Kimberly Johnson, Counselor, Pace University, Pace Plaza, New York, New York 10038; 212-346-1225, fax: 212-346-1821, e-mail address: kjohnson@pace.edu

# Penn State University Park
## University Park, Pennsylvania

State-related, coed. Small town campus. Total enrollment: 43,252. Theater program established 1935.
**Degrees** Bachelor of Fine Arts. Majors and concentrations: design technology, music theater, stage management. Graduate degrees offered: Master of Fine Arts in the areas of acting, costume, scene design. Program accredited by NAST.
**Enrollment** 185 total; 71 undergraduate, 33 graduate, 81 nonprofessional degree.
**Theater Student Profile** 63% females, 37% males, 9% minorities, 1% international.
**Theater Faculty** 21 total (full-time), 5 total (part-time). 98% of full-time faculty have terminal degrees. Graduate students teach a few undergraduate courses. Undergraduate student–faculty ratio: 8:1.
**Student Life** Student groups/activities include University Park Ensemble, Minority Theatre Workshop, Drama Duo. Special housing available for theater students.
**Expenses for 2007–2008** Application fee: $50. State resident tuition: $12,284 full-time. Nonresident tuition: $23,152 full-time. Mandatory fees: $560 full-time. Full-time tuition and fees vary according to course level, location, program, and student level. College room and board: $7180. College room only: $3820. Room and board charges vary according to board plan, housing facility, and location.
**Financial Aid** Program-specific awards: 1 Mona Shibley Bird Scholarship for above-average students ($862), 2 Gallu Scholarships for freshmen ($820), 2 Lethbridge-Jackson Awards for outstanding achievement ($466), 25 Mabel Reed Knight Scholarships for those demonstrating financial need ($350–$1500), 2 Irene Richards Scholarships for sophomores demonstrating high academic achievement ($1609).
**Application Procedures** Students admitted directly into the professional program freshman year. Deadline for freshmen and transfers: March 1. Notification date for freshmen and transfers: continuous. Required: essay, high school transcript, college transcript(s) for transfer students, minimum 2.0 high school GPA, 2 letters of recommendation, interview, audition, portfolio, SAT or ACT test scores. Auditions held 7-8 times on campus and off campus in Chicago, IL; Irvine, CA; New York, NY; videotaped performances are permissible as a substitute for live auditions if distance is prohibitive or scheduling is difficult. Portfolio reviews held 7-8 times on campus and off campus in Chicago, IL; New York, NY; San Francisco, CA; the submission of slides may be substituted for portfolios only if accompanied by an interview.
**Web Site** http://www.theatre.psu.edu
**Undergraduate Contact** Ms. Paula Wheland, Staff Specialist, School of Theatre, Penn State University Park, 133 Arts Building, University Park, Pennsylvania 16802; 814-863-6819, fax: 814-865-5754, e-mail address: paw23@psu.edu
**Graduate Contact** Ms. Sue Carson, Staff Assistant, School of Theatre, Penn State University Park, 103 Arts Building, University Park, Pennsylvania 16802; 814-865-7586, fax: 814-865-5754, e-mail address: msc1@psu.edu

# Point Park University
## Pittsburgh, Pennsylvania

Independent, coed. Urban campus. Total enrollment: 3,592. Theater program established 1968.
**Degrees** Bachelor of Arts/Bachelor of Fine Arts in the areas of theatre arts, musical theatre, acting. Majors and concentrations: acting, music theater, stage management, technical theatre/design. Graduate degrees offered: Master of Fine Arts in the area of theatre arts. Cross-registration with Carnegie Mellon University, University of Pittsburgh, Chatham College, Robert Morris College, Duquesne University, Carlow College.
**Enrollment** 312 total; 306 undergraduate, 6 graduate.
**Theater Student Profile** 59% females, 41% males, 11% minorities.
**Theater Faculty** 11 undergraduate (full-time), 23 undergraduate (part-time), 2 graduate (full-time), 1 graduate (part-time). 100% of full-time faculty have terminal degrees. Graduate students teach a few undergraduate courses. Undergraduate student–faculty ratio: 10:1.
**Student Life** Student groups/activities include American College Theatre Festival.
**Expenses for 2007–2008** Application fee: $40. Comprehensive fee: $27,430 includes full-time tuition ($18,460), mandatory fees ($530), and college room and board ($8440). College room only: $3980. Full-time tuition and fees vary according to program. Room and board charges vary according to board plan and housing facility. Special program-related fees: $450 per term for voice/piano private lessons.
**Financial Aid** Program-specific awards: 35 apprenticeships for those demonstrating talent ($500–$3000), 35 talent scholarships for those demonstrating academic achievement and talent ($500–$5000).
**Application Procedures** Students admitted directly into the professional program freshman year. Deadline for freshmen and transfers: May 1. Required: high school transcript, college transcript(s) for transfer students, minimum 2.0 high school GPA, 2 letters of recommendation, interview, ACT test score only, theater questionnaire and 2 photos, portfolio for technical theater and stage management applicants, audition for acting and musical theater applicants. Auditions held 8 times on campus and off campus in New York, NY; Louisville, KY; state conferences in Pennsylvania, Arizona, Maryland, Atlanta, Southeastern Theatre Conference sites; recorded music is permissible as a substitute for live auditions if a live audition is impossible and videotaped performances are permissible as a substitute for live auditions by prior arrangement. Portfolio reviews held 8 times on campus and off campus in Louisville, KY; state conferences in Pennsylvania, Arizona, Maryland, and New York; the submission of slides may be substituted for portfolios whenever needed.
**Web Site** http://www.pointpark.edu
**Undergraduate Contact** Mr. Joseph McGoldrick, Director of Artistic Recruitment, Conservatory of Performing Arts, Point Park University, 201 Wood Street, Pittsburgh, Pennsylvania 15222-1984; 412-392-3450, fax: 412-391-2424, e-mail address: jmcgoldrick@pointpark.edu

*More About the Program*

The Conservatory of Performing Arts confers Bachelor of Arts and Bachelor of Fine Arts degrees in dance, dance pedagogy, and theater arts and offers conservatory training within a liberal arts context. Students receive intense training in their concentration as well as a thorough academic education. Because the faculty members believe that performing arts majors develop best in front of a live audience, the program offers varied performing opportunities for students at the Pittsburgh Playhouse of Point Park University.

Nationally renowned, the Pittsburgh Playhouse is the performance facility for the Conservatory of Performing Arts. Here students participate in live-theater/dance experiences before a subscription audience. Consisting of three working theaters, this 70-year-old facility is fully staffed by a production team of designers and artisans who train and supervise student apprentices in building, designing, lighting, and managing shows. The front-of-house staff members as well as the box office and public relations personnel engage all students in the business aspect of running a theater. The season, which features student actors, dancers, designers, and stage managers, consists of five Playhouse Jr. productions for children and five Conservatory Company dramas/musicals.

Dance students may perform in one of five Playhouse Dance Company productions and a Playhouse Jr. Children's Dance Show as well as a public school outreach program.

The Bachelor of Arts degree in cinema and digital arts is an innovatively designed program, with an emphasis on professional education and liberal arts—both in theory and in practice. Exploring the integration of media and the arts in society as well as the impact of technology on culture, the curriculum provides practical, professional training while developing a sound foundation in the arts and humanities. Theory and aesthetics are taught as an integral part of developing communication and production skills.

In the Conservatory of Performing Arts, it is the mission to educate, train, and artistically equip students with the skills necessary to compete in the commercial media industry. The degree offered is a four-year, 120-credit Bachelor of Arts in cinema and digital arts, with concentrations in cinematography, directing, editing and sound, producing, and screenwriting.

This well-rounded educational experience culminates with the annual Point Park Digital Film Festival presented to showcase graduating senior thesis production projects. Admission to the Film and Electronic Arts program is based on self-discipline, professional attitude, and a commitment to the craft as demonstrated through an interview with the Director of Film.

The B.F.A. degree in film and video production is offered in collaboration with Pittsburgh Filmmakers. Students take their academic courses at Point Park University and their film and video requirements at Pittsburgh Filmmakers' newly built facility in the Oakland section of Pittsburgh. Both institutions work together to ensure that students receive a challenging educational experience.

Conservatory faculty members are working professionals in acting, singing, dancing, writing, composing, painting, designing, choreography, and other specialties. Guest artists and master teachers in musical theater, voice and speech, and dance are regularly featured. Past guests include Chita Rivera, Michael Rupert, Jeff Shade, Rob Ashford, Sherry Zunker-Dow, Cicely Berry, Paul Gavert, Patricia Wilde, Albert Poland, Barbara Pontecorvo, Edward Villella, Maxine Sherman, Marshall Swiney, and Claire Bataille. The program also offers many workshops and collaborative efforts of an interdisciplinary nature with other University programs.

During the summer, the Conservatory offers an International Summer Dance program (open by audition) featuring renowned names in the world of dance. The International Summer Dance program offers training in jazz, ballet, and modern dance. The program culminates in a recital performance.

The community of Pittsburgh itself is an arts and education center with the Pittsburgh Symphony, Opera, Ballet, and Dance Council and the Pittsburgh Public Theaters supplemented by eight other institutions of higher learning within a 15-minute drive. The whole city is truly the campus of the programs.

Prospective applicants must apply and be accepted by the University. An audition for and an interview with faculty members is required for all prospective majors. Scholarships/apprenticeships from $1000 to $5000 are based on either talent or academics or both. Presidential and special academic full- and part-time awards are highly competitive.

Off-campus auditions are possible at Thespian State Conferences and dance auditions in Chicago; New York; Dayton, Ohio; and Louisville, Kentucky. Videotaped auditions are acceptable; prospective students should contact the Conservatory for procedures.

For more information and audition guidelines, interested students should contact Joseph McGoldrick, Director of Artistic Recruitment, Point Park University, 201 Wood Street, Pittsburgh, Pennsylvania 15222; jmcgoldrick@pointpark.edu; 800-321-0129 (toll-free).

**Program Facilities and Features** At the Conservatory of Performing Arts, facilities include ten dance studios as well as the three-theater complex at the Pittsburgh Playhouse of Point Park University, which offers performance opportunities for students in front of a subscription audience. In addition, students can take advantage of the on-site costume/set construction apprenticeships, 11 private singing and piano instructors; art and design classes; more than 100 dance classes per week, acting classes with a ratio of 1 instructor to 15 students, and the Point Park University Singers. Point Park University is central to many educational, arts, and entertainment activities, and it is within walking distance of boating, swimming, and parks.

**Alumni** The Conservatory has numerous graduates performing in touring companies, on Broadway, in dance companies, in movies, on television, and in other theaters. Many more alumni are teaching in schools, on faculties, choreographing, writing, directing, and stage managing across the world. Broadway and national touring productions of *Contact, Cabaret, 42nd St.,* and *Kiss Me Kate* as well as movie and television credits, including *Pulp Fiction, Inspector Gadget, Wonder Boys, NYPD Blue, Due South, The Guiding Light, Providence, CSI: NYC,* and *Leaving L.A.* are just a few of the vehicles showcasing Conservatory graduates of theater and dance.

# Potter College of Arts, Humanities, and Social Sciences

See Western Kentucky University

# Purchase College, State University of New York

### Purchase, New York

State-supported, coed. Small town campus. Total enrollment: 4,265.

**Degrees** Bachelor of Fine Arts in the areas of acting, design technology, film, dramatic writing. Majors and concentrations: acting, costume construction, costume design, design technology, dramatic writing, film, lighting design, playwriting, scenic design, screenwriting, stage management, technical direction. Graduate degrees offered: Master of Fine Arts in the areas of theater design, theater technology.

**Enrollment** 338 total; 330 undergraduate, 8 graduate.

**Theater Student Profile** 48% females, 52% males, 16% minorities, 2% international.

**Theater Faculty** 11 undergraduate (full-time), 34 undergraduate (part-time). 100% of full-time faculty have terminal degrees. Graduate students do not teach undergraduate courses.

*Purchase College, State University of New York (continued)*

**Student Life** Student groups/activities include Downtown Cabaret.
**Expenses for 2008–2009** Application fee: $40. State resident tuition: $4350 full-time. Nonresident tuition: $10,610 full-time. Mandatory fees: $1647 full-time. College room and board: $9484. College room only: $5886.
**Financial Aid** Program-specific awards: 124 theater scholarships/ awards ($1122).
**Application Procedures** Students admitted directly into the professional program freshman year. Deadline for freshmen and transfers: March 1. Notification date for freshmen: April 1; transfers: May 1. Required: high school transcript, college transcript(s) for transfer students, essay for film applicants, audition for acting applicants, portfolio for design and technical theater applicants, minimum TOEFL score of 550 for international applicants. Recommended: letter of recommendation, SAT or ACT test scores, picture and resumé for acting applicants, interview for design, technical theater applicants. Auditions held on campus and off campus in various locations once per year; videotaped performances are permissible as a substitute for live auditions for international applicants or with approval from the department for domestic applicants. Portfolio reviews held at various times on campus and off campus in various locations; the submission of slides may be substituted for portfolios with some original work.
**Web Site** http://www.purchase.edu/taf
**Undergraduate Contact** Ms. Shirley Williams, Admissions Counselor, Purchase College, State University of New York, 735 Anderson Hill Road, Purchase, New York 10577-1400; 914-251-6315, fax: 914-251-6314, e-mail address: shirley.williams@purchase.edu
**Graduate Contact** Ms. Sabrina Johnston, Admissions Counselor, Purchase College, State University of New York, 735 Anderson Hill Road, Purchase, New York 10577; 914-251-6479, fax: 914-251-6314, e-mail address: sabrina.johnston@purchase.edu

## *More About the College*

Professional training for a professional career in acting, design/technology, dramatic writing, and film is the dominant goal of the program. Young artists are selected for the intensity of both their interest and potential in becoming professionals. The program offers focused and in-depth training in theater and film with a faculty that is itself working, creating, and succeeding in New York's professional world.

The community of students and faculty members is constantly enriched by the creative bustle and aesthetic influence of New York City, just 35 minutes away. Students and teachers work and thrive together on the modern Purchase campus and Performing Arts Center located in Westchester County, a beautiful and elegant suburb of New York City.

All classes, rehearsals, and productions are supervised by men and women who are contributing participants in the professional artistic life of New York City, the United States, and international arts communities. These artist-teachers have a common goal: to thoroughly train young artists so that the individual creativity of each student is preserved and augmented by the most strenuous and critical practice and performance standards possible. Practical learning and practical experience become core components of the daily life of the student artist at Purchase. State-of-the-art equipment, theaters, and work spaces for every aspect of training abound in this woods-surrounded center of contemporary art and learning.

In addition to this serious concentration in the arts, each student fulfills a SUNY-mandated 30-credit core in liberal arts and sciences. Life at Purchase consists of a rich social intermix of the performing and visual arts with the more traditional academic life of the liberal arts and sciences.

The student's life after graduation is a powerfully active concern of the training program. Therefore, as the student gains proficiency, his or her work has gradually been presented to the professional community. By the time of graduation when the work is formally introduced to that professional community—using New York City presentations for the actors and writers; internships, portfolio reviews, and faculty personal contacts for

the designers; and completed student films for filmmakers— Purchase students find that an extraordinary number of doors open for them. Agents, producers, theaters, film companies, and television producers are available for the next creative and working step of the Purchase graduate.

The Conservatory of Theatre Arts and Film is now graduating some of the most exciting and successful young actors, designers, technical directors, stage managers, filmmakers, and writers in America. It is not only the flagship program of the State University of New York but also among the finest and most prestigious of the conservatory programs offered in the disciplines of theater and film in the United States.

The Purchase College Conservatory of Theatre Arts and Film is a member of the Consortium of Undergraduate Professional Theatre Training Programs.

# Rockford College
## Rockford, Illinois

Independent, coed. Suburban campus. Total enrollment: 1,566. Theater program established 1994.
**Degrees** Bachelor of Fine Arts in the area of musical theatre. Majors and concentrations: music theater.
**Theater Student Profile** 60% females, 40% males, 16% minorities, 1% international.
**Theater Faculty** 8 undergraduate (full-time). 100% of full-time faculty have terminal degrees. Graduate students do not teach undergraduate courses. Undergraduate student–faculty ratio: 11:1.
**Student Life** Student groups/activities include master classes, theater and musical productions, dance studio performances.
**Expenses for 2008–2009** Application fee: $35. Comprehensive fee: $30,250 includes full-time tuition ($23,500) and college room and board ($6750). College room only: $3850.
**Financial Aid** Program-specific awards: 1 Aqua Aerobics Scholarship, 5 Talent scholarships for incoming students ($1000).
**Application Procedures** Students admitted directly into the professional program freshman year. Deadline for freshmen and transfers: continuous. Required: high school transcript, college transcript(s) for transfer students, audition, SAT or ACT test scores (minimum composite ACT score of 19), minimum 2.65 high school GPA, minimum 2.3 cumulative college GPA for transfer students, top 1/2 of graduating class for first-years. Recommended: 2 letters of recommendation, interview. Auditions held twice, with other dates available upon request on campus; videotaped performances are permissible as a substitute for live auditions when distance is prohibitive.
**Web Site** http://www.rockford.edu
**Undergraduate Contact** Cassie Swanson, Assistant Director of Admissions, Rockford College, 5050 East State Street, Burpee Center, Rockford, Illinois 61108; 800-892-2984, fax: 815-226-2822, e-mail address: rcadmissions@rockford.edu

### *Feinstein College of Arts and Sciences*
# Roger Williams University
## Bristol, Rhode Island

Independent, coed. Total enrollment: 5,166. Theater program established 1972.
**Web Site** http://www.rwu.edu/

### *Chicago College of Performing Arts - The Theatre Conservatory*
# Roosevelt University
## Chicago, Illinois

Independent, coed. Urban campus. Total enrollment: 7,163. Theater program established 1988.
**Degrees** Bachelor of Fine Arts in the areas of acting, musical theatre. Majors and concentrations: acting, music theater.

Graduate degrees offered: Master of Arts in the area of directing (fast-track summer program); Master of Fine Arts in the area of theatre.

**Enrollment** 190 total; 170 undergraduate, 20 graduate.

**Theater Student Profile** 50% females, 50% males, 20% minorities, 10% international.

**Theater Faculty** 12 total (full-time), 24 total (part-time). 100% of full-time faculty have terminal degrees. Graduate students do not teach undergraduate courses. Undergraduate student–faculty ratio: 12:1.

**Expenses for 2007–2008** Application fee: $25. Comprehensive fee: $26,828 includes full-time tuition ($16,680), mandatory fees ($300), and college room and board ($9848). College room only: $6824. Full-time tuition and fees vary according to course load and program. Room and board charges vary according to board plan and housing facility.

**Financial Aid** Program-specific awards: 150 theatre award scholarships ($2000–$15,000).

**Application Procedures** Students admitted directly into the professional program freshman year. Deadline for freshmen and transfers: January 15. Notification date for freshmen and transfers: April 1. Required: essay, high school transcript, college transcript(s) for transfer students, minimum 2.0 high school GPA, 3 letters of recommendation, interview, audition, SAT or ACT test scores (minimum combined SAT score of 1260, minimum composite ACT score of 20), minimum 2.0 college GPA for transfer students. Recommended: minimum 3.0 high school GPA. Auditions held 9 times on campus and off campus in Los Angeles, CA; Chicago, IL; New York, NY; Las Vegas, NV.

**Web Site** http://ccpa.roosevelt.edu/theatre

**Contact** Heather McCowen, Assistant Dean for Enrollment and Student Services, Roosevelt University, 430 South Michigan Avenue, Chicago, Illinois 60605; 312-341-3789, fax: 312-341-6358, e-mail address: theatre@roosevelt.edu

### More About the University

The Theatre Conservatory of the Chicago College of Performing Arts (CCPA) at Roosevelt University provides training and education within the context of a vibrant university in a world-class city. It is a place where the energies of one discipline spill over to enliven other artistic endeavors and where students come to enhance their unique talents and polish them to perfection. At CCPA, students experience a professional program of study with a faculty that is committed to a comprehensive theater education.

Chicago College of Performing Arts at Roosevelt University is well situated on the top floors of the historic landmark Auditorium Building, designed by world-famous architects Dankmar Adler and Louis Sullivan. The building includes the 3,800-seat Auditorium Theatre, renowned for its beauty and exquisite acoustics. Located on the corner of Michigan Avenue and Congress Parkway, this edifice is now an integral part of the "educational corridor" of more than 50,000 students enrolled in various institutions in the famous downtown Loop. Across the street are Pritzker Music Pavilion of Millennium Park, the magnificent Buckingham Fountain, and the sparkling beauty of Lake Michigan. The new state-of-the-art residence hall, the University Center of Chicago, is located just one block away on the corner of State Street and Congress Parkway.

Within walking distance are many of the city's major cultural institutions, including the Goodman, Chicago, Oriental, and Cadillac theaters; Symphony Center, home of the Chicago Symphony Orchestra; the Lyric Opera, the Jazz Showcase; the Art Institute; the Field Museum of Natural History; and the Magnificent Mile of shops and galleries. This ideal location provides opportunities for learning from some of the most accomplished actors in Chicago, as well as interning with some of the literally hundreds of small theater companies in the city.

**Faculty** Joel G. Fink (Director of the Theatre Conservatory/Associate Dean); Christine Adaire (Assistant Professor of Theatre); June Compton (Associate Professor of Theatre); Ray Frewen (Assistant Professor of Theatre); Sean Ryan Kelley (Associate Professor of Theatre); Stephen Kruse (Technical Director); Michael Lasswell (Instructor of Theatre); Kestutis Nakas (Associate Professor of Theatre); Luis Perez (Assistant Professor of Theatre); Keland Scher (Assistant Professor of Theatre); Bonnie Shadrake (Musical Theatre Director); and Emily Humphreys (Production Coordinator).

Part-time professional faculty: Jane Alderman (audition and theater business); Belinda Bremmer (dialects, theater business); Philip Caldwell (musical theater); Lou Conte Dance Studio Staff; Chuck Coyl (stage combat and fight choreography); Joseph Drummond (stage management); Luis Galvez (musical theater voice); Nadine Gomez (musical theater voice); Catherine Head (acting on camera); Ted Hoerl (acting); Patrick Holland (musical theater piano); Kendall Kelley (assistant to the director and theater business); Jason K. Martin (dialects); Neil Massey (fight choreography); Molly McGrath (makeup); James Morehead (musical theater piano); Tina Paul (musical theater); Karen Petratos (master electrical and lighting instruction); Jerry Proffit (Fast Track Administrator); Meera Sanghani (yoga); Steve Scott (Shakespeare in Performance); Rebecca Simone Schorsch (vocal performance); Craig Springer (musical theater voice) and Dan Stetzel (musical theater/cabaret). There are additional voice faculty members for private voice lessons.

**Student Performance Opportunities** There are fourteen to sixteen productions each year. Freshmen present showcases in their first year and audition with the entire conservatory thereafter. As an integral part of students' training, the Theatre Conservatory encourages advanced students to work with professional theater companies through specially arranged internships. In the past two years, theaters have included the Goodman Theatre, Steppenwolf Theatre Company, Chicago Shakespeare Theatre, Lookingglass Theatre, and Northlight Theatre. Students have interned in the areas of acting, directing, stage and arts management, design, theater technology, business and marketing, public relations, and development/front of house.

**Programs and Additional Information** Undergraduate degree programs include the B.F.A. in acting and B.F.A. in musical theatre. Graduate degree programs include the M.F.A. in acting and M.A. Fast Track in directing (summer program designed for high school theater teachers).

A 320-bed residence hall is connected to the main building, and an eighteen-story facility opened in fall 2004.

# Russell Sage College
## Troy, New York

Independent, Urban campus. Total enrollment: 682. Theater program established 1916.

**Degrees** Bachelor of Arts. Majors and concentrations: theater arts/drama. Program accredited by NASAD.

**Enrollment** 18 total; all undergraduate.

**Theater Student Profile** 100% females, 6% minorities.

**Theater Faculty** 4 undergraduate (full-time), 2 undergraduate (part-time). 81% of full-time faculty have terminal degrees. Graduate students do not teach undergraduate courses. Undergraduate student–faculty ratio: 11:1.

**Student Life** Student groups/activities include New York State Theatre Institute.

**Expenses for 2007–2008** Application fee: $30. Comprehensive fee: $34,790 includes full-time tuition ($25,000), mandatory fees ($990), and college room and board ($8800). College room only: $4500. Special program-related fees: $250 per one-time internship fee for internship with New York State Theatre Institute.

**Application Procedures** Students admitted directly into the professional program freshman year. Deadline for freshmen: August 1; transfers: continuous. Required: essay, high school transcript, college transcript(s) for transfer students, minimum 2.0 high school GPA, 2 letters of recommendation, SAT or ACT test scores. Recommended: interview, audition, portfolio. Auditions held on an individual basis on campus; recorded music is permissible as a substitute for live auditions and videotaped performances are permissible as a substitute for live auditions. Portfolio reviews

*Russell Sage College (continued)*

held on an individual basis on campus; the submission of slides may be substituted for portfolios.
**Web Site** http://www.sage.edu
**Undergraduate Contact** Kathy Rusch, Director of Admissions, Admissions, Russell Sage College, 45 Ferry Street, Troy, New York 12180; 518-244-2217, fax: 518-244-6880, e-mail address: ruschk@sage.edu

# Rutgers, The State University of New Jersey

See Mason Gross School of the Arts

# Salem State College

## Salem, Massachusetts

State-supported, coed. Suburban campus. Total enrollment: 10,085. Theater program established 1984.
**Degrees** Bachelor of Fine Arts in the area of theater. Majors and concentrations: acting, costume design, lighting design, set design, stage management, technical theater. Program accredited by NAST.
**Enrollment** 162 total; 48 undergraduate, 114 nonprofessional degree.
**Theater Student Profile** 75% females, 25% males, 2% minorities, 2% international.
**Theater Faculty** 9 undergraduate (full-time), 2 undergraduate (part-time). 75% of full-time faculty have terminal degrees. Graduate students do not teach undergraduate courses. Undergraduate student–faculty ratio: 10:1.
**Student Life** Student groups/activities include Student Theater Ensemble, Salem State Summer Theater, Repertory Dance Theater.
**Expenses for 2007–2008** Application fee: $25. State resident tuition: $910 full-time. Nonresident tuition: $7050 full-time. Mandatory fees: $5300 full-time. Full-time tuition and fees vary according to class time. College room only: $5545. Room charges vary according to housing facility.
**Financial Aid** Program-specific awards: 5–7 Presidential Arts Scholarships for program majors ($1000), 1 Ettinger Scholarship for program majors ($500), 1 David Allen George Scholarship for program majors ($500).
**Application Procedures** Students apply for admission into the professional program by freshman year. Deadline for freshmen and transfers: continuous. Required: high school transcript, college transcript(s) for transfer students, minimum 3.0 high school GPA, SAT or ACT test scores (minimum composite ACT score of 24), audition for acting majors, portfolio for design/technical theater majors. Recommended: essay, 2 letters of recommendation, interview, video. Auditions held twice on campus; recorded music is permissible as a substitute for live auditions if applicant is outside of the New England six-state region and videotaped performances are permissible as a substitute for live auditions if applicant is outside of the New England six-state region. Portfolio reviews held twice on campus; the submission of slides may be substituted for portfolios if applicant is outside of the New England six-state region.
**Web Site** http://www.salemstate.edu
**Undergraduate Contact** Mr. William Cunningham, Chairperson, Department of Theatre and Speech Communication, Salem State College, Salem, Massachusetts 01970; 978-542-6464, fax: 978-542-6291, e-mail address: wcunningham@salemstate.edu

# Sarofim School of Fine Arts

See Southwestern University

# Shenandoah Conservatory

See Shenandoah University

*Shenandoah Conservatory*

# Shenandoah University

## Winchester, Virginia

Independent United Methodist, coed. Total enrollment: 3,393.
**Degrees** Bachelor of Fine Arts in the areas of musical theater, theater for youth, acting, costume design, scenic lighting and design. Majors and concentrations: acting, costume design, music theater, scenic lighting and design, theater for youth. Program accredited by NASM.
**Enrollment** 185 total; 181 undergraduate, 4 nonprofessional degree.
**Theater Student Profile** 64% females, 36% males, 3% minorities, 1% international.
**Theater Faculty** 8 undergraduate (full-time), 4 undergraduate (part-time). 89% of full-time faculty have terminal degrees. Graduate students do not teach undergraduate courses. Undergraduate student–faculty ratio: 15:1.
**Student Life** Student groups/activities include Alpha Psi Omega fraternity shows, special workshops, Children's Theater.
**Expenses for 2008–2009** Application fee: $30. Comprehensive fee: $31,690 includes full-time tuition ($23,040), mandatory fees ($300), and college room and board ($8350).
**Financial Aid** Program-specific awards: 186 talent and academic scholarships for program students ($3758).
**Application Procedures** Students admitted directly into the professional program freshman year. Deadline for freshmen and transfers: continuous. Required: high school transcript, college transcript(s) for transfer students, minimum 2.0 high school GPA, letter of recommendation, interview, video, audition, SAT or ACT test scores, portfolio for costume design, portfolio for scenic lighting and design. Auditions held 10 times on campus and off campus in various cities; recorded music is permissible as a substitute for live auditions with permission and videotaped performances are permissible as a substitute for live auditions with permission. Portfolio reviews held 10 times on campus and off campus in various cities; the submission of slides may be substituted for portfolios as part of portfolio.
**Web Site** http://www.su.edu/conservatory
**Undergraduate Contact** Mr. David Anthony, Dean, Admissions Office, Shenandoah University, 1460 University Drive, Winchester, Virginia 22601-5195; 540-665-4581, fax: 540-665-4627, e-mail address: admit@su.edu

# Shorter College

## Rome, Georgia

Independent Baptist, coed. Small town campus. Total enrollment: 1,394.
**Degrees** Bachelor of Fine Arts in the areas of theatre, musical theatre, musical direction. Majors and concentrations: music theater, musical direction, theater arts/drama. Program accredited by NASM.
**Enrollment** 40 total; all undergraduate.
**Theater Student Profile** 60% females, 40% males, 5% minorities.
**Theater Faculty** 3 undergraduate (full-time), 4 undergraduate (part-time). 100% of full-time faculty have terminal degrees. Graduate students do not teach undergraduate courses.
**Student Life** Student groups/activities include Shorter Players.
**Expenses for 2007–2008** Application fee: $25. Comprehensive fee: $22,160 includes full-time tuition ($14,850), mandatory fees ($310), and college room and board ($7000). College room only: $3800. Full-time tuition and fees vary according to course load. Room and board charges vary according to board plan and housing facility.
**Financial Aid** Program-specific awards: 10–12 theater scholarships for theater majors ($500–$1250).
**Application Procedures** Students admitted directly into the professional program freshman year. Deadline for freshmen and transfers: continuous. Required: high school transcript, college transcript(s) for transfer students, interview, audition, SAT or ACT test scores, two-minute monologue (video), dance audition. Recommended: 2 letters of recommendation. Auditions held 4 times on campus. Portfolio reviews held 4 times on campus.
**Web Site** http://shorter.edu

**Undergraduate Contact** Dr. Alan B. Wingard, Dean, School of the Arts, Shorter College, 315 Shorter Avenue, Rome, Georgia 30165; 706-233-7248, fax: 706-236-1517, e-mail address: awingard@shorter.edu

# Simon Fraser University
**Burnaby, British Columbia, Canada**

Province-supported, coed. Suburban campus. Total enrollment: 26,128. Theater program established 1992.
**Web Site** http://www.sfu.ca/

## *Meadows School of the Arts*
# Southern Methodist University
**Dallas, Texas**

Independent, coed. Suburban campus. Total enrollment: 10,829. Theater program established 1964.
**Degrees** Bachelor of Fine Arts in the area of theater. Majors and concentrations: acting, theater studies. Graduate degrees offered: Master of Fine Arts in the areas of acting, design, directing. Program accredited by NAST.
**Enrollment** 124 total; 101 undergraduate, 23 graduate.
**Theater Student Profile** 45% females, 55% males, 27% minorities, 1% international.
**Theater Faculty** 17 total (full-time), 8 total (part-time). 89% of full-time faculty have terminal degrees. Graduate students teach a few undergraduate courses. Undergraduate student–faculty ratio: 8:1.
**Student Life** Special housing available for theater students.
**Expenses for 2008–2009** Application fee: $60. Comprehensive fee: $45,073 includes full-time tuition ($29,430), mandatory fees ($3768), and college room and board ($11,875). College room only: $7655.
**Financial Aid** Program-specific awards: 20–25 Meadows Artistic Scholarships for talented program majors ($1000–$10,000).
**Application Procedures** Students admitted directly into the professional program freshman year. Deadline for freshmen and transfers: March 2. Required: essay, high school transcript, college transcript(s) for transfer students, letter of recommendation, audition, SAT or ACT test scores. Recommended: interview. Auditions held 37 times on campus and off campus in various locations. Portfolio reviews held twice on campus and off campus; the submission of slides may be substituted for portfolios in special circumstances.
**Web Site** http://www.smu.edu/meadows/
**Undergraduate Contact** Dr. Charley Helfert, Professor, Division of Theatre, Southern Methodist University, Meadows School of the Arts, PO Box 750356, Dallas, Texas 75275-0356; 214-768-2417, fax: 214-768-1136, e-mail address: chelfert@smu.edu
**Graduate Contact** Jean Cherry, Graduate Advisor, MSA Graduate Admissions/Records, Southern Methodist University, Meadows School of the Arts, PO Box 750356, Dallas, Texas 75275-0356; 214-768-3765, fax: 214-768-1136, e-mail address: jcherry@smu.edu

# Southern Oregon University
**Ashland, Oregon**

State-supported, coed. Small town campus. Total enrollment: 4,801. Theater program established 1982.
**Degrees** Bachelor of Fine Arts in the area of theater arts. Majors and concentrations: acting, costume design, design, directing, performance, scenic design, stage management, technical theater, theater business management.
**Enrollment** 139 total; 27 undergraduate, 112 nonprofessional degree.
**Theater Student Profile** 56% females, 44% males.
**Theater Faculty** 8 undergraduate (full-time), 2 undergraduate (part-time). 100% of full-time faculty have terminal degrees. Graduate students do not teach undergraduate courses.
**Expenses for 2007–2008** Application fee: $50. State resident tuition: $5409 full-time. Nonresident tuition: $17,988 full-time.

Full-time tuition varies according to course load, location, and reciprocity agreements. College room and board: $7941. Room and board charges vary according to board plan and housing facility.
**Financial Aid** Program-specific awards: 2 Angus Bowmer Theatre Arts Scholarships for acting, directing, and design majors ($500), 2 Beverly Bartell Scholarships for actors ($600), 1 Leon Mulling Scholarship for program majors ($500), departmental awards for program majors, Schneider Award for program majors, 2 E. Mulling Scholarships for program majors ($350), 1 Jeffrey Allen Staver Memorial Award for scenic design majors ($1000).
**Application Procedures** Students apply for admission into the professional program by sophomore year. Deadline for freshmen and transfers: continuous. Required: high school transcript, college transcript(s) for transfer students, minimum 3.0 high school GPA, 3 letters of recommendation, interview, audition, SAT or ACT test scores. Recommended: portfolio. Auditions held once in fall and spring on campus. Portfolio reviews held twice on campus; the submission of slides may be substituted for portfolios for applicants in technical areas.
**Web Site** http://www.sou.edu/thtr
**Undergraduate Contact** Associate Director of Admissions, Southern Oregon University, 1250 Siskiyou Boulevard, Ashland, Oregon 97520; 541-552-6411, fax: 541-552-6329, e-mail address: admissions@sou.edu

## *Sarofim School of Fine Arts*
# Southwestern University
**Georgetown, Texas**

Independent Methodist, coed. Suburban campus. Total enrollment: 1,294.
**Degrees** Bachelor of Fine Arts in the area of theater. Majors and concentrations: acting, music theater, technical theatre/design.
**Enrollment** 55 total; 15 undergraduate, 40 nonprofessional degree.
**Theater Student Profile** 60% females, 40% males, 10% minorities.
**Theater Faculty** 6 undergraduate (full-time), 3 undergraduate (part-time). 100% of full-time faculty have terminal degrees. Graduate students do not teach undergraduate courses. Undergraduate student–faculty ratio: 4:1.
**Student Life** Student groups/activities include Alpha Psi Omega, Mask and Wig Players.
**Expenses for 2007–2008** Application fee: $40. Comprehensive fee: $33,870 includes full-time tuition ($25,740) and college room and board ($8130). College room only: $4410. Room and board charges vary according to board plan and housing facility.
**Financial Aid** Program-specific awards: 10–20 departmental scholarships for program students ($5000).
**Application Procedures** Students apply for admission into the professional program by sophomore year. Deadline for freshmen: February 15; transfers: April 1. Required: essay, high school transcript, college transcript(s) for transfer students, minimum 3.0 high school GPA, letter of recommendation, interview, audition, SAT or ACT test scores, portfolio and/or audition for scholarship consideration. Auditions held by appointment (spring) on campus and off campus in various locations; recorded music is permissible as a substitute for live auditions. Portfolio reviews held on campus and off campus in various locations in Texas; the submission of slides may be substituted for portfolios.
**Web Site** http://www.southwestern.edu
**Undergraduate Contact** Dr. Rick Roemer, Chair/Artistic Director, Department of Theater, Southwestern University, 1001 East University Avenue, Georgetown, Texas 78626; 512-863-1548, fax: 512-863-1422, e-mail address: roemerr@southwestern.edu

# State University of New York at Fredonia
**Fredonia, New York**

State-supported, coed. Small town campus. Total enrollment: 5,404. Theater program established 1970.

*State University of New York at Fredonia (continued)*

**Degrees** Bachelor of Fine Arts. Majors and concentrations: acting, music theater, production/design. Program accredited by NAST, NASM.

**Enrollment** 153 total; 88 undergraduate, 65 nonprofessional degree.

**Theater Student Profile** 60% females, 40% males, 19% minorities, 2% international.

**Theater Faculty** 10 undergraduate (full-time), 4 undergraduate (part-time). 100% of full-time faculty have terminal degrees. Graduate students do not teach undergraduate courses. Undergraduate student–faculty ratio: 7:1.

**Student Life** Student groups/activities include Performing Arts Company (student run), Walter Gloor Mainstage Series, Orchesis Dance (student dance organization).

**Expenses for 2007–2008** Application fee: $40. State resident tuition: $4350 full-time. Nonresident tuition: $10,610 full-time. Mandatory fees: $1192 full-time. College room and board: $8380. College room only: $5050. Room and board charges vary according to board plan and housing facility. Special program-related fees: $20 per course for stagecraft materials fee, $35 per program for theatre major fees, $40 per program for BFA production and design CADD lab fee, $50 per course for audition techniques class accompanist, $100 per program for BFA music theater freshman/sophomore School of Music fee.

**Financial Aid** Program-specific awards: 6 Jack Cogdill Scholarships for program majors ($1250), 3 Gertrude Prushaw Maytum Scholarships for program majors ($1250).

**Application Procedures** Students admitted directly into the professional program freshman year. Deadline for freshmen and transfers: continuous. Required: high school transcript, college transcript(s) for transfer students, 2 letters of recommendation, interview, portfolio, SAT or ACT test scores, portfolio for production design applicants, audition for acting and music theater applicants. Recommended: minimum 3.0 high school GPA. Auditions held 8 times throughout the year by appointment on campus; videotaped performances are permissible as a substitute for live auditions if a live audition is impossible. Portfolio reviews held 4 times and throughout the year by appointment on campus; the submission of slides may be substituted for portfolios (CD/DVD preferred) if a campus visit is impossible.

**Web Site** http://www.fredonia.edu

**Undergraduate Contact** Prof. Stephen E. Rees, Chair, Department of Theatre and Dance, State University of New York at Fredonia, Rockefeller Arts Center, Fredonia, New York 14063; 716-673-3596, fax: 716-673-3621, e-mail address: stephen.rees@fredonia.edu

# Steinhardt School of Culture, Education, and Human Development, Department of Music and Performing Arts Professions

See New York University

# Stephen F. Austin State University
## Nacogdoches, Texas

State-supported, coed. Small town campus. Total enrollment: 11,607. Theater program established 1972.

**Degrees** Bachelor of Fine Arts in the area of theater. Majors and concentrations: acting, design technology, directing, stage management. Cross-registration with Rose Bruford College (United Kingdom). Program accredited by NAST.

**Enrollment** 181 total; 40 undergraduate, 141 nonprofessional degree.

**Theater Student Profile** 65% females, 35% males, 3% minorities, 10% international.

**Theater Faculty** 10 undergraduate (full-time), 4 undergraduate (part-time). 80% of full-time faculty have terminal degrees.

Graduate students do not teach undergraduate courses. Undergraduate student–faculty ratio: 18:1.

**Student Life** Student groups/activities include Beta Phi Chapter of Alpha Psi Omega.

**Expenses for 2007–2008** Application fee: $35. State resident tuition: $4410 full-time. Nonresident tuition: $12,750 full-time. Mandatory fees: $1752 full-time. Full-time tuition and fees vary according to course load. College room and board: $6885. Room and board charges vary according to board plan and housing facility. Special program-related fees: $5 for theater admission, $7–$15 per course for supplies.

**Financial Aid** Program-specific awards: 8–10 departmental scholarships for incoming students passing audition evaluations ($750–$1000), 1 Gray Scholarship for Nacogdoches County, TX residents ($500), 5–8 Stokes Foundation Scholarships for enrolled students ($600–$1000), 1 Cochran Scholarship for enrolled students ($700), 1 alumni scholarship for enrolled students ($500), 1 McGrath Scholarship for enrolled students ($700).

**Application Procedures** Students apply for admission into the professional program by sophomore year. Deadline for freshmen and transfers: continuous. Required: high school transcript, college transcript(s) for transfer students, minimum 2.0 high school GPA, interview, SAT or ACT test scores, audition for acting applicants, portfolio for design/technology applicants. Auditions held 4 times on campus and off campus in Texas Educational Theatre Association Convention location; videotaped performances are permissible as a substitute for live auditions when distance is prohibitive. Portfolio reviews held 4 times for design and technology applicants on campus and off campus in Texas Educational Theatre Association Convention; the submission of slides may be substituted for portfolios if a campus visit is impossible.

**Web Site** http://www.sfasu.edu/theatre/

**Undergraduate Contact** Mr. Scott Shattuck, Director, School of Theatre, Stephen F. Austin State University, PO Box 6090 SFA Station, Nacogdoches, Texas 75962-6090; 936-468-4003, fax: 936-468-7601, e-mail address: sshattuck@sfasu.edu

# Stephens College
## Columbia, Missouri

Independent, Urban campus. Total enrollment: 1,050. Theater program established 1899.

**Degrees** Bachelor of Fine Arts in the area of theater arts. Majors and concentrations: acting, costume design, design, directing, music theatre/dance, technical theater, theater management. Cross-registration with Mid-Missouri Associated Colleges and Universities.

**Enrollment** 104 total; all undergraduate.

**Theater Student Profile** 99% females, 1% males, 17% minorities, 4% international.

**Theater Faculty** 10 undergraduate (full-time). 80% of full-time faculty have terminal degrees. Graduate students do not teach undergraduate courses. Undergraduate student–faculty ratio: 12:1.

**Student Life** Student groups/activities include Warehouse Theatre, Velvetones (vocal group), Okoboji Summer Theatre.

**Expenses for 2008–2009** Application fee: $25. Comprehensive fee: $31,730 includes full-time tuition ($23,000) and college room and board ($8730). College room only: $5080.

**Financial Aid** Program-specific awards: 2 musical theater awards for vocalists ($500–$1500), 1 Patricia Barry Award for actors ($1500), 1 Maude Adams Award for actors ($1000), Leadership Awards for program majors ($1000–$2000).

**Application Procedures** Students admitted directly into the professional program freshman year. Deadline for freshmen and transfers: July 31. Notification date for freshmen and transfers: continuous. Required: essay, high school transcript, college transcript(s) for transfer students, minimum 2.0 high school GPA, letter of recommendation, SAT or ACT test scores, portfolio for design/technical applicants. Recommended: minimum 3.0 high school GPA, interview, video. Portfolio reviews held as needed on campus and off campus in various locations.

**Web Site** http://www.stephens.edu

**Undergraduate Contact** Office of Admission, Stephens College, Box 2121, Columbia, Missouri 65215; 800-876-7207, fax: 573-876-7237, e-mail address: apply@stephens.edu

# Syracuse University
### Syracuse, New York

Independent, coed. Urban campus. Total enrollment: 17,677. Theater program established 1921.

**Degrees** Bachelor of Fine Arts in the areas of drama, musical theater, design/technical theater, stage management; Bachelor of Science in the area of drama. Majors and concentrations: acting, design/technical theater, music theater, stage management.

**Enrollment** 297 total; all undergraduate.

**Theater Student Profile** 57% females, 43% males, 13% minorities.

**Theater Faculty** 15 total (full-time), 10 total (part-time). 77% of full-time faculty have terminal degrees. Graduate students do not teach undergraduate courses. Undergraduate student–faculty ratio: 14:1.

**Student Life** Student groups/activities include Danceworks, Black Box Players.

**Expenses for 2007–2008** Application fee: $70. Comprehensive fee: $42,626 includes full-time tuition ($30,470), mandatory fees ($1216), and college room and board ($10,940). College room only: $5660. Room and board charges vary according to board plan and housing facility. Special program-related fees: $15 per semester for piano maintenance, $25 for performances and subscriptions, $350–$700 per credit hour for private music lessons.

**Application Procedures** Students admitted directly into the professional program freshman year. Deadline for freshmen and transfers: January 1. Notification date for freshmen: March 15; transfers: August 15. Required: essay, high school transcript, college transcript(s) for transfer students, minimum 3.0 high school GPA, 2 letters of recommendation, SAT or ACT test scores, audition for acting and musical theater applicants, high school counselor evaluation, portfolio for design/technical theater and stage management applicants. Recommended: interview. Auditions held 10 times on campus and off campus in New York, NY; Washington, DC; Los Angeles CA; Chicago, IL; videotaped performances are permissible as a substitute for live auditions if a live audition is not possible. Portfolio reviews held 7 times on campus; the submission of slides may be substituted for portfolios if original work is not available or if a campus visit is impossible (for design/technical applicants only).

**Web Site** http://vpa.syr.edu/drama

**Undergraduate Contact** Director, CVPA Recruitment and Admissions, College of Visual and Performing Arts, Syracuse University, 202P Crouse College, Syracuse, New York 13244-1010; 315-443-2769, fax: 315-443-1935, e-mail address: admissu@syr.edu

# Tisch School of the Arts, Department of Drama, Undergraduate
See New York University

# Tisch School of the Arts, Rita and Burton Goldberg Department of Dramatic Writing
See New York University

# Tulane University
### New Orleans, Louisiana

Independent, coed. Urban campus. Total enrollment: 10,519. Theater program established 1937.

**Degrees** Bachelor of Fine Arts in the areas of acting, design/technical theatre. Majors and concentrations: acting, design/technical theater. Graduate degrees offered: Master of Fine Arts in the area of design/technical theater. Cross-registration with Loyola University New Orleans.

**Enrollment** 59 total; 6 undergraduate, 3 graduate, 50 nonprofessional degree.

**Theater Student Profile** 60% females, 40% males, 5% international.

**Theater Faculty** 19 total (full-time), 4 total (part-time). 100% of full-time faculty have terminal degrees. Graduate students teach a few undergraduate courses. Undergraduate student–faculty ratio: 10:1.

**Student Life** Student groups/activities include American College Theatre Festival, United States Institute for Theatre Technology, Southeastern Theatre Conference.

**Expenses for 2007–2008** Application fee: $0. Comprehensive fee: $45,550 includes full-time tuition ($33,500), mandatory fees ($3110), and college room and board ($8940). College room only: $5140. Room and board charges vary according to board plan and housing facility. Special program-related fees: $35 per semester for design studio fee.

**Application Procedures** Students apply for admission into the professional program by sophomore year. Deadline for freshmen: January 15; transfers: June 1. Notification date for freshmen: April 1; transfers: continuous. Required: essay, high school transcript, college transcript(s) for transfer students, minimum 2.0 high school GPA, SAT or ACT test scores, minimum 3.0 college GPA for transfer students, 1 recommendation from high school counselor, audition for acting applicants, portfolio for design/technical applicants. Recommended: 2 letters of recommendation, interview, SAT. Auditions held once on campus. Portfolio reviews held twice on campus and off campus in United States Institute for Theatre Technology; the submission of slides may be substituted for portfolios when scheduling is difficult.

**Web Site** http://www.tulane.edu/~theatre

**Undergraduate Contact** Prof. Martin Sachs, Chair, Department of Theatre and Dance, Tulane University, McWilliams Hall, New Orleans, Louisiana 70118; 504-314-7744 ext. 1757, fax: 504-865-6737, e-mail address: msachs@tulane.edu

**Graduate Contact** Prof. Martin Sachs, Head, MFA Design Program, Department of Theatre and Dance, Tulane University, McWilliams Hall, New Orleans, Louisiana 70118; 504-314-7744, fax: 504-865-6737, e-mail address: msachs@tulane.edu

# The University of British Columbia
### Vancouver, British Columbia, Canada

Province-supported, coed. Urban campus. Total enrollment: 43,720. Theater program established 1951.

**Web Site** http://www.ubc.ca/

# University of California, Santa Barbara
### Santa Barbara, California

State-supported, coed. Suburban campus. Total enrollment: 21,410. Theater program established 1984.

**Web Site** http://www.ucsb.edu/

# University of Central Florida
### Orlando, Florida

State-supported, coed. Suburban campus. Total enrollment: 48,497. Theater program established 1968.

**Degrees** Bachelor of Fine Arts in the areas of acting, musical theatre, design and technology stage management. Majors and concentrations: acting, music theater, performance, stage management. Graduate degrees offered: Master of Fine Arts in the areas of acting, design, musical theatre, theatre for young audiences.

**Enrollment** 407 total; 224 undergraduate, 43 graduate, 140 nonprofessional degree.

**Theater Student Profile** 55% females, 45% males, 15% minorities.

**Theater Faculty** 34 total (full-time), 6 total (part-time). 100% of full-time faculty have terminal degrees. Graduate students teach a few undergraduate courses. Undergraduate student–faculty ratio: 10:1.

**Student Life** Student groups/activities include Alpha Psi Omega, Florida Theatre Association.

*University of Central Florida (continued)*

**Expenses for 2007–2008** Application fee: $30. State resident tuition: $3020 full time. Nonresident tuition: $17,821 full-time. Full-time tuition varies according to course load. College room and board: $8164. College room only: $4600. Room and board charges vary according to board plan and housing facility. Special program-related fees: $15 per credit hour for equipment; lab fee.

**Financial Aid** Program-specific awards: 32 talent grants for program majors ($1000), 24 Disney Scholarships for design/technology and stage management majors ($2200), 1 James Cali Award for BFA majors ($1500), 6 Florida Theatrical Awards for BFA majors ($1000).

**Application Procedures** Students admitted directly into the professional program freshman year. Deadline for freshmen and transfers: August 1. Notification date for freshmen and transfers: August 15. Required: high school transcript, college transcript(s) for transfer students, minimum 3.0 high school GPA, 3 letters of recommendation, interview, audition, portfolio, SAT or ACT test scores. Auditions held 3 times on campus; videotaped performances are permissible as a substitute for live auditions when distance is prohibitive. Portfolio reviews held 6 times on campus; the submission of slides may be substituted for portfolios when distance is prohibitive.

**Web Site** http://www.theatre.ucf.edu

**Undergraduate Contact** Office of Admissions, University of Central Florida, PO Box 160111, Orlando, Florida 32816; 407-823-3180, e-mail address: admission@mail.ucf.edu

**Graduate Contact** Dr. Julia Listengarten, Associate Professor, Department of Theatre, University of Central Florida, PO Box 162372, Orlando, Florida 32816; 407-823-3858, fax: 407-823-6446, e-mail address: jlisteng@mail.ucf.edu

# University of Cincinnati

See University of Cincinnati College Conservatory of Music

*University of Cincinnati*

# University of Cincinnati College Conservatory of Music

**Cincinnati, Ohio**

State-supported, coed. Urban campus. Total enrollment: 29,319. Theater program established 1970.

**Degrees** Bachelor of Fine Arts in the areas of musical theater, dramatic performance, theater design and production. Majors and concentrations: costume design, dramatic performance, lighting design, makeup, music theater, set design, sound design, stage management. Graduate degrees offered: Master of Fine Arts in the areas of directing, theater design and production. Cross-registration with Greater Cincinnati Consortium of Colleges and Universities. Program accredited by NAST, NASM, NASD.

**Enrollment** 229 total; 202 undergraduate, 27 graduate.

**Theater Student Profile** 49% females, 51% males, 7% minorities, 1% international.

**Theater Faculty** 15 total (full-time), 11 total (part-time). 95% of full-time faculty have terminal degrees. Graduate students teach a few undergraduate courses. Undergraduate student–faculty ratio: 7:1.

**Student Life** Student groups/activities include Student Artist Program. Special housing available for theater students.

**Expenses for 2007–2008** Application fee: $40. State resident tuition: $7896 full-time. Nonresident tuition: $22,419 full-time. Mandatory fees: $1503 full-time. Full-time tuition and fees vary according to course load, degree level, location, program, and reciprocity agreements. College room and board: $8799. College room only: $5259. Room and board charges vary according to board plan and housing facility.

**Financial Aid** Program-specific awards: 86 honors awards for program majors ($3700), 21 Cincinnatus Awards for those in top

5% of graduating class with minimum 26 ACT score or minimum 1170 SAT score ($2000–$20,000).

**Application Procedures** Students admitted directly into the professional program freshman year. Deadline for freshmen and transfers: February 1. Notification date for freshmen and transfers: continuous. Required: high school transcript, college transcript(s) for transfer students, letter of recommendation, audition, SAT or ACT test scores, portfolio, interview, essay, and 3 letters of recommendation for theater design and production applicants. Recommended: minimum 3.0 high school GPA. Auditions held 10 times on campus and off campus in Atlanta, GA; New York, NY; Chicago, IL; Los Angeles, CA; San Francisco, CA; Seattle, WA; Southeastern Theatre Conference sites. Portfolio reviews held 8 times for theater design and production applicants on campus and off campus in New York, NY; Chicago, IL; Los Angeles, CA; CA; Atlanta, GA; Seattle, WA; Southeastern Theatre Conference sites; the submission of slides may be substituted for portfolios with approval from the department.

**Web Site** http://www.ccm.uc.edu

**Undergraduate Contact** Ms. P.J. Woolston, Senior Admissions Officer, College-Conservatory of Music, University of Cincinnati, PO Box 210003, Cincinnati, Ohio 45221-0003; 513-556-9479, fax: 513-556-1028, e-mail address: pj.woolston@uc.edu

**Graduate Contact** Mr. Paul R. Hillner, Assistant Dean, College-Conservatory of Music, University of Cincinnati, PO Box 210003, Cincinnati, Ohio 45221-0003; 513-556-9478, fax: 513-556-1028, e-mail address: paul.hillner@uc.edu

# University of Colorado at Boulder

**Boulder, Colorado**

State-supported, coed. Suburban campus. Total enrollment: 31,470. Theater program established 1962.

**Degrees** Bachelor of Fine Arts in the area of theater. Majors and concentrations: design/technical theater, music theater, performance. Graduate degrees offered: Doctor of Philosophy in the area of theater.

**Enrollment** 214 total; 53 undergraduate, 29 graduate, 132 nonprofessional degree.

**Theater Student Profile** 66% females, 34% males, 12% minorities, 2% international.

**Theater Faculty** 14 total (full-time), 3 total (part-time). 100% of full-time faculty have terminal degrees. Graduate students teach a few undergraduate courses. Undergraduate student–faculty ratio: 4:1.

**Student Life** Student groups/activities include On Stage, Colorado Shakespeare Festival. Special housing available for theater students.

**Expenses for 2008–2009** Application fee: $50. One-time mandatory fee: $112. State resident tuition: $5922 full-time. Nonresident tuition: $25,400 full-time. Mandatory fees: $1356 full-time. College room and board: $9860. Special program-related fees: $25 per course for instructional support in selected courses.

**Financial Aid** Program-specific awards: 14 Technical Assistant Awards for program students ($4400), 5 University Theatre Awards for theatre majors ($550), 2 University Theatre Awards for incoming freshmen ($1000), 1–3 David A. Busse Scholarships for upperclass design students ($1000), 1 Dorothy and Anthony Riddle Scholarship for actors/students ($900), 1 Mabel Gaiser Borgmann Scholarship for female drama students ($700), 2 Katherine J. Lamont Scholarships for junior and senior theater and dance majors ($1300).

**Application Procedures** Students apply for admission into the professional program by sophomore year. Deadline for freshmen: January 15; transfers: April 1. Required: essay, high school transcript, college transcript(s) for transfer students, SAT or ACT test scores, audition for music theater applicants. Recommended: minimum 3.0 high school GPA. Auditions held once on campus.

**Web Site** http://www.colorado.edu/TheatreDance/

**Undergraduate Contact** Dr. Bud Coleman, Chair, Department of Theatre and Dance, University of Colorado at Boulder, CB 261, Boulder, Colorado 80309-0261; 303-492-2793, fax: 303-492-7722, e-mail address: bud.coleman@colorado.edu

**Graduate Contact** Michelle Gipner, Theater Studies Assistant, Department of Theatre and Dance, University of Colorado at

Boulder, CB 261, Boulder, Colorado 80309-0261; 303-492-7356, fax: 303-492-7722, e-mail address: gipner@colorado.edu

# University of Connecticut
## Storrs, Connecticut

State-supported, coed. Rural campus. Total enrollment: 23,692. Theater program established 1960.

**Degrees** Bachelor of Fine Arts in the areas of acting, design, puppetry, technical direction. Majors and concentrations: acting, design/technical theater, puppetry. Graduate degrees offered: Master of Arts in the area of production-puppetry; Master of Fine Arts in the areas of acting, design, puppetry, technical direction. Program accredited by NAST.

**Enrollment** 163 total; 121 undergraduate, 30 graduate, 12 nonprofessional degree.

**Theater Student Profile** 53% females, 47% males.

**Theater Faculty** 15 total (full-time), 3 total (part-time). 85% of full-time faculty have terminal degrees. Graduate students teach a few undergraduate courses. Undergraduate student–faculty ratio: 5:1.

**Student Life** Student groups/activities include Connecticut Repertory Theatre. Special housing available for theater students.

**Expenses for 2008–2009** Application fee: $70. State resident tuition: $7200 full-time. Nonresident tuition: $21,912 full-time. Mandatory fees: $2138 full-time. College room and board: $9300. College room only: $4210. Special program-related fees: $60 for supplemental materials costs.

**Financial Aid** Program-specific awards: 15 University Drama Scholarships for incoming students ($1000).

**Application Procedures** Students admitted directly into the professional program freshman year. Deadline for freshmen and transfers: March 6. Notification date for freshmen and transfers: continuous. Required: essay, high school transcript, college transcript(s) for transfer students, interview, audition, portfolio, SAT or ACT test scores, interview and portfolio for design/technical theater applicants, audition for acting applicants, audition and interview for puppetry applicants. Recommended: 2 letters of recommendation. Auditions held 4 times by appointment for acting and puppetry majors on campus. Portfolio reviews held by appointment on campus; the submission of slides may be substituted for portfolios if a campus visit is impossible.

**Web Site** http://www.drama.uconn.edu

**Undergraduate Contact** Admissions Assistant, Department of Dramatic Arts, University of Connecticut, U-127, 802 Bolton Road, Storrs, Connecticut 06269-1127; 860-486-2281, fax: 860-486-3110, e-mail address: daoffice@uconn.edu

**Graduate Contact** Ms. Mary Tellier, Administrative Assistant, Department of Dramatic Arts, University of Connecticut, U-127, 802 Bolton Road, Storrs, Connecticut 06269-1127; 860-486-2281, fax: 860-486-3110, e-mail address: mary.tellier@uconn.edu

# University of Florida
## Gainesville, Florida

State-supported, coed. Suburban campus. Total enrollment: 51,725. Theater program established 1975.

**Degrees** Bachelor of Fine Arts in the areas of theater performance, acting, musical theater, theater production, costume design, costume technology, light design, scene design. Majors and concentrations: acting, costume design, lighting design, music theater, scenic design. Graduate degrees offered: Master of Fine Arts in the areas of theater performance, theater production. Cross-registration with Florida State University System. Program accredited by NAST.

**Enrollment** 224 total; 66 undergraduate, 36 graduate, 122 nonprofessional degree.

**Theater Student Profile** 70% females, 30% males, 20% minorities, 1% international.

**Theater Faculty** 17 total (full-time), 4 total (part-time). 100% of full-time faculty have terminal degrees. Graduate students teach a few undergraduate courses. Undergraduate student–faculty ratio: 4:1.

**Student Life** Student groups/activities include International Production Program, Florida Players, Theatre Strike Force. Special housing available for theater students.

**Expenses for 2007–2008** Application fee: $30. State resident tuition: $3257 full-time. Nonresident tuition: $17,841 full-time. College room and board: $7020. College room only: $4530. Room and board charges vary according to board plan. Special program-related fees: $15–$45 for lab fees.

**Financial Aid** Program-specific awards: 5 Constans Theater and Dance Scholarships for program majors ($500), 5 Ingram Scholarships for program majors ($500), 2 Richardson Scholarships for program majors ($1000), 8 Stoughton Scholarships for program majors ($500), 3 Outstanding Senior Awards for graduating seniors ($500), Hubbell Scholarships for program majors ($1000), 1 Gator Tones Musical Theatre Award for musical theatre majors ($200).

**Application Procedures** Students admitted directly into the professional program freshman year. Deadline for freshmen: January 7; transfers: June 7. Required: essay, high school transcript, college transcript(s) for transfer students, minimum 2.0 high school GPA, audition, portfolio, SAT or ACT test scores. Recommended: minimum 3.0 high school GPA, letter of recommendation. Auditions held twice on campus and off campus in New York, NY; Chicago, IL. Portfolio reviews held twice on campus and off campus in Southeastern Theatre Conference, American College Theatre Festival, University Resident Theatre Association; the submission of slides may be substituted for portfolios with permission from the school.

**Web Site** http://www.arts.ufl.edu/theatreanddance

**Undergraduate Contact** Prof. Kevin Austin, Director, School of Theatre and Dance, University of Florida, PO Box 115900, Gainesville, Florida 32611-5900; 352-273-0519, fax: 352-392-5114, e-mail address: kaustin@ufl.edu

**Graduate Contact** Dr. Mikell Pinkney, Graduate Coordinator, School of Theatre and Dance, University of Florida, PO Box 115900, Gainesville, Florida 32611-5900; 352-273-0512, fax: 352-392-5114, e-mail address: mpinkney@ufl.edu

# *The Hartt School*
# University of Hartford
## West Hartford, Connecticut

Independent, coed. Suburban campus. Total enrollment: 7,290. Theater program established 1996.

**Web Site** http://www.hartford.edu/

# University of Houston
## Houston, Texas

State-supported, coed. Urban campus. Total enrollment: 34,663. Theater program established 1970.

**Degrees** Bachelor of Arts in the area of theater. Majors and concentrations: acting, dance, design, directing, music theater, playwriting. Graduate degrees offered: Master of Arts in the area of theater; Master of Fine Arts in the area of theater.

**Enrollment** 290 total; 237 undergraduate, 53 graduate.

**Theater Student Profile** 67% females, 33% males, 26% minorities, 2% international.

**Theater Faculty** 11 total (full-time), 4 total (part-time). 100% of full-time faculty have terminal degrees. Graduate students teach a few undergraduate courses. Undergraduate student–faculty ratio: 16:1.

**Student Life** Student groups/activities include Alpha Psi Omega.

**Expenses for 2007–2008** Application fee: $50. State resident tuition: $4826 full-time. Nonresident tuition: $13,166 full-time. Mandatory fees: $2624 full-time. Full-time tuition and fees vary according to course level, course load, degree level, location, program, reciprocity agreements, and student level. College room and board: $6651. College room only: $3778. Room and board charges vary according to board plan and housing facility. Special program-related fees: $20–$50 per course for equipment maintenance and supplies fee.

**Financial Aid** Program-specific awards: 5 theater scholarships for all theater students ($750), 1 Trey Wilson Award for all theater

*University of Houston (continued)*

students ($1000), 1 Robert Bullard Award for all theater students ($500), 1 Cecil Pickett Award for all theater students ($1000), 1 Joseph Michael Adamo Award for all theater students ($500), 1 Jose Quintero Award for all theater students ($1000).
**Application Procedures** Students admitted directly into the professional program freshman year. Deadline for freshmen and transfers: July 1. Required: high school transcript, college transcript(s) for transfer students, minimum 3.0 high school GPA, 3 letters of recommendation, SAT test score only.
**Web Site** http://www.hfac.uh.edu/theatre/home.html
**Undergraduate Contact** Molly Dean, Academic Advisor, Admission Office, University of Houston, 4800 Calhoun, Wortham Theatre, Houston, Texas 77204-4016; 713-743-2913, fax: 713-749-1420, e-mail address: mcdean@uh.edu
**Graduate Contact** Dr. Sidney Berger, Director, School of Theatre, University of Houston, 4800 Calhoun, Wortham Theatre, Houston, Texas 77204-4016; 713-743-2930, fax: 713-749-4016, e-mail address: sberger@uh.edu

# University of Illinois at Urbana–Champaign
## Champaign, Illinois

State-supported, coed. Urban campus. Total enrollment: 42,326. Theater program established 1969.
**Degrees** Bachelor of Fine Arts in the areas of acting, design, technology and management, theater studies. Majors and concentrations: acting, costume design, costume technology, lighting design, scenic design, scenic technology, sound design and technology, stage management, theater studies. Graduate degrees offered: Master of Fine Arts in the areas of acting, design, technology and management. Doctor of Philosophy. Cross-registration with Parkland College. Program accredited by NAST.
**Enrollment** 185 total; 126 undergraduate, 59 graduate.
**Theater Student Profile** 48% females, 52% males, 10% minorities, 1% international.
**Theater Faculty** 20 total (full-time), 13 total (part-time). 100% of full-time faculty have terminal degrees. Graduate students teach a few undergraduate courses. Undergraduate student–faculty ratio: 8:1.
**Student Life** Student groups/activities include KCPA season productions, Armory Free Theatre.
**Expenses for 2007–2008** Application fee: $40. State resident tuition: $8440 full-time. Nonresident tuition: $22,526 full-time. Mandatory fees: $2690 full-time. Full-time tuition and fees vary according to course load, program, and student level. College room and board: $8196. Room and board charges vary according to board plan and housing facility. Entering degree-seeking students are guaranteed the same tuition rates for 4 years.
**Financial Aid** Program-specific awards: 50 talented student tuition waivers for program students ($500–$1000), 6 Bernard Gold Awards for program students ($1000).
**Application Procedures** Students admitted directly into the professional program freshman year. Deadline for freshmen and transfers: continuous. Notification date for freshmen and transfers: April 15. Required: high school transcript, college transcript(s) for transfer students, minimum 2.0 high school GPA, interview, audition, portfolio, SAT or ACT test scores (minimum combined SAT score of 920, minimum composite ACT score of 19), audition for acting applicants, portfolio for design applicants, statement of purpose for theater studies applicants and interview. Recommended: essay, minimum 3.0 high school GPA. Auditions held 6 times on campus and off campus in Chicago, IL; videotaped performances are permissible as a substitute for live auditions if a campus visit is impossible. Portfolio reviews held 6 times on campus; the submission of slides may be substituted for portfolios for international applicants.
**Web Site** http://www.theatre.uiuc.edu/
**Undergraduate Contact** Mr. David Swinford, Admissions and Records Representative, Department of Theatre, University of Illinois at Urbana–Champaign, 4-122KCPA, 500 South Goodwin Avenue, Urbana, Illinois 61801; 217-244-6189, fax: 217-244-1861, e-mail address: dswinfor@uiuc.edu

**Graduate Contact** Mr. David Swinford, Admissions and Records Representative, Department of Theatre, University of Illinois at Urbana–Champaign, 4-122 Krannert Center for the Performing Arts, 500 South Goodwin Avenue, Urbana, Illinois 61801; 217-244-6189, fax: 217-244-1861, e-mail address: dswinfor@uiuc.edu

# University of Kentucky
## Lexington, Kentucky

State-supported, coed. Urban campus. Total enrollment: 25,856. Theater program established 1928.
**Web Site** http://www.uky.edu/

# University of Memphis
## Memphis, Tennessee

State-supported, coed. Urban campus. Total enrollment: 20,379. Theater program established 1950.
**Web Site** http://www.memphis.edu/

# University of Miami
## Coral Gables, Florida

Independent, coed. Suburban campus. Total enrollment: 15,462. Theater program established 1936.
**Degrees** Bachelor of Fine Arts in the area of theater arts. Majors and concentrations: design production, music theater, performance, stage management, theater management.
**Enrollment** 130 total; 60 undergraduate, 70 nonprofessional degree.
**Theater Student Profile** 60% females, 40% males, 17% minorities.
**Theater Faculty** 19 undergraduate (full-time), 2 undergraduate (part-time). 100% of full-time faculty have terminal degrees. Graduate students do not teach undergraduate courses. Undergraduate student–faculty ratio: 6:1.
**Student Life** Student groups/activities include Jerry Herman Ring Theatre, TAG-Theatre Action Group.
**Expenses for 2007–2008** Application fee: $65. Comprehensive fee: $42,724 includes full-time tuition ($32,422), mandatory fees ($696), and college room and board ($9606). College room only: $5762.
**Financial Aid** Program-specific awards: 12 departmental scholarships for program majors demonstrating need/talent ($1000–$3000).
**Application Procedures** Students admitted directly into the professional program freshman year. Deadline for freshmen: February 15; transfers: continuous. Notification date for freshmen: May 1; transfers: continuous. Required: essay, high school transcript, college transcript(s) for transfer students, minimum 3.0 high school GPA, letter of recommendation, interview, audition, portfolio, SAT or ACT test scores (minimum composite ACT score of 24). Auditions held by appointment on campus and off campus in New York, NY; Chicago, IL; Southeastern Theatre Conference sites; International Thespian Conference sites; videotaped performances are permissible as a substitute for live auditions if a campus visit is impossible. Portfolio reviews held by appointment on campus and off campus in New York, NY; Chicago, IL; Southeastern Theatre Conference sites; International Thespian Conference sites; the submission of slides may be substituted for portfolios for design, production, management applicants.
**Web Site** http://www.miami.edu/tha/
**Undergraduate Contact** Ms. Doris Thompson, Staff Associate, Department of Theatre Arts, University of Miami, PO Box 248273, Coral Gables, Florida 33124-4820; 305-284-4474, fax: 305-284-5702, e-mail address: dthompson@miami.edu

# University of Michigan
## Ann Arbor, Michigan

State-supported, coed. Suburban campus. Total enrollment: 41,042. Theater program established 1915.

**Degrees** Bachelor of Fine Arts in the areas of theatre performance, acting or directing, theatre design and production; Bachelor in Theater Arts. Majors and concentrations: acting, directing, production/design, theater arts/drama, theater design and production.
**Enrollment** 147 total; 125 undergraduate, 22 nonprofessional degree.
**Theater Student Profile** 58% females, 42% males, 7% minorities.
**Theater Faculty** 17 total (full-time), 14 total (part-time). 80% of full-time faculty have terminal degrees. Graduate students do not teach undergraduate courses. Undergraduate student–faculty ratio: 5:1.
**Student Life** Student groups/activities include Basement Arts Productions, university productions.
**Expenses for 2007–2008** Application fee: $40. State resident tuition: $10,258 full-time. Nonresident tuition: $31,112 full-time. Mandatory fees: $189 full-time. Full-time tuition and fees vary according to course load, degree level, location, program, and student level. College room and board: $8190. Room and board charges vary according to board plan and housing facility.
**Financial Aid** Program-specific awards: 16–18 merit awards for continuing students ($800–$5000), 25 scholarships for continuing students ($500–$12,000).
**Application Procedures** Students admitted directly into the professional program freshman year. Deadline for freshmen and transfers: December 1. Required: essay, high school transcript, college transcript(s) for transfer students, minimum 3.0 high school GPA, 2 letters of recommendation, interview, SAT or ACT test scores (minimum combined SAT score of 1650, minimum composite ACT score of 24), portfolio for design, production, and directing applicants, audition for acting applicants. Recommended: production photos for design and production applicants. Auditions held 10 times on campus and off campus in Chicago, IL; New York, NY; Los Angeles, CA; San Francisco, CA. Portfolio reviews held 6 times and by appointment on campus; the submission of slides may be substituted for portfolios when distance is prohibitive.
**Web Site** http://www.music.umich.edu
**Undergraduate Contact** Ms. Laura Strozeski, Assistant Dean for Enrollment Management & Student Services, Office of Admissions and Student Services, University of Michigan, 1100 Baits Drive, Ann Arbor, Michigan 48109-2085; 734-764-0593, fax: 734-763-5097, e-mail address: music.admissions@umich.edu

# University of Michigan–Flint
## Flint, Michigan

State-supported, coed. Urban campus. Total enrollment: 6,883. Theater program established 1975.
**Degrees** Bachelor of Fine Arts in the area of performance; Bachelor of Science in the area of design and technology. Majors and concentrations: performance.
**Enrollment** 55 total; 7 undergraduate, 48 nonprofessional degree.
**Theater Student Profile** 50% females, 50% males, 10% minorities.
**Theater Faculty** 7 undergraduate (full-time), 4 undergraduate (part-time). 100% of full-time faculty have terminal degrees. Graduate students do not teach undergraduate courses. Undergraduate student–faculty ratio: 9:1.
**Student Life** Student groups/activities include American College Theatre Festival.
**Expenses for 2007–2008** Application fee: $30. State resident tuition: $6994 full-time. Nonresident tuition: $13,650 full-time. Mandatory fees: $348 full-time. Full-time tuition and fees vary according to course level, course load, degree level, program, and student level.
**Financial Aid** Program-specific awards: 3 Carl and Sarah Morgan Trust Awards for theater majors ($1000–$3300), 1 Jeffrey F. Garfield Scholarship for theater majors ($1000–$3300), 14 departmental awards for theater majors ($1000–$3300), 1 Kay Kelly Award for theatre majors ($500).
**Application Procedures** Students apply for admission into the professional program by sophomore year. Deadline for freshmen and transfers: continuous. Required: high school transcript, college transcript(s) for transfer students, minimum 3.0 high school GPA, interview, audition, portfolio, SAT or ACT test scores, minimum 2.7 high school GPA in academic courses in

grades 10-12. Recommended: letter of recommendation. Auditions held once in March on campus. Portfolio reviews held once on campus.
**Web Site** http://www.flint.umich.edu
**Undergraduate Contact** Dr. Lauren Friesen, Chair, Department of Theater, University of Michigan–Flint, 303 East Kearsley Street, Flint, Michigan 48502-1950; 810-762-3349, fax: 810-766-6630, e-mail address: lfriesen@umich.edu

# University of Minnesota, Twin Cities Campus
## Minneapolis, Minnesota

State-supported, coed. Urban campus. Total enrollment: 50,883. Theater program established 1999.
**Degrees** Bachelor of Fine Arts in the area of acting. Majors and concentrations: acting. Graduate degrees offered: Master of Fine Arts in the area of design and technology. Program accredited by NAST.
**Enrollment** 384 total; 68 undergraduate, 12 graduate, 304 nonprofessional degree.
**Theater Student Profile** 60% females, 40% males, 5% minorities, 5% international.
**Theater Faculty** 5 undergraduate (full-time), 6 undergraduate (part-time), 7 graduate (full-time), 1 graduate (part-time). 100% of full-time faculty have terminal degrees. Graduate students do not teach undergraduate courses. Undergraduate student–faculty ratio: 15:1.
**Student Life** Student groups/activities include partnership with Guthrie Theater. Special housing available for theater students.
**Expenses for 2007–2008** Application fee: $45. One-time mandatory fee: $1000. State resident tuition: $7950 full-time. Nonresident tuition: $19,580 full-time. Full-time tuition varies according to program and reciprocity agreements. College room and board: $7062. College room only: $4184. Room and board charges vary according to board plan, housing facility, and location.
**Financial Aid** Program-specific awards: department scholarships.
**Application Procedures** Students admitted directly into the professional program freshman year. Deadline for freshmen and transfers: continuous. Notification date for freshmen and transfers: April 15. Required: high school transcript, college transcript(s) for transfer students, audition, SAT or ACT test scores. Recommended: minimum 3.0 high school GPA, 2 letters of recommendation. Auditions held once in each city in January and February on campus and off campus in New York, NY; Chicago, IL; San Francisco, CA, Las Vegas, NV.
**Web Site** http://theatre.umn.edu/
**Undergraduate Contact** Afton McNitt, Undergraduate Studies Secretary, Department of Theatre Arts and Dance, University of Minnesota, Twin Cities Campus, 580 Rarig Center, 330 21st Avenue South, Minneapolis, Minnesota 55455; 612-624-1257, fax: 612-625-6334, e-mail address: theatre@umn.edu
**Graduate Contact** Virginia Arons, Secretary for Graduate Studies, 580 Rarig Centre, University of Minnesota, Twin Cities Campus, 330 21st Avenue South, Minneapolis, Minnesota 55455; 612-625-5029, fax: 612-625-6334, e-mail address: theatre@umn.edu

# The University of Montana
## Missoula, Montana

State-supported, coed. Total enrollment: 13,858. Theater program established 1950.
**Degrees** Bachelor of Fine Arts in the area of drama. Majors and concentrations: acting, design technology. Graduate degrees offered: Master of Fine Arts in the area of drama. Program accredited by NAST.
**Enrollment** 199 total; 74 undergraduate, 9 graduate, 116 nonprofessional degree.
**Theater Student Profile** 54% females, 46% males, 1% minorities.
**Theater Faculty** 9 total (full-time), 7 total (part-time). 100% of full-time faculty have terminal degrees. Graduate students teach a few undergraduate courses. Undergraduate student–faculty ratio: 15:1.

*The University of Montana (continued)*

**Student Life** Student groups/activities include Montana Repertory Theatre, Montana Repertory Missoula.

**Expenses for 2008–2009** Application fee: $30. State resident tuition: $3739 full-time. Nonresident tuition: $15,014 full-time. Mandatory fees: $1441 full-time. College room and board: $6258. College room only: $2808. Special program-related fees: $20–$60 per course for class materials/performance tickets (selected classes).

**Financial Aid** Program-specific awards: 15 departmental scholarships for program majors ($250–$1000), 1 Gordon Scholarship for program majors ($300), 8 Dean Awards for program majors ($500–$800), 1 Mary Carol Zeman Award for program majors ($1000), 2 Kliber Memorial Awards for program majors ($1000), 1 William Gillespie Award for program majors ($1000), 12 Odyssey Scholarships for program majors ($200–$1000), 3 Moore and Cardell Awards for program majors ($100–$400).

**Application Procedures** Students apply for admission into the professional program by freshman, sophomore year. Deadline for freshmen and transfers: March 1. Notification date for freshmen and transfers: continuous. Required: high school transcript, college transcript(s) for transfer students, SAT or ACT test scores (minimum combined SAT score of 1540, minimum composite ACT score of 22). Recommended: minimum 2.0 high school GPA.

**Web Site** http://www.sfa.umt.edu/drama

**Contact** Erin McDaniel, Administrative Assistant, Department of Drama/Dance, The University of Montana, PARTV 196, Missoula, Montana 59812-8136; 406-243-4481, fax: 406-243-5726, e-mail address: umtheatredance@umontana.edu

# University of Montevallo

## Montevallo, Alabama

State-supported, coed. Small town campus. Total enrollment: 2,948. Theater program established 1923.

**Degrees** Bachelor of Fine Arts in the areas of acting/directing, design, musical theatre. Majors and concentrations: acting, directing, music theater, technical theatre/design. Cross-registration with Birmingham Area Consortium for Higher Education (BACHE): Samford University, Birmingham-Southern College, Miles College, University of Alabama at Birmingham.

**Enrollment** 75 total; all undergraduate.

**Theater Student Profile** 60% females, 40% males, 10% minorities.

**Theater Faculty** 5 undergraduate (full-time), 6 undergraduate (part-time). 100% of full-time faculty have terminal degrees. Graduate students teach a few undergraduate courses. Undergraduate student–faculty ratio: 15:1.

**Student Life** Student groups/activities include Joint Music-Theatre Musicals, College of Fine Arts fundraising gala.

**Expenses for 2007–2008** Application fee: $25. State resident tuition: $5850 full-time. Nonresident tuition: $11,700 full-time. Mandatory fees: $230 full-time. Full-time tuition and fees vary according to course load. College room and board: $4360. Special program-related fees: $100–$150 per semester for dance shoes, make-up, and art supplies.

**Financial Aid** Program-specific awards: 4–10 Dean of Fine Arts Awards for talented students with high GPA ($1000), 15 endowed awards for talented students ($500–$1000), 4 President's Scholarships for talented students with high GPA ($3600).

**Application Procedures** Students apply for admission into the professional program by sophomore year. Deadline for freshmen and transfers: August 15. Notification date for freshmen and transfers: continuous. Required: high school transcript, college transcript(s) for transfer students, minimum 3.0 high school GPA, 2 letters of recommendation, interview, audition, portfolio, SAT or ACT test scores (minimum composite ACT score of 18), interview for acting, directing and technical theater applicants. Auditions held twice on campus. Portfolio reviews held twice on campus; the submission of slides may be substituted for portfolios as part of interview.

**Web Site** http://www.montevallo.edu/thea/

**Undergraduate Contact** Pam Lucas, Division Secretary, Communication Art Department, University of Montevallo, Station 6210, Montevallo, Alabama 35115; 205-665-6210, fax: 205-665-6211, e-mail address: lucasp@montevallo.edu

*Johnny Carson School of Theatre and Film*

# University of Nebraska–Lincoln

## Lincoln, Nebraska

State-supported, coed. Urban campus. Total enrollment: 22,973. Theater program established 1900.

**Degrees** Bachelor of Fine Arts in the areas of design/technical theatre, film and new media. Majors and concentrations: film and new media, theater design/technology. Graduate degrees offered: Master of Fine Arts in the areas of acting, design/technical theater, directing for stage and screen. Program accredited by NAST.

**Enrollment** 120 total; 106 undergraduate, 14 graduate.

**Theater Student Profile** 10% minorities.

**Theater Faculty** 14 total (full-time), 2 total (part-time). 100% of full-time faculty have terminal degrees. Graduate students teach a few undergraduate courses. Undergraduate student–faculty ratio: 7:1.

**Student Life** Student groups/activities include American College Theatre Festival, University/Resident Theatre Association.

**Expenses for 2007–2008** Application fee: $45. State resident tuition: $5085 full-time. Nonresident tuition: $15,105 full-time. Mandatory fees: $1130 full-time. Full-time tuition and fees vary according to course load. College room and board: $6523. College room only: $3441. Room and board charges vary according to board plan and housing facility. Special program-related fees: $25–$100 per course for scene painting, CAD, combat, film and new media classes.

**Financial Aid** Program-specific awards: 1–2 Williams-H. Alice Howell Awards for upperclass program majors ($750–$1500), 1 Dame Judith Anderson Award for sophomores ($100), 4 Eunice Vivian Peterson Memorial Scholarships for freshmen ($400–$550), 1–2 Helen Hayes MacArthur Scholarships for upperclass program majors ($1000), 4 Felton-Alice Howell Awards for theater students ($2500), 1–2 Ann Keyser Rawley Scholarships for upperclass program majors ($500–$1500), 1–2 Louise E. Mundy Scholarships ($500–$1000), 3–4 Nelle Powley Hills and John Hills Scholarships ($500–$1250).

**Application Procedures** Students admitted directly into the professional program freshman year. Deadline for freshmen and transfers: continuous. Notification date for freshmen and transfers: April 1. Required: essay, high school transcript, college transcript(s) for transfer students, interview, audition, portfolio, SAT or ACT test scores (minimum composite ACT score of 22), audition for scholarship consideration, application packet (contact Admissions Coordinator). Recommended: minimum 3.0 high school GPA, 3 letters of recommendation, portfolio for design/technical theater applicants (scholarship consideration). Auditions held twice on campus and off campus in Chicago, IL; Los Angeles, CA; New York, NY. Portfolio reviews held twice on campus and off campus in Chicago, IL; Los Angeles, CA; New York, NY.

**Web Site** http://www.unl.edu/TheatreArts

**Undergraduate Contact** Mr. Todd Cuddy, Admissions Coordinator, Johnny Carson School of Theatre and Film, University of Nebraska–Lincoln, PO Box 880201, 215 Temple Building, Lincoln, Nebraska 68588-0201; 402-472-2072 ext. 1, fax: 402-472-9055, e-mail address: theatrearts@unl.edu

**Graduate Contact** Dr. William Grange, Chair, Graduate Committee, Johnny Carson School of Theatre and Film, University of Nebraska–Lincoln, PO Box 880201, 215 Temple Building, Lincoln, Nebraska 68588-0201; 402-472-1604, fax: 402-472-9055, e-mail address: wgrange1@unl.edu

# University of Nevada, Reno

## Reno, Nevada

State-supported, coed. Urban campus. Total enrollment: 16,681. Theater program established 1988.

**Degrees** Bachelor of Fine Arts. Majors and concentrations: design technology, performance.

**Enrollment** 40 total; 10 undergraduate, 30 nonprofessional degree.

**Theater Student Profile** 50% females, 50% males, 25% minorities, 13% international.

**Theater Faculty** 5 total (full-time), 3 total (part-time). 100% of full-time faculty have terminal degrees. Graduate students do not teach undergraduate courses. Undergraduate student–faculty ratio: 2:1.

**Expenses for 2008–2009** Application fee: $60. State resident tuition: $4005 full-time. Nonresident tuition: $15,100 full-time. Mandatory fees: $406 full-time. College room and board: $9989. College room only: $5890.

**Application Procedures** Students apply for admission into the professional program by junior year. Deadline for freshmen and transfers: continuous. Notification date for freshmen and transfers: continuous. Required: high school transcript, college transcript(s) for transfer students, SAT or ACT test scores, minimum 2.5 high school GPA, minimum 2.0 college GPA for transfer students.

**Web Site** http://www.unr.edu/cla/spth/

**Undergraduate Contact** Dr. Jim Bernardi, Director, University of Nevada, Reno, Department of Theatre/ 228 UNR, Reno, Nevada 89557; 775-784-6659, e-mail address: bernardi@unr.nevada.edu

# The University of North Carolina at Greensboro

## Greensboro, North Carolina

State-supported, coed. Urban campus. Total enrollment: 17,157. Theater program established 1953.

**Degrees** Bachelor of Arts in the area of drama; Bachelor of Fine Arts in the areas of acting, design and technical production, theatre education. Majors and concentrations: acting, design, technical theater, theater education. Graduate degrees offered: Master of Education in the area of drama; Master of Fine Arts in the areas of acting, design, directing, theater for youth. Cross-registration with North Carolina Agricultural and Technical State University, Greensboro College, Guilford College, and others. Program accredited by NAST.

**Enrollment** 282 total; 178 undergraduate, 26 graduate, 78 nonprofessional degree.

**Theater Student Profile** 63% females, 37% males, 15% minorities.

**Theater Faculty** 14 total (full-time), 6 total (part-time). 100% of full-time faculty have terminal degrees. Graduate students teach a few undergraduate courses. Undergraduate student–faculty ratio: 15:1.

**Student Life** Student groups/activities include Alpha Psi Omega, North Carolina Theatre for Young People, North Carolina Theatre Conference.

**Expenses for 2007–2008** Application fee: $45. State resident tuition: $2458 full-time. Nonresident tuition: $13,726 full-time. Mandatory fees: $1571 full-time. College room and board: $6051. College room only: $3427.

**Financial Aid** Program-specific awards: 1 W. Raymond Taylor Scholarship for drama majors ($500).

**Application Procedures** Students apply for admission into the professional program by freshman year. Deadline for freshmen and transfers: August 1. Notification date for freshmen and transfers: continuous. Required: high school transcript, minimum 2.0 high school GPA, SAT test score only, portfolio review for design students, audition for acting students. Recommended: 3 letters of recommendation. Auditions held twice on campus and off campus in Southeastern Theatre Conference sites; videotaped performances are permissible as a substitute for live auditions if a campus visit is impossible. Portfolio reviews held twice on campus; the submission of slides may be substituted for portfolios when distance is prohibitive.

**Web Site** http://www.uncg.edu/the

**Undergraduate Contact** Tom Humphrey, Head, Department of Theatre, The University of North Carolina at Greensboro, 201 Taylor, Greensboro, North Carolina 27412; 336-334-5576, fax: 336-334-5100, e-mail address: twhumphrey@uncg.edu

**Graduate Contact** Deb Bell, Professor, Department of Theatre, The University of North Carolina at Greensboro, 201 Taylor, Greensboro, North Carolina 27412; 336-334-5576, fax: 336-334-5100, e-mail address: deb_bell@uncg.edu

# University of North Dakota

## Grand Forks, North Dakota

State-supported, coed. Urban campus. Total enrollment: 12,559. Theater program established 1980.

**Degrees** Bachelor of Fine Arts in the area of performance. Majors and concentrations: performance, theater arts/drama. Program accredited by NAST.

**Enrollment** 38 total; 8 undergraduate, 30 nonprofessional degree.

**Theater Student Profile** 60% females, 40% males.

**Theater Faculty** 6 undergraduate (full-time), 1 undergraduate (part-time). 100% of full-time faculty have terminal degrees. Graduate students do not teach undergraduate courses. Undergraduate student–faculty ratio: 4:1.

**Expenses for 2007–2008** Application fee: $35. State resident tuition: $5025 full-time. Nonresident tuition: $13,418 full-time. Mandatory fees: $1105 full-time. Full-time tuition and fees vary according to degree level, program, and reciprocity agreements. College room and board: $5203. College room only: $2137. Room and board charges vary according to board plan and housing facility. Special program-related fees: $15 per semester for makeup class fees.

**Financial Aid** Program-specific awards: 2–3 Donors Awards for program majors ($1200), 10–15 departmental awards for program majors ($600).

**Application Procedures** Students admitted directly into the professional program freshman year. Deadline for freshmen and transfers: continuous. Required: high school transcript, minimum 2.0 high school GPA. Recommended: 2 letters of recommendation, interview, audition for performance applicants, portfolio for design/technology applicants. Auditions held once on campus; videotaped performances are permissible as a substitute for live auditions when distance is prohibitive. Portfolio reviews held once on campus.

**Web Site** http://www.theatre.und.edu

**Undergraduate Contact** Kathleen McLennan, Chair, Department of Theatre Arts, University of North Dakota, Box 8136, Grand Forks, North Dakota 58202; 701-777-3446, fax: 701-777-3522.

# University of Oklahoma

## Norman, Oklahoma

State-supported, coed. Suburban campus. Total enrollment: 26,205. Theater program established 1923.

**Degrees** Bachelor of Fine Arts in the area of drama. Majors and concentrations: design, design technology, dramaturgy, performance, stage management. Graduate degrees offered: Master of Arts in the area of drama; Master of Fine Arts in the area of drama (directing or design). Program accredited by NAST.

**Enrollment** 175 total; 150 undergraduate, 25 graduate.

**Theater Student Profile** 55% females, 45% males, 10% minorities, 3% international.

**Theater Faculty** 11 total (full-time), 4 total (part-time). 100% of full-time faculty have terminal degrees. Graduate students teach a few undergraduate courses. Undergraduate student–faculty ratio: 15:1.

**Student Life** Student groups/activities include Drama Student Senate, Alpha Psi Omega.

**Expenses for 2007–2008** Application fee: $40. State resident tuition: $2609 full-time. Nonresident tuition: $9900 full-time. Mandatory fees: $1925 full-time. Full-time tuition and fees vary according to course load, location, program, and reciprocity agreements. College room and board: $7058. College room only: $3854. Room and board charges vary according to board plan and housing facility. Special program-related fees: $5–$95 per course for lab fees.

**Financial Aid** Program-specific awards: 55 departmental scholarships for program majors ($500–$1500), 10 assistantships for program majors ($3300).

**Application Procedures** Students admitted directly into the professional program freshman year. Deadline for freshmen and transfers: June 1. Required: high school transcript, college transcript(s) for transfer students, 3 letters of recommendation, interview, audition, SAT or ACT test scores (minimum composite ACT score of 24), minimum 2.5 high school GPA, portfolio for

*University of Oklahoma (continued)*

design applicants. Recommended: essay, minimum 3.0 high school GPA. Auditions held 3 times and as needed on campus and off campus in University Resident Theatre Association locations, Texas Educational Theatre Association locations, and various other theater association sites; videotaped performances are permissible as a substitute for live auditions with permission of the director. Portfolio reviews held 3 times and as needed on campus and off campus in University Resident Theatre Association locations, Texas Educational Theatre Association locations, and various other theater association sites; the submission of slides may be substituted for portfolios (slides preferred).
**Web Site** http://www.ou.edu/finearts/drama
**Undergraduate Contact** Charlotte Chandler, Administrative Assistant, School of Drama, University of Oklahoma, 729 Elm Street, Hester Hall 165, Norman, Oklahoma 73019-0310; 405-325-4021, fax: 405-325-0400, e-mail address: cchandler@ou.edu
**Graduate Contact** Dr. Judith Midyett Pender, Graduate Liaison, School of Drama, University of Oklahoma, 729 Elm Street, Hester Hall 165, Norman, Oklahoma 73019-0310; 405-325-5328, fax: 405-325-0400, e-mail address: jmpender@ou.edu

# University of Rhode Island
## Kingston, Rhode Island

State-supported, coed. Small town campus. Total enrollment: 15,650. Theater program established 1966.
**Degrees** Bachelor of Fine Arts in the areas of acting, directing, stage management, theatre design and technology. Majors and concentrations: acting, design/technical theater, directing, stage management. Cross-registration with Rhode Island College, Community College of Rhode Island. Program accredited by NAST.
**Enrollment** 100 total; all undergraduate.
**Theater Student Profile** 54% females, 46% males, 1% minorities.
**Theater Faculty** 5 undergraduate (full-time), 10 undergraduate (part-time). 100% of full-time faculty have terminal degrees. Graduate students do not teach undergraduate courses. Undergraduate student–faculty ratio: 12:1.
**Expenses for 2007–2008** Application fee: $50. State resident tuition: $6440 full-time. Nonresident tuition: $21,294 full-time. Mandatory fees: $1744 full-time. Full-time tuition and fees vary according to reciprocity agreements. College room and board: $8732. College room only: $5016. Room and board charges vary according to board plan and housing facility. Special program-related fees: $5–$35 per course for lab/materials fees.
**Financial Aid** Program-specific awards: 1–2 Theatre Freshmen Scholarships for theater majors ($750), 4 Theatre Department Merit Awards for theater majors ($500), 1–2 Thomas Pezzullo Scholarships for theater majors ($1000), 1–2 Theatre Department Talent Awards for theater majors ($750).
**Application Procedures** Students admitted directly into the professional program freshman year. Deadline for freshmen: April 1; transfers: May 1. Notification date for freshmen: May 1. Required: essay, high school transcript, college transcript(s) for transfer students, SAT or ACT test scores, minimum 2.5 high school GPA. Recommended: interview, audition, portfolio. Auditions held once in January on campus; recorded music is permissible as a substitute for live auditions and videotaped performances are permissible as a substitute for live auditions. Portfolio reviews held as needed on campus; the submission of slides may be substituted for portfolios.
**Web Site** http://www.uri.edu
**Undergraduate Contact** Paula McGlasson, Chair, Department of Theatre, University of Rhode Island, 105 Upper College Road, Suite 3, Kingston, Rhode Island 02881; 401-874-2712, fax: 401-874-5618, e-mail address: paulam@uri.edu

# University of South Alabama
## Mobile, Alabama

State-supported, coed. Suburban campus. Total enrollment: 13,779. Theater program established 1968.

**Degrees** Bachelor of Fine Arts in the area of theater arts/drama. Majors and concentrations: acting, design technology, music theater.
**Enrollment** 53 total; 27 undergraduate, 26 nonprofessional degree.
**Theater Student Profile** 60% females, 40% males, 20% minorities, 1% international.
**Theater Faculty** 4 undergraduate (full-time), 4 undergraduate (part-time). 100% of full-time faculty have terminal degrees. Graduate students do not teach undergraduate courses. Undergraduate student–faculty ratio: 12:1.
**Student Life** Student groups/activities include department play productions.
**Expenses for 2007–2008** Application fee: $35. State resident tuition: $4020 full-time. Nonresident tuition: $8040 full-time. Mandatory fees: $802 full-time. College room and board: $4820. College room only: $2590. Room and board charges vary according to board plan, housing facility, and location.
**Financial Aid** Program-specific awards: 10 assistantship awards for drama majors ($2000), 12 acting grants for actors ($1000).
**Application Procedures** Students admitted directly into the professional program freshman year. Deadline for freshmen and transfers: continuous. Required: essay, college transcript(s) for transfer students, 2 letters of recommendation, SAT or ACT test scores (minimum composite ACT score of 20). Recommended: high school transcript, minimum 2.0 high school GPA, interview, audition, portfolio. Auditions held 5 times on campus and off campus in ACTS and Southeastern Theatre Conference high school audition sites; recorded music is permissible as a substitute for live auditions when distance is prohibitive and videotaped performances are permissible as a substitute for live auditions when distance is prohibitive. Portfolio reviews held periodically on campus; the submission of slides may be substituted for portfolios.
**Web Site** http://www.southalabama.edu/drama
**Undergraduate Contact** Dr. Leon J. Van Dyke, Chairman, Department of Dramatic Arts, University of South Alabama, 1052 PAC, USA, Mobile, Alabama 36688-0002; 251-460-6305, fax: 251-461-1511.

# The University of South Dakota
## Vermillion, South Dakota

State-supported, coed. Small town campus. Total enrollment: 9,243. Theater program established 1935.
**Degrees** Bachelor of Fine Arts in the areas of acting, design/technology, musical theatre, theatre. Majors and concentrations: acting, costume design, design technology, lighting/sound design, music theater, set design, technical theater, theater. Graduate degrees offered: Master of Fine Arts in the areas of directing, design/technology. Program accredited by NAST.
**Enrollment** 78 total; 62 undergraduate, 8 graduate, 8 nonprofessional degree.
**Theater Student Profile** 55% females, 45% males, 1% minorities.
**Theater Faculty** 11 total (full-time), 1 total (part-time). 100% of full-time faculty have terminal degrees. Graduate students do not teach undergraduate courses. Undergraduate student–faculty ratio: 10:1.
**Student Life** Student groups/activities include Strollers, Coyote Capers, Student Theatre Cooperative.
**Expenses for 2007–2008** Application fee: $20. State resident tuition: $2478 full-time. Nonresident tuition: $7872 full-time. Mandatory fees: $2914 full-time. Full-time tuition and fees vary according to course load and reciprocity agreements. College room and board: $5174. College room only: $2503. Room and board charges vary according to board plan and housing facility.
**Financial Aid** Program-specific awards: 1–10 freshman talent scholarships for entering freshmen theatre majors ($400–$1500), 10–12 endowed scholarships for sophomore/junior/senior theatre majors ($200–$750), 15 student technical assistant awards for all theatre majors ($250–$800).
**Application Procedures** Students admitted directly into the professional program freshman year. Deadline for freshmen and transfers: continuous. Required: high school transcript, college transcript(s) for transfer students, minimum 2.0 high school GPA, interview, audition, portfolio, SAT or ACT test scores (minimum

combined SAT score of 910, minimum composite ACT score of 19), standing in top 50% of graduating class or minimum ACT/SAT score of 19/910 or minimum 2.6 high school GPA (contact program for additional curriculum details). Auditions held during December, February, and April off campus in several thespian festivals; videotaped performances are permissible as a substitute for live auditions when distance is prohibitive (more than 300 miles from campus). Portfolio reviews held during December, February, and April in United States Institute for Theatre Technology venues, several thespian festivals; the submission of slides may be substituted for portfolios when distance is prohibitive (more than 300 miles from campus).
**Web Site** http://www.usd.edu/cfa/Theatre/
**Contact** Department of Theatre, The University of South Dakota, 414 East Clark Street, Vermillion, South Dakota 57069-2390; 605-677-5418, fax: 605-677-5988, e-mail address: theatre@usd.edu

# University of Southern California
## Los Angeles, California

Independent, coed. Urban campus. Total enrollment: 33,408. Theater program established 1990.
**Degrees** Bachelor of Fine Arts in the areas of acting, design, stage management, technical direction. Majors and concentrations: acting, design, stage management, technical direction. Graduate degrees offered: Master of Fine Arts in the areas of acting, dramatic writing. Cross-registration with University of Kent (England), British American Drama Academy.
**Enrollment** 501 total; 100 undergraduate, 34 graduate, 367 nonprofessional degree.
**Theater Student Profile** 69% females, 31% males, 12% minorities, 2% international.
**Theater Faculty** 26 total (full-time), 48 total (part-time). 100% of full-time faculty have terminal degrees. Graduate students do not teach undergraduate courses. Undergraduate student–faculty ratio: 25:1.
**Student Life** Student groups/activities include community-based theater lab, Theatre for Youth, Theater Representative Council.
**Expenses for 2007–2008** Application fee: $65. Comprehensive fee: $46,668 includes full-time tuition ($35,212), mandatory fees ($598), and college room and board ($10,858). College room only: $5992. Full-time tuition and fees vary according to program. Room and board charges vary according to board plan and housing facility.
**Financial Aid** Program-specific awards: 3–5 Trustee Scholarships for program majors demonstrating talent and academic achievement ($24,000), 10–11 Dean's Scholarships for program majors demonstrating talent and academic achievement ($6000), 2 Jack Nicholson Awards for performers demonstrating talent and academic achievement ($8000), 2 Stanley Musgrove Awards for those demonstrating talent and academic achievement ($2500), 2 John Blankenship/William C. White Awards for those demonstrating talent and academic achievement ($2000), 1 James Pendleton Award for program majors demonstrating talent and academic achievement ($2500), 3–5 Presidential Scholarships for program majors demonstrating talent and academic achievement ($12,000), 1 David Dukes Memorial Scholarship for performers demonstrating talent and academic achievement ($5500).
**Application Procedures** Students admitted directly into the professional program freshman year. Deadline for freshmen: January 10; transfers: February 1. Notification date for freshmen and transfers: continuous. Required: essay, high school transcript, college transcript(s) for transfer students, minimum 3.0 high school GPA, 2 letters of recommendation, interview, audition, SAT or ACT test scores, portfolio for stage management, technical and design applicants. Auditions held 4 times on campus and off campus in New York, NY; Chicago, IL; Los Angeles, CA; San Francisco, CA; videotaped performances are permissible as a substitute for live auditions. Portfolio reviews held on campus and off campus in New York, NY; Chicago, IL; Los Angeles, CA; San Francisco, CA.
**Web Site** http://theatre.usc.edu/
**Undergraduate Contact** Phyllis Lemons, Assistant Director Theatre Admissions, School of Theatre, University of Southern California,

1029 Childs Way, DRC 116, Los Angeles, California 90089-0791; 213-740-1286, fax: 213-821-1193, e-mail address: thtrinfo@usc.edu
**Graduate Contact** Sergio Ramirez, Director of Graduate Student Services, School of Theatre, University of Southern California, 1029 Childs Way, DRC 116, Los Angeles, California 90089-0791; 213-821-4163, fax: 213-821-1193, e-mail address: sergio.ramirez@usc.edu

### More About the University

Founded in 1945 by playwright and director William C. DeMille, the University of Southern California (USC) School of Theatre is recognized internationally as a leader in theater education. Ranked among the top five undergraduate theater programs in the nation, the School blends artistic training in a conservatory environment with all the academic advantages of a major research university.

The School offers Bachelor of Arts (B.A.) and Bachelor of Fine Arts (B.F.A.) programs in acting, design, stage management, and technical direction. The B.F.A. offers a conservatory approach, while the B.A. offers more flexibility and the opportunity to double major or minor in another discipline. The School of Theatre also offers minors in applied theatre arts, dance, performing arts, and playwriting.

The School of Theatre has intentionally kept classes small to maintain a close student interaction with faculty members. Every student is also assigned an academic adviser to guide his or her course selection throughout the undergraduate's four years.

The School offers educational and performance opportunities overseas. Students can study abroad at the British American Drama Academy (BADA) for course credit, working with leading actors and directors. The School of Theatre holds the distinction of having created the first American university theatrical troupe—Festival Theatre USC-USA—to be invited to perform at the prestigious Fringe of the International Theatre Festival in Edinburgh, Scotland.

**Unique Opportunities for Students** On campus, performance opportunities abound. USC's School of Theatre produces more than twelve main stage shows each season. The School also encourages independent student productions. Students can participate in Brand New Theatre, which presents plays written, produced, acted, and directed by students. The School's partnership with the USC School of Cinematic Arts allows theater students the opportunity to collaborate with film students on a variety of projects.

The location of the campus in Los Angeles—in the heart of the entertainment industry near major motion picture studios, performing arts centers, museums, and vibrant resident theaters—offers enrichment for the artist and the young professional that makes the USC School of Theatre distinctive among colleges and universities in the United States.

The School encourages students to gain professional experience and academic credit through internships and has created a partnership with Center Theatre Group—one of the country's leading professional theaters that runs the Tony Award-winning Mark Taper Forum, the Ahmanson Theatre, and the Kirk Douglas Theatre—that offers internships to students who receive professional experience and academic credit in such varied departments as production, development, marketing, press, and casting, as well as performance opportunities. In the last two years, over 50 students have benefited from this unique relationship. Additional internship opportunities can be arranged for students through the School's association with other theaters as well as various film and television production companies and entertainment agencies.

The many performance and production opportunities, the quality of programs, and the lasting relationships students forge with faculty members and peers make USC a nurturing environment for developing theater skills and knowledge. Whether a student chooses to major or minor in theater or to pursue studies in acting, dance, theatrical design, or dramatic writing, a theater education at the University of Southern California is a unique and invaluable experience.

*University of Southern California (continued)*

**Program Facilities** In addition to studio spaces, the School of Theatre's active production program utilizes four main facilities. The Bing Theatre is a traditional proscenium house with seating for 550. The Massman Theatre is a flexible performance space, comparable to Equity Waiver and off-Broadway theatres, with seating for 50 to 75 individuals. The Scene Dock Theatre is also a flexible performance space, with seating for up to 99 people, while the Village Gate Theatre is a cabaret-style performance space with seating for 70.

**Faculty, Visiting Artists, and Alumni** Comprised of first-rate master teachers and theater professionals working at the highest level in their respective fields, the School of Theatre's faculty members have strong ties in the theater world and are sought out by leaders in the industry, the arts, and the media for their expertise. Faculty members include Tony Award-winning designer and director of production Christopher Akerlind, MacArthur "Genius" Grant-recipient playwright Luis Alfaro, award-winning stage/film/television actor Andrew J. Robinson, Royal National Theatre and Royal Shakespeare Company member actress Charlotte Cornwell, Tony Award-nominee Mary-Joan Negro, author Angus Fletcher, and Applied Theatre Arts founding director Brent Blair.

The USC School of Theatre also attracts a wide range of guest artists who are some of the most distinguished talents from stage, film, and television, including Academy and Emmy Award-winners Tim Robbins and Christine Lahti; Tony Award-winners playwright David Edgar, composer/lyricist Jason Robert Brown, actors Brian Stokes Mitchell and Bill Irwin, director Peter Hall, and director/choreographer Twyla Tharp; as well as hip-hop artist Danny Hock, world-renown director Peter Sellars, internationally-acclaimed actresses Kathleen Turner and Fiona Shaw, and four-time Olympic gold medalist Greg Louganis.

The School of Theatre's alumni have gone on to establish careers in all aspects of theater, film, and television, including Academy Award-winner Forest Whitaker, Golden Globe-winner Kyra Sedgwick, Emmy Award-winner LeVar Burton, as well as Eric Stoltz, Tate Donovan, Anthony Edwards, James Lesure, Jonathan Silverman, Sophia Bush, writer/actor Grant Heslov, director Andy Tennant, producer/director Jack Bender, and producer Todd Black. Recent graduates starring on Broadway include Stark Sands in *Journey's End*, for which he received a Tony Award nomination as Best Featured Actor in a Play, and James Snyder who has the title role in the new musical *Cry-Baby*.

# University of Southern Mississippi
## Hattiesburg, Mississippi

State-supported, coed. Suburban campus. Total enrollment: 14,592. Theater program established 1956.
**Degrees** Bachelor of Fine Arts in the areas of performance, design and technology. Majors and concentrations: acting, design/technical theater, theater. Graduate degrees offered: Master of Fine Arts in the areas of performance, design and technical theater, directing. Program accredited by NAST.
**Enrollment** 128 total; 16 undergraduate, 20 graduate, 92 nonprofessional degree.
**Theater Student Profile** 53% females, 47% males, 2% minorities.
**Theater Faculty** 8 total (full-time). 100% of full-time faculty have terminal degrees. Graduate students teach a few undergraduate courses. Undergraduate student–faculty ratio: 2:1.
**Student Life** Student groups/activities include Southern Arena Theater, "At the Door" events.
**Expenses for 2008–2009** Application fee: $25. State resident tuition: $4914 full-time. Nonresident tuition: $11,692 full-time. College room and board: $5040. College room only: $2826.
**Financial Aid** Program-specific awards: 15–20 service awards for talented students with high test scores ($300).
**Application Procedures** Students apply for admission into the professional program by sophomore year. Deadline for freshmen and transfers: August 15. Required: high school transcript,

college transcript(s) for transfer students, minimum 2.0 high school GPA, SAT or ACT test scores. Recommended: 3 letters of recommendation, interview, audition, portfolio. Auditions held twice on campus; recorded music is permissible as a substitute for live auditions when no accompanist is available and videotaped performances are permissible as a substitute for live auditions if a campus visit is impossible. Portfolio reviews held twice on campus; the submission of slides may be substituted for portfolios slides or discs preferred.
**Web Site** http://www.usm.edu/colleges/coal
**Undergraduate Contact** Mr. Louis Rackoff, Chair, Department of Theatre and Dance, University of Southern Mississippi, Box 5052, Hattiesburg, Mississippi 39406-5052; 601-266-4994, fax: 601-266-6423, e-mail address: louis.rackoff@usm.edu
**Graduate Contact** Mr. Louis Rackhoff, Chair, Department of Theatre and Dance, University of Southern Mississippi, Box 5052, Hattiesburg, Mississippi 39406-5052; 601-266-4994, fax: 601-266-6423, e-mail address: louis.rackoff@usm.edu

# University of South Florida
## Tampa, Florida

State-supported, coed. Urban campus. Total enrollment: 44,870.
**Web Site** http://www.usf.edu

# The University of Tennessee at Martin
## Martin, Tennessee

State-supported, coed. Small town campus. Total enrollment: 7,173. Theater program established 1999.
**Degrees** Bachelor of Fine Arts in the area of fine and performing arts. Majors and concentrations: theater arts/drama.
**Enrollment** 10 total; all undergraduate.
**Theater Student Profile** 30% females, 70% males.
**Theater Faculty** 4 undergraduate (full-time). 25% of full-time faculty have terminal degrees. Graduate students do not teach undergraduate courses.
**Student Life** Student groups/activities include Vanguard Theatre, Alpha Psi Omega Theatre Honor Society.
**Expenses for 2007–2008** Application fee: $30. State resident tuition: $4150 full-time. Nonresident tuition: $14,190 full-time. Mandatory fees: $855 full-time. College room and board: $4446. College room only: $2160. Room and board charges vary according to board plan and housing facility.
**Financial Aid** Program-specific awards: 2 Endowment for the Arts scholarships for freshman theater majors ($1000), 1 William Snyder Scholarship for upperclass theater majors ($500), 1 Bill Williams Scholarship for upperclass theater majors ($500), 1 Joan Methany McGraw Scholarship for upperclass theater majors ($1500).
**Application Procedures** Students admitted directly into the professional program freshman year. Deadline for freshmen and transfers: continuous. Required: high school transcript, college transcript(s) for transfer students, SAT or ACT test scores, ACT score of 21 and high school GPA of 2.50 or ACT score of 18 and high school GPA of 2.85.
**Web Site** http://www.utm.edu/departments/chfa/finearts/
**Undergraduate Contact** Mr. Douglas J. Cook, Chair, Department of Visual and Theatre Arts, The University of Tennessee at Martin, 102 Fine Arts Building, Martin, Tennessee 38238; 731-881-7400, fax: 731-881-7415, e-mail address: dcook@utm.edu

# The University of Texas at Austin
## Austin, Texas

State-supported, coed. Urban campus. Total enrollment: 50,170. Theater program established 1938.
**Degrees** Bachelor of Fine Arts in the area of theater studies. Majors and concentrations: theater arts/drama, theater design and production, theater studies, theater technology. Graduate degrees offered: Master of Fine Arts in the areas of acting, creative drama, directing, playwriting, theater technology, design. Doctor of Philosophy in the area of theater history. Program accredited by NAST.

**Enrollment** 60 undergraduate, 100 graduate, 290 nonprofessional degree.

**Theater Student Profile** 55% females, 45% males, 18% minorities, 1% international.

**Theater Faculty** 35 total (full-time), 8 total (part-time). 99% of full-time faculty have terminal degrees. Graduate students teach a few undergraduate courses. Undergraduate student–faculty ratio: 12:1.

**Student Life** Student groups/activities include Drama Education Organization, Student Advisory Council, Fine Arts Advisory Council.

**Expenses for 2007–2008** Application fee: $60. State resident tuition: $7670 full-time. Nonresident tuition: $24,544 full-time. Full-time tuition varies according to course load and program. College room and board: $8576. Room and board charges vary according to board plan, housing facility, and location. Special program-related fees: $87 per course for production and performance fee.

**Financial Aid** Program-specific awards: 1 Barton-Berry Scholarship for theater students ($2000), 2 Crain Scholarships for theater students ($2000), 2 Denney Scholarships for theater students ($2000), 1 Hanna CES in Drama Scholarship for theater students ($8600), 2 Hexter Scholarships for theater students ($5000), 1 Hingle Scholarship for theater students ($2000), 1 McGriff Scholarship for theater students ($8000).

**Application Procedures** Students admitted directly into the professional program freshman year. Deadline for freshmen: February 8; transfers: March 8. Notification date for freshmen and transfers: May 9. Required: essay, high school transcript, college transcript(s) for transfer students, SAT or ACT test scores, resumé for transfer students. Auditions held 3-10 times on campus.

**Web Site** http://www.finearts.utexas.edu/tad/

**Undergraduate Contact** Kristen Hotopp, Academic Advisor II, Department of Theatre and Dance, The University of Texas at Austin, WIN 1.120, Austin, Texas 78712; 512-471-5793, e-mail address: khotopp@mail.utexas.edu

**Graduate Contact** Dr. Charlotte Canning, Graduate Coordinator, Department of Theatre and Dance, The University of Texas at Austin, WIN 2.160, Austin, Texas 78712; 512-471-5793.

## The University of the Arts

### Philadelphia, Pennsylvania

Independent, coed. Total enrollment: 2,396. Theater program established 1983.

**Degrees** Bachelor of Fine Arts in the areas of acting, musical theater, theater management production, theater design and technology. Majors and concentrations: acting, music theater, theater design, theater design/technology, theater management.

**Enrollment** 252 total; all undergraduate.

**Theater Student Profile** 55% females, 45% males, 20% minorities, 1% international.

**Theater Faculty** 11 undergraduate (full-time), 40 undergraduate (part-time). 55% of full-time faculty have terminal degrees. Graduate students do not teach undergraduate courses. Undergraduate student–faculty ratio: 5:1.

**Student Life** Student groups/activities include Student Government. Special housing available for theater students.

**Expenses for 2008–2009** Application fee: $60. Tuition: $29,500 full-time. Mandatory fees: $1100 full-time. College room only: $7047.

**Financial Aid** Program-specific awards: 40 merit scholarships for incoming students ($1000–$12,000).

**Application Procedures** Students admitted directly into the professional program freshman year. Deadline for freshmen and transfers: continuous. Notification date for freshmen and transfers: September 1. Required: essay, high school transcript, college transcript(s) for transfer students, minimum 2.0 high school GPA, letter of recommendation, audition, SAT or ACT test scores, resume and photograph. Recommended: minimum 3.0 high school GPA, interview. Auditions held 9 times on campus and off campus in various thespian festival locations and in California; videotaped performances are permissible as a substitute for live auditions when applicant lives more than 200 miles from Philadelphia.

**Web Site** http://www.uarts.edu

**Undergraduate Contact** Susan Gandy, Director of Admission, The University of the Arts, 320 South Broad Street, Philadelphia, Pennsylvania 19102; 800-616-ARTS ext. 6049, fax: 215-717-6045, e-mail address: admissions@uarts.edu

## University of Utah

### Salt Lake City, Utah

State-supported, coed. Urban campus. Total enrollment: 28,025. Theater program established 1947.

**Degrees** Bachelor of Fine Arts in the areas of actor training, teaching, design, stage management. Majors and concentrations: acting, design, stage management.

**Enrollment** 200 total; all undergraduate.

**Theater Student Profile** 55% females, 45% males, 5% minorities, 5% international.

**Theater Faculty** 10 total (full-time), 15 total (part-time). 100% of full-time faculty have terminal degrees. Graduate students do not teach undergraduate courses. Undergraduate student–faculty ratio: 12:1.

**Student Life** Student groups/activities include Theatre School for Youth, American College Theatre Festival, Utah Theater Association. Special housing available for theater students.

**Expenses for 2007–2008** Application fee: $35. State resident tuition: $4269 full-time. Nonresident tuition: $14,945 full-time. Mandatory fees: $717 full-time. Full-time tuition and fees vary according to course level, course load, degree level, program, reciprocity agreements, and student level. College room and board: $5778. College room only: $2890. Room and board charges vary according to board plan and housing facility. Contact university directly for part-time tuition costs.

**Financial Aid** Program-specific awards: 4 special departmental scholarships for resident incoming freshmen ($2000), continuing student scholarships for continuing students, 30 endowed scholarship funds for continuing students ($750).

**Application Procedures** Students admitted directly into the professional program freshman year. Deadline for freshmen: August 1; transfers: continuous. Required: high school transcript, college transcript(s) for transfer students, minimum 2.0 high school GPA, 2 letters of recommendation, SAT or ACT test scores, audition for actor training program. Recommended: essay, minimum 3.0 high school GPA, interview, video, portfolio for design applicants. Auditions held once on campus and off campus at National Unified Auditions (New York, NY; Chicago, IL; Las Vegas, NV; San Francisco, CA; Los Angeles, CA). Portfolio reviews held twice on campus.

**Web Site** http://www.theatre.utah.edu/

**Undergraduate Contact** Faye Barron, Administrative Assistant, Department of Theatre, University of Utah, 240 South 1500 East, Room 206, Salt Lake City, Utah 84112-0170; 801-581-6448, fax: 801-585-6154, e-mail address: faye.barron@m.cc.utah.edu

## University of Windsor

### Windsor, Ontario, Canada

Province-supported, coed. Urban campus. Total enrollment: 15,999. Theater program established 1958.

**Degrees** Bachelor of Arts in the area of drama in education and community; Bachelor of Fine Arts in the area of acting. Majors and concentrations: acting, drama in education and community.

**Enrollment** 417 total; 219 undergraduate, 198 nonprofessional degree.

**Theater Student Profile** 60% females, 40% males, 4% minorities, 1% international.

**Theater Faculty** 14 undergraduate (full-time), 8 undergraduate (part-time). 65% of full-time faculty have terminal degrees. Graduate students do not teach undergraduate courses. Undergraduate student–faculty ratio: 20:1.

**Student Life** Student groups/activities include University Players, Club Soda Playfest.

**Expenses for 2008–2009** Application fee: $60 Canadian dollars. Province resident tuition: $4660 full-time. Mandatory fees: $733 full-time. College room and board: $8290. College room only: $4601. International student tuition: $14,330 full-time.

*University of Windsor (continued)*

**Financial Aid** Program-specific awards: 5 School of Dramatic Art Scholarships for top 5 GPA ($200), 1 Frances Hyland Entrance Award for acting majors ($1000), 1 Claire Kire Memorial Bursary for 2nd- or 3rd-year dramatic art students ($100), 1 Myrtle Kennedy Memorial Award for 2nd-year and dramatic art students, 1 Jessica Sue Rogers Pauze Award for drama in education majors ($100), 1 Theatre Alive Scholarship for upperclass acting majors ($1000), 1 Daniel Patrick Kelly Award in Dramatic Art for 4th-year dramatic art students, 1 University of Windsor Women's Auxiliary of Dramatic Art Fund Award for dramatic art students.

**Application Procedures** Students admitted directly into the professional program freshman year. Deadline for freshmen and transfers: continuous. Required: high school transcript, college transcript(s) for transfer students, minimum 2.0 high school GPA, 3 letters of recommendation, application form, resumé, interview for drama in education and community applicants, audition for acting applicants. Recommended: minimum 3.0 high school GPA. Auditions held twice on campus and off campus in Toronto, ON; Halifax, NS; Vancouver, BC; videotaped performances are permissible as a substitute for live auditions when distance is prohibitive.

**Web Site** http://www.uwindsor.ca/drama

**Undergraduate Contact** Brenda Bourque, Secretary, School of Dramatic Art, University of Windsor, 401 Sunset Avenue, Windsor, Ontario N9B 3P4, Canada; 519-253-3000 ext. 2804, fax: 519-971-3629, e-mail address: drama@uwindsor.ca

# University of Wisconsin–Milwaukee
## Milwaukee, Wisconsin

State-supported, coed. Urban campus. Total enrollment: 29,338. Theater program established 1978.

**Degrees** Bachelor of Fine Arts in the area of theater. Majors and concentrations: acting, costume production, stage management, technical production.

**Enrollment** 205 total; 48 undergraduate, 157 nonprofessional degree.

**Theater Student Profile** 50% females, 50% males, 5% minorities.

**Theater Faculty** 15 undergraduate (full-time). 60% of full-time faculty have terminal degrees. Graduate students do not teach undergraduate courses. Undergraduate student–faculty ratio: 7:1.

**Student Life** Student groups/activities include Players Guild. Special housing available for theater students.

**Expenses for 2007–2008** Application fee: $35. State resident tuition: $6960 full-time. Nonresident tuition: $16,686 full-time. Mandatory fees: $767 full-time. Full-time tuition and fees vary according to location, program, and reciprocity agreements. College room only: $3620. Room charges vary according to housing facility. Special program-related fees: $15 per credit for differential tuition.

**Financial Aid** Program-specific awards: 8–10 Corliss Philabaum Scholarships for sophomores and juniors ($500–$1500), Cindy Poulson Scholarship for sophomores and juniors ($500–$1500), Schoenloker Awards for sophomores and juniors ($500–$1000), theatre awards for sophomores and juniors ($500–$1000).

**Application Procedures** Students apply for admission into the professional program by freshman year. Deadline for freshmen and transfers: April 1. Notification date for freshmen and transfers: April 15. Required: high school transcript, college transcript(s) for transfer students, minimum 2.0 high school GPA, 2 letters of recommendation, interview, audition, SAT or ACT test scores. Recommended: essay, portfolio. Auditions held once a year (spring) on campus. Portfolio reviews held once in the spring on campus; the submission of slides may be substituted for portfolios upon request of student.

**Web Site** http://www.uwm.edu/psoa

**Undergraduate Contact** Department of Enrollment Services, University of Wisconsin–Milwaukee, PO Box 749, Milwaukee, Wisconsin 53201; 414-229-5932, fax: 414-229-6940, e-mail address: desadmin@uwm.edu

# University of Wisconsin–Stevens Point
## Stevens Point, Wisconsin

State-supported, coed. Small town campus. Total enrollment: 8,888. Theater program established 1985.

**Web Site** http://www.uwsp.edu/

# University of Wisconsin–Superior
## Superior, Wisconsin

State-supported, coed. Suburban campus. Total enrollment: 2,753. Theater program established 1952.

**Degrees** Bachelor of Fine Arts in the area of theater. Majors and concentrations: performance, technical theater. Cross-registration with University of Minnesota-Duluth.

**Enrollment** 33 total; 6 undergraduate, 3 graduate, 24 nonprofessional degree.

**Theater Student Profile** 40% females, 60% males, 5% minorities.

**Theater Faculty** 2 total (full-time), 3 total (part-time). 100% of full-time faculty have terminal degrees. Graduate students do not teach undergraduate courses. Undergraduate student–faculty ratio: 4:1.

**Student Life** Student groups/activities include student-directed shows, Drama Honorary Organization, Guerilla Theatre.

**Expenses for 2007–2008** Application fee: $35. State resident tuition: $4969 full-time. Nonresident tuition: $12,572 full-time. Mandatory fees: $938 full-time. Full-time tuition and fees vary according to reciprocity agreements. College room and board: $4720. College room only: $2770. Room and board charges vary according to board plan and housing facility.

**Financial Aid** Program-specific awards: 5 departmental scholarships for program students ($100–$1000).

**Application Procedures** Students apply for admission into the professional program by sophomore year. Deadline for freshmen and transfers: continuous. Notification date for freshmen and transfers: continuous. Required: high school transcript, college transcript(s) for transfer students, minimum 2.0 high school GPA, audition, portfolio, SAT or ACT test scores. Auditions held once on campus. Portfolio reviews held on campus.

**Web Site** http://www.uwsuper.edu/wb/~comm/

**Undergraduate Contact** Dr. Martha Einerson, Chair, Department of Communicating Arts, University of Wisconsin–Superior, Holden Fine Arts Building, Belknap and Catlin, Superior, Wisconsin 54880-4500; 715-394-8369, fax: 715-394-8065, e-mail address: meinerson@uwsuper.edu

# University of Wisconsin–Whitewater
## Whitewater, Wisconsin

State-supported, coed. Small town campus. Total enrollment: 10,737.

**Degrees** Bachelor of Fine Arts in the areas of performance, design/technology, stage management, management/promotions. Majors and concentrations: design technology, management promotions, performance, stage management. Cross-registration with University of Wisconsin System. Program accredited by NAST.

**Enrollment** 90 total; 47 undergraduate, 43 nonprofessional degree.

**Theater Student Profile** 60% females, 40% males, 5% minorities.

**Theater Faculty** 5 undergraduate (full-time), 6 undergraduate (part-time). 100% of full-time faculty have terminal degrees. Graduate students do not teach undergraduate courses. Undergraduate student–faculty ratio: 5:1.

**Student Life** Student groups/activities include University Players, Theta Alpha Phi, Dance Company.

**Expenses for 2007–2008** Application fee: $35. State resident tuition: $5859 full-time. Nonresident tuition: $13,432 full-time. Mandatory fees: $871 full-time. Full-time tuition and fees vary according to degree level and reciprocity agreements. College room and board: $4474. College room only: $2768. Room and

board charges vary according to board plan. Special program-related fees: $23–$40 per semester for makeup.
**Financial Aid** Program-specific awards: 2–4 freshmen scholarships ($200–$500), 1 Richard Elkow Award for design/technology students ($200), 1 Greenhill Scholarship for freshmen with GPA of 3.85 or ACT score of 30 ($1000).
**Application Procedures** Students apply for admission into the professional program by sophomore year. Deadline for freshmen: March 15. Required: high school transcript, SAT or ACT test scores, standing in upper 50% of graduating class, minimum 2.5 college GPA for entrance into BFA program, audition for scholarship consideration, portfolio for design/technology applicants for scholarship consideration. Auditions held once on campus; recorded music is permissible as a substitute for live auditions. Portfolio reviews held once on campus; the submission of slides may be substituted for portfolios.
**Web Site** http://www.uww.edu
**Undergraduate Contact** Mr. Marshall B. Anderson, Chairperson, Theatre/Dance Department, University of Wisconsin–Whitewater, 800 West Main Street, Whitewater, Wisconsin 53190-1790; 262-472-1566, fax: 262-472-2808, e-mail address: andersom@uww.edu

# University of Wyoming
## Laramie, Wyoming

State-supported, coed. Total enrollment: 12,875. Theater program established 1972.
**Degrees** Bachelor of Fine Arts in the areas of theater, performance, design, theater/English, directing/playwriting. Majors and concentrations: acting, costume design, directing, lighting design, playwriting, set design, technical direction, theater/English.
**Enrollment** 100 total; 80 undergraduate, 20 nonprofessional degree.
**Theater Student Profile** 50% females, 50% males, 17% minorities.
**Theater Faculty** 13 undergraduate (full-time), 1 undergraduate (part-time). 90% of full-time faculty have terminal degrees. Graduate students do not teach undergraduate courses. Undergraduate student–faculty ratio: 10:1.
**Student Life** Student groups/activities include Associated Students of the Performing Arts.
**Expenses for 2007–2008** Application fee: $40. One-time mandatory fee: $40. State resident tuition: $2820 full-time. Nonresident tuition: $9660 full-time. Mandatory fees: $734 full-time. Full-time tuition and fees vary according to course load, location, program, and reciprocity agreements. College room and board: $7274. College room only: $3158. Room and board charges vary according to board plan and housing facility.
**Financial Aid** Program-specific awards: 21 departmental awards for program majors ($2575).
**Application Procedures** Students admitted directly into the professional program freshman year. Deadline for freshmen and transfers: August 31. Required: high school transcript, college transcript(s) for transfer students, SAT or ACT test scores, audition for scholarship consideration, minimum 2.5 high school GPA. Recommended: letter of recommendation, interview, audition, portfolio. Auditions held twice on campus and off campus in Rocky Mountain Theatre Association Festival locations; recorded music is permissible as a substitute for live auditions and videotaped performances are permissible as a substitute for live auditions if a campus visit is impossible. Portfolio reviews held twice on campus and off campus in Rocky Mountain Theatre Association Festival locations, Wyoming State Drama Festival; the submission of slides may be substituted for portfolios if a campus visit is impossible.
**Web Site** http://www.uwyo.edu/th&d/
**Undergraduate Contact** Leigh Selting, Head, Department of Theatre and Dance, University of Wyoming, Department 3951, 1000 East University Avenue, Laramie, Wyoming 82071-3951; 307-766-2198, fax: 307-766-2197, e-mail address: selting@uwyo.edu

# Utah State University
## Logan, Utah

State-supported, coed. Urban campus. Total enrollment: 14,893. Theater program established 1967.
**Web Site** http://www.usu.edu/

# Valdosta State University
## Valdosta, Georgia

State-supported, coed. Small town campus. Total enrollment: 11,280. Theater program established 1964.
**Web Site** http://www.valdosta.edu/

# Virginia Commonwealth University
## Richmond, Virginia

State-supported, coed. Urban campus. Total enrollment: 31,907. Theater program established 1940.
**Degrees** Bachelor of Arts in the area of theatre; Bachelor of Fine Arts in the areas of theater, theater education. Majors and concentrations: costume design, lighting design, performance, scenic design, stage management, theater education. Graduate degrees offered: Master of Fine Arts in the areas of theater pedagogy (with emphasis in stage movement, voice and speech, acting, directing, history and literature). Program accredited by NAST.
**Enrollment** 271 total; 227 undergraduate, 44 graduate.
**Theater Student Profile** 60% females, 40% males, 27% minorities.
**Theater Faculty** 14 total (full-time), 5 total (part-time). 100% of full-time faculty have terminal degrees. Graduate students teach a few undergraduate courses. Undergraduate student–faculty ratio: 20:1.
**Student Life** Student groups/activities include Four Main Stage Productions per academic year, Senior Showcase in NYC, Student Voices for incoming freshmen.
**Expenses for 2007–2008** Application fee: $40. State resident tuition: $4482 full-time. Nonresident tuition: $16,858 full-time. Mandatory fees: $1714 full-time. College room and board: $7567. College room only: $4497. Room and board charges vary according to board plan. Special program-related fees: $30 per course for theater course fee, $75–$265 per semester for art major fee.
**Financial Aid** Program-specific awards: 4 Bobby Chandler Awards in Theatre for outstanding seniors ($300), Theatre VCU Alumnae Scholarship for theatre majors.
**Application Procedures** Students admitted directly into the professional program freshman year. Deadline for freshmen: February 1; transfers: May 1. Notification date for freshmen and transfers: continuous. Required: high school transcript, college transcript(s) for transfer students, minimum 2.0 high school GPA, letter of recommendation, interview, audition, portfolio, SAT or ACT test scores (minimum combined SAT score of 910, minimum composite ACT score of 20), portfolio for design applicants, audition for performance and theater education applicants. Recommended: essay. Auditions held 6 times on campus and off campus in Southeastern Theatre Conference sites; Virginia Theater Association sites; videotaped performances are permissible as a substitute for live auditions for International Applicants only. Portfolio reviews held 6 times on campus and off campus in Virginia Theater Association sites, southeastern Theatre Conference sites; the submission of slides may be substituted for portfolios with some original work.
**Web Site** http://www.vcu.edu/artweb/Theatre
**Undergraduate Contact** Kathleen Legault, Administrator, Theatre Department, Virginia Commonwealth University, Box 842524, Richmond, Virginia 23284-2524; 804-828-1514, fax: 804-828-6741, e-mail address: klegault@vcu.edu
**Graduate Contact** Dr. Noreen Barnes, Director of Graduate Studies, Theatre Department, Virginia Commonwealth University, Box 842524, Richmond, Virginia 23284-2524; 804-827-1677, fax: 804-828-6741, e-mail address: nbarnesm@vcu.edu

# Virginia Intermont College
### Bristol, Virginia

Independent, coed. Small town campus. Total enrollment: 635.
**Degrees** Bachelor of Fine Arts in the area of theatre. Majors and concentrations: acting, music theater. Cross-registration with King College.
**Enrollment** 4 total; all undergraduate.
**Theater Student Profile** 75% females, 25% males.
**Theater Faculty** 1 undergraduate (full-time), 3 undergraduate (part-time). 100% of full-time faculty have terminal degrees. Graduate students do not teach undergraduate courses. Undergraduate student–faculty ratio: 4:1.
**Student Life** Student groups/activities include Southeastern Theatre Conference.
**Expenses for 2007–2008** Application fee: $25. Comprehensive fee: $28,645 includes full-time tuition ($21,200), mandatory fees ($950), and college room and board ($6495). College room only: $3100. Full-time tuition and fees vary according to class time and program. Room and board charges vary according to housing facility.
**Financial Aid** Program-specific awards: performance scholarships for program majors ($500–$1500), departmental scholarships for program majors ($1200).
**Application Procedures** Students admitted directly into the professional program freshman year. Deadline for freshmen and transfers: continuous. Notification date for freshmen and transfers: continuous. Required: high school transcript, college transcript(s) for transfer students, minimum 2.0 high school GPA, SAT or ACT test scores, audition for scholarship consideration. Recommended: letter of recommendation, interview, video, audition, portfolio. Auditions held 5 times and by request on campus and off campus in Southwestern Theatre Conference sites; videotaped performances are permissible as a substitute for live auditions for extreme distance/foreign students. Portfolio reviews held 5 times and by request on campus and off campus in Southeastern Theatre Conference.
**Web Site** http://www.vic.edu
**Undergraduate Contact** Mr. Tony England, Vice President of Enrollment Services, Admissions, Virginia Intermont College, 1013 Moore Street, Bristol, Virginia 24201; 276-466-7873, fax: 276-466-7855, e-mail address: viadmit@vic.edu

# Viterbo University
### La Crosse, Wisconsin

Independent Roman Catholic, coed. Suburban campus. Total enrollment: 3,088. Theater program established 1944.
**Degrees** Bachelor of Fine Arts. Majors and concentrations: acting, arts administration, design/technical theater, music theater, stage management.
**Enrollment** 70 total; all undergraduate.
**Theater Student Profile** 60% females, 40% males, 7% minorities, 2% international.
**Theater Faculty** 9 undergraduate (full-time), 1 undergraduate (part-time). 90% of full-time faculty have terminal degrees. Graduate students do not teach undergraduate courses. Undergraduate student–faculty ratio: 7:1.
**Expenses for 2008–2009** Application fee: $25. Comprehensive fee: $25,870 includes full-time tuition ($19,000), mandatory fees ($490), and college room and board ($6380). College room only: $2910. Special program-related fees: $265 per credit for applied music fee for music theater.
**Financial Aid** Program-specific awards: 10 Fine Arts Scholarships for program majors ($1000).
**Application Procedures** Students apply for admission into the professional program by freshman year. Deadline for freshmen and transfers: August 1. Required: high school transcript, college transcript(s) for transfer students, minimum 2.0 high school GPA, 3 letters of recommendation, interview, audition, SAT or ACT test scores. Recommended: minimum 3.0 high school GPA, portfolio for design/technical applicants. Auditions held 6 times on campus and off campus in Lincoln, NE; recorded music is permissible as a substitute for live auditions and videotaped performances are permissible as a substitute for live auditions.

Portfolio reviews held 6 times on campus and off campus in Lincoln, NE; the submission of slides may be substituted for portfolios when distance is prohibitive.
**Web Site** http://www.viterbo.edu/SchoolofFineArts.aspx
**Undergraduate Contact** Dr. Roland Nelson, Director of Admissions, Viterbo University, 900 Viterbo Drive, La Crosse, Wisconsin 54601; 608-796-3012, fax: 608-796-3020.

# Wayne State University
### Detroit, Michigan

State-supported, coed. Urban campus. Total enrollment: 33,240. Theater program established 1967.
**Degrees** Bachelor of Fine Arts. Majors and concentrations: theater arts/drama. Graduate degrees offered: Master of Fine Arts in the areas of acting, lighting design, costuming design, management, scene design, stage management. Doctor of Arts in the areas of theater history, criticism. Program accredited by NAST.
**Enrollment** 267 total; 192 undergraduate, 75 graduate.
**Theater Student Profile** 42% females, 58% males, 10% minorities, 1% international.
**Theater Faculty** 16 total (full-time), 4 total (part-time). 90% of full-time faculty have terminal degrees. Graduate students teach a few undergraduate courses. Undergraduate student–faculty ratio: 16:1.
**Expenses for 2007–2008** Application fee: $30. State resident tuition: $6783 full-time. Nonresident tuition: $15,534 full-time. Mandatory fees: $1061 full-time. Full-time tuition and fees vary according to course load and student level. College room and board: $6702. Room and board charges vary according to board plan and housing facility.
**Financial Aid** Program-specific awards: 10 freshman incentive awards for incoming freshmen ($1800).
**Application Procedures** Students apply for admission into the professional program by junior year. Deadline for freshmen and transfers: August 1. Notification date for freshmen and transfers: continuous. Required: college transcript(s) for transfer students, minimum 2.0 high school GPA. Recommended: minimum 3.0 high school GPA.
**Web Site** http://www.theatre.wayne.edu
**Undergraduate Contact** Undergraduate Admissions, Wayne State University, 42 West Warren, Suite 436, Detroit, Michigan 48202; 313-577-3577, fax: 313-577-7536.
**Graduate Contact** Blair Anderson, Chair, Department of Theatre, Wayne State University, 4841 Cass Avenue, Suite 3225, Detroit, Michigan 48202; 313-577-3511, fax: 313-577-0935, e-mail address: ad5298@wayne.edu

### *Leigh Gerdine College of Fine Arts*
# Webster University
### St. Louis, Missouri

Independent, coed. Suburban campus. Total enrollment: 8,430. Theater program established 1967.
**Degrees** Bachelor of Arts in the area of directing; Bachelor of Fine Arts in the areas of acting, musical theater, design/tech, stage management. Majors and concentrations: acting, costume design, directing, lighting design, makeup and wig design, music theater, scene painting, scenic design, sound design, technical direction, technical production. Cross-registration with various colleges in St. Louis.
**Enrollment** 150 total; all undergraduate.
**Theater Student Profile** 50% females, 50% males, 10% minorities, 1% international.
**Theater Faculty** 12 undergraduate (full-time), 20 undergraduate (part-time). 100% of full-time faculty have terminal degrees. Graduate students do not teach undergraduate courses. Undergraduate student–faculty ratio: 12:1.
**Student Life** Student groups/activities include United States Institute for Theatre Technology.
**Expenses for 2007–2008** Application fee: $35. Comprehensive fee: $27,550 includes full-time tuition ($19,330) and college room and board ($8220). College room only: $4100. Full-time tuition

varies according to program. Room and board charges vary according to board plan and housing facility. Special program-related fees: $300 per year for technical theater materials.

**Financial Aid** Program-specific awards: 5 endowed scholarships for talented juniors and seniors ($1500).

**Application Procedures** Students admitted directly into the professional program freshman year. Deadline for freshmen and transfers: March 15. Notification date for freshmen and transfers: April 1. Required: essay, high school transcript, college transcript(s) for transfer students, minimum 2.0 high school GPA, letter of recommendation, audition, portfolio, SAT or ACT test scores (minimum combined SAT score of 1500, minimum composite ACT score of 21). Recommended: minimum 3.0 high school GPA. Auditions held 12 times on campus and off campus in New York, NY; San Francisco, CA; Los Angeles, CA; Chicago, IL. Portfolio reviews held by arrangement on campus and off campus in New York, NY; San Francisco, CA; Los Angeles, CA; Chicago, IL; the submission of slides may be substituted for portfolios when distance is prohibitive (for design/tech only).

**Web Site** http://www.webster.edu

**Undergraduate Contact** Ms. Carrie George, Auditions Coordinator, Office of Admissions, Webster University, 470 East Lockwood Avenue, St. Louis, Missouri 63119-3194; 314-968-7001, fax: 314-968-7115, e-mail address: cgeorge@webster.edu

# Western Carolina University

## Cullowhee, North Carolina

State-supported, coed. Rural campus. Total enrollment: 9,056. Theater program established 1975.

**Degrees** Bachelor of Fine Arts in the area of theater arts. Majors and concentrations: acting, design technology, music theater. Program accredited by NAST.

**Enrollment** 48 total; 31 undergraduate, 17 nonprofessional degree.

**Theater Student Profile** 60% females, 40% males.

**Theater Faculty** 5 undergraduate (full-time), 4 undergraduate (part-time). 100% of full-time faculty have terminal degrees. Graduate students do not teach undergraduate courses. Undergraduate student–faculty ratio: 7:1.

**Student Life** Student groups/activities include Alpha Psi Omega, University Players, Black Theatre Ensemble.

**Expenses for 2008–2009** Application fee: $40. State resident tuition: $2078 full time. Nonresident tuition: $11,661 full-time. Mandatory fees: $2336 full-time. College room and board: $5626. College room only: $2916.

**Financial Aid** Program-specific awards: Josephina Niggli Scholarships for those demonstrating talent and academic achievement.

**Application Procedures** Students apply for admission into the professional program by sophomore year. Deadline for freshmen and transfers: continuous. Required: essay, high school transcript, college transcript(s) for transfer students, 3 letters of recommendation, interview, audition, portfolio, SAT or ACT test scores. Auditions held 3-4 times on campus and off campus in Southeastern Theatre Conference sites, North Carolina Theatre Conference sites; videotaped performances are permissible as a substitute for live auditions with prior approval. Portfolio reviews held by appointment on campus; the submission of slides may be substituted for portfolios (digital portfolio can be sent as e-mail attachment).

**Web Site** http://www.wcu.edu

**Undergraduate Contact** Ms. Susan Brown-Strauss, Head, Department of Theatre, Dance, Motion Picture and Television Production, Western Carolina University, Stillwell 233, Cullowhee, North Carolina 28723; 828-227-7491, fax: 828-227-7647, e-mail address: bstrauss@wcu.edu

## *Potter College of Arts, Humanities, and Social Sciences*

# Western Kentucky University

## Bowling Green, Kentucky

State-supported, coed. Suburban campus. Total enrollment: 19,258. Theater program established 1987.

**Web Site** http://www.wku.edu/

# Western Michigan University

## Kalamazoo, Michigan

State-supported, coed. Urban campus. Total enrollment: 24,433. Theater program established 1976.

**Degrees** Bachelor of Fine Arts in the area of music theater performance. Majors and concentrations: arts management, design technology, music theater, performance. Cross-registration with Kalamazoo Valley Community College, Kalamazoo College. Program accredited by NAST.

**Enrollment** 175 total; 40 undergraduate, 135 nonprofessional degree.

**Theater Student Profile** 55% females, 45% males, 9% minorities, 2% international.

**Theater Faculty** 12 undergraduate (full-time), 3 undergraduate (part-time). 100% of full-time faculty have terminal degrees. Graduate students do not teach undergraduate courses. Undergraduate student–faculty ratio: 13:1.

**Student Life** Student groups/activities include United States Institute for Theatre Technology, American College Theatre Festival, Theatre Kalamazoo.

**Expenses for 2007–2008** Application fee: $35. One-time mandatory fee: $300. State resident tuition: $6570 full-time. Nonresident tuition: $16,116 full-time. Mandatory fees: $690 full-time. Full-time tuition and fees vary according to course load, location, and student level. College room and board: $7042. College room only: $3725. Room and board charges vary according to board plan. Special program-related fees: $10 for lighting/sound, $10 for scenic design, $25 for introduction to theater, $40 per course for stagecraft fee, $60 per course for accompanist, $75 per credit hour for practicum lab fee.

**Financial Aid** Program-specific awards: 6 music theater scholarships for music theater majors ($500–$4000), 6 theater scholarships for theater majors ($500–$4000).

**Application Procedures** Students admitted directly into the professional program freshman year. Deadline for freshmen and transfers: March 1. Notification date for freshmen and transfers: April 1. Required: high school transcript, college transcript(s) for transfer students, minimum 2.0 high school GPA, 2 letters of recommendation, interview, audition, portfolio, SAT or ACT test scores (minimum composite ACT score of 20), resumé, photo. Recommended: essay, minimum 3.0 high school GPA. Auditions held 2 times on campus; videotaped performances are permissible as a substitute for live auditions when the video is of adequate quality. Portfolio reviews held twice on campus.

**Web Site** http://www.wmich.edu/theatre/

**Undergraduate Contact** Dr. Joan Herrington, Chair, Department of Theatre, Western Michigan University, Kalamazoo, Michigan 49008; 269-387-3224, fax: 269-387-3222, e-mail address: joan.herrington@umich.edu

# West Virginia University

## Morgantown, West Virginia

State-supported, coed. Small town campus. Total enrollment: 28,113. Theater program established 1970.

**Degrees** Bachelor of Fine Arts. Majors and concentrations: acting, creative dramatics and puppetry, design technology. Graduate degrees offered: Master of Fine Arts in the areas of acting, design. Program accredited by NAST.

**Enrollment** 127 total; 121 undergraduate, 6 graduate.

**Theater Student Profile** 70% females, 30% males, 4% minorities.

**Theater Faculty** 16 total (full-time). 98% of full-time faculty have terminal degrees. Graduate students teach a few undergraduate courses. Undergraduate student–faculty ratio: 8:1.

**Student Life** Student groups/activities include Student Actors and Technicians Organization, Puppetry Touring Program. Special housing available for theater students.

**Expenses for 2007–2008** Application fee: $25. State resident tuition: $4722 full-time. Nonresident tuition: $14,600 full-time. Full-time tuition varies according to location, program, and reciprocity agreements. College room and board: $7046. Room and board charges vary according to board plan, housing facility, and location. Special program-related fees: $75 per semester for related classroom expenses.

*West Virginia University (continued)*

**Financial Aid** Program-specific awards: 15 performance grants for incoming freshmen program majors ($1750–$4800), 1 Tanner Scholarship for state resident program majors ($500–$2000), 1–2 Boyd Scholarships for program majors ($500–$1000), 1–4 Tate-Ensley Scholarships for program majors ($500–$2000), 1 Selby Scholarship for program juniors ($750).
**Application Procedures** Students admitted directly into the professional program freshman year. Deadline for freshmen and transfers: continuous. Notification date for freshmen and transfers: continuous. Required: high school transcript, college transcript(s) for transfer students, minimum 2.0 high school GPA, 2 letters of recommendation, interview, audition, portfolio, SAT or ACT test scores (minimum composite ACT score of 19). Auditions held 3 times and by appointment on campus and off campus in University Resident Theatre Association regional auditions, Southeastern Theatre Conference auditions; videotaped performances are permissible as a substitute for live auditions when distance is prohibitive (beyond a 500-mile radius). Portfolio reviews held 3 times and by appointment on campus and off campus in University Resident Theatre Association regional reviews, Southeastern Theatre Conference reviews; the submission of slides may be substituted for portfolios when distance is prohibitive (beyond a 500 mile radius).
**Web Site** http://www.wvu.edu/~theatre/
**Contact** Carol Kurcaba, Senior Administrative Secretary, Division of Theatre and Dance, West Virginia University, PO Box 6111, Morgantown, West Virginia 26506-6111; 304-293-4841 ext. 3120, fax: 304-293-2533, e-mail address: carol.kurcaba@mail.wvu.edu

## Wichita State University
### Wichita, Kansas

State-supported, coed. Urban campus. Total enrollment: 14,442. Theater program established 1924.
**Degrees** Bachelor of Fine Arts. Majors and concentrations: design/technical theater, music theater, performance. Program accredited by NAST, NASM.
**Enrollment** 135 total; 120 undergraduate, 15 nonprofessional degree.
**Theater Student Profile** 60% females, 40% males, 2% minorities.
**Theater Faculty** 6 undergraduate (full-time), 6 undergraduate (part-time). 100% of full-time faculty have terminal degrees. Graduate students do not teach undergraduate courses. Undergraduate student–faculty ratio: 23:1.
**Student Life** Student groups/activities include Kennedy Center American College Theatre Festival, Arts Partners/Wichita, Kansas Bureau of Investigation's "Finding Words". Special housing available for theater students.
**Expenses for 2007–2008** Application fee: $30. State resident tuition: $3912 full-time. Nonresident tuition: $11,259 full-time. Mandatory fees: $858 full-time. Full-time tuition and fees vary according to course load. College room and board: $5580. Room and board charges vary according to board plan and housing facility. Special program-related fees: $30 per lighting design I & II for drafting supplies, $30 per scene design I & II for drafting supplies, $30 per design/tech for drafting supplies, $45 per adv. stagecraft for supplies, $45 per stage makeup for makeup supplies/photography.
**Financial Aid** Program-specific awards: 25 Miller Theatre Scholarships for incoming students and continuing majors ($650–$1500), 25 musical theater scholarships (various) for incoming students and continuing majors ($500), 5 Randall M. Jones Scholarships for incoming students and continuing majors ($2000), 1 Mildred McCoy Armstrong Award for continuing majors ($275), 1 Julianne Weaver Masters Award for continuing students juniors ($1000), 2 Heriford Awards for continuing majors ($700), 1 June M. Lair Award for continuing juniors ($1000), 1 Eleanor Doty Clair Award for continuing majors ($600), 1 George Wilner Award for continuing majors ($675), 1 Brett Neff Scholarship for continuing majors ($400), 5 Graham Scholarships for technical theater and design majors ($800–$1000), 4 Buck Scholarships for continuing majors ($1000–$1500), 2 Heriford Scholarships for continuing majors ($500–$1000), 1 Needles Scholarship for majors junior/senior ($250), 3 Perry Scholarships for continuing majors ($700).

**Application Procedures** Students admitted directly into the professional program freshman year. Deadline for freshmen and transfers: continuous. Required: high school transcript, college transcript(s) for transfer students, minimum 2.0 high school GPA, SAT or ACT test scores, portfolio or audition for scholarship consideration. Recommended: interview. Auditions held 3 times and by appointment on campus and off campus in Kansas State Thespian Conference sites. Portfolio reviews held 3 times and by appointment on campus; the submission of slides may be substituted for portfolios.
**Web Site** http://finearts.wichita.edu
**Undergraduate Contact** Ms. Christine Schneikart-Luebbe, Director of Admissions, Wichita State University, 1845 Fairmount, Wichita, Kansas 67260-0124; 316-978-3085, fax: 316-978-3174.

## William Carey University
### Hattiesburg, Mississippi

Independent Southern Baptist, coed. Small town campus. Total enrollment: 2,493 (2007).
**Degrees** Bachelor of Fine Arts in the area of theater. Majors and concentrations: music theater, theater arts/drama.
**Enrollment** 30 total; all undergraduate.
**Theater Student Profile** 47% females, 53% males, 3% minorities, 3% international.
**Theater Faculty** 3 undergraduate (full-time), 2 undergraduate (part-time). 100% of full-time faculty have terminal degrees. Graduate students do not teach undergraduate courses. Undergraduate student–faculty ratio: 8:1.
**Student Life** Student groups/activities include Alpha Psi Omega, Serampore Players.
**Expenses for 2007–2008** Application fee: $20. Comprehensive fee: $12,825 includes full-time tuition ($8700), mandatory fees ($315), and college room and board ($3810). College room only: $1500. Full-time tuition and fees vary according to degree level and location. Room and board charges vary according to board plan, housing facility, and location.
**Financial Aid** Program-specific awards: 6 named scholarships for enrolled program students ($500–$5000), 26 theater talent awards for program majors ($500–$5000).
**Application Procedures** Students admitted directly into the professional program freshman year. Deadline for freshmen and transfers: July 1. Notification date for freshmen and transfers: August 1. Required: high school transcript, college transcript(s) for transfer students, minimum 2.0 high school GPA, letter of recommendation, SAT or ACT test scores. Recommended: interview, video, audition, portfolio. Auditions held at various times on campus; recorded music is permissible as a substitute for live auditions and videotaped performances are permissible as a substitute for live auditions when distance is prohibitive. Portfolio reviews held at various times on campus; the submission of slides may be substituted for portfolios whenever needed.
**Web Site** http://www.wmcarey.edu
**Undergraduate Contact** Charles Bosworth, Director of Theatre, Department of Theatre and Communication, William Carey University, 498 Tuscan Avenue, Hattiesburg, Mississippi 39401-5461; 601-381-6218, fax: 601-381-6145, e-mail address: thecom@wmcarey.edu

## Wright State University
### Dayton, Ohio

State-supported, coed. Suburban campus. Total enrollment: 16,151.
**Degrees** Bachelor of Fine Arts in the areas of acting, musical theatre, theatre design/technology/stage management. Majors and concentrations: acting, film production, music theater, stage management, theater arts/drama, theater design/technology.
**Enrollment** 340 total; all undergraduate.
**Theater Student Profile** 50% females, 50% males, 5% minorities, 5% international.
**Theater Faculty** 17 undergraduate (full-time), 10 undergraduate (part-time). 75% of full-time faculty have terminal degrees. Graduate students do not teach undergraduate courses.

**Student Life** Special housing available for theater students.

**Expenses for 2007–2008** Application fee: $30. State resident tuition: $7278 full-time. Nonresident tuition: $14,004 full-time. College room and board: $7180. Special program-related fees: $20–$40 per quarter for certification, $100 for film lab fees, $190 per quarter for private voice lessons.

**Financial Aid** Program-specific awards: theater arts talent awards for incoming program students ($500–$2000), Milton Augsburger and Francisco Estevez Scholarships for incoming program students ($500–$2000), Faculty Academic scholarships for out-of-state incoming program students ($6400), merit scholarships for continuing students, Rising Star Scholarships for incoming/continuing students ($500–$1000), Arts Gala Scholarships for incoming/continuing students ($500–$2000), Tom Hanks Scholarship and Visiting Artist Funds for incoming students.

**Application Procedures** Students admitted directly into the professional program freshman year. Deadline for freshmen and transfers: March 1. Required: high school transcript, college transcript(s) for transfer students, interview, audition, SAT or ACT test scores, photograph, audition for acting and musical theater applicants, portfolio for scholarship consideration. Auditions held 6-8 times on campus and off campus in Louisville, KY; Atlanta, GA; videotaped performances are permissible as a substitute for live auditions. Portfolio reviews held on campus.

**Web Site** http://www.wright.edu/tdmp/

**Undergraduate Contact** Ms. Victoria Oleen, Managing Director, Department of Theatre, Dance & Motion Pictures, Wright State University, 3640 Colonel Glenn Highway, T148 CAC, Dayton, Ohio 45435; 937-775-3072, fax: 937-775-3787, e-mail address: victoria.oleen@wright.edu

### More About the University

Wright State University (WSU) is a dynamic and diverse institution, with nearly 15,000 students pursuing studies in more than 100 undergraduate majors and forty graduate and professional degree programs. Named after aviation pioneers Orville and Wilbur Wright, the University seeks excellence in all of its academic programs, many of which receive national recognition. The Department of Theatre, Dance, and Motion Pictures is recognized as one of the premier performing arts programs for undergraduate training and performance in the nation. The department has established a growing reputation for superior theatrical production of musicals and dramas and has been repeatedly spotlighted. Some of these spotlights include winning a record fourteen awards from the American College Theatre Festival (ACTF) in 1997 for *1913: The Great Dayton Flood*; being the only university in a four-state region to take two productions to the XXI Kennedy Center ACTF regional competition in 1998; the department's design/technology area winning the USITT National Olympics in 1995, 1997, 1999, and 2002; and, in the area of film, winning awards at the Los Angeles Independence Film Festival and the Sundance Festival.

**Campus and Surroundings** Wright State campus is adjacent to downtown Dayton, which is home to the Dayton Contemporary Dance Company, Dayton Ballet, Victoria Theatre, Human Race Theatre Company, Benjamin & Marian Schuster Performing Arts Center, Dayton Opera, and others. Wright State is also within an hour of Columbus and Cincinnati, which have many performing arts organizations.

**Program Facilities** The Department of Theatre, Dance, and Motion Pictures is housed in a state-of-the-art facility that includes acting and dance studios, a movement studio, a lighting and graphics lab, and motion-picture production facilities. Main-stage theater productions are held in the newly renovated Festival Playhouse, a 380-seat proscenium theater. Studio productions are in a 100-seat black box theater, and a student-performance theater that seats 92. The department has access to a comprehensive collection of play scripts, musical theater scores and soundtracks, and a videotape library.

**Faculty, Resident Artists, Guest Artists and Alumni** Chair W. Stuart McDowell is the founder and former artistic director of the Riverside Shakespeare Company in New York City and director of numerous professional productions across the country. Faculty members have worked with leading theater and dance companies throughout the country. Guest artists have included Austin Pendleton, Tom Jones, Shirley Jones, Ricky Ian Gordon, Jason Robert Brown, and Michael-John LaChuisa. Current notable alumni include Brad Sherwood (*Whose Line Is It Anyway?*), Erik Bork (recipient of two Emmy Awards), Nicole Scherzinger (lead singer of Pussycat Dolls), Chauncey Jenkins (*Color Purple*, National Tour and Broadway production), Heather Douglas (*Chicago*-London), Martin Fahrer (Art Director, Nickelodeon Television), and Carrie Hill (Master Electrician, Court Theatre). There are numerous recent graduates on national tours. The winners of the first annual Roger Sturtevant Award, given by Actors Equity, were Meegan Midkiff (2001 WSU) and Nick Verina (2005). This national award was given to 1 female actor and 1 male actor who demonstrated outstanding abilities in musical theater.

**Student Performance Opportunities** Students may work on six main-stage and three studio productions as actors, designers, dancers, or technicians. Students are also offered directing, design, choreography, acting, and dance opportunities in student productions in the directing lab and studio theater. Students majoring in motion picture production are required to complete a fully realized film prior to graduation.

In 2005, a Tom Hanks Scholarship and Guest Artist funds were established to enhance programs in the department.

**Cooperative Agreements** Performance opportunities are also offered with the Human Race Theatre Company, Dayton Opera, the Dayton Ballet, and the Dayton Contemporary Dance Company.

**Career Placement** Acting/Musical Theatre students may perform a "Showcase" in New York City. Auditions for professional companies are held on campus.

## York University
### Toronto, Ontario, Canada

Province-supported, coed. Urban campus. Total enrollment: 51,420. Theater program established 1969.

**Degrees** Bachelor of Fine Arts in the area of theater. Majors and concentrations: acting, design production, directing, playwriting. Graduate degrees offered: Master of Fine Arts in the area of theater.

**Enrollment** 483 total; 227 undergraduate, 18 graduate, 238 nonprofessional degree.

**Theater Student Profile** 67% females, 33% males, 2% international.

**Theater Faculty** 20 total (full-time), 14 total (part-time). 72% of full-time faculty have terminal degrees. Graduate students teach a few undergraduate courses. Undergraduate student–faculty ratio: 11:1.

**Student Life** Student groups/activities include Theatre Students Association, Creative Arts Students Association.

**Expenses for 2007–2008** Application fee: $175 Canadian dollars. Tuition, fee, and room and board charges are reported in Canadian dollars. Comprehensive fee: $11,664 includes full-time tuition ($5278) and college room and board ($6386). College room only: $3986. Full-time tuition varies according to course load, degree level, and program. Room and board charges vary according to board plan and housing facility. International student tuition: $15,278 full-time. Special program-related fees: $10–$40 per course for materials and supplies.

**Financial Aid** Program-specific awards: 3 talent awards for applicants with outstanding auditions ($1000), 5 Harry Rowe Bursaries for those demonstrating achievement or potential in artistic or scholarly work ($1000–$2000), Fine Arts Bursaries for academically qualified students demonstrating financial need, 1 Cheryl Rosen Bursary for upperclassmen demonstrating need ($400), 1 Fitzhenry-Weatherhead Theatre Award for 3rd- or 4th-year students demonstrating achievement in theater sound ($500), Friends of Theatre Bursaries for those demonstrating need, 4 Theatre Department Bursaries for those demonstrating need ($500), 1 Jean Gascon Award for 3rd- or 4th- year students

*York University (continued)*

demonstrating need and originality and creativity in acting ($500), 10 IMASCO Performing Arts Awards for 2nd- or 3rd-year students demonstrating outstanding ability and sound academic standing ($3000), 1 Kenneth Ford Award for 3rd- or 4th- year students demonstrating talent in production and financial need ($350).

**Application Procedures** Students apply for admission into the professional program by freshman year. Deadline for freshmen and transfers: February 1. Notification date for freshmen: June 16; transfers: continuous. Required: high school transcript, college transcript(s) for transfer students, minimum 3.0 high school GPA, 2 letters of recommendation, interview, audition, SAT, ACT or Canadian equivalent. Recommended: essay, portfo-

lio for theater production applicants. Auditions held 10 times, or as needed on campus and off campus; videotaped performances are permissible as a substitute for live auditions when distance is prohibitive. Portfolio reviews held by appointment on campus; the submission of slides may be substituted for portfolios when distance is prohibitive.

**Web Site** http://www.yorku.ca/finearts/theatre

**Undergraduate Contact** Susan Wessels, Coordinator, Recruitment and Liaison, Student and Academic Services, York University, 201R GCFA, Faculty of Fine Arts, Toronto, Ontario M3J 1P3, Canada; fax: 416-736-5447, e-mail address: finearts@yorku.ca

**Graduate Contact** Paul Lampert, Graduate Program Director, Department of Theatre, York University, 324 CFT, Toronto, Ontario M3J 1P3, Canada; 416-736-2100 ext. 22202.

# Appendixes

# Summer Programs in the Performing Arts

This list of summer programs is not exhaustive but will help you in thinking about some wonderful opportunities in the performing arts, since taking advantage of summer study is important.

**ACTEEN**

**ACTeen June Academy**

**ACTeen July Academy**

**ACTeen August Academy**

**ACTeen Summer Saturday Academy**

Rita Litton
ACTeen Director
35 West 45th Street
New York, NY 10036
*Phone:* 212-391-5915
*Fax:* 212-768-8918
*E-mail:* rita@acteen.com
*Web site:* www.acteen.com

**THE AILEY SCHOOL**

**Summer Intensive Program**

The Ailey School
Admissions Office
405 West 55th Street (at 9th Avenue)
New York, NY 10019
*Phone:* 212-405-9000
*Fax:* 212-405-9001
*E-mail:* info@alvinalley.org
*Web site:* www.theaileyschool.edu

**AMERICAN ACADEMY OF DRAMATIC ARTS**

**American Academy of Dramatic Arts Summer Program at Los Angeles, California**

Dan Justin
Director of Admissions
1336 North LaBrea Avenue
Hollywood, CA 90028
*Phone:* 800-222-2867
*E-mail:* admissions-ca@aada.org
*Web site:* www.aada.org

**American Academy of Dramatic Arts Summer Program at New York**

Ms. Karen Higginbotham
Director of Admissions
120 Madison Avenue
New York, NY 10016
*Phone:* 800-463-8990
*Fax:* 212-685-8093
*E-mail:* admissions-ny@aada.org
*Web site:* www.aada.org

**AMERICAN CONSERVATORY THEATER (A.C.T.)**

**Summer Training Congress**

Director
30 Grant Avenue
San Francisco, CA 94108
*Phone:* 415-439-2350
*Fax:* 415-834-3300
*E-mail:* jsharrar@act-sf.org
*Web site:* www.ACTactortraining.org

**APPEL FARM ARTS AND MUSIC CENTER**

**Appel Farm Summer Arts Camp**

Ms. Jennie Quinn
Camp Director
PO Box 888
457 Shirley Road
Elmer, NJ 08318-0888
*Phone:* 856-358-2472
*Fax:* 856-358-6513
*E-mail:* appelcamp@aol.com
*Web site:* www.appelfarm.org

Performing Arts

### ASPEN MUSIC FESTIVAL AND SCHOOL

Student Services
2 Music School Road
Aspen, CO 81611
*Phone:* 970-925-3254
*Fax:* 970-925-3802
*E-mail:* studentservices@aspenmusic.org
*Web site:* www.aspenmusicfestival.com

### ATELIER DES ARTS

Francia Tobacman
Director
55 Bethune Street, B645
New York, NY 10014
*Phone:* 212-727-1756
*Fax:* 212-691-0631
*E-mail:* info@atelierdesarts.org
*Web site:* www.atelierdesarts.org

### ATLANTA BALLET

**Centre for Dance Education**

Jen Apgar
1400 W. Peachtree Street, NW
Atlanta, GA 30309
*Phone:* 404-873-5811 Ext. 212
*Fax:* 404-874-7905
*E-mail:* japgar@atlantaballet.com
*Web site:* www.atlantaballet.com/centre/
summer.php

### THE BANFF CENTRE

**Summer Arts Programs**

Arts, Office of the Registrar
Box 1020
Banff, Alberta
Canada T1L 1H5
*Phone:* 800-565-9989
*Fax:* 403-762-6345
*E-mail:* arts_info@banffcentre.ca
*Web site:* www.banffcentre.ca

### BELVOIR TERRACE

Summer Contact: Ms. Nancy S. Goldberg
Director
80 Cliffwood Street
Lenox, MA 01240
*Phone:* 413-637-0555
*Fax:* 413-637-4651
*E-mail:* info@belvoirterrace.com
*Web site:* www.belvoirterrace.com

Winter Contact: Ms. Nancy S. Goldberg
Director
101 West 79th Street
New York, NY 10024
*Phone:* 212-580-3398
*Fax:* 212-579-7282
*E-mail:* info@belvoirterrace.com
*Web site:* www.belvoirterrace.com

### BERKLEE COLLEGE OF MUSIC

**Berklee Business of Music Program**

**Berklee College of Music Summer Performance Program**

**Berklee Gospel Workshop**

**Berklee in L.A. Summer Performance Program**

**Berklee Music Production Workshop**

**Berklee Percussion Festival**

**Berklee Summer Brass Lines Program**

**Berklee Summer Brass Weekend**

**Berklee Summer Guitar Sessions**

**Berklee Summer Saxophone Weekend**

**Berklee Summer Songwriting Workshop**

**Berklee Summer String Fling**

Office of Special Programs
1140 Boylston Street
MS-155 SP
Boston, MA 02215-3693
*Phone:* 617-747-2245
877-237-5533 (toll-free in U.S. and Canada)
*Fax:* 617-262-5419
*E-mail:* summer@berklee.edu
*Web site:* www.berklee.edu/summer/

### BOSTON BALLET

**Summer Dance Program—Boston**

**Summer Dance Program—Newton**

**Summer Dance Workshop**

Boston Ballet
19 Clarendon Street
Boston, MA 02116
*Phone:* 617-456-6298
*E-mail:* summerprograms@bostonballet.
com
*Web site:* www.bostonballet.org

**THE BOSTON CONSERVATORY**

**Summer Dance**

**Vocal/Choral Intensive**

**Eli Epstein Horn Intensive**

Summer Programs Coordinator
The Boston Conservatory
8 The Fenway
Boston, MA 02215
*Phone:* 617-912-9166
*Fax:* 617-912-9101
*E-mail:* summer@bostonconservatory.edu
*Web site:* www.bostonconservatory.edu

**BOSTON UNIVERSITY
TANGLEWOOD INSTITUTE**

Admissions
855 Commonwealth Avenue
Boston, MA 02215
*Phone:* 800-643-4796
*Fax:* 617-353-7455
*E-mail:* tanglewd@bu.edu
*Web site:* www.bu.edu/tanglewood

**BRANT LAKE CAMP**

**Brant Lake Camp's Dance Centre**

Ms. Kirstin Been Spielman
Director
7586 State Route 8
Brant Lake, NY 12815-2256
*Phone:* 518-494-2406
*Fax:* 518-494-7372
*E-mail:* brantlakec@aol.com
*Web site:* www.blcdance.com

**BREVARD MUSIC CENTER**

**Summer Institute & Festival**

Dorothy Knowles
Admissions Coordinator and Registrar
PO Box 312
Brevard, NC 28712
*Phone:* 828-862-2140
*Fax:* 828-884-2036
*E-mail:* bmcadmission@brevardmusic.org
*Web site:* www.brevardmusic.org

**BRIANSKY SARATOGA BALLET**

**Summer Program at Skidmore College,
Saratoga Springs, NY**

Admissions
220 West 93rd Street
New York, NY 10025-7446
*Phone:* 212-799-0341
*Fax:* 212-799-0341
*E-mail:* olegbriansky@msn.com
*Web site:* www.briansky.org

**BUCK'S ROCK PERFORMING AND CREATIVE
ARTS CAMP**

Ms. Laura Morris
Director
59 Buck's Rock Road
New Milford, CT 06776
*Phone:* 860-354-5030
*Fax:* 860-354-1355
*E-mail:* info@bucksrockcamp.com
*Web site:* www.bucksrockcamp.com

**BUTLER UNIVERSITY–JORDAN COLLEGE OF
FINE ARTS**

**Summer Dance Workshop**

Stephen Laurent
Department of Dance
4600 Sunset Avenue
Indianapolis, IN 46208
*Phone:* 317-940-9346
*E-mail:* e-slaurent@butler.edu
*Web site:* www.butler.edu/dance

**CALIFORNIA STATE SUMMER SCHOOL FOR
THE ARTS/INNER SPARK**

Summer Contact: Neil Brillante
Office Technician
1010 Hurley
Suite 185
Sacramento, CA 95825
*Phone:* 916-274-5815
*Fax:* 916-274-5814
*E-mail:* application@innerspark.us
*Web site:* www.innerspark.us

Performing *Arts*

Winter Contact: Neil Brillante
Office Technician
PO Box 1077
Sacramento, CA 95812-1077
*Phone:* 916-274-5815
*Fax:* 916-274-5814
*E-mail:* application@innerspark.us
*Web site:* www.innerspark.us

### CAMP ENCORE-CODA

Summer Contact: James Saltman
Director
50 Encore/Coda Lane
Sweden, ME 04040
*Phone:* 207-647-3947
*Fax:* 207-647-3259
*E-mail:* jamie@encore-coda.com
*Web site:* www.encore-coda.com

Winter Contact: James Saltman
Director
32 Grassmere Road
Brookline, MA 02467
*Phone:* 617-325-1541
*Fax:* 617-325-7278
*E-mail:* jamie@encore-coda.com
*Web site:* www.encore-coda.com

### CAPITOL REGION EDUCATION COUNCIL
**Center for Creative Youth**

Nancy Wolfe
Director
Wesleyan University
350 High Street
Middletown, CT 06459
*Phone:* 860-685-3307
*Fax:* 860-685-3311
*E-mail:* ccy@wesleyan.edu
*Web site:* www.wesleyan.edu/CCY/home.
html

### CAZADERO PERFORMING ARTS CAMP
**Youth Music Summer Camp**

Summer Contact: Jim Mazzaferro
Artistic Director
5385 Cazadero Highway
Cazadero, CA 95421
*Phone:* 707-632-5159
*Fax:* 707-632-5260
*E-mail:* info@cazadero.org
*Web site:* www.cazadero.org

Winter Contact: Administrative Office
P.O. Box 7908
Berkeley, CA 94707
*Phone:* 510-527-7500
*Fax:* 510-527-2790
*E-mail:* info@cazadero.org
*Web site:* www.cazadero.org

### CENTRAL PENNSYLVANIA YOUTH BALLET

CPYB Summer Program
5 North Orange Street
Suite 3
Carlisle, PA 17013
*Phone:* 717-254-8998
*Fax:* 717-245-1189
*E-mail:* info@cpyb.org
*Web site:* www.cpyb.org

### CHAUTAUQUA INSTITUTION
**Chautauqua Summer Schools of Fine and Performing Arts**

Sarah Malinoski
Coordinator of Student Services
PO Box 1098
1 Ames Avenue
Chautauqua, NY 14722
*Phone:* 800–836-ARTS
716-357-6233
*Fax:* 716-357-9014
*E-mail:* dance@ciweb.org; music@ciweb.
org; theater@ciweb.org
*Web site:* www.ciweb.org/schools.html

### CHOATE ROSEMARY HALL
**Choate Rosemary Hall Summer Arts Conservatory–Theater**

Mrs. Randi J. Brandt
Admissions Director, Arts Conservatory
Paul Mellon Arts Center
333 Christian Street
Wallingford, CT 06492
*Phone:* 203-697-2423
*Fax:* 203-697-2396
*E-mail:* rbrandt@choate.edu
*Web site:* www.choate.edu/pmac

## CIRCLE IN THE SQUARE THEATRE SCHOOL

### Summer Workshop—Acting and Musical

Admissions
1633 Broadway at 50th Street
New York, NY 10019
*Phone:* 212-307-0388
*Fax:* 212-307-0257
*E-mail:* circleinthesquare@att.net
*Web site:* www.circlesquare.org

## CROSSROADS SCHOOL FOR ARTS AND SCIENCES

### Crossroads School–Jazz Workshop

Angela Smith
Director, Summer Program
1714 21st Street
Santa Monica, CA 90404
*Phone:* 310-829-7391 ext. 506
*Fax:* 310-828-8147
*E-mail:* summer@xrds.org
*Web site:* www.xrds.org

## CUSHING ACADEMY

### Summer Session

Admissions
39 School Street
Ashvurnham, MA 01430-8000
*Phone:* 978-827-7700
*Fax:* 978-827-6927
*E-mail:* admission@cushing.org
*Web site:* www.cushing.org

## DUKE YOUTH PROGRAMS–DUKE UNIVERSITY CONTINUING STUDIES

### Duke Drama Workshop

Duke Continuing Studies
201 Bishop's House
Box 90700
Durham, NC 27708-0700
*Phone:* 919-684-6259
*Fax:* 919-681-8235
*E-mail:* learnmore@duke.edu
*Web site:* www.learnmore.duke.edu/youth

## EASTERN U.S. MUSIC CAMP, INC. AT COLGATE UNIVERSITY

Summer Contact: Dr. Thomas A. Brown
Director
Dana Arts Center
Hamilton, NY 13346-1398
*Phone:* 315-228-7041
*Fax:* 315-228-7557
*E-mail:* summer@EasternUSMusicCamp.com
*Web site:* www.EasternUSMusicCamp.com

Winter Contact: Dr. Thomas A. Brown
Director
7 Brook Hollow Road
Ballston Lake, NY 12019
*Phone:* 866-777-7841
*Fax:* 518-877-4943
*E-mail:* eusmc@EasternUSMusicCamp.com
*Web site:* www.EasternUSMusicCamp.com

## EASTMAN SCHOOL OF MUSIC

### Programs for High School Students

### Collegiate Institutes for High School Students

Summer Session Office
26 Gibbs Street
Rochester, NY 14604
*Phone:* 800-246-4706
*Fax:* 585-274-1005
*E-mail:* summer@esm.rochester.edu
*Web site:* www.esm.rochester.edu/summer

## EDUCATION UNLIMITED

### California Actor's Workshop by Education Unlimited

### Ashland Shakespeare Seminar

Director
1700 Shattuck Avenue, #305
Berkeley, CA 94709
*Phone:* 510-548-6612
*Fax:* 510-548-0212
*E-mail:* camps@educationunlimited.com
*Web site:* www.educationunlimited.com

Performing Arts

**EMMA WILLARD SCHOOL**
*GirlSummer at Emma Willard School*

Director
285 Pawling Avenue
Troy, NY 12180
*Phone:* 866-397-2267 (toll-free)
*Fax:* 718-237-8862
*E-mail:* girlsummer@emmawillard.org
*Web site:* www.emmawillard.org/summer/
residential

**ENSEMBLE THEATRE COMMUNITY SCHOOL**

Summer Contact: Seth Orbach
Program Director
PO Box 188
Eagles Mere, PA 17731
*Phone:* 570-525-3043
*Fax:* 570-525-3548
*E-mail:* info@etcschool.org
*Web site:* www.etcschool.org

Winter Contact: Seth Orbach
Program Director
43 Lyman Circle
Shaker Heights, OH 44122
*Phone:* 216-464-1688
*E-mail:* info@etcschool.org
*Web site:* www.etcschool.org

**THE EXPERIMENT IN INTERNATIONAL LIVING–
WORLD LEARNING**

**The Experiment in International Living–The
Arts Theme**

**The Experiment in International Living–
Brazil: The Rhythm of Bahia–Dance, Music,
and Capoeira**

**The Experiment in International Living–
France: A Festival of Theater**

**The Experiment in International Living–
United Kingdom: A Midsummer
Theatrical Journey**

Enrollment Director
Summer Abroad
1 Kipling Road
PO Box 676
Brattleboro, VT 05302-0676
*Phone:* 800-345-2929
*Fax:* 802-258-3428
*E-mail:* info@worldlearning.org
*Web site:* www.usexperiment.org

**HARAND CAMP OF THE THEATRE ARTS**

Summer Contact: Sulie Harand
Director
Carthage on the Lake
2001 Alford Park Drive
Kenosha, WI 53140-1994
*Phone:* 262-551-2140
*E-mail:* info@HarandCamp.com
*Web site:* www.harandcamp.com

Winter Contact: Sulie Harand
Director
708 Church Street, #231
Evanston, IL 60201
*Phone:* 847-864-1500
*E-mail:* info@HarandCamp.com
*Web site:* www.harandcamp.com

**THE HARID CONSERVATORY**
**Summer School**

The Harid Conservatory
2285 Potomac Road
Boca Raton, FL 33431-5518
*Phone:* 561-997-2677
*Fax:* 561-997-8920
*E-mail:* info@harid.edu
*Web site:* www.harid.edu

**HOLLINS UNIVERSITY**
**Hollinsummer Program**

Director of Admissions
PO Box 9707
Roanoke, VA 24020-1707
*Phone:* 800-456-9595
*Fax:* 540-362-6218
*E-mail:* huadm@hollins.edu
*Web site:* www.hollins.edu/

**THE HOTCHKISS SCHOOL**
**Hotchkiss School Summer Music Studies**

Christie Gurney Rawlings
Director of Admission and Residential Life
11 Interlaken Road
PO Box 800
Lakeville, CT 06039-0800
*Phone:* 860-435-3173
*Fax:* 860-435-4413
*E-mail:* summer@hotchkiss.org
*Web site:* www.hotchkiss.org/summer

Performing Arts

## HUMANITIES SPRING IN ASSISI
**Interdisciplinary Travel-Study Programs in New York and Assisi, Italy**

Ms. Jane R. Oliensis
Director
Santa Maria di Lignano, 2
Assisi 06081, Italy
*Phone:* 39–075–802400
*Fax:* 39–075–802400
*E-mail:* info@humanitiesspring.com
*Web site:* www.humanitiesspring.com

## HYDE SCHOOL
**Hyde School Summer Challenge Program–Bath, ME**

Director of Admission
616 High Street
Bath, ME 04530-5002
*Phone:* 207-443-7101
*Fax:* 207-442-9346
*E-mail:* bath.admissions@hyde.edu
*Web site:* www.hyde.edu

**Hyde School Summer Challenge Program–Woodstock, CT**

Director of Admissions
PO Box 237
Woodstock, CT 06281-0237
*Phone:* 860-963-4736
*Fax:* 860-928-0612
*E-mail:* woodstock.admissions@hyde.edu
*Web site:* www.hyde.edu

## IDYLLWILD ARTS FOUNDATION
**Idyllwild Arts Summer Program–American Experience for International Students**

Ms. Diane Dennis
Summer Program Registrar
PO Box 38
Idyllwild, CA 92549
*Phone:* 951-659-2171 ext. 2365
*Fax:* 951-659-4552
*E-mail:* summer@idyllwildarts.org
*Web site:* www.idyllwildarts.org

## INTERLOCHEN CENTER FOR THE ARTS
**Interlochen Arts Camp**

Kellye Modarelli
Director of Admissions
PO Box 199
Interlochen, MI 49643
*Phone:* 231-276-7472
*Fax:* 231-276-7464
*E-mail:* admissions@interlochen.org
*Web site:* www.interlochen.org/

## INTERN EXCHANGE INTERNATIONAL, LTD.
**IEI–Theatre Plus Programme**

**Video Production/Acting for the Camera**

Nina Miller Glickman
Director
1858 Mallard Lane
Villanova, PA 19085
*Phone:* 610-527-6066
*Fax:* 610-527-5499
*E-mail:* info@internexchange.com
*Web site:* www.internexchange.com

## ITHACA COLLEGE DIVISION OF CONTINUING EDUCATION AND SUMMER SESSIONS
**Ithaca College Summer Piano Institute**

Mr. E. Kimball Milling
Director of Continuing Education and
    Summer Sessions
120 Towers Concourse
Ithaca, NY 14850-7141
*Phone:* 607-274-3143
*Fax:* 607-274-1263
*E-mail:* cess@ithaca.edu
*Web site:* www.ithaca.edu/cess

## JACOB'S PILLOW DANCE
**Summer Programs**

Director of Education
358 George Carter Road
Becket, MA 01223
*Phone:* 413-243-9919
*Fax:* 413-243-4744
*E-mail:* info@jacobspillow.org
*Web site:* www.jacobspillow.org

Performing Arts

**THE JUILLIARD SCHOOL**

**Summer Programs**

**Complete Choral Musician**

**Interpreting for the Theater Institute**

**Juilliard String Quartet Seminar**

**Starling-DeLay Symposium on Violin Studies**

**Summer Dance Intensive**

**Summer Percussion Seminar**

Summer Programs
60 Lincoln Center Plaza
New York, NY 10023-6588
*Phone:* 610-527-6066
*Fax:* 212-799-5000
*E-mail:* admissions@juilliard.edu
*Web site:* www.juilliard.edu

**KINHAVEN MUSIC SCHOOL**

Kinhaven Admissions Office
1704 Sycamore Street
Bethlehem, PA 18017
*Phone:* 610-868-9200
*E-mail:* kinhavenmusic@aol.com
*Web site:* www.kinhaven.org

**LEARNING THEATRE, INC.**

**Encore! Ensemble Theatre Workshop**

Program Administrator
4661 Sweetmeadow Circle
Sarasota, FL 34238
*Phone:* 941-926-3244
*Fax:* 941-926-3254
*E-mail:* susanb@learntheatre.org
*Web site:* www.learntheatre.org

**THE LEE STRASBERG THEATRE & FILM INSTITUTE**

**Summer Intensive Program–New York**

Admissions
115 East 15th Street
New York, NY 10003
*Phone:* 212-533-5500
*Fax:* 212-473-1727
*E-mail:* newyork@strasberg.com
*Web site:* www.strasberg.com

**Summer Program–Los Angeles**

Admissions
7936 Santa Monica Boulevard
Los Angeles, CA 90046
*Telephone:* 323-650-7777
*Fax:* 323-650-7770
*E-mail:* losangeles@strasberg.com
*Web site:* www.strasberg.com

**LEYSIN AMERICAN SCHOOL IN SWITZERLAND**

**Summer in Switzerland**

SIS Admissions Office
Leysin American School
Leysin 1854, Switzerland
*Phone:* 41–24–493–3979
*Fax:* 41–24–494–1585
*E-mail:* admissions@las.ch
*Web site:* www.las.ch/summer

**THE LIMÓN INSTITUTE**

**Summer Dance Workshop with the Limón Dance Company**

Admissions
307 West 38th Street, Suite 1105
New York, NY 10018
*Phone:* 212-777-3353
*Fax:* 212-777-4764
*E-mail:* info@limon.org
*Web site:* www.limon.org

**MEADOWMOUNT SCHOOL OF MUSIC**

Mary McGowan-Welp
Admissions Director
1424 County Route 10
Westport, New York 12993
*Phone:* 518- 962–2400
*Fax:* 518-962-2310 (summer use only)
*E-mail:* admissions@meadowmount.com
*Web site:* www.meadowmount.com

## MERCERSBURG ACADEMY SUMMER AND EXTENDED PROGRAMS

**Mercersburg Onstage! Young Actors Workshop**

Director
Office of Summer and Extended Programs
300 East Seminary Street
Mercersburg, PA 17236
*Phone:* 717-328-6225
*Fax:* 717-328-9072
*E-mail:* summerprograms@mercersburg.edu
*Web site:* www.mercersburg.edu/summer_programs

## MICHIGAN TECHNOLOGICAL UNIVERSITY

**Michigan Technological University Orchestra Fellowship Program**

Rose Martell
Youth Programs Administrative Aide
1400 Townsend Drive
Houghton, MI 49931-1295
*Phone:* 906-487-2219
*Fax:* 906-487-3101
*E-mail:* yp@mtu.edu
*Web site:* www.mtu.edu/

## NATIONAL STUDENT LEADERSHIP CONFERENCE

**Inside the Arts–New York City**

Admissions
414 North Orleans Street
Suite LL8
Chicago, IL 60610-1087
*Phone:* 312-322-9999
800-994-6752 (toll-free)
*Fax:* 312-765-0081
*E-mail:* info@nslcleaders.org
*Web site:* www.nslcleaders.org

## NEW YORK FILM ACADEMY

**The New York Film Academy, Universal Studios, Hollywood, CA**

Admissions
100 East 17th Street
New York, NY 10003
*Phone:* 212-674-4300
800–611-FILM (toll-free)
*Fax:* 212-477-1414
*E-mail:* film@nyfa.com
*Web site:* www.nyfa.com

## NEW YORK UNIVERSITY, TISCH SCHOOL OF THE ARTS

**Tisch School of the Arts–International High School Program–Dublin**

**Tisch School of the Arts–International High School Program–Paris**

**Tisch School of the Arts–Summer High School Programs**

Mr. Josh Murray
Assistant Director of Recruitment
Special Programs
721 Broadway
12th Floor
New York, NY 10003
*Phone:* 212-998-1500
*Fax:* 212-995-4610
*E-mail:* tisch.special.info@nyu.edu
*Web site:* specialprograms.tisch.nyu.edu

## NORTHWESTERN UNIVERSITY

**National High School Institute at Northwestern University**

Summer Programs for High School Students
Northwestern University
617 Noyes St.
Evanston, IL 60208-4165
*Phone:* 847-491-3026
*Fax:* 847-467-1057
*E-mail:* nhsi@northwestern.edu
*Web site:* www.northwestern.edu/nhsi

## OXBRIDGE ACADEMIC PROGRAMS

**The Cambridge Tradition**

**La Academia de España**

**L'Académie de France**

**L'Académie de Paris**

**The Oxford Tradition**

Admissions
601 Cathedral Parkway, Suite 7R
New York, NY 10025-2186
*Phone:* 212-932-3049
800-828-8349 (toll-free in U.S. and Canada)
*Fax:* 212-663-8169
*E-mail:* info@oxbridgeprograms.com
*Web site:* www.oxbridgeprograms.com

Performing Arts

**PERIDANCE CENTER**

**International Dance School**

Admissions
890 Broadway, Sixth Floor
New York, NY 10003
*Phone:* 212-505-0886
*Fax:* 212-674-2239
*E-mail:* info@peridance.com
*Web site:* www. peridance.com

**PERRY-MANSFIELD PERFORMING ARTS SCHOOL AND CAMP**

Executive Director
40755 Routt County Road 36
Steamboat Springs, CO 80487
*Phone:* 800-430-2787
*Fax:* 970-879-5823
*E-mail:* p-m@perry-mansfield.org
*Web site:* www.perry-mansfield.org

**POWER CHORD ACADEMY**

**Power Chord Academy Summer Sessions**

Summer Session
7336 Santa Monica Boulevard, #107
Los Angeles, CA 90046
*Phone:* 800-897-6677 Ext. 80
*Fax:* 775-306-7923
*E-mail:* info@powerchordacademy.com
*Web site:* www.powerchordacademy.com

**THE PUTNEY SCHOOL**

**The Putney School Summer Arts Program**

Susan Farber
Administrative Coordinator
Elm Lea Farm
418 Houghton Brook Road
Putney, VT 05346
*Phone:* 802-387-6276
*Fax:* 802-387-6216
*E-mail:* summer@putneyschool.org
*Web site:* www.putneyschool.org/summer

**PUTNEY STUDENT TRAVEL**

**Excel at Amherst College**

**Putney Student Travel–Cultural Exploration–Theatre in Britain**

Director
345 Hickory Ridge Road
Putney, VT 05346
*Phone:* 802-387-5000
*Fax:* 802-387-4276
*E-mail:* info@goputney.com
*Web site:* www.goputney.com

**RENSSELAER POLYTECHNIC INSTITUTE–OUTREACH PROGRAMS**

**Summer@Rensselaer**

Mr. Michael L. Gunther
Program Manager for Recruitment
CII Low Center, Suite 4011
110 Eighth Street
Troy, NY 12180-3590
*Phone:* 518-276-8351
*Fax:* 518-276-8738
*E-mail:* gunthm@rpi.edu
*Web site:* http://summer.rpi.edu

**SAGE SUMMER LEARNING ADVENTURES**

**Arts and Religions of India**

Summer SAGE Program
19 Old Town Square
Suite 238
Fort Collins, CO 80524
*Phone:* 888–997-SAGE (toll-free)
*Fax:* 970-482-0251
*E-mail:* info@sageprogram.org
*Web site:* http://sageprogram.org

**SALEM ACADEMY AND COLLEGE**

**Salem Spotlight**

Douglas Murphy
Executive Director
PO Box 10578
Winston-Salem, NC 27108-1753
*Phone:* 800-883-1753
*E-mail:* spotlight@salem.edu
*Web site:* http://spotlight.salem.edu

Performing

Arts

### SARAH LAWRENCE COLLEGE

**Sarah Lawrence College Summer High School Programs**

Liz Irmiter
Director of Special Programs
1 Mead Way
Bronxville, NY 10708
*Phone:* 914-395-2693
*E-mail:* specialprograms@sarahlawrence.
edu
*Web site:* www.sarahlawrence.edu/summer

### THE SCHOOL OF TORONTO DANCE THEATRE

**Summer School in Contemporary Dance**

Patricia Fraser
Director
80 Winchester Street
Toronto, Ontario
Canada M4X 1B2
*Phone:* 416-967-6887
*Fax:* 416-967-4379
*E-mail:* info@schooloftdt.org
*Web site:* www.schooloftdt.org

### SIGNATURE MUSIC CAMP, INC.

**Signature Music Teen Camp at Ithaca College**

Signature Music Camp
118 Julian Place, #229
Syracuse, NY 13210
*Phone:* 315-478-7480
*Fax:* 315-478-0962
*E-mail:* contact@signaturemusic.org
*Web site:* www.signaturemusic.org

### SKIDMORE COLLEGE

**SITI Summer Theater Workshop**

**Skidmore Jazz Institute**

**Skidmore Summer Flute Institute**

**Summer Dance Workshop**

Office of the Dean of Special Programs
Skidmore College
815 North Broadway
Saratoga Springs, NY 12866-1632
*Phone:* 518-580-5590
E-mail: mmccoll@skidmore.edu
*Web site:* www.skidmore.edu/summer

### SPOLETO ARTS SYMPOSIA

**Spoleto Vocal Arts Symposium**

**Spoleto Vocal Jazz Symposium**

C.J. Everett
Executive Director
760 West End Avenue, #3A
New York, NY 10025
*Phone:* 212-665-3544
*E-mail:* clintoneve@aol.com
*Web site:* www.spoletoarts.com

### SPOLETO STUDY ABROAD

**Summer Arts and Humanities Programs**

Nancy Langston
Marketing Director
PO Box 13389
Charleston, SC 29422-3389
*Phone:* 843-822-1248
*E-mail:* spoleto@mindspring.com
*Web site:* www.spoletostudyabroad.com

### STAGEDOOR MANOR PERFORMING ARTS TRAINING CENTER/THEATRE AND DANCE CAMP

Summer Contact: Barbara Martin
Director
116 Karmel Road
Loch Sheldrake, NY 12759-5308
*Phone:* 888-STAGE 88
*Fax:* 888-STAGE 88
*Web site:* www.stagedoormanor.com

Winter Contact: Barbara Martin
Director
8 Wingate Road
Lexington, MA 02421
*Phone:* 888-STAGE 88
*Fax:* 888-STAGE 88
*E-mail:* stagedoormanor@aol.com
*Web site:* www.stagedoormanor.com

Performing *Arts*

**STELLA ADLER STUDIO OF ACTING**

**Summer Conservatory**

**Chekov Intensive**

**Physical Theater Intensive**

**Shakespeare Intensive**

Admissions
31 West 27th Street, 3rd Floor
New York, NY 10001
*Phone:* 212-689-0087
800-112-1111 (toll-free)
*Fax:* 212-689-6110
*E-mail:* info@stellaadler.com
*Web site:* www.stellaadler.com

**SUMMER THEATRE INSTITUTE NEW YORK CITY**

**Summer Theatre Institute**

Ms. Allyn Sitjar
Artistic Director
23 Tomahawk Trail
Sparta, NJ 07871
*Phone:* 201-415-5329
973-729-6026 (evenings and weekends)
*E-mail:* youththeatreallyn@yahoo.com
*Web site:* www.youththeatreinstitutes.org

**SYRACUSE UNIVERSITY**

**Syracuse University Summer College**

Program Manager
700 University Avenue
Syracuse, NY 13244-2530
*Phone:* 315-443-3225
*Fax:* 315-443-4174
*E-mail:* sumcoll@syr.edu
*Web site:* www.summercollege.syr.edu/

**TANGLEWOOD INSTITUTE**

**Boston University Tanglewood Institute Summer Programs**

College of Fine Arts
Boston University
855 Commonwealth Avenue
Boston, MA 02215.
*Phone:* 617-353-3350
*E-mail:* tanglwd@bu.edu
*Web site:* www.bu.edu/cfa/music/
tanglewood/

**TASIS**

**The TASIS Summer Programs in England, France, and Switzerland**

The TASIS Schools, U.S. Office
1640 Wisconsin Avenue, NW
Washington, D.C. 20007
*Phone:* 202-965-5800
800-442-6005 (toll-free)
*Fax:* 202-965-5816
*E-mail:* usadmissions@tasis.com
*Web site:* http://summer.tasis.com

**UCLA SUMMER SESSIONS AND SPECIAL PROGRAMS**

**UCLA Summer Experience: Institutes**

Dr. Susan Pertel Jain
Director of Academic Program Development
Box 951418
Los Angeles, CA 90095
*Phone:* 310-825-4101
*Fax:* 310-825-1528
*E-mail:* info@summer.ucla.edu
*Web site:* www.summer.ucla.edu

**THE UNIVERSITY OF THE ARTS**

**Pre-College Summer Institute**

Pre-College Programs
320 South Broad Street
Philadelphia, PA 19102
*Phone:* 215-717-6430
800–616-ARTS (toll-free outside Pennsylvania)
*Fax:* 215-717-6433
*E-mail:* precollege@uarts.edu
*Web site:* www.uarts.edu/precollege

**USDAN CENTER FOR THE CREATIVE AND PERFORMING ARTS**

Dale Lewis
Executive Director
Usdan Long Island Office
185 Colonial Springs Road
Wheatley Heights, NY 11798
*Phone:* 631–643–7900
212-772-6060
*Web site:* www.usdan.org

Performing

*Arts*

**WALNUT HILL SCHOOL**

**Summer at Walnut Hill**

Office of Admission and Placement
12 Highland Street
Natick, MA 01760
*Phone:* 508-653-4312
*Fax:* 508-655-3726
*Web site:* www.walnuthillarts.org

**WESTMINSTER COLLEGE OF THE ARTS OF RIDER UNIVERSITY**

Princeton Campus
101 Walnut Lane
Princeton, NJ 08540-3899
*Phone:* 800-257-9026 (admissions)
609-896-5000 (main)
*E-mail:* woce@rider.edu
*Web site:* www.rider.edu

Lawrenceville Campus
2083 Lawrenceville Road
Lawrenceville, NJ 08648
*Phone:* 800-257-9026 (admissions)
609-896-5000 (main)
*Fax:* 888-STAGE 88
*E-mail:* woce@rider.edu
*Web site:* www.rider.edu

**WILDERNESS DANCE CAMP, INC.**

**Wilderness Dance Camp**

Ms. Chandra Saign
Director
10251 Lyndale Avenue South
Bloomington, MN 55420
*Phone:* 952-884-6009
*E-mail:* info@dancecamp.org
*Web site:* www.dancecamp.org/

**WORLD HORIZONS INTERNATIONAL**

**United Kingdom: Service and Arts Program**

Mr. Stuart L. Rabinowitz
Executive Director
PO Box 662
Bethelem, CT 06751-0662
*Phone:* 800-262-5874
*Fax:* 203-266-6227
*E-mail:* worldhorizons@att.net
*Web site:* www.world-horizons.com

**WYOMING SEMINARY COLLEGE PREPARATORY SCHOOL**

**The Performing Arts Institute of Wyoming Seminary**

Nancy Sanderson, Director
201 North Sprague Avenue
Kingston, PA 18704
*Phone:* 570-270-2186
*Fax:* 570-270-2198
*E-mail:* onstage@wyomingseminary.org
*Web site:* www.wyomingseminary.org/pai

Performing *Arts*

# Scholarships for Performing Artists

**ACADEMY OF TELEVISION ARTS AND SCIENCES FOUNDATION**

**Academy of Television Arts and Sciences College Television Awards**

Nancy Robinson, Programs Coordinator
Academy of Television Arts and Sciences Foundation
5220 Lankershim Boulevard
North Hollywood, CA 91601
*Phone:* 818-754-2839
*Fax:* 818-761-8524
*E-mail:* collegeawards@emmys.org
*Web site:* http://www.emmysfoundation.org

**ACTORS THEATRE OF LOUISVILLE**

**National Ten-Minute Play Contest**

Ms. Adrien-Alice Hansel, New Play Development Director
Actors Theatre of Louisville
316 West Main Street
Louisville, KY 40202-4218
*Phone:* 502-584-1265 Ext. 3031
*Fax:* 502-561-3300
*E-mail:* ahansel@actorstheatre.org
*Web site:* http://www.actorstheatre.org

**AMERICAN COLLEGE OF MUSICIANS/NATIONAL GUILD OF PIANO TEACHERS**

**American College of Musicians/National Guild of Piano Teachers $200 Scholarships**

Scholarship Committee
American College of Musicians/National Guild of Piano Teachers
PO Box 1807
Austin, TX 78767-1807
*Web site:* http://www.pianoguild.com

**AMERICAN COUNCIL FOR POLISH CULTURE**

**Marcella Kochanska Sembrich Vocal Competition**

Mr. Jaroslaw Golembiowski, ACPC Music Committee Chair
American Council for Polish Culture
1532 N. Artesian
Chicago, IL 60622-1750
*Phone:* 773-862-4686
*E-mail:* yaromusic@dsl.polel.us
*Web site:* http://www.polishcultureacpc.org

**AMERICAN FOUNDATION FOR THE BLIND**

**R.L. Gillette Scholarship**

Dawn Bodrogi, Information Center and Library Coordinator
American Foundation for the Blind
11 Penn Plaza, Suite 300
New York, NY 10001
*Phone:* 212-502-7661
*Fax:* 212-502-7771
*E-mail:* afbinfo@afb.net
*Web site:* http://www.afb.org

**AMERICAN LEGION DEPARTMENT OF KANSAS**

**Music Committee Scholarship**

Jim Gravenstein, Chairman, Scholarship Committee
American Legion Department of Kansas
1314 Topeka Boulevard, SW
Topeka, KS 66612
*Phone:* 785-232-9315
*Fax:* 782-232-1399
*Web site:* http://www.ksamlegion.org

Performing Arts

## AMERICAN STRING TEACHERS ASSOCIATION
**National Solo Competition**

Laura Kobayashi, Committee Chair
American String Teachers Association
4153 Chain Bridge Road
Fairfax, VA 22030
*Phone:* 703-279-2113
*Fax:* 703-279-2114
*E-mail:* lkobayas@myway.com
*Web site:* http://www.astaweb.com

## AMERICAN THEATRE ORGAN SOCIETY INC.
**American Theatre Organ Society Organ Performance Scholarship**

Carlton B. Smith, Chairperson, Scholarship
  Program
American Theatre Organ Society Inc.
2175 North Irwin Street
Indianapolis, IN 46219-2220
*Phone:* 317-356-1270
*Fax:* 317-322-9379
*E-mail:* smith@atos.org
*Web site:* http://www.atos.org

## BALTIMORE CHAPTER OF THE AMERICAN MARKETING ASSOCIATION
**Undergraduate Marketing Education Merit Scholarships**

Marisa O'Brien, Scholarship Committee
Baltimore Chapter of the American
  Marketing Association
22 West Road, Suite 301
Towson, MD 21204
*Phone:* 410-467-2529
*E-mail:* scholarship@amabaltimore.org
*Web site:* http://www.amabaltimore.org

## BMI FOUNDATION INC.
**BMI Student Composer Awards**

**John Lennon Scholarship Program**

**Peermusic Latin Scholarship**

Mr. Ralph N. Jackson, President
BMI Foundation Inc.
320 West 57th Street
New York, NY 10019
*Phone:* 212-586-2000
*Fax:* 212-245-8986
*E-mail:* rjackson@bmi.com
*Web site:* http://www.bmifoundation.org

## CARMEL MUSIC SOCIETY
**Carmel Music Society Competition**

Competition Chair
Carmel Music Society
PO Box 22783
Carmel, CA 93922
*Phone:* 831-625-9938
*Fax:* 831-625-6823
*E-mail:* carmelmusic@sbcglobal.net
*Web site:* http://www.carmelmusic.org

## CHOPIN FOUNDATION OF THE UNITED STATES
**Chopin Foundation of the United States Scholarship**

Jadwiga Gewert, Executive Director
Chopin Foundation of the United States
1440 79th Street Causeway, Suite 117
Miami, FL 33141
*Phone:* 305-868-0624
*Fax:* 305-865-5150
*E-mail:* info@chopin.org
*Web site:* http://www.chopin.org

## CHRISTOPHER PETTIET SCHOLARSHIP FUND
**Christopher Pettiet Memorial Fund**

Scholarship Committee
Christopher Pettiet Scholarship Fund
The Actors Circle
4475 Sepulveda Boulevard
Culver City, CA 90230
*Phone:* 310-837-4536
*E-mail:* workshops@theactorscircle.com
*Web site:* http://www.theactorscircle.com/
  chris.html

## THE CIRI FOUNDATION (TCF)
**CIRI Foundation Susie Qimmiqsak Bevins Endowment Scholarship Fund**

Susan Anderson, President and Chief
  Executive Officer
CIRI Foundation (TCF)
3600 San Jeronimo Drive, Suite 256
Anchorage, AK 99508-2870
*Phone:* 907-793-3575
*Fax:* 907-793-3585
*E-mail:* tcf@thecirifoundation.org
*Web site:* http://www.thecirifoundation.
  org

## COLLEGEBOUND FOUNDATION
### Janet B. Sondheim Scholarship

Jamie Crouse, Scholarship Program
Administrator
CollegeBound Foundation
300 Water Street, Suite 300
Baltimore, MD 21202
*Phone:* 410-783-2905 Ext. 207
*Fax:* 410-727-5786
*E-mail:* jcrouse@collegeboundfoundation.
org
*Web site:* http://www.
collegeboundfoundation.org

## COLUMBIA UNIVERSITY, DEPARTMENT OF MUSIC
### Joseph H. Bearns Prize in Music

Department, Music
Columbia University, Department of Music
621 Dodge Hall, MC No. 1813
2960 Broadway
New York, NY 10027
*Phone:* 212-854-3825
*Fax:* 212-854-8191
*Web site:* http://www.music.columbia.edu

## COMMUNITY FOUNDATION FOR GREATER ATLANTA INC.
### James M. and Virginia M. Smyth Scholarship

Kristina Morris, Program Associate
Community Foundation for Greater
Atlanta Inc.
50 Hurt Plaza, Suite 449
Atlanta, GA 30303
*Phone:* 404-688-5525
*Fax:* 404-688-3060
*E-mail:* scholarships@atlcf.org
*Web site:* http://www.atlcf.org

## CONCERT ARTISTS GUILD
### Concert Artists Guild Competition

Amy Frawley, Competition Manager
Concert Artists Guild
850 Seventh Avenue, Suite 1205
New York, NY 10019-5230
*Phone:* 212-333-5200 Ext. 14
*Fax:* 212-977-7149
*E-mail:* caguild@concertartists.org
*Web site:* http://www.concertartists.org

## CONGRESSIONAL BLACK CAUCUS SPOUSES PROGRAM
### Congressional Black Caucus Spouses Performing Arts Scholarship

Janet Carter, Scholarship Coordinator
Congressional Black Caucus Spouses
Program
1720 Massachusetts Avenue, NW
Washington, DC 20036
*Phone:* 202-263-2840
*Fax:* 202-263-0844
*E-mail:* jcarter@cbcfinc.org
*Web site:* http://www.cbcfinc.org

## CONTEMPORARY RECORD SOCIETY
### Contemporary Record Society National Competition for Performing Artists

Jack Shusterman, Artist Representative
Contemporary Record Society
724 Winchester Road
Broomall, PA 19008
*Phone:* 610-544-5920
*Fax:* 610-544-5921
*E-mail:* crsnews@verizon.net
*Web site:* http://www.crsnews.org

### National Competition for Composers' Recordings

Jack Shusterman, Artist Representative
Contemporary Record Society
724 Winchester Road
Broomall, PA 19008
*Phone:* 610-544-5920
*Fax:* 610-544-5921
*E-mail:* crsnews@verizon.net
*Web site:* http://www.crsnews.org

## COSTUME SOCIETY OF AMERICA
### Adele Filene Travel Award
### Stella Blum Research Grant

Noel Liccardi, Program Contact
Costume Society of America
203 Towne Center Drive
Hillsborough, NJ 08844
*Phone:* 800-272-9447
*Fax:* 908-450-1118
*E-mail:* national.
office@costumesocietyamerica.com
*Web site:* http://www.
costumesocietyamerica.com

Performing *Arts*

### DAVIDSON INSTITUTE FOR TALENT DEVELOPMENT
**Davidson Fellows**

Tacie Moessner, Davidson Fellows Program Manager
Davidson Institute for Talent Development
9665 Gateway Drive, Suite B
Reno, NV 89521
*Phone:* 775-852-3483 Ext. 423
*Fax:* 775-852-2184
*E-mail:* davidsonfellows@ditd.org
*Web site:* http://www.davidsoninstitute.org

### DAYTON FOUNDATION
**Mu Phi Epsilon Scholarship Fund**

Diane Timmons, Director Grants and Programs
Dayton Foundation
2300 Kettering Tower
Dayton, OH 45423
*Phone:* 937-225-9966
*E-mail:* dtimmons@daytonfoundation.org
*Web site:* http://www.daytonfoundation.org

### DELTA OMICRON INTERNATIONAL MUSIC FRATERNITY/DELTA OMICRON FOUNDATION INC.
**Delta Omicron Froundation Educational Grants in Music**

Kay C. Wideman, President
Delta Omicron International Music Fraternity/Delta Omicron Foundation Inc.
503 Greystone Lane
Douglasville, GA 30134
*Phone:* 770-920-2417
*Fax:* 770-577-5863
*E-mail:* widemans@bellsouth.net
*Web site:* http://www.delta-omicron.org

**Delta Omicron Summer Scholarships**

Ms. Michelle A. May, Chair, Summer Scholarships
Delta Omicron International Music Fraternity/Delta Omicron Foundation Inc.
1635 West Boston Boulevard
Detroit, MI 48206
*Phone:* 313-865-1149
*E-mail:* maybiz@aol.com
*Web site:* http://www.delta-omicron.org

### DOMENIC TROIANO GUITAR SCHOLARSHIP
**Domenic Troiano Guitar Scholarship**

Clinton Somerton, Administrator
Domenic Troiano Guitar Scholarship
18 Sherbourne Street
Toronto, ON M5A 2R2
Canada
*Phone:* 416-367-0178
*Fax:* 416-367-0178
*E-mail:* clinton@domenictroiano.com
*Web site:* http://www.domenictroiano.com

### DONNA REED FOUNDATION FOR THE PERFORMING ARTS
**Donna Reed Performing Arts Scholarships**

Kenny Kahl, Festival Coordinator
Donna Reed Foundation for the Performing Arts
1305 Broadway
Denison, IA 51442
*Phone:* 712-263-3334
*Fax:* 712-263-8026
*E-mail:* info@donnareed.org
*Web site:* http://www.donnareed.org

### FOREST ROBERTS THEATRE
**Mildred and Albert Panowski Playwriting Award**

Matt Hudson, Playwriting Award Coordinator
Forest Roberts Theatre
Northern Michigan University
1401 Presque Isle Avenue
Marquette, MI 49855-5364
*Phone:* 906-227-2559
*Fax:* 906-227-2567
*Web site:* http://www.nmu.edu

**FORT COLLINS SYMPHONY ASSOCIATION**

**Adeline Rosenberg Memorial Prize**

Carol Kauffman, Office Manager
Fort Collins Symphony Association
214 South College Avenue
PO Box 1963
Fort Collins, CO 80524
*Phone:* 970-482-4823
*Fax:* 970-482-4858
*E-mail:* yac@fcsymphony.org
*Web site:* http://www.fcsymphony.org

**GENERAL FEDERATION OF WOMEN'S CLUBS OF MASSACHUSETTS**

**Dorchester Women's Club Music Scholarship**

**General Federation of Women's Clubs of Massachusetts Nickel for Notes Music Scholarship**

Joan Korslund, Music Chairman
General Federation of Women's Clubs of Massachusetts
25 Apple Lane
Wrentham, MA 02093
*E-mail:* nonnalda@aol.com
*Web site:* http://www.gfwcma.org

**GLENN MILLER BIRTHPLACE SOCIETY**

**Glenn Miller Instrumental Scholarship**

**Jack Pullan Memorial Scholarship**

**Ralph Brewster Vocal Scholarship**

Arlene Leonard, Secretary
Glenn Miller Birthplace Society
107 East Main Street, PO Box 61
Clarinda, IA 51632-0061
*Phone:* 712-542-2461
*Fax:* 712-542-2461
*E-mail:* gmbs@heartland.net
*Web site:* http://www.glennmiller.org

**GRAND RAPIDS COMMUNITY FOUNDATION**

**Llewellyn L. Cayvan String Instrument Scholarship**

Ruth Bishop, Education Program Officer
Grand Rapids Community Foundation
161 Ottawa Avenue, NW, 209 C
Grand Rapids, MI 49503-2757
*Phone:* 616-454-1751 Ext. 103
*Fax:* 616-454-6455
*E-mail:* rbishop@grfoundation.org
*Web site:* http://www.grfoundation.org

**HAPCO MUSIC FOUNDATION INC.**

**Traditional Marching Band Extravaganza Scholarship Award**

Joseph McMullen, President
HapCo Music Foundation Inc.
PO Box 784581
Winter Garden, FL 34778-4581
*Phone:* 407-877-2262
*Fax:* 407-654-0308
*E-mail:* hapcopromo@aol.com
*Web site:* http://www.hapcopromo.org

**HARTFORD JAZZ SOCIETY INC.**

**Hartford Jazz Society Scholarships**

Scholarship Committee Chair
Hartford Jazz Society Inc.
116 Cottage Grove Road
Bloomfield, CT 06002
*Phone:* 860-242-6688
*Fax:* 860-243-8871
*E-mail:* hartjazzsocinc@aol.com
*Web site:* http://www.hartfordjazzsociety.com

**HEMOPHILIA FEDERATION OF AMERICA**

**Artistic Encouragement Grant**

Scholarship Committee
Hemophilia Federation of America
1405 West Pinhook Road, Suite 101
Lafayette, LA 70503
*Phone:* 337-261-9787
*E-mail:* info@hemophiliafed.org
*Web site:* http://www.hemophiliaed.org

Performing *Arts*

**HISPANIC SCHOLARSHIP FUND**

**HSF/McNamara Family Creative Arts Project Grant**

John Schmucker, Scholarship Coordinator
Hispanic Scholarship Fund
55 Second Street, Suite 1500
San Francisco, CA 94105
*Phone:* 877-473-4636
*E-mail:* scholar1@hsf.net
*Web site:* http://www.hsf.net

**HOSTESS COMMITTEE SCHOLARSHIPS/ MISS AMERICA PAGEANT**

**Eugenia Vellner Fischer Award for Performing Arts**

Doreen Lindell Gordon, Controller and
Scholarship Administrator
Hostess Committee Scholarships/
Miss America Pageant
Two Miss America Way, Suite 1000
Atlantic City, NJ 08401
*Phone:* 609-345-7571 Ext. 27
*Fax:* 609-653-8740
*E-mail:* doreen@missamerica.org
*Web site:* http://www.missamerica.org

**HOUSTON SYMPHONY**

**Houston Symphony Ima Hogg Young Artist Competition**

**Houston Symphony League Concerto Competition**

Carol Wilson, Education Coordinator
Houston Symphony
615 Louisiana Street, Suite 102
Houston, TX 77002
*Phone:* 713-238-1449
*Fax:* 713-224-0453
*E-mail:* e&o@houstonsymphony.org
*Web site:* http://www.houstonsymphony.org

**ILLUMINATING ENGINEERING SOCIETY OF NORTH AMERICA**

**Robert W. Thunen Memorial Scholarships**

Phil Hall, Chairman
Illuminating Engineering Society of North
America
120 Wall Street
New York, NY 10005-4001
*Phone:* 510-864-0204
*Fax:* 510-864-8511
*E-mail:* mrcatisbac@aol.com
*Web site:* http://www.iesna.org

**JACK J. ISGUR FOUNDATION**

*Jack J. Isgur Foundation Scholarship*

Charles Jensen, Attorney at Law
Jack J. Isgur Foundation
c/o Charles F. Jensen, Stinson, Morrison,
Hecker LLP
1201 Walnut Street, 28th Floor
Kansas City, MO 64106
*Phone:* 816-691-2760
*Fax:* 816-691-3495
*E-mail:* cjensen@stinson.com
*Web site:* http://www.iesna.org

**KARMEL SCHOLARSHIP**

**KarMel Scholarship**

Scholarship Committee
KarMel Scholarship
PO Box 70382
Sunnyvale, CA 94086
*E-mail:* karen@karenandmelody.com
*Web site:* http://www.karenandmelody.com

**KE ALI'I PAUAHI FOUNDATION**

**Edwin Mahiai Copp Beamer Scholarship**

Elizabeth Stevenson, Development
Manager
Ke Ali'I Pauahi Foundation
567 South King Street, Suite 160
Honolulu, HI 96813
*Phone:* 808-534-3966
*Fax:* 808-534-3890
*E-mail:* scholarships@pauahi.org
*Web site:* http://www.pauahi.org

Performing

*Arts*

## KOSCIUSZKO FOUNDATION

**Kosciuszko Foundation Chopin Piano Competition**

**Marcella Sembrich Voice Competition**

Tom Pniewski, Director of Cultural Programs
Kosciuszko Foundation
15 East 65th Street
New York, NY 10021-6595
*Phone:* 212-734-2130
*Fax:* 212-628-4552
*E-mail:* tompkf@aol.com
*Web site:* http://www.kosciuszkofoundation.org

## KURT WEILL FOUNDATION FOR MUSIC

**Kurt Weill Foundation for Music Grants Program**

**Lotte Lenya Competition for Singers**

Carolyn Weber, Director
Kurt Weill Foundation for Music
Seven East 20th Street
New York, NY 10003-1106
*Phone:* 212-505-5240
*Fax:* 212-353-9663
*E-mail:* cweber@kwf.org
*Web site:* http://www.kwf.org

## LIEDERKRANZ FOUNDATION

**Liederkranz Foundation Scholarship Award for Voice**

Manager
Liederkranz Foundation
Six East 87th Street
New York, NY 10128
*Phone:* 212-534-0880
*Fax:* 212-828-5372
*E-mail:* contactus@liederkranznycity.org
*Web site:* http://www.liederkranznycity.org

## LOS ANGELES PHILHARMONIC

**Bronislaw Kaper Awards for Young Artists**

Karl Montezirgen, Program Manager
Los Angeles Philharmonic
151 South Grand Avenue
Los Angeles, CA 90012
*Phone:* 213-972-0705
*Fax:* 213-972-7650
*E-mail:* education@laphil.org
*Web site:* http://www.laphil.com

## MELLON NEW ENGLAND

**Susan Glover Hitchcock Scholarship**

Sandra Brown-McMullen, Vice President
Mellon New England
1 Boston Place, 024-0084
Boston, MA 02108
*Phone:* 617-722-3891
*E-mail:* brown-mcmullen.s@mellon.com
*Web site:* http://www.mellon.com

## NATIONAL ASSOCIATION OF PASTORAL MUSICIANS

**Dan Schutte Scholarship**

Kathleen Haley, Director of Membership Services
National Association of Pastoral Musicians
962 Wayne Avenue, Suite 210
Silver Spring, MD 20910 4461
*Phone:* 240-247-3000
*Fax:* 240-247 3001
*E-mail:* haley@npm.org
*Web site:* http://www.npm.org

**Elaine Rendler-Rene Dosogne-Georgetown Chorale Scholarship**

J. Michael McMahon, President
National Association of Pastoral Musicians
962 Wayne Avenue, Suite 210
Silver Spring, MD 20910
*Phone:* 240-247-3000
*Fax:* 240-247-3001
*E-mail:* npmsing@npm.org
*Web site:* http://www.npm.org

Performing *Arts*

Funk Family Memorial Scholarship

GIA Publication Pastoral Musician Scholarship

MuSonics Scholarship

National Association of Pastoral Musicians Members' Scholarship

NPM Board of Directors Scholarship

NPM Composers and Authors Scholarship

NPM Koinonia/Board of Directors Scholarship

NPM Miami Valley Catholic Church Musicians Scholarship

NPM Perrot Scholarship

Oregon Catholic Press Scholarship

Paluch Family Foundation/World Library Publications Scholarship

**Steven C. Warner Scholarship**

Kathleen Haley, Director of Membership Services
National Association of Pastoral Musicians
962 Wayne Avenue, Suite 210
Silver Spring, MD 20910-4461
*Phone:* 240-247-3000
*Fax:* 240-247-3001
*E-mail:* haley@npm.org
*Web site:* http://www.npm.org

## NATIONAL FOUNDATION FOR ADVANCEMENT IN THE ARTS
### youngARTS

Carla Hill, Programs Department
National Foundation for Advancement in the Arts
444 Brickell Avenue, Suite R14
Miami, FL 33133
*Phone:* 800-970-2787
*Fax:* 305-377-1149
*E-mail:* nfaa@nfaa.org
*Web site:* http://www.youngARTS.org

## NATIONAL OPERA ASSOCIATION
### NOA Vocal Competition/Legacy Award Program

Robert Hansen, Executive Secretary
National Opera Association
2403 Russell Long Boulevard, PO Box 60869
Canyon, TX 79016-0001
*Phone:* 806-651-2857
*Fax:* 806-651-2958
*E-mail:* hansen@mail.wtamu.edu
*Web site:* http://www.noa.org

## PI LAMBDA THETA INC.
### Nadeen Burkeholder Williams Music Scholarship

Pam Todd, Manager, Member Services
Pi Lambda Theta Inc.
4101 East Third Street, PO Box 6626
Bloomington, IN 47407-6626
*Phone:* 812-339-3411
*Fax:* 812-339-3462
*E-mail:* office@pilambda.org
*Web site:* http://www.pilambda.org

## PLAYWRIGHTS' CENTER
### Many Voices Residency Program

Kevin McLaughlin, Fellowships Technology and Space Manager
Playwrights' Center
2301 East Franklin Avenue
Minneapolis, MN 55406-1099
*Phone:* 612-332-7481 Ext. 15
*Fax:* 612-332-6037
*E-mail:* info@pwcenter.org
*Web site:* http://www.pwcenter.org

## POLISH ARTS CLUB OF BUFFALO SCHOLARSHIP FOUNDATION
### Polish Arts Club of Buffalo Scholarship Foundation Trust

Anne Flansburg, Selection Chair
Polish Arts Club of Buffalo Scholarship Foundation
PO Box 1362
Williamsville, NY 14231-1362
*Phone:* 716-626-9083
*E-mail:* anneflanswz@aol.com
*Web site:* http://www.pacb.bfn.org

Performing

*Arts*

### PRINCESS GRACE FOUNDATION-USA
**Princess Grace Scholarships in Dance, Theater, and Film**

Kathleen Richards, Program Manager
Princess Grace Foundation-USA
150 East 58th Street, 25th Floor
New York, NY 10155
*Phone:* 212-317-1470
*Fax:* 212-317-1473
*E-mail:* grants@pgfusa.org
*Web site:* http://www.pgfusa.org

### QUEEN ELISABETH INTERNATIONAL MUSIC COMPETITION OF BELGIUM
**Queen Elisabeth Competition**

Michel-Etienne Van Neste, Secretary General
Queen Elisabeth International Music Competition of Belgium
Rue Aux Laines 20
Brussels 1000
Belgium
*Phone:* 32 2 213 40 50
*Fax:* 32 2 514 32 97
*E-mail:* info@qeimc.be
*Web site:* http://www.qeimc.be

### RHODE ISLAND FOUNDATION
**Bach Organ and Keyboard Music Scholarship**

**Constant Memorial Scholarship for Aquidneck Island Residents**

Libby Monahan, Funds Administrator
Rhode Island Foundation
One Union Station
Providence, RI 02903
*Phone:* 401-274-4564 Ext. 3117
*Fax:* 401-751-7983
*E-mail:* libbym@rifoundation.org
*Web site:* http://www.rifoundation.org

### SAN ANGELO SYMPHONY SOCIETY
**Sorantin Young Artist Award**

Jennifer Odom, Executive Director
San Angelo Symphony Society
PO Box 5922
San Angelo, TX 76902-5922
*Phone:* 325-658-5877
*Fax:* 325-653-1045
*E-mail:* assistant@sanangelosymphony.org
*Web site:* http://www.sanangelosymphony.org

### SAN DIEGO FOUNDATION
**Dr. Barta-Lehman Musical Scholarship**

Shryl Helvie, Scholarship Coordinator
San Diego Foundation
2508 Historic Decatur Road, Suite 200
San Diego, CA 92106
*Phone:* 619-814-1307
*Fax:* 619-239-1710
*E-mail:* shryl@sdfoundation.org
*Web site:* http://www.sdfoundation.org

### SERVICE EMPLOYEES INTERNATIONAL UNION (SEIU)
**SEIU Moe Foner Scholarship Program for Visual and Performing Arts**

c/o Scholarship Program Administrators, Inc.
Service Employees International Union (SEIU)
PO Box 23737
Nashville, TN 37202-3737
*Phone:* 615-320-3149
*Fax:* 615-320-3151
*E-mail:* info@spaprog.com
*Web site:* http://www.seiu.org

### SIGMA ALPHA IOTA PHILANTHROPIES INC.
**Sigma Alpha Iota Jazz Performance Awards**

**Sigma Alpha Iota Jazz Studies Scholarship**

Jaide Fried Massen, Project Director
Sigma Alpha Iota Philanthropies Inc.
One Tunnel Road
Asheville, NC 28805
*Phone:* 828-251-0606
*Fax:* 828-251-0644
*E-mail:* toffuti@hotmail.com
*Web site:* http://www.sigmaalphaiota.org

Performing Arts

### Sigma Alpha Iota Music Business/Technology Scholarship

Kim L. Wangler, Director
Sigma Alpha Iota Philanthropies Inc.
One Tunnel Road
Asheville, NC 28805
*Phone:* 828-251-0606
*Fax:* 828-251-0644
*E-mail:* wanglerkl@appstate.edu
*Web site:* http://www.sigmaalphaiota.org

### Sigma Alpha Iota Musicians with Special Needs Scholarship

Karen Louise Gearreald, Director
Sigma Alpha Iota Philanthropies Inc.
One Tunnel Road
Asheville, NC 28805
*Phone:* 828-251-0606
*Fax:* 828-251-0644
*E-mail:* hadley@exis.net
*Web site:* http://www.sigmaalphaiota.org

### Sigma Alpha Iota Music Therapy Scholarship

Michelle Gaddis Kennemer, Director
Sigma Alpha Iota Philanthropies Inc.
One Tunnel Road
Asheville, NC 28805
*Phone:* 828-251-0606
*Fax:* 828-251-0644
*E-mail:* jmichelle17@hotmail.com
*Web site:* http://www.sigmaalphaiota.org

### Sigma Alpha Iota Summer Music Scholarships in the U.S. or Abroad

Mary Jennings, Director
Sigma Alpha Iota Philanthropies Inc.
One Tunnel Road
Asheville, NC 28805
*Phone:* 828-251-0606
*Fax:* 828-251-0644
*E-mail:* maryj10101@aol.com
*Web site:* http://www.sigmaalphaiota.org

### Sigma Alpha Iota Undergraduate Performance Scholarships

Dr. Emily White, Director
Sigma Alpha Iota Philanthropies Inc.
One Tunnel Road
Asheville, NC 28805
*Phone:* 828-251-0606
*Fax:* 828-251-0644
*E-mail:* hornstein1@aol.com
*Web site:* http://www.sigmaalphaiota.org

### Sigma Alpha Iota Undergraduate Scholarships

Eleanor B. Tapscott, Project Director
Sigma Alpha Iota Philanthropies Inc.
One Tunnel Road
Asheville, NC 28805
*Phone:* 828-251-0606
*Fax:* 828-251-0644
*E-mail:* saiphxalum@joetapscott.com
*Web site:* http://www.sigmaalphaiota.org

## SINFONIA FOUNDATION

### Delta Iota Alumni Scholarship

### Sinfonia Educational Foundation Scholarship

Matthew Garber, Director of Development
Sinfonia Foundation
10600 Old State Road
Evansville, IN 47711
*Phone:* 812-867-2433 Ext. 110
*Fax:* 812-867-0633
*E-mail:* garber@sinfonia.org
*Web site:* http://www.sinfonia.org

## SUZUKI ASSOCIATION OF THE AMERICAS

### Suzuki Association of the Americas Teacher Development Scholarships

Pam Brasch, Director
Suzuki Association of the Americas
PO Box 17310
Boulder, CO 80308
*Phone:* 303-444-0948
*E-mail:* info@suzukiassociation.org
*Web site:* http://www.suzukiassociation.org

## UNICO NATIONAL INC.

### Theodore Mazza Scholarship

Ann Tichenor, Secretary
UNICO National Inc.
271 U.S. Highway 46 West, Suite A-108
Fairfield, NJ 07004
*Phone:* 973-808-0035
*Fax:* 973-808-0043
*Web site:* http://www.unico.org

**UNITED NEGRO COLLEGE FUND**

**Jimi Hendrix Endowment Fund Scholarship**

Director, Program Services
United Negro College Fund
8260 Willow Oaks Corporate Drive
PO Box 10444
Fairfax, VA 22031-8044
*Phone:* 800-331-2244
*E-mail:* rebecca.bennett@uncf.org
*Web site:* http://www.uncf.org

**John Lennon Endowed Scholarship**

William Dunham, Program Services
     Department
United Negro College Fund
8260 Willow Oaks Corporate Drive, PO Box
     10444
Fairfax, VA 22031
*Phone:* 703-205-3486
*Web site:* http://www.uncf.org

**VSA ARTS**

**VSA Arts-International Young Soloist Award**

**VSA arts Playwright Discovery Award**

Liz McCloskey, Performing Arts Manager
VSA arts
818 Connecticut Avenue, NW, Suite 600
Washington, DC 20006
*Phone:* 800-933-8721
*Fax:* 202-429-0868
*E-mail:* info@vsarts.org
*Web site:* http://www.vsarts.org

**WALTER W. NAUMBURG FOUNDATION**

**International Violoncello Competition**

Lucy Mann, Executive Director
Walter W. Naumburg Foundation
120 Claremont Avenue
New York, NY 10027-4698
*Phone:* 212-362-9877
*Fax:* 212-362-9877
*E-mail:* luciamann@aol.com
*Web site:* http://www.naumburg.org

**WAMSO-MINNESOTA ORCHESTRA VOLUNTEER ASSOCIATION**

**Young Artist Competition**

Eloise Breikjern, Executive Director
WAMSO-Minnesota Orchestra Volunteer
     Association
1111 Nicollet Mall, Orchestra Hall
Minneapolis, MN 55403-2477
*Phone:* 612-371-5654
*Fax:* 612-371-7176
*E-mail:* wamso@mnorch.org
*Web site:* http://www.wamso.org

**WATERBURY FOUNDATION**

**Michael and Jane Sendzimir Fund Scholarship**

Josh Carey, Program Officer
Waterbury Foundation
43 Field Street
Waterbury, CT 06702-1216
*Phone:* 203-753-1315
*Fax:* 203-756-3054
*E-mail:* jcarey@conncf.org
*Web site:* http://www.conncf.org

**WOMEN BAND DIRECTORS INTERNATIONAL**

**Charlotte Plummer Owen Memorial Scholarship**

**Helen May Butler Memorial Scholarship**

**Martha Ann Stark Memorial Scholarship**

**Volkwein Memorial Scholarship**

Nicole Aakre-Rubis, Scholarship Chair
Women Band Directors International
16085 Excel Way
Rosemount, MN 55068
*Web site:* http://www.
     womenbanddirectors.org

Performing *Arts*

# Additional Resources

**AMERICAN SYMPHONY ORCHESTRA LEAGUE (ASOL)**

New York Headquarters
33 West 60th Street, 5th Floor
New York, NY 10023-7905
*Phone:* 212-262-5161
*Fax:* 212-262-5198
*E-mail:* league@symphony.org
*Web site:* www.symphony.org

Washington Office
910 17th Street N.W.
Washington, D.C. 20006
*Phone:* 202-776-0215
*Fax:* 202-776-0224
*E-mail:* heatherw@symphony.org

**ASSOCIATION FOR THEATRE IN HIGHER EDUCATION (ATHE)**

P.O. Box 1290
Boulder, CO 80306-1290
*Phone:* 888-284-3737
        303-530-2167
*Fax:* 303-530-2168
*E-mail:* info@athe.org
*Web site:* www.athe.org

**EDUCATIONAL THEATER ASSOCIATION**

2343 Auburn Avenue
Cincinnati, OH 45219
*Phone:* 513-421-3900
*Web site:* www.edta.org

**NATIONAL ASSOCIATION FOR MUSIC EDUCATION (NAME)**

1806 Robert Fulton Drive
Reston, VA 20191
*Phone:* 703-860-4000
        800-336-3768
*Fax:* 703-860-1531
*Web site:* www.menc.org

**NATIONAL ASSOCIATION OF SCHOOLS OF DANCE**

**NATIONAL ASSOCIATION OF SCHOOLS OF MUSIC (NASM)**

**NATIONAL ASSOCIATION OF SCHOOLS OF THEATRE**

11250 Roger Bacon Drive, Suite 21
Reston, VA 20190
*Phone:* 703-437-0700
*Fax:* 703-860-1531
*E-mail:* info@arts-accredit.org
*Web site:* http://nast.arts-accredit.org

**NATIONAL DANCE EDUCATION ORGANIZATION**

4948 St. Elmo Avenue, Suite 301
Bethesda, Maryland 20814
*Phone:* 301-657-2880
        301-657-2881
*Fax:* 301-657-2882
*E-mail:* info@ndeo.org
*Web site:* www.ndeo.org

**VISUAL AND PERFORMING ARTS COLLEGE FAIRS**

National Association for College Admission
    Counseling (NACAC)
1631 Prince Street
Alexandria, Virginia 22314
*Phone:* 703-836-2222
        800-822-6285
*Fax:* 703-836-8015
*E-mail:* info@nacac.com
*Web site:* www.nacac.org

Performing Arts

# Indexes

# Majors and Concentrations

## Dance

### Arts management
Long Island University, C.W. Post Campus 203

### Ballet
Belhaven College 195
Cornish College of the Arts 200
East Carolina University 200
Indiana University Bloomington 201
North Carolina School of the Arts 205
Point Park University 206
Purchase College, State University of New York 207
Radford University 208
Southern Methodist University 210
Texas Christian University 211
University of Cincinnati 212
University of Oklahoma 215
The University of the Arts 216
University of Utah 217
University of Wyoming 218
York University 220

### Choreography
Columbia College 199
Columbia College Chicago 200

### Choreography and performance
Cornish College of the Arts 200
University of Colorado at Boulder 212
University of Florida 212
University of Illinois at Urbana–Champaign 213
University of Michigan 214
The University of Montana 215

### Composition
Purchase College, State University of New York 207
York University 220

### Contemporary dance
North Carolina School of the Arts 205
Radford University 208
San Diego State University 209
University of Colorado at Boulder 212
University of Wisconsin–Milwaukee 218

### Dance
The Boston Conservatory 195
Brenau University 196
California Institute of the Arts 197
California State University, Long Beach 198
The College at Brockport, State University of New York 199
Florida State University 201
Fordham University 201
Jacksonville University 202

The Juilliard School 202
Long Island University, C.W. Post Campus 203
Marymount Manhattan College 203
Montclair State University 204
New York University 205
The Ohio State University 205
Ohio University 206
Ryerson University 209
Shenandoah University 209
Slippery Rock University of Pennsylvania 210
State University of New York at Fredonia 210
Tulane University 211
The University of Akron 211
University of Idaho 213
University of Illinois at Urbana–Champaign 213
The University of Iowa 213
University of Massachusetts Amherst 214
University of Minnesota, Twin Cities Campus 214
University of Missouri–Kansas City 215
The University of the Arts 216
Webster University 218
Western Michigan University 219
West Texas A&M University 219
Wichita State University 219
Wright State University 220

### Dance arts administration
Butler University 196

### Dance education
Arizona State University 195
Brenau University 196
Columbia College Chicago 200
East Carolina University 200
Kent State University 203
Shenandoah University 209
The University of Montana 215
The University of Tennessee at Martin 216
The University of the Arts 216
University of Wisconsin–Milwaukee 218

### Dance in medicine
University of Florida 212

### Dance pedagogy
Butler University 196
Point Park University 206

### Dance performance
Butler University 196
Columbia College 199
Kent State University 203
Missouri State University 204

### Dance studies
Missouri State University 204

### Dance theater
University of Florida 212
University of Hawaii at Manoa 213

### Jazz dance
East Carolina University 200
Point Park University 206
Southern Methodist University 210
The University of the Arts 216
University of Wyoming 218

### Modern dance
Belhaven College 195
Cornish College of the Arts 200
East Carolina University 200
Point Park University 206
Purchase College, State University of New York 207
Rutgers, The State University of New Jersey, Mason Gross School of the Arts 204
Southern Methodist University 210
Texas Christian University 211
University of Michigan 214
University of Oklahoma 215
The University of the Arts 216
University of Utah 217
University of Wyoming 218
Virginia Commonwealth University 218
York University 220

### Music theater
University of Wisconsin–Milwaukee 218

### Performance
Chapman University 199
Columbia College Chicago 200
New World School of the Arts 204
Purchase College, State University of New York 207

### Production
Purchase College, State University of New York 207

### Teacher certification
Columbia College Chicago 200
Texas Christian University 211

### World dance
University of Florida 212

# Music

**Accompanying**
Howard Payne University *260*
James Madison University *266*
Oberlin College *247*

**Accordion**
The College of New Jersey *245*
University of Denver *323*

**Acoustic recording**
City College of the City University of New York *242*

**Applied music**
Butler University *233*
Lee University *272*
University of Rochester *340*

**Arranging**
University of Denver *323*

**Arts administration**
Acadia University *221*

**Arts management**
Baldwin-Wallace College *225*
Shenandoah University *305*

**Audio production**
University of Denver *323*

**Audio recording technology**
Cleveland Institute of Music *243*
Five Towns College *254*
Indiana University Bloomington *262*

**Band**
Southeastern Louisiana University *308*

**Bass**
Musicians Institute *283*
New World School of the Arts *287*
Purchase College, State University of New York *297*
St. Francis Xavier University *301*
University of Wisconsin–Green Bay *348*
Walla Walla University *353*

**Bassoon**
Indiana University Bloomington *262*
The Juilliard School *268*
New World School of the Arts *287*
University of California, Irvine *318*

**Brass**
Baldwin-Wallace College *225*
The Boston Conservatory *229*
Boston University *230*
Bowling Green State University *230*
Butler University *233*
The Curtis Institute of Music *250*
Dalhousie University *250*
DePaul University *251*
Houghton College *260*
Ithaca College *263*

Longwood University *274*
North Park University *291*
Oberlin College *247*
Queens College of the City University of New York *298*
St. Francis Xavier University *301*
Simpson College *306*
State University of New York at Fredonia *311*
Susquehanna University *312*
Truman State University *315*
University at Buffalo, the State University of New York *315*
University of Central Arkansas *319*
University of Colorado at Boulder *321*
University of Regina *339*
University of Rochester *340*
The University of South Dakota *342*
University of the Incarnate Word *346*
University of the Pacific *346*
University of Utah *347*
University of Wisconsin–Madison *348*
University of Wisconsin–Milwaukee *349*
University of Wisconsin–Oshkosh *349*
Walla Walla University *353*
West Virginia University *358*

**Brass instruments performance**
Cedarville University *240*
Illinois Wesleyan University *262*
Kentucky Wesleyan College *269*
North Carolina Central University *289*

**Cello**
Indiana University Bloomington *262*
New World School of the Arts *287*
Purchase College, State University of New York *297*
Walla Walla University *353*

**Choral music**
Chowan University *241*
Lawrence University *270*

**Choral music education**
Anderson University *222*
Armstrong Atlantic State University *223*
Auburn University *224*
Brenau University *231*
The Catholic University of America *239*
Christopher Newport University *242*
Georgia College & State University *257*
Howard Payne University *260*
Indiana University Bloomington *262*
Northern Arizona University *290*
Northern Michigan University *291*
Silver Lake College *306*
University of Maryland, College Park *328*
VanderCook College of Music *352*
William Carey University *359*

**Church music**
The Baptist College of Florida *226*
Belmont University *226*

Birmingham-Southern College *228*
Calvary Bible College and Theological Seminary *237*
Carson-Newman College *238*
Cedarville University *240*
Crown College *249*
Furman University *256*
Georgetown College *256*
Hardin-Simmons University *259*
Howard Payne University *260*
Huntington University *261*
Jackson State University *265*
Lambuth University *270*
Lee University *272*
Oklahoma City University *294*
Ouachita Baptist University *295*
Palm Beach Atlantic University *296*
Philadelphia Biblical University *296*
St. Olaf College *302*
Samford University *302*
Shenandoah University *305*
Shorter College *306*
Tennessee Wesleyan College *314*
Texas Christian University *314*
University of Mobile *333*
University of the Cumberlands *345*
Valparaiso University *351*
William Carey University *359*

**Clarinet**
Indiana University Bloomington *262*
The Juilliard School *268*
New World School of the Arts *287*
University of California, Irvine *318*

**Classical guitar**
Baldwin-Wallace College *225*
California State University, Northridge *236*
Cleveland Institute of Music *243*
Dalhousie University *250*
Illinois State University *261*
Indiana University Bloomington *262*
Lawrence University *270*
Mannes College The New School for Music *276*
Purchase College, State University of New York *297*
San Francisco Conservatory of Music *303*
Simpson College *306*
University at Buffalo, the State University of New York *315*
University of Cincinnati *319*
University of Evansville *324*
University of Southern California *342*
The University of Texas at San Antonio *345*

**Classical music**
Baylor University *226*
Birmingham-Southern College *228*
Brooklyn College of the City University of New York *232*
California Institute of the Arts *234*
California State University, Long Beach *235*
Carleton University *238*

University of Colorado Denver *322*
University of Evansville *324*
University of the Pacific *346*

**Music marketing**
The University of Texas at San Antonio *345*

**Music media**
Capital University *237*
Carleton University *238*
Norfolk State University *289*
University of Louisiana at Lafayette *326*

**Music merchandising**
Capital University *237*
South Dakota State University *307*
Southern Illinois University
    Edwardsville *309*

**Music pedagogy**
Acadia University *221*
Viterbo University *353*

**Music performance**
Augsburg College *224*
Capital University *237*
Duquesne University *252*
Georgia College & State University *257*
Hardin-Simmons University *259*
Mansfield University of Pennsylvania *277*
Marylhurst University *278*
Nebraska Wesleyan University *284*
Ohio Northern University *293*
Ohio Wesleyan University *293*
Seton Hill University *305*
University of Colorado Denver *322*
University of Evansville *324*
University of Louisville *327*
University of Nebraska at Omaha *334*
University of Rhode Island *340*
The University of Tampa *343*
University of Wyoming *350*
West Virginia University *358*

**Music production and recording technology**
Shenandoah University *305*
The University of Toledo *347*

**Music recording**
Youngstown State University *361*

**Music scholarship**
The University of British Columbia *318*

**Music studies**
University of Massachusetts Lowell *329*

**Music synthesis**
Berklee College of Music *227*

**Music teaching**
Brevard College *232*

**Music technology**
Acadia University *221*
California Institute of the Arts *234*
Capital University *237*

Carleton University *238*
Duquesne University *252*
Florida Atlantic University *255*
Jackson State University *265*
Lebanon Valley College *272*
New York University *288*
Stetson University *312*
University of Central Missouri *319*
University of Colorado Denver *322*
University of Michigan *331*
The University of Montana *333*
University of Nebraska at Omaha *334*
Wayne State University *354*

**Music theater**
Acadia University *221*
Arizona State University *223*
Baldwin-Wallace College *225*
Belmont University *226*
The Catholic University of America *239*
East Carolina University *252*
Florida State University *255*
Illinois State University *261*
James Madison University *266*
Kansas State University *268*
Manhattanville College *275*
Missouri State University *281*
Montclair State University *282*
Oklahoma City University *294*
Otterbein College *295*
Ouachita Baptist University *295*
Samford University *302*
Shorter College *306*
Southern Illinois University
    Edwardsville *309*
University of Idaho *325*
University of Miami *329*
University of Michigan *331*
University of Mobile *333*
University of South Alabama *341*
University of Southern Maine *343*
Westminster Choir College of Rider
    University *357*

**Music theater accompanying**
Shenandoah University *305*

**Music theory**
Acadia University *221*
Baldwin-Wallace College *225*
Belmont University *226*
Butler University *233*
Carson-Newman College *238*
Christopher Newport University *242*
Concordia College *247*
Florida State University *255*
Furman University *256*
Ithaca College *263*
Kent State University *268*
Mannes College The New School for
    Music *276*
McGill University *279*
Mercer University *279*
Nazareth College of Rochester *284*
New England Conservatory of Music *284*
Oberlin College *247*
Rice University *299*

Southwestern Oklahoma State
    University *310*
Temple University *313*
University of Arkansas *317*
University of Cincinnati *319*
University of Georgia *324*
University of Houston *325*
University of Illinois at
    Urbana–Champaign *326*
University of Maryland, College Park *328*
University of Michigan *331*
University of Mississippi *332*
University of Missouri–Columbia *332*
University of Missouri–Kansas City *333*
University of Nebraska–Lincoln *334*
University of North Texas *337*
University of Regina *339*
University of Rochester *340*
University of Utah *347*
University of Washington *348*

**Music theory and composition**
Arizona State University *223*
California State University, Sacramento *236*
Central Michigan University *240*
Central Washington University *241*
Coe College *244*
East Carolina University *252*
Fort Hays State University *256*
Hardin-Simmons University *259*
Jacksonville University *265*
Lawrence University *270*
Marygrove College *277*
Montclair State University *282*
New York University *288*
Oklahoma Baptist University *293*
St. Cloud State University *301*
St. Olaf College *302*
Samford University *302*
Sam Houston State University *303*
Southern Illinois University Carbondale *308*
Southern Illinois University
    Edwardsville *309*
Stephen F. Austin State University *311*
Stetson University *312*
Texas Christian University *314*
University of Alberta *316*
University of Delaware *323*
University of Louisiana at Lafayette *326*
University of Louisville *327*
University of Minnesota, Duluth *331*
University of New Mexico *335*
University of Prince Edward Island *338*
University of South Carolina *342*
The University of Tennessee *344*
The University of Tennessee at
    Chattanooga *344*
Vanderbilt University *352*
Wayne State University *354*
Westminster Choir College of Rider
    University *357*
Youngstown State University *361*

**Music therapy**
Acadia University *221*
Alverno College *221*
Anna Maria College *222*

## Voice pedagogy

## Voice performance

## Wind and percussion instruments

# Theater

University of Southern Mississippi *402*
The University of the Arts *403*
University of Utah *403*
University of Windsor *403*
University of Wisconsin–Milwaukee *404*
University of Wyoming *405*
Virginia Intermont College *406*
Viterbo University *406*
Webster University *406*
Western Carolina University *407*
West Virginia University *407*
Wright State University *408*
York University *409*

**Acting and directing**
Catawba College *370*
Northern Kentucky University *384*

**Arts administration**
Viterbo University *406*

**Arts management**
Brenau University *367*
Lindenwood University *379*
Long Island University, C.W. Post
    Campus *379*
Western Michigan University *407*

**Audio recording technology**
Five Towns College *374*

**Costume construction**
Purchase College, State University of New
    York *387*

**Costume design**
Boston University *366*
California Institute of the Arts *369*
Catawba College *370*
Central Connecticut State University *370*
Columbia College Chicago *371*
Cornish College of the Arts *372*
DePaul University *372*
North Carolina School of the Arts *384*
Purchase College, State University of New
    York *387*
Salem State College *390*
Shenandoah University *390*
Southern Oregon University *391*
Stephens College *392*
University of Cincinnati *394*
University of Florida *395*
University of Illinois at
    Urbana–Champaign *396*
The University of South Dakota *400*
University of Wyoming *405*
Virginia Commonwealth University *405*
Webster University *406*

**Costume production**
Boston University *366*
University of Wisconsin–Milwaukee *404*

**Costume technology**
DePaul University *372*
North Carolina School of the Arts *384*
University of Illinois at
    Urbana–Champaign *396*

**Creative dramatics and puppetry**
West Virginia University *407*

**Creative writing**
Nebraska Wesleyan University *381*

**Dance**
Central Connecticut State University *370*
Illinois State University *375*
Long Island University, C.W. Post
    Campus *379*
Northern Kentucky University *384*
Northwestern State University of
    Louisiana *384*
University of Houston *395*

**Dance arts**
Howard University *375*

**Design**
Baylor University *365*
Lindenwood University *379*
Southern Oregon University *391*
Stephens College *392*
University of Houston *395*
The University of North Carolina at
    Greensboro *399*
University of Oklahoma *399*
University of Southern California *401*
University of Utah *403*

**Design production**
East Carolina University *372*
University of Miami *396*
York University *409*

**Design technology**
Arkansas State University *364*
Auburn University *365*
Kent State University *379*
Northern Kentucky University *384*
Otterbein College *385*
Penn State University Park *386*
Purchase College, State University of New
    York *387*
Rutgers, The State University of New
    Jersey, Mason Gross School of the
    Arts *381*
Stephen F. Austin State University *392*
The University of Montana *397*
University of Nevada, Reno *398*
University of Oklahoma *399*
University of South Alabama *400*
The University of South Dakota *400*
University of Wisconsin–Whitewater *404*
Western Carolina University *407*
Western Michigan University *407*
West Virginia University *407*

**Design/technical theater**
Syracuse University *393*
Tulane University *393*
University of Colorado at Boulder *394*
University of Connecticut *395*
University of Rhode Island *400*
University of Southern Mississippi *402*
Viterbo University *406*
Wichita State University *408*

**Directing**
Arkansas State University *364*
Central Connecticut State University *370*
Columbia College Chicago *371*
Fordham University *375*
Lindenwood University *379*
Nebraska Wesleyan University *381*
Pace University *385*
Southern Oregon University *391*
Stephen F. Austin State University *392*
Stephens College *392*
University of Houston *395*
University of Michigan *396*
University of Montevallo *398*
University of Rhode Island *400*
University of Wyoming *405*
Webster University *406*
York University *409*

**Drama in education and community**
University of Windsor *403*

**Dramatic performance**
University of Cincinnati *394*

**Dramatic writing**
New York University *383*
Purchase College, State University of New
    York *387*

**Dramaturgy**
University of Oklahoma *399*

**Dramaturgy/criticism**
DePaul University *372*

**Educational theater**
Central Connecticut State University *370*
New York University *383*

**Entertainment arts**
Kent State University *379*

**Film**
Long Island University, C.W. Post
    Campus *379*
Purchase College, State University of New
    York *387*

**Film and new media**
University of Nebraska–Lincoln *398*

**Film and video production**
Five Towns College *374*

**Film production**
Wright State University *408*

**International theatre production**
Ohio Northern University *385*

**Lighting design**
Boston University *366*
California Institute of the Arts *369*
Columbia College Chicago *371*
Cornish College of the Arts *372*
DePaul University *372*
North Carolina School of the Arts *384*

*Lighting design (continued)*
Purchase College, State University of New
York *387*
Salem State College *390*
University of Cincinnati *394*
University of Florida *395*
University of Illinois at
Urbana–Champaign *396*
University of Wyoming *405*
Virginia Commonwealth University *405*
Webster University *406*

**Lighting/sound design**
Catawba College *370*
The University of South Dakota *400*

**Makeup**
University of Cincinnati *394*

**Makeup and wig design**
North Carolina School of the Arts *384*
Webster University *406*

**Management promotions**
University of Wisconsin–Whitewater *404*

**Music theater**
Arkansas State University *364*
The Boston Conservatory *365*
Brenau University *367*
Catawba College *370*
East Carolina University *372*
Emerson College *373*
Five Towns College *374*
Florida State University *374*
Howard University *375*
Illinois Wesleyan University *376*
Ithaca College *377*
Kent State University *379*
Lindenwood University *379*
Millikin University *381*
Nebraska Wesleyan University *381*
New World School of the Arts *382*
Niagara University *383*
Northern Kentucky University *384*
Northwestern State University of
Louisiana *384*
Ohio Northern University *385*
Otterbein College *385*
Pace University *385*
Penn State University Park *386*
Point Park University *386*
Rockford College *388*
Roosevelt University *388*
Shenandoah University *390*
Shorter College *390*
Southwestern University *391*
State University of New York at
Fredonia *391*
Syracuse University *393*
University of Central Florida *393*
University of Cincinnati *394*
University of Colorado at Boulder *394*
University of Florida *395*
University of Houston *395*
University of Miami *396*
University of Montevallo *398*

University of South Alabama *400*
The University of South Dakota *400*
The University of the Arts *403*
Virginia Intermont College *406*
Viterbo University *406*
Webster University *406*
Western Carolina University *407*
Western Michigan University *407*
Wichita State University *408*
William Carey University *408*
Wright State University *408*

**Music theater performance**
Auburn University *365*

**Music theatre/dance**
Otterbein College *385*
Stephens College *392*

**Musical direction**
Shorter College *390*

**Original works**
Cornish College of the Arts *372*

**Performance**
Albertus Magnus College *363*
Auburn University *365*
Baylor University *365*
Bradley University *367*
Chapman University *371*
Longwood University *380*
Marshall University *380*
Ohio University *385*
Southern Oregon University *391*
University of Central Florida *393*
University of Colorado at Boulder *394*
University of Miami *396*
University of Michigan–Flint *397*
University of Nevada, Reno *398*
University of North Dakota *399*
University of Oklahoma *399*
University of Wisconsin–Superior *404*
University of Wisconsin–Whitewater *404*
Virginia Commonwealth University *405*
Western Michigan University *407*
Wichita State University *408*

**Performance/directing**
Northwestern State University of
Louisiana *384*

**Performing arts**
Cornish College of the Arts *372*

**Playwriting**
Columbia College Chicago *371*
DePaul University *372*
Fordham University *375*
Northern Kentucky University *384*
Ohio University *385*
Purchase College, State University of New
York *387*
University of Houston *395*
University of Wyoming *405*
York University *409*

**Production and management
specialties**
Rutgers, The State University of New
Jersey, Mason Gross School of the
Arts *381*

**Production management**
Auburn University *365*
Emerson College *373*
Nebraska Wesleyan University *381*

**Production/design**
Illinois State University *375*
Long Island University, C.W. Post
Campus *379*
State University of New York at
Fredonia *391*
University of Michigan *396*

**Puppetry**
California Institute of the Arts *369*
University of Connecticut *395*

**Scene painting**
North Carolina School of the Arts *384*
Webster University *406*

**Scenic design**
Catawba College *370*
DePaul University *372*
North Carolina School of the Arts *384*
Purchase College, State University of New
York *387*
Southern Oregon University *391*
University of Florida *395*
University of Illinois at
Urbana–Champaign *396*
Virginia Commonwealth University *405*
Webster University *406*

**Scenic lighting and design**
Shenandoah University *390*

**Scenic technology**
University of Illinois at
Urbana–Champaign *396*

**Screenwriting**
Purchase College, State University of New
York *387*

**Set design**
Boston University *366*
California Institute of the Arts *369*
Columbia College Chicago *371*
Cornish College of the Arts *372*
Pace University *385*
Salem State College *390*
University of Cincinnati *394*
The University of South Dakota *400*
University of Wyoming *405*

**Sound design**
Boston University *366*
California Institute of the Arts *369*
Cornish College of the Arts *372*
North Carolina School of the Arts *384*
University of Cincinnati *394*

Webster University *406*

**Sound design and technology**
University of Illinois at
Urbana–Champaign *396*

**Stage automation**
North Carolina School of the Arts *384*

**Stage management**
Boston University *366*
California Institute of the Arts *369*
Cornish College of the Arts *372*
DePaul University *372*
East Carolina University *372*
Emerson College *373*
Millikin University *381*
North Carolina School of the Arts *384*
Northern Kentucky University *384*
Penn State University Park *386*
Point Park University *386*
Purchase College, State University of New
York *387*
Rutgers, The State University of New
Jersey, Mason Gross School of the
Arts *381*
Salem State College *390*
Southern Oregon University *391*
Stephen F. Austin State University *392*
Syracuse University *393*
University of Central Florida *393*
University of Cincinnati *394*
University of Illinois at
Urbana–Champaign *396*
University of Miami *396*
University of Oklahoma *399*
University of Rhode Island *400*
University of Southern California *401*
University of Utah *403*
University of Wisconsin–Milwaukee *404*
University of Wisconsin–Whitewater *404*
Virginia Commonwealth University *405*
Viterbo University *406*
Wright State University *408*

**Technical direction**
California Institute of the Arts *369*
Cornish College of the Arts *372*
North Carolina School of the Arts *384*
Purchase College, State University of New
York *387*
University of Southern California *401*
University of Wyoming *405*
Webster University *406*

**Technical production**
Boston University *366*
University of Wisconsin–Milwaukee *404*
Webster University *406*

**Technical theater**
Adelphi University *363*
Central Connecticut State University *370*
Lindenwood University *379*

Niagara University *383*
Salem State College *390*
Southern Oregon University *391*
Stephens College *392*
The University of North Carolina at
Greensboro *399*
The University of South Dakota *400*
University of Wisconsin–Superior *404*

**Technical theater/stage management**
Longwood University *380*

**Technical theatre/design**
Columbia College Chicago *371*
Point Park University *386*
Southwestern University *391*
University of Montevallo *398*

**Theater**
Butler University *368*
Emporia State University *373*
New York University *383*
Northern Kentucky University *384*
The University of South Dakota *400*
University of Southern Mississippi *402*

**Theater arts administration**
Butler University *368*
Howard University *375*
Millikin University *381*

**Theater arts studies**
Boston University *366*
DePaul University *372*
Illinois Wesleyan University *376*
Jacksonville University *378*

**Theater arts/drama**
Catawba College *370*
Fairleigh Dickinson University, College at
Florham *373*
Illinois State University *375*
The Juilliard School *378*
Kent State University *379*
Long Island University, C.W. Post
Campus *379*
Millikin University *381*
Niagara University *383*
Ohio Northern University *385*
Russell Sage College *389*
Shorter College *390*
University of Michigan *396*
University of North Dakota *399*
The University of Tennessee at Martin *402*
The University of Texas at Austin *402*
Wayne State University *406*
William Carey University *408*
Wright State University *408*

**Theater business management**
Southern Oregon University *391*

**Theater design**
Columbia College Chicago *371*
Ithaca College *377*
The University of the Arts *403*

**Theater design and production**
Fordham University *375*
Ohio University *385*
University of Michigan *396*
The University of Texas at Austin *402*

**Theater design/technology**
Emerson College *373*
Illinois Wesleyan University *376*
Millikin University *381*
Nebraska Wesleyan University *381*
Northwestern State University of
Louisiana *384*
University of Nebraska–Lincoln *398*
The University of the Arts *403*
Wright State University *408*

**Theater education**
Brigham Young University *368*
East Carolina University *372*
Howard University *375*
Illinois State University *375*
Lindenwood University *379*
Longwood University *380*
The University of North Carolina at
Greensboro *399*
Virginia Commonwealth University *405*

**Theater for youth**
Shenandoah University *390*

**Theater management**
Catawba College *370*
DePaul University *372*
Nebraska Wesleyan University *381*
Ohio University *385*
Pace University *385*
Stephens College *392*
University of Miami *396*
The University of the Arts *403*

**Theater production**
Bradley University *367*
Ithaca College *377*
Marshall University *380*

**Theater studies**
Southern Methodist University *391*
University of Illinois at
Urbana–Champaign *396*
The University of Texas at Austin *402*

**Theater technology**
DePaul University *372*
Howard University *375*
Ithaca College *377*
North Carolina Agricultural and Technical
State University *383*
Ohio University *385*
The University of Texas at Austin *402*

**Theater/English**
University of Wyoming *405*

# Alphabetical Listing of Schools

# NOTES

# NOTES

# Peterson's
# Book Satisfaction Survey

## Give Us Your Feedback

Thank you for choosing Peterson's as your source for personalized solutions for your education and career achievement. Please take a few minutes to answer the following questions. Your answers will go a long way in helping us to produce the most user-friendly and comprehensive resources to meet your individual needs.

When completed, please tear out this page and mail it to us at:

Publishing Department
Peterson's, a Nelnet company
2000 Lenox Drive
Lawrenceville, NJ 08648

You can also complete this survey online at **www.petersons.com/booksurvey.**

1. **What is the ISBN of the book you have purchased? (The ISBN can be found on the book's back cover in the lower right-hand corner. )** _____

2. **Where did you purchase this book?**
   - ❑ Retailer, such as Barnes & Noble
   - ❑ Online reseller, such as Amazon.com
   - ❑ Petersons.com
   - ❑ Other (please specify) _____

3. **If you purchased this book on Petersons.com, please rate the following aspects of your online purchasing experience on a scale of 4 to 1 (4 = Excellent and 1 = Poor).**

| | 4 | 3 | 2 | 1 |
|---|---|---|---|---|
| Comprehensiveness of Peterson's Online Bookstore page | ❑ | ❑ | ❑ | ❑ |
| Overall online customer experience | ❑ | ❑ | ❑ | ❑ |

4. **Which category best describes you?**
   - ❑ High school student
   - ❑ Parent of high school student
   - ❑ College student
   - ❑ Graduate/professional student
   - ❑ Returning adult student
   - ❑ Teacher
   - ❑ Counselor
   - ❑ Working professional/military
   - ❑ Other (please specify) _____

5. **Rate your overall satisfaction with this book.**

| Extremely Satisfied | Satisfied | Not Satisfied |
|---|---|---|
| ❑ | ❑ | ❑ |

6. **Rate each of the following aspects of this book on a scale of 4 to 1 (4 = Excellent and 1 = Poor).**

|  | 4 | 3 | 2 | 1 |
|---|---|---|---|---|
| Comprehensiveness of the information | ❑ | ❑ | ❑ | ❑ |
| Accuracy of the information | ❑ | ❑ | ❑ | ❑ |
| Usability | ❑ | ❑ | ❑ | ❑ |
| Cover design | ❑ | ❑ | ❑ | ❑ |
| Book layout | ❑ | ❑ | ❑ | ❑ |
| Special features (e.g., CD, flashcards, charts, etc.) | ❑ | ❑ | ❑ | ❑ |
| Value for the money | ❑ | ❑ | ❑ | ❑ |

7. **This book was recommended by:**
   - ❑ Guidance counselor
   - ❑ Parent/guardian
   - ❑ Family member/relative
   - ❑ Friend
   - ❑ Teacher
   - ❑ Not recommended by anyone—I found the book on my own
   - ❑ Other (please specify) _____

8. **Would you recommend this book to others?**

   | Yes | Not Sure | No |
   |---|---|---|
   | ❑ | ❑ | ❑ |

9. **Please provide any additional comments.**

   _____

   _____

   _____

   _____

   _____

Remember, you can tear out this page and mail it to us at:

   Publishing Department
   Peterson's, a Nelnet company
   2000 Lenox Drive
   Lawrenceville, NJ 08648

or you can complete the survey online at **www.petersons.com/booksurvey.**

Your feedback is important to us at Peterson's, and we thank you for your time!

If you would like us to keep in touch with you about new products and services, please include your e-mail address here: _____